CODE OF FEDERAL REGULATIONS

Title 30
Mineral Resources

Parts 1 to 199

Revised as of July 1, 2023

Containing a codification of documents
of general applicability and future effect

As of July 1, 2023

Published by the Office of the Federal Register
National Archives and Records Administration
as a Special Edition of the Federal Register

Table of Contents

	Page
Explanation	v

Title 30:

    Chapter I—Mine Safety and Health Administration, Department of Labor 3

Finding Aids:

    Table of CFR Titles and Chapters 765

    Alphabetical List of Agencies Appearing in the CFR 785

    List of CFR Sections Affected 795

Cite this Code: **CFR**

To cite the regulations in this volume use title, part and section number. Thus, 30 CFR 1.1 *refers to title 30, part 1, section 1.*

Explanation

The Code of Federal Regulations is a codification of the general and permanent rules published in the Federal Register by the Executive departments and agencies of the Federal Government. The Code is divided into 50 titles which represent broad areas subject to Federal regulation. Each title is divided into chapters which usually bear the name of the issuing agency. Each chapter is further subdivided into parts covering specific regulatory areas.

Each volume of the Code is revised at least once each calendar year and issued on a quarterly basis approximately as follows:

Title 1 through Title 16...as of January 1
Title 17 through Title 27 ....as of April 1
Title 28 through Title 41 ....as of July 1
Title 42 through Title 50..as of October 1

The appropriate revision date is printed on the cover of each volume.

LEGAL STATUS

The contents of the Federal Register are required to be judicially noticed (44 U.S.C. 1507). The Code of Federal Regulations is prima facie evidence of the text of the original documents (44 U.S.C. 1510).

HOW TO USE THE CODE OF FEDERAL REGULATIONS

The Code of Federal Regulations is kept up to date by the individual issues of the Federal Register. These two publications must be used together to determine the latest version of any given rule.

To determine whether a Code volume has been amended since its revision date (in this case, July 1, 2023), consult the "List of CFR Sections Affected (LSA)," which is issued monthly, and the "Cumulative List of Parts Affected," which appears in the Reader Aids section of the daily Federal Register. These two lists will identify the Federal Register page number of the latest amendment of any given rule.

EFFECTIVE AND EXPIRATION DATES

Each volume of the Code contains amendments published in the Federal Register since the last revision of that volume of the Code. Source citations for the regulations are referred to by volume number and page number of the Federal Register and date of publication. Publication dates and effective dates are usually not the same and care must be exercised by the user in determining the actual effective date. In instances where the effective date is beyond the cut-off date for the Code a note has been inserted to reflect the future effective date. In those instances where a regulation published in the Federal Register states a date certain for expiration, an appropriate note will be inserted following the text.

OMB CONTROL NUMBERS

The Paperwork Reduction Act of 1980 (Pub. L. 96–511) requires Federal agencies to display an OMB control number with their information collection request.

Many agencies have begun publishing numerous OMB control numbers as amendments to existing regulations in the CFR. These OMB numbers are placed as close as possible to the applicable recordkeeping or reporting requirements.

PAST PROVISIONS OF THE CODE

Provisions of the Code that are no longer in force and effect as of the revision date stated on the cover of each volume are not carried. Code users may find the text of provisions in effect on any given date in the past by using the appropriate List of CFR Sections Affected (LSA). For the convenience of the reader, a "List of CFR Sections Affected" is published at the end of each CFR volume. For changes to the Code prior to the LSA listings at the end of the volume, consult previous annual editions of the LSA. For changes to the Code prior to 2001, consult the List of CFR Sections Affected compilations, published for 1949-1963, 1964-1972, 1973-1985, and 1986-2000.

"[RESERVED]" TERMINOLOGY

The term "[Reserved]" is used as a place holder within the Code of Federal Regulations. An agency may add regulatory information at a "[Reserved]" location at any time. Occasionally "[Reserved]" is used editorially to indicate that a portion of the CFR was left vacant and not dropped in error.

INCORPORATION BY REFERENCE

What is incorporation by reference? Incorporation by reference was established by statute and allows Federal agencies to meet the requirement to publish regulations in the Federal Register by referring to materials already published elsewhere. For an incorporation to be valid, the Director of the Federal Register must approve it. The legal effect of incorporation by reference is that the material is treated as if it were published in full in the Federal Register (5 U.S.C. 552(a)). This material, like any other properly issued regulation, has the force of law.

What is a proper incorporation by reference? The Director of the Federal Register will approve an incorporation by reference only when the requirements of 1 CFR part 51 are met. Some of the elements on which approval is based are:

(a) The incorporation will substantially reduce the volume of material published in the Federal Register.

(b) The matter incorporated is in fact available to the extent necessary to afford fairness and uniformity in the administrative process.

(c) The incorporating document is drafted and submitted for publication in accordance with 1 CFR part 51.

What if the material incorporated by reference cannot be found? If you have any problem locating or obtaining a copy of material listed as an approved incorporation by reference, please contact the agency that issued the regulation containing that incorporation. If, after contacting the agency, you find the material is not available, please notify the Director of the Federal Register, National Archives and Records Administration, 8601 Adelphi Road, College Park, MD 20740-6001, or call 202-741-6010.

CFR INDEXES AND TABULAR GUIDES

A subject index to the Code of Federal Regulations is contained in a separate volume, revised annually as of January 1, entitled CFR INDEX AND FINDING AIDS. This volume contains the Parallel Table of Authorities and Rules. A list of CFR titles, chapters, subchapters, and parts and an alphabetical list of agencies publishing in the CFR are also included in this volume.

An index to the text of "Title 3—The President" is carried within that volume.

The Federal Register Index is issued monthly in cumulative form. This index is based on a consolidation of the "Contents" entries in the daily Federal Register.

A List of CFR Sections Affected (LSA) is published monthly, keyed to the revision dates of the 50 CFR titles.

REPUBLICATION OF MATERIAL

There are no restrictions on the republication of material appearing in the Code of Federal Regulations.

INQUIRIES

For a legal interpretation or explanation of any regulation in this volume, contact the issuing agency. The issuing agency's name appears at the top of odd-numbered pages.

For inquiries concerning CFR reference assistance, call 202-741-6000 or write to the Director, Office of the Federal Register, National Archives and Records Administration, 8601 Adelphi Road, College Park, MD 20740-6001 or e-mail *fedreg.info@nara.gov*.

THIS TITLE

Title 30—MINERAL RESOURCES is composed of three volumes. The parts in these volumes are arranged in the following order: parts 1—199, parts 200—699, and part 700 to end. The contents of these volumes represent all current regulations codified under this title of the CFR as of July 1, 2023.

For this volume, Gabrielle E. Burns was Chief Editor. The Code of Federal Regulations publication program is under the direction of John Hyrum Martinez, assisted by Stephen J. Frattini.

Title 30—Mineral Resources

(This book contains parts 1 to 199)

	Part
CHAPTER I—Mine Safety and Health Administration, Department of Labor	1

CHAPTER I—MINE SAFETY AND HEALTH ADMINISTRATION, DEPARTMENT OF LABOR

EDITORIAL NOTE: Nomenclature changes to chapter I appear at 69 FR 18803, Apr. 9, 2004.

SUBCHAPTER A—OFFICIAL EMBLEM AND OMB CONTROL NUMBERS FOR RECORDKEEPING AND REPORTING

Part		Page
1	Mine Safety and Health Administration; establishment and use of official emblem	7
3	OMB Control Numbers under the Paperwork Reduction Act	7

SUBCHAPTER B—TESTING, EVALUATION, AND APPROVAL OF MINING PRODUCTS

5	Fees for testing, evaluation, and approval of mining products	11
6	Testing and evaluation by independent laboratories and non-MSHA product safety standards	12
7	Testing by applicant or third party	14
14	Requirements for the approval of flame-resistant conveyor belts	90
15	Requirements for approval of explosives and sheathed explosive units	94
18	Electric motor-driven mine equipment and accessories	101
19	Electric cap lamps	143
20	Electric mine lamps other than standard cap lamps	148
22	Portable methane detectors	153
23	Telephones and signaling devices	157
27	Methane-monitoring systems	162
28	Fuses for use with direct current in providing short-circuit protection for trailing cables in coal mines	170
33	Dust collectors for use in connection with rock drilling in coal mines	175
35	Fire-resistant hydraulic fluids	182

Part		Page
36	Approval requirements for permissible mobile diesel-powered transportation equipment	189

SUBCHAPTERS C–F [RESERVED]

SUBCHAPTER G—FILING AND OTHER ADMINISTRATIVE REQUIREMENTS

40	Representative of miners	203
41	Notification of legal identity	204
42	National Mine Health and Safety Academy	206
43	Procedures for processing hazardous conditions complaints	207
44	Rules of practice for petitions for modification of mandatory safety standards	210
45	Independent contractors	222

SUBCHAPTER H—EDUCATION AND TRAINING

46	Training and retraining of miners engaged in shell dredging or employed at sand, gravel, surface stone, surface clay, colloidal phosphate, or surface limestone mines	224
47	Hazard Communication (HazCom)	232
48	Training and retraining of miners	240
49	Mine rescue teams	260

SUBCHAPTER I—ACCIDENTS, INJURIES, ILLNESSES, EMPLOYMENT, AND PRODUCTION IN MINES

50	Notification, investigation, reports and records of accidents, injuries, illnesses, employment, and coal production in mines	274

SUBCHAPTER J [RESERVED]

SUBCHAPTER K—METAL AND NONMETAL MINE SAFETY AND HEALTH

56	Safety and health standards—surface metal and nonmetal mines	285
57	Safety and health standards—underground metal and nonmetal mines	341

Mine Safety and Health Admin., Labor

Part		Page
58	Health standards for metal and nonmetal mines	443

SUBCHAPTER L [RESERVED]

SUBCHAPTER M—UNIFORM MINE HEALTH REGULATIONS

| 62 | Occupational noise exposure .... | 444 |

SUBCHAPTER N [RESERVED]

SUBCHAPTER O—COAL MINE SAFETY AND HEALTH

70	Mandatory health standards—underground coal mines	452
71	Mandatory health standards—surface coal mines and surface work areas of underground coal mines	466
72	Health standards for coal mines	480
74	Coal mine dust sampling devices	485
75	Mandatory safety standards—underground coal mines	496
77	Mandatory safety standards, surface coal mines and surface work areas of underground coal mines	679
90	Mandatory health standards—coal miners who have evidence of the development of pneumoconiosis	735

SUBCHAPTER P—CIVIL PENALTIES FOR VIOLATIONS OF THE FEDERAL MINE SAFETY AND HEALTH ACT OF 1977

| 100 | Criteria and procedures for proposed assessment of civil penalties .... | 747 |
| 101–103 | [Reserved] | |

SUBCHAPTER Q—PATTERN OF VIOLATIONS

| 104 | Pattern of violations .... | 761 |
| 105–199 | [Reserved] | |

SUBCHAPTER A—OFFICIAL EMBLEM AND OMB CONTROL NUMBERS FOR RECORDKEEPING AND REPORTING

PART 1—MINE SAFETY AND HEALTH ADMINISTRATION; ESTABLISHMENT AND USE OF OFFICIAL EMBLEM

Sec.
1.1 Official emblem.
1.2 Description.
1.3 Use of letters and acronym MSHA.

AUTHORITY: Sec. 508, Federal Coal Mine Health and Safety Act of 1969; sec. 301 of Title 5, United States Code; secs. 301(a) and 302(a), Federal Mine Safety and Health Amendments Act of 1977, Pub. L. 95–164, 30 U.S.C. 961 and 951 and 29 U.S.C. 577a, 91 Stat. 1317 and 91 Stat. 1319; sec. 508, Federal Mine Safety and Health Act of 1977, Pub. L. 91–173 as amended by Pub. L. 95–164, 30 U.S.C. 957, 83 Stat. 803.

SOURCE: 39 FR 23997, June 28, 1974, unless otherwise noted.

§ 1.1 Official emblem.

The following emblem is established and shall be used as the official emblem of the Mine Safety and Health Administration, except where use of the Departmental Seal is required:

[39 FR 23997, June 28, 1974, as amended at 43 FR 12312, Mar. 24, 1978]

§ 1.2 Description.

The emblem of the Mine Safety and Health Administration is of contemporary design with the letters and acronym of the Administration delineated as MSHA appearing in large letters in the middle of the emblem. Above the letters and acronym appear the words "United States Department of Labor" and below the letters and acronym appear the words "Mine Safety and Health Administration."

[39 FR 23997, June 28, 1974, as amended at 43 FR 12312, Mar. 24, 1978]

§ 1.3 Use of letters and acronym MSHA.

The letters and acronym MSHA may be used and substituted for the words "Mine Safety and Health Administration" in correspondence, rules, regulations, and in certificates of approval, approval plates, labels, and markings prescribed by the Mine Safety and Health Administration to designate and denote equipment, devices, and apparatus approved as "permissible" and suitable for use in mines under the applicable parts of Chapter I of this title, and in such other documents, publications, and pamphlets, and on signs, clothing and uniforms, and offices of the Administration and at such times and locations as may be deemed appropriate by the Assistant Secretary of Labor for Mine Safety and Health.

[39 FR 23997, June 28, 1974, as amended at 43 FR 12312, Mar. 24, 1978]

PART 3—OMB CONTROL NUMBERS UNDER THE PAPERWORK REDUCTION ACT

AUTHORITY: 30 U.S.C. 957; 44 U.S.C. 3501–3520.

§ 3.1 OMB control numbers.

The collection of information requirements in MSHA regulation sections in this chapter have been approved and assigned control numbers by the Office of Management and Budget (OMB) under the Paperwork Reduction Act. Regulation sections in this chapter containing paperwork requirements and their respective OMB control numbers are displayed in the following table:

TABLE 1—OMB CONTROL NUMBERS

30 CFR Citation	OMB Control No.
Subchapter B—Testing, Evaluation, and Approval of Mining Products	
6.10	1219–0066
7.3	1219–0066
7.4	1219–0066
7.6	1219–0066
7.7	1219–0066

§ 3.1

TABLE 1—OMB CONTROL NUMBERS—Continued

30 CFR Citation	OMB Control No.
7.23	1219–0066
7.27	1219–0066
7.28	1219–0066
7.29	1219–0066
7.30	1219–0066
7.43	1219–0066
7.46	1219–0066
7.47	1219–0066
7.48	1219–0066
7.49	1219–0066
7.51	1219–0066
7.63	1219–0066
7.69	1219–0066
7.71	1219–0066
7.83	1219–0066
7.90	1219–0066
7.97	1219–0066
7.105	1219–0066
7.108	1219–0066
7.303	1219–0066
7.306	1219–0066
7.309	1219–0066
7.311	1219–0066
7.403	1219–0066
7.407	1219–0066
7.408	1219–0066
7.409	1219–0066
7.411	1219–0066
15.4	1219–0066
15.8	1219–0066
18.6	1219–0066
18.15	1219–0066
18.53	1219–0066, –0116
18.81	1219–0066
18.82	1219–0066
18.93	1219–0066
18.94	1219–0066
19.3	1219–0066
19.13	1219–0066
20.3	1219–0066
20.14	1219–0066
22.4	1219–0066
22.8	1219–0066
22.11	1219–0066
23.3	1219–0066
23.7	1219–0066
23.10	1219–0066
23.12	1219–0066
23.14	1219–0066
27.4	1219–0066
27.6	1219–0066
27.11	1219–0066
28.10	1219–0066
28.23	1219–0066
28.25	1219–0066
28.30	1219–0066
28.31	1219–0066
33.6	1219–0066
33.12	1219–0066
35.6	1219–0066
35.10	1219–0066
35.12	1219–0066
36.6	1219–0066
36.12	1219–0066

Subchapter G—Filing and Other Administrative Requirements

30 CFR Citation	OMB Control No.
40.3	1219–0042
40.4	1219–0042
40.5	1219–0042

30 CFR Ch. I (7–1–23 Edition)

TABLE 1—OMB CONTROL NUMBERS—Continued

30 CFR Citation	OMB Control No.
41.20	1219–0042
43.4	1219–0014
43.7	1219–0014
44.9	1219–0065
44.10	1219–0065
44.11	1219–0065
45.3	1219–0040
45.4	1219–0040

Subchapter H—Education and Training

30 CFR Citation	OMB Control No.
46.3	1219–0131
46.5	1219–0131
46.6	1219–0131
46.7	1219–0131
46.8	1219–0131
46.9	1219–0131
46.11	1219–0131
47.31	1219–0133
47.32	1219–0133
47.32(a)(4)	1219–0133
47.41	1219–0133
47.51	1219–0133
47.71	1219–0133
47.73	1219–0133
48.3	1219–0009, –0141
48.9	1219–0009
48.23	1219–0009
48.29	1219–0009
49.2	1219–0078
49.3	1219–0078
49.4	1219–0078
49.6	1219–0078
49.7	1219–0078
49.8	1219–0078
49.9	1219–0078
49.12	1219–0144
49.16	1219–0144
49.18	1219–0144
49.50	1219–0144

Subchapter I—Accidents, Injuries, Illnesses, Employment, and Production in Mines

30 CFR Citation	OMB Control No.
50.10	1219–0007, –0141
50.11	1219–0007, –0141
50.20	1219–0007
50.30	1219–0007

Subchapter K—Metal and Nonmetal Mine Safety and Health

30 CFR Citation	OMB Control No.
56.1000	1219–0042
56.3203(a)	1219–0121
56.5005	1219–0048
56.13015	1219–0089
56.13030	1219–0089
56.14100	1219–0089
56.18002	1219–0089
56.19022	1219–0034
56.19023	1219–0034
56.19057	1219–0049
56.19121	1219–0034
57.1000	1219–0042
57.3203(a)	1219–0121
57.3461	1219–0097
57.5005	1219–0048
57.5037	1219–0003
57.5040	1219–0003
57.5047	1219–0039
57.5060	1219–0135

Mine Safety and Health Admin., Labor §3.1

TABLE 1—OMB CONTROL NUMBERS—Continued

30 CFR Citation	OMB Control No.
57.5065	1219–0135
57.5066	1219–0135
57.5067	1219–0135
57.5070	1219–0135
57.5071	1219–0135
57.5075	1219–0135
57.8520	1219–0016
57.8525	1219–0016
57.11053	1219–0046
57.13015	1219–0089
57.13030	1219–0089
57.14100	1219–0089
57.18002	1219–0089
57.19022	1219–0034
57.19023	1219–0034
57.19057	1219–0049
57.19121	1219–0034
57.22004(c)	1219–0103
57.22204	1219–0030
57.22229	1219–0103
57.22230	1219–0103
57.22231	1219–0103
57.22239	1219–0103
57.22401	1219–0096
57.22606	1219–0095

Subchapter M—Uniform Mine Health Regulations

30 CFR Citation	OMB Control No.
62.110	1219–0120
62.130	1219–0120
62.170	1219–0120
62.171	1219–0120
62.172	1219–0120
62.173	1219–0120
62.174	1219–0120
62.175	1219–0120
62.180	1219–0120
62.190	1219–0120

Subchapter O—Coal Mine Safety and Health

30 CFR Citation	OMB Control No.
70.201(c)	1219–0011
70.202(b)	1219–0011
70.204	1219–0011
70.209	1219–0011
70.210	1219–0011
70.220	1219–0011
70.220(a)	1219–0011
71.201(c)	1219–0011
71.202(b)	1219–0011
71.204	1219–0011
71.209	1219–0011
71.210	1219–0011
71.220	1219–0011
71.220(a)	1219–0011
71.300	1219–0011
71.301	1219–0011
71.301(d)	1219–0011
71.403	1219–0024
71.404	1219–0024
72.500	1219–0124
72.503	1219–0124
72.510	1219–0124
72.520	1219–0124
75.100	1219–0127
75.153(a)(2)	1219–0001
75.155	1219–0127
75.159	1219–0127
75.160	1219–0127
75.161	1219–0127
75.204(a)	1219–0121

TABLE 1—OMB CONTROL NUMBERS—Continued

30 CFR Citation	OMB Control No.
75.215	1219–0004
75.220	1219–0004
75.221	1219–0004
75.222	1219–0004
75.223	1219–0004
75.310	1219–0088
75.312	1219–0088
75.335	1219–0142
75.336	1219–0142
75.337	1219–0142
75.338	1219–0142
75.342	1219–0088
75.350	1219–0138
75.351	1219–0088, –0116, –0138
75.352	1219–0138
75.360	1219–0088
75.361	1219–0088
75.362	1219–0088
75.363	1219–0088
75.364	1219–0088
75.370	1219–0088
75.371	1219–0088, –0138
75.372	1219–0073
75.373	1219–0073
75.382	1219–0088
75.512	1219–0116
75.703	1219–0116
75.703–3	1219–0116
75.800	1219–0116
75.800–4	1219–0116
75.820	1210–0116
75.821	1219–0116
75.900	1219–0116
75.900–4	1219–0116
75.1001–1	1219–0116
75.1100–3	1219–0054
75.1103–8	1219–0054
75.1103–11	1219–0054
75.1200	1219–0073
75.1200–1	1219–0073
75.1201	1219–0073
75.1202	1219–0073
75.1202–1	1219–0073
75.1203	1219–0073
75.1204	1219–0073
75.1204–1	1219–0073
75.1321	1219–0025
75.1327	1219–0025
75.1400–2	1219–0034
75.1400–4	1219–0034
75.1432	1219–0034
75.1433	1219–0034
75.1501	1219–0054
75.1502	1219–0054, –0141
75.1504	1219–0141
75.1505	1219–0141
75.1702	1219–0041
75.1712–4	1219–0024
75.1712–5	1219–0024
75.1713–1	1219–0078
75.1714–3	1219–0141
75.1714–3(e)	1219–0044
75.1714–4	1219–0044
75.1714–5	1219–0141
75.1714–8	1219–0141
75.1716	1219–0020
75.1716–1	1219–0020
75.1716–3	1219–0020
75.1721	1219–0073
75.1901	1219–0119

§ 3.1

TABLE 1—OMB CONTROL NUMBERS—Continued

30 CFR Citation	OMB Control No.
75.1904	1219–0119
75.1911	1219–0119
75.1912	1219–0119
75.1914	1219–0119
75.1915	1219–0119, –0124
77.100	1219–0127
77.103(a)(2)	1219–0001
77.105	1219–0127
77.106	1219–0127
77.107	1219–0127
77.107–1	1219–0127
77.215	1219–0015
77.215–2	1219–0015
77.215–3	1219–0015
77.215–4	1219–0015
77.216–2	1219–0015
77.216–3	1219–0015
77.216–4	1219–0015
77.216–5	1219–0015
77.502	1219–0116
77.800	1219–0116
77.800–2	1219–0116
77.900	1219–0116
77.900–2	1219–0116
77.1000	1219–0026

TABLE 1—OMB CONTROL NUMBERS—Continued

30 CFR Citation	OMB Control No.
77.1000–1	1219–0026
77.1101	1219–0051
77.1200	1219–0073
77.1201	1219–0073
77.1202	1219–0073
77.1404	1219–0034
77.1432	1219–0034
77.1433	1219–0034
77.1702	1219–0078
77.1713	1219–0083
77.1900	1219–0019
77.1901	1219–0082
77.1906	1219–0034
77.1909–1	1219–0025
90.201(c)	1219–0011
90.202(b)	1219–0011
90.204	1219–0011
90.209	1219–0011
90.220	1219–0011
90.300	1219–0011
90.301	1219–0011
90.301(d)	1219–0011

[73 FR 36790, June 30, 2008]

SUBCHAPTER B—TESTING, EVALUATION, AND APPROVAL OF MINING PRODUCTS

PART 5—FEES FOR TESTING, EVALUATION, AND APPROVAL OF MINING PRODUCTS

Sec.
5.10 Purpose and scope.
5.30 Fee calculation.
5.40 Fee administration.
5.50 Fee revisions.

AUTHORITY: 30 U.S.C. 957.

SOURCE: 80 FR 45056, July 29, 2015, unless otherwise noted.

§ 5.10 Purpose and scope.

This part establishes a system under which MSHA charges a fee for services provided. This part includes the management and calculation of fees for the approval program, which includes: Application processing, testing and evaluation, approval decisions, post-approval activities, and termination of approvals.

§ 5.30 Fee calculation.

(a) *Fee calculation.* MSHA charges a fee based on an hourly rate for Approval and Certification Center (A&CC) approval program activities and other associated costs, such as travel expenses and part 15 fees. Part 15 fees for services provided to MSHA by other organizations may be set by those organizations.

(b) *Hourly rate calculation.* The hourly rate consists of direct and indirect costs of the A&CC's approval program divided by the number of direct hours worked on all approval program activities.

(1) Direct costs are compensation and benefit costs for hours worked on approval program activities.

(2) Indirect costs are a proportionate share of the following A&CC costs:

(i) Compensation and benefit hours worked in support of all A&CC activities;

(ii) A&CC building and equipment depreciation costs;

(iii) A&CC utilities, facility and equipment maintenance, and supplies and materials; and

(iv) Information Technology and other services the Department of Labor provides to the A&CC.

(c) *Fees are charged for—*

(1) Application processing (*e.g.*, administrative and technical review of applications, computer tracking, and status reporting);

(2) Testing and evaluation (*e.g.*, analysis of drawings, technical evaluation, testing, test set up and test tear down, and internal quality control activities);

(3) Approval decisions (*e.g.*, consultation on applications, records control and security, document preparation); and

(4) Two post-approval activities: changes to approvals and post-approval product audits.

(d) *Fees are not charged for—*

(1) Technical assistance not related to processing an approval application;

(2) Technical programs, including development of new technology programs;

(3) Participation in research conducted by other government agencies or private organizations; and

(4) Regulatory review activities, including participation in the development of health and safety standards, regulations, and legislation.

(e) *Fee estimate.* Except as provided in paragraphs (e)(1) and (2) of this section, on completion of an initial administrative review of the application, the A&CC will prepare a maximum fee estimate for each application. A&CC will begin the technical evaluation after the applicant authorizes the fee estimate.

(1) The applicant may pre-authorize an expenditure for services, and may further choose to pre-authorize either a maximum dollar amount or an expenditure without a specified maximum amount.

(i) All applications containing a pre-authorization statement will be put in the queue for the technical evaluation on completion of an initial administrative review.

§ 5.40

(ii) MSHA will concurrently prepare a maximum fee estimate for applications containing a statement pre-authorizing a maximum dollar amount, and will provide the applicant with this estimate.

(2) Where MSHA's estimated maximum fee exceeds the pre-authorized maximum dollar amount, the applicant has the choice of cancelling the action and paying for all work done up to the time of the cancellation, or authorizing MSHA's estimate.

(3) Under the Revised Acceptance Modification Program (RAMP), MSHA expedites applications for acceptance of minor changes to previously approved, certified, accepted, or evaluated products. The applicant must pre-authorize a fixed dollar amount, set by MSHA, for processing the application.

(f) If unforeseen circumstances are discovered during the evaluation, and MSHA determines that these circumstances would result in the actual costs exceeding either the pre-authorized expenditure or the authorized maximum fee estimate, as appropriate, MSHA will prepare a revised maximum fee estimate for completing the evaluation. The applicant will have the option of either cancelling the action and paying for services rendered or authorizing MSHA's revised estimate, in which case MSHA will continue to test and evaluate the product.

(g) If the actual cost of processing the application is less than MSHA's maximum fee estimate, MSHA will charge the actual cost.

§ 5.40 Fee administration.

Applicants and approval holders will be billed for all fees, including actual travel expenses, if any, when approval program activities are completed. Invoices will contain specific payment instruction, including the address to mail payments and authorized methods of payment.

§ 5.50 Fee revisions.

The hourly rate will remain in effect for at least one year and be subject to revision at least once every three years.

PART 6—TESTING AND EVALUATION BY INDEPENDENT LABORATORIES AND NON-MSHA PRODUCT SAFETY STANDARDS

Sec.
6.1 Purpose and effective date.
6.2 Definitions.
6.10 Use of independent laboratories.
6.20 MSHA acceptance of equivalent non-MSHA product safety standards.
6.30 MSHA listing of equivalent non-MSHA product safety standards.

AUTHORITY: 30 U.S.C. 957.

SOURCE: 68 FR 36417, June 17, 2003, unless otherwise noted.

§ 6.1 Purpose and effective date.

This part sets out alternate requirements for testing and evaluation of products MSHA approves for use in gassy underground mines. It permits manufacturers of certain products who seek MSHA approval to use an independent laboratory to perform, in whole or part, the necessary testing and evaluation for approval. It also permits manufacturers to have their products approved based on non-MSHA product safety standards once MSHA has determined that the non-MSHA standards are equivalent to MSHA's applicable product approval requirements or can be modified to provide at least the same degree of protection as those MSHA requirements. The provisions of this part may be used by applicants for product approval under parts 18, 19, 20, 22, 23, 27, 33, 35, and 36. This rule is effective August 18, 2003.

§ 6.2 Definitions.

The following definitions apply in this part.

Applicant. An individual or organization that manufactures or controls the assembly of a product and applies to MSHA for approval of that product.

Approval. A written document issued by MSHA which states that a product has met the applicable requirements of part 18, 19, 20, 22, 23, 27, 33, 35, or 36. The definition is based on the existing definitions of "approval" in the parts specified above. It is expanded to include "certification" and "acceptance" because these terms also are used to denote MSHA approval.

Mine Safety and Health Admin., Labor §6.20

Approval holder. An applicant whose application for approval of a product under part 18, 19, 20, 22, 23, 27, 33, 35 or 36 of this chapter has been approved by MSHA.

Equivalent non-MSHA product safety standards. A non-MSHA product safety standard, or group of standards, determined by MSHA to provide at least the same degree of protection as the applicable MSHA product approval requirements in parts 14, 18, 19, 20, 22, 23, 27, 33, 35, and 36, or which in modified form provide at least the same degree of protection.

Independent laboratory. A laboratory that:

(1) has been recognized by a laboratory accrediting organization to test and evaluate products to a product safety standard, and

(2) is free from commercial, financial, and other pressures that may influence the results of the testing and evaluation process.

Post-approval product audit. The examination, testing, or both, by MSHA of approved products selected by MSHA to determine whether those products meet the applicable product approval requirements and have been manufactured as approved.

Product safety standard. A document, or group of documents, that specifies the requirements for the testing and evaluation of a product for use in explosive gas and dust atmospheres, and, when appropriate, includes documents addressing the flammability properties of products.

[68 FR 36417, June 17, 2003, as amended at 73 FR 80609, Dec. 31, 2008]

§6.10 Use of independent laboratories.

(a) MSHA will accept testing and evaluation performed by an independent laboratory for purposes of MSHA product approval provided that MSHA receives as part of the application:

(1) Written evidence of the laboratory's independence and current recognition by a laboratory accrediting organization;

(2) Complete technical explanation of how the product complies with each requirement in the applicable MSHA product approval requirements;

(3) Identification of components or features of the product that are critical to the safety of the product; and

(4) All documentation, including drawings and specifications, as submitted to the independent laboratory by the applicant and as required by the applicable part under this chapter.

(b) Product testing and evaluation performed by independent laboratories for purposes of MSHA approval must comply with the applicable MSHA product approval requirements.

(c) Product testing and evaluation must be conducted or witnessed by the laboratory's personnel.

(d) After review of the information required under paragraphs (a)(1) through (a)(4) of this section, MSHA will notify the applicant if additional information or testing is required. The applicant must provide this information, arrange any additional or repeat tests and notify MSHA of the location, date, and time of the test(s). MSHA may observe any additional testing conducted by an independent laboratory. Further, MSHA may decide to conduct the additional or repeated tests at the applicant's expense. The applicant must supply any additional components necessary for testing and evaluation.

(e) Upon request by MSHA, but not more than once a year, except for cause, approval holders of products approved based on independent laboratory testing and evaluation must make such products available for post-approval audit at a mutually agreeable site at no cost to MSHA.

(f) Once the product is approved, the approval holder must notify MSHA of all product defects of which they become aware.

§6.20 MSHA acceptance of equivalent non-MSHA product safety standards.

(a) MSHA will accept non-MSHA product safety standards, or groups of standards, as equivalent after determining that they:

(1) Provide at least the same degree of protection as MSHA's product approval requirements in parts 14, 18, 19, 20, 33, 35 and 36 of this chapter; or

§ 6.30

(2) Can be modified to provide at least the same degree of protection as those MSHA requirements.

(b) MSHA will publish its intent to review any non-MSHA product safety standard for equivalency in the FEDERAL REGISTER for the purpose of soliciting public input.

(c) A listing of all equivalency determinations will be published in this part 6 and the applicable approval parts. The listing will state whether MSHA accepts the non-MSHA product safety standards in their original form, or whether MSHA will require modifications to demonstrate equivalency. If modifications are required, they will be provided in the listing. MSHA will notify the public of each equivalency determination and will publish a summary of the basis for its determination. MSHA will provide equivalency determination reports to the public upon request to the Approval and Certification Center.

(d) After MSHA has determined that non-MSHA product safety standards are equivalent and has notified the public of such determinations, applicants may seek MSHA product approval based on such non-MSHA product safety standards.

[68 FR 36417, June 17, 2003, as amended at 73 FR 80609, Dec. 31, 2008]

§ 6.30 MSHA listing of equivalent non-MSHA product safety standards.

MSHA evaluated the following non-MSHA product safety standards and determined that they provide at least the same degree of protection as current MSHA requirements with or without modifications as indicated:

(a) The International Electrotechnical Commission's (IEC) standards for Electrical Apparatus for Explosive Gas Atmospheres, Part 0, General Requirements (IEC 60079–0, Fourth Edition, 2004–01) and Part 1, Electrical Apparatus for Explosive Gas Atmospheres, Flameproof Enclosures ''d'' (IEC 60079–1, Fifth Edition, 2003–11) must be modified in order to provide at least the same degree of protection as MSHA explosion-proof enclosure requirements included in parts 7 and 18 of this chapter. Refer to §§ 7.10(c)(1) and 18.6(a)(3)(i) for a list of the required modifications. The IEC standards may be inspected at the U.S. Department of Labor, Mine Safety and Health Administration, Electrical Safety Division, Approval and Certification Center, 765 Technology Drive, Triadelphia, WV 26059, and may be purchased from International Electrical Commission, Central Office 3, rue de Varembé, P.O. Box 131, CH–1211 GENEVA 20, Switzerland.

(b) [Reserved]

[71 FR 28583, May 17, 2006, as amended at 73 FR 52210, Sept. 9, 2008]

PART 7—TESTING BY APPLICANT OR THIRD PARTY

Subpart A—General

Sec.
7.1 Purpose and scope.
7.2 Definitions.
7.3 Application procedures and requirements.
7.4 Product testing.
7.5 Issuance of approval.
7.6 Approval marking and distribution record.
7.7 Quality assurance.
7.8 Post-approval product audit.
7.9 Revocation.
7.10 MSHA acceptance of equivalent non—MSHA product safety standards.

Subpart B—Brattice Cloth and Ventilation Tubing

7.21 Purpose and effective date.
7.22 Definitions.
7.23 Application requirements.
7.24 Technical requirements.
7.25 Critical characteristics.
7.26 Flame test apparatus.
7.27 Test for flame resistance of brattice cloth.
7.28 Test for flame resistance of rigid ventilation tubing.
7.29 Approval marking.
7.30 Post-approval product audit.
7.31 New technology.

Subpart C—Battery Assemblies

7.41 Purpose and effective date.
7.42 Definitions.
7.43 Application requirements.
7.44 Technical requirements.
7.45 Critical characteristics.
7.46 Impact test.
7.47 Deflection temperature test.
7.48 Acid resistance test.
7.49 Approval marking.
7.50 Post-approval product audit.
7.51 Approval checklist.

Mine Safety and Health Admin., Labor § 7.2

7.52 New technology.

Subpart D—Multiple-Shot Blasting Units

7.61 Purpose and effective date.
7.62 Definitions.
7.63 Application requirements.
7.64 Technical requirements.
7.65 Critical characteristics.
7.66 Output energy test.
7.67 Construction test.
7.68 Firing line terminals test.
7.69 Approval marking.
7.70 Post-approval product audit.
7.71 Approval checklist.
7.72 New technology.

Subpart E—Diesel Engines Intended for Use in Underground Coal Mines

7.81 Purpose and effective date.
7.82 Definitions.
7.83 Application requirements.
7.84 Technical requirements.
7.85 Critical characteristics.
7.86 Test equipment and specifications.
7.87 Test to determine the maximum fuel-air ratio.
7.88 Test to determine the gaseous ventilation rate.
7.89 Test to determine the particulate index.
7.90 Approval marking.
7.91 Post-approval product audit.
7.92 New technology.

Subpart F—Diesel Power Packages Intended for Use in Areas of Underground Coal Mines Where Permissible Electric Equipment Is Required

7.95 Purpose and effective date.
7.96 Definitions.
7.97 Application requirements.
7.98 Technical requirements.
7.99 Critical characteristics.
7.100 Explosion tests.
7.101 Surface temperature tests.
7.102 Exhaust gas cooling efficiency test.
7.103 Safety system control test.
7.104 Internal static pressure test.
7.105 Approval marking.
7.106 Post-approval product audit.
7.107 New technology.
7.108 Power package checklist.

Subpart J—Electric Motor Assemblies

7.301 Purpose and effective date.
7.302 Definitions.
7.303 Application requirements.
7.304 Technical requirements.
7.305 Critical characteristics.
7.306 Explosion tests.
7.307 Static pressure test.
7.308 Lockwasher equivalency test.
7.309 Approval marking.
7.310 Post-approval product audit.
7.311 Approval checklist.

APPENDIX I TO SUBPART J OF PART 7

Subpart K—Electric Cables, Signaling Cables, and Cable Splice Kits

7.401 Purpose and effective date.
7.402 Definitions.
7.403 Application requirements.
7.404 Technical requirements.
7.405 Critical characteristics.
7.406 Flame test apparatus.
7.407 Test for flame resistance of electric cables and cable splices.
7.408 Test for flame resistance of signaling cables.
7.409 Approval markings.
7.410 Post-approval product audit.
7.411 New technology.

Subpart L—Refuge Alternatives

7.501 Purpose and scope.
7.502 Definitions.
7.503 Application requirements.
7.504 Refuge alternatives and components; general requirements.
7.505 Structural components.
7.506 Breathable air components.
7.507 Air-monitoring components.
7.508 Harmful gas removal components.
7.509 Approval markings.
7.510 New technology.

AUTHORITY: 30 U.S.C. 957.

SOURCE: 53 FR 23500, June 22, 1988, unless otherwise noted.

Subpart A—General

§ 7.1 Purpose and scope.

This part sets out requirements for MSHA approval of certain equipment and materials for use in underground mines whose product testing and evaluation does not involve subjective analysis. These requirements apply to products listed in the subparts following this Subpart A. After the dates specified in the following subparts, requests for approval of products shall be made in accordance with this Subpart A and the applicable subpart.

§ 7.2 Definitions.

The following definitions apply in this part.

Applicant. An individual or organization that manufactures or controls the assembly of a product and that applies to MSHA for approval of that product.

§ 7.3

Approval. A document issued by MSHA which states that a product has met the requirements of this part and which authorizes an approval marking identifying the product as approved.

Authorized company official. An individual designated by applicant who has the authority to bind the company.

Critical characteristic. A feature of a product that, if not manufactured as approved, could have a direct adverse effect on safety and for which testing or inspection is required prior to shipment to ensure conformity with the technical requirements under which the approval was issued.

Equivalent non-MSHA product safety standards. A non-MSHA product safety standard, or group of standards, that is determined by MSHA to provide at least the same degree of protection as the applicable MSHA product technical requirements in the subparts of this part, or can be modified to provide at least the same degree of protection as those MSHA requirements.

Extension of approval. A document issued by MSHA which states that the change to a product previously approved by MSHA under this part meets the requirements of this part and which authorizes the continued use of the approval marking after the appropriate extension number has been added.

Post-approval product audit. Examination, testing, or both, by MSHA of approved products selected by MSHA to determine whether those products meet the applicable technical requirements and have been manufactured as approved.

Technical requirements. The design and performance requirements for a product, as specified in a subpart of this part.

Test procedures. The methods specified in a subpart of this part used to determine whether a product meet the performance portion of the technical requirements.

[53 FR 23500, June 22, 1988; 53 FR 25569, July 7, 1988, as amended at 68 FR 36418, June 17, 2003]

§ 7.3 Application procedures and requirements.

(a) *Application.* Requests for an approval or extension of approval shall be sent to: U.S. Department of Labor, Mine Safety and Health Administration, Approval and Certification Center, 765 Technology Drive, Triadelphia, WV 26059.

(b) *Fees.* Fees calculated in accordance with part 5 of this title shall be submitted in accordance with § 5.40.

(c) *Original approval.* Each application for approval of a product shall include—

(1) A brief description of the product;

(2) The documentation specified in the appropriate subpart of this part;

(3) The name, address, and telephone number of the applicant's representative responsible for answering any questions regarding the application;

(4) If appropriate, a statement indicating whether, in the applicant's opinion, testing is required. If testing is not proposed, the applicant shall explain the reasons for not testing; and

(5) If appropriate, the place and date for product testing.

(d) *Subsequent approval of a similar product.* Each application for a product similar to one for which the applicant already holds an approval shall include—

(1) The approval number for the product which most closely resembles the new one;

(2) The information specified in paragraph (c) of this section for the new product, except that any document which is the same as one listed by MSHA in prior approvals need not be submitted, but shall be noted in the application;

(3) An explanation of any change from the existing approval; and

(4) A statement as to whether, in the applicant's opinion, the change requires product testing. If testing is not proposed, the applicant shall explain the reasons for not testing.

(e) *Extension of an approval.* Any change in the approved product from the documentation on file at MSHA that affects the technical requirements of this part shall be submitted to MSHA for approval prior to implementing the change. Each application for an extension of approval shall include—

(1) The MSHA-assigned approval number for the product for which the extension is sought;

(2) A brief description of the proposed change to the previously approved product;

(3) Drawings and specifications which show the change in detail;

(4) A statement as to whether, in the applicant's opinion, the change requires product testing. If testing is not proposed, the applicant shall explain the reasons for not testing;

(5) The place and date for product testing, if testing will be conducted; and

(6) The name, address, and telephone number of the applicant's representative responsible for answering any questions regarding the application.

(f) *Certification statement.* (1) Each application for original approval, subsequent approval, or extension of approval of a product shall include a certification by the applicant that the product meets the design portion of the technical requirements, as specified in the appropriate subpart, and that the applicant will perform the quality assurance functions specified in §7.7. For a subsequent approval or extension of approval, the applicant shall also certify that the proposed change cited in the application is the only change that affects the technical requirements.

(2) After completion of the required product testing, the applicant shall certify that the product has been tested and meets the performance portion of the technical requirements, as specified in the appropriate subpart.

(3) All certification statements shall be signed by an authorized company official.

[53 FR 23500, June 22, 1988, as amended at 60 FR 33722, June 29, 1995; 73 FR 52210, Sept. 9, 2008]

§ 7.4 Product testing.

(a) All products submitted for approval under this part shall be tested using the test procedures specified in the appropriate subpart unless MSHA determines, upon review of the documentation submitted, that testing is not required. Applicants shall maintain records of test results and procedures for three years.

(b) Unless otherwise specified in the subpart, test instruments shall be calibrated at least as frequently as, and according to, the instrument manufacturer's specifications, using calibration standards traceable to those set by the National Bureau of Standards, U.S. Department of Commerce or other nationally recognized standards and accurate to at least one significant figure beyond the desired accuracy.

(c) When MSHA elects to observe product testing, the applicant shall permit an MSHA official to be present at a mutually agreeable date, time, and place.

(d) MSHA will accept product testing conducted outside the United States where such acceptance is specifically required by international agreement.

[53 FR 23500, June 22, 1988; 53 FR 25569, July 7, 1988; 60 FR 33722, June 29, 1995]

§ 7.5 Issuance of approval.

(a) An applicant shall not advertise or otherwise represent a product as approved until MSHA has issued the applicant an approval.

(b) MSHA will issue an approval or a notice of the reasons for denying approval after reviewing the application, and the results of product testing, when applicable. An approval will identify the documents upon which the approval is based.

§ 7.6 Approval marking and distribution record.

(a) Each approved product shall have an approval marking, as specified in the appropriate subpart of this part.

(b) For an extension of approval, the extension number shall be added to the original approval number on the approval marking.

(c) Applicants shall maintain records of the initial sale of each unit having an approval marking. The record retention period shall be at least the expected shelf life and service life of the product.

[53 FR 23500, June 22, 1988, as amended at 60 FR 33722, June 29, 1995]

§ 7.7 Quality assurance.

Applicants granted an approval or an extension of approval under this part shall—

(a) Inspect or test, or both, the critical characteristics in accordance with the appropriate subpart of this part;

§ 7.8

(b) Unless otherwise specified in the subparts, calibrate instruments used for the inspection and testing of critical characteristics at least as frequently as, and according to, the instrument manufacturer's specifications, using calibration standards traceable to those set by the National Bureau of Standards, U.S. Department of Commerce or other nationally recognized standards and use instruments accurate to at least one significant figure beyond the desired accuracy.

(c) Control production documentation so that the product is manufactured as approved;

(d) Immediately report to the MSHA Approval and Certification Center, any knowledge of a product distributed with critical characteristics not in accordance with the approval specifications.

[53 FR 23500, June 22, 1988, as amended at 60 FR 33722, June 29, 1995]

§ 7.8 Post-approval product audit.

(a) Approved products shall be subject to periodic audits by MSHA for the purpose of determining conformity with the technical requirements upon which the approval was based. Any approved product which is to be audited shall be selected by MSHA and be representative of those distributed for use in mines. The approval-holder may obtain any final report resulting from such audit.

(b) No more than once a year except for cause, the approval-holder, at MSHA's request, shall make an approved product available at no cost to MSHA for an audit to be conducted at a mutually agreeable site and time. The approval-holder may observe any tests conducted during this audit.

(c) An approved product shall be subject to audit for cause at any time MSHA believes that it is not in compliance with the technical requirements upon which the approval was based.

§ 7.9 Revocation.

(a) MSHA may revoke for cause an approval issued under this part if the product:
(1) Fails to meet the applicable technical requirements; or
(2) Creates a hazard when used in a mine.

(b) Prior to revoking an approval, the approval-holder shall be informed in writing of MSHA's intention to revoke approval. The notice shall:
(1) Explain the specific reasons for the proposed revocation; and
(2) Provide the approval-holder an opportunity to demonstrate or achieve compliance with the product approval requirements.

(c) Upon request, the approval-holder shall be afforded an opportunity for a hearing.

(d) If a product poses an imminent hazard to the safety or health of miners, the approval may be immediately suspended without a written notice of the agency's intention to revoke. The suspension may continue until the revocation proceedings are completed.

§ 7.10 MSHA acceptance of equivalent non-MSHA product safety standards.

(a) MSHA will accept non-MSHA product safety standards, or groups of standards, as equivalent after determining that they:
(1) Provide at least the same degree of protection as MSHA's applicable technical requirements for a product in the subparts of this part; or
(2) Can be modified to provide at least the same degree of protection as those MSHA requirements.

(b) MSHA will publish its intent to review any non-MSHA product safety standard for equivalency in the FEDERAL REGISTER for the purpose of soliciting public input.

(c) A listing of all equivalency determinations will be published in this part 7. The listing will state whether MSHA accepts the non-MSHA product safety standards in their original form, or whether MSHA will require modifications to demonstrate equivalency. If modifications are required, they will be provided in the listing. MSHA will notify the public of each equivalency determination and will publish a summary of the basis for its determination. MSHA will provide equivalency determination reports to the public upon request to the Approval and Certification Center. MSHA has made the following equivalency determinations applicable to this part 7.

(1) MSHA will accept applications for motors under Subpart J designed and tested to the International Electrotechnical Commission's (IEC) standards for Electrical Apparatus for Explosive Gas Atmospheres, Part 0, General Requirements (IEC 60079–0, Fourth Edition, 2004–01) and Part 1, Electrical Apparatus for Explosive Gas Atmospheres, Flameproof Enclosures "d" (IEC 60079–1, Fifth Edition, 2003–11) (which are hereby incorporated by reference and made a part hereof) provided the modifications to the IEC standards specified in §7.10(c)(1)(i) through (ix) are met. The Director of the Federal Register approves this incorporation by reference in accordance with 5 U.S.C. 552(a) and 1 CFR part 51. The IEC standards may be inspected at the U.S. Department of Labor, Mine Safety and Health Administration, Electrical Safety Division, Approval and Certification Center, 765 Technology Drive, Triadelphia, WV 26059, or at the National Archives and Records Administration (NARA). For information on the availability of this material at NARA, call 202–741–6030, or go to: http://www.archives.gov/federal_register/code_of_federal_regulations/ibr_locations.html. These IEC standards may be obtained from International Electrical Commission, Central Office 3, rue de Varembé, P.O. Box 131, CH–1211 GENEVA 20, Switzerland.

(i) Enclosures associated with an electric motor assembly shall be made of metal and not have a compartment exceeding ten (10) feet in length. External surfaces of enclosures shall not exceed 150 °C (302 °F) in normal operation.

(ii) Enclosures shall be rugged in construction and should meet existing requirements for minimum bolt size and spacing and for minimum wall, cover, and flange thicknesses specified in paragraph (g)(19) of §7.304 Technical requirements. Enclosure fasteners should be uniform in size and length, be provided at all corners, and be secured from loosening by lockwashers or equivalent. An engineering analysis shall be provided for enclosure designs that deviate from the existing requirements. The analysis shall show that the proposed enclosure design meets or exceeds the mechanical strength of a comparable enclosure designed to 150 psig according to existing requirements, and that flamepath clearances in excess of existing requirements will not be produced at an internal pressure of 150 psig. This shall be verified by explosion testing the enclosure at a minimum of 150 psig.

(iii) Enclosures shall be designed to withstand a minimum pressure of at least 150 psig without leakage through any welds or castings, rupture of any part that affects explosion-proof integrity, clearances exceeding those permitted under existing requirements along flame-arresting paths, or permanent distortion exceeding 0.040-inch per linear foot.

(iv) Flamepath clearances, including clearances between fasteners and the holes through which they pass, shall not exceed those specified in existing requirements. No intentional gaps in flamepaths are permitted.

(v) The minimum lengths of the flame arresting paths, based on enclosure volume, shall conform to those specified in existing requirements to the nearest metric equivalent value (e.g., 12.5 mm, 19 mm, and 25 mm are considered equivalent to ½ inch, ¾ inch and 1 inch respectively for plane and cylindrical joints). The widths of any grooves for o-rings shall be deducted in measuring the widths of flame-arresting paths.

(vi) Gaskets shall not be used to form any part of a flame-arresting path. If o-rings are installed within a flamepath, the location of the o-rings shall meet existing requirements.

(vii) Cable entries into enclosures shall be of a type that utilizes either flame-resistant rope packing material or sealing rings (grommets). If plugs and mating receptacles are mounted to an enclosure wall, they shall be of explosion-proof construction. Insulated bushings or studs shall not be installed in the outside walls of enclosures. Lead entrances utilizing sealing compounds and flexible or rigid metallic conduit are not permitted.

(viii) Unused lead entrances shall be closed with a metal plug that is secured by spot welding, brazing, or equivalent.

(ix) Special explosion tests are required for electric motor assemblies that share leads (electric conductors)

§ 7.21

through a common wall with another explosion-proof enclosure, such as a motor winding compartment and a conduit box. These tests are required to determine the presence of any pressure piling conditions in either enclosure when one or more of the insulating barriers, sectionalizing terminals, or other isolating parts are sequentially removed from the common wall between the enclosures. Enclosures that exhibit pressures during these tests that exceed those specified in existing requirements must be provided with a warning tag. The durable warning tag must indicate that the insulating barriers, sectionalizing terminals, or other isolating parts be maintained in order to insure the explosion-proof integrity for either enclosure sharing a common wall. A warning tag is not required if the enclosures withstand a static pressure of twice the maximum value observed in the explosion tests.

(2) [Reserved]

(d) After MSHA has determined that non-MSHA product safety standards are equivalent and has notified the public of such determinations, applicants may seek MSHA product approval based on such non-MSHA product safety standards.

[68 FR 36418, June 17, 2003, as amended at 71 FR 28583, May 17, 2006; 73 FR 52210, Sept. 9, 2008]

Subpart B—Brattice Cloth and Ventilation Tubing

§ 7.21 Purpose and effective date.

This subpart establishes the specific requirements for approval of brattice cloth and ventilation tubing. It is effective August 22, 1988. Applications for approval or extension of approval submitted after August 22, 1989, shall meet the requirements of this part.

§ 7.22 Definitions.

The following definitions apply in this subpart:

Brattice cloth. A curtain of jute, plastic, or similar material used to control or direct ventilating air.

Denier. A unit of yarn size indicating the fineness of fiber of material based on the number of grams in a length of 9,000 meters.

Film. A sheet of flexible material applied to a scrim by pressure, temperature, adhesion, or other method.

Scrim. A substrate material of plastic or fabric laminated between or coated with a film.

Ventilation tubing. Rigid or flexible tubing used to convey ventilating air.

§ 7.23 Application requirements.

(a) *Brattice cloth.* A single application may address two or more products if the products differ only in: weight of the finished product; weight or weave of the same fabric or scrim; or thickness or layers of the same film. Applications shall include the following information:

(1) Trade name.

(2) Product designations (for example, style and code number).

(3) Color.

(4) Type of brattice (for example, plastic or jute).

(5) Weight of finished product.

(6) Film: type, weight, thickness, supplier, supplier's stock number or designation, and percent of finished product by weight.

(7) Scrim: Type, denier, weight, weave, the supplier, supplier's stock number or designation, and percent of finished product by weight.

(8) Adhesive: type, supplier, supplier's stock number or designation, and percent of finished product by weight.

(b) *Flexible ventilation tubing.* Applications shall include the product description information in paragraph (a) of this section and list the type of supporting structure, if applicable; inside diameters; and configurations.

(c) *Rigid ventilation tubing.* A single application may address two or more products if the products differ only in diameters, lengths, configuration, or average wall thickness. Applications shall include the following information:

(1) Trade name.

(2) Product designations (for example, style and code numbers).

(3) Color.

(4) Type of ventilation tubing (for example, fiberglass, plastic, or polyethylene).

(5) Inside diameter, configuration, and average wall thickness.

Mine Safety and Health Admin., Labor §7.27

(6) Suspension system (for example, metal hooks).

(7) Base material: type, supplier, the supplier's stock number, and percent of finished product by weight.

(8) Resin: type, supplier, the supplier's stock number, and percent of finished product by weight.

(9) Flame retardant, if added during manufacturing: type, supplier, the supplier's stock number, and percent of finished product by weight.

[53 FR 23500, June 22, 1988, as amended at 60 FR 33722, June 29, 1995]

§7.24 Technical requirements.

(a) Brattice cloth shall be flame resistant when tested in accordance with the flame resistance test in §7.27.

(b) Flexible ventilation tubing shall be manufactured using an MSHA-approved brattice cloth. If a supporting structure is used, it shall be metal or other noncombustible material which will not ignite, burn, support combustion or release flammable vapors when subjected to fire or heat.

(c) Rigid ventilation tubing shall be flame resistant when tested in accordance with the flame resistance test in §7.28.

§7.25 Critical characteristics.

A sample of each batch or lot of brattice cloth and ventilation tubing shall be flame tested or a sample of each batch or lot of the materials that contribute to the flame-resistance characteristic shall be inspected or tested to ensure that the finished product will meet the flame-resistance test.

§7.26 Flame test apparatus.

The principal parts of the apparatus used to test for flame-resistance of brattice cloth and ventilation tubing shall be constructed as follows:

(a) A 16-gauge stainless steel gallery lined on the top, bottom and both sides with ½ inch thick Marinite or equivalent insulating material yielding inside dimensions approximately 58 inches long, 41 inches high, and 30 inches wide;

(b) Two ⅜-inch diameter steel J hooks and a 9/16-inch diameter steel rod to support the sample located approximately 2 3/16-inches from the front and back ends of the test gallery, 1½-inches from the ceiling insulation and centrally located in the gallery along its length. Samples shall be suspended to preclude folds or wrinkles;

(c) A tapered 16-gauge stainless steel duct section tapering from a cross sectional area measuring 2 feet 7 inches wide by 3 feet 6 inches high at the test gallery to a cross-sectional area 1 foot 6 inches square over a length of 3 feet. The tapered duct section must be tightly connected to the test gallery;

(d) A 16-gauge stainless steel fan housing, consisting of a 1 foot 6 inches square section 6 inches long followed by a 10 inch long section which tapers from 1 foot 16 inches square to 12 inches diameter round and concluding with a 12 inch diameter round collar 3 inches long. A variable speed fan capable of producing an air velocity of 125 ft./min. in the test gallery must be secured in the fan housing. The fan housing must be tightly connected to the tapered duct section;

(e) A methane-fueled impinged jet burner igniting source, measuring 12 inches long from the threaded ends of the first and last jets and 4 inches wide with 12 impinged jets, approximately 1⅜-inches long and spaced alternately along the length of the burner tube. The burner jets must be canted so that they point toward each other in pairs and the flame from these pairs impinge upon each other.

§7.27 Test for flame resistance of brattice cloth.

(a) *Test procedures.* (1) Prepare 6 samples of brattice cloth 40 inches wide by 48 inches long.

(2) Prior to testing, condition each sample for a minimum of 24 hours at a temperature of 70 ±10 °F (21 ±5.5 °C) and a relative humidity of 55 ±10%.

(3) For each test, suspend the sample in the gallery by wrapping the brattice cloth around the rod and clamping each end and the center. The brattice cloth must hang 4 inches from the gallery floor.

(4) Use a front exhaust system to remove smoke escaping from the gallery. The exhaust system must remain on during all testing, but not affect the air flow in the gallery.

(5) Set the methane-fueled impinged jet burner to yield a flame height of 12

inches as measured at the outermost tip of the flame.

(6) Apply the burner to the front lower edge of the brattice cloth and keep it in contact with the material for 25 seconds or until 1 foot of material, measured horizontally, is consumed, whichever occurs first. If the material shrinks during application of the burner flame, move the burner flame to maintain contact with 1 foot of the material. If melting material might clog the burner orifices, rotate the burner slightly during application of the flame.

(7) Test 3 samples in still air and 3 samples with an average of 125 ft./min. of air flowing past the sample.

(8) Record the propagation length and duration of burning for each of the 6 samples. The duration of burning is the total burning time of the specimen during the flame test. This includes the burn time of any material that falls on the floor of the test gallery during the igniting period. However, the suspended specimen is considered burning only after the burner is removed. Should the burning time of a suspended specimen and a specimen on the floor coincide, count the coinciding burning time only once.

(9) Calculate the average duration of burning for the first 3 samples (still air) and the second 3 samples (125 ft./min. air flow).

(b) *Acceptable performance.* The brattice cloth shall meet each of the following criteria:

(1) Flame propagation of less than 4 feet in each of the six tests.

(2) An average duration of burning of less than 1 minute in both groups of three tests.

(3) A duration of burning not exceeding two minutes in each of the six tests.

[53 FR 23500, June 22, 1988, as amended at 60 FR 33723, June 29, 1995]

§ 7.28 Test for flame resistance of rigid ventilation tubing.

(a) *Test procedures.* (1) Prepare 6 samples of ventilation tubing 48 inches in length with all flared or thickened ends removed. Any sample with a cross-sectional dimension greater than 24 inches must be tested in a 24-inch size.

(2) For each test, suspend the sample in the center of the gallery by running a wire through the 48-inch length of tubing.

(3) Use a front exhaust system to remove smoke escaping from the gallery. The exhaust system must remain on during all testing but not affect the air flow in the gallery.

(4) Set the methane-fueled impinged jet burner to yield a flame height of 12 inches as measured at the outermost tip of the flame.

(5) Apply the burner to the front lower edge of the tubing so that two-thirds of the burner is under the tubing and the remaining third is exposed to allow the flames to curl onto the inside of the tubing. Keep the burner in contact with the material for 60 seconds. If melting material might clog the burner orifices, rotate the burner slightly during application of the flame.

(6) Test 3 samples in still air and 3 samples with an average of 125 ft./min. of air flowing past the sample.

(7) Record the propagation length and duration of burning for each of the 6 samples. The duration of burn is the total burning time of the specimen during the flame test. This includes the burning time of any material that falls on the floor of the test gallery during the igniting period. However, the suspended specimen is considered burning only after the burner is removed. Should the burning time of a suspended specimen and a specimen on the floor coincide, count the coinciding burn time only once.

(8) Calculate the average duration of burning for the first 3 samples (still air) and the second 3 samples (125 ft./min. air flow).

(b) *Acceptable performance.* The ventilation tubing shall meet each of the following criteria:

(1) Flame propagation of less than 4 feet in each of the 6 tests.

(2) An average duration of burning of less than 1 minute in both groups of 3 tests.

(3) A duration of burning not exceeding 2 minutes in each of the 6 tests.

[53 FR 23500, June 22, 1988, as amended at 60 FR 33723, June 29, 1995]

Mine Safety and Health Admin., Labor § 7.44

§ 7.29 Approval marking.

(a) Approved brattice cloth shall be legibly and permanently marked with the assigned MSHA approval number at intervals not exceeding ten feet. If the nature of the material or method of processing makes such marking impractical, permanent paint or ink may be used to mark the edge with an MSHA-assigned color code.

(b) Approved ventilation tubing shall be legibly and permanently marked on each section with the assigned MSHA approval number.

(c) An approved product shall be marketed only under a brand or trade name that has been furnished to MSHA.

§ 7.30 Post-approval product audit.

Upon request by MSHA but no more than once a year except for cause, the approval-holder shall supply to MSHA at no cost up to fifty feet of each approved design of brattice cloth and ventilation tubing for audit.

§ 7.31 New technology.

MSHA may approve brattice cloth and ventilation tubing that incorporates technology for which the requirements of this subpart are not applicable, if the Agency determines that the product is as safe as those which meet the requirements of this subpart.

Subpart C—Battery Assemblies

§ 7.41 Purpose and effective date.

This subpart establishes the specific requirements for MSHA approval of battery assemblies intended for incorporation in approved equipment in underground mines. It is effective August 22, 1988. Applications for approval or extensions of approval submitted after August 22, 1989, shall meet the requirements of this part.

§ 7.42 Definitions.

The following definitions apply in this subpart:

Battery assembly. A unit or units consisting of cells and their electrical connections, assembled in a battery box or boxes with covers.

Battery box. The exterior sides, bottom, and connector receptacle compartment, if any, of a battery assembly, excluding internal partitions.

§ 7.43 Application requirements.

(a) An application for approval of a battery assembly shall contain sufficient information to document compliance with the technical requirements of this subpart and include a composite drawing with the following information:

(1) Overall dimensions of the battery assembly, including the minimum distance from the underside of the cover to the top of the terminals and caps.

(2) Composition and thicknesses of the battery box and cover.

(3) Provision for securing covers.

(4) Documentation of flame-resistance of insulating materials and cables.

(5) Number, type, and rating of the battery cells.

(6) Diagram of battery connections between cells and between battery boxes, except when connections between battery boxes are a part of the machine's electrical system.

(7) Total weight of the battery, charged and ready for service.

(8) Documentation of materials and configurations for battery cells, intercell connectors, filler caps, and battery top:

(i) If nonmetallic cover designs are used with cover support blocks; or

(ii) If the cover comes into contact with any portion of the cells, caps, filler material, battery top, or intercell connectors during the impact test specified by § 7.46.

(b) All drawings shall be titled, dated, numbered, and include the latest revision number.

[53 FR 23500, June 22, 1988, as amended at 60 FR 33723, June 29, 1995]

§ 7.44 Technical requirements.

(a)(1) Battery boxes and covers constructed of AISI 1010 hot rolled steel shall have the following minimum thicknesses based on the total weight of a unit of the battery assembly charged and ready for service:

Weight of battery unit	Minimum required thickness
1,000 lbs. maximum	10 gauge or ⅛″ nominal
1,001 to 2,000 lbs	7 gauge or 3/16″ nominal
2,001 to 4,500 lbs	3 gauge or ¼″ nominal

§ 7.45

Weight of battery unit	Minimum required thickness
Over 4,500 lbs	0 gauge or 5⁄16″ nominal

(2) Battery boxes not constructed of AISI 1010 hot rolled steel shall have at least the tensile strength and impact resistance of battery boxes for the same weight class, as listed in paragraph (a)(1) of this section.

(3) Battery box covers constructed of materials with less than the tensile strength and impact resistance of AISI 1010 hot rolled steel or constructed of nonmetallic materials shall meet the acceptable performance criteria for the impact test in § 7.46. Nonmetallic covers shall be used only in the battery assembly configuration in which they pass the impact test.

(4) Nonmetallic materials for boxes and covers shall—

(i) Be accepted by MSHA as flame-resistant material under part 18 of this chapter; and

(ii) Meet the acceptable performance criteria for the deflection temperature test in § 7.47.

(b) All insulating material shall have a minimum resistance of 100 megohms at 500 volts d.c. and be accepted by MSHA as flame resistant under part 18 of this chapter.

(c) Battery box and cover insulating material shall meet the acceptable performance criteria for the acid resistance test in § 7.48.

(d) Covers shall be lined with insulating material permanently attached to the underside of the cover, unless the cover is constructed of insulating material.

(e) Covers, including those used over connector receptacle housings, shall be provided with a means of securing them in a closed position.

(f) Battery boxes shall be provided with vent openings to prevent the accumulation of flammable or toxic gases or vapors within the battery assembly. The size and location of openings shall prevent direct access to cell terminals and other uninsulated current carrying parts. The total minimum unobstructed cross-sectional area of the ventilation openings shall be no less than the value determined by the following formula:

$$\frac{(N)(R)}{950} = M$$

N = Number of cells in battery box.
R = Rated 6 hour battery capacity in ampere hours.
M = Total minimum ventilation area in square inches per battery box.

(g) Battery boxes shall have drainage holes to prevent accumulation of water or electrolyte.

(h) Battery cells shall be insulated from the battery box walls, partitions and bottom by insulating material, unless such part of the battery box is constructed of insulating material. Battery box wall insulating material shall extend to the top of the wall.

(i) Cell terminals shall be burned on, except that bolted connectors using two or more bolts may be used on end terminals.

(j) Battery connections shall be designed so that total battery potential is not available between adjacent cells.

(k) Cables within a battery box shall be accepted by MSHA as flame resistant under part 18 of this chapter or approved under subpart K of this part. The cables shall be protected against abrasion by insulation, location, clamping, or other effective means.

(l) When the battery plug and receptacle are not located on or within the battery box, strain on the battery terminals shall be prevented by a strain-relief device on the cable. Insulating material shall be placed between the strain-relief device and cable, unless the device is constructed of insulating material.

(m) At least a ½-inch air space shall be provided between the underside of the battery cover and the top of the battery, including the terminals and connectors.

[53 FR 23500, June 22, 1988, as amended at 57 FR 61220, Dec. 23, 1992]

§ 7.45 Critical characteristics

The following critical characteristics shall be inspected or tested on each battery assembly to which an approval marking is affixed:

(a) Thickness of covers and boxes.

(b) Application and resistance of insulating material.

(c) Size and location of ventilation openings.

(d) Method of cell terminations.
(e) Strain relief devices for cables leaving boxes.
(f) Type, location, and physical protection of cables.

§ 7.46 Impact test.

(a) *Test procedures.* (1) Prepare four covers for testing by conditioning two covers at −13 °F (−25 °C) and two covers at 122 °F (50 °C) for a period of 48 hours.

(2) Mount the covers on a battery box of the same design with which the covers are to be approved, including any support blocks, with the battery cells completely assembled. If used, support blocks must contact only the filler material or partitions between the individual cells. At the test temperature range of 65 °F–80 °F (18.3 °C–26.7 °C), apply a dynamic force of 200 ft. lbs. to the following areas using a hemispherical weight with a 6″ maximum radius:

(i) The center of the two largest unsupported areas;
(ii) The areas above at least two support blocks, if used;
(iii) The areas above at least two intercell connectors, one cell, and one filler cap; and
(iv) Areas on at least two corners. If the design consists of both inside and outside corners, test one of each.

(3) Record the condition of the covers, supports, intercell connectors, filler caps, cell covers, and filler material.

(b) *Acceptable performance.* Impact tests of any of the four covers shall not result in any of the following:

(1) Bent intercell connectors.
(2) Cracked or broken filler caps, except plastic tabs which extend from the body of the filler caps.
(3) Cracks in the cell cover, cells, or filler material.
(4) Cracked or bent supports.
(5) Cracked or splintered battery covers.

[53 FR 23500, June 22, 1988, as amended at 60 FR 33723, June 29, 1995]

§ 7.47 Deflection temperature test.

(a) *Test procedures.* (1) Prepare two samples for testing that measure 5 inches by ½ inch, by the thickness of the material as it will be used. Prior to testing, condition the samples at 73.4 ±3.6 °F (23 ±2 °C) and 50 ±5% relative humidity for at least 40 hours.

(2) Place a sample on supports which are 4 inches apart and immersed in a heat transfer medium at a test temperature range of 65 °F–80 °F (18.3 °C–26.7 °C). The heat transfer medium must be a liquid which will not chemically affect the sample. The testing apparatus must be constructed so that expansion of any components during heating of the medium does not result in deflection of the sample.

(3) Place a temperature measuring device with an accuracy of 1% into the heat transfer medium within ⅛ inch of, but not touching, the sample.

(4) Apply a total load, in pounds, numerically equivalent to 11 times the thickness of the sample, in inches, to the sample midway between the supports using a ⅛ inch radius, rounded contact. The total load includes that weight used to apply the load and any force exerted by the deflection measurement device.

(5) Use a deflection measuring device with an accuracy of ±.001 inches to measure the deflection of the sample at the point of loading as the temperature of the medium is increased at a uniform rate of 3.6 ±.36 °F/min. (2 ±0.2 °C/min.). Apply the load to the sample for 5 minutes prior to heating, to allow compensation for creep in the sample due to the loading.

(6) Record the deflection of the sample due to heating at 180 °F (82 °C).

(7) Repeat steps 2 through 6 for the other sample.

(b) *Acceptable performance.* Neither sample shall have a deflection greater than .010 inch at 180 °F (82 °C).

[53 FR 23500, June 22, 1988; 53 FR 25569, July 7, 1988; 60 FR 33723, June 29, 1995]

§ 7.48 Acid resistance test.

(a) *Test procedures.* (1) Prepare one sample each of the insulated surfaces of the battery box and of the cover that measure at least 4 inches by 8 inches, by the thickness of the sample which includes the insulation plus the battery cover or box material. The insulation thickness shall be representative of that used on the battery box and cover. If the insulation material and thickness of material are identical for

§ 7.49

the battery box and cover, only one sample need be prepared and tested.

(2) Prepare a 30 percent solution of sulfuric acid (H_2SO_4) by mixing 853 ml of water with 199 ml of sulfuric acid (H_2SO_4) with a specific gravity of 1.84. Completely cover the samples with the acid solution at the test temperature range of 65 °F – 80 °F (18.3 °C – 26.7 °C) and maintain these conditions for 7 days.

(3) After 7 days, record the condition of the samples.

(b) *Acceptable performance.* At the end of the test, the insulation shall not exhibit any blistering, discoloration, cracking, swelling, tackiness, rubberiness, or loss of bond.

[53 FR 23500, June 22, 1988, as amended at 60 FR 33723, June 29, 1995]

§ 7.49 Approval marking.

Each approved battery assembly shall be identified by a legible and permanent approval plate inscribed with the assigned MSHA approval number and securely attached to the battery box.

§ 7.50 Post-approval product audit.

Upon request by MSHA, but no more than once a year except for cause, the approval-holder shall make an approved battery assembly available for audit at no cost to MSHA.

§ 7.51 Approval checklist.

Each battery assembly bearing an MSHA approval plate shall be accompanied by a description of what is necessary to maintain the battery assembly as approved.

[53 FR 23500, June 22, 1988, as amended at 60 FR 33723, June 29, 1995]

§ 7.52 New technology.

MSHA may approve a battery assembly that incorporates technology for which the requirements of this subpart are not applicable, if the Agency determines that the battery assembly is as safe as those which meet the requirements of this subpart.

Subpart D—Multiple-Shot Blasting Units

SOURCE: 54 FR 48210, Nov. 21, 1989, unless otherwise noted.

§ 7.61 Purpose and effective date.

This subpart establishes the specific requirements for MSHA approval of multiple-shot blasting units. It is effective January 22, 1990. Applications for approval or extensions of approval submitted after January 22, 1991 shall meet the requirements of this subpart.

§ 7.62 Definitions.

The following definitions apply in this subpart:

Blasting circuit. A circuit that includes one or more electric detonators connected in a single series and the firing cable used to connect the detonators to the blasting unit.

Blasting unit. An electric device used to initiate electric detonators.

Normal operation. Operation of the unit according to the manufacturer's instructions with fully-charged batteries, with electric components at any value within their specified tolerances, and with adjustable electric components set to any value within their range.

§ 7.63 Application requirements.

(a) Each application for approval of a blasting unit shall include the following:

(1) An overall assembly drawing showing the physical construction of the blasting unit.

(2) A schematic diagram of the electric circuit.

(3) A parts list specifying each electric component and its electrical ratings, including tolerances.

(4) A layout drawing showing the location of each component and wiring.

(5) The model number or other manufacturer's designation of the blasting unit.

(b) All drawings shall be titled, numbered, dated, and include the latest revision number. The drawings may be combined into one or more composite drawings.

(c) The application shall contain a list of all the drawings submitted, including drawing titles, numbers, and revisions.

(d) A detailed technical description of the operation and use of the blasting unit shall be submitted with the application.

[54 FR 48210, Nov. 21, 1989, as amended at 60 FR 33723, June 29, 1995]

§ 7.64 Technical requirements.

(a) *Energy output.* Blasting units shall meet the acceptable performance criteria of the output energy test in § 7.66.

(b) *Maximum blasting circuit resistance.* The maximum value of the resistance of the blasting circuit that can be connected to the firing line terminals of the blasting unit, without exceeding its capacity, shall be specified by the applicant. The specified maximum blasting circuit resistance shall be at least 150 ohms.

(c) *Visual indicator.* The blasting unit shall provide a visual indication to the user prior to the operation of the firing switch when the voltage necessary to produce the required firing current is attained.

(d) *Firing switch.* The switch used to initiate the application of energy to the blasting circuit shall—

(1) Require deliberate action for its operation to prevent accidental firing; and

(2) Operate only when the voltage necessary to produce the required firing current is available to the blasting circuit.

(e) *Firing line terminals.* The terminals used to connect the blasting circuit to the blasting unit shall—

(1) Provide a secure, low-resistance connection to the blasting circuit as demonstrated by the firing line terminals test in § 7.68;

(2) Be corrosion-resistant;

(3) Be insulated to protect the user from electrical shock; and

(4) Be separated from each other by an insulated barrier.

(f) *Ratings of electric components.* No electric component of the blasting unit, other than batteries, shall be operated at more than 90 percent of any of its electrical ratings in the normal operation of the blasting unit.

(g) *Non-incendive electric contacts.* In the normal operation of a blasting unit, the electric energy discharged by making and breaking electric contacts shall not be capable of igniting a methane-air atmosphere, as determined by the following:

(1) The electric current through an electric contact shall not be greater than that determined from Figure D-1.

(2) The maximum voltage that can be applied across an electric contact that discharges a capacitor shall not be greater than that determined from Figure D-2.

(3) The electric current through an electric contact that interrupts a circuit containing inductive components shall not be greater than that determined from Figure D-3. Inductive components include inductors, chokes, relay coils, motors, transformers, and similar electric components that have an inductance greater than 100 microhenries. No inductive component in a circuit with making and breaking electric contacts shall have an inductance value greater than 100 millihenries.

FIGURE D-1

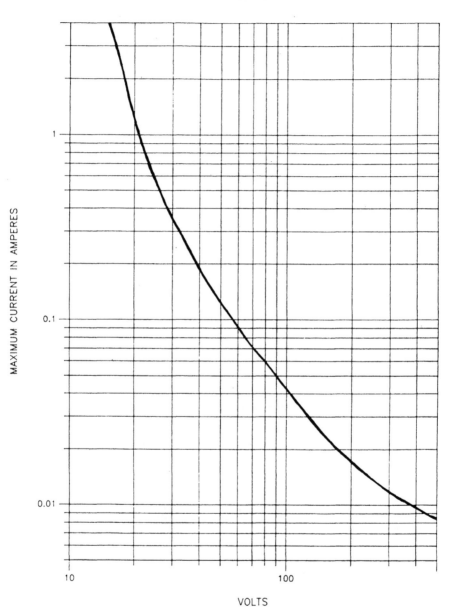

FIGURE D-2

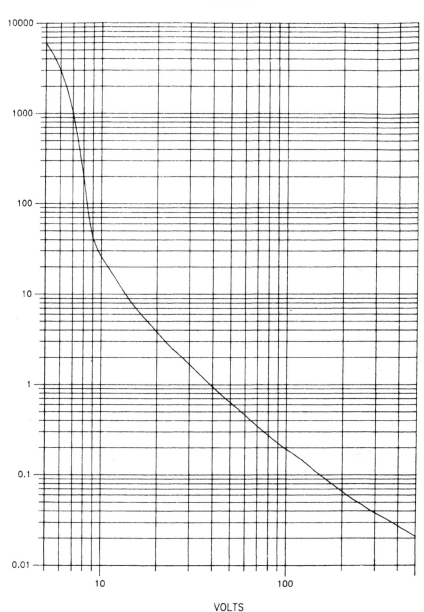

FIGURE D-3

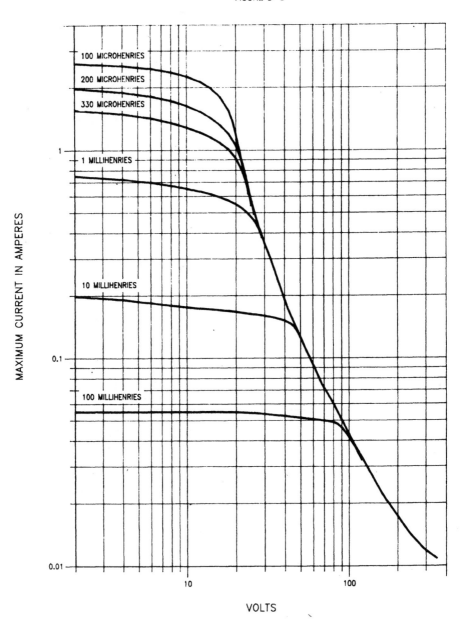

(h) *Maximum temperature.* In the normal operation of the blasting unit, the maximum temperature of any electric component shall not exceed 302 °F (150 °C).

(i) *Capacitor discharge.* The blasting unit shall include an automatic means to dissipate any electric charge remaining in any capacitor after the blasting unit is deenergized and not in use.

(j) *Construction.* Blasting units shall meet the acceptable performance criteria of the construction test of § 7.67.

(k) *Locking device.* The blasting unit shall be equipped with a locking device to prevent unauthorized use.

(l) *Enclosure.* The blasting unit enclosure shall be protected against tampering by—

(1) Sealing the enclosure, except the battery compartment, using continuous welding, brazing, soldering, or equivalent methods; or

(2) Sealing the electric components, other than batteries, in a solidified insulating material and assembling the enclosure with tamper-resistant hardware.

(m) *Battery charging.* Blasting units that contain rechargeable batteries shall have the following:

(1) A blocking diode, or equivalent device, in series with the battery to prevent electric energy in the battery from being available at the charging connector.

(2) The charging connector recessed into the enclosure.

§ 7.65 Critical characteristics.

The following critical characteristics shall be inspected or tested on each blasting unit to which an approval marking is affixed:

(a) The output current.
(b) The voltage cut-off time.
(c) The components that control voltage and current through each making and breaking electric contact.
(d) Operation of the visual indicator and the firing switch.

§ 7.66 Output energy test.

(a) *Test procedures.* The blasting unit shall be tested by firing into each of the following resistive loads, within a tolerance of ±1%:

(1) The maximum blasting circuit resistance.
(2) Any resistive load between 3 ohms and the maximum blasting circuit resistance.
(3) One ohm.

(b) *Acceptable performance.* (1) The voltage shall be zero at the firing line terminals 10 milliseconds after operation of the firing switch.

(2) The electric current from the blasting unit shall be:

(i) Less than 50 milliamperes except during firing of the blasting unit.

(ii) Available only through the firing line terminals.

(iii) At least an average of 2 amperes during the first 5 milliseconds following operation of the firing switch.

(iv) Not exceed an average of 100 amperes during the first 10 milliseconds following operation of the firing switch.

§ 7.67 Construction test.

The construction test is to be performed on the blasting unit subsequent to the output energy test of § 7.66.

(a) *Test procedures.* (1) The blasting unit shall be dropped 20 times from a height of 3 feet onto a horizontal concrete floor. When dropped, the orientation of the blasting unit shall be varied each time in an attempt to have a different surface, corner, or edge strike the floor first for each drop.

(2) After the blasting unit has been drop tested in accordance with paragraph (a)(1) above, it shall be submerged in 1 foot of water for 1 hour in each of 3 tests. The water temperature shall be maintained within ±5 °F (±2.8 °C) of 40 °F (4.4 °C), 70 °F (21.1 °C) and 100 °F (37.8 °C) during the tests.

(3) Immediately after removing the blasting unit from the water at each temperature, the unit shall be operated first with the firing line terminals open circuited, then operated again with the firing line terminals short circuited, and last, the output energy tested in accordance with the output energy test of § 7.66.

(b) *Acceptable performance.* (1) The blasting unit shall meet the acceptable performance criteria of the output energy test in § 7.66 each time it is performed.

(2) There shall be no damage to the firing line terminals that exposes an electric conductor.

(3) The visual indicator shall be operational.

(4) The batteries shall not be separated from the blasting unit.

(g) There shall be no water inside the blasting unit enclosure, except for the battery compartment.

§ 7.68 Firing line terminals test.

(a) *Test procedures.* (1) The contact resistance through each firing line terminal shall be determined.

(2) A 10-pound pull shall be applied to a No. 18 gauge wire that has been connected to each firing line terminal according to the manufacturer's instructions.

(b) *Acceptable performance.* (1) The contact resistance shall not be greater than 1 ohm.

(2) The No. 18 gauge wire shall not become disconnected from either firing line terminal.

§ 7.69 Approval marking.

Each approved blasting unit shall be identified as permissible by a legible and permanent marking securely attached, stamped, or molded to the outside of the unit. This marking shall include the following:

(a) The assigned MSHA approval number.

(b) The maximum blasting circuit resistance.

(c) A warning that the unit's components must not be disassembled or removed.

(d) The replacement battery types if the unit has replaceable batteries.

(e) A warning placed next to the charging connector that the battery only be charged in a fresh air location if rechargeable batteries are used.

(f) A warning that the unit is compatible only with detonators that will—

(1) Fire when an average of 1.5 amperes is applied for 5 milliseconds;

(2) Not misfire when up to an average 100 amperes is applied for 10 milliseconds; and

(3) Not fire when a current of 250 milliamperes or less is applied.

§ 7.70 Post-approval product audit.

Upon request by MSHA, but not more than once a year except for cause, the approval holder shall make an approved blasting unit available for audit at no cost to MSHA.

§ 7.71 Approval checklist.

Each blasting unit bearing an MSHA approval marking shall be accompanied by a description of what is necessary to maintain the blasting unit as approved.

[54 FR 48210, Nov. 21, 1989, as amended at 60 FR 33723, June 29, 1995]

§ 7.72 New technology.

MSHA may approve a blasting unit that incorporates technology for which the requirements of this subpart are not applicable if the Agency determines that the blasting unit is as safe as those which meet the requirements of this subpart.

Subpart E—Diesel Engines Intended for Use in Underground Coal Mines

SOURCE: 61 FR 55504, Oct. 25, 1996, unless otherwise noted.

§ 7.81 Purpose and effective date.

Subpart A general provisions of this part apply to this subpart E. Subpart E establishes the specific engine performance and exhaust emission requirements for MSHA approval of diesel engines for use in areas of underground coal mines where permissible electric equipment is required and areas where non-permissible electric equipment is allowed. It is effective November 25, 1996.

§ 7.82 Definitions.

In addition to subpart A definitions of this part, the following definitions apply in this subpart.

Brake Power. The observed power measured at the crankshaft or its equivalent when the engine is equipped only with standard auxiliaries necessary for its operation on the test bed.

Category A engines. Diesel engines intended for use in areas of underground coal mines where permissible electric equipment is required.

Category B engines. Diesel engines intended for use in areas of underground coal mines where nonpermissible electric equipment is allowed.

Corrosion-resistant material. Material that has at least the corrosion-resistant properties of type 304 stainless steel.

Diesel engine. Any compression ignition internal combustion engine using the basic diesel cycle where combustion results from the spraying of fuel into air heated by compression.

Exhaust emission. Any substance emitted to the atmosphere from the exhaust port of the combustion chamber of a diesel engine.

Intermediate speed. Maximum torque speed if it occurs between 60 percent and 75 percent of rated speed. If the maximum torque speed is less than 60 percent of rated speed, then the intermediate speed shall be 60 percent of the rated speed. If the maximum torque speed is greater than 75 percent of the rated speed, then the intermediate speed shall be 75 percent of rated speed.

Low idle speed. The minimum no load speed as specified by the engine manufacturer.

Maximum torque speed. The speed at which an engine develops maximum torque.

Operational range. All speed and load (including percent loads) combinations from the rated speed to the minimum permitted engine speed at full load as specified by the engine manufacturer.

Particulates. Any material collected on a specified filter medium after diluting exhaust gases with clean, filtered air at a temperature of less than or equal to 125 °F (52 °C), as measured at a point immediately upstream of the primary filter. This is primarily carbon, condensed hydrocarbons, sulfates, and associated water.

Percent load. The fraction of the maximum available torque at an engine speed.

Rated horsepower. The nominal brake power output of a diesel engine as specified by the engine manufacturer with a specified production tolerance. For laboratory test purposes, the fuel pump calibration for the rated horsepower must be set between the nominal and the maximum fuel tolerance specification.

Rated speed. Speed at which the rated power is delivered, as specified by the engine manufacturer.

Steady-state condition. Diesel engine operating condition which is at a constant speed and load and at stabilized temperatures and pressures.

Total oxides of nitrogen. The sum total of the measured parts per millions (ppm) of nitric oxide (NO) plus the measured ppm of nitrogen dioxide (NO_2).

§7.83 Application requirements.

(a) An application for approval of a diesel engine shall contain sufficient information to document compliance with the technical requirements of this subpart and specify whether the application is for a category A engine or category B engine.

(b) The application shall include the following engine specifications—

(1) Model number;

(2) Number of cylinders, cylinder bore diameter, piston stroke, engine displacement;

(3) Maximum recommended air inlet restriction and exhaust backpressure;

(4) Rated speed(s), rated horsepower(s) at rated speed(s), maximum torque speed, maximum rated torque, high idle, minimum permitted engine speed at full load, low idle;

(5) Fuel consumption at rated horsepower(s) and at the maximum rated torque;

(6) Fuel injection timing; and

(7) Performance specifications of turbocharger, if applicable.

(c) The application shall include dimensional drawings (including tolerances) of the following components specifying all details affecting the technical requirements of this subpart. Composite drawings specifying the required construction details may be submitted instead of individual drawings of the following components—

(1) Cylinder head;
(2) Piston;
(3) Inlet valve;
(4) Exhaust valve;
(5) Cam shaft—profile;
(6) Fuel cam shaft, if applicable;
(7) Injector body;
(8) Injector nozzle;
(9) Injection fuel pump;
(10) Governor;
(11) Turbocharger, if applicable;
(12) Aftercooler, if applicable;
(13) Valve guide;

(14) Cylinder head gasket; and
(15) Precombustion chamber, if applicable.

(d) The application shall include a drawing showing the general arrangement of the engine.

(e) All drawings shall be titled, dated, numbered, and include the latest revision number.

(f) When all necessary testing has been completed, the following information shall be submitted:

(1) The gaseous ventilation rate for the rated speed and horsepower.

(2) The particulate index for the rated speed and horsepower.

(3) A fuel deration chart for altitudes for each rated speed and horsepower.

§ 7.84 Technical requirements.

(a) *Fuel injection adjustment.* The fuel injection system of the engine shall be constructed so that the quantity of fuel injected can be controlled at a desired maximum value. This adjustment shall be changeable only after breaking a seal or by altering the design.

(b) *Maximum fuel-air ratio.* At the maximum fuel-air ratio determined by § 7.87 of this part, the concentrations (by volume, dry basis) of carbon monoxide (CO) and oxides of nitrogen (NO_X) in the undiluted exhaust gas shall not exceed the following:

(1) There shall be no more than 0.30 percent CO and no more than 0.20 percent NO_X for category A engines.

(2) There shall be no more than 0.25 percent CO and no more than 0.20 percent NO_X for category B engines.

(c) *Gaseous emissions ventilation rate.* Ventilation rates necessary to dilute gaseous exhaust emissions to the following values shall be determined under § 7.88 of this part:

Carbon dioxide	−5000 ppm
Carbon monoxide	−50 ppm
Nitric oxide	−25 ppm
Nitrogen dioxide	−5 ppm

A gaseous ventilation rate shall be determined for each requested speed and horsepower rating as described in § 7.88(b) of this part.

(d) *Fuel deration.* The fuel rates specified in the fuel deration chart shall be based on the tests conducted under paragraphs (b) and (c) of this section and shall ensure that the maximum fuel:air (f/a) ratio determined under paragraph (b) of this section is not exceeded at the altitudes specified in the fuel deration chart.

(e) *Particulate index.* For each rated speed and horsepower requested, the particulate index necessary to dilute the exhaust particulate emissions to 1 mg/m^3 shall be determined under § 7.89 of this part.

§ 7.85 Critical characteristics.

The following critical characteristics shall be inspected or tested on each diesel engine to which an approval marking is affixed—

(a) Fuel rate is set properly; and

(b) Fuel injection pump adjustment is sealed, if applicable.

§ 7.86 Test equipment and specifications.

(a) Dynamometer test cell shall be used in determining the maximum f/a ratio, gaseous ventilation rates, and the particulate index.

(1) The following testing devices shall be provided:

(i) An apparatus for measuring torque that provides an accuracy of ±2.0 percent based on the engine's maximum value;

(ii) An apparatus for measuring revolutions per minute (rpm) that provides an accuracy of ±2.0 percent based on the engine's maximum value;

(iii) An apparatus for measuring temperature that provides an accuracy of ±4 °F (2 °C) of the absolute value except for the exhaust gas temperature device that provides an accuracy of ±27 °F (15 °C);

(iv) An apparatus for measuring intake and exhaust restriction pressures that provides an accuracy of ±5 percent of maximum;

(v) An apparatus for measuring atmospheric pressure that provides an accuracy of ±0.5 percent of reading;

(vi) An apparatus for measuring fuel flow that provides an accuracy of ±2 percent based on the engine's maximum value;

(vii) An apparatus for measuring the inlet air flow rate of the diesel engine that provides an accuracy of ±2 percent based on the engine's maximum value; and

(viii) For testing category A engines, an apparatus for metering in 1.0 ±0.1

Mine Safety and Health Admin., Labor § 7.86

percent, by volume, of methane (CH_4) into the intake air system shall be provided.

(2) The test fuel specified in Table E-1 shall be a low volatile hydrocarbon fuel commercially designated as "Type 2-D" grade diesel fuel. The fuel may contain nonmetallic additives as follows: Cetane improver, metal deactivator, antioxidant, dehazer, antirust, pour depressant, dye, dispersant, and biocide.

TABLE E-1—DIESEL TEST FUEL SPECIFICATIONS

Item	ASTM	Type 2-D
Cetane number	D613	40–48.
Cetane index	D976	40–48.
Distillation range:		
IBP °F	D86	340–400.
(°C)		(171.1–204.4).
10 pct. point, °F	D86	400–460.
(°C)		(204.4–237.8).
50 pct. point, °F	D86	470.540.
(°C)		(243.3–282.2).
90 pct. point, °F	D86	560–630.
(°C)		(293.3–332.2).
EP, °F	D86	610–690.
(°C)		(321.1–365.6).
Gravity, °API	D287	32–37.
Total sulfur, pct.	D2622	0.03–0.05.
Hydrocarbon composition:		
Aromatics, pct.	D1319	27 minimum.
Paraffins, naphthenes, olefins.	D1319	Remainder.
Flashpoint, minimum, °F	93	130.
(°C)		(54.4).
Viscosity, centistokes	445	2.0–3.2.

(3) The test fuel temperature at the inlet to the diesel engine's fuel injection pump shall be controlled to the engine manufacturer's specification.

(4) The engine coolant temperature (if applicable) shall be maintained at normal operating temperatures as specified by the engine manufacturer.

(5) The charge air temperature and cooler pressure drop (if applicable) shall be set to within ±7 °F(4 °C) and ±0.59 inches Hg (2kPa) respectively, of the manufacturer's specification.

(b) Gaseous emission sampling system shall be used in determining the gaseous ventilation rates.

(1) The schematic of the gaseous sampling system shown in Figure E–1 shall be used for testing category A engines. Various configurations of Figure E–1 may produce equivalent results. The components in Figure E–1 are designated as follows—

(i) Filters—F1, F2, F3, and F4;

(ii) Flowmeters—FL1, FL2, FL3, FL4, FL5, FL6, and FL7;

(iii) Upstream Gauges—G1, G2, and G5;

(iv) Downstream Gauges—G3, G4, and G6;

(v) Pressure Gauges—P1, P2, P3, P4, P5, and P6;

(vi) Regulators—R1, R2, R3, R4, R5, R6, and R7;

(vii) Selector Valves—V1, V2, V3, V4, V6, V7, V8, V15, and V19;

(viii) Heated Selector Valves—V5, V13, V16, and V17;

(ix) Flow Control Valves—V9, V10, V11 and V12;

(x) Heated Flow Control Valves—V14 and V18;

(xi) Pump—Sample Transfer Pump;

(xii) Temperature Sensor—(T1);

(xiii) Dryer—D1 and D2; and

(xiv) Water traps—WT1 and WT2.

(A) Water removal from the sample shall be done by condensation.

(B) The sample gas temperature or dew point shall be monitored either within the water trap or downstream of the water trap and shall not exceed 45 °F (7 °C).

(C) Chemical dryers are not permitted.

§ 7.86

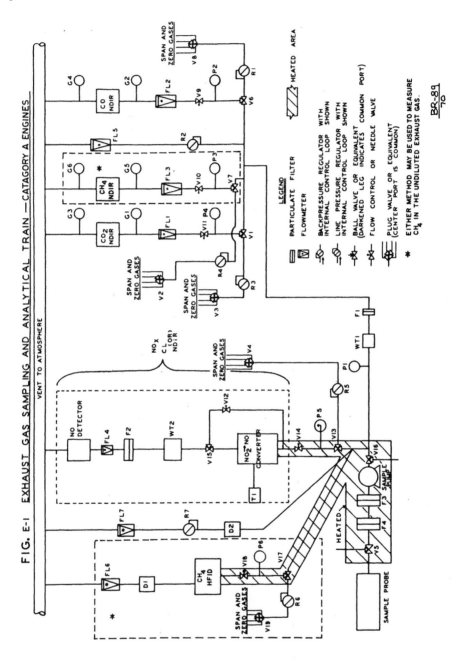

FIG. E-1 EXHAUST GAS SAMPLING AND ANALYTICAL TRAIN—CATAGORY A ENGINES

(2) The schematic of the gaseous sampling system shown in Figure E-2 shall be used for testing category B engines. Various configurations of Figure E-2 may produce equivalent results. The components are designated as follows—
(i) Filters—F1, F2, F3, and F4;

Mine Safety and Health Admin., Labor § 7.86

(ii) Flowmeters—FL1, FL2, FL3, and FL4;

(iii) Upstream Gauges—G1, and G2;

(iv) Downstream Gauges—G3, and G4;

(v) Pressure Gauges—P1, P2, P3, and P4;

(vi) Regulators—R1, R2, R3, and R4;

(vii) Selector Valves—V1, V2, V3, V4, V6, and V7;

(viii) Heated Selector Valves—V5, V8, and V12;

(ix) Flow Control Valves—V9, V10, V11;

(x) Heated Flow Control Valves—V13;

(xi) Pump—Sample Transfer Pump;

(xii) Temperature Sensor—(T1); and

(xiii) Water traps—WT1 and WT2.

(A) Water removal from the sample shall be done by condensation.

(B) The sample gas temperature or dew point shall be monitored either within the water trap or downstream of the water trap and shall not exceed 45 °F (7 °C).

(C) Chemical dryers are not permitted.

(3) All components or parts of components that are in contact with the sample gas or corrosive calibration gases shall be corrosion-resistant material.

§ 7.86

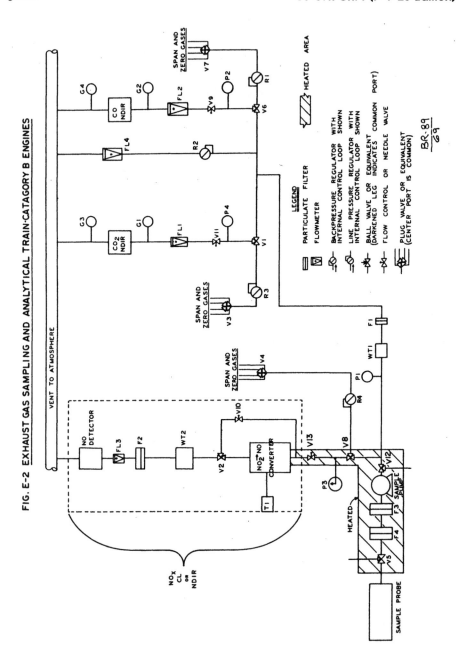

FIG. E-2 EXHAUST GAS SAMPLING AND ANALYTICAL TRAIN-CATAGORY B ENGINES

(4) All analyzers shall obtain the sample to be analyzed from the same sample probe.

(5) CO and CO_2 measurements shall be made on a dry basis.

Mine Safety and Health Admin., Labor §7.86

(6) Calibration or span gases for the NO_X measurement system shall pass through the NO_2 to NO converter.

(7) A stainless steel sample probe shall be straight, closed-end, multi-holed, and shall be placed inside the exhaust pipe.

(i) The probe length shall be at least 80 percent of the diameter of the exhaust pipe.

(ii) The inside diameter of the sample probe shall not be greater than the inside diameter of the sample line.

(iii) The heated sample line shall have a 0.197 inch (5 mm) minimum and a 0.53 inch (13.5 mm) maximum inside diameter.

(iv) The wall thickness of the probe shall not be greater than 0.040 inch (1 mm).

(v) There shall be a minimum of 3 holes in 3 different radial planes sized to sample approximately the same flow.

(8) The sample probe shall be located in the exhaust pipe at a minimum distance of 1.6 feet (0.5 meters) or 3 times the diameter of the exhaust pipe, whichever is the larger, from the exhaust manifold outlet flange or the outlet of the turbocharger. The exhaust gas temperature at the sample probe shall be a minimum of 158 °F (70 °C).

(9) The maximum allowable leakage rate on the vacuum side of the analyzer pump shall be 0.5 percent of the in-use flow rate for the portion of the system being checked.

(10) *General analyzer specifications.* (i) The total measurement error, including the cross sensitivity to other gases, (paragraphs (b)(11)(ii), (b)(12)(iii), (b)(13)(iii), and (b)(13)(iv) of this section), shall not exceed ±5 percent of the reading or ±3.5 percent of full scale, whichever is smaller. For concentrations of less than 100 ppm the measurement error shall not exceed ±4 ppm.

(ii) The repeatability, defined as 2.5 times the standard deviation of 10 repetitive responses to a given calibration or span gas, must be no greater than ±1 percent of full scale concentration for each range used above 155 parts per million (ppm) or parts per million equivalent carbon (ppmC) or ±2 percent of each range used below 155 ppm (or ppmC).

(iii) The analyzer peak to peak response to zero and calibration or span gases over any 10 second period shall not exceed 2 percent of full scale on all ranges used.

(iv) The analyzer zero drift during a 1-hour period shall be less than 2 percent of full scale on the lowest range used. The zero-response is the mean response, including noise, to a zero gas during a 30-second time interval.

(v) The analyzer span drift during a 1-hour period shall be less than 2 percent of full scale on the lowest range used. The analyzer span is defined as the difference between the span response and the zero response. The span response is the mean response, including noise, to a span gas during a 30-second time interval.

(11) *CO and CO_2* analyzer specifications. (i) Measurements shall be made with nondispersive infrared (NDIR) analyzers.

(ii) For the CO analyzer, the water and CO_2 interference shall be less than 1 percent of full scale for ranges equal to or greater than 300 ppm (3 ppm for ranges below 300 ppm) when a CO_2 span gas concentration of 80 percent to 100 percent of full scale of the maximum operating range used during testing is bubbled through water at room temperature.

(12) For NO_X analysis using a chemiluminescence (CL) analyzer the following parameters shall apply:

(i) From the sample point to the NO_2 to NO converter, the NO_X sample shall be maintained between 131 °F (55 °C) and 392 °F (200 °C).

(ii) The NO_2 to NO converter efficiency shall be at least 90 percent.

(iii) The quench interference from CO_2 and water vapor must be less than 3.0 percent.

(13) For NO_X analysis using an NDIR analyzer system the following parameters shall apply:

(i) The system shall include a NO_2 to NO converter, a water trap, and a NDIR analyzer.

(ii) From the sample point to the NO_2 to NO converter, the NO_X sample shall be maintained between 131 °F (55 °C) and 392 °F (200 °C).

(iii) The minimum water rejection ratio (maximum water interference)

§ 7.86

for the NO_X NDIR analyzer shall be 5,000:1.

(iv) The minimum CO_2 rejection ratio (maximum CO_2 interference) for the NO_X NDIR analyzer shall be 30,000:1.

(14) When CH_4 is measured using a heated flame ionization detector (HFID) the following shall apply:

(i) The analyzer shall be equipped with a constant temperature oven that houses the detector and sample-handling components.

(ii) The detector, oven, and sample-handling components shall be suitable for continuous operation at temperatures of 374 °F (190 °C) ±18 °F (10 °C).

(iii) The analyzer fuel shall contain 40 ±2 percent hydrogen. The balance shall be helium. The mixture shall contain ≤1 part per million equivalent carbon (ppmC), and ≤400 ppm CO.

(iv) The burner air shall contain <2 ppmC hydrocarbon.

(v) The percent of oxygen interference shall be less than 5 percent.

(15) An NDIR analyzer for measuring CH_4 may be used in place of the HFID specified in paragraph (b)(14) of this section and shall conform to the requirements of paragraph (b)(10) of this section. Methane measurements shall be made on a dry basis.

(16) Calibration gas values shall be traceable to the National Institute for Standards and Testing (NIST), "Standard Reference Materials" (SRM's). The analytical accuracy of the calibration gas values shall be within 2.0 percent of NIST gas standards.

(17) Span gas values shall be traceable to NIST SRM's. The analytical accuracy of the span gas values shall be within 2.0 percent of NIST gas standards.

(18) Calibration or span gases for the CO and CO_2 analyzers shall have purified nitrogen as a diluent. Calibration or span gases for the CH_4 analyzer shall be CH_4 with purified synthetic air or purified nitrogen as diluent.

(19) Calibration or span gases for the NO_X analyzer shall be NO with a maximum NO_2 concentration of 5 percent of the NO content. Purified nitrogen shall be the diluent.

(20) Zero-grade gases for the CO, CO_2, CH_4, and NO_X analyzers shall be either purified synthetic air or purified nitrogen.

(21) The allowable zero-grade gas (purified synthetic air or purified nitrogen) impurity concentrations shall not exceed ≤1ppm C, ≤1 ppm CO, ≤400 ppm CO_2, and ≤0.1 ppm NO.

(22) The calibration and span gases may also be obtained by means of a gas divider. The accuracy of the mixing device must be such that the concentration of the diluted calibration gases are within 2 percent.

(c) Particulate sampling system shall be used in determining the particulate index. A schematic of a full flow (single dilution) particulate sampling system for testing under this subpart is shown in Figures E-3 and E-4.

(1) The dilution system shall meet the following parameters:

(i) Either a positive displacement pump (PDP) or a critical flow venturi (CFV) shall be used as the pump/mass measurement device shown in Figure E-3.

(ii) The total volume of the mixture of exhaust and dilution air shall be measured.

(iii) All parts of the system from the exhaust pipe up to the filter holder, which are in contact with raw and diluted exhaust gas, shall be designed to minimize deposition or alteration of the particulate.

(iv) All parts shall be made of electrically conductive materials that do not react with exhaust gas components.

(v) All parts shall be electrically grounded to prevent electrostatic effects.

(vi) Systems other than full flow systems may also be used provided they yield equivalent results where:

(A) A seven sample pair (or larger) correlation study between the system under consideration and a full flow dilution system shall be run concurrently.

(B) Correlation testing is to be performed at the same laboratory, test cell, and on the same engine.

(C) The equivalency criterion is defined as a ±5 percent agreement of the sample pair averages.

(2) The mass of particulate in the exhaust shall be collected by filtration. The exhaust temperature immediately

before the primary particulate filter shall not exceed 125 °F (52.0 °C).

(3) Exhaust system backpressure shall not be artificially lowered by the PDP, CFV systems or dilution air inlet system. Static exhaust backpressure measured with the PDP or CFV system operating shall remain within ±0.44 inches Hg (1.5 kPa) of the static pressure measured without being connected to the PDP or CFV at identical engine speed and load.

(4) The gas mixture temperature shall be measured at a point immediately ahead of the pump or mass measurement device.

(i) Using PDP, the gas mixture temperature shall be maintained within ±10 °F (6.0 °C) of the average operating temperature observed during the test, when no flow compensation is used.

(ii) Flow compensation can be used provided that the temperature at the inlet to the PDP does not exceed 122 °F (50 °C).

(iii) Using CFV, the gas mixture temperature shall be maintained within ±20 °F (11 °C) of the average operating temperature observed during the test, when no flow compensation is used.

(5) The heat exchanger shall be of sufficient capacity to maintain the temperature within the limits required above and is optional if electronic flow compensation is used.

(6) When the temperature at the inlet of either the PDP or CFV exceeds the limits stated in either paragraphs (c)(4)(i) or (c)(4)(iii) of this section, an electronic flow compensation system shall be required for continuous measurement of the flow rate and control of the proportional sampling in the particulate sampling system.

(7) The flow capacity of the system shall be large enough to eliminate water condensation.

FIG. E-3 DILUTION TUNNEL/CONSTANT VOLUME SYSTEM

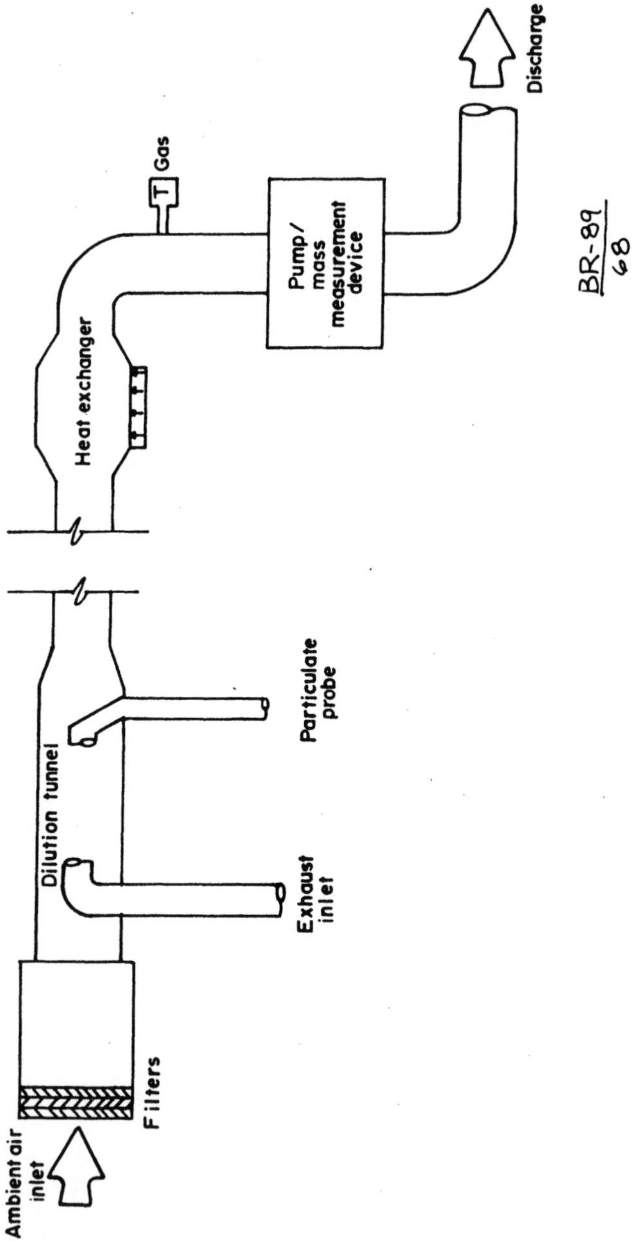

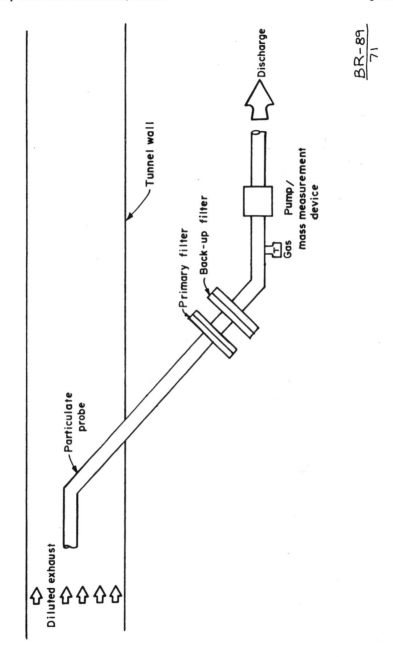

FIG. E-4 PARTICULATE SAMPLING SYSTEM

(8) The flow capacity of the PDP or CFV system using single dilution shall maintain the diluted exhaust at 125 °F (52.0 °C) or less immediately before the primary particulate filter.

(9) The flow capacity of the PDP or CFV system using a double dilution

§ 7.86

system shall be sufficient to maintain the diluted exhaust in the dilution tunnel at 375 °F (191 °C) or less at the sampling zone.

(10) The secondary dilution system shall provide sufficient secondary dilution air to maintain the double-diluted exhaust stream at 125 °F (52.0 °C) or less immediately before the primary particulate filter.

(11) The gas flow meters or the mass flow measurement instrumentation shall have a maximum error of the measured value within ±2 percent of reading.

(12) The dilution air shall have a temperature of 77 °F ±9 °F (25 °C ±5 °C), and be—

(i) Filtered at the air inlet; or

(ii) Sampled to determine background particulate levels, which can then be subtracted from the values measured in the exhaust stream.

(13) The dilution tunnel shall have the following specifications:

(i) Be small enough in diameter to cause turbulent flow (Reynolds number greater than 4,000) and of sufficient length to cause complete mixing of the exhaust and dilution air;

(ii) Be at least 3 inches (75 mm) in diameter; and

(iii) Be configured to direct the engine exhaust downstream at the point where it is introduced into the dilution tunnel for thorough mixing.

(14) The exhaust pipe length from the exit of the engine exhaust manifold or turbocharger outlet to the dilution tunnel shall not exceed a total length of 32 feet (10 m).

(i) When the exhaust pipe exceeds 12 feet (4 m), then all pipe in excess of 12 feet (4 m) shall be insulated with a radial thickness of at least 1.0 inch (25 mm) and the thermal conductivity of the insulating material shall be no greater than 0.1 W/mK measured at 752 °F (400 °C).

(ii) To reduce the thermal inertia of the exhaust pipe, the thickness to diameter ratio shall be 0.015 or less.

(iii) The use of flexible sections shall be limited to the length to diameter ratio of 12 or less.

(15) The particulate sample probe shall—

(i) Be installed in the dilution tunnel facing upstream, on the dilution tunnel centerline, and approximately 10 dilution tunnel diameters downstream of the point where the engine's exhaust enters the dilution tunnel; and

(ii) Have 0.5 inches (12 mm) minimum inside diameter.

(16) The inlet gas temperature to the particulate sample pump or mass measurement device shall remain a constant temperature of ±5 °F (3.0 °C) if flow compensation is not used.

(17) The secondary dilution portion of the double dilution system shall have:

(i) A particulate transfer tube shall have a 0.5 inch (12 mm) minimum inside diameter not to exceed 40 inches (1020 mm) in length measured from the probe tip to the secondary dilution tunnel has:

(A) An inlet with the transfer tube facing upstream in the primary dilution tunnel, centerline, and approximately 10 dilution tunnel diameters downstream of the point where the engine's exhaust enters the dilution tunnel.

(B) An outlet where the transfer tube exits on the centerline of the secondary tunnel and points downstream.

(ii) A secondary tunnel that has a minimum diameter of 3.0 inches (75 mm), and of sufficient length to provide a residence time of at least 0.25 seconds for the double-diluted sample.

(iii) Secondary dilution air supplied at a temperature of 77 °F ±9 °F (25 °C ±5 °C).

(iv) A primary filter holder located within 12.0 inches (300 mm) of the exit of the secondary tunnel.

(18) The particulate sampling filters shall—

(i) Be fluorocarbon-coated glass fiber filters or fluorocarbon-based (membrane) filters and have a 0.3 µm dioctylphthalate (DOP) collection efficiency of at least 95 percent at a gas face velocity between 35 and 80 cm/s.;

(ii) Have a minimum diameter of 1.85 inches (47 mm), 1.46 inches (37 mm) stain diameter;

(iii) Have a minimum filter loading ratio of 0.5mg/1075 mm^2 stain area for the single filter method.

(iv) Have minimum filter loading such that the sum of all eight (8) multiple filters is equal to the minimum loading value (mg) for a single filter multiplied by the square root of eight (8).

(v) Be sampled at the same time by a pair of filters in series (one primary and one backup filter) so that:

(A) The backup filter holder shall be located no more than 4 inches (100 mm) downstream of the primary filter holder.

(B) The primary and backup filters shall not be in contact with each other.

(C) The filters may be weighed separately or as a pair with the filters placed stain side to stain side.

(D) The single filter method incorporates a bypass system for passing the sample through the filters at the desired time.

(vi) Have a pressure drop increase between the beginning and end of the test of no more than 7.4 in Hg (25kPa).

(vii) Filters of identical quality shall be used when performing correlation tests specified in paragraph (c)(1)(vi) of this section.

(19) *Weighing chamber specifications.* (i) The temperature of the chamber (room) in which the particulate filters are conditioned and weighed shall be maintained to within 72 °F ±5 °F (22 °C ±3 °C) during all filter conditioning and weighing.

(ii) The humidity of the chamber (room) in which the particulate filters are conditioned and weighed shall be maintained to a dewpoint of 49 °F ±5 °F (9.5 °C ±3 °C) and a relative humidity of 45 percent ±8 percent during all filter conditioning and weighing.

(iii) The chamber (room) environment shall be free of any ambient contaminants (such as dust) that would settle on the particulate filters during their stabilization. This shall be determined as follows:

(A) At least two unused reference filters or reference filter pairs shall be weighed within four (4) hours of, but preferably at the same time as the sample filter (pair) weighings.

(B) The reference filters are to be the same size and material as the sample filters.

(C) If the average weight of reference filters (reference filter pairs) changes between sample filter weighings by more than ±5.0 percent (±7.5 percent for the filter pair respectively) of the recommended minimum filter loading in paragraphs (c)(18)(iii) or (c)(18)(iv) of this section, then all sample filters shall be discarded and the tests repeated.

(20) The analytical balance used to determine the weights of all filters shall have a precision (standard deviation) of 20 µg and resolution of 10 µg. For filters less than 70 mm diameter, the precision and resolution shall be 2 µg and 1 µg, respectively.

(21) All filters shall be neutralized to eliminate the effects of static electricity prior to weighing.

§ 7.87 **Test to determine the maximum fuel-air ratio.**

(a) *Test procedure.* (1) Couple the diesel engine to the dynamometer and connect the sampling and measurement devices specified in § 7.86.

(2) Prior to testing, zero and span the CO and NO_X analyzers to the lowest analyzer range that will be used during this test.

(3) While running the engine, the following shall apply:

(i) The parameter for the laboratory atmospheric factor, f_a, shall be: $0.98 \leq f_a \leq 1.02$;

(A) The equation is $f_a = (99/P_s) * ((T_a + 273)/298)^{0.7}$ for a naturally aspirated and mechanically supercharged engines; or

(B) The equation is $f_a = (99/P_s)^{0.7} * ((T_a + 273)/298)^{1.5}$ for a turbocharged engine with or without cooling of the intake air.

Where:

P_s = dry atmospheric pressure (kPa)
T_a = intake air temperature (°C)

(ii) The air inlet restriction shall be set within ±10 percent of the recommended maximum air inlet restriction as specified by the engine manufacturer at the engine operating condition giving maximum air flow to determine the concentration of CO as specified in paragraph (a)(6) of this section.

(iii) The exhaust backpressure restriction shall be set within ±10 percent of the maximum exhaust backpressure as specified by the engine manufacturer at the engine operating condition giving maximum rated horsepower to determine the concentrations of CO and NO_X as specified in paragraph (a)(6) of this section.

§ 7.88

(iv) The air inlet restriction shall be set within ±10 percent of a recommended clean air filter at the engine operating condition giving maximum air flow as specified by the engine manufacturer to determine the concentration of NO_X as specified in paragraph (a)(6) of this section.

(4) The engine shall be at a steady-state condition when the exhaust gas samples are collected and other test data is measured.

(5) In a category A engine, 1.0 ±0.1 percent CH_4 shall be injected into the engine's intake air.

(6) Operate the engine at several speed/torque conditions to determine the concentrations of CO and NO_X, dry basis, in the raw exhaust.

(b) *Acceptable performance.* The CO and NO_X concentrations in the raw exhaust shall not exceed the limits specified in § 7.84(b) throughout the specified operational range of the engine.

§ 7.88 Test to determine the gaseous ventilation rate.

The test shall be performed in the order listed in Table E-2. The test for determination of the particulate index described in § 7.89 may be done simultaneously with this test.

(a) *Test procedure.* (1) Couple the diesel engine to the dynamometer and attach the sampling and measurement devices specified in § 7.86.

(2) A minimum time of 10 minutes is required for each test mode.

(3) CO, CO_2, NO_X, and CH_4 analyzers shall be zeroed and spanned at the analyzer range to be used prior to testing.

(4) Run the engine.

(i) The parameter for f_a shall be calculated in accordance with § 7.87(a)(3).

(ii) The air inlet and exhaust backpressure restrictions on the engine shall be set as specified in §§ 7.87(a)(3) (iii) and (iv).

(5) The engine shall be at a steady-state condition before starting the test modes.

(i) The output from the gas analyzers shall be measured and recorded with exhaust gas flowing through the analyzers a minimum of the last three (3) minutes of each mode.

(ii) To evaluate the gaseous emissions, the last 60 seconds of each mode shall be averaged.

(iii) A 1.0 ±0.1 percent CH_4, by volume, shall be injected into the engine's intake air for category A engines.

(iv) The engine speed and torque shall be measured and recorded at each test mode.

(v) The data required for use in the gaseous ventilation calculations specified in paragraph (a)(9) of this section shall be measured and recorded at each test mode.

(6) Operate the engine at each rated speed and horsepower rating requested by the applicant according to Table E-2 in order to measure the raw exhaust gas concentration, dry basis, of CO, CO_2, NO, and NO_2, and CH_4- exhaust (category A engines only).

(i) Test speeds shall be maintained within ±1 percent of rated speed or ±3 RPM, which ever is greater, except for low idle which shall be within the tolerances established by the manufacturer.

(ii) The specified torque shall be held so that the average over the period during which the measurements are taken is within ±2 percent of the maximum torque at the test speed.

(7) The concentration of CH_4 in the intake air shall be measured for category A engines.

TABLE E-2—GASEOUS TEST MODES

Speed	Rated speed				Intermediate speed			Low-idle speed
% Torque	100	75	50	10	100	75	50	0

(8) After completion of the test modes, the following shall be done:

(i) Zero and span the analyzers at the ranges used during the test.

(ii) The gaseous emission test shall be acceptable if the difference in the zero and span results taken before the test and after the test are less than 2 percent.

(9) The gaseous ventilation rate for each exhaust gas contaminant shall be calculated as follows—

(i) The following abbreviations shall apply to both category A and category B engine calculations as appropriate:

cfm—Cubic feet per min (ft³/min)
Exh—Exhaust
A—Air (lbs/hr)
H—Grains of water per lb. of dry intake air
J—Conversion factor
m—Mass flow rate (mass/hr)
TI—Intake air temperature (°F)
PCAir—Percent Air
PCCH$_4$—Percent CH$_4$ (intake air)
UCH$_4$—Unburned CH$_4$
PCECH$_4$—Percent Exhaust CH$_4$

(ii) Exhaust gas flow calculation for category B engines shall be (m Exh) = (A) + (m fuel).

(iii) Fuel/air ratio for category B engines shall be (f/a) = (m fuel) / (A).

(iv) Methane flow through category A engines shall be determined by the following:

PCAir = 100 − PCCH$_4$
Y = (PCAir)(0.289) + (PCCH$_4$)(0.16)
Z = (0.16)(PCCH$_4$) + Y
mCH$_4$ = (A)(Z) ÷ (1 − Z)

(v) Exhaust gas flow calculation for category A engines shall be (m Exh) = (A) + (m fuel) + (m CH$_4$)

(vi) Unburned CH$_4$ (lbs/hr) calculation for category A engines shall be mUCH$_4$ = (m Exh)(0.0052)(PCECH$_4$)

(vii) Fuel/air ratio for category A engines shall be (f/a) = ((m fuel) + (m CH$_4$) − (m UCH$_4$)) ÷ (A)

(viii) Conversion from dry to wet basis for both category A and category B engines shall be:

(NO wet basis) = (NO dry basis)(J)
(NO$_2$ wet basis) = (NO$_2$ dry basis)(J)
(CO$_2$ wet basis) = (CO$_2$ dry basis)(J)
(CO wet basis) = (CO dry basis)(10^{-4})(J)

Where:

J = (f/a)(−1.87) + (1 − (0.00022)(H))

(ix) NO and NO$_2$ correction for humidity and temperature for category A and category B engines shall be:

(NO corr) = (NO wet basis) ÷ (E)
(NO$_2$ corr) = (NO$_2$ wet basis) ÷ (E)

Where:

E = 1.0 + (R)(H − 75) + (G)(TI − 77)
R = (f/a)(0.044) − (0.0038)
G = (f/a)(−0.116) + (0.0053)

(x) The calculations to determine the m of each exhaust gas contaminant in grams per hour at each test point shall be as follows for category A and category B engines:

(m NO) = (NO corr)(0.000470)(m Exh)
(m NO$_2$) = (NO$_2$ corr)(0.000720)(m Exh)
(m CO$_2$) = (CO$_2$ wet basis)(6.89)(m Exh)
(m CO) = (CO wet basis)(4.38)(m Exh)

(xi) The calculations to determine the ventilation rate for each exhaust gas contaminant at each test point shall be as follows for category A and category B engines:

(cfm NO) = (m NO)(K)
(cfm NO$_2$) = (m NO$_2$)(K)
(cfm CO$_2$) = (m CO$_2$)(K)
(cfm CO) = (m CO)(K)

Where:

K = 13,913.4/ (pollutant grams/mole) (pollutant dilution value specified in §7.84(c)).

(b) The gaseous ventilation rate for each requested rated speed and horsepower shall be the highest ventilation rate calculated in paragraph (a)(9)(xi) of this section.

(1) Ventilation rates less than 20,000 cfm shall be rounded up to the next 500 cfm.

Example: 10,432 cfm shall be listed 10,500 cfm.

(2) Ventilation rates greater than 20,000 cfm shall be rounded up to the next 1,000 cfm.

Example: 26,382 cfm shall be listed 27,000 cfm.

[61 FR 55504, Oct. 25, 1996; 62 FR 34640, June 27, 1997]

§ 7.89 Test to determine the particulate index.

The test shall be performed in the order listed in Table E–3.

(a) *Test procedure.* (1) Couple the diesel engine to the dynamometer and connect the sampling and measurement devices specified in § 7.86.

(2) A minimum time of 10 minutes is required for each measuring point.

(3) Prior to testing, condition and weigh the particulate filters as follows:

(i) At least 1 hour before the test, each filter (pair) shall be placed in a closed, but unsealed, petri dish and placed in a weighing chamber (room) for stabilization.

§ 7.89

(ii) At the end of the stabilization period, each filter (pair) shall be weighed. The reading is the tare weight.

(iii) The filter (pair) shall then be stored in a closed petri dish or a filter holder, both of which shall remain in the weighing chamber (room) until needed for testing.

(iv) The filter (pair) must be reweighed if not used within 8 hours of its removal from the weighing chamber (room).

(4) Run the engine.

(i) The parameter for f_a shall be calculated in accordance with § 7.87(a)(3).

(ii) The air inlet and exhaust backpressure restrictions on the engine shall be set as specified in §§ 7.87(a)(3) (iii) and (iv).

(iii) The dilution air shall be set to obtain a maximum filter face temperature of 125 °F (52 °C) or less at each test mode.

(iv) The total dilution ratio shall not be less than 4.

(5) The engine shall be at a steady state condition before starting the test modes.

(i) The engine speed and torque shall be measured and recorded at each test mode.

(ii) The data required for use in the particulate index calculation specified in paragraph (a)(9) of this section shall be measured and recorded at each test mode.

(6) A 1.0 ±0.1 percent CH_4, by volume shall be injected into the engine's intake air for category A engines.

(7) Operate the engine at each rated speed and horsepower rating requested by the applicant according to Table E-3 to collect particulate on the primary filter.

(i) One pair of single filters shall be collected or eight multiple filter pairs shall be collected.

(ii) Particulate sampling shall be started after the engine has reached a steady-state condition.

(iii) The sampling time required per mode shall be either a minimum of 20 seconds for the single filter method or a minimum of 60 seconds for the multiple filter method.

(iv) The minimum particulate loading specified in §§ 7.86(c)(18) (iii) or (iv) shall be done.

TABLE E–3—PARTICULATE TEST MODES

Speed	Rated speed				Intermediate speed			Low-idle speed
% Torque	100	75	50	10	100	75	50	0
Weighting factor	0.15	0.15	0.15	0.1	0.1	0.1	0.1	0.15

(v) Test speeds shall be maintained within ±percent of rated speed or ±3 RPM, which ever is greater, except for low idle which shall be within the tolerances set by the manufacturer.

(vi) The specified torque shall be held so that the average over the period during which the measurements are being taken is within ±2 percent of the maximum torque at the test speed.

(vii) The modal weighting factors (WF) given in Table E-3 shall be applied to the multiple filter method during the calculations as shown in paragraph (a)(9)(iii)(B) of this section.

(viii) For the single filter method, the modal WF shall be taken into account during sampling by taking a sample proportional to the exhaust mass flow for each mode of the cycle.

(8) After completion of the test, condition and weigh the particulate filters in the weighing chamber (room) as follows:

(i) Condition the filters for at least 1 hour, but not more than 80 hours.

(ii) At the end of the stabilization period, weigh each filter. The reading is the gross weight.

(iii) The particulate mass of each filter is its gross weight minus its tare weight.

(iv) The particulate mass (P_F for the single filter method; $P_{F,i}$ for the multiple filter method) is the sum of the particulate masses collected on the primary and back-up filters.

(v) The test is void and must be rerun if the sample on the filter contacts the petri dish or any other surface.

(9) The particulate index for the mass particulate shall be calculated from the equations listed below—
(i) The following abbreviations shall be:

cfm—Cubic feet per min (ft³ min)
PT—Particulate (gr/hr)
m mix—Diluted exhaust gas mass flow rate on wet basis (kg/hr)
m sample—Mass of the diluted exhaust sample passed through the particulate sampling filters (kg)
P_f—Particulate sample mass collected on a filter (mg) at each test mode as determined in Table E-3.
K_p—Humidity correction factor for particulate
WF—Weighting factor
i-Subscript denoting an individual mode, i = 1, ... n
PI—Particulate Index (cfm)

(ii) When calculating ambient humidity correction for the particulate concentration (P_f part), the equation shall be:

$P_{fcorr} = (P_f)(K_p)$
$K_p = 1 / (1 + 0.0133 * (H - 10.71))$

Where:

H_a = humidity of the intake air, g water per kg dry air
$H_a = (6.220 * R_a * p_a) / (p_B - p_a - R_a * 10^{-2})$
R_a = relative humidity of the intake air, %
p_a = saturation vapor pressure of the intake air, kPa
p_B = total barometric pressure, kPa

(iii) When the multiple filter method is used, the following equations shall be used.
(A) Mass of particulate emitted is calculated as follows:

$$\text{PT gr}/\text{hr}_i = \frac{(P_{fcorr}\, mg_i)(m\ mix\ kg/hr_i)}{(m\ sample\ kg_i)(1000\ mg/gr)}$$

(B) Determination of weighted particulate average is calculated as follows:

$$\text{PT gr}/\text{hr} = \sum_{i=1}^{i=n} (\text{PT gr}/\text{hr}_i)(WF_i)$$

(C) Determination of particulate index for the mass particulate from the average of the test modes shall be calculated as follows:

$$PI = \frac{(\text{PT gr}/\text{hr})(1000\ mg/gr)(1\ hr/60\ min)(35.31\ ft^3/m^3)}{(1/1\ mg/m^3)}$$

(iv) When the single filter method is used, the following equations shall be used.

(A) Mass of particulate emitted:

$$\text{PT gr/hr} = \frac{(P_{fcorr}\ mg)(m\ mix\ kg/hr)\,avg.}{(m\ sample\ kg)(1000\ mg/gr)}$$

§ 7.90

Where:

$$(\text{m mix kg / hr}) \text{ avg.} = \sum_{i=1}^{i=n} (\text{m mix kg / hr}_i)(WF_i)$$

$$(\text{m sample kg}) = \sum_{i=1}^{i=n} (\text{m sample kg}_i)$$

(B) Determination of particulate index for the mass particulate from the average of the test modes shall be as follows:

$$PI = \frac{(PT \text{ gr /hr})(1000 \text{ mg /gr})(1 \text{ hr /60 min})(35.31 \text{ ft}^3 / m^3)}{(1/1 \text{ mg /m}^3)}$$

(v) When the effective weighting factor, $WF_{E,i}$, for each mode is calculated for the single filter method, the following shall apply.

(A) $$WF_{E,i} = \frac{(\text{m sample kg}_i)(\text{m mix kg /hr avg})}{(\text{m sample kg})(\text{m mix kg /hr}_i)}$$

(B) The value of the effective weighting factors shall be within ±0.005 (absolute value) of the weighting factors listed in Table E-3.

(b) A particulate index for each requested rated speed and horsepower shall be the value determined in paragraph (a)(9)(iii)(C) of this section for the multiple filter method or paragraph (a)(9)(iv)(B) of this section for the single filter method.

(1) Particulate indices less than 20,000 cfm shall be rounded up to the next 500 cfm. Example: 10,432 cfm shall be listed 10,500 cfm.

(2) Particulate indices greater than 20,000 cfm shall be rounded up to the nearest thousand 1,000 cfm. Example: 26,382 cfm shall be listed 27,000 cfm.

[61 FR 55504, Oct. 25, 1996; 62 FR 34640, June 27, 1997]

§ 7.90 Approval marking.

Each approved diesel engine shall be identified by a legible and permanent approval marking inscribed with the assigned MSHA approval number and securely attached to the diesel engine. The marking shall also contain the following information:

(a) Ventilation rate.
(b) Rated power.
(c) Rated speed.
(d) High idle.
(e) Maximum altitude before deration.
(f) Engine model number.

§ 7.91 Post-approval product audit.

Upon request by MSHA, but no more than once a year except for cause, the approval holder shall make a diesel engine available for audit at no cost to MSHA.

§ 7.92 New technology.

MSHA may approve a diesel engine that incorporates technology for which the requirements of this subpart are not applicable if MSHA determines that the diesel engine is as safe as those which meet the requirements of this subpart.

Subpart F—Diesel Power Packages Intended for Use in Areas of Underground Coal Mines Where Permissible Electric Equipment is Required

SOURCE: 61 FR 55518, Oct. 25, 1996, unless otherwise noted.

§ 7.95 Purpose and effective date.

Part 7, subpart A general provisions apply to subpart F. Subpart F establishes the specific requirements for MSHA approval of diesel power packages intended for use in approved equipment in areas of underground coal mines where electric equipment is required to be permissible. It is effective November 25, 1996.

§ 7.96 Definitions.

In addition to the definitions in subparts A and E of this part, the following definitions apply in this subpart.

Cylindrical joint. A joint comprised of two contiguous, concentric, cylindrical surfaces.

Diesel power package. A diesel engine with an intake system, exhaust system, and a safety shutdown system installed.

Dry exhaust conditioner. An exhaust conditioner that cools the exhaust gas without direct contact with water.

Exhaust conditioner. An enclosure, containing a cooling system, through which the exhaust gases pass.

Exhaust system. A system connected to the outlet of the diesel engine which includes, but is not limited to, the exhaust manifold, the exhaust pipe, the exhaust conditioner, the exhaust flame arrester, and any adapters between the exhaust manifold and exhaust flame arrester.

Fastening. A bolt, screw, or stud used to secure adjoining parts to prevent the escape of flame from the diesel power package.

Flame arrester. A device so constructed that flame or sparks from the diesel engine cannot propagate an explosion of a flammable mixture through it.

Flame arresting path (explosion-proof joint). Two or more adjoining or adjacent surfaces between which the escape of flame is prevented.

Flammable mixture. A mixture of methane or natural gas with normal air, that will propagate flame or explode when ignited.

Grade. The slope of an incline expressed as a percent.

High idle speed. The maximum no load speed specified by the engine manufacturer.

Intake system. A system connected to the inlet of the diesel engine which includes, but is not limited to, the intake manifold, the intake flame arrester, the emergency intake air shutoff device, the air cleaner, and all piping and adapters between the intake manifold and air cleaner.

Plane joint. A joint comprised of two adjoining surfaces in parallel planes.

Safety shutdown system. A system which, in response to signals from various safety sensors, recognizes the existence of a potential hazardous condition and automatically shuts off the fuel supply to the engine.

Step (rabbet) joint. A joint comprised of two adjoining surfaces with a change or changes in direction between its inner and outer edges. A step joint may be composed of a cylindrical portion and a plane portion or of two or more plane portions.

Threaded joint. A joint consisting of a male- and female-threaded member, both of which are the same type and gauge.

Wet exhaust conditioner. An exhaust conditioner that cools the exhaust gas through direct contact with water, commonly called a water scrubber.

§ 7.97 Application requirements.

(a) An application for approval of a diesel power package shall contain sufficient information to document compliance with the technical requirements of this subpart and include:

§ 7.97

drawings, specifications, and descriptions with dimensions (including tolerances) demonstrating compliance with the technical requirements of § 7.98. The specifications and descriptions shall include the materials of construction and quantity. These shall include the following—

(1) A general arrangement drawing showing the diesel power package and the location and identification of the intake system, exhaust system, safety shutdown system sensors, flame arresters, exhaust conditioner, emergency intake air shutoff device, automatic fuel shutoff device and the engine.

(2) Diesel engine specifications including the MSHA approval number, the engine manufacturer, the engine model number, and the rated speed, rated horsepower, and fuel rate.

(3) A drawing(s) which includes the fan blade material specifications, the location and identification of all water-cooled components, coolant lines, radiator, surge tank, temperature sensors, and orifices; arrows indicating proper flow direction; the height relationship of water-cooled components to the surge tank; and the proper procedure for filling the cooling system.

(4) A drawing(s) showing the relative location, identification of components, and design of the safety shutdown system.

(5) Specific component identification, or specific information including detail drawings that identify the characteristics of the cooling system and safety shutdown system that ensures compliance with the technical requirements.

(6) Detail drawings of gaskets used to form flame-arresting paths.

(7) An assembly drawing showing the location and identification of all intake system components from the air cleaner to the engine head.

(8) An assembly drawing showing the location and identification of all exhaust system components from the engine head to the exhaust outlet.

(9) Detail drawings of those intake and exhaust system components identified in paragraphs (a)(7) and (a)(8) of this section that ensure compliance with the technical requirements. An exhaust conditioner assembly drawing shall be provided showing the location, dimensions, and identification of all internal parts, exhaust inlet and outlet, sensors, and the exhaust gas path through the exhaust conditioner. If a wet exhaust conditioner is used, the exhaust conditioner assembly drawing must also show the location, dimensions, and identification of the fill port, drain port, low water check port; high or normal operating water level; minimum allowable low water level; and the maximum allowable grade that maintains explosion-proof operations.

(10) A power package checklist which shall consist of a list of specific features that must be checked and tests that must be performed to determine if a previously approved diesel power package is in approved condition. Test procedures shall be specified in sufficient detail to allow the evaluation to be made without reference to other documents. Illustrations shall be used to fully identify the approved configuration of the diesel power package.

(11) Information showing that the electrical systems and components meet the requirements of § 7.98.

(12) A drawing list consisting of a complete list of those drawings and specifications which show the details of the construction and design of the diesel power package.

(b) Composite drawings specifying the required construction details may be submitted instead of the individual drawings in paragraph (a) of this section.

(c) All documents shall be titled, dated, numbered, and include the latest revision.

(d) When all testing has been completed, the following information shall be submitted and become part of the approval documentation:

(1) The settings of any adjustable devices used to meet the performance requirements of this subpart.

(2) The coolant temperature sensor setting and exhaust gas temperature sensor setting used to meet the performance requirements of this subpart.

(3) The minimum allowable low water level and the low water sensor setting used to meet the performance requirements of this subpart for systems using a wet exhaust conditioner as the exhaust flame arrester.

Mine Safety and Health Admin., Labor § 7.98

(4) The maximum grade on which the wet exhaust conditioner can be operated retaining the flame arresting characteristics.

(5) A finalized version of the power package checklist.

§ 7.98 Technical requirements.

(a) The diesel power package shall use a category A diesel engine approved under subpart E of this part with the following additional requirements:

(1) A hydraulic, pneumatic, or other mechanically actuated starting mechanism. Other means of starting shall be evaluated in accordance with the provisions of § 7.107.

(2) If an air compressor is provided, the intake air line shall be connected to the engine intake system between the air cleaner and the flame arrester. If the air compressor's inlet air line is not connected to the engine's intake system, it shall have an integral air filter.

(b) The temperature of any external surface of the diesel power package shall not exceed 302 °F (150 °C).

(1) Diesel power package designs using water jacketing to meet this requirement shall be tested in accordance with § 7.101.

(2) Diesel power packages using other techniques will be evaluated under the provisions of § 7.107.

(3) When using water-jacketed components, provisions shall be made for positive circulation of coolant, venting of the system to prevent the accumulation of air pockets, and effective activation of the safety shutdown system before the temperature of the coolant in the jackets exceeds the manufacturer's specifications or 212 °F (100 °C), whichever is lower.

(c) External rotating parts shall not be constructed of aluminum alloys containing more than 0.6 percent magnesium.

(d) If nonmetallic rotating parts are used, they shall be provided with a means to prevent an accumulation of static electricity. Static conducting materials shall have a total resistance of 1 megohm or less, measured with an applied potential of 500 volts or more. Static conducting materials having a total resistance greater than 1 megohm will be evaluated under the provisions of § 7.107.

(e) All V-belts shall be static conducting and have a resistance not exceeding 6 megohms, when measured with a direct current potential of 500 volts or more.

(f) The engine crankcase breather shall not be connected to the air intake system of the engine. The discharge from the breather shall be directed away from hot surfaces of the engine and exhaust system.

(g) Electrical components on diesel power packages shall be certified or approved by MSHA under parts 7, 18, 20, and 27 of this chapter.

(h) Electrical systems on diesel power packages consisting of electrical components, interconnecting wiring, and mechanical and electrical protection shall meet the requirements of parts 7, 18, and 27 of this chapter, as applicable.

(i) The diesel power package shall be equipped with a safety shutdown system which will automatically shut off the fuel supply and stop the engine in response to signals from sensors indicating—

(1) The coolant temperature limit specified in paragraph (b) of this section;

(2) The exhaust gas temperature limit specified in paragraph (s)(4) of this section;

(3) The minimum allowable low water level, for a wet exhaust conditioner, as established by tests in § 7.100. Restarting of the engine shall be prevented until the water level in the wet exhaust conditioner has been replenished above the minimum allowable low water level; and

(4) The presence of other safety hazards such as high methane concentration, actuation of the fire suppression system, etc., if such sensors are included in the safety shutdown system.

(j) The safety shutdown system shall have the following features:

(1) A means to automatically disable the starting circuit and prevent engagement of the starting mechanism while the engine is running, or a starting mechanism constructed of non-sparking materials.

(2) If the design of the safety shutdown system requires that the lack of

§ 7.98

engine oil pressure must be overridden to start the engine, the override shall not be capable of overriding any of the safety shutdown sensors specified in paragraph (i) of this section.

(k) The diesel power package shall be explosion-proof as determined by the tests set out in § 7.100.

(l) Engine joints that directly or indirectly connect the combustion chamber to the surrounding atmosphere shall be explosion-proof in accordance with paragraphs (m) through (q) of this section and § 7.100. This paragraph does not apply to the following:

(1) Pistons to piston rings;
(2) Pistons to cylinder walls;
(3) Piston rings to cylinder walls;
(4) Cylinder head to cylinder block;
(5) Valve stem to valve guide; or
(6) Injector body to cylinder head.

(m) Each segment of the intake system and exhaust system required to provide explosion-proof features shall be constructed of metal and designed to withstand a minimum internal pressure equal to four times the maximum pressure observed in that segment in tests under § 7.100 or a pressure of 150 psig, whichever is less. Castings shall be free from blowholes.

(n) Welded joints forming the explosion-proof intake and exhaust systems shall be continuous and gas-tight. At a minimum, they shall be made in accordance with American Welding Society Standard D14.4–77 or meet the test requirements of § 7.104 with the internal pressure equal to four times the maximum pressure observed in tests under § 7.100 or a pressure of 150 psig, whichever is less.

(o) Flexible connections shall be permitted in segments of the intake and exhaust systems required to provide explosion-proof features, provided that failure of the connection activates the safety shutdown system before the explosion-proof characteristics are lost.

(p) Flame-arresting paths in the intake and exhaust systems shall be formed either by—

(1) Flanged metal to metal joints meeting the requirements of paragraph (q) of this section; or

(2) Metal flanges fitted with metal gaskets and meeting the following requirements:

30 CFR Ch. I (7–1–23 Edition)

(i) Flat surfaces between bolt holes that form any part of a flame-arresting path shall be planed to within a maximum deviation of one-half the maximum clearance specified in paragraph (q)(7) of this section. All metal surfaces forming a flame-arresting path shall be finished during the manufacturing process to not more than 250 microinches.

(ii) A means shall be provided to ensure that fastenings maintain the tightness of joints. The means provided shall not lose its effectiveness through repeated assembly and disassembly.

(iii) Fastenings shall be as uniform in size as practicable to preclude improper assembly.

(iv) Holes for fastenings shall not penetrate to the interior of an intake or exhaust system and shall be threaded to ensure that all specified bolts or screws will not bottom even if the washers are omitted.

(v) Fastenings used for joints of flame-arresting paths on intake or exhaust systems shall be used only for attaching parts that are essential in maintaining the explosion-proof integrity. They shall not be used for attaching brackets or other parts.

(vi) The minimum thickness of material for flanges shall be ½-inch, except that a final thickness of $7/16$-inch is allowed after machining rolled plate.

(vii) The maximum fastening spacing shall be 6 inches.

(viii) The minimum diameter of fastenings shall be ⅜-inch, except smaller diameter fastenings may be used if the joint first meets the requirements of the static pressure test in § 7.104, and the explosion test in § 7.100.

(ix) The minimum thread engagement of fastenings shall be equal to or greater than the nominal diameter of the fastenings specified, or the intake or exhaust system must meet the test requirements of the explosion tests in § 7.100 and the static pressure test in § 7.104.

(x) The minimum contact surface of gaskets forming flame-arresting paths shall be ⅜-inch, and the thickness of the gaskets shall be no greater than $1/16$-inch. The minimum distance from the interior edge of a gasket to the edge of a fastening hole shall be ⅜-inch. The gaskets shall be positively

Mine Safety and Health Admin., Labor § 7.98

positioned, and a means shall be provided to preclude improper installation. When the joint is completely assembled, it shall be impossible to insert a 0.0015-inch thickness gauge to a depth exceeding ⅛-inch between the gasket and mating flanges. Other gasket designs shall be evaluated in accordance with § 7.107.

(q) The following construction requirements shall apply to flame-arresting paths formed without gaskets:

(1) Flat surfaces between fastening holes that form any part of a flame-arresting path shall be planed to within a maximum deviation of one-half the maximum clearance specified in paragraph (q)(7) of this section. All metal surfaces forming a flame-arresting path shall be finished during the manufacturing process to not more than 250 microinches. A thin film of nonhardening preparation to inhibit rusting may be applied to these finished metal surfaces, as long as the final surface can be readily wiped free of any foreign materials.

(2) A means shall be provided to ensure that fastenings maintain the tightness of joints. The means provided shall not lose its effectiveness through repeated assembly and disassembly.

(3) Fastenings shall be as uniform in size as practicable to preclude improper assembly.

(4) Holes for fastenings shall not penetrate to the interior of an intake or exhaust system and shall be threaded to ensure that all specified bolts or screws will not bottom even if the washers are omitted.

(5) Fastenings used for joints of flame-arresting paths on intake or exhaust systems shall be used only for attaching parts that are essential in maintaining the explosion-proof integrity. They shall not be used for attaching brackets or other parts.

(6) The flame-arresting path of threaded joints shall conform to the requirements of paragraph (q)(7) of this section.

(7) Intake and exhaust systems joints shall meet the specifications set out in Table F–1.

TABLE F–1—DIMENSIONAL REQUIREMENTS FOR EXPLOSION-PROOF INTAKE AND EXHAUST SYSTEM JOINTS

Minimum thickness of material for flanges	½″[1]
Minimum width of joint; all in one plane	1″
Maximum clearance; joint all in one plane	0.004″
Minimum width of joint, portions of which are different planes; cylinders or equivalent	¾″[2]
Maximum clearances; joint in two or more planes, cylinders or equivalent:	
Portion perpendicular to plane	0.008″[3]
Plane portion	0.006″
Maximum fastening [4] spacing; joints all in one plane [5]	6″
Maximum fastening spacing; joints, portions of which are in different planes	8″
Minimum diameter of fastening (without regard to type of joint) [6]	⅜″
Minimum thread engagement of fastening [7]	⅜″
Maximum diametrical clearance between fastening body and unthreaded holes through which it passes [8][9][10].	1/16″
Minimum distance from interior of the intake or exhaust system to the edge of a fastening hole: [11]	
Joint-minimum width 1″	7/16″[8][12]
Shafts centered by ball or roller bearings:	
Minimum length of flame-arresting path	1″
Maximum diametrical clearance	0.030″
Other cylindrical joints:	
Minimum length of flame-arresting path	1″
Maximum diametrical clearance	0.010″

[1] 1/16-inch less is allowable for machining rolled plate.
[2] If only two planes are involved, neither portion of a joint shall be less than ⅛-inch wide, unless the wider portion conforms to the same requirements as those for a joint that is all in one plane. If more than two planes are involved (as in labyrinths or tongue-in-groove joints), the combined lengths of those portions having prescribed clearances are considered.
[3] The allowable diametrical clearance is 0.008-inch when the portion perpendicular to the plane portion is ⅛-inch or greater in length. If the perpendicular portion is more than ⅛-inch but less than ¼-inch wide, the diametrical clearance shall not exceed 0.006-inch.
[4] Studs, when provided, shall bottom in blind holes, be completely welded in place, or have the bottom of the hole closed with a plug secured by weld or braze. Fastenings shall be provided at all corners.

§ 7.98

30 CFR Ch. I (7–1–23 Edition)

⁵ The requirements as to diametrical clearance around the fastening and minimum distance from the fastening hole to the inside of the intake or exhaust system apply to steel dowel pins. In addition, when such pins are used, the spacing between centers of the fastenings on either side of the pin shall not exceed 5 inches.
⁶ Fastening diameters smaller than specified may be used if the joint or assembly meets the test requirements of § 7.104.
⁷ Minimum thread engagement shall be equal to or greater than the nominal diameter of the fastening specified, or the intake or exhaust system must meet the test requirements of § 7.104.
⁸ The requirements as to diametrical clearance around the fastening and minimum distance from the fastening hole to the inside of the intake or exhaust system apply to steel dowel pins. In addition, when such pins are used, the spacing between centers of the fastenings on either side of the pin shall not exceed 5 inches.
⁹ This maximum clearance only applies when the fastening is located within the flame-arresting path.
¹⁰ Threaded holes for fastenings shall be machined to remove burrs or projections that affect planarity of a surface forming a flame-arresting path.
¹¹ Edge of the fastening hole shall include any edge of any machining done to the fastening hole, such as chamfering.
¹² If the diametrical clearance for fastenings does not exceed 1/32-inch, then the minimum distance shall be 1/4-inch.

(r) *Intake system.* (1) The intake system shall include a device between the air cleaner and intake flame arrester, operable from the equipment operator's compartment, to shut off the air supply to the engine for emergency purposes. Upon activation, the device must operate immediately and the engine shall stop within 15 seconds.

(2) The intake system shall include a flame arrester that will prevent an explosion within the system from propagating to a surrounding flammable mixture when tested in accordance with the explosion tests in § 7.100. The flame arrester shall be located between the air cleaner and the intake manifold and shall be attached so that it can be removed for inspection or cleaning. The flame arrester shall be constructed of corrosion-resistant metal and meet the following requirements:

(i) Two intake flame arrester designs, the spaced-plate type and the crimped ribbon type, will be tested in accordance with the requirements of § 7.100. Variations to these designs or other intake flame arrester designs will be evaluated under the provisions of § 7.107.

(ii) In flame arresters of the spaced-plate type, the thickness of the plates shall be at least 0.125-inch; spacing between the plates shall not exceed 0.018-inch; and the flame-arresting path formed by the plates shall be at least 1 inch wide. The unsupported length of the plates shall be short enough that permanent deformation resulting from explosion tests shall not exceed 0.002-inch. The plates and flame arrester housing shall be an integral unit which cannot be disassembled.

(iii) In flame arresters of the crimped ribbon type, the dimensions of the core openings shall be such that a plug gauge 0.018-inch in diameter shall not pass through, and the flame-arresting path core thickness shall be at least 1 inch. The core and flame arrester housing shall be an integral unit which cannot be disassembled.

(3) The intake system shall be designed so that improper installation of the flame arrester is impossible.

(4) The intake system shall include an air cleaner service indicator. The air cleaner shall be installed so that only filtered air will enter the flame arrester. The air cleaner shall be sized and the service indicator set in accordance with the engine manufacturer's recommendations. Unless the service indicator is explosion-proof, it shall be located between the air cleaner and flame arrester, and the service indicator setting shall be reduced to account for the additional restriction imposed by the flame arrester.

(5) The intake system shall include a connection between the intake flame arrester and the engine head for temporary attachment of a device to indicate the total vacuum in the system. This opening shall be closed by a plug or other suitable device that is sealed or locked in place except when in use.

(s) *Exhaust system.* (1) The exhaust system shall include a flame arrester that will prevent propagation of flame or discharge of glowing particles to a surrounding flammable mixture. The flame arrester shall be constructed of corrosion-resistant metal.

(i) If a mechanical flame arrester is used, it shall be positioned so that only cooled exhaust gas at a maximum temperature of 302 °F (150 °C) will be discharged through it.

(ii) If a mechanical flame arrester of the spaced-plate type is used, it must meet the requirements of paragraph (r)(2)(ii) of this section and the test requirements of § 7.100. Variations to the spaced-plate flame arrester design and other mechanical flame arrester designs shall be evaluated under the provisions of §7.107. The flame arrester shall be designed and attached so that it can be removed for inspection and cleaning.

(2) The exhaust system shall allow a wet exhaust conditioner to be used as the exhaust flame arrester provided that the explosion tests of §7.100 demonstrate that the wet exhaust conditioner will arrest flame. When used as a flame arrester, the wet exhaust conditioner shall be equipped with a sensor to automatically activate the safety shutdown system at or above the minimum allowable low water level established by §7.100. Restarting of the engine shall be prevented until the water supply in the wet exhaust conditioner has been replenished above the minimum allowable low water level. All parts of the wet exhaust conditioner and associated components that come in contact with contaminated exhaust conditioner water shall be constructed of corrosion-resistant material. The wet exhaust conditioner shall include a means for verifying that the safety shutdown system operates at the proper water level. A means shall be provided for draining and cleaning the wet exhaust conditioner. The final exhaust gas temperature at discharge from the wet exhaust conditioner shall not exceed 170 °F (76 °C) under test conditions specified in §7.102. A sensor shall be provided that activates the safety shutdown system before the exhaust gas temperature at discharge from the wet exhaust conditioner exceeds 185 °F (85 °C) under test conditions specified in §7.103(a)(4).

(3) The exhaust system shall be designed so that improper installation of the flame arrester is impossible.

(4) The exhaust system shall provide a means to cool the exhaust gas and prevent discharge of glowing particles.

(i) When a wet exhaust conditioner is used to cool the exhaust gas and prevent the discharge of glowing particles, the temperature of the exhaust gas at the discharge from the exhaust conditioner shall not exceed 170 °F (76 °C) when tested in accordance with the exhaust gas cooling efficiency test in §7.102. A sensor shall be provided that activates the safety shutdown system before the exhaust gas temperature at discharge from the wet exhaust conditioner exceeds 185 °F (85 °C) when tested in accordance with the safety system controls test in §7.103. All parts of the wet exhaust conditioner and associated components that come in contact with contaminated exhaust conditioner water shall be constructed of corrosion-resistant material.

(ii) When a dry exhaust conditioner is used to cool the exhaust gas, the temperature of the exhaust gas at discharge from the diesel power package shall not exceed 302 °F (150 °C) when tested in accordance with the exhaust gas cooling efficiency test of §7.102. A sensor shall be provided that activates the safety shutdown system before the exhaust gas exceeds 302 °F (150 °C) when tested in accordance with the safety system control test in §7.103. A means shall be provided to prevent the discharge of glowing particles, and it shall be evaluated under the provisions of §7.107.

(5) Other means for cooling the exhaust gas and preventing the propagation of flame or discharge of glowing particles shall be evaluated under the provisions of §7.107.

(6) There shall be a connection in the exhaust system for temporary attachment of a device to indicate the total backpressure in the system and collection of exhaust gas samples. This opening shall be closed by a plug or other suitable device that is sealed or locked in place except when in use.

[61 FR 55518, Oct. 25, 1996, 62 FR 34640, 34641, June 27, 1997]

§7.99 Critical characteristics.

The following critical characteristics shall be inspected or tested on each diesel power package to which an approval marking is affixed:

(a) Finish, width, planarity, and clearances of surfaces that form any part of a flame-arresting path.

(b) Thickness of walls and flanges that are essential in maintaining the explosion-proof integrity of the diesel power package.

(c) Size, spacing, and tightness of fastenings.

(d) The means provided to maintain tightness of fastenings.

(e) Length of thread engagement on fastenings and threaded parts that ensure the explosion-proof integrity of the diesel power package.

(f) Diesel engine approval marking.

(g) Fuel rate setting to ensure that it is appropriate for the intended application, or a warning tag shall be affixed to the fuel system notifying the purchaser of the need to make proper adjustments.

(h) Material and dimensions of gaskets that are essential in maintaining the explosion-proof integrity of the diesel power package.

(i) Dimensions and assembly of flame arresters.

(j) Materials of construction to ensure that the intake system, exhaust system, cooling fans, and belts have been fabricated from the required material.

(k) Proper interconnection of the coolant system components and use of specified components.

(l) Proper interconnection of the safety shutdown system components and use of specified components.

(m) All plugs and covers to ensure that they are tightly installed.

(n) The inspections and tests described in the diesel power package checklist shall be performed and all requirements shall be met.

§ 7.100 Explosion tests.

(a) *Test procedures.* (1) Prepare to test the diesel power package as follows:

(i) Perform a detailed check of parts against the drawings and specifications submitted under § 7.97 to determine that the parts and drawings agree.

(ii) Remove all parts that do not contribute to the operation or ensure the explosion-proof integrity of the diesel power package such as the air cleaner and exhaust gas dilution system.

(iii) Fill coolant system fluid and engine oil to the engine manufacturer's recommended levels.

(iv) Interrupt fuel supply to the injector pump.

(v) Establish a preliminary low water level for systems using the wet exhaust conditioner as a flame arrester.

(2) Perform static and dynamic tests of the intake system as follows:

(i) Install the diesel power package in an explosion test chamber which is large enough to contain the complete diesel power package. The chamber must be sufficiently darkened and provide viewing capabilities of the flame-arresting paths to allow observation during testing of any discharge of flame or ignition of the flammable mixture surrounding the diesel power package. Couple the diesel power package to an auxiliary drive mechanism. Attach a pressure measuring device, a temperature measuring device, and an ignition source to the intake system. The pressure measuring device shall be capable of indicating the peak pressure accurate to ±1 pound-per-square inch gauge (psig) at 100 psig static pressure and shall have a frequency response of 40 Hertz or greater. The ignition source shall be an electric spark with a minimum energy of 100 millijoules. The ignition source shall be located immediately adjacent to the intake manifold and the pressure and temperature devices shall be located immediately adjacent to the flame arrester.

(ii) For systems using the wet exhaust conditioner as an exhaust flame arrester, fill the exhaust conditioner to the specified high or normal operating water level.

(iii) Fill the test chamber with a mixture of natural gas and air or methane and air. If natural gas is used, the content of combustible hydrocarbons shall total at least 98.0 percent, by volume, with the remainder being inert. At least 80.0 percent, by volume, of the gas shall be methane. For all tests, the methane or natural gas concentration shall be 8.5 ±1.8 percent, by volume, and the oxygen concentration shall be no less than 18 percent, by volume.

(iv) Using the auxiliary drive mechanism, motor the engine to fill the intake and exhaust systems with the flammable mixture. The intake system, exhaust system, and test chamber gas concentration shall not differ by more than ±0.3 percent, by volume, at the time of ignition.

(v) For static tests, stop the engine, actuate the ignition source, and observe the peak pressure. The peak pressure shall not exceed 110 psig. If the peak pressure exceeds 110 psig, construction changes shall be made that result in a reduction of pressure to 110 psig or less, or the system shall be tested in accordance with the static pressure test of §7.104 with the pressure parameter replaced with a static pressure of twice the highest value recorded.

(vi) If the peak pressure does not exceed 110 psig or if the system meets the static pressure test requirements of this section and there is no discharge of visible flames or glowing particles or ignition of the flammable mixture in the chamber, a total of 20 tests shall be conducted in accordance with the explosion test specified above.

(vii) For dynamic tests, follow the same procedures for static tests, except actuate the ignition source while motoring the engine. Forty dynamic tests shall be conducted at two speeds, twenty at 1800 ±200 RPM and twenty at 1000 ±200 RPM. Under some circumstances, during dynamic testing the flammable mixture may continue to burn within the diesel power package after ignition. This condition can be recognized by the presence of a rumbling noise and a rapid increase in temperature. This can cause the flame-arrester to reach temperatures which can ignite the surrounding flammable mixture. Ignition of the flammable mixture in the test chamber under these circumstances does not constitute failure of the flame arrester. However; if this condition is observed, the test operator should immediately stop the engine and allow components to cool to prevent damage to the components.

(3) Perform static and dynamic tests of the exhaust system as follows:

(i) Prepare the diesel power package for explosion tests according to §7.100(a)(2)(i) as follows:

(A) Install the ignition source immediately adjacent to the exhaust manifold.

(B) Install pressure measuring devices in each segment as follows: immediately adjacent to the exhaust conditioner inlet; in the exhaust conditioner; and immediately adjacent to the flame arrester, if applicable.

(C) Install a temperature device immediately adjacent to the exhaust conditioner inlet.

(ii) If the exhaust system is provided with a spaced-plate flame arrester in addition to an exhaust conditioner, explosion tests of the exhaust system shall be performed as described for the intake system in accordance with this section. Water shall not be present in a wet exhaust conditioner for the tests.

(iii) If the wet exhaust conditioner is used as the exhaust flame arrester, explosion testing of this type of system shall be performed as described for the intake system in accordance with this section with the following modifications:

(A) Twenty static tests, twenty dynamic tests at 1800 ±200 RPM, and twenty dynamic tests at 1000 ±200 RPM shall be conducted at 2 inches below the minimum allowable low water level. All entrances in the wet exhaust conditioner which do not form explosion-proof joints shall be opened. These openings may include lines which connect the reserve water supply to the wet exhaust conditioner, insert flanges, float flanges, and cover plates. These entrances are opened during this test to verify that they are not flame paths.

(B) Twenty static tests, twenty dynamic tests at 1800 ±200 RPM, and twenty dynamic tests at 1000 ±200 RPM shall be conducted at 2 inches below the minimum allowable low water level. All entrances in the wet exhaust conditioner (except the exhaust conditioner outlet) which do not form explosion-proof joints shall be closed. These openings are closed to simulate normal operation.

(C) Twenty static tests, twenty dynamic tests at 1800 ±200 RPM, and twenty dynamic tests at 1000 ±200 RPM shall be conducted at the specified high or normal operating water level. All entrances in the wet exhaust conditioner which do not form explosion-proof joints shall be opened.

(D) Twenty static tests, twenty dynamic tests at 1800 ±200 RPM, and twenty dynamic tests at 1000 ±200 RPM shall be conducted at the specified high or normal operating water level. All entrances in the wet exhaust conditioner (except the exhaust conditioner outlet) which do not form explosion-proof joints shall be closed.

(iv) After successful completion of the explosion tests of the exhaust system, the minimum allowable low water level, for a wet exhaust conditioner used as the exhaust flame arrester, shall be determined by adding two

§ 7.101

inches to the lowest water level that passed the explosion tests.

(v) A determination shall be made of the maximum grade on which the wet exhaust conditioner can be operated retaining the flame-arresting characteristics.

(b) *Acceptable performance.* The explosion tests shall not result in any of the following—

(1) Discharge of flame or glowing particles.

(2) Visible discharge of gas through gasketed joints.

(3) Ignition of the flammable mixture in the test chamber.

(4) Rupture of any part that affects the explosion-proof integrity.

(5) Clearances, in excess of those specified in this subpart, along accessible flame-arresting paths, following any necessary retightening of fastenings.

(6) Pressure exceeding 110 psig, unless the intake system or exhaust system has withstood a static pressure of twice the highest value recorded in the explosion tests of this section following the static pressure test procedures of § 7.104.

(7) Permanent distortion of any planar surface of the diesel power package exceeding 0.04-inches/linear foot.

(8) Permanent deformation exceeding 0.002-inch between the plates of spaced-plate flame arrester designs.

[61 FR 55518, Oct. 25, 1996; 62 FR 34641, June 27, 1997]

§ 7.101 Surface temperature tests.

The test for determination of exhaust gas cooling efficiency described in § 7.102 may be done simultaneously with this test.

(a) *Test procedures.* (1) Prepare to test the diesel power package as follows:

(i) Perform a detailed check of parts against the drawings and specifications submitted to MSHA under compliance with § 7.97 to determine that the parts and drawings agree.

(ii) Fill the coolant system with a mixture of equal parts of antifreeze and water, following the procedures specified in the application, § 7.97(a)(3).

(iii) If a wet exhaust conditioner is used to cool the exhaust gas, fill the exhaust conditioner to the high or normal operating water level and have a reserve water supply available, if applicable.

(2) Tests shall be conducted as follows:

(i) The engine shall be set to the rated horsepower specified in § 7.97(a)(2).

(ii) Install sufficient temperature measuring devices to determine the location of the highest coolant temperature. The temperature measuring devices shall be accurate to ±4 °F (±2 °C).

(iii) Operate the engine at rated horsepower and with 0.5 ±0.1 percent, by volume, of methane in the intake air mixture until all parts of the engine, exhaust coolant system, and other components reach their respective equilibrium temperatures. The liquid fuel temperature into the engine shall be maintained at 100 °F (38 °C) ±10 °F (6 °C) and the intake air temperature shall be maintained at 70 °F (21 °C) ±5 °F (3 °C).

(iv) Increase the coolant system temperatures until the highest coolant temperature is 205 °F to 212 °F (96 °C to 100 °C), or to the maximum temperature specified by the applicant, if lower.

(v) After all coolant system temperatures stabilize, operate the engine for 1 hour.

(vi) The ambient temperature shall be between 50 °F (10 °C) and 104 °F (40 °C) throughout the tests.

(b) *Acceptable performance.* The surface temperature of any external surface of the diesel power package shall not exceed 302 °F (150 °C) during the test.

§ 7.102 Exhaust gas cooling efficiency test.

(a) *Test procedures.* (1) Follow the procedures specified in § 7.101(a).

(2) Install a temperature measuring device to measure the exhaust gas temperature at discharge from the exhaust conditioner. The temperature measuring device shall be accurate to ±4 °F (±2 °C).

(3) Determine the exhaust gas temperature at discharge from the exhaust conditioner before the exhaust gas is diluted with air.

(b) *Acceptable performance.* (1) The exhaust gas temperature at discharge from a wet exhaust conditioner before the exhaust gas is diluted with air shall not exceed 170 °F (76 °C).

(2) The exhaust gas temperature at discharge from a dry exhaust conditioner before the gas is diluted with air shall not exceed 302 °F (150 °C).

§ 7.103 Safety system control test.

(a) *Test procedures.* (1) Prior to testing, perform the tasks specified in § 7.101(a)(1) and install sufficient temperature measuring devices to measure the highest coolant temperature and exhaust gas temperature at discharge from the exhaust conditioner. The temperature measuring devices shall be accurate to ±4 °F (±2 °C).

(2) Determine the effectiveness of the coolant system temperature shutdown sensors which will automatically activate the safety shutdown system and stop the engine before the coolant temperature in the cooling jackets exceeds manufacturer's specifications or 212 °F (100 °C), whichever is lower, by operating the engine and causing the coolant in the cooling jackets to exceed the specified temperature.

(3) For systems using a dry exhaust gas conditioner, determine the effectiveness of the temperature sensor in the exhaust gas stream which will automatically activate the safety shutdown system and stop the engine before the cooled exhaust gas temperature exceeds 302 °F (150 °C), by operating the engine and causing the cooled exhaust gas to exceed the specified temperature.

(4) For systems using a wet exhaust conditioner, determine the effectiveness of the temperature sensor in the exhaust gas stream which will automatically activate the safety shutdown system and stop the engine before the cooled exhaust gas temperature exceeds 185 °F (85 °C), with the engine operating at a high idle speed condition. Temporarily disable the reserve water supply, if applicable, and any safety shutdown system control that might interfere with the evaluation of the operation of the exhaust gas temperature sensor. Prior to testing, set the water level in the wet exhaust conditioner to a level just above the minimum allowable low water level. Run the engine until the exhaust gas temperature sensor activates the safety shutdown system and stops the engine.

(5) For systems using a wet exhaust conditioner as an exhaust flame arrester, determine the effectiveness of the low water sensor which will automatically activate the safety shutdown system and stop the engine at or above the minimum allowable low water level established from results of the explosion tests in § 7.100 with the engine operating at a high idle speed condition. Temporarily disable the reserve water supply, if applicable, and any safety shutdown system control that might interfere with the evaluation of the operation of the low water sensor. Prior to testing, set the water level in the wet exhaust conditioner to a level just above the minimum allowable low water level. Run the engine until the low water sensor activates the safety shutdown system and stops the engine. Measure the low water level. Attempt to restart the engine.

(6) Determine the effectiveness of the device in the intake system which is designed to shut off the air supply and stop the engine for emergency purposes with the engine operating at both a high idle speed condition and a low idle speed condition. Run the engine and activate the emergency intake air shutoff device.

(7) Determine the total air inlet restriction of the complete intake system, including the air cleaner, as measured between the intake flame arrester and the engine head with the engine operating at maximum air flow.

(8) Determine the total exhaust backpressure with the engine operating at rated horsepower as specified in § 7.103(a)(7). If a wet exhaust conditioner is used, it must be filled to the high or normal operating water level during this test.

(9) The starting mechanism shall be tested to ensure that engagement is not possible while the engine is running. Operate the engine and attempt to engage the starting mechanism.

(10) Where the lack of engine oil pressure must be overridden in order to start the engine, test the override to ensure that it does not override any of the safety shutdown sensors specified in § 7.98(i). After each safety shutdown sensor test specified in paragraphs

§ 7.104

(a)(2) through (a)(5) of this section, immediately override the engine oil pressure and attempt to restart the engine.

(b) *Acceptable performance.* Tests of the safety system controls shall result in the following:

(1) The coolant system temperature shutdown sensor shall automatically activate the safety shutdown system and stop the engine before the water temperature in the cooling jackets exceeds manufacturer's specifications or 212 °F (100 °C), whichever is lower.

(2) The temperature sensor in the exhaust gas stream of a system using a dry exhaust conditioner shall automatically activate the safety shutdown system and stop the engine before the cooled exhaust gas exceeds 302 °F (150 °C).

(3) The temperature sensor in the exhaust gas stream of a system using a wet exhaust conditioner shall automatically activate the safety shutdown system and stop the engine before the cooled exhaust gas exceeds 185 °F (85 °C).

(4) The low water sensor for systems using a wet exhaust conditioner shall automatically activate the safety shutdown system and stop the engine at or above the minimum allowable low water level and prevent restarting of the engine.

(5) The emergency intake air shutoff device shall operate immediately when activated and stop the engine within 15 seconds.

(6) The total intake air inlet restriction and the total exhaust backpressure shall not exceed the engine manufacturer's specifications.

(7) It shall not be possible to engage the starting mechanism while the engine is running, unless the starting mechanism is constructed of non-sparking material.

(8) The engine oil pressure override shall not override any of the shutdown sensors.

§ 7.104 **Internal static pressure test.**

(a) *Test procedures.* (1) Isolate and seal each segment of the intake system or exhaust system to allow pressurization.

(2) Internally pressurize each segment of the intake system or exhaust system to four times the maximum pressure observed in each segment during the tests of § 7.100, or 150 psig ±5 psig, whichever is less. Maintain the pressure for a minimum of 10 seconds.

(3) Following the pressure hold, the pressure shall be removed and the pressurizing agent removed from the intake system or exhaust system.

(b) *Acceptable performance.* (1) The intake system or exhaust system, during pressurization, shall not exhibit—

(i) Leakage through welds and gasketed joints; or

(ii) Leakage other than along joints meeting the explosion-proof requirements of § 7.98(q).

(2) Following removal of the pressurizing agent, the intake system or exhaust system shall not exhibit any—

(i) Changes in fastening torque;

(ii) Visible cracks in welds;

(iii) Permanent deformation affecting the length or gap of any flame-arresting paths;

(iv) Stretched or bent fastenings;

(v) Damaged threads of parts affecting the explosion-proof integrity of the intake system or exhaust system; or

(vi) Permanent distortion of any planar surface of the diesel power package exceeding 0.04-inches/linear foot.

§ 7.105 **Approval marking.**

Each approved diesel power package shall be identified by a legible and permanent approval plate inscribed with the assigned MSHA approval number and securely attached to the diesel power package in a manner that does not impair any explosion-proof characteristics. The grade limitation of a wet exhaust conditioner used as an exhaust flame arrester shall be included on the approval marking.

§ 7.106 **Post-approval product audit.**

Upon request by MSHA, but not more than once a year except for cause, the approval-holder shall make an approved diesel power package available for audit at no cost to MSHA.

§ 7.107 **New technology.**

MSHA may approve a diesel power package that incorporates technology for which the requirements of this subpart are not applicable if MSHA determines that the diesel power package is

Mine Safety and Health Admin., Labor § 7.303

as safe as those which meet the requirements of this subpart.

§ 7.108 Power package checklist.

Each diesel power package bearing an MSHA approval plate shall be accompanied by a power package checklist. The power package checklist shall consist of a list of specific features that must be checked and tests that must be performed to determine if a previously approved diesel power package is in approved condition. Test procedures shall be specified in sufficient detail to allow evaluation to be made without reference to other documents. Illustrations shall be used to fully identify the approved configuration of the diesel power package.

Subpart J—Electric Motor Assemblies

SOURCE: 57 FR 61193, Dec. 23, 1992, unless otherwise noted.

§ 7.301 Purpose and effective date.

This subpart establishes the specific requirements for MSHA approval of certain explosion-proof electric motor assemblies intended for use in approved equipment in underground mines. Applications for approval or extensions of approval submitted after February 22, 1996 shall meet the requirements of this part. Those motors that incorporate features not specifically addressed in this subpart will continue to be evaluated under part 18 of this chapter.

§ 7.302 Definitions.

The following definitions apply in this subpart:

Afterburning. The combustion of any flammable mixture that is drawn into an enclosure after an internal explosion in the enclosure. This condition is determined through detection of secondary pressure peaks occurring subsequent to the initial explosion.

Cylindrical joint. A joint comprised of two contiguous, concentric, cylindrical surfaces.

Explosion-proof enclosure. A metallic enclosure used as a winding compartment, conduit box, or a combination of both that complies with the applicable requirements of § 7.304 of this part and is constructed so that it will withstand the explosion tests of § 7.306 of this part.

Fastening. A bolt, screw, or stud used to secure adjoining parts to prevent the escape of flame from an explosion-proof enclosure.

Flame-arresting path. Two or more adjoining or adjacent surfaces between which the escape of flame is prevented.

Internal free volume (of an empty enclosure). The volume remaining after deducting the volume of any part that is essential in maintaining the explosion-proof integrity of the enclosure or necessary for operation of the motor. Essential parts include the parts that constitute the flame-arresting path and those necessary to secure parts that constitute a flame-arresting path.

Motor assembly. The winding compartment including a conduit box when specified. A motor assembly is comprised of one or more explosion-proof enclosures.

Plane joint. A joint comprised of two adjoining surfaces in parallel planes.

Step (rabbet) joint. A joint comprised of two adjoining surfaces with a change or changes in direction between its inner and outer edges. A step joint may be composed of a cylindrical portion and a plane portion or of two or more plane portions.

Stuffing box. An entrance with a recess filled with packing material for cables extending through a wall of an explosion-proof enclosure.

Threaded joint. A joint consisting of a male- and a female-threaded member, both of which are the same type and gauge.

§ 7.303 Application requirements.

(a) An application for approval of a motor assembly shall include a composite drawing or drawings with the following information:

(1) Model (type), frame size, and rating of the motor assembly.

(2) Overall dimensions of the motor assembly, including conduit box if applicable, and internal free volume.

(3) Material and quantity for each of the component parts that form the explosion-proof enclosure or enclosures.

(4) All dimensions (including tolerances) and specifications required to

§ 7.304

ascertain compliance with the requirements of § 7.304 of this part.

(b) All drawings shall be titled, dated, numbered, and include the latest revision.

§ 7.304 Technical requirements.

(a) Voltage rating of the motor shall not exceed 4160 volts.

(b) The temperature of the external surfaces of the motor assembly shall not exceed 150 °C (302 °F) when operated at the manufacturers' specified ratings.

(c) Minimum clearances between uninsulated electrical conductor surfaces, or between uninsulated conductor surfaces and grounded metal surfaces, within the enclosure shall meet the requirements of table J–1 of this section.

TABLE J–1—MINIMUM CLEARANCES BETWEEN UNINSULATED SURFACES

Phase-to-phase voltage (rms)	Clearances (inches)	
	Phase-to-phase	Phase-to-ground or control circuit
0 to 250	0.25	0.25
251 to 600	0.28	0.25
601 to 1000	0.61	0.25
1001 to 2400	1.4	0.6
2401 to 4160	3.0	1.4

(d) Parts whose dimensions can change with the motor operation, such as ball and roller bearings and oil seals, shall not be used as flame-arresting paths.

(e) The widths of any grooves, such as grooves for holding oil seals or o-rings, shall be deducted in measuring the widths of flame-arresting paths.

(f) An outer bearing cap shall not be considered as forming any part of a flame-arresting path unless the cap is used as a bearing cartridge.

(g) Requirements for explosion-proof enclosures of motor assemblies.

(1) Enclosures shall be—

(i) Constructed of metal;

(ii) Designed to withstand a minimum internal pressure of 150 pounds per square inch (gauge);

(iii) Free from blowholes when cast; and

(iv) Explosion proof as determined by the tests set out in § 7.306 of this part.

(2) Welded joints forming an enclosure shall be—

(i) Continuous and gas-tight; and

(ii) Made in accordance with or exceed the American Welding Society Standard AWS D14.4–77, "Classification and Application of Welded Joints for Machinery and Equipment," or meet the test requirements set out in § 7.307 of this part. AWS D14.4–77 is incorporated by reference and has been approved by the Director of the Federal Register in accordance with 5 U.S.C. 552(a) and 1 CFR part 51. Copies may be obtained from the American Welding Society, Inc., 2501 NW 7th Street, Miami, FL 33125. Copies may be inspected at the U.S. Department of Labor, Mine Safety and Health Administration, Approval and Certification Center, 765 Technology Drive, Triadelphia, WV 26059, or at the National Archives and Records Administration (NARA). For information on the availability of this material at NARA, call 202–741–6030, or go to: *http://www.archives.gov/federal_register/code_of_federal_regulations/ibr_locations.html*.

(3) External rotating parts shall not be constructed of aluminum alloys containing more than 0.6 percent magnesium. Non-metallic rotating parts shall be provided with a means to prevent an accumulation of static electricity.

(4) Threaded covers and mating parts shall be designed with Class 1A and 1B (coarse, loose fitting) threads. The covers shall be secured against loosening.

(5) Flat surfaces between fastening holes that form any part of a flame-arresting path shall be plane to within a maximum deviation of one-half the maximum clearance specified in paragraph (g)(19) of this section. All surfaces forming a flame-arresting path shall be finished during the manufacturing process to not more than 250 microinches. A thin film of nonhardening preparation to inhibit rusting may be applied to these finished metal surfaces as long as the final surface can be readily wiped free of any foreign materials.

(6) For a laminated stator frame, it shall be impossible to insert a 0.0015 inch thickness gauge to a depth exceeding 1/8 inch between adjacent laminations or between end rings and laminations.

Mine Safety and Health Admin., Labor § 7.304

(7) Lockwashers, or equivalent, shall be provided for all fastenings. Devices other than lockwashers shall meet the requirements of § 7.308 of this part. Equivalent devices shall only be used in the configuration in which they were tested.

(8) Fastenings shall be as uniform in size as practicable to preclude improper installation.

(9) Holes for fastenings in an explosion-proof enclosure shall be threaded to ensure that all specified bolts or screws will not bottom even if the washers are omitted.

(10) Holes for fastenings shall not penetrate to the interior of an explosion-proof enclosure, except holes made through motor casings for bolts, studs, or screws to hold essential parts, such as pole pieces, brush rigging, and bearing cartridges. The attachments of such parts shall be secured against loosening. The threaded holes in these parts shall be blind unless the fastenings are inserted from the inside, in which case the fastenings shall not be accessible with the rotor in place.

(11) For direct current motor assemblies with narrow interpoles, the distance from the edge of the pole piece to any bolt hole in the frame shall be at least 1/8 inch. If the distance is 1/8 to 1/4 inch, the diametrical clearance for the pole bolt shall not exceed 1/64 inch for not less than 1/2 inch through the frame. Furthermore, the pole piece shall have the same radius as the inner surface of the frame. Pole pieces may be shimmed as necessary. If used, the total resulting thickness of the shims shall be specified. The shim assembly shall meet the same requirements as the pole piece.

(12) Coil-thread inserts, if used in holes for fastenings, shall meet the following:

(i) The inserts shall have internal screw threads.

(ii) The holes for the inserts shall be drilled and tapped consistent with the insert manufacturer's specifications.

(iii) The inserts shall be installed consistent with the insert manufacturer's specifications.

(iv) The insert shall be of sufficient length to ensure the minimum thread engagement of fastening specified in paragraph (g)(19) of this section.

(13) A minimum of 1/8 inch of stock shall be left at the center of the bottom of each blind hole that could penetrate into the interior of an explosion-proof enclosure.

(14) Fastenings shall be used only for attaching parts that are essential in maintaining the explosion-proof integrity of the enclosure, or necessary for the operation of the motor. They shall not be used for making electrical connections.

(15) Through holes not in use shall be closed with a metal plug. Plugs, including eyebolts, in through holes where future access is desired shall meet the flame-arresting paths, lengths, and clearances of paragraph (g)(19) of this section and be secured by spot welding or brazing. The spot weld or braze may be on a plug, clamp, or fastening (for example see figure J–1). Plugs for holes where future access is not desired shall be secured all around by a continuous gas-tight weld.

(16) O-rings, if used in a flame-arresting path, shall meet the following:

(i) When the flame-arresting path is in one plane, the o-ring shall be located at least one-half the acceptable flame-arresting path length specified in paragraph (g)(19) of this section from within the outside edge of the path (see figure J–2).

(ii) When the flame-arresting path is one of the plane-cylindrical type (step joint), the o-ring shall be located at least 1/2 inch from within the outer edge of the plane portion (see figure J–3), or at the junction of the plane and cylindrical portion of the joint (see figure J–4), or in the cylindrical portion (see figure J–5).

(17) Mating parts comprising a pressed fit shall result in a minimum interference of 0.001 inch between the parts. The minimum length of the pressed fit shall be equal to the minimum thickness requirement of paragraph (g)(19) of this section for the material in which the fit is made.

(18) The flame-arresting path of threaded joints shall conform to the requirements of paragraph (g)(19) of this section.

(19) Explosion-proof enclosures shall meet the requirements set out in table

§ 7.304

J-2 of this section, based on the internal free volume of the empty enclosure.

TABLE J-2—EXPLOSION-PROOF REQUIREMENTS BASED ON VOLUME

	Volume of empty enclosure		
	Less than 45 cu. ins.	45 to 124 cu. ins. inclusive	More than 124 cu. ins.
Minimum thickness of material for walls [1]	1/8″	3/16″	1/4″
Minimum thickness of material for flanges and covers	2 1/4″	3 3/8″	3 1/2″
Minimum width of joint; all in one plane	1/2″	3/4″	1″
Maximum clearance; joint all in one plane	0.002″	0.003″	0.004″
Minimum width of joint, portions of which are in different planes; cylinders or equivalent	4 3/8″	4 5/8″	4 3/4″
Maximum clearances; joint in two or more planes, cylinders or equivalent: [5]			
(a) Portion perpendicular to plane [6]	0.008″	0.008″	0.008″
(b) Plane portion	0.006″	0.006″	0.006″
Maximum fastening [7] [8] spacing; joints all in one plane	([16])	([16])	([16])
Maximum fastening spacing; joints, portions of which are in different planes	([17])	([17])	([17])
Minimum diameter of fastening [9] (without regard to type of joint)	1/4″	1/4″	3/8″
Minimum thread engagement of fastening [10]	1/4″	1/4″	3/8″
Maximum diametrical clearance between fastening body and unthreaded holes through which it passes [8] [11] [12]	1/64″	1/32″	1/16″
Minimum distance from interior of enclosure to the edge of a fastening hole: [8] [13]			
Joint—minimum width 1″	....	....	[14] 7/16″
Joint—less than 1″ wide	1/8″	3/16″	
Cylindrical Joints			
Shaft centered by ball or roller bearings:			
Minimum length of flame-arresting path	1/2″	3/4″	1″
Maximum diametrical clearance	0.020″	0.025″	0.030″
Other cylindrical joints: [15]			
Minimum length of flame-arresting path	1/2″	3/4″	1″
Maximum diametrical clearance	0.006″	0.008″	0.010″

[1] This is the minimal nominal dimension when applied to standard steel plate.
[2] 1/32 inch less is allowable for machining rolled plate.
[3] 1/16 inch less is allowable for machining rolled plate.
[4] If only two planes are involved, neither portion of a joint shall be less than 1/8 inch wide, unless the wider portion conforms to the same requirements as those for a joint that is all in one plane. If more than two planes are involved (as in labyrinths or tongue-and-groove joints) the combined lengths of those portions having prescribed clearances are considered.
[5] For winding compartments having internal free volume not exceeding 350 cubic inches and joints not exceeding 32 inches in outer circumference and provided with step joints between the stator frame and the end bracket the following dimensions shall apply:

DIMENSIONS OF RABBET (STEP) JOINTS-INCHES
[See figure J-6 in appendix]

Minimum total width	Minimum width of clamped radial portion	Maximum clearance of radial portion	Maximum diametrical clearance at axial portion
3/8	3/64	0.0015	0.003
1/2	3/64	0.002	0.003
1/2	3/32	0.002	0.004

[6] The allowable diametrical clearance is 0.008 inch when the portion perpendicular to the plane portion is 1/4 inch or greater in length. If the perpendicular portion is more than 1/8 inch but less than 1/4 inch wide, the diametrical clearance shall not exceed 0.006 inch.
[7] Studs, when provided, shall bottom in blind holes, be completely welded in place, or have the bottom of the hole closed with a plug secured by weld or braze. Fastenings shall be provided at all corners.
[8] The requirements as to diametrical clearance around the fastening and minimum distance from the fastening hole to the inside of the explosion-proof enclosure apply to steel dowel pins. In addition, when such pins are used, the spacing between centers of the fastenings on either side of the pin shall not exceed 5 inches.
[9] Fastening diameters smaller than specified may be used if the enclosure meets the test requirements of 30 CFR 7.307 and then 7.306 in that order.
[10] Minimum thread engagement shall be equal to or greater than the diameter of the fastening specified, or the enclosure must meet the test requirements of 30 CFR 7.307 and then 7.306 in that order.
[11] This maximum clearance applies only when the fastening is located within the flame-arresting path.
[12] Threaded holes for fastening bolts shall be machined to remove burrs or projections that affect planarity of a surface forming a flame-arresting path.
[13] Edge of the fastening hole shall include the edge of any machining done to the fastening hole, such as chamfering.
[14] If the diametrical clearance for fastenings does not exceed 1/32 inch, then the minimum distance shall be 1/4 inch.

Mine Safety and Health Admin., Labor § 7.306

[15] Shafts or operating rods through journal bearings shall be at least 1/4" in diameter. The length of the flame-arresting path shall not be reduced when a pushbutton is depressed. Operating rods shall have a shoulder or head on the portion inside the enclosure. Essential parts riveted or bolted to the inside portion are acceptable in lieu of a head or shoulder, but cotter pins and similar devices shall not be used.
[16] 6" with a minimum of 4 fastenings.
[17] 8" with a minimum of 4 fastenings.

(h) *Lead entrances.* (1) Each cable, which extends through an outside wall of the motor assembly, shall pass through a stuffing-box lead entrance (see figure J–7). All sharp edges shall be removed from stuffing boxes, packing nuts, and other lead entrance (gland) parts, so that the cable jacket is not damaged.

(2) When the packing is properly compressed, the gland nut shall have—

(i) A clearance distance of 1/8 inch or more, with no maximum, to travel without interference by parts other than packing; and

(ii) A minimum of three effective threads engaged (see figures J–8, J–9, and J–10).

(3) Packing nuts (see figure J–7) and stuffing boxes shall be secured against loosening (see figure J–11).

(4) Compressed packing material shall be in contact with the cable jacket for a length of not less than 1/2 inch.

(5) Requirements for lead entrances in which MSHA accepted rope packing material is specified, are:

(i) Rope packing material shall be acceptable under § 18.37(e) of this chapter.

(ii) The width of the space for packing material shall not exceed by more than 50 percent the diameter or width of the uncompressed packing material (see figure J–12).

(iii) The maximum diametrical clearance, using the specified tolerances, between the cable and the through holes in the gland parts adjacent to the packing (stuffing box, packing nut, hose tube, or bushings) shall not exceed 75 percent of the nominal diameter or width of the packing material (see figure J–13).

(6) Requirements for lead entrances in which grommet packing made of compressible material is specified, are:

(i) The grommet packing material shall be accepted by MSHA as flame-resistant material under § 18.37(f)(1) of this chapter.

(ii) The diametrical clearance between the cable jacket and the nominal inside diameter of the grommet shall not exceed 1/16 inch, based on the nominal specified diameter of the cable (see figure J–14).

(iii) The diametrical clearance between the nominal outside diameter of the grommet and the inside wall of the stuffing box shall not exceed 1/16 inch (see figure J–14).

(i) *Combustible gases from insulating material.* (1) Insulating materials that give off flammable or explosive gases when decomposed electrically shall not be used within explosion-proof enclosures where the materials are subjected to destructive electrical action.

(2) Parts coated or impregnated with insulating materials shall be treated to remove any combustible solvent before assembly in an explosion-proof enclosure.

[57 FR 61193, Dec. 23, 1992, as amended at 73 FR 52210, Sept. 9, 2008]

§ 7.305 Critical characteristics.

The following critical characteristics shall be inspected on each motor assembly to which an approval marking is affixed:

(a) Finish, width, and planarity of surfaces that form any part of a flame-arresting path.

(b) Clearances between mating parts that form flame-arresting paths.

(c) Thickness of walls, flanges, and covers that are essential in maintaining the explosion-proof integrity of the enclosure.

(d) Spacing of fastenings.

(e) Length of thread engagement on fastenings and threaded parts that assure the explosion-proof integrity of the enclosure.

(f) Use of lockwasher or equivalent with all fastenings.

(g) Dimensions which affect compliance with the requirements for packing gland parts in § 7.304 of this part.

§ 7.306 Explosion tests.

(a) The following shall be used for conducting an explosion test:

(1) An explosion test chamber designed and constructed to contain an

§ 7.306

explosive gas mixture to surround and fill the motor assembly being tested. The chamber must be sufficiently darkened and provide viewing capabilities of the flame-arresting paths to allow observation during testing of any discharge of flame or ignition of the explosive mixture surrounding the motor assembly.

(2) A methane gas supply with at least 98 by volume per centum of combustible hydrocarbons, with the remainder being inert. At least 80 percent by volume of the gas shall be methane.

(3) Coal dust having a minimum of 22 percent dry volatile matter and a minimum heat constant of 11,000 moist BTU (coal containing natural bed moisture but not visible surface water) ground to a fineness of minus 200 mesh U.S. Standard sieve series.

(4) An electric spark ignition source with a minimum of 100 millijoules of energy.

(5) A pressure recording system that will indicate the pressure peaks resulting from the ignition and combustion of explosive gas mixtures within the enclosure being tested.

(b) *General test procedures.* (1) Motor assemblies being tested shall—

(i) Be equipped with unshielded bearings regardless of the type of bearings specified; and

(ii) Have all parts that do not contribute to the operation or assure the explosion-proof integrity of the enclosure, such as oil seals, grease fittings, hose conduit, cable clamps, and outer bearing caps (which do not house the bearings) removed from the motor assembly.

(2) Each motor assembly shall be placed in the explosion test chamber and tested as follows:

(i) The motor assembly shall be filled with and surrounded by an explosive mixture of the natural gas supply and air. The chamber gas concentrations shall be between 6.0 by volume per centum and the motor assembly natural gas concentration just before ignition of each test. Each externally visible flame-arresting path fit shall be observed for discharge of flames for at least two of the tests, including one with coal dust added.

(ii) A single spark source is used for all testing. Pressure shall be measured at each end of the winding compartment simultaneously during all tests. Quantity and location of test holes shall permit ignition on each end of the winding compartment and recording of pressure on the same and opposite ends as the ignition.

(iii) Motor assemblies incorporating a conduit box shall have the pressure in the conduit box recorded simultaneously with the other measured pressures during all tests. Quantity and location of test holes in the conduit box shall permit ignition and recording of pressure as required in paragraphs (c)(1) and (c)(4)(i) of this section.

(iv) The motor assembly shall be completely purged and recharged with a fresh explosive gas mixture from the chamber or by injection after each test. The chamber shall be completely purged and recharged with a fresh explosive gas mixture as necessary. The oxygen level of the chamber gas mixture shall be no less than 18 percent by volume for testing. In the absence of oxygen monitoring equipment, the maximum number of tests conducted before purging shall be less than or equal to the chamber volume divided by forty times the volume occupied by the motor assembly.

(c) *Test procedures.* (1) Eight tests at 9.4 ±0.4 percent methane by volume within the winding compartment shall be conducted, with the rotor stationary during four tests and rotating at rated speed (rpm) during four tests. The ignition shall be at one end of the winding compartment for two stationary and two rotating tests, and then switched to the opposite end for the remaining four tests. If a nonisolated conduit box is used, then two additional tests, one stationary and one rotating, shall be conducted with ignition in the conduit box at a point furthest away from the opening between the conduit box and the winding compartment.

(2) Four tests at 7.0 ±0.3 percent methane by volume within the winding compartment shall be conducted with the rotor stationary, 2 ignitions at each end.

(3) Four tests at 9.4 ±0.4 percent methane by volume plus coal dust shall be conducted. A quantity of coal dust

Mine Safety and Health Admin., Labor § 7.306

equal to 0.05 ounces per cubic foot of internal free volume of the winding compartment plus the nonisolated conduit box shall be introduced into each end of the winding compartment and nonisolated conduit box to coat the interior surface before conducting the first of the four tests. The coal dust introduced into the conduit box shall be proportional to its volume. The remaining coal dust shall be equally divided between the winding compartment ends. For two tests, one stationary and one rotating, the ignition shall be either in the conduit box or one end of the connected winding compartment, whichever produced the highest pressure in the previous tests. The two remaining tests, one stationary and one rotating, shall be conducted with the ignition in the winding compartment end furthest away from the conduit box.

(4) For motor assemblies incorporating a conduit box which is isolated from the winding compartment by an isolating barrier the following additional tests shall be conducted—

(i) For conduit boxes with an internal free volume greater than 150 cubic inches, two ignition points shall be used, one as close to the geometric center of the conduit box as practical and the other at the furthest point away from the isolating barrier between the conduit box and the winding compartment. Recording of pressure shall be on the same and opposite sides as the ignition point furthest from the isolating barrier between the conduit box and the winding compartment. Conduit boxes with an internal free volume of 150 cubic inches or less shall have one test hole for ignition located as close to the geometric center of the conduit box as practical and one for recording of pressure located on a side of the conduit box.

(ii) The conduit box shall be tested separately. Six tests at 9.4 ±0.4 percent methane by volume within the conduit box shall be conducted followed by two tests at 7.0 ±0.3 percent methane by volume. Then two tests at 9.4 ±0.4 percent methane by volume with a quantity of coal dust equal to 0.05 ounces per cubic foot of internal free volume of the conduit box and meeting the specifications in paragraph (c)(3) of this section shall be conducted. For conduit boxes with an internal free volume of more than 150 cubic inches, the number of tests shall be evenly divided between each ignition point.

(iii) The motor assembly shall be tested following removal of the isolating barrier or one sectionalizing terminal (as applicable). Six tests at 9.4 ±0.4 percent methane by volume in the winding compartment and conduit box shall be conducted using three ignition locations. The ignition shall be at one end of the winding compartment for one stationary and one rotating test; the opposite end for one stationary and one rotating test; and at the ignition point that produced the highest pressure on the previous test in paragraph (c)(4)(ii) of this section in the conduit box for one stationary and one rotating test. Motor assemblies that use multiple sectionalizing terminals shall have one test conducted as each additional terminal is removed. Each of these tests shall use the rotor state and ignition location that produced the highest pressure in the previous tests.

(d) A motor assembly incorporating a conduit box that is isolated from the winding compartment that exhibits pressures exceeding 110 psig, while testing during removal of any or all isolating barriers as specified in paragraph (c)(4) of this section, shall have a warning statement on the approval plate. This statement shall warn that the isolating barrier must be maintained to ensure the explosion-proof integrity of the motor assembly. A statement is not required when the motor assembly has withstood a static pressure of twice the maximum pressure recorded in the explosion tests of paragraph (c)(4) of this section. The static pressure test shall be conducted on the motor assembly with all isolating barriers removed, and in accordance with § 7.307 of this part.

(e) *Acceptable performance.* Explosion tests of a motor assembly shall not result in—

(1) Discharge of flames.

(2) Ignition of the explosive mixture surrounding the motor assembly in the chamber.

(3) Development of afterburning.

§ 7.307

(4) Rupture of any part of the motor assembly or any panel or divider within the motor assembly.

(5) Clearances, in excess of those specified in this subpart, along accessible flame-arresting paths, following any necessary retightening of fastenings.

(6) Pressure exceeding 110 psig, except as provided in paragraph (d) of this section unless the motor assembly has withstood a static pressure of twice the maximum pressure recorded in the explosion tests of this section following the static pressure test procedures of § 7.307 of this part.

(7) Permanent deformation greater than 0.040 inches per linear foot.

§ 7.307 Static pressure test.

(a) *Test procedure.* (1) The enclosure shall be internally pressurized to a minimum of 150 psig and the pressure maintained for a minimum of 10 seconds.

(2) Following the pressure hold, the pressure shall be removed and the pressurizing agent removed from the enclosure.

(b) *Acceptable performance.* (1) The enclosure during pressurization shall not exhibit—

(i) Leakage through welds or casting; or

(ii) Rupture of any part that affects the explosion-proof integrity of the enclosure.

(2) The enclosure following removal of the pressurizing agent shall not exhibit—

(i) Visible cracks in welds;

(ii) Permanent deformation exceeding 0.040 inches per linear foot; or

(iii) Clearances, in excess of those specified in this subpart, along accessible flame-arresting paths, following any necessary retightening of fastenings.

§ 7.308 Lockwasher equivalency test.

(a) *Test procedure.* (1) Each test sample shall be an assembly consisting of a fastening with a locking device. Each standard sample shall be an assembly consisting of a fastening with a lockwasher.

(2) Five standard samples and five test samples shall be tested.

(3) Each standard and test sample shall use a new fastening of the same specifications as being used on the motor assembly.

(4) A new tapped hole shall be used for each standard and test sample. The hole shall be of the same specifications as used on the motor assembly.

(5) Each standard and test sample shall be inserted in the tapped hole and continuously and uniformly tightened at a speed not to exceed 30 rpm until the fastening's proof load is achieved. The torquing device shall not contact the locking device or the threaded portion of the fastening.

(6) Each standard and test sample shall be engaged and disengaged for 15 full cycles.

(b) *Acceptable performance.* The minimum torque value required to start removal of the fastening from the installed position (minimum breakaway torque) for any cycle of any test sample shall be greater than or equal to the average breakaway torque of each removal cycle of every standard sample.

§ 7.309 Approval marking.

Each approved motor assembly shall be identified by a legible and permanent approval plate inscribed with the assigned MSHA approval number and a warning statement as specified in § 7.306(d) of this part. The plate shall be securely attached to the motor assembly in a manner that does not impair any explosion-proof characteristics.

§ 7.310 Post-approval product audit.

Upon request by MSHA but not more than once a year, except for cause, the approval holder shall make a motor assembly available for audit at no cost.

§ 7.311 Approval checklist.

Each motor assembly bearing an MSHA approval marking shall be accompanied by a list of items necessary for maintenance of the motor assembly as approved.

Appendix I to Subpart J of Part 7

Appendix I to Subpart J—Figures J-1 through J-14

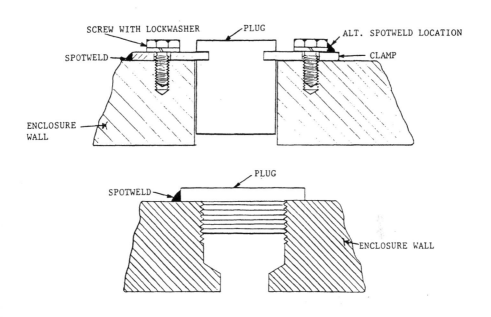

WELD (OR BRAZE) MAY BE ON PLUG, CLAMP, OR FASTENING

FIGURE J-1

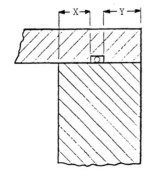

X + Y = MIN. ACCEPTABLE FLAME-ARRESTING PATH LENGTH

$Y = \dfrac{X + Y}{2}$

FIGURE J-2

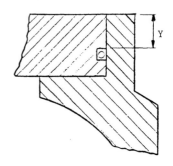

Y = 1/2" MIN.

FIGURE J-3

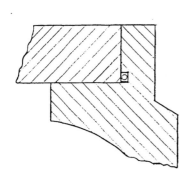

FIGURE J-4

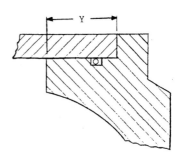

O-RING CAN BE LOCATED ANYWHERE ALONG LENGTH OF (Y).

FIGURE J-5

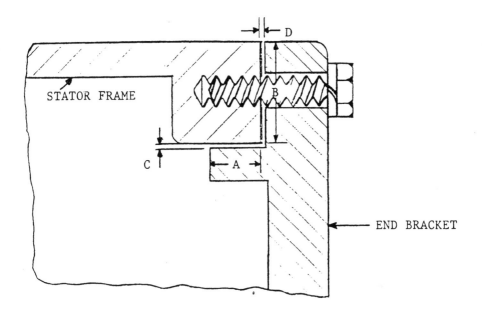

A = Width of Axial Portion

B = Width of Clamped Radial Portion

C = Clearance of Axial Portion

D = Clearance of Radial Portion

Total Width of Flamepath = A + B

FIGURE J-6

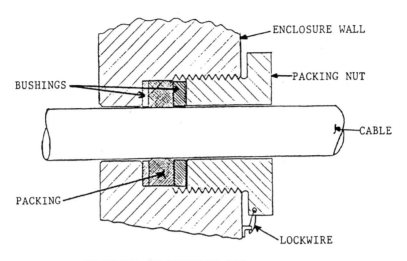

MACHINED-IN STUFFING BOX

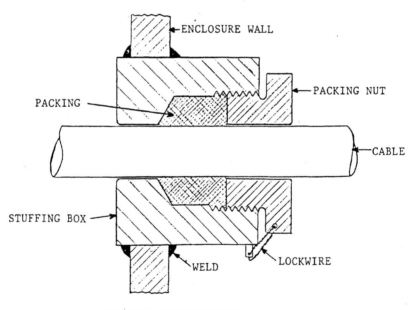

WELD-IN STUFFING BOX

FIGURE J-7

Mine Safety and Health Admin., Labor   Pt. 7, Subpt. J, App. I

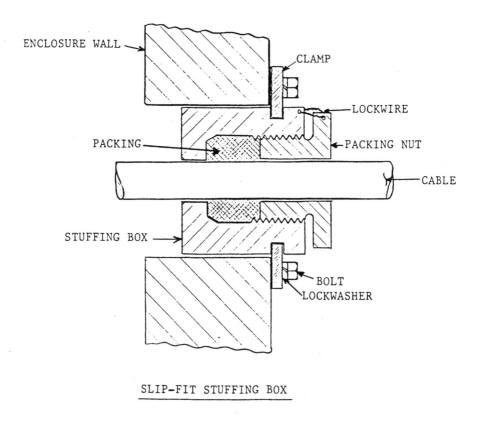

SLIP-FIT STUFFING BOX

FIGURE J-7

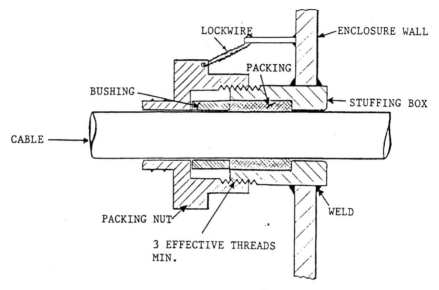

FIGURE J-8

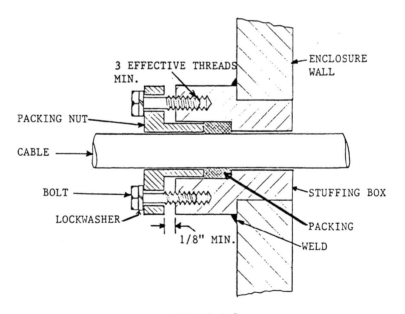

FIGURE J-9

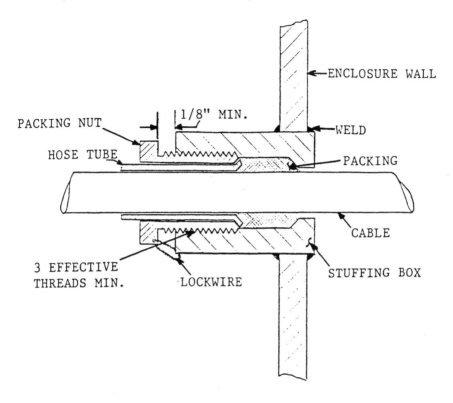

FIGURE J-10

Pt. 7, Subpt. J, App. I   **30 CFR Ch. I (7-1-23 Edition)**

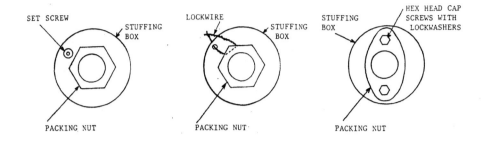

FIGURE J-11

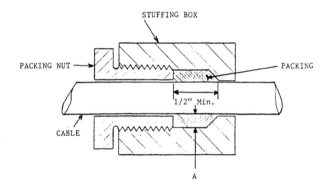

A ≦ 150% of Packing Material Diameter or Width

FIGURE J-12

Mine Safety and Health Admin., Labor Pt. 7, Subpt. J, App. I

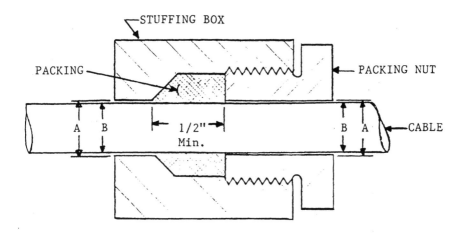

A − B ≤ 75% of Packing Material Diameter or Width

FIGURE J-13

§ 7.401

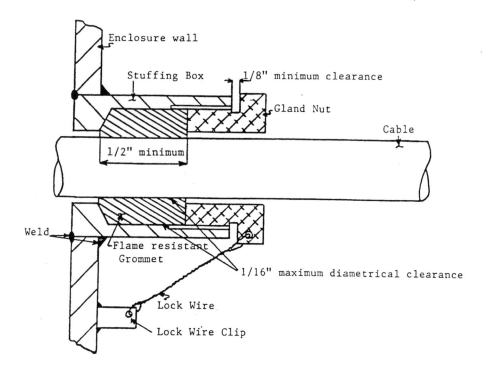

FIGURE J-14

Subpart K—Electric Cables, Signaling Cables, and Cable Splice Kits

SOURCE: 57 FR 61220, Dec. 23, 1992, unless otherwise noted.

§ 7.401 Purpose and effective date.

This subpart establishes the flame-resistant requirements for approval of electric cables, signaling cables and cable splice kit designs. Applications for approval or extension of approval submitted after February 22, 1994 shall meet the requirements of this subpart.

§ 7.402 Definitions.

The following definitions apply in this subpart.

Component. Any material in a cable splice kit which becomes part of a splice.

Conductor. A bare or insulated wire or combination of wires not insulated from one another, suitable for carrying an electric current.

Electric Cable. An assembly of one or more insulated conductors of electric current under a common or integral jacket. A cable may also contain one or more uninsulated conductors.

Jacket. A nonmetallic abrasion-resistant outer covering of a cable or splice.

Power Conductor. An insulated conductor of a cable assembly through which the primary electric current or power is transmitted.

Signaling Cable. A fiber optic cable, or a cable containing electric conductors of a cross-sectional area less than #14 AWG used where the circuit cannot deliver currents which would increase conductor temperatures beyond that established for the current-carrying capacity of the conductors.

Mine Safety and Health Admin., Labor § 7.406

Splice. The mechanical joining of one or more severed conductors in a single length of a cable including the replacement of insulation and jacket.

Splice Kit. A group of materials and related instructions which clearly identify all components and detail procedures used in safely making a flame-resistant splice in an electric cable.

§ 7.403 Application requirements.

(a) *Electric cables and signaling cables.* A single application may address two or more sizes, types, and constructions if the products do not differ in composition of materials or basic design. Applications shall include the following information for each product:

(1) Product information:

(i) Cable type (for example, G or G-GC).

(ii) Construction (for example, round or flat).

(iii) Number and size (gauge) of each conductor.

(iv) Voltage rating for all cables containing electric conductors.

(v) For electric cables, current-carrying capacity of each conductor, with corresponding ambient temperature upon which the current rating (ampacity) is based, of each power conductor.

(2) Design standard. Specify any published consensus standard used and fully describe any deviations from it, or fully describe any nonstandard design used.

(3) Materials. Type and identifying numbers for each material comprising the finished assembly.

(b) *Splice kit.* A single application may address two or more sizes, types, and constructions if the products do not differ in composition of materials or basic design. Applications shall include the following information for each product:

(1) Product information:

(i) Trade name or designation (for example, style or code number).

(ii) Type or kit (for example, shielded or nonshielded).

(iii) Voltage rating.

(2) Design standard. Specify any published design standard used and fully describe any deviations from it, or provide complete final assembly dimensions for all components for each cable that the splice kit is designed to repair.

(3) Materials. Type of materials, supplier, supplier's stock number or designation for each component.

(4) Complete splice assembly instructions which clearly identify all components and detail procedures used in making the splice.

§ 7.404 Technical requirements.

(a) Electric cables and splices shall be flame resistant when tested in accordance with § 7.407.

(b) Signaling cables shall be flame resistant when tested in accordance with § 7.408.

§ 7.405 Critical characteristics.

(a) A sample from each production run, batch, or lot of manufactured electric cable, signaling cable, or splice made from a splice kit shall be flame tested, or

(b) A sample of the materials that contribute to the flame-resistant characteristic of the cable or splice and a sample of the cable or splice kit assembly shall be visually inspected or tested through other means for each production run, batch, or lot to ensure that the finished product meets the flame-resistance test.

§ 7.406 Flame test apparatus.

The principal parts of the apparatus used to test for flame resistance of electric cables, signaling cables and splices shall include#:

(a) *Test chamber.* A rectangular enclosure measuring 17 inches deep by 14½ inches high by 39 inches wide and completely open at the top and front. The floor or base of the chamber shall be fabricated or lined with a noncombustible material that will not extinguish burning matter which may fall from the test specimen during testing. The chamber shall have permanent connections mounted to the back wall, sides, or floor of the chamber which extend to the sample end location. These are used to energize the electric cable and splice specimens. They are not used, but may stay in place, when testing signaling cables.

(b) *Specimen holder (support).* A specimen holder (support) consisting of three separate metal rods each measuring approximately ³⁄₁₆ inch in diameter (nominal) to support the specimen. The horizontal portion of the rod which contacts the test specimen shall be approximately 12 inches in length.

(c) *Gas ignition source.* A standard natural gas type Tirrill burner, with a nominal inside diameter of ⅜ inch, to apply the flame to the test specimen. The fuel for the burner shall be natural gas composed of at least 96 percent combustible hydrocarbons, with at least 80 percent being methane.

(d) *Current source.* (For electric cables and splices only). A source of electric current (either alternating current or direct current) for heating the power conductors of the test specimen. The current source shall have a means to regulate current flow through the test specimen and have an open circuit voltage not exceeding the voltage rating of the test specimen.

(e) *Current measuring device.* (For electric cables and splices only). An instrument to monitor the effective value of heating current flow through the power conductors of the specimen within an accuracy of ±1 percent.

(f) *Temperature measuring device.* (For electric cables and splices only). An instrument to measure conductor temperature within an accuracy of ±2 percent without the necessity of removing material from the test specimen in order to measure the temperature.

§ 7.407 Test for flame resistance of electric cables and cable splices.

(a) *Test procedure.* (1) For electric cables, prepare 3 specimens of cable, each 3 feet in length, by removing 5 inches of jacket material and 2½ inches of conductor insulation from both ends of each test specimen. For splices, prepare a splice specimen in each of 3 sections of MSHA-approved flame-resistant cable. The cable shall be of the type that the splice kit is designed to repair. The finished splice shall not exceed 18 inches or be less than 6 inches in length for test purposes. The spliced cables shall be 3 feet in length with the midpoint of the splice located 14 inches from one end. Both ends of each of the spliced cables shall be prepared by removing 5 inches of jacket material and 2½ inches of conductor insulation. The type, amperage, voltage rating, and construction of the cable shall be compatible with the splice kit design. Each splice shall be made in accordance with the instructions provided with the splice kit.

(2) Prior to testing, condition each test specimen for a minimum of 24 hours at a temperature of 70 ±10 °F (21.1 ±5.5 °C) and a relative humidity of 55 ±10 percent. These environmental conditions shall be maintained during testing.

(3) For electric cables, locate the sensing element of the temperature measuring device 26 inches from one end of each test specimen. For splices, locate the sensing element 12 inches from the midpoint of the splice and 10 inches from the end of the cable. The sensing element must be secured so that it remains in direct contact with the metallic portion of the power conductor for the duration of the flame-resistant test. If a thermocouple-type temperature measuring instrument is used, connect the sensing element through the cable jacket and power conductor insulation. Other means for monitoring conductor temperature may be used, provided the temperature measurement is made at the same location. If the jacket and conductor insulation must be disturbed to insert the temperature measuring device, each must be restored as closely as possible to its original location and maintained there for the duration of the testing.

(4) Center the test specimen horizontally in the test chamber on the three rods. The three rods shall be positioned perpendicular to the longitudinal axis of the test specimen and at the same height, which permits the tip of the inner cone from the flame of the gas burner, when adjusted in accordance with the test procedure, to touch the jacket of the test specimen. The specimen shall be maintained at this level for the duration of the flame test. The two outermost rods shall be placed so that 1 inch of cable jacket extends beyond each rod. For electric cables, the third rod shall be placed 14 inches from the end of the test specimen nearer the temperature monitoring location on the specimen. For splices, the third rod shall be placed between the splice and the temperature monitoring

location at a distance 8 inches from the midpoint of the splice. The specimen shall be free from external air currents during testing.

(5) Adjust the gas burner to give an overall blue flame 5 inches high with a 3-inch inner cone. There shall be no persistence of yellow coloration.

(6) Connect all power conductors of the test specimen to the current source. The connections shall be secure and compatible with the size of the cable's power conductors in order to reduce contact resistance.

(7) Energize all power conductors of the test specimen with an effective heating current value of 5 times the power conductor ampacity rating (to the nearest whole ampere) at an ambient temperature of 104 °F (40 °C).

(8) Monitor the electric current through the power conductors of the test specimen with the current measuring device. Adjust the amount of heating current, as required, to maintain the proper effective heating current value within ±5 percent until the power conductors reach a temperature of 400 °F (204.4 °C).

(9) For electric cables, apply the tip of the inner cone from the flame of the gas burner directly beneath the test specimen for 60 seconds at a location 14 inches from one end of the cable and between the supports separated by a 16-inch distance. For splices, apply the tip of the inner cone from the flame of a gas burner for 60 seconds beneath the midpoint of the splice jacket.

(10) After subjecting the test specimen to external flame for the specified time, fully remove the flame of the gas from beneath the specimen without disturbing air currents within the test chamber. Simultaneously turn off the heating current.

(11) Record the amount of time the test specimen continues to burn after the flame from the gas burner has been removed. The duration of burning includes the burn time of any material that falls from the test specimen after the flame from the gas has been removed.

(12) Record the length of burned (charred) area of each test specimen measured longitudinally along the cable axis.

(13) Repeat the procedure for the remaining two specimens.

(b) *Acceptable performance.* Each of the three test specimens shall meet the following criteria:

(1) The duration of burning shall not exceed 240 seconds.

(2) The length of the burned (charred) area shall not exceed 6 inches.

§ 7.408 **Test for flame resistance of signaling cables.**

(a) *Test procedure.* (1) Prepare 3 samples of cable each 2 feet long.

(2) Prior to testing, condition each test specimen for a minimum of 24 hours at a temperature of 70 ±10 °F (21.1 ±5.5 °C) and relative humidity of 55 ±10 percent. These environmental conditions shall be maintained during testing.

(3) Center the test specimen horizontally in the test chamber on the three rods. The three rods shall be positioned perpendicular to the longitudinal axis of the test specimen and at the same height, which permits the tip of the inner cone from the flame of the gas burner, when adjusted in accordance with the test procedure, to touch the test specimen. The specimen shall be maintained at this height for the duration of the flame test. The two outermost rods shall be placed so that 1 inch of cable extends beyond each rod. The third rod shall be placed at the midpoint of the cable. The specimen shall be free from external air currents during testing.

(4) Adjust the gas burner to give an overall blue flame 5 inches high with a 3-inch inner cone. There shall be no persistence of yellow coloration.

(5) Apply the tip of the inner cone from the flame of the gas burner for 30 seconds directly beneath the specimen centered between either and support and the center support.

(6) After subjecting the test specimen to external flame for the specified time, fully remove the flame of the gas from beneath the specimen without disturbing air currents within the test chamber.

(7) Record the amount of time the test specimen continues to burn after the flame from the gas burner has been removed. The duration of burning includes the burn time of any material

§ 7.409

that falls from the test specimen after the flame from the gas has been removed.

(8) Record the length of burned (charred) area of each test specimen measured longitudinally along the cable axis.

(9) Repeat the procedure for the remaining two specimens.

(b) *Acceptable performance.* Each of the three test specimens shall meet the following criteria:

(1) The duration of burning shall not exceed 60 seconds.

(2) The length of the burned (charred) area shall not exceed 6 inches.

§ 7.409 Approval marking.

Approved electric cables, signaling cables, and splices shall be legibly and permanently marked with the MSHA-assigned approval marking. For electric cables and signaling cables, the marking shall appear at intervals not exceeding 3 feet and shall include the MSHA-assigned approval number in addition to the number and size (gauge) of conductors and cable type. For cables containing electric conductors, the marking shall also include the voltage rating. For splices, the marking shall be placed on the jacket so that it will appear at least once on the assembled splice.

§ 7.410 Post-approval product audit.

Upon request by MSHA, but no more than once a year except for cause, the approval holder shall supply to MSHA for audit at no cost—

(a) 12 feet of an approved electric cable or approved signaling cable; or

(b) 3 splice kits of one approved splice kit design and 12 feet of MSHA-assigned cable that the splice kit is designed to repair.

§ 7.411 New technology.

MSHA may approve cable products or splice kits that incorporate technology for which the requirements of this subpart are not applicable if the Agency determines that they are as safe as those which meet the requirements of this subpart.

Subpart L—Refuge Alternatives

Source: 74 FR 80694, Dec. 31, 2008, unless otherwise noted.

§ 7.501 Purpose and scope.

This subpart L establishes requirements for MSHA approval of refuge alternatives and components for use in underground coal mines. Refuge alternatives are intended to provide a life-sustaining environment for persons trapped underground when escape is impossible.

§ 7.502 Definitions.

The following definitions apply in this subpart:

Apparent temperature. A measure of relative discomfort due to the combined effects of air movement, heat, and humidity on the human body.

Breathable oxygen. Oxygen that is at least 99 percent pure with no harmful contaminants.

Flash fire. A fire that rapidly spreads through a diffuse fuel, such as airborne coal dust or methane, without producing damaging pressure.

Noncombustible material. Material, such as concrete or steel, that will not ignite, burn, support combustion, or release flammable vapors when subjected to fire or heat.

Overpressure. The highest pressure over the background atmospheric pressure that could result from an explosion, which includes the impact of the pressure wave on an object.

Refuge alternative. A protected, secure space with an isolated atmosphere and integrated components that create a life-sustaining environment for persons trapped in an underground coal mine.

§ 7.503 Application requirements.

(a) An application for approval of a refuge alternative or component shall include:

(1) The refuge alternative's or component's make and model number, if applicable.

(2) A list of the refuge alternative's or component's parts that includes—

(i) The MSHA approval number for electric-powered equipment;

(ii) Each component's or part's in-mine shelf life, service life, and recommended replacement schedule;

Mine Safety and Health Admin., Labor §7.504

(iii) Materials that have a potential to ignite used in each component or part with their MSHA approval number; and

(iv) A statement that the component or part is compatible with other components and, upon replacement, is equivalent to the original component or part.

(3) The capacity and duration (the number of persons it is designed to maintain and for how long) of the refuge alternative or component on a per-person per-hour basis.

(4) The length, width, and height of the space required for storage of each component.

(b) The application for approval of the refuge alternative shall include the following:

(1) A description of the breathable air component, including drawings, air-supply sources, piping, regulators, and controls.

(2) The maximum volume, excluding the airlock; the dimensions of floor space and volume provided for each person using the refuge alternative; and the floor space and volume of the airlock.

(3) The maximum positive pressures in the interior space and the airlock and a description of the means used to limit or control the positive pressure.

(4) The maximum allowable apparent temperature of the interior space and the airlock and the means to control the apparent temperature.

(5) The maximum mine air temperature under which the refuge alternative is designed to operate when the unit is fully occupied.

(6) Drawings that show the features of each component and contain sufficient information to document compliance with the technical requirements.

(7) A manual that contains sufficient detail for each refuge alternative or component addressing in-mine transportation, operation, and maintenance of the unit.

(8) A summary of the procedures for deploying refuge alternatives.

(9) A summary of the procedures for using the refuge alternative.

(10) The results of inspections, evaluations, calculations, and tests conducted under this subpart.

(c) The application for approval of the air-monitoring component shall specify the following:

(1) The operating range, type of sensor, gas or gases measured, and environmental limitations, including the cross-sensitivity to other gases, of each detector or device in the air-monitoring component.

(2) The procedure for operation of the individual devices so that they function as necessary to test gas concentrations over a 96-hour period.

(3) The procedures for monitoring and maintaining breathable air in the airlock, before and after purging.

(4) The instructions for determining the quality of the atmosphere in the airlock and refuge alternative interior and a means to maintain breathable air in the airlock.

(d) The application for approval of the harmful gas removal component shall specify the following:

(1) The volume of breathable air available for removing harmful gas both at start-up and while persons enter through the airlock.

(2) The maximum volume of each gas that the component is designed to remove on a per-person per-hour basis.

§7.504 Refuge alternatives and components; general requirements.

(a) *Refuge alternatives and components:* (1) Electrical components that are exposed to the mine atmosphere shall be approved as intrinsically safe for use. Electrical components located inside the refuge alternative shall be either approved as intrinsically safe or approved as permissible.

(2) Shall not produce continuous noise levels in excess of 85 dBA in the structure's interior.

(3) Shall not liberate harmful or irritating gases or particulates into the structure's interior or airlock.

(4) Shall be designed so that the refuge alternative can be safely moved with the use of appropriate devices such as tow bars.

(5) Shall be designed to withstand forces from collision of the refuge alternative structure during transport or handling.

(b) The apparent temperature in the structure shall be controlled as follows:

(1) When used in accordance with the manufacturer's instructions and defined limitations, the apparent temperature in the fully occupied refuge alternative shall not exceed 95 degrees Fahrenheit (°F).

(2) Tests shall be conducted to determine the maximum apparent temperature in the refuge alternative when used at maximum occupancy and in conjunction with required components. Test results including calculations shall be reported in the application.

(c) The refuge alternative shall include:

(1) A two-way communication facility that is a part of the mine communication system, which can be used from inside the refuge alternative; and accommodations for an additional communication system and other requirements as defined in the communications portion of the operator's approved Emergency Response Plan.

(2) Lighting sufficient for persons to perform tasks.

(3) A means to contain human waste effectively and minimize objectionable odors.

(4) First aid supplies.

(5) Materials, parts, and tools for repair of components.

(6) A fire extinguisher that—

(i) Meets the requirements for portable fire extinguishers used in underground coal mines under part 75;

(ii) Is appropriate for extinguishing fires involving the chemicals used for harmful gas removal; and

(iii) Uses a low-toxicity extinguishing agent that does not produce a hazardous by-product when deployed.

(d) Containers used for storage of refuge alternative components or provisions shall be—

(1) Airtight, waterproof, and rodent-proof;

(2) Easy to open and close without the use of tools; and

(3) Conspicuously marked with an expiration date and instructions for use.

§ 7.505 Structural components.

(a) The structure shall—

(1) Provide at least 15 square feet of floor space per person and 30 to 60 cubic feet of volume per person according to the following chart. The airlock can be included in the space and volume if waste is disposed outside the refuge alternative.

Mining height (inches)	Unrestricted volume (cubic feet) per person*
36 or less	30
>36–≤42	37.5
>42–≤48	45
>48–≤54	52.5
>54	60

*Includes an adjustment of 12 inches for clearances.

(2) Include storage space that secures and protects the components during transportation and that permits ready access to components for maintenance examinations.

(3) Include an airlock that creates a barrier and isolates the interior space from the mine atmosphere, except for a refuge alternative capable of maintaining adequate positive pressure.

(i) The airlock shall be designed for multiple uses to accommodate the structure's maximum occupancy.

(ii) The airlock shall be configured to accommodate a stretcher without compromising its function.

(4) Be designed and made to withstand 15 pounds per square inch (psi) overpressure for 0.2 seconds prior to deployment.

(5) Be designed and made to withstand exposure to a flash fire of 300 °F for 3 seconds prior to deployment.

(6) Be made with materials that do not have a potential to ignite or are MSHA-approved.

(7) Be made from reinforced material that has sufficient durability to withstand routine handling and resist puncture and tearing during deployment and use.

(8) Be guarded or reinforced to prevent damage to the structure that would hinder deployment, entry, or use.

(9) Permit measurement of outside gas concentrations without exiting the structure or allowing entry of the outside atmosphere.

(b) Inspections or tests shall be conducted as follows:

(1) A test shall be conducted to demonstrate that trained persons can fully deploy the structure, without the use of tools, within 10 minutes of reaching the refuge alternative.

(2) A test shall be conducted to demonstrate that an overpressure of 15 psi applied to the pre-deployed refuge alternative structure for 0.2 seconds does not allow gases to pass through the structure separating the interior and exterior atmospheres.

(3) A test shall be conducted to demonstrate that a flash fire of 300 °F for 3 seconds does not allow gases to pass from the outside to the inside of the structure.

(4) An inspection shall be conducted to determine that the overpressure forces of 15 psi applied to the pre-deployed refuge alternative structure for 0.2 seconds does not prevent the stored components from operating.

(5) An inspection shall be conducted to determine that a flash fire of 300 °F for 3 seconds does not prevent the stored components from operating.

(6) A test shall be conducted to demonstrate that each structure resists puncture and tearing when tested in accordance with ASTM D2582–07 "Standard Test Method for Puncture-Propagation Tear Resistance of Plastic Film and Thin Sheeting." This publication is incorporated by reference. The Director of the Federal Register approves this incorporation by reference in accordance with 5 U.S.C. 552(a) and 1 CFR part 51. A copy may be obtained from the American Society for Testing and Materials (ASTM), 100 Barr Harbor Drive, P.O. Box C700, West Conshohocken, PA 19428–2959; 610–832–9500; *http://www.astm.org*. A copy may be inspected at any MSHA Coal Mine Safety and Health District Office; or at MSHA's Office of Standards, Regulations, and Variances, 201 12th Street South, Arlington, VA 22202–5452; 202–693–9440; or at the National Archives and Records Administration (NARA). For information on the availability of this material at NARA, call 202–741–6030, or go to: *http://www.archives.gov/ federal_register/ code_of_federal_regulations/ ibr_locations.html*.

(7) A test shall be conducted to demonstrate that each reasonably anticipated repair can be completed within 10 minutes of opening the storage space for repair materials and tools.

(8) A test shall be conducted to demonstrate that no harmful gases or noticeable odors are released from nonmetallic materials before or after the flash fire test. The test shall identify the gases released and determine their concentrations.

(c) If pressurized air is used to deploy the structure or maintain its shape, the structure shall—

(1) Include a pressure regulator or other means to prevent over pressurization of the structure, and

(2) Provide a means to repair and repressurize the structure in case of failure of the structure or loss of air pressure.

(d) The refuge alternative structure shall provide a means—

(1) To conduct a preshift examination, without entering the structure, of components critical for deployment; and

(2) To indicate unauthorized entry or tampering.

[73 FR 80694, Dec. 31, 2008, as amended at 80 FR 52985, Sept. 2, 2015]

§ 7.506 **Breathable air components.**

(a) Breathable air shall be supplied by compressed air cylinders, compressed breathable-oxygen cylinders, or boreholes with fans installed on the surface or compressors installed on the surface. Only uncontaminated breathable air shall be supplied to the refuge alternative.

(b) Mechanisms shall be provided and procedures shall be included so that, within the refuge alternative,—

(1) The breathable air sustains each person for 96 hours,

(2) The oxygen concentration is maintained at levels between 18.5 and 23 percent, and

(3) The average carbon dioxide concentration is 1.0 percent or less and excursions do not exceed 2.5 percent.

(c) Breathable air supplied by compressed air from cylinders, fans, or compressors shall provide a minimum flow rate of 12.5 cubic feet per minute of breathable air for each person.

(1) Fans or compressors shall meet the following:

(i) Be equipped with a carbon monoxide detector located at the surface that automatically provides a visual and audible alarm if carbon monoxide in supplied air exceeds 10 parts per million (ppm).

§ 7.507

(ii) Provide in-line air-purifying sorbent beds and filters or other equivalent means to assure the breathing air quality and prevent condensation, and include maintenance instructions that provide specifications for periodic replacement or refurbishment.

(iii) Provide positive pressure and an automatic means to assure that the pressure is relieved at 0.18 psi, or as specified by the manufacturer, above mine atmospheric pressure in the refuge alternative.

(iv) Include warnings to assure that only uncontaminated breathable air is supplied to the refuge alternative.

(v) Include air lines to supply breathable air from the fan or compressor to the refuge alternative.

(A) Air lines shall be capable of preventing or removing water accumulation.

(B) Air lines shall be designed and protected to prevent damage during normal mining operations, a flash fire of 300 °F for 3 seconds, a pressure wave of 15 psi overpressure for 0.2 seconds, and ground failure.

(vi) Assure that harmful or explosive gases, water, and other materials cannot enter the breathable air.

(2) Redundant fans or compressors and power sources shall be provided to permit prompt re-activation of equipment in the event of failure.

(d) Compressed breathable oxygen shall—

(1) Include instructions for deployment and operation;

(2) Provide oxygen at a minimum flow rate of 1.32 cubic feet per hour per person;

(3) Include a means to readily regulate the pressure and volume of the compressed oxygen;

(4) Include an independent regulator as a backup in case of failure; and

(5) Be used only with regulators, piping, and other equipment that is certified and maintained to prevent ignition or combustion.

(e) The applicant shall prepare and submit an analysis or study demonstrating that the breathable air component will not cause an ignition.

(1) The analysis or study shall specifically address oxygen fire hazards and fire hazards from chemicals used for removal of carbon dioxide.

(2) The analysis or study shall identify the means used to prevent any ignition source.

§ 7.507 Air-monitoring components.

(a) Each refuge alternative shall have an air-monitoring component that provides persons inside with the ability to determine the concentrations of carbon dioxide, carbon monoxide, oxygen, and methane, inside and outside the structure, including the airlock.

(b) Refuge alternatives designed for use in mines with a history of harmful gases, other than carbon monoxide, carbon dioxide, and methane, shall be equipped to measure the harmful gases' concentrations.

(c) The air-monitoring component shall be inspected or tested and the test results shall be included in the application.

(d) The air-monitoring component shall meet the following:

(1) The total measurement error, including the cross-sensitivity to other gases, shall not exceed ±10 percent of the reading, except as specified in the approval.

(2) The measurement error limits shall not be exceeded after start-up, after 8 hours of continuous operation, after 96 hours of storage, and after exposure to atmospheres with a carbon monoxide concentration of 999 ppm (full-scale), a carbon dioxide concentration of 3 percent, and full-scale concentrations of other gases.

(3) Calibration gas values shall be traceable to the National Institute for Standards and Technology (NIST) "Standard Reference Materials" (SRMs).

(4) The analytical accuracy of the calibration gas and span gas values shall be within 2.0 percent of NIST gas standards.

(5) The detectors shall be capable of being kept fully charged and ready for immediate use.

§ 7.508 Harmful gas removal components.

(a) Each refuge alternative shall include means for removing harmful gases.

(1) Purging or other effective procedures shall be provided for the airlock

to dilute the carbon monoxide concentration to 25 ppm or less and the methane concentration to 1.0 percent or less as persons enter, within 20 minutes of persons deploying the refuge alternative.

(2) Chemical scrubbing or other effective procedures shall be provided so that the average carbon dioxide concentration in the occupied structure shall not exceed 1.0 percent over the rated duration, and excursions shall not exceed 2.5 percent.

(i) Carbon dioxide removal components shall be used with breathable air cylinders or oxygen cylinders.

(ii) Carbon dioxide removal components shall remove carbon dioxide at a rate of 1.08 cubic feet per hour per person.

(3) Instructions shall be provided for deployment and operation of the harmful gas removal component.

(b) The harmful gas removal component shall meet the following requirements: Each chemical used for removal of harmful gas shall be—

(1) Contained such that when stored or used it cannot come in contact with persons, and it cannot release airborne particles.

(2) Provided with all materials; parts, such as hangers, racks, and clips; equipment; and instructions necessary for deployment and use.

(3) Stored in an approved container that is conspicuously marked with the manufacturer's instructions for disposal of used chemical.

(c) Each harmful gas removal component shall be tested to determine its ability to remove harmful gases.

(1) The component shall be tested in a refuge alternative structure that is representative of the configuration and maximum volume for which the component is designed.

(i) The test shall include three sampling points located vertically along the centerlines of the length and width of the structure and equally spaced over the horizontal centerline of the height of the structure.

(ii) The structure shall be sealed airtight.

(iii) The operating gas sampling instruments shall be placed inside the structure and continuously exposed to the test atmosphere.

(iv) Sampling instruments shall simultaneously measure the gas concentrations at the three sampling points.

(2) For testing the component's ability to remove carbon monoxide, the structure shall be filled with a test gas of either purified synthetic air or purified nitrogen that contains 400 ppm carbon monoxide, ±5 percent.

(i) After a stable concentration of 400 ppm, ±5 percent, carbon monoxide has been obtained for 5 minutes at all three sampling points, a timer shall be started and the structure shall be purged or carbon monoxide otherwise removed.

(ii) Carbon monoxide concentration readings from each of the three sampling instruments shall be recorded every 2 minutes.

(iii) The time shall be recorded from the start of harmful gas removal until the readings of the three sampling instruments all indicate a carbon monoxide concentration of 25 ppm or less.

(3) For testing the component's ability to remove carbon dioxide, the carbon dioxide concentration shall not exceed 1.0 percent over the rated duration and excursions shall not exceed 2.5 percent under the following conditions:

(i) At 55 °F (±4 °F), 1 atmosphere (±1 percent), and 50 percent (±5 percent) relative humidity.

(ii) At 55 °F (±4 °F), 1 atmosphere (±1 percent), and 100 percent (±5 percent) relative humidity.

(iii) At 90 °F (±4 °F), 1 atmosphere (±1 percent), and 50 percent (±5 percent) relative humidity.

(iv) At 82 °F (±4 °F), 1 atmosphere (±1 percent), and 100 percent (±5 percent) relative humidity.

(4) Testing shall demonstrate the component's continued ability to remove harmful gases effectively throughout its designated shelf-life, specifically addressing the effects of storage and transportation.

(d) Alternate performance tests may be conducted if the tests provide the same level of assurance of the harmful gas removal component's capability as the tests specified in paragraph (c) of this section. Alternate tests shall be specified in the approval application.

§ 7.509 Approval markings.

(a) Each approved refuge alternative or component shall be identified by a legible, permanent approval marking that is securely and conspicuously attached to the component or its container.

(b) The approval marking shall be inscribed with the component's MSHA approval number and any additional markings required by the approval.

(c) The refuge alternative structure shall provide a conspicuous means for indicating an out-of-service status, including the reason it is out of service.

(d) The airlock shall be conspicuously marked with the recommended maximum number of persons that can use it at one time.

§ 7.510 New technology.

MSHA may approve a refuge alternative or a component that incorporates new knowledge or technology, if the applicant demonstrates that the refuge alternative or component provides no less protection than those meeting the requirements of this subpart.

PART 14—REQUIREMENTS FOR THE APPROVAL OF FLAME-RESISTANT CONVEYOR BELTS

Subpart A—General Provisions

Sec.
14.1 Purpose, effective date for approval holders.
14.2 Definitions.
14.3 Observers at tests and evaluations.
14.4 Application procedures and requirements.
14.5 Test samples.
14.6 Issuance of approval.
14.7 Approval marking and distribution records.
14.8 Quality assurance.
14.9 Disclosure of information.
14.10 Post-approval product audit.
14.11 Revocation.

Subpart B—Technical Requirements

14.20 Flame resistance.
14.21 Laboratory-scale flame test apparatus.
14.22 Test for flame resistance of conveyor belts.
14.23 New technology.

AUTHORITY: 30 U.S.C. 957.

SOURCE: 73 FR 80609, Dec. 31, 2008, unless otherwise noted.

Subpart A—General Provisions

§ 14.1 Purpose, effective date for approval holders.

This Part establishes the flame resistance requirements for MSHA approval of conveyor belts for use in underground coal mines. Applications for approval or extensions of approval submitted after December 31, 2008, must meet the requirements of this Part.

§ 14.2 Definitions.

The following definitions apply in this part:

Applicant. An individual or organization that manufactures or controls the production of a conveyor belt and applies to MSHA for approval of conveyor belt for use in underground coal mines.

Approval. A document issued by MSHA, which states that a conveyor belt has met the requirements of this Part and which authorizes an approval marking identifying the conveyor belt as approved.

Extension of approval. A document issued by MSHA, which states that a change to a product previously approved by MSHA meets the requirements of this Part and which authorizes the continued use of the approval marking after the appropriate extension number has been added.

Flame-retardant ingredient. A material that inhibits ignition or flame propagation.

Flammable ingredient. A material that is capable of combustion.

Inert ingredient. A material that does not contribute to combustion.

Post-approval product audit. An examination, testing, or both, by MSHA of an approved conveyor belt selected by MSHA to determine if it meets the technical requirements and has been manufactured as approved.

Similar conveyor belt. A conveyor belt that shares the same cover compound, general carcass construction, and fabric type as another approved conveyor belt.

Mine Safety and Health Admin., Labor § 14.4

§ 14.3 Observers at tests and evaluations.

Representatives of the applicant and other persons agreed upon by MSHA and the applicant may be present during tests and evaluations conducted under this Part. However, if MSHA receives a request from others to observe tests, the Agency will consider it.

§ 14.4 Application procedures and requirements.

(a) *Application address.* Applications for approvals or extensions of approval under this Part may be sent to: U.S. Department of Labor, Mine Safety and Health Administration, Chief, Approval and Certification Center, 765 Technology Drive, Triadelphia, West Virginia 26059. Alternatively, applications for approval or extensions of approval may be filed online at *http://www.msha.gov* or faxed to: Chief, Mine Safety and Health Administration Approval and Certification Center at 304-547-2044.

(b) *Approval application.* Each application for approval of a conveyor belt for use in underground coal mines must include the information below, except any information submitted in a prior approval application need not be resubmitted, but must be noted in the application.

(1) A technical description of the conveyor belt, which includes:

(i) Trade name or identification number;

(ii) Cover compound type and designation number;

(iii) Belt thickness and thickness of top and bottom covers;

(iv) Presence and type of skim coat;

(v) Presence and type of friction coat;

(vi) Carcass construction (number of plies, solid woven);

(vii) Carcass fabric by textile type and weight (ounces per square yard);

(viii) Presence and type of breaker or floated ply; and

(ix) The number, type, and size of cords and fabric for metal cord belts.

(2) The name, address, and telephone number of the applicant's representative responsible for answering any questions regarding the application.

(c) *Similar belts and extensions of approval* may be evaluated for approval without testing using the BELT method if the following information is provided in the application:

(1) Formulation information on the compounds in the conveyor belt indicated by either:

(i) Specifying each ingredient by its chemical name along with its percentage (weight) and tolerance or percentage range; or

(ii) Specifying each flame-retardant ingredient by its chemical or generic name with its percentage and tolerance or percentage range or its minimum percent. List each flammable ingredient and inert ingredient by chemical, generic, or trade name along with the total percentage of all flammable and inert ingredients.

(2) Identification of any similar approved conveyor belt for which the applicant already holds an approval, and the formulation specifications for that belt if it has not previously been submitted to the Agency.

(i) The MSHA assigned approval number of the conveyor belt that most closely resembles the new one; and

(ii) An explanation of any changes from the existing approval.

(d) *Extension of approval.* Any change in an approved conveyor belt from the documentation on file at MSHA that affects the technical requirements of this Part must be submitted for approval prior to implementing the change. Each application for an extension of approval must include:

(1) The MSHA-assigned approval number for the conveyor belt for which the extension is sought;

(2) A description of the proposed change to the conveyor belt; and

(3) The name, address, and telephone number of the applicant's representative responsible for answering any questions regarding the application.

(e) MSHA will determine if testing, additional information, samples, or material is required to evaluate an application. If the applicant believes that flame testing is not required, a statement explaining the rationale must be included in the application.

(f) *Equivalent non-MSHA product safety standard.* An applicant may request an equivalency determination to this part under § 6.20 of this chapter, for a non-MSHA product safety standard.

§ 14.5

(g) *Fees.* Fees calculated in accordance with Part 5 of this chapter must be submitted in accordance with § 5.40.

§ 14.5 Test samples.

Upon request by MSHA, the applicant must submit 3 precut, unrolled, flat conveyor belt samples for flame testing. Each sample must be 60 ±¼ inches long (152.4 ±0.6 cm) by 9 ±⅛ inches (22.9 ±0.3 cm) wide.

§ 14.6 Issuance of approval.

(a) MSHA will issue an approval or notice of the reasons for denying approval after completing the evaluation and testing provided in this part.

(b) An applicant must not advertise or otherwise represent a conveyor belt as approved until MSHA has issued an approval.

§ 14.7 Approval marking and distribution records.

(a) An approved conveyor belt must be marketed only under the name specified in the approval.

(b) Approved conveyor belt must be legibly and permanently marked with the assigned MSHA approval number for the service life of the product. The approval marking must be at least ½ inch (1.27 cm) high, placed at intervals not to exceed 60 feet (18.3 m) and repeated at least once every foot (0.3 m) across the width of the belt.

(c) Where the construction of a conveyor belt does not permit marking as prescribed above, other permanent marking may be accepted by MSHA.

(d) Applicants granted approval must maintain records of the initial sale of each belt having an approval marking. The records must be retained for at least 5 years following the initial sale.

§ 14.8 Quality assurance.

Applicants granted an approval or an extension of approval under this Part must:

(a) In order to assure that the finished conveyor belt will meet the flame-resistance test—

(1) Flame test a sample of each batch, lot, or slab of conveyor belts; or

(2) Flame test or inspect a sample of each batch or lot of the materials that contribute to the flame-resistance characteristic.

30 CFR Ch. I (7–1–23 Edition)

(b) Calibrate instruments used for the inspection and testing in paragraph (a) of this section according to the instrument manufacturer's specifications. Instruments must be calibrated using standards set by the National Institute of Standards and Technology, U.S. Department of Commerce or other nationally or internationally recognized standards. The instruments used must be accurate to at least one significant figure beyond the desired accuracy.

(c) Control production so that the conveyor belt is manufactured in accordance with the approval document. If a third party is assembling or manufacturing all or part of an approved belt, the approval holder shall assure that the product is manufactured as approved.

(d) Immediately notify the MSHA Approval and Certification Center of any information that a conveyor belt has been distributed that does not meet the specifications of the approval. This notification must include a description of the nature and extent of the problem, the locations where the conveyor belt has been distributed, and the approval holder's plans for corrective action.

§ 14.9 Disclosure of information.

(a) All proprietary information concerning product specifications and performance submitted to MSHA by the applicant will be protected.

(b) MSHA will notify the applicant or approval holder of requests for disclosure of information concerning its conveyor belts, and provide an opportunity to present its position prior to any decision on disclosure.

§ 14.10 Post-approval product audit.

(a) Approved conveyor belts will be subject to periodic audits by MSHA to determine conformity with the technical requirements upon which the approval was based. MSHA will select an approved conveyor belt to be audited; the selected belt will be representative of that distributed for use in mines. Upon request to MSHA, the approval holder may obtain any final report resulting from the audit.

(b) No more than once a year, except for cause, the approval holder, at

MSHA's request, must make 3 samples of an approved conveyor belt of the size specified in § 14.5 available at no cost to MSHA for an audit. If a product is not available because it is not currently in production, the manufacturer will notify MSHA when it is available. Representatives of the applicant and other persons agreed upon by MSHA and the applicant may be present during audit tests and evaluations. MSHA will also consider requests by others to observe tests.

(c) A conveyor belt will be subject to audit for cause at any time MSHA believes the approval holder product is not in compliance with the technical requirements of the approval.

§ 14.11 Revocation.

(a) MSHA may revoke for cause an approval issued under this Part if the conveyor belt—

(1) Fails to meet the technical requirements; or

(2) Creates a danger or hazard when used in a mine.

(b) Prior to revoking an approval, the approval holder will be informed in writing of MSHA's intention to revoke. The notice will—

(1) Explain the reasons for the proposed revocation; and

(2) Provide the approval holder an opportunity to demonstrate or achieve compliance with the product approval requirements.

(c) Upon request to MSHA, the approval holder will be given the opportunity for a hearing.

(d) If a conveyor belt poses an imminent danger to the safety or health of miners, an approval may be immediately suspended without written notice of the Agency's intention to revoke.

Subpart B—Technical Requirements

§ 14.20 Flame resistance.

Conveyor belts for use in underground coal mines must be flame-resistant and:

(a) Tested in accordance with § 14.22 of this part; or

(b) Tested in accordance with an alternate test determined by MSHA to be equivalent under 30 CFR §§ 6.20 and 14.4(e).

§ 14.21 Laboratory-scale flame test apparatus.

The principal parts of the apparatus used to test for flame resistance of conveyor belts are as follows—

(a) A horizontal test chamber 66 inches (167.6 cm) long by 18 inches (45.7 cm) square (inside dimensions) constructed from 1 inch (2.5 cm) thick Marinite I®, or equivalent insulating material.

(b) A 16-gauge (0.16 cm) stainless steel duct section which tapers over a length of at least 24 inches (61 cm) from a 20 inch (51 cm) square cross-sectional area at the test chamber connection to a 12 inch (30.5 cm) diameter exhaust duct, or equivalent. The interior surface of the tapered duct section must be lined with ½ inch (1.27 cm) thick ceramic blanket insulation, or equivalent insulating material. The tapered duct must be tightly connected to the test chamber.

(c) A U-shaped gas-fueled impinged jet burner ignition source, measuring 12 inches (30.5 cm) long and 4 inches (10.2 cm) wide, with two parallel rows of 6 jets each. Each jet is spaced alternately along the U-shaped burner tube. The 2 rows of jets are slanted so that they point toward each other and the flame from each jet impinges upon each other in pairs. The burner fuel must be at least 98 percent methane (technical grade) or natural gas containing at least 96 percent combustible gases, which includes not less than 93 percent methane.

(d) A removable steel rack, consisting of 2 parallel rails and supports that form a 7 ±⅛ inches (17.8 ±0.3 cm) wide by 60 ±⅛ inches (152.4 ±0.3 cm) long assembly to hold a belt sample.

(1) The 2 parallel rails, with a 5 ±⅛ inches (12.7 ±0.3 cm) space between them, comprise the top of the rack. The rails and supports must be constructed of slotted angle iron with holes along the top surface.

(2) The top surface of the rack must be 8 ±⅛ inches (20.3 ±0.3 cm) from the inside roof of the test chamber.

§ 14.22 Test for flame resistance of conveyor belts.

(a) *Test procedures.* The test must be conducted in the following sequence using a flame test apparatus meeting the specifications of § 14.21:

(1) Lay three samples of the belt, 60 ±¼ inches (152.4 ±0.6 cm) long by 9 ±⅛ inches (22.9 ±0.3 cm) wide, flat at a temperature of 70 ±10 °Fahrenheit (21 ±5 °Centigrade) for at least 24 hours prior to the test;

(2) For each of three tests, place one belt sample with the load-carrying surface facing up on the rails of the rack so that the sample extends 1 ±⅛ inch (2.5 ±0.3 cm) beyond the front of the rails and 1 ±⅛ inch (2.5 ±0.3 cm) from the outer lengthwise edge of each rail;

(3) Fasten the sample to the rails of the rack with steel washers and cotter pins. The cotter pins shall extend at least ¾ inch (1.9 cm) below the rails. Equivalent fasteners may be used. Make a series of 5 holes approximately 9/32 inch (0.7 cm) in diameter along both edges of the belt sample, starting at the first rail hole within 2 inches (5.1 cm) from the front edge of the sample. Make the next hole 5 ±¼ inches (12.7 ±0.6 cm) from the first, the third hole 5 ±¼ inches (12.7 ±0.6 cm) from the second, the fourth hole approximately midway along the length of the sample, and the fifth hole near the end of the sample. After placing a washer over each sample hole, insert a cotter pin through the hole and spread it apart to secure the sample to the rail;

(4) Center the rack and sample in the test chamber with the front end of the sample 6 ±½ inches (15.2 ±1.27 cm) from the entrance;

(5) Measure the airflow with a 4-inch (10.2 cm) diameter vane anemometer, or an equivalent device, placed on the centerline of the belt sample 12 ±½ inches (30.5 ±1.27 cm) from the chamber entrance. Adjust the airflow passing through the chamber to 200 ±20 ft/min (61 ±6 m/min);

(6) Before starting the test on each sample, the inner surface temperature of the chamber roof measured at points 6 ±½, 30 ±½, and 60 ±½ inches (15.2 ±1.27, 76.2 ±1.27, and 152.4 ±1.27 cm) from the front entrance of the chamber must not exceed 95 °Fahrenheit (35 °Centigrade) at any of these points with the specified airflow passing through the chamber. The temperature of the air entering the chamber during the test on each sample must not be less than 50 °Fahrenheit (10 °Centigrade);

(7) Center the burner in front of the sample's leading edge with the plane, defined by the tips of the burner jets, ¾ ±⅛ inch (1.9 ±0.3 cm) from the front edge of the belt;

(8) With the burner lowered away from the sample, set the gas flow at 1.2 ±0.1 standard cubic feet per minute (SCFM) (34 ±2.8 liters per minute) and then ignite the gas burner. Maintain the gas flow to the burner throughout the 5 to 5.1 minute ignition period;

(9) After applying the burner flame to the front edge of the sample for a 5 to 5.1 minute ignition period, lower the burner away from the sample and extinguish the burner flame;

(10) After completion of each test, determine the undamaged portion across the entire width of the sample. Blistering without charring does not constitute damage.

(b) *Acceptable performance.* Each tested sample must exhibit an undamaged portion across its entire width.

(c) MSHA may modify the procedures of the flammability test for belts constructed of thicknesses more than ¾ inch (1.9 cm).

§ 14.23 New technology.

MSHA may approve a conveyor belt that incorporates technology for which the requirements of this part are not applicable if the Agency determines that the conveyor belt is as safe as those which meet the requirements of this part.

PART 15—REQUIREMENTS FOR APPROVAL OF EXPLOSIVES AND SHEATHED EXPLOSIVE UNITS

Subpart A—General Provisions

Sec.
15.1 Purpose and effective dates.
15.2 Definitions.
15.3 Observers at tests and evaluation.
15.4 Application procedures and requirements.
15.5 Test samples.
15.6 Issuance of approval.
15.7 Approval marking.

Mine Safety and Health Admin., Labor § 15.3

15.8 Quality assurance.
15.9 Disclosure of information.
15.10 Post-approval product audit.
15.11 Revocation.

Subpart B—Requirements for Approval of Explosives

15.20 Technical requirements.
15.21 Tolerances for ingredients.
15.22 Tolerances for performance, wrapper, and specific gravity.

Subpart C—Requirements for Approval of Sheathed Explosive Units or Other Explosive Units Designed to be Fired Outside the Confines of a Borehole

15.30 Technical requirements.
15.31 Tolerances for ingredients.
15.32 Tolerances for weight of explosive, sheath, wrapper, and specific gravity.

AUTHORITY: 30 U.S.C. 957.

SOURCE: 53 FR 46761, Nov. 18, 1988, unless otherwise noted.

Subpart A—General Provisions

§ 15.1 Purpose and effective dates.

This part sets forth the requirements for approval of explosives and sheathed explosive units to be used in underground coal mines and certain underground metal and nonmetal gassy mines and is effective January 17, 1989. Those manufacturers proceeding under the provisions of the previous regulation may file requests for approval or extension of approval of explosives under that regulation until January 17, 1990. After January 17, 1990, all requests for approval or extension of approval of explosives or sheathed explosive units shall be made in accordance with Subpart A and the applicable subpart of this part. Explosives issued an approval under regulations in place prior to January 17, 1989, and in compliance with those regulations, may continue to be manufactured and marked as approved as long as no change to the explosive is made.

[53 FR 46761, Nov. 18, 1988; 54 FR 351, Jan. 5, 1989]

§ 15.2 Definitions.

The following definitions apply in this part.

Applicant. An individual or organization that manufactures or controls the production of an explosive or an explosive unit and that applies to MSHA for approval of that explosive or explosive unit.

Approval. A document issued by MSHA which states that an explosive or explosive unit has met the requirements of this part and which authorizes an approval marking identifying the explosive or explosive unit as approved as permissible.

Explosive. A substance, compound, or mixture, the primary purpose of which is to function by explosion.

Extension of approval. A document issued by MSHA which states that the change to an explosive or explosive unit previously approved by MSHA under this part meets the requirements of this part and which authorizes the continued use of the approval marking after the appropriate extension number has been added.

Minimum product firing temperature. The lowest product temperature at which the explosive or explosive unit is approved for use under this part.

Post-approval product audit. Examination, testing, or both, by MSHA of approved explosives or explosive units selected by MSHA to determine whether they meet the technical requirements and have been manufactured as approved.

Sheath. A chemical compound or mixture incorporated in a sheathed explosive unit and which forms a flame inhibiting cloud on detonation of the explosive.

Sheathed explosive unit. A device consisting of an approved or permissible explosive covered by a sheath encased in a sealed covering and designed to be fired outside the confines of a borehole.

Test detonator. An instantaneous detonator that has a strength equivalent to that of a detonator with a base charge of 0.40–0.45 grams PETN.

[53 FR 46761, Nov. 18, 1988; 54 FR 351, Jan. 5, 1989]

§ 15.3 Observers at tests and evaluation.

Only personnel of MSHA, designees of MSHA, representatives of the applicant, and such other persons as agreed upon by MSHA and the applicant shall

§ 15.4

be present during tests and evaluations conducted under this part.

[70 FR 46342, Aug. 9, 2005]

§ 15.4 Application procedures and requirements.

(a) *Application.* Requests for an approval or an extension of approval under this part shall be sent to: U.S. Department of Labor, Mine Safety and Health Administration, Approval and Certification Center, 765 Technology Drive, Triadelphia, WV 26059.

(b) *Fees.* Fees calculated in accordance with Part 5 of this Title shall be submitted in accordance with § 5.40.

(c) *Original approval for explosives.* Each application for approval of an explosive shall include—

(1) A technical description of the explosive, including the chemical composition of the explosive with tolerances for each ingredient;

(2) A laboratory number or other suitable designation identifying the explosive. The applicant shall provide the brand or trade name under which the explosive will be marketed prior to issuance of the approval;

(3) The lengths and diameters of explosive cartridges for which approval is requested;

(4) The proposed minimum product firing temperature of the explosive; and

(5) The name, address, and telephone number of the applicant's representative responsible for answering any questions regarding the application.

(d) *Original approval for sheathed explosive units.* Each application for approval of a sheathed explosive unit shall include—

(1) A technical description of the sheathed explosive unit which includes the chemical composition of the sheath, with tolerances for each ingredient, and the types of material used for the outer covering;

(2) The minimum thickness weight, and specific gravity of the sheath and outer covering;

(3) The brand or trade name, weight, specific gravity, and minimum product firing temperature of the approved explosive to be used in the unit;

(4) The ratio of the weight of the sheath to the weight of the explosive; and

(5) The name, address and telephone number of the applicant's representative responsible for answering any questions regarding the application.

(e) *Subsequent approval of a similar explosive or sheathed explosive unit.* Each application for approval of an explosive or sheathed explosive unit similar to one for which the applicant already holds an approval shall include—

(1) The approval number of the explosive or sheathed explosive unit which most closely resembles the new one;

(2) The information specified in paragraphs (c) and (d) of this section for an original approval, as applicable, except that any document which is the same as the one listed by MSHA in the prior approval need not be submitted but shall be noted in the application; and

(3) An explanation of all changes from the existing approval.

(f) *Extension of the approval.* Any change in an approved explosive or sheathed explosive unit from the documentation on file at MSHA that affects the technical requirements of this Part shall be submitted for approval prior to implementing the change.

(1) Each application for an extension of approval shall include—

(i) The MSHA-assigned approval number for the explosive or sheathed explosive unit for which the extension is sought;

(ii) A description of the proposed change to the approved explosive or sheathed explosive unit; and

(iii) The name, address, and telephone number of the applicant's representative responsible for answering any questions regarding the application.

(2) MSHA will determine what tests, additional information, samples, or material, if any, are required to evaluate the proposed change.

(3) When a change involves the chemical composition of an approved explosive or sheathed explosive unit which affects the firing characteristics, MSHA may require the explosive or sheathed explosive unit to be distinguished from those associated with the former composition.

[53 FR 46761, Nov. 18, 1988; 54 FR 351, Jan. 5, 1989; 60 FR 33723, June 29, 1995; 73 FR 52211, Sept. 9, 2008]

§ 15.5 Test samples.

(a) *Submission of test samples.* (1) The applicant shall not submit explosives or sheathed explosive units to be tested until requested to do so by MSHA.

(2) The applicant shall submit 70 pounds of 1¼-inch diameter explosives and additional cartridges in the amount of 3200 divided by the length in inches, except for cartridges 12, 20 and greater than 36 inches long. The applicant shall submit 70 pounds and additional cartridges in the amount of 3800 divided by the length in inches for cartridges 12, 20 and greater than 36 inches long.

(3) If approval is requested for cartridges in diameters less than 1-¼ inches, the applicant shall submit a number of cartridges equal to 1800 divided by the length in inches, except for cartridges 12, 20 and greater than 36 inches long. The applicant shall submit cartridges in the amount of 2200 divided by the length in inches for cartridges 12, 20 and greater than 36 inches long.

(4) If approval is requested for cartridges in diameters larger than 1-¼ inches, the applicant shall submit an additional 10 cartridges of each larger diameter.

(5) If approval is requested for cartridges in more than one length, the applicant shall submit an additional 10 cartridges for each additional length and diameter combination.

(6) Each applicant seeking approval of sheathed explosive units shall submit 140 units.

(b) *Condition and composition.* Explosives and sheathed explosive units will not be tested that—

(1) Contain chlorites, chlorates, or substances that will react over an extended time and cause degradation of the explosive or sheathed explosive unit;

(2) Are chemically unstable;

(3) Show leakage;

(4) Use aluminum clips to seal the cartridge;

(5) Contain any combination of perchlorate and aluminum;

(6) Contain more than 5 percent perchlorate; or

(7) Contain any perchlorate and less than 5 percent water.

(c) *Storage.* Explosives and sheathed explosive units shall be stored in a magazine for at least 30 days before gallery tests are conducted.

§ 15.6 Issuance of approval.

(a) MSHA will issue an approval or a notice of the reasons for denying approval after completing the evaluation and testing provided for by this part.

(b) An applicant shall not advertise or otherwise represent an explosive or sheathed explosive unit as approved until MSHA has issued an approval.

§ 15.7 Approval marking.

(a) An approved explosive or sheathed explosive unit shall be marketed only under the brand or trade name specified in the approval.

(b) The wrapper of each cartridge and each case of approved explosives shall be legibly labeled with the following: the brand or trade name, "MSHA Approved Explosive", the test detonator strength, and the minimum product firing temperature.

(c) The outer covering of each sheathed explosive unit and each case of approved sheathed explosive units shall be legibly labeled with the following: the brand or trade name, "MSHA Approved Sheathed Explosive Unit", the test detonator strength, and the minimum product firing temperature.

[53 FR 46761, Nov. 18, 1988; 54 FR 351, Jan. 5, 1989; 54 FR 27641, June 30, 1989; 60 FR 33723, June 29, 1995]

§ 15.8 Quality assurance.

(a) Applicants granted an approval or an extension of approval under this part shall manufacture the explosive or sheathed explosive unit as approved.

(b) Applicants shall immediately report to the MSHA Approval and Certification Center, any knowledge of explosives or sheathed explosive units that have been distributed that do not meet the specifications of the approval.

[53 53 FR 46761, Nov. 18, 1988, as amended at 60 FR 33723, June 29, 1995]

§ 15.9 Disclosure of information.

(a) All information concerning product specifications and performance submitted to MSHA by the applicant shall be considered proprietary information.

(b) MSHA will notify the applicants of requests for disclosure of information concerning its explosives or sheathed explosive units and shall give the applicant an opportunity to provide MSHA with a statement of its position prior to any disclosure.

§ 15.10 Post-approval product audit.

(a) Approved explosives and sheathed explosive units shall be subject to periodic audits by MSHA for the purpose of determining conformity with the technical requirements upon which the approval was based. Any approved explosive or sheathed explosive unit which is to be audited shall be selected by MSHA and be representative of those distributed for use in mines. The approval-holder may obtain any final report resulting from such audit.

(b) No more than once a year, except for cause, the approval-holder, at MSHA's request, shall make one case of explosives or 25 sheathed explosive units available at no cost to MSHA for an audit. The approval-holder may observe any tests conducted during this audit.

(c) An approved explosive or sheathed explosive unit shall be subject to audit for cause at any time MSHA believes that it is not in compliance with the technical requirements upon which the approval was based.

(d) Explosives approved under regulations in effect prior to January 17, 1989, shall conform to the provisions on field samples set out in those regulations (See 30 CFR part 15, 1987 edition).

§ 15.11 Revocation.

(a) MSHA may revoke for cause an approval issued under this part if the explosive or sheathed explosive unit—

(1) Fails to meet the applicable technical requirements; or

(2) Creates a hazard when used in a mine.

(b) Prior to revoking an approval, the approval-holder shall be informed in writing of MSHA's intention to revoke. The notice shall—

(1) Explain the specific reasons for the proposed revocation; and

(2) Provide the approval-holder an opportunity to demonstrate or achieve compliance with the product approval requirements.

(c) Upon request, the approval-holder shall be afforded an opportunity for a hearing.

(d) If an explosive or sheathed explosive unit poses an imminent hazard to the safety or health of miners, the approval may be immediately suspended without a written notice of the agency's intention to revoke. The suspension may continue until the revocation proceedings are completed.

Subpart B—Requirements for Approval of Explosives

§ 15.20 Technical requirements.

(a) *Chemical composition.* The chemical composition of the explosive shall be within the tolerances furnished by the applicant.

(b) *Rate-of-detonation test.* The explosive shall propagate completely in the rate-of-detonation test. The test is conducted at an ambient temperature between 68 and 86 °F. Nongelatinous explosives are initiated with a test detonator only, while gelatinous explosives are initiated with a test detonator and a 60-gram tetryl pellet booster. The test is conducted on—

(1) A 50-inch column of 1¼ inch diameter cartridges; and

(2) A 50-inch column of the smallest diameter cartridges less than 1¼ inches submitted for testing.

(c) *Air-gap sensitivity.* The air-gap sensitivity of the explosive shall be at least 2 inches at the minimum product firing temperature and 3 inches at a temperature between 68 and 86 °F, and the explosive shall propagate completely.

(1) Air-gap sensitivity of the explosive is determined in the explosion-by-influence test using the 7-inch cartridge method. The air-gap sensitivity is determined for 1¼ inch diameter cartridges and each cartridge diameter smaller than 1¼ inches. Explosives are initiated with a test detonator.

(2) The 7-inch cartridge method is conducted with two 8-inch cartridges. One inch is cut off the end of each cartridge. The cartridges are placed in a paper tube, the cut ends facing each other, with the appropriate 2-inch or 3-inch air gap between them. The test is

conducted at a temperature between 68 and 86 °F and at the minimum product firing temperature proposed by the applicant, or 41 °F, whichever is lower. The test temperature at which the explosive propagates completely will be specified in the approval as the minimum product firing temperature at which the explosive is approved for use.

(d) *Gallery Test 7.* The explosive shall yield a value of at least 450 grams for the lower 95 percent confidence limit (L_{95}) on the weight for 50 percent probability of ignition (W_{50}) in gallery test 7 and shall propagate completely. The L_{95} and W_{50} values for the explosive are determined by using the Bruceton up-and-down method. A minimum of 20 trials are made with explosive charges of varying weights, including wrapper and seals. Each charge is primed with a test detonator, then tamped and stemmed with one pound of dry-milled fire clay into the borehole of a steel cannon. The cannon is fired into air containing 7.7 to 8.3 percent of natural gas. The air temperature is between 68 and 86 °F.

(e) *Gallery Test 8.* The explosive shall yield a value of at least 350 grams for the weight for 50 percent probability of ignition (W_{CDG}) in gallery test 8 and shall propagate completely. The (W_{CDG}) value for the explosive is determined using the Bruceton up-and-down method. A minimum of 10 tests are made with explosive charges of varying weights, including wrapper and seals. Each charge is primed with a test detonator, then tamped into the borehole of a steel cannon. The cannon is fired into a mixture of 8 pounds of bituminous coal dust predispersed into 640 cubic feet of air containing 3.8 to 4.2 percent of natural gas. The air temperature is between 68 and 86 °F.

(f) *Pendulum-friction test.* The explosive shall show no perceptible reaction in the pendulum-friction test with the hard fiber-faced shoe. Ten trials of the test are conducted by releasing the steel shoe from a height of 59 inches. If there is evidence of sensitivity, the test is repeated with the hard fiber-faced shoe.

(g) *Toxic gases.* The total volume equivalent to carbon monoxide (CO) of toxic gases produced by detonation of the explosive shall not exceed 2.5 cubic feet per pound of explosive as determined in the large chamber test. The explosive shall propagate completely.

(1) The large chamber test is conducted with a one-pound explosive charge, including wrapper and seal, primed with a test detonator. The explosive charge is loaded into the borehole of a steel cannon, then tamped and stemmed with one pound of dry-milled fire clay. The cannon is fired into the large chamber and the gaseous products resulting from detonation of the explosive are collected and analyzed for toxic gases. At least two trials are conducted.

(2) The equivalent volume of each toxic gas produced, relative to CO, is determined by multiplying the measured volume of the gas by a conversion factor. The conversion factor is equal to the threshold limit value, time weighted average (TLV-TWA) in parts-per-million for CO divided by the TLV-TWA for the toxic gas. The TLV-TWA conversion factor for each gas for which MSHA shall test is specified in Table I of this subpart. The total volume equivalent to CO of the toxic gases produced by detonation of the explosive is the sum of the equivalent volumes of the individual toxic gases.

TABLE I—CONVERSION FACTORS FOR TOXIC GASES

[For Equivalent Volume Relative to Carbon Monoxide]

Toxic Gas	Conversion Factor	TLV-TWA (PPM)
Ammonia	2	25
Carbon Dioxide	0.01	5000
Carbon Monoxide	1	50
Hydrogen Sulfide	5	10
Nitric Oxide	2	25
Nitrogen Dioxide	17	3
Sulfur Dioxide	25	2

(h) *Cartridge diameter and length changes.* (1) For proposed changes to an approved explosive involving only cartridge diameter or length, MSHA will determine what tests, if any, will be required.

(2) When a proposed change to an approved explosive involves a smaller diameter than that specified in the approval, the rate-of-detonation and air-gap sensitivity tests will be conducted.

§ 15.21

(3) No test will be conducted on cartridges with diameters the same as or smaller than those that previously failed to detonate in the rate-of-detonation test.

(i) *New technology.* MSHA may approve an explosive that incorporates technology for which the requirements of this subpart are not applicable if MSHA determines that the explosive is as safe as those which meet the requirements of this subpart.

§ 15.21 Tolerances for ingredients.

Tolerances for each ingredient in an explosive, which are expressed as a percentage of the total explosive, shall not exceed the following:

(a) Physical sensitizers: The tolerances established by the applicant;

(b) Aluminum: ±0.7 percent;

(c) Carbonaceous materials: ±3 percent; and

(d) Moisture and ingredients other than specified in paragraphs (a), (b), and (c) of this section: The tolerances specified in Table II.

TABLE II—TOLERANCES FOR MOISTURE AND OTHER INGREDIENTS

Quantity of ingredients (as percent of total explosive or sheath)	Tolerance percent
0 to 5.0	1.2
5.1 to 10.0	1.5
10.1 to 20.0	1.7
20.1 to 30.0	2.0
30.1 to 40.0	2.3
40.1 to 50.0	2.5
50.1 to 55.0	2.8
55.1 to 100.0	3.0

§ 15.22 Tolerances for performance, wrapper, and specific gravity.

(a) The rate of detonation of the explosive shall be within ±15 percent of that specified in the approval.

(b) The weight of wrapper per 100 grams of explosive shall be within ±2 grams of that specified in the approval.

(c) The apparent specific gravity of the explosive shall be within ±7.5 percent of that specified in the approval.

Subpart C—Requirements for Approval of Sheathed Explosive Units or Other Explosive Units Designed to be Fired Outside the Confines of a Borehole

§ 15.30 Technical requirements.

(a) *Quantity of explosive.* The sheathed explosive unit shall contain not more than 1½ pounds of an approved or permissible explosive.

(b) *Chemical composition.* The chemical composition of the sheath shall be within the tolerances furnished by the applicant.

(c) *Detonator well.* The sheathed explosive unit shall have a detonator well that—

(1) Is protected by a sealed covering;

(2) Permits an instantaneous detonator to be inserted in the unit with the detonator completely embedded in the well;

(3) Is provided with a means of securing the detonator in the well; and

(4) Is clearly marked.

(d) *Drop test.* The outer covering of the sheathed explosive unit shall not tear or rupture and the internal components shall not shift position or be damaged in the drop test.

(1) The drop test is conducted on at least 10 sheathed explosive units. Each unit is dropped on its top, bottom, and edge from a height of 6 feet onto a concrete surface. For units with explosives approved with a minimum product firing temperature, the drop test is performed with the unit at the minimum product firing temperature established for the explosive in the unit. For units with explosives approved under regulations in effect prior to January 17, 1989, the drop test is performed with the unit at 41 °F.

(2) At least four units which have been drop-tested shall be cut-open and examined.

(3) At least six units which have been drop-tested shall be subjected to gallery tests 9 and 10 as provided in paragraphs (e)(1) and (e)(2) of this section.

(e) *Gallery tests.* No sheathed explosive unit shall cause an ignition in gallery tests 9, 10, 11, or 12. Ten trials in each gallery test shall be conducted and each sheathed explosive unit shall propagate completely in all tests.

(1) Gallery test 9 is conducted in each trial with three sheathed explosive units placed in a row 2 feet apart. One of the trials is conducted with sheathed explosive units which have been subjected to the drop test as provided in paragraph (d)(3) of this section. The units are placed on a concrete slab, primed with test detonators and fired in air containing 7.7 to 8.3 percent natural gas or 8.7 to 9.3 percent methane. The air temperature is between 41 and 86 °F.

(2) Gallery test 10 is conducted in each trial with three sheathed explosive units placed in a row 2 feet apart. One of the trials is conducted with sheathed explosive units which have been subjected to the drop test as provided in paragraph (d)(3) of this section. The units are placed on a concrete slab, primed with test detonators and fired in air containing 3.8 to 4.2 percent natural gas, or 4.3 to 4.7 percent methane, mixed with 0.2 ounces per cubic foot of predispersed bituminous coal dust. The air temperature is between 41 and 86 °F.

(3) Gallery test 11 is conducted in each trial with three sheathed explosive units arranged in a triangular pattern with the units in contact with each other. The units are placed in a simulated crevice formed between two square concrete slabs, each measuring 24 inches on a side and 2 inches in thickness. The crevice is formed by placing one slab on top of the other and raising the edge of the upper slab at least 4 inches. The sheathed explosive units are primed with test detonators and fired in air containing 7.7 to 8.3 percent natural gas or 8.7 to 9.3 percent methane. The air temperature is between 41 and 86 °F.

(4) Gallery test 12 is conducted in each trial with three sheathed explosive units arranged in a triangular pattern with the units in contact with each other. The units are placed in a corner formed by three square steel plates, each measuring 24 inches on a side and one inch in thickness. The sheathed explosive units are primed with test detonators and fired in air containing 7.7 to 8.3 percent natural gas or 8.7 to 9.3 percent methane. The air temperature is between 41 and 86 °F.

(f) *Detonation test.* Each of ten sheathed explosive units shall propagate completely when fired at the minimum product firing temperature for the explosive used in the unit or 41 °F for units with explosives approved under regulations in effect prior to January 17, 1989. The units are initiated with test detonators.

(g) *New technology.* MSHA may approve an explosive unit designed to be fired outside the confines of a borehole that incorporates technology for which the requirements of this subpart are not applicable if MSHA determines that such explosive unit is as safe as those which meet the requirements of this subpart.

[53 FR 46761, Nov. 18, 1988; 54 FR 351, Jan. 5, 1989]

§ 15.31   **Tolerances for ingredients.**

Tolerances established by the applicant for each ingredient in the sheath shall not exceed the tolerances specified in Table II § 15.21 of this part.

§ 15.32   **Tolerances for weight of explosive, sheath, wrapper, and specific gravity.**

(a) The weight of the explosive, the sheath, and the outer covering shall each be within ±7.5 percent of that specified in the approval.

(b) The ratio of the weight of the sheath to that of the explosive shall be within ±7.5 percent of that specified in the approval.

(c) The specific gravity of the explosive and sheath shall be within ±7.5 percent of that specified in the approval.

PART 18—ELECTRIC MOTOR-DRIVEN MINE EQUIPMENT AND ACCESSORIES

Subpart A—General Provisions

Sec.
18.1   Purpose.
18.2   Definitions.
18.3   Consultation.
18.4   Electrical equipment for which approval is issued.
18.5   Equipment for which certification will be issued.
18.6   Applications.
18.7   [Reserved]
18.8   Date for conducting investigation and tests.

§ 18.1

18.9 Conduct of investigations and tests.
18.10 Notice of approval or disapproval.
18.11 Approval plate.
18.12 Letter of certification.
18.13 Certification plate.
18.14 Identification of tested noncertified explosion-proof enclosures.
18.15 Changes after approval or certification.
18.16 Withdrawal of approval, certification, or acceptance.

Subpart B—Construction and Design Requirements

18.20 Quality of material, workmanship, and design.
18.21 Machines equipped with powered dust collectors.
18.22 Boring-type machines equipped for auxiliary face ventilation.
18.23 Limitation of external surface temperatures.
18.24 Electrical clearances.
18.25 Combustible gases from insulating material.
18.26 Static electricity.
18.27 Gaskets.
18.28 Devices for pressure relief, ventilation, or drainage.
18.29 Access openings and covers, including unused lead-entrance holes.
18.30 Windows and lenses.
18.31 Enclosures—joints and fastenings.
18.32 Fastenings—additional requirements.
18.33 Finish of surface joints.
18.34 Motors.
18.35 Portable (trailing) cables and cords.
18.36 Cables between machine components.
18.37 Lead entrances.
18.38 Leads through common walls.
18.39 Hose conduit.
18.40 Cable clamps and grips.
18.41 Plug and receptacle-type connectors.
18.42 Explosion-proof distribution boxes.
18.43 Explosion-proof splice boxes.
18.44 Non-intrinsically safe battery-powered equipment.
18.45 Cable reels.
18.46 Headlights.
18.47 Voltage limitation.
18.48 Circuit-interrupting devices.
18.49 Connection boxes on machines.
18.50 Protection against external arcs and sparks.
18.51 Electrical protection of circuits and equipment.
18.52 Renewal of fuses.
18.53 High-voltage longwall mining systems.
18.54 High-voltage continuous mining machines.

Subpart C—Inspections and Tests

18.60 Detailed inspection of components.
18.61 Final inspection of complete machine.
18.62 Tests to determine explosion-proof characteristics.

30 CFR Ch. I (7–1–23 Edition)

18.63 [Reserved]
18.65 Flame test of hose.
18.66 Tests of windows and lenses.
18.67 Static-pressure tests.
18.68 Tests for intrinsic safety.
18.69 Adequacy tests.

Subpart D—Machines Assembled With Certified or Explosion-Proof Components, Field Modifications of Approved Machines, and Permits To Use Experimental Equipment

18.80 Approval of machines assembled with certified or explosion-proof components.
18.81 Field modification of approved (permissible) equipment; application for approval of modification; approval of plans for modification before modification.
18.82 Permit to use experimental electric face equipment in a gassy mine or tunnel.

APPENDIX I TO SUBPART D OF PART 18—LIST OF TABLES
APPENDIX II TO SUBPART D OF PART 18—LIST OF FIGURES

Subpart E—Field Approval of Electrically Operated Mining Equipment

18.90 Purpose.
18.91 Electric equipment for which field approvals will be issued.
18.92 Quality of material and design.
18.93 Application for field approval; filing procedures.
18.94 Application for field approval; contents of application.
18.95 Approval of machines constructed of components approved, accepted or certified under Bureau of Mines Schedule 2D, 2E, 2F, or 2G.
18.96 Preparation of machines for inspection; requirements.
18.97 Inspection of machines; minimum requirements.
18.98 Enclosures, joints, and fastenings; pressure testing.
18.99 Notice of approval or disapproval; letters of approval and approval plates.

AUTHORITY: 30 U.S.C. 957, 961.

SOURCE: 33 FR 4660, Mar. 19, 1968, unless otherwise noted.

Subpart A—General Provisions

§ 18.1 Purpose.

The regulations in this part set forth the requirements to obtain MSHA: Approval of electrically operated machines and accessories intended for use in gassy mines or tunnels, certification of components intended for use on or with approved machines, permission to

Mine Safety and Health Admin., Labor § 18.2

modify the design of an approved machine or certified component, acceptance of flame-resistant hoses, sanction for use of experimental machines and accessories in gassy mines or tunnels; also, procedures for applying for such approval, certification, acceptance for listing.

[43 FR 12313, Mar. 24, 1978, as amended at 52 FR 17514, May 8, 1987; 57 FR 61223, Dec. 23, 1992; 73 FR 80611, Dec. 31, 2008]

§ 18.2 Definitions.

As used in this part—

Acceptance means written notification by MSHA that a hose has met the applicable requirements of this part and will be listed by MSHA as acceptable flame-resistant auxiliary equipment.

Acceptance marking means an identifying marking indicating that the hose has been accepted by MSHA for listing as flame resistant.

Accessory means associated electrical equipment, such as a distribution or splice box, that is not an integral part of an approved (permissible) machine.

Afterburning means the combustion of a flammable mixture that is drawn into a machine compartment after an internal explosion in the compartment.

Applicant means an individual, partnership, company, corporation, organization, or association that designs, manufactures, assembles, or controls the assembly of an electrical machine or accessory and seeks approval, certification, or permit, or MSHA acceptance for listing of flame-resistant hose.

Approval means a formal document issued by MSHA which states that a completely assembled electrical machine or accessory has met the applicable requirements of this part and which authorizes the attachment of an approval plate so indicating.

Approval plate means a metal plate, the design of which meets MSHA's requirements, for attachment to an approved machine or accessory, identifying it as permissible for use in gassy mines or tunnels.

Assistant Secretary means the Assistant Secretary of Labor for Mine Safety and Health.

Branch circuit means an electrical circuit connected to the main circuit, the conductors of which are of smaller size than the main circuit.

Bureau means the U.S. Bureau of Mines.

Certification means a formal written notification, issued by MSHA, which states that an electrical component complies with the applicable requirements of this part and, therefore, is suitable for incorporation in approved (permissible) equipment.

Certification label means a plate, label, or marking, the design of which meets MSHA's requirements, for attachment to a certified component identifying the component as having met the MSHA's requirements for incorporation in a machine to be submitted for approval.

Component means an integral part of an electrical machine or accessory that is essential to the functioning of the machine or accessory.

Connection box (also known as conduit or terminal box) means an enclosure mounted on an electrical machine or accessory to facilitate wiring, without the use of external splices. (Such boxes may have a joint common with an explosion-proof enclosure provided the adjoining surfaces conform to the requirements of subpart B of this part.)

Cylindrical joint means a joint comprised of two contiguous, concentric, cylindrical surfaces.

Distribution box means an enclosure through which one or more portable cables may be connected to a source of electrical energy, and which contains a short-circuit protective device for each outgoing cable.

Experimental equipment means any electrical machine or accessory that an applicant or MSHA may desire to operate experimentally for a limited time in a gassy mine or tunnel. (For example, this might include a machine constructed at a mine, an imported machine, or a machine or device designed and developed by MSHA.)

Explosion-proof enclosure means an enclosure that complies with the applicable design requirements in subpart B of this part and is so constructed that it will withstand internal explosions of methane-air mixtures: (1) Without damage to or excessive distortion of its

103

walls or cover(s), and (2) without ignition of surrounding methane-air mixtures or discharge of flame from inside to outside the enclosure.

Flame-arresting path means two or more adjoining or adjacent surfaces between which the escape of flame is prevented.

Flame resistant as applied to cable, hose, and insulating materials means material that will burn when held in a flame but will cease burning when the flame is removed.

Flammable mixture means a mixture of methane or natural gas and air that when ignited will propagate flame. Natural gas containing a high percentage of methane is a satisfactory substitute for pure methane in most tests.

Gassy mine means a coal mine classed as "gassy" by MESA or by the State in which the mine is situated.

Incendive arc or spark means an arc or spark releasing enough electrical or thermal energy to ignite a flammable mixture of the most easily ignitable composition.

Intrinsically safe means incapable of releasing enough electrical or thermal energy under normal or abnormal conditions to cause ignition of a flammable mixture of methane or natural gas and air of the most easily ignitable composition.

MESA means the United States Department of the Interior, Mining Enforcement and Safety Administration. Predecessor organization to MSHA, prior to March 9, 1978.

Mobile equipment means equipment that is self-propelled.

MSHA means the United States Department of Labor, Mine Safety and Health Administration.

Normal operation means the regular performance of those functions for which a machine or accessory was designed.

Permissible equipment means a completely assembled electrical machine or accessory for which a formal approval has been issued, as authorized by the Administrator, Mining Enforcement and Safety Administration under the Federal Coal Mine Health and Safety Act of 1969 (Pub. L. 91–173, 30 U.S.C. 801 or, after March 9, 1978, by the Assistant Secretary under the Federal Mine Safety and Health Act of 1977 (Pub. L. 91–173, as amended by Pub. L. 95–164, 30 U.S.C. 801).

Permit means a formal document, signed by the Assistant Secretary, authorizing the operation of specific experimental equipment in a gassy mine or tunnel under prescribed conditions.

Plane joint means two adjoining surfaces in parallel planes.

Portable cable, or *trailing cable* means a flame-resistant, flexible cable or cord through which electrical energy is transmitted to a permissible machine or accessory. (A portable cable is that portion of the power-supply system between the last short-circuit protective device, acceptable to MSHA, in the system and the machine or accessory to which it transmits electrical energy.)

Portable equipment means equipment that may be moved frequently and is constructed or mounted to facilitate such movement.

Potted component means a component that is entirely embedded in a solidified insulating material within an enclosure.

Pressure piling means the development of abnormal pressure as a result of accelerated rate of burning of a gas-air mixture. (Frequently caused by restricted configurations within enclosures.)

Qualified representative means a person authorized by MSHA to determine whether the applicable requirements of this part have been complied with in the original manufacture, rebuilding, or repairing of equipment for which approval, certification, or a permit is sought.

Splice box means a portable enclosure in which electrical conductors may be joined.

Step (rabbet) joint means a joint comprised of two adjoining surfaces with a change(s) in direction between its inner and outer edges. (A step joint may be composed of a cylindrical portion and a plane portion or of two or more plane portions.)

Threaded joint means a joint consisting of a male- and a female-threaded member, both of which are of the same type and gage.

[33 FR 4660, Mar. 19, 1968, as amended at 39 FR 23999, June 28, 1974; 43 FR 12314, Mar. 24, 1978; 57 FR 61223, Dec. 23, 1992; 73 FR 80611, Dec. 31, 2008]

Mine Safety and Health Admin., Labor §18.6

§18.3 Consultation.

By appointment, applicants or their representatives may visit the U.S. Department of Labor, Mine Safety and Health Administration, Approval and Certification Center, 765 Technology Drive, Triadelphia, WV 26059, to discuss a proposed design to be submitted for approval, certification, or acceptance for listing. No charge is made for such consultation and no written report thereof will be made to the applicant.

[33 FR 4660, Mar. 19, 1968, as amended at 43 FR 12314, Mar. 24, 1978; 73 FR 52211, Sept. 9, 2008]

§18.4 Electrical equipment for which approval is issued.

An approval will be issued only for a complete electrical machine or accessory. Only components meeting the requirements of subpart B of this part or those approved under part 7 of this chapter, unless they contain intrinsically safe circuits, shall be included in the assemblies.

[57 FR 61209, Dec. 23, 1992]

§18.5 Equipment for which certification will be issued.

Certification will be issued for a component or subassembly suitable to incorporate in an approved machine. Certification may be issued for such components as explosion-proof enclosures, battery trays, and connectors.

§18.6 Applications.

(a)(1) Investigation leading to approval, certification, extension thereof, or acceptance of hose will be undertaken by MSHA only pursuant to a written application. The application shall be accompanied by all necessary drawings, specifications, descriptions, and related materials, as set out in this part. Fees calculated in accordance with part 5 of this title shall be submitted in accordance with §5.40.

(2) Where the applicant for approval has used an independent testing laboratory under part 6 of this chapter to perform, in whole or in part, the necessary testing and evaluation for approval under this part, the applicant must provide to MSHA as part of the approval application:

(i) Written evidence of the laboratory's independence and current recognition by a laboratory accrediting organization;

(ii) Complete technical explanation of how the product complies with each requirement in the applicable MSHA product approval requirements;

(iii) Identification of components or features of the product that are critical to the safety of the product; and

(iv) All documentation, including drawings and specifications, as submitted to the independent laboratory by the applicant and as required by this part.

(3) An applicant may request testing and evaluation to non-MSHA product safety standards which have been determined by MSHA to be equivalent, under §6.20 of this chapter, to MSHA's product approval requirements under this part. A listing of all equivalency determinations will be published in 30 CFR part 6 and the applicable approval parts. The listing will state whether MSHA accepts the non-MSHA product safety standards in their original form, or whether MSHA will require modifications to demonstrate equivalency. If modifications are required, they will be provided in the listing. MSHA will notify the public of each equivalency determination and will publish a summary of the basis for its determination. MSHA will provide equivalency determination reports to the public upon request to the Approval and Certification Center. MSHA has made the following equivalency determinations applicable to this part 18.

(i) MSHA will accept applications for explosion-proof enclosures under part 18 designed and tested to the International Electrotechnical Commission's (IEC) standards for Electrical Apparatus for Explosive Gas Atmospheres, Part 0, General Requirements (IEC 60079-0, Fourth Edition, 2004-01); and Part 1, Electrical Apparatus for Explosive Gas Atmospheres, Flameproof Enclosures "d" (IEC 60079-1, Fifth Edition, 2003-11) (which are hereby incorporated by reference and made a part hereof) provided the modifications to the IEC standards specified in §18.6(a)(3)(i)(A) through (I) are met. The Director of the Federal Register

§ 18.6

30 CFR Ch. I (7-1-23 Edition)

approves this incorporation by reference in accordance with 5 U.S.C. 552(a) and 1 CFR part 51. The IEC standards may be inspected at the U.S. Department of Labor, Mine Safety and Health Administration, Electrical Safety Division, Approval and Certification Center, 765 Technology Drive, Triadelphia, WV 26059, or at the National Archives and Records Administration (NARA). For information on the availability of this material at NARA, call 202-741-6030, or go to: *http:// www.archives.gov/federal_register/ code_of_federal_regulations/ ibr_locations.html.* These IEC standards may be obtained from International Electrical Commission, Central Office 3, rue de Varembé, P.O. Box 131, CH-1211 GENEVA 20, Switzerland.

(A) Enclosures shall be made of metal and not have a compartment exceeding ten (10) feet in length. Glass or polycarbonate materials shall be the only materials utilized in the construction of windows and lenses. External surfaces of enclosures shall not exceed 150 °C (302 °F) and internal surface temperatures of enclosures with polycarbonate windows and lenses shall not exceed 115 °C (240 °F), in normal operation. Other non-metallic materials for enclosures or parts of enclosures will be evaluated, on a case-by-case basis, under the new technology provisions in § 18.20(b) of this part.

(B) Enclosures shall be rugged in construction and should meet existing requirements for minimum bolt size and spacing and for minimum wall, cover, and flange thicknesses specified in paragraph (g)(19) of § 7.304 Technical requirements. Enclosure fasteners should be uniform in size and length, be provided at all corners, and be secured from loosening by lockwashers or equivalent. An engineering analysis shall be provided for enclosure designs that deviate from the existing requirements. The analysis shall show that the proposed enclosure design meets or exceeds the mechanical strength of a comparable enclosure designed to 150 psig according to existing requirements, and that flamepath clearances in excess of existing requirements will not be produced at an internal pressure of 150 psig. This shall be verified by explosion testing the enclosure at a minimum of 150 psig.

(C) Enclosures shall be designed to withstand a minimum pressure of at least 150 psig without leakage through any welds or castings, rupture of any part that affects explosion-proof integrity, clearances exceeding those permitted under existing requirements along flame-arresting paths, or permanent distortion exceeding 0.040-inch per linear foot.

(D) Flamepath clearances, including clearances between fasteners and the holes through which they pass, shall not exceed those specified in existing requirements. No intentional gaps in flamepaths are permitted.

(E) The minimum lengths of the flame arresting paths, based on enclosure volume, shall conform to those specified in existing requirements to the nearest metric equivalent value (*e.g.*, 12.5 mm, 19 mm, and 25 mm are considered equivalent to ½ inch, ¾ inch and 1 inch respectively for plane and cylindrical joints). The widths of any grooves for o-rings shall be deducted in measuring the widths of flame-arresting paths.

(F) Gaskets shall not be used to form any part of a flame-arresting path. If o-rings are installed within a flamepath, the location of the o-rings shall meet existing requirements.

(G) Cable entries into enclosures shall be of a type that utilizes either flame-resistant rope packing material or sealing rings (grommets). If plugs and mating receptacles are mounted to an enclosure wall, they shall be of explosion-proof construction. Insulated bushings or studs shall not be installed in the outside walls of enclosures. Lead entrances utilizing sealing compounds and flexible or rigid metallic conduit are not permitted.

(H) Unused lead entrances shall be closed with a metal plug that is secured by spot welding, brazing, or equivalent.

(I) Special explosion tests are required for explosion-proof enclosures that share leads (electric conductors) through a common wall with another explosion-proof enclosure. These tests are required to determine the presence of pressure piling conditions in either

106

enclosure when one or more of the insulating barriers, sectionalizing terminals, or other isolating parts are sequentially removed from the common wall between the enclosures. Enclosures that exhibit pressures during these tests that exceed those specified in existing requirements must be provided with a warning tag. The durable warning tag must indicate that the insulating barriers, sectionalizing terminals, or other isolating parts be maintained in order to insure the explosion-proof integrity for either enclosure sharing a common wall. A warning tag is not required if the enclosures withstand a static pressure of twice the maximum value observed in the explosion tests.

(ii) [Reserved]

(4) The application, all related documents, and all correspondence concerning it shall be addressed to the U.S. Department of Labor, Mine Safety and Health Administration, Approval and Certification Center, 765 Technology Drive, Triadelphia, WV 26059.

(b)–(c) [Reserved]

(d) Applications for acceptance of hose as flame resistant shall include the following information: Trade name of hose, identification of materials used, including compound numbers, thickness of cover, thickness of tube, and number and weight of plies. The applicant shall provide other description or specifications as may be subsequently required.

(e) Drawings, drawing lists, specifications, wiring diagram, and descriptions shall be adequate in number and detail to identify fully the complete assembly, component parts, and subassemblies. Drawings shall be titled, numbered, dated and shall show the latest revision. Each drawing shall include a warning statement that changes in design must be authorized by MSHA before they are applied to approved equipment. When intrinsically safe circuits are incorporated in a machine or accessory, the wiring diagram shall include a warning statement that any change(s) in the intrinsically safe circuitry or components may result in an unsafe condition. The specifications shall include an assembly drawing(s) (see Figure 1 in Appendix II) showing the overall dimensions of the machine and the identity of each component part which may be listed thereon or separately, as in a bill of material (see Figure 2 in Appendix II). MSHA may accept photographs (minimum size 8″ × 10½″) in lieu of assembly drawing(s). Purchased parts shall be identified by the manufacturer's name, catalog number(s), and rating(s). In the case of standard hardware and miscellaneous parts, such as insulating pieces, size and kind of material shall be specified. All drawings of component parts submitted to MSHA shall be identical to those used in the manufacture of the parts. Dimensions of parts designed to prevent the passage of flame shall specify allowable tolerances. A notation "Do Not Drill Through" or equivalent should appear on drawings with the specifications for all "blind" holes.

(f) MSHA reserves the right to require the applicant to furnish supplementary drawings showing sections through complex flame-arresting paths, such as labyrinths used in conjunction with ball or roller bearings, and also drawings containing dimensions not indicated on other drawings submitted to MSHA.

(g) The applicant may ship his equipment to MSHA for investigation at the time of filing his application and payment of the required fees. Shipping charges shall be prepaid by the applicant.

(h) For a complete investigation leading to approval or certification the applicant shall furnish MSHA with the components necessary for inspection and testing. Expendable components shall be supplied by the applicant to permit continuous operation of the equipment while being tested. If special tools are necessary to assemble or disassemble any component for inspection or test, the applicant shall furnish them with the equipment to be tested.

(i) For investigation of a hose, the applicant shall furnish samples as follows:

Hose—a sample having a minimum length of 2 feet

(j) The applicant shall submit a sample caution statement (see Figure 3 in Appendix II) specifying the conditions for maintaining permissibility of the equipment.

§ 18.7

(k) The applicant shall submit a factory-inspection form (see Figure 4 in Appendix II) used to maintain quality control at the place of manufacture or assembly to insure that component parts are made and assembled in strict accordance with the drawings and specifications covering a design submitted to MSHA for approval or certification.

(l) MSHA will accept an application for an approval, a letter of certification, or an acceptance for listing of a product that is manufactured in a country other than the United States provided: (1) All correspondence, specifications, lettering on drawings (metric-system dimensions acceptable), instructions, and related information are in English; and (2) all other requirements of this part are met the same as for a domestic applicant.

[33 FR 4660, Mar. 19, 1968, as amended at 43 FR 12314, Mar. 24, 1978; 47 FR 14696, Apr. 6, 1982; 57 FR 61223, Dec. 23, 1992; 60 FR 33723, June 29, 1995; 60 FR 35693, July 11, 1995; 68 FR 36419, June 17, 2003; 70 FR 46343, Aug. 9, 2005; 71 FR 28584, May 17, 2006; 73 FR 52211, Sept. 9, 2008; 73 FR 80611, Dec. 31, 2008]

§ 18.7 [Reserved]

§ 18.8 Date for conducting investigation and tests.

The date of receipt of an application will determine the order of precedence for investigation and testing. If an electrical machine component or accessory fails to meet any of the requirements, it shall lose its order of precedence. If an application is submitted to resume investigation and testing after correction of the cause of failure, it will be treated as a new application and the order of precedence for investigation and testing will be so determined.

§ 18.9 Conduct of investigations and tests.

(a) Prior to the issuance of an approval, certification, or acceptance of a hose, only MSHA personnel, representative(s) of the applicant, and such other person(s) as may be mutually agreed upon may observe any part of the investigation or tests. The MSHA will hold as confidential and will not disclose principles or patentable features; nor will it disclose to persons other than the applicant the results of tests, chemical analysis of materials or any details of the applicant's drawings, specifications, instructions, and related material.

(b) Unless notified to the contrary by MSHA, the applicant shall provide assistance in disassembling parts for inspection, preparing parts for testing, and preparing equipment for return shipment. Explosion-proof enclosures shall be drilled and tapped for pipe connections in accordance with instructions supplied by MSHA.

(c) MSHA reserves the right to inspect a complete machine, component part, or accessory at a place other than the Bureau's premises, such as the assembly plant or other location acceptable to MSHA, at the applicant's expense.

(d) Applicants shall be responsible for their representatives present during tests and for observers admitted at their request and shall save the Government harmless in the event of damage to applicant's property or injury to applicant's representatives or to observers admitted at their request.

[33 FR 4660, Mar. 19, 1968; 33 FR 6345, Apr. 26, 1968, as amended at 57 FR 61223, Dec. 23, 1992; 73 FR 80612, Dec. 31, 2008]

§ 18.10 Notice of approval or disapproval.

(a) Upon completing investigation of a complete assembly of an electrical machine or accessory, MSHA will issue to the applicant either a written notice of approval or a written notice of disapproval, as the case may require. No informal notification of approval will be issued. If a notice of disapproval is issued, it will be accompanied by details of the defects, with recommendations for possible correction. MSHA will not disclose, except to the applicant, any information upon which a notice of disapproval has been issued.

(b) A formal notice of approval will be accompanied by a list of drawings, specifications, and related material, covering the details of design and construction of the equipment upon which the approval is based. Applicants shall keep exact duplicates of the drawings, specifications, and descriptions that relate to equipment for which an approval has been issued, and the drawings and specifications shall be adhered to exactly in production of the approved equipment.

(c) An applicant shall not advertise or otherwise represent his equipment as approved (permissible) until he has received MSHA's formal notice of approval.

§ 18.11 Approval plate.

(a)(1) The notice of approval will be accompanied by a photograph of an approval plate, bearing the emblem of Mine Safety and Health Administration, the name of the complete assembly, the name of the applicant, and spaces for the approval number, serial number, and the type or model of machine.

(2) An extension of approval will not affect the original approval number except that the extension number shall be added to the original approval number on the approval plate. (Example: Original approval No. 2G–3000; seventh extension No. 2G–3000–7.)

(b) The applicant shall reproduce the design on a separate plate, which shall be attached in a suitable place, on each complete assembly to which it relates. The size, type, location, and method of attaching an approval plate are subject to MSHA's concurrence. The method for affixing the approval plate shall not impair any explosion-proof feature of the equipment.

(c) The approval plate identifies as permissible the machine or accessory to which it is attached, and use of the approval plate obligates the applicant to whom the approval was issued to maintain in his plant the quality of each complete assembly and guarantees that the equipment is manufactured and assembled according to the drawings, specifications, and descriptions upon which the approval and subsequent extension(s) of approval were based.

(d) A completely assembled approved machine with an integral dust collector shall bear an approval plate indicating that the requirements of part 33 of this chapter (Bureau of Mines Schedule 25B), have been complied with. Approval numbers will be assigned under each part of such joint approvals.

[33 FR 4660, Mar. 19, 1968, as amended at 43 FR 12314, Mar. 24, 1978]

§ 18.12 Letter of certification.

(a) A letter of certification may be issued by MSHA for a component intended for incorporation in a complete machine or accessory for which an approval may be subsequently issued. A letter of certification will be issued to an applicant when a component has met all the applicable requirements of this part. Included in the letter of certification will be an assigned MSHA certification number that will identify the certified component.

(b) A letter of certification will be accompanied by a list of drawings, specifications, and related material covering the details of design and construction of a component upon which the letter of certification is based. Applicants shall keep exact duplicates of the drawings, specifications, and descriptions that relate to the component for which a letter of certification has been issued; and the drawings and specifications shall be adhered to exactly in production of the certified component.

(c) A component shall not be represented as certified until the applicant has received MSHA's letter of certification for the component. Certified components are not to be represented as "approved" or "permissible" because such terms apply only to completely assembled machines or accessories.

§ 18.13 Certification plate.

Each certified component shall be identified by a certification plate attached to the component in a manner acceptable to MSHA. The method of attachment shall not impair any explosion-proof characteristics of the component. The plate shall be of serviceable material, acceptable, to MSHA, and shall contain the following:

Certified as complying with the applicable requirements of 30 CFR part _____.
Certification No._____.

The blank spaces shall be filled with appropriate designations. Inclusion of the information on a company name plate will be permitted provided the plate is made of material acceptable to MSHA.

§ 18.14 Identification of tested noncertified explosion-proof enclosures.

An enclosure that meets all applicable requirements of this part, but has not been certified by MSHA, shall be identified by a permanent marking on it in a conspicuous location. The design of such marking shall consist of capital letters USMSHA not less than ¼ inch in height, enclosed in a circle not less than 1 inch in diameter.

[33 FR 4660, Mar. 19, 1968, as amended at 43 FR 12314, Mar. 24, 1978]

§ 18.15 Changes after approval or certification.

If an applicant desires to change any feature of approved equipment or a certified component, he shall first obtain MSHA's concurrence pursuant to the following procedure:

(a)(1) Application shall be made as for an original approval or letter of certification requesting that the existing approval or certification be extended to cover the proposed changes and shall be accompanied by drawings, specifications, and related information, showing the changes in detail.

(2) Where the applicant for approval has used an independent laboratory under part 6 of this chapter to perform, in whole or in part, the necessary testing and evaluation for approval of changes to an approved or certified product under this part, the applicant must provide to MSHA as part of the approval application:

(i) Written evidence of the laboratory's independence and current recognition by a laboratory accrediting organization;

(ii) Complete technical explanation of how the product complies with each requirement in the applicable MSHA product approval requirements;

(iii) Identification of components or features of the product that are critical to the safety of the product; and

(iv) All documentation, including drawings and specifications, as submitted to the independent laboratory by the applicant and as required by this part.

(b) The application will be examined by MSHA to determine whether inspection or testing will be required. Testing will be required if there is a possibility that the change(s) may adversely affect safety.

(c) If the change(s) meets the requirements of this part, a formal extension of approval or certification will be issued, accompanied by a list of new or revised drawings, specifications, and related information to be added to those already on file for the original approval or certification.

(d) Revisions in drawings or specifications that do not involve actual change in the explosion-proof features of equipment may be handled informally.

[43 FR 12313, Mar. 24, 1978, as amended at 52 FR 17514, May 8, 1987; 68 FR 36419, June 17, 2003]

§ 18.16 Withdrawal of approval, certification, or acceptance.

MSHA reserves the right to rescind, for cause, any approval, certification, acceptance, or extension thereof, issued under this part.

Subpart B—Construction and Design Requirements

§ 18.20 Quality of material, workmanship, and design.

(a) Electrically operated equipment intended for use in coal mines shall be rugged in construction and shall be designed to facilitate inspection and maintenance.

(b) MSHA will test only electrical equipment that in the opinion of its qualified representatives is constructed of suitable materials, is of good quality workmanship, based on sound engineering principles, and is safe for its intended use. Since all possible designs, circuits, arrangements, or combinations of components and materials cannot be foreseen, MSHA reserves the right to modify design, construction, and test requirements to obtain the same degree of protection as provided by the tests described in Subpart C of this part.

(c) Moving parts, such as rotating saws, gears, and chain drives, shall be guarded to prevent personal injury.

(d) Flange joints and lead entrances shall be accessible for field inspection, where practicable.

(e) An audible warning device shall be provided on each mobile machine

Mine Safety and Health Admin., Labor § 18.28

that travels at a speed greater than 2.5 miles per hour.

(f) Brakes shall be provided for each wheel-mounted machine, unless design of the driving mechanism will preclude accidental movement of the machine when parked.

(g) A headlight and red light-reflecting material shall be provided on both front and rear of each mobile transportation unit that travels at a speed greater than 2.5 miles per hour. Red light-reflecting material should be provided on each end of other mobile machines.

§ 18.21 Machines equipped with powered dust collectors.

Powered dust collectors on machines submitted for approval shall meet the applicable requirements of Part 33 of this chapter (Bureau of Mines Schedule 25B), and shall bear the approval number assigned by MSHA.

§ 18.22 Boring-type machines equipped for auxiliary face ventilation.

Each boring-type continuous-mining machine that is submitted for approval shall be constructed with an unobstructed continuous space(s) of not less than 200 square inches total cross-sectional area on or within the machine to which flexible tubing may be attached to facilitate auxiliary face ventilation.

§ 18.23 Limitation of external surface temperatures.

The temperature of the external surfaces of mechanical or electrical components shall not exceed 150 °C. (302 °F.) under normal operating conditions.

§ 18.24 Electrical clearances.

Minimum clearances between uninsulated electrical conductor surfaces, or between uninsulated conductor surfaces and grounded metal surfaces, within the enclosure shall be as follows:

MINIMUM CLEARANCES BETWEEN UNINSULATED SURFACES

Phase-to-Phase Voltage (rms)	Clearances (inches)	
	Phase-to-Phase	Phase-to-Ground or Control Circuit
0 to 250	0.25	0.25

MINIMUM CLEARANCES BETWEEN UNINSULATED SURFACES—Continued

Phase-to-Phase Voltage (rms)	Clearances (inches)	
	Phase-to-Phase	Phase-to-Ground or Control Circuit
251 to 600	0.28	0.25
601 to 1000	0.61	0.25
1001 to 2400	1.4	0.6
2401 to 4160	3.0	1.4

[57 FR 61209, Dec. 23, 1992]

§ 18.25 Combustible gases from insulating material.

(a) Insulating materials that give off flammable or explosive gases when decomposed electrically shall not be used within enclosures where the materials are subjected to destructive electrical action.

(b) Parts coated or impregnated with insulating materials shall be heat-treated to remove any combustible solvent(s) before assembly in an explosion-proof enclosure. Air-drying insulating materials are excepted.

§ 18.26 Static electricity.

Nonmetallic rotating parts, such as belts and fans, shall be provided with a means to prevent an accumulation of static electricity.

§ 18.27 Gaskets.

A gasket(s) shall not be used between any two surfaces forming a flame-arresting path except as follows:

(a) A gasket of lead, elastomer, or equivalent will be acceptable provided the gasket does not interfere with an acceptable metal-to-metal joint.

(b) A lead gasket(s) or equivalent will be acceptable between glass and a hard metal to form all or a part of a flame-arresting path.

§ 18.28 Devices for pressure relief, ventilation, or drainage.

(a) Devices for installation on explosion-proof enclosures to relieve pressure, ventilate, or drain will be acceptable provided the length of the flame-arresting path and the clearances or size of holes in perforated metal will prevent discharge of flame in explosion tests.

§ 18.29

(b) Devices for pressure relief, ventilation, or drainage shall be constructed of materials that resist corrosion and distortion, and be so designed that they can be cleaned readily. Provision shall be made for secure attachment of such devices.

(c) Devices for pressure relief, ventilation, or drainage will be acceptable for application only on enclosures with which they are explosion tested.

§ 18.29 Access openings and covers, including unused lead-entrance holes.

(a) Access openings in explosion-proof enclosures will be permitted only where necessary for maintenance of internal parts such as motor brushes and fuses.

(b) Covers for access openings shall meet the same requirements as any other part of an enclosure except that threaded covers shall be secured against loosening, preferably with screws having heads requiring a special tool. (See Figure 1 in Appendix II.)

(c) Holes in enclosures that are provided for lead entrances but which are not in use shall be closed with metal plugs secured by spot welding, brazing, or equivalent. (See Figure 10 in Appendix II.)

§ 18.30 Windows and lenses.

(a) MSHA may waive testing of materials for windows or lenses except headlight lenses. When tested, material for windows or lenses shall meet the test requirements prescribed in § 18.66 and shall be sealed in place or provided with flange joints in accordance with § 18.31.

(b) Windows or lenses shall be protected from mechanical damage by structural design, location, or guarding. Windows or lenses, other than headlight lenses, having an exposed area greater than 8 square inches, shall be provided with guarding or equivalent.

§ 18.31 Enclosures—joints and fastenings.

(a) Explosion-proof enclosures:

(1) Cast or welded enclosures shall be designed to withstand a minimum internal pressure of 150 pounds per square inch (gage). Castings shall be free from blowholes.

(2) Welded joints forming an enclosure shall have continuous gas-tight welds. All welds shall be made in accordance with American Welding Society standards.

(3) External rotating parts shall not be constructed of aluminum alloys containing more than 0.6 percent magnesium.

(4) MSHA reserves the right to require the applicant to conduct static-pressure tests on each enclosure when MSHA determines that the particular design will not permit complete visual inspection or when the joint(s) forming an enclosure is welded on one side only (see § 18.67).

(5) Threaded covers and mating parts shall be designed with Class 1A and 1B (coarse, loose-fitting) threads. The flame-arresting path of threaded joints shall conform to the requirements of paragraph (a)(6) of this section.

(6) Enclosure requirements shall be based on the internal volumes of the empty enclosure. The internal volume is the volume remaining after deducting the volume of any part that is essential in maintaining the explosion-proof integrity of the enclosure or necessary for the operation. Essential parts include the parts that constitute the flame-arresting path and those necessary to secure parts that constitute a flame-arresting path. Enclosures shall meet the following requirements:

EXPLOSION-PROOF REQUIREMENTS BASED ON VOLUME

	Volume of empty enclosure		
	Less than 45 cu. in.	45 to 124 cu. in. inclusive	More than 124 cu. in.
Minimum thickness of material for walls [1]	1/8″	3/16″	1/4″
Minimum thickness of material for flanges and covers	2 1/4″	3 3/8″	3 1/2″
Minimum width of joint; all in one plane [4]	1/2″	3/4″	1″
Maximum clearance; joint all in one plane	0.002″	0.003″	0.004″
Minimum width of joint, portions of which are in different planes; cylinders or equivalent [4] [5]	3/8″	5/8″	3/4″

Mine Safety and Health Admin., Labor § 18.31

EXPLOSION-PROOF REQUIREMENTS BASED ON VOLUME—Continued

	Volume of empty enclosure		
	Less than 45 cu. in.	45 to 124 cu. in. inclusive	More than 124 cu. in.
Maximum clearances; joint in two or more planes, cylinders or equivalent:			
(a) Portion perpendicular to plane [6]	0.008″	0.008″	0.008″
(b) Plane portion	0.006″	0.006″	0.006″
Maximum bolt [7] [8] spacing; joints all in one plane	([16])	([16])	([16])
Maximum bolt spacing; joints, portions of which are in different planes	([9])	([9])	([9])
Minimum diameter of bolt (without regard to type of joint)	¼″	¼″	⅜″
Minimum thread engagement [10]	¼″	¼″	⅜″
Maximum diametrical clearance between bolt body and unthreaded holes through which it passes [8] [11] [12]	1/64″	1/32″	1/16″
Minimum distance from interior of enclosure to the edge of a bolt hole: [8] [13]			
Joint—minimum width 1″	....	....	[14] 7/16″
Joint—less than 1″ wide	⅛″	3/16″	....
Cylindrical joints			
Shaft centered by ball or roller bearings:			
Minimum length of flame-arresting path	½″	¾″	1″
Maximum diametrical clearance	0.020″	0.025″	0.030″
Other cylindrical joints: [15]			
Minimum length of flame-arresting path	½″	¾″	1″
Maximum diametrical clearance	0.006″	0.008″	0.010″

[1] This is the minimal nominal dimension when applied to standard steel plate.
[2] 1/32 inch less is allowable for machining rolled plate.
[3] 1/16 inch less is allowable for machining rolled plate.
[4] The widths of any grooves, such as grooves for holding oil seals or O-rings, shall be deducted in measuring the widths of flame-arresting paths.
[5] If only two planes are involved, neither portion of a joint shall be less than ⅛ inch wide, unless the wider portion conforms to the same requirements as those for a joint that is all in one plane. If more than two planes are involved (as in labyrinths or tongue-and-groove joints) the combined lengths of those portions having prescribed clearances are considered.
[6] The allowable diametrical clearance is 0.008 inch when the portion perpendicular to the plane portion is ¼ inch or greater in length. If the perpendicular portion is more than ⅛ inch but less than ¼ inch wide, the diametrical clearance shall not exceed 0.006 inch.
[7] Where the term "bolt" is used, it refers to a machine bolt or a cap screw, and for either of these studs may be substituted provided the studs, bottom in blind holes, are completely welded in place, or the bottom of the hole is closed with a plug secured by weld or braze. Bolts shall be provided at all corners.
[8] The requirements as to diametrical clearance around the bolt and minimum distance from the bolt hole to the inside of the explosion-proof enclosure apply to steel dowel pins. In addition, when such pins are used, the spacing between centers of the bolts on either side of the pin shall not exceed 5 inches.
[9] Adequacy of bolt spacing will be judged on the basis of size and configuration of the enclosure, strength of materials, and explosion test results.
[10] In general, minimum thread engagement shall be equal to or greater than the diameter of the bolt specified.
[11] Threaded holes for fastening bolts shall be machined to remove burrs or projections that affect planarity of a surface forming a flame-arresting path.
[12] This maximum clearance applies only when the bolt is located within the flamepath.
[13] The edge of the bolt hole shall include the edge of any machining done to the bolt hole, such as chamfering.
[14] Less than 7/16″ (¼″ minimum) will be acceptable provided the diametrical clearance for fastening bolts does not exceed 1/32″.
[15] Shafts or operating rods through journal bearings shall be at least ¼″ in diameter. The length of fit shall not be reduced when a push button is depressed. Operating rods shall have a shoulder or head on the portion inside the enclosure. Essential parts riveted or bolted to the inside portion are acceptable in lieu of a head or shoulder, but cotter pins and similar devices shall not be used.
[16] 6″ with a minimum of 4 bolts.

(7) O-rings, if used in a flame-arresting path, shall meet the following:

(i) When the flame-arresting path is in one plane, the o-ring shall be located at least one-half the acceptable flame-arresting path length specified in paragraph (a)(6) of this section within the outside edge of the path (see figure J–2 in the appendix to subpart J of part 7 of this chapter).

(ii) When the flame-arresting path is one of the plane-cylindrical type (step joint), the o-ring shall be located at least ½ inch within the outer edge of the plane portion (see figure J–3 in the appendix to subpart J of part 7 of this chapter), or at the junction of the plane and cylindrical portion of the joint (see figure J–4 in the appendix to subpart J of part 7 of this chapter); or in the cylindrical portion (see figure J–5 in the appendix to subpart J of part 7 of this chapter).

(8) Mating parts comprising a pressed fit shall result in a minimum interference of 0.001 inch between the parts. The minimum length of the pressed fit

shall be equal to the minimum thickness requirement of paragraph (a)(6) of this section for the material in which the fit is made.

(b) Enclosures for potted components: Enclosures shall be rugged and constructed with materials having 75 percent, or greater, of the thickness and flange width specified in paragraph (a) of this section. These enclosures shall be provided with means for attaching hose conduit, unless energy carried by the cable is intrinsically safe.

(c) No assembly will be approved that requires the opening of an explosion-proof enclosure to operate a switch, rheostat, or other device during normal operation of a machine.

[33 FR 4660, Mar. 19, 1968, as amended at 57 FR 61209, Dec. 23, 1992]

§ 18.32 Fastenings—additional requirements.

(a) Bolts, screws, or studs shall be used for fastening adjoining parts to prevent the escape of flame from an enclosure. Hinge pins or clamps will be acceptable for this purpose provided MSHA determines them to be equally effective.

(b) Lockwashers shall be provided for all bolts, screws, and studs that secure parts of explosion-proof enclosures. Special fastenings designed to prevent loosening will be acceptable in lieu of lockwashers, provided MSHA determines them to be equally effective.

(c) Fastenings shall be as uniform in size as practicable to preclude improper assembly.

(d) Holes for fastenings shall not penetrate to the interior of an explosion-proof enclosure, except as provided in paragraph (a)(9) of § 18.34, and shall be threaded to insure that a specified bolt or screw will not bottom even if its lockwasher is omitted.

(e) A minimum of ⅛-inch of stock shall be left at the center of the bottom of each hole drilled for fastenings.

(f) Fastenings used for joints on explosion-proof enclosures shall not be used for attaching nonessential parts or for making electrical connections.

(g) The acceptable sizes for and spacings of fastenings shall be determined by the size of the enclosure, as indicated in § 18.31.

(h) MSHA reserves the right to conduct explosion tests with standard bolts, nuts, cap screws, or studs substituted for any special high-tensile strength fastening(s) specified by the applicant.

(i) Coil-thread inserts, if used in holes for fastenings, shall meet the following:

(1) The inserts shall have internal screw threads.

(2) The holes for the inserts shall be drilled and tapped consistent with the insert manufacturer's specifications.

(3) The inserts shall be installed consistent with the insert manufacturer's specifications.

(4) The insert shall be of sufficient length to ensure the minimum thread engagement of fastening specified in § 18.31(a)(6) of this part.

[33 FR 4660, Mar. 19, 1968, as amended at 57 FR 61210, Dec. 23, 1992]

§ 18.33 Finish of surface joints.

Flat surfaces between bolt holes that form any part of a flame-arresting path shall be plane to within a maximum deviation of one-half the maximum clearance specified in § 18.31(a)(6). All metal surfaces forming a flame-arresting path shall be finished during the manufacturing process to not more than 250 microinches. A thin film of nonhardening preparation to inhibit rusting may be applied to these finished metal surfaces as long as the final surface can be readily wiped free of any foreign materials.

[57 FR 61210, Dec. 23, 1992]

§ 18.34 Motors.

Explosion-proof electric motor assemblies intended for use in approved equipment in underground mines that are specifically addressed in part 7 of this chapter shall be approved under part 7 of this chapter after February 22, 1996. Those motor assemblies not specifically addressed under part 7 of this chapter shall be accepted or certified under this part.

(a) *General.* (1) Motors shall have explosion-proof enclosures.

(2) Motors submitted to MSHA for test shall be equipped with unshielded bearings regardless of whether that type of bearing is specified.

(3) MSHA reserves the right to test motors with the maximum clearance specified between the shaft and the mating part which forms the required flame-arresting path. Also reserved is the right to remachine these parts, at the applicant's expense, to specified dimensions to provide the maximum clearance.

NOTE: For example, a shaft with a diameter greater than 2 inches at the flame-arresting portion might require such machining.

(4) Ball and roller bearings and oil seals will not be acceptable as flame-arresting paths; therefore, a separate path shall be provided between the shaft and another part, preferably inby the bearing. The length and clearances of such flame-arresting path shall conform to the requirements of § 18.31.

(5) Labyrinths or other arrangements that provide change(s) in direction of escaping gases will be acceptable but the use of small detachable pieces shall not be permitted unless structurally unavoidable. The lengths of flame-arresting path(s) and clearance(s) shall conform to the requirements of § 18.31.

(6) Oil seals shall be removed from motors prior to submission for explosion tests.

NOTE: Oil seals will be removed from motors prior to explosion tests and therefore may be omitted from motors submitted for investigation.

(7) Openings for filling and draining bearing lubricants shall be so located as to prevent escape of flame through them.

(8) An outer bearing cap will not be considered as forming any part of a flame-arresting path unless the cap is used as a bearing cartridge.

NOTE: The outer bearing cap will be omitted during explosion tests unless it houses the bearing.

(9) If unavoidable, holes may be made through motor casings for bolts, studs, or screws to hold essential parts such as pole pieces, brush rigging, and bearing cartridges. Such parts shall be attached to the casing by at least two fastenings. The threaded holes in these parts shall be blind, unless the fastenings are inserted from the inside, in which case the fastenings shall not be accessible with the armature of the motor in place.

(b) *Direct-current motors.* For direct-current motors with narrow interpoles, the distance from the edge of the pole piece to any bolt hole in the frame shall be not less than ⅛ inch. If the distance is ⅛ to ¼ inch, the diametrical clearance for the pole bolt shall not exceed ¹⁄₆₄ inch for not less than ½ inch through the frame. Furthermore, the pole piece shall have the same radius as the inner surface of the frame. Pole pieces may be shimmed as necessary.

(c) *Alternating-current motors.* Stator laminations that form a part of an explosion-proof enclosure will be acceptable provided: (1) The laminations and their end rings are fastened together under pressure; (2) the joint between the end rings and the laminations is not less than ¼ inch, but preferably as close to 1 inch as possible; and (3) it shall be impossible to insert a 0.0015-inch thickness gage to a depth exceeding ⅛ inch between adjacent laminations or between end rings and laminations.

(d) *Small motors (alternating- and direct-current).* Motors having internal free volume not exceeding 350 cubic inches and joints not exceeding 32 inches in outer circumference will be acceptable for investigation if provided with rabbet joints between the stator frame and the end bracket having the following dimensions:

DIMENSIONS OF RABBET JOINTS—INCHES

Minimum total width	Min. width of clamped radial portion	Max. clearance of radial portion	Max. diametrical clearance at axial portion
⅜	³⁄₆₄	0.0015	0.003
½	³⁄₆₄	.002	.003
½	³⁄₃₂	.002	.004

[33 FR 4660, Mar. 19, 1968, as amended at 57 FR 61210, Dec. 23, 1992]

§ 18.35 Portable (trailing) cables and cords.

(a) Portable cables and cords used to conduct electrical energy to face equipment shall conform to the following:

(1) Have each conductor of a current-carrying capacity consistent with the Insulated Power Cable Engineers Association (IPCEA) standards. (See Tables 1 and 2 in Appendix I.)

(2) Have current-carrying conductors not smaller than No. 14 (AWG). Cords with sizes 14 to 10 (AWG) conductors

§ 18.36

shall be constructed with heavy jackets, the diameters of which are given in Table 6 in Appendix I.

(3) Be accepted as flame resistant under this part or approved under subpart K of part 7 of this chapter.

(4) Have short-circuit protection at the outby (circuit-connecting) end of ungrounded conductors. (See Table 8 in Appendix I.) The fuse rating or trip setting shall be included in the assembler's specifications.

(5) Ordinarily the length of a portable (trailing) cable shall not exceed 500 feet. Where the method of mining requires the length of a portable (trailing) cable to be more than 500 feet, such length of cable shall be permitted only under the following prescribed conditions:

(i) The lengths of portable (trailing) cables shall not exceed those specified in Table 9, Appendix I, titled "Specifications for Portable Cables Longer Than 500 Feet."

(ii) Short-circuit protection shall be provided by a protective device with an instantaneous trip setting as near as practicable to the maximum starting-current-inrush value, but the setting shall not exceed the trip value specified in MSHA approval for the equipment for which the portable (trailing) cable furnishes electric power.

(6) Have nominal outside dimensions consistent with IPCEA standards. (See Tables 4, 5, 6, and 7 in Appendix I.)

(7) Have conductors of No. 4 (AWG) minimum for direct-current mobile haulage units or No. 6 (AWG) minimum for alternating-current mobile haulage units.

(8) Have not more than five well-made temporary splices in a single length of portable cable.

(b) Sectionalized portable cables will be acceptable provided the connectors used inby the last open crosscut in a gassy mine meet the requirements of § 18.41.

(c) A portable cable having conductors smaller than No. 6 (AWG), when used with a trolley tap and a rail clamp, shall have well insulated single conductors not smaller than No. 6 (AWG) spliced to the outby end of each conductor. All splices shall be made in a workmanlike manner to insure good electrical conductivity, insulation, and mechanical strength.

(d) Suitable provisions shall be made to facilitate disconnection of portable cable quickly and conveniently for replacement.

[33 FR 4660, Mar. 19, 1968; 33 FR 6343, Apr. 26, 1968, as amended at 57 FR 61223, Dec. 23, 1992]

§ 18.36 Cables between machine components.

(a) Cables between machine components shall have: (1) Adequate current-carrying capacity for the loads involved, (2) short-circuit protection, (3) insulation compatible with the impressed voltage, and (4) flame-resistant properties unless totally enclosed within a flame-resistant hose conduit or other flame-resistant material.

(b) Cables between machine components shall be: (1) Clamped in place to prevent undue movement, (2) protected from mechanical damage by position, flame-resistant hose conduit, metal tubing, or troughs (flexible or threaded rigid metal conduit will not be acceptable), (3) isolated from hydraulic lines, and (4) protected from abrasion by removing all sharp edges which they might contact.

(c) Cables (cords) for remote-control circuits extending from permissible equipment will be exempted from the requirements of conduit enclosure provided the total electrical energy carried is intrinsically safe or that the cables are constructed with heavy jackets, the sizes of which are stated in Table 6 of Appendix I. Cables (cords) provided with hose-conduit protection shall have a tensile strength not less than No. 16 (AWG) three-conductor, type SO cord. (Reference: 7.7.7 IPCEA Pub. No. S–19–81, Fourth Edition.) Cables (cords) constructed with heavy jackets shall consist of conductors not smaller than No. 14 (AWG) regardless of the number of conductors.

§ 18.37 Lead entrances.

(a) Insulated cable(s), which must extend through an outside wall of an explosion-proof enclosure, shall pass through a stuffing-box lead entrance. All sharp edges that might damage insulation shall be removed from stuffing boxes and packing nuts.

(b) Stuffing boxes shall be so designed, and the amount of packing used shall be such, that with the packing properly compressed, the gland nut still has a clearance distance of 1/8 inch or more to travel without meeting interference by parts other than packing. In addition, the gland nut shall have a minimum of three effective threads engaged. (See figures 8, 9 and 10 in appendix II.)

(c) Packing nuts and stuffing boxes shall be secured against loosening.

(d) Compressed packing material shall be in contact with the cable jacket for a length of not less than 1/2 inch.

(e) Special requirements for glands in which asbestos-packing material is specified are:

(1) Asbestos-packing material shall be untreated, not less than 3/16-inch diameter if round, or not less than 3/16 by 3/16 inch if square. The width of the space for packing material shall not exceed by more than 50 percent the diameter or width of the uncompressed packing material.

(2) The allowable diametrical clearance between the cable and the holes in the stuffing box and packing nut shall not exceed 75 percent of the nominal diameter or width of the packing material.

(f) Special requirements for glands in which a compressible material (example—synthetic elastomers) other than asbestos is specified, are:

(1) The packing material shall be flame resistant.

(2) The radial clearance between the cable jacket and the nominal inside diameter of the packing material shall not exceed 1/32-inch, based on the nominal specified diameter of the cable.

(3) The radial clearance between the nominal outside diameter of the packing material and the inside wall of the stuffing box (that portion into which the packing material fits) shall not exceed 1/32-inch.

[33 FR 4660, Mar. 19, 1968, as amended at 57 FR 61210, Dec. 23, 1992]

§ 18.38 Leads through common walls.

(a) Insulated studs will be acceptable for use in a common wall between two explosion-proof enclosures.

(b) When insulated wires or cables are extended through a common wall between two explosion-proof enclosures in insulating bushings, such bushings shall be not less than 1-inch long and the diametrical clearance between the wire or cable insulation and the holes in the bushings shall not exceed 1/16-inch (based on the nominal specified diameter of the cable). The insulating bushings shall be secured in the metal wall.

(c) Insulated wires or cables conducted from one explosion-proof enclosure to another through conduit, tubing, piping, or other solid-wall passageways will be acceptable provided one end of the passageway is plugged, thus isolating one enclosure from the other. Glands of secured bushings with close-fitting holes through which the wires or cables are conducted will be acceptable for plugging. The tubing or duct specified for the passageway shall be brazed or welded into the walls of both explosion-proof enclosures with continuous gas-tight welds.

(d) If wires and cables are taken through openings closed with sealing compounds, the design of the opening and characteristics of the compounds shall be such as to hold the sealing material in place without tendency of the material to crack or flow out of its place. The material also must withstand explosion tests without cracking or loosening.

(e) Openings through common walls between explosion-proof enclosures not provided with bushings or sealing compound, shall be large enough to prevent pressure piling.

§ 18.39 Hose conduit.

Hose conduit shall be provided for mechanical protection of all machine cables that are exposed to damage. Hose conduit shall be flame resistant and have a minimum wall thickness of 3/16 inch. The flame resistance of hose conduit will be determined in accordance with the requirements of § 18.65.

§ 18.40 Cable clamps and grips.

Insulated clamps shall be provided for all portable (trailing) cables to prevent strain on the cable terminals of a machine. Also insulated clamps shall be provided to prevent strain on both ends of each cable or cord leading from a machine to a detached or separately mounted component. Cable grips anchored to the cable may be used in lieu of insulated strain clamps. Supporting clamps for cables used for wiring around machines shall be provided in a manner acceptable to MSHA.

§ 18.41 **Plug and receptacle-type connectors.**

(a) Plug and receptacle-type connectors for use inby the last open crosscut in a gassy mine shall be so designed that insertion or withdrawal of a plug cannot cause incendive arcing or sparking. Also, connectors shall be so designed that no live terminals, except as hereinafter provided, are exposed upon withdrawal of a plug. The following types will be acceptable:

(1) Connectors in which the mating or separation of the male and female electrodes is accomplished within an explosion-proof enclosure.

(2) Connectors that are mechanically or electrically interlocked with an automatic circuit-interrupting device.

(i) *Mechanically interlocked connectors.* If a mechanical interlock is provided, the design shall be such that the plug cannot be withdrawn before the circuit has been interrupted and the circuit cannot be established with the plug partially withdrawn.

(ii) *Electrically interlocked connectors.* If an electrical interlock is provided, the total load shall be removed before the plug can be withdrawn and the electrical energy in the interlocking pilot circuit shall be intrinsically safe, unless the pilot circuit is opened within an explosion-proof enclosure.

(3) Single-pole connectors for individual conductors of a circuit used at terminal points shall be so designed that all plugs must be completely inserted before the control circuit of the machine can be energized.

(b) Plug and receptacle-type connectors used for sectionalizing the cables outby the last open crosscut in a gassy mine need not be explosion-proof or electrically interlocked provided such connectors are designed and constructed to prevent accidental separation.

(c) Conductors shall be securely attached to the electrodes in a plug or receptacle and the connections shall be totally enclosed.

(d) Molded-elastomer connectors will be acceptable provided:

(1) Any free space within the plug or receptacle is isolated from the exterior of the plug.

(2) Joints between the elastomer and metal parts are not less than 1 inch wide and the elastomer is either bonded to or fits tightly with metal parts.

(e) The contacts of all line-side connectors shall be shielded or recessed adequately.

(f) For a mobile battery-powered machine, a plug and receptacle-type connector will be acceptable in lieu of an interlock provided:

(1) The plug is padlocked to the receptacle and is held in place by a threaded ring or equivalent mechanical fastening in addition to a padlock. A connector within a padlocked enclosure will be acceptable; or,

(2) The plug is held in place by a threaded ring or equivalent mechanical fastening, in addition to the use of a device that is captive and requires a special tool to disengage and allow for the separation of the connector. All connectors using this means of compliance shall have a clearly visible warning tag that states: "DO NOT DISENGAGE UNDER LOAD," or an equivalent statement; or,

(3) The plug is held in place by a spring-loaded or other locking device, that maintains constant pressure against a threaded ring or equivalent mechanical fastening, to secure the plug from accidental separation. All connectors using this means of compliance shall have a clearly visible warning tag that states: "DO NOT DISENGAGE UNDER LOAD," or an equivalent statement.

[33 FR 4660, Mar. 19, 1968, as amended at 68 FR 37082, June 23, 2003]

§ 18.42 **Explosion-proof distribution boxes.**

(a) A cable passing through an outside wall(s) of a distribution box shall be conducted either through a packing gland or an interlocked plug and receptacle.

(b) Short-circuit protection shall be provided for each branch circuit connected to a distribution box. The current-carrying capacity of the specified connector shall be compatible with the automatic circuit-interrupting device.

(c) Each branch receptacle shall be plainly and permanently marked to indicate its current-carrying capacity and each receptacle shall be such that it will accommodate only an appropriate plug.

(d) Provision shall be made to relieve mechanical strain on all connectors to distribution boxes.

§ 18.43 Explosion-proof splice boxes.

Internal connections shall be rigidly held and adequately insulated. Strain clamps shall be provided for all cables entering a splice box.

§ 18.44 Non-intrinsically safe battery-powered equipment.

(a) Battery-powered equipment shall use battery assemblies approved under Part 7 of this chapter, or battery assemblies accepted or certified under this part prior to August 22, 1989.

(b) Battery box covers shall be secured in a closed position.

(c) Each wire or cable leaving a battery box on storage battery-operated equipment shall have short-circuit protection in an explosion-proof enclosure located as close as practicable to the battery terminals. A short-circuit protection device installed within a nearby explosion-proof enclosure will be acceptable. In no case shall the exposed portion of the cable from the battery box to the enclosure exceed 36 inches in length. Each wire or cable shall be protected from damage.

[53 FR 23500, June 22, 1988]

§ 18.45 Cable reels.

(a) A self-propelled machine, that receives electrical energy through a portable cable and is designed to travel at speeds exceeding 2.5 miles per hour, shall have a mechanically, hydraulically, or electrically driven reel upon which to wind the portable cable.

(b) The enclosure for moving contacts or slip rings of a cable reel shall be explosion-proof.

(c) Cable-reel bearings shall not constitute an integral part of a circuit for transmitting electrical energy.

(d) Cable reels for shuttle cars and locomotives shall maintain positive tension on the portable cable during reeling and unreeling. Such tension shall only be high enough to prevent a machine from running over its own cable(s).

(e) Cable reels and spooling devices shall be insulated with flame-resistant material.

(f) The maximum speed of travel of a machine when receiving power through a portable (trailing) cable shall not exceed 6 miles per hour.

(g) Diameters of cable reel drums and sheaves should be large enough to prevent undue bending strain on cables.

§ 18.46 Headlights.

(a) Headlights shall be constructed as explosion-proof enclosures.

(b) Headlights shall be mounted to provide illumination where it will be most effective. They shall be protected from damage by guarding or location.

(c) Lenses for headlights shall be glass or other suitable material with physical characteristics equivalent to ½-inch thick tempered glass, such as "Pyrex." Lenses shall meet the requirements of the tests prescribed in § 18.66.

(d) Lenses permanently fixed in a ring with lead, epoxy, or equivalent will be acceptable provided only lens assemblies meeting the original manufacturer's specifications are used as replacements.

(e) If a single lead gasket is used, the contact surface of the opposite side of the lens shall be plane within a maximum deviation of 0.002 inch.

§ 18.47 Voltage limitation.

(a) A tool or switch held in the operator's hand or supported against his body will not be approved with a nameplate rating exceeding 300 volts direct current or alternating current.

(b) A battery-powered machine shall not have a nameplate rating exceeding 240 volts, nominal (120 lead-acid cells or equivalent).

(c) Other direct-current machines shall not have a nameplate rating exceeding 550 volts.

(d) An alternating-current machine shall not have a nameplate rating exceeding 660 volts, except that a machine may have a nameplate rating

§ 18.48

greater than 660 volts but not exceeding 4,160 volts when the following conditions are complied with:

(1) Adequate clearances and insulation for the particular voltage(s) are provided in the design and construction of the equipment, its wiring, and accessories.

(2) A continuously monitored, failsafe grounding system is provided that will maintain the frame of the equipment and the frames of all accessory equipment at ground potential. Also, the equipment, including its controls and portable (trailing) cable, will be deenergized automatically upon the occurrence of an incipient ground fault. The ground-fault-tripping current shall be limited by grounding resistor(s) to that necessary for dependable relaying. The maximum ground-fault-tripping current shall not exceed 25 amperes.

(3) All high voltage switch gear and control for equipment having a nameplate rating exceeding 1,000 volts are located remotely and operated by remote control at the main equipment. Potential for remote control shall not exceed 120 volts.

(4) Portable (trailing) cable for equipment with nameplate ratings from 661 volts through 1,000 volts shall include grounding conductors, a ground check conductor, and grounded metallic shields around each power conductor or a grounded metallic shield over the assembly; except that on machines employing cable reels, cables without shields may be used if the insulation is rated 2,000 volts or more.

(5) Portable (trailing) cable for equipment with nameplate ratings from 1,001 volts through 4,160 volts shall include grounding conductors, a ground check conductor, and grounded metallic shields around each power conductor.

(6) MSHA reserves the right to require additional safeguards for high-voltage equipment, or modify the requirements to recognize improved technology.

§ 18.48 Circuit-interrupting devices.

(a) Each machine shall be equipped with a circuit-interrupting device by means of which all power conductors can be deenergized at the machine. A manually operated controller will not be acceptable as a service switch.

(b) When impracticable to mount the main-circuit-interrupting device on a machine, a remote enclosure will be acceptable. When contacts are used as a main-circuit-interrupting device, a means for opening the circuit shall be provided at the machine and at the remote contactors.

(c) Separate two-pole switches shall be provided to deenergize power conductors for headlights or floodlights.

(d) Each handheld tool shall be provided with a two-pole switch of the "dead-man-control" type that must be held closed by hand and will open when hand pressure is released.

(e) A machine designed to operate from both trolley wire and portable cable shall be provided with a transfer switch, or equivalent, which prevents energizing one from the other. Such a switch shall be designed to prevent electrical connection to the machine frame when the cable is energized.

(f) Belt conveyors shall be equipped with control switches to automatically stop the driving motor in the event the belt is stopped, or abnormally slowed down.

NOTE: Short transfer-type conveyors will be exempted from this requirement when attended.

§ 18.49 Connection boxes on machines.

Connection boxes used to facilitate replacement of cables or machine components shall be explosion-proof. Portable-cable terminals on cable reels need not be in explosion-proof enclosures provided that connections are well made, adequately insulated, protected from damage by location, and securely clamped to prevent mechanical strain on the connections.

§ 18.50 Protection against external arcs and sparks.

Provision shall be made for maintaining the frames of all off-track machines and the enclosures of related detached components at safe voltages by using one or a combination of the following:

(a) A separate conductor(s) in the portable cable in addition to the power conductors by which the machine

Mine Safety and Health Admin., Labor § 18.53

frame can be connected to an acceptable grounding medium, and a separate conductor in all cables connecting related components not on a common chassis. The cross-sectional area of the additional conductor(s) shall not be less than 50 percent of that of one power conductor unless a ground-fault tripping relay is used, in which case the minimum size may be No. 8 (AWG). Cables smaller than No. 6 (AWG) shall have an additional conductor(s) of the same size as one power conductor.

(b) A means of actuating a circuit-interrupting device, preferably at the outby end of the portable cable.

NOTE: The frame to ground potential shall not exceed 40 volts.

(c) A device(s) such as a diode(s) of adequate peak inverse voltage rating and current-carrying capacity to conduct possible fault current through the grounded power conductor. Diode installations shall include: (1) An overcurrent device in series with the diode, the contacts of which are in the machine's control circuit; and (2) a blocking diode in the control circuit to prevent operation of the machine with the polarity reversed.

§ 18.51 Electrical protection of circuits and equipment.

(a) An automatic circuit-interrupting device(s) shall be used to protect each ungrounded conductor of a branch circuit at the junction with the main circuit when the branch-circuit conductor(s) has a current carrying capacity less than 50 percent of the main circuit conductor(s), unless the protective device(s) in the main circuit will also provide adequate protection for the branch circuit. The setting of each device shall be specified. For headlight and control circuits, each conductor shall be protected by a fuse or equivalent. Any circuit that is entirely contained in an explosion-proof enclosure shall be exempt from these requirements.

(b) Each motor shall be protected by an automatic overcurrent device. One protective device will be acceptable when two motors of the same rating operate simultaneously and perform virtually the same duty.

(1) If the overcurrent-protective device in a direct-current circuit does not open both lines, particular attention shall be given to marking the polarity at the terminals or otherwise preventing the possibility of reversing connections which would result in changing the circuit interrupter to the grounded line.

(2) Three-phase alternating-current motors shall have an overcurrent-protective device in at least two phases such that actuation of a device in one phase will cause the opening of all three phases.

(c) Circuit-interrupting devices shall be so designed that they can be reset without opening the compartment in which they are enclosed.

(d) All magnetic circuit-interrupting devices shall be mounted in a manner to preclude the possibility of their closing by gravity.

§ 18.52 Renewal of fuses.

Enclosure covers that provide access to fuses, other than headlight, control-circuit, and handheld-tool fuses, shall be interlocked with a circuit-interrupting device. Fuses shall be inserted on the load side of the circuit interrupter.

§ 18.53 High-voltage longwall mining systems.

(a) In each high-voltage motor-starter enclosure, with the exception of a controller on a high-voltage shearer, the disconnect device compartment, control/communications compartment, and motor contactor compartment must be separated by barriers or partitions to prevent exposure of personnel to energized high-voltage conductors or parts. In each motor-starter enclosure on a high-voltage shearer, the high-voltage components must be separated from lower voltage components by barriers or partitions to prevent exposure of personnel to energized high-voltage conductors or parts. Barriers or partitions must be constructed of grounded metal or nonconductive insulating board.

(b) Each cover of a compartment in the high-voltage motor-starter enclosure containing high-voltage components must be equipped with at least two interlock switches arranged to automatically deenergize the high-

§ 18.53

voltage components within that compartment when the cover is removed.

(c) Circuit-interrupting devices must be designed and installed to prevent automatic reclosure.

(d) Transformers with high-voltage primary windings that supply control voltages must incorporate grounded electrostatic (Faraday) shielding between the primary and secondary windings. The shielding must be connected to equipment ground by a minimum No. 12 AWG grounding conductor. The secondary nominal voltage must not exceed 120 volts, line to line.

(e) Test circuits must be provided for checking the condition of ground-wire monitors and ground-fault protection without exposing personnel to energized circuits. Each ground-test circuit must inject a primary current of 50 percent or less of the current rating of the grounding resistor through the current transformer and cause each corresponding circuit-interrupting device to open.

(f) Each motor-starter enclosure, with the exception of a controller on a high-voltage shearer, must be equipped with a disconnect device installed to deenergize all high-voltage power conductors extending from the enclosure when the device is in the "open" position.

(1) When multiple disconnect devices located in the same enclosure are used to satisfy the above requirement they must be mechanically connected to provide simultaneous operation by one handle.

(2) The disconnect device must be rated for the maximum phase-to-phase voltage and the full-load current of the circuit in which it is located, and installed so that—

(i) Visual observation determines that the contacts are open without removing any cover;

(ii) The load-side power conductors are grounded when the device is in the "open" position;

(iii) The device can be locked in the "open" position;

(iv) When located in an explosion-proof enclosure, the device must be designed and installed to cause the current to be interrupted automatically prior to the opening of the contacts; and

(v) When located in a non-explosion-proof enclosure, the device must be designed and installed to cause the current to be interrupted automatically prior to the opening of the contacts, or the device must be capable of interrupting the full-load current of the circuit.

(g) Control circuits for the high-voltage motor starters must be interlocked with the disconnect device so that—

(1) The control circuit can be operated with an auxiliary switch in the "test" position only when the disconnect device is in the open and grounded position; and

(2) The control circuit can be operated with the auxiliary switch in the "normal" position only when the disconnect switch is in the closed position.

(h) A study to determine the minimum available fault current must be submitted to MSHA to ensure adequate protection for the length and conductor size of the longwall motor, shearer and trailing cables.

(i) Longwall motor and shearer cables with nominal voltages greater than 660 volts must be made of a shielded construction with a grounded metallic shield around each power conductor.

(j) High-voltage motor and shearer circuits must be provided with instantaneous ground-fault protection of not more than 0.125-amperes. Current transformers used for this protection must be of the single-window type and must be installed to encircle all three phase conductors.

(k) Safeguards against corona must be provided on all 4,160 voltage circuits in explosion-proof enclosures.

(l) The maximum pressure rise within an explosion-proof enclosure containing high-voltage switchgear must be limited to 0.83 times the design pressure.

(m) High-voltage electrical components located in high-voltage explosion-proof enclosures must not be coplanar with a single plane flame-arresting path.

(n) Rigid insulation between high-voltage terminals (Phase-to-Phase or Phase-to-Ground) must be designed with creepage distances in accordance with the following table:

Mine Safety and Health Admin., Labor   § 18.53

MINIMUM CREEPAGE DISTANCES

Phase to phase voltage	Points of measure	Minimum creepage distances (inches) for comparative tracking index (CTI) range [1]			
		CTI≥500	380≤CTI<500	175≤CTI<380	CTI<175
2,400	0–0	1.50	1.95	2.40	2.90
	0–G	1.00	1.25	1.55	1.85
4,160	0–0	2.40	3.15	3.90	4.65
	0–G	1.50	1.95	2.40	2.90

[1] Assumes that all insulation is rated for the applied voltage or higher.

(o) Explosion-proof motor-starter enclosures must be designed to establish the minimum free distance (MFD) between the wall or cover of the enclosure and uninsulated electrical conductors inside the enclosure in accordance with the following table:

HIGH-VOLTAGE MINIMUM FREE DISTANCES (MFD)

Wall/cover thickness (in)	Steel MFD (in)			Aluminum MFD (in)		
	A [1]	B [2]	C [3]	A	B	C
¼	2.8	4.3	5.8	[4] NA	[4] NA	[4] NA
⅜	1.8	2.3	3.9	8.6	12.8	18.1
½	*1.2	2.0	2.7	6.5	9.8	13.0
⅝	*0.9	1.5	2.1	5.1	7.7	10.4
¾	*0.6	*1.1	1.6	4.1	6.3	8.6
1	(*)	*0.6	*1.0	2.9	4.5	6.2

NOTE: * The minimum electrical clearances must still be maintained.
[1] Column A specifies the MFD for enclosures that have available 3-phase bolted short-circuit currents of 10,000 amperes rms or less.
[2] Column B specifies the MFD for enclosures that have a maximum available 3-phase bolted short-circuit currents greater than 10,000 and less than or equal to 15,000 amperes rms.
[3] Column C specifies the MFD for enclosures that have a maximum available 3-phase bolted short-circuit currents greater than 15,000 and less than or equal to 20,000 amperes rms.
[4] Not Applicable—MSHA doesn't allow aluminum wall or covers to be ¼ inch or less in thickness (Section 18.31).

(1) For values not included in the table, the following formulas on which the table is based may be used to determine the minimum free distance.

(i) Steel Wall/Cover:

$$\text{MFD} = 2.296 \times 10^{-6} \frac{(35 + 105 \, (C)) \, (I_{sc}) \, (t)}{(C) \, (d)} - \frac{d}{2}$$

(ii) Aluminum Wall/Cover:

$$\text{MFD} = 1.032 \times 10^{-5} \frac{(35 + 105 \, (C)) \, (I_{sc}) \, (t)}{(C) \, (d)} - \frac{d}{2}$$

Where C is 1.4 for 2,400 volt systems or 3.0 for 4,160 volt systems, I_{sc} is the 3-phase short circuit current in amperes of the system, t is the clearing time in seconds of the outby circuit-interrupting device and d is the thickness in inches of the metal wall/cover adjacent to an area of potential arcing.

(2) The minimum free distance must be increased by 1.5 inches for 4,160 volt systems and 0.7 inches for 2,400 volt systems when the adjacent wall area is the top of the enclosure. If a steel shield is mounted in conjunction with

§ 18.54

an aluminum wall or cover, the thickness of the steel shield is used to determine the minimum free distances.

(p) The following static pressure test must be performed on each prototype design of explosion-proof enclosures containing high-voltage switchgear prior to the explosion tests. The static pressure test must also be performed on every explosion-proof enclosure containing high-voltage switchgear, at the time of manufacture, unless the manufacturer uses an MSHA accepted quality assurance procedure covering inspection of the enclosure. Procedures must include a detailed check of parts against the drawings to determine that the parts and the drawings coincide and that the minimum requirements stated in part 18 have been followed with respect to materials, dimensions, configuration and workmanship.

(1) *Test procedure.* (i) The enclosure must be internally pressurized to at least the design pressure, maintaining the pressure for a minimum of 10 seconds.

(ii) Following the pressure hold, the pressure must be removed and the pressurizing agent removed from the enclosure.

(2) *Acceptable performance.* (i) The enclosure during pressurization must not exhibit—

(A) Leakage through welds or casting; or

(B) Rupture of any part that affects the explosion-proof integrity of the enclosure.

(ii) The enclosure following removal of the pressurizing agents must not exhibit—

(A) Visible cracks in welds;

(B) Permanent deformation exceeding 0.040 inches per linear foot; or

(C) Excessive clearances along flame-arresting paths following retightening of fastenings, as necessary.

[67 FR 10999, Mar. 11, 2002; 69 FR 68078, Nov. 23, 2004; 69 FR 70752, Dec. 7, 2004]

§ 18.54 High-voltage continuous mining machines.

(a) *Separation of high-voltage components from lower voltage components.* In each motor-starter enclosure, barriers, partitions, and covers must be provided and arranged so that personnel can test and troubleshoot low- and medium-voltage circuits without being exposed to energized high-voltage circuits. Barriers or partitions must be constructed of grounded metal or nonconductive insulating board.

(b) *Interlock switches.* Each removable cover, barrier, or partition of a compartment in the motor-starter enclosure providing direct access to high-voltage components must be equipped with at least two interlock switches arranged to automatically de-energize the high-voltage components within that compartment when the cover, barrier, or partition is removed.

(c) *Circuit-interrupting devices.* Circuit-interrupting devices must be designed and installed to prevent automatic re-closure.

(d) *Transformers supplying control voltages.* (1) Transformers supplying control voltages must not exceed 120 volts line to line.

(2) Transformers with high-voltage primary windings that supply control voltages must incorporate a grounded electrostatic (Faraday) shield between the primary and secondary windings. Grounding of the shield must be as follows:

(i) Transformers with an external grounding terminal must have the shield grounded by a minimum of No. 12 A.W.G. grounding conductor extending from the grounding terminal to the equipment ground.

(ii) Transformers with no external grounding terminal must have the shield grounded internally through the transformer frame to the equipment ground.

(e) *Onboard ungrounded, three-phase power circuit.* A continuous mining machine designed with an onboard ungrounded, three-phase power circuit must:

(1) Be equipped with a light that will indicate a grounded-phase condition;

(2) Have the indicator light installed so that it can be observed by the operator from any location where the continuous mining machine is normally operated; and

(3) Have a test circuit for the grounded-phase indicator light circuit to assure that the circuit is operating properly. The test circuit must be designed

Mine Safety and Health Admin., Labor §18.54

so that, when activated, it does not require removal of any electrical enclosure cover or create a double-phase-to-ground fault.

(f) *High-voltage trailing cable(s).* High-voltage trailing cable(s) must conform to the ampacity and outer dimensions specified in Table 10 of Appendix I to Subpart D of this part. In addition, the cable must be constructed with:

(1) 100 percent semi-conductive tape shielding over each insulated power conductor;

(2) A grounded metallic braid shielding over each insulated power conductor;

(3) A ground-check conductor not smaller than a No. 10 A.W.G.; or if a center ground-check conductor is used, not smaller than a No. 16 A.W.G. stranded conductor; and

(4) Either a double-jacketed or single-jacketed cable as follows:

(i) *Double jacket.* A double-jacketed cable consisting of reinforced outer and inner protective layers. The inner layer must be a distinctive color from the outer layer. The color black must not be used for either protective layer. The tear strength for each layer must be more than 40 pounds per inch thickness and the tensile strength must be more than 2,400 pounds per square inch.

(ii) *Single jacket.* A single-jacketed cable consisting of one protective layer. The tear strength must be more than 100 pounds per inch thickness, and the tensile strength must be more than 4,000 pounds per square inch. The cable jacket must not be black in color.

(g) *Safeguards against corona.* Safeguards against corona must be provided on all 4,160-voltage circuits in explosion-proof enclosures.

(h) *Explosion-proof enclosure design.* The maximum pressure rise within an explosion-proof enclosure containing high-voltage switchgear must be limited to 0.83 times the design pressure.

(i) *Location of high-voltage electrical components near flame paths.* High-voltage electrical components located in high-voltage explosion-proof enclosures must not be coplanar with a single plane flame-arresting path.

(j) *Minimum creepage distances.* Rigid insulation between high-voltage terminals (Phase-to-Phase or Phase-to-Ground) must be designed with creepage distances in accordance with the following table:

Phase-to-phase voltage	Points of measure	Minimum creepage distances (inches) for comparative tracking index (CTI) range [1]			
		CTI ≥500	380 ≤CTI <500	175 ≤CTI <380	CTI <175
2,400	0–0	1.50	1.95	2.40	2.90
	0–G	1.00	1.25	1.55	1.85
4,160	0–0	2.40	3.15	3.90	4.65
	0–G	1.50	1.95	2.40	2.90

[1] Assumes that all insulation is rated for the applied voltage or higher.

(k) *Minimum free distances.* Motor-starter enclosures must be designed to establish the minimum free distance (MFD) between the wall or cover of the enclosure and uninsulated electrical conductors inside the enclosure in accordance with the following table:

Wall/cover thickness (in)	Steel MFD (in)			Aluminum MFD (in)		
	A[1]	B[2]	C[3]	A[1]	B[2]	C[3]
¼	2.8	4.3	5.8	[4]NA	[4]NA	[4]NA
⅜	1.8	2.3	3.9	8.6	12.8	18.1
½	*1.2	2.0	2.7	6.5	9.8	13.0
⅝	*0.9	1.5	2.1	5.1	7.7	10.4
¾	*0.6	*1.1	1.6	4.1	6.3	8.6
1	*	*0.6	*1.0	2.9	4.5	6.2

*Note: The minimum electrical clearances must still be maintained in accordance with the minimum clearance table of §18.24.
[1] Column A specifies the MFD for enclosures that have available three-phase, bolted, short-circuit currents of 10,000 amperes root-mean-square (rms) value or less.
[2] Column B specifies the MFD for enclosures that have maximum available three-phase, bolted, short-circuit currents greater than 10,000 and less than or equal to 15,000 amperes rms.
[3] Column C specifies the MFD for enclosures that have maximum available three-phase, bolted, short-circuit currents greater than 15,000 and less than or equal to 20,000 amperes rms.

[4] Not Applicable—MSHA does not allow aluminum wall or covers to be ¼ inch or less in thickness. (See also § 18.31.)

(1) For values not included in the table, the following formulas, on which the table is based, may be used to determine the minimum free distance.

(i) Steel Wall/Cover:

$$\text{MFD} = 2.296 \times 10^{-6} \frac{(35 + 105(C))\left(I_{sc}\right)(t)}{(C)(d)} - \frac{d}{2}$$

(ii) Aluminum Wall/Cover:

$$\text{MFD} = 1.032 \times 10^{-5} \frac{(35 + 105(C))\left(I_{sc}\right)(t)}{(C)(d)} - \frac{d}{2}$$

Where "C" is 1.4 for 2,400 volt systems or 3.0 for 4,160 volt systems; "I_{sc}" is the three-phase, short-circuit current in amperes of the system; "t" is the clearing time in seconds of the outby circuit-interrupting device; and "d" is the thickness in inches of the metal wall/cover adjacent to an area of potential arcing.

(2) The minimum free distance must be increased by 1.5 inches for 4,160 volt systems and 0.7 inches for 2,400 volt systems when the adjacent wall area is the top of the enclosure. If a steel shield is mounted in conjunction with an aluminum wall or cover, the thickness of the steel shield is used to determine the minimum free distances.

(l) *Static pressure testing of explosion-proof enclosures containing high-voltage switchgear*—(1) *Prototype enclosures.* The following static pressure test must be performed on each prototype design of an explosion-proof enclosure containing high-voltage switchgear prior to the explosion tests.

(i) *Test procedure.* (A) The enclosure must be internally pressurized to at least the design pressure, maintaining the pressure for a minimum of 10 seconds.

(B) Following the pressure hold, the pressure must be removed and the pressurizing agent removed from the enclosure.

(ii) *Acceptable performance.* (A) During pressurization, the enclosure must not exhibit:

(*1*) Leakage through welds or casting; or

(*2*) Rupture of any part that affects the explosion-proof integrity of the enclosure.

(B) Following removal of the pressurizing agents, the enclosure must not exhibit:

(*1*) Cracks in welds visible to the naked eye;

(*2*) Permanent deformation exceeding 0.040 inches per linear foot; or

(*3*) Excessive clearances along flame-arresting paths following retightening of fastenings, as necessary.

(2) *Enclosures for production.* Every explosion-proof enclosure containing high-voltage switchgear manufactured after the prototype was tested must undergo one of the following tests or procedures:

(i) The static pressure test specified in paragraph (l)(1)(i) of this section; or

(ii) An MSHA-accepted quality assurance procedure covering inspection of the enclosure.

(A) The quality assurance procedure must include a detailed check of parts against the drawings to determine that—

(*1*) The parts and the drawings coincide; and

(2) The requirements stated in part 18 have been followed with respect to materials, dimensions, configuration and workmanship.

(B) [Reserved]

[75 FR 17547, Apr. 6, 2010]

Subpart C—Inspections and Tests

§ 18.60 Detailed inspection of components.

An inspection of each electrical component shall include the following:

(a) A detailed check of parts against the drawings submitted by the applicant to determine that: (1) The parts and drawings coincide; and (2) the minimum requirements stated in this part have been met with respect to materials, dimensions, configuration, workmanship, and adequacy of drawings and specifications.

(b) Exact measurement of joints, journal bearings, and other flame-arresting paths.

(c) Examination for unnecessary through holes.

(d) Examination for adequacy of lead-entrance design and construction.

(e) Examination for adequacy of electrical insulation and clearances between live parts and between live parts and the enclosure.

(f) Examination for weaknesses in welds and flaws in castings.

(g) Examination for distortion of enclosures before tests.

(h) Examination for adequacy of fastenings, including size, spacing, security, and possibility of bottoming.

§ 18.61 Final inspection of complete machine.

(a) A completely assembled new machine or a substantially modified design of a previously approved one shall be inspected by a qualified representative(s) of MSHA. When such inspection discloses any unsafe condition or any feature not in strict conformance with the requirements of this part it shall be corrected before an approval of the machine will be issued. A final inspection will be conducted at the site of manufacture, rebuilding, or other locations at the option of MSHA.

(b) Complete machines shall be inspected for:

(1) Compliance with the requirements of this part with respect to joints, lead entrances, and other pertinent features.

(2) Wiring between components, adequacy of mechanical protection for cables, adequacy of clamping of cables, positioning of cables, particularly with respect to proximity to hydraulic components.

(3) Adequacy of protection against damage to headlights, push buttons, and any other vulnerable component.

(4) Settings of overload- and short-circuit protective devices.

(5) Adequacy of means for connecting and protecting portable cable.

§ 18.62 Tests to determine explosion-proof characteristics.

(a) In testing for explosion-proof characteristics of an enclosure, it shall be filled and surrounded with various explosive mixtures of natural gas and air. The explosive mixture within the enclosure will be ignited electrically and the explosion pressure developed therefrom recorded. The point of ignition within the enclosure will be varied. Motor armatures and/or rotors will be stationary in some tests and revolving in others. Coal dust having a minimum of 22 percent dry volatile matter and a minimum heat constant of 11,000 moist BTU (coal containing natural bed moisture but not visible surface water) ground to a fineness of minus 200 mesh U.S. Standard sieve series. At MSHA's discretion dummies may be substituted for internal electrical components during some of the tests. Not less than 16 explosion tests shall be conducted; however, the nature of the enclosure and the results obtained during the tests will determine whether additional tests shall be made.

(b) Explosion tests of an enclosure shall not result in:

(1) Discharge of flame.

(2) Ignition of an explosive mixture surrounding the enclosure.

(3) Development of afterburning.

(4) Rupture of any part of the enclosure or any panel or divider within the enclosure.

(5) Permanent distortion of the enclosure exceeding 0.040 inch per linear foot.

§ 18.63

(c) When a pressure exceeding 125 pounds per square inch (gage) is developed during explosion tests, MSHA reserves the right to reject an enclosure(s) unless (1) constructional changes are made that result in a reduction of pressure to 125 pounds per square inch (gage) or less, or (2) the enclosure withstands a dynamic pressure of twice the highest value recorded in the initial test.

[33 FR 4660, Mar. 19, 1968, as amended at 57 FR 61210, Dec. 23, 1992]

§ 18.63 [Reserved]

§ 18.65 Flame test of hose.

(a) *Size of test specimen.* (1) [Reserved]

(2) Hose—four specimens each 6 inches long by ½-inch wide by thickness of the hose.

(b) *Flame-test apparatus.* The principal parts of the apparatus within and/or appended to a 21-inch cubical test gallery are:

(1) A support stand with a ring clamp and wire gauze.

(2) A Pittsburgh-Universal Bunsen-type burner (inside diameter of burner tube 11 mm.), or equivalent, mounted in a burner placement guide in such a manner that the burner may be placed beneath the test specimen, or pulled away from it by an external knob on the front panel of the test gallery.

(3) A variable-speed electric fan and an ASME flow nozzle (16–8½ inches reduction) to attain constant air velocities at any speed between 50–500 feet a minute.

(4) An electric timer or stopwatch to measure the duration of the tests.

(5) A mirror mounted inside the test gallery to permit a rear view of the test specimen through the viewing door.

(c) *Mounting of test specimen.* The specimen shall be clamped in a support with its free end centered 1 inch above the burner top. The longitudinal axis shall be horizontal and the transverse axis inclined at 45° to the horizontal. Under the test specimen shall be clamped a piece of 20-mesh iron-wire gauze, 5 inches square, in a horizontal position ¼-inch below the pulley cover edge of the specimen and with about ½-inch of the specimen extending beyond the edge of the gauze.

(d) *Procedure for flame tests.* (1) The Bunsen burner, retracted from the test position, shall be adjusted to give a blue flame 3 inches in height with natural gas.

(2) The observation door of the gallery shall be closed for the entire test.

(3) The burner flame shall be applied to the free end of the specimen for 1 minute in still air.

(4) At the end of 1 minute the burner flame shall be removed, the ventilating fan turned on to give an air current having a velocity of 300 feet per minute, and the duration of flame measured.

(5) After the test specimen ceases to flame, it shall remain in the air current for at least 3 minutes to determine the presence and duration of afterglow. If a glowing specimen exhibits flame within 3 minutes the duration of flame shall be added to the duration of flame obtained according to paragraph (d) (4) of this section.

(e) *Test requirements.* The tests of the four specimens cut from any sample shall not result in either duration of flame exceeding an average of 1 minute after removal of the applied flame or afterglow exceeding an average of 3 minutes duration.

(f) *Acceptance markings.* (1) [Reserved]

(2) Hose—hose conduit accepted by MSHA as flame-resistant shall be marked as follows: Impressed letters, raised letters on depressed background, or printed letters with the words "Flame-Resistant, USMSHA No. ___" at intervals not exceeding 3 feet. This number will be assigned to the manufacturer after the sample has passed the tests. The letters and numbers shall be at least ¼-inch high.

[33 FR 4660, Mar. 19, 1968, as amended at 43 FR 12314, Mar. 24, 1978; 73 FR 80612, Dec. 31, 2008]

§ 18.66 Tests of windows and lenses.

(a) *Impact tests.* A 4-pound cylindrical weight with a 1-inch-diameter hemispherical striking surface shall be dropped (free fall) to strike the window or lens in its mounting, or the equivalent thereof, at or near the center. Three of four samples shall withstand without breakage the impact according to the following table:

Lens diameter, (D), inches	Height of fall, inches
D<4	6
4≤D<5	9
5≤D<6	15
6≤D	24

Windows or lenses of smaller diameter than 1 inch may be tested by alternate methods at the discretion of MSHA.

(b) *Thermal-shock tests.* Four samples of the window or lens will be heated in an oven for 15 minutes to a temperature of 150 °C. (302 °F.) and immediately upon withdrawal of the samples from the oven they will be immersed in water having a temperature between 15 °C. (59 °F) and 20 °C. (68 °F.). Three of the four samples shall show no defect or breakage from this thermal-shock test.

§ 18.67 Static-pressure tests.

Static-pressure tests shall be conducted by the applicant on each enclosure of a specific design when MSHA determines that visual inspection will not reveal defects in castings or in single-seam welds. Such test procedure shall be submitted to MSHA for approval and the specifications on file with MSHA shall include a statement assuring that such tests will be conducted. The static pressure to be applied shall be 150 pounds per square inch (gage) or one and one-half times the maximum pressure recorded in MSHA's explosion tests, whichever is greater.

§ 18.68 Tests for intrinsic safety.

(a) General:

(1) Tests for intrinsic safety will be conducted under the general concepts of "intrinsically safe" as defined in Subpart A of this part. Further tests or requirements may be added at any time if features of construction or use or both indicate them to be necessary. Some tests included in these requirements may be omitted on the basis of previous experience.

(2) Intrinsically safe circuits and/or components will be subjected to tests consisting of making and breaking the intrinsically safe circuit under conditions judged to simulate the most hazardous probable faults or malfunctions. Tests will be made in the most easily ignitable mixture of methane or natural gas and air. The method of making and breaking the circuit may be varied to meet a particular condition.

(3) Those components which affect intrinsic safety must meet the following requirements:

(i) Current limiting components shall consist of two equivalent devices each of which singly will provide intrinsic safety. They shall not be operated at more than 50 percent of their ratings.

(ii) Components of reliable construction shall be used and they shall be so mounted as to provide protection against shock and vibration in normal use.

(iii) Semiconductors shall be amply sized. Rectifiers and transistors shall be operated at not more than two-thirds of their rated current and permissible peak inverse voltage. Zener diodes shall be operated at not more than one-half of their rated current and shall short under abnormal conditions.

(iv) Electrolytic capacitors shall be operated at not more than two-thirds of their rated voltage. They shall be designed to withstand a test voltage of 1,500 volts.

(4) Intrinsically safe circuits shall be so designed that after failure of a single component, and subsequent failures resulting from this first failure, the circuit will remain intrinsically safe.

(5) The circuit will be considered as intrinsically safe if in the course of testing no ignitions occur.

(b) Complete intrinsically safe equipment powered by low energy batteries:

(1) Short-circuit tests shall be conducted on batteries at normal operating temperature. Tests may be made on batteries at elevated temperature if such tests are deemed necessary.

(2) Resistance devices for limiting short-circuit current shall be an integral part of the battery, or installed as close to the battery terminal as practicable.

(3) Transistors of battery-operated equipment may be subjected to thermal "run-away" tests to determine that they will not ignite an explosive atmosphere.

(4) A minimum of 1,000 make-break sparks will be produced in each test for

§ 18.69

direct current circuits with consideration given to reversed polarity.

(5) Tests on batteries shall include series and/or parallel combinations of twice the normal battery complement, and the effect of capacitance and inductance, added to that normally present in the circuit.

(6) No ignition shall occur when approximately ½-inch of a single wire strand representative of the wire used in the equipment or device is shorted across the intrinsically safe circuit.

(7) Consideration shall be given to insure against accidental reversal of polarity.

(c) Line-powered equipment and devices:

(1) Line-powered equipment shall meet all applicable provisions specified for battery-powered equipment.

(2) Nonintrinsically safe components supplying power for intrinsically safe circuits shall be housed in explosion-proof enclosures and be provided with energy limiting components in the enclosure.

(3) Wiring for nonintrinsically safe circuits shall not be intermingled with wiring for intrinsically safe circuits.

(4) Transformers that supply power for intrinsically safe circuits shall have the primary and secondary windings physically separated. They shall be designed to withstand a test voltage of 1,500 volts when rated 125 volts or less and 2,500 volts when rated more than 125 volts.

(5) The line voltage shall be increased to 120 percent of nominal rated voltage to cover power line voltage variations.

(6) In investigations of alternating current circuits a minimum of 5,000 make-break sparks will be produced in each test.

(d) The design of intrinsically safe circuits shall preclude extraneous voltages caused by insufficient isolation or inductive coupling. The investigation shall determine the effect of ground faults where applicable.

(e) Identification markings: Circuits and components of intrinsically safe equipment and devices shall be adequately identified by marking or labeling. Battery-powered equipment shall be marked to indicate the manufacturer, type designation, ratings, and size of batteries used.

§ 18.69 Adequacy tests.

MSHA reserves the right to conduct appropriate test(s) to verify the adequacy of equipment for its intended service.

Subpart D—Machines Assembled With Certified or Explosion-Proof Components, Field Modifications of Approved Machines, and Permits To Use Experimental Equipment

§ 18.80 Approval of machines assembled with certified or explosion-proof components.

(a) A machine may be a new assembly, or a machine rebuilt to perform a service that is different from the original function, or a machine converted from nonpermissible to permissible status, or a machine converted from direct- to alternating-current power or vice versa. Properly identified components that have been investigated and accepted for application on approved machines will be accepted in lieu of certified components.

(b) A single layout drawing (see Figure 1 in Appendix II) or photographs will be acceptable to identify a machine that was assembled with certified or explosion-proof components. The following information shall be furnished:

(1) Overall dimensions.

(2) Wiring diagram.

(3) List of all components (see Figure 2 in Appendix II) identifying each according to its certification number or the approval number of the machine of which the component was a part.

(4) Specifications for:

(i) Overcurrent protection of motors.

(ii) All wiring between components, including mechanical protection such as hose conduits and clamps.

(iii) Portable cable, including the type, length, outside diameter, and number and size of conductors.

(iv) Insulated strain clamp for machine end of portable cable.

(v) Short-circuit protection to be provided at outby end of portable cable.

(c) MSHA reserves the right to inspect and to retest any component(s) that had been in previous service, as it deems appropriate.

(d) When MSHA has determined that all applicable requirements of this part have been met, the applicant will be authorized to attach an approval plate to each machine that is built in strict accordance with the drawings and specifications filed with MSHA and listed with MSHA's formal approval. A design of the approval plate will accompany the notification of approval. (Refer to §§ 18.10 and 18.11.)

(e) Approvals are issued only by the U.S. Department of Labor, Mine Safety and Health Administration, Approval and Certification Center, 765 Technology Drive, Triadelphia, WV 26059.

[33 FR 4660, Mar. 19, 1968, as amended at 43 FR 12314, Mar. 24, 1978; 52 FR 17514, May 8, 1987; 73 FR 52211, Sept. 9, 2008]

§ 18.81 Field modification of approved (permissible) equipment; application for approval of modification; approval of plans for modification before modification.

(a) An owner of approved (permissible) equipment who desires to make modifications in such equipment shall apply in writing to make such modifications. The application, together with the plans of modifications, shall be filed with the U.S. Department of Labor, Mine Safety and Health Administration, Approval and Certification Center, 765 Technology Drive, Triadelphia, WV 26059.

(b) Proposed modifications shall conform with the applicable requirements of subpart B of this part, and shall not substantially alter the basic functional design that was originally approved for the equipment.

(c) Upon receipt of the application for modification, and after such examination and investigation as may be deemed necessary by MSHA, MSHA will notify the owner and the District office of the mine workers' organization having jurisdiction at the mine where such equipment is to be operated stating the modifications which are proposed to be made and MSHA's action thereon.

[33 FR 4660, Mar. 19, 1968, as amended at 43 FR 12314, Mar. 24, 1978; 60 FR 35693, July 11, 1995; 73 FR 52211, Sept. 9, 2008]

§ 18.82 Permit to use experimental electric face equipment in a gassy mine or tunnel.

(a) *Application for permit.* An application for a permit to use experimental electric face equipment in a gassy mine or tunnel will be considered only when submitted by the user of the equipment. The user shall submit a written application to the Assistant Secretary of Labor for Mine Safety and Health, 201 12th Street South, Arlington, VA 22202–5452, and send a copy to the U.S. Department of Labor, Mine Safety and Health Administration, Approval and Certification Center, 765 Technology Drive, Triadelphia, WV 26059.

(b) *Requirements*—(1) *Constructional.* (i) Experimental equipment shall be so constructed that it will not constitute a fire or explosion hazard.

(ii) Enclosures designed as explosion-proof, unless already certified, or components of previously approved (permissible) machines, shall be submitted to MSHA for inspection and test and shall meet the applicable design requirements of subpart B of this part. Components designed as intrinsically safe also shall be submitted to MSHA for investigation.

(iii) MSHA may, at its discretion, waive the requirements for detailed drawings of component parts, inspections, and tests provided satisfactory evidence is submitted that an enclosure has been certified, or otherwise accepted by a reputable testing agency whose standards are substantially equivalent to those set forth in subpart B of this part.

(2) *Specifications.* The specifications for experimental equipment shall include a layout drawing (see Figure 1 in Appendix II) or photograph(s) with the components, including overcurrent-protective device(s) with setting(s) identified thereon or separately; a wiring diagram; and descriptive material necessary to insure safe operation of the equipment. Drawings already filed with MSHA need not be duplicated by the applicant, but shall be properly identified.

(c) *Final inspection.* Unless equipment is delivered to MSHA for investigation, the applicant shall notify the U.S. Department of Labor, Mine Safety and Health Administration, Approval and

Certification Center, 765 Technology Drive, Triadelphia, WV 26059, when and where the experimental equipment will be ready for inspection by a representative of MSHA before installing it on a trial basis. Such inspection shall be completed before a permit will be issued.

(d) *Issuance of permit.* When the inspection discloses full compliance with the applicable requirements of this subpart, the Assistant Secretary will issue a permit sanctioning the operation of a single unit in a gassy mine or tunnel, as designated in the application. If the applicant is not the assembler of the equipment, a copy of the permit also may be sent to the assembler.

(e) *Duration of permit.* A permit will be effective for a period of 6 months. For a valid reason, to be stated in a written application, the Administrator of MSHA may grant an extension of a permit for an additional period, not exceeding 6 months. Further extension will be granted only where, after investigation, the Assistant Secretary finds that for reasons beyond the control of the user, it has not been possible to complete the experiment within the period covered by the extended permit.

(f) *Permit label.* With the notification granting a permit, the applicant will receive a photographic copy of a permit label bearing the following:

(1) Emblem of the Mine Safety and Health Administration.
(2) Permit number.
(3) Expiration date of the permit.
(4) Name of machine.
(5) Name of the user and mine or tunnel.

The applicant shall attach the photographic copy of the permit label, or replica thereof, to the experimental equipment. If a photograph is used, a clear plastic covering shall be provided for it.

(g) *Withdrawal of permit.* The Assistant Secretary may rescind, for cause, any permit granted under this subpart.

[33 FR 4660, Mar. 19, 1968, as amended at 43 FR 12314, Mar. 24, 1978; 52 FR 17514, May 8, 1987; 60 FR 35693, July 11, 1995; 67 FR 38384, June 4, 2002; 73 FR 52211, Sept. 9, 2008; 80 FR 52985, Sept. 2, 2015]

APPENDIX I TO SUBPART D OF PART 18
LIST OF TABLES

Table No.	Title
1	Portable power cable ampacities—600 volts.
2	Portable cord ampacities—600 volts.
3	Portable power cable ampacities—601 to 5,000 volts.
4	Normal diameter of round cables with tolerances in inches—600 volts.
5	Nominal dimension of flat cables with tolerances in inches—600 volts.
6	Nominal diameter of heavy jacketed cords with tolerances in inches—600 volts.
7	Nominal diameter of three-conductor portable power cables with tolerances in inches—601 to 5,000 volts.
8	Fuse ratings or instantaneous settings of circuit breakers for short-circuit protection of portable cables.
9	Specifications for portable cables longer than 500 feet.
10	High voltage trailing cable ampacities and outside diameters.

TABLE 1—PORTABLE POWER CABLE AMPACITIES—600 VOLTS (AMPERES PER CONDUCTOR BASED ON 60 °C. COPPER TEMPERATURE—40 °C. AMBIENT)

Conductor size—AWG or MCM	Single conductor	2-conductor, round or flat	3-conductor, round or flat	4-conductor	5-conductor	6-conductor
8	45	40	35	30	25	20
6	60	50	50	40	35	30
4	85	70	65	55	45	35
3	95	80	75	65	55	45
2	110	95	90	75	65	55
1	130	110	100	85	75	65
1/0	150	130	120	100	90	80
2/0	175	150	135	115	105	95
3/0	205	175	155	130	120	110
4/0	235	200	180	150	140	130
250	275	220	200	160	....	....
300	305	240	220	175	....	....

Mine Safety and Health Admin., Labor   Pt. 18, Subpt. D, App. I

TABLE 1—PORTABLE POWER CABLE AMPACITIES—600 VOLTS (AMPERES PER CONDUCTOR BASED ON 60 °C. COPPER TEMPERATURE—40 °C. AMBIENT)—Continued

Conductor size—AWG or MCM	Single conductor	2-conductor, round or flat	3-conductor, round or flat	4-conductor	5-conductor	6-conductor
350	345	240	235	190		
400	375	280	250	200		
450	400	300	270	215		
500	425	320	290	230		

TABLE 2—PORTABLE CORD AMPACITIES—600 VOLTS (AMPERES PER CONDUCTOR BASED ON 60 °C. COPPER TEMPERATURE—40 °C. AMBIENT)

Conductor size—AWG	1–3 conductor	4–6 conductor	7–9 conductor
14	15	12	8
12	20	16	11
10	25	20	14

TABLE 3—PORTABLE POWER CABLE AMPACITIES—601 TO 5,000 VOLTS (AMPERES PER CONDUCTOR BASED ON 75 °C. COPPER TEMPERATURE—40 °C. AMBIENT)

Conductor size—AWG or MCM	3-conductor types G-GC and SIIC-GC 2,000 volts	3-conductor type SHD-GC 2,001–5,000 volts
6	65	65
4	85	85
3	100	100
2	115	115
1	130	130
1/0	145	145
2/0	170	170
3/0	195	195
4/0	220	220
250	245	245
300	275	275
350	305	305

TABLE 4—NOMINAL DIAMETERS OF ROUND CABLES WITH TOLERANCES IN INCHES—600 VOLTS

Conductor size—AWG or MCM	Single conductor	2-conductor			3-conductor			4-conductor—Types W & G	5-conductor—Types W & G	6-conductor	
		Types W & G twisted	Type PG, 2 power	Type PCG, 3 power, ground	Types W & G	Type PG, 3 power, ground	Type PCG, 3 power, 2 control, ground			Type w	Tolerance
8	0.44	0.81	0.84	0.94	0.91	0.93	1.03	0.99	1.07	1.18	±0.03
6	.51	.93	.93	.98	1.01	1.03	1.18	1.10	1.21	1.31	±.03
4	.57	1.08	1.08	1.10	1.17	1.20	1.29	1.27	1.40	1.52	±.03
3	.63	1.17	1.17	1.20	1.24	1.27	1.31	1.34	1.48	1.61	±.03
2	.66	1.27	1.27	1.29	1.34	1.34	1.39	1.48	1.61	1.75	±.03
1	.74	1.44	1.44	1.44	1.51	1.52	1.52	1.68	1.88	2.05	±.03
1/0	.77	1.52	1.52	1.52	1.65	1.68	1.68	1.79	1.96	2.13	±.04
2/0	.82	1.65	1.65	1.65	1.75	1.79	1.79	1.93	2.13	2.32	±.04
3/0	.87	1.77	1.77	1.77	1.89	1.93	1.93	2.07	2.26	2.49	±.05
4/0	.93	1.92	1.92	1.92	2.04	2.13	2.13	2.26	2.46	2.71	±.05
250	1.03	2.16	2.16	2.16	2.39	2.39	2.39	2.66			±.06
300	1.09	2.32			2.56			2.84			±.06
350	1.15	2.43			2.68			2.98			±.06
400	1.20	2.57			2.82			3.14			±.06
450	1.26	2.67			2.94			3.26			±.06
500	1.31	2.76			3.03			3.40			±.06

TABLE 5—NOMINAL DIMENSIONS OF FLAT CABLES WITH TOLERANCES IN INCHES—600 VOLTS

Conductor size—AWG	2-conductor								3-conductor—Type G			
	Type W				Type G				Major		Minor	
	Major		Minor		Major		Minor		O.D.	Tolerance	O.D.	Tolerance
	O.D.	Tolerance	O.D.	Tolerance	O.D.	Tolerance	O.D.	Tolerance				
8	0.84	±0.04	0.51	±0.03								
6	.93	±.04	.56	±.03	1.02	±.04	0.56	±.03	1.65	±0.06	0.67	±0.05
4	1.05	±.04	.61	±.03	1.15	±.04	.61	±.03	1.85	±.06	.75	±.05
3	1.14	±.04	.68	±.03	1.26	±.04	.68	±.03	1.99	±.06	.77	±.05
2	1.24	±.04	.73	±.03	1.35	±.04	.73	±.06	2.10	±.06	.81	±.05
1	1.40	±.04	.81	±.03	1.55	±.04	.81	±.03	2.43	±.06	.97	±.05
1/0	1.51	±.04	.93	±.03	1.67	±.04	.93	±.03				
2/0	1.63	±.04	.99	±.03	1.85	±.04	.99	±.03				
3/0	1.77	±.04	1.03	±.03	2.00	±.04	1.03	±.03				
4/0	1.89	±.04	1.10	±.03	2.10	±.04	1.10	±.03				

TABLE 6—NOMINAL DIAMETERS OF HEAVY JACKETED CORDS WITH TOLERANCES IN INCHES—600 VOLTS

Conductor size—AWG	2-conductor		3-conductor		4-conductor		5-conductor		6-conductor		7-conductor	
	Diameter	Tolerance	Diameter	Tolerance	Diameter	Tolerance	Diameter	Tolerance	Diameter	Tolerance	Diameter	Tolerance
14	0.64	±0.02	0.67	±0.02	0.71	±0.02	0.78	±0.03	0.83	±0.03	0.89	±0.03
12	.68	±.02	.72	±.03	.76	±.03	.83	±.03	.89	±.03	.98	±.03
10	.73	±.03	.80	±.03	.84	±.03	.90	±.03	1.00	±.03	1.07	±.03

TABLE 7—NOMINAL DIAMETERS OF THREE-CONDUCTOR PORTABLE POWER CABLES WITH TOLERANCES IN INCHES—601 TO 5,000 VOLTS

Conductor size—AWG or MCM	Type G-GC (non-shielded) 2,000 volts		Type SHC-GC (shielded overall) 2,000 volts		Type SHD-GC (individually shielded power conductors) 2,001–3,000 volts		Type SHD-GC (individually shielded power conductors) 3,001–5,000 volts	
	Diameter	Tolerance	Diameter	Tolerance	Diameter	Tolerance	Diameter	Tolerance
6	1.25	+ 0.10, − 0.06	1.39	+ 0.11, − 0.07	1.62	+ 0.13, − 0.08	1.78	+ 0.14, − 0.09
4	1.40	+ .11, − .07	1.55	+ .12, − .08	1.77	+ .14, − .09	1.90	+ .15, − .10
3	1.48	+ .12, − .07	1.62	+ .13, − .08	1.84	+ .15, − .10	1.98	+ .16, − .10
2	1.55	+ .12, − .08	1.71	+ .14, − .09	1.92	+ .15, − .10	2.09	+ .17, − .11
1	1.74	+ .14, − .09	1.89	+ .15, − .09	2.04	+ .16, − .10	2.18	+ .17, − .11
1/0	1.84	+ .15, − .09	2.02	+ .16, − .10	2.18	+ .17, − .11	2.34	+ .19, − .12
2/0	1.99	+ .16, − .10	2.16	+ .17, − .10	2.29	+ .18, − .12	2.46	+ .20, − .12
3/0	2.12	+ .17, − .11	2.30	+ .18, − .11	2.45	+ .20, − .12	2.62	+ .21, − .13
4/0	2.30	+ .18, − .12	2.48	+ .20, − .12	2.62	+ .21, − .13	2.76	+ .22, − .14
250	2.46	+ .20, − .12	2.70	+ .22, − .13				
300	2.63	+ .21, − .13	2.84	+ .23, − .14				
350	2.75	+ .22, − .14	2.97	+ .24, − .15				

TABLE 8—FUSE RATINGS OR INSTANTANEOUS SETTING OF CIRCUIT BREAKERS FOR SHORT-CIRCUIT PROTECTION OF PORTABLE CABLES AND CORDS

Conductor size—AWG or MCM	Ohms/1,000 ft. at 25 °C.	Maximum allowable fuse rating (amperes)	Maximum allowable circuit breaker instantaneous setting (amperes) [1]
14	2.62	20	50
12	1.65	30	75
10	1.04	40	150
8	.654	80	200
6	.410	100	300
4	.259	200	500
3	.205	250	600
2	.162	300	800

Mine Safety and Health Admin., Labor — Pt. 18, Subpt. D, App. I

TABLE 8—FUSE RATINGS OR INSTANTANEOUS SETTING OF CIRCUIT BREAKERS FOR SHORT-CIRCUIT PROTECTION OF PORTABLE CABLES AND CORDS—Continued

Conductor size—AWG or MCM	Ohms/1,000 ft. at 25 °C.	Maximum allowable fuse rating (amperes)	Maximum allowable circuit breaker instantaneous setting (amperes) [1]
1	.129	375	1,000
1/0	.102	500	1,250
2/0	.081		1,500
3/0	.064		2,000
4/0	.051		2,500
250	.043		2,500
300	.036		2,500
350	.031		2,500
400	.027		2,500
450	.024		2,500
500	.022		2,500

[1] Higher circuit-breaker settings may be permitted for special applications when justified.

TABLE 9—SPECIFICATIONS FOR PORTABLE CABLES LONGER THAN 500 FEET [1]

Conductor size—AWG or MCM	Max. allowable length (feet)	Normal ampacity at 60 °C. copper temperature (40 °C. ambient)	Resistance at 60 °C. copper temperature (ohms)
6	550	50	0.512
4	600	70	.353
3	650	80	.302
2	700	95	.258
1	750	110	.220
1/0	800	130	.185
2/0	850	150	.157
3/0	900	175	.130
4/0	1,000	200	.116
250	1,000	220	.098
300	1,000	240	.082
350	1,000	260	.070
400	1,000	280	.061
450	1,000	300	.054
500	1,000	320	.050

[1] Fuses shall not be used for short-circuit protection of these cables. Circuit breakers shall be used with the instantaneous trip settings not to exceed the values given in Table 8.

TABLE 10—HIGH VOLTAGE TRAILING CABLE AMPACITIES AND OUTSIDE DIAMETERS

Power conductor Size AWG or kcmil	Ampacity* Amperes per conductor	Outside diameter** (inches)		
		SHD–GC 2001 to 5000 volts	SHD–CGC 2001 to 5000 volts	SHD–PCG 2001 to 5000 volts
6	93	1.56	1.62	
4	122	1.68	1.73	
3	140	1.78	1.82	1.94
2	159	1.87	1.91	2.03
1	184	1.95	1.98	2.12
1/0	211	2.08	2.10	2.26
2/0	243	2.20	2.20	2.40
3/0	279	2.36	2.36	2.58
4/0	321	2.50	2.50	2.76
250	355	2.69	2.69	
300	398	2.81	2.81	
350	435	2.95	2.95	
500	536	3.31	3.31	

*These ampacities are based on single isolated conductor in air, operated with open-circuited shield for a 90 °C conductor temperature and an ambient temperature of 40 °C.
**Tolerances for the outside diameter are + 8%/ − 5%.

[33 FR 4660, Mar. 19, 1968; 33 FR 6345, Apr. 26, 1968, as amended at 42 FR 8373, Feb. 10, 1977; 75 FR 17549, Apr. 6, 2010; 75 FR 20918, Apr. 22, 2010]

Pt. 18, Subpt. D, App. II   **30 CFR Ch. I (7-1-23 Edition)**

APPENDIX II TO SUBPART D OF PART 18
LIST OF FIGURES

Figure No.	Title
1	Typical layout drawing of a machine.
2	Sample bill of material (to accompany layout drawing shown on figure 1)
3	Material to be included with the operating instructions on or with the wiring diagram submitted to each customer.
4	Sample factory inspection form.
5	Typical plane joint.
6	Typical combination joint.
7	Typical threaded joint.
8	Typical threaded straight stuffing box and packing gland lead entrance with provision for hose conduit.
9	Typical slip-fit straight-type and angle-type stuffing box and packing gland lead entrance.
10	Typical slip-fit angle-type stuffing box and packing gland lead entrance and typical plug for spare lead entrance hole.

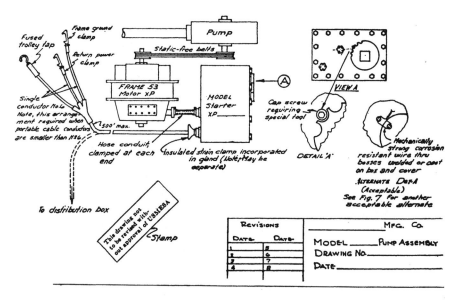

FIGURE 2—SAMPLE BILL OF MATERIAL

B. of M. No. _____
     Date _____

Revision   Date
       1. _____
       2. _____
       3. _____
       4. _____
       5. _____

Bill of Material (Electrical)

          (Manufacturing Company)
Model: _____
             (Unit Name)
Approval 2G– _____

Motor: _____
       (Manufacturing Company)
Frame _____
_____ Hp., _____ Volts, _____ Ph.,
_____ Cy., _____ R.P.M.
X/P_____(Date).
_____(Date) Extension.
Starter: _____
         (Manufacturing Company)
Model _____
_____Hp., _____Volts.
X/P _____
                             (Date)
_____ Extension.
 (Date)
Cable—Motor to Starter:
 Cond. No. _____, _____"
 O.D., _____' Long
Hose—Motor to Starter Cable:
 _____" I.D., _____" O.D., _____' Long
Portable (Trailing) Cable—
Type: _____
 Cond. No. _____, _____"
 O.D., _____' Long
Hose—for Portable Cable:
 _____" I.D., _____" O.D., _____' Long
Hose Clamps—
 2 for Motor-Starter Hose conduit _____" D
 1 for Portable Cable Hose conduit _____" D*
 *Only when short length of hose is used. Trolley Tap—
     (Manufacturing Company)
 Model _____ with _____-ampere fuse.
Rail Clamps, 2.
 1 Ground Clamp, Cat. No. _____
     (Manufacturing Company)
 1 Return Power Conductor, Cat. No. _____
     (Manufacturing Company)
     or—as Optional
Plug on outby end of potable cable for insertion into receptacle on distribution box or equivalent with short-circuit protective device set at _____ amperes.
Static-free Belt
 Model
 Style
 Catalog No. _____,
     (Manufacturing Company)
Guard for Belt—
Material _____
 Overall Dimensions _____" Long × _____"
 Wide × _____" High
NOTE: The foregoing is intended as a guide. Additional electrical components used shall be completely identified.

FIGURE 3—MATERIAL TO BE INCLUDED WITH THE OPERATING INSTRUCTIONS—ON OR WITH THE WIRING DIAGRAM SUBMITTED TO EACH CUSTOMER

(SOMETIMES REFERRED TO AS "CAUTION STATEMENT")

CAUTION

To retain "permissibility" of this equipment the following conditions shall be satisfied:
1. *General safety.* Frequent inspection shall be made. All electrical parts, including the portable cable and wiring, shall be kept in a safe condition. There shall be no openings into the casings of the electrical parts. A permissible distribution box shall be used for connection to the power circuit unless connection is made in fresh intake air. To maintain the overload protection on direct-current machines, the ungrounded conductor of the portable cable shall

be connected to the proper terminal. The machine frame shall be effectively grounded. The power wires shall not be used for grounding except in conjunction with diode(s) or equivalent. The operating voltage should match the voltage rating of the motor(s).

2. *Servicing.* Explosion-proof enclosures shall be restored to the state of original safety with respect to all flame arresting paths, lead entrances, etc., following disassembly for repair or rebuilding, whether by the owner or an independent shop.

3. *Fastenings.* All bolts, nuts, screws, and other means of fastening, and also threaded covers, shall be in place, properly tightened and secured.

4. *Renewals and repairs.* Inspections, repairs, or renewals of electrical parts shall not be made unless the portable cable is disconnected from the circuit furnishing power, and the cable shall not be connected again until all parts are properly reassembled. Special care shall be taken in making renewals or repairs. Leave no parts off. Use replacement parts exactly like those furnished by the manufacturer. When any lead entrance is disturbed, the original leads or exact duplicates thereof shall be used and stuffing boxes shall be repacked in the approved manner.

5. *Cable requirements.* A flame-resistant portable cable bearing a MSHA assigned identification number, adequately protected by an automatic circuit-interrupting device shall be used. Special care shall be taken in handling the cable to guard against mechanical injury and wear. Splices in portable cables shall be made in a workmanlike manner, mechanically strong, and well insulated. Not more than five temporary splices are permitted in a portable cable regardless of length. Connections and wiring to the outby end of the cable shall be in accordance with recognized standards of safety.

FIGURE 4—SAMPLE FACTORY INSPECTION FORM

Date _____
Inspector _____

MACHINE

Designation: _____
Type: _____ Serial No. _____

MOTOR

Manufacturer: _____
Serial No.: _____ Type: _____
Frame: _____
Hp.___ F.L. Speed:___ Volts:___ Amps.__
Winding: _____ X/P No. _____ (or parts list designation).

STARTER

Manufacturer: _____
Serial No. _____ Type: _____
Hp. _____ Volts: _____ X/P No. _____ (or parts list designation).
Short-circuit protection _____ amps.
Overload-current protection _____ amps.

PORTABLE CABLE

Manufacturer: _____
Type: _____ Conductors: _____
Length: _____ O.D. _____ MSHA No. _____
Is all wiring around machine adequately protected from mechanical damage?
By hose conduit_____, Troughs _____
Metal tubing _____, Other _____
By removal of all sharp corners or edges? _____
Is wiring separated from hydraulic components? _____
Is an adequate insulated strain clamp provided for the portable cable? _____
Are all packing glands properly packed so that ⅛-inch clearance remains between packing nut and stuffing box? _____
Are lockwashers (or equivalent) provided for all explosion-proof enclosure fastenings? _____
Are all plane joints securely fastened so that an 0.005-inch feeler gage cannot be inserted? ____
Are all threaded covers secured? _____
How? _____
Are all electrical connections secure _____ and properly insulated where necessary? _____

NOTE: Add appropriate material for each explosion-proof enclosure when more than a motor and starter are on a machine.

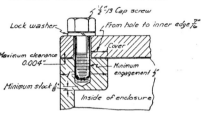

Figure 5

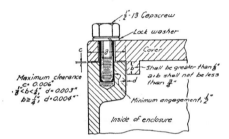

Figure 6

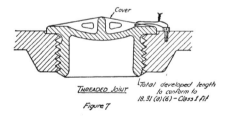

Figure 7

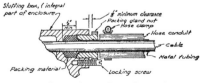

Figure 8

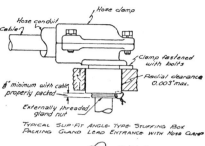

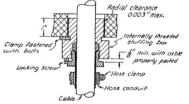

Figure 9

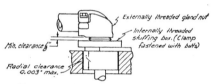

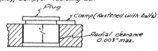

Figure 10

[33 FR 4660, Mar. 19, 1968, as amended at 42 FR 8373, Feb. 10, 1977; 42 FR 25855, May 20, 1977]

Subpart E—Field Approval of Electrically Operated Mining Equipment

SOURCE: 36 FR 7007, Apr. 13, 1971, unless otherwise noted.

§ 18.90 Purpose.

The regulations of this subpart E set forth the procedures and requirements

§ 18.91

for permissibility which must be met to obtain MSHA field approval of electrically operated machinery used or intended for use in by the last open crosscut of a coal mine which has not been otherwise approved, certified or accepted under the provisions of this part 18, chapter I, title 30, Code of Federal Regulations (Bureau of Mines Schedule 2G).

§ 18.91 Electric equipment for which field approvals will be issued.

(a) Individual field approvals will be issued by MSHA under the provisions of this subpart E for electrically operated machines commercially built, or constructed, by the owner-coal mine operator of such machines including any associated electrical equipment, electrical components, and electrical accessories.

(b) Approvals will not be issued under the provisions of this subpart E for electrically operated mining equipment manufactured or rebuilt primarily for sale or resale to any operator of a coal mine, or for small electrically operated equipment which consumes less than 2,250 watts of electricity, or for instruments and other small devices which employ electric power.

§ 18.92 Quality of material and design.

(a) Electrically operated machinery approved under the provisions of this subpart E shall be rugged in construction and shall be designed to facilitate maintenance and inspection.

(b) MSHA shall conduct field investigations and, where necessary, field test electric machinery only where such machinery is found to be constructed of suitable materials and safe for its intended use.

§ 18.93 Application for field approval; filing procedures.

(a)(1) Investigation and testing leading to field approval shall be undertaken by MSHA only pursuant to individual written applications for each machine submitted in triplicate on MSHA Form No. 6–1481, by the owner-coal mine operator of the machine.

(2) Except as provided in paragraph (b) of this section, each application shall be accompanied by appropriate photographs, drawings, specifications, and descriptions as required under the provisions of § 18.94 and each such application shall be filed with the Coal Mine Health and Safety District Manager for the District in which such machine will be employed.

(b) The Coal Mine Health and Safety District Manager may, upon receipt of any application filed pursuant to paragraph (a) of this section, waive the requirements of § 18.94 with respect to such application if he determines that the submission of photographs, drawings, specifications, or descriptions will place an undue financial burden upon the applicant. In the event a waiver is granted in accordance with this paragraph (b), initial review of the application will be waived and the applicant shall be notified on MSHA Form 6–1481 of such waiver and the date, time, and location at which field inspection of the equipment described in the application will be conducted.

(c) Following receipt of an application filed in accordance with paragraph (a) of this section, the Coal Mine Health and Safety District Manager shall determine whether the application has been filed in accordance with § 18.91, and cause the application to be reviewed by a qualified electrical representative to determine compliance with § 18.92:

(1) If it is determined on the basis of the application or the data submitted in accordance with § 18.94 that further consideration of a field approval is warranted under this subpart E or that the machine appears suitable and safe for its intended use, the Coal Mine Health and Safety District Manager shall advise the applicant in writing that further investigation and inspection of the machine will be necessary. The notice issued by the Coal Mine Health and Safety District Manager shall set forth the time and place at which such inspection will be conducted and specify the location and size of any tapped holes required to be made by the applicant to facilitate the pressure testing of enclosures.

(2) If it is determined on the basis of data submitted in accordance with § 18.94 that the applicant is not qualified to receive an approval or that the machine does not appear to be suitable

Mine Safety and Health Admin., Labor § 18.96

and safe for its intended use, the Coal Mine Health and Safety District Manager shall so advise the applicant in writing, setting forth the reasons for his denial of the application, and where applicable, the deficiencies in the machine which rendered it unsuitable or unsafe for use.

(3) Rejected applications, together with attached photographs, drawings, specifications and descriptions shall be forwarded by the Coal Mine Health and Safety District Manager to Approval and Certification Center which shall record all pertinent data with respect to the machine for which field approval was sought.

[33 FR 4660, Mar. 19, 1968, as amended at 43 FR 12314, Mar. 24, 1978]

§ 18.94 Application for field approval; contents of application.

(a) Each application for field approval shall, except as provided in § 18.93(b), include the following information with respect to the electrically operated machine for which field approval is sought:

(1) The trade name and the certification number or other means of identifying any explosion-proof compartment or intrinsically-safe component installed on the machine for which a prior approval or certification has been issued under the provisions of Bureau of Mines Schedules 2D, 2E, 2F, or 2G.

(2) The trade name and the flame-resistance acceptance or approval number of any cable, cord, hose, or conveyor belt installed on the machine for which prior acceptance or approval by MSHA has been issued.

(b) Each application for field approval shall be accompanied by:

(1) If the machine is constructed or assembled entirely from components which have been certified or removed from machines approved under Bureau of Mines Schedule 2D, 2E, 2F, or 2G, photographs or a single layout drawing which clearly depicts and identifies each of the permissible components and its location on the machine.

(2) If the machine contains one or more components required to be permissible which has not been approved or certified under Bureau of Mines Schedule 2D, 2E, 2F, or 2G, a single layout drawing which clearly identifies all of the components from which it was assembled.

(3) All applications shall include specifications for:

(i) Overcurrent protection of motors;

(ii) All wiring between components, including mechanical protection such as hose conduit and clamps;

(iii) Portable trailing cable for use with the machine, including the type, length, diameter, and number and size of conductors;

(iv) Insulated strain clamp for machine end of portable trailing cable;

(v) Short-circuit protection to be provided at outby end of portable trailing cable.

[33 FR 4660, Mar. 19, 1968, as amended at 57 FR 61223, Dec. 23, 1992]

§ 18.95 Approval of machines constructed of components approved, accepted or certified under Bureau of Mines Schedule 2D, 2E, 2F, or 2G.

Machines for which field approval is sought which are constructed entirely from properly identified components that have been investigated and accepted or certified for applications on approved machines under the Bureau of Mines Schedule 2D, 2E, 2F, or 2G, shall be approved following a determination by the electrical representative that the construction of the entire machine is permissible and conforms to the data submitted in accordance with § 18.94.

§ 18.96 Preparation of machines for inspection; requirements.

(a) Upon receipt of written notice from the Health and Safety District Manager of the time and place at which a field approval investigation will be conducted with respect to any machine, the applicant will prepare the machine for inspection in the following manner:

(1) The machine shall be in fresh air out by the last open crosscut and free from obstructions, or, if the machine is located on the surface, moved to a clear area;

(2) All enclosure covers shall be removed;

(3) The flanges and interior of each enclosure, including the cover, shall be cleaned thoroughly;

(4) All hoses, cables, cord, and conveyor belts shall be wiped clean to expose surface markings;

(5) All electrical components shall be cleaned to reveal all stampings, identification plates, certification numbers, or explosion test markings.

§ 18.97 Inspection of machines; minimum requirements.

(a) Except as provided in § 18.95, all machines approved under the provisions of this subpart E shall, where practicable, meet the minimum design and performance requirements set forth in subpart B of this part 18 and, where necessary, the requirements of § 18.98.

(b) The inspection of each machine shall be conducted by an electrical representative and such inspection shall include:

(1) Examination of all electrical components for materials, workmanship, design, and construction;

(2) Examination of all components of the machine which have been approved or certified under Bureau of Mines Schedule 2D, 2E, 2F, or 2G to determine whether such components have been maintained in permissible conditions;

(3) Comparison of the location of components on the machine with the drawings or photographs submitted to determine that each of them is properly located, identified and marked;

(4) Pressure testing of explosion-proof compartments, when necessary, shall be conducted in accordance with § 18.98; and:

(i) Where the results of pressure testing are acceptable, the applicant shall be advised;

(ii) Where the explosion-proof enclosure is found unacceptable, the applicant shall be so informed;

(iii) If the performance of the explosion-proof enclosure is questionable, the qualified electrical representative may, at the request of the applicant, conduct a further detailed examination of the enclosure after disassembly and record his additional findings on MSHA Form No. 6–1481 under Results of Field Inspections.

[33 FR 4660, Mar. 19, 1968, as amended at 42 FR 8373, Feb. 10, 1977]

§ 18.98 Enclosures, joints, and fastenings; pressure testing.

(a) Cast or welded enclosures shall be designed to withstand a minimum internal pressure of 150 pounds per square inch (gage). Castings shall be free from blowholes.

(b) Pneumatic field testing of explosion-proof enclosures shall be conducted by determining:

(1) Leak performance with a peak dynamic or static pressure of 150 pounds per square inch (gage); or

(2) A pressure rise and rate of decay consistent with unyielding components during a pressure-time history as derived from a series of oscillograms.

(c) Welded joints forming an enclosure shall have continuous gastight welds.

§ 18.99 Notice of approval or disapproval; letters of approval and approval plates.

Upon completion of each inspection conducted in accordance with § 18.97(b), the electrical representative conducting such inspection shall record his findings with respect to the machine examined on MSHA Form No. 6–1481 together with his recommendation of approval or disapproval of the machine.

(a) If the qualified electrical representative recommends field approval of the machine, the Coal Mine Health and Safety District Manager shall forward the completed application form together with all attached photographs, drawings, specifications, and descriptions to Approval and Certification Center. Approval and Certification Center shall record all pertinent data with respect to such machine, issue a letter of approval with a copy to the Coal Mine Health and Safety District Manager who authorized its issuance and send the field approval plate to the applicant. The approval plate shall be affixed to the machine by the applicant in such a manner so as not to impair its explosion-proof characteristics.

(b) If the electrical representative recommends disapproval of the machine, he shall record the reasons for such disapproval and the Coal Mine Health and Safety District Manager shall forward the completed application form and other data to Approval and Certification Center which shall record all pertinent data with respect to such machine and notify the applicant that the application for approval has been rejected and the reasons for the rejection.

[33 FR 4660, Mar. 19, 1968, as amended at 42 FR 8373, Feb. 10, 1977; 43 FR 12314, Mar. 24, 1978]

PART 19—ELECTRIC CAP LAMPS

Sec.
19.1 Purpose.
19.2 [Reserved]
19.3 Application procedures and requirements.
19.4 Conditions governing investigations.
19.5 General requirements for approval.
19.6 Specific requirements for approval.
19.7 Protection against explosion hazard.
19.8 Protection against bodily hazard.
19.9 Performance.
19.10 Material required for MSHA records.
19.11 How approvals are granted.
19.12 Wording, purpose, and use of approval plate.
19.13 Instructions for handling future changes in lamp design.

AUTHORITY: 30 U.S.C. 957, 961.
Secs. 19.1(b) and 19.7(a) also issued under 30 U.S.C. 811.

SOURCE: Schedule 6D, 4 FR 4003, Sept. 21, 1939, unless otherwise noted.

§ 19.1 Purpose.

(a) The purpose of investigations made under this part is to promote the development of electric cap lamps that may be used in mines, especially in mines that may contain dangerous concentrations of methane. Lists of such lamps will be published from time to time in order that State mine-inspection departments, compensation bureaus, mine operators, miners, and others interested in safe equipment for mines may have information in regard to available permissible electric cap lamps. This part supersedes Schedule 6C issued under date of December 21, 1935, and goes into effect August 26, 1939.

(b) Any electric cap lamp that meets the requirements set forth in this part will be termed "permissible" by MSHA and, if actively marketed, will be listed as such in publications relating to permissible electric cap lamps. MSHA will test only electrical equipment that in the opinion of its qualified representatives is constructed of suitable materials, is of good quality workmanship, is based on sound engineering principles, and is safe for its intended use. MSHA reserves the right to modify design, construction, and test requirements to obtain the same degree of protection as provided by the tests described in this part.

(c) *Definition of permissible.* Completely assembled and conforming in every respect with the design formally approved by the MSHA under this part. (Approvals under this part are given only to equipment for use in gassy and dusty mines.)

NOTE: Paragraph (b) of this section is issued under the authority of Sec. 101 of the Federal Mine Safety and Health Act of 1977, Pub. L. 91–173 as amended by Pub. L. 95–164, 91 Stat. 1291 (30 U.S.C. 811). All other paragraphs in this section continue under the original authority.

(Sec. 101, Federal Mine Safety and Health Act of 1977, 91 Stat. 1291 (30 U.S.C. 811))

[Sched. 6D, 4 FR 4003, Sept. 21, 1939, as amended by Supp. 1, 20 FR 2718, Apr. 23, 1955; 47 FR 11369, Mar. 16, 1982]

§ 19.2 [Reserved]

§ 19.3 Application procedures and requirements.

(a) Before MSHA will undertake the active investigation leading to approval of any lamp, the applicant shall make application by letter for an investigation leading to approval of the lamp. This application shall be sent to: U.S. Department of Labor, Mine Safety and Health Administration, Approval and Certification Center, 765 Technology Drive, Triadelphia, WV 26059, together with the required drawings, one complete lamp, and instructions for its operation. Fees calculated in accordance with part 5 of this title shall be submitted in accordance with § 5.40.

(b) Where the applicant for approval has used an independent laboratory under part 6 of this chapter to perform, in whole or in part, the necessary testing and evaluation for approval under this part, the applicant must provide to MSHA as part of the approval application:

(1) Written evidence of the laboratory's independence and current recognition by a laboratory accrediting organization;

(2) Complete technical explanation of how the product complies with each requirement in the applicable MSHA product approval requirements;

(3) Identification of components or features of the product that are critical to the safety of the product; and

(4) All documentation, including drawings and specifications, as submitted to the independent laboratory by the applicant and as required by this part.

(c) An applicant may request testing and evaluation to non-MSHA product safety standards which have been determined by MSHA to be equivalent, under § 6.20 of this chapter, to MSHA's product approval requirements under this part.

[68 FR 36419, June 17, 2003, as amended at 70 FR 46342, Aug. 9, 2005; 73 FR 52211, Sept. 9, 2008]

§ 19.4 Conditions governing investigations.

(a) One complete lamp, with the assembly and detail drawings that show the construction of the lamp and the materials of which it is made, should be submitted at the time the application for test is made. This material should be sent prepaid to the U.S. Department of Labor, Mine Safety and Health Administration, Approval and Certification Center, 765 Technology Drive, Triadelphia, WV 26059.

(b) When this lamp has been inspected by MSHA, the applicant will be notified as to the amount of material that will be required for the tests. In general, the material required will be as follows: (1) Thirty complete lamps; (2) 500 bulbs; (3) 50 feet of cord; (4) a battery discharge rack for 20 batteries; and (5) a 50-bulb rack. Specifications for items (4) and (5) will be furnished by MSHA.

(c) The applicant will be notified of the date on which the tests will start and will be given an opportunity to witness them.

(d) *Observers at formal investigations and demonstrations.* No one shall be present during any part of the formal investigation conducted by MSHA which leads to approval for permissibility except the necessary Government personnel, representatives of the applicant, and such other persons as may be mutually agreed upon by the applicant and MSHA. Upon granting approval for permissibility, MSHA will announce that such approval has been granted to the device and may thereafter conduct, from time to time in its discretion, public demonstrations of the tests conducted on the approved device. Those who attend any part of the investigation, or any public demonstration, shall be present solely as observers; the conduct of the investigation and of any public demonstration shall be controlled by MSHA. Results of chemical analyses of material and all information contained in the drawings, specifications, and instructions shall be deemed confidential and their disclosure will be appropriately safeguarded by MSHA.

(e) Permissibility tests will not be made unless the lamp has been completely developed and is in a form that can be marketed.

(f) The results of the tests shall be regarded as confidential by all present at the tests and shall not be made public in any way prior to the formal approval of the lamp by MSHA.

(g) No verbal report of approval or disapproval will be made to the applicant. After MSHA has considered the results of the tests, a formal report of the approval or disapproval will be made to the applicant in writing by Approval and Certification Center. The applicant shall not advertise the lamp as being permissible or as having passed the tests prior to receipt of formal notice of approval.

[Sched. 6D, 4 FR 4003, Sept. 21, 1939, as amended by Supp. 1, 20 FR 2718, Apr. 23, 1955; 43 FR 12314, Mar. 24, 1978; 60 FR 35693, July 11, 1996; 73 FR 52211, Sept. 9, 2008]

§ 19.5 General requirements for approval.

Electric cap lamps shall be complete units. They shall be durable in construction, practical in operation, and suitable for the conditions of underground service. They shall offer no probable explosion hazard if used in gassy or dusty mine atmospheres or bodily hazard from the spilling of the battery electrolyte. They shall exhibit, under laboratory test conditions, the various minimum performance requirements specified in this part.

§ 19.6 Specific requirements for approval.

(a) *Design*. In the determination of the adequacy of the lamp, with respect to design, the following points will be considered: (1) The materials used; (2) construction; (3) weight; (4) amount of light; (5) distribution of light; and (6) exclusion of dust from the headpiece. The suitability of the materials and the construction shall be determined by preliminary inspection, by dropping tests,[1] by durability tests of the cord and cord armor,[2] and by the general behavior of the lamp equipment during the investigation. The amount and distribution of the light shall be judged both by observation of the illumination on a white screen and by photometric measurements.

(b) *Angle of light beam*. MSHA recommends that the angle of the light beam be at least 130 degrees horizontally to insure that the contrast edge of the beam is away from the more sensitive sector of the wearer's vision; however, to allow for manufacturing and assembly tolerances and the use of multiple filament bulbs, MSHA will approve lamps giving a minimum beam angle of 120 degrees. If the bulb has more than one major filament, the one giving the smaller angle will be used in the determination.

(c) *Light distribution, visual*. Excepting special headpieces for inspection purposes, the area illuminated by the beam shall be free from sharp gradations in light intensity and spectral shadows.

(d) *Light distribution, photometric*. (1) Excepting special headpieces for inspection purposes, the maximum candlepower of the light beam shall not be greater than 25 times the average or mean candlepower of the beam.[3]

(2) The minimum candlepower of the beam based upon readings at the design voltage of the bulb shall not be less than 1.

§ 19.7 Protection against explosion hazard.

Unless properly designed, electric cap lamps may present two sources of probable explosion hazards: Ignition of an explosive atmosphere by the heated filament of the bulb in case the bulb glass is accidentally broken, and ignition by sparks or flashes from the battery. MSHA therefore requires the following safeguards:

(a) *Safety device or design*. The headpiece shall have a safety device to prevent the ignition of explosive mixtures of methane and air if the bulb glass surrounding the filament is broken. Alternatively, if the lamp is designed and constructed to prevent the ignition of explosive mixtures of methane and air by protecting the bulb from breakage and preventing exposure of the hot filament, no safety device is required.

(b) *Headpiece lock or seal*. The headpiece shall be provided with a lock or seal to prevent unauthorized removal of the lens and tampering with the safety device, the bulb, or the electrical contacts.

(c) *Locks on charging terminals*. Lamps shall be equipped with a magnetic or other equally effective lock at the battery, the headpiece, or the cord assembly to prevent unauthorized access to live charging terminals.

(d) *Protection of battery terminals*. The battery covers of lamps that are recharged through the cord shall be so constructed and assembled as to prevent unauthorized access to the battery terminals.

(e) *Battery current restricted*. The amount of current flow between the conductors of the cord, if short-circuited just outside of the battery casing or cord armor, shall be limited by the design of the battery or by a

---

[1] Batteries are dropped 3 feet, at least 20 times onto an oak floor. Headpieces are dropped 6 feet, at least 20 times, onto concrete.

[2] Ten cords, assembled with the cord armor and outlet of the lamp with which it is to be used, are slatted at least 100,000 times through an arc of 50 degrees at approximately 90 slattings per minute.

[3] The minimum allowable angle of 120 degrees will be used in determining the mean candlepower of the beam.

fuse to such a value[4] as will not produce sparks that will ignite an explosive mixture of methane and air.

(f) It shall not be possible to obtain a difference of potential between any two accessible points of the cap lamp when assembled for use.

NOTE: Paragraph (a) of this section is issued under the authority of Sec. 101 of the Federal Mine Safety and Health Act of 1977, Pub. L. 91–173 as amended by Pub. L. 95–164, 91 Stat. 1291 (30 U.S.C. 811). All other paragraphs in this section continue under the original authority.

(Sec. 101, Federal Mine Safety and Health Act of 1977, 91 Stat. 1291 (30 U.S.C. 811))

[Sched. 6D, 4 FR 4003, Sept. 21, 1939, as amended at 47 FR 11369, Mar. 16, 1982]

§ 19.8 Protection against bodily hazard.

This hazard is chiefly due to the possible burning of the wearer by electrolyte spilled from the battery. MSHA therefore requires that:

(a) *Spilling of electrolyte.* The lamp shall be so designed and constructed that, when properly filled, the battery will neither leak nor spill electrolyte under actual service conditions. Lamps passing a laboratory spilling test will be considered satisfactory in this respect, contingent upon satisfactory performance in service.

(b) *Corrosion of battery container.* The material of which the container is made shall resist corrosion under conditions of use.

§ 19.9 Performance.

In addition to the general design and the safety features, MSHA considers that a lamp of permissible type should meet certain minimum requirements with respect to performance, as follows:

(a) *Time of burning and candlepower.* Permissible electric cap lamps shall burn for at least 10 consecutive hours on one charge of the battery and shall give during that period a mean candlepower of light beam of not less than 1.

(b) *Bulb life.* The average life of the bulbs shall be not less than 200 hours, and at least 92 percent of the bulbs shall have a life of 150 hours. The life of a bulb is the number of hours its main filament will burn in the cap lamp or its equivalent.

The life of a bulb having main filaments in parallel is considered ended when the first filament ceases to burn; the life of a bulb having independent main filament is considered ended when the last filament ceases to burn.

(c) *Bulb uniformity.* (1) The bulbs submitted shall meet the following minimum requirements for variation in current consumption and candlepower:

(2) The current consumption of at least 94 percent of the bulbs shall not exceed the average current by more than 6 percent. The candlepower (s. cp.) of at least 90 percent of the bulbs shall not fall short of the average candlepower by more than 30 percent.

(d) *Corrosion of contacts.* Battery terminals and leads therefrom, as well as the battery gas vents, shall be designed to minimize corrosion of the electrical contacts.

[Sched. 6D, 4 FR 4003, Sept. 21, 1939, as amended at 47 FR 11369, Mar. 16, 1982]

§ 19.10 Material required for MSHA records.

In order that MSHA may know exactly what it has tested and approved, detailed records are kept covering each investigation. These include drawings and actual equipment, as follows:

(a) *Drawings.* The original drawings submitted with the application for the tests and the final drawings, which the manufacturer must submit to MSHA before the approval is granted, to show the details of the lamp as approved. These drawings are used to identify the lamp in the approval and as a means of checking the future commercial product of the manufacturer.

(b) *Actual equipment.* (1) If MSHA so desires, parts of the lamps which are used in the tests will be retained as a permanent record of the investigation and of the lamps submitted.

(2) If the lamp is approved, MSHA will require the manufacturer, as soon as his first manufactured lamps are available, to submit one complete

---

[4] The following maximum short-circuit current values may be used as a guide in the design of cap lamp batteries: 100 amperes for a 4-volt battery; 75 amperes for a 6-volt battery; 50 amperes for an 8-volt battery.

lamp, bearing the approval plate, as a record of his commercial product.

§ 19.11 How approvals are granted.

(a) All approvals are granted by official letter from MSHA. A lamp will be approved under this part only when the testing engineers judge that the lamp has met the requirements of the part and MSHA's records concerning the lamp are complete, including drawings from the manufacturer that show the lamp as it is to be commercially made. No verbal reports of MSHA's decisions, concerning the investigation will be given, and no informal approvals will be granted.

(b) As soon as the manufacturer has received the formal approval he shall be free to advertise his lamps as permissible.

[Sched. 6D, 4 FR 4003, Sept. 21, 1939, as amended by Supp. 1, 20 FR 2718, Apr. 23, 1955]

§ 19.12 Wording, purpose, and use of approval plate.

(a) *Approval plate.* The manufacturer shall attach, stamp, or mold an approval plate on the battery container of each permissible lamp. The plate shall bear the emblem of the Mine Safety and Health Administration and be inscribed as follows: "Permissible Electric Cap Lamp. Approval No. _____ issued to the _____ Company." When deemed necessary, an appropriate caution statement shall be added. The size and position of the approval plate shall be satisfactory to MSHA.

(b) *Purpose of approval plate.* The approval plate is a label which identifies the lamp so that anyone can tell at a glance whether or not the lamp is of the permissible type. By it, the manufacturer can point out that his lamp complies with specifications of MSHA and that it has been judged as suitable for use in gassy mines.

(c) *Use of approval plate.* Permission to place MSHA's approval plate on his lamp obligates the manufacturer to maintain the quality of his product and to see that each lamp is constructed according to the drawings which have been accepted by MSHA for this lamp and which are in MSHA's files. Lamps exhibiting changes in design which have not been approved are not permissible lamps and must not bear MSHA's approval plate.

(d) *Withdrawal of approval.* MSHA reserves the right to rescind, for cause, at any time any approval granted under this part.

[Sched. 6D, 4 FR 4003, Sept. 21, 1939, as amended at 43 FR 12314, Mar. 24, 1978]

§ 19.13 Instructions for handling future changes in lamp design.

All approvals are granted with the understanding that the manufacturer will make his lamp according to the drawings which he has submitted to MSHA and which have been considered and included in the approval. Therefore, when he desires to make any change in the design of the lamp, he should first of all obtain MSHA's approval of the change. The procedure is as follows:

(a)(1) The manufacturer shall write to the U.S. Department of Labor, Mine Safety and Health Administration, Approval and Certification Center, 765 Technology Drive, Triadelphia, WV 26059, requesting an extension of the original approval and stating the change or changes desired. With this letter the manufacturer should submit a revised drawing or drawings showing the changes in detail, and one of each of the changed lamp parts.

(2) Where the applicant for approval has used an independent laboratory under part 6 of this chapter to perform, in whole or in part, the necessary testing and evaluation for approval of changes to an approved product under this part, the applicant must provide to MSHA as part of the approval application:

(i) Written evidence of the laboratory's independence and current recognition by a laboratory accrediting organization;

(ii) Complete technical explanation of how the product complies with each requirement in the applicable MSHA product approval requirements;

(iii) Identification of components or features of the product that are critical to the safety of the product; and

(iv) All documentation, including drawings and specifications, as submitted to the independent laboratory by the applicant and as required by this part.

(b) MSHA will consider the application and inspect the drawings and parts to determine whether it will be necessary to make any tests.

(c) If no tests are necessary, the applicant will be advised of the approval or disapproval of the change by letter from MSHA.

(d) If tests are judged necessary, the applicant will be advised of the material that will be required.

[Sched. 6D, 4 FR 4003, Sept. 21, 1939, as amended by Supp. 1, 20 FR 2718, Apr. 23, 1955; 43 FR 12314, Mar. 24, 1978; 52 FR 17514, May 8, 1987; 60 FR 35693, July 11, 1995; 68 FR 36419, June 17, 2003; 73 FR 52211, Sept. 9, 2008]

PART 20—ELECTRIC MINE LAMPS OTHER THAN STANDARD CAP LAMPS

Sec.
20.0 Compliance with the requirements necessary for obtaining approval.
20.1 Purpose.
20.2 Definitions.
20.3 Application procedures and requirements.
20.4 [Reserved]
20.5 Conditions governing investigations.
20.6 General requirements.
20.7 Specific requirements.
20.8 Class 1 lamps.
20.9 Class 2 lamps.
20.10 Tests (class 1 and 2 lamps).
20.11 Material required for MSHA records.
20.12 How approvals are granted.
20.13 Approval plate.
20.14 Instructions for handling future changes in lamp design.

AUTHORITY: 30 U.S.C. 957, 961.

SOURCE: Schedule 10C, May 17, 1938, as amended at 5 FR 3467, Aug. 30, 1940, unless otherwise noted.

§ 20.0 Compliance with the requirements necessary for obtaining approval.

To receive approval of MSHA for any electric mine lamps other than standard cap lamps a manufacturer must comply with the requirements specified in this part.

§ 20.1 Purpose.

(a) The purpose of the investigations made under this part is to aid in the development and use of electric lamps, other than standard cap lamps, that may be used in mines, especially in mines that may contain dangerous proportions of methane.

(b) This part supersedes Schedule 10B, issued under date of June 1, 1932, and Schedule 11A, issued under date of January 13, 1936, and goes into effect May 17, 1938.

(c)(1) Electric lamps and flashlights that meet the requirements set forth in this part will be termed "permissible" by MSHA, and if actively marketed will be listed as such in publications relating to permissible equipment, in order that State mine inspection departments, compensation bureaus, mine operators, miners, and others interested in safety equipment for mines may have information in regard to electric lamps and flashlights approved by MSHA.

(2) MSHA May approve electric lamps and flashlights that incorporate technology for which the requirements of this part are not applicable if MSHA determines by testing that the electric lamps or flashlights are as safe as those which meet the requirements of this part.

[Sched. 10C, May 17, 1938, as amended at 5 FR 3467, Aug. 30, 1940; 54 FR 30513, July 20, 1989]

§ 20.2 Definitions.

(a) *Adequate.* Appropriate and sufficient as determined by mutual agreement between the manufacturer and MSHA.

(b) *Approval.* Official notification in writing from MSHA to a responsible organization, stating that upon investigation its lamp has been adjudged satisfactory under the requirements of this part.

(c) *Explosion-proof compartment.* An enclosure that withstands internal explosions of methane-air mixtures without damage to itself or discharge of flame and without ignition of surrounding explosive methane-air mixtures.

(d) *Permissible.* Completely assembled and conforming in every respect with the design formally approved by MSHA under this part. (Approvals under this part are given only to equipment for use in gassy and dusty mines.)

[Sched. 10C, May 17, 1938, as amended by Supp. 1, 20 FR 2718, Apr. 23, 1955]

Mine Safety and Health Admin., Labor § 20.5

§ 20.3 Application procedures and requirements.

(a) Before MSHA will undertake the active investigation of any lamp, the applicant shall make application by letter for an investigation of the lamp. This application shall be sent to: U.S. Department of Labor, Mine Safety and Health Administration, Approval and Certification Center, 765 Technology Drive, Triadelphia, WV 26059, together with the required drawings, one complete lamp, and instructions for its operation. Fees calculated in accordance with part 5 of this title shall be submitted in accordance with § 5.40.

(b) Where the applicant for approval has used an independent laboratory under part 6 of this chapter to perform, in whole or in part, the necessary testing and evaluation for approval under this part, the applicant must provide to MSHA as part of the approval application:

(1) Written evidence of the laboratory's independence and current recognition by a laboratory accrediting organization;

(2) Complete technical explanation of how the product complies with each requirement in the applicable MSHA product approval requirements;

(3) Identification of components or features of the product that are critical to the safety of the product; and

(4) All documentation, including drawings and specifications, as submitted to the independent laboratory by the applicant and as required under this part.

(c) An applicant may request testing and evaluation to non-MSHA product safety standards which have been determined by MSHA to be equivalent, under § 6.20 of this chapter, to MSHA's product approval requirements under this part.

[68 FR 36420, June 17, 2003, as amended at 70 FR 46343, Aug. 9, 2005; 73 FR 52211, Sept. 9, 2008]

§ 20.4 [Reserved]

§ 20.5 Conditions governing investigations.

(a) One complete lamp, with assembly and detail drawings that show the construction of the lamp and the materials of which it is made, should be submitted at the time the application for investigation is made. This material should be sent prepaid to the U.S. Department of Labor, Mine Safety and Health Administration, Approval and Certification Center, 765 Technology Drive, Triadelphia, WV 26059.

(b) When the lamp has been inspected by MSHA, the applicant will be notified as to the amount of material that will be required for the test. He will also be notified of the date on which the tests will start and will be given an opportunity to witness the tests.

(c) *Observers at formal investigations and demonstrations.* No one shall be present during any part of the formal investigation conducted by MSHA which leads to approval for permissibility except the necessary Government personnel, representatives of the applicant, and such other persons as may be mutually agreed upon by the applicant and MSHA. Upon granting approval for permissibility, MSHA will announce that such approval has been granted to the device and may thereafter conduct, from time to time in its discretion, public demonstrations of the tests conducted on the approved device. Those who attend any part of the investigation, or any public demonstration, shall be present solely as observers; the conduct of the investigation and of any public demonstration shall be controlled by MSHA. Results of chemical analyses of material and all information contained of material and all information contained in the drawings, specifications, and instructions shall be deemed confidential and their disclosure will be appropriately safeguarded by MSHA.

(d) Permissibility tests will not be made unless the lamp is complete and in a form that can be marketed.

(e) The results of the tests shall be regarded as confidential by all present at the tests and shall not be made public in any way prior to the formal approval of the lamp by MSHA.

(f) No verbal report of approval or disapproval will be made to the applicant. Approval will be made only in writing by MSHA. The applicant shall not be free to advertise the lamp as being permissible, or as having passed the tests, prior to receipt of formal notice of approval.

[Sched. 10C, May 17, 1938, as amended by Supp. 1, 20 FR 2719, Apr. 23, 1955; 43 FR 12314, Mar. 24, 1978; 60 FR 35693, July 11, 1995; 73 FR 52212, Sept. 9, 2008]

§ 20.6 General requirements.

(a) The lamps shall be durable in construction, practical in operation, and suitable for the service for which they are designed and approved.

(b) The intensity of light, distribution of light, and battery capacity shall be adequate for the use for which the lamp is intended.

(c) Battery terminals and leads therefrom, as well as the battery gas vents, shall be designed to minimize corrosion of the electrical contacts.

(d) Bulbs and other replacement parts of the lamps shall be adequately marked as a means of identification.

§ 20.7 Specific requirements.

Two general classes of electric lamps are recognized in these requirements, namely: Class 1, those that are self-contained and easily carried by hand, and class 2, those that may or may not be self-contained and not so readily portable as the first class.

(a) *Class 1.* Class 1 includes hand lamps, signal lamps, inspection lamps, flashlights, and animal lamps which are operated by small storage batteries or dry cells.

(b) *Class 2.* Class 2 includes lamps such as the pneumatic-electric types and large battery lamps.

§ 20.8 Class 1 lamps.

(a) *Protection against explosion hazards.* Unless properly designed, class 1 lamps present two sources of probable explosion hazards: Ignition of an explosive atmosphere by the heated filament of the bulb in case the bulb glass is accidentally broken, and ignition by electric sparks or arcs from the battery or connections thereto. MSHA's therefore, requires the following safeguards:

(1) *Safety device or design.* The lighting unit shall have a safety device to prevent the ignition of explosive mixtures of methane and air if the bulb glass surrounding the filament is broken. Alternatively, if the lamp is designed and constructed of materials that will prevent the ignition of explosive mixtures of methane and air by protecting the bulb from breakage and preventing exposure of the hot filament, no separate safety device is required. Alternative designs will be evaluated by mechanical impact tests, temperature tests and thermal shock tests to determine that the protection provided is no less effective than a safety device.

(2) *Safety device (protection).* The design of the safety device and the housing which protects it shall be such that the action of the safety device is positive; yet the lamp shall not be too readily extinguished during normal service by the unnecessary operation of the device.

(3) *Locks or seals.* For lamps other than flashlights, all parts, such as bulb housing and battery container, through which access may be had to live terminals or contacts shall be adequately sealed or equipped with magnetic or other equally reliable locks to prevent opening by unauthorized persons. For flashlights, provision shall be made for sealing the battery container.

(4) *Battery current restricted.* Unless all current-carrying parts including conductors, are adequately covered and protected by the sealed or locked compartments, the maximum possible current flow through that part shall be limited by battery design, or by an enclosed-type fuse inside the sealed or locked container, to values that will not produce sparks or arcs sufficient to ignite an explosive mixture of methane and air.

(b) *Protection against bodily hazard.* This hazard is chiefly due to the possible burning of the user by electrolyte spilled from the battery. MSHA, therefore, requires that:

(1) *Spilling of electrolyte.* The lamp shall be so designed and constructed that when properly filled the battery will neither leak nor spill electrolyte under conditions of normal use. Lamps passing a laboratory spilling test will be considered satisfactory in this respect, contingent upon satisfactory performance in service.

(2) *Corrosion of battery container.* The material of which the container is

Mine Safety and Health Admin., Labor § 20.10

made shall resist corrosion under conditions of normal use.

[Sched. 10C, May 17, 1938, as amended at 5 FR 3467, Aug. 30, 1940; 54 FR 30513, July 20, 1989]

§ 20.9 Class 2 lamps.

(a) *Safety.* (1) Unless special features of the lamp prevent ignition of explosive mixtures of methane and air by the broken bulb or other igniting sources within the lamp, the bulb and all spark-producing parts must be enclosed in explosion-proof compartments.

(2) Explosion-proof compartments will be tested while filled and surrounded with explosive mixtures of Pittsburgh natural gas[1] and air. A sufficient number of tests of each compartment will be made to prove that there is no danger of ignition of the mixture surrounding the lamp by explosions within the compartment. The lamp will not pass the above tests, even though the surrounding explosive mixtures are not ignited, if external flame is observed, if excessive pressures are developed, or if excessive distortion of any part of the compartment takes place.

(3) Glass-enclosed parts of such compartments must be guarded and be of extra-heavy glass to withstand pick blows, and be adequately protected by shrouds or by an automatic cut-out that opens the lamp circuit if the enclosure is broken.

(4) When an explosion-proof enclosure consists of two or more parts that are held together securely by bolts or some suitable means to permit assembly, the flanges comprising the joints between parts shall have surfaces with metal-to-metal contact, except enclosures requiring glass, in which case glass-to-metal joints are permitted. Gaskets, if adequate, may be used to obtain a firm seat for the glass but not elsewhere. Rubber, putty, and plaster of paris are not acceptable as material for gaskets. For enclosures having an unoccupied volume (air space) of more than 60 cubic inches the width of the joint measured along the shortest flame path from the inside to the outside of the enclosure shall not be less than 1 inch. When the unoccupied volume (air space) is less than 60 cubic inches, this path shall not be less than three-fourths inch.

(b) *Locks and seals (lighting attachment).* Explosion-proof compartments shall be equipped with seals or locks that prevent unauthorized and unsafe opening of the compartments in a mine.

(c) *Locks or seals (battery).* The battery shall be enclosed in a locked or sealed container that will prevent exposure of live terminals.

(d) *Temperature of lamp.* The temperature of the lamp under conditions of use shall not be such that a person may be burned in handling it.

(e) *Cable and connection.* (1) The cable or cord connecting the lamp to its battery shall be of high-grade design and materials, comparable to the specially recommended trailing cables as listed by MSHA, and shall be not more than 15 feet in length.

(2) The cable (or cord) shall be adequately protected at the battery end by a fuse in the locked battery box or housing. The cable (or cord) and the fuse shall be considered parts of the lamp, and specifications for them shall be submitted by the lamp manufacturer.

(3) The method of terminating the cable (or cord) at the lamp and at the battery housing shall be adequate, but in no case shall the cable or cord be detachable.

MSHA reserves the right to make minor changes in the requirements outlined in paragraphs (e) (1), (2), and (3) of this section (No. 9, class 2 lamps), as experience and service prove to be necessary in the interests of safety.

§ 20.10 Tests (class 1 and 2 lamps).

Such tests will be made as are necessary to prove the adequacy of a lamp or any of its parts in fulfilling the purposes for which it was designed. These tests include the following:

(a) Safety tests, including tests of safety devices, electrical contacts, and explosion-proof features.

(b) Photometric tests.

(c) Tests to demonstrate adequacy of mechanical strength.

---

[1] Investigation has shown that for practical purposes Pittsburgh natural gas (containing a high percentage of methane) is a satisfactory substitute for pure methane.

§ 20.11

(d) Tests of nonspilling features (storage-battery lamps of class 1).

(e) Temperature tests.

§ 20.11 Material required for MSHA records.

In order that MSHA may know exactly what it has tested and approved, detailed records are kept covering each investigation. These include drawings and actual equipment, as follows:

(a) *Drawings.* The original drawings submitted with the application for the tests and the final drawings which the manufacturer must submit to MSHA before approval is granted, to show the details of the lamp as approved, are retained. These drawings are used to identify the lamp and its parts in the approval and as a means of checking the future commercial product of the manufacturer.

(b) *Equipment.* (1) If MSHA so desires, parts of the lamps which are used in the tests will be retained as a permanent record of the investigation and of the lamps submitted.

(2) If the lamp is approved, MSHA will require the manufacturer, as soon as his first manufactured lamps are available, to submit one complete lamp, with the approval plate attached, as a record of his commercial product.

§ 20.12 How approvals are granted.

(a) All approvals are granted by official letter from MSHA. A lamp will be approved under this part only when the testing engineers judge that the lamp has met the requirements of this part and after MSHA's records concerning the lamp are complete, including manufacturer's drawings that show the lamp as it is to be made commercially. No verbal reports of MSHA's decision concerning the investigation will be given, and no informal approvals will be granted.

(b) As soon as the manufacturer has received the formal approval he shall be free to advertise his lamp as permissible.

[Sched. 10C, May 17, 1938, as amended by Supp. 1, 20 FR 2719, Apr. 23, 1955]

§ 20.13 Approval plate.

The manufacturer shall attach, stamp, or mold an approval plate on the battery container or housing of each permissible lamp. The plate shall bear the emblem of the Mine Safety and Health Administration, and be inscribed as follows: "Permissible _____ Lamp. Approval No. _____ issued to the _____ Company." When deemed necessary, an appropriate caution statement shall be added. The size, material, and position of the approval plate shall be satisfactory to MSHA.

(a) *Purpose of approval plate.* The approval plate is a label which identifies the lamp so that anyone can tell at a glance whether the lamp is of the permissible type or not. By it the manufacturer can point out that his lamp complies with specifications of MSHA and that it has been adjudged safe for use in gassy and dusty mines.

(b) *Use of approval plate.* Permission to place MSHA's approval plate on his lamp obligates the manufacturer to maintain the quality of his product and to see that each lamp is constructed according to the drawings which have been accepted by MSHA for this lamp and which are in the MSHA files. Lamps exhibiting changes in design which have not been approved are not permissible lamps and must not bear MSHA's approval plate.

(c) *Withdrawal of approval.* MSHA reserves the right to rescind for cause at any time any approval granted under this part.

[Sched. 10C, May 17, 1938, as amended at 5 FR 3467, Aug. 30, 1940; 43 FR 12314, Mar. 24, 1978]

§ 20.14 Instructions for handling future changes in lamp design.

All approvals are granted with the understanding that the manufacturer will make the lamp according to the drawings submitted to MSHA, which have been considered and included in the approval. Therefore, when the manufacturer desires to make any change in the design of the lamp, the manufacturer should first obtain an extension of the original approval to cover the change. The procedure is as follows:

(a)(1) The manufacturer shall write to the U.S. Department of Labor, Mine Safety and Health Administration, Approval and Certification Center, 765 Technology Drive, Triadelphia, WV 26059, requesting an extension of the original approval and describing the change or changes proposed. With this letter the manufacturer should submit a revised drawing or drawings showing the changes in detail, and one of each of the changed lamp parts.

(2) Where the applicant for approval has used an independent laboratory under part 6 of this chapter to perform, in whole or in part, the necessary testing and evaluation for approval of changes to an approved product under this part, the applicant must provide to MSHA as part of the approval application:

(i) Written evidence of the laboratory's independence and current recognition by a laboratory accrediting organization;

(ii) Complete technical explanation of how the product complies with each requirement in the applicable MSHA product approval requirements;

(iii) Identification of components or features of the product that are critical to the safety of the product; and

(iv) All documentation, including drawings and specifications, as submitted to the independent laboratory by the applicant and as required by this part.

(b) MSHA will consider the application and inspect the drawings and parts to determine whether it will be necessary to make any tests.

(c) If no tests are necessary, the applicant will be advised of the acceptance or rejection of the proposed change by letter from MSHA.

(d) If tests are judged necessary, the applicant will be advised of the material that will be required.

[Sched. 10C, May 17, 1938, as amended by Supp. 1, 20 FR 2719, Apr. 23, 1955; 43 FR 12314, Mar. 24, 1978; 52 FR 17514, May 8, 1987; 60 FR 35693, July 11, 1995; 68 FR 36420, June 17, 2003; 73 FR 52212, Sept. 9, 2008]

PART 22—PORTABLE METHANE DETECTORS

Sec.
22.0 Compliance with the requirements necessary for obtaining approval.
22.1 Purpose.
22.2 Definitions.
22.3 [Reserved]
22.4 Application procedures and requirements.
22.5 Conditions governing investigations.
22.6 General requirements.
22.7 Specific requirements.
22.8 Material required for MSHA records.
22.9 How approvals are granted.
22.10 Approval plate.
22.11 Instructions on handling future changes in design.

AUTHORITY: 30 U.S.C. 957, 961.

SOURCE: Schedule 8C, Oct. 31, 1935, unless otherwise noted.

§ 22.0 Compliance with the requirements necessary for obtaining approval.

To receive approval of MSHA for any portable methane detectors a manufacturer must comply with the requirements specified in this part.

§ 22.1 Purpose.

(a) The purpose of investigations under this part is to provide portable methane detectors that may be safely used in mines. Lists of such detectors will be published from time to time in order that State mine-inspection departments, compensation bureaus, mine operators, miners, and others interested in safe equipment for mines may have information in regard to permissible methane detectors. This part supersedes Schedule 8B, issued under date of November 17, 1926, and goes into effect October 31, 1935.

(b) Any methane detector that meets the requirements set forth in this part will be termed permissible by MSHA and if actively marketed will be listed as such in publications relating to permissible mining equipment.

§ 22.2 Definitions.

(a) *Methane detector.* A methane detector is a device that may be used to detect the presence of methane in a gassy mine.

(b) *Methane-indicating detector.* A methane-indicating detector is a device that will show, within certain limits of error, on an adequate scale, the percentage of methane in a gassy atmosphere.

(c) *Permissible.* Completely assembled and conforming in every respect with the design formally approved by MSHA under this part. (Approvals under this part are given only to equipment for use in gassy and dusty mines.)

[Sched. 8C, Oct. 31, 1955, as amended by Supp. 1, 20 FR 2575, Apr. 19, 1955]

§ 22.3 [Reserved]

§ 22.4 Application procedures and requirements.

(a) Before MSHA will undertake an active investigation leading to approval of any methane detector, the applicant shall make application by letter for an investigation leading to approval of the detector. This application shall be sent to: U.S. Department of Labor, Mine Safety and Health Administration, Approval and Certification Center, 765 Technology Drive, Triadelphia, WV 26059, together with the required drawings, one complete detector, and instructions for its operation. Fees calculated in accordance with part 5 of this title shall be submitted in accordance with § 5.40.

(b) Where the applicant for approval has used an independent laboratory under part 6 of this chapter to perform, in whole or in part, the necessary testing and evaluation for approval under this part, the applicant must provide to MSHA as part of the approval application:

(1) Written evidence of the laboratory's independence and current recognition by a laboratory accrediting organization;

(2) Complete technical explanation of how the product complies with each requirement in the applicable MSHA product approval requirements;

(3) Identification of components or features of the product that are critical to the safety of the product; and

(4) All documentation, including drawings and specifications, as submitted to the independent laboratory by the applicant and as required by this part.

(c) An applicant may request testing and evaluation to non-MSHA product safety standards which have been determined by MSHA to be equivalent, under § 6.20 of this chapter, to MSHA's product approval requirements under this part.

[68 FR 36420, June 17, 2003, as amended at 70 FR 46343, Aug. 9, 2005; 70 FR 48872, Aug. 22, 2005; 73 FR 52212, Sept. 9, 2008]

§ 22.5 Conditions governing investigations.

(a) One complete detector, with assembly and detail drawings that show the construction of the device and the materials of which it is made, should be forwarded prepaid to the U.S. Department of Labor, Mine Safety and Health Administration, Approval and Certification Center, 765 Technology Drive, Triadelphia, WV 26059, at the time the application for tests is made.

(b) When this has been inspected by MSHA, the applicant will be notified as to the amount of material that will be required for the tests. The manufacturer will be notified of the date on which the tests will be started and will be given an opportunity to witness the tests.

(c) *Observers at formal investigations and demonstrations.* No one shall be present during any part of the formal investigation conducted by MSHA which leads to approval for permissibility except the necessary Government personnel, representatives of the applicant, and such other persons as may be mutually agreed upon by the applicant and MSHA. Upon granting approval for permissibility, MSHA will announce that such approval has been granted to the device and may thereafter conduct, from time to time in its discretion, public demonstrations of the tests conducted on the approved device. Those who attend any part of the investigation, or any public demonstration, shall be present solely as observers; the conduct of the investigation and of any public demonstration shall be controlled by MSHA. Results of chemical analyses of material and all information contained in the drawings, specifications, and instructions shall be deemed confidential and their disclosure will be appropriately safeguarded by MSHA.

[Sched. 8C, Oct. 31, 1935, as amended by Supp. 1, 20 FR 2575, Apr. 19, 1955; 43 FR 12315, Mar. 24, 1978; 60 FR 35694, July 11, 1995; 73 FR 52212, Sept. 9, 2008]

§ 22.6 General requirements.

Methane detectors approved under this part shall be portable. They shall be durable in construction, practical in operation, and suitable for service conditions underground. They shall offer no probable explosion hazard if used in gaseous mine atmospheres nor any bodily hazard, such as spilling of battery electrolyte. They shall exhibit under

Mine Safety and Health Admin., Labor § 22.7

laboratory test conditions various requirements of minimum performance that are specified in this part.

§ 22.7 Specific requirements.

(a) *Design.* In the determination of adequacy of design, the following points will be considered: (1) Materials used, (2) construction, (3) accuracy, (4) size and shape, (5) range of detection (or indication), (6) life of the active parts, and (7) attention required. The suitability of the materials and the construction shall be determined by preliminary inspection, by dropping tests, by laboratory and field tests in gas and air mixtures, and by the general behavior of the equipment during the investigation.

(b) *Safety against explosion hazard*—(1) *Detectors.* Detectors shall be constructed so that they will not cause external ignitions when used in gaseous mine atmospheres.

(2) *Seals or locks.* All parts through which external ignitions might result shall be covered and protected adequately. All covers shall be sealed adequately or equipped with magnetic or other equally reliable locks to prevent their being opened by unauthorized persons.

(3) *Glasses.* Glasses or glass windows shall be of good-quality glass and protected adequately against breakage. Unguarded windows may be considered adequate in this respect, provided they are of small diameter and are of reasonably thick glass.

(4) *Battery.* If the detector is equipped with a battery, it shall be of such design that it will not produce sparks that will ignite an explosive mixture of methane and air.

(5) *Detectors of the flame type.* Methane detectors of the flame type shall be subject to the requirements of the flame-lamp schedule then in force.

(c) *Safety against bodily hazard.* Bodily hazard with battery-type detectors is due chiefly to possible burning of the user by electrolyte that has spilled from the battery. MSHA, therefore, requires that:

(1) *Spilling of electrolyte.* The battery shall be so designed and constructed that when properly filled it will not spill electrolyte under actual service conditions.

(2) *Corrosion of battery container.* The material of which the container is made shall resist corrosion under conditions of use.

(d) *Performance.* In addition to the general design and safety features, MSHA considers that permissible types of methane detectors should meet certain minimum requirements with respect to their performance, as follows:

(1) *Detectors.* (i) When the detector is operated according to the manufacturer's instructions, it shall be possible to detect at least 1 percent methane in air, and increasing percentages up to 5 percent shall be shown by continuously increasing evidence.

(ii) The average number of determinations that may be made in approximately 2-percent methane mixtures without recharging a battery or replacing a chemical accessory shall not be less than 25, and the average number of such determinations that may be made without replacing any other part shall be not less than 100.

(2) *Indicating detectors.* Indicating detectors shall give indications of as low as 0.25 percent methane. Detectors having an upper scale limit of 2 percent may be approved, but it is recommended that the detector be designed to give indications of as high as 4 percent methane. The indications for these percentages shall be within the limits of error specified in the following table:

ALLOWABLE VARIATIONS IN SCALE READING
[In percent]

Methane in mixtures	Minimum indication	Maximum indication
0.25	0.10	0.40
.50	.35	.65
1.00	.80	1.20
2.00	1.80	2.20
3.00	2.70	3.30
4.00	3.70	4.30

(i) Tests shall be made at several percentages within the range of the indicating detector and at temperatures between the limits of 50° and 70 °F. by increments of 5°. Ten determinations shall be made at each percentage. Neither the average of the 10 readings nor more than 2 readings for each percentage shall exceed the limits of error given in the table.

155

§ 22.8

(ii) The average number of determinations that may be made with an indicating detector without replacement of any part shall be not less than 30, and the average number that may be made without recharging the battery shall be not less than 15.

(iii) The scale shall not be subdivided into smaller divisions than the general accuracy of the indicating detector warrants.

(3) *Mechanical strength.* Detectors and indicating detectors shall be subjected to the following mechanical tests: Four of each of those parts or groups of assembled parts that are not normally strapped to the user shall be dropped 20 times on a wood floor from a height of 3 feet. Parts that are strapped to the user may be subjected to a jarring or bumping test to demonstrate adequate strength. The average number of times that any one of the detectors can be dropped before breakage or material distortion of essential parts shall be not less than 10.

(e) *Attachments for illumination.* If detectors are provided with attachments for illuminating purposes, such attachments shall be subject to the same requirements as those applying to that type of lamp under the lamp schedule then in force.

§ 22.8 Material required for MSHA records.

In order that MSHA may know exactly what it has tested and approved, it keeps detailed records covering each investigation. These records include drawings and actual equipment as follows:

(a) *Drawings.* The original drawings submitted with the application for the tests and the final drawings which the manufacturer must submit to MSHA before the approval is granted to show the details of the detector as approved, are retained. These drawings are used to identify the detector in the approval and as a means of checking the future commercial product of the manufacturer.

(b) *Actual equipment.* If MSHA so desires, parts of the detectors that are used in the tests will be retained as records of the equipment submitted. If the detector is approved, MSHA will require the manufacturer to submit one of his detectors, with the approval plate attached, as a record of his commercial product.

§ 22.9 How approvals are granted.

All approvals are granted by official letter from MSHA. A detector will be approved under this part only when the testing engineers have judged that it has met the requirements of the schedule and MSHA's records are complete, including drawings from the manufacturer that show the detector as it is to be commercially made. No verbal reports of the investigation will be given and no informal approvals will be granted. As soon as the manufacturer has received the formal approval, he shall be free to advertise his detector as permissible.

[Sched. 8C, Oct. 31, 1935, as amended by Supp. 1, 20 FR 2575, Apr. 19, 1955]

§ 22.10 Approval plate.

(a) *Attachment to be made by manufacturers.* (1) Manufacturers shall attach, stamp, or mold an approval plate on each permissible methane detector. The plate shall bear the emblem of the Mines Safety and Health Administration and be inscribed as follows:

Permissible Methane Detector (or Permissible Methane Indicating Detector) Approval No. _____ issued to the _____ Company.

(2) When deemed necessary, an appropriate caution statement shall be added. The size and position of the approval plate shall be satisfactory to MSHA.

(b) *Purpose of approval plate.* The approval plate is a label that identifies the device so that anyone can tell at a glance whether it is of the permissible type or not. By the plate, the manufacturer can point out that his detector complies with MSHA's requirements and that it has been approved for use in gassy mines.

(c) *Use of approval plate.* Permission to place MSHA's approval plate on his detector obligates the manufacturer to maintain the quality of his product and to see that each detector is constructed according to the drawings that have been accepted by MSHA and are in MSHA's files. Detectors exhibiting changes in design that have not been approved are not permissible and must not bear MSHA's approval plate.

(d) *Withdrawal of approval.* MSHA reserves the right to rescind for cause at any time any approval granted under this part.

[Sched. 8C, Oct. 31, 1935, as amended at 43 FR 12315, Mar. 24, 1978]

§ 22.11 Instructions on handling future changes in design.

All approvals are granted with the understanding that the manufacturer will make the detector according to the drawings submitted to MSHA which have been considered and included in the approval. Therefore, when the manufacturer desires to make any changes in the design, the manufacturer should first obtain MSHA's approval of the change. The procedure is as follows:

(a)(1) The manufacturer must write to the U.S. Department of Labor, Mine Safety and Health Administration, Approval and Certification Center, 765 Technology Drive, Triadelphia, WV 26059, requesting an extension of the original approval and stating the change or changes desired. With this request, the manufacturer should submit a revised drawing or drawings showing changes in detail, together with one of each of the parts affected.

(2) Where the applicant for approval has used an independent laboratory under part 6 of this chapter to perform, in whole or in part, the necessary testing and evaluation for approval of changes to an approved product under this part, the applicant must provide to MSHA as part of the approval application:

(i) Written evidence of the laboratory's independence and current recognition by a laboratory accrediting organization;

(ii) Complete technical explanation of how the product complies with each requirement in the applicable MSHA product approval requirements;

(iii) Identification of components or features of the product that are critical to the safety of the product; and

(iv) All documentation, including drawings and specifications, as submitted to the independent laboratory by the applicant and as required by this part.

(b) MSHA will consider the application and inspect the drawings and parts to determine whether it will be necessary to make any tests.

(c) If no tests are necessary, the applicant will be advised of the approval or disapproval of the change by letter from MSHA.

(d) If tests are judged necessary, the applicant will be advised of the material that will be required.

[Sched. 8C, Oct. 31, 1935, as amended by Supp. 1, 20 FR 2575, Apr. 19, 1955; 43 FR 12315, Mar. 24, 1978; 52 FR 17514, May 8, 1987; 60 FR 35694, July 11, 1995; 68 FR 36420, June 17, 2003; 73 FR 52212, Sept. 9, 2008]

PART 23—TELEPHONES AND SIGNALING DEVICES

Sec.
23.1 Purpose.
23.2 Definitions.
23.3 Application procedures and requirements.
23.4 [Reserved]
23.5 Conditions governing investigations.
23.6 General requirements for approval.
23.7 Specific requirements for approval.
23.8 Inspection and tests.
23.9 Special requirements for complete devices.
23.10 Material required for MSHA records.
23.11 How approvals are granted.
23.12 Wording, purpose, and use of approval plate.
23.13 Withdrawal of approval.
23.14 Instructions for handling future changes in design.

AUTHORITY: 30 U.S.C. 957, 961.
Sec. 23.2(f) also issued under 30 U.S.C. 811.

SOURCE: Schedule 9B, 4 FR 1555, Apr. 11, 1939, unless otherwise noted.

§ 23.1 Purpose.

(a) The purpose of investigations under this part is to promote the development of telephones and signaling devices that may be used safely in mines, especially in coal mines that may have gassy or dust-laden atmospheres. This schedule supersedes Schedule 9A, issued under date of December 5, 1922, and becomes effective October 18, 1938.

(b) Telephones and signaling devices approved under the requirements of this part will be termed "permissible" by MSHA, and if actively marketed will be listed as such in publications relating to permissible equipment, for the information of State mine inspection departments, compensation bureaus, mine operators, miners, and others interested in safety equipment for mines.

§ 23.2 Definitions.

(a) *Adequate* means appropriate and sufficient, as determined by mutual agreement of the manufacturer, operators, and MSHA.

(b) *Approval* means official notification by letter, from MSHA to a responsible organization, stating that the device under consideration has been judged to meet the requirements of this part.

(c) *Normal operation* means the performance by each part of the device of those functions for which the part was designed.

(d) *Permissible* as used in this part means completely assembled and conforming in every respect with the design formally approved by MSHA under this part. (Approvals under this part are given only to equipment for use in gassy and dusty mines.)

(e) *Protected* means effectively covered, enclosed, or otherwise guarded by adequate covers.

(f) *Signaling device.* As used in this part, a signaling device is one that gives visual or audible signals.

(g) *MESA* means the United States Department of the Interior, Mining Enforcement and Safety Administration. Predecessor organization to MSHA, prior to March 9, 1978.

(h) *MSHA* means the U.S. Department of Labor, Mine Safety and Health Administration.

NOTE: Paragraph (f) of this section is issued under the authority of Sec. 101 of the Federal Mine Safety and Health Act of 1977, Pub. L. 91-173 as amended by Pub. L. 95-164, 91 Stat. 1291 (30 U.S.C. 811). All other paragraphs in this section continue under the original authority.

[Sched. 9B, 4 FR 1555, Apr. 11, 1939, as amended by Supp. 1, 20 FR 2975, May 4, 1955; 39 FR 24001, June 28, 1974; 43 FR 12315, Mar. 24, 1978; 47 FR 11370, Mar. 16, 1982]

§ 23.3 Application procedures and requirements.

(a) Before MSHA will undertake an active investigation leading to approval of any telephone or signaling device, the applicant shall make application by letter for an investigation leading to approval of the device. This application shall be sent to: U.S. Department of Labor, Mine Safety and Health Administration, Approval and Certification Center, 765 Technology Drive, Triadelphia, WV 26059, together with the required drawings, one complete telephone or signaling device, and instructions for its operation. Fees calculated in accordance with part 5 of this title shall be submitted in accordance with § 5.40.

(b) Where the applicant for approval has used an independent laboratory under part 6 of this chapter, to perform, in whole or in part, the necessary testing and evaluation for approval under this part, the applicant must provide to MSHA as part of the approval application:

(1) Written evidence of the laboratory's independence and current recognition by a laboratory accrediting organization;

(2) Complete technical explanation of how the product complies with each requirement in the applicable MSHA product approval requirements;

(3) Identification of components or features of the product that are critical to the safety of the product; and

(4) All documentation, including drawings and specifications, as submitted to the independent laboratory by the applicant and as required by this part.

(c) An applicant may request testing and evaluation to non-MSHA product safety standards which have been determined by MSHA to be equivalent, under § 6.20 of this chapter, to MSHA's product approval requirements under this part.

[68 FR 36421, June 17, 2003, as amended at 70 FR 46343, Aug. 9, 2005; 70 FR 48872, Aug. 22, 2005; 73 FR 52212, Sept. 9, 2008]

§ 23.4 [Reserved]

§ 23.5 Conditions governing investigations.

(a) One complete device together with assembly and detail drawings that show its construction and the materials of which the parts are made, shall be submitted preferably at the time the application for test is made. These

Mine Safety and Health Admin., Labor

shall be sent prepaid to: Approval and Certification Center, 765 Technology Drive, Triadelphia, WV 26059.

(b) After the device has been inspected by MSHA, the applicant will be notified as to the amount of material that he will be required to supply for the tests and of the date on which testing will be started.

(c) *Observers at formal investigations and demonstrations.* No one shall be present during any part of the formal investigation conducted by MSHA which leads to approval for permissibility except the necessary Government personnel, representatives of the applicant, and such other persons as may be mutually agreed upon by the applicant and MSHA. Upon granting approval for permissibility, MSHA will announce that such approval has been granted to the device and may thereafter conduct, from time to time in its discretion, public demonstrations of the tests conducted on the approved device. Those who attend any part of the investigation, or any public demonstration, shall be present solely as observers; the conduct of the investigation and of any public demonstration shall be controlled by MSHA. Results of chemical analyses of material and all information contained in the drawings, specifications, and instructions shall be deemed confidential and their disclosure will be appropriately safeguarded by MSHA.

(d) Formal tests will not be made unless the device has been completely developed and is in a form that can be marketed.

(e) The results of the tests shall be regarded as confidential by all present at the tests and shall not be made public in any way prior to the formal approval of the device by MSHA.

(f) No verbal report of approval or disapproval will be made to the applicant. After MSHA has considered the results of the inspections and tests, a formal written report of the approval or disapproval will be made to the applicant by MSHA. The applicant shall not advertise his device as being permissible or approved, or as having passed the tests, prior to receipt of the formal notice of approval.

[Sched. 9B, 4 FR 1555, Apr. 11, 1939, as amended by Supp. 1, 20 FR 2975, May 4, 1955; 43 FR 12315, Mar. 24, 1978; 73 FR 52212, Sept. 9, 2008]

§ 23.6 General requirements for approval.

Telephones and signaling devices shall be durable in construction, practical in operation, and suitable for conditions of underground service. They shall offer no probable explosion hazard under normal operation if use in gassy or dusty mine atmospheres.

§ 23.7 Specific requirements for approval.

(a) The circuits external to telephones and signal devices shall be intrinsically safe; that is, the electrical design and construction of telephones and signal devices shall be such that neither contact between wires comprising the external circuits nor contact of tools or other metal objects with external terminals and circuits will result in electrical sparks capable of igniting explosive methane-air mixtures (or such mixtures with coal dust in suspension) during normal operation of the telephones or signal devices.

(b) All parts which, during normal operation, are capable of producing sparks that might ignite explosive methane-air mixtures shall be enclosed in explosion-proof compartments. All openings in the casings of such compartments shall be adequately protected. It is desirable that openings be as few as possible. All joints in the casings of an explosion-proof compartment shall be metal-to-metal so designed as to have a width of contact, measured along the shortest path from the inside to the outside of the compartment, of not less than 1 inch if the unoccupied volume (air space) in the compartment is more than 60 cubic inches. For unoccupied volume of 60 cubic inches or less, a ⅜-inch width of contact will be acceptable.

(c) All bolts and screw holes shall be "blind" or bottomed if the omission of a bolt or screw would otherwise leave an opening into the compartment. An adequate lock or seal shall be provided to prevent tampering and exposure of spark-producing parts by unauthorized persons.

(d) Battery cells shall be placed in an explosion-proof compartment or else in one that is locked or sealed, and the terminals and the connections thereto shall be so arranged and protected as to preclude meddling, tampering, or making other electrical connections with them.

(e) Manufacturers shall furnish adequate instructions for the installation and connection of telephones and signal devices in order that the safety of these devices and other circuits shall not be diminished by improper installation. MSHA reserves the right to require the attachment of wiring diagrams to the cases of telephones and signal devices.

(f) If electric light bulbs are used in signaling devices, they shall be either equipped with effective safety devices, such as are required for permissible electric mine lamps,[1] or enclosed in explosion-proof compartments.

(g) Line powered telephones and signaling devices or systems shall be equipped with standby power sources that have the capacity to enable the devices or systems to continue functioning in the event the line power fails or is cut off. Manufacturers shall furnish instructions for the proper maintenance of standby power sources.

NOTE: Paragraph (g) of this section is issued under the authority of Sec. 101 of the Federal Mine Safety and Health Act of 1977, Pub. L. 91–173 as amended by Pub. L. 95–164, 91 Stat. 1291 (30 U.S.C. 811). All other paragraphs in this section continue under the original authority.

[Sched. 9B, 4 FR 1555, Apr. 11, 1939, as amended at 47 FR 11370, Mar. 16, 1982]

§ 23.8 Inspection and tests.

(a) A thorough inspection of the telephone or signaling device will be made to determine its adequacy and permissibility. Tests may be made to check the electrical characteristics and constants of the various parts, and determine the adequacy of the insulation and other parts of features of the device.

(b) In addition, compartments of explosion-proof design will be tested while filled and surrounded with explosive mixtures containing varying percentages of Pittsburgh natural gas[2] and air, the mixture within the compartment being ignited by a spark plug or other suitable means. For some of the tests bituminous-coal dust will be introduced into the compartment in addition to the explosive mixtures, and the effects will be noted. A sufficient number of tests will be made under the foregoing conditions to determine the ability of the compartment to retain flame without bursting. Even though the surrounding mixtures are not ignited, the compartment will not be considered as having passed the tests, if flames are discharged from any joint or opening; if excessive pressures are developed or if serious distortion of the compartment walls take place.

§ 23.9 Special requirements for complete devices.

Telephones and signaling devices will be considered nonpermissible if used under any of the followings conditions:

(a) Without the approval plate, mentioned hereafter.

(b) With unprotected openings in any of the explosion-proof compartments. This condition refers to any openings in these compartments, but especially to those equipped with removable covers.

(c) If not complete with all of the parts considered in the approval.

(d) If installed or connected otherwise than in accordance with the instructions furnished by the manufacturer.

(e) If modified in any manner not authorized by MSHA.

§ 23.10 Material required for MSHA records.

In order that MSHA may know exactly what it has tested and approved, it keeps detailed records covering each investigation. These records include drawings and actual equipment as follows:

---

[1] In this case, the requirements of the current schedule for mine lamps will apply.

[2] Investigation has shown that for test purposes Pittsburgh natural gas (containing a high percentage of methane) is a satisfactory substitute for pure methane.

(a) *Drawings.* The original drawings submitted with the application for the tests and the final drawings which the manufacturer must submit to MSHA before the approval is granted, to show the details of the device as approved. These drawings are used to identify the device in the approval and as a means of checking the future commercial product of the manufacturer.

(b) *Actual equipment.* If MSHA so desires, parts of the devices that are used in the tests will be retained as records of the equipment submitted. If the device is approved, MSHA reserves the right to require the manufacturer to submit one, with the approval plate attached and without cost to MSHA, as a record of his commercial product.

§ 23.11 How approvals are granted.

All approvals are granted by official letter from MSHA. A device will be approved under this part only when the testing engineers have judged that it has met the requirements of the part and MSHA's records are complete, including drawings from the manufacturer that show the device as it is to be commercially made. Individual parts of devices will not be approved. No verbal reports of the investigation will be given and no informal approvals will be granted. As soon as the manufacturer has received the formal approval, he shall be free to advertise his device as permissible.

[Sched. 9B, 4 FR 1555, Apr. 11, 1939, as amended by Supp. 1, 20 FR 2975, May 4, 1955]

§ 23.12 Wording, purpose, and use of approval plate.

(a) *Approval plate.* (1) Manufacturers shall attach, stamp, or mold an approval plate on each permissible device. The plate shall bear the emblem of the Mine Safety and Health Administration and be inscribed as follows:

Permissible Telephone (or Permissible Signaling Device) Approval No.____Issued to the _____
Company.

(2) When deemed necessary, an appropriate caution statement shall be added. The size and position of the approval plate shall be satisfactory to MSHA.

(b) *Purpose.* The approval plate is a label that identifies the device so that anyone can tell at a glance whether or not it is of the permissible type. By the plate, the manufacturer can point out that his device complies with MSHA's requirements and that it has been approved for use in gassy or dusty mines.

(c) *Use.* Permission to place MSHA's approval plate on his device obligates the manufacturer to maintain the quality of his product and to see that each device is constructed according to the drawings that have been accepted by MSHA and are in MSHA's files. Devices exhibiting changes in design that have not been authorized are not permissible and must not bear MSHA's approval plate.

[Sched. 9B, 4 FR 1555, Apr. 11, 1939, as amended at 43 FR 12315, Mar. 24, 1978]

§ 23.13 Withdrawal of approval.

MSHA reserves the right to rescind for cause at any time any approval granted under this part.

§ 23.14 Instructions for handling future changes in design.

All approvals are granted with the understanding that the manufacturer will make his device according to the drawings that he has submitted to MSHA and that have been considered and included in the approval. Therefore, before making any changes in the design he shall obtain MSHA's authorization of the change. The procedure is as follows:

(a)(1) The manufacturer shall write to the U.S. Department of Labor, Mine Safety and Health Administration, Approval and Certification Center, 765 Technology Drive, Triadelphia, WV 26059, requesting an extension of the original approval and stating the change or changes desired. With this request, the manufacturer should submit a revised drawing or drawings showing the changes in detail, together with one of each of the parts affected.

(2) Where the applicant for approval has used an independent laboratory under part 6 of this chapter to perform, in whole or in part, the necessary testing and evaluation for approval of changes to an approved product under this part, the applicant must provide

to MSHA as part of the approval application:

(i) Written evidence of the laboratory's independence and current recognition by a laboratory accrediting organization;

(ii) Complete technical explanation of how the product complies with each requirement in the applicable MSHA product approval requirements;

(iii) Identification of components or features of the product that are critical to the safety of the product; and

(iv) All documentation, including drawings and specifications, as submitted to the independent laboratory by the applicant and as required by this part.

(b) MSHA will consider the application and inspect the drawings and parts to determine whether it will be necessary to make any tests.

(c) If no tests are necessary, and the change meets the requirements, the applicant will be officially advised by MSHA that his original approval has been extended to include the change.

(d) If tests are judged necessary, the applicant will be advised of the material that will be required. In this case extension of approval will be granted upon satisfactory completion of the tests and full compliance with the requirements.

[Sched. 9B, 4 FR 1555, Apr. 11, 1939, as amended by Supp. 1, 20 FR 2975, May 4, 1955; 43 FR 12315, Mar. 24, 1978; 52 FR 17514, May 8, 1987; 68 FR 36421, June 17, 2003; 73 FR 52212, Sept. 9, 2008]

PART 27—METHANE-MONITORING SYSTEMS

Subpart A—General Provisions

Sec.
27.1 Purpose.
27.2 Definitions.
27.3 Consultation.
27.4 Application procedures and requirements.
27.5 Letter of certification.
27.6 Certification of components.
27.7 Certification plate or label.
27.8 [Reserved]
27.9 Date for conducting tests.
27.10 Conduct of investigations, tests, and demonstrations.
27.11 Extension of certification.
27.12 Withdrawal of certification.

Subpart B—Construction and Design Requirements

27.20 Quality of material, workmanship, and design.
27.21 Methane-monitoring system.
27.22 Methane detector component.
27.23 Automatic warning device.
27.24 Power-shutoff component.

Subpart C—Test Requirements

27.30 Inspection.
27.31 Testing methods.
27.32 Tests to determine performance of the system.
27.33 Tests to determine explosion-proof construction.
27.34 Test for intrinsic safety.
27.35 Tests to determine life of critical components and subassemblies.
27.36 Test for adequacy of electrical insulation and clearances.
27.37 Tests to determine adequacy of safety devices for bulbs.
27.38 Tests to determine adequacy of windows and lenses.
27.39 Tests to determine resistance to vibration.
27.40 Test to determine resistance to dust.
27.41 Tests to determine resistance to moisture.

AUTHORITY: 30 U.S.C. 957, 961.

SOURCE: 31 FR 10607, Aug. 9, 1966, unless otherwise noted.

Subpart A—General Provisions

§ 27.1 Purpose.

The regulations in this part set forth the requirements for methane-monitoring systems or components thereof to procure certification for their incorporation in or with permissible equipment that is used in gassy mines, tunnels, or other underground workings and procedures for applying for such certification.

[31 FR 10607, Aug. 9, 1966, as amended at 52 FR 17515, May 8, 1987]

§ 27.2 Definitions.

As used in this part:

(a) *MSHA* means the United States Department of Labor, Mine Safety and Health Administration.

(b) *Applicant* means an individual, partnership, company, corporation, association, or other organization that designs, manufactures, or assembles and that seeks certification or preliminary testing of a methane-monitoring system or component.

(c) *Methane-monitoring system* means a complete assembly of one or more methane detectors and all other components required for measuring and signalling the presence of methane in the atmosphere of a mine, tunnel, or other underground workings, and shall include a power-shutoff component.

(d) *Methane detector* means a component for a methane-monitoring system that functions in a gassy mine, tunnel, or other underground workings to sample the atmosphere continuously and responds to the presence of methane.

(e) *Power-shutoff component* means a component of a methane-monitoring system, such as a relay, switch, or switching mechanism, that will cause a control circuit to deenergize a machine, equipment, or power circuit when actuated by the methane detector.

(f) *Flammable mixture* means a mixture of a gas, such as methane, natural gas, or similar hydrocarbon gas with normal air, that can be ignited.

(g) *Gassy mine or tunnel* means a mine, tunnel, or other underground workings in which a flammable mixture has been ignited, or has been found with a permissible flame safety lamp, or has been determined by air analysis to contain 0.25 percent or more (by volume) of methane in any open workings when tested at a point not less than 12 inches from the roof, face, or rib.

(h) *Letter of certification* means a formal document issued by MSHA stating that a methane-monitoring system or subassembly or component thereof:

(1) Has met the requirements of this part, and

(2) Is certified for incorporation in or with permissible or approved equipment that is used in gassy mines and tunnels.

(i) *Component* means a part of a methane-monitoring system that is essential to its operation as a certified methane-monitoring system.

(j) *Explosion-proof* means that a component or group of components (subassembly) is so constructed and protected by an enclosure with or without a flame arrester(s) that, if a flammable mixture of gas is ignited within the enclosure, it will withstand the resultant pressure without damage to the enclosure and/or flame arrester(s). Also the enclosure and/or flame arrester(s) shall prevent the discharge of flame from within either the enclosure or the flame arrester, or the ignition of any flammable mixture that surrounds the enclosure and/or flame arrester.[1]

(k) *Normal operation* means that performance of each component as well as of the entire assembly of the methane-monitoring system is in conformance with the functions for which it was designed and for which it was tested by MSHA.

(l) *Flame arrester* means a device so constructed that it will prevent propagation of flame or explosion from within the unit of which it is part to a surrounding flammable mixture.

(m) *Intrinsically safe equipment and circuitry* means equipment and circuitry that are incapable of releasing enough electrical or thermal energy under normal or abnormal conditions to cause ignition of a flammable mixture of the most easily ignitable composition.

(n) *Fail safe* means that the circuitry of a methane-monitoring system shall be so designed that electrical failure of a component which is critical in MSHA's opinion will result in deenergizing the methane-monitoring system and the machine or equipment of which it is a part.

[31 FR 10607, Aug. 9, 1966, as amended at 39 FR 24003, June 28, 1974; 43 FR 12316, Mar. 24, 1978]

§ 27.3 Consultation.

By appointment, applicants or their representatives may visit the U.S. Department of Labor, Mine Safety and Health Administration, Approval and Certification Center, 765 Technology Drive, Triadelphia, WV 26059, to discuss with qualified MSHA personnel proposed methane-monitoring systems to be submitted in accordance with the regulations of this part. No charge is made for such consultation and no

---

[1] Explosion-proof components or subassemblies shall be constructed in accordance with the requirements of Part 18 of this subchapter.

§ 27.4

written report thereof will be made to the applicant.

[31 FR 10607, Aug. 9, 1966, as amended at 43 FR 12316, Mar. 24, 1978; 60 FR 35694, July 11, 1995; 73 FR 52212, Sept. 9, 2008]

§ 27.4 Application procedures and requirements.

(a)(1) No investigation or testing for certification will be undertaken by MSHA except pursuant to a written application, accompanied by all drawings, specifications, descriptions, and related materials. The application and all related matters and correspondence shall be addressed to: U.S. Department of Labor, Mine Safety and Health Administration, Approval and Certification Center, 765 Technology Drive, Triadelphia, WV 26059. Fees calculated in accordance with part 5 of this title shall be submitted in accordance with § 5.40.

(2) Where the applicant for approval has used an independent laboratory under part 6 of this chapter to perform, in whole or in part, the necessary testing and evaluation for approval under this part, the applicant must provide to MSHA as part of the approval application:

(i) Written evidence of the laboratory's independence and current recognition by a laboratory accrediting organization;

(ii) Complete technical explanation of how the product complies with each requirement in the applicable MSHA product approval requirements;

(iii) Identification of components or features of the product that are critical to the safety of the product; and

(iv) All documentation, including drawings and specifications, as submitted to the independent laboratory by the applicant and as required by this part.

(3) An applicant may request testing and evaluation to non-MSHA product safety standards which have been determined by MSHA to be equivalent, under § 6.20 of this chapter, to the product approval requirements under this part.

(b) Drawings, specifications, and descriptions shall be adequate in detail to identify fully all components and subassemblies that are submitted for investigation, and shall include wiring and block diagrams. All drawings shall include title, number, and date; any revision dates and the purpose of each revision shall also be shown on the drawing.

(c) For a complete investigation leading to certification, the applicant shall furnish all necessary components and material to MSHA. MSHA reserves the right to require more than one of each component, subassembly, or assembly for the investigation. Spare parts and expendable components, subject to wear in normal operation, shall be supplied by the applicant to permit continuous operation during test periods. The applicant shall furnish special tools necessary to assemble or disassemble any component or subassembly for inspection or test.

(d) The applicant shall submit a plan of inspection of components at the place of manufacture or assembly. The applicant shall furnish to MSHA a copy of any factory-inspection form or equivalent with the application. The form shall direct attention to the points that must be checked to make certain that all components or subassemblies of the complete assembly are in proper condition, complete in all respects, and in agreement with the drawings, specifications, and descriptions filed with MSHA.

(e) The applicant shall furnish to MSHA complete instructions for operating the assembly and servicing components. After completion of MSHA's investigation, and before certification, if any revision of the instructions is required, a revised copy thereof shall be submitted to MSHA for inclusion with the drawings and specifications.

[31 FR 10607, Aug. 9, 1966, as amended at 43 FR 12316, Mar. 24, 1978; 60 FR 35694, July 11, 1995; 68 FR 36421, June 17, 2003; 70 FR 46343, Aug. 9, 2005; 73 FR 52212, Sept. 9, 2008]

§ 27.5 Letter of certification.

(a) Upon completion of investigation of a methane-monitoring system, or component or subassembly thereof, MSHA will issue to the applicant either a letter of certification or a written notice of disapproval, as the case may require If a letter of certification is issued, no test data or detailed results of tests will accompany it. If a notice of disapproval is issued, it will be accompanied by details of the defects, with a view to possible correction. MSHA will not disclose except to the applicant or his authorized representative, any information because of which a notice of disapproval has been issued.

(b) A letter of certification will be accompanied by an appropriate cautionary statement specifying the conditions to be observed for operating and maintaining the device(s) and to preserve its certified status.

§ 27.6 Certification of components.

In accordance with § 27.4, manufacturers of components may apply to MSHA to issue a letter of certification. To qualify for certification, electrical components shall conform to the prescribed inspection and test requirements and the construction thereof shall be adequately covered by specifications officially recorded and filed with MSHA. Letters of certification may be cited to fabricators of equipment intended for use in a certified methane-monitoring system as evidence that further inspection and test of the components will not be required.

§ 27.7 Certification plate or label.

A certified methane-monitoring system or component thereof shall be identified with a certification plate or label which is attached to the system or component in a manner acceptable to MSHA. The method of attachment shall not impair the explosion-proof characteristics of any enclosure. The plate or label shall be of serviceable material, acceptable to MSHA, and shall contain the following inscription with spaces for appropriate identification of the system or component and assigned certificate number:

Manufacturer's Name _____
Description _____
(Name)
Model or Type No _____
Certified as complying with the applicable requirements of Schedule 32A. _____
Certificate No _____

§ 27.8 [Reserved]

§ 27.9 Date for conducting tests.

The date of receipt of an application will determine the order of precedence for investigation and testing. The applicant will be notified of the date on which tests will begin.

NOTE: If an assembly, subassembly, or component fails to meet any of the requirements, testing of it may be suspended and other items may be tested. However, if the cause of failure is corrected, testing will be resumed after completing such other test work as may be in progress.

[31 FR 10607, Aug. 9, 1966, as amended at 70 FR 46343, Aug. 9, 2005]

§ 27.10 Conduct of investigations, tests, and demonstrations.

MSHA shall hold as confidential and shall not disclose principles or patentable features, nor shall it disclose any details of drawings, specifications, or related materials. The conduct of all investigations, tests, and demonstrations shall be under the direction and control of MSHA, and any other persons shall be present only as observers, except as noted in paragraph (b) of this section.

(a) Prior to the issuance of a letter of certification, necessary Government personnel, representatives of the applicant, and such other persons as are mutually agreed upon may observe the investigations or tests.

(b) When requested by MSHA the applicant shall provide assistance in assembling or disassembling components, subassemblies, or assemblies for testing, preparing components, subassemblies, or assemblies for testing, and operating the system during the tests.

(c) After the issuance of a letter of certification, MSHA may conduct such public demonstrations and tests of the certified methane-monitoring system or components as it deems appropriate.

[31 FR 10607, Aug. 9, 1966, as amended at 39 FR 24003, June 28, 1974]

§ 27.11 Extension of certification.

If an applicant desires to change any feature of a certified system or component, he shall first obtain MSHA's approval of the change, pursuant to the following procedure:

(a)(1) Application shall be made as for an original certification, requesting that the existing certification be extended to cover the proposed changes. The application shall include complete drawings, specifications, and related data, showing the changes in detail.

(2) Where the applicant for approval has used an independent laboratory under part 6 of this chapter to perform, in whole or in part, the necessary testing and evaluation for approval of changes to an approved product under this part, the applicant must provide to MSHA as part of the approval application:

(i) Written evidence of the laboratory's independence and current recognition by a laboratory accrediting organization;

(ii) Complete technical explanation of how the product complies with each requirement in the applicable MSHA product approval requirements;

(iii) Identification of components or features of the product that are critical to the safety of the product; and

(iv) All documentation, including drawings and specifications, as submitted to the independent laboratory by the applicant and as required by this part.

(b) The application will be examined by MSHA to determine whether inspection and testing of the modified system or component or of a part will be required. MSHA will inform the applicant whether testing is required and the component or components and related material to be submitted for that purpose.

(c) If the proposed modification meets the requirements of this part, a formal extension of certification will be issued, accompanied by a list of revised drawings and specifications which MSHA has added to those already on file.

[31 FR 10607, Aug. 9, 1966, as amended at 52 FR 17515, May 8, 1987; 68 FR 36421, June 17, 2003]

§ 27.12 Withdrawal of certification.

MSHA reserves the right to rescind for cause any certification issued under this part.

Subpart B—Construction and Design Requirements

§ 27.20 Quality of material, workmanship, and design.

(a) MSHA will test only equipment that, in its opinion, is constructed of suitable materials, is of good workmanship, is based on sound engineering principles, and is safe for its intended use. Since all possible designs, arrangements, or combinations of components cannot be foreseen, MSHA reserves the right to modify the construction and design requirements of components or subassemblies and the tests to obtain the degree of protection intended by the tests described in Subpart C of this part.

(b) Unless otherwise noted, the requirements stated in this part shall apply to explosion-proof enclosures and intrinsically safe circuits.

(c) All components, subassemblies, and assemblies shall be designed and constructed in a manner that will not create an explosion or fire hazard.

(d) All assemblies or enclosures—explosion-proof or intrinsically safe—shall be so designed that the temperatures of the external surfaces, during continuous operation, do not exceed 150 °C. (302 °F.) at any point.

(e) Lenses or globes shall be protected against damage by guards or by location.

(f) If MSHA determines that an explosion hazard can be created by breakage of a bulb having an incandescent filament, the bulb mounting shall be so constructed that the bulb will be ejected if the bulb glass enclosing the filament is broken.

NOTE: Other methods that provide equivalent protection against explosion hazards from incandescent filaments may be considered satisfactory at the discretion of MSHA.

§ 27.21 Methane-monitoring system.

(a) A methane-monitoring system shall be so designed that any machine or equipment, which is controlled by the system, cannot be operated unless the electrical components of the methane-monitoring system are functioning normally.

(b) A methane-monitoring system shall be rugged in construction so that its operation will not be affected by vibration or physical shock, such as normally encountered in mining operations.

(c) Insulating materials that give off flammable or explosive gases when decomposed shall not be used within enclosures where they might be subjected to destructive electrical action.

(d) An enclosure shall be equipped with a lock, seal, or acceptable equivalent when MSHA deems such protection necessary for safety.

(e) A component or subassembly of a methane-monitoring system shall be constructed as a package unit or otherwise in a manner acceptable to MSHA. Such components or subassemblies shall be readily replaceable or removable without creating an ignition hazard.

(f) The complete system shall "fail safe" in a manner acceptable to MSHA.

§ 27.22 Methane detector component.

(a) A methane detector component shall be suitably constructed for incorporation in or with permissible and approved equipment that is operated in gassy mines and tunnels.

(b) A methane detector shall include:

(1) A method of continuous sampling of the atmosphere in which it functions.

(2) A method for actuating a warning device which shall function automatically at a methane content of the mine atmosphere between 1.0 to 1.5 volume percent. The warning device shall also function automatically at all higher concentrations of methane in the mine atmosphere.

(3) A method for actuating a power-shutoff component, which shall function automatically when the methane content of the mine atmosphere is 2.0 volume percent and at all higher concentrations of methane.

(4) A suitable filter on the sampling intake to prevent dust and moisture from entering and interfering with normal operation.

NOTE: This requirement for the methane detector may be waived if the design is such as to preclude the need of a filter.

(c) A methane detector may provide means for sampling at more than one point; provided, the methane detector shall separately detect the methane in the atmosphere at each sampling point with, in MSHA's opinion, sufficient frequency.

§ 27.23 Automatic warning device.

(a) An automatic warning device shall be suitably constructed for incorporation in or with permissible and approved equipment that is operated in gassy mines and tunnels.

(b) An automatic warning device shall include an alarm signal (audible or colored light), which shall be made to function automatically at a methane content of the mine atmosphere between 1.0 to 1.5 volume percent and at all higher concentrations of methane.

(c) It is recommended that the automatic warning device be supplemented by a meter calibrated in volume percent of methane.

§ 27.24 Power-shutoff component.

(a) A power-shutoff component shall be suitably constructed for incorporation in or with permissible and approved equipment that is operated in gassy mines and tunnels.

(b) The power-shutoff component shall include:

(1) A means which shall be made to function automatically to deenergize the machine or equipment when actuated by the methane detector at a methane concentration of 2.0 volume percent and at all higher concentrations in the mine atmosphere.

(i) For an electric-powered machine or equipment energized by means of a trailing cable, the power-shutoff component shall, when actuated by the methane detector, cause a control circuit to shut down the machine or equipment on which it is installed; or it shall cause a control circuit to deenergize both the machine or equipment and the trailing cable.

NOTE: It is not necessary that power be controlled both at the machine and at the outby end of the trailing cable.

(ii) For a battery-powered machine or equipment, the methane-monitor power-shutoff component shall, when actuated by the methane detector, cause a control circuit to deenergize the machine or equipment as near as possible to the battery terminals.

(iii) For a diesel-powered machine or equipment, the power-shutoff component, when actuated by the methane detector, shall shut down the prime mover and deenergize all electrical

§ 27.30

components of the machine or equipment. Batteries are to be disconnected as near as possible to the battery terminals. Headlights which are approved under Part 20 of this subchapter (Schedule 10, or any revision thereof) are specifically exempted from this requirement.

(2) An arrangement for testing the power-shutoff characteristic to determine whether the power-shutoff component is functioning properly.

Subpart C—Test Requirements

§ 27.30 Inspection.

A detailed inspection shall be made by MSHA of the equipment and all components and functions related to safety in operation, which shall include:

(a) Examining materials, workmanship, and design to determine conformance with paragraph (a) of § 27.20.

(b) Comparing components and subassemblies with the drawings and specifications to verify conformance with the requirements of this part.

§ 27.31 Testing methods.

A methane-monitoring system shall be tested by MSHA to determine its functional performance, and its explosion-proof and other safety characteristics. Since all possible designs, arrangements, or combinations cannot be foreseen, MSHA reserves the right to make any tests or to place any limitations on equipment, or components or subassemblies thereof, not specifically covered herein, to determine and assure the safety of such equipment with regard to explosion and fire hazards.

§ 27.32 Tests to determine performance of the system.

(a) *Laboratory tests for reliability and durability.* Five hundred successful consecutive tests[2] for gas detection, alarm action, and power shutoff in natural gas-air mixtures[3] shall be conducted to demonstrate acceptable performance as to reliability and durability of a methane-monitoring system. The tests shall be conducted as follows:

(1) The methane detector component shall be placed in a test gallery into which natural gas shall be made to enter at various rates with sufficient turbulence for proper mixing with the air in the gallery. To comply with the requirements of this test, the detector shall provide an impulse to actuate an alarm at a predetermined percentage of gas and also provide an impulse to actuate a power shutoff at a second predetermined percentage of gas. (See §§ 27.21, 27.22, 27.23, and 27.24.)[4]

(b) *Field tests.* MSHA reserves the right to conduct tests, similar to those stated in paragraph (a) of this section, in underground workings to verify reliability and durability of a methane-monitoring system installed in connection with a piece of mining equipment.

§ 27.33 Test to determine explosion-proof construction.

Any assembly, subassembly, or component which, in the opinion of MSHA, requires explosion-proof construction shall be tested in accordance with the procedures stated in Part 18 of this subchapter.

§ 27.34 Test for intrinsic safety.

Assemblies, subassemblies, or components that are designed for intrinsic safety shall be tested by introducing into the circuit(s) thereof a circuit-interrupting device which produces an electric spark from the current in the circuit. The circuit-interrupting device shall be placed in a gallery containing various flammable natural gas-air mixtures. To meet the requirements of this test, the spark shall not ignite the flammable mixture. For this test the circuit-interrupting device shall be operated not less than 100 times at 125 percent of the normal operating voltage of the particular circuit.

---

[2] Normal replacements and adjustments shall not constitute a failure.

[3] Investigation has shown that, for practical purposes, natural gas (containing a high percentage of methane) is a satisfactory substitute for pure methane in these tests.

[4] At the option of MSHA, these tests will be conducted with dust or moisture added to the atmosphere within the gallery.

§ 27.35 Tests to determine life of critical components and subassemblies.

Replaceable components may be subjected to appropriate life tests at the discretion of MSHA.

§ 27.36 Test for adequacy of electrical insulation and clearances.

MSHA shall examine, and test in a manner it deems suitable, electrical insulation and clearances between electrical conductors to determine adequacy for the intended service.

§ 27.37 Tests to determine adequacy of safety devices for bulbs.

The glass envelope of bulbs with the filament incandescent at normal operating voltage shall be broken in flammable methane-air or natural gas-air mixtures in a gallery to determine that the safety device will prevent ignition of the flammable mixtures.

§ 27.38 Tests to determine adequacy of windows and lenses.

Impact tests. A 4-pound cylindrical weight with a one-inch diameter hemispherical striking surface will be dropped (free fall) to strike the window or lens in its mounting or the equivalent thereof at or near the center. At least three out of four samples shall withstand the impact according to the following table:

Overall lens diameter (inches)	Height of fall (inches)
Less than 4	6
4 to 5	9
5 to 6	15
Greater than 6	24

Lenses or windows of smaller diameter than 1 inch may be tested by alternate methods at the discretion of MSHA.

§ 27.39 Tests to determine resistance to vibration.

(a) *Laboratory tests for reliability and durability.* Components, subassemblies, or assemblies that are to be mounted on permissible and approved equipment shall be subjected to two separate vibration tests, each of one-hour duration. The first test shall be conducted at a frequency of 30 cycles per second with a total movement per cycle of $\frac{1}{16}$-inch. The second test shall be conducted at a frequency of 15 cycles per second with a total movement per cycle of $\frac{1}{8}$-inch. Components, subassemblies, and assemblies shall be secured to the vibration testing equipment in their normal operating positions (with shock mounts, if regularly provided with shock mounts). Each component, subassembly and assembly shall function normally during and after each vibration test.

NOTE: The vibrating equipment is designed to impart a circular motion in a plane inclined 45° to the vertical or horizontal.

(b) *Field tests.* MSHA reserves the right to conduct tests to determine resistance to vibration in underground workings to verify the reliability and durability of a methane-monitoring system or component(s) thereof where installed in connection with a piece of mining equipment.

§ 27.40 Test to determine resistance to dust.

Components, subassemblies, or assemblies, the normal functioning of which might be affected by dust, such as coal or rock dust, shall be tested in an atmosphere containing an average concentration (50 million minus 40 micron particles per cubic foot) of such dust(s) for a continuous period of 4 hours. The component, subassembly, or assembly shall function normally after being subjected to this test.

NOTE: Dust measurements, when necessary, shall be made by impinger sampling and light-field counting technique.

§ 27.41 Test to determine resistance to moisture.

Components, subassemblies, or assemblies, the normal functioning of which might be affected by moisture, shall be tested in atmospheres of high relative humidity (80 percent or more at 65°–75 °F.) for continuous operating and idle periods of 4 hours each. The component or subassembly or assembly shall function normally after being subjected to those tests.

PART 28—FUSES FOR USE WITH DIRECT CURRENT IN PROVIDING SHORT-CIRCUIT PROTECTION FOR TRAILING CABLES IN COAL MINES

Subpart A—General Provisions

Sec.
28.1 Purpose.
28.2 Approved fuses.
28.3 Installation, use, and maintenance of approved fuses.
28.4 Definitions.

Subpart B—Application for Approval

28.10 Application procedures.

Subpart C—Approval and Disapproval

28.20 Certificates of approval; scope of approval.
28.21 Certificates of approval; contents.
28.22 Notice of disapproval.
28.23 Approval labels or markings; approval of contents; use.
28.24 Revocation of certificates of approval.
28.25 Changes or modifications of approved fuses; issuance of modification of certificate of approval.

Subpart D—Quality Control

28.30 Quality control plans; filing requirements.
28.31 Quality control plans; contents.
28.32 Proposed quality control plans; approval by MSHA.
28.33 Quality control test methods, equipment, and records; review by MSHA: revocation of approval.

Subpart E—Construction, Performance and Testing Requirements

28.40 Construction and performance requirements; general.
28.41 Testing requirements; general.

AUTHORITY: 30 U.S.C. 957, 961.

SOURCE: 37 FR 7562, Apr. 15, 1972, unless otherwise noted.

Subpart A—General Provisions

§ 28.1 Purpose.

The purpose of the regulations contained in this Part 28 is: (a) To establish procedures and prescribe requirements which must be met in filing applications for the approval of fuses for use with direct current in providing short-circuit protection for trailing cables in coal mines, or the approval of changes or modifications of approved fuses; (b) to specify minimum performance requirements and to prescribe methods to be employed in conducting inspections, examinations, and tests to determine the effectiveness of fuses for use with direct current in providing short-circuit protection for trailing cables in coal mines; and (c) to provide for the issuance of certificates of approval or modifications of certificates of approval for fuses which have met the minimum requirements for performance and short-circuit protection set forth in this part.

§ 28.2 Approved fuses.

(a) On and after the effective date of this part, fuses shall be considered to be approved for use with direct current in providing short-circuit protection for trailing cables in coal mines only where such fuses are: (1) The same in all respects as those fuses which have been approved after meeting the minimum requirements for performance and short-circuit protection prescribed in this Part 28; and (2) maintained in an approved condition.

§ 28.3 Installation, use, and maintenance of approved fuses.

Approved fuses shall be installed and maintained in accordance with the specifications prescribed by the manufacturer of the fuses, and shall be selected and used in accordance with the standards prescribed for short-circuit protective devices for trailing cables in Parts 75 and 77, Subchapter O of this chapter.

§ 28.4 Definitions.

As used in this part—

(a) *Applicant* means an individual, partnership, company, corporation, association, or other organization that designs, manufactures, assembles, or fabricates, or controls the design, manufacture, assembly, or fabrication of a fuse, and who seeks to obtain a certificate of approval for such fuse.

(b) *Approval* means a certificate or formal document issued by MSHA stating that an individual fuse or combination of fuses has met the minimum requirements of this Part 28, and that the applicant is authorized to use and attach an approval label or other equivalent marking to any fuse manufactured, assembled, or fabricated in conformance with the plans and specifications upon which the approval was based, as evidence of such approval.

(c) *Approved* means conforming to the minimum requirements of this Part 28.

(d) *MESA* means the United States Department of the Interior, Mining Enforcement and Safety Administration. Predecessor organization to MSHA, prior to March 9, 1978.

(e) *MSHA* means the United States Department of Labor, Mine Safety and Health Administration.

(f) *Fuse* means a device, no less effective than an automatic circuit breaker, for use with direct current which provides short-circuit protection for trailing cables in coal mines by interrupting an excessive current in the circuit.

[37 FR 7562, Apr. 15, 1972, as amended at 39 FR 24003, June 28, 1974; 43 FR 12316, Mar. 24, 1978]

Subpart B—Application for Approval

§ 28.10 Application procedures.

(a) Each applicant seeking approval of a fuse for use with direct current in providing short-circuit protection for trailing cables shall arrange for submission, at applicant's own expense, of the number of fuses necessary for testing to a nationally recognized independent testing laboratory capable of performing the examination, inspection, and testing requirements of this part.

(b) The applicant shall insure, at his own expense, that the examination, inspection, and testing requirements of this part are properly and thoroughly performed by the independent testing laboratory of his choice.

(c) Upon satisfactory completion by the independent testing laboratory of the examination, inspection, and testing requirements of this part, the data and results of such examination, inspection, and tests shall be certified by both the applicant and the laboratory and shall be sent for evaluation of such data and results to the U.S. Department of Labor, Mine Safety and Health Administration, Approval and Certification Center, 765 Technology Drive, Triadelphia, WV 26059. Fees calculated in accordance with part 5 of this title shall be submitted in accordance with § 5.40.

(d) The certified data and results of the examinations, inspections, and tests required by this part and submitted to MSHA for evaluation shall be accompanied by a proposed plan for quality control which meets the minimum requirements set forth in Subpart D of this part.

(e) Each applicant shall deliver to MSHA at his own expense, three fuses of each size and type which may be necessary for evaluation of the examination, inspection, and test results by the Bureau.

(f) Applicants or their representatives may visit or communicate with Approval and Certification Center in order to discuss the requirements for approval of any fuse, or to obtain criticism of proposed designs; no charge shall be made for such consultation and no written report shall be issued by MSHA as a result of such consultation.

[37 FR 7562, Apr. 15, 1972, as amended at 43 FR 12316, Mar. 24, 1978; 52 FR 17515, May 8, 1987; 60 FR 35694, July 11, 1995; 70 FR 46343, Aug. 9, 2005; 73 FR 52212, Sept. 9, 2008]

Subpart C—Approval and Disapproval

§ 28.20 Certificates of approval; scope of approval.

(a) MSHA shall issue certificates of approval pursuant to the provisions of this subpart only for individual, completely fabricated fuses which have been examined, inspected, and tested as specified in § 28.10, and have been evaluated by MSHA to ensure that they meet the minimum requirements prescribed in this part.

(b) MSHA shall not issue an informal notification of approval.

§ 28.21 Certificates of approval; contents.

(a) Each certificate of approval shall contain a description of the fuse and a classification of its current-interrupting capacity and current rating.

(b) The certificate of approval shall specifically set forth any restrictions or limitations on the use of the fuse in providing short-circuit protection for trailing cables.

(c) Each certificate of approval shall be accompanied by a reproduction of the approval label or marking design, as appropriate, to be employed by the applicant with each approved fuse as provided in § 28.23.

(d) No test data or specific laboratory findings will accompany any certificate of approval; however, MSHA will release analyses of pertinent test data and specific findings upon receipt of a written request by the applicant, or when required by statute or regulation.

(e) Each certificate of approval shall also contain the approved quality control plan as specified in § 28.31.

§ 28.22 Notice of disapproval.

(a) If, upon completion of the evaluation by MSHA conducted in accordance with § 28.10, it is determined that the fuse does not meet the minimum requirements set forth in this part, MSHA shall issue a written notice of disapproval to the applicant.

(b) Each notice of disapproval shall be accompanied by all available findings with respect to the defects of the fuse for which approval was sought with a view to the possible correction of any such defects.

(c) MSHA shall not disclose, except to the applicant upon written request or when required by statute or regulation, any data, findings, or other information with respect to any fuse for which a notice of disapproval is issued.

§ 28.23 Approval labels or markings; approval of contents; use.

(a) Approval labels shall bear the emblem of the Mine Safety and Health Administration, an approval number, the restrictions, if any, placed upon the use of the fuse by MSHA, and where appropriate, the applicant's name and address.

(b) Upon receipt of a certificate of approval, the applicant shall submit to MSHA, for approval of contents, full-scale reproductions of approval labels or markings, as appropriate, and a sketch or description of the method of application and position on the fuse, together with instructions for the installation, use, and maintenance of the fuse.

(c) Legible reproductions or abbreviated forms of the label or markings approved by MSHA shall be attached to or printed on each fuse.

(d) Each fuse shall be marked with the rating of the Underwriters Laboratories, Inc.

(e) MSHA shall, where necessary, notify the applicant when additional labels, markings, or instructions will be required.

(f) Approval labels or markings shall only be used by the applicant to whom they were issued.

(g) The use of any MSHA approval label or marking obligates the applicant to whom it is issued to maintain or cause to be maintained the approved quality control sampling procedure and the acceptable quality level for each characteristic tested, and to guarantee that the approved fuse is manufactured according to the specifications upon which the certificate of approval is based.

(h) The use of any MSHA approval label or marking obligates the applicant to whom it is issued to retest the approved fuse within a 2-year period from the date of the certificate of approval, and every 2 years thereafter, in accordance with the provisions of § 28.10.

[37 FR 7562, Apr. 15, 1972, as amended at 43 FR 12316, Mar. 24, 1978; 45 FR 68935, Oct. 17, 1980]

§ 28.24 Revocation of certificates of approval.

MSHA reserves the right to revoke, for cause, any certificate of approval issued pursuant to the provisions of this part. Such causes include, but are not limited to, misuse of approval labels and markings, misleading advertising, violations of section 110(h) of the Federal Mine Safety and Health Act of 1977 and failure to maintain or cause to be maintained the quality control requirements of the certificate of approval.

[37 FR 7562, Apr. 15, 1972, as amended at 43 FR 12316, Mar. 24, 1978]

Mine Safety and Health Admin., Labor § 28.32

§ 28.25 Changes or modifications of approved fuses; issuance of modification of certificate of approval.

(a) Each applicant may, if he desires to change any feature of an approved fuse, request a modification of the original certificate of approval issued by MSHA for such fuse by filing an application for modification in accordance with the provisions of this section.

(b) Applications, including fees, shall be submitted as specified in § 28.10 for an original certificate of approval, with a request for a modification of the existing certificate to cover any proposed change.

(c) The application for modification, together with the examination, inspection, and test results prescribed by § 28.10 shall be examined and evaluated by MSHA to determine if the proposed modification meets the requirements of this part.

(d) If the proposed modification meets the requirements of this part, a formal modification of approval will be issued, accompanied, where necessary, by reproductions of revised approval labels or markings.

Subpart D—Quality Control

§ 28.30 Quality control plans; filing requirements.

As a part of each application for approval or modification of approval submitted pursuant to this part, each applicant shall file with MSHA a proposed quality control plan which shall be designed to assure the quality of short-circuit protection provided by the fuse for which approval is sought.

§ 28.31 Quality control plans; contents.

(a) Each quality control plan shall contain provisions for the management of quality, including:

(1) Requirements for the production of quality data and the use of quality control records;

(2) Control of engineering drawings, documentations, and changes;

(3) Control and calibration of measuring and test equipment;

(4) Control of purchased material to include incoming inspection;

(5) Lot identification, control of processes, manufacturing, fabrication, and assembly work conducted in the applicant's plant;

(6) Audit or final inspection of the completed product; and,

(7) The organizational structure necessary to carry out these provisions.

(b) The sampling plan shall include inspection tests and sampling procedures developed in accordance with Military Specification MIL-F-15160D, "Fuses; Instrument, Power, and Telephone" (which is hereby incorporated by reference and made a part hereof), Group A tests and Group B tests, except that the continuity and/or resistance characteristics of each fuse shall be tested. Military Specification MIL-F-15160D is available for examination at the U.S. Department of Labor, Mine Safety and Health Administration, Approval and Certification Center, 765 Technology Drive, Triadelphia, WV 26059. Copies of the document may be purchased from Information Dissemination (Superintendent of Documents), P.O. Box 371954, Pittsburgh, PA 15250-7954; Telephone: 866-512-1800, *http://bookstore.gpo.gov*.

(c) The sampling procedure shall include a list of the characteristics to be tested by the applicant or his agent and shall include but not be limited to:

(1) Continuity and/or resistance determination for each fuse;

(2) Carry current capability (not less than 110 percent of the rated current); and,

(3) Overload current interruption capability (not less than 135 percent of the rated current).

(d) The quality control inspection test method to be used by the applicant or his agent for each characteristic required to be tested shall be described in detail.

[37 FR 7562, Apr. 15, 1972, as amended at 43 FR 12316, Mar. 24, 1978; 60 FR 35694, July 11, 1995; 71 FR 16666, Apr. 3, 2006; 73 FR 52212, Sept. 9, 2008]

§ 28.32 Proposed quality control plans; approval by MSHA.

(a) Each proposed quality control plan submitted in accordance with this subpart shall be reviewed by MSHA to determine its effectiveness in insuring the quality of short-circuit protection provided by the fuse for which an approval is sought.

§ 28.33

(b) If MSHA determines that the proposed quality control plan submitted by the applicant will not insure adequate quality control, MSHA shall require the applicant to modify the procedures and testing requirements of the plan prior to approval of the plan and issuance of any certificate of approval.

(c) Approved quality control plans shall constitute a part of and be incorporated into any certificate of approval issued by MSHA, and compliance with such plans by the applicant shall be a condition of approval.

§ 28.33 Quality control test methods, equipment, and records; review by MSHA; revocation of approval.

(a) MSHA reserves the right to have its representatives inspect the applicant's quality control test methods, equipment, and records, and to interview any employee or agent of the applicant in regard to quality control test methods, equipment, and records.

(b) MSHA reserves the right to revoke, for cause, any certificate of approval where it finds that the applicant's quality control test methods, equipment, or records do not ensure effective quality control over the fuse for which the approval was issued.

Subpart E—Construction, Performance, and Testing Requirements

§ 28.40 Construction and performance requirements; general.

(a) MSHA shall issue approvals for fuses for use with direct current in providing short-circuit protection for trailing cables, when such fuses have met the minimum construction, performance, and testing requirements set forth in this subpart.

(b) Fuses submitted to MSHA for approval will not be accepted unless they are designed on sound engineering and scientific principles, constructed of suitable materials, and evidence good workmanship.

(c) Fuses may be single-element or dual-element in type, however, they shall be capable of interrupting any direct current within a range from the ampere rating of the fuse under consideration for approval up to 20,000 amperes.

(d) MSHA shall accept the fuse size and ampere rating as specified in the Underwriters Laboratories, Inc., standard for alternating current fuses (UL-198), which is hereby incorporated by reference and made a part hereof. This document is available for examination at the U.S. Department of Labor, Mine Safety and Health Administration, Approval and Certification Center, 765 Technology Drive, Triadelphia, WV 26059, and copies of the document are available from COMM 2000, 1414 Brook Drive, Downers Grove, IL 60515; Telephone: 888–853–3512 (toll free); *http:// ulstandardsinfonet.ul.com.*

(e) Fuses shall be capable of completely interrupting a current within 30 milliseconds after initial current interruption, and shall not show any evidence of restriking after 30 milliseconds.

(f) The blown fuse shall show only superficial damage.

[37 FR 7562, Apr. 15, 1972, as amended at 43 FR 12316, Mar. 24, 1978; 60 FR 35694, July 11, 1995; 71 FR 16666, Apr. 3, 2006; 73 FR 52213, Sept. 9, 2008]

§ 28.41 Testing requirements; general.

(a) The open circuit voltage of the test circuit shall be 300 volts d.c., or 600 volts d.c., depending on the voltage rating of the fuse being tested.

(b) Time constant of the circuit (defined as $T = L/R$, where T is the time in seconds, L is the inductance in henries, and R is the resistance in ohms) shall be as follows:

(1) For 10,000 amperes and greater currents, $T = 0.016$ second or more;

(2) For 1,000 amperes to 10,000 amperes, $T = 0.008$ second or more;

(3) For 100 amperes to 1,000 amperes, $T = 0.006$ second or more; and

(4) For less than 100 amperes, $T = 0.002$ seconds or more.

(c) Test currents shall be as follows:

(1) 200 percent of rated current for fuses having 200 or less ampere rating, or 300 percent of rated current for fuses having greater than 200 ampere rating;

(2) 900 percent of rated current;

(3) 10,000 amperes; and

(4) 20,000 amperes.

Mine Safety and Health Admin., Labor § 33.2

(d) The voltage shall continue to be applied for at least 30 seconds after completion of circuit interruption.

(e) Five fuses of each case size shall be tested at each test current specified in paragraph (c) of this section, with the value of the fuse being the maximum value for the case size.

(f) Three of each lot of five fuses shall be preconditioned at 95 ±5 percent RH for not less than 5 days immediately prior to testing; and the other two fuses of each lot of five shall be preconditioned by heating to 90 °C. for 24 hours, and tested within 1 hour after removal from the preconditioning chamber.

(g) At least three of each lot of five fuses shall be tested in a fuse holder of a trolley-tap type, and the fuse holder shall remain intact and shall readily accept and retain a replacement fuse.

PART 33—DUST COLLECTORS FOR USE IN CONNECTION WITH ROCK DRILLING IN COAL MINES

Subpart A—General Provisions

Sec.
33.1 Purpose.
33.2 Definitions.
33.3 Consultation.
33.4 Types of dust collectors for which certificates of approval may be granted.
33.5 [Reserved]
33.6 Application procedures and requirements.
33.7 Date for conducting tests.
33.8 Conduct of investigations, tests, and demonstrations.
33.9 Certification of dust-collecting systems.
33.10 Certificates of approval or performance.
33.11 Approval plates.
33.12 Changes after certification.
33.13 Withdrawal of certification.

Subpart B—Dust-Collector Requirements

33.20 Design and construction.
33.21 Modification of test equipment.
33.22 Mode of use.
33.23 Mechanical positioning of parts.

Subpart C—Test Requirements

33.30 Test site.
33.31 Test space.
33.32 Determination of dust concentration.
33.33 Allowable limits of dust concentration.
33.34 Drilling test.
33.35 Methods of drilling; dust-collector unit.
33.36 Method of drilling; combination unit or dust-collecting system.
33.37 Test procedure.
33.38 Electrical parts.

AUTHORITY: 30 U.S.C. 957, 961.

SOURCE: Schedule 25B, 25 FR 6473, July 9, 1960, unless otherwise noted.

Subpart A—General Provisions

§ 33.1 Purpose.

The regulations in this part set forth the requirements for dust collectors used in connection with rock drilling in coal mines to procure their certification as permissible for use in coal mines; procedures for applying for such certification; and fees.

§ 33.2 Definitions.

As used in this part:

(a) *Permissible*, as applied to a dust collector, means that it conforms to the requirements of this part, and that a certificate of approval to that effect has been issued.

(b) *Bureau* means the United States Bureau of Mines.

(c) *Certificate of approval* means a formal document issued by MSHA stating that the dust collector unit or combination unit has met the requirements of this part, and authorizing the use and attachment of an official approval plate or a marking so indicating.

(d) *Certificate of performance* means a formal document issued by MSHA stating that a dust-collecting system has met the test requirements of Subpart C of this part and therefore is suitable for use as part of permissible units.

(e) *Dust-collector unit* means a complete assembly of parts comprising apparatus for collecting the dust that results from drilling in rock in coal mines, and is independent of the drilling equipment.

(f) *Combination unit* means a rock-drilling device with an integral dust-collecting system, or mining equipment with an integral rock-drilling device and dust-collecting system.

(g) *Dust-collecting system* means an assembly of parts comprising apparatus for collecting the dust that results from drilling in rock and is dependent

§ 33.3

upon attachment to other equipment for its operation.

(h) *Applicant* means an individual, partnership, company, corporation, association, or other organization that designs and manufactures, assembles or controls the assembly of a dust-collecting system, dust-collector unit, or a combination unit, and seeks certification thereof.

(i) *MSHA* means the United States Department of Labor, Mine Safety and Health Administration.

[Sched. 25B, 25 FR 6473, July 9, 1960, as amended at 39 FR 24005, June 28, 1974; 43 FR 12317, Mar. 24, 1978]

§ 33.3 Consultation.

By appointment, applicants or their representatives may visit the U.S. Department of Labor, Mine Safety and Health Administration, Approval and Certification Center, 765 Technology Drive, Triadelphia, WV 26059, to discuss with MSHA personnel proposed designs of equipment to be submitted in accordance with the regulations of this part. No charge is made for such consultation and no written report thereof will be made to the applicant.

[70 FR 46343, Aug. 9, 2005, as amended at 73 FR 52213, Sept. 9, 2008]

§ 33.4 Types of dust collectors for which certificates of approval may be granted.

(a) Certificates of approval will be granted only for completely assembled dust-collector or combination units; parts or subassemblies will not be approved.

(b) The following types of equipment may be approved: Dust-collector or combination units having components designed specifically to prevent dissemination of airborne dust generated by drilling into coal-mine rock strata in concentrations in excess of those hereinafter stated in § 33.33 as allowable, and to confine or control the collected dust in such manner that it may be removed or disposed of without dissemination into the mine atmosphere in quantities that would create unhygienic conditions.

§ 33.5 [Reserved]

§ 33.6 Application procedures and requirements.

(a)(1) No investigation or testing for certification will be undertaken by MSHA except pursuant to a written application (except as provided in paragraph (e) of this section), accompanied by all prescribed drawings, specifications, and related materials. The application and all related matters and correspondence shall be addressed to: U.S. Department of Labor, Mine Safety and Health Administration, Approval and Certification Center, 765 Technology Drive, Triadelphia, WV 26059. Fees calculated in accordance with part 5 of this title shall be submitted in accordance with § 5.40.

(2) Where the applicant for approval has used an independent laboratory under part 6 of this chapter to perform, in whole or in part, the necessary testing and evaluation for approval under this part, the applicant must provide to MSHA as part of the approval application:

(i) Written evidence of the laboratory's independence and current recognition by a laboratory accrediting organization;

(ii) Complete technical explanation of how the product complies with each requirement in the applicable MSHA product approval requirements;

(iii) Identification of components or features of the product that are critical to the safety of the product; and

(iv) All documentation, including drawings and specifications, as submitted to the independent laboratory by the applicant and as required by this part.

(3) An applicant may request testing and evaluation to non-MSHA product safety standards which have been determined by MSHA to be equivalent, under § 6.20 of this chapter, to MSHA's product approval requirements under this part.

(b) The application shall specify the operating conditions (see § 33.22) for which certification is requested.

(c) Shipment of the equipment to be tested shall be deferred until MSHA has notified the applicant that the application will be accepted. Shipping instructions will be issued by MSHA and shipping charges shall be prepaid by the applicant. Upon completion of the investigation and notification thereof to the applicant by MSHA, the applicant shall remove his equipment promptly from the test site (see § 33.30).

(d) Drawings and specifications shall be adequate in number and detail to identify fully the design of the unit or system and to disclose its materials and detailed dimensions of all component parts. Drawings must be numbered and dated to insure accurate identification and reference to records, and must show the latest revision. Specifications and drawings, including a complete assembly drawing with each part that affects dust collection identified thereon, shall include:

(1) Details of all dust-collector parts. A manufacturer who supplies the applicant with component parts or sub- assemblies may submit drawings and specifications of such parts or sub-assemblies direct to MSHA instead of to the applicant. If the unit or system is certified, MSHA will supply the applicant with a list, in duplicate, of drawing numbers pertaining to such parts or subassemblies for identification purposes only.

(2) Details of the electrical parts of units designed to operate as face equipment (see § 33.38) in accordance with the provisions of Part 18 of Subchapter D of this chapter. (Bureau of Mines Schedule 2, revised, the current revision of which is Schedule 2F).

(3) Storage capacity of the various stages of dust collection in the dust separator.

(4) Net filter area in the dust separator, and complete specifications of the filtering material.

(e) If an application is made for certification of a dust-collector unit or a combination unit that includes electrical parts, and is designed to operate as electric face equipment, as defined in § 33.38, the application shall be in triplicate.

(f) The application shall state that the unit or system is completely developed and of the design and materials which the applicant believes to be suitable for a finished marketable product.

(g) The applicant shall furnish a complete unit or system for inspection and testing. Spare parts, such as gaskets and other expendable components subject to wear in normal operation, shall be supplied by the applicant to permit continuous operation during test periods. If special tools are necessary to disassemble any part for inspection or test, they shall be furnished by the applicant.

(h) Each unit or system shall be carefully inspected before it is shipped from the place of manufacture or assembly and the results of the inspection shall be recorded on a factory-inspection form. The applicant shall furnish MSHA with a copy of the factory-inspection form with his application. The form shall direct attention to the points that must be checked to make certain that all parts are in proper condition, complete in all respects, and in agreement with the drawings and specifications filed with MSHA.

(i) With the application the applicant shall furnish MSHA with complete instructions for operating and servicing the unit or system and information as to the kind of power required. After MSHA's investigation, if any revision of the instructions is required a revised copy thereof shall be submitted to MSHA for inclusion with the drawings and specifications.

[Sched. 25B, 25 FR 6473, July 9, 1960, as amended at 43 FR 12317, Mar. 24, 1978; 47 FR 14696, Apr. 6, 1982; 47 FR 28095, June 29, 1982; 60 FR 33723, June 29, 1995; 68 FR 36422, June 17, 2003; 70 FR 46343, Aug. 9, 2005; 73 FR 52213, Sept. 9, 2008]

§ 33.7 Date for conducting tests.

The date of acceptance of an application will determine the order of precedence for testing when more than one application is pending, and the applicant will be notified of the date on which tests will begin. If a unit or system fails to meet any of the requirements, it shall lose its order of precedence. If an application is submitted to resume testing after correction of the cause of failure, it will be treated as a new application and the order of precedence for testing will be so determined.

§ 33.8 Conduct of investigations, tests, and demonstrations.

(a) Prior to the issuance of a certificate of approval or performance, necessary government personnel, representatives of the applicant, and such other persons as may be mutually agreed upon, may observe the investigations or tests. MSHA shall hold as confidential and shall not disclose principles or patentable features, nor shall it disclose any details of drawings, specifications, and related materials. After the issuance of a certificate, MSHA may conduct such public demonstrations and tests of the unit or system as it deems appropriate. The conduct of all investigations, tests, and demonstrations shall be under the direction and control of MSHA, and any other persons shall be present only as observers, except as noted in paragraph (b) of this section.

(b) When requested by MSHA, the applicant shall provide assistance in disassembling parts for inspection, preparing parts for testing, and operating combination units.

[Sched. 25B, 25 FR 6473, July 9, 1960, as amended at 39 FR 24005, June 28, 1974]

§ 33.9 Certification of dust-collecting systems.

Manufacturers of dust-collecting systems that are designed for integral use on machines with drilling equipment may apply to MSHA to issue a certificate of performance for such systems. To qualify for a certificate of performance, the dust-collecting system shall have met satisfactorily the test requirements of Subpart C under specified operating conditions, such as type of drilling equipment, drilling speed, and power requirements and the construction thereof shall be adequately covered by specifications and drawings officially recorded and filed with MSHA. Individual parts of dust-collecting systems will not be certified for performance. Certificates of performance may be cited to fabricators of combination units as evidence that further inspection and testing of the dust-collecting system will not be required, provided the dust-collecting requirements of the drilling equipment do not exceed the limits of performance for which the system was certified. Since MSHA does not sanction the use of the words "permissible" or "approved" except as applying to completely assembled equipment, dust-collecting systems, which have been certified only as to performance, shall not be advertised or labeled in a manner inferring that such systems themselves are permissible or approved by MSHA. However, a certified system may be advertised as suitable for use on combination units for which certification may be desired if the limits of its performance are cited. Certified dust-collecting systems shall bear labels or tags which shall contain the following: "Performance-tested Dust Collecting, System, MSHA File No. P/T_____," and name of manufacturer, identifying numbers of the dust-collector parts, and description of the limitations for which performance is certified. MSHA will assign a P/T file number in the certification letter.

§ 33.10 Certificates of approval or performance.

(a) Upon completion of an investigation, MSHA will issue to the applicant either a certificate or a written notice of disapproval, as they case may require. No informal notification of approval will be issued. If a certificate is issued, no test data or detailed results of tests will accompany it. If a notice of disapproval is issued, it will be accompanied by details of the defects, with a view to possible correction. MSHA will not disclose, except to the applicant, any information on a unit or system upon which a notice of disapproval has been issued.

(b) A certificate will be accompanied by a list of the drawings and specifications covering the details of design and construction of the unit or system, including the electrical parts, if applicable, upon which the certificate is based. Applicants shall keep exact duplicates of the drawings and specifications submitted and the list of drawing numbers referred to in § 33.6(d)(1) that relate to the certified unit or system, and these are to be adhered to exactly in production.

§ 33.11 Approval plates.

(a) A certificate of approval will be accompanied by a photograph of a design for an approval plate, bearing the emblem of the Mine Safety and Health Administration, the name of the applicant, the name of the unit, the approval number or space for the approval number (or numbers if permissibility of electrical parts is involved), spaces for the type and the serial numbers of the unit, conditions of approval, and identifying numbers of the dust-collector parts. When deemed necessary by MSHA, an appropriate statement shall be added, giving the precautions to be observed in maintaining the unit in an approved condition.

(b) An approval plate for a unit designed for use in a nongassy coal mine shall state that any electrical parts are not certified for use in a gassy coal mine. (See § 33.38(c).)

(c) The applicant shall reproduce the design either as a separate plate or by stamping or molding it in some suitable place on each unit to which it relates. The size, type, and method of attaching and location of an approval plate are subject to the approval of MSHA. The method of affixing the plate shall not impair the dust-collection or explosion-proof features of the unit.

(d) The approval plate identifies the unit, to which it is attached, as permissible, and is the applicant's guarantee that the unit complies with the requirements of this part. Without an approval plate, no unit has the status of "permissible" under the provisions of this part.

(e) Use of the approval plate obligates the applicant to whom the certificate of approval was granted to maintain the quality of each unit bearing it and guarantees that it is manufactured and assembled according to the drawings and specifications upon which a certificate of approval was based. Use of the approval plate is not authorized except on units that conform strictly with the drawings and specifications upon which the certificate of approval was based.

[Sched. 25B, 25 FR 6473, July 9, 1960, as amended at 43 FR 12317, Mar. 24, 1978]

§ 33.12 Changes after certification.

If an applicant desires to change any feature of a certified unit or system, he shall first obtain MSHA's approval of the change, pursuant to the following procedure:

(a)(1) Application shall be made as for an original certificate, requesting that the existing certification be extended to cover the proposed changes, and shall be accompanied by drawings, specifications, and related data showing the changes in detail.

(2) Where the applicant for approval has used an independent laboratory under part 6 of this chapter to perform, in whole or in part, the necessary testing and evaluation for approval of changes to an approved product under this part, the applicant must provide to MSHA as part of the approval application:

(i) Written evidence of the laboratory's independence and current recognition by a laboratory accrediting organization;

(ii) Complete technical explanation of how the product complies with each requirement in the applicable MSHA product approval requirements;

(iii) Identification of components or features of the product that are critical to the safety of the product; and

(iv) All documentation, including drawings and specifications, as submitted to the independent laboratory by the applicant and as required by this part.

(b) The application will be examined by MSHA to determine whether inspection and testing will be required. Testing will be necessary if there is a possibility that the modification may affect adversely the performance of the unit or system. MSHA will inform the applicant whether such testing is required and the components or materials to be submitted for that purpose.

(c) If the proposed modification meets the requirements of this part and Part 18 of Subchapter D of this chapter (Bureau of Mines Schedule 2, revised, the current revision of which is Schedule 2F) if applicable, a formal extension of certification will be issued, accompanied by a list of new and corrected drawings and specifications to be added to those already on

§ 33.13

file as the basis for the extension of certification.

[Sched. 25B, 25 FR 6473, July 9, 1960, as amended at 52 FR 17515, May 8, 1987; 68 FR 36422, June 17, 2003]

§ 33.13 Withdrawal of certification.

MSHA reserves the right to rescind for cause, at any time, any certification granted under this part.

Subpart B—Dust-Collector Requirements

§ 33.20 Design and construction.

(a) MSHA will not test or investigate any dust collector that in its opinion is not constructed of suitable materials, that evidences faulty workmanship, or that is not designed upon sound engineering principles. Since all possible designs, arrangements, or combinations of components and materials cannot be foreseen, MSHA reserves the right to modify the tests specified in this part in such manner to obtain substantially the same information and degree of protection as provided by the tests described in Subpart C of this part.

(b) Adequacy of design and construction of a unit or system will be determined in accordance with its ability (1) to prevent the dissemination of objectionable or harmful concentrations of dust into a mine atmosphere, and (2) to protect against explosion and/or fire hazards of electrical equipment, except as provided in § 33.38(b).

§ 33.21 Modification of test equipment.

For test purposes the unit or system may be modified, such as by attaching instruments or measuring devices, at MSHA's discretion; but such modification shall not alter its performance.

§ 33.22 Mode of use.

(a) A unit or system may be designed for use in connection with percussion and/or rotary drilling in any combination of the following drilling positions: (1) Vertically upward, (2) upward at angles to the vertical, (3) horizontally, and (4) downward.

(b) Dust-collector units may be designed for use with specific drilling equipment or at specific drilling speeds.

§ 33.23 Mechanical positioning of parts.

All parts of a unit that are essential to the dust-collection feature shall be provided with suitable mechanical means for positioning and maintaining such parts properly in relation to the stratum being drilled.

Subpart C—Test Requirements

§ 33.30 Test site.

Tests shall be conducted at an appropriate location determined by MSHA.

[39 FR 24005, June 28, 1974]

§ 33.31 Test space.

(a) Drilling tests shall be conducted in a test space formed by two curtains suspended across a mine opening in such a manner that the volume of the test space shall be approximately 2,000 cubic feet.

(b) No mechanical ventilation shall be provided in the test space during a drilling test, except such air movement as may be induced by operation of drilling- or dust-collecting equipment.

(c) All parts of a unit or system shall be within the test space during a drilling test.

§ 33.32 Determination of dust concentration.

(a) Concentrations of airborne dust in the test space shall be determined by sampling with a midget impinger apparatus, and a light-field microscopic technique shall be employed in determining concentrations of dust in terms of millions of particles (5 microns or less in diameter) per cubic foot of air sampled.

(b) Before a drilling test is started the surfaces of the test space shall be wetted; the test space shall be cleared of air-borne dust insofar as practicable by mechanical ventilation or other means; and an atmospheric sample, designated as a control sample, shall be collected during a 5-minute period to determine residual airborne dust in the test space.

(c) A sample of airborne dust, designated as a test sample, shall be collected in the breathing zone of the drill operators during the drilling of each test hole. Time consumed in changing drill steel shall not be considered as drilling time and sampling shall be discontinued during such periods.

[Sched. 25B, 25 FR 6473, July 9, 1960, as amended at 26 FR 2599, Mar. 28, 1961]

§ 33.33 Allowable limits of dust concentration.

(a) The concentration of dust determined by the control sample shall be subtracted from the average concentration of dust determined by the test samples collected at each drill operator's position, and the difference shall be designated as the net concentration of airborne dust. Calculations of the average concentration of dust determined from the test samples shall be based upon the results of not less than 80 percent of each set of test samples.

(b) Under each prescribed test condition, the net concentration of airborne dust at each drill operator's position shall not exceed 10 million particles (5 microns or less in diameter) per cubic foot of air when determined in accordance with the method given in § 33.32(a).

[Sched. 25B, 25 FR 6473, July 9, 1960, as amended at 26 FR 2599, Mar. 28, 1961]

§ 33.34 Drilling test.

(a) A drilling test shall consist of drilling a set of 10 test holes, without undue delay, under specified operating conditions. When the test involves the control of dust from more than one drill, all the drills shall be used in the intended manner to complete the set of test holes.

(b) Holes shall be drilled to a depth of 4 feet plus or minus 2 inches and shall be spaced so as not to interfere with adjacent holes. Each hole may be plugged after completion.

(c) Receptacles and filters for collecting drill cuttings shall be emptied and cleaned before each drilling test is started.

(d) Holes designated as "vertical" shall be drilled to incline not more than 10 degrees to the vertical. Holes designated as "angle" shall be drilled to incline not less than 30 and not more than 45 degrees to the vertical. Holes designated as "horizontal" shall be drilled to incline not more than 15 degrees to the horizontal.

[Sched. 25B, 25 FR 6473, July 9, 1960, as amended at 26 FR 2599, Mar. 28, 1961]

§ 33.35 Methods of drilling; dust-collector unit.

(a) *General.* All drilling shall be done with conventional, commercial drilling equipment—pneumatic-percussion, hydraulic-rotary, and/or electric-rotary types—in accordance with the applicant's specifications.

(b) *Pneumatic-percussion drilling.* A stoper-type drill with a piston diameter of 2½ to 3 inches shall be used for roof drilling, A hand-held, sinker-type drill with a piston diameter of 2½ to 3 inches shall be used for down drilling and also for horizontal drilling, except that the drill shall be supported mechanically. Compressed air for operating the drill shall be supplied at a gage pressure of 85–95 pounds per square inch. Drill bits shall be detachable, cross type with hard inserts, and shall be sharp when starting to drill each set of 10 holes. In roof drilling, 1¼- and 1½-inch diameter drill bits shall be used; in horizontal and down drilling, 1¾-inch diameter bits shall be used. The drill steel shall be ⅞-inch hexagonal and of hollow type to permit the introduction of compressed air through the drill steel when necessary to clean a hole during drilling.

(c) *Rotary drilling.* A hydraulic-rotary drill with a rated drilling speed of 18 feet per minute free lift, capable of rotating drill steel at 900 revolutions per minute with 100 foot-pounds torque, and having a feed force of 7,000 pounds, shall be used for roof drilling. An electric-rotary drill, supported by a post mounting, with a rated drilling speed of 30 inches per minute and powered by a 2.25 horsepower motor, shall be used for horizontal drilling. For roof drilling, the bits shall be hard-tipped, 1⅜ and 1½ inches outside diameter, and 1¼-inch auger-type drill steel shall be used. For horizontal drilling, the bits shall be hard-tipped, 2 inches outside diameter, and 1¾-inch auger-type drill steel shall be used. Drill bits shall be sharp when starting to drill each set of 10 holes.

§ 33.36 Method of drilling; combination unit or dust-collecting system.

Drilling shall be conducted in accordance with the applicant's specifications and operating instructions. If special drill bits or drill steel are required, they shall be furnished to MSHA by the applicant. Otherwise the drill bit and drill steel requirements stated in paragraphs (b) and (c) of § 33.35 shall be complied with for all types of combination units or dust-collecting systems.

§ 33.37 Test procedure.

(a) Roof drilling: Drilling shall be done in friable strata, similar to the roof in the Bureau's Experimental Mine, which tends to produce large scale-like cuttings.

(b) Horizontal drilling: Drilling shall be done in strata comparable in hardness to that of coal-mine draw slate. Holes shall be started near the roof of the test space under conditions simulating the drilling of draw slate in coal mining.

(c) Down drilling: Drilling shall be done in typical mine floor strata with a pneumatic percussion-type drill. Five holes shall be drilled vertically and five holes shall be drilled at an angle.

(d) At MSHA's discretion drilling in "on site" strata may be acceptable in lieu of strata requirements in paragraphs (a), (b), and (c) of this section. (See § 33.20(a).)

§ 33.38 Electrical parts.

(a) Units with electrical parts and designed to operate as electric face equipment (see definition, § 45.44–1 of this chapter) in gassy coal mines shall meet the requirements of Part 18 of Subchapter D of this chapter (Bureau of Mines Schedule 2, revised, the current revision of which is Schedule 2F), and the examination and testing of the electrical parts shall be entirely separate from the examination and testing of dust-collecting equipment as such.

(b) Units with electrical parts designed to operate only outby the last open crosscut in a gassy coal-mine entry, room, or other opening (including electric-drive units with their controls and push buttons) are not required to comply with the provisions of Part 18 of Subchapter D of this chapter (Bureau of Mines Schedule 2, revised, the current revision of which is Schedule 2F).

(c) Units with electrical parts and designed for operation only in nongassy coal mines are not required to comply with the provisions of Part 18 of Subchapter D of this chapter (Bureau of Mines Schedule 2, revised, the current revision of which is Schedule 2F). (See § 33.11(b).)

PART 35—FIRE-RESISTANT HYDRAULIC FLUIDS

Subpart A—General Provisions

Sec.
35.1 Purpose.
35.2 Definitions.
35.3 Consultation.
35.4 Types of hydraulic fluid for which certificates of approval may be granted.
35.5 [Reserved]
35.6 Application procedures and requirements.
35.7 Date for conducting tests.
35.8 Conduct of investigations, tests, and demonstrations.
35.9 Certificates of approval.
35.10 Approval labels or markings.
35.11 Material required for record.
35.12 Changes after certification.
35.13 Withdrawal of certification.

Subpart B—Test Requirements

35.20 Autogenous-ignition temperature test.
35.21 Temperature-pressure spray-ignition test.
35.22 Test to determine effect of evaporation on flammability.
35.23 Performance required for certification.

AUTHORITY: 30 U.S.C. 957, 961.

SOURCE: Schedule 30, 24 FR 10201, Dec. 17, 1959, unless otherwise noted.

Subpart A—General Provisions

§ 35.1 Purpose.

The regulations in this part set forth the requirements for fire-resistant hydraulic fluids and concentrates for the production thereof to procure their certification as approved for use in machines and devices that are operated in

Mine Safety and Health Admin., Labor § 35.6

coal mines and procedures for applying for such certification.

[Sched. 30, 24 FR 10201, Dec. 17, 1959, as amended at 52 FR 17515, May 8, 1987]

§ 35.2 Definitions.

As used in this part—

(a) *Permissible*, as applied to hydraulic fluids, means that the fluid conforms to the requirements of this part, and that a certificate of approval to that effect has been issued.

(b) *MSHA* means the United States Department of Labor, Mine Safety and Health Administration.

(c) *Certificate of approval* means a formal document issued by MESA stating that the fluid has met the requirements of this part for fire-resistant hydraulic fluids and authorizing the use of an official identifying marking so indicating.

(d) *Fire-resistant hydraulic fluid* means a fluid of such chemical composition and physical characteristics that it will resist the propagation of flame.

(e) *Concentrate* means a substance in concentrated form that might not be fire resistant as such but when mixed with water or other vehicle in accordance with instructions furnished by the applicant will constitute a fire-resistant hydraulic fluid.

(f) *Applicant* means an individual, partnership, company, corporation, association, or other organization that manufactures, compounds, refines, or otherwise produces, a fire-resistant hydraulic fluid or a concentrate for the production thereof, and seeks a certificate of approval.

[Sched. 30, 24 FR 10201, Dec. 17, 1959, as amended at 39 FR 24005, June 28, 1974; 43 FR 12317, Mar. 24, 1978]

§ 35.3 Consultation.

By appointment, applicants or their representatives may visit the U.S. Department of Labor, Mine Safety and Health Administration, Approval and Certification Center, 765 Technology Drive, Triadelphia, WV 26059, to discuss with qualified MSHA personnel proposed fluids to be submitted in accordance with the regulations of this part.. No charge is made for such consultation and no written report thereof will be submitted to the applicant.

[Sched. 30, 24 FR 10201, Dec. 17, 1959, as amended at 43 FR 12317, Mar. 24, 1978; 60 FR 35694, July 11, 1995; 73 FR 52213, Sept. 9, 2008]

§ 35.4 Types of hydraulic fluid for which certificates of approval may be granted.

Certificates of approval will be granted for completely compounded or mixed fluids and not for individual ingredients; except that when a concentrate is submitted for testing, complete instructions for mixing with water or other vehicle shall be furnished to MSHA, together with the vehicle other than water, and the approval will cover only the specific mixture that constitutes the hydraulic fluid for use in coal mines.

§ 35.5 [Reserved]

§ 35.6 Application procedures and requirements.

(a)(1) No investigation or testing will be undertaken by MSHA except pursuant to a written application accompanied by all descriptions, specifications, test samples, and related materials. The application and all related matters and correspondence shall be addressed to: U.S. Department of Labor, Mine Safety and Health Administration, Approval and Certification Center, 765 Technology Drive, Triadelphia, WV 26059. Fees calculated in accordance with part 5 of this title shall be submitted in accordance with § 5.40.

(2) Where the applicant for approval has used an independent laboratory under part 6 of this chapter to perform, in whole or in part, the necessary testing and evaluation for approval under this part, the applicant must provide to MSHA as part of the approval application:

(i) Written evidence of the laboratory's independence and current recognition by a laboratory accrediting organization;

(ii) Complete technical explanation of how the product complies with each requirement in the applicable MSHA product approval requirements;

§ 35.7

(iii) Identification of components or features of the product that are critical to the safety of the product; and

(iv) All documentation, including drawings and specifications, as submitted to the independent laboratory by the applicant and as required by this part.

(3) An applicant may request testing and evaluation to non-MSHA product safety standards which have been determined by MSHA to be equivalent, under § 6.20 of this chapter, to MSHA's product approval requirements under this part.

(b) Descriptions and specifications shall be adequate in detail to identify fully the composition of the hydraulic fluid and to disclose its characteristics. Descriptions and specifications shall include:

(1) An identifying name or number of the fluid or concentrate for the production thereof.

(2) Pour point, °F.; freezing point, °F.; color; neutralization number or pH; viscosity at 100 °F., 150 °F., 175 °F. (Saybolt or Furol); viscosity index; specific gravity.

(3) A statement of the water or other vehicle content in percent by weight or volume and how it affects fire resistance of the hydraulic fluid. If water is the vehicle, the statement shall include the applicant's method for determining water content quickly in the field.

(c) The application shall state whether the fluid submitted for test is toxic or irritating to the skin and what precautions are necessary in handling it.

(d) The application shall state that the applicant has tested the fluid which he believes to have fire-resistant properties, the basis for such determination, and submit with his application the data resulting from the applicant's use or laboratory tests to determine the fire-resistant properties of the fluid.

(e) The application shall contain evidence that the fluid has lubricating and hydraulic properties and is satisfactory for use in underground mining machinery; and shall state that the fluid, or concentrate for the production thereof, is fully developed and is of the composition that the applicant believes to be a suitable marketable product.

(f) The application shall state the nature, adequacy, and continuity of control of the constituents of the fluid to maintain its fire-resistant characteristics and how each lot will be sampled and tested to maintain its protective qualities. MSHA reserves the right to have its qualified representative(s) inspect the applicant's control-test equipment, procedures, and records, and to interview the personnel who conduct the control tests to satisfy MSHA that the proper procedure is being followed to insure that the fire-resistant qualities of the hydraulic fluid are maintained.

(g) When MSHA notifies the applicant that the application will be accepted, it will also notify him as to the number of samples and related materials that will be required for testing. Ordinarily a 5-gallon sample of hydraulic fluid will be required provided that it is a finished product or, if in concentrate form, enough shall be furnished to make a 5-gallon sample when mixed with water or other vehicle according to the applicant's instructions. All samples and related materials required for testing must be delivered (charges prepaid) to: U.S. Department of Labor, Mine Safety and Health Administration, Approval and Certification Center, 765 Technology Drive, Triadelphia, WV 26059.

[Sched. 30, 24 FR 10201, Dec. 17, 1959, as amended at 43 FR 12317, Mar. 24, 1978; 60 FR 35694, July 11, 1995; 68 FR 36422, June 17, 2003; 70 FR 46344, Aug. 9, 2005; 73 FR 52213, Sept. 9, 2008]

§ 35.7 Date for conducting tests.

The date of acceptance of an application will determine the order of precedence for testing when more than one application is pending, and the applicant will be notified of the date on which tests will begin. However, not more than two fluids will be tested consecutively for one applicant provided other applications are pending. If a fluid fails to meet any of the requirements, it shall lose its order of precedence. If an application is submitted to resume testing after correction of the course of failure, it will be treated as a new application and the order of precedence for testing will be so determined.

§ 35.8 Conduct of investigations, tests, and demonstrations.

Prior to the issuance of a certificate of approval, necessary Government personnel, representatives of the applicant, and such other persons as may be mutually agreed upon, may observe the investigations or tests. MSHA shall hold as confidential and shall not disclose features of this hydraulic fluid such as the chemical analysis, specifications, descriptions, and related material. After issuing a certificate of approval MSHA may conduct such public demonstrations and tests of the approved hydraulic fluid as it deems appropriate. The conduct of all investigations, tests, and demonstrations shall be under the direction and control of MSHA, and any other persons shall be present only as observers.

[Sched. 30, 24 FR 10201, Dec. 17, 1959, as amended at 39 FR 24005, June 28, 1974]

§ 35.9 Certificates of approval.

(a) Upon completion of an investigation of a hydraulic fluid MSHA will issue to the applicant either a certificate of approval or a written notice of disapproval as the case may require. No informal notification of approval will be issued. If a certificate of approval is issued, no test data or detailed results of tests will accompany it. If a notice of disapproval is issued, it will be accompanied by details of the defect(s), with a view to possible correction. MSHA will not disclose, except to the applicant, any information on a fluid upon which a notice of disapproval has been issued.

(b) A certificate of approval will be accompanied by a list of specifications covering the characteristics of a hydraulic fluid upon which the certificate of approval is based. In addition to the applicant's record of control in maintaining the fire-resistant characteristics, applicants shall keep exact duplicates of the specifications that have been submitted to MSHA and that relate to any fluid which has received a certificate of approval; and these are to be adhered to exactly in production of the certified fluid for commercial purposes.

§ 35.10 Approval labels or markings.

(a) A certificate of approval will be accompanied by a photograph of a design for an approval label or marking, which shall bear the emblem of the Mine Safety and Health Administration and shall be inscribed substantially as follows:

PERMISSIBLE FIRE-RESISTANT HYDRAULIC FLUID

MSHA Approval No. _____
Issued to _____
(Name of Applicant)

(b) A label so inscribed shall be attached to each fluid container in such a manner that it cannot be easily removed or containers may be so marked with a metal stencil. The letters and numbers shall be at least ½ inch in height and of a color which contrasts with that of the container.

(c) For a concentrate the label or marking shall clearly indicate that the certification thereof applies only when the concentrate is used in exact conformance with the instructions on such label or marking. The label or marking shall clearly indicate the exact amount of water or other vehicle to make the fire-resistant hydraulic fluid upon which the certificate of approval was based.

(d) Appropriate instructions and caution statements on the handling of the hydraulic fluid or concentrate shall be included on the approval label or marking.

(e) Use of MSHA's approval label or marking obligates the applicant to whom the certificate of approval was granted to maintain the fire-resistant characteristics of the hydraulic fluid and guarantees that it is manufactured according to the specifications upon which the certificate of approval was based. Use of the approval label or marking is not authorized except on containers of hydraulic fluids that conform strictly with the specifications and characteristics upon which the certificate of approval was based.

[Sched. 30, 24 FR 10201, Dec. 17, 1959, as amended at 43 FR 12317, Mar. 24, 1978]

§ 35.11 Material required for record.

MSHA may retain for record all or part of the material submitted for testing. Any material that MSHA does not require will be returned to the applicant at his expense upon receipt of his written request and shipping instructions not more than 6 months after the termination or completion of the tests. Thereafter MSHA will dispose of such surplus material as it deems appropriate.

§ 35.12 Changes after certification.

If an applicant desires to change any specification or characteristic of a certified hydraulic fluid, he shall first obtain MSHA's approval of the change, pursuant to the following procedures:

(a)(1) Application shall be made, as for an original certificate of approval, requesting that the existing certification be extended to cover the proposed change. The application shall be accompanied by specifications and related material as in the case of an original application.

(2) Where the applicant for approval has used an independent laboratory under part 6 of this chapter to perform, in whole or in part, the necessary testing and evaluation for approval of changes to an approved product under this part, the applicant must provide to MSHA as part of the approval application:

(i) Written evidence of the laboratory's independence and current recognition by a laboratory accrediting organization;

(ii) Complete technical explanation of how the product complies with each requirement in the applicable MSHA product approval requirements;

(iii) Identification of components or features of the product that are critical to the safety of the product; and

(iv) All documentation, including drawings and specifications, as submitted to the independent laboratory by the applicant and as required by this part.

(b) The application and related material(s) will be examined by MSHA to determine whether testing of the modified hydraulic fluid will be required. Testing will be necessary if there is a possibility that the modification may affect adversely the performance characteristics of the fluid. MSHA will inform the applicant in writing whether such testing is required.

(c) If the proposed modification meets the requirements of this part, a formal extension of certification will be issued, accompanied by a list of new and corrected specifications to be added to those already on file, as the basis for the extension of certification.

[Sched, 30, 24 FR 10201, Dec. 17, 1959, as amended at 52 FR 17515, May 8, 1987; 68 FR 36422, June 17, 2003]

§ 35.13 Withdrawal of certification.

MSHA reserves the right to rescind for cause, at any time, any certificate of approval granted under this part.

Subpart B—Test Requirements

§ 35.20 Autogenous-ignition temperature test.

(a) *Purpose.* The purpose of this test, referred to hereinafter as the ignition-temperature test, is to determine the lowest autogenous-ignition temperature of a hydraulic fluid at atmospheric pressure when using the syringe-injection method.

(b) *Description of apparatus*—(1) *Test flask.* The test flask, which is heated and into which the test sample is injected, shall be a commercial 200 ml. borosilicate glass Erlenmeyer flask.

(2) *Thermocouples.* Calibrated thermocouples—iron-constantan or chromelalumel—and a potentiometer shall be used for all temperature measurements.

(3) *Syringe.* A hypodermic syringe (0.25 or 1 cc. capacity) equipped with a 2-inch No. 18 stainless steel needle and calibrated in hundredths of a cubic centimeter (0.01 cc.) shall be used to inject samples into the heated test flask.

(4) *Timer.* An electric timer or stopwatch calibrated in not more than 0.2 second intervals shall be used to determine the time lag before ignition.

NOTE: Time lag is the time that elapses between the instant of injection and that of ignition of the test sample, as evidenced by flame.

(5) *Furnace.* The furnace in which the ignition-temperature test is conducted shall consist of a refractory (alundum or equivalent) cylinder 5 inches in internal diameter and 5 inches in height;

a transite-ring top and a transite-disk bottom, each of which is attached to a metal cylinder. The furnace is heated by three elements as follows: (i) A circumferential heater embedded in the refractory cylinder; (ii) a top or toroidal-neck heater that surrounds the neck of the test flask; and (iii) a flat base heater on which the test flask rests. The temperature of each heating element shall be controlled independently by an autotransformer. Means shall be provided for applying thermocouples at the neck, mid-section, and base of the test flask, which shall be inserted upright in the furnace.

(c) *Test procedures*—(1) *Temperature control.* Each autotransformer shall be so adjusted that the temperature at the neck, mid-section, and base of the test flask is uniform within ±2 °F. of the desired test temperature.

(2) *Sample injection and timing.* A 0.07 cc. test sample shall be injected into the heated test flask with the hypodermic syringe, and the syringe shall be withdrawn immediately. Measurement of time shall start at the instant the sample is injected.

(3) *Observations.* (i) If flame does not result in 5 minutes or more after injection of the test sample, the sample shall be considered nonflammable at the test temperature, and the timer shall be stopped. The test flask shall then be flushed well with clean dry air and, after a lapse of 15 minutes or more, the test shall be repeated with the test flask temperature raised 50 °F. ±2 °F. above the first test temperature.

(ii) If ignition (flame) is observed in 5 minutes or less after the injection of the test sample (0.07 cc.), the time lag (time interval) shall be noted. After an ignition occurs the temperature of the test flask shall be reduced 5 °F., and the test procedure repeated in decrements of 5 °F. until ignition no longer occurs and this temperature shall be noted as the first nonignition test temperature for the 0.07 cc. sample.

(iii) The temperature shall be increased 50 °F. ±2 °F. above the first nonignition test temperature, and the ignition-temperature test procedure shall be repeated with a 0.10 cc. test sample injected into the heated test flask.

(iv) If the lowest temperature at which ignition occurs with the 0.10 cc. sample (in decrements of 5 °F.) is lower than that obtained with the 0.07 cc. sample, the ignition-temperature test procedure shall be repeated using a test sample of 0.12 cc., then 0.15 cc., and so on by increments of 0.03 cc. until the lowest ignition temperature is obtained.

(v) If the lowest temperature at which ignition is obtained with the 0.10 cc. sample is greater than that obtained with the 0.07 cc. sample, the ignition temperature test procedure shall be repeated by reducing the test sample to 0.05 cc. and then to 0.03 cc. until the lowest ignition temperature is obtained.

(d) *Appraisal of test.* A fluid shall be considered fire-resistant, according to the test requirements of this section: *Provided,* That in no instance of the ignition-temperature test procedure, as stated in this section, shall the ignition temperature of the test sample be less than 600 °F.

§ 35.21 **Temperature-pressure spray-ignition tests.**

(a) *Purpose.* The purpose of this test shall be to determine the flammability of a hydraulic fluid when it is sprayed over three different sources of ignition which are described in paragraph (b)(4) of this section.

(b) *Description of apparatus.* (1) A 3-quart pressure vessel, with the necessary connections, valves, and heating elements, shall be used for containing and heating the fluid under the test conditions as specified hereinafter.

(2) An atomizing round-spray nozzle, having a discharge orifice of 0.025-inch diameter, capable of discharging 3.28 gallons of water per hour with a spray angle of 90 degrees at a pressure of 100 p.s.i., shall be connected to the pressure vessel.

(3) A commercial pressurized cylinder, containing nitrogen with the customary regulators, valves, tubing, and connectors, shall be used to supply nitrogen to the pressure vessel described in paragraph (b)(1) of this section.

(4) Three igniting devices shall provide three different sources of ignition as follows:

(i) A metal trough with a metal cover in which cotton waste soaked in kerosene is ignited.

(ii) An electric arcing device in which the arc is produced by a 12,000-volt transformer.

(iii) A propane torch—Bernzomatic or equivalent.

(5) A means of measuring distances from the nozzle tip to the igniting device shall be provided.

(c) *Test procedures.* (1) A 2½-quart sample of the fluid shall be poured into the pressure vessel and heated to a temperature of 150 °F. The temperature shall be maintained at not less than 145 °F. or not more than 155 °F. during the test.

(2) Nitrogen shall be introduced into the vessel at 150 p.s.i.g.

(3) The fluid shall be sprayed at each igniting device, described in paragraph (b) (4) of this section, which is moved along the trajectory of the spray. Each igniting device shall be held in the spray at different distances from the nozzle tip for one minute or until the flame or arc is extinguished (if less than one minute) to determine this fire-resistant characteristic of the fluid.

(d) *Appraisal of tests.* If the test procedures in paragraph (c) of this section do not result in an ignition of any sample of fluid or if an ignition of a sample does not result in flame propagation for a time interval not exceeding 6 seconds at a distance of 18 inches or more from the nozzle tip to the center of each igniting device, it shall be considered fire resistant, according to the test requirements of this section.

§ 35.22 Test to determine effect of evaporation on flammability.

(a) *Purpose.* The purpose of this test shall be to determine the effect of evaporation on the reduction of fire resistance of a hydraulic fluid.

(b) *Description of apparatus*—(1) *Petri dish.* Standard laboratory Petri dishes, approximately 90 mm. by 16 mm., shall be used to contain the test samples.

(2) *Oven.* A gravity convection air oven, capable of maintaining the specified evaporation temperature constant within ±2 °F., shall be used in the test.

(3) *Pipe cleaner.* An ordinary smoker's pipe cleaner (U.S. Tobacco Co., Dill's or equivalent) shall be used in the test procedure, described in paragraph (c) of this section.

(c) *Test procedures.* (1) Three 30-milliliter samples of the fluid shall be placed in uncovered Petri dishes. Two of these samples shall be inserted in the oven, that shall have been heated to a temperature of 150 °F., ±2 °F., which shall be maintained throughout this test. The third sample shall remain at room temperature.

(2) An electrically operated cycling device, such as an automobile windshield wiper mechanism, shall be oscillated in a horizontal plane, 25 ±2 cycles per minute. A pipe cleaner shall be attached to the device so that it will enter and leave a flame of a standard (Bunsen or equivalent) laboratory burner, which is adjusted to provide a nonluminous flame approximately 4 inches in height without forming a sharp inner cone. The cycling device shall be so arranged that when a 2-inch length of pipe cleaner is attached thereto the exposed end shall describe an arc with a radius of 4 inches ±⅛ inch. The cycling device shall be so arranged that when the 2-inch length of pipe cleaner is attached thereto, its midpoint shall be in the center of the flame at one extreme end of the cycle.

(3) Each of five 2-inch lengths of pipe cleaner shall be soaked separately for a period of 2 minutes in the test sample that remained at room temperature. Each pipe cleaner shall then be removed from the test sample and permitted to drain freely until all excess fluid is expelled from it. Each soaked pipe cleaner shall be attached to the cycling device, the mechanism started, and the pipe cleaner permitted to enter and leave the burner flame, as described in paragraph (c) (2) of this section, until a self-sustaining flame shall be observed on the pipe cleaner. The number of cycles necessary to obtain a self-sustaining flame shall be noted and averaged for each of the five soaked pipe cleaners.

(4) After one test sample has remained in the oven for a period of 2 hours, the Petri dish containing it

Mine Safety and Health Admin., Labor

shall be removed from the oven and allowed to cool to room temperature, after which 5 lengths of 2-inch pipe cleaner shall be soaked separately in the test sample for a period of 2 minutes. Then the test procedure stated in paragraph (c) (3) of this section shall be repeated.

(5) After one test sample has remained in the oven for a period of 4 hours, the Petri dish containing it shall be removed from the oven and allowed to cool to room temperature, after which 5 lengths of 2-inch pipe cleaner shall be soaked separately in the test sample for a period of 2 minutes. Then the test procedure stated in paragraph (c) (3) of this section shall be repeated.

(d) *Appraisal of tests.* To be determined as fire resistant according to the test requirements of this section, the three following results shall be achieved:

(1) The average number of cycles before attaining a self-sustaining flame in the test described in paragraph (c) (3) of this section shall be 24 or more.

(2) The average number of cycles before attaining a self-sustaining flame in the test described in paragraph (c) (4) of this section shall be 18 or more.

(3) The average number of cycles before attaining a self-sustaining flame in the test described in paragraph (c) (5) of this section shall be 12 or more.

§ 35.23 Performance required for certification.

To qualify as fire-resistant under the regulations of this part, a hydraulic fluid shall meet each performance requirement and stated in §§ 35.20(d), 35.21(d), and 35.22(d).

PART 36—APPROVAL REQUIREMENTS FOR PERMISSIBLE MOBILE DIESEL-POWERED TRANSPORTATION EQUIPMENT

Subpart A—General Provisions

Sec.
36.1 Purpose.
36.2 Definitions.
36.3 Consultation.
36.4 Mobile diesel-powered transportation equipment for which certificates of approval may be granted.
36.5 Letters of certification.
36.6 Application procedures and requirements.
36.7 [Reserved]
36.8 Date for conducting tests.
36.9 Conduct of investigations, tests, and demonstrations.
36.10 Certificate of approval.
36.11 Approval plates.
36.12 Changes after certification.
36.13 Withdrawal of certification.

Subpart B—Construction and Design Requirements

36.20 Quality of material, workmanship, and design.
36.21 Engine for equipment considered for certification.
36.22 Fuel-injection system.
36.23 Engine intake system.
36.24 Engine joints.
36.25 Engine exhaust system.
36.26 Composition of exhaust gas.
36.27 Fuel-supply system.
36.28 Signal or warning device.
36.29 Brakes.
36.30 Rerailing device.
36.31 Fire extinguisher.
36.32 Electrical components and systems.
36.33 Headlights and fixtures.

Subpart C—Test Requirements

36.40 Test site.
36.41 Testing methods.
36.42 Inspection.
36.43 Determination of exhaust-gas composition.
36.44 Maximum allowable fuel:air ratio.
36.45 Quantity of ventilating air.
36.46 Explosion tests of intake and exhaust systems.
36.47 Tests of exhaust-gas cooling system.
36.48 Tests of surface temperature of engine and components of the cooling system.
36.49 Tests of exhaust-gas dilution system.
36.50 Tests of fuel tank.

AUTHORITY: 30 U.S.C. 957, 961.

SOURCE: Schedule 31, 26 FR 645, Jan. 24, 1961, unless otherwise noted.

Subpart A—General Provisions

§ 36.1 Purpose.

The regulations in this part set forth the requirements for mobile diesel-powered transportation equipment to procure their approval and certification as permissible; procedures for applying for such certification; and fees.

[61 FR 55525, Oct. 25, 1996]

§ 36.2 Definitions.

The following definitions apply in this part.

Applicant An individual, partnership, company, corporation, association, or other organization, that designs, manufactures, assembles, or controls the assembly and that seeks a certificate of approval or preliminary testing of mobile diesel-powered transportation equipment as permissible.

Certificate of approval. A formal document issued by MSHA stating that the complete assembly has met the requirements of this part for mobile diesel-powered transportation equipment and authorizing the use and attachment of an official approval plate so indicating.

Component. A piece, part, or fixture of mobile diesel-powered transportation equipment that is essential to its operation as a permissible assembly.

Diesel engine. A compression-ignition, internal-combustion engine that utilizes diesel fuel.

Explosion proof. A component or subassembly that is so constructed and protected by an enclosure and/or flame arrester (s) that if a flammable mixture of gas is ignited within the enclosure it will withstand the resultant pressure without damage to the enclosure and/or flame arrester(s). Also the enclosure and/or flame arrester(s) shall prevent the discharge of flame or ignition of any flammable mixture that surrounds the enclosure.

Flame arrester. A device so constructed that flame or sparks from the diesel engine cannot propagate an explosion of a flammable mixture through it.

Flammable mixture. A mixture of gas, such as methane, natural gas, or similar hydrocarbon gas with normal air, that will propagate flame or explode violently when initiated by an incendive source.

Fuel-air ratio. The composition of the mixture of fuel and air in the combustion chamber of the diesel engine expressed as weight-pound of fuel per pound of air.

MSHA. The United States Department of Labor, Mine Safety and Health Administration.

Mobile diesel-powered transportation equipment. Equipment that is:

(1) Used for transporting the product being mined or excavated, or for transporting materials and supplies used in mining or excavating operations;

(2) Mounted on wheels or crawler treads (tracks); and

(3) Powered by a diesel engine as the prime mover.

Normal operation. When each component and the entire assembly of the mobile diesel-powered transportation equipment performs the functions for which they were designed.

Permissible. As applied to mobile diesel-powered transportation equipment, this means that the complete assembly conforms to the requirements of this part, and that a certificate of approval to that effect has been issued.

Subassembly. A group or combination of components.

[61 FR 55525, Oct. 25, 1996]

§ 36.3 Consultation.

By appointment, applicants or their representatives may visit the U.S. Department of Labor, Mine Safety and Health Administration, Approval and Certification Center, 765 Technology Drive, Triadelphia, WV 26059, to discuss with qualified MSHA personnel proposed mobile diesel-powered transportation equipment to be submitted in accordance with the regulations of this part. No charge is made for such consultation and no written report thereof will be submitted to the applicant.

[Sched. 31, 26 FR 645, Jan. 24, 1961, as amended at 43 FR 12318, Mar. 24, 1978; 60 FR 35695, July 11, 1995; 73 FR 52213, Sept. 9, 2008]

§ 36.4 Mobile diesel-powered transportation equipment for which certificates of approval may be granted.

Certificates of approval will be granted for completely assembled mobile diesel-powered transportation equipment only. Subassemblies or components may be granted letters of certification in accordance with § 36.5.

§ 36.5 Letters of certification.

When a component or subassembly meets all of the applicable requirements of Subparts B and C of this part, and also its normal operation will not

Mine Safety and Health Admin., Labor § 36.6

be affected by connection to adjacent components or subassemblies, MSHA will issue to the applicant, upon his request, a letter of certification informing him that additional inspection or tests of the component or subassembly will not be required when it is incorporated without modification in a piece of completely assembled mobile diesel-powered transportation equipment. The applicant may cite this letter of certification to another applicant who seeks approval and certification of his completely assembled mobile diesel-powered transportation equipment and who desires to incorporate the component or subassembly in such equipment.

§ 36.6 Application procedures and requirements.

(a)(1) No investigation or testing will be undertaken by MSHA except pursuant to a written application accompanied by all descriptions, specifications, test samples, and related materials. The application and all related matters and correspondence shall be addressed to: U.S. Department of Labor, Mine Safety and Health Administration, Approval and Certification Center, 765 Technology Drive, Triadelphia, WV 26059. Fees calculated in accordance with part 5 of this title shall be submitted in accordance with § 5.40.

(2) Where the applicant for approval has used an independent laboratory under part 6 of this chapter to perform, in whole or in part, the necessary testing and evaluation for approval under this part, the applicant must provide to MSHA as part of the approval application:

(i) Written evidence of the laboratory's independence and current recognition by a laboratory accrediting organization;

(ii) Complete technical explanation of how the product complies with each requirement in the applicable MSHA product approval requirements;

(iii) Identification of components or features of the product that are critical to the safety of the product; and

(iv) All documentation, including drawings and specifications, as submitted to the independent laboratory by the applicant and as required by this part.

(3) An applicant may request testing and evaluation to non-MSHA product safety standards which have been determined by MSHA to be equivalent, under § 6.20 of this chapter, to MSHA's product approval requirements under this part.

(b) Drawings, specifications, and descriptions shall be adequate in detail to identify fully the complete assembly, components, and subassemblies. Drawings, specifications, and descriptions shall include:

(1) Assembly drawing(s) showing the overall dimensions of the equipment, location and capacity of the fuel tank, location of flame arresters, exhaust-gas conditioner and its water-supply tank, if applicable, exhaust-gas dilution system, and other details that are essential to the functioning of the equipment.

(2) Except for equipment utilizing part 7, subpart F power packages, detailed drawings showing the intake, combustion, and exhaust systems of the diesel engine, including joints and gaskets; the turbulence or precombustion chamber, if applicable; injector assembly and nozzle details; and any surfaces that form the combustion chamber or part thereof, such as the cylinder head, piston and cylinder liner; and other features that may affect permissibility, such as exhaust-gas conditioner and flame arresters.

(3) Except for equipment utilizing part 7, subpart F power packages, a schematic drawing of the fuel system showing piping, connections, fuel filters, fuel-injection pump, and mechanical governor assembly. All components shall be identified to permit adjustment, as necessary, and the location of seals or locks to prevent tampering shall be indicated.

(4) Except for equipment utilizing part 7, subpart F power packages, drawing(s) specifying the kind of material and detailed dimensions of the components of explosion-proof enclosures, including joints and openings.

(5) Drawing(s) showing the construction of headlights, battery boxes, including seals or locks, and method of mounting.

§ 36.7

(6) Other drawings, specifications, or descriptions identifying any feature that MSHA considers necessary for certification of the particular mobile diesel-powered transportation equipment.

(c) Shipment of the mobile diesel-powered transportation equipment or component part or subassembly as the case may be, shall be deferred until MSHA has notified the applicant that the application will be accepted. Shipping instructions will be issued by MSHA and shipping charges shall be prepaid by the application. Upon completion of the investigation and notification thereof to the applicant by MSHA, the applicant shall remove his equipment promptly from the test site (see § 36.40).

(d) The application shall state that the equipment is completely developed and of the design and materials that the applicant believes to be suitable for a finished marketable product or is a completely developed component or subassembly suitable for incorporation in a finished marketable complete assembly of mobile diesel-powered transportation equipment. If the final design of a component depends upon results of MSHA's tests, this shall be so stated in the application.

(e) For a complete investigation leading to approval and certification, the applicant shall furnish a complete operable assembly for inspecting and testing. Spare parts and expendable components, subject to wear in normal operation, shall be supplied by the applicant to permit continuous operation of the equipment during test periods. If special tools are necessary to disassembly any component for inspection or test, the applicant shall furnish these with the equipment to be tested.

(f) With each application, the applicant shall submit evidence of how he proposes to inspect his completely assembled mobile diesel-powered transportation equipment at the place of manufacture or assembly before shipment to purchasers. Ordinarily such inspection is recorded on a factory inspection form and the applicant shall furnish to MSHA a copy of his factory inspection form or equivalent with his application. The form shall direct attention to the points that must be checked to make certain that all components of the assembly are in proper condition, complete in all respects, and in agreement with the drawings, specifications, and descriptions filed with MSHA.

(g) With the application, the applicant shall furnish to MSHA complete instructions for operating and servicing his equipment. After completing MSHA's investigation, if any revision of the instructions is required, a revised copy thereof shall be submitted to MSHA for inclusion with the drawings and specifications.

[Sched. 31, 26 FR 645, Jan. 24, 1961, as amended at 43 FR 12318, Mar. 24, 1978; 47 FR 14696, Apr. 6, 1982; 60 FR 33723, June 29, 1995; 60 FR 35695, July 11, 1995; 61 FR 55526, Oct. 25, 1996; 68 FR 36422, June 17, 2003; 70 FR 46344, Aug. 9, 2005; 73 FR 52213, Sept. 9, 2008]

§ 36.7 [Reserved]

§ 36.8 Date for conducting tests.

The date for acceptance of an application will determine the order of precedence for testing when more than one application is pending, and the applicant will be notified of the date on which tests will begin. If a complete assembly, or component, or subassembly fails to meet any of the requirements, it shall lose its order of precedence. However, if the cause of failure is corrected, testing will be resumed after completing such test work as may be in progress.

§ 36.9 Conduct of investigations, tests, and demonstrations.

(a) Prior to the issuance of a certificate of approval or a letter of certification, as the case may require, necessary Government personnel, representatives of the applicant, and such other persons as may be mutually agreed upon may observe the investigations or tests. MSHA shall hold as confidential and shall not disclose principles or patentable features prior to certification, nor shall it disclose any details of drawings, specifications, descriptions, or related materials. After the issuance of a certificate of approval, MSHA may conduct such public demonstrations and tests of the approved mobile diesel-powered transportation equipment as it deems appropriate. The conduct of all investigations, tests, and demonstrations shall be under the direction and control of MSHA, and any other persons shall be present only as observers, except as noted in paragraph (b) of this section.

(b) When requested by MSHA, the applicant shall provide assistance in disassembling parts for inspection, preparing parts for testing, and operating equipment during the tests.

[Sched. 31, 26 FR 645, Jan. 24, 1961, as amended at 39 FR 24006, June 28, 1974; 61 FR 55526, Oct. 25, 1996]

§ 36.10 Certificate of approval.

(a) Upon completion of investigation of a complete assembly of mobile diesel-powered transportation equipment, MSHA will issue to the applicant either a certificate of approval or a written notice of disapproval, as the case may require. No informal notification of approval will be issued. If a certificate of approval is issued, no test data or detailed results of tests will accompany it. If a notice of disapproval is issued, it will be accompanied by details of the defects, with a view to possible correction. MSHA will not disclose, except to the applicant, any information on mobile diesel-powered transportation equipment upon which a notice of disapproval has been issued.

(b) A certificate of approval will be accompanied by a list of drawings, specifications, and related material covering the details of design and construction of equipment upon which the certificate of approval is based. Applicants shall keep exact duplicates of the drawings, specifications, and descriptions that relate to equipment which has received a certificate of approval, and these are to be adhered to exactly in production of the certified equipment.

(c) A certificate of approval will be accompanied by an appropriate caution statement specifying the conditions to be observed for operating and maintaining the equipment and to preserve its permissible status.

§ 36.11 Approval plates.

(a) A certificate of approval will be accompanied by a photograph of an approval plate, bearing the emblem of the Mine Safety and Health Administration and spaces for the approval number, the type, the serial number, and ventilation requirement; the name of the complete assembly; and the name of the applicant.

(b) The applicant shall reproduce the design as a separate plate, which shall be attached, in a suitable place, on each complete assembly to which it relates. The size, type, and method of attaching and location of an approval plate are subject to MSHA's approval. The method of affixing the approval plate shall not impair the permissibility (explosion-proof) features of the complete assembly of mobile diesel-powered transportation equipment.

(c) The approval plate identifies the equipment, to which it is attached, as permissible and is the applicant's guarantee that the equipment complies with the requirements of this part. Without an approval plate no equipment is considered permissible under the provisions of this part.

(d) Use of the approval plate obligates the applicant to whom the certificate of approval was granted to maintain in his plant the quality of each complete assembly bearing it and guarantees that it is manufactured and assembled according to the drawings, specifications, and descriptions upon which a certificate of approval was based.

[Sched. 31, 26 FR 645, Jan. 24, 1961, as amended at 43 FR 12318, Mar. 24, 1978]

§ 36.12 Changes after certification.

If an applicant desires to change any feature of certified equipment, he shall first obtain MSHA's approval of the change, pursuant to the following procedure:

(a)(1) Application shall be made, as for an original certificate of approval, requesting that the existing certification be extended to cover the proposed change. The application shall be accompanied by specifications and related material as in the case of an original application.

§ 36.13

(2) Where the applicant for approval has used an independent laboratory under part 6 of this chapter to perform, in whole or in part, the necessary testing and evaluation for approval of changes to an approved product under this part, the applicant must provide to MSHA as part of the approval application:

(i) Written evidence of the laboratory's independence and current recognition by a laboratory accrediting organization;

(ii) Complete technical explanation of how the product complies with each requirement in the applicable MSHA product approval requirements;

(iii) Identification of components or features of the product that are critical to the safety of the product; and

(iv) All documentation, including drawings and specifications, as submitted to the independent laboratory by the applicant and as required by this part.

(b) The application will be examined by MSHA to determine whether inspection and testing of the modified equipment or component or subassembly will be required. Testing will be necessary if there is a possibility that the modification may affect adversely the performance of the equipment. MSHA will inform the applicant whether such testing is required and the component, subassembly, and related material to be submitted for that purpose.

(c) If the proposed modification meets the requirements of this part, a formal extension of certification will be issued, accompanied by a list of new and corrected drawings and specifications to be added to those already on file as the basis for the extension of certification.

[Sched. 31, 26 FR 645, Jan. 24, 1961, as amended at 52 FR 17516, May 8, 1987; 68 FR 36423, June 17, 2003]

§ 36.13 Withdrawal of certification.

MSHA reserves the right to rescind for cause any certificate of approval granted under this part.

Subpart B—Construction and Design Requirements

§ 36.20 Quality of material, workmanship, and design.

(a) MSHA will test only equipment that in the opinion of its qualified representatives is constructed of suitable materials, is of good quality workmanship, based on sound engineering principles, and is safe for its intended use. Since all possible designs, arrangements, or combinations of components and materials cannot be foreseen, MSHA reserves the right to modify the construction and design requirements of subassemblies or components and tests thereof to obtain the same degree of protection as provided by the tests described in Subpart C of this part.

(b) The quality of material, workmanship, and design shall conform to the requirements of § 7.98(q) of this chapter.

(c) Power packages approved under part 7, subpart F of this chapter are considered to be acceptable for use in equipment submitted for approval under this part. Sections 36.21 through 36.26 (except § 36.25(f)) and §§ 36.43 through 36.48 are not applicable to equipment utilizing part 7, subpart F power packages, since these requirements have already been satisfied.

[Sched. 31, 26 FR 645, Jan. 24, 1961, as amended at 61 FR 55526, Oct. 25, 1996]

§ 36.21 Engine for equipment considered for certification.

Only equipment powered by a compression-ignition (diesel) engine and burning diesel fuel will be considered for approval and certification. The starting mechanism shall be actuated pneumatically, hydraulically, or by other methods acceptable to MSHA. Electric starting shall not be accepted. Engines burning other fuels or utilizing volatile fuel starting aids will not be investigated.

[Sched. 31, 26 FR 645, Jan. 24, 1961, as amended at 61 FR 55526, Oct. 25, 1996]

§ 36.22 Fuel-injection system.

This system shall be so constructed that the quantity of fuel injected can be controlled at a desired maximum value and shall be so arranged that this

Mine Safety and Health Admin., Labor §36.24

adjustment can be changed only after breaking a seal or unlocking a compartment. Provision shall be made for convenient adjustment of the maximum fuel-injection rate to that required for safe operation at different altitudes (elevations above sea level). The governor, controlling engine speed and fuel injection, shall not directly affect airflow to the engine and provision shall be made to seal or lock its adjustment compartment. Filters shall be provided to insure that only clean fuel will reach the injection pump or injectors.

§36.23 Engine intake system.

(a) *Construction.* The intake system (exclusive of the air cleaner) shall be designed to withstand an internal pressure equal to 4 times the maximum pressure observed in explosion tests, which are described in §36.46, or a pressure of 125 pounds per square inch, whichever is the lesser. Joints in the intake system shall be formed by metal flanges fitted with metal or metal-clad gaskets, positively positioned by through bolts or other suitable means for secure assembly, or shall meet the requirements for flanged metal-to-metal flame-proof joints as required in §36.20(b). Either type of joint shall withstand repeated explosions within the intake system without permanent deformation and shall prevent the propagation of flame through the joint into a surrounding flammable mixture.

(b) *Intake flame arrester.* (1) The intake system shall include a flame arrester that will prevent an explosion within the system from propagating to a surrounding flammable mixture. This flame arrester shall be between the air cleaner and the intake manifold and shall be attached so that it may be removed for inspecting, cleaning, or repairing. Its construction shall be such that it may be cleaned readily. The flame arrester shall be of rugged construction to withstand the effects of repeated explosions within the intake system, and the material of construction shall resist deterioration in service. It shall be so mounted in the equipment assembly that it is protected from accidental external damage.

(2) The parts of any flame arrester shall be positively positioned to produce a flame path that will arrest the propagation of an explosion and shall be so designed that improper assembly is impossible. In flame arresters of the spaced-plate type, the thickness of the plates shall be at least 0.125 inch; spacing between the plates shall not exceed 0.018 inch; and the plates forming the flame path shall be at least 1 inch wide. The unsupported length of the plates shall be short enough that deformation during the explosion tests shall not exceed 0.002 inch. Corrosion-resistant metal shall be used to construct flame arresters.

(c) *Air shutoff valve.* The intake system shall include a valve, operable from the operator's compartment, to shut off the air supply to the engine. This valve shall be constructed to permit its operation only after the fuel supply to the engine is shut off. In reverse operation the valve must open fully before fuel can be supplied to the engine.

(d) *Air cleaner.* An air cleaner shall be included in the engine intake system and so arranged that only clean air will enter the flame arrester. The resistance to airflow shall not increase rapidly in dusty atmospheres. Filters of the self-cleansing (oil-bath) type will be considered satisfactory for this application. Provision, satisfactory to MSHA, shall be made to prevent overfilling the oil-bath air cleaner.

(e) *Vacuum-gage connection.* A connection shall be provided in the intake system for temporary attachment of a vacuum gage to indicate the pressure drop under flow conditions. This opening shall be closed by a plug or other suitable device that is sealed or locked in place except when a gage is attached.

§36.24 Engine joints.

(a) *Cylinder head.* The joint between the cylinder head and block of the engine shall be fitted with a metal or metal-clad gasket satisfactory to MSHA held securely in position by through bolts or other suitable means to prevent a change in alignment. This joint shall provide an adequate flame barrier with the gasket in place.

(b) *Valve guides.* Valve guides shall be long enough to form an adequate flame barrier along the valve stem.

§ 36.25

(c) *Gaskets.* All metal or metal-clad gaskets shall maintain their tightness during repeated explosions within the engine and its intake and exhaust systems to prevent the propagation of flame.

§ 36.25 Engine exhaust system.

(a) *Construction.* The exhaust system of the engine shall be designed to withstand an internal pressure equal to 4 times the maximum pressure observed in explosion tests, which are described in § 36.46, or a pressure of 125 pounds per square inch, whichever is the lesser. The system shall withstand repeated internal explosions without permanent deformation or deterioration.

(b) *Exhaust flame arrester.* (1) The exhaust system of the engine shall be provided with a flame arrester to prevent propagation of flame or discharge of heated particles to a surrounding flammable mixture. The flame arrester shall be so positioned that only cooled exhaust gas will discharge through it and shall be so designed and attached that it can be removed for inspecting, cleaning, or repairing. Its construction shall be such that it can be cleaned readily. The flame arrester shall be of rugged construction to withstand the effects of repeated explosions within the exhaust system, and the material of construction shall resist deterioration in service. It shall be so mounted in the equipment assembly that it is protected from accidental external damage.

(2) A spaced-plate flame arrester for the exhaust system shall meet the same requirements as flame arresters for the intake system (see § 36.23(b)(2)).

(3) In lieu of a space-place flame arrester, an exhaust-gas cooling box or conditioner may be used as the exhaust flame arrester provided that explosion tests demonstrate that the cooling box will arrest flame. When used as a flame arrester the cooling box shall be equipped with a device to shut off automatically the fuel supply to the engine at a safe minimum water level. A cooling box used as a flame arrester shall withstand repeated explosion tests without permanent deformation. It shall be constructed of material, satisfactory to MSHA, that will resist deterioration in service.

(c) *Exhaust cooling system.* (1) A cooling system shall be provided for the engine exhaust gas. The heat-dissipation capacity shall be capable of reducing the temperature of the undiluted exhaust gas to less than 170 °F. at the point of discharge from the cooling system under any condition of engine operation acceptable to MSHA. A device shall be provided that will automatically shut off the fuel supply to the engine immediately if the temperature of the exhaust gas exceeds 185 °F. at the point of discharge from the cooling system. Provision shall be made, acceptable to MSHA, to prevent restarting the engine after the fuel supply has been shut off automatically until the water supply in the cooling box has been replenished. When the cooling box is used as a flame arrester, one safety device may be accepted provided it controls a safe minimum water level in the cooling box and also prevents the final exhaust temperature from exceeding 185 °F.

(2) Cooling shall be obtained by passing the exhaust gas through water or a dilute aqueous chemical solution held in a cooling box or conditioner, or by a spray of water or a dilute aqueous chemical solution that will enter the exhaust system near the outlet of the exhaust manifold, or a combination of the two methods. When a spray is used it shall be provided with a filtering device to protect the nozzle from clogging. Provisions shall be made for draining and cleaning all parts of the exhaust cooling system. Openings for draining and cleaning shall be closed and sealed or locked by a method satisfactory to MSHA.

(3) The cooling system shall be constructed of corrosion-resistant metal suitable for the intended application.

(4) The cooling system shall store enough water or aqueous solution to permit operation of the engine at one-third load factor for eight hours. The minimum quantity of usable water or aqueous solution available for cooling shall equal the consumption for one hour with the engine operating at maximum load and speed multiplied by 8 and this product divided by 3.

(d) *Surface temperature of engine and exhaust system.* (1) The temperature of any external surface of the engine or exhaust system shall not exceed 400 °F. under any condition of engine operation prescribed by MSHA. Water-jacketed components shall have integral jackets and provision shall be made for positive circulation of water in the jackets and to automatically shut off the engine when the temperature in the cooling jacket(s) exceeds 212 °F. Insulated coverings to control surface temperature are not acceptable.

(2) When a spray is used to reduce the temperature of the exhaust gas, it shall be located as near as practicable to the outlet of the exhaust manifold.

(3) Exterior surfaces of the exhaust system shall be designed to minimize accumulation and lodgement of dust or combustible substances and to permit ready access for cleaning.

(e) *Tightness of exhaust system.* All joints in the exhaust system shall be tight to prevent the flow of exhaust gas through them under any condition of engine operation prescribed by MSHA. A tight system shall be obtained by the use of ground joints, or thin metal or metal-clad gaskets. All such joints shall be fitted with adequate through bolts and all gaskets shall be aligned and held firmly in position by the bolts or other suitable means. Such joints shall remain tight to prevent passage of flame or propagation of repeated internal explosions to a surrounding flammable mixture.

(f) *Dilution of exhaust gas.* (1) Provision shall be made to dilute the exhaust gas with and before it is discharged into the surrounding atmosphere. The discharged exhaust gas shall be so diluted with air that the mixture shall not contain more than 0.5 percent, by volume, of carbon dioxide; 0.01 percent, by volume, of carbon monoxide; 0.0025 percent, by volume, of oxides of nitrogen (calculated as equivalent nitrogen dioxide); or 0.0010 percent, by volume, of aldehydes (calculated as equivalent formaldehyde) under any condition of engine operation prescribed by MSHA.

(2) The final diluted exhaust mixture shall be discharged in such a manner that it is directed away from the operator's compartment and also away from the breathing zones of persons required to be alongside the equipment.

(g) *Pressure-gage connection.* A connection shall be provided in the exhaust system for convenient, temporary attachment of a pressure gage at a point suitable for measuring the total back pressure in the system. The connection also shall be suitable for temporary attachment of gas-sampling equipment to the exhaust system. This opening shall be closed by a plug or other suitable device that is sealed or locked in place except when a gage or sampling tube is attached.

§ 36.26   Composition of exhaust gas.

(a) *Preliminary engine adjustment.* The engine shall be submitted to MSHA by the applicant in such condition that it can be tested immediately at full load and speed. The preliminary liquid-fuel-injection rate shall be such that the exhaust will not contain black smoke and the applicant shall adjust the injection rate promptly to correct any adverse conditions disclosed by preliminary tests.

(b) *Final engine adjustment.* The liquid fuel supply to the engine shall be adjusted so that the undiluted exhaust gas shall contain not more than 0.30 percent, by volume, of carbon monoxide or 0.20 percent, by volume, of oxides of nitrogen (calculated as equivalent nitrogen dioxide, NO_2) under any conditions of engine operation prescribed by MSHA when the intake air mixture to the engine contains 1.5 ±0.1 percent, by volume, of Pittsburgh natural gas.[3]

(c) *Coupling or adapter.* The applicant shall provide the coupling or adapter for connecting the engine to MSHA's dynamometer.

NOTE: Preferably this coupling or adapter should be attached to the flywheel of the engine.

Clutches, transmissions, or torque converters ordinarily are not required in the coupling train.

---

[3] Investigation has shown that for practical purposes, Pittsburgh natural gas (containing a high percentage of methane) is a satisfactory substitute for pure methane in these tests.

§ 36.27 Fuel-supply system.

(a) *Fuel tank.* (1) The fuel tank shall not leak and shall be fabricated of metal at least 1/16 inch thick, welded at all seams, except that tanks of 5 gallons or less capacity may have thinner walls which shall be preformed or reinforced to provide good resistance to deflection. A drain plug (not a valve or petcock) shall be provided and locked in position. A vent opening shall be provided in the fuel filler cap of such design that atmospheric pressure is maintained inside the tank. The size of the vent opening shall be restricted to prevent fuel from splashing through it. The filler opening shall be so arranged that fuel can be added only through a self-closing valve at least 1 foot from the exhaust manifold of the engine, preferably below it. The self-closing valve shall constitute a fuel-tight closure when fuel is not being added. Any part of the self-closing valve that might become detached during the addition of fuel shall be secured to the tank by a chain or other fastening to prevent loss.

(2) The fuel tank shall have a definite position in the equipment assembly, and no provision shall be made for attachment of separate or auxiliary fuel tanks.

(3) Capacity of the fuel tank shall not exceed the amount of fuel necessary to operate the engine continuously at full load for approximately four hours.

(b) *Fuel lines.* All fuel lines shall be installed to protect them against damage in ordinary use and they shall be designed, fabricated, and secured to resist breakage from vibration.

(c) *Valve in fuel line.* A shutoff valve shall be provided in the fuel system, installed in a manner acceptable to MSHA.

NOTE: This shutoff valve is in addition to the normal shutoff provided in the fuel-injection system and also in addition to the air-shutoff valve.

§ 36.28 Signal or warning device.

All mobile diesel-powered transportation equipment shall be provided with a bell, horn, or other suitable warning device convenient to the operator. Warning devices shall be operated manually or pneumatically.

§ 36.29 Brakes.

All mobile diesel-powered transportation equipment shall be equipped with adequate brakes acceptable to MSHA.

§ 36.30 Rerailing device.

All mobile diesel-powered transportation equipment designed to travel on rails in haulage service shall carry a suitable rerailing device.

§ 36.31 Fire extinguisher.

Each unit of mobile diesel-powered transportation equipment shall be fitted with a fire extinguisher carried in a location easily accessible to the operator and protected by position from external damage. Liquid carbon dioxide extinguishers shall contain an active charge of not less than 4 pounds. Pressurized dry chemical extinguishers shall contain an active charge of not less than 2½ pounds.

§ 36.32 Electrical components and systems.

(a) Electrical components on mobile diesel-powered transportation equipment shall be certified or approved under Part 18, 20 or 27 of this chapter, as applicable, and shall bear the certification number assigned by MSHA.

(b) Electrical systems on mobile diesel-powered transportation equipment shall meet the requirements of Part 18 or 27 of this chapter, as applicable.

[47 FR 11372, Mar. 16, 1982]

§ 36.33 Headlights and fixtures.

(a) Headlights and lighting fixtures on mobile diesel-powered transportation equipment shall be protected from external damage by recessing them in the equipment frame, enclosing them within a shield of substantial construction, or by any other method that provides equivalent protection.

(b) Mobile diesel-powered transportation equipment shall be equipped with at least one headlight on each end.

[47 FR 11372, Mar. 16, 1982]

Subpart C—Test Requirements

§ 36.40 Test site.

Tests shall be conducted at MSHA's Diesel Testing Laboratory or other appropriate place(s) determined by MSHA.

[39 FR 24006, June 28, 1974, as amended at 43 FR 12318, Mar. 24, 1978]

§ 36.41 Testing methods.

Mobile diesel-powered transportation equipment submitted for certification and approval shall be tested to determine its combustion, explosion-proof, and other safety characteristics. MSHA shall prescribe the tests and reserves the right to modify the procedure(s) to attain these objectives (see § 36.20).

§ 36.42 Inspection.

A detailed inspection shall be made of the equipment and all components and features related to safety in operation. The inspection shall include:

(a) Investigating the materials, workmanship, and design to determine their adequacy.

(b) Checking the parts and assemblies against the drawings and specifications with respect to materials, dimensions, and locations to verify their conformance.

(c) Inspecting and measuring joints, flanges, and other possible flame paths in the intake and exhaust systems to determine whether they will prevent the issuance of flame or propagation of an internal explosion.

(d) Inspecting and measuring flame arresters to determine whether they will prevent the issuance of flame or propagation of an internal explosion.

§ 36.43 Determination of exhaust-gas composition.

(a) Samples shall be taken to determine the composition of the exhaust gas while the engine is operated at loads and speeds prescribed by MSHA to determine the volume of air (ventilation) required to dilute the exhaust gas (see § 36.45). The engine shall be at temperature equilibrium before exhaust-gas samples are collected or other test data are observed. At all test conditions the intake mixture shall contain 1.5 ±0.1 percent, by volume, of Pittsburgh natural gas (see footnote 3) in the air. Test observations shall include the rate of fuel consumption, pressures, temperatures, and other data significant in the safe operation of diesel equipment.

(b) Exhaust-gas samples shall be analyzed for carbon dioxide, oxygen, carbon monoxide, hydrogen, methane, nitrogen, oxides of nitrogen, and aldehydes, or any other constituent prescribed by MSHA.

(c) The intake and exhaust systems shall be complete with all component equipment such as air cleaners, flame arresters, and exhaust cooling systems. The performance of component equipment shall be observed to determine whether it functions properly.

[Sched. 31, 26 FR 645, Jan. 24, 1961, as amended at 61 FR 55526, Oct. 25, 1996]

§ 36.44 Maximum allowable fuel:air ratio.

(a) When an engine is delivered to MSHA with the fuel-injection system adjusted by the applicant and tests of the exhaust-gas composition (see § 36.43) show not more than 0.30 percent, by volume, of carbon monoxide, the applicant's adjustment of the fuel-injection system shall be accepted. The maximum fuel:air ratio determined from the exhaust-gas composition shall be designated as the maximum allowable fuel:air ratio. The maximum liquid fuel rate (pounds per hour) that produces the maximum allowable fuel:air ratio shall be designated as the maximum allowable fuel rate for operating the equipment at elevations not exceeding 1,000 feet above sea level.

(b) When the carbon monoxide content of the exhaust exceeds 0.30 percent, by volume, only near maximum power output, the maximum fuel:air ratio at which carbon monoxide does not exceed 0.30 percent shall be calculated and designated as the maximum allowable fuel:air ratio. The corresponding calculated liquid fuel rate shall be designated as the maximum allowable fuel rate at elevations not exceeding 1,000 feet above sea level.

NOTE: The applicant may be requested to adjust the liquid fuel rate during tests to determine the maximum allowable fuel:air ratio.

§ 36.45

(c) The maximum allowable fuel:air ratio and maximum liquid fuel rates shall be used to calculate a liquid fuel rate-altitude table that shall govern the liquid fuel rate of engines operated at elevations exceeding 1,000 feet above sea level.

§ 36.45 Quantity of ventilating air.

(a) Results of the engine tests shall be used to calculate ventilation (cubic feet of air per minute) that shall be supplied by positive air movement when the permissible mobile diesel-powered transportation equipment is used underground. This quantity shall be stamped on the approval plate. The quantity so determined shall apply when only one machine is operated.

(b) Determination of the ventilation rate shall be based upon dilution of the exhaust gas with normal air. The most undesirable and hazardous condition of engine operation prescribed by MSHA shall be used in the calculations. The concentration of any of the following individual constituents in the diluted mixture shall not exceed:

0.25 percent, by volume, of carbon dioxide (CO_2).
0.005 percent, by volume, of carbon monoxide (CO).
0.00125 percent, by volume, of oxides of nitrogen (calculated as equivalent nitrogen dioxide, NO_2).

The oxygen (O_2) content of the diluted mixture shall be not less than 20 percent, by volume. The maximum quantity of normal air to produce the above dilution shall be designated the ventilation rate.

NOTE: This ventilation rate will provide a factor of safety for exposure of persons to air mixtures containing harmful or objectionable gases and for minor variations in engine performance.

§ 36.46 Explosion tests of intake and exhaust systems.

(a) Explosion tests to determine the strength of the intake and exhaust systems to withstand internal explosions and the adequacy of the flame arresters to prevent the propagation of an explosion shall be made with the systems connected to the engine or the systems simulated as connected to the engine. The system shall be filled with and surrounded by an explosive natural gas-air mixture. The mixture within the intake and exhaust systems shall be ignited by suitable means and the internal pressure developed by the resultant explosion shall be determined. Tests shall be conducted with the ignition source in several different locations to determine the maximum pressure developed by an internal explosion.

(b) Explosion tests shall be made with the engine at rest and with the flammable natural gas-air mixtures in the intake and exhaust systems. In other tests with the flammable mixture in motion, the engine shall be driven (externally) at speeds prescribed by MSHA but no liquid fuel shall be supplied to the injection valves.

(c) The temperature of the flame arresters in the intake or exhaust systems shall not exceed 212 °F. when an explosion test is conducted. Any water-spray cooling for the exhaust system shall not be operated and water shall not be present in the exhaust cooling boxes except when water is the cooling agent for a cooling box designed to act as a flame arrester, in which case MSHA will prescribe the test conditions.

(d) The explosion tests of the intake and exhaust systems shall not result in:

(1) Discharge of visible flame from any joint or opening.

(2) Ignition of surrounding flammable gas-air mixture.

(3) Development of dangerous afterburning.[4]

(4) Excessive pressures.

§ 36.47 Tests of exhaust-gas cooling system.

(a) The adequacy of the exhaust-gas cooling system and its components shall be determined with the engine operating at the maximum allowable liquid fuel rate and governed speed with 0.5 ±0.1 percent, by volume, of natural gas in the intake air mixture. All parts of the engine and exhaust-gas cooling system shall be at their respective equilibrium temperatures. The cooling spray, if any, shall be operated, and all

---

[4] The term "afterburning" as used in this part is applied to combustion of a flammable gas-air mixture drawn into the system under test by the cooling of the products from an explosion in the system.

compartments designed to hold cooling water shall be filled with the quantity of water recommended by the applicant. No cooling air shall be circulated over the engine or components in the cooling system during the test.

(b) Determinations shall be made during the test to establish the cooling performance of the system, the cooling water consumption, high-water level when the system sprays excess water, and low-water level when the cooling system fails.

(c) The final exhaust-gas temperature at discharge from the cooling system, and before the exhaust gas is diluted with air, shall not exceed 170 °F. or the temperature of adiabatic saturation, if this temperature is lower.

(d) Water consumed in cooling the exhaust gas under the test conditions shall not exceed by more than 15 percent that required for adiabatic saturation of the exhaust-gas at the final temperature. Water in excess of that required for adiabatic saturation shall be considered as entrained water. Enough water shall be available in the cooling system or in reserve supply compartments for sustained satisfactory operation for at least 2⅔ hours under the test conditions.

NOTE: This amount is enough to cool the exhaust for an 8-hour shift at one-third load factor.

(e) The adequacy of the automatic fuel shutoff actuated by the temperature of the final exhaust shall be determined with the engine operating under test conditions by withdrawing water until the cooling system fails to function. The final exhaust-gas temperature at which the liquid fuel to the engine is automatically shut off shall be noted. This temperature shall not exceed 185 °F.

(f) Following the automatic fuel shutoff test in paragraph (e) of this section, the temperature of the control point shall be allowed to fall to 170 °F. At this temperature and with the water replenished in the cooling system, it shall be possible to start the engine.

NOTE: If the cooling system includes a reserve supply water tank, the line or lines connecting it to the cooling compartment may require a suitable flame arrester.

(g) The effectiveness of the automatic engine shut-off, which will operate when the water in the cooling jacket(s) exceeds 212 °F., shall be determined by causing the jacket temperature to exceed 212 °F.

§ 36.48 Tests of surface temperature of engine and components of the cooling system.

(a) The surface temperatures of the engine, exhaust cooling system, and other components subject to heating by engine operation shall be determined with the engine operated as prescribed by MSHA. All parts of the engine, cooling system, and other components shall have reached their respective equilibrium temperatures. The exhaust cooling system shall be operated, but air shall not be circulated over the engine or components. Surface temperatures shall be measured at various places prescribed by MSHA to determine where maximum temperatures develop.

(b) The temperature of any surface shall not exceed 400 °F.

NOTE TO § 36.48: The engine may be operated under test conditions prescribed by MSHA while completely surrounded by a flammable mixture. MSHA reserves the right to apply combustible materials to any surface for test. Operation under such conditions shall not ignite the flammable mixture.

[Sched. 31, 26 FR 645, Jan. 24, 1961, as amended at 61 FR 55526, Oct. 25, 1996]

§ 36.49 Tests of exhaust-gas dilution system.

The performance and adequacy of the exhaust-gas dilution system shall be determined in tests of the complete equipment. The engine, at temperature equilibrium, shall be operated in normal air as prescribed by MSHA. Samples of the undiluted exhaust gas and of the diluted exhaust gas, at location(s) prescribed by MSHA, shall be considered with the data obtained from the engine test (see § 36.43) to determine that the concentrations of carbon dioxide, carbon monoxide, oxides of nitrogen, and aldehydes in the diluted exhaust shall be below the required concentrations specified in § 36.25(f)(1).

§ 36.50 Tests of fuel tank.

The fuel tank shall be inspected and tested to determine whether: (a) It is fuel-tight, (b) the vent maintains atmospheric pressure within the tank, and (c) the vent and closure restrict the outflow of liquid fuel.

SUBCHAPTERS C–F [RESERVED]

SUBCHAPTER G—FILING AND OTHER ADMINISTRATIVE REQUIREMENTS

PART 40—REPRESENTATIVE OF MINERS

Sec.
40.1 Definitions.
40.2 Requirements.
40.3 Filing procedures.
40.4 Posting at mine.
40.5 Termination of designation as representative of miners.

AUTHORITY: Secs. 5(f)(1), 101(c) and (e), 103(c), (f), (g)(1) and (g)(2), 104(c), 105(a), (b)(1), (c)(1), (c)(2), (c)(3), and (d), 107(b)(1) and (e)(1), 109(b), 115(a)(1) and (a)(2), 302(a), 305(b), 312(b), 505 and 508, Federal Mine Safety and Health Act of 1977, Pub. L. 91–173 as amended by Pub. L. 95–164, 83 Stat. 745, 91 Stat. 1294, 1295, 1298, 1299, 1301, 1303, 1304, 1305, 1308, 1310 and 1316, 83 Stat. 766, 777, 785, 802, and 803 (30 U.S.C. 804(f)(1), 811(c) and (e), 813(c), (f), (g)(1) and (g)(2), 814(c), 815(a), (b)(1), (c)(1), (c)(2), (c)(3) and (d), 817(b)(1) and (e)(1), 819(b), 825(a)(1) and (a)(2), 862(a), 865(b), 872(b), 954 and 957); sec. 307, Federal Mine Safety and Health Amendments Act of 1977, Pub. L. 95–164, 91 Stat. 1322 (30 U.S.C. 801 note).

SOURCE: 43 FR 29509, July 7, 1978, unless otherwise noted.

§ 40.1 Definitions.

As used in this Part 40:

(a) *Act* means the Federal Mine Safety and Health Act of 1977.

(b) *Representative of miners* means:

(1) Any person or organization which represents two or more miners at a coal or other mine for the purposes of the Act, and

(2) *Representatives authorized by the miners, miners or their representative, authorized miner representative,* and other similar terms as they appear in the Act.

§ 40.2 Requirements.

(a) A representative of miners shall file with the Mine Safety and Health Administration District Manager for the district in which the mine is located the information required by § 40.3 of this part. Concurrently, a copy of this information shall be provided to the operator of the mine by the representative of miners.

(b) Miners or their representative organization may appoint or designate different persons to represent them under various sections of the act relating to representatives of miners.

(c) All information filed pursuant to this part shall be maintained by the appropriate Mine Safety and Health Administration District Office and shall be made available for public inspection.

(Pub. L. No. 96–511, 94 Stat. 2812 (44 U.S.C. 3501 et seq.))

[43 FR 29509, July 7, 1978, as amended at 47 FR 14696, Apr. 6, 1982; 60 FR 33722, June 29, 1995]

§ 40.3 Filing procedures.

(a) The following information shall be filed by a representative of miners with the appropriate District Manager, with copies to the operators of the affected mines. This information shall be kept current:

(1) The name, address, and telephone number of the representative of miners. If the representative is an organization, the name, address, and telephone number of the organization and the title of the official or position, who is to serve as the representative and his or her telephone number.

(2) The name and address of the operator of the mine where the represented miners work and the name, address, and Mine Safety and Health Administration identification number, if known, of the mine.

(3) A copy of the document evidencing the designation of the representative of miners.

(4) A statement that the person or position named as the representative of miners is the representative for all purposes of the Act; or if the representative's authority is limited, a statement of the limitation.

(5) The names, addresses, and telephone numbers, of any representative to serve in his absence.

(6) A statement that copies of all information filed pursuant to this section have been delivered to the operator of the affected mine, prior to or concurrently with the filing of this statement.

§ 40.4

(7) A statement certifying that all information filed is true and correct followed by the signature of the representative of miners.

(b) The representative of miners shall be responsible for ensuring that the appropriate District Manager and operator have received all of the information required by this part and informing such District Manager and operator of any subsequent changes in the information.

§ 40.4 Posting at mine.

A copy of the information provided the operator pursuant to § 40.3 of this part shall be posted upon receipt by the operator on the mine bulletin board and maintained in a current status.

§ 40.5 Termination of designation as representative of miners.

(a) A representative of miners who becomes unable to comply with the requirements of this part shall file a statement with the appropriate District Manager terminating his or her designation.

(b) The Mine Safety and Health Administration shall terminate and remove from its files all designations of representatives of miners which have been terminated pursuant to paragraph (a) of this section or which are not in compliance with the requirements of this part. The Mine Safety and Health Administration shall notify the operator of such termination.

PART 41—NOTIFICATION OF LEGAL IDENTITY

Subpart A—Definitions

Sec.
41.1 Definitions.

Subpart B—Notification of Legal Identity

41.10 Scope.
41.11 Notification by operator.
41.12 Changes; notification by operator.
41.13 Failure to notify.

Subpart C—Operator's Report to the Mine Safety and Health Administration

41.20 Legal identity report.
41.30 Address of record and telephone number.

AUTHORITY: Secs. 103(h), 109(d) and 508, Federal Mine Safety and Health Act of 1977, Pub. L. 91–173 as amended by Pub. L. 95–164, 91 Stat. 1299 and 1310, 83 Stat. 803 (30 U.S.C. 813(h), 819(d) and 957); sec. 307, Federal Mine Safety and Health Amendments Act of 1977, Pub. L. 95–164, 91 Stat. 1322 (30 U.S.C. 801 note).

SOURCE: 43 FR 29512, July 7, 1978, unless otherwise noted.

Subpart A—Definitions

§ 41.1 Definitions.

As used in this part:

(a) *Operator* means any owner, lessee, or other person who operates, controls, or supervises a coal or other mine or any designated independent contractor performing services or construction at such mine.

(b) *Person* means any individual, sole proprietor, partnership, association, corporation, firm, subsidiary of a corporation, or other organization.

(c) *Coal or other mine* means (a) an area of land from which minerals are extracted in nonliquid form or, if in liquid form, are extracted with workers underground, (b) private ways and roads appurtenant to such area, and (c) lands, excavations, underground passageways, shafts, slopes, tunnels and workings, structures, facilities, equipment, machines, tools, or other property including impoundments, retention dams, and tailings ponds, on the surface or underground, used in, or to be used in, or resulting from, the work of extracting such minerals from their natural deposits in nonliquid form, or if in liquid form, with workers underground, or used in, or to be used in, the milling of such minerals, or the work of preparing coal or other minerals, and includes custom coal preparation facilities. In making a determination of what constitutes mineral milling for purposes of this act, the Secretary shall give due consideration to the convenience of administration resulting from the delegation to one Assistant Secretary of all authority with respect to the health and safety of miners employed at one physical establishment.

Subpart B—Notification of Legal Identity

§ 41.10 Scope.

Section 109(d) of the Federal Mine Safety and Health Act of 1977 (Pub. L. 91–173, as amended by Pub. L. 95–164), requires each operator of a coal or other mine to file with the Secretary of Labor the name and address of such mine, the name and address of the person who controls or operates the mine, and any revisions in such names and addresses. Section 103(h) of the act requires the operator of a coal or other mine to provide such information as the Secretary of Labor may reasonably require from time to time to enable the Secretary to perform his functions under the act. The regulations in this Subpart B provide for the notification to the Mine Safety and Health Administration of the legal identity of the operator of a coal or other mine and the reporting of all changes in the legal identity of the operator as they occur. The submission of a properly completed Legal Identity Report Form No. 2000–7 required under Subpart C of this part will constitute adequate notification of legal identity to the Mine Safety and Health Administration.

§ 41.11 Notification by operator.

(a) Not later than 30 days after (1) the effective date of this part, and (2) the opening of a new mine thereafter, the operator of a coal or other mine shall, in writing, notify the appropriate district manager of the Mine Safety and Health Administration in the district in which the mine is located of the legal identity of the operator in accordance with the applicable provisions of paragraph (b), (c), (d), or (e) of this section.

(b) If the operator is a sole proprietorship, the operator shall state: (1) His full name and address; (2) the name and address of the mine and the Federal mine identification number; (3) the name and address of the person at the mine in charge of health and safety; (4) the name and address of the person with overall responsibility for a health and safety program at all of the operator's mines, if the operator is not directly involved in the daily operation of the mine; (5) the Federal mine identification numbers of all other mines in which the sole proprietor has a 20 percent or greater ownership interest; and (6) the trade name, if any, and the full name, address of record and telephone number of the proprietorship.

(c) If the operator is a partnership, the operator shall state: (1) The name and address of the mine and the Federal mine identification number; (2) the name and address of the person at the mine in charge of health and safety; (3) the name and address of the person with overall responsibility for a health and safety program at all of the operator's mines, if the operator is not directly involved in the daily operation of the mine; (4) the Federal mine identification numbers of all other mines in which the partnership has a 20 percent or greater ownership interest; (5) the full name and address of all partners; (6) the trade name, if any, and the full name and address of record and telephone number of the partnership; and (7) the Federal mine identification numbers of all other mines in which any partner has a 20 percent or greater ownership interest.

(d) If the operator is a corporation, the operator shall state: (1) The name and address of the mine and the Federal mine identification number; (2) the name and address of the person at the mine in charge of health and safety; (3) the name and address of the person with overall responsibility for a health and safety program at all of the operator's mines, if the operator is not directly involved in the daily operation of the mine; (4) the Federal mine identification numbers of all other mines in which the corporation has a 20 percent or greater ownership interest; (5) the full name, address of record and telephone number of the corporation and the State of incorporation; (6) the full name and address of each officer and director of the corporation; (7) whether such corporation is a domestic or foreign corporation in the State in which the mine is located; (8) if the corporation is a subsidiary corporation, the operator shall state the full name, address, and State of incorporation of the parent corporation; and (9) the Federal mine identification numbers of all

§ 41.12

other mines in which any corporate officer has a 20 percent or greater ownership interest.

(e) If the operator is any organization other than a sole proprietorship, partnership, or corporation, the operator shall state: (1) The nature and type, or legal identity of the organization; (2) the name and address of the mine and the Federal mine identification number; (3) the name and address of the person at the mine in charge of health and safety; (4) the name and address of the person with overall responsibility for a health and safety program at all of the operator's mines, if the operator is not directly involved in the daily operation of the mine; (5) the Federal mine identification numbers of all other mines in which the organization has a 20 percent or greater ownership interest; (6) the full name, address of record and telephone number of the organization; (7) the name and address of each individual who has an ownership interest in the organization; (8) the name and address of the principal organization officials or members; and (9) the Federal mine identification numbers of all other mines in which any official or member has a 20 percent or greater ownership interest.

§ 41.12 Changes; notification by operator.

Within 30 days after the occurrence of any change in the information required by § 41.11, the operator of a coal or other mine shall, in writing, notify the appropriate district manager of the Mine Safety and Health Administration in the district in which the mine is located of such change.

§ 41.13 Failure to notify.

Failure of the operator to notify the Mine Safety and Health Administration, in writing, of the legal identity of the operator or any changes thereof within the time required under this part will be considered to be a violation of section 109(d) of the Act and shall be subject to penalties as provided in section 110 of the Act.

Subpart C—Operator's Report to the Mine Safety and Health Administration

§ 41.20 Legal identity report.

Each operator of a coal or other mine shall file notification of legal identity and every change thereof with the appropriate district manager of the Mine Safety and Health Administration by properly completing, mailing, or otherwise delivering form 2000–7 "legal identity report" which shall be provided by the Mine Safety and Health Administration for this purpose. If additional space is required, the operator may use a separate sheet or sheets.

§ 41.30 Address of record and telephone number.

The address of record and telephone number required under this part shall be considered the operator's official address and telephone number for purposes of the Act. Service of documents upon the operator may be proved by a post office return receipt showing that the documents could not be delivered to such operator at the address of record because the operator had moved without leaving a forwarding address or because delivery was not accepted at that address, or because no such address existed. However, operators may request service by delivery to another appropriate address provided by the operator. The telephone number required under this part will be used in connection with proposed civil penalty assessments as provided in 30 CFR part 100.

PART 42—NATIONAL MINE HEALTH AND SAFETY ACADEMY

Subpart A [Reserved]

Subpart B—Tuition Fees

Sec.
42.10 Tuition fees.
42.20 Schedule of fees.
42.30 Procedure for payment.
42.40 Refunds.

Subpart C—Room and Board

42.50 Charges for room and board.

AUTHORITY: 30 U.S.C. 957.

SOURCE: 50 FR 11643, Mar. 22, 1985, unless otherwise noted. Redesignated at 67 FR 42382, June 21, 2002.

Subpart A [Reserved]

Subpart B—Tuition Fees

§ 42.10 Tuition fees.

The National Mine Health and Safety Academy, located in Beckley, West Virginia, will charge tuition fees to all persons attending Academy courses, except employees of Federal, State, or local governments, persons attending the Academy under a program supported through an MSHA State grant, and persons performing a direct service. Also, subject to available resources, MSHA may waive all or part of fees for students, or persons employed by a non-profit organization, who are invited by MSHA to attend an Academy course which would, in the Agency's judgment, contribute to improved conduct, supervision, or management of a function or activity under the Federal Mine Safety and Health Act of 1977 or a function related to an MSHA appropriation. requests for waivers must be in writing.

[62 FR 60985, Nov. 13, 1997]

§ 42.20 Schedule of fees.

(a) Tuition fees will be computed on the basis of the cost to the Government for the Academy to conduct the course, as determined by the Superintendent of the Academy.

(b) The tuition fee for each course will be stated in the course announcement and will be reassessed on an annual basis.

§ 42.30 Procedure for payment.

When notified of acceptance for a course by the Academy, applicants shall submit a check or money order to the Academy, payable to the "Mine Safety and Health Administration" in the amount indicated by the course announcement prior to the commencement of the course.

§ 42.40 Refunds.

An applicant may withdraw an application and receive a full refund of tuition fees provided that written notification to the Academy's Student Services Branch is mailed no later than 14 days before the course begins.

Subpart C—Room and Board

§ 42.50 Charges for room and board.

The Academy will charge room and board to all persons staying at the Academy, except MSHA personnel, persons attending the Academy under a program supported through an MSHA State grant, and persons performing a direct service. Also, subject to available resources, MSHA may waive all or part of fees for students, or persons employed by a non-profit organization, who are invited by MSHA to attend an MSHA-sponsored training or meeting which would, in the Agency's judgment, contribute to improved conduct, supervision, or management of a function or activity under the Federal Mine Safety and Health Act of 1977 or a function related to an MSHA appropriation. Requests for waivers must be in writing. Charges for room and board will be based upon the average cost per person of the lodging, meals, and services provided and will be reassessed on an annual basis.

[62 FR 60985, Nov. 13, 1997]

PART 43—PROCEDURES FOR PROCESSING HAZARDOUS CONDITIONS COMPLAINTS

Subpart A—General

Sec.
43.1 Definitions.
43.2 General.
43.3 Purpose and scope of this part.

Subpart B—Special Inspections

43.4 Requirements for giving notice.
43.5 Action by the Secretary.
43.6 Notice of negative finding.

Subpart C—Informal Review

43.7 Informal review upon written notice given to an inspector on the mine premises.
43.8 Informal review upon the issuance of a notice of negative finding.

AUTHORITY: Secs. 103(g), and 508, Federal Mine Safety and Health Act of 1977 Pub. L. 91–173 as amended by Pub. L. 95–164, 91 Stat. 1298 83 Stat. 803 (30 U.S.C. 813(g) and 957); sec.

§ 43.1

307, Federal Mine Safety and Health Amendments Act of 1977, Pub. L. 95–164, 91 Stat. 1322 (30 U.S.C. 801 note).

SOURCE: 43 FR 29515, July 7, 1978, unless otherwise noted.

Subpart A—General

§ 43.1 Definitions.

For purposes of this part, *Act* means the Federal Mine Safety and Health Act of 1977, Pub. L. 91–173, as amended by Pub. L. 95–164, and "Secretary" means the Secretary of Labor or his designee.

§ 43.2 General.

(a) Under section 103(g)(1) of the Act, a representative of miners, or where there is no such representative, a miner, who has reasonable grounds to believe that a violation of the act or a mandatory health or safety standard exists, or an imminent danger exists, has a right to obtain a special inspection if he or she gives notice of such violation to the Secretary or his duly authorized representative. The notice shall be reduced to writing and signed by the miners' representative or miner, and a copy that does not reveal the name of the person giving the notice must be served on the operator no later than at the time of the inspection. If the Secretary determines that a violation or danger does not exist, he must so notify the miners' representative or miner in writing.

(b) Under section 103(g)(2) of the Act, a representative of miners or, if there is no such representative, a miner, may notify in writing an authorized representative of the Secretary who is on mine premises prior to or during an inspection, of any violation or imminent danger which he or she has reason to believe exists in the mine. There shall be procedures for the informal review of any refusal by the Secretary's authorized representative to issue a citation with respect to such alleged violation or danger, including notification to the miners' representative or miner of the reasons for his disposition of the case.

(Pub. L. No. 96–511, 94 Stat. 2812 (44 U.S.C. 3501 *et seq.*))

[43 FR 29515, July 7, 1978, as amended at 47 FR 14696, Apr. 6, 1982; 60 FR 33722, June 29, 1995]

§ 43.3 Purpose and scope of this part.

This part sets forth the procedures for giving notice to the Secretary under section 103(g)(1) of the Act, for responding to such notices and for reviewing refusals by authorized representatives of the Secretary to issue citations or orders under section 103 (g)(1) or (g)(2). Specifically, Subpart B details the steps to be taken by a representative of miners or a miner in making a request for a special inspection and by the Secretary in processing and taking action on such a request under section 103(g)(1). Subpart C sets forth informal review procedures which a representative of miners or a miner may request under sections 103 (g)(1) and (g)(2) where no citation or order is issued under those sections.

Subpart B—Special Inspections

§ 43.4 Requirements for giving notice.

(a) A representative of miners or, where there is no such representative, a miner, who has reasonable grounds to believe that a violation of the act or a mandatory health or safety standard exists, or that an imminent danger exists, may obtain a special inspection by giving notice to the Secretary or any authorized representative of the Secretary of such violation or danger.

(b) Any such notice shall set forth the alleged violation or imminent danger and the location of such violation or danger and shall be reduced to a writing signed by the representative of miners or miner giving such notice.

(c) A copy of such written notice shall be provided to the operator or his agent by the Secretary or his authorized representative no later than the time that the inspection begins. In addition, if the notice indicates that an imminent danger exists, the operator or his agent shall be notified as quickly as possible of the alleged danger. The name of the person giving such notice and the names of any individual miners referred to therein shall not appear in the copy of the written notice or in a notification provided to the operator.

§ 43.5 Action by the Secretary.

(a) As soon as possible after the receipt of a notice of alleged violation or imminent danger under this subpart, the Secretary or his authorized representative shall make a special inspection to determine if a citation or withdrawal order should be issued, unless on the face of the notice, the condition complained of, even if it were found to exist, would clearly not constitute a violation or imminent danger.

(b) Where the Secretary or his authorized representative makes a special inspection under this subpart and finds a violation or imminent danger, a citation or withdrawal order, as appropriate, shall be issued.

§ 43.6 Notice of negative finding.

(a) If it is determined that a special inspection is not warranted, a written notice of negative finding shall be issued as soon as possible following such determination.

(b) If it is determined that an inspection is warranted and upon such inspection it is determined that neither a citation nor a withdrawal order should be issued for the alleged violation or imminent danger, a written notice of negative finding shall be issued by the authorized representative of the Secretary prior to leaving the mine premises.

(c) Any notice of negative finding issued under this part shall be issued to the representative of miners or miner seeking the special inspection and a copy shall be served upon the operator.

Subpart C—Informal Review

§ 43.7 Informal review upon written notice given to an inspector on the mine premises.

(a) A representative of miners or, where there is no such representative, a miner, who has reason to believe that a violation of the Act or a mandatory health or safety standard exists, or an imminent danger exists, may notify an authorized representative of the Secretary in writing prior to or during an inspection conducted by such representative of any violation of the Act or mandatory health or safety standard or of any imminent danger which he or she has reason to believe exists in the mine being inspected. Where the authorized representative or the Secretary refuses to issue a citation or order with respect to such alleged violation or imminent danger, the representative of miners or miner may obtain review of such refusal in accordance with paragraphs (b) through (d) of this section.

(b) A request for informal review shall be sent in writing to the appropriate district manager within 10 days of the date of the refusal to issue a citation or order and shall be accompanied by any supporting information the person requesting review wishes to submit.

(c) After receipt of the request for informal review, the district manager or his agent may hold, at his or her discretion, an informal conference where the person requesting review can present his views.

(d) After review of all written and oral statements submitted, the district manager may either affirm the refusal to issue a citation or order or may direct that a new inspection be conducted with respect to the alleged violation or imminent danger. The district manager shall furnish the person requesting review with a written statement of the reasons for his or her final disposition of the request as soon thereafter as possible. A copy of such statement shall be furnished the operator. The district manager's determination in the matter shall be final.

§ 43.8 Informal review upon issuance of a notice of negative finding.

A person to whom a notice of negative finding has been issued pursuant to § 43.6 of this part may request informal review of such finding in accordance with the provisions of § 43.7(b)–(d) of this subpart.

PART 44—RULES OF PRACTICE FOR PETITIONS FOR MODIFICATION OF MANDATORY SAFETY STANDARDS

Subpart A—General

Sec.
44.1 Scope and construction.
44.2 Definitions.
44.3 Parties.
44.4 Standard of evaluation of petitions; effect of petitions granted.
44.5 Notice of a granted petition for modification.
44.6 Service.
44.7 Filing.
44.8 Ex parte communication.
44.9 Posting of petition.

Subpart B—Initial Procedure for Petitions for Modification

44.10 Filing of petition; service.
44.11 Contents of petition.
44.12 Procedure for public notice of petition received.
44.13 Proposed decision.
44.14 Request for hearing.
44.15 Referral to Chief Administrative Law Judge.
44.16 Application for temporary relief; relief to give effect to the proposed decision and order.

Subpart C—Hearings

44.20 Designation of administrative law judge.
44.21 Filing and form of documents.
44.22 Administrative law judges; powers and duties.
44.23 Prehearing conferences.
44.24 Discovery.
44.25 Depositions.
44.26 Subpoenas; witness fees.
44.27 Consent findings and rules or orders.
44.28 Notice of hearing.
44.29 Motions.
44.30 Hearing procedures.
44.31 Proposed findings of fact, conclusions, and orders.
44.32 Initial decision.
44.33 Departmental review.
44.34 Transmission of record.
44.35 Decision of the Assistant Secretary.

Subpart D—Summary Decisions

44.40 Motion for summary decision.
44.41 Summary decision.

Subpart E—Effect of Initial Decision

44.50 Effect of appeal on initial decision.
44.51 Finality for purposes of judicial review.
44.52 Revocation of modification.
44.53 Amended modification.

AUTHORITY: 30 U.S.C. 957.

SOURCE: 43 FR 29518, July 7, 1978, unless otherwise noted.

Subpart A—General

§ 44.1 Scope and construction.

(a) The procedures and rules of practice set forth in this part shall govern petitions for modification of mandatory safety standards filed under section 101(c) of the Act.

(b) These rules shall be liberally construed to carry out the purpose of the Act by assuring adequate protection of miners and to secure just and prompt determination of all proceedings consistent with adequate consideration of the issues involved.

[43 FR 29518, July 7, 1978, as amended at 55 FR 53440, Dec. 28, 1990]

§ 44.2 Definitions.

As used in this part, unless the context clearly requires otherwise, the term—

(a) *Act* means the Federal Mine Safety and Health Act of 1977, Pub. L. 91–173, as amended by Pub. L. 95–164.

(b) *Secretary, operator, agent, person, miner,* and *coal or other mine,* have the meanings set forth in section 3 of the act.

(c) *Assistant Secretary* means the Assistant Secretary of Labor for Mine Safety and Health.

(d) *Administrative law judge* means an administrative law judge of the Department of Labor appointed under section 3105 of title 5 of the United States Code.

(e) *Representative of miners* means a person or organization designated by two or more miners to act as their representative for purposes of the act and who is in compliance with 30 CFR part 40.

[43 FR 29518, July 7, 1978, as amended at 55 FR 53440, Dec. 28, 1990]

§ 44.3 Parties.

Parties to proceedings under this part shall include the Mine Safety and Health Administration, the operator of the mine, and any representative of the miners in the affected mine. Any other person claiming a right of participation as an interested party in a proceeding may become a party upon application to the Assistant Secretary and the granting of such application. After referral of a petition to the Chief Administrative Law Judge, all applications for status as a party shall be made to the Chief Administrative Law Judge for his disposition.

§ 44.4 Standard of evaluation of petitions; effect of petitions granted.

(a) A petition for modification of application of a mandatory safety standard may be granted upon a determination that—

(1) An alternative method of achieving the result of the standard exists that will at all times guarantee no less than the same measure of protection afforded by the standard, or

(2) Application of the standard will result in a diminution of safety to the miners.

(b) Except as may be provided in § 44.16 for relief to give effect to a proposed decision and order, a decision of an Administrator or an administrative law judge granting or denying a petition for modification shall not be effective until time for appeal has expired under § 44.14 or § 44.33, as appropriate.

(c) All petitions for modification granted pursuant to this part shall have only future effect: *Provided,* That the granting of the modification under this part shall be considered as a factor in the resolution of any enforcement action previously initiated for claimed violation of the subsequently modified mandatory safety standard. Orders granting petitions for modification may contain special terms and conditions to assure adequate protection to miners. The modification, together with any conditions, shall have the same effect as a mandatory safety standard.

[43 FR 29518, July 7, 1978, as amended at 55 FR 53440, Dec. 28, 1990]

§ 44.5 Notice of a granted petition for modification.

(a) Every final action granting a petition for modification under this part shall be published in the FEDERAL REGISTER. Every such final action published shall specify the statutory grounds upon which the modification is based and a summary of the facts which warranted the modification.

(b) Every final action or a summary thereof granting a petition for modification under this part shall be posted by the operator on the mine bulletin board at the affected mine and shall remain posted as long as the modification is effective. If a summary of the final action is posted on the mine bulletin board, a copy of the full decision shall be kept at the affected mine office and made available to the miners.

§ 44.6 Service.

(a) Copies of all documents filed in any proceeding described in this part and copies of all notices pertinent to such proceeding shall be served by the filing party on all other persons made parties to the proceeding under § 44.3. If a request for hearing has been filed by any party, a copy of all subsequent documents filed shall be served upon the Mine Safety and Health Administration through its representative, the Office of the Solicitor, Department of Labor.

(b) All documents filed subsequent to a petition for modification may be served personally or by first class mail to the last known address of the party. Service may also be completed by telecopier or other electronic means.

(c) Whenever a party is represented by an attorney who has signed any document filed on behalf of such party or otherwise entered an appearance on behalf of such party, service thereafter shall be made upon the attorney.

(d) Any party filing a petition for modification under these rules shall file proof of service in the form of a return receipt where service is by registered or certified mail or an acknowledgment by the party served or a verified return where service is made personally. A certificate of service shall accompany all other documents filed by a party under these rules.

(e) Service by mail shall be complete upon mailing. Service by telecopier or other electronic means shall be complete upon receipt.

(f) Whenever a party has the right to do some act within a prescribed period after the service of a document or other material upon the party and the document or other material is served upon the party by mail, 5 days shall be added to the prescribed period: *Provided*, that specific provisions may, for good cause, be made otherwise by an order of an administrative law judge or the Assistant Secretary in a particular proceeding pending before that person.

[43 FR 29518, July 7, 1978, as amended at 55 FR 53440, Dec. 28, 1990]

§ 44.7 Filing.

For purposes of this part, a petition, request for hearing, notice of appeal, or other document shall be considered to be filed when received, or when mailed by certified mail, return receipt requested. Such documents may be filed by telecopier or other electronic means.

[55 FR 53440, Dec. 28, 1990]

§ 44.8 Ex parte communication.

There shall be no ex parte communication with respect to the merits of any case not concluded between the Assistant Secretary or the administrative law judge, including any employee or agent of the Assistant Secretary or of the administrative law judge, and any of the parties, intervenors, representatives, or other interested parties.

[55 FR 53440, Dec. 28, 1990]

§ 44.9 Posting of petition.

An operator of a mine for which there is no representative of miners shall post a copy of each petition concerning the mine on the mine bulletin board and shall maintain the posting until a ruling on the petition becomes final.

Subpart B—Initial Procedure for Petitions for Modification

§ 44.10 Filing of petition; service.

A petition for modification of the application of a mandatory safety standard under section 101(c) of the Act may be filed only by the operator of the affected mine or any representative of the miners at such mine. All petitions must be in writing and must be filed with the Director, Office of Standards, Regulations, and Variances, Mine Safety and Health Administration, 201 12th Street South, Arlington, VA 22202–5452. If the petition is filed by a mine operator, a copy of the petition shall be served by the mine operator upon a representative of miners at the affected mine. If the petition is filed by a representative of the miners, a copy of the petition shall be served by the representative of miners upon the mine operator. Service shall be accomplished personally or by registered or certified mail, return receipt requested.

[55 FR 53440, Dec. 28, 1990, as amended at 67 FR 38384, June 4, 2002; 80 FR 52985, Sept. 2, 2015]

§ 44.11 Contents of petition.

(a) A petition for modification filed pursuant to § 44.10 shall contain:

(1) The name and address of the petitioner.

(2) The mailing address and mine identification number of the mine or mines affected.

(3) The mandatory safety standard to which the petition is directed.

(4) A concise statement of the modification requested, and whether the petitioner proposes to establish an alternate method in lieu of the mandatory safety standard or alleges that application of the standard will result in diminution of safety to the miners affected or requests relief based on both grounds.

(5) A detailed statement of the facts the petitioner would show to establish the grounds upon which it is claimed a modification is warranted.

(6) Identification of any representative of the miners at the affected mine, if the petitioner is a mine operator.

(b) A petition for modification shall not include a request for modification of the application of more than one mandatory safety standard. A petition for modification shall not request relief for more than one operator. However, an operator may file a petition for modification pertaining to more than one mine where it can be shown that identical issues of law and fact exist as to the petition for each mine.

§ 44.12 Procedure for public notice of petition received.

(a) Within 15 days from the filing of a petition for modification, the Mine Safety and Health Administration will give notice of the petition to each known representative of miners or the operator of the affected mine, as appropriate, and shall publish notice of the petition in the FEDERAL REGISTER.

(b) The FEDERAL REGISTER notice shall contain a statement that the petition has been filed, identify the petitioner and the mine or mines to which the petition relates, cite the mandatory safety standard for which modification is sought, and describe the requested relief.

(c) All such notices shall advise interested parties that they may, within 30 days from the date of publication in the FEDERAL REGISTER, in writing, comment upon or provide information relative to the proposed modification.

[43 FR 29518, July 7, 1978, as amended at 55 FR 53440, Dec. 28, 1990]

§ 44.13 Proposed decision.

(a) Upon receipt of a petition for modification, the Mine Safety and Health Administration shall cause an investigation to be made as to the merits of the petition. Any party may request that the investigation of the petition for modification be expedited, or that the time period for investigating the petition be extended. Such requests shall be granted in the discretion of the Administrator upon good cause shown.

(b) As soon as is practicable after the investigation is completed, the appropriate Administrator shall make a proposed decision and order, which shall be served upon all parties to the proceeding. The proposed decision shall become final upon the 30th day after service thereof, unless a request for hearing has been filed with the appropriate Administrator, as provided in § 44.14 of this part.

(c) Service of the proposed decision is complete upon mailing.

[55 FR 53440, Dec. 28, 1990]

§ 44.14 Request for hearing.

A request for hearing filed in accordance with § 44.13 of this part must be filed within 30 days after service of the proposed decision and shall include:

(a) A concise summary of position on the issues of fact or law desired to be raised by the party requesting the hearing, including specific objections to the proposed decision. A party other than petitioner who has requested a hearing shall also comment upon all issues of fact or law presented in the petition, and

(b) An indication of a desired hearing site.

(c) *Partial appeal.* (1) If the Administrator has issued a proposed decision and order granting the requested modification, a request for hearing on the proposed decision and order may be made by any party based upon objection to one or more of the terms and conditions of the Administrator's proposed decision and order. If such a request for hearing is made, the request should specify which of the terms and conditions should be the subject of the hearing.

(2) During the pendency of the partial appeal, the proposed decision and order of the Administrator will become final on the 30th day after service thereof, unless a request for hearing on the proposed decision and order is filed in accordance with paragraph (a) of this section by any other party. The decision and order will remain in effect as proposed by the Administrator until the terms and conditions for which the hearing was requested are modified, affirmed, or set aside by a final order of the presiding administrative law judge or the Assistant Secretary. The presiding administrative law judge shall take such action upon a determination of whether—

(i) The terms and conditions for which the hearing was requested are necessary to ensure that the alternative method of achieving the result of the standard will at all times guarantee to the miners at the mine at least the same measure of protection afforded to the miners at the mine by such standard; or

(ii) In the case of a petition involving a finding by the Administrator of a diminution of safety to the miners caused by application of the standard at the mine, whether the terms and conditions for which the hearing was requested are necessary to provide equivalent protection to the miners at the mine from the hazard against which the standard is directed.

[43 FR 29518, July 7, 1978, as amended at 55 FR 53441, Dec. 28, 1990]

§ 44.15 Referral to Chief Administrative Law Judge.

Upon receipt of a request for hearing as provided in § 44.14 of this part, the Administrator shall, within 5 days, refer to the Chief Administrative Law Judge the original petition, the proposed decision and order, all information upon which the proposed decision was based, any written request for a hearing on the petition filed, any other written comments or information received and considered in making the proposed decision. The MSHA investigation report shall be made part of the record on the petition.

[55 FR 53441, Dec. 28, 1990]

§ 44.16 Application for temporary relief; relief to give effect to the proposed decision and order.

(a) *Time for filing.* An application for temporary relief from enforcement of a mandatory standard may be filed at any time before a proposed decision and order is issued on a petition for modification and shall be served upon all parties to the proceeding.

(b) *With whom filed.* The application shall be filed with and decided by the appropriate Administrator.

(c) *Investigation and decision.* Upon receipt of an application for temporary relief, the Administrator shall cause an investigation to be made as to the merits of the application. As soon thereafter as practicable, but in no event greater than 60 days from filing of the application, the Administrator shall issue a decision. If the Administrator does not issue a decision within 60 days of filing of the application, the application shall be deemed to be denied.

(d) *Contents of application.* An application for temporary relief shall comply with applicable general requirements of this part, state the specific relief requested, and include specific evidence showing how the applicant meets the criteria set forth in paragraph (e) of this section.

(e) *Criteria.* Before temporary relief is granted, the applicant must clearly show that—

(1) The application was filed in good faith;

(2) The requested relief will not adversely affect the health or safety of miners in the affected mine;

(3) An identifiable hazard to miners exists in the mine which is caused by application of the standard at the mine;

(4) Other means will be used to reasonably address the hazard against which the original standard was designed to protect; and

(5) Compliance with the standard while the petition for modification is pending will expose miners to the identifiable hazard upon which the application is based.

(f) *Response.* All parties to the proceeding in which an application for temporary relief has been filed shall have 15 days from receipt of the application to file a written response with the Administrator.

(g) *Evidence.* An application for temporary relief or a response to such an application may be supported by affidavits or other evidentiary matter.

(h) *Findings.* Temporary relief may be granted by the Administrator upon a finding that application of the standard at the mine will result in a diminution of safety to the miners at such mine.

(i) *Appeal to the Office of the Administrative Law Judges.* If the application for temporary relief is granted by the Administrator, any other party may request a hearing within 15 days of the Administrator's decision. The request shall be addressed to the Administrator and shall be referred by the Administrator, along with the petition for modification, to the Chief Administrative Law Judge in accordance with § 44.15. The hearing and decision of the presiding administrative law judge shall be in accordance with subparts C through E of this part. After referral of the petition for modification and application for temporary relief, no further decision shall be rendered by the Administrator.

(j) *Duration of relief.* An order granting temporary relief shall be effective until superseded by the Administrator's proposed decision and order, unless a hearing is requested in accordance with paragraph (i) of this section. If such hearing is requested, the temporary relief shall remain in effect until modified, affirmed or set aside by the presiding administrative law judge.

Mine Safety and Health Admin., Labor § 44.22

In no case, however, shall the Administrator's order remain in effect for more than one year, unless renewed or affirmed by the presiding administrative law judge.

(k) *Application for relief to give effect to the proposed decision and order.* At any time following the proposed decision and order of the Administrator on the accompanying petition for modification, any party may request relief to give effect to the proposed decision and order until it becomes final.

(l) An application for relief under paragraph (k) shall be filed with the Administrator and shall include a good faith representation that no party is expected to contest the granting of the petition for modification.

(m) A decision to grant relief requested under paragraph (k) will take effect on the seventh day following the decision. If a request for hearing on the proposed decision and order is filed in accordance with § 44.14 prior to the seventh day following the granting of such relief, the relief will not become effective. If such request for hearing on the proposed decision and order is filed after relief becomes effective, the relief will expire immediately.

[55 FR 53441, Dec. 28, 1990]

Subpart C—Hearings

§ 44.20 Designation of administrative law judge.

Within 5 days after receipt of a referral of a request for hearing in a petition for modification proceeding, the Chief Administrative Law Judge shall designate an administrative law judge appointed under section 3105 of Title 5 of the United States Code to preside over the hearing.

[55 FR 53442, Dec. 28, 1990]

§ 44.21 Filing and form of documents.

(a) *Where to file.* After a petition has been referred to the Office of the Chief Administrative Law Judge, the parties will be notified of the name and address of the administrative law judge assigned to the case. All further documents shall be filed with the administrative law judge at the address designated or with the Chief Administrative Law Judge, if the assignment has not been made. While the petition is before the Assistant Secretary at any stage of the proceeding, all documents should be filed with the Assistant Secretary of Labor for Mine Safety and Health, 201 12th Street South, Arlington, VA 22202–5452.

(b) *Caption, title and signature.* (1) The documents filed in any proceeding under this part shall be captioned in the name of the operator of the mine to which the proceeding relates and in the name of the mine or mines affected. After a docket number has been assigned to the proceeding by the Office of the Chief Administrative Law Judge, the caption shall contain such docket number.

(2) After the caption each such document shall contain a title which shall be descriptive of the document and which shall identify the party by whom the document is submitted.

(3) The original of all documents filed shall be signed at the end by the party submitting the document or, if the party is represented by an attorney, by such attorney. The address of the party or the attorney shall appear beneath the signature.

[43 FR 29518, July 7, 1978, as amended at 67 FR 38384, June 4, 2002; 80 FR 52985, Sept. 2, 2015]

§ 44.22 Administrative law judges; powers and duties.

(a) *Powers.* An administrative law judge designated to preside over a hearing shall have all powers necessary or appropriate to conduct a fair, full, and impartial hearing, including the following:

(1) To administer oaths and affirmations;

(2) To issue subpoenas on his own motion or upon written application of a party;

(3) To rule upon offers of proof and receive relevant evidence;

(4) To take depositions or have depositions taken when the ends of justice would be served;

(5) To provide for discovery and determine its scope;

(6) To regulate the course of the hearing and the conduct of parties and their counsel;

(7) To consider and rule upon procedural requests;

(8) To hold conferences for settlement or simplification of issues by consent of the parties;

(9) To make decisions in accordance with the Act, this part, and section 557 of title 5 of the United States Code; and

(10) To take any other appropriate action authorized by this part, section 556 of title 5 of the United States Code, or the Act.

(b) *Disqualification.* (1) When an administrative law judge deems himself disqualified to preside over a particular hearing, he shall withdraw therefrom by notice on the record directed to the Chief Administrative Law Judge.

(2) Any party who deems an administrative law judge for any reason to be disqualified to preside or continue to preside over a particular hearing, may file with the Chief Administrative Law Judge of the Department of Labor a motion to be supported by affidavits setting forth the alleged grounds for disqualification. The Chief Administrative Law Judge shall rule upon the motion.

(c) *Contumacious conduct; failure or refusal to appear or obey rulings of a presiding administrative law judge.* (1) Contumacious conduct at any hearing before the administrative law judge shall be grounds for exclusion from the hearing.

(2) If a witness or party refuses to answer a question after being directed to do so or refuses to obey an order to provide or permit discovery, the administrative law judge may make such orders with regard to the refusal as are just and appropriate, including an order denying the application of a petitioner or regulating the contents of the record of the hearing.

(d) *Referral to Federal Rules of Civil Procedure and Evidence.* On any procedural question not regulated by this part, the act, or the Administrative Procedure Act, an administrative law judge shall be guided to the extent practicable by any pertinent provisions of the Federal Rules of Civil Procedure or Federal Rules of Evidence, as appropriate.

(e) *Remand.* The presiding administrative law judge shall be authorized to remand the petition for modification proceeding to the appropriate Administrator based upon new evidence which was not available to the Administrator and which may have materially affected the Administrator's proposed decision and order. Remand may be upon the judge's own motion or the motion of any party, and shall be granted in the discretion of the presiding administrative law judge.

[43 FR 29518, July 7, 1978, as amended at 55 FR 53442, Dec. 28, 1990]

§ 44.23 Prehearing conferences.

(a) *Convening a conference.* Upon his own motion or the motion of a party, the administrative law judge may direct the parties or their counsel to meet with him for a conference to consider:

(1) Simplification of issues;

(2) Necessity or desirability of amendments to documents for clarification, simplification, or limitation;

(3) Stipulations and admissions of facts;

(4) Limitation of the number of parties and expert witnesses; and

(5) Such other matters as may tend to expedite the disposition of the proceeding and assure a just conclusion thereof.

(b) *Record of conference.* The administrative law judge may, where appropriate, issue an order which recites the action taken at the conference, amendments allowed to any filed documents, and agreements made between the parties as to any of the matters considered. The order shall limit the issues for hearing to those not disposed of by admissions or agreements. Such an order controls the subsequent course of the hearing, unless modified at the hearing to prevent manifest injustice.

§ 44.24 Discovery.

Parties shall be governed in their conduct of discovery by appropriate provisions of the Federal Rules of Civil Procedure, except as provided in § 44.25 of this part. After consultation with the parties, the administrative law judge shall prescribe a time of not more than 45 days to complete discovery. Alternative periods of time for discovery may be prescribed by the presiding administrative law judge upon the request of any party. As soon as is practicable after completion of discovery, the administrative law judge shall schedule a hearing in accordance with § 44.28 of this part.

[55 FR 53442, Dec. 28, 1990]

§ 44.25 Depositions.

(a) *Purpose.* For reasons of unavailability or for purpose of discovery, the testimony of any witness may be taken by deposition.

(b) *Form.* Depositions may be taken before any person having the power to administer oaths. Each witness testifying upon deposition shall be sworn, and the parties not calling him shall have the right to cross-examine him. Questions propounded and answers thereto, together with all objections made, shall be reduced to writing, read to or by the witness, subscribed by him, and certified by the officer before whom the deposition is taken. The officer shall send copies by registered mail to the Chief Administrative Law Judge or the presiding administrative law judge.

§ 44.26 Subpoenas; witness fees.

(a) Except as provided in paragraph (b) of this section, the Chief Administrative Law Judge or the presiding administrative law judge, as appropriate, shall issue subpoenas upon written application of a party requiring attendance of witnesses and production of relevant papers, books, documents, or tangible things in their possession and under their control. A subpoena may be served by any person who is not a party and is not less than 18 years of age, and the original subpoena bearing a certificate of service shall be filed with the administrative law judge. A witness may be required to attend a deposition or hearing at a place not more than 100 miles from the place of service.

(b) If a party's written application for subpoena is submitted 3 working days or less before the hearing to which it relates, a subpoena shall issue at the discretion of the Chief Administrative Law Judge or presiding administrative law judge, as appropriate.

(c) Any person served with a subpoena may move in writing to revoke or modify the subpoena. All motions to revoke or modify shall be served on the party at whose request the subpoena was issued. The administrative law judge shall revoke or modify the subpoena if in his opinion the evidence required to be produced does not relate to any matter under investigation or in question in the proceedings; the subpoena does not describe with sufficient particularity the evidence required to be produced; or if for any other reason, sufficient in law, the subpoena is found to be invalid or unreasonable. The administrative law judge shall make a simple statement of procedural or other grounds for the ruling on the motion to revoke or modify. The motion to revoke or modify, any answer filed thereto, and any ruling thereon shall become a part of the record.

(d) Witnesses subpoenaed by any party shall be paid the same fees for attendance and mileage as are paid in the District Courts of the United States. The fees shall be paid by the party at whose instance the witness appears.

§ 44.27 Consent findings and rules or orders.

(a) *General.* At any time after a request for hearing is filed in accordance with § 44.14, a reasonable opportunity may be afforded to permit negotiation by the parties of an agreement containing consent findings and a rule or order disposing of the whole or any part of the proceedings. Allowance of such opportunity and the duration thereof shall be in the discretion of the Chief Administrative Law Judge, if no administrative law judge has been assigned, or of the presiding administrative law judge. In deciding whether to afford such an opportunity, the administrative law judge shall consider the nature of the proceeding, requirements of the public interest, representations of the parties, and probability of an agreement which will result in a just disposition of the issues involved.

(b) *Contents.* Any agreement containing consent findings and rule or order disposing of a proceeding shall also provide:

(1) That the rule or order shall have the same effect as if made after a full hearing;

(2) That the record on which any rule or order may be based shall consist of the petition and agreement, and all other pertinent information, including: any request for hearing on the petition; the investigation report; discovery;

§ 44.28

motions and requests, filed in written form and rulings thereon; any documents or papers filed in connection with prehearing conferences; and, if a hearing has been held, the transcript of testimony and any proposed findings, conclusions, rules or orders, and supporting reasons as may have been filed.

(3) A waiver of further procedural steps before the administrative law judge and Assistant Secretary; and

(4) A waiver of any right to challenge or contest the validity of the findings and rule or order made in accordance with the agreement.

(c) *Submission.* On or before expiration of the time granted for negotiations, the parties or their counsel may:

(1) Submit the proposed agreement to the Chief Administrative Law Judge or presiding administrative law judge, as appropriate, for his consideration; or

(2) Inform the Chief Administrative Law Judge or presiding administrative law judge, as appropriate, that agreement cannot be reached.

(d) *Disposition.* In the event an agreement containing consent findings and rule or order is submitted within the time allowed, the Chief Administrative Law Judge or presiding administrative law judge, as appropriate, may accept the agreement by issuing his decision based upon the agreed findings.

[43 FR 29518, July 7, 1978, as amended at 55 FR 53442, Dec. 28, 1990]

§ 44.28 Notice of hearing.

(a) The administrative law judge shall fix a place and date for the hearing and notify all parties at least 30 days in advance of the date set, unless at least one party requests and all parties consent to an earlier date, or the hearing date has been otherwise advanced in accordance with this part. The notice shall include:

(1) The time, place, and nature of the hearing; and

(2) The legal authority under which the hearing is to be held.

(b) In accordance with the provisions of section 554 of title 5 of the United States Code, a party may move for transfer of a hearing on the basis of convenience to parties and witnesses. Such motion should be filed with the administrative law judge assigned to the case.

§ 44.29 Motions.

Each motion filed shall be in writing and shall contain a short and plain statement of the grounds upon which it is based. A statement in opposition to the motion may be filed by any party within 10 days after the date of service. The administrative law judge may permit oral motions during proceedings.

§ 44.30 Hearing procedures.

(a) *Order of proceeding.* Except as may be ordered otherwise by the administrative law judge, the petitioner shall proceed first at a hearing.

(b) *Burden of proof.* The petitioner shall have the burden of proving his case by a preponderance of the evidence.

(c) *Evidence*—(1) *Admissibility.* A party shall be entitled to present its case or defense by oral or documentary evidence, to submit rebuttal evidence, and to conduct such cross-examination as may be required for full and true disclosure of the facts. Any oral or documentary evidence may be received, but the administrative law judge shall exclude evidence which is irrelevant, immaterial, or unduly repetitious.

(2) *Testimony of witnesses.* The testimony of a witness shall be upon oath or affirmation administered by the administrative law judge.

(3) *Objections.* If a party objects to admission or rejection of any evidence, limitation of the scope of any examination or cross-examination, or failure to limit such scope, he shall state briefly the grounds for such objection. Rulings on such objections shall appear in the record.

(4) *Exceptions.* Formal exception to an adverse ruling is not required.

(d) *Official notice.* Official notice may be taken of any material fact not appearing in evidence in the record, which is among the traditional matters of judicial notice or concerning which the Department of Labor by reason of its functions is presumed to be expert: *Provided,* That the parties shall be given adequate notice at the hearing or by reference in the presiding administrative law judge's decision of the matters so noticed and shall be given adequate opportunity to show the contrary.

(e) *Transcript.* Copies of the transcript of the hearing may be obtained by the parties upon written application filed with the reporter and payment of fees at the rate provided in the agreement with the reporter.

§ 44.31 Proposed findings of fact, conclusions, and orders.

After consultation with the parties, the administrative law judge may prescribe a time period of 30 days within which each party may file proposed findings of fact, conclusions of law, and rule or order, together with a supporting brief expressing the reasons for such proposals. Such time may be expedited or extended upon request and at the discretion of the Administrative Law Judge. Proposals and briefs shall be served on all other parties and shall refer to all portions of the record and to all authorities relied upon in support of each proposal.

[55 FR 53442, Dec. 28, 1990]

§ 44.32 Initial decision.

(a) Within 60 days after the time allowed for the filing of proposed findings of fact and conclusions of law, the administrative law judge shall make and serve upon each party a decision, which shall become final upon the 30th day after service thereof, unless an appeal is filed as provided in § 44.33 of this part. After consultation with the parties, the administrative law judge may expedite or extend the time for issuing the decision. The decision of the administrative law judge shall include:

(1) A statement of findings of fact and conclusions of law, with reasons therefor, upon each material issue of fact, law, or discretion presented on the record; and

(2) The appropriate rule, order, relief, or denial thereof.

(b) The decision of the administrative law judge shall be based upon a consideration of the whole record and shall state all facts officially noticed and relied upon. It shall be made on the basis of a preponderance of reliable and probative evidence.

[43 FR 29518, July 7, 1978, as amended at 55 FR 53442, Dec. 28, 1990]

§ 44.33 Departmental review.

(a) *Notice of appeal.* Any party may appeal from the initial decision of the administrative law judge by filing with the Assistant Secretary a notice of appeal within 30 days after service of the initial decision. The Assistant Secretary may consolidate related appeals. Copies of a notice of appeal shall be served on all parties to the proceeding in accordance with § 44.6 of this part.

(b) *Statement of objections.* Within 20 days after filing the notice of appeal, the appellant shall file his statement of objections to the decision of the administrative law judge and serve copies on all other parties to the proceeding. The statement shall refer to the specific findings of fact, conclusions of law, or terms of the order objected to in the initial decision. Where any objection is based upon evidence of record, the objection need not be considered by the Assistant Secretary if specific record citations to the pertinent evidence are not contained in the statement of objections.

(c) *Responding statements.* Within 20 days after service of the statement of objections, any other party to the proceeding may file a statement in response.

[43 FR 29518, July 7, 1978, as amended at 55 FR 53442, Dec. 28, 1990]

§ 44.34 Transmission of record.

If an appeal is filed, the administrative law judge shall, as soon thereafter as is practicable, transmit the record of the proceeding to the Assistant Secretary for review. The record shall include: the petition; the MSHA investigation report; any request for hearing on the petition; the transcript of testimony taken at the hearing, together with exhibits admitted in evidence; any documents or papers filed in connection with prehearing conferences; such proposed findings of fact, conclusions of law, rules or orders, and supporting reasons, as may have been filed; and the administrative law judge's decision.

[55 FR 53442, Dec. 28, 1990]

§ 44.35 Decision of the Assistant Secretary.

Appeals from a decision rendered pursuant to § 44.32 of this part shall be decided by the Assistant Secretary within 120 days after the time for filing responding statements under § 44.33 of this part. The Assistant Secretary's decision shall be based upon consideration of the entire record of the proceedings transmitted, together with the statements submitted by the parties. The decision may affirm, modify, or set aside, in whole or part, the findings, conclusions, and rule or order contained in the decision of the presiding administrative law judge and shall include a statement of reasons for the action taken. The Assistant Secretary may also remand the petition to the administrative law judge for additional legal or factual determinations. Any party may request that the time for the Assistant Secretary's decision be expedited. Such requests shall be granted in the discretion of the Assistant Secretary.

[55 FR 53442, Dec. 28, 1990]

Subpart D—Summary Decisions

§ 44.40 Motion for summary decision.

(a) Any party may, at least 20 days before the date fixed for any hearing under Subpart C of this part, move with or without supporting affidavits for a summary decision on all or any part of the proceeding. Any other party may, within 10 days after service of the motion, serve opposing affidavits or countermove for summary decision. The administrative law judge may set the matter for argument and call for submission of briefs.

(b) Filing of any documents under paragraph (a) of this section shall be with the administrative law judge, and copies of such documents shall be served in accordance with § 44.6 of this part.

(c) Any affidavits submitted with the motion shall set forth such facts as would be admissible in evidence in a proceeding subject to 5 U.S.C. 556 and 557 and shall show affirmatively that the affiant is competent to testify to the matters stated therein. When a motion for summary decision is made and supported as provided in this section, a party opposing the motion may not rest upon the mere allegations or denials of such pleading. Such response must set forth specific facts showing that there is a genuine issue of fact for the hearing.

(d) The administrative law judge may grant the motion if the pleadings, affidavits, material obtained by discovery or otherwise, or matters officially noticed show that there is no genuine issue as to any material fact and a party is entitled to summary decision. The administrative law judge may deny the motion whenever the moving party denies access to information by means of discovery to a party opposing the motion.

(e) The denial of all or part of a motion for summary decision by the administrative law judge shall not be subject to interlocutory appeal to the Assistant Secretary unless the administrative law judge certifies in writing that (1) the ruling involves an important question of law or policy as to which there are substantial grounds for difference of opinion, and (2) an immediate appeal from the ruling may materially advance termination of the proceeding. The allowance of an interlocutory appeal shall not stay the proceedings before the administrative law judge unless ordered by the Assistant Secretary.

§ 44.41 Summary decision.

(a) *No genuine issue of material fact.* (1) Where no genuine issue of a material fact is found to have been raised, the administrative law judge may issue an initial decision to become final 30 days after service thereof, unless, within such time, any party has filed an appeal with the Assistant Secretary. Thereafter, the Assistant Secretary, after consideration of the entire record, may issue a final decision.

(2) An initial decision and a final decision made under this paragraph shall include a statement of—

(i) Findings and conclusions, and the reasons therefor, on all issues presented; and

(ii) Any terms and conditions of the rule or order.

(3) A copy of an initial decision and final decision under this paragraph shall be served on each party.

(b) *Hearings on issues of fact.* Where a genuine question of material fact is raised, the administrative law judge shall, and in any other case may, set the case for an evidentiary hearing in accordance with Subpart C of this part.

Subpart E—Effect of Initial Decision

§ 44.50 Effect of appeal on initial decision.

Except as provided in § 44.14(c), a proposed decision and order of an Administrator is not operative pending appeal to an administrative law judge, and a decision of an administrative law judge is not operative pending appeal to the Assistant Secretary.

[55 FR 53443, Dec. 28, 1990]

§ 44.51 Finality for purposes of judicial review.

Only a decision by the Assistant Secretary shall be deemed final agency action for purposes of judicial review. A decision by an Administrator or administrative law judge which becomes final for lack of appeal is not deemed final agency action for purposes of 5 U.S.C. 704.

§ 44.52 Revocation of modification.

(a) *Petition for revocation.* Any party to a proceeding under this part in which a petition for modification of a mandatory safety standard was granted by an Administrator, administrative law judge, or the Assistant Secretary may petition that the modification be revoked. Such petition shall be filed with the Chief Administrative Law Judge for disposition.

(b) *Revocation by the Administrator.* The appropriate Administrator may propose to revoke a modification previously granted by the Administrator, an administrative law judge, or the Assistant Secretary, by issuing a proposed decision and order revoking the modification. Such proposed revocation and a statement of reasons supporting the proposal must be served upon all parties to the proceeding, and shall become final on the 30th day after service thereof unless a hearing is requested in accordance with § 44.14.

(c) Revocation of a granted modification must be based upon a change in circumstances or because findings which originally supported the modification are no longer valid.

(d) Disposition of the revocation shall be subject to all procedures of subparts C through E of this part.

[55 FR 53443, Dec. 28, 1990]

§ 44.53 Amended modification.

(a) The Administrator may propose to revise the terms and conditions of a granted modification by issuing an amended proposed decision and order, along with a statement of reasons for the amended proposed decision and order, when one or both of the following occurs:

(1) A change in circumstances which originally supported the terms and conditions of the modification.

(2) The Administrator determines that findings which originally supported the terms and conditions of the modification are no longer valid.

(b) The Administrator's amended proposed decision and order shall be served upon all parties to the proceeding and shall become final upon the 30th day after service thereof, unless a request for hearing on the proposed amendments is filed under § 44.14. If a request for hearing is filed, the amended proposed decision and order shall be subject to all procedures of subparts C through E of this part as if it were a proposed decision and order of the Administrator issued in accordance with § 44.13. The original modification shall remain in effect until superseded by a final amended modification.

(c) In cases where the original decision and order was based upon an alternative method of achieving the result of the standard, the amended decision and order shall at all times provide to miners at the mine at least the same measure of protection afforded to the miners at the mine by such standard. In cases where the original decision and order was based upon a diminution of safety to the miners resulting from application of the standard at such time, the amended decision and order shall not reduce the protection afforded miners by the original decision and order.

[55 FR 53443, Dec. 28, 1990]

PART 45—INDEPENDENT CONTRACTORS

Sec.
45.1 Scope and purpose.
45.2 Definitions.
45.3 Identification of independent contractors.
45.4 Independent contractor register.
45.5 Service of documents; independent contractors.
45.6 Address of record and telephone number; independent contractors.

AUTHORITY: 30 U.S.C. 802(d), 957.

SOURCE: 45 FR 44496, July 1, 1980, unless otherwise noted.

§ 45.1 Scope and purpose.

This part sets forth information requirements and procedures for independent contractors to obtain an MSHA identification number and procedures for service of documents upon independent contractors. Production-operators are required to maintain certain information for each independent contractor at the mine. The purpose of this rule is to facilitate implementation of MSHA's enforcement policy of holding independent contractors responsible for violations committed by them and their employees.

§ 45.2 Definitions.

As used in this part:

(a) *Act* means the Federal Mine Safety and Health Act of 1977, Pub. L. 91-173, as amended by Pub. L. 95-164;

(b) *District Manager* means the District Manager of the Mine Safety and Health Administration District in which the independent contractor is located;

(c) *Independent contractor* means any person, partnership, corporation, subsidiary of a corporation, firm, association or other organization that contracts to perform services or construction at a mine; and,

(d) *Production-operator* means any owner, lessee, or other person who operates, controls or supervises a coal or other mine.

§ 45.3 Identification of independent contractors.

(a) Any independent contractor may obtain a permanent MSHA identification number. To obtain an identification number, an independent contractor shall submit to the District Manager in writing the following information:

(1) The trade name and business address of the independent contractor;

(2) An address of record for service of documents;

(3) A telephone number at which the independent contractor can be contacted during regular business hours; and

(4) The estimated annual hours worked on mine property by the independent contractor in the previous calendar year, or in the instance of a business operating less than one full calendar year, prorated to an annual basis.

(Pub. L. No. 96-511, 94 Stat. 2812 (44 U.S.C. 3501 et seq.))

[45 FR 44496, July 1, 1980, as amended at 47 FR 14696, Apr. 6, 1982; 60 FR 33722, June 29, 1995]

§ 45.4 Independent contractor register.

(a) Each independent contractor shall provide the production-operator in writing the following information:

(1) The independent contractor's trade name, business address and business telephone number;

(2) A description of the nature of the work to be performed by the independent contractor and where at the mine the work is to be performed;

(3) The independent contractor's MSHA identification number, if any; and

(4) The independent contractor's address of record for service of citations, or other documents involving the independent contractor.

(b) Each production-operator shall maintain in writing at the mine the information required by paragraph (a) of this section for each independent contractor at the mine. The production-operator shall make this information available to any authorized representative of the Secretary upon request.

§ 45.5 Service of documents; independent contractors.

Service of citations, orders and other documents upon independent contractors shall be completed upon delivery to the independent contractor or mailing to the independent contractor's address of record.

§ 45.6 Address of record and telephone number; independent contractors.

(a) The address and telephone number required under this part shall be the independent contractor's official address and telephone number for purposes of the Act. Service of documents upon independent contractors may be proved by a Post Office return receipt showing that the documents were delivered to the address of record or that the documents could not be delivered to the address of record because the independent contractor is no longer at that address and has established no forwarding address; because delivery was not accepted at that address; or because no such address exists. Independent contractors may request service by delivery to another appropriate address of record provided by the independent contractor. The telephone number required under this part will be used in connection with the proposed penalty assessment procedures in 30 CFR part 100.

SUBCHAPTER H—EDUCATION AND TRAINING

PART 46—TRAINING AND RETRAINING OF MINERS ENGAGED IN SHELL DREDGING OR EMPLOYED AT SAND, GRAVEL, SURFACE STONE, SURFACE CLAY, COLLOIDAL PHOSPHATE, OR SURFACE LIMESTONE MINES.

Sec.
46.1 Scope.
46.2 Definitions.
46.3 Training plans.
46.4 Training plan implementation.
46.5 New miner training.
46.6 Newly hired experienced miner training.
46.7 New task training.
46.8 Annual refresher training.
46.9 Records of training.
46.10 Compensation for training.
46.11 Site-specific hazard awareness training.
46.12 Responsibility for independent contractor training.

AUTHORITY: 30 U.S.C. 811, 825.

SOURCE: 64 FR 53130, Sept. 30, 1999, unless otherwise noted.

§ 46.1 Scope.

The provisions of this part set forth the mandatory requirements for training and retraining miners and other persons at shell dredging, sand, gravel, surface stone, surface clay, colloidal phosphate, and surface limestone mines.

§ 46.2 Definitions.

The following definitions apply in this part:

(a) *Act* means the Federal Mine Safety and Health Act of 1977.

(b) *Competent person* means a person designated by the production-operator or independent contractor who has the ability, training, knowledge, or experience to provide training to miners in his or her area of expertise. The competent person must be able both to effectively communicate the training subject to miners and to evaluate whether the training given to miners is effective.

(c) *Equivalent experience* means work experience where the person performed duties similar to duties performed in mining operations at surface mines. Such experience may include, but is not limited to, work as a heavy equipment operator, truck driver, skilled craftsman, or plant operator.

(d)(1) *Experienced miner* means:
(i) A person who is employed as a miner on April 14, 1999;
(ii) A person who has at least 12 months of cumulative surface mining or equivalent experience on or before October 2, 2000;
(iii) A person who began employment as a miner after April 14, 1999, but before October 2, 2000, and who has received new miner training under § 48.25 of this chapter or under proposed requirements published April 14, 1999, which are available from the Office of Standards, Regulations, and Variances, MSHA, 201 12th Street South, Arlington, VA 22202-5452; or,
(iv) A person employed as a miner on or after October 2, 2000 who has completed 24 hours of new miner training under § 46.5 of this part or under § 48.25 of this title and who has at least 12 cumulative months of surface mining or equivalent experience.

(2) Once a miner is an experienced miner under this section, the miner will retain that status permanently.

(e) *Independent contractor* means any person, partnership, corporation, subsidiary of a corporation, firm, association, or other organization that contracts to perform services at a mine under this part.

(f) *Mine site* means an area of the mine where mining operations occur.

(g)(1) *Miner* means:
(i) Any person, including any operator or supervisor, who works at a mine and who is engaged in mining operations. This definition includes independent contractors and employees of independent contractors who are engaged in mining operations; and
(ii) Any construction worker who is exposed to hazards of mining operations.

(2) The definition of "miner" does not include scientific workers; delivery workers; customers (including commercial over-the-road truck drivers); vendors; or visitors. This definition

also does not include maintenance or service workers who do not work at a mine site for frequent or extended periods.

(h) *Mining operations* means mine development, drilling, blasting, extraction, milling, crushing, screening, or sizing of minerals at a mine; maintenance and repair of mining equipment; and associated haulage of materials within the mine from these activities.

(i) *New miner* means a person who is beginning employment as a miner with a production-operator or independent contractor and who is not an experienced miner.

(j) *Newly hired experienced miner* means an experienced miner who is beginning employment with a production-operator or independent contractor. Experienced miners who move from one mine to another, such as drillers and blasters, but who remain employed by the same production-operator or independent contractor are not considered newly hired experienced miners.

(k) *Normal working hours* means a period of time during which a miner is otherwise scheduled to work, including the sixth or seventh working day if such a work schedule has been established for a sufficient period of time to be accepted as the common practice of the production-operator or independent contractor, as applicable.

(l) *Operator* means any production-operator, or any independent contractor whose employees perform services at a mine.

(m) *Production-operator* means any owner, lessee, or other person who operates, controls, or supervises a mine under this part.

(n) *Task* means a work assignment or component of a job that requires specific job knowledge or experience.

(o) *We* or *us* means the Mine Safety and Health Administration (MSHA).

(p) *You* means production-operators and independent contractors.

[64 FR 53130, Sept. 30, 1999, as amended at 67 FR 38384, June 4, 2002; 80 FR 52985, Sept. 2, 2015]

§ 46.3 Training plans.

(a) You must develop and implement a written plan, approved by us under either paragraph (b) or (c) of this section, that contains effective programs for training new miners and newly hired experienced miners, training miners for new tasks, annual refresher training, and site-specific hazard awareness training.

(b) A training plan is considered approved by us if it contains, at a minimum, the following information:

(1) The name of the production-operator or independent contractor, mine name(s), and MSHA mine identification number(s) or independent contractor identification number(s);

(2) The name and position of the person designated by you who is responsible for the health and safety training at the mine. This person may be the production-operator or independent contractor;

(3) A general description of the teaching methods and the course materials that are to be used in the training program, including the subject areas to be covered and the approximate time or range of time to be spent on each subject area.

(4) A list of the persons and/or organizations who will provide the training, and the subject areas in which each person and/or organization is competent to instruct; and

(5) The evaluation procedures used to determine the effectiveness of training.

(c) A plan that does not include the minimum information specified in paragraphs (b)(1) through (b)(5) of this section must be submitted to and approved by the Regional Manager, Educational Field Services Division, or designee, for the region in which the mine is located. You also may voluntarily submit a plan for Regional Manager approval. You must notify miners or their representatives when you submit a plan for Regional Manager approval. Within two weeks of receipt or posting of the plan, miners and their representatives may also request review and approval of the plan by the Regional Manager and must notify the production-operator or independent contractor of such request.

(d) You must provide the miners' representative, if any, with a copy of the plan at least 2 weeks before the plan is implemented or, if you request MSHA approval of your plan, at least two weeks before you submit the plan to

§ 46.4

the Regional Manager for approval. At mines where no miners' representative has been designated, you must post a copy of the plan at the mine or provide a copy to each miner at least 2 weeks before you implement the plan or submit it to the Regional Manager for approval.

(e) Within 2 weeks following the receipt or posting of the training plan under paragraph (d) of this section, miners or their representatives may submit written comments on the plan to you, or to the Regional Manager, as appropriate.

(f) The Regional Manager must notify you and miners or their representatives in writing of the approval, or status of the approval, of the training plan within 30 calendar days of the date we received the training plan for approval, or within 30 calendar days of the date we received the request by a miner or miners' representative that we approve your plan.

(g) You must provide the miners' representative, if any, with a copy of the approved plan within one week after approval. At mines where no miners' representative has been designated, you must post a copy of the plan at the mine or provide a copy to each miner within one week after approval.

(h) If you, miners, or miners' representatives wish to appeal a decision of the Regional Manager, you must send the appeal, in writing, to the Director for Educational Policy and Development, MSHA, 201 12th Street South, Arlington, VA 22202–5452, within 30 calendar days after notification of the Regional Manager's decision. The Director will issue a final decision of the Agency within 30 calendar days after receipt of the appeal.

(i) You must make available at the mine a copy of the current training plan for inspection by us and for examination by miners and their representatives. If the training plan is not maintained at the mine, you must have the capability to provide the plan within one business day upon request by us, miners, or their representatives.

(j) You must comply with the procedures for plan approval under this section whenever the plan undergoes revisions.

(k) The addresses for the EFS Regional Managers are as follows. Current information on the EFS organization is available on MSHA's Internet Home Page at *http://www.msha.gov.*

Eastern Regional Manager

Educational Field Services, National Mine Health and Safety Academy, 1301 Airport Road, Beaver, WV 25813–9426, Telephone: (304) 256–3223, FAX: (304) 256–3319, E-mail: *EFS_EAST@MSHA.GOV*

Western Regional Manager

Educational Field Services, P.O. Box 25367, Denver, CO 80225–0367, Telephone: (303) 231–5434, FAX: (304) 231–5474, E-mail: *EFS_WEST@MSHA.GOV*

[64 FR 53130, Sept. 30, 1999, as amended at 67 FR 38384, June 4, 2002; 80 FR 52986, Sept. 2, 2015]

§ 46.4 Training plan implementation.

(a) You must ensure that each program, course of instruction, or training session is:

(1) Conducted in accordance with the written training plan;

(2) Presented by a competent person; and

(3) Presented in language understood by the miners who are receiving the training.

(b) You may conduct your own training programs or may arrange for training to be conducted by: state or federal agencies; associations of production-operators or independent contractors; miners' representatives; consultants; manufacturers' representatives; private associations; educational institutions; or other training providers.

(c) You may substitute, as applicable, health and safety training required by the Occupational Safety and Health Administration (OSHA), or other federal or state agencies to meet requirements under this part. This training must be relevant to training subjects required in this part. You must document the training in accordance with § 46.9 of this part.

(d) Training methods may consist of classroom instruction, instruction at the mine, interactive computer-based instruction or other innovative training methods, alternative training technologies, or any combination of training methods.

Mine Safety and Health Admin., Labor §46.5

(e) Employee health and safety meetings, including informal health and safety talks and instruction, may be credited under this part toward either new miner training, newly hired experienced miner training, or annual refresher training requirements, as appropriate, provided that you document each training session in accordance with §46.9 of this part. In recording the duration of training, you must include only the portion of the session actually spent in training.

§ 46.5 New miner training.

(a) Except as provided in paragraphs (f) and (g) of this section, you must provide each new miner with no less than 24 hours of training as prescribed by paragraphs (b), (c), and (d). Miners who have not yet received the full 24 hours of new miner training must work where an experienced miner can observe that the new miner is performing his or her work in a safe and healthful manner.

(b) Before a new miner begins work at the mine—	You must provide the miner with no less than 4 hours of training in the following subjects, which must also address site-specific hazards: (1) An introduction to the work environment, including a visit and tour of the mine, or portions of the mine that are representative of the entire mine (walkaround training). The method of mining or operation utilized must be explained and observed; (2) Instruction on the recognition and avoidance of electrical hazards and other hazards present at the mine, such as traffic patterns and control, mobile equipment (e.g., haul trucks and front-end loaders), and loose or unstable ground conditions; (3) A review of the emergency medical procedures, escape and emergency evacuation plans, in effect at the mine, and instruction on the firewarning signals and firefighting procedures; (4) Instruction on the health and safety aspects of the tasks to be assigned, including the safe work procedures of such tasks, the mandatory health and safety standards pertinent to such tasks, information about the physical and health hazards of chemicals in the miner's work area, the protective measures a miner can take against these hazards, and the contents of the mine's HazCom program; (5) Instruction on the statutory rights of miners and their representatives under the Act; (6) A review and description of the line of authority of supervisors and miners' representatives and the responsibilities of such supervisors and miners' representatives; and (7) An introduction to your rules and procedures for reporting hazards.
(c) No later than 60 calendar days after a new miner begins work at the mine—	You must provide the miner with training in the following subject: (1) Instruction and demonstration on the use, care, and maintenance of self-rescue and respiratory devices, if used at the mine; and (2) A review of first aid methods.
(d) No later than 90 calendar days after a new miner begins work at the mine—	You must provide the miner with the balance, if any, of the 24 hours of training on any other subjects that promote occupational health and safety for miners at the mine.

(e) Practice under the close observation of a competent person may be used to fulfill the requirement for training on the health and safety aspects of an

§ 46.6

assigned task in paragraph (b)(4) of this section, if hazard recognition training specific to the assigned task is given before the miner performs the task.

(f) A new miner who has less than 12 cumulative months of surface mining or equivalent experience and has completed new miner training under this section or under § 48.25 of this title within 36 months before beginning work at the mine does not have to repeat new miner training. However, you must provide the miner with training specified in paragraph (b) of this section before the miner begins work at the mine.

(g) A new miner training course completed under § 48.5 or § 48.25 of this title may be used to satisfy the requirements of paragraphs (a), (b), and (c) of this section, if the course was completed by the miner within 36 months before beginning work at the mine; and the course is relevant to the subjects specified in paragraphs (b) and (c) of this section.

[64 FR 53130, Sept. 30, 1999, as amended at 67 FR 42382, June 21, 2002]

§ 46.6 Newly hired experienced miner training.

(a) Except as provided in paragraph (f) of this section, you must provide each newly hired experienced miner with training as prescribed by paragraphs (b) and (c).

(b) Before a newly hired experienced miner begins work at the mine—	You must provide the miner with training in the following subjects, which must also address site-specific hazards: (1) An introduction to the work environment, including a visit and tour of the mine, or portions of the mine that are representative of the entire mine (walkaround training). The method of mining or operation utilized must be explained and observed; (2) Instruction on the recognition and avoidance of electrical hazards and other hazards present at the mine, such as traffic patterns and control, mobile equipment (e.g., haul trucks and front-end loaders), and loose or unstable ground conditions; (3) A review of the emergency medical procedures, escape and emergency evacuation plans, in effect at the mine, and instruction on the firewarning signals and firefighting procedures; (4) Instruction on the health and safety aspects of the tasks to be assigned, including the safe work procedures of such tasks, the mandatory health and safety standards pertinent to such tasks, information about the physical and health hazards of chemicals in the miner's work area, the protective measures a miner can take against these hazards, and the contents of the mine's HazCom program; (5) Instruction on the statutory rights of miners and their representatives under the Act; (6) A review and description of the line of authority of supervisors and miners' representatives and the responsibilities of such supervisors and miners' representatives; and (7) An introduction to your rules and procedures for reporting hazards.
(c) No later than 60 calendar days after a newly hired experienced miner begins work at the mine—	You must provide the miner with an instruction and demonstration on the use, care, and maintenance of self-rescue and respiratory devices, if used at the mine.

(d) Practice under the close observation of a competent person may be used to fulfill the requirement for training on the health and safety aspects of an assigned task in paragraph (b)(4) of this section, if hazard recognition training specific to the assigned task is given before the miner performs the task.

(e) In addition to subjects specified in paragraphs (b) and (c) of this section, you may provide training on any other subjects that promote occupational health and safety for miners.

(f) You are not required to provide a newly hired experienced miner who returns to the same mine, following an absence of 12 months or less, with the training specified in paragraphs (b) and (c) of this section. Instead you must provide such miner with training on any changes at the mine that occurred during the miner's absence that could adversely affect the miner's health or safety. This training must be given before the miner begins work at the mine. If the miner missed any part of annual refresher training under §46.8 of this part during the absence, you must provide the miner with the missed training no later than 90 calendar days after the miner begins work at the mine.

[64 FR 53130, Sept. 30, 1999, as amended at 67 FR 42382, June 21, 2002]

§46.7 New task training.

(a) You must provide any miner who is reassigned to a new task in which he or she has no previous work experience with training in the health and safety aspects of the task to be assigned, including the safe work procedures of such task, information about the physical and health hazards of chemicals in the miner's work area, the protective measures a miner can take against these hazards, and the contents of the mine's HazCom program. This training must be provided before the miner performs the new task.

(b) If a change occurs in a miner's assigned task that affects the health and safety risks encountered by the miner, you must provide the miner with training under paragraph (a) of this section that addresses the change.

(c) You are not required to provide new task training under paragraphs (a) and (b) of this section to miners who have received training in a similar task or who have previous work experience in the task, and who can demonstrate the necessary skills to perform the task in a safe and healthful manner. To determine whether task training under this section is required, you must observe that the miner can perform the task in a safe and healthful manner.

(d) Practice under the close observation of a competent person may be used to fulfill the requirement for task training under this section, if hazard recognition training specific to the assigned task is given before the miner performs the task.

(e) Training provided under this section may be credited toward new miner training, as appropriate.

[64 FR 53130, Sept. 30, 1999, as amended at 67 FR 42382, June 21, 2002]

§46.8 Annual refresher training.

(a) You must provide each miner with no less than 8 hours of annual refresher training—

(1) No later than 12 months after the miner begins work at the mine, or no later than March 30, 2001, whichever is later; and

(2) Thereafter, no later than 12 months after the previous annual refresher training was completed.

(b) The refresher training must include instruction on changes at the mine that could adversely affect the miner's health or safety.

(c) Refresher training must also address other health and safety subjects that are relevant to mining operations at the mine. Recommended subjects include, but are not limited to: applicable health and safety requirements, including mandatory health and safety standards; information about the physical and health hazards of chemicals in the miner's work area, the protective measures a miner can take against these hazards, and the contents of the mine's HazCom program; transportation controls and communication systems; escape and emergency evacuation plans, firewarning and firefighting; ground conditions and control; traffic patterns and control; working in areas of highwalls; water hazards, pits, and spoil banks; illumination and night work; first aid; electrical hazards; prevention of accidents; health; explosives; and respiratory devices. Training is also recommended on the hazards associated with the equipment that has accounted for the most fatalities and serious injuries at the mines covered by this rule, including: mobile equipment (haulage and service trucks, front-end loaders and tractors); conveyor systems; cranes; crushers; excavators; and dredges. Other recommended subjects include: maintenance and repair (use of hand tools and welding equipment); material handling; fall prevention and protection; and working around moving objects (machine guarding).

[64 FR 53130, Sept. 30, 1999, as amended at 67 FR 42382, June 21, 2002]

§ 46.9 Records of training.

(a) You must record and certify on MSHA Form 5000–23, or on a form that contains the information listed in paragraph (b) of this section, that each miner has received training required under this part.

(b) The form must include:

(1) The printed full name of the person trained;

(2) The type of training, the duration of the training, the date the training was received, the name of the competent person who provided the training;

(3) The name of the mine or independent contractor, MSHA mine identification number or independent contractor identification number, and location of training (if an institution, the name and address of the institution).

(4) The statement, "False certification is punishable under §110(a) and (f) of the Federal Mine Safety and Health Act," printed in bold letters and in a conspicuous manner; and

(5) A statement signed by the person designated in the MSHA-approved training plan for the mine as responsible for health and safety training, that states "I certify that the above training has been completed."

(c) You must make a record of training under paragraphs (b)(1) through (b)(4) of this section—

(1) For new miner training under § 46.5, no later than—

(i) when the miner begins work at the mine as required under § 46.5(b);

(ii) 60 calendar days after the miner begins work at the mine as required under § 46.5(c); and

(iii) 90 calendar days after the miner begins work at the mine as required under § 46.5(d), if applicable.

(2) For newly hired experienced miner training under § 46.6, no later than—

(i) when the miner begins work at the mine; and

(ii) 60 calendar days after the miner begins work at the mine.

(3) Upon completion of new task training under § 46.7;

(4) After each session of annual refresher training under § 46.8; and

(5) Upon completion by miners of site-specific hazard awareness training under § 46.11.

(d) You must ensure that all records of training under paragraphs (c)(1) through (c)(5) of this section are certified under paragraph (b)(5) of this section and a copy provided to the miner—

(1) Upon completion of the 24 hours of new miner training;

(2) Upon completion of newly hired experienced miner training;

(3) At least once every 12 months for new task training, or upon request by the miner, if applicable;

(4) Upon completion of the 8 hours of annual refresher training; and

(5) Upon completion by miners of site-specific hazard awareness training.

(e) False certification that training was completed is punishable under § 110(a) and (f) of the Act.

(f) When a miner leaves your employ, you must provide each miner with a copy of his or her training records and certificates upon request.

(g) You must make available at the mine a copy of each miner's training records and certificates for inspection by us and for examination by miners and their representatives. If training certificates are not maintained at the mine, you must be able to provide the certificates upon request by us, miners, or their representatives.

(h) You must maintain copies of training certificates and training records for each currently employed miner during his or her employment, except records and certificates of annual refresher training under § 46.8, which you must maintain for only two years. You must maintain copies of training certificates and training records for at least 60 calendar days after a miner terminates employment.

(i) You are not required to make records under this section of site-specific hazard awareness training you provide under § 46.11 of this part to persons who are not miners under § 46.2. However, you must be able to provide evidence to us, upon request, that the training was provided, such as the training materials that are used; copies of written information distributed to persons upon their arrival at the mine; or visitor log books that indicate that training has been provided.

§ 46.10 Compensation for training.

(a) Training must be conducted during normal working hours. Persons required to receive training must be paid at a rate of pay that corresponds to the rate of pay they would have received had they been performing their normal work tasks.

(b) If training is given at a location other than the normal place of work, persons required to receive such training must be compensated for the additional costs, including mileage, meals, and lodging, they may incur in attending such training sessions.

§ 46.11 Site-specific hazard awareness training.

(a) You must provide site-specific hazard awareness training before any person specified under this section is exposed to mine hazards.

(b) You must provide site-specific hazard awareness training, as appropriate, to any person who is not a miner as defined by § 46.2 of this part but is present at a mine site, including:

(1) Office or staff personnel;
(2) Scientific workers;
(3) Delivery workers;
(4) Customers, including commercial over-the-road truck drivers;
(5) Construction workers or employees of independent contractors who are not miners under § 46.2 of this part;
(6) Maintenance or service workers who do not work at the mine site for frequent or extended periods; and
(7) Vendors or visitors.

(c) You must provide miners, such as drillers or blasters, who move from one mine to another mine while remaining employed by the same production-operator or independent contractor with site-specific hazard awareness training for each mine.

(d) Site-specific hazard awareness training is information or instructions on the hazards a person could be exposed to while at the mine, as well as applicable emergency procedures. The training must address site-specific health and safety risks, such as unique geologic or environmental conditions, recognition and avoidance of hazards such as electrical and powered-haulage hazards, traffic patterns and control, and restricted areas; and warning and evacuation signals, evacuation and emergency procedures, or other special safety procedures.

(e) You may provide site-specific hazard awareness training through the use of written hazard warnings, oral instruction, signs and posted warnings, walkaround training, or other appropriate means that alert persons to site-specific hazards at the mine.

(f) Site-specific hazard awareness training is not required for any person who is accompanied at all times by an experienced miner who is familiar with hazards specific to the mine site.

§ 46.12 Responsibility for independent contractor training.

(a)(1) Each production-operator has primary responsibility for ensuring that site-specific hazard awareness training is given to employees of independent contractors who are required to receive such training under § 46.11 of this part.

(2) Each production-operator must provide information to each independent contractor who employs a person at the mine on site-specific mine hazards and the obligation of the contractor to comply with our regulations, including the requirements of this part.

(b)(1) Each independent contractor who employs a miner, as defined in § 46.2, at the mine has primary responsibility for complying with §§ 46.3 through 46.10 of this part, including providing new miner training, newly hired experienced miner training, new task training, and annual refresher training.

(2) The independent contractor must inform the production-operator of any

hazards of which the contractor is aware that may be created by the performance of the contractor's work at the mine.

PART 47—HAZARD COMMUNICATION (HazCom)

Subpart A—Purpose, Scope, Applicability, and Initial Miner Training

Sec.
47.1 Purpose of a HazCom standard; applicability.
47.2 Operators and chemicals covered; initial miner training.

Subpart B—Definitions

47.11 Definitions of terms used in this part.

Subpart C—Hazard Determination

47.21 Identifying hazardous chemicals.

Subpart D—HazCom Program

47.31 Requirement for a HazCom program.
47.32 HazCom program contents.

Subpart E—Container Labels and Other Forms of Warning

47.41 Requirement for container labels.
47.42 Label contents.
47.43 Label alternatives.
47.44 Temporary, portable containers.

Subpart F—Material Safety Data Sheets (MSDS)

47.51 Requirement for an MSDS.
47.52 MSDS contents.
47.53 Alternative for hazardous waste.
47.54 Availability of an MSDS.
47.55 Retaining an MSDS.

Subpart G [Reserved]

Subpart H—Making HazCom Information Available

47.71 Access to HazCom materials.
47.72 Cost for copies.
47.73 Providing labels and MSDSs to customers.

Subpart I—Trade Secret Hazardous Chemical

47.81 Provisions for withholding trade secrets.
47.82 Disclosure of information to MSHA.
47.83 Disclosure in a medical emergency.
47.84 Non-emergency disclosure.
47.85 Confidentiality agreement and remedies.
47.86 Denial of a written request for disclosure.
47.87 Review of denial.

Subpart J—Exemptions

47.91 Exemptions from the HazCom standard.
47.92 Exemptions from labeling.

AUTHORITY: 30 U.S.C. 811, 825.

SOURCE: 67 FR 42383, June 21, 2002, unless otherwise noted.

Subpart A—Purpose, Scope, Applicability, and Initial Miner Training

§ 47.1 Purpose of a HazCom standard; applicability.

The purpose of this part is to reduce injuries and illnesses by ensuring that each operator—

(a) Identifies the chemicals at the mine,

(b) Determines which chemicals are hazardous,

(c) Establishes a HazCom program, and

(d) Informs each miner who can be exposed, and other on-site operators whose miners can be exposed, about chemical hazards and appropriate protective measures.

(e) As of September 23, 2002, all mines employing six or more miners are required to comply with this part.

(f) As of March 21, 2003, all mines employing five or fewer miners are required to comply with this part.

§ 47.2 Operators and chemicals covered; initial miner training.

(a) This part applies to any operator producing or using a hazardous chemical to which a miner can be exposed under normal conditions of use or in a foreseeable emergency. (Subpart J of this part lists exemptions from coverage.)

(b) Operators of mines which employ six or more miners must instruct each miner with information about the physical and health hazards of chemicals in the miner's work area, the protective measures a miner can take against these hazards, and the contents of the mine's HazCom program by September 23, 2002. Operators of mines that employ five or fewer miners must instruct each miner with information about the physical and health hazards of chemicals in the miner's work area, the protective measures a miner can take against these hazards, and the contents of the mine's HazCom program by March 21, 2003.

Subpart B—Definitions

§ 47.11 Definitions of terms used in this part.

The definitions in Table 47.11 apply in this part as follows:

TABLE 47.11—DEFINITIONS

Term	Definition for purposes of HazCom
Access	The right to examine and copy records.
Article	A manufactured item, other than a fluid or particle, that— (1) Is formed to a specific shape or design during manufacture, and (2) Has end-use functions dependent on its shape or design.
Chemical	Any element, chemical compound, or mixture of these.
Chemical name	(1) The scientific designation of a chemical in accordance with the nomenclature system of either the International Union of Pure and Applied Chemistry (IUPAC) or the Chemical Abstracts Service (CAS), or (2) A name that will clearly identify the chemical for the purpose of conducting a hazard evaluation.
Common name	Any designation or identification (such as a code name, code number, trade name, brand name, or generic name) used to identify a chemical other than by its chemical name.
Consumer product	A product or component of a product that is packaged, labeled, and distributed in the same form and concentration as it is sold for use by the general public.
Container	(1) Any bag, barrel, bottle, box, can, cylinder, drum, reaction vessel, storage tank, or the like. (2) The following are not considered to be containers for the purpose of compliance with this part: (i) Pipes or piping systems; (ii) Conveyors; and (iii) Engines, fuel tanks, or other operating systems or parts in a vehicle.
Cosmetics and drugs	(1) Cosmetics are any article applied to the human body for cleansing, beautifying, promoting attractiveness, or altering appearance. (2) Drugs are any article used to affect the structure or any function of the body of humans or other animals.
CPSC	The U.S. Consumer Product Safety Commission.
Designated representative	(1) Any individual or organization to whom a miner gives written authorization to exercise the miner's rights under this part, or (2) A representative of miners under part 40 of this chapter.
EPA	The U.S. Environmental Protection Agency.
Exposed	Subjected, or potentially subjected, to a physical or health hazard in the course of employment. "Subjected," in terms of health hazards, includes any route of entry, such as through the lungs (inhalation), the stomach (ingestion), or the skin (skin absorption).
Foreseeable emergency	Any potential occurrence that could result in an uncontrolled release of a hazardous chemical into the mine.
Hazard warning	Any words, pictures, or symbols, appearing on a label or other form of warning, that convey the specific physical and health hazards of the chemical. (See the definitions for *physical hazard* and *health hazard* for examples of the hazards that the warning must convey.)
Hazardous chemical	Any chemical that can present a physical or health hazard.
Hazardous substance	Regulated by CPSC under the Federal Hazardous Substances Act or EPA under the Comprehensive Environmental Response, Compensation, and Liability Act.
Hazardous waste	Chemicals regulated by EPA under the Solid Waste Disposal Act as amended by the Resource Conservation and Recovery Act.
Health hazard	A chemical for which there is statistically significant evidence that it can cause acute or chronic health effects in exposed persons. *Health hazard* includes chemicals which— (1) Cause cancer; (2) Damage the reproductive system or cause birth defects; (3) Are irritants, corrosives, or sensitizers; (4) Damage the liver; (5) Damage the kidneys; (6) Damage the nervous system; (7) Damage the blood or lymphatic systems; (8) Damage the stomach or intestines; (9) Damage the lungs, skin, eyes, or mucous membranes; or (10) Are toxic or highly toxic agents.
Health professional	A physician, physician's assistant, nurse, emergency medical technician, or other person qualified to provide medical or occupational health services.
Identity	A chemical's *common name* or *chemical name*.
Label	Any written, printed, or graphic material displayed on or affixed to a container to identify its contents and convey other relevant information.
Material safety data sheet (MSDS)	Written or printed material concerning a hazardous chemical which—

§ 47.21

30 CFR Ch. I (7-1-23 Edition)

TABLE 47.11—DEFINITIONS—Continued

Term	Definition for purposes of HazCom
	(1) An operator prepares in accordance with Table 47.52—Contents of MSDS; or
	(2) An employer prepares in accordance with 29 CFR 1910.1200, 1915.1200, 1917.28, 1918.90, 1926.59, or 1928.21 (OSHA Hazard Communication regulations); or
	(3) An independent source prepares which contains equivalent information, such as International Chemical Safety Cards (ICSC) and Workplace Hazardous Material Information Sheets (WHMIS).
Mixture	Any combination of two or more chemicals which is not the result of a chemical reaction.
Ordinary consumer use	Household, family, school, recreation, or other personal use or enjoyment, as opposed to business use.
OSHA	The Occupational Safety and Health Administration, U.S. Department of Labor.
Physical hazard	A chemical for which there is scientifically valid evidence that it is—
	(1) *Combustible liquid:*
	(i) A liquid having a flash point at or above 100 °F (37.8 °C) and below 200 °F (93.3 °C); or
	(ii) A liquid mixture having components with flashpoints of 200 °F (93.3 °C) or higher, the total volume of which make up 99% or more of the mixture.
	(2) *Compressed gas:*
	(i) A contained gas or mixture of gases with an absolute pressure exceeding:
	(A) 40 psi (276 kPa) at 70 °F (21.1 °C); or
	(B) 104 psi (717 kPa) at 130 °F (54.4 °C) regardless of pressure at 70 °F.
	(ii) A liquid having a vapor pressure exceeding 40 psi (276 kPa) at 100 °F (37.8 °C) as determined by ASTM D-323-82.
	(3) *Explosive:* A chemical that undergoes a rapid chemical change causing a sudden, almost instantaneous release of pressure, gas, and heat when subjected to sudden shock, pressure, or high temperature.
	(4) *Flammable:* A chemical that will readily ignite and, when ignited, will burn persistently at ambient temperature and pressure in the normal concentration of oxygen in the air.
	(5) *Organic peroxide:* An explosive, shock sensitive, organic compound or an oxide that contains a high proportion of oxygen-superoxide.
	(6) *Oxidizer:* A chemical, other than an explosive, that initiates or promotes combustion in other materials, thereby causing fire either of itself or through the release of oxygen or other gases.
	(7) *Pyrophoric:* Capable of igniting spontaneously in air at a temperature of 130 °F (54.4 °C) or below.
	(8) *Unstable (reactive):* A chemical which in the pure state, or as produced or transported, will vigorously polymerize, decompose, condense, or become self-reactive under conditions of shock, pressure, or temperature.
	(9) *Water-reactive:* A chemical that reacts with water to release a gas that is either flammable or a health hazard.
Produce	To manufacture, process, formulate, generate, or repackage.
Raw material	Ore, valuable minerals, worthless material or gangue, overburden, or a combination of these, that is removed from natural deposits by mining or is upgraded through milling.
Trade secret	Any confidential formula, pattern, process, device, information, or compilation of information that is used by the operator and that gives the operator an opportunity to obtain an advantage over competitors who do not know about it or use it.
Use	To package, handle, react, or transfer.
Work area	Any place in or about a mine where a miner works.

[67 FR 42383, June 21, 2002; 67 FR 57635, Sept. 11, 2002]

Subpart C—Hazard Determination

§ 47.21 Identifying hazardous chemicals.

The operator must evaluate each chemical brought on mine property and each chemical produced on mine property to determine if it is hazardous as specified in Table 47.21 as follows:

TABLE 47.21—IDENTIFYING HAZARDOUS CHEMICALS

Category	Basis for determining if a chemical is hazardous
(a) Chemical brought to the mine	The chemical is hazardous when its MSDS or container label indicates it is a physical or health hazard; or the operator may choose to evaluate the chemical using the criteria in paragraphs (b) and (c) of this table.
(b) Chemical produced at the mine	The chemical is hazardous if any one of the following is true that it is a hazard:
	(1) Available evidence concerning its physical or health hazards.
	(2) MSHA standards in 30 CFR chapter I.
	(3) Occupational Safety and Health Administration (OSHA), 29 CFR part 1910, subpart Z, *Toxic and Hazardous Substances.*

Mine Safety and Health Admin., Labor §47.41

TABLE 47.21—IDENTIFYING HAZARDOUS CHEMICALS—Continued

Category	Basis for determining if a chemical is hazardous
	(4) American Conference of Governmental Industrial Hygienists (ACGIH), *Threshold Limit Values and Biological Exposure Indices* (2001). (5) U.S. Department of Health and Human Services, National Toxicology Program (NTP), *Ninth Annual Report on Carcinogens*, January 2001. (6) International Agency for Research on Cancer (IARC), Monographs and related supplements, Volumes 1 through 77.
(c) Mixture produced at the mine	(1) If a mixture has been tested as a whole to determine its hazards, use the results of that testing. (2) If a mixture has not been tested as a whole to determine its hazards— (i) Use available, scientifically valid evidence to determine its physical hazard potential; (ii) Assume that it presents the same health hazard as a non-carcinogenic component that makes up 1% or more (by weight or volume) of the mixture; and (iii) Assume that it presents a carcinogenic health hazard if a component considered carcinogenic by NTP or IARC makes up 0.1% or more (by weight or volume) of the mixture. (3) If evidence indicates that a component could be released from a mixture in a concentration that could present a health risk to miners, assume that the mixture presents the same hazard.

Subpart D—HazCom Program

§47.31 Requirement for a HazCom program.

Each operator must—
(a) Develop and implement a written HazCom program,
(b) Maintain it for as long as a hazardous chemical is known to be at the mine, and
(c) Share relevant HazCom information with other on-site operators whose miners can be affected.

§47.32 HazCom program contents.

The HazCom program must include the following:
(a) How this part is put into practice at the mine through the use of—
(1) Hazard determination,
(2) Labels and other forms of warning,
(3) Material safety data sheets (MSDSs), and
(4) Miner training.
(b) A list or other record identifying all hazardous chemicals known to be at the mine. The list must—
(1) Use a chemical identity that permits cross-referencing between the list, a chemical's label, and its MSDS; and
(2) Be compiled for the whole mine or by individual work areas.
(c) At mines with more than one operator, the methods for—
(1) Providing other operators with access to MSDSs, and
(2) Informing other operators about—

(i) Hazardous chemicals to which their miners can be exposed,
(ii) The labeling system on the containers of these chemicals, and
(iii) Appropriate protective measures.

[67 FR 42383, June 21, 2002; 67 FR 57635, Sept. 11, 2002]

Subpart E—Container Labels and Other Forms of Warning

§47.41 Requirement for container labels.

(a) The operator must ensure that each container of a hazardous chemical has a label. If a container is tagged or marked with the appropriate information, it is labeled.
(1) The operator must replace a container label immediately if it is missing or if the hazard information on the label is unreadable.
(2) The operator must not remove or deface existing labels on containers of hazardous chemicals.
(b) For each hazardous chemical produced at the mine, the operator must prepare a container label and update this label with any significant, new information about the chemical's hazards within 3 months of becoming aware of this information.
(c) For each hazardous chemical brought to the mine, the operator must

§ 47.42

replace an outdated label when a revised label is received from the chemical's manufacturer or supplier. The operator is not responsible for an inaccurate label obtained from the chemical's manufacturer or supplier.

§ 47.42 Label contents.

When an operator must make a label, the label must—

(a) Be prominently displayed, legible, accurate, and in English;

(b) Display appropriate hazard warnings;

(c) Use a chemical identity that permits cross-referencing between the list of hazardous chemicals, a chemical's label, and its MSDS; and

(d) Include on labels for customers, the name and address of the operator or another responsible party who can provide additional information about the hazardous chemical.

[67 FR 42383, June 21, 2002; 67 FR 63255, Oct. 11, 2002]

§ 47.43 Label alternatives.

The operator may use signs, placards, process sheets, batch tickets, operating procedures, or other label alternatives for individual, stationary process containers, provided that the alternative—

(a) Identifies the container to which it applies;

(b) Communicates the same information as required on the label, and

(c) Is readily available throughout each work shift to miners in the work area.

§ 47.44 Temporary, portable containers.

(a) The operator does not have to label a temporary, portable container if he or she ensures that the miner using the portable container—

(1) Knows the identity of the chemical, its hazards, and any protective measures needed, and

(2) Leaves the container empty at the end of the shift.

(b) Otherwise, the operator must mark the temporary, portable container with at least the common name of its contents.

Subpart F—Material Safety Data Sheets (MSDS)

§ 47.51 Requirement for an MSDS.

Operators must have an MSDS for each hazardous chemical which they produce or use. The MSDS may be in any medium, such as paper or electronic, that does not restrict availability.

(a) For each hazardous chemical produced at the mine, the operator must prepare an MSDS, and update it with significant, new information about the chemical's hazards or protective measures within 3 months of becoming aware of this information.

(b) For each hazardous chemical brought to the mine, the operator must rely on the MSDS received from the chemical manufacturer or supplier, develop their own MSDS, or obtain one from another source.

(c) Although the operator is not responsible for an inaccurate MSDS obtained from the chemical's manufacturer, supplier, or other source, the operator must—

(1) Replace an outdated MSDS upon receipt of an updated revision, and

(2) Obtain an accurate MSDS as soon as possible after becoming aware of an inaccuracy.

(d) The operator is not required to prepare an MSDS for an intermediate chemical or by-product resulting from mining or milling if its hazards are already addressed on the MSDS of the source chemical.

§ 47.52 MSDS contents.

When an operator must prepare an MSDS for a hazardous chemical produced at the mine, the MSDS must—

(a) Be legible, accurate, and in English;

(b) Use a chemical identity that permits cross-referencing between the list of hazardous chemicals, the chemical's label, and its MSDS; and

(c) Contain information, or indicate if no information is available, for the categories listed in Table 47.52 as follows:

Mine Safety and Health Admin., Labor § 47.73

TABLE 47.52—CONTENTS OF MSDS

Category	Requirements, descriptions, and exceptions
(1) Identity	The identity of the chemical or, if the chemical is a mixture, the identities of all hazardous ingredients. See § 47.21 (Identifying hazardous chemicals).
(2) Properties	The physical and chemical characteristics of the chemical, such as vapor pressure and solubility in water.
(3) Physical	The physical hazards of the chemical including the potential for fire, explosion, and reactivity.
(4) Health hazards	The health hazards of the chemical including— (i) Signs and symptoms of exposure, (ii) Any medical conditions which are generally recognized as being aggravated by exposure to the chemical, and (iii) The primary routes of entry for the chemical, such as lungs, stomach, or skin.
(5) Exposure limits	For the chemical or the ingredients of a mixture— (i) The MSHA or OSHA permissible limit, if there is one, and (ii) Any other exposure limit recommended by the preparer of the MSDS.
(6) Carcinogenicity	Whether the chemical is a carcinogen or potential carcinogen. See the sources specified in § 47.21 (Identifying hazardous chemicals).
(7) Safe use	Precautions for safe handling and use including— (i) Appropriate hygienic practices, (ii) Protective measures during repair and maintenance of contaminated equipment, and (iii) Procedures for clean-up of spills and leaks.
(8) Control measures	Generally applicable control measures such as engineering controls, work practices, and personal protective equipment.
(9) Emergency information	(i) Emergency medical and first-aid procedures; and (ii) The name, address, and telephone number of the operator or other responsible party who can provide additional information on the hazardous chemical and appropriate emergency procedures.
(10) Date prepared	The date the MSDS was prepared or last changed.

[67 FR 42383, June 21, 2002; 67 FR 57635, Sept. 11, 2002]

§ 47.53 Alternative for hazardous waste.

If the mine produces or uses hazardous waste, the operator must provide potentially exposed miners and designated representatives access to available information for the hazardous waste that—

(a) Identifies its hazardous chemical components,

(b) Describes its physical or health hazards, or

(c) Specifies appropriate protective measures.

§ 47.54 Availability of an MSDS.

The operator must make MSDSs accessible to miners during each work shift for each hazardous chemical to which they may be exposed either—

(a) At each work area where the hazardous chemical is produced or used, or

(b) At an alternative location, provided that the MSDS is readily available to miners in an emergency.

§ 47.55 Retaining an MSDS.

The operator must—

(a) Retain its MSDS for as long as the hazardous chemical is known to be at the mine, and

(b) Notify miners at least 3 months before disposing of the MSDS.

Subpart G [Reserved]

Subpart H—Making HazCom Information Available

§ 47.71 Access to HazCom materials.

Upon request, the operator must provide access to all HazCom materials required by this part to miners and designated representatives, except as provided in § 47.81 through § 47.87 (provisions for trade secrets).

§ 47.72 Cost for copies.

(a) The operator must provide the first copy and each revision of the HazCom material without cost.

(b) Fees for a subsequent copy of the HazCom material must be non-discriminatory and reasonable.

§ 47.73 Providing labels and MSDSs to customers.

For a hazardous chemical produced at the mine, the operator must provide customers, upon request, with the

237

§ 47.81

chemical's label or a copy of the label information, and the chemical's MSDS.

Subpart I—Trade Secret Hazardous Chemical

§ 47.81 Provisions for withholding trade secrets.

(a) Operators may withhold the identity of a trade secret chemical, including the name and other specific identification, from the written list of hazardous chemicals, the label, and the MSDS, provided that the operator—

(1) Can support the claim that the chemical's identity is a trade secret,

(2) Identifies the chemical in a way that it can be referred to without disclosing the secret,

(3) Indicates in the MSDS that the chemical's identity is withheld as a trade secret, and

(4) Discloses in the MSDS information on the properties and effects of the hazardous chemical.

(b) The operator must make the chemical's identity available to miners, designated representatives, and health professionals in accordance with the provisions of this subpart.

(c) This subpart does not require the operator to disclose process or percentage of mixture information, which is a trade secret, under any circumstances.

§ 47.82 Disclosure of information to MSHA.

(a) Even if the operator has a trade secret claim, the operator must disclose to MSHA, upon request, any information which this subpart requires the operator to make available.

(b) The operator must make a trade secret claim, no later than at the time the information is provided to MSHA, so that MSHA can determine the trade secret status and implement the necessary protection.

§ 47.83 Disclosure in a medical emergency.

(a) Upon request and regardless of the existence of a written statement of need or a confidentiality agreement, the operator must immediately disclose the identity of a trade secret chemical to the treating health professional when that person determines that—

(1) A medical emergency exists, and

(2) The identity of the hazardous chemical is necessary for emergency or first-aid treatment.

(b) The operator may require a written statement of need and confidentiality agreement in accordance with the provisions of § 47.84 and § 47.85 as soon as circumstances permit.

§ 47.84 Non-emergency disclosure.

Upon request, the operator must disclose the identity of a trade secret chemical in a non-emergency situation to an exposed miner, the miner's designated representative, or a health professional providing services to the miner, if the following conditions are met.

(a) The request is in writing.

(b) The request describes in reasonable detail an occupational health need for the information, as follows:

(1) To assess the chemical hazards to which the miner will be exposed.

(2) To conduct or assess health sampling to determine the miner's exposure levels.

(3) To conduct reassignment or periodic medical surveillance of the exposed miner.

(4) To provide medical treatment to the exposed miner.

(5) To select or assess appropriate personal protective equipment for the exposed miner.

(6) To design or assess engineering controls or other protective measures for the exposed miner.

(7) To conduct studies to determine the health effects of exposure.

(c) The request explains in detail why the disclosure of the following information would not satisfy the purpose described in paragraph (b) of this section:

(1) The properties and effects of the chemical.

(2) Measures for controlling the miner's exposure to the chemical.

(3) Methods of monitoring and analyzing the miner's exposure to the chemical.

(4) Methods of diagnosing and treating harmful exposures to the chemical.

(d) The request describes the procedures to be used to maintain the confidentiality of the disclosed information.

(e) The person making the request enters a written confidentiality agreement that he or she will not use the information for any purpose other than the health needs asserted and agrees not to release the information under any circumstances, except as authorized by §47.85, by the terms of the agreement, or by the operator.

§47.85 Confidentiality agreement and remedies.

(a) The confidentiality agreement authorized by §47.84—

(1) May restrict the use of the trade secret chemical identity to the health purposes indicated in the written statement of need;

(2) May provide for appropriate legal remedies in the event of a breach of the agreement, including stipulation of a reasonable pre-estimate of likely damages;

(3) Must allow the exposed miner, the miner's designated representative, or the health professional to disclose the trade secret chemical identity to MSHA;

(4) May provide that the exposed miner, the miner's designated representative, or the health professional inform the operator who provided the trade secret chemical identity prior to or at the same time as its disclosure to MSHA; and

(5) May not include requirements for the posting of a penalty bond.

(b) Nothing in this subpart precludes the parties from pursuing non-contractual remedies to the extent permitted by law.

§47.86 Denial of a written request for disclosure.

To deny a written request for disclosure of the identity of a trade secret chemical, the operator must—

(a) Put the denial in writing,

(1) Including evidence to substantiate the claim that the chemical's identity is a trade secret,

(2) Stating the specific reasons why the request is being denied, and

(3) Explaining how alternative information will satisfy the specific medical or occupational health need without revealing the chemical's identity.

(b) Provide the denial to the health professional, miner, or designated representative within 30 days of the request.

§47.87 Review of denial.

(a) The health professional, miner, or designated representative may refer the written denial to MSHA for review. The request for review must include a copy of—

(1) The request for disclosure of the identity of the trade secret chemical,

(2) The confidentiality agreement, and

(3) The operator's written denial.

(b) If MSHA determines that the identity of the trade secret chemical should have been disclosed, the operator will be subject to citation by MSHA.

(c) If MSHA determines that the confidentiality agreement would not sufficiently protect against unauthorized disclosure of the trade secret, MSHA may impose additional conditions to ensure that the occupational health services are provided without an undue risk of harm to the operator.

(d) If the operator contests a citation for a failure to release the identity of a trade secret chemical, the matter will be adjudicated by the Federal Mine Safety and Health Review Commission. The Administrative Law Judge may review the citation and supporting documentation "in camera" or issue appropriate orders to protect the trade secret.

Subpart J—Exemptions

§47.91 Exemptions from the HazCom standard.

A hazardous chemical is exempt from this part under the conditions described in Table 47.91 as follows:

TABLE 47.91—CHEMICALS AND PRODUCTS EXEMPT FROM THIS HAZCOM STANDARD

Exemption	Conditions for exemption
Article	If, under normal conditions of use, it— (1) Releases no more than insignificant amounts of a hazardous chemical, and

§ 47.92

TABLE 47.91—CHEMICALS AND PRODUCTS EXEMPT FROM THIS HAZCOM STANDARD—Continued

Exemption	Conditions for exemption
Biological hazards	(2) Poses no physical or health risk to exposed miners. All biological hazards, such as poisonous plants, insects, and micro-organisms.
Consumer product or hazardous substance regulated by CPSC.	(1) If the miner uses it for the purpose the manufacturer intended; and
	(2) Such use does not expose the miner more often and for longer periods than *ordinary consumer use*.
Cosmetics, drugs, food, food additive, color additive, drinks, alcoholic beverages, tobacco and tobacco products, or medical or veterinary device or product, including materials intended for use as ingredients in such products (such as flavors and fragrances).	When intended for personal consumption or use.
Radiation	All ionizing or non-ionizing radiation, such as alpha or gamma, microwaves, or x-rays.
Wood or wood products, including lumber	If they do not release or otherwise result in exposure to a hazardous chemical under normal conditions of use. For example, wood is not exempt if it is treated with a hazardous chemical or if it will be subsequently cut or sanded.

§ 47.92 Exemptions from labeling.

A hazardous chemical is exempt from subpart E of this part under the conditions described in Table 47.92 as follows:

TABLE 47.92—HAZARDOUS CHEMICALS EXEMPT FROM LABELING

Exemption	Conditions for exemption
Chemical substance, consumer product, hazardous substance, or pesticide.	When kept in its manufacturer's or supplier's original packaging labeled under other federal labeling requirements.
Hazardous substance	When the subject of remedial or removal action under the Comprehensive Environmental Response, Compensation and Liability Act (CERCLA) in accordance with EPA regulations.
Hazardous waste	When regulated by EPA under the Solid Waste Disposal Act as amended by the Resource Conservation and Recovery Act.
Raw material being mined or processed	While on mine property, except when the container holds a mixture of the raw material and another hazardous chemical and the mixture is found to be hazardous under § 47.21—Identifying hazardous chemicals.
Wood or wood products, including lumber	Wood or wood products are always exempt from labeling.

[67 FR 42383, June 21, 2002; 67 FR 42366, Sept. 11, 2002; 67 FR 63655, Oct. 11, 2002]

PART 48—TRAINING AND RETRAINING OF MINERS

Subpart A—Training and Retraining of Underground Miners

Sec.
48.1 Scope.
48.2 Definitions.
48.3 Training plans; time of submission; where filed; information required; time for approval; method for disapproval; commencement of training; approval of instructors.
48.4 Cooperative training program.
48.5 Training of new miners; minimum courses of instruction; hours of instruction.
48.6 Experienced miner training.
48.7 Training of miners assigned to a task in which they have had no previous experience; minimum courses of instruction.
48.8 Annual refresher training of miners; minimum courses of instruction; hours of instruction.
48.9 Records of training.
48.10 Compensation for training.
48.11 Hazard training.
48.12 Appeals procedures.

Subpart B—Training and Retraining of Miners Working at Surface Mines and Surface Areas of Underground Mines

48.21 Scope.
48.22 Definitions.
48.23 Training plans; time of submission; where filed; information required; time for approval; method for disapproval;

commencement of training; approval of instructors.
48.24 Cooperative training program.
48.25 Training of new miners; minimum courses of instruction; hours of instruction.
48.26 Experienced miner training.
48.27 Training of miners assigned to a task in which they have had no previous experience; minimum courses of instruction.
48.28 Annual refresher training of miners; minimum courses of instruction; hours of instruction.
48.29 Records of training.
48.30 Compensation for training.
48.31 Hazard training.
48.32 Appeals procedures.

AUTHORITY: 30 U.S.C. 811, 825.

SOURCE: 43 FR 47459, Oct. 13, 1978, unless otherwise noted.

Subpart A—Training and Retraining of Underground Miners

§ 48.1 Scope.

The provisions of this subpart A set forth the mandatory requirements for submitting and obtaining approval of programs for training and retraining miners working in underground mines. Requirements regarding compensation for training and retraining are also included. The requirements for training and retraining miners working at surface mines and surface areas of underground mines are set forth in subpart B of this part.

§ 48.2 Definitions.

For the purposes of this subpart A—

(a)(1) *Miner* means, for purposes of §§ 48.3 through 48.10 of this subpart A, any person working in an underground mine and who is engaged in the extraction and production process, or engaged in shaft or slope construction, or who is regularly exposed to mine hazards, or who is a maintenance or service worker employed by the operator or a maintenance or service worker contracted by the operator to work at the mine for frequent or extended periods. This definition shall include the operator if the operator works underground on a continuing, even if irregular basis. Short-term, specialized contract workers, such as drillers and blasters, who are engaged in the extraction and production process or engaged in shaft or slope construction and who have received training under § 48.6 (Experienced miner training) of this subpart A may, in lieu of subsequent training under that section for each new employment, receive training under § 48.11 (Hazard training) of this subpart A. This definition does not include:

(i) Workers under subpart C of this part 48, engaged in the construction of major additions to an existing mine which requires the mine to cease operations;

(ii) Any person covered under paragraph (a)(2) of this section.

(2) *Miner* means, for purposes of § 48.11 (Hazard training) of this subpart A, any person working in an underground mine, including any delivery, office, or scientific worker or occasional, short-term maintenance or service worker contracted by the operator, and any student engaged in academic projects involving his or her extended presence at the mine. This definition excludes persons covered under paragraph (a)(1) of this section and subpart C of this part.

(b) *Experienced miner* means:

(1) A miner who has completed MSHA-approved new miner training for underground miners or training acceptable to MSHA from a State agency and who has had at least 12 months of underground mining experience; or

(2) A supervisor who is certified under an MSHA-approved State certification program and who is employed as an underground supervisor on October 6, 1998; or

(3) An experienced underground miner on February 3, 1999.

(4)(i) A person employed as an underground shaft or slope construction worker on June 28, 2006; or

(ii) A person who has six months of underground shaft or slope experience within 24 months before June 28, 2006.

(c) *New miner* means a miner who is not an experienced miner.

(d) *Normal working hours* means a period of time during which a miner is otherwise scheduled to work. This definition does not preclude scheduling training classes on the sixth or seventh working day if such a work schedule has been established for a sufficient period of time to be accepted as the operator's common practice. Miners shall

§ 48.3

be paid at a rate of pay which shall correspond to the rate of pay they would have received had they been performing their normal work tasks.

(e) *Operator* means any owner, lessee, or other person who operates, controls or supervises an underground mine; or any independent contractor identified as an operator performing services or construction at such mine.

(f) *Task* means a work assignment that includes duties of a job that occur on a regular basis and which requires physical abilities and job knowledge.

(g) *Act* means the Federal Mine Safety and Health Act of 1977.

[43 FR 47459, Oct. 13, 1978, as amended at 63 FR 53759, Oct. 6, 1998; 70 FR 77727, Dec. 30, 2005]

§ 48.3 Training plans; time of submission; where filed; information required; time for approval; method for disapproval; commencement of training; approval of instructors.

(a) Except as provided in paragraphs (o) and (p) of this section, each operator of an underground mine shall have an MSHA approved plan containing programs for training new miners, training experienced miners, training miners for new tasks, annual refresher training, and hazard training for miners as follows:

(1) In the case of an underground mine which is operating on the effective date of this subpart A, the operator of the mine shall submit such plan for approval within 90 days after the effective date of this subpart A.

(2) Within 60 days after the operator submits the plan for approval, unless extended by MSHA, the operator shall have an approved plan for the mine.

(3) In the case of a new underground mine which is to be opened or a mine which is to be reopened or reactivated after the effective date of this subpart A, the operator shall have an approved plan prior to opening the new mine, or reopening or reactivating the mine.

(b) The training plan shall be filed with the District Manager for the area in which the mine is located.

(c) Each operator shall submit to the District Manager the following information:

(1) The company name, mine name, and MSHA identification number of the mine.

(2) The name and position of the person designated by the operator who is responsible for health and safety training at the mine. This person may be the operator.

(3) A list of MSHA approved instructors with whom the operator proposes to make arrangements to teach the courses, and the courses each instructor is qualified to teach.

(4) The location where training will be given for each course.

(5) A description of the teaching methods and the course materials which are to be used in training.

(6) The approximate number of miners employed at the mine and the maximum number who will attend each session of training.

(7) The predicted time or periods of time when regularly scheduled refresher training will be given. This schedule shall include the titles of courses to be taught, the total number of instruction hours for each course, and the predicted time and length of each session of training.

(8) For the purposes of § 48.7 (New task training of miners) of this subpart A, the operator shall submit:

(i) A complete list of task assignments to correspond with the definition of "task" in § 48.2 (f) of this subpart A.

(ii) The titles of personnel conducting the training for this section.

(iii) The outline of training procedures used in training miners in those work assignments listed according to paragraph (c)(8)(i) of this section.

(iv) The evaluation procedures used to determine the effectiveness of training under § 48.7 of this subpart A.

(d) The operator shall furnish to the representative of the miners a copy of the training plan two weeks prior to its submission to the District Manager. Where a miners' representative is not designated, a copy of the plan shall be posted on the mine bulletin board 2 weeks prior to its submission to the District Manager. Written comments received by the operator from miners or their representatives shall be submitted to the District Manager. Miners or their representatives may submit

Mine Safety and Health Admin., Labor § 48.3

written comments directly to the District Manager.

(e) All training required by the training plan submitted to and approved by the District Manager as required by this subpart A shall be subject to evaluation by the District Manager to determine the effectiveness of the training programs. If it is deemed necessary, the District Manager may require changes in, or additions to, programs. Upon request from the District Manager the operator shall make available for evaluation the instructional materials, handouts, visual aids and other teaching accessories used or to be used in the training programs. Upon request from the District Manager the operator shall provide information concerning the schedules of upcoming training.

(f) The operator shall make a copy of the MSHA approved training plan available at the mine site for MSHA inspection and for examination by the miners and their representatives.

(g) Except as provided in § 48.7 (New task training of miners) and § 48.11 (Hazard training) of this subpart A, all courses shall be conducted by MSHA approved instructors.

(h) Instructors shall be approved by the District Manager in one or more of the following ways:

(1) Instructors shall take an instructor's training course conducted by the District Manager or given by persons designated by the District Manager to give such instruction; and instructors shall have satisfactorily completed a program of instruction approved by the Office of Educational Policy and Development, MSHA, in the subject matter to be taught.

(2) Instructors may be designated by MSHA as approved instructors to teach specific courses based on written evidence of the instructors' qualifications and teaching experience.

(3) At the discretion of the District Manager, instructors may be designated by MSHA as approved instructors to teach specific courses based on the performance of the instructors while teaching classes monitored by MSHA. Operators shall indicate in the training plans submitted for approval whether they want to have instructors approved based on monitored performance. The District Manager shall consider such factors as the size of the mine, the number of employees, the mine safety record and remoteness from a training facility when determining whether instructor approval based on monitored performance is appropriate.

(4) On the effective date of this subpart A, cooperative instructors who have been designated by MSHA to teach MSHA approved courses and who have taught such courses within the 24 months prior to the effective date of this subpart A shall be considered approved instructors for such courses.

(i) Instructors may have their approval revoked by MSHA for good cause which may include not teaching a course at least once every 24 months. Before any revocation is effective, the District Manager must send written reasons for revocation to the instructor and the instructor shall be given an opportunity to demonstrate or achieve compliance before the District Manager on the matter. A decision by the District Manager to revoke an instructor's approval may be appealed by the instructor to the Administrator for Coal Mine Safety and Health or Administrator for Metal and Nonmetal Mine Safety and Health, as appropriate, MSHA, 201 12th Street South, Arlington, VA 22202–5452. Such an appeal shall be submitted to the Administrator within 5 days of notification of the District Manager's decision. Upon revocation of an instructor's approval, the District Manager shall immediately notify operators who use the instructor for training.

(j) The District Manager for the area in which the mine is located shall notify the operator and the miners' representative, in writing, within 60 days from the date on which the training plan is filed, of the approval or status of the approval of the training programs.

(1) If revisions are required for approval, or to retain approval thereafter, the revisions required shall be specified to the operator and the miners' representative and the operator and the miners' representative shall be afforded an opportunity to discuss the revisions with the District Manager, or to propose alternate revisions or

changes. The District Manager, in consultation with the operator and the representative of the miners, shall fix a time within which the discussion will be held, or alternate revisions or changes submitted, before final approval is made.

(2) The District Manager may approve separate programs of the training plan and withhold approval of other programs, pending discussion of revisions or submission of alternate revisions or changes.

(k) Except as provided under §48.8(c) (Annual refresher training of miners) of this subpart A, the operator shall commence training of miners within 60 days after approval of the training plan, or approved programs of the training plan.

(l) The operator shall notify the District Manager of the area in which the mine is located, and the miners' representative of any changes or modifications the operator proposes to make in the approved training plan. The operator shall obtain the approval of the District Manager for such changes or modifications.

(m) In the event the District Manager disapproves a training plan or a proposed modification of a training plan or requires changes in a training plan or modification, the District Manager shall notify the operator and the miners' representative in writing of:

(1) The specific changes or items of deficiency.

(2) The action necessary to effect the changes or bring the disapproved training plan or modification into compliance.

(3) The deadline for completion of remedial action to effect compliance, which shall serve to suspend punitive action under the provisions of sections 104 and 110 of the Act and other related regulations until that established deadline date, except that no such suspension shall take place in imminent danger situations.

(n) The operator shall post on the mine bulletin board, and provide to the miners' representative, a copy of all MSHA revisions and decisions which concern the training plan at the mine and which are issued by the District Manager.

(o) Each operator engaged in shaft or slope construction shall have an MSHA-approved training plan, as outlined in this section, containing programs for training new miners, training experienced miners, training miners for new tasks, annual refresher training, and hazard training for miners as follows:

(1) In the case of an operator engaged in shaft or slope construction on December 30, 2005, the operator shall submit a plan for approval by May 1, 2006, unless extended by MSHA.

(2) In the case of a new shaft or slope construction operator after June 28, 2006, the operator shall have an approved plan prior to commencing shaft or slope construction.

(p) Each underground coal operator, who is required to submit a revised program of instruction for 30 CFR 75.1502, shall also submit a revised training plan under this part 48.

(Pub. L. No. 96–511, 94 Stat. 2812 (44 U.S.C. 3501 et seq.))

[43 FR 47459, Oct. 13, 1978; 44 FR 1980, Jan. 9, 1979, as amended at 47 FR 14696, Apr. 6, 1982; 47 FR 23640, May 28, 1982; 47 FR 28095, June 29, 1982; 60 FR 33722, June 29, 1995; 63 FR 53759, Oct. 6, 1998; 67 FR 38384, June 4, 2002; 70 FR 77727, Dec. 30, 2005; 71 FR 12268, Mar. 9, 2006; 71 FR 71451, Dec. 8, 2006; 80 FR 52986, Sept. 2, 2015]

§ 48.4 Cooperative training program.

(a) An operator of a mine may conduct his own training programs, or may participate in training programs conducted by MSHA, or may participate in MSHA approved training programs conducted by State or other Federal agencies, or associations of mine operators, miners' representatives, other mine operators, private associations, or educational institutions.

(b) Each program and course of instruction shall be given by instructors who have been approved by MSHA to instruct in the courses which are given, and such courses and the training programs shall be adapted to the mining operations and practices existing at the mine and shall be approved by the District Manager for the area in which the mine is located.

[43 FR 47459, Oct. 13, 1978, as amended at 47 FR 23640, May 28, 1982]

§ 48.5 Training of new miners; minimum courses of instruction; hours of instruction.

(a) Each new miner shall receive no less than 40 hours of training as prescribed in this section before such miner is assigned to work duties. Such training shall be conducted in conditions which as closely as practicable duplicate actual underground conditions, and approximately 8 hours of training shall be given at the minesite.

(b) The training program for new miners shall include the following courses:

(1) *Instruction in the statutory rights of miners and their representatives under the Act; authority and responsibility of supervisors.* The course shall include instruction in the statutory rights of miners and their representatives under the Act, including a discussion of section 2 of the Act; a review and description of the line of authority of supervisors and miners' representatives and the responsibilities of such supervisors and miners' representatives; and an introduction to the operator's rules and the procedures for reporting hazards.

(2) *Self-rescue and respiratory devices.* The course shall be given before a new miner goes underground and shall include—

(i) Instruction and demonstration in the use, care, and maintenance of self-rescue and respiratory devices used at the mine;

(ii) Hands-on training in the complete donning of all types of self-contained self-rescue devices used at the mine, which includes assuming a donning position, opening the device, activating the device, inserting the mouthpiece, and putting on the nose clip; and

(iii) Hands-on training in transferring between all applicable self-rescue devices.

(3) *Entering and leaving the mine; transportation; communications.* The course shall include instruction on the procedures in effect for entering and leaving the mine; the check-in and checkout system in effect at the mine; the procedures for riding on and in mine conveyances; the controls in effect for the transportation of miners and materials; and the use of the mine communication systems, warning signals, and directional signs.

(4) *Introduction to the work environment.* The course shall include a visit and tour of the mine, or portions of the mine which are representative of the entire mine. A method of mining utilized at the mine shall be observed and explained.

(5) *Mine map; escapeways; emergency evacuation; barricading.* The program of instruction for mine emergency evacuation and firefighting approved by the District Manager under 30 CFR 75.1502 or the escape and evacuation plan under 30 CFR 57.11053, as applicable, shall be used for this course. The course shall include—

(i) A review of the mine map; the escapeway system; the escape, firefighting, and emergency evacuation plans in effect at the mine; and the location of abandoned areas; and

(ii) An introduction to the methods of barricading and the locations of the barricading materials, where applicable.

(6) *Roof or ground control and ventilation plans.* The course shall include an introduction to and instruction on the roof or ground control plan in effect at the mine and procedures for roof and rib or ground control; and an introduction to and instruction on the ventilation plan in effect at the mine and the procedures for maintaining and controlling ventilation.

(7) *Health.* The course shall include instruction on the purpose of taking dust, noise, and other health measurements, and any health control plan in effect at the mine shall be explained. The health provisions of the act and warning labels shall also be explained.

(8) *Cleanup; rock dusting.* The course shall include instruction on the purpose of rock dusting and the cleanup and rock dusting program in effect at the mine, where applicable.

(9) *Hazard recognition.* The course shall include the recognition and avoidance of hazards present in the mine, particularly any hazards related to explosives where explosives are used or stored at the mine.

(10) *Electrical hazards.* The course shall include recognition and avoidance of electrical hazards.

(11) *First aid.* The course shall include instruction in first aid methods acceptable to MSHA.

§ 48.6

(12) *Mine gases.* The course shall include instruction in the detection and avoidance of hazards associated with mine gases.

(13) *Health and safety aspects of the tasks to which the new miner will be assigned.* The course shall include instruction in the health and safety aspects of the tasks to be assigned, including the safe work procedures of such tasks, the mandatory health and safety standards pertinent to such tasks, information about the physical and health hazards of chemicals in the miner's work area, the protective measures a miner can take against these hazards, and the contents of the mine's HazCom program.

(14) Such other courses as may be required by the District Manager based on circumstances and conditions at the mine.

(c) Methods, including oral, written, or practical demonstration, to determine successful completion of the training shall be included in the training plan. The methods for determining such completion shall be administered to the miner before he is assigned work duties.

(d) A newly employed miner who has less than 12 months of mining experience and has received the courses and hours of instruction in paragraphs (a) and (b) of this section, within 36 months preceding employment at a mine, does not have to repeat this training. Before the miner starts work, the operator must provide the miner with the experienced miner training in § 48.6(b) of this part and, if applicable, the new task training in § 48.7 of this part. The operator must also provide the miner with annual refresher training and additional new task training, as applicable.

[43 FR 47459, Oct. 13, 1978, as amended at 47 FR 23640, May 28, 1982; 53 FR 10335, Mar. 30, 1988; 63 FR 53760, Oct. 6, 1998; 67 FR 42388, June 21, 2002; 71 FR 12268, Mar. 9, 2006; 71 FR 71451, Dec. 8, 2006]

§ 48.6 Experienced miner training.

(a) Except as provided in paragraph (e), this section applies to experienced miners who are—

(1) Newly employed by the operator;

(2) Transferred to the mine;

(3) Experienced underground miners transferred from surface to underground; or

(4) Returning to the mine after an absence of more than 12 months.

(b) Experienced miners must complete the training prescribed in this section before beginning work duties. Each experienced miner returning to mining following an absence of 5 years or more, must receive at least 8 hours of training. The training must include the following instruction:

(1) *Introduction to work environment.* The course shall include a visit and tour of the mine. The methods of mining utilized at the mine shall be observed and explained.

(2) *Mandatory health and safety standards.* The course shall include the mandatory health and safety standards pertinent to the tasks to be assigned.

(3) *Authority and responsibility of supervisors and miners' representatives.* The course shall include a review and description of the line of authority of supervisors and miners' representatives and the responsibilities of such supervisors and miners' representatives; and an introduction to the operator's rules and the procedures for reporting hazards.

(4) *Entering and leaving the mine; transportation; communications.* The course shall include instruction in the procedures in effect for entering and leaving the mine; the check-in and checkout system in effect at the mine; the procedures for riding on and in mine conveyances; the controls in effect for the transportation of miners and materials; and the use of the mine communication systems, warning signals, and directional signs.

(5) *Mine map; escapeways; emergency evacuation; barricading.* The program of instruction for mine emergency evacuation and firefighting approved by the District Manager under 30 CFR 75.1502 or the escape and evacuation plan under 30 CFR 57.11053, as applicable, shall be used for this course. The course shall include—

(i) A review of the mine map; the escapeway system; the escape, firefighting, and emergency evacuation plans in effect at the mine; and the location of abandoned areas; and

Mine Safety and Health Admin., Labor § 48.7

(ii) Methods of barricading and the locations of barricading materials, where applicable.

(6) *Roof or ground control and ventilation plans.* The course shall include an introduction to and instruction on the roof or ground control plan in effect at the mine and procedures for roof and rib or ground control; and an introduction to and instruction on the ventilation plan in effect at the mine and the procedures for maintaining and controlling ventilation.

(7) *Hazard recognition.* The course must include the recognition and avoidance of hazards present in the mine.

(8) *Prevention of accidents.* The course must include a review of the general causes of accidents applicable to the mine environment, causes of specific accidents at the mine, and instruction in accident prevention in the work environment.

(9) *Emergency medical procedures.* The course must include instruction on the mine's emergency medical arrangements and the location of the mine's first aid equipment and supplies.

(10) *Health.* The course must include instruction on the purpose of taking dust, noise, and other health measurements, where applicable; must review the health provisions of the Act; and must explain warning labels and any health control plan in effect at the mine.

(11) *Health and safety aspects of the tasks to which the experienced miner is assigned.* The course must include instruction in the health and safety aspects of the tasks assigned, including the safe work procedures of such tasks, information about the physical and health hazards of chemicals in the miner's work area, the protective measures a miner can take against these hazards, and the contents of the mine's HazCom program. Experienced miners who must complete new task training under §48.7 do not need to take training under this paragraph.

(12) *Self-rescue and respiratory devices.* The course shall be given before the miner goes underground and shall include—

(i) Instruction and demonstration in the use, care, and maintenance of self-rescue and respiratory devices used at the mine;

(ii) Hands-on training in the complete donning of all types of self-contained self-rescue devices used at the mine, which includes assuming a donning position, opening the device, activating the device, inserting the mouthpiece, and putting on the nose clip; and

(iii) Hands-on training in transferring between all applicable self-rescue devices.

(13) Such other courses as may be required by the District Manager based on circumstances and conditions at the mine.

(c) The operator may include instruction on additional safety and health subjects based on circumstances and conditions at the mine.

(d) The training time spent on individual subjects must vary depending upon the training needs of the miners.

(e) Any miner returning to the same mine, following an absence of 12 months or less, must receive training on any major changes to the mine environment that have occurred during the miner's absence and that could adversely affect the miner's health or safety.

(1) A person designated by the operator who is knowledgeable of these changes must conduct the training in this paragraph. An MSHA approved instructor is not required to conduct the training outlined in this paragraph.

(2) No record of this training is required.

(3) The miner must also complete annual refresher training as required in §48.8, if the miner missed taking that training during the absence.

[43 FR 47459, Oct. 13, 1978, as amended at 47 FR 23640, May 28, 1982; 53 FR 10335, Mar. 30, 1988; 53 FR 12415, Apr. 14, 1988; 63 FR 53760, Oct. 6, 1998; 67 FR 42388, June 21, 2002; 71 FR 12268, Mar. 9, 2006; 71 FR 71451, Dec. 8, 2006]

§ 48.7 Training of miners assigned to a task in which they have had no previous experience; minimum courses of instruction.

(a) Miners assigned to new work tasks as mobile equipment operators, drilling machine operators, haulage and conveyor systems operators, roof and ground control machine operators, and those in blasting operations shall not perform new work tasks in these

§ 48.8

categories until training prescribed in this paragraph and paragraph (b) of this section has been completed. This training shall not be required for miners who have been trained and who have demonstrated safe operating procedures for such new work tasks within 12 months preceding assignment. This training shall also not be required for miners who have performed the new work tasks and who have demonstrated safe operating procedures for such new work tasks within 12 months preceding assignment. The training program shall include the following:

(1) *Health and safety aspects and safe operating procedures for work tasks, equipment, and machinery.* The training shall include instruction in the health and safety aspects and the safe operating procedures related to the assigned tasks, including information about the physical and health hazards of chemicals in the miner's work area, the protective measures a miner can take against these hazards, and the contents of the mine's HazCom program. The training shall be given in an on-the-job environment; and

(2)(i) *Supervised practice during nonproduction.* The training shall include supervised practice in the assigned tasks, and the performance of work duties at times or places where production is not the primary objective; on

(ii) *Supervised operation during production.* The training shall include, while under direct and immediate supervision and production is in progress, operation of the machine or equipment and the performance of work duties.

(3) *New or modified machines and equipment.* Equipment and machine operators shall be instructed in safe operating procedures applicable to new or modified machines or equipment to be installed or put into operation in the mine, which require new or different operating procedures.

(4) Such other courses as may be required by the District Manager based on circumstances and conditions at the mine.

(b) Miners under paragraph (a) of this section shall not operate the equipment or machine or engage in blasting operations without direction and immediate supervision until such miners have demonstrated safe operating procedures for the equipment or machine or blasting operation to the operator or the operator's agent.

(c) Miners assigned a new task not covered in paragraph (a) of this section shall be instructed in the safety and health aspects and safe work procedures of the task, including information about the physical and health hazards of chemicals in the miner's work area, the protective measures a miner can take against these hazards, and the contents of the mine's HazCom program, prior to performing such task.

(d) Any person who controls or directs haulage operations at a mine shall receive and complete training courses in safe haulage procedures related to the haulage system, ventilation system, firefighting procedures, and emergency evacuation procedures in effect at the mine before assignment to such duties.

(e) All training and supervised practice and operation required by this section shall be given by a qualified trainer, or a supervisor experienced in the assigned tasks, or other person experienced in the assigned tasks.

[43 FR 47459, Oct. 13, 1978, as amended at 44 FR 1980, Jan. 9, 1979; 47 FR 23640, May 28, 1982; 67 FR 42388, June 21, 2002]

§ 48.8 Annual refresher training of miners; minimum courses of instruction; hours of instruction.

(a) Each miner shall receive a minimum of 8 hours of annual refresher training as prescribed in this section.

(b) The annual refresher training program for all miners shall include the following courses of instruction:

(1) *Mandatory health and safety standards.* The course shall include mandatory health and safety standard requirements which are related to the miner's tasks.

(2) *Transportation controls and communication systems.* The course shall include instruction on the procedures for riding on and in mine conveyances; the controls in effect for the transportation of miners and materials; and the use of the mine communication systems, warning signals, and directional signs.

(3) *Barricading.* The course shall include a review of the methods of barricading and locations of barricading materials, where applicable.

(4) *Roof or ground control, ventilation, emergency evacuation and firefighting plans.* The course shall include a review of roof or ground control plans in effect at the mine and the procedures for maintaining and controlling ventilation. In addition, for underground coal mines, except for miners who receive this training under 30 CFR 75.1504, the course shall include a review of the emergency evacuation and firefighting program of instruction in effect at the mine.

(5) *First aid.* The course shall include a review of first aid methods acceptable to MSHA.

(6) *Electrical hazards.* The course shall include recognition and avoidance of electrical hazards.

(7) *Prevention of accidents.* The course shall include a review of accidents and causes of accidents, and instruction in accident prevention in the work environment.

(8) *Self-rescue and respiratory devices.* The course shall include instruction and demonstration in the use, care, and maintenance of self-rescue and respiratory devices used at the mine. In addition, except for miners who receive this training under 30 CFR 75.1504, the training for self-contained self-rescue (SCSR) devices shall include:

(i) Hands-on training in the complete donning of all types of self-contained self-rescue devices used at the mine, which includes assuming a donning position, opening the device, activating the device, inserting the mouthpiece, and putting on the nose clip; and

(ii) Hands-on training in transferring between all applicable self-rescue devices.

(9) *Explosives.* The course shall include a review and instruction on the hazards related to explosives. The only exception to this course component is when there are no explosives used or stored on the mine property.

(10) *Mine gases.* The course shall include instruction in the detection and avoidance of hazards associated with mine gases.

(11) *Health.* The course shall include instruction on the purpose of taking dust, noise, and other health measurements and any health control plan in effect at the mine shall be explained. The health provisions of the Act and warning labels shall also be explained.

(12) Such other courses as may be required by the District Manager based on circumstances and conditions at the mine.

(c) Refresher training may include other health and safety subjects that are relevant to mining operations at the mine. Recommended subjects include, but are not limited to, information about the physical and health hazards of chemicals in the miner's work area, the protective measures a miner can take against these hazards, and the contents of the mine's HazCom program.

(d) All persons employed as shaft or slope construction workers on June 28, 2006 must receive annual refresher training within 12 months of June 2006.

(e) Where annual refresher training is conducted periodically, such sessions shall not be less than 30 minutes of actual instruction time and the miners shall be notified that the session is part of annual refresher training.

[43 FR 47459, Oct. 13, 1978, as amended at 47 FR 23640, May 28, 1982; 53 FR 10336, Mar. 30, 1988; 63 FR 53760, Oct. 6, 1998; 67 FR 42389, June 21, 2002; 67 FR 76665, Dec. 12, 2002; 68 FR 53049, Sept. 9, 2003; 71 FR 12269, Mar. 9, 2006; 70 FR 77727, Dec. 30, 2005; 71 FR 71451, Dec. 8, 2006]

§ 48.9 Records of training.

(a) Upon a miner's completion of each MSHA approved training program, the operator shall record and certify on MSHA form 5000–23 that the miner has received the specified training. A copy of the training certificate shall be given to the miner at the completion of the training. The training certificates for each miner shall be available at the minesite for inspection by MSHA and for examination by the miners, the miner's representative, and State inspection agencies. When a miner leaves the operator's employ, the miner shall be entitled to a copy of his training certificates.

(b) False certification that training was given shall be punishable under section 110 (a) and (f) of the Act.

§ 48.10

(c) Copies of training certificates for currently employed miners shall be kept at the minesite for 2 years, or for 60 days after termination of employment.

(Pub. L. No. 96–511, 94 Stat. 2812 (44 U.S.C. 3501 et seq.))

[43 FR 47459, Oct. 13, 1978, as amended at 47 FR 14706, Apr. 6, 1982; 60 FR 33722, June 29, 1995]

§ 48.10 Compensation for training.

(a) Training shall be conducted during normal working hours; miners attending such training shall receive the rate of pay as provided in § 48.2(d) (Definition of normal working hours) of this subpart A.

(b) If such training shall be given at a location other than the normal place of work, miners shall be compensated for the additional cost, such as mileage, meals, and lodging, they may incur in attending such training sessions.

§ 48.11 Hazard training.

(a) Operators shall provide to those miners, as defined in § 48.2(a)(2) (Definition of miner) of this subpart A, a training program before such miners commence their work duties. This training program shall include the following instruction, which is applicable to the duties of such miners:

(1) Hazard recognition and avoidance;

(2) Emergency and evacuation procedures;

(3) Health and safety standards, safety rules, and safe working procedures;

(4) Use of self-rescue and respiratory devices, including:

(i) Hands-on training in the complete donning of all types of self-contained self-rescue devices used at the mine, which includes assuming a donning position, opening the device, activating the device, inserting the mouthpiece, and putting on the nose clip; and

(ii) Hands-on training in transferring between all applicable self-rescue devices; and

(5) Such other instruction as may be required by the District Manager based on circumstances and conditions at the mine.

(b) Miners shall receive the instruction required by this section at least once every 12 months.

(c) The training program required by this section shall be submitted with the training plan required by § 48.3(a) (Training plans: Submission and approval) of this subpart A and shall include a statement on the methods of instruction to be used.

(d) In accordance with § 48.9 (Records of training) of this subpart A, the operator shall maintain and make available for inspection certificates that miners have received the hazard training required by this section.

(e) Miners subject to hazard training shall be accompanied at all times while underground by an experienced miner, as defined in § 48.2(b) (Definition of miner) of this subpart A.

[43 FR 47459, Oct. 13, 1978, as amended at 47 FR 23640, May 25, 1982; 53 FR 10336, Mar. 30, 1988; 71 FR 12269, Mar. 9, 2006; 71 FR 71452, Dec. 8, 2006]

§ 48.12 Appeals procedures.

The operator, miner, and miners' representative shall have the right of appeal from a decision of the District Manager.

(a) In the event an operator, miner, or miners' representative decides to appeal a decision by a District Manager, such an appeal shall be submitted, in writing, to the Administrator for Coal Mine Safety and Health or the Administrator for Metal and Nonmetal Mine Safety and Health, as appropriate, MSHA, 201 12th Street South, Arlington, VA 22202–5452, within 30 days of notification of the District Manager's decision.

(b) The Administrator may require additional information from the operator, the miners, or their representatives, and the District Manager, if the Administrator determines such information is necessary.

(c) The Administrator shall render a decision on the appeal within 30 days after receipt of the appeal.

[43 FR 47459, Oct. 13, 1978, as amended at 47 FR 23640, May 28, 1982; 71 FR 16666, Apr. 3, 2006; 80 FR 52986, Sept. 2, 2015]

Subpart B—Training and Retraining of Miners Working at Surface Mines and Surface Areas of Underground Mines

§ 48.21 Scope.

The provisions of this subpart B set forth the mandatory requirements for submitting and obtaining approval of programs for training and retraining miners working at surface mines and surface areas of underground mines. Requirements regarding compensation for training and retraining are also included. The requirements for training and retraining miners working in underground mines are set forth in subpart A of this part. This part does not apply to training and retraining of miners at shell dredging, sand, gravel, surface stone, surface clay, colloidal phosphate, and surface limestone mines, which are covered under 30 CFR Part 46.

[43 FR 47459, Oct. 13, 1978, as amended at 64 FR 53130, Sept. 30, 1999]

§ 48.22 Definitions.

For the purposes of this subpart B—

(a)(1) *Miner* means, for purposes of §§ 48.23 through 48.30 of this subpart B, any person working in a surface mine or surface areas of an underground mine and who is engaged in the extraction and production process, or engaged in shaft or slope construction, or who is regularly exposed to mine hazards, or who is a maintenance or service worker employed by the operator or a maintenance or service worker contracted by the operator to work at the mine for frequent or extended periods. This definition shall include the operator if the operator works at the mine on a continuing, even if irregular, basis. Short-term, specialized contract workers, such as drillers and blasters, who are engaged in the extraction and production process or engaged in shaft or slope construction and who have received training under § 48.26 (Experienced miner training) of this subpart B, may in lieu of subsequent training under that section for each new employment, receive training under § 48.31 (Hazard training) of this subpart B. This definition does not include:

(i) Construction workers under subpart C of this Part 48;

(ii) Any person covered under paragraph (a)(2) of this section.

(2) *Miner* means, for purposes of § 48.31 (Hazard training) of this subpart B, any person working in a surface mine, including any delivery, office, or scientific worker or occasional, short-term maintenance or service worker contracted by the operator, and any student engaged in academic projects involving his or her extended presence at the mine. This definition excludes persons covered under paragraph (a)(1) of this section and subpart C of this part.

(b) *Experienced miner* means:

(1) A miner who has completed MSHA-approved new miner training for surface miners or training acceptable to MSHA from a State agency and who has had at least 12 months of surface mining experience; or

(2) A supervisor who is certified under an MSHA-approved State certification program and who is employed as a surface supervisor on October 6, 1998; or

(3) An experienced surface miner on February 3, 1999.

(4)(i) A person employed as a surface shaft or slope construction worker on the June 28, 2006; or,

(ii) A person who has six months of surface shaft or slope experience within 24 months before June 28, 2006.

(c) *New miner* means a miner who is not an experienced miner.

(d) *Normal working hours* means a period of time during which a miner is otherwise scheduled to work. This definition does not preclude scheduling training classes on the sixth or seventh working day if such a work schedule has been established for a sufficient period of time to be accepted as the operator's common practice. Miners shall be paid at a rate of pay which shall correspond to the rate of pay they would have received had they been performing their normal work tasks.

(e) *Operator* means any owner, lessee, or other person who operates, controls, or supervises a surface mine or surface area of an underground mine; or any independent contractor identified as an operator performing services or construction at such time.

§ 48.23

(f) *Task* means a work assignment that includes duties of a job that occur on a regular basis and which requires physical abilities and job knowledge.

(g) *Act* means the Federal Mine Safety and Health Act of 1977.

[43 FR 47459, Oct. 13, 1978; 44 FR 1980, Jan. 9, 1979, as amended at 63 FR 53759, 53760, Oct. 6, 1998; 70 FR 77727, Dec. 30, 2005]

§ 48.23 Training plans; time of submission; where filed; information required; time for approval; method for disapproval; commencement of training; approval of instructors.

(a) Except as provided in paragraph (o) of this section, each operator of a surface mine shall have an MSHA-approved plan containing programs for training new miners, training experienced miners, training miners for new tasks, annual refresher training, and hazard training for miners as follows:

(1) In the case of a mine which is operating on the effective date of this subpart B, the operator of the mine shall submit such plan for approval within 150 days after the effective date of this subpart B.

(2) Within 60 days after the operator submits the plan for approval, unless extended by MSHA, the operator shall have an approved plan for the mine.

(3) In the case of a new mine which is to be opened or a mine which is to be reopened or reactivated after the effective date of this subpart B, the operator shall have an approved plan prior to opening the new mine, or reopening or reactivating the mine unless the mine is reopened or reactivated periodically using portable equipment and mobile teams of miners as a normal method of operation by the operator. The operator to be so excepted shall maintain an approved plan for training covering all mine locations which are operated with portable equipment and mobile teams of miners.

(b) The training plan shall be filed with the District Manager for the area in which the mine is located.

(c) Each operator shall submit to the District Manager the following information:

(1) The company name, mine name, and MSHA identification number of the mine.

(2) The name and position of the person designated by the operator who is responsible for health and safety training at the mine. This person may be the operator.

(3) A list of MSHA approved instructors with whom the operator proposes to make arrangements to teach the courses, and the courses each instructor is qualified to teach.

(4) The location where training will be given for each course.

(5) A description of the teaching methods and the course materials which are to be used in training.

(6) The approximate number of miners employed at the mine and the maximum number who will attend each session of training.

(7) The predicted time or periods of time when regularly scheduled refresher training will be given. This schedule shall include the titles of courses to be taught, the total number of instruction hours for each course, and the predicted time and length of each session of training.

(8) For the purposes of § 48.27 (New task training of miners) of this subpart B, the operator shall submit:

(i) A complete list of task assignments to correspond with the definition of "task" in § 48.22(f) of this subpart B.

(ii) The titles of personnel conducting the training for this section.

(iii) The outline of training procedures used in training miners in those work assignments listed according to paragraph (c)(8)(i) of this section.

(iv) The evaluation procedures used to determine the effectiveness of training under § 48.27 of this subpart B.

(d) The operator shall furnish to the representative of the miners a copy of the training plan 2 weeks prior to its submission to the District Manager. Where a miners' representative is not designated, a copy of the plan shall be posted on the mine bulletin board 2 weeks prior to its submission to the District Manager. Written comments received by the operator from miners or their representatives shall be submitted to the District Manager. Miners or their representatives may submit written comments directly to the District Manager.

Mine Safety and Health Admin., Labor § 48.23

(e) All training required by the training plan submitted to and approved by the District Manager as required by this subpart B shall be subject to evaluation by the District Manager to determine the effectiveness of the training programs. If it is deemed necessary, the District Manager may require changes in, or additions to, programs. Upon request from the District Manager the operator shall make available for evaluation the instructional materials, handouts, visual aids, and other teaching accessories used or to be used in the training programs. Upon request from the District Manager the operator shall provide information concerning schedules of upcoming training.

(f) The operator shall make a copy of the MSHA approved training plan available at the mine site for MSHA inspection and examination by the miners and their representatives.

(g) Except as provided in § 48.27 (New task training of miners) and § 48.31 (Hazard training) of this subpart B, all courses shall be conducted by MSHA approved instructors.

(h) Instructors shall be approved by the District Manager in one or more of the following ways:

(1) Instructors shall take an instructor's training course conducted by the District Manager or given by persons designated by the District Manager to give such instruction; and instructors shall have satisfactorily completed a program of instruction approved by the Office of Educational Policy and Development, MSHA, in the subject matter to be taught.

(2) Instructors may be designated by MSHA as approved instructors to teach specific courses based on written evidence of the instructors' qualifications and teaching experience.

(3) At the discretion of the District Manager, instructors may be designated by MSHA as approved instructors to teach specific courses based on the performance of the instructors while teaching classes monitored by MSHA. Operators shall indicate in training plans submitted for approval whether they want to have instructors approved based on monitored performance. The District Manager shall consider such factors as the size of the mine, the number of employees, the mine safety record and remoteness from a training facility when determining whether instructor approval based on monitored performance is appropriate.

(4) On the effective date of this subpart B, cooperative instructors who have been designated by MSHA to teach MSHA approved courses and who have taught such courses within 24 months prior to the effective date of this subpart shall be considered approved instructors for such courses.

(i) Instructors may have their approval revoked by MSHA for good cause which may include not teaching a course at least once every 24 months. Before any revocation is effective, the District Manager must send written reasons for revocation to the instructor and the instructor shall be given an opportunity to demonstrate or achieve compliance before the District Manager on the matter. A decision by the District Manager to revoke an instructor's approval may be appealed by the instructor to the Administrator for Coal Mine Safety and Health or the Administrator for Metal and Nonmetal Mine Safety and Health, as appropriate, MSHA, 201 12th Street South, Arlington, VA 22202-5452. Such an appeal shall be submitted to the Administrator within 5 days of notification of the District Manager's decision. Upon revocation of an instructor's approval, the District Manager shall immediately notify operators who use the instructor for training.

(j) The District Manager for the area in which the mine is located shall notify the operator and the miners' representative, in writing, within 60 days from the date on which the training plan is filed, of the approval or status of the approval of the training programs.

(1) If revisions are required for approval, or to retain approval thereafter, the revisions required shall be specified to the operator and the miners' representative and the operator and the miners' representative shall be afforded an opportunity to discuss the revisions with the District Manager, or propose alternate revisions or changes. The District Manager, in consultation with the operator and the representative of miners, shall fix a time within

which the discussion will be held, or alternate revisions or changes submitted, before final approval is made.

(2) The District Manager may approve separate programs of the training plan and withhold approval of other programs, pending discussion of revisions or submission of alternate revisions or changes.

(k) Except as provided under §48.28(c) (Annual refresher training of miners) of this subpart B, the operator shall commence training of miners within 60 days after approval of the training plan, or approved programs of the training plan.

(l) The operator shall notify the District Manager of the area in which the mine is located and the miners' representative of any changes of modifications which the operator proposes to make in the approval training plan. The operator shall obtain the approval of the District Manager for such changes or modifications.

(m) In the event the District Manager disapproves a training plan or a proposed modification of a training plan or requires changes in a training plan or modification, the District Manager shall notify the operator and the miners' representative in writing of:

(1) The specific changes or items of deficiency.

(2) The action necessary to effect the changes or bring the disapproved training plan or modification into compliance.

(3) The deadline for completion of remedial action to effect compliance, which shall serve to suspend punitive action under the provisions of sections 104 and 110 of the Act and other related regulations until that established deadline date, except that no such suspension shall take place in imminent danger situations.

(n) The operator shall post on the mine bulletin board, and provide to the miners' representative, a copy of all MSHA revisions and decisions which concern the training plan at the mine and which are issued by the District Manager.

(o) Each operator engaged in shaft or slope construction shall have an MSHA-approved training plan, as outlined in this section, containing programs for training new miners, training experienced miners, training miners for new tasks, annual refresher training, and hazard training for miners as follows:

(1) In the case of an operator engaged in shaft or slope construction on December 30, 2005, the operator shall submit a plan for approval by May 1, 2006, unless extended by MSHA.

(2) In the case of a new shaft or slope construction operator after June 28, 2006, the operator shall have an approved plan prior to commencing shaft or slope construction.

(Pub. L. No. 96–511, 94 Stat. 2812 (44 U.S.C. 3501 et seq.))

[43 FR 47459, Oct. 13, 1978, as amended at 47 FR 14696, Apr. 6, 1982; 47 FR 23640, May 28, 1982; 47 FR 28095, June 29, 1982; 60 FR 33723, June 29, 1995; 63 FR 52759, Oct. 6, 1998; 67 FR 38384, June 4, 2002; 70 FR 77727, Dec. 30, 2005; 80 FR 52986, Sept. 2, 2015]

§ 48.24 Cooperative training program.

(a) An operator of a mine may conduct his own training programs, or may participate in training programs conducted by MSHA, or may participate in MSHA approved training programs conducted by State or other Federal agencies, or associations of mine operators, miners' representatives, other mine operators, private associations, or educational institutions.

(b) Each program and course of instruction shall be given by instructors who have been approved by MSHA to instruct in the courses which are given, and such courses and the training programs shall be adapted to the mining operations and practices existing at the mine and shall be approved by the District Manager for the area in which the mine is located.

[43 FR 47459, Oct. 13, 1978, as amended at 47 FR 23641, May 28, 1982]

§ 48.25 Training of new miners; minimum courses of instruction; hours of instruction.

(a) Each new miner shall receive no less than 24 hours of training as prescribed in this section. Except as otherwise provided in this paragraph, new miners shall receive this training before they are assigned to work duties. At the discretion of the District Manager, new miners may receive a portion of this training after assignment to work duties: *Provided,* That no less than 8 hours of training shall in all cases be given to new miners before they are assigned to work duties. The following courses shall be included in the 8 hours of training: Introduction to work environment, hazard recognition, and health and safety aspects of the tasks to which the new miners will be assigned. Following the completion of this preassignment training, new miners shall then receive the remainder of the required 24 hours of training, or up to 16 hours, within 60 days. Operators shall indicate in the training plans submitted for approval whether they want to train new miners after assignment to duties and for how many hours. In determining whether new miners may be given this training after they are assigned duties, the District Manager shall consider such factors as the mine safety record, rate of employee turnover and mine size. Miners who have not received the full 24 hours of new miner training shall be required to work under the close supervision of an experienced miner.

(b) The training program for new miners shall include the following courses:

(1) *Instruction in the statutory rights of miners and their representatives under the Act; authority and responsibility of supervisors.* The course shall include instruction in the statutory rights of miners and their representatives under the Act, including a discussion of section 2 of the Act; a review and description of the line of authority of supervisors and miners' representatives and the responsibilities of such supervisors and miners' representatives; and an introduction to the operator's rules and the procedures for reporting hazards.

(2) *Self-rescue and respiratory devices.* The course shall include instruction and demonstration in the use, care, and maintenance of self-rescue and respiratory devices, where applicable.

(3) *Transportation controls and communication systems.* The course shall include instruction on the procedures in effect for riding on and in mine conveyances where applicable; the controls for the transportation of miners and materials; and the use of mine communication systems, warning signals, and directional signs.

(4) *Introduction to work environment.* The course shall include a visit and tour of the mine, or portions of the mine which are representative of the entire mine. The method of mining or operation utilized shall be observed and explained.

(5) *Escape and emergency evacuation plans; firewarning and firefighting.* The course shall include a review of the mine escape system, and escape and emergency evacuation plans in effect at the mine; and instruction in the firewarning signals and firefighting procedures.

(6) *Ground control; working in areas of highwalls, water hazards, pits and spoil banks; illumination and night work.* The course shall include, where applicable, and introduction to and instruction on the highwall and ground control plans in effect at the mine; procedures for working safely in areas of highwalls, water hazards, pits and spoil banks; the illumination of work areas; and safe work procedures during the hours of darkness.

(7) *Health.* The course shall include instruction on the purpose of taking dust measurements, where applicable, and noise and other health measurements, and any health control plan in effect at the mine shall be explained. The health provisions of the Act and warning labels shall also be explained.

(8) *Hazard recognition.* The course shall include the recognition and avoidance of hazards present in the mine.

(9) *Electrical hazards.* The course shall include recognition and avoidance of electrical hazards.

(10) *First aid.* The course shall include instruction in first aid methods acceptable to MSHA.

(11) *Explosives.* The course shall include a review and instruction on the hazards related to explosives. The only exception to this course component is when no explosives are used or stored on mine property.

(12) *Health and safety aspects of the tasks to which the new miner will be assigned.* The course shall include instructions in the health and safety aspects of the tasks to be assigned, including the safe work procedures of such tasks, the mandatory health and safety standards pertinent to such

tasks, information about the physical and health hazards of chemicals in the miner's work area, the protective measures a miner can take against these hazards, and the contents of the mine's HazCom program.

(13) Such other courses as may be required by the District Manager based on circumstances and conditions at the mine.

(c) Methods, including oral, written or practical demonstration, to determine successful completion of the training shall be included in the training plan. Upon completion of training, the methods for determining successful completion shall be administered to the miner. The method for determining successful completion of pre-assignment training under paragraph (a) of this section shall be administered to the miner before he is assigned to work duties.

(d) A newly employed miner who has less than 12 months of mining experience and has received the courses and hours of instruction in paragraphs (a) and (b) of this section, within 36 months preceding employment at a mine, does not have to repeat this training. Before the miner starts work, the operator must provide the miner with the experienced miner training in § 48.26(b) of this part and, if applicable, the new task training in § 48.27 of this part. The operator must also provide the miner with annual refresher training and additional new task training, as applicable.

[43 FR 47459, Oct. 13, 1978, as amended at 47 FR 23641, May 28, 1982; 63 FR 53760, Oct. 6, 1998; 67 FR 42389, June 21, 2002]

§ 48.26 Experienced miner training.

(a) Except as provided in paragraph (e), this section applies to experienced miners who are—
(1) Newly employed by the operator;
(2) Transferred to the mine;
(3) Experienced surface miners transferred from underground to surface; or
(4) Returning to the mine after an absence of more than 12 months.

(b) Experienced miners must complete the training prescribed in this section before beginning work duties. Each experienced miner returning to mining following an absence of 5 years or more, must receive at least 8 hours of training. The training must include the following instruction:

(1) *Introduction to work environment.* The course shall include a visit and tour of the mine. The methods of mining or operations utilized at the mine shall be observed and explained.

(2) *Mandatory health and safety standards.* The course shall include the mandatory health and safety standards pertinent to the tasks to be assigned.

(3) *Authority and responsibility of supervisors and miners' representatives.* The course shall include a review and description of the line of authority of supervisors and miners' representatives and the responsibilities of such supervisors and miners' representatives; and an introduction to the operator's rules and the procedures for reporting hazards.

(4) *Transportation controls and communication systems.* The course shall include instruction on the procedures in effect for riding on and in mine conveyances; the controls for the transportation of miners and materials; and the use of the mine communication systems, warning signals, and directional signs.

(5) *Escape and emergency evacuation plans; firewarning and firefighting.* The course must include a review of the mine escape system and the escape and emergency evacuation plans in effect at the mine, and instruction in the firewarning signals and firefighting procedures in effect at the mine.

(6) *Ground controls; working in areas of highwalls, water hazards, pits, and spoil banks; illumination and night work.* The course shall include, where applicable, an introduction to and instruction on the highwall and ground control plans in effect at the mine; procedures for working safely in areas of highwalls, water hazards, pits, and spoil banks, the illumination of work areas, and safe work procedures for miners during hours of darkness.

(7) *Hazard recognition.* The course must include the recognition and avoidance of hazards present in the mine.

(8) *Prevention of accidents.* The course must include a review of the general causes of accidents applicable to the mine environment, causes of specific accidents at the mine, and instruction

Mine Safety and Health Admin., Labor §48.27

in accident prevention in the work environment.

(9) *Emergency medical procedures.* The course must include instruction on the mine's emergency medical arrangements and the location of the mine's first aid equipment and supplies.

(10) *Health.* The course must include instruction on the purpose of taking dust, noise, and other health measurements, where applicable; must review the health provisions of the Act; and must explain warning labels and any health control plan in effect at the mine.

(11) *Health and safety aspects of the tasks to which the experienced miner is assigned.* The course must include instruction in the health and safety aspects of the tasks assigned, including the safe work procedures of such tasks, information about the physical and health hazards of chemicals in the miner's work area, the protective measures a miner can take against these hazards, and the contents of the mine's HazCom program. Experienced miners who must complete new task training under § 48.27 do not need to take training under this paragraph.

(12) Such other courses as may be required by the District Manager based on circumstances and conditions at the mine.

(c) The operator may include instruction in additional safety and health subjects based on circumstances and conditions at the mine.

(d) The training time spent on individual subjects must vary depending upon the training needs of the miners.

(e) Any miner returning to the same mine, following an absence of 12 months or less, must receive training on any major changes to the mine environment that have occurred during the miner's absence and that could adversely affect the miner's health or safety.

(1) A person designated by the operator who is knowledgeable of these changes must conduct the training in this paragraph. An MSHA approved instructor is not required to conduct the training outlined in this paragraph.

(2) No record of this training is required.

(3) The miner must complete annual refresher training as required in § 48.28, if the miner missed taking that training during the absence.

[43 FR 47459, Oct. 13, 1978, as amended at 47 FR 23641, May 28, 1982; 63 FR 53760, Oct. 6, 1998; 67 FR 42389, June 21, 2002]

§ 48.27 Training of miners assigned to a task in which they have had no previous experience; minimum courses of instruction.

(a) Miners assigned to new work tasks as mobile equipment operators, drilling machine operators, haulage and conveyor systems operators, ground control machine operators, AMS operators, and those in blasting operations shall not perform new work tasks in these categories until training prescribed in this paragraph and paragraph (b) of this section has been completed. This training shall not be required for miners who have been trained and who have demonstrated safe operating procedures for such new work tasks within 12 months preceding assignment. This training shall also not be required for miners who have performed the new work tasks and who have demonstrated safe operating procedures for such new work tasks within 12 months preceding assignment. The training program shall include the following:

(1) *Health and safety aspects and safe operating procedures for work tasks, equipment, and machinery.* The training shall include instruction in the health and safety aspects and safe operating procedures related to the assigned task, including information about the physical and health hazards of chemicals in the miner's work area, the protective measures a miner can take against these hazards, and the contents of the mine's HazCom program. The training shall be given in an on-the-job environment; and

(2)(i) *Supervised practice during nonproduction.* The training shall include supervised practice in the assigned tasks, and the performance of work duties at times or places where production is not the primary objective; or,

(ii) *Supervised operation during production.* The training shall include, while under direct and immediate supervision and production is in progress, operation of the machine or equipment and the performance of work duties.

(3) *New or modified machines and equipment.* Equipment and machine operators shall be instructed in safe operating procedures applicable to new or modified machines or equipment to be installed or put into operation in the mine, which require new or different operating procedures.

(4) Such other courses as may be required by the District Manager based on circumstances and conditions at the mine.

(b) Miners under paragraph (a) of this section shall not operate the equipment or machine or engage in blasting operations without direction and immediate supervision until such miners have demonstrated safe operating procedures for the equipment or machine or blasting operation to the operator or the operator's agent.

(c) Miners assigned a new task not covered in paragraph (a) of this section shall be instructed in the safety and health aspects and safe work procedures of the task, including information about the physical and health hazards of chemicals in the miner's work area, the protective measures a miner can take against these hazards, and the contents of the mine's HazCom program, prior to performing such task.

(d) All training and supervised practice and operation required by this section shall be given by a qualified trainer, or a supervisor experienced in the assigned tasks, or other person experienced in the assigned tasks.

[43 FR 47459, Oct. 13, 1978, as amended at 47 FR 23640, May 28, 1982; 67 FR 42389, June 21, 2002; 73 FR 80612, Dec. 31, 2008]

§ 48.28 **Annual refresher training of miners; minimum courses of instruction; hours of instruction.**

(a) Each miner shall receive a minimum of 8 hours of annual refresher training as prescribed in this section.

(b) The annual refresher training program for all miners shall include the following courses of instruction:

(1) *Mandatory health and safety standards.* The course shall include mandatory health and safety standard requirements which are related to the miner's tasks.

(2) *Transportation controls and communication systems.* The course shall include instruction on the procedures for riding on and in mine conveyances; the controls in effect for the transportation of miners and materials; and the use of the mine communication systems, warning signals, and directional signs.

(3) *Escape and emergency evacuation plans; firewarning and firefighting.* The course shall include a review of the mine escape system; escape and emergency evacuation plans in effect at the mine; and instruction in the firewarning signals and firefighting procedures.

(4) *Ground control; working in areas of highwalls, water hazards, pits, and spoil banks; illumination and night work.* The course shall include, where applicable, a review and instruction on the highwall and ground control plans in effect at the mine; procedures for working safely in areas of highwalls, water hazards, pits, and spoil banks; the illumination of work areas; and safe work procedures during hours of darkness.

(5) *First aid.* The course shall include a review of first aid methods acceptable to MSHA.

(6) *Electrical hazards.* The course shall include recognition and avoidance of electrical hazards.

(7) *Prevention of accidents.* the course shall include a review of accidents and causes of accidents, and instruction in accident prevention in the work environment.

(8) *Health.* The course shall include instruction on the purpose of taking dust measurements, where applicable, and noise and other health measurements, and any health control plan in effect at the mine shall be explained. The health provisions of the Act and warning labels shall also be explained.

(9) *Explosives.* The course shall include a review and instruction on the hazards related to explosives. The only exception to this course component is when there are no explosives used or stored on the mine property.

(10) *Self-rescue and respiratory devices.* The course shall include instruction and demonstration in the use, care, and maintenance of self-rescue and respiratory devices, where applicable.

(11) Such other courses as may be required by the District Manager based

on circumstances and conditions at the mine.

(c) Refresher training may include other health and safety subjects that are relevant to mining operations at the mine. Recommended subjects include, but are not limited to, information about the physical and health hazards of chemicals in the miner's work area, the protective measures a miner can take against these hazards, and the contents of the mine's HazCom program.

(d) All persons employed as shaft or slope construction workers on June 28, 2006 must receive annual refresher training within 12 months of June 2006.

(e) Where annual refresher training is conducted periodically, such sessions shall not be less than 30 minutes of actual instruction time and the miners shall be notified that the session is part of annual refresher training.

[43 FR 47459, Oct. 13, 1978, as amended at 47 FR 23641, May 28, 1982; 63 FR 53761, Oct. 6, 1998; 70 FR 77728, Dec. 30, 2005]

§ 48.29 Records of training.

(a) Upon a miner's completion of each MSHA approved training program, the operator shall record and certify on MSHA form 5000-23 that the miner has received the specified training. A copy of the training certificate shall be given to the miner at the completion of the training. The training certificates for each miner shall be available at the mine site for inspection by MSHA and for examination by the miners, the miners' representative and State inspection agencies. When a miner leaves the operator's employ, the miner shall be entitled to a copy of his training certificates.

(b) False certification that training was given shall be punishable under section 110 (a) and (f) of the Act.

(c) Copies of training certificates for currently employed miners shall be kept at the mine site for 2 years, or for 60 days after termination of employment.

(Pub. L. No. 96-511, 94 Stat. 2812 (44 U.S.C. 3501 et seq.))

[43 FR 47459, Oct. 13, 1978, as amended at 47 FR 14706, Apr. 6, 1982; 60 FR 33723, June 29, 1995]

§ 48.30 Compensation for training.

(a) Training shall be conducted during normal working hours; miners attending such training shall receive the rate of pay as provided in § 48.22(d) (Definition of normal working hours) of this subpart B.

(b) If such training shall be given at a location other than the normal place of work, miners shall be compensated for the additional costs, such a mileage, meals, and lodging, they may incur in attending such training sessions.

§ 48.31 Hazard training.

(a) Operators shall provide to those miners, as defined in § 48.22(a) (2) (Definition of miner) of this subpart B, a training program before such miners commence their work duties. This training program shall include the following instruction, which is applicable to the duties of such miners:

(1) Hazard recognition and avoidance;

(2) Emergency and evacuation procedures;

(3) Health and safety standards, safety rules and safe working procedures;

(4) Self-rescue and respiratory devices; and,

(5) Such other instruction as may be required by the District Manager based on circumstances and conditions at the mine.

(b) Miners shall receive the instruction required by this section at least once every 12 months.

(c) The training program required by this section shall be submitted with the training plan required by § 48.23(a) (Training plans: Submission and approval) of this subpart B and shall include a statement on the methods of instruction to be used.

(d) In accordance with § 48.29 (Records of training) of this subpart B, the operator shall maintain and make available for inspection, certificates that miners have received the instruction required by this section.

[43 FR 47459, Oct. 13, 1978, as amended at 47 FR 23641, May 28, 1982]

§ 48.32 Appeals procedures.

The operator, miner, and miners' representative shall have the right of appeal from a decision of the District Manager.

(a) In the event an operator, miner, or miners' representative decides to appeal a decision by the District Manager, such an appeal shall be submitted, in writing, to the Administrator for Coal Mine Safety and Health or the Administrator for Metal and Nonmetal Mine Safety and Health, as appropriate, MSHA, 201 12th Street South, Arlington, VA 22202–5452, within 30 days of notification of the District Manager's decision.

(b) The Administrator may require additional information from the operator, the miners or their representatives, and the District Manager, if the Administrator determines such information is necessary.

(c) The Administrator shall render a decision on the appeal within 30 days after receipt of the appeal.

[43 FR 47459, Oct. 13, 1978, as amended at 47 FR 23641, May 28, 1982; 67 FR 38384, June 4, 2002; 80 FR 52986, Sept. 2, 2015]

PART 49—MINE RESCUE TEAMS

Subpart A—Mine Rescue Teams for Underground Metal and Nonmetal Mines

Sec.
49.1 Purpose and scope.
49.2 Availability of mine rescue teams.
49.3 Alternative mine rescue capability for small and remote mines.
49.4 Alternative mine rescue capability for special mining conditions.
49.5 Mine rescue station.
49.6 Equipment and maintenance requirements.
49.7 Physical requirements for mine rescue team.
49.8 Training for mine rescue teams.
49.9 Mine emergency notification plan.

Subpart B—Mine Rescue Teams for Underground Coal Mines

49.11 Purpose and scope.
49.12 Availability of mine rescue teams.
49.13 Alternative mine rescue capability for small and remote mines.
49.14 [Reserved]
49.15 Mine rescue station.
49.16 Equipment and maintenance requirements.
49.17 Physical requirements for mine rescue team.
49.18 Training for mine rescue teams.
49.19 Mine emergency notification plan.
49.20 Requirements for all coal mines.
49.30 Requirements for small coal mines.
49.40 Requirements for large coal mines.
49.50 Certification of coal mine rescue teams.
49.60 Requirements for a local mine rescue contest.

APPENDIX TO SUBPART B OF PART 49—OPTIONAL FORM FOR CERTIFYING MINE RESCUE TEAMS

AUTHORITY: 30 U.S.C. 811, 825(e).

SOURCE: 45 FR 47002, July 11, 1980, unless otherwise noted.

Subpart A—Mine Rescue Teams for Underground Metal and Nonmetal Mines

§ 49.1 Purpose and scope.

This part implements the provisions of Section 115(e) of the Federal Mine Safety and Health Act of 1977. Every operator of an underground mine shall assure the availability of mine rescue capability for purposes of emergency rescue and recovery.

§ 49.2 Availability of mine rescue teams.

(a) Except where alternative compliance is permitted for small and remote mines (§ 49.3) or those mines operating under special mining conditions (§ 49.4), every operator of an underground mine shall:

(1) Establish at least two mine rescue teams which are available at all times when miners are underground; or

(2) Enter into an arrangement for mine rescue services which assures that at least two mine rescue teams are available at all times when miners are underground.

(b) Each mine rescue team shall consist of five members and one alternate, who are fully qualified, trained, and equipped for providing emergency mine rescue service.

(c) To be considered for membership on a mine rescue team, each person must have been employed in an underground mine for a minimum of one year within the past five years. For the purpose of mine rescue work only, miners who are employed on the surface but work regularly underground shall meet the experience requirement. The underground experience requirement is waived for those miners on a mine rescue team on the effective date of this rule.

(d) Each operator shall arrange, in advance, ground transportation for rescue teams and equipment to the mine or mines served.

(e) Upon the effective date of this part, the required rescue capability shall be present at all existing underground mines, upon initial excavation of a new underground mine entrance, or the re-opening of an existing underground mine.

(f) Except where alternative compliance is permitted under §49.3 or §49.4, no mine served by a mine rescue team shall be located more than two hours ground travel time from the mine rescue station with which the rescue team is associated.

(g) As used in this part, mine rescue teams shall be considered available where teams are capable presenting themselves at the mine site(s) within a reasonable time after notification of an occurrence which might require their services. Rescue team members will be considered available even though performing regular work duties or in an off-duty capacity. The requirement that mine rescue teams be available shall not apply when teams are participating in mine rescue contests or providing services to another mine.

(h) Each operator of an underground mine who provides rescue teams under this section shall send the District Manager a statement describing the mine's method of compliance with this part. The statement shall disclose whether the operator has independently provided mine rescue teams or entered into an agreement for the services of mine rescue teams. The name of the provider and the location of the services shall be included in the statement. A copy of the statement shall be posted at the mine for the miners' information. Where a miners' representative has been designated, the operator shall also provide the representative with a copy of the statement.

§ 49.3 **Alternative mine rescue capability for small and remote mines.**

(a) If an underground mine is small and remote, an operator may provide for an alternative mine rescue capability. For the purposes of this part only, consideration for small and remote shall be given where the total underground employment of the operator's mine and any surrounding mine(s) within two hours ground travel time of the operator's mine is less than 36.

(b) An application for alternative mine rescue capability shall be submitted to the District Manager for the district in which the mine is located for review and approval.

(c) Each application for an alternative mine rescue capability shall contain:

(1) The number of miners employed underground at the mine on each shift;

(2) The distances from the two nearest mine rescue stations;

(3) The total underground employment of mines within two hours ground travel time of the operator's mine;

(4) The operator's mine fire, ground, and roof control history;

(5) The operator's established escape and evacuation plan;

(6) A statement by the operator evaluating the usefulness of additional refuge chambers to supplement those which may exist;

(7) A statement by the operator as to the number of miners willing to serve on a mine rescue team;

(8) The operator's alternative plan for assuring that a suitable mine rescue capability is provided at all times when miners are underground; and

(9) Other relevant information about the operator's mine which may be requested by the District Manager.

(d) A copy of the operator's application shall be posted at the mine. Where a miners' representative has been designated, the operator shall also provide the representative with a copy of the application.

(e) In determining whether to approve an application for alternative compliance, the District Manager shall consider:

(1) The individual circumstances of the small and remote mine;

(2) Comments submitted by, or on behalf of, any affected miner; and

§ 49.4

(3) Whether the alternative mine rescue plan provides a suitable rescue capability at the operator's mine.

(f) Where alternative compliance is approved by MSHA, the operator shall adopt the alternative plan and post a copy of the approved plan (with appropriate MSHA mine emergency telephone numbers) at the mine for the miners' information. Where a miners' representative has been designated, the operator shall also provide the representative with a copy of the approved plan.

(g) The operator shall notify the District Manager of any changed condition or factor materially affecting information submitted in the application for alternative mine rescue capability.

(h)(1) An approved plan for alternative mine rescue capability shall be subject to revocation or modification for cause by MSHA, where it is determined that a condition or factor has changed which would materially alter the operator's mine rescue capability. If such action is contemplated, the operator will be notified, and given an opportunity to be heard before the appropriate District Manager.

(2) If an application for alternative compliance is denied or revoked, the District Manager shall provide the reason for such denial or revocation in writing to the operator. The operator may appeal this decision in writing to the Administrator for Metal and Nonmetal Mine Safety and Health, 201 12th Street South, Arlington, VA 22202–5452.

[45 FR 47002, July 11, 1980, as amended at 67 FR 38385, June 4, 2002; 80 FR 52986, Sept. 2, 2015]

§ 49.4 Alternative mine rescue capability for special mining conditions.

(a) If an underground mine is operating under special mining conditions, the operator may provide an alternative mine rescue capability.

(b) An application for alternative mine rescue capability shall be submitted to the District Manager for the district in which the mine is located for review and approval.

(c) To be considered "operating under special mining conditions," the operator must show that all of the following conditions are present:

(1) The mine has multiple adits or entries;

(2) The mined substance is noncombustible and the mining atmosphere nonexplosive;

(3) There are multiple vehicular openings to all active mine areas, sufficient to allow fire and rescue vehicles full access to all parts of the mine in which miners work or travel;

(4) Roadways or other openings are not supported or lined with combustible materials;

(5) The mine shall not have a history of flammable-gas emission or accumulation, and the mined substance shall not have a history associated with flammable or toxic gas problems; and

(6) Any reported gas or oil well or exploratory drill hole shall be plugged to within 100 feet above and below the horizon of the ore body or seam.

(d) Each application shall contain:

(1) An explanation of the special mining conditions;

(2) The number of miners employed underground at the mine on each shift;

(3) The distances from the two nearest mine rescue stations;

(4) The operator's mine fire history;

(5) The operator's established escape and evacuation plan;

(6) The operator's alternative plan for assuring that a suitable mine rescue capability is provided at all times when miners are underground; and

(7) Other relevant information about the operator's mine which may be requested by the District Manager.

(e) A copy of the operator's application shall be posted at the mine. Where a miners' representative has been designated, the operator shall also provide the representative with a copy of the application.

(f) In determining whether to approve an application for alternative compliance, the District Manager shall consider:

(1) The individual circumstances of the mine operating under special mining conditions;

(2) Comments submitted by, or on behalf of, any affected miner; and

(3) Whether the alternative mine rescue plan provides a suitable rescue capability at the operator's mine.

(g) Where alternative compliance is approved by MSHA the operator shall

Mine Safety and Health Admin., Labor § 49.6

adopt the alternative plan and post a copy of the approved plan (with appropriate MSHA mine emergency telephone numbers) at the mine for the miners' information. Where a miners' representative has been designated, the operator shall also provide the representative with a copy of the alternative plan.

(h) The operator shall notify the District Manager of any changed condition or factor materially affecting information submitted in the application for alternative mine rescue capability.

(i)(1) An approved plan for alternative mine rescue capability shall be subject be to revocation or modification by MSHA, where it is determined that a condition or factor has changed which would materially alter the operator's mine rescue capability. If such action is contemplated, the operator will be notified and given an opportunity to be heard before the appropriate District Manager.

(2) If an application for alternative compliance is denied or revoked, the District Manager shall provide the reason for such denial or revocation in writing to the operator. The operator may appeal this decision in writing to the Administrator for Metal and Nonmetal Mine Safety and Health, 201 12th Street South, Arlington, VA 22202–5452.

[45 FR 47002, July 11, 1980, as amended at 67 FR 38385, June 4, 2002; 80 FR 52986, Sept. 2, 2015]

§ 49.5 Mine rescue station.

(a) Except where alternative compliance is permitted, every operator of an underground mine shall designate, in advance, the location of the mine rescue station serving the mine.

(b) Mine rescue stations are to provide a centralized storage location for rescue equipment. This centralized storage location may be either at the mine site, affiliated mines, or a separate mine rescue structure.

(c) Mine rescue stations shall provide a proper storage environment to assure equipment readiness for immediate use.

(d) Authorized representatives of the Secretary shall have the right of entry to inspect any designated mine rescue station.

§ 49.6 Equipment and maintenance requirements.

(a) Each mine rescue station shall be provided with at least the following equipment:

(1) Twelve self-contained breathing apparatus, each with a minimum of 4 hours capacity (approved by MSHA and NIOSH under 42 CFR Part 84, Subpart H), and any necessary equipment for testing such breathing apparatus;

(2) A portable supply of liquid air, liquid oxygen, pressurized oxygen, or oxygen generating chemicals, and carbon dioxide absorbent chemicals, applicable to the supplied breathing apparatus and sufficient to sustain each team for eight hours while using the breathing apparatus during rescue operations.

(3) Two extra, fully-charged oxygen bottles for every six self-contained breathing apparatus;

(4) One oxygen pump or a cascading system, compatible with the supplied breathing apparatus;

(5) Twelve permissible cap lamps and a charging rack;

(6) Four gas detectors appropriate for each type of gas that may be encountered at the mines served. Gas detectors must measure concentrations of methane from 0.0 percent to 100 percent of volume, oxygen from 0.0 percent to at least 20 percent of volume, and carbon monoxide from 0.0 parts per million to at least 9,999 parts per million.

(7) [Reserved]

(8) One portable mine rescue communication system (approved under part 23 of this title) or a sound-powered communication system.

(i) The wires or cable to the communication system shall be of sufficient tensile strength to be used as a manual communication system.

(ii) These communication systems shall be at least 1,000 feet in length.

(9) Necessary spare parts and tools for repairing the breathing apparatus and communication system.

(b) Mine rescue apparatus and equipment shall be maintained in a manner that will ensure readiness for immediate use.

(1) A person trained in the use and care of breathing apparatus shall inspect and test the apparatus at intervals not exceeding 30 days and shall

§ 49.7

certify by signature and date that the inspections and tests were done.

(2) When the inspection indicates that a corrective action is necessary, the corrective action shall be made and the person shall record the corrective action taken.

(3) The certification and the record of corrective action shall be maintained at the mine rescue station for a period of one year and made available on request to an authorized representative of the Secretary.

[73 FR 53123, Sept. 15, 2008]

§ 49.7 Physical requirements for mine rescue team.

(a) Each member of a mine rescue team shall be examined annually by a physician who shall certify that each person is physically fit to perform mine rescue and recovery work for prolonged periods under strenuous conditions. The first such physical examination shall be completed within 60 days prior to scheduled initial training. A team member requiring corrective eyeglasses will not be disqualified provided the eyeglasses can be worn securely within an approved facepiece.

(b) In determining whether a miner is physically capable of performing mine rescue duties, the physician shall take the following conditions into consideration:

(1) Seizure disorder;
(2) Perforated eardrum;
(3) Hearing loss without a hearing aid greater than 40 decibels at 400, 1,000 and 2,000 Hz;
(4) Repeated blood pressure (controlled or uncontrolled by medication) reading which exceeds 160 systolic, or 100 diastolic, or which is less than 105 systolic, or 60 diastolic;
(5) Distant visual acuity (without glasses) less than 20/50 Snellen scale in one eye, and 20/70 in the other;
(6) Heart disease;
(7) Hernia;
(8) Absence of a limb or hand; or
(9) Any other condition which the examining physician determines is relevant to the question of whether the miner is fit for rescue team service;

(c) The operator shall have MSHA Form 5000-3 certifying medical fitness completed and signed by the examining physician for each member of a mine rescue team. These forms shall be kept on file at the mine rescue station for a period of one year.

§ 49.8 Training for mine rescue teams.

(a) Prior to serving on a mine rescue team each member shall complete, at a minimum, an initial 20-hour course of instruction as prescribed by MSHA's Office of Educational Policy and Development, in the use, care, and maintenance of the type of breathing apparatus which will be used by the mine rescue team. The initial training requirement is waived for those miners on a mine rescue team on the effective date of this rule.

(b) Upon completion of the initial training, all team members shall receive at least 40 hours of refresher training annually. This training shall be given at least 4 hours each month, or for a period of 8 hours every two months. This training shall include:

(1) Sessions underground at least once each 6 months;
(2) The wearing and use of the breathing apparatus by team members for a period of at least two hours while under oxygen every two months;
(3) Where applicable, the use, care, capabilities, and limitations of auxiliary mine rescue equipment, or a different breathing apparatus;
(4) Advanced mine rescue training and procedures; as prescribed by MSHA's Office of Educational Policy and Development; and
(5) Mine map training and ventilation procedures.

(c) A mine rescue team member will be ineligible to serve on a team if more than 8 hours of training is missed during one year, unless additional training is received to make up for the time missed.

(d) The training courses required by this section shall be conducted by instructors who have been employed in an underground mine for a minimum of one year within the past five years, and who have received MSHA approval through:

(1) Completion of an MSHA or State approved instructor's training course and the program of instruction in the subject matter to be taught.
(2) Designation by the District Manager as approved instructors to teach

specific courses, based on their qualifications and teaching experience. Previously approved instructors need not be re-designated to teach the approved courses as long as they have taught those courses within the 24 months prior to the effective date of this part. Where individuals are designated, the District Manager may waive the underground experience requirement.

(e) The District Manager may revoke an instructor's approval for good cause. A written statement revoking the approval together with reasons for revocation shall be provided the instructor. The affected instructor may appeal the decision of the District Manager by writing to the Administrator for Metal and Nonmetal Mine Safety and Health, MSHA, 201 12th Street South, Arlington, VA 22202–5452. The Administrator shall issue a decision on the appeal.

(f) Upon request from the District Manager, the operator shall provide information concerning the schedule of upcoming training.

(g) A record of training of each team member shall be on file at the mine rescue station for a period of one year.

[45 FR 47002, July 11, 1980, as amended at 47 FR 23641, May 28, 1982; 47 FR 28095, June 29, 1982; 67 FR 38385, June 4, 2002; 80 FR 52986, Sept. 2, 2015]

§ 49.9 Mine emergency notification plan.

(a) Each underground mine shall have a mine rescue notification plan outlining the procedures to follow in notifying the mine rescue teams when there is an emergency that requires their services.

(b) A copy of the mine rescue notification plan shall be posted at the mine for the miners' information. Where a miners' representative has been designated, the operator shall also provide the representative with a copy of the plan.

Subpart B—Mine Rescue Teams for Underground Coal Mines

SOURCE: 73 FR 7648, Feb. 8, 2008, unless otherwise noted.

§ 49.11 Purpose and scope.

(a) This subpart implements the provisions of section 115(e) of the Federal Mine Safety and Health Act of 1977, as amended by the Mine Improvement and New Emergency Response (MINER) Act of 2006. Every operator of an underground coal mine shall assure the availability of mine rescue capability for purposes of emergency rescue and recovery.

(b) The following Table 49.11 summarizes the new requirements for mine rescue teams contained in section 4 of the MINER Act.

TABLE 49.11—SUMMARY OF NEW MINER ACT REQUIREMENTS FOR UNDERGROUND COAL MINE OPERATORS AND MINE RESCUE TEAMS

Requirement	Type of mine rescue team			
	Mine-site	Composite	Contract	State-sponsored
Team members must participate at least annually in two local mine rescue contests.	YES	YES	YES	YES.
Team members must participate in mine rescue training at each mine covered by the mine rescue team. A portion of the training must be conducted underground.	Annually at Large Mines; Semi-annually at Small Mines.	Semi-annually	Quarterly at Large Mines; Semi-annually at Small Mines.	Annually at Large Mines; Semi-annually at Small Mines.
Team must be available at the mine within 1 hour ground travel time from the mine rescue station.	YES	YES	YES	YES.
Team members must be knowledgeable about the operations and ventilation of each covered mine.	YES	YES	YES	YES.

TABLE 49.11—SUMMARY OF NEW MINER ACT REQUIREMENTS FOR UNDERGROUND COAL MINE OPERATORS AND MINE RESCUE TEAMS—Continued

Requirement	Type of mine rescue team			
	Mine-site	Composite	Contract	State-sponsored
Team must include at least two active employees from each covered large mine and at least one active employee from each covered small mine.		YES		
Team must be comprised of persons with a minimum of 3 years underground coal mine experience that shall have occurred within the 10-year period preceding their employment on the contract mine rescue team.			YES	

All mine operators must provide for two certified mine rescue teams. Large mine operators shall provide one team that is either an individual mine-site mine rescue team or a composite team.

Team members of State-sponsored teams who are full-time State employees whose primary job duties include (1) inspecting underground mines for compliance with State safety laws or (2) training mine rescue teams or (3) other similar duties that would enhance their mine rescue knowledge may substitute their regular job experience for 50 percent of the training requirements for non-State employee mine rescue team members, except these team members must participate in two local mine rescue contests and train at the covered mine in accordance with § 49.20(b).

[73 FR 7648, Feb. 8, 2008, as amended at 74 FR 28608, June 17, 2009]

§ 49.12 Availability of mine rescue teams.

(a) Except where alternative compliance is permitted for small and remote mines (§ 49.13), every operator of an underground mine shall:

(1) Establish at least two mine rescue teams which are available at all times when miners are underground; or

(2) Enter into an arrangement for mine rescue services which assures that at least two mine rescue teams are available at all times when miners are underground.

(b) Each mine rescue team shall consist of five members and one alternate who are fully qualified, trained, and equipped for providing emergency mine rescue service. Mine rescue teams for anthracite coal mines, which have no electrical equipment at the face or working section, shall consist of at least three members per team and one alternate that may be shared between both teams.

(c) To be considered for membership on a mine rescue team, each person must have been employed in an underground mine for a minimum of 1 year within the past 5 years, except that members of contract mine rescue teams shall have a minimum of 3 years underground coal mine experience that shall have occurred within the 10-year period preceding their employment on the contract mine rescue team. For the purpose of mine rescue work only, miners who are employed on the surface but work regularly underground shall meet the experience requirement. The underground experience requirement is waived for those miners on a mine rescue team on February 8, 2008.

(d) Each operator shall arrange, in advance, ground transportation for rescue teams and equipment to the mine or mines served.

(e) The required rescue capability shall be present at all existing underground mines, upon initial excavation of a new underground mine entrance, or the re-opening of an existing underground mine.

(f) No mine served by a mine rescue team shall be located more than 1 hour ground travel time from the mine rescue station with which the rescue team is associated.

(g) As used in this subpart, mine rescue teams shall be considered available where teams are capable of presenting themselves at the mine site(s) within a reasonable time after notification of an occurrence which might require their services. Rescue team members will be considered available even though performing regular work duties or in an off-duty capacity. The requirement that mine rescue teams be available shall not apply when teams are participating in mine rescue contests or providing services to another mine.

(h) Each operator of an underground mine who provides rescue teams under this section shall send the District Manager a statement describing the mine's method of compliance with this subpart. The statement shall disclose whether the operator has independently provided mine rescue teams or entered into an agreement for the services of mine rescue teams. The name of the provider and the location of the services shall be included in the statement. A copy of the statement shall be posted at the mine for the miners' information. Where a miners' representative has been designated, the operator shall also provide the representative with a copy of the statement.

§ 49.13 Alternative mine rescue capability for small and remote mines.

(a) If an underground mine is small and remote, an operator may provide for an alternative mine rescue capability consistent with statutory requirements. For the purposes of this subpart only, consideration for small and remote shall be given where the total underground employment of the operator's mine and any surrounding mine(s) within 1 hour ground travel time of the operator's mine is less than 36.

(b) An application for alternative mine rescue capability shall be submitted to the District Manager for the district in which the mine is located for review and approval.

(c) Each application for an alternative mine rescue capability shall contain:

(1) The number of miners employed underground at the mine on each shift;
(2) The location of the designated mine rescue station serving the mine;
(3) The total underground employment of mines within 1 hour ground travel time of the operator's mine;
(4) The operator's mine fire, ground, and roof control history;
(5) The operator's established escape and evacuation plan;
(6) A statement by the operator evaluating the usefulness of additional refuge chambers to supplement those which may exist;

(7) A statement by the operator as to the number of miners willing to serve on a mine rescue team;
(8) The operator's alternative plan for assuring that a suitable mine rescue capability is provided at all times when miners are underground; and
(9) Other relevant information about the operator's mine which may be requested by the District Manager.

(d) A copy of the operator's application shall be posted at the mine. Where a miners' representative has been designated, the operator shall also provide the representative with a copy of the application.

(e) In determining whether to approve an application for alternative compliance, the District Manager shall consider:

(1) The individual circumstances of the small and remote mine;
(2) Comments submitted by, or on behalf of, any affected miner; and
(3) Whether the alternative mine rescue plan provides a suitable rescue capability at the operator's mine.

(f) Where alternative compliance is approved by MSHA, the operator shall adopt the alternative plan and post a copy of the approved plan (with appropriate MSHA mine emergency telephone numbers) at the mine for the miners' information. Where a miners' representative has been designated, the operator shall also provide the representative with a copy of the approved plan.

(g) The operator shall notify the District Manager of any changed condition or factor materially affecting information submitted in the application for alternative mine rescue capability.

(h)(1) An approved plan for alternative mine rescue capability shall be subject to revocation or modification for cause by MSHA, where it is determined that a condition or factor has changed which would materially alter the operator's mine rescue capability. If such action is contemplated, the operator will be notified, and given an opportunity to be heard before the appropriate District Manager.

(2) If an application for alternative compliance is denied or revoked, the District Manager shall provide the reason for such denial or revocation in writing to the operator. The operator

§ 49.14

may appeal this decision in writing to the Administrator for Coal Mine Safety and Health.

§ 49.14 [Reserved]

§ 49.15 Mine rescue station.

(a) Every operator of an underground mine shall designate, in advance, the location of the mine rescue station serving the mine.

(b) Mine rescue stations are to provide a centralized storage location for rescue equipment. This centralized storage location may be either at the mine site, affiliated mines, or a separate mine rescue structure.

(c) Mine rescue stations shall provide a proper storage environment to assure equipment readiness for immediate use.

(d) Authorized representatives of the Secretary shall have the right of entry to inspect any designated mine rescue station.

§ 49.16 Equipment and maintenance requirements.

(a) Each mine rescue station shall be provided with at least the following equipment. Mine rescue stations serving underground anthracite coal mines, which have no electrical equipment at the face or working section, shall have at least the amount of equipment appropriate for the number of mine rescue team members.

(1) Twelve self-contained breathing apparatus, each with a minimum of 4 hours capacity (approved by MSHA and NIOSH under 42 CFR part 84, subpart H), and any necessary equipment for testing such breathing apparatus.

(2) A portable supply of liquid air, liquid oxygen, pressurized oxygen, or oxygen generating chemicals, and carbon dioxide absorbent chemicals, as applicable to the supplied breathing apparatus and sufficient to sustain each team for 8 hours while using the breathing apparatus during rescue operations.

(3) Two extra, fully-charged oxygen bottles for every six self-contained breathing apparatus.

(4) One oxygen pump or a cascading system, compatible with the supplied breathing apparatus.

(5) Twelve permissible cap lamps and a charging rack.

(6) Four gas detectors appropriate for each type of gas that may be encountered at the mines served. Gas detectors must measure concentrations of methane from 0.0 percent to 100 percent of volume, oxygen from 0.0 percent to at least 20 percent of volume, and carbon monoxide from 0.0 parts per million to at least 9,999 parts per million.

(7) [Reserved]

(8) One portable mine rescue communication system (approved under part 23 of this title) or a sound-powered communication system.

(i) The wires or cable to the communication system shall be of sufficient tensile strength to be used as a manual communication system.

(ii) These communication systems shall be at least 1,000 feet in length.

(9) Necessary spare parts and tools for repairing the breathing apparatus and communication system.

(b) Mine rescue apparatus and equipment shall be maintained in a manner that will ensure readiness for immediate use.

(1) A person trained in the use and care of breathing apparatus shall inspect and test the apparatus at intervals not exceeding 30 days and shall certify by signature and date that the inspections and tests were done.

(2) When the inspection indicates that a corrective action is necessary, the corrective action shall be made and the person shall record the corrective action taken.

(3) The certification and the record of corrective action shall be maintained at the mine rescue station for a period of 1 year and made available on request to an authorized representative of the Secretary.

[73 FR 53123, Sept. 15, 2008]

§ 49.17 Physical requirements for mine rescue team.

(a) Each member of a mine rescue team shall be examined annually by a physician who shall certify that each person is physically fit to perform mine rescue and recovery work for prolonged periods under strenuous conditions. The first such physical examination shall be completed within 60 days prior to scheduled initial training. A team member requiring corrective eyeglasses will not be disqualified provided the eyeglasses can be worn securely within an approved facepiece.

(b) In determining whether a miner is physically capable of performing mine rescue duties, the physician shall take the following conditions into consideration:

(1) Seizure disorder;

(2) Perforated eardrum;

(3) Hearing loss without a hearing aid greater than 40 decibels at 400, 1000, and 2000 Hz;

(4) Repeated blood pressure (controlled or uncontrolled by medication) reading which exceeds 160 systolic, or 100 diastolic, or which is less than 105 systolic, or 60 diastolic;

(5) Distant visual acuity (without glasses) less than 20/50 Snellen scale in one eye, and 20/70 in the other;

(6) Heart disease;

(7) Hernia;

(8) Absence of a limb or hand; or

(9) Any other condition which the examining physician determines is relevant to the question of whether the miner is fit for rescue team service.

(c) The operator shall have MSHA Form 5000–3 (available at *http://www.msha.gov*) certifying medical fitness completed and signed by the examining physician for each member of a mine rescue team. These forms shall be kept on file at the mine rescue station for a period of 1 year.

§ 49.18 Training for mine rescue teams.

(a) Prior to serving on a mine rescue team each member shall complete, at a minimum, an initial 20-hour course of instruction as prescribed by MSHA's Office of Educational Policy and Development, in the use, care, and maintenance of the type of breathing apparatus which will be used by the mine rescue team.

(b) Upon completion of the initial training, all team members shall receive at least 96 hours of refresher training annually, which shall include participation in local mine rescue contests and training at the covered mine. Training shall be given at least 8 hours every 2 months and shall consist of:

(1) Sessions underground at least once each 6 months;

(2) The wearing and use of the breathing apparatus by team members for a period of at least 2 hours while under oxygen every 2 months;

(3) Where applicable, the use, care, capabilities, and limitations of auxiliary mine rescue equipment, or a different breathing apparatus;

(4) Advanced mine rescue training and procedures, as prescribed by MSHA's Office of Educational Policy and Development;

(5) Mine map training and ventilation procedures; and

(6) The wearing of mine rescue apparatus while in smoke, simulated smoke, or an equivalent environment at least once during each 12-month period.

(c) A mine rescue team member will be ineligible to serve on a team if more than 8 hours of training is missed during 1 year, unless additional training is received to make up for the time missed.

(d) The training courses required by this section shall be conducted by instructors who have been employed in an underground mine and have had a minimum of 1 year experience as a mine rescue team member or a mine rescue instructor within the past 5 years, and who have received MSHA approval through:

(1) Completion of an MSHA or State approved instructor's training course and the program of instruction in the subject matter to be taught.

(2) Designation by the District Manager as approved instructors to teach specific courses, based on their qualifications and teaching experience outlined above. Previously approved instructors need not be re-designated to teach the approved courses as long as they have taught those courses within the 24 months prior to the effective date of this part.

(e) The District Manager may revoke an instructor's approval for good cause. A written statement revoking the approval together with reasons for revocation shall be provided the instructor. The affected instructor may appeal the decision of the District Manager by writing to the Administrator for Coal Safety and Health. The Administrator shall issue a decision on the appeal.

(f) Upon request from the District Manager, the operator shall provide information concerning the schedule of upcoming training.

(g) A record of training of each team member shall be on file at the mine rescue station for a period of 1 year.

§ 49.19 Mine emergency notification plan.

(a) Each underground mine shall have a mine rescue notification plan outlining the procedures to follow in notifying the mine rescue teams when there is an emergency that requires their services.

(b) A copy of the mine rescue notification plan shall be posted at the mine for the miners' information. Where a miners' representative has been designated, the operator shall also provide the representative with a copy of the plan.

§ 49.20 Requirements for all coal mines.

(a) The operator of each underground coal mine shall make available two certified mine rescue teams whose members—

(1) Are familiar with the operations of the mine, and

(2) Participate at least annually in two local mine rescue contests.

(b) Team members shall meet the following:

(1) *Mine-site team.* Members who work at the mine and participate in mine rescue training at the mine at least annually at large mines and at least semi-annually at small mines.

(2) *Composite team.* A mine rescue team that covers multiple mines and whose members—

(i) Include at least two members from each covered large mine and at least one member from each covered small mine,

(ii) Are knowledgeable about the operations and ventilation of each covered underground coal mine, and

(iii) Participate in mine rescue training at each covered mine at least semi-annually.

(3) *Contract team.* A mine rescue team that is provided by an arrangement with another coal mine or with a third party and whose members—

(i) Are knowledgeable about the operations and ventilation of each covered underground coal mine, and

(ii) Participate in mine rescue training at each covered large mine at least quarterly and at each covered small mine at least semi-annually.

(4) *State-sponsored team.* Members who are state employees and participate in mine rescue training at each covered mine at least annually at large mines and at least semi-annually at small mines.

(c) For the purpose of mine rescue team membership, a member employed by an operator of multiple mines is considered to be an employee of each mine at which the member regularly works.

(d) For the purpose of mine rescue team training at each covered mine, a portion of the training must be conducted underground.

[73 FR 7648, Feb. 8, 2008, as amended at 74 FR 28609, June 17, 2009]

§ 49.30 Requirements for small coal mines.

At mines with 36 or fewer underground employees, mine rescue team members shall be knowledgeable about the operations and ventilation of each covered mine.

§ 49.40 Requirements for large coal mines.

At mines with more than 36 underground employees, one of the two certified mine rescue teams shall be an individual mine-site team or a composite team.

§ 49.50 Certification of coal mine rescue teams.

(a) For each mine rescue team designated to provide mine rescue coverage at an underground coal mine, the mine operator shall send the District Manager an annual statement certifying that each team meets the requirements of this subpart as listed in the following Table 49.50–A and Table 49.50–B.

(b) The operator shall notify the District Manager within 60 days of any change in team membership.

TABLE 49.50–A—INITIAL CRITERIA TO CERTIFY THE QUALIFICATIONS OF MINE RESCUE TEAMS

Qualification	Criteria (30 CFR)
(1) Team is available at all times when miners are underground	49.12(a); 49.12(g)
(2) Except where alternative compliance is permitted, team has five members and one alternate	49.12(b)
(3) Members have experience working in an underground coal mine	49.12(c)
(4) Team is available within 1-hour ground travel time from the mine rescue station to the mine	49.12(f)
(5) Appropriate mine rescue equipment is provided, inspected, tested, and maintained	49.16
(6) Members are physically fit	49.17
(7) Members have completed initial training	49.18(a)

TABLE 49.50–B—ANNUAL CRITERIA TO MAINTAIN MINE RESCUE TEAM CERTIFICATION

Qualification	Criteria (30 CFR)
(1) Members are properly trained annually	49.18(b)
(2) Members are familiar with the operations of each covered mine	49.20(a)(1)
(3) Members participate in at least two local mine rescue contests annually. Judges certify results	49.20(a)(2)
(4) Members participate in mine rescue training at each covered mine	49.20(b)(1); 49.20(b)(2)(iii); 49.20(b)(3)(ii); 49.20(b)(4)
(5) Members are knowledgeable about the operations and ventilation of each covered mine	49.20(b)(2)(ii); 49.20(b)(3)(i); 49.30

§ 49.60 Requirements for a local mine rescue contest.

(a) A local mine rescue contest is one that—

(1) Is conducted in the United States;

(2) Uses MSHA-recognized rules;

(3) Has a minimum of three mine rescue teams competing;

(4) Has one or more problems conducted on one or more days with a determined winner;

(5) Includes team members who—

(i) Have the necessary equipment to participate in a simulated mine rescue team exercise,

(ii) Participate in a simulated mine rescue team exercise while being timed and observed by trained judges who evaluate the performance of each team and provide written feedback, and

(iii) Wear oxygen breathing apparatus while participating in a simulated mine rescue team exercise; and

(6) Includes contest judges who have completed annual training for mine rescue contest judges.

(b) A local mine rescue contest is training that provides an objective evaluation of demonstrated mine rescue team skills and can be a Mine Emergency Response Development (MERD) exercise or a practical simulation exercise, such as a fire or explosion drill, where the team participates in simulated mine rescue team exercises and wears breathing apparatus.

(c) Upon request from the District Manager, the operator shall provide information concerning each designated team's schedule of participation in upcoming local mine rescue contests.

Pt. 49, Subpt. B, App.   30 CFR Ch. I (7-1-23 Edition)

APPENDIX TO SUBPART B OF PART 49—OPTIONAL FORM FOR CERTIFYING MINE RESCUE TEAMS

Operator's Annual Certification of Mine Rescue Team Qualifications

MSHA Mine ID No.:   Contractor ID No.:   Company Name:

Mine Name:

Team Name:

Mine size: ○ Large   ○ Small

Type of Team: ○ Mine-site   ○ Composite   ○ Contract   ○ State-sponsored

○ Mine Rescue Team is available within 1-hour ground travel time from the Mine Rescue Station

Address of Mine Rescue Station:

○ Team is available at all times when miners are underground

○ Appropriate mine rescue equipment is provided, inspected, tested, & maintained

	1	2	3	4	5 Alternate
Member's name					
Employer's name					
Experience working in underground coal mine	○	○	○	○	○
Physically fit	○	○	○	○	○
New member training	○ Initial 20 hr	○ Initial 20 hr	○ Initial 20 hr	○ Initial 20 hr	○ Initial 20 hr
Annual training	○ Refresher training totals 96 hr or more	○ Refresher training totals 96 hr or more	○ Refresher training totals 96 hr or more	○ Refresher training totals 96 hr or more	○ Refresher training totals 96 hr or more
8 hr training every 2 mos; includes wearing apparatus for 2 hr	○ Jan-Feb ○ Mar-Apr ○ May-Jun ○ Jul-Aug ○ Sep-Oct ○ Nov-Dec	○ Jan-Feb ○ Mar-Apr ○ May-Jun ○ Jul-Aug ○ Sep-Oct ○ Nov-Dec	○ Jan-Feb ○ Mar-Apr ○ May-Jun ○ Jul-Aug ○ Sep-Oct ○ Nov-Dec	○ Jan-Feb ○ Mar-Apr ○ May-Jun ○ Jul-Aug ○ Sep-Oct ○ Nov-Dec	○ Jan-Feb ○ Mar-Apr ○ May-Jun ○ Jul-Aug ○ Sep-Oct ○ Nov-Dec
Trains underground every 6 mos	○ Jan-Jun ○ Jul-Dec	○ Jan-Jun ○ Jul-Dec	○ Jan-Jun ○ Jul-Dec	○ Jan-Jun ○ Jul-Dec	○ Jan-Jun ○ Jul-Dec
Wears apparatus in smoke annually	○	○	○	○	○

Mine Safety and Health Admin., Labor — Pt. 49, Subpt. B, App.

Familiar with operations of mine	O	O	O	O	O	O
Knowledge of operations & ventilation of mine	O	O	O	O	O	O
Participates in two local mine rescue contests (Insert dates)						
Trains at this mine (Insert dates)						

MSHA Form No. _____   OMB Control No. _____

I certify the information above is true and accurate to the best of my knowledge.

Printed Name & Signature: _____   Position held at the mine: _____
Date: _____

Use of this form is optional.

An underground coal mine operator may file a copy of this form with the appropriate District Manager for each of the two designated mine rescue teams, that provide coverage for this mine, to certify that each team meets the requirements of 30 CFR Part 49 Subpart B.

273

SUBCHAPTER I—ACCIDENTS, INJURIES, ILLNESSES, EMPLOYMENT, AND PRODUCTION IN MINES

PART 50—NOTIFICATION, INVESTIGATION, REPORTS AND RECORDS OF ACCIDENTS, INJURIES, ILLNESSES, EMPLOYMENT, AND COAL PRODUCTION IN MINES

Subpart A—General

Sec.
50.1 Purpose and scope.
50.2 Definitions.

Subpart B—Notification, Investigation, Preservation of Evidence

50.10 Immediate notification.
50.11 Investigation.
50.12 Preservation of evidence.

Subpart C—Reporting of Accidents, Injuries, and Illnesses

50.20 Preparation and submission of MSHA Report Form 7000–1—Mine Accident, Injury, and Illness Report.
50.20–1 General instructions for completing MSHA Form 7000–1.
50.20–2 Criteria—"Transfer to another job".
50.20–3 Criteria—Differences between medical treatment and first aid.
50.20–4 Criteria—MSHA Form 7000–1, Section A.
50.20–5 Criteria—MSHA Form 7000–1, Section B.
50.20–6 Criteria—MSHA Form 7000–1, Section C.
50.20–7 Criteria—MSHA Form 7000–1, Section D.

Subpart D—Quarterly Employment and Coal Production Report

50.30 Preparation and submission of MSHA Form 7000–2—Quarterly Employment and Coal Production Report.
50.30–1 General instructions for completing MSHA Form 7000–2.

Subpart E—Maintenance of Records; Verification of Information

50.40 Maintenance of records.
50.41 Verification of reports.

AUTHORITY: 29 U.S.C. 557(a); 30 U.S.C. 811, 813(j), 951, 957, 961.

SOURCE: 42 FR 65535, Dec. 30, 1977, unless otherwise noted.

Subpart A—General

§50.1 Purpose and scope.

This part 50 implements sections 103(e) and 111 of the Federal Coal Mine Health and Safety Act of 1969, 30 U.S.C. 801 *et seq.*, and sections 4 and 13 of the Federal Metal and Nonmetallic Mine Safety Act, 30 U.S.C. 721 *et seq.*, and applies to operators of coal, metal, and nonmetallic mines. It requires operators to immediately notify the Mine Safety and Health Administration (MSHA) of accidents, requires operators to investigate accidents, and restricts disturbance of accident related areas. This part also requires operators to file reports pertaining to accidents, occupational injuries and occupational illnesses, as well as employment and coal production data, with MSHA, and requires operators to maintain copies of reports at relevant mine offices. The purpose of this part is to implement MSHA's authority to investigate, and to obtain and utilize information pertaining to, accidents, injuries, and illnesses occurring or originating in mines. In utilizing information received under part 50, MSHA will develop rates of injury occurrence (incident rates or IR), on the basis of 200,000 hours of employee exposure (equivalent to 100 employees working 2,000 hours per year). The incidence rate for a particular injury category will be based on the formula:

IR = (number of cases × 200,000) divided by hours of employee exposure.

MSHA will develop data respecting injury severity using days away from work or days of restricted work activity and the 200,000 hour base as criteria. The severity measure (SM) for a particular injury category will be based on the formula:

SM = (sum of days × 200,000) divided by hours of employee exposure.

[42 FR 65535, Dec. 30, 1977; 43 FR 1617, Jan. 11, 1978, as amended at 43 FR 12318, Mar. 24, 1978; 71 FR 16666, Apr. 3, 2006]

§ 50.2 Definitions.

As used in this part:

(a) *Mine* means: (1) An area of land from which minerals are extracted in nonliquid form or, if in liquid form, are extracted with workers underground (2) private ways and roads appurtenant to such area, and (3) lands, excavations, underground passageways, shafts, slopes, tunnels and workings, structures, facilities, equipment, machines, tools, or other property including impoundments, retention dams, and tailings ponds, on the surface or underground, used in, or to be used in, or resulting from, the work of extracting such minerals from their natural deposits in nonliquid form, or if in liquid form, with workers underground, or used in, or to be used in, the milling of such minerals, or the work of preparing coal or other minerals, and includes custom coal preparation facilities.

(b) *Work of preparing the coal* means the breaking, crushing, sizing, cleaning, washing, drying, mixing, storing, and loading of bituminous coal, lignite, or anthracite, and such other work of preparing such coal as is usually done by the operator of the coal mine.

(c) *Operator* means

(1) Any owner, lessee, or other person who operates, controls, or supervises a coal mine; or,

(2) The person, partnership, association, or corporation, or subsidiary of a corporation operating a metal or nonmetal mine, and owning the right to do so, and includes any agent thereof charged with responsibility for the operation of such mine.

(d) *Miner* means any individual working in a mine.

(e) *Occupational injury* means any injury to a miner which occurs at a mine for which medical treatment is administered, or which results in death or loss of consciousness, inability to perform all job duties on any day after an injury, temporary assignment to other duties, or transfer to another job.

(f) *Occupational illness* means an illness or disease of a miner which may have resulted from work at a mine or for which an award of compensation is made.

(g) *First aid* means one-time treatment, and any follow-up visit for observational purposes, of a minor injury.

(h) *Accident* means:

(1) A death of an individual at a mine;

(2) An injury to an individual at a mine which has a reasonable potential to cause death;

(3) An entrapment of an individual for more than 30 minutes or which has a reasonable potential to cause death;

(4) An unplanned inundation of a mine by a liquid or gas;

(5) An unplanned ignition or explosion of gas or dust;

(6) In underground mines, an unplanned fire not extinguished within 10 minutes of discovery; in surface mines and surface areas of underground mines, an unplanned fire not extinguished within 30 minutes of discovery;

(7) An unplanned ignition or explosion of a blasting agent or an explosive;

(8) An unplanned roof fall at or above the anchorage zone in active workings where roof bolts are in use; or, an unplanned roof or rib fall in active workings that impairs ventilation or impedes passage;

(9) A coal or rock outburst that causes withdrawal of miners or which disrupts regular mining activity for more than one hour;

(10) An unstable condition at an impoundment, refuse pile, or culm bank which requires emergency action in order to prevent failure, or which causes individuals to evacuate an area; or, failure of an impoundment, refuse pile, or culm bank;

(11) Damage to hoisting equipment in a shaft or slope which endangers an individual or which interferes with use of the equipment for more than thirty minutes; and

(12) An event at a mine which causes death or bodily injury to an individual not at the mine at the time the event occurs.

[42 FR 65535, Dec. 30, 1977; 43 FR 1617, Jan. 11, 1978, as amended at 43 FR 12318, Mar. 24, 1978; 69 FR 26499, May 13, 2004; 71 FR 71452, Dec. 8, 2006]

Subpart B—Notification, Investigation, Preservation of Evidence

§ 50.10 Immediate notification.

The operator shall immediately contact MSHA at once without delay and

§ 50.11

within 15 minutes at the toll-free number, 1-800-746-1553, once the operator knows or should know that an accident has occurred involving:

(a) A death of an individual at the mine;

(b) An injury of an individual at the mine which has a reasonable potential to cause death;

(c) An entrapment of an individual at the mine which has a reasonable potential to cause death; or

(d) Any other accident.

[74 FR 68919, Dec. 29, 2009]

§ 50.11 Investigation.

(a) After notification of an accident by an operator, the MSHA District Manager will promptly decide whether to conduct an accident investigation and will promptly inform the operator of his decision. If MSHA decides to investigate an accident, it will initiate the investigation within 24 hours of notification.

(b) Each operator of a mine shall investigate each accident and each occupational injury at the mine. Each operator of a mine shall develop a report of each investigation. No operator may use Form 7000-1 as a report, except that an operator of a mine at which fewer than twenty miners are employed may, with respect to that mine, use Form 7000-1 as an investigation report respecting an occupational injury not related to an accident. No operator may use an investigation or an investigation report conducted or prepared by MSHA to comply with this paragraph. An operator shall submit a copy of any investigation report to MSHA at its request. Each report prepared by the operator shall include,

(1) The date and hour of occurrence;

(2) The date the investigation began;

(3) The names of individuals participating in the investigation;

(4) A description of the site;

(5) An explanation of the accident or injury, including a description of any equipment involved and relevant events before and after the occurrence, and any explanation of the cause of any injury, the cause of any accident or cause of any other event which caused an injury;

(6) The name, occupation, and experience of any miner involved;

(7) A sketch, where pertinent, including dimensions depicting the occurrence;

(8) A description of steps taken to prevent a similar occurrence in the future; and

(9) Identification of any report submitted under § 50.20 of this part.

[42 FR 65535, Dec. 30, 1977, as amended at 69 FR 26499, May 13, 2004]

§ 50.12 Preservation of evidence.

Unless granted permission by a MSHA District Manager, no operator may alter an accident site or an accident related area until completion of all investigations pertaining to the accident except to the extent necessary to rescue or recover an individual, prevent or eliminate an imminent danger, or prevent destruction of mining equipment.

[42 FR 65535, Dec. 30, 1977; 43 FR 1617, Jan. 11, 1978, as amended at 69 FR 26499, May 13, 2004]

Subpart C—Reporting of Accidents, Injuries, and Illnesses

§ 50.20 Preparation and submission of MSHA Report Form 7000-1—Mine Accident, Injury, and Illness Report.

(a) Each operator shall maintain at the mine office a supply of MSHA Mine Accident, Injury, and Illness Report Form 7000-1. These may be obtained from the MSHA District Office. Each operator shall report each accident, occupational injury, or occupational illness at the mine. The principal officer in charge of health and safety at the mine or the supervisor of the mine area in which an accident or occupational injury occurs, or an occupational illness may have originated, shall complete or review the form in accordance with the instructions and criteria in §§ 50.20-1 through 50.20-7. If an occupational illness is diagnosed as being one of those listed in § 50.20-6(b)(7), the operator must report it under this part. The operator shall mail completed forms to MSHA within ten working days after an accident or occupational injury occurs or an occupational illness is diagnosed. When an accident specified in § 50.10 occurs, which does not involve an occupational injury, sections

A, B, and items 5 through 12 of section C of Form 7000–1 shall be completed and mailed to MSHA in accordance with the instructions in §50.20–1 and criteria contained in §§50.20–4 through 50.20–6.

(b) Each operator shall report each occupational injury or occupational illness on one set of forms. If more than one miner is injured in the same accident or is affected simultaneously with the same occupational illness, an operator shall complete a separate set of forms for each miner affected. To the extent that the form is not self-explanatory, an operator shall complete the form in accordance with the instructions in §50.20–1 and criteria contained in §§50.20–2 through 50.20–7.

(Secs. 103 (a) and (h), and 508, Pub. L. 91–173, as amended by Pub. L. 95–164, 91 Stat. 1297, 1299, 83 Stat. 803 (30 U.S.C. 801, 813, 957))

[42 FR 65535, Dec. 30, 1977, as amended at 44 FR 52828, Sept. 11, 1979; 60 FR 35695, July 11, 1995; 69 FR 26499, May 13, 2004]

§ 50.20–1 General instructions for completing MSHA Form 7000–1.

Each Form 7000–1 consists of four sheets, an original and three copies. The original form shall be mailed to: MSHA Office of Injury and Employment Information, P.O. Box 25367, Denver Federal Center, Denver, Colo. 80225, within ten working days after an accident, occupational injury or occupational illness. At the same time, the first copy shall be mailed to the appropriate local MSHA district office. If the first copy does not contain a completed Section D—Return to Duty Information—the second copy shall be retained by the operator until the miner returns to work or a final disposition is made respecting the miner. When the miner returns to work or a final disposition is made, the operator shall, within five days, complete Section D and mail the second copy to the MSHA Office of Injury and Employment Information at the above address. A third copy, containing all the information in the first and second copies shall be retained at the mine office closest to the mine for a period of five years. You may also submit reports by facsimile, 888–231–5515. To file electronically, follow the instructions on MSHA Internet site, *http://www.msha.gov*. For assistance in electronic filing, contact the MSHA help desk at 877–778–6055.

[42 FR 65535, Dec. 30, 1977; 43 FR 1617, Jan. 11, 1978; 60 FR 35695, July 11, 1995, as amended at 69 FR 26499, May 13, 2004; 71 FR 16666, Apr. 3, 2006]

§ 50.20–2 Criteria—"Transfer to another job."

"Transfer to another job" means transfers, either temporary, or permanent, which are occasioned by a work-related injury or illness. Permanent or temporary transfers to remove miners from further exposure to health hazards are considered preventative in nature and are not required to be reported. Controlling the amount of exposure to radiation during some period of time is one example. Transfer of a coal miner to a less dusty area of a mine when the miner elects to exercise rights under Section 203(b) of the Federal Coal Mine Health and Safety Act of 1969 is another example.

§ 50.20–3 Criteria—Differences between medical treatment and first aid.

(a) Medical treatment includes, but is not limited to, the suturing of any wound, treatment of fractures, application of a cast or other professional means of immobilizing an injured part of the body, treatment of infection arising out of an injury, treatment of bruise by the drainage of blood, surgical removal of dead or damaged skin (debridement), amputation or permanent loss of use of any part of the body, treatment of second and third degree burns. Procedures which are diagnostic in nature are not considered by themselves to constitute medical treatments. Visits to a physician, physical examinations, X-ray examinations, and hospitalization for observations, where no evidence of injury or illness is found and no medical treatment given, do not in themselves constitute medical treatment. Procedures which are preventive in nature also are not considered by themselves to constitute medical treatment. Tetanus and flu shots are considered preventative in nature. First aid includes any one-time treatment, and follow-up visit for the purpose of observation, of minor injuries such as, cuts, scratches, first degree burns and splinters. Ointments, salves, antiseptics, and dressings to minor injuries are considered to be first aid.

(1) *Abrasion.* (i) First aid treatment is limited to cleaning a wound, soaking, applying antiseptic and nonprescription medication and bandages on the first visit and follow-up visits limited to observation including changing dressing and bandages. Additional cleaning and application of antiseptic constitutes first aid where it is required by work duties that soil the bandage.

(ii) Medical treatment includes examination for removal of imbedded foreign material, multiple soakings, whirlpool treatment, treatment of infection, or other professional treatments and any treatment involving more than a minor spot-type injury. Treatment of abrasions occurring to greater than full skin depth is considered medical treatment.

(2) *Bruises.* (i) First aid treatment is limited to a single soaking or application of cold compresses, and follow-up visits if they are limited only to observation.

(ii) Medical treatment includes multiple soakings, draining of collected blood, or other treatment beyond observation.

(3) *Burns, Thermal and Chemical (resulting in destruction of tissue by direct contact).* (i) First aid treatment is limited to cleaning or flushing the surface, soaking, applying cold compresses, antiseptics or nonprescription medications, and bandaging on the first visit, and follow-up visits restricted to observation, changing bandages, or additional cleaning. Most first degree burns are amenable to first aid treatment.

(ii) Medical treatment includes a series of treatments including soaks, whirlpool, skin grafts, and surgical debridement (cutting away dead skin). Most second and third degree burns require medical treatment.

(4) *Cuts and Lacerations.* (i) First aid treatment is the same as for abrasions except the application of butterfly closures for cosmetic purposes only can be considered first aid.

(ii) Medical treatment includes the application of butterfly closures for non-cosmetic purposes, sutures, (stitches), surgical debridement, treatment of infection, or other professional treatment.

(5) *Eye Injuries.* (i) First aid treatment is limited to irrigation, removal of foreign material not imbedded in eye, and application of nonprescription medications. A precautionary visit (special examination) to a physician is considered as first aid if treatment is limited to above items, and follow-up visits if they are limited to observation only.

(ii) Medical treatment cases involve removal of imbedded foreign objects, use of prescription medications, or other professional treatment.

(6) *Inhalation of Toxic or Corrosive Gases.* (i) First aid treatment is limited to removal of the miner to fresh air or the one-time administration of oxygen for several minutes.

(ii) Medical treatment consists of any professional treatment beyond that mentioned under first aid and all cases involving loss of consciousness.

(7) *Foreign Objects.* (i) First aid treatment is limited to cleaning the wound, removal of any foreign object by tweezers or other simple techniques, application of antiseptics and nonprescription medications, and bandaging on the first visit. Follow-up visits are limited to observation including changing of bandages. Additional cleaning and applications of antiseptic constitute first aid where it is required by work duties that soil the bandage.

(ii) Medical treatment consists of removal of any foreign object by physician due to depth of imbedment, size or shape of object, or location of wound. Treatment for infection, treatment of a reaction to tetanus booster, or other professional treatment, is considered medical treatment.

(8) *Sprains and Strains.* (i) First aid treatment is limited to soaking, application of cold compresses, and use of elastic bandages on the first visit. Follow-up visits for observation, including reapplying bandage, are first aid.

(ii) Medical treatment includes a series of hot and cold soaks, use of whirlpools, diathermy treatment, or other professional treatment.

[42 FR 65535, Dec. 30, 1977; 43 FR 12318, Mar. 24, 1978]

Mine Safety and Health Admin., Labor § 50.20-6

§ 50.20-4 Criteria—MSHA Form 7000-1, Section A.

(a) *MSHA I.D. number.* Enter the seven digit number assigned to the mine operation by MSHA. If the number is unknown, the nearest MSHA District Office should be contacted.

(b) *Mine name.* Enter the exact name of the operation to which the MSHA I.D. number was assigned.

(c) *Company name.* Enter the name of the mining company submitting this report or, if not a company, the operator's name.

[42 FR 65535, Dec. 30, 1977, as amended at 69 FR 26499, May 13, 2004]

§ 50.20-5 Criteria—MSHA Form 7000-1, Section B.

(a) This section shall be completed for all accidents immediately reported to MSHA as defined in § 50.10. Circle the code from the following list which best defines the accident:

Code 01—A death of an individual at a mine;
Code 02—An injury to an individual at a mine which has a reasonable potential to cause death;
Code 03—An entrapment of an individual for more than 30 minutes;
Code 04—An unplanned mine inundation by a liquid or gas;
Code 05—An unplanned ignition or explosion of dust or gas;
Code 06—An unplanned mine fire not extinguished within 30 minutes of discovery;
Code 07—An unplanned ignition of a blasting agent or an explosive;
Code 08—An unplanned roof fall at or above the anchorage zone in active workings where roof bolts are in use; or a roof or rib fall on active workings that impairs ventilation or impedes passage;
Code 09—A coal or rock outburst that causes withdrawal of miners or which disrupts regular mining activity for more than one hour;
Code 10—An unstable condition at an impoundment, refuse pile, or culm bank which requires emergency action in order to prevent failure, or which causes individuals to evacuate an area; or, failure of an impoundment, refuse pile, or culm bank;
Code 11—Damage to hoisting equipment in a shaft or slope which endangers an individual or which interferes with use of the equipment for more than thirty minutes; and
Code 12—An event at a mine which causes death or bodily injury to an individual not at the mine at the time the event occurs.

§ 50.20-6 Criteria—MSHA Form 7000-1, Section C.

(a) Complete items 5 through 12 for each accident, occupational injury, or occupational illness.

(1) Item 5. Location and mining method. Circle the appropriate location code that was nearest to the location of the accident injury or illness. If the accident injury or illness occurred at the surface, circle only the surface location code in column (a). If the accident injury or illness occurred underground, circle only the underground location code in column (b). Where applicable, circle the underground mining method code in column (c). Applicable codes for columns (a), (b), and (c) are as follows:

(i) Column (a)—Surface location codes. If the accident injury or illness occurred at the surface of a mine, circle one of the following codes which best describes where the accident injury or illness occurred and ignore columns (b) and (c):

Code 02—Surface shop, yard, etc., at an underground mine;
Code 30—Mill operation, preparation plant, or breaker, including associated shops and yards;
Code 03—Surface strip or open pit mine, including shop and yard;
Code 04—Surface auger coal operation on a coal mine, including shop and yard;
Code 05—Surface culm bank or refuse pile at a coal mine, including shop and yard;
Code 06—Dredge mining, including shop and yard;
Code 12—Other surface mining;
Code 17—Independent shops;
Code 99—Office facilities.

(ii) Column (b)—Underground location codes. If the accident injury or illness occurred underground, circle the one code which best describes where the accident injury or illness occurred:

Code 01—Vertical shaft;
Code 02—Slope/Inclined shaft;
Code 03—Face;
Code 04—Intersection;
Code 05—Underground Shop/Office;
Code 06—Other.

(iii) Column (c)—Underground mining method. If the underground accident injury or illness occurred on a working section or working place, enter the code for the mining method

§ 50.20–6

at that working section or working place:

Code 01—Longwall;
Code 02—Shortwall;
Code 03—Conventional/stoping;
Code 05—Continuous Miners;
Code 06—Hand Loading;
Code 07—Caving;
Code 08—Other.

(2) Item 6. Date of accident injury or illness. Enter the date the accident injury or illness occurred.

(3) Item 9. Describe fully the conditions contributing to the accident injury or illness and quantify the damage or impairment. Describe what happened and the reasons therefor, identify the factors which led or contributed to the accident, injury or illness and identify any damage or impairment to the mining operation. The narrative shall clearly specify the actual cause or causes of the accident injury or illness and shall include the following:

(i) Whether the accident injury or illness involved any aspect of compliance with rules and regulations;

(ii) Whether the accident injury or illness involved mine equipment or the mining system;

(iii) Whether the accident injury or illness involved job skills and miner proficiency, training and attitude; and

(iv) Whether the accident injury or illness involved protective items relating to clothing, or protective devices on equipment.

(4) Item 10. If equipment was involved in the accident, injury or illness specify type (loader, shuttle car, dozer, etc.), name of manufacturer, and equipment model number.

(5) Item 11. Name of witness to accident injury or illness. If any miner witnessed the accident injury or illness, enter the name.

(b) Complete items 13–27 for each occupational injury, or occupational illness.

(1) Item 13. Name of injured/ill miner. Enter the miner's name (first, middle initial, and last).

(2) Item 17. Regular job title. Enter the miner's regular job title. For example: "shuttle car operator".

(3) Item 19. Check if this injury/illness resulted in permanent total or partial disability.

(i) "Permanent total disability." The classification for any injury or illness other than death which permanently and totally incapacitates an employee from following any gainful occupation or which results in the loss, or the complete loss of use, of any of the following in one accident injury or illness:

(A) Both eyes;
(B) One eye and one hand, or arm, or leg, or foot;
(C) Any two of the following not on the same limb: hand, arm, foot, or leg.

(ii) "Permanent partial disability." The classification for any injury or illness other than death or permanent total disability which results in the loss, or complete loss of use, of any member or part of a member of the body, or any permanent impairment of functions of the body or part thereof, regardless of any preexisting disability of the affected member or impaired body function.

(4) Item 20. What directly inflicted injury or illness. Name the object or substance which directly affected the miner. For example: the machine or thing struck against or which struck the miner; the vapor or poison inhaled or swallowed; the chemical or non-ionizing radiation which irritated the skin; or in cases of strains or hernias, the thing lifted or pulled.

(5) Item 21. Nature of injury or illness. For injuries, use commonly used medical terms to answer this question such as puncture wound, third degree burn, fracture, dislocation, amputation. For multiple injuries, enter the injury which was the most serious. For illness, name the illness, such as pneumoconiosis, silicosis. Avoid general terms such as "hurt", "sore", "sick".

(6) Item 22. Part of body injured or affected. Name the part of the body with the most serious injury. For example, if an injured employee has a bruised finger and a broken ankle, write "ankle". If amputation, enter part of the body lost.

(7) Item 23. Occupational Illness. Circle the code from the list below which most accurately describes the illness. These are typical examples and are not to be considered the complete listing of the types of illnesses and disorders

that should be included under each category. In cases where the time of onset of illness is in doubt, the day of diagnosis of illness will be considered as the first day of illness.

(i) Code 21—*Occupational Skin Diseases or Disorders*. Examples: Contact dermatitis, eczema, or rash caused by primary irritants and sensitizers or poisonous plants; oil acne; chrome ulcers; chemical burns or inflammations.

(ii) Code 22—*Dust Diseases of the Lungs (Pneumoconioses)*. Examples: Silicosis, asbestosis, coal worker's pneumoconiosis, and other pneumoconioses.

(iii) Code 23—*Respiratory Conditions due to Toxic Agents*. Examples: Pneumonitis, pharyngitis, rhinitis, or acute congestion due to chemicals, dusts, gases, or fumes.

(iv) Code 24—*Poisoning (Systemic Effects of Toxic Materials)*. Examples: Poisoning by lead, mercury, cadmium, arsenic, or other metals, poisoning by carbon monoxide, hydrogen sulfide or other gases; poisoning by benzol, carbon tetrachloride, or other organic solvents; poisoning by insecticide sprays such as parathion, lead arsenate; poisoning by other chemicals such as formaldehyde, plastics and resins.

(v) Code 25—*Disorders Due to Physical Agents (Other than Toxic Materials)*. Examples: Heatstroke, sunstroke, heat exhaustion and other effects of environmental heat; freezing, frostbite and effects of exposure to low temperatures; caisson disease; effects of ionizing radiation (radon daughters, non-medical, non-therapeutic X-rays, radium); effects of nonionizing radiation (welding flash, ultra-violet rays, microwaves, sunburn).

(vi) Code 26—*Disorders Associated with Repeated Trauma*. Examples: Noise-induced hearing loss; synovitis, tenosynovitis, and bursitis; Raynaud's phenomena; and other conditions due to repeated motion, vibration or pressure.

(vii) Code 29—*All Other Occupational Illnesses*. Examples: Infectious hepatitis, malignant and benign tumors, any form of cancer, kidney diseases, food poisoning, histoplasmosis.

(8) Item 24. Miner's work activity when injury or illness occurred. Describe exactly the activity of the injured miner when the occupational injury or occupational illness occurred. For example: "Setting temporary support prior to drilling holes for roof bolts."

(Secs. 103 (a) and (h), and 508, Pub. L. 91–173, as amended by Pub. L. 95–164, 91 Stat. 1297, 1299, 83 Stat. 803 (30 U. S. C. 801, 813, 957))

[42 FR 65535, Dec. 30, 1977; 43 FR 1617, Jan. 11, 1978, as amended at 44 FR 52828, Sept. 11, 1979; 69 FR 26499, May 13, 2004]

§ 50.20-7 Criteria—MSHA Form 7000-1, Section D.

This section requires information concerning the miner's return to duty.

(a) Item 28. Permanently transferred or terminated. Check this block if the miner's employment was terminated or if the miner was permanently transferred to another regular job as a direct result of the occupational injury or occupational illness.

(b) Item 29. Show the date that the injured person returned to his regular job at full capacity (not to restricted work activity) or was transferred or terminated.

(c) Item 30. Number of days away from work. Enter the number of workdays, consecutive or not, on which the miner would have worked but could not because of occupational injury or occupational illness. The number of days away from work shall not include the day of injury or onset of illness or any days on which the miner would not have worked even though able to work. If an employee loses a day from work solely because of the unavailability of professional medical personnel for initial observation or treatment and not as a direct consequence of the injury or illness, the day should not be counted as a day away from work.

(d) Item 31. Number of days of restricted work activity. Enter the number of workdays, consecutive or not, on which because of occupational injury or occupational illness:

(1) The miner was assigned to another job on a temporary basis;

(2) The miner worked at a permanent job less than full time; or

(3) The miner worked at a permanently assigned job but could not perform all duties normally connected with it. The number of days of restricted work activity shall not include the day of injury or onset of illness, or

§ 50.30

any days the miner did not work even though able to work.

If an injured or ill employee receives scheduled follow-up medical treatment or observation which results in the loss of a full workday solely because of the unavailability of professional medical personnel, it will not be counted as a day of restricted work activity. Days of restricted work activity end as the result of any of the following:

(i) The miner returns to his regularly scheduled job and performs all of its duties for a full day or shift;

(ii) The miner is permanently transferred to another permanent job (which shall be reported under Item 28, Permanently Transferred or Terminated). If this happens, even though the miner could not perform this original job any longer, the Days of Restricted Work Activity will stop; or

(iii) The miner is terminated or leaves the mine. (Termination shall also be reported under Item 28, Permanently Transferred or Terminated).

Subpart D—Quarterly Employment and Coal Production Report

§ 50.30 Preparation and submission of MSHA Form 7000–2—Quarterly Employment and Coal Production Report.

(a) Each operator of a mine in which an individual worked during any day of a calendar quarter shall complete a MSHA Form 7000–2 in accordance with the instructions and criteria in § 50.30–1 and submit the original to the MSHA Office of Injury and Employment Information, P.O. Box 25367, Denver Federal Center, Denver, Colo. 80225, within 15 days after the end of each calendar quarter. These forms may be obtained from the MSHA District Office. Each operator shall retain an operator's copy at the mine office nearest the mine for 5 years after the submission date. You may also submit reports by facsimile, 888–231–5515. To file electronically, follow the instructions on MSHA Internet site, *http://www.msha.gov*. For assistance in electronic filing, contact the MSHA help desk at 877–778–6055.

(b) Each operator of a coal mine in which an individual worked during any day of a calendar quarter shall report coal production on Form 7000–2.

[42 FR 65535, Dec. 30, 1977, as amended at 60 FR 35695, July 11, 1995; 69 FR 26499, May 13, 2004]

§ 50.30–1 General instructions for completing MSHA Form 7000–2.

(a) *MSHA I.D. Number* is the 7-digit number assigned to the mine operation by MSHA. Any questions regarding the appropriate I.D. number to use should be directed to your local MSHA District Office.

(b) *Calendar Quarter:* First quarter is January, February, and March. Second quarter is April, May, and June. Third quarter is July, August, and September. Fourth quarter is October, November, and December.

(c) *County* is the name of the county, borough, or independent city in which the operation is located.

(d) *Operation Name* is the specific name of the mine or plant to which the MSHA I.D. number was assigned and for which the quarterly employment report is being submitted.

(e) *Company Name* is the name of the operating company that this report pertains to.

(f) *Mailing Address* is the address of the mine office where the quarterly employment report is to be retained. This should be as near the operation as possible.

(g) *Employment, Employee Hours, and Coal Production*—(1) *Operation Sub-Unit:* (i) Underground Mine: Report data for your underground workers on the first line. If you have personnel working at the surface of your underground mine, report data for those persons on the second line;

(ii) Surface Mine (Including Shops and Yards): Report on the appropriate line, employment and coal production for the mining operation. For surface mining sub-units 03, 04, 05 and 06, include all work associated with shops and yards;

(iii) Mill Operations, Preparation Plants, Breakers: Report data on all persons employed at your milling (crushing, sizing, grinding, concentrating, etc.) operation, preparation plant, or breaker, including those working in associated shops and yards. (Do not include personnel reported in shops and yards associated with other sub-units.);

(iv) Office: Include in this category employees who work principally at the mine or preparation facility office.

(2) *Average number of persons working during quarter:* Show the average number of employees on the payroll during all active periods in the quarter. Include all classes of employees (supervisory, professional, technical proprietors, owners, operators, partners, and service personnel) on your payroll, full or part-time, Report Each Employee Under One Activity Only. For example: If one or more persons work both in the mine and the mill, report these employees under the activity where they spend most of their time. If necessary, estimate for the major activity. The average number may be computed by adding together the number of employees working during each pay period and then dividing by the number of pay periods. Do not include pay periods where no one worked. For example, during the quarter you had 5 pay periods where employees worked. The number of employees in each pay period was 10, 12, 13, 14 and 15 respectively. To compute the average, add the number of employees working each pay period (10 + 12 + 13 + 14 + 15 = 64). Then divide by the number of pay periods (64 divided by 5 = 12.8). Rounding this to the nearest whole number, we get 13 as the average number of persons working.

(3) *Total employee-hours worked during the quarter:* Show the total hours worked by all employees during the quarter covered. Include all time where the employee was actually on duty, but exclude vacation, holiday, sick leave, and all other off-duty time, even though paid for. Make certain that each overtime hour is reported as one hour, and not as the overtime pay multiple for an hour of work. The hours reported should be obtained from payroll or other time records. If actual hours are not available, they may be estimated on the basis of scheduled hours. Make certain not to include hours paid but not worked.

(4) *Production of clean coal (short tons):* This section is to be compiled only by operators of underground or surface mines, but not by operators of central or independent coal preparation plants or operators of metal or nonmetal mines. Enter the total production of clean coal from the mine. This must include coal shipped from the mine and coal used for fuel at the mine, but exclude refuse and coal produced at another mine and purchased for use at the mine.

(h) *Other Reportable Data.* Indicate the number of reportable injuries or illnesses occurring at your operation during the quarter covered by this report. Show the name, title, and telephone number of the person to be contacted regarding this report, and show the date that this report was completed.

[42 FR 65535, Dec. 30, 1977, as amended at 69 FR 26500, May 13, 2004]

Subpart E—Maintenance of Records; Verification of Information

§ 50.40 Maintenance of records.

(a) Each operator of a mine shall maintain a copy of each investigation report required to be prepared under § 50.11 at the mine office closest to the mine for five years after the concurrence.

(b) Each operator shall maintain a copy of each report submitted under § 50.20 or § 50.30 at the mine office closest to the mine for five years after submission. Upon request by the Mine Safety and Health Administration, an operator shall make a copy of any report submitted under § 50.20 or § 50.30 available to MSHA for inspection or copying.

[42 FR 65535, Dec. 30, 1977, as amended at 43 FR 12318, Mar. 24, 1978]

§ 50.41 Verification of reports.

Upon request by MSHA, an operator shall allow MSHA to inspect and copy information related to an accident, injury or illnesses which MSHA considers relevant and necessary to verify a report of investigation required by § 50.11 of this part or relevant and necessary to a determination of compliance with the reporting requirements of this part.

SUBCHAPTER J [RESERVED]

SUBCHAPTER K—METAL AND NONMETAL MINE SAFETY AND HEALTH

PART 56—SAFETY AND HEALTH STANDARDS—SURFACE METAL AND NONMETAL MINES

Subpart A—General

Sec.
56.1 Purpose and scope.
56.2 Definitions.

PROCEDURES

56.1000 Notification of commencement of operations and closing of mines.

Subpart B—Ground Control

56.3000 Definitions.

MINING METHODS

56.3130 Wall, bank, and slope stability.
56.3131 Pit or quarry wall perimeter.

SCALING AND SUPPORT

56.3200 Correction of hazardous conditions.
56.3201 Location for performing scaling.
56.3202 Scaling tools.
56.3203 Rock fixtures.

PRECAUTIONS

56.3400 Secondary breakage.
56.3401 Examination of ground conditions.
56.3430 Activity between machinery or equipment and the highwall or bank.

Subpart C—Fire Prevention and Control

56.4000 Definitions.
56.4011 Abandoned electric circuits.

PROHIBITIONS/PRECAUTIONS/HOUSEKEEPING

56.4100 Smoking and use of open flames.
56.4101 Warning signs.
56.4102 Spillage and leakage.
56.4103 Fueling internal combustion engines.
56.4104 Combustible waste.
56.4130 Electric substations and liquid storage facilities.

FIREFIGHTING EQUIPMENT

56.4200 General requirements.
56.4201 Inspection.
56.4202 Fire hydrants.
56.4203 Extinguisher recharging or replacement.
56.4230 Self-propelled equipment.

FIREFIGHTING PROCEDURES/ALARMS/DRILLS

56.4330 Firefighting, evacuation, and rescue procedures.
56.4331 Firefighting drills.

FLAMMABLE AND COMBUSTIBLE LIQUIDS AND GASES

56.4400 Use restrictions.
56.4401 Storage tank foundations.
56.4402 Safety can use.
56.4430 Storage facilities.

INSTALLATION/CONSTRUCTION/MAINTENANCE

56.4500 Heat sources.
56.4501 Fuel lines.
56.4502 Battery-charging stations.
56.4503 Conveyor belt slippage.
56.4530 Exits.
56.4531 Flammable or combustible liquid storage buildings or rooms.

WELDING/CUTTING/COMPRESSED GASES

56.4600 Extinguishing equipment.
56.4601 Oxygen cylinder storage.
56.4602 Gauges and regulators.
56.4603 Closure of valves.
56.4604 Preparation of pipelines or containers.

APPENDIX I TO SUBPART C OF PART 56—NATIONAL CONSENSUS STANDARDS

Subpart D—Air Quality and Physical Agents

AIR QUALITY

56.5001 Exposure limits for airborne contaminants.
56.5002 Exposure monitoring.
56.5005 Control of exposure to airborne contaminants.
56.5006 Restricted use of chemicals.

Subpart E—Explosives

56.6000 Definitions.

STORAGE

56.6100 Separation of stored explosive material.
56.6101 Areas around explosive material storage facilities.
56.6102 Explosive material storage practices.
56.6130 Explosive material storage facilities.
56.6131 Location of explosive material storage facilities.
56.6132 Magazine requirements.
56.6133 Powder chests.

TRANSPORTATION

56.6200 Delivery to storage or blast site areas.

56.6201	Separation of transported explosive material.
56.6202	Vehicles.
56.6203	Locomotives.
56.6204	Hoists.
56.6205	Conveying explosives by hand.

USE

56.6300	Control of blasting operations.
56.6301	Blasthole obstruction check.
56.6302	Separation of explosive material.
56.6303	Initiation preparation.
56.6304	Primer protection.
56.6305	Unused explosive material.
56.6306	Loading, blasting, and security.
56.6307	Drill stem loading.
56.6308	Initiation systems.
56.6309	Fuel oil requirements for ANFO.
56.6310	Misfire waiting period.
56.6311	Handling of misfires.
56.6312	Secondary blasting.

ELECTRIC BLASTING

56.6400	Compatibility of electric detonators.
56.6401	Shunting.
56.6402	Deenergized circuits near detonators.
56.6403	Branch circuits.
56.6404	Separation of blasting circuits from power source.
56.6405	Firing devices.
56.6406	Duration of current flow.
56.6407	Circuit testing.

NONELECTRIC BLASTING

56.6500	Damaged initiating material.
56.6501	Nonelectric initiation systems.
56.6502	Safety fuse.

EXTRANEOUS ELECTRICITY

56.6600	Loading practices.
56.6601	Grounding.
56.6602	Static electricity dissipation during loading.
56.6603	Air gap.
56.6604	Precautions during storms.
56.6605	Isolation of blasting circuits.

EQUIPMENT/TOOLS

56.6700	Nonsparking tools.
56.6701	Tamping and loading pole requirements.

MAINTENANCE

56.6800	Storage facilities.
56.6801	Vehicle repair.
56.6802	Bulk delivery vehicles.
56.6803	Blasting lines.

GENERAL REQUIREMENTS

56.6900	Damaged or deteriorated explosive material.
56.6901	Black powder.
56.6902	Excessive temperatures.
56.6903	Burning explosive material.
56.6904	Smoking and open flames.
57.6905	Protection of explosive material.

Subpart F—Drilling and Rotary Jet Piercing

DRILLING

56.7002	Equipment defects.
56.7003	Drill area inspection.
56.7004	Drill mast.
56.7005	Augers and drill stems.
56.7008	Moving the drill.
56.7009	Drill helpers.
56.7010	Power failures.
56.7011	Straightening crossed cables.
56.7012	Tending drills in operation.
56.7013	Covering or guarding drill holes.
56.7018	Hand clearance.
56.7050	Tool and drill steel racks.
56.7051	Loose objects on the mast or drill platform.
56.7052	Drilling positions.
56.7053	Moving hand-held drills.
56.7055	Intersecting holes.
56.7056	Collaring in bootlegs.

ROTARY JET PIERCING

56.7801	Jet drills.
56.7802	Oxygen hose lines.
56.7803	Lighting the burner.
56.7804	Refueling.
56.7805	Smoking and open flames.
56.7806	Oxygen intake coupling.
56.7807	Flushing the combustion chamber.

Subpart G [Reserved]

Subpart H—Loading, Hauling, and Dumping

TRAFFIC SAFETY

56.9100	Traffic control.
56.9101	Operating speeds and control of equipment.
56.9102	Movement of independently operating rail equipment.
56.9103	Clearance on adjacent tracks.
56.9104	Railroad crossings.

TRANSPORTATION OF PERSONS AND MATERIALS

56.9200	Transporting persons.
56.9201	Loading, hauling, and unloading of equipment or supplies.
56.9202	Loading and hauling large rocks.

SAFETY DEVICES, PROVISIONS, AND PROCEDURES FOR ROADWAYS, RAILROADS, AND LOADING AND DUMPING SITES

56.9300	Berms or guardrails.
56.9301	Dump site restraints.
56.9302	Protection against moving or runaway railroad equipment.
56.9303	Construction of ramps and dumping facilities.
56.9304	Unstable ground.
56.9305	Truck spotters.

Mine Safety and Health Admin., Labor

Pt. 56

56.9306 Warning devices for restricted clearances.
56.9307 Design, installation, and maintenance of railroads.
56.9308 Switch throws.
56.9309 Chute design.
56.9310 Chute hazards.
56.9311 Anchoring stationary sizing devices.
56.9312 Working around drawholes.
56.9313 Roadway maintenance.
56.9314 Trimming stockpile and muckpile faces.
56.9315 Dust control.
56.9316 Notifying the equipment operator.
56.9317 Suspended loads.
56.9318 Getting on or off moving equipment.
56.9319 Going over, under, or between railcars.
56.9330 Clearance for surface equipment.

Subpart I—Aerial Tramways

56.10001 Filling buckets.
56.10002 Inspection and maintenance.
56.10003 Correction of defects.
56.10004 Brakes.
56.10005 Track cable connections.
56.10006 Tower guards.
56.10007 Falling object protection.
56.10008 Riding tramways.
56.10009 Riding loaded buckets.
56.10010 Starting precautions.

Subpart J—Travelways

56.11001 Safe access.
56.11002 Handrails and toeboards.
56.11003 Construction and maintenance of ladders.
56.11004 Portable rigid ladders.
56.11005 Fixed ladder anchorage and toe clearance.
56.11006 Fixed ladder landings.
56.11007 Wooden components of ladders.
56.11008 Restricted clearance.
56.11009 Walkways along conveyors.
56.11010 Stairstep clearance.
56.11011 Use of ladders.
56.11012 Protection for openings around travelways.
56.11013 Conveyor crossovers.
56.11014 Crossing moving conveyors.
56.11016 Snow and ice on walkways and travelways.
56.11017 Inclined fixed ladders.
56.11025 Railed landings, backguards, and other protection for fixed ladders.
56.11026 Protection for inclined fixed ladders.
56.11027 Scaffolds and working platforms.

Subpart K—Electricity

56.12001 Circuit overload protection.
56.12002 Controls and switches.
56.12003 Trailing cable overload protection.
56.12004 Electrical conductors.
56.12005 Protection of power conductors from mobile equipment.
56.12006 Distribution boxes.
56.12007 Junction box connection procedures.
56.12008 Insulation and fittings for power wires and cables.
56.12010 Isolation or insulation of communication conductors.
56.12011 High-potential electrical conductors.
56.12012 Bare signal wires.
56.12013 Splices and repairs of power cables.
56.12014 Handling energized power cables.
56.12016 Work on electrically-powered equipment.
56.12017 Work on power circuits.
56.12018 Identification of power switches.
56.12019 Access to stationary electrical equipment or switchgear.
56.12020 Protection of persons at switchgear.
56.12021 Danger signs.
56.12022 Authorized persons at major electrical installations.
56.12023 Guarding electrical connections and resistor grids.
56.12025 Grounding circuit enclosures.
56.12026 Grounding transformer and switchgear enclosures.
56.12027 Grounding mobile equipment.
56.12028 Testing grounding systems.
56.12030 Correction of dangerous conditions.
56.12032 Inspection and cover plates.
56.12033 Hand-held electric tools.
56.12034 Guarding around lights.
56.12035 Weatherproof lamp sockets.
56.12036 Fuse removal or replacement.
56.12037 Fuses in high-potential circuits.
56.12038 Attachment of trailing cables.
56.12039 Protection of surplus trailing cables.
56.12040 Installation of operating controls.
56.12041 Design of switches and starting boxes.
56.12042 Track bonding.
56.12045 Overhead powerlines.
56.12047 Guy wires.
56.12048 Communication conductors on power poles.
56.12050 Installation of trolley wires.
56.12053 Circuits powered from trolley wires.
56.12065 Short circuit and lightning protection.
56.12066 Guarding trolley wires and bare powerlines.
56.12067 Installation of transformers.
56.12068 Locking transformer enclosures.
56.12069 Lightning protection for telephone wires and ungrounded conductors.
56.12071 Movement or operation of equipment near high-voltage power lines.

Subpart L—Compressed Air and Boilers

56.13001 General requirements for boilers and pressure vessels.

287

56.13010 Reciprocating-type air compressors.
56.13011 Air receiver tanks.
56.13012 Compressor air intakes.
56.13015 Inspection of compressed-air receivers and other unfired pressure vessels.
56.13017 Compressor discharge pipes.
56.13019 Pressure system repairs.
56.13020 Use of compressed air.
56.13021 High-pressure hose connections.
56.13030 Boilers.

Subpart M—Machinery and Equipment

56.14000 Definitions.

SAFETY DEVICES AND MAINTENANCE REQUIREMENTS

56.14100 Safety defects; examination, correction and records.
56.14101 Brakes.
56.14102 Brakes for rail equipment.
56.14103 Operators' stations.
56.14104 Tire repairs.
56.14105 Procedures during repairs or maintenance.
56.14106 Falling object protection.
56.14107 Moving machine parts.
56.14108 Overhead drive belts.
56.14109 Unguarded conveyors with adjacent travelways.
56.14110 Flying or falling materials.
56.14111 Slusher, backlash guards and securing.
56.14112 Construction and maintenance of guards.
56.14113 Inclined conveyors: backstops or brakes.
56.14114 Air valves for pneumatic equipment.
56.14115 Stationary grinding machines.
56.14116 Hand-held power tools.
56.14130 Roll-over protective structures (ROPS) and seat belts.
56.14131 Seat belts for haulage trucks.
56.14132 Horns and back-up alarms.

SAFETY PRACTICES AND OPERATIONAL PROCEDURES

56.14200 Warnings prior to starting or moving equipment.
56.14201 Conveyor start-up warnings.
56.14202 Manual cleaning of conveyor pulleys.
56.14203 Application of belt dressing.
56.14204 Machinery lubrication.
56.14205 Machinery, equipment, and tools.
56.14206 Securing movable parts.
56.14207 Parking procedures for unattended equipment.
56.14208 Warning devices.
56.14209 Safety procedures for towing.
56.14210 Movement of dippers, buckets, loading booms, or suspended loads.
56.14211 Blocking equipment in a raised position.
56.14212 Chains, ropes, and drive belts.
56.14213 Ventilation and shielding for welding.
56.14214 Train warnings.
56.14215 Coupling or uncoupling cars.
56.14216 Backpoling.
56.14217 Securing parked railcars.
56.14218 Movement of equipment on adjacent tracks.
56.14219 Brakeman signals.

APPENDIX I TO SUBPART M OF PART 56—NATIONAL CONSENSUS STANDARDS

Subpart N—Personal Protection

56.15001 First aid materials.
56.15002 Hard hats.
56.15003 Protective footwear.
56.15004 Eye protection.
56.15005 Safety belts and lines.
56.15006 Protective equipment and clothing for hazards and irritants.
56.15007 Protective equipment or clothing for welding, cutting, or working with molten metal.
56.15014 Eye protection when operating grinding wheels.
56.15020 Life jackets and belts.

Subpart O—Materials Storage and Handling

56.16001 Stacking and storage of materials.
56.16002 Bins, hoppers, silos, tanks, and surge piles.
56.16003 Storage of hazardous materials.
56.16004 Containers for hazardous materials.
56.16005 Securing gas cylinders.
56.16006 Protection of gas cylinder valves.
56.16007 Taglines, hitches, and slings.
56.16009 Suspended loads.
56.16010 Dropping materials from overhead.
56.16011 Riding hoisted loads or on the hoist hook.
56.16012 Storage of incompatible substances.
56.16013 Working with molten metal.
56.16014 Operator-carrying overhead cranes.
56.16015 Work or travel on overhead crane bridges.
56.16016 Lift trucks.

Subpart P—Illumination

56.17001 Illumination of surface working areas.

Subpart Q—Safety Programs

56.18002 Examination of working places.
56.18006 New employees.
56.18009 Designation of person in charge.
56.18010 First aid.
56.18012 Emergency telephone numbers.
56.18013 Emergency communications system.
56.18014 Emergency medical assistance and transportation.
56.18020 Working alone.

Mine Safety and Health Admin., Labor

Subpart R—Personnel Hoisting

56.19000 Application.

Hoists

56.19001 Rated capacities.
56.19002 Anchoring.
56.19003 Driving mechanism connections.
56.19004 Brakes.
56.19005 Locking mechanism for clutch.
56.19006 Automatic hoist braking devices.
56.19007 Overtravel and overspeed devices.
56.19008 Friction hoist synchronizing mechanisms.
56.19009 Position indicator.
56.19010 Location of hoist controls.
56.19011 Drum flanges.
56.19012 Grooved drums.
56.19013 Diesel- and other fuel-injection-powered hoists.
56.19014 Friction hoist overtravel protection.
56.19017 Emergency braking for electric hoists.
56.19018 Overtravel by-pass switches.

Wire Ropes

56.19021 Minimum rope strength.
56.19022 Initial measurement.
56.19023 Examinations.
56.19024 Retirement criteria.
56.19025 Load end attachments.
56.19026 Drum end attachment.
56.19027 End attachment retermination.
56.19028 End attachment replacement.
56.19030 Safety device attachments.

Headframes and Sheaves

56.19035 Headframe design.
56.19036 Headframe height.
56.19037 Fleet angles.
56.19038 Platforms around elevated head sheaves.

Conveyances

56.19045 Metal bonnets.
56.19049 Hoisting persons in buckets.
56.19050 Bucket requirements.
56.19054 Rope guides.

Hoisting Procedures

56.19055 Availability of hoist operator for manual hoists.
56.19056 Availability of hoist operator for automatic hoists.
56.19057 Hoist operator's physical fitness.
56.19058 Experienced hoist operators.
56.19061 Maximum hoisting speeds.
56.19062 Maximum acceleration and deceleration.
56.19063 Persons allowed in hoist room.
56.19065 Lowering conveyances by the brakes.
56.19066 Maximum riders in a conveyance.
56.19067 Trips during shift changes.
56.19068 Orderly conduct in conveyances.
56.19069 Entering and leaving conveyances.
56.19070 Closing cage doors or gates.
56.19071 Riding in skips or buckets.
56.19072 Skips and cages in same compartment.
56.19073 Hoisting during shift changes.
56.19074 Riding the bail, rim, bonnet, or crosshead.
56.19075 Use of open hooks.
56.19076 Maximum speeds for hoisting persons in buckets.
56.19077 Lowering buckets.
56.19078 Hoisting buckets from the shaft bottom.
56.19079 Blocking mine cars.
56.19080 Hoisting tools, timbers, and other materials.
56.19081 Conveyances not in use.
56.19083 Overtravel backout device.

Signaling

56.19090 Dual signaling systems.
56.19091 Signaling instructions to hoist operator.
56.19092 Signaling from conveyances.
56.19093 Standard signal code.
56.19094 Posting signal code.
56.19095 Location of signal devices.
56.19096 Familiarity with signal code.

Shafts

56.19100 Shaft landing gates.
56.19101 Stopblocks and derail switches.
56.19102 Shaft guides.
56.19103 Dumping facilities and loading pockets.
56.19104 Clearance at shaft stations.
56.19105 Landings with more than one shaft entrance.
56.19106 Shaft sets.
56.19107 Precautions for work in compartment affected by hoisting operation.
56.19108 Posting warning signs during shaft work.
56.19109 Shaft inspection and repair.
56.19110 Overhead protection for shaft deepening work.
56.191111 Shaft-sinking ladders.

Inspection and Maintenance

56.19120 Procedures for inspection, testing, and maintenance.
56.19121 Recordkeeping.
56.19122 Replacement parts.
56.19129 Examinations and tests at beginning of shift.
56.19130 Conveyance shaft test.
56.19131 Hoist conveyance connections.
56.19132 Safety catches.
56.19133 Shaft.
56.19134 Sheaves.
56.19135 Rollers in inclined shafts.

Subpart S—Miscellaneous

56.20001 Intoxicating beverages and narcotics.

§ 56.1

56.20002 Potable water.
56.20003 Housekeeping.
56.20005 Carbon tetrachloride.
56.20008 Toilet facilities.
56.20009 Tests for explosive dusts.
56.20010 Retaining dams.
56.20011 Barricades and warning signs.
56.20013 Waste receptacles.
56.20014 Prohibited areas for food and beverages.

AUTHORITY: 30 U.S.C. 811.

SOURCE: 50 FR 4054, Jan. 29, 1985, unless otherwise noted.

Subpart A—General

§ 56.1 Purpose and scope.

This part 56 sets forth mandatory safety and health standards for each surface metal or nonmetal mine, including open pit mines, subject to the Federal Mine Safety and Health Act of 1977. The purpose of these standards is the protection of life, the promotion of health and safety, and the prevention of accidents.

§ 56.2 Definitions.

The following definitions apply in this part. In addition definitions contained in any subpart of part 56 apply in that subpart. If inconsistent with the general definitions in this section, the definition in the subpart will apply in that subpart:

American Table of Distances means the current edition of "The American Table of Distances for Storage of Explosives" published by the Institute of Makers of Explosives.

Approved means tested and accepted for a specific purpose by a nationally recognized agency.

Attended means presence of an individual or continuous monitoring to prevent unauthorized entry or access.

Authorized person means a person approved or assigned by mine management to perform a specific type of duty or duties or to be at a specific location or locations in the mine.

Barricaded means obstructed to prevent the passage of persons, vehicles, or flying materials.

Barrier means a material object, or objects that separates, keeps apart, or demarcates in a conspicuous manner such as cones, a warning sign, or tape.

Berm means a pile or mound of material along an elevated roadway capable of moderating or limiting the force of a vehicle in order to impede the vehicle's passage over the bank of the roadway.

Blast area means the area in which concussion (shock wave), flying material, or gases from an explosion may cause injury to persons. In determining the blast area, the following factors shall be considered:

(1) Geology or material to be blasted.
(2) Blast pattern.
(3) Burden, depth, diameter, and angle of the holes.
(4) Blasting experience of the mine.
(5) Delay system, powder factor, and pounds per delay.
(6) Type and amount of explosive material.
(7) Type and amount of stemming.

Blast site means the area where explosive material is handled during loading, including the perimeter formed by the loaded blastholes and 50 feet (15.2 meters) in all directions from loaded holes. A minimum distance of 30 feet (9.1 meters) may replace the 50-foot (15.2-meter) requirement if the perimeter of loaded holes is demarcated with a barrier. The 50-foot (15.2-meter) and alternative 30-foot (9.1-meter) requirement also apply in all directions along the full depth of the hole.

Blasting agent means any substance classified as a blasting agent by the Department of Transportation in 49 CFR 173.114(a) (44 FR 31182, May 31, 1979) which is incorporated by reference. This document is available for inspection at each Metal and Nonmetal Safety and Health District Office of the Mine Safety and Health Administration, and may be obtained from the U.S. Government Printing Office, Washington, DC 20402.

Blasting area means the area near the blasting operations in which concussion or flying material can reasonably be expected to cause injury.

Blasting cap means a detonator which is initiated by a safety fuse.

Blasting circuit means the electrical circuit used to fire one or more electric blasting caps.

Blasting switch means a switch used to connect a power source to a blasting circuit.

Booster means any unit of explosive or blasting agent used for the purpose of perpetuating or intensifying an initial detonation.

Capped fuse means a length of safety fuse to which a blasting cap has been attached.

Capped primer means a package or cartridge of explosives which is specifically designed to transmit detonation to other explosives and which contains a detonator.

Circuit breaker means a device designed to open and close a circuit by nonautomatic means and to open the circuit automatically on a predetermined overcurrent setting without injury to itself when properly applied within its rating.

Combustible means capable of being ignited and consumed by fire.

Combustible liquids means liquids having a flash point at or above 100 °F (37.8 °C). They are divided into the following classes:

(1) Class II liquids—those having flash points at or above 100 °F (37.8 °C) and below 140 °F (60 °C).

(2) Class IIIA liquids—those having flash points at or above 140 °F (60 °C) and below 200 °F (93.4 °C).

(3) Class IIIB liquids—those having flash points at or above 200 °F (93.4 °C).

Combustible material means a material that, in the form in which it is used and under the conditions anticipated, will ignite, burn, support combustion, or release flammable vapors when subjected to fire or heat. Wood, paper, rubber, and plastics are examples of combustible materials.

Company official means a member of the company supervisory or technical staff.

Competent person means a person having abilities and experience that fully qualify him to perform the duty to which he is assigned.

Conductor means a material, usually in the form of a wire, cable, or bus bar, capable of carrying an electric current.

Delay connector means a non-electric short interval delay device for use in delaying blasts which are initiated by detonating cord.

Detonating cord means a flexible cord containing a solid core of high explosives.

Detonator means any device containing a detonating charge that is used to initiate an explosive and includes but is not limited to blasting caps, electric blasting caps and nonelectric instantaneous or delay blasting caps.

Distribution box means a portable apparatus with an enclosure through which an electric circuit is carried to one or more cables from a single incoming feed line, each cable circuit being connected through individual overcurrent protective devices.

Electric blasting cap means a detonator designed for and capable of being initiated by means of an electric current.

Electrical grounding means to connect with the ground to make the earth part of the circuit.

Employee means a person who works for wages or salary in the service of an employer.

Employer means a person or organization which hires one or more persons to work for wages or salary.

Emulsion means an explosive material containing substantial amounts of oxidizers dissolved in water droplets, surrounded by an immiscible fuel.

Explosive means any substance classified as an explosive by the Department of Transportation in 49 CFR 173.53, 173.88, and 173.100 which are incorporated by reference. Title 49 CFR is available for inspection at each Metal and Nonmetal Safety and Health district office of the Mine Safety and Health Administration, and may be obtained from the U.S. Government Printing Office, Washington, DC 20402.

Explosive material means explosives, blasting agents, and detonators.

Face or bank means that part of any mine where excavating is progressing or was last done.

Fire resistance rating means the time, in minutes or hours, that an assembly of materials will retain its protective characteristics or structural integrity upon exposure to fire.

Flammable means capable of being easily ignited and of burning rapidly.

Flammable gas means a gas that will burn in the normal concentrations of oxygen in the air.

Flammable liquid means a liquid that has a flash point below 100 °F (37.8 °C),

§ 56.2

a vapor pressure not exceeding 40 pounds per square inch (absolute) at 100 °F (37.8 °C), and is known as a Class I liquid.

Flash point means the minimum temperature at which sufficient vapor is released by a liquid or solid to form a flammable vapor-air mixture at atmospheric pressure.

High potential means more than 650 volts.

Highway means any public street, public alley, or public road.

Hoist means a power driven windlass or drum used for raising ore, rock, or other material from a mine, and for lowering or raising persons and material.

Igniter cord means a fuse, cordlike in appearance, which burns progressively along its length with an external flame at the zone of burning, and is used for lighting a series of safety fuses in the desired sequence.

Insulated means separated from other conducting surfaces by a dielectric substance permanently offering a high resistance to the passage of current and to disruptive discharge through the substance. When any substance is said to be insulated, it is understood to be insulated in a manner suitable for the conditions to which it is subjected. Otherwise, it is, within the purpose of this definition, uninsulated. Insulating covering is one means for making the conductor insulated.

Insulation means a dielectric substance offering a high resistance to the passage of current and to a disruptive discharge through the substance.

Laminated partition means a partition composed of the following material and minimum nominal dimensions: ½-inch-thick plywood, ½-inch-thick gypsum wallboard, ⅛-inch-thick low carbon steel, and ¼-inch-thick plywood, bonded together in that order (IME-22 Box). A laminated partition also includes alternative construction materials described in the Institute of Makers of Explosives (IME) Safety Library Publication No. 22, "Recommendations for the Safe Transportation of Detonators in a Vehicle with Other Explosive Materials" (May 1993), and the "Generic Loading Guide for the IME-22 Container" (October 1993). The IME is located at 1120 19th Street NW., Suite 310, Washington, DC 20036-3605; 202-429-9280; *https://www.ime.org*. This incorporation by reference has been approved by the Director of the Federal Register in accordance with 5 U.S.C. 552(a) and 1 CFR part 51. Copies are available at MSHA's Office of Standards, Regulations, and Variances, 201 12th Street South, Arlington, VA 22202-5452; 202-693-9440; and at all Metal and Nonmetal Mine Safety and Health District Offices, or available for inspection at the National Archives and Records Administration (NARA). For information on the availability of this material at NARA, call 202-741-6030, or go to: *http://www.archives.gov/federal_register/code_of_federal_regulations/ibr_locations.html*.

Lay means the distance parallel to the axis of the rope in which a strand makes one complete turn about the axis of the rope.

Loading means placing explosive material either in a blasthole or against the material to be blasted.

Low potential means 650 volts or less.

Magazine means a facility for the storage of explosives, blasting agents, or detonators.

Major electrical installation means an assemblage of stationary electrical equipment for the generation, transmission, distribution, or conversion of electrical power.

Mantrip means a trip on which persons are transported to and from a work area.

Mill includes any ore mill, sampling works, concentrator, and any crushing, grinding, or screening plant used at, and in connection with, an excavation or mine.

Misfire means the complete or partial failure of a blasting charge to explode as planned.

Mobile equipment means wheeled, skid-mounted, track-mounted, or rail-mounted equipment capable of moving or being moved.

Multipurpose dry-chemical fire extinguisher means an extinguisher having a rating of at least 2-A:10-B:C and containing a nominal 4.5 pounds or more of dry-chemical agent.

Noncombustible material means a material that, in the form in which it is used and under the conditions anticipated, will not ignite, burn, support combustion, or release flammable vapors when subjected to fire or heat. Concrete, masonry block, brick, and steel are examples of noncombustible materials.

Non-electric delay blasting cap means a detonator with an integral delay element and capable of being initiated by miniaturized detonating cord.

Overburden means material of any nature, consolidated or unconsolidated, that overlies a deposit of useful materials or ores that are to be mined.

Overload means that current which will cause an excessive or dangerous temperature in the conductor or conductor insulation.

Permissible means a machine, material, apparatus, or device that has been investigated, tested, and approved by the Bureau of Mines or the Mine Safety and Health Administration and is maintained in permissible condition.

Potable water means water which shall meet the applicable minimum health requirements for drinking water established by the State or community in which the mine is located or by the Environmental Protection Agency in 40 CFR part 141, pages 169–182 revised as of July 1, 1977. Where no such requirements are applicable, the drinking water provided shall conform with the Public Health Service Drinking Water Standards, 42 CFR part 72, subpart J, pages 527–533, revised as of October 1, 1976. Publications to which references are made in this definition are hereby made a part hereof. These incorporated publications are available for inspection at each Metal and Nonmetal Mine Safety and Health District Office of the Mine Safety and Health Administration.

Powder chest means a substantial, nonconductive portable container equipped with a lid and used at blasting sites for explosives other than blasting agents.

Primer means a unit, package, or cartridge of explosives used to initiate other explosives or blasting agents, and which contains a detonator.

Reverse-current protection means a method or device used on direct-current circuits or equipment to prevent the flow of current in the reverse direction.

Rock fixture means any tensioned or nontensioned device or material inserted into the ground to strengthen or support the ground.

Roll protection means a framework, safety canopy or similar protection for the operator when equipment overturns.

Safety can means an approved container, of not over five gallons capacity, having a spring-closing lid and spout cover.

Safety fuse means a flexible cord containing an internal burning medium by which fire is conveyed at a continuous and uniform rate for the purpose of firing blasting caps or a black powder charge.

Safety switch means a sectionalizing switch that also provides shunt protection in blasting circuits between the blasting switch and the shot area.

Scaling means removal of insecure material from a face or highwall.

Secondary safety connection means a second connection between a conveyance and rope, intended to prevent the conveyance from running away or falling in the event the primary connection fails.

Shaft means a vertical or inclined shaft, a slope, incline or winze.

Short circuit means an abnormal connection of relatively low resistance, whether made accidentally or intentionally, between two points of different potential in a circuit.

Slurry (as applied to blasting). See "Water gel."

Storage facility means the entire class of structures used to store explosive materials. A "storage facility" used to store blasting agents corresponds to a BATF Type 4 or 5 storage facility.

Storage tank means a container exceeding 60 gallons in capacity used for the storage of flammable or combustible liquids.

Stray current means that portion of a total electric current that flows through paths other than the intended circuit.

Substantial construction means construction of such strength, material, and workmanship that the object will withstand all reasonable shock, wear, and usage, to which it will be subjected.

§ 56.1000

Suitable means that which fits, and has the qualities or qualifications to meet a given purpose, occasion, condition, function, or circumstance.

Travelway means a passage, walk or way regularly used and designated for persons to go from one place to another.

Water gel or *Slurry* (as applied to blasting) means an explosive or blasting agent containing substantial portions of water.

Wet drilling means the continuous application of water through the central hole of hollow drill steel to the bottom of the drill hole.

Working place means any place in or about a mine where work is being performed.

[69 FR 38837, June 29, 2004, as amended at 80 FR 52986, Sept. 2, 2015]

PROCEDURES

§ 56.1000 Notification of commencement of operations and closing of mines.

The owner, operator, or person in charge of any metal and nonmetal mine shall notify the nearest MSHA Metal and Nonmetal Mine Safety and Health district office before starting operations, of the approximate or actual date mine operation will commence. The notification shall include the mine name, location, the company name, mailing address, person in charge, and whether operations will be continuous or intermittent.

When any mine is closed, the person in charge shall notify the nearest district office as provided above and indicate whether the closure is temporary or permanent.

[50 FR 4054, Jan. 29, 1985, as amended at 60 FR 33723, June 29, 1995; 60 FR 35695, July 11, 1995; 71 FR 16667, Apr. 3, 2006]

Subpart B—Ground Control

AUTHORITY: 30 U.S.C. 811

SOURCE: 51 FR 36197, Oct. 8, 1986, unless otherwise noted.

§ 56.3000 Definitions.

The following definitions apply in this subpart.

Travelway. A passage, walk, or way regularly used or designated for persons to go from one place to another.

[51 FR 36197, Oct. 8, 1986, as amended at 69 FR 38840, June 29, 2004]

MINING METHODS

§ 56.3130 Wall, bank, and slope stability.

Mining methods shall be used that will maintain wall, bank, and slope stability in places where persons work or travel in performing their assigned tasks. When benching is necessary, the width and height shall be based on the type of equipment used for cleaning of benches or for scaling of walls, banks, and slopes.

§ 56.3131 Pit or quarry wall perimeter.

In places where persons work or travel in performing their assigned tasks, loose or unconsolidated material shall be sloped to the angle of repose or stripped back for at least 10 feet from the top of the pit or quarry wall. Other conditions at or near the perimeter of the pit or quarry wall which create a fall-of-material hazard to persons shall be corrected.

SCALING AND SUPPORT

§ 56.3200 Correction of hazardous conditions.

Ground conditions that create a hazard to persons shall be taken down or supported before other work or travel is permitted in the affected area. Until corrective work is completed, the area shall be posted with a warning against entry and, when left unattended, a barrier shall be installed to impede unauthorized entry.

§ 56.3201 Location for performing scaling.

Scaling shall be performed from a location which will not expose persons to injury from falling material, or other protection from falling material shall be provided.

§ 56.3202 Scaling tools.

Where manual scaling is performed, a scaling bar shall be provided. This bar shall be of a length and design that will allow the removal of loose material without exposing the person performing this work to injury.

§ 56.3203 Rock fixtures.

(a) For rock bolts and accessories addressed in ASTM F432–95, "Standard Specification for Roof and Rock Bolts and Accessories," the mine operator shall—

(1) Obtain a manufacturer's certification that the material was manufactured and tested in accordance with the specifications of ASTM F432–95; and

(2) Make this certification available to an authorized representative of the Secretary and to the representative of miners.

(b) Fixtures and accessories not addressed in ASTM F432–95 may be used for ground support provided they—

(1) Have been successful in supporting the ground in an area with similar strata, opening dimensions and ground stresses in any mine; or

(2) Have been tested and shown to be effective in supporting ground in an area of the affected mine which has similar strata, opening dimensions, and ground stresses as the area where the fixtures are expected to be used. During the test process, access to the test area shall be limited to persons necessary to conduct the test.

(c) Bearing plates shall be used with fixtures when necessary for effective ground support.

(d) The diameter of finishing bits shall be within a tolerance of plus or minus 0.030 inch of the manufacturer's recommended hole diameter for the anchor used. When separate finishing bits are used, they shall be distinguishable from other bits.

(e) Damaged or deteriorated cartridges of grouting material shall not be used.

(f) When rock bolts tensioned by torquing are used as a means of ground support,

(1) Selected tension level shall be—

(i) At least 50 percent of either the yield point of the bolt or anchorage capacity of the rock, whichever is less; and

(ii) No greater than the yield point of the bolt or anchorage capacity of the rock.

(2) The torque of the first bolt, every tenth bolt, and the last bolt installed in each work area during the shift shall be accurately determined immediately after installation. If the torque of any fixture tested does not fall within the installation torque range, corrective action shall be taken.

(g) When grouted fixtures can be tested by applying torque, the first fixture installed in each work place shall be tested to withstand 150 foot-pounds of torque. Should it rotate in the hole, a second fixture shall be tested in the same manner. If the second fixture also turns, corrective action shall be taken.

(h) When other tensioned and nontensioned fixtures are used, test methods shall be established to verify their effectiveness.

(i) The mine operator shall certify that tests were conducted and make the certification available to an authorized representative of the Secretary.

[51 FR 36197, Oct. 8, 1986, as amended at 51 FR 36804, Oct. 16, 1986; 63 FR 20030, Apr. 22, 1998]

PRECAUTIONS

§ 56.3400 Secondary breakage.

Prior to secondary breakage operations, material to be broken, other than hanging material, shall be positioned or blocked to prevent movement which would endanger persons in the work area. Secondary breakage shall be performed from a location which would not expose persons to danger.

§ 56.3401 Examination of ground conditions.

Persons experienced in examining and testing for loose ground shall be designated by the mine operator. Appropriate supervisors or other designated persons shall examine and, where applicable, test ground conditions in areas where work is to be performed prior to work commencing, after blasting, and as ground conditions warrant during the work shift. Highwalls and banks adjoining travelways shall be examined weekly or more often if changing ground conditions warrant.

§ 56.3430 Activity between machinery or equipment and the highwall or bank.

Persons shall not work or travel between machinery or equipment and the highwall or bank where the machinery or equipment may hinder escape from falls or slides of the highwall or bank. Travel is permitted when necessary for persons to dismount.

Subpart C—Fire Prevention and Control

AUTHORITY: Sec. 101, Federal Mine Safety and Health Act of 1977, Pub. L. 91–173, as amended by Pub. L. 95–164, 91 Stat. 1291 (30 U.S.C. 811).

§ 56.4000 Definitions.

The following definitions apply in this subpart.

Flash point. The minimum temperature at which sufficient vapor is released by a liquid to form a flammable vapor-air mixture near the surface of the liquid.

Safety can. A container of not over five gallons capacity that is designed to safely relieve internal pressure when exposed to heat and has a spring-closing lid and spout cover.

[50 FR 4054, Jan. 29, 1985, as amended at 68 FR 32361, May 30, 2003; 69 FR 38840, June 29, 2004]

§ 56.4011 Abandoned electric circuits.

Abandoned electric circuits shall be deenergized and isolated so that they cannot become energized inadvertently.

PROHIBITIONS/PRECAUTIONS/ HOUSEKEEPING

§ 56.4100 Smoking and use of open flames.

No person shall smoke or use an open flame where flammable or combustible liquids, including greases, or flammable gases are—

(a) Used or transported in a manner that could create a fire hazard; or

(b) Stored or handled.

§ 56.4101 Warning signs.

Readily visible signs prohibiting smoking and open flames shall be posted where a fire or explosion hazard exists.

§ 56.4102 Spillage and leakage.

Flammable or combustible liquid spillage or leakage shall be removed in a timely manner or controlled to prevent a fire hazard.

§ 56.4103 Fueling internal combustion engines.

Internal combustion engines shall be switched off before refueling if the fuel tanks are integral parts of the equipment. This standard does not apply to diesel-powered equipment.

§ 56.4104 Combustible waste.

(a) Waste materials, including liquids, shall not accumulate in quantities that could create a fire hazard.

(b) Until disposed of properly, waste or rags containing flammable or combustible liquids that could create a fire hazard shall be placed in covered metal containers or other equivalent containers with flame containment characteristics.

§ 56.4130 Electric substations and liquid storage facilities.

(a) If a hazard to persons could be created, no combustible materials shall be stored or allowed to accumulate within 25 feet of the following:

(1) Electric substations.

(2) Unburied, flammable or combustible liquid storage tanks.

(3) Any group of containers used for storage of more than 60 gallons of flammable or combustible liquids.

(b) The area within the 25-foot perimeter shall be kept free of dry vegetation.

FIREFIGHTING EQUIPMENT

§ 56.4200 General requirements.

(a) For fighting fires that could endanger persons, each mine shall have—

(1) Onsite firefighting equipment for fighting fires in their early stages; and

(2) Onsite firefighting equipment for fighting fires beyond their early stages, or the mine shall have made prior arrangements with a local fire department to fight such fires.

(b) This onsite firefighting equipment shall be—

(1) Of the type, size, and quantity that can extinguish fires of any class which could occur as a result of the hazards present; and

(2) Strategically located, readily accessible, plainly marked, and maintained in fire-ready condition.

[50 FR 4054, Jan. 29, 1985, as amended at 50 FR 20100, May 14, 1985]

§ 56.4201 Inspection.

(a) Firefighting equipment shall be inspected according to the following schedules:

(1) Fire extinguishers shall be inspected visually at least once a month to determine that they are fully charged and operable.

(2) At least once every twelve months, maintenance checks shall be made of mechanical parts, the amount and condition of extinguishing agent and expellant, and the condition of the hose, nozzle, and vessel to determine that the fire extinguishers will operate effectively.

(3) Fire extinguishers shall be hydrostatically tested according to Table C-1 or a schedule based on the manufacturer's specifications to determine the integrity of extinguishing agent vessels.

(4) Water pipes, valves, outlets, hydrants, and hoses that are part of the mine's firefighting system shall be visually inspected at least once every three months for damage or deterioration and use-tested at least once every twelve months to determine that they remain functional.

(5) Fire suppression systems shall be inspected at least once every twelve months. An inspection schedule based on the manufacturer's specifications or the equivalent shall be established for individual components of a system and followed to determine that the system remains functional. Surface fire suppression systems are exempt from these inspection requirements if the systems are used solely for the protection of property and no persons would be affected by a fire.

(b) At the completion of each inspection or test required by this standard, the person making the inspection or test shall certify that the inspection or test has been made and the date on which it was made. Certifications of hydrostatic testing shall be retained until the fire extinguisher is retested or permanently removed from service. Other certifications shall be retained for one year.

TABLE C-1—HYDROSTATIC TEST INTERVALS FOR FIRE EXTINGUISHERS

Extinguisher type	Test interval (years)
Soda Acid	5
Cartridge-Operated Water and/or Antifreeze	5
Stored-Pressure Water and/or Antifreeze	5
Wetting Agent	5
Foam	5
AFFF (Aqueous Film Forming Foam)	5
Loaded Stream	5
Dry-Chemical with Stainless Steel Shells	5
Carbon Dioxide	5
Dry-Chemical, Stored Pressure, with Mild Steel Shells, Brazed Brass Shells, or Aluminum Shells	12
Dry-Chemical, Cartridge or Cylinder Operated, with Mild Steel Shells	12
Bromotrifluoromethane—Halon 1301	12
Bromochlorodifluoromethane—Halon 1211	12
Dry-Powder, Cartridge or Cylinder-Operated, with Mild Steel Shells [1]	12

[1] Except for stainless steel and steel used for compressed gas cylinders, all other steel shells are defined as "mild steel" shells.

§ 56.4202 Fire hydrants.

If fire hydrants are part of the mine's firefighting system, the hydrants shall be provided with—

(a) Uniform fittings or readily available adapters for onsite firefighting equipment;

(b) Readily available wrenches or keys to open the valves; and

(c) Readily available adapters capable of connecting hydrant fittings to the hose equipment of any firefighting organization relied upon by the mine.

§ 56.4203 Extinguisher recharging or replacement.

Fire extinguishers shall be recharged or replaced with a fully charged extinguisher promptly after any discharge.

§ 56.4230 Self-propelled equipment.

(a)(1) Whenever a fire or its effects could impede escape from self-propelled equipment, a fire extinguisher shall be on the equipment.

(2) Whenever a fire or its effects would not impede escape from the equipment but could affect the escape

§ 56.4330

of other persons in the area, a fire extinguisher shall be on the equipment or within 100 feet of the equipment.

(b) A fire suppression system may be used as an alternative to fire extinguishers if the system can be manually activated.

(c) Fire extinguishers or fire suppression systems shall be of a type and size that can extinguish fires of any class in their early stages which could originate from the equipment's inherent fire hazards. Fire extinguishers or manual actuators for the suppression system shall be located to permit their use by persons whose escape could be impeded by fire.

FIREFIGHTING PROCEDURES/ALARMS/DRILLS

§ 56.4330 Firefighting, evacuation, and rescue procedures.

(a) Mine operators shall establish emergency firefighting, evacuation, and rescue procedures. These procedures shall be coordinated in advance with available firefighting organizations.

(b) Fire alarm procedures or systems shall be established to promptly warn every person who could be endangered by a fire.

(c) Fire alarm systems shall be maintained in operable condition.

§ 56.4331 Firefighting drills.

Emergency firefighting drills shall be held at least once every six months for persons assigned firefighting responsibilities by the mine operator.

FLAMMABLE AND COMBUSTIBLE LIQUIDS AND GASES

§ 56.4400 Use restrictions.

(a) Flammable liquids shall not be used for cleaning.

(b) Solvents shall not be used near an open flame or other ignition source, near any source of heat, or in an atmosphere that can elevate the temperature of the solvent above the flash point.

§ 56.4401 Storage tank foundations.

Fixed, unburied, flammable or combustible liquid storage tanks shall be securely mounted on firm foundations. Piping shall be provided with flexible connections or other special fittings where necessary to prevent leaks caused by tanks settling.

§ 56.4402 Safety can use.

Small quantities of flammable liquids drawn from storage shall be kept in safety cans labeled to indicate the contents.

§ 56.4430 Storage facilities.

(a) Storage tanks for flammable or combustible liquids shall be—

(1) Capable of withstanding working pressures and stresses and compatible with the type of liquid stored;

(2) Maintained in a manner that prevents leakage;

(3) Isolated or separated from ignition sources to prevent fire or explosion; and

(4) Vented or otherwise constructed to prevent development of pressure or vacuum as a result of filling, emptying, or atmospheric temperature changes. Vents for storage of Class I, II, or IIIA liquids shall be isolated or separated from ignition sources. These pressure relief requirements do not apply to tanks used for storage of Class IIIB liquids that are larger than 12,000 gallons in capacity.

(b) All piping, valves, and fittings shall be—

(1) Capable of withstanding working pressures and stresses;

(2) Compatible with the type of liquid stored; and

(3) Maintained in a manner that prevents leakage.

(c) Fixed, unburied tanks located where escaping liquid could present a hazard to persons shall be provided with—

(1) Containment for the entire capacity of the largest tank; or

(2) Drainage of a remote impoundment area that does not endanger persons. However, storage of only Class IIIB liquids does not require containment or drainage to remote impoundment.

Installation/Construction/Maintenance

§ 56.4500 Heat sources.

Heat sources capable of producing combustion shall be separated from combustible materials if a fire hazard could be created.

§ 56.4501 Fuel lines.

Fuel lines shall be equipped with valves capable of stopping the flow of fuel at the source and shall be located and maintained to minimize fire hazards. This standard does not apply to fuel lines on self-propelled equipment.

§ 56.4502 Battery-charging stations.

(a) Battery-charging stations shall be ventilated with a sufficient volume of air to prevent the accumulation of hydrogen gas.

(b) Smoking, use of open flames, or other activities that could create an ignition source shall be prohibited at the battery charging station during battery charging.

(c) Readily visible signs prohibiting smoking or open flames shall be posted at battery-charging stations during battery charging.

§ 56.4503 Conveyor belt slippage.

Belt conveyors within confined areas where evacuation would be restricted in the event of a fire resulting from belt-slippage shall be equipped with a detection system capable of automatically stopping the drive pulley. A person shall attend the belt at the drive pulley when it is necessary to operate the conveyor while temporarily bypassing the automatic function.

§ 56.4530 Exits.

Buildings or structures in which persons work shall have a sufficient number of exits to permit prompt escape in case of fire.

§ 56.4531 Flammable or combustible liquid storage buildings or rooms.

(a) Storage buildings or storage rooms in which flammable or combustible liquids, including grease, are stored and that are within 100 feet of any person's work station shall be ventilated with a sufficient volume of air to prevent the accumulation of flammable vapors.

(b) In addition, the buildings or rooms shall be—

(1) Constructed to meet a fire resistance rating of at least one hour; or

(2) Equipped with an automatic fire suppression system; or

(3) Equipped with an early warning fire detection device that will alert any person who could be endangered by a fire, provided that no person's work station is in the building.

(c) Flammable or combustible liquids in use for day-to-day maintenance and operational activities are not considered in storage under this standard.

Welding/Cutting/Compressed Gases

§ 56.4600 Extinguishing equipment.

(a) When welding, cutting, soldering, thawing, or bending—

(1) With an electric arc or with an open flame where an electrically conductive extinguishing agent could create an electrical hazard, a multipurpose dry-chemical fire extinguisher or other extinguisher with at least a 2–A:10–B:C rating shall be at the worksite.

(2) With an open flame in an area where no electrical hazard exists, a multipurpose dry-chemical fire extinguisher or equivalent fire extinguishing equipment for the class of fire hazard present shall be at the worksite.

(b) Use of halogenated fire extinguishing agents to meet the requirements of this standard shall be limited to Halon 1211 ($CBrClF_2$) and Halon 1301 ($CBrF_3$). When these agents are used in confined or unventilated areas, precautions based on the manufacturer's use instructions shall be taken so that the gases produced by thermal decompostion of the agents are not inhaled.

§ 56.4601 Oxygen cylinder storage.

Oxygen cylinders shall not be stored in rooms or areas used or designated for storage of flammable or combustible liquids, including grease.

§ 56.4602 Gauges and regulators.

Gauges and regulators used with oxygen or acetylene cylinders shall be kept clean and free of oil and grease.

§ 56.4603 Closure of valves.

To prevent accidental release of gases from hoses and torches attached to oxygen and acetylene cylinders or to manifold systems, cylinder or manifold system valves shall be closed when—
(a) The cylinders are moved;
(b) The torch and hoses are left unattended; or
(c) The task or series of tasks is completed.

§ 56.4604 Preparation of pipelines or containers.

Before welding, cutting, or applying heat with an open flame to pipelines or containers that have contained flammable or combustible liquids, flammable gases, or explosive solids, the pipelines or containers shall be—
(a) Drained, ventilated, and thoroughly cleaned of any residue;
(b) Vented to prevent pressure build-up during the application of heat; and
(c)(1) Filled with an inert gas or water, where compatible; or
(2) Determined to be free of flammable gases by a flammable gas detection device prior to and at frequent intervals during the application of heat.

APPENDIX I TO SUBPART C OF PART 56—NATIONAL CONSENSUS STANDARDS

Mine operators seeking further information in the area of fire prevention and control may consult the following national consensus standards.

MSHA standard	National consensus standard
§§ 56.4200, 56.4201.	NFPA No. 10—Portable Fire Extinguisher.
	NFPA No. 11—Low Expansion Foam and Combined Agent Systems.
	NFPA No. 11A—High Expansion Foam Systems.
	NFPA No. 12—Carbon Dioxide Extinguishing Systems.
	NFPA No. 12A—Halon 1301 Extinguishing Systems.
	NFPA No. 13—Water Sprinkler Systems.
	NFPA No. 14—Standpipe and Hose Systems.
	NFPA No. 15—Water Spray Fixed Systems.
	NFPA No. 16—Foam Water Spray Systems.
	NFPA No. 17—Dry-Chemical Extinguishing Systems.
	NFPA No. 121—Mobile Surface Mining Equipment.
	NFPA No. 291—Testing and Marketing Hydrants.
	NFPA No. 1962—Care, Use, and Maintenance of Fire Hose, Connections, and Nozzles.
§ 56.4202 ..	NFPA No. 14—Standpipe and Hose Systems.
	NFPA No. 291—Testing and Marketing Hydrants.
§ 56.4203 ..	NFPA No. 10—Portable Fire Extinguishers.
§ 56.4230 ..	NFPA No. 10—Portable Fire Extinguishers.
	NFPA No. 121—Mobile Surface Mining Equipment.

Subpart D—Air Quality and Physical Agents

AIR QUALITY

§ 56.5001 Exposure limits for airborne contaminants.

Except as permitted by § 56.5005—
(a) Except as provided in paragraph (b) of this section, the exposure to airborne contaminants shall not exceed, on the basis of a time weighted average, the threshold limit values adopted by the American Conference of Governmental Industrial Hygienists, as set forth and explained in the 1973 edition of the Conference's publication, entitled "TLV's Threshold Limit Values for Chemical Substances in Workroom Air Adopted by ACGIH for 1973," pages 1 through 54, which are hereby incorporated by reference and made a part hereof. This publication may be obtained from the American Conference of Governmental industrial Hygienists by writing to 1330 Kemper Meadow Drive, Attn: Customer Service, Cincinnati, OH 45240; *http://www.acgih.org*", or may be examined in any Metal and Nonmetal Mine Safety and Health District Office of the Mine Safety and Health Administration. Excursions above the listed thresholds shall not be of a greater magnitude than is characterized as permissible by the Conference.

(b) *Asbestos standard*—(1) *Definitions.* Asbestos is a generic term for a number of asbestiform hydrated silicates that, when crushed or processed, separate into flexible fibers made up of fibrils.

Asbestos means chrysotile, cummingtonite-grunerite asbestos (amosite), crocidolite, anthophylite asbestos, tremolite asbestos, and actinolite asbestos.

Asbestos fiber means a fiber of asbestos that meets the criteria of a fiber.

Fiber means a particle longer than 5 micrometers (μm) with a length-to-diameter ratio of at least 3-to-1.

(2) *Permissible Exposure Limits (PELs)*—(i) *Full-shift limit.* A miner's personal exposure to asbestos shall not exceed an 8-hour time-weighted average full-shift airborne concentration of 0.1 fiber per cubic centimeter of air (f/cc).

(ii) *Excursion limit.* No miner shall be exposed at any time to airborne concentrations of asbestos in excess of 1 fiber per cubic centimeter of air (f/cc) as averaged over a sampling period of 30 minutes.

(3) *Measurement of airborne asbestos fiber concentration.* Potential asbestos fiber concentration shall be determined by phase contrast microscopy (PCM) using the OSHA Reference Method in OSHA's asbestos standard found in 29 CFR 1910.1001, Appendix A, or a method at least equivalent to that method in identifying a potential asbestos exposure exceeding the 0.1 f/cc full-shift limit or the 1 f/cc excursion limit. When PCM results indicate a potential exposure exceeding the 0.1 f/cc full-shift limit or the 1 f/cc excursion limit, samples shall be further analyzed using transmission electron microscopy according to NIOSH Method 7402 or a method at least equivalent to that method.

(c) Employees shall be withdrawn from areas where there is present an airborne contaminant given a "C" designation by the Conference and the concentration exceeds the threshold limit value listed for that contaminant.

[50 FR 4054, Jan. 29, 1985, as amended at 60 FR 35695, July 11, 1995; 71 FR 16667, Apr. 3, 2006; 73 FR 11303, Feb. 29, 2008; 73 FR 66172, Nov. 7, 2008]

§ 56.5002 Exposure monitoring.

Dust, gas, mist, and fume surveys shall be conducted as frequently as necessary to determine the adequacy of control measures.

§ 56.5005 Control of exposure to airborne contaminants.

Control of employee exposure to harmful airborne contaminants shall be, insofar as feasible, by prevention of contamination, removal by exhaust ventilation, or by dilution with uncontaminated air. However, where accepted, engineering control measures have not been developed or when necessary by the nature of work involved (for example, while establishing controls or occasional entry into hazardous atmospheres to perform maintenance or investigation), employees may work for reasonable periods of time in concentrations of airborne contaminants exceeding permissible levels if they are protected by appropriate respiratory protective equipment. Whenever respiratory protective equipment is used a program for selection, maintenance, training, fitting, supervision, cleaning, and use shall meet the following minimum requirements:

(a) Respirators approved by NIOSH under 42 CFR part 84 which are applicable and suitable for the purpose intended shall be furnished and miners shall use the protective equipment in accordance with training and instruction.

(b) A respirator program consistent with the requirements of ANSI Z88.2–1969, published by the American National Standards Institute and entitled "American National Standards Practices for Respiratory Protection ANSI Z88.2–1969," approved August 11, 1969, which is hereby incorporated by reference and made a part hereof. This publication may be obtained from the American National Standards Institute, Inc., 25 W. 43rd Street, 4th Floor, New York, NY 10036; *http://www.ansi.org*", or may be examined in any Metal and Nonmetal Mine Safety and Health District Office of the Mine Safety and Health Administration.

(c) When respiratory protection is used in atmospheres immediately harmful to life, the presence of at least one other person with backup equipment and rescue capability shall be required in the event of failure of the respiratory equipment.

[50 FR 4054, Jan. 29, 1985, as amended at 60 FR 30400, June 8, 1995; 60 FR 33723, June 29, 1995; 60 FR 35695, July 11, 1995; 71 FR 16667, Apr. 3, 2006]

§ 56.5006 Restricted use of chemicals.

The following chemical substances shall not be used or stored except by competent persons under laboratory conditions approved by a nationally recognized agency acceptable to the Secretary.

§ 56.6000

(a) Carbon tetrachloride.
(b) Phenol,
(c) 4-Nitrobiphenyl,
(d) Alpha-naphthylamine,
(e) 4,4-Methylene Bis (2-chloroaniline),
(f) Methyl-chloromethyl ether,
(g) 3,3 Dichlorobenzidine,
(h) Bis (chloromethyl) ether,
(i) Beta-napthylamine,
(j) Benzidine,
(k) 4-Aminodiphenyl,
(l) Ethyleneimine,
(m) Beta-propiolactone,
(n) 2-Acetylaminofluorene,
(o) 4-Dimethylaminobenzene, and
(p) N-Nitrosodimethylamine.

Subpart E—Explosives

SOURCE: 61 FR 36795, July 12, 1996, unless otherwise noted.

§ 56.6000 Definitions.

The following definitions apply in this subpart.

Blasting agent. Any substance classified as a blasting agent by the Department of Transportation in 49 CFR 173.114a(a). This document is available at any MSHA Metal and Nonmetal Safety and Health district office.

Detonating cord. A flexible cord containing a center core of high explosives which may be used to initiate other explosives.

Detonator. Any device containing a detonating charge used to initiate an explosive. These devices include electronic detonators, electric or nonelectric instantaneous or delay blasting caps, and delay connectors. The term "detonator" does not include detonating cord. Detonators may be either "Class A" detonators or "Class C" detonators, as classified by the Department of Transportation in 49 CFR 173.53 and 173.100, which is available at any MSHA Metal and Nonmetal Safety and Health district office.

Flash point. The minimum temperature at which sufficient vapor is released by a liquid to form a flammable vapor-air mixture near the surface of the liquid.

Igniter cord. A fuse that burns progressively along its length with an external flame at the zone of burning, used for lighting a series of safety fuses in a desired sequence.

Magazine. A bullet-resistant, theft-resistant, fire-resistant, weather-resistant, ventilated facility for the storage of explosives and detonators (BATF Type 1 or Type 2 facility).

Misfire. The complete or partial failure of explosive material to detonate as planned. The term also is used to describe the explosive material itself that has failed to detonate.

Primer. A unit, package, or cartridge of explosives which contains a detonator and is used to initiate other explosives or blasting agents.

Safety switch. A switch that provides shunt protection in blasting circuits between the blast site and the switch used to connect a power source to the blasting circuit.

Slurry. An explosive material containing substantial portions of a liquid, oxidizers, and fuel, plus a thickener.

Water gel. An explosive material containing substantial portions of water, oxidizers, and fuel, plus a cross-linking agent.

[50 FR 4054, Jan. 29, 1985, as amended at 67 FR 38385, June 4, 2002; 68 FR 32361, May 30, 2003; 69 FR 38840, June 29, 2004; 85 FR 2027, Jan. 14, 2020]

STORAGE

§ 56.6100 Separation of stored explosive material.

(a) Detonators shall not be stored in the same magazine with other explosive material.

(b) When stored in the same magazine, blasting agents shall be separated from explosives, safety fuse, and detonating cord to prevent contamination.

§ 56.6101 Areas around explosive material storage facilities.

(a) Areas surrounding storage facilities for explosive material shall be clear of rubbish, brush, dry grass, and trees for 25 feet in all directions, except that live trees 10 feet or taller need not be removed.

(b) Other combustibles shall not be stored or allowed to accumulate within 50 feet of explosive material. Combustible liquids shall be stored in a manner that ensures drainage will occur away from the explosive material storage facility in case of tank rupture.

§ 56.6102 Explosive material storage practices.

(a) Explosive material shall be—
(1) Stored in a manner to facilitate use of oldest stocks first;
(2) Stored according to brand and grade in such a manner as to facilitate identification; and
(3) Stacked in a stable manner but not more than 8 feet high.

(b) Explosives and detonators shall be stored in closed nonconductive containers except that nonelectric detonating devices may be stored on nonconductive racks provided the case-insert instructions and the date-plant-shift code are maintained with the product.

§ 56.6130 Explosive material storage facilities.

(a) Detonators and explosives shall be stored in magazines.

(b) Packaged blasting agents shall be stored in a magazine or other facility which is ventilated to prevent dampness and excessive heating, weather-resistant, and locked or attended. Drop trailers do not have to be ventilated if they are currently licensed by the Federal, State, or local authorities for over-the-road use. Facilities other than magazines used to store blasting agents shall contain only blasting agents.

(c) Bulk blasting agents shall be stored in weather-resistant bins or tanks which are locked, attended, or otherwise inaccessible to unauthorized entry.

(d) Facilities, bins or tanks shall be posted with the appropriate United States Department of Transportation placards or other appropriate warning signs that indicate the contents and are visible from each approach.

§ 56.6131 Location of explosive material storage facilities.

(a) Storage facilities for any explosive material shall be—
(1) Located so that the forces generated by a storage facility explosion will not create a hazard to occupants in mine buildings and will not damage dams or electric substations; and
(2) Detached structures located outside the blast area and a sufficient distance from powerlines so that the powerlines, if damaged, would not contact the magazines.

(b) Operators should also be aware of regulations affecting storage facilities in 27 CFR part 55, in particular, 27 CFR 55.218 and 55.220. This document is available at any MSHA Metal and Nonmetal Safety and Health district office.

§ 56.6132 Magazine requirements.

(a) Magazines shall be—
(1) Structurally sound;
(2) Noncombustible or the exterior covered with fire-resistant material;
(3) Bullet resistant;
(4) Made of nonsparking material on the inside;
(5) Ventilated to control dampness and excessive heating within the magazine;
(6) Posted with the appropriate United States Department of Transportation placards or other appropriate warning signs that indicate the contents and are visible from each approach, so located that a bullet passing through any of the signs will not strike the magazine;
(7) Kept clean and dry inside;
(8) Unlighted or lighted by devices that are specifically designed for use in magazines and which do not create a fire or explosion hazard;
(9) Unheated or heated only with devices that do not create a fire or explosion hazard;
(10) Locked when unattended; and
(11) Used exclusively for the storage of explosive material except for essential nonsparking equipment used for the operation of the magazine.

(b) Metal magazines shall be equipped with electrical bonding connections between all conductive portions so the entire structure is at the same electrical potential. Suitable electrical bonding methods include welding, riveting, or the use of securely tightened bolts where individual metal portions are joined. Conductive portions of nonmetal magazines shall be grounded.

(c) Electrical switches and outlets shall be located on the outside of the magazine.

§ 56.6133 Powder chests.

(a) Powder chests (day boxes) shall be—

(1) Structurally sound, weather-resistant, equipped with a lid or cover, and with only nonsparking material on the inside;

(2) Posted with the appropriate United States Department of Transportation placards or other appropriate warning signs that indicate the contents and are visible from each approach;

(3) Located out of the blast area once loading has been completed;

(4) Locked or attended when containing explosive material; and

(5) Emptied at the end of each shift with the contents returned to a magazine or other storage facility, or attended.

(b) Detonators shall be kept in chests separate from explosives or blasting agents, unless separated by 4 inches of hardwood or equivalent, or a laminated partition. When a laminated partition is used, operators must follow the provisions of the Institute of Makers of Explosives (IME) Safety Library Publication No. 22, "Recommendations for the Safe Transportation of Detonators in a Vehicle with Other Explosive Materials" (May 1993), and the "Generic Loading Guide for the IME–22 Container" (October 1993). The IME is located at 1120 19th Street NW., Suite 310, Washington, DC 20036–3605; 202–429–9280; *https://www.ime.org*. This incorporation by reference has been approved by the Director of the Federal Register in accordance with 5 U.S.C. 552(a) and 1 CFR part 51. Copies are available at MSHA's Office of Standards, Regulations, and Variances, 201 12th Street South, Arlington, VA 22202–5452; 202–693–9440; and at all Metal and Nonmetal Mine Safety and Health District Offices, or available for inspection at the National Archives and Records Administration (NARA). For information on the availability of this material at NARA, call 202–741–6030, or go to: *http://www.archives.gov/federal_register/code_of_federal_regulations/ibr_locations.html*.

[50 FR 4054, Jan. 29, 1985, as amended at 67 FR 38385, June 4, 2002; 80 FR 52987, Sept. 2, 2015]

TRANSPORTATION

§ 56.6200 Delivery to storage or blast site areas.

Explosive material shall be transported without undue delay to the storage area or blast site.

§ 56.6201 Separation of transported explosive material.

Detonators shall not be transported on the same vehicle or conveyance with other explosives except as follows:

(a) Detonators in quantities of more than 1000 may be transported in a vehicle or conveyance with explosives or blasting agents provided the detonators are—

(1) Maintained in the original packaging as shipped from the manufacturer; and

(2) Separated from explosives or blasting agents by 4 inches of hardwood or equivalent, or a laminated partition. The hardwood or equivalent shall be fastened to the vehicle or conveyance. When a laminated partition is used, operators must follow the provisions of the Institute of Makers of Explosives (IME) Safety Library Publication No.22, "Recommendations for the Safe Transportation of Detonators in a Vehicle with Other Explosive Materials" (May 1993), and the "Generic Loading Guide for the IME–22 Container" (October 1993). The IME is located at 1120 19th Street NW., Suite 310, Washington, DC 20036–3605; 202–429–9280; *https://www.ime.org*. This incorporation by reference has been approved by the Director of the Federal Register in accordance with 5 U.S.C. 552(a) and 1 CFR part 51. Copies are available at MSHA's Office of Standards, Regulations, and Variances, 201 12th Street South, Arlington, VA 22202–5452; 202–693–9440; and at all Metal and Nonmetal Mine Safety and Health District Offices, or available for inspection at the National Archives and Records Administration (NARA). For information on the availability of this material at NARA, call 202–741–6030, or go to: *http://www.archives.gov/federal_register/code_of_federal_regulations/ibr_locations.html*.

(b) Detonators in quantities of 1000 or fewer may be transported with explosives or blasting agents provided the detonators are—

(1) Kept in closed containers; and

(2) Separated from explosives or blasting agents by 4 inches of hardwood or equivalent, or a laminated partition. The hardwood or equivalent shall be fastened to the vehicle or conveyance. When a laminated partition is used, operators must follow the provisions of IME Safety Library Publication No. 22, "Recommendations for the Safe Transportation of Detonators in a Vehicle with Other Explosive Materials" (May 1993), and the "Generic Loading Guide for the IME–22 Container" (October 1993). The IME is located at 1120 19th Street NW., Suite 310, Washington, DC 20036–3605; 202–429–9280; https://www.ime.org. This incorporation by reference has been approved by the Director of the Federal Register in accordance with 5 U.S.C. 552(a) and 1 CFR part 51. Copies are available at MSHA's Office of Standards, Regulations, and Variances, 201 12th Street South, Arlington, VA 22202–5452; 202–693–9440; and at all Metal and Nonmetal Mine Safety and Health District Offices, or available for inspection at the National Archives and Records Administration (NARA). For information on the availability of this material at NARA, call 202–741–6030, or go to: http://www.archives.gov/federal_register/code_of_federal_regulations/ibr_locations.html.

[50 FR 4054, Jan. 29, 1985, as amended at 67 FR 38385, June 4, 2002; 80 FR 52987, Sept. 2, 2015]

§ 56.6202 Vehicles.

(a) Vehicles containing explosive material shall be—

(1) Maintained in good condition and shall comply with the requirements of subpart M of this part;

(2) Equipped with sides and enclosures higher than the explosive material being transported or have the explosive material secured to a nonconductive pallet;

(3) Equipped with a cargo space that shall contain the explosive material (passenger areas shall not be considered cargo space);

(4) Equipped with at least two multi-purpose dry-chemical fire extinguishers or one such extinguisher and an automatic fire suppression system;

(5) Posted with warning signs that indicate the contents and are visible from each approach;

(6) Occupied only by persons necessary for handling the explosive material;

(7) Attended or the cargo compartment locked, except when parked at the blast site and loading is in progress; and

(8) Secured while parked by having—

(i) The brakes set;

(ii) The wheels chocked if movement could occur; and

(iii) The engine shut off unless powering a device being used in the loading operation.

(b) Vehicles containing explosives shall have—

(1) No sparking material exposed in the cargo space; and

(2) Only properly secured non-sparking equipment in the cargo space with the explosives.

(c) Vehicles used for dispensing bulk explosive material shall—

(1) Have no zinc or copper exposed in the cargo space; and

(2) Provide any enclosed screw-type conveyors with protection against internal pressure and frictional heat.

§ 56.6203 Locomotives.

Explosive material shall not be transported on a locomotive. When explosive material is hauled by trolley locomotive, covered, electrically insulated cars shall be used.

§ 56.6204 Hoists.

(a) Before explosive material is transported in hoist conveyances, the hoist operator shall be notified.

(b) Explosive material transported in hoist conveyances shall be placed within a container which prevents shifting of the cargo that could cause detonation of the container by impact or by sparks. The manufacturer's container may be used if secured to a nonconductive pallet. When explosives are transported, they shall be secured so as not to contact any sparking material.

(c) No explosive material shall be transported during a mantrip.

§ 56.6205 Conveying explosives by hand.

Closed, nonconductive containers shall be used to carry explosives and detonators to and from blast sites. Separate containers shall be used for explosives and detonators.

USE

§ 56.6300 Control of blasting operations.

(a) Only persons trained and experienced in the handling and use of explosive material shall direct blasting operations and related activities.

(b) Trainees and inexperienced persons shall work only in the immediate presence of persons trained and experienced in the handling and use of explosive material.

§ 56.6301 Blasthole obstruction check.

Before loading, blastholes shall be checked and, wherever possible, cleared of obstructions.

§ 56.6302 Separation of explosive material.

Explosives and blasting agents shall be kept separated from detonators until loading begins.

§ 56.6303 Initiation preparation.

(a) Primers shall be made up only at the time of use and as close to the blast site as conditions allow.

(b) Primers shall be prepared with the detonator contained securely and completely within the explosive or contained securely and appropriately for its design in the tunnel or cap well.

(c) When using detonating cord to initiate another explosive, a connection shall be prepared with the detonating cord threaded through, attached securely to, or otherwise in contact with the explosive.

§ 56.6304 Primer protection.

(a) Tamping shall not be done directly on a primer.

(b) Rigid cartridges of explosives or blasting agents that are 4 inches (100 millimeters) in diameter or larger shall not be dropped on the primer except where the blasthole contains sufficient depth of water to protect the primer from impact. Slit packages of prill, water gel, or emulsions are not considered rigid cartridges and may be drop loaded.

§ 56.6305 Unused explosive material.

Unused explosive material shall be moved to a protected location as soon as practical after loading operations are completed.

§ 56.6306 Loading, blasting, and security.

(a) When explosive materials or initiating systems are brought to the blast site, the blast site shall be attended; barricaded and posted with warning signs, such as "Danger," "Explosives," or "Keep Out;" or flagged against unauthorized entry.

(b) Vehicles and equipment shall not be driven over explosive material or initiating systems in a manner which could contact the material or systems, or create other hazards.

(c) Once loading begins, the only activities permitted within the blast site shall be those activities directly related to the blasting operation and the activities of surveying, stemming, sampling of geology, and reopening of holes, provided that reasonable care is exercised. Haulage activity is permitted near the base of a highwall being loaded or awaiting firing, provided no other haulage access exists.

(d) Loading and blasting shall be conducted in a manner designed to facilitate a continuous process, with the blast fired as soon as possible following the completion of loading. If blasting a loaded round may be delayed for more than 72 hours, the operator shall notify the appropriate MSHA district office.

(e) In electric blasting prior to connecting to the power source, and in nonelectric blasting prior to attaching an initiating device, all persons shall leave the blast area except persons in a blasting shelter or other location that protects them from concussion (shock wave), flying material, and gases.

(f) Before firing a blast—

(1) Ample warning shall be given to allow all persons to be evacuated;

(2) Clear exit routes shall be provided for persons firing the round; and

(3) All access routes to the blast area shall be guarded or barricaded to prevent the passage of persons or vehicles.

Mine Safety and Health Admin., Labor § 56.6403

(g) Work shall not resume in the blast area until a post-blast examination addressing potential blast-related hazards has been conducted by a person with the ability and experience to perform the examination.

§ 56.6307 Drill stem loading.

Explosive material shall not be loaded into blastholes with drill stem equipment or other devices that could be extracted while containing explosive material. The use of loading hose, collar sleeves, or collar pipes is permitted.

§ 56.6308 Initiation systems.

Initiation systems shall be used in accordance with the manufacturer's instructions.

§ 56.6309 Fuel oil requirements for ANFO.

(a) Liquid hydrocarbon fuels with flash points lower than that of No. 2 diesel oil (125 °F) shall not be used to prepare ammonium nitrate-fuel oil, except that diesel fuels with flash points no lower than 100 °F may be used at ambient air temperatures below 45 °F.

(b) Waste oil, including crankcase oil, shall not be used to prepare ammonium nitrate-fuel oil.

§ 56.6310 Misfire waiting period.

When a misfire is suspected, persons shall not enter the blast area—
(a) For 30 minutes if safety fuse and blasting caps are used;
(b) For 15 minutes if any other type detonators are used; or
(c) For 30 minutes if electronic detonators are used, or for the manufacturer-recommended time, whichever is longer.

[61 FR 36795, July 12, 1996, as amended at 85 FR 2027, Jan. 14, 2020]

§ 56.6311 Handling of misfires.

(a) Faces and muck piles shall be examined for misfires after each blasting operation.

(b) Only work necessary to remove a misfire and protect the safety of miners engaged in the removal shall be permitted in the affected area until the misfire is disposed of in a safe manner.

(c) When a misfire cannot be disposed of safely, each approach to the area affected by the misfire shall be posted with a warning sign at a conspicuous location to prohibit entry, and the condition shall be reported immediately to mine management.

(d) Misfires occurring during the shift shall be reported to mine management not later than the end of the shift.

§ 56.6312 Secondary blasting.

Secondary blasts fired at the same time in the same work area shall be initiated from one source.

ELECTRIC BLASTING

§ 56.6400 Compatibility of electric detonators.

All electric detonators to be fired in a round shall be from the same manufacturer and shall have similar electrical firing characteristics.

§ 56.6401 Shunting.

Except during testing—
(a) Electric detonators shall be kept shunted until connected to the blasting line or wired into a blasting round;
(b) Wired rounds shall be kept shunted until connected to the blasting line; and
(c) Blasting lines shall be kept shunted until immediately before blasting.

§ 56.6402 Deenergized circuits near detonators.

Electrical distribution circuits within 50 feet of electric detonators at the blast site shall be deenergized. Such circuits need not be deenergized between 25 to 50 feet of the electric detonators if stray current tests, conducted as frequently as necessary, indicate a maximum stray current of less than 0.05 amperes through a 1-ohm resistor as measured at the blast site.

§ 56.6403 Branch circuits.

(a) If electric blasting includes the use of branch circuits, each branch shall be equipped with a safety switch or equivalent method to isolate the circuits to be used.

(b) At least one safety switch or equivalent method of protection shall be located outside the blast area and shall be in the open position until persons are withdrawn.

§ 56.6404 Separation of blasting circuits from power source.

(a) Switches used to connect the power source to a blasting circuit shall be locked in the open position except when closed to fire the blast.

(b) Lead wires shall not be connected to the blasting switch until the shot is ready to be fired.

§ 56.6405 Firing devices.

(a) Power sources shall be capable of delivering sufficient current to energize all electric detonators to be fired with the type of circuits used. Storage or dry cell batteries are not permitted as power sources.

(b) Blasting machines shall be tested, repaired, and maintained in accordance with manufacturer's instructions.

(c) Only the blaster shall have the key or other control to an electrical firing device.

§ 56.6406 Duration of current flow.

If any part of a blast is connected in parallel and is to be initiated from powerlines or lighting circuits, the time of current flow shall be limited to a maximum of 25 milliseconds. This can be accomplished by incorporating an arcing control device in the blasting circuit or by interrupting the circuit with an explosive device attached to one or both lead lines and initiated by a 25-millisecond delay electric detonator.

§ 56.6407 Circuit testing.

A blasting galvanometer or other instrument designed for testing blasting circuits shall be used to test each of the following:

(a) Continuity of each electric or electronic detonator in the blasthole prior to stemming and connection to the blasting line.

(b) Resistance of individual series or the resistance of multiple balanced series to be connected in parallel prior to their connection to the blasting line.

(c) Continuity of blasting lines prior to the connection of electric or electronic detonator series.

(d) Total blasting circuit resistance prior to connection to the power source.

[61 FR 36795, July 12, 1996, as amended at 85 FR 2027, Jan. 14, 2020]

NONELECTRIC BLASTING

§ 56.6500 Damaged initiating material.

A visual check of the completed circuit shall be made to ensure that the components are properly aligned and connected. Safety fuse, igniter cord, detonating cord, shock or gas tubing, and similar material which is kinked, bent sharply, or damaged shall not be used.

§ 56.6501 Nonelectric initiation systems.

(a) When the nonelectric initiation system uses shock tube—

(1) Connections with other initiation devices shall be secured in a manner which provides for uninterrupted propagation;

(2) Factory-made units shall be used as assembled and shall not be cut except that a single splice is permitted on the lead-in trunkline during dry conditions; and

(3) Connections between blastholes shall not be made until immediately prior to clearing the blast site when surface delay detonators are used.

(b) When the nonelectric initiation system uses detonating cord—

(1) The line of detonating cord extending out of a blasthole shall be cut from the supply spool immediately after the attached explosive is correctly positioned in the hole;

(2) In multiple row blasts, the trunkline layout shall be designed so that the detonation can reach each blasthole from at least two directions;

(3) Connections shall be tight and kept at right angles to the trunkline;

(4) Detonators shall be attached securely to the side of the detonating cord and pointed in the direction in which detonation is to proceed;

(5) Connections between blastholes shall not be made until immediately prior to clearing the blast site when surface delay detonators are used; and

(6) Lead-in lines shall be manually unreeled if connected to the trunklines at the blast site.

(c) When the nonelectric initiation system uses gas tube, continuity of the circuit shall be tested prior to blasting.

§ 56.6502 Safety fuse.

(a) The burning rate of each spool of safety fuse to be used shall be measured, posted in locations which will be conspicuous to safety fuse users, and brought to the attention of all persons involved with the blasting operation.

(b) When firing with safety fuse ignited individually using handheld lighters, the safety fuse shall be of lengths which provide at least the minimum burning time for a particular size round, as specified in the following table:

TABLE E–1—SAFETY FUSE—MINIMUM BURNING TIME

Number of holes in a round	Minimum burning time
1	2 min.[1]
2–5	2 min. 40 sec.
6–10	3 min. 20 sec.
11 to 15	5 min.

[1] For example, at least a 36-inch length of 40-second-per-foot safety fuse or at least a 48-inch length of 30-second-per-foot safety fuse would have to be used to allow sufficient time to evacuate the area.

(c) Where flyrock might damage exposed safety fuse, the blast shall be timed so that all safety fuses are burning within the blastholes before any blasthole detonates.

(d) Fuse shall be cut and capped in dry locations.

(e) Blasting caps shall be crimped to fuse only with implements designed for that purpose.

(f) Safety fuse shall be ignited only after the primer and the explosive material are securely in place.

(g) Safety fuse shall be ignited only with devices designed for that purpose. Carbide lights, liquefied petroleum gas torches, and cigarette lighters shall not be used to light safety fuse.

(h) At least two persons shall be present when lighting safety fuse, and no one shall light more than 15 individual fuses. If more than 15 holes per person are to be fired, electric initiation systems, igniter cord and connectors, or other nonelectric initiation systems shall be used.

EXTRANEOUS ELECTRICITY

§ 56.6600 Loading practices.

If extraneous electricity is suspected in an area where electric detonators are used, loading shall be suspended until tests determine that stray current does not exceed 0.05 amperes through a 1-ohm resister when measured at the location of the electric detonators. If greater levels of extraneous electricity are found, the source shall be determined and no loading shall take place until the condition is corrected.

§ 56.6601 Grounding.

Electric blasting circuits, including powerline sources when used, shall not be grounded.

§ 56.6602 Static electricity dissipation during loading.

When explosive material is loaded pneumatically into a blasthole in a manner that generates a static electricity hazard—

(a) An evaluation of the potential static electricity hazard shall be made and any hazard shall be eliminated before loading begins;

(b) The loading hose shall be of a semiconductive type, have a total of not more than 2 megohms of resistance over its entire length and not less than 1000 ohms of resistance per foot;

(c) Wire-countered hoses shall not be used;

(d) Conductive parts of the loading equipment shall be bonded and grounded and grounds shall not be made to other potential sources of extraneous electricity; and

(e) Plastic tubes shall not be used as hole liners if the hole contains an electric detonator.

§ 56.6603 Air gap.

At least a 15-foot air gap shall be provided between the blasting circuit and the electric power source.

§ 56.6604 Precautions during storms.

During the approach and progress of an electrical storm, blasting operations shall be suspended and persons withdrawn from the blast area or to a safe location.

§ 56.6605 Isolation of blasting circuits.

Lead wires and blasting lines shall be isolated and insulated from power conductors, pipelines, and railroad tracks, and shall be protected from sources of stray or static electricity. Blasting circuits shall be protected from any contact between firing lines and overhead powerlines which could result from the force of a blast.

EQUIPMENT/TOOLS

§ 56.6700 Nonsparking tools.

Only nonsparking tools shall be used to open containers of explosive material or to punch holes in explosive cartridges.

§ 56.6701 Tamping and loading pole requirements.

Tamping and loading poles shall be of wood or other nonconductive, nonsparking material. Couplings for poles shall be nonsparking.

MAINTENANCE

§ 56.6800 Storage facilities.

When repair work which could produce a spark or flame is to be performed on a storage facility—

(a) The explosive material shall be moved to another facility, or moved at least 50 feet from the repair activity and monitored; and

(b) The facility shall be cleaned to prevent accidental detonation.

§ 56.6801 Vehicle repair.

Vehicles containing explosive material and oxidizers shall not be taken into a repair garage or shop.

§ 56.6802 Bulk delivery vehicles.

No welding or cutting shall be performed on a bulk delivery vehicle until the vehicle has been washed down and all explosive material has been removed. Before welding or cutting on a hollow shaft, the shaft shall be thoroughly cleaned inside and out and vented with a minimum ½-inch diameter opening to allow for sufficient ventilation.

§ 56.6803 Blasting lines.

Permanent blasting lines shall be properly supported. All blasting lines shall be insulated and kept in good repair.

GENERAL REQUIREMENTS

§ 56.6900 Damaged or deteriorated explosive material.

Damaged or deteriorated explosive material shall be disposed of in a safe manner in accordance with the instructions of the manufacturer.

§ 56.6901 Black powder.

(a) Black powder shall be used for blasting only when a desired result cannot be obtained with another type of explosive, such as in quarrying certain types of dimension stone.

(b) Containers of black powder shall be—

(1) Nonsparking;

(2) Kept in a totally enclosed cargo space while being transported by a vehicle;

(3) Securely closed at all times when—

(i) Within 50 feet of any magazine or open flame;

(ii) Within any building in which a fuel-fired or exposed-element electric heater is operating; or

(iii) In an area where electrical or incandescent-particle sparks could result in powder ignition; and

(4) Opened only when the powder is being transferred to a blasthole or another container and only in locations not listed in paragraph (b)(3) of this section.

(c) Black powder shall be transferred from containers only by pouring.

(d) Spills shall be cleaned up promptly with nonsparking equipment. Contaminated powder shall be put into a container of water and shall be disposed of promptly after the granules have disintegrated, or the spill area shall be flushed promptly with water until the granules have disintegrated completely.

(e) Misfires shall be disposed of by washing the stemming and powder charge from the blasthole, and removing and disposing of the initiator in accordance with the requirement for damaged explosives.

(f) Holes shall not be reloaded for at least 12 hours when the blastholes have failed to break as planned.

§ 56.6902 Excessive temperatures.

(a) Where heat could cause premature detonation, explosive material shall not be loaded into hot areas, such as kilns or sprung holes.

(b) When blasting sulfide ores where hot holes occur that may react with explosive material in blastholes, operators shall—

(1) Measure an appropriate number of blasthole temperatures in order to assess the specific mine conditions prior to the introduction of explosive material;

(2) Limit the time between the completion of loading and the initiation of the blast to no more than 12 hours; and

(3) Take other special precautions to address the specific conditions at the mine to prevent premature detonation.

§ 56.6903 Burning explosive material.

If explosive material is suspected of burning at the blast site, persons shall be evacuated from the endangered area and shall not return for at least one hour after the burning or suspected burning has stopped.

§ 56.6904 Smoking and open flames.

Smoking and use of open flames shall not be permitted within 50 feet of explosive material except when separated by permanent noncombustible barriers. This standard does not apply to devices designed to ignite safety fuse or to heating devices which do not create a fire or explosion hazard.

§ 56.6905 Protection of explosive material.

(a) Explosive material shall be protected from temperatures in excess of 150 degrees Fahrenheit.

(b) Explosive material shall be protected from impact, except for tamping and dropping during loading.

Subpart F—Drilling and Rotary Jet Piercing

DRILLING

§ 56.7002 Equipment defects.

Equipment defects affecting safety shall be corrected before the equipment is used.

§ 56.7003 Drill area inspection.

The drilling area shall be inspected for hazards before starting the drilling operations.

§ 56.7004 Drill mast.

Persons shall not be on a mast while the drill-bit is in operation unless they are provided with a safe platform from which to work and they are required to use safety belts to avoid falling.

§ 56.7005 Augers and drill stems.

Drill crews and others shall stay clear of augers or drill stems that are in motion. Persons shall not pass under or step over a moving stem or auger.

§ 56.7008 Moving the drill.

When a drill is being moved from one drilling area to another, drill steel, tools, and other equipment shall be secured and the mast placed in a safe position.

§ 56.7009 Drill helpers.

If a drill helper assists the drill operator during movement of a drill to a new location, the helper shall be in sight of, or in communication with, the operator at all times.

§ 56.7010 Power failures.

In the event of power failure, drill controls shall be placed in the neutral position until power is restored.

§ 56.7011 Straightening crossed cables.

The drill stem shall be resting on the bottom of the hole or on the platform with the stem secured to the mast before attempts are made to straighten a crossed cable on a reel.

§ 56.7012 Tending drills in operation.

While in operation, drills shall be attended at all times.

§ 56.7013 Covering or guarding drill holes.

Drill holes large enough to constitute a hazard shall be covered or guarded.

§ 56.7018 Hand clearance.

Persons shall not hold the drill steel while collaring holes, or rest their hands on the chuck or centralizer while drilling.

§ 56.7050 Tool and drill steel racks.

Receptacles or racks shall be provided for drill steel and tools stored or carried on drills.

§ 56.7051 Loose objects on the mast or drill platform.

To prevent injury to personnel, tools and other objects shall not be left loose on the mast or drill platform.

§ 56.7052 Drilling positions.

Persons shall not drill from—
(a) Positions which hinder their access to the control levers;
(b) Insecure footing or insecure staging; or
(c) Atop equipment not suitable for drilling.

§ 56.7053 Moving hand-held drills.

Before hand-held drills are moved from one working area to another, air shall be turned off and bled from the hose.

§ 56.7055 Intersecting holes.

Holes shall not be drilled where there is a danger of intersecting a misfired hole or a hole containing explosives blasting agents, or detonators.

[56 FR 46508, Sept. 12, 1991]

§ 56.7056 Collaring in bootlegs.

Holes shall not be collared in bootlegs.

[56 FR 46508, Sept. 12, 1991]

ROTARY JET PIERCING

§ 56.7801 Jet drills.

Jet piercing drills shall be provided with—
(a) A system to pressurize the equipment operator's cab, when a cab is provided; and
(b) A protective cover over the oxygen flow indicator.

§ 56.7802 Oxygen hose lines.

Safety chains or other suitable locking devices shall be provided across connections to and between high pressure oxygen hose lines of 1-inch inside diameter or larger.

§ 56.7803 Lighting the burner.

A suitable means of protection shall be provided for the employee when lighting the burner.

§ 56.7804 Refueling.

When rotary jet piercing equipment requires refueling at locations other than fueling stations, a system for fueling without spillage shall be provided.

§ 56.7805 Smoking and open flames.

Persons shall not smoke and open flames shall not be used in the vicinity of the oxygen storage and supply lines. Signs warning against smoking and open flames shall be posted in these areas.

§ 56.7806 Oxygen intake coupling.

The oxygen intake coupling on jet-piercing drills shall be constructed so that only the oxygen hose can be coupled to it.

§ 56.7807 Flushing the combustion chamber.

The combustion chamber of a jet drill stem which has been sitting unoperated in a drill hole shall be flushed with a suitable solvent after the stem is pulled up.

Subpart G [Reserved]

Subpart H—Loading, Hauling, and Dumping

SOURCE: 53 FR 32520, Aug. 25, 1988, unless otherwise noted.

TRAFFIC SAFETY

§ 56.9100 Traffic control.

To provide for the safe movement of self-propelled mobile equipment—
(a) Rules governing speed, right-of-way, direction of movement, and the use of headlights to assure appropriate visibility, shall be established and followed at each mine; and
(b) Signs or signals that warn of hazardous conditions shall be placed at appropriate locations at each mine.

§ 56.9101 Operating speeds and control of equipment.

Operators of self-propelled mobile equipment shall maintain control of the equipment while it is in motion. Operating speeds shall be consistent with conditions of roadways, tracks, grades, clearance, visibility, and traffic, and the type of equipment used.

§ 56.9102 Movement of independently operating rail equipment.

Movement of two or more pieces of rail equipment operating independently on the same track shall be controlled for safe operation.

§ 56.9103 Clearance on adjacent tracks.

Railcars shall not be left on side tracks unless clearance is provided for traffic on adjacent tracks.

§ 56.9104 Railroad crossings.

Designated railroad crossings shall be posted with warning signs or signals, or shall be guarded when trains are passing. These crossings shall also be planked or filled between the rails.

TRANSPORTATION OF PERSONS AND MATERIALS

§ 56.9200 Transporting persons.

Persons shall not be transported—

(a) In or on dippers, forks, clamshells, or buckets except shaft buckets during shaft-sinking operations or during inspection, maintenance and repair of shafts.

(b) In beds of mobile equipment or railcars, unless—

(1) Provisions are made for secure travel, and

(2) Means are taken to prevent accidental unloading if the equipment is provided with unloading devices;

(c) On top of loads in mobile equipment;

(d) Outside cabs, equipment operators' stations, and beds of mobile equipment, except when necessary for maintenance, testing, or training purposes, and provisions are made for secure travel. This provision does not apply to rail equipment.

(e) Between cars of trains, on the leading end of trains, on the leading end of a single railcar, or in other locations on trains that expose persons to hazards from train movement.

(1) This paragraph does not apply to car droppers if they are secured with safety belts and lines which prevent them from falling off the work platform.

(2) Brakemen and trainmen are prohibited from riding between cars of moving trains, but may ride on the leading end of trains or other locations when necessary to perform their duties;

(f) To and from work areas in overcrowded mobile equipment;

(g) In mobile equipment with materials or equipment unless the items are secured or are small and can be carried safely by hand without creating a hazard to persons; or

(h) On conveyors unless the conveyors are designed to provide for their safe transportation.

§ 56.9201 Loading, hauling, and unloading of equipment or supplies.

Equipment and supplies shall be loaded, transported, and unloaded in a manner which does not create a hazard to persons from falling or shifting equipment or supplies.

§ 56.9202 Loading and hauling large rocks.

Large rocks shall be broken before loading if they could endanger persons or affect the stability of mobile equipment. Mobile equipment used for haulage of mined material shall be loaded to minimize spillage where a hazard to persons could be created.

SAFETY DEVICES, PROVISIONS, AND PROCEDURES FOR ROADWAYS, RAILROADS, AND LOADING AND DUMPING SITES

§ 56.9300 Berms or guardrails.

(a) Berms or guardrails shall be provided and maintained on the banks of roadways where a drop-off exists of sufficient grade or depth to cause a vehicle to overturn or endanger persons in equipment.

(b) Berms or guardrails shall be at least mid-axle height of the largest self-propelled mobile equipment which usually travels the roadway.

(c) Berms may have openings to the extent necessary for roadway drainage.

§ 56.9301

(d) Where elevated roadways are infrequently traveled and used only by service or maintenance vehicles, berms or guardrails are not required when all of the following are met:

(1) Locked gates are installed at the entrance points to the roadway.

(2) Signs are posted warning that the roadway is not bermed.

(3) Delineators are installed along the perimeter of the elevated roadway so that, for both directions of travel, the reflective surfaces of at least three delineators along each elevated shoulder are always visible to the driver and spaced at intervals sufficient to indicate the edges and attitude of the roadway.

(4) A maximum speed limit is posted and observed for the elevated unbermed portions of the roadway. Factors to consider when establishing the maximum speed limit shall include the width, slope and alignment of the road, the type of equipment using the road, the road material, and any hazardous conditions which may exist.

(5) Road surface traction is not impaired by weather conditions, such as sleet and snow, unless corrective measures are taken to improve traction.

(e) This standard is not applicable to rail beds.

[53 FR 32520, Aug. 25, 1988, as amended at 55 FR 37218, Sept. 7, 1990]

§ 56.9301 Dump site restraints.

Berms, bumper blocks, safety hooks, or similar impeding devices shall be provided at dumping locations where there is a hazard of overtravel or overturning.

§ 56.9302 Protection against moving or runaway railroad equipment.

Stopblocks, derail devices, or other devices that protect against moving or runaway rail equipment shall be installed wherever necessary to protect persons.

§ 56.9303 Construction of ramps and dumping facilities.

Ramps and dumping facilities shall be designed and constructed of materials capable of supporting the loads to which they will be subjected. The ramps and dumping facilities shall provide width, clearance, and headroom to safely accommodate the mobile equipment using the facilities.

§ 56.9304 Unstable ground.

(a) Dumping locations shall be visually inspected prior to work commencing and as ground conditions warrant.

(b) Where there is evidence that the ground at a dumping location may fail to support the mobile equipment, loads shall be dumped a safe distance back from the edge of the unstable area of the bank.

§ 56.9305 Truck spotters.

(a) If truck spotters are used, they shall be in the clear while trucks are backing into dumping position or dumping.

(b) Spotters shall use signal lights to direct trucks where visibility is limited.

(c) When a truck operator cannot clearly recognize the spotter's signals, the truck shall be stopped.

§ 56.9306 Warning devices for restricted clearances.

Where restricted clearance creates a hazard to persons on mobile equipment, warning devices shall be installed in advance of the restricted area and the restricted area shall be conspicuously marked.

§ 56.9307 Design, installation, and maintenance of railroads.

Roadbeds and all elements of the railroad tracks shall be designed, installed, and maintained to provide safe operation consistent with the speed and type of haulage used.

§ 56.9308 Switch throws.

Switch throws shall be installed to provide clearance to protect switchmen from contact with moving trains.

§ 56.9309 Chute design.

Chute-loading installations shall be designed to provide a safe location for persons pulling chutes.

§ 56.9310 Chute hazards.

(a) Prior to chute-pulling, persons who could be affected by the draw or otherwise exposed to danger shall be

Mine Safety and Health Admin., Labor §56.10006

warned and given time to clear the hazardous area.

(b) Persons attempting to free chute hangups shall be experienced and familiar with the task, know the hazards involved, and use the proper tools to free material.

(c) When broken rock or material is dumped into an empty chute, the chute shall be equipped with a guard or all persons shall be isolated from the hazard of flying rock or material.

§56.9311 Anchoring stationary sizing devices.

Grizzlies and other stationary sizing devices shall be securely anchored.

§56.9312 Working around drawholes.

Unless platforms or safety lines are used, persons shall not position themselves over drawholes if there is danger that broken rock or material may be withdrawn or bridged.

§56.9313 Roadway maintenance.

Water, debris, or spilled material on roadways which creates hazards to the operation of mobile equipment shall be removed.

§56.9314 Trimming stockpile and muckpile faces.

Stockpile and muckpile faces shall be trimmed to prevent hazards to persons.

§56.9315 Dust control.

Dust shall be controlled at muck piles, material transfer points, crushers, and on haulage roads where hazards to persons would be created as a result of impaired visibility.

§56.9316 Notifying the equipment operator.

When an operator of self-propelled mobile equipment is present, persons shall notify the equipment operator before getting on or off that equipment.

§56.9317 Suspended loads.

Persons shall not work or pass under the buckets or booms of loaders in operation.

§56.9318 Getting on or off moving equipment.

Persons shall not get on or off moving mobile equipment. This provision does not apply to trainmen, brakemen, and car droppers who are required to get on or off slowly moving trains in the performance of their work duties.

§56.9319 Going over, under, or between railcars.

Persons shall not go over, under, or between railcars unless:

(a) The train is stopped; and

(b) The train operator, when present, is notified and the notice acknowledged.

§56.9330 Clearance for surface equipment.

Continuous clearance of at least 30 inches from the farthest projection of moving railroad equipment shall be provided on at least one side of the tracks at all locations where possible or the area shall be marked conspicuously.

Subpart I—Aerial Tramways

§56.10001 Filling buckets.

Buckets shall not be overloaded, and feed shall be regulated to prevent spillage.

§56.10002 Inspection and maintenance.

Inspection and maintenance of carriers (including loading and unloading mechanisms), ropes and supports, and brakes shall be performed by competent persons according to the recommendations of the manufacturer.

§56.10003 Correction of defects.

Any hazardous defects shall be corrected before the equipment is used.

§56.10004 Brakes.

Positive-action-type brakes and devices which apply the brakes automatically in the event of a power failure shall be provided on aerial tramways.

§56.10005 Track cable connections.

Track cable connections shall not obstruct the passage of carriage wheels.

§56.10006 Tower guards.

Towers shall be suitably protected from swaying buckets.

§ 56.10007 Falling object protection.

Guard nets or other suitable protection shall be provided where tramways pass over roadways, walkways, or buildings.

§ 56.10008 Riding tramways.

Persons other than maintenance persons shall not ride aerial tramways unless the following features are provided:

(a) Two independent brakes, each capable of holding the maximum load;

(b) Direct communication between terminals;

(c) Power drives with emergency power available in case of primary power failure; and

(d) Buckets equipped with positive locks to prevent accidental tripping or dumping.

§ 56.10009 Riding loaded buckets.

Persons shall not ride loaded buckets.

§ 56.10010 Starting precautions.

Where possible, aerial tramways shall not be started until the operator has ascertained that everyone is in the clear.

Subpart J—Travelways

§ 56.11001 Safe access.

Safe means of access shall be provided and maintained to all working places.

§ 56.11002 Handrails and toeboards.

Crossovers, elevated walkways, elevated ramps, and stairways shall be of substantial construction provided with handrails, and maintained in good condition. Where necessary, toeboards shall be provided.

§ 56.11003 Construction and maintenance of ladders.

Ladders shall be of substantial construction and maintained in good condition.

§ 56.11004 Portable rigid ladders.

Portable rigid ladders shall be provided with suitable bases and placed securely when used.

§ 56.11005 Fixed ladder anchorage and toe clearance.

Fixed ladders shall be anchored securely and installed to provide at least 3 inches of toe clearance.

§ 56.11006 Fixed ladder landings.

Fixed ladders shall project at least 3 feet above landings, or substantial handholds shall be provided above the landings.

§ 56.11007 Wooden components of ladders.

Wooden components of ladders shall not be painted except with a transparent finish.

§ 56.11008 Restricted clearance.

Where restricted clearance creates a hazard to persons, the restricted clearance shall be conspicuously marked.

[53 FR 32521, Aug. 25, 1988]

§ 56.11009 Walkways along conveyors.

Walkways with outboard railings shall be provided wherever persons are required to walk alongside elevated conveyor belts. Inclined railed walkways shall be nonskid or provided with cleats.

§ 56.11010 Stairstep clearance.

Vertical clearance above stair steps shall be a minimum of seven feet, or suitable warning signs or similar devices shall be provided to indicate an impaired clearance.

§ 56.11011 Use of ladders.

Persons using ladders shall face the ladders and have both hands free for climbing and descending.

§ 56.11012 Protection for openings around travelways.

Openings above, below, or near travelways through which persons or materials may fall shall be protected by railings, barriers, or covers. Where it is impractical to install such protective devices, adequate warning signals shall be installed.

§ 56.11013 Conveyor crossovers.

Crossovers shall be provided where it is necessary to cross conveyors.

Mine Safety and Health Admin., Labor

§ 56.11014 Crossing moving conveyors.

Moving conveyors shall be crossed only at designated crossover points.

§ 56.11016 Snow and ice on walkways and travelways.

Regularly used walkways and travelways shall be sanded, salted, or cleared of snow and ice as soon as practicable.

§ 56.11017 Inclined fixed ladders.

Fixed ladders shall not incline backwards.

§ 56.11025 Railed landings, backguards, and other protection for fixed ladders.

Fixed ladders, except on mobile equipment, shall be offset and have substantial railed landings at least every 30 feet unless backguards or equivalent protection, such as safety belts and safety lines, are provided.

§ 56.11026 Protection for inclined fixed ladders.

Fixed ladders 70 degrees to 90 degrees from the horizontal and 30 feet or more in length shall have backguards, cages or equivalent protection, starting at a point not more than seven feet from the bottom of the ladders.

§ 56.11027 Scaffolds and working platforms.

Scaffolds and working platforms shall be of substantial construction and provided with handrails and maintained in good condition. Floor boards shall be laid properly and the scaffolds and working platforms shall not be overloaded. Working platforms shall be provided with toeboards when necessary.

Subpart K—Electricity

§ 56.12001 Circuit overload protection.

Circuits shall be protected against excessive overload by fuses or circuit breakers of the correct type and capacity.

§ 56.12002 Controls and switches.

Electric equipment and circuits shall be provided with switches or other controls. Such switches or controls shall be of approved design and construction and shall be properly installed.

§ 56.12003 Trailing cable overload protection.

Individual overload protection or short circuit protection shall be provided for the trailing cables of mobile equipment.

§ 56.12004 Electrical conductors.

Electrical conductors shall be of a sufficient size and current-carrying capacity to ensure that a rise in temperature resulting from normal operations will not damage the insulating materials. Electrical conductors exposed to mechanical damage shall be protected.

§ 56.12005 Protection of power conductors from mobile equipment.

Mobile equipment shall not run over power conductors, nor shall loads be dragged over power conductors, unless the conductors are properly bridged or protected.

§ 56.12006 Distribution boxes.

Distribution boxes shall be provided with a disconnecting device for each branch circuit. Such disconnecting devices shall be equipped or designed in such a manner that it can be determined by visual observation when such a device is open and that the circuit is deenergized, the distribution box shall be labeled to show which circuit each device controls.

§ 56.12007 Junction box connection procedures.

Trailing cable and power-cable connections to junction boxes shall not be made or broken under load.

§ 56.12008 Insulation and fittings for power wires and cables.

Power wires and cables shall be insulated adequately where they pass into or out of electrical compartments. Cables shall enter metal frames of motors, splice boxes, and electrical compartments only through proper fittings. When insulated wires, other than cables, pass through metal frames, the holes shall be substantially bushed with insulated bushings.

§ 56.12010 Isolation or insulation of communication conductors.

Telephone and low-potential signal wire shall be protected, by isolation or suitable insulation, or both, from contacting energized power conductors or any other power source.

§ 56.12011 High-potential electrical conductors.

High-potential electrical conductors shall be covered, insulated, or placed to prevent contact with low potential conductors.

§ 56.12012 Bare signal wires.

The potential on bare signal wires accessible to contact by persons shall not exceed 48 volts.

§ 56.12013 Splices and repairs of power cables.

Permanent splices and repairs made in power cables, including the ground conductor where provided, shall be:

(a) Mechanically strong with electrical conductivity as near as possible to that of the original;

(b) Insulated to a degree at least equal to that of the original, and sealed to exclude moisture; and

(c) Provided with damage protection as near as possible to that of the original, including good bonding to the outer jacket.

§ 56.12014 Handling energized power cables.

Power cables energized to potentials in excess of 150 volts, phase-to-ground, shall not be moved with equipment unless sleds or slings, insulated from such equipment, are used. When such energized cables are moved manually, insulated hooks, tongs, ropes, or slings shall be used unless suitable protection for persons is provided by other means. This does not prohibit pulling or dragging of cable by the equipment it powers when the cable is physically attached to the equipment by suitable mechanical devices, and the cable is insulated from the equipment in conformance with other standards in this part.

§ 56.12016 Work on electrically-powered equipment.

Electrically powered equipment shall be deenergized before mechanical work is done on such equipment. Power switches shall be locked out or other measures taken which shall prevent the equipment from being energized without the knowledge of the individuals working on it. Suitable warning notices shall be posted at the power switch and signed by the individuals who are to do the work. Such locks or preventive devices shall be removed only by the persons who installed them or by authorized personnel.

§ 56.12017 Work on power circuits.

Power circuits shall be deenergized before work is done on such circuits unless hot-line tools are used. Suitable warning signs shall be posted by the individuals who are to do the work. Switches shall be locked out or other measures taken which shall prevent the power circuits from being energized without the knowledge of the individuals working on them. Such locks, signs, or preventative devices shall be removed only by the person who installed them or by authorized personnel.

§ 56.12018 Identification of power switches.

Principal power switches shall be labeled to show which units they control, unless identification can be made readily by location.

§ 56.12019 Access to stationary electrical equipment or switchgear.

Where access is necessary, suitable clearance shall be provided at stationary electrical equipment or switchgear.

§ 56.12020 Protection of persons at switchgear.

Dry wooden platforms, insulating mats, or other electrically nonconductive material shall be kept in place at all switchboards and power-control switches where shock hazards exist. However, metal plates on which a person normally would stand and which are kept at the same potential as the grounded, metal, non-current-carrying

Mine Safety and Health Admin., Labor

parts of the power switches to be operated may be used.

§ 56.12021 Danger signs.

Suitable danger signs shall be posted at all major electrical installations.

§ 56.12022 Authorized persons at major electrical installations.

Areas containing major electrical installations shall be entered only by authorized persons.

§ 56.12023 Guarding electrical connections and resistor grids.

Electrical connections and resistor grids that are difficult or impractical to insulate shall be guarded, unless protection is provided by location.

§ 56.12025 Grounding circuit enclosures.

All metal enclosing or encasing electrical circuits shall be grounded or provided with equivalent protection. This requirement does not apply to battery-operated equipment.

§ 56.12026 Grounding transformer and switchgear enclosures.

Metal fencing and metal buildings enclosing transformers and switchgear shall be grounded.

§ 56.12027 Grounding mobile equipment.

Frame grounding or equivalent protection shall be provided for mobile equipment powered through trailing cables.

§ 56.12028 Testing grounding systems.

Continuity and resistance of grounding systems shall be tested immediately after installation, repair, and modification; and annually thereafter. A record of the resistance measured during the most recent tests shall be made available on a request by the Secretary or his duly authorized representative.

§ 56.12030 Correction of dangerous conditions.

When a potentially dangerous condition is found it shall be corrected before equipment or wiring is energized.

§ 56.12032 Inspection and cover plates.

Inspection and cover plates on electrical equipment and junction boxes shall be kept in place at all times except during testing or repairs.

§ 56.12033 Hand-held electric tools.

Hand-held electric tools shall not be operated at high potential voltages.

§ 56.12034 Guarding around lights.

Portable extension lights, and other lights that by their location present a shock or burn hazard, shall be guarded.

§ 56.12035 Weatherproof lamp sockets.

Lamp sockets shall be of a weatherproof type where they are exposed to weather or wet conditions that may interfere with illumination or create a shock hazard.

§ 56.12036 Fuse removal or replacement.

Fuses shall not be removed or replaced by hand in an energized circuit, and they shall not otherwise be removed or replaced in an energized circuit unless equipment and techniques especially designed to prevent electrical shock are provided and used for such purpose.

§ 56.12037 Fuses in high-potential circuits.

Fuse tongs or hot line tools shall be used when fuses are removed or replaced in high-potential circuits.

§ 56.12038 Attachment of trailing cables.

Trailing cables shall be attached to machines in a suitable manner to protect the cable from damage and to prevent strain on the electrical connections.

§ 56.12039 Protection of surplus trailing cables.

Surplus trailing cables to shovels, cranes and similar equipment shall be—
(a) Stored in cable boats;
(b) Stored on reels mounted on the equipment; or
(c) Otherwise protected from mechanical damage.

§ 56.12040 Installation of operating controls.

Operating controls shall be installed so that they can be operated without danger of contact with energized conductors.

§ 56.12041 Design of switches and starting boxes.

Switches and starting boxes shall be of safe design and capacity.

§ 56.12042 Track bonding.

Both rails shall be bonded or welded at every joint and rails shall be crossbonded at least every 200 feet if the track serves as the return trolley circuit. When rails are moved, replaced, or broken bonds are discovered, they shall be rebonded within three working shifts.

§ 56.12045 Overhead powerlines.

Overhead high-potential powerlines shall be installed as specified by the National Electrical Code.

§ 56.12047 Guy wires.

Guy wires of poles supporting high-voltage transmission lines shall meet the requirements for grounding or insulator protection of the National Electrical Safety Code, part 2, entitled "Safety Rules for the Installation and Maintenance of Electric Supply and Communication Lines" (also referred to as National Bureau of Standards Handbook 81, November 1, 1961) and Supplement 2 thereof issued March 1968, which are hereby incorporated by reference and made a part hereof. These publications and documents may be obtained from the National Institute of Science and Technology, 100 Bureau Drive, Stop 3460, Gaithersburg, MD 20899–3460. Telephone: 301–975–6478 (not a toll free number); http://ts.nist.gov/nvl; or from the Government Printing Office, Information Dissemination (Superintendent of Documents), P.O. Box 371954, Pittsburgh, PA 15250–7954; Telephone: 866–512–1800 (toll free) or 202–512–1800, http://bookstore.gpo.gov, or may be examined in any Metal and Nonmetal Mine Safety and Health District Office of the Mine Safety and Health Administration.

[50 FR 4054, Jan. 29, 1985, as amended at 60 FR 35695, July 11, 1995; 71 FR 16667, Apr. 3, 2006]

§ 56.12048 Communication conductors on power poles.

Telegraph, telephone, or signal wires shall not be installed on the same crossarm with power conductors. When carried on poles supporting powerlines, they shall be installed as specified by the National Electrical Code.

§ 56.12050 Installation of trolley wires.

Trolley wires shall be installed at least seven feet above rails where height permits, and aligned and supported to suitably control sway and sag.

§ 56.12053 Circuits powered from trolley wires.

Ground wires for lighting circuits powered from trolley wires shall be connected securely to the ground-return circuit.

§ 56.12065 Short circuit and lightning protection.

Powerlines, including trolley wires, and telephone circuits shall be protected against short circuits and lightning.

§ 56.12066 Guarding trolley wires and bare powerlines.

Where metallic tools or equipment can come in contact with trolley wires or bare powerlines, the lines shall be guarded or deenergized.

§ 56.12067 Installation of transformers.

Transformers shall be totally enclosed, or shall be placed at least 8 feet above the ground, or installed in a transformer house, or surrounded by a substantial fence at least 6 feet high and at least 3 feet from any energized parts, casings, or wiring.

§ 56.12068 Locking transformer enclosures.

Transformer enclosures shall be kept locked against unauthorized entry.

Mine Safety and Health Admin., Labor § 56.13019

§ 56.12069 Lightning protection for telephone wires and ungrounded conductors.

Each ungrounded power conductor or telephone wire that leads underground and is directly exposed to lightning shall be equipped with suitable lightning arrestors of approved type within 100 feet of the point where the circuit enters the mine. Lightning arrestors shall be connected to a low resistance grounding medium on the surface and shall be separated from neutral grounds by a distance of not less than 25 feet.

§ 56.12071 Movement or operation of equipment near high-voltage power lines.

When equipment must be moved or operated near energized high-voltage powerlines (other than trolley lines) and the clearance is less than 10 feet, the lines shall be deenergized or other precautionary measures shall be taken.

Subpart L—Compressed Air and Boilers

§ 56.13001 General requirements for boilers and pressure vessels.

All boilers and pressure vessels shall be constructed, installed, and maintained in accordance with the standards and specifications of the American Society of Mechanical Engineers Boiler and Pressure Vessel Code.

§ 56.13010 Reciprocating-type air compressors.

(a) Reciprocating-type air compressors rated over 10 horsepower shall be equipped with automatic temperature-actuated shutoff mechanisms which shall be set or adjusted to the compressor when the normal operating temperature is exceeded by more than 25 percent.

(b) However, this standard does not apply to reciprocating-type air compressors rated over 10 horsepower that were equipped with fusible plugs that were installed in the compressor discharge lines before November 15, 1979, and designed to melt at temperatures at least 50 degrees below the flash point of the compressors' lubricating oil.

§ 56.13011 Air receiver tanks.

Air receiver tanks shall be equipped with one or more automatic pressure-relief valves. The total relieving capacity of the relief valves shall prevent pressure from exceeding the maximum allowable working pressure in a receiver tank by not more than 10 percent. Air receiver tanks also shall be equipped with indicating pressure gauges which accurately measure the pressure within the air receiver tanks.

§ 56.13012 Compressor air intakes.

Compressor air intakes shall be installed to ensure that only clean, uncontaminated air enters the compressors.

§ 56.13015 Inspection of compressed-air receivers and other unfired pressure vessels.

(a) Compressed-air receivers and other unfired pressure vessels shall be inspected by inspectors holding a valid National Board Commission and in accordance with the applicable chapters of the National Board Inspection Code, a Manual for Boiler and Pressure Vessel Inspectors, 1979. This code is incorporated by reference and made a part of this standard. It may be examined at any Metal and Nonmetal Mine Safety and Health District Office of the Mine Safety and Health Administration, and may be obtained from the publisher, the National Board of Boiler and Pressure Vessel Inspector, 1055 Crupper Avenue, Columbus, Ohio 43229.

(b) Records of inspections shall be kept in accordance with requirements of the National Board Inspection Code, and the records shall be made available to the Secretary or his authorized representative.

§ 56.13017 Compressor discharge pipes.

Compressor discharge pipes where carbon build-up may occur shall be cleaned periodically as recommended by the manufacturer, but no less frequently than once every two years.

§ 56.13019 Pressure system repairs.

Repairs involving the pressure system of compressors, receivers, or compressed-air-powered equipment shall

§ 56.13020

not be attempted until the pressure has been bled off.

§ 56.13020 Use of compressed air.

At no time shall compressed air be directed toward a person. When compressed air is used, all necessary precautions shall be taken to protect persons from injury.

§ 56.13021 High-pressure hose connections.

Except where automatic shutoff valves are used, safety chains or other suitable locking devices shall be used at connections to machines of high-pressure hose lines of ¾-inch inside diameter or larger, and between high-pressure hose lines of ¾-inch inside diameter or larger, where a connection failure would create a hazard.

§ 56.13030 Boilers.

(a) Fired pressure vessels (boilers) shall be equipped with water level gauges, pressure gauges, automatic pressure-relief valves, blowdown piping, and other safety devices approved by the American Society of Mechanical Engineers to protect against hazards from overpressure, flameouts, fuel interruptions and low water level, all as required by the appropriate sections, chapters and appendices listed in paragraphs (b) (1) and (2) of this section.

(b) These gauges, devices and piping shall be designed, installed, operated, maintained, repaired, altered, inspected, and tested by inspectors holding a valid National Board Commission and in accordance with the following listed sections, chapters and appendices:

(1) The ASME Boiler and Pressure Vessel Code, 1977, Published by the American Society of Mechanical Engineers.

SECTION AND TITLE

I Power Boilers.
II Material Specifications—Part A—Ferrous.
II Material Specifications—Part B—Nonferrous.
II Material Specifications—Part C—Welding Rods, Electrodes, and Filler Metals.
IV Heating Boilers
V Nondestructive Examination
VI Recommended Rules for Care and Operation of Heating Boilers

VII Recommended Rules for Care of Power Boilers

(2) The National Board Inspection Code, a Manual for Boiler and Pressure Vessel Inspectors, 1979, published by the National Board of Boiler and Pressure Vessel Inspectors.

CHAPTER AND TITLE

I Glossary of Terms
II Inspection of Boilers and Pressure Vessels
III Repairs and Alterations to Boiler and Pressure Vessels by Welding
IV Shop Inspection of Boilers and Pressure Vessels
V Inservice Inspection of Pressure Vessels by Authorized Owner-User Inspection Agencies

APPENDIX AND TITLE

A Safety and Safety Relief Valves
B Non-ASME Code Boilers and Pressure Vessels
C Storage of Mild Steel Covered Arc Welding Electrodes
D-R National Board "R" (Repair) Symbol Stamp
D-VR National Board "VR" (Repair of Safety and Safety Relief Valve) Symbol Stamp
D-VR1 Certificate of Authorization for Repair Symbol Stamp for Safety and Safety Relief Valves
D-VR2 Outline of Basic Elements of Written Quality Control System for Repairers of ASME Safety and Safety Relief Valves
D-VR3 Nameplate Stamping for "VR"
E Owner-user Inspection Agencies
F Inspection Forms

(c) Records of inspections and repairs shall be kept in accordance with the requirements of the ASME Boiler and Pressure Vessel Code and the National Board Inspection Code. The records shall be made available to the Secretary or his authorized representative.

(d) Sections of the ASME Boiler and Pressure Vessel Code, 1977, listed in paragraph (b)(1) of this section, and chapters and appendices of the National Board Inspection Code, 1979, listed in paragraph (b)(2) of this section, are incorporated by reference and made a part of this standard. These publications may be obtained from the publishers, the American Society of Mechanical Engineers, 22 Law Drive, P.O. Box 2900, Fairfield, New Jersey 07007, Phone: 800–843–2763 (toll free); *http://www.asme.org*, and the National Board of Boiler and Pressure Vessel Inspectors, 1055 Crupper Avenue, Columbus, Ohio 43229. The publications may be examined at any Metal and Nonmetal Mine Safety and Health District Office of the Mine Safety and Health Administration.

[50 FR 4054, Jan. 29, 1985, as amended at 71 FR 16667, Apr. 3, 2006]

Subpart M—Machinery and Equipment

SOURCE: 53 FR 32521, Aug. 25, 1988, unless otherwise noted.

§ 56.14000 Definitions.

The following definitions apply in this subpart.

Travelway. A passage, walk, or way regularly used or designated for persons to go from one place to another.

[53 FR 32521, Aug. 25, 1988, as amended at 69 FR 38840, June 29, 2004]

SAFETY DEVICES AND MAINTENANCE REQUIREMENTS

§ 56.14100 Safety defects; examination, correction and records.

(a) Self-propelled mobile equipment to be used during a shift shall be inspected by the equipment operator before being placed in operation on that shift.

(b) Defects on any equipment, machinery, and tools that affect safety shall be corrected in a timely manner to prevent the creation of a hazard to persons.

(c) When defects make continued operation hazardous to persons, the defective items including self-propelled mobile equipment shall be taken out of service and placed in a designated area posted for that purpose, or a tag or other effective method of marking the defective items shall be used to prohibit further use until the defects are corrected.

(d) Defects on self-propelled mobile equipment affecting safety, which are not corrected immediately, shall be reported to and recorded by the mine operator. The records shall be kept at the mine or nearest mine office from the date the defects are recorded, until the defects are corrected. Such records shall be made available for inspection by an authorized representative of the Secretary.

§ 56.14101 Brakes.

(a) *Minimum requirements.* (1) Self-propelled mobile equipment shall be equipped with a service brake system capable of stopping and holding the equipment with its typical load on the maximum grade it travels. This standard does not apply to equipment which is not originally equipped with brakes unless the manner in which the equipment is being operated requires the use of brakes for safe operation. This standard does not apply to rail equipment.

(2) If equipped on self-propelled mobile equipment, parking brakes shall be capable of holding the equipment with its typical load on the maximum grade it travels.

(3) All braking systems installed on the equipment shall be maintained in functional condition.

(b) *Testing.* (1) Service brake tests shall be conducted when an MSHA inspector has reasonable cause to believe that the service brake system does not function as required, unless the mine operator removes the equipment from service for the appropriate repair;

(2) The performance of the service brakes shall be evaluated according to Table M–1.

TABLE M–1

Gross vehicle weight lbs.	Equipment speed, MPH										
	10	11	12	13	14	15	16	17	18	19	20
	Service Brake Maximum Stopping Distance—Feet										
0–36000	34	38	43	48	53	59	64	70	76	83	89
36000–70000	41	46	52	58	62	70	76	83	90	97	104
70000–140000	48	54	61	67	74	81	88	95	103	111	119
140000–250000	56	62	69	77	84	92	100	108	116	125	133
250000–400000	59	66	74	81	89	97	105	114	123	132	141

§ 56.14101

TABLE M-1—Continued

Gross vehicle weight lbs.	Equipment speed, MPH										
	10	11	12	13	14	15	16	17	18	19	20
Over 400000	63	71	78	86	94	103	111	120	129	139	148

Stopping distances are computed using a constant deceleration of 9.66 FPS^2 and system response times of .5.1, 1.5, 2, 2.25 and 2.5 seconds for each increasing weight category respectively. Stopping distance values include a one-second operator response time.

TABLE M-2—THE SPEED OF A VEHICLE CAN BE DETERMINED BY CLOCKING IT THROUGH A 100-FOOT MEASURED COURSE AT CONSTANT VELOCITY USING TABLE M-2. WHEN THE SERVICE BRAKES ARE APPLIED AT THE END OF THE COURSE, STOPPING DISTANCE CAN BE MEASURED AND COMPARED TO TABLE M-1.

Miles per hour	10	11	12	13	14	15	16	17	18	19	20
Seconds Required to Travel 100 Feet	6.8	6.2	5.7	5.2	4.9	4.5	4.3	4.0	3.8	3.6	3.4

(3) Service brake tests shall be conducted under the direction of the mine operator in cooperation with an according to the instructions provided by the MSHA inspector as follows:

(i) Equipment capable of traveling at least 10 miles per hour shall be tested with a typical load for that particular piece of equipment. Front-end loaders shall be tested with the loader bucket empty. Equipment shall not be tested when carrying hazardous loads, such as explosives.

(ii) The approach shall be sufficient length to allow the equipment operator to reach and maintain a constant speed between 10 and 20 miles per hour prior to entering the 100 foot measured area. The constant speed shall be maintained up to the point when the equipment operator receives the signal to apply the brakes. The roadway shall be wide enough to accommodate the size of the equipment being tested. The ground shall be generally level, packed, and dry in the braking portion of the test course. Ground moisture may be present to the extent that it does not adversely affect the braking surface.

(iii) Braking is to be performed using only those braking systems, including auxiliary retarders, which are designed to bring the equipment to a stop under normal operating conditions. Parking or emergency (secondary) brakes are not to be actuated during the test.

(iv) The tests shall be conducted with the transmission in the gear appropriate for the speed the equipment is traveling except for equipment which is designed for the power train to be disengaged during braking.

(v) Testing speeds shall be a minimum of 10 miles per hour and a maximum of 20 miles per hour.

(vi) Stopping distances shall be measured from the point at which the equipment operator receives the signal to apply the service brakes to the final stopped position.

(4) Test results shall be evaluated as follows:

(i) If the initial test run is valid and the stopping distance does not exceed the corresponding stopping distance listed in Table 1, the performance of the service brakes shall be considered acceptable. For tests to be considered valid, the equipment shall not slide sideways or exhibit other lateral motion during the braking portion of the test.

(ii) If the equipment exceeds the maximum stopping distance in the initial test run, the mine operator may request from the inspector up to four additional test runs with two runs to be conducted in each direction. The performance of the service brakes shall be considered acceptable if the equipment does not exceed the maximum stopping distance on at least three of the additional tests.

(5) Where there is not an appropriate test site at the mine or the equipment is not capable or traveling at least 10 miles per hour, service brake tests will not be conducted. In such cases, the inspector will rely upon other available evidence to determine whether the

service brake system meets the performance requirement of this standard.

[53 FR 32521, Aug. 25, 1988; 53 FR 44588, Nov. 4, 1988]

§ 56.14102 Brakes for rail equipment.

Braking systems on railroad cars and locomotives shall be maintained in functional condition.

§ 56.14103 Operators stations.

(a) If windows are provided on operators' stations of self-propelled mobile equipment, the windows shall be made of safety glass or material with equivalent safety characteristics. The windows shall be maintained to provide visibility for safe operation.

(b) If damaged windows obscure visibility necessary for safe operation, or create a hazard to the equipment operator, the windows shall be replaced or removed. Damaged windows shall be replaced if absence of a window would expose the equipment operator to hazardous environmental conditions which would affect the ability of the equipment operator to safely operate the equipment.

(c) The operator's stations of self-propelled mobile equipment shall—

(1) Be free of materials that could create a hazard to persons by impairing the safe operation of the equipment; and

(2) Not be modified, in a manner that obscures visibility necessary for safe operation.

§ 56.14104 Tire repairs.

(a) Before a tire is removed from a vehicle for tire repair, the valve core shall be partially removed to allow for gradual deflation and then removed. During deflation, to the extent possible, persons shall stand outside of the potential trajectory of the lock ring of a multi-piece wheel rim.

(b) To prevent injury from wheel rims during tire inflation, one of the following shall be used:

(1) A wheel cage or other restraining device that will constrain all wheel rim components during an explosive separation of a multi-piece wheel rim, or during the sudden release of contained air in a single piece rim wheel; or

(2) A stand-off inflation device which permits persons to stand outside of the potential trajectory of wheel components.

§ 56.14105 Procedures during repairs or maintenance.

Repairs or maintenance of machinery or equipment shall be performed only after the power is off, and the machinery or equipment blocked against hazardous motion. Machinery or equipment motion or activation is permitted to the extent that adjustments or testing cannot be performed without motion or activation, provided that persons are effectively protected from hazardous motion.

§ 56.14106 Falling object protection.

(a) Fork-lift trucks, front-end loaders, and bulldozers shall be provided with falling object protective structures if used in an area where falling objects could create a hazard to the equipment operator.

(b) The protective structure shall be capable of withstanding the falling object loads to which it would be subjected.

§ 56.14107 Moving machine parts.

(a) Moving machine parts shall be guarded to protect persons from contacting gears, sprockets, chains, drive, head, tail, and takeup pulleys, flywheels, couplings, shafts, fan blades, and similar moving parts that can cause injury.

(b) Guards shall not be required where the exposed moving parts are at least seven feet away from walking or working surfaces.

§ 56.14108 Overhead drive belts.

Overhead drive belts shall be guarded to contain the whipping action of a broken belt if that action could be hazardous to persons.

§ 56.14109 Unguarded conveyors with adjacent travelways.

Unguarded conveyors next to the travelways shall be equipped with—

(a) Emergency stop devices which are located so that a person falling on or against the conveyor can readily deactivate the conveyor drive motor; or

(b) Railings which—

(1) Are positioned to prevent persons from falling on or against the conveyor;

(2) Will be able to withstand the vibration, shock, and wear to which they will be subjected during normal operation; and

(3) Are constructed and maintained so that they will not create a hazard.

§ 56.14110 Flying or falling materials.

In areas where flying or falling materials generated from the operation of screens, crushers, or conveyors present a hazard, guards, shields, or other devices that provide protection against such flying or falling materials shall be provided to protect persons.

§ 56.14111 Slusher, backlash guards and securing.

(a) When persons are exposed to slushing operations, the slushers shall be equipped with rollers and drum covers and anchored securely before slushing operations are started.

(b) Slushers rated over 10 horsepower shall be equipped with backlash guards, unless the equipment operator is otherwise protected.

(c) This standard does not apply to air tuggers of 10 horsepower or less that have only one cable and one drum.

§ 56.14112 Construction and maintenance of guards.

(a) Guards shall be constructed and maintained to—

(1) Withstand the vibration, shock, and wear to which they will be subjected during normal operation; and

(2) Not create a hazard by their use.

(b) Guards shall be securely in place while machinery is being operated, except when testing or making adjustments which cannot be performed without removal of the guard.

§ 56.14113 Inclined conveyors: backstops or brakes.

Backstops or brakes shall be installed on drive units of inclined conveyors to prevent the conveyors from running in reverse, creating a hazard to persons.

§ 56.14114 Air valves for pneumatic equipment.

A manual master quick-close type air valve shall be installed on all pneumatic-powered equipment if there is a hazard of uncontrolled movement when the air supply is activated. The valve shall be closed except when the equipment is being operated.

§ 56.14115 Stationary grinding machines.

Stationary grinding machines, other than special bit grinders, shall be equipped with—

(a) Peripheral hoods capable of withstanding the force of a bursting wheel and enclosing not less than 270° of the periphery of the wheel;

(b) Adjustable tool rests set so that the distance between the grinding surface of the wheel and the tool rest in not greater than ⅛ inch; and

(c) A safety washer on each side of the wheel.

[53 FR 32521, Aug. 25, 1988; 53 FR 44588, Nov. 4, 1988]

§ 56.14116 Hand-held power tools.

(a) Power drills, disc sanders, grinders and circular and chain saws, when used in the hand-held mode shall be operated with controls which require constant hand or finger pressure.

(b) Circular saws and chain saws shall not be equipped with devices which lock-on the operating controls.

§ 56.14130 Roll-over protective structures (ROPS) and seat belts.

(a) *Equipment included.* Roll-over protective structures (ROPS) and seat belts shall be installed on—

(1) Crawler tractors and crawler loaders;

(2) Graders;

(3) Wheel loaders and wheel tractors;

(4) The tractor portion of semi-mounted scrapers, dumpers, water wagons, bottom-dump wagons, rear-dump wagons, and towed fifth wheel attachments;

(5) Skid-steer loaders; and

(6) Agricultural tractors.

(b) *ROPS construction.* ROPS shall meet the requirements of the following Society of Automotive Engineers (SAE) publications, as applicable, which are incorporated by reference:

(1) SAE J1040, "Performance Criteria for Roll-Over Protective Structures (ROPS) for Construction, Earthmoving, Forestry, and Mining Machines,", 1986; or

(2) SAE J1194, "Roll-Over Protective Structures (ROPS) for Wheeled Agricultural Tractors", 1983.

(c) *ROPS labelling.* ROPS shall have a label permanently affixed to the structure identifying—

(1) The manufacturer's name and address;

(2) The ROPS model number; and

(3) The make and model number of the equipment for which the ROPS is designed.

(d) *ROPS installation.* ROPS shall be installed on the equipment in accordance with the recommendations of the ROPS manufacturer.

(e) *ROPS maintenance.* (1) ROPS shall be maintained in a condition that meets the performance requirements applicable to the equipment. If the ROPS is subjected to roll-over an abnormal structural loading, the equipment manufacturer or a registered professional engineer with knowledge and experience in ROPS design shall recertify that the ROPS meets the applicable performance requirements before it is returned to service.

(2) Alterations or repairs on ROPS shall be performed only with approval from the ROPS manufacturer or under the instructions of a registered professional engineer with knowledge and experience in ROPS design. The manufacturer or engineer shall certify that the ROPS meets the applicable performance requirements.

(f) *Exemptions.* (1) This standard does not apply to—

(i) Self-propelled mobile equipment manufactured prior to July 1, 1969;

(ii) Over-the-road type tractors that pull trailers or vans on highways;

(iii) Equipment that is only operated by remote control; and

(2) Self-propelled mobile equipment manufactured prior to October 24, 1988, that is equipped with ROPS and seat belts that meet the installation and performance requirements of 30 CFR 56.9088 (1986 edition) shall be considered in compliance with paragraphs (b) and (h) of this section.

(g) *Wearing seat belts.* Seat belts shall be worn by the equipment operator except that when operating graders from a standing position, the grader operator shall wear safety lines and a harness in place of a seat belt.

(h) *Seat belts construction.* Seat belts required under this section shall meet the requirement of SAE J386, "Operator Restraint System for Off-Road Work Machines" (1985, 1993, or 1997), or SAE J1194, "Roll-Over Protective Structures (ROPS) for Wheeled Agricultural Tractors" (1983, 1989, 1994, or 1999), as applicable, which are incorporated by reference.

(i) *Seat belt maintenance.* Seat belts shall be maintained in functional condition, and replaced when necessary to assure proper performance.

(j) *Publications.* The incorporation by reference of these publications is approved by the Director of the Federal Register in accordance with 5 U.S.C. 552(a) and 1 CFR part 51. Copies of these publications may be examined at any Metal and Nonmetal Mine Safety and Health District Office; at MSHA's Office of Standards, Regulations, and Variances, 201 12th Street South, Arlington, VA 22202–5452; 202–693–9440; or at the National Archives and Records Administration (NARA). For information on the availability of this material at NARA, call 202–741–6030, or go to: *http://www.archives.gov/federal_register/code_of_federal_regulations/ibr_locations.html.* Copies may be purchased from the Society of Automotive Engineers, 400 Commonwealth Drive, Warrendale, PA 15096–0001; 724–776–4841; *http://www.sae.org.*

[53 FR 32521, Aug. 25, 1988; 53 FR 44588, Nov. 4, 1988, as amended at 60 FR 33723, June 29, 1995; 67 FR 38385, June 4, 2002; 68 FR 19347, Apr. 21, 2003; 80 FR 52987, Sept. 2, 2015]

§ 56.14131 Seat belts for haulage trucks.

(a) Seat belts shall be provided and worn in haulage trucks.

(b) Seat belts shall be maintained in functional condition, and replaced when necessary to assure proper performance.

(c) Seat belts required under this section shall meet the requirements of SAE J386, "Operator Restraint System for Off-Road Work Machines" (1985,

§ 56.14132

1993, or 1997), which are incorporated by reference.

(d) The incorporation by reference of these publications is approved by the Director of the Federal Register in accordance with 5 U.S.C. 552(a) and 1 CFR part 51. Copies of these publications may be examined at any Metal and Nonmetal Mine Safety and Health District Office; at MSHA's Office of Standards, Regulations, and Variances, 201 12th Street South, Arlington, VA 22202–5452; 202–693–9440; or at the National Archives and Records Administration (NARA). For information on the availability of this material at NARA, call 202–741–6030, or go to: *http://www.archives.gov/federal_register/code_of_federal_regulations/ibr_locations.html*. Copies may be purchased from the Society of Automotive Engineers, 400 Commonwealth Drive, Warrendale, PA 15096–0001; 724–776–4841; *http://www.sae.org*.

[50 FR 4054, Jan. 29, 1985, as amended at 67 FR 38385, June 4, 2002; 68 FR 19347, Apr. 21, 2003; 80 FR 52987, Sept. 2, 2015]

§ 56.14132 Horns and backup alarms.

(a) Manually-operated horns or other audible warning devices provided on self-propelled mobile equipment as a safety feature shall be maintained in functional condition.

(b)(1) When the operator has an obstructed view to the rear, self-propelled mobile equipment shall have—

(i) An automatic reverse-activated signal alarm;

(ii) A wheel-mounted bell alarm which sounds at least once for each three feet of reverse movement;

(iii) A discriminating backup alarm that covers the area of obstructed view; or

(iv) An observer to signal when it is safe to back up.

(2) Alarms shall be audible above the surrounding noise level.

(3) An automatic reverse-activated strobe light may be used at night in lieu of an audible reverse alarm.

(c) This standard does not apply to rail equipment.

SAFETY PRACTICES AND OPERATIONAL PROCEDURES

§ 56.14200 Warnings prior to starting or moving equipment.

Before starting crushers or moving self-propelled mobile equipment, equipment operators shall sound a warning that is audible above the surrounding noise level or use other effective means to warn all persons who could be exposed to a hazard from the equipment.

§ 56.14201 Conveyor start-up warnings.

(a) When the entire length of a conveyor is visible from the starting switch, the conveyor operator shall visually check to make certain that all persons are in the clear before starting the conveyor.

(b) When the entire length of the conveyor is not visible from the starting switch, a system which provides visible or audible warning shall be installed and operated to warn persons that the conveyor will be started. Within 30 seconds after the warning is given, the conveyor shall be started or a second warning shall be given.

§ 56.14202 Manual cleaning of conveyor pulleys.

Pulleys of conveyors shall not be cleaned manually while the conveyor is in motion.

§ 56.14203 Application of belt dressing.

Belt dressings shall not be applied manually while belts are in motion unless a pressurized-type applicator is used that allows the dressing to be applied from outside the guards.

§ 56.14204 Machinery lubrication.

Machinery or equipment shall not be lubricated manually while it is in motion where application of the lubricant may expose persons to injury.

§ 56.14205 Machinery, equipment, and tools.

Machinery, equipment, and tools shall not be used beyond the design capacity intended by the manufacturer where such use may create a hazard to persons.

§ 56.14206 Securing movable parts.

(a) When moving mobile equipment between workplaces, booms, forks, buckets, beds, and similar movable parts of the equipment shall be positioned in the travel mode and, if required for safe travel, mechanically secured.

(b) When mobile equipment is unattended or not in use, dippers, buckets and scraper blades shall be lowered to the ground. Other movable parts, such as booms, shall be mechanically secured or positioned to prevent movement which would create a hazard to persons.

[53 FR 32521, Aug. 25, 1988; 53 FR 44588, Nov. 4, 1988]

§ 56.14207 Parking procedures for unattended equipment.

Mobile equipment shall not be left unattended unless the controls are placed in the park position and the parking brake, if provided, is set. When parked on a grade, the wheels or tracks of mobile equipment shall be either chocked or turned into a bank.

§ 56.14208 Warning devices.

(a) Visible warning devices shall be used when parked mobile equipment creates a hazard to persons in other mobile equipment.

(b) Mobile equipment, other than forklifts, carrying loads that project beyond the sides or more than four feet beyond the rear of the equipment shall have a warning flag at the end of the projection. Under conditions of limited visibility these loads shall have a warning light at the end of the projection. Such flag or lights shall be attached to the end of the projection or be carried by persons walking beside or behind the projection.

§ 56.14209 Safety procedures for towing.

(a) A properly sized tow bar or other effective means of control shall be used to tow mobile equipment.

(b) Unless steering and braking are under the control of the equipment operator on the towed equipment, a safety chain or wire rope capable of withstanding the loads to which it could be subjected shall be used in conjunction with any primary rigging.

(c) This provision does not apply to rail equipment.

§ 56.14210 Movement of dippers, buckets, loading booms, or suspended loads.

(a) Dippers, buckets, loading booms, or suspended loads shall not be swung over the operators' stations of self-propelled mobile equipment until the equipment operator is out of the operator's station and in a safe location.

(b) This section does not apply when the equipment is specifically designed to protect the equipment operator from falling objects.

§ 56.14211 Blocking equipment in a raised position.

(a) Persons shall not work on top of, under, or work from mobile equipment in a raised position until the equipment has been blocked or mechanically secured to prevent it from rolling or falling accidentally.

(b) Persons shall not work on top of, under, or work from a raised component of mobile equipment until the component has been blocked or mechanically secured to prevent accidental lowering. The equipment must also be blocked or secured to prevent rolling.

(c) A raised component must be secured to prevent accidental lowering when persons are working on or around mobile equipment and are exposed to the hazard of accidental lowering of the component.

(d) Under this section, a raised component of mobile equipment is considered to be blocked or mechanically secured if provided with a functional load-locking device or a device which prevents free and uncontrolled descent.

(e) Blocking or mechanical securing of the raised component is required during repair or maintenance of elevated mobile work platforms.

§ 56.14212 Chains, ropes, and drive belts.

Chains, ropes, and drive belts shall be guided mechanically onto moving pulleys, sprockets, or drums except where equipment is designed specifically for hand feeding.

§ 56.14213 Ventilation and shielding for welding.

(a) Welding operations shall be shielded when performed at locations where arc flash could be hazardous to persons.

(b) All welding operations shall be well-ventilated.

§ 56.14214 Train warnings.

A warning that is audible above the surrounding noise level shall be sounded—

(a) Immediately prior to moving trains;

(b) When trains approach persons, crossings, other trains on adjacent tracks; and

(c) Any place where the train operator's vision is obscured.

§ 56.14215 Coupling or uncoupling cars.

Prior to coupling or uncoupling cars manually, trains shall be brought to a complete stop, and then moved at minimum tram speed until the coupling or uncoupling activity is completed. Coupling or uncoupling shall not be attempted from the inside of curves unless the railroad and cars are designed to eliminate hazards to persons.

§ 56.14216 Backpoling.

Backpoling of trolleys is prohibited except where there is inadequate clearance to reverse the trolley pole. Where backpoling is required, it shall be done only at the minimum tram speed of the trolley.

§ 56.14217 Securing parked railcars.

Parked railcars shall be blocked securely unless held effectively by brakes.

§ 56.14218 Movement of equipment on adjacent tracks.

When a locomotive on one track is used to move rail equipment on adjacent tracks, a chain, cable, or drawbar shall be used which is capable of meeting the loads to which it could be subjected.

§ 56.14219 Brakeman signals.

When a train is under the direction of a brakeman and the train operator cannot clearly recognize the brakeman's signals, the train operator shall bring the train to a stop.

APPENDIX I TO SUBPART M OF PART 56—NATIONAL CONSENSUS STANDARDS

Mine operators seeking further information regarding the construction and installation of falling object protective structures (FOPS) may consult the following national consensus standards, as applicable.

MSHA STANDARD 56.14106, FALLING OBJECT PROTECTION.

Equipment	National consensus standard
Front-end loaders and bulldozers.	Society of Automotive Engineers (SAE) minimum performance criteria for falling object protective structures (FOPS) SAE J231—January, 1981.
Fork-lift trucks	American National Standards Institute (ANSI) safety standard for low lift and high lift trucks, B 56.1, section 7.27—1983; or, American National Standards Institute (ANSI) standard, rough terrain fork lift trucks, B56.6—1987.

Subpart N—Personal Protection

§ 56.15001 First-aid materials.

Adequate first-aid materials, including stretchers and blankets, shall be provided at places convenient to all working areas. Water or neutralizing agents shall be available where corrosive chemicals or other harmful substances are stored, handled, or used.

§ 56.15002 Hard hats.

All persons shall wear suitable hard hats when in or around a mine or plant where falling objects may create a hazard.

§ 56.15003 Protective footwear.

All persons shall wear suitable protective footwear when in or around an area of a mine or plant where a hazard exists which could cause an injury to the feet.

§ 56.15004 Eye protection.

All persons shall wear safety glasses, goggles, or face shields or other suitable protective devices when in or around an area of a mine or plant where a hazard exists which could cause injury to unprotected eyes.

Mine Safety and Health Admin., Labor § 56.16007

§ 56.15005 Safety belts and lines.

Safety belts and lines shall be worn when persons work where there is danger of falling; a second person shall tend the lifeline when bins, tanks, or other dangerous areas are entered.

§ 56.15006 Protective equipment and clothing for hazards and irritants.

Special protective equipment and special protective clothing shall be provided, maintained in a sanitary and reliable condition and used whenever hazards of process or environment, chemical hazards, radiological hazards, or mechanical irritants are encountered in a manner capable of causing injury or impairment.

§ 56.15007 Protective equipment or clothing for welding, cutting, or working with molten metal.

Protective clothing or equipment and face shields, or goggles shall be worn when welding, cutting, or working with molten metal.

§ 56.15014 Eye protection when operating grinding wheels.

Face shields or goggles in good condition shall be worn when operating a grinding wheel.

[53 FR 32526, Aug. 25, 1988]

§ 56.15020 Life jackets and belts.

Life jackets or belts shall be worn where there is danger from falling into water.

Subpart O—Materials Storage and Handling

§ 56.16001 Stacking and storage of materials.

Supplies shall not be stacked or stored in a manner which creates tripping or fall-of-material hazards.

§ 56.16002 Bins, hoppers, silos, tanks, and surge piles.

(a) Bins, hoppers, silos, tanks, and surge piles, where loose unconsolidated materials are stored, handled or transferred shall be—

(1) Equipped with mechanical devices or other effective means of handling materials so that during normal operations persons are not required to enter or work where they are exposed to entrapment by the caving or sliding of materials; and

(2) Equipped with supply and discharge operating controls. The controls shall be located so that spills or overruns will not endanger persons.

(b) Where persons are required to move around or over any facility listed in this standard, suitable walkways or passageways shall be provided.

(c) Where persons are required to enter any facility listed in this standard for maintenance or inspection purposes, ladders, platforms, or staging shall be provided. No person shall enter the facility until the supply and discharge of materials have ceased and the supply and discharge equipment is locked out. Persons entering the facility shall wear a safety belt or harness equipped with a lifeline suitably fastened. A second person, similarly equipped, shall be stationed near where the lifeline is fastened and shall constantly adjust it or keep it tight as needed, with minimum slack.

§ 56.16003 Storage of hazardous materials.

Materials that can create hazards if accidentally liberated from their containers shall be stored in a manner that minimizes the dangers.

§ 56.16004 Containers for hazardous materials.

Containers holding hazardous materials must be of a type approved for such use by recognized agencies.

[67 FR 42389, June 21, 2002]

§ 56.16005 Securing gas cylinders.

Compressed and liquid gas cylinders shall be secured in a safe manner.

§ 56.16006 Protection of gas cylinder valves.

Valves on compressed gas cylinders shall be protected by covers when being transported or stored, and by a safe location when the cylinders are in use.

§ 56.16007 Taglines, hitches, and slings.

(a) Taglines shall be attached to loads that may require steadying or guidance while suspended.

(b) Hitches and slings used to hoist materials shall be suitable for the particular material handled.

§ 56.16009 Suspended loads.

Persons shall stay clear of suspended loads.

§ 56.16010 Dropping materials from overhead.

To protect personnel, material shall not be dropped from an overhead elevation until the drop area is first cleared of personnel and the area is then either guarded or a suitable warning is given.

§ 56.16011 Riding hoisted loads or on the hoist hook.

Persons shall not ride on loads being moved by cranes or derricks, nor shall they ride the hoisting hooks unless such method eliminates a greater hazard.

§ 56.16012 Storage of incompatible substances.

Chemical substances, including concentrated acids and alkalies, shall be stored to prevent inadvertent contact with each other or with other substances, where such contact could cause a violent reaction or the liberation of harmful fumes or gases.

§ 56.16013 Working with molten metal.

Suitable warning shall be given before molten metal is poured and before a container of molten metal is moved.

§ 56.16014 Operator-carrying overhead cranes.

Operator-carrying overhead cranes shall be provided with—
(a) Bumpers at each end of each rail;
(b) Automatic switches to halt uptravel of the blocks before they strike the hoist;
(c) Effective audible warning signals within easy reach of the operator; and
(d) A means to lock out the disconnect switch.

§ 56.16015 Work or travel on overhead crane bridges.

No person shall work from or travel on the bridge of an overhead crane unless the bridge is provided with substantial footwalks with toeboards and railings the length of the bridge.

§ 56.16016 Lift trucks.

Fork and other similar types of lift trucks shall be operated with the—
(a) Upright tilted back to steady and secure the load;
(b) Load in the upgrade position when ascending or descending grades in excess of 10 percent;
(c) Load not raised or lowered enroute except for minor adjustments; and
(d) Load-engaging device downgrade when traveling unloaded on all grades.

Subpart P—Illumination

§ 56.17001 Illumination of surface working areas.

Illumination sufficient to provide safe working conditions shall be provided in and on all surface structures, paths, walkways, stairways, switch panels, loading and dumping sites, and work areas.

Subpart Q—Safety Programs

§ 56.18002 Examination of working places.

(a) A competent person designated by the operator shall examine each working place at least once each shift before miners begin work in that place, for conditions that may adversely affect safety or health.

(1) The operator shall promptly notify miners in any affected areas of any conditions found that may adversely affect safety or health and promptly initiate appropriate action to correct such conditions.

(2) Conditions noted by the person conducting the examination that may present an imminent danger shall be brought to the immediate attention of the operator who shall withdraw all persons from the area affected (except persons referred to in section 104(c) of the Federal Mine Safety and Health Act of 1977) until the danger is abated.

(b) A record of each examination shall be made before the end of the shift for which the examination was conducted. The record shall contain the name of the person conducting the examination; date of the examination;

location of all areas examined; and description of each condition found that may adversely affect the safety or health of miners.

(c) When a condition that may adversely affect safety or health is corrected, the examination record shall include, or be supplemented to include, the date of the corrective action.

(d) The operator shall maintain the examination records for at least one year, make the records available for inspection by authorized representatives of the Secretary and the representatives of miners, and provide these representatives a copy on request.

[84 FR 51401, Sept. 30, 2019]

§ 56.18006 New employees.

New employees shall be indoctrinated in safety rules and safe work procedures.

§ 56.18009 Designation of person in charge.

When persons are working at the mine, a competent person designated by the mine operator shall be in attendance to take charge in case of an emergency.

§ 56.18010 First aid.

An individual capable of providing first aid shall be available on all shifts. The individual shall be currently trained and have the skills to perform patient assessment and artificial respiration; control bleeding; and treat shock, wounds, burns, and musculoskeletal injuries. First aid training shall be made available to all interested miners.

[61 FR 50436, Sept. 26, 1996]

§ 56.18012 Emergency telephone numbers.

Emergency telephone numbers shall be posted at appropriate telephones.

§ 56.18013 Emergency communications system.

A suitable communication system shall be provided at the mine to obtain assistance in the event of an emergency.

§ 56.18014 Emergency medical assistance and transportation.

Arrangements shall be made in advance for obtaining emergency medical assistance and transportation for injured persons.

§ 56.18020 Working alone.

No employee shall be assigned, or allowed, or be required to perform work alone in any area where hazardous conditions exist that would endanger his safety unless he can communicate with others, can be heard, or can be seen.

Subpart R—Personnel Hoisting

§ 56.19000 Application.

(a) The hoisting standards in this subpart apply to those hoists and appurtenances used for hoisting persons. However, where persons may be endangered by hoists and appurtenances used solely for handling ore, rock, and materials, the appropriate standards should be applied.

(b) Standards 56.19021 through 56.19028 apply to wire ropes in service used to hoist persons with an incline hoist on the surface.

(c) Emergency hoisting facilities should conform to the extent possible to safety requirements for other hoists, and should be adequate to remove the persons from the mine with a minimum of delay.

HOISTS

§ 56.19001 Rated capacities.

Hoists shall have rated capacities consistent with the loads handled and the recommended safety factors of the ropes used.

§ 56.19002 Anchoring.

Hoists shall be anchored securely.

§ 56.19003 Driving mechanism connections.

Belt, rope, or chains shall not be used to connect driving mechanisms to man hoists.

§ 56.19004 Brakes.

Any hoist used to hoist persons shall be equipped with a brake or brakes which shall be capable of holding its

§ 56.19005

fully loaded cage, skip, or bucket at any point in the shaft.

§ 56.19005 Locking mechanism for clutch.

The operating mechanism of the clutch of every man-hoist drum shall be provided with a locking mechanism, or interlocked electrically or mechanically with the brake to prevent accidental withdrawal of the clutch.

§ 56.19006 Automatic hoist braking devices.

Automatic hoists shall be provided with devices that automatically apply the brakes in the event of power failure.

§ 56.19007 Overtravel and overspeed devices.

All man hoists shall be provided with devices to prevent overtravel. When utilized in shafts exceeding 100 feet in depth, such hoists shall also be provided with overspeed devices.

§ 56.19008 Friction hoist synchronizing mechanisms.

Where creep or slip may alter the effective position of safety devices, friction hoists shall be equipped with synchronizing mechanisms that recalibrate the overtravel devices and position indicators.

§ 56.19009 Position indicator.

An accurate and reliable indicator of the position of the cage, skip, bucket, or cars in the shaft shall be provided.

§ 56.19010 Location of hoist controls.

Hoist controls shall be placed or housed so that the noise from machinery or other sources will not prevent hoistmen from hearing signals.

§ 56.19011 Drum flanges.

Flanges on drums shall extend radially a minimum of 4 inches or three rope diameters beyond the last wrap, whichever is the lesser.

§ 56.19012 Grooved drums.

Where grooved drums are used, the grooves shall be of suitable size and pitch for the ropes used.

§ 56.19013 Diesel- and other fuel-injection-powered hoists.

Where any diesel or similar fuel-injection engine is used to power a hoist, the engine shall be equipped with a damper or other cutoff in its air intake system. The control handle shall be clearly labeled to indicate that its intended function is for emergency stopping only.

§ 56.19014 Friction hoist overtravel protection.

In a friction hoist installation, tapered guides or other approved devices shall be installed above and below the limits of regular travel of the conveyance and arranged to prevent overtravel in the event of failure of other devices.

§ 56.19017 Emergency braking for electric hoists.

Each electric hoist shall be equipped with a manually-operable switch that will initiate emergency braking action to bring the conveyance and the counterbalance safely to rest. This switch shall be located within reach of the hoistman in case the manual controls of the hoist fail.

§ 56.19018 Overtravel by-pass switches.

When an overtravel by-pass switch is installed, the switch shall function so as to allow the conveyance to be moved through the overtravel position when the switch is held in the closed position by the hoistman. The overtravel by-pass switch shall return automatically to the open position when released by the hoistman.

[50 FR 4054, Jan. 29, 1985; 50 FR 20100, May 14, 1985]

WIRE ROPES

AUTHORITY: Sec. 101, Federal Mine Safety and Health Act of 1977, Pub. L. 91–173 as amended by Pub. L. 95–164, 91 Stat. 1291 (30 U.S.C. 811).

§ 56.19021 Minimum rope strength.

At installation, the nominal strength (manufacturer's published catalog strength) of wire ropes used for hoisting shall meet the minimum rope strength values obtained by the following formulas in which "L" equals the maximum suspended rope length in feet:

(a) *Winding drum ropes* (all constructions, including rotation resistant).

For rope lengths less than 3,000 feet:
Minimum Value = Static Load × (7.0−0.001L)
For rope lengths 3,000 feet or greater:
Minimum Value = Static Load × 4.0

(b) *Friction drum ropes.*

For rope lengths less than 4,000 feet:
Minimum Value = Static Load × (7.0−0.0005L)
For rope lengths 4,000 feet or greater:
Minimum Value = Static Load × 5.0

(c) *Tail ropes* (balance ropes).
Minimum Value = Weight of Rope × 7.0

§ 56.19022 Initial measurement.

After initial rope stretch but before visible wear occurs, the rope diameter of newly installed wire ropes shall be measured at least once in every third interval of active length and the measurements averaged to establish a baseline for subsequent measurements. A record of the measurements and the date shall be made by the person taking the measurements. This record shall be retained until the rope is retired from service.

[50 FR 4054, Jan. 29, 1985, as amended at 60 FR 33723, June 29, 1995]

§ 56.19023 Examinations.

(a) At least once every fourteen calendar days, each wire rope in service shall be visually examined along its entire active length for visible structural damage, corrosion, and improper lubrication or dressing. In addition, visual examination for wear and broken wires shall be made at stress points, including the area near attachments, where the rope rests on sheaves, where the rope leaves the drum, at drum crossovers, and at change-of-layer regions. When any visible condition that results in a reduction of rope strength is present, the affected portion of the rope shall be examined on a daily basis.

(b) Before any person is hoisted with a newly installed wire rope or any wire rope that has not been examined in the previous fourteen calendar days, the wire rope shall be examined in accordance with paragraph (a) of this section.

(c) At least once every six months, nondestructive tests shall be conducted of the active length of the rope, or rope diameter measurements shall be made—

(1) Wherever wear is evident;

(2) Where the hoist rope rests on sheaves at regular stopping points;

(3) Where the hoist rope leaves the drum at regular stopping points; and

(4) At drum crossover and change-of-layer regions.

(d) At the completion of each examination required by paragraph (a) of this section, the person making the examination shall certify, by signature and date, that the examination has been made. If any condition listed in paragraph (a) of this section is present, the person conducting the examination shall make a record of the condition and the date. Certifications and records of examinations shall be retained for one year.

(e) The person making the measurements or nondestructive tests as required by paragraph (c) of this section shall record the measurements or test results and the date. This record shall be retained until the rope is retired from service.

[50 FR 4054, Jan. 29, 1985, as amended at 60 FR 33723, June 29, 1995]

§ 56.19024 Retirement criteria.

Unless damage or deterioration is removed by cutoff, wire ropes shall be removed from service when any of the following conditions occurs:

(a) The number of broken wires within a rope lay length, excluding filler wires, exceeds either—

(1) Five percent of the total number of wires; or

(2) Fifteen percent of the total number of wires within any strand.

(b) On a regular lay rope, more than one broken wire in the valley between strands in one rope lay length.

(c) A loss of more than one-third of the original diameter of the outer wires.

(d) Rope deterioration from corrosion.

(e) Distortion of the rope structure.

(f) Heat damage from any source.

(g) Diameter reduction due to wear that exceeds six percent of the baseline diameter measurement.

§ 56.19025

(h) Loss of more than ten percent of rope strength as determined by nondestructive testing.

§ 56.19025 Load end attachments.

(a) Wire rope shall be attached to the load by a method that develops at least 80 percent of the nominal strength of the rope.

(b) Except for terminations where use of other materials is a design feature, zinc (spelter) shall be used for socketing wire ropes. Design feature means either the manufacturer's original design or a design approved by a registered professional engineer.

(c) Load end attachment methods using splices are prohibited.

§ 56.19026 Drum end attachment.

(a) For drum end attachment, wire rope shall be attached—

(1) Securely by clips after making one full turn around the drum spoke;

(2) Securely by clips after making one full turn around the shaft, if the drum is fixed to the shaft; or

(3) By properly assembled anchor bolts, clamps, or wedges, provided that the attachment is a design feature of the hoist drum. Design feature means either the manufacturer's original design or a design approved by a registered professional engineer.

(b) A minimum of three full turns of wire rope shall be on the drum when the rope is extended to its maximum working length.

§ 56.19027 End attachment retermination.

Damaged or deteriorated wire rope shall be removed by cutoff and the rope reterminated where there is—

(a) More than one broken wire at an attachment;

(b) Improper installation of an attachment;

(c) Slippage at an attachment; or

(d) Evidence of deterioration from corrosion at an attachment.

§ 56.19028 End attachment replacement.

Wire rope attachments shall be replaced when cracked, deformed, or excessively worn.

§ 56.19030 Safety device attachments.

Safety device attachments to hoist ropes shall be selected, installed, and maintained according to manufacturers' specifications to minimize internal corrosion and weakening of the hoist rope.

HEADFRAMES AND SHEAVES

§ 56.19035 Headframe design.

All headframes shall be constructed with suitable design considerations to allow for all dead loads, live loads, and wind loads.

§ 56.19036 Headframe height.

Headframes shall be high enough to provide clearance for overtravel and safe stopping of the conveyance.

§ 56.19037 Fleet angles.

Fleet angles on hoists installed after November 15, 1979, shall not be greater than one and one-half degrees for smooth drums or two degrees for grooved drums.

§ 56.19038 Platforms around elevated head sheaves.

Platforms with toeboards and handrails shall be provided around elevated head sheaves.

CONVEYANCES

§ 56.19045 Metal bonnets.

Man cages and skips used for hoisting or lowering employees or other persons in any vertical shaft or any inclineshaft with an angle of inclination of forty-five degrees from the horizontal, shall be covered with a metal bonnet.

§ 56.19049 Hoisting persons in buckets.

Buckets shall not be used to hoist persons except during shaft sinking operations, inspection, maintenance, and repairs.

§ 56.19050 Bucket requirements.

Buckets used to hoist persons during vertical shaft sinking operations shall—

(a) Be securely attached to a crosshead when traveling in either direction between the lower and upper crosshead parking locations;

(b) Have overhead protection when the shaft depth exceeds 50 feet;
(c) Have sufficient depth or a suitably designed platform to transport persons safely in a standing position; and
(d) Have devices to prevent accidental dumping where the bucket is supported by a bail attached to its lower half.

§ 56.19054 Rope guides.

Where rope guides are used in shafts other than in shaft sinking operations, the rope guides shall be a type of lock coil construction.

HOISTING PROCEDURES

§ 56.19055 Availability of hoist operator for manual hoists.

When a manually operated hoist is used, a qualified hoistman shall remain within hearing of the telephone or signal device at all times while any person is underground.

§ 56.19056 Availability of hoist operator for automatic hoists.

When automatic hoisting is used, a competent operator of the hoist shall be readily available at or near the hoisting device while any person is underground.

§ 56.19057 Hoist operator's physical fitness.

No person shall operate a hoist unless within the preceding 12 months he has had a medical examination by a qualified, licensed physician who shall certify his fitness to perform this duty. Such certification shall be available at the mine.

§ 56.19058 Experienced hoist operators.

Only experienced hoistmen shall operate the hoist except in cases of emergency and in the training of new hoistmen.

§ 56.19061 Maximum hoisting speeds.

The safe speed for hoisting persons shall be determined for each shaft, and this speed shall not be exceeded. Persons should not be hoisted at a speed faster than 2,500 feet per minute, except in an emergency.

§ 56.19062 Maximum acceleration and deceleration.

Maximum normal operating acceleration and deceleration shall not exceed 6 feet per second per second. During emergency braking, the deceleration shall not exceed 16 feet per second per second.

§ 56.19063 Persons allowed in hoist room.

Only authorized persons shall be in hoist rooms.

§ 56.19065 Lowering conveyances by the brakes.

Conveyances shall not be lowered by the brakes alone except during emergencies.

§ 56.19066 Maximum riders in a conveyance.

In shafts inclined over 45 degrees, the operator shall determine and post in the conveyance or at each shaft station the maximum number of persons permitted to ride in a hoisting conveyance at any one time. Each person shall be provided a minimum of 1.5 square feet of floor space.

§ 56.19067 Trips during shift changes.

During shift changes, an authorized person shall be in charge of each trip in which persons are hoisted.

§ 56.19068 Orderly conduct in conveyances.

Persons shall enter, ride, and leave conveyances in an orderly manner.

§ 56.19069 Entering and leaving conveyances.

Persons shall not enter or leave conveyances which are in motion or after a signal to move the conveyance has been given to the hoistman.

§ 56.19070 Closing cage doors or gates.

Cage doors or gates shall be closed while persons are being hoisted; they shall not be opened until the cage has come to a stop.

§ 56.19071 Riding in skips or buckets.

Persons shall not ride in skips or buckets with muck, supplies, materials, or tools other than small hand tools.

§ 56.19072 Skips and cages in same compartment.

When combinations of cages and skips are used in the same compartment, the cages shall be enclosed to protect personnel from flying material and the hoist speed reduced to manspeed as defined in standard 56.19061, but not to exceed 1,000 feet per minute. Muck shall not be hoisted with personnel during shift changes.

§ 56.19073 Hoisting during shift changes.

Rock or supplies shall not be hoisted in the same shaft as persons during shift changes, unless the compartments and dumping bins are partitioned to prevent spillage into the cage compartment.

§ 56.19074 Riding the bail, rim, bonnet, or crosshead.

Persons shall not ride the bail, rim, bonnet, or crosshead of any shaft conveyance except when necessary for inspection and maintenance, and then only when suitable protection for persons is provided.

§ 56.19075 Use of open hooks.

Open hooks shall not be used to hoist buckets or other conveyances.

§ 56.19076 Maximum speeds for hoisting persons in buckets.

When persons are hoisted in buckets, speeds shall not exceed 500 feet per minute and shall not exceed 200 feet per minute when within 100 feet of the intended station.

§ 56.19077 Lowering buckets.

Buckets shall be stopped about 15 feet from the shaft bottom to await a signal from one of the crew on the bottom for further lowering.

§ 56.19078 Hoisting buckets from the shaft bottom.

All buckets shall be stopped after being raised about 3 feet above the shaft bottom. A bucket shall be stabilized before a hoisting signal is given to continue hoisting the bucket to the crosshead. After a hoisting signal is given, hoisting to the crosshead shall be at a minimum speed. The signaling device shall be attended constantly until a bucket reaches the guides. When persons are hoisted, the signaling devices shall be attended until the crosshead has been engaged.

§ 56.19079 Blocking mine cars.

Where mine cars are hoisted by cage or skip, means for blocking cars shall be provided at all landings and also on the cage.

§ 56.19080 Hoisting tools, timbers, and other materials.

When tools, timbers, or other materials are being lowered or raised in a shaft by means of a bucket, skip, or cage, they shall be secured or so placed that they will not strike the sides of the shaft.

§ 56.19081 Conveyances not in use.

When conveyances controlled by a hoist operator are not in use, they shall be released and the conveyances shall be raised or lowered a suitable distance to prevent persons from boarding or loading the conveyances.

§ 56.19083 Overtravel backout device.

A manually operated device shall be installed on each electric hoist that will allow the conveyance or counterbalance to be removed from an overtravel position. Such device shall not release the brake, or brakes, holding the overtravelled conveyance or counterbalance until sufficient drive motor torque has been developed to assure movement of the conveyance or counterbalance in the correct direction only.

SIGNALING

§ 56.19090 Dual signaling systems.

There shall be at least two effective approved methods of signaling between each of the shaft stations and the hoist room, one of which shall be a telephone or speaking tube.

§ 56.19091 Signaling instructions to hoist operator.

Hoist operators shall accept hoisting instructions only by the regular signaling system unless it is out of order. In such an event, and during other emergencies, the hoist operator shall accept instructions to direct movement of the conveyances only from authorized persons.

§ 56.19092 **Signaling from conveyances.**

A method shall be provided to signal the hoist operator from cages or other conveyances at any point in the shaft.

§ 56.19093 **Standard signal code.**

A standard code of hoisting signals shall be adopted and used at each mine. The movement of a shaft conveyance on a "one bell" signal is prohibited.

§ 56.19094 **Posting signal code.**

A legible signal code shall be posted prominently in the hoist house within easy view of the hoistman, and at each place where signals are given or received.

§ 56.19095 **Location of signal devices.**

Hoisting signal devices shall be positioned within easy reach of persons on the shaft bottom or constantly attended by a person stationed on the lower deck of the sinking platform.

§ 56.19096 **Familiarity with signal code.**

Any person responsible for receiving or giving signals for cages, skips, and mantrips when persons or materials are being transported shall be familiar with the posted signaling code.

SHAFTS

§ 56.19100 **Shaft landing gates.**

Shaft landings shall be equipped with substantial safety gates so constructed that materials will not go through or under them; gates shall be closed except when loading or unloading shaft conveyances.

§ 56.19101 **Stopblocks and derail switches.**

Positive stopblocks or a derail switch shall be installed on all tracks leading to a shaft collar or landing.

§ 56.19102 **Shaft guides.**

A means shall be provided to guide the movement of a shaft conveyance.

§ 56.19103 **Dumping facilities and loading pockets.**

Dumping facilities and loading pockets shall be constructed so as to minimize spillage into the shaft.

§ 56.19104 **Clearance at shaft stations.**

Suitable clearance at shaft stations shall be provided to allow safe movement of persons, equipment, and materials.

§ 56.19105 **Landings with more than one shaft entrance.**

A safe means of passage around open shaft compartments shall be provided on landings with more than one entrance to the shaft.

§ 56.19106 **Shaft sets.**

Shaft sets shall be kept in good repair and clean of hazardous material.

§ 56.19107 **Precautions for work in compartment affected by hoisting operation.**

Hoistmen shall be informed when persons are working in a compartment affected by that hoisting operation and a "Men Working in Shaft" sign shall be posted at the hoist.

§ 56.19108 **Posting warning signs during shaft work.**

When persons are working in a shaft "Men Working in Shaft" signs shall be posted at all devices controlling hoisting operations that may endanger such persons.

§ 56.19109 **Shaft inspection and repair.**

Shaft inspection and repair work in vertical shafts shall be performed from substantial platforms equipped with bonnets or equivalent overhead protection.

§ 56.19110 **Overhead protection for shaft deepening work.**

A substantial bulkhead or equivalent protection shall be provided above persons at work deepening a shaft.

§ 56.19111 **Shaft-sinking ladders.**

Substantial fixed ladders shall be provided from the collar to as near the shaft bottom as practical during shaft-sinking operations, or an escape hoist powered by an emergency power source shall be provided. When persons are on the shaft bottom, a chain ladder, wire rope ladder, or other extension ladders shall be used from the fixed ladder or lower limit of the escape hoist to the shaft bottom.

INSPECTION AND MAINTENANCE

§ 56.19120 Procedures for inspection, testing, and maintenance.

A systematic procedure of inspection, testing, and maintenance of shafts and hoisting equipment shall be developed and followed. If it is found or suspected that any part is not functioning properly, the hoist shall not be used until the malfunction has been located and repaired or adjustments have been made.

§ 56.19121 Recordkeeping.

At the time of completion, the person performing inspections, tests, and maintenance of hoisting equipment required in standard 56.19120 shall certify, by signature and date, that they have been done. A record of any part that is not functioning properly shall be made and dated. Certifications and records shall be retained for one year.

(Sec. 101, Pub. L. 91-173 as amended by Pub. L. 95-164, 91 Stat. 1291 (30 U.S.C. 811))

[50 FR 4054, Jan. 29, 1985, as amended at 60 FR 33723, June 29, 1995]

§ 56.19122 Replacement parts.

Parts used to repair hoists shall have properties that will ensure the proper and safe function of the hoist.

§ 56.19129 Examinations and tests at beginning of shift.

Hoistmen shall examine their hoists and shall test overtravel, deadman controls, position indicators, and braking mechanisms at the beginning of each shift.

§ 56.19130 Conveyance shaft test.

Before hoisting persons and to assure that the hoisting compartments are clear of obstructions, empty hoist conveyances shall be operated at least one round trip after:

(a) Any hoist or shaft repairs or related equipment repairs that might restrict or obstruct conveyance clearance;

(b) Any oversize or overweight material or equipment trips that might restrict or obstruct conveyance clearance;

(c) Blasting in or near the shaft that might restrict or obstruct conveyance clearance; or

(d) Remaining idle for one shift or longer.

§ 56.19131 Hoist conveyance connections.

Hoist conveyance connections shall be inspected at least once during any 24-hour period that the conveyance is used for hoisting persons.

§ 56.19132 Safety catches.

(a) A performance drop test of hoist conveyance safety catches shall be made at the time of installation, or prior to installation, in a mockup of the actual installation. The test shall be certified to in writing by the manufacturer or by a registered professional engineer performing the test.

(b) After installation and before use, and at the beginning of any seven day period during which the conveyance is to be used, the conveyance shall be suitably rested and the hoist rope slackened to test for the unrestricted functioning of the safety catches and their activating mechanisms.

(c) The safety catches shall be inspected by a competent person at the beginning of any 24-hour period that the conveyance is to be used.

§ 56.19133 Shaft.

Shafts that have not been inspected within the past 7 days shall not be used until an inspection has been conducted by a competent person.

§ 56.19134 Sheaves.

Sheaves in operating shafts shall be inspected weekly and kept properly lubricated.

§ 56.19135 Rollers in inclined shafts.

Rollers used in operating inclined shafts shall be lubricated, properly aligned, and kept in good repair.

Subpart S—Miscellaneous

§ 56.20001 Intoxicating beverages and narcotics.

Intoxicating beverages and narcotics shall not be permitted or used in or around mines. Persons under the influence of alcohol or narcotics shall not be permitted on the job.

§ 56.20002 Potable water.

(a) An adequate supply of potable drinking water shall be provided at all active working areas.

(b) The common drinking cup and containers from which drinking water must be dipped or poured are prohibited.

(c) Where single service cups are supplied, a sanitary container for unused cups and a receptacle for used cups shall be provided.

(d) When water is cooled by ice, the ice shall either be of potable water or shall not come in contact with the water.

(e) Potable water outlets shall be posted.

(f) Potable water systems shall be constructed to prevent backflow or backsiphonage of non-potable water.

§ 56.20003 Housekeeping.

At all mining operations—

(a) Workplaces, passageways, storerooms, and service rooms shall be kept clean and orderly;

(b) The floor of every workplace shall be maintained in a clean and, so far as possible, dry condition. Where wet processes are used, drainage shall be maintained, and false floors, platforms, mats, or other dry standing places shall be provided where practicable; and

(c) Every floor, working place, and passageway shall be kept free from protruding nails, splinters, holes, or loose boards, as practicable.

§ 56.20005 Carbon tetrachloride.

Carbon tetrachloride shall not be used.

§ 56.20008 Toilet facilities.

(a) Toilet facilities shall be provided at locations that are compatible with the mine operations and that are readily accessible to mine personnel.

(b) The facilities shall be kept clean and sanitary. Separate toilet facilities shall be provided for each sex except where toilet rooms will be occupied by no more than one person at a time and can be locked from the inside.

§ 56.20009 Tests for explosive dusts.

Dusts suspected of being explosive shall be tested for explosibility. If tests prove positive, appropriate control measures shall be taken.

§ 56.20010 Retaining dams.

If failure of a water or silt retaining dam will create a hazard, it shall be of substantial construction and inspected at regular intervals.

§ 56.20011 Barricades and warning signs.

Areas where health or safety hazards exist that are not immediately obvious to employees shall be barricaded, or warning signs shall be posted at all approaches. Warning signs shall be readily visible, legible, and display the nature of the hazard and any protective action required.

§ 56.20013 Waste receptacles.

Receptacles with covers shall be provided at suitable locations and used for the disposal of waste food and associated materials. They shall be emptied frequently and shall be maintained in a clean and sanitary condition.

§ 56.20014 Prohibited areas for food and beverages.

No person shall be allowed to consume or store food or beverages in a toilet room or in any area exposed to a toxic material.

PART 57—SAFETY AND HEALTH STANDARDS—UNDERGROUND METAL AND NONMETAL MINES

Subpart A—General

Sec.
57.1 Purpose and scope.
57.2 Definitions.

PROCEDURES

57.1000 Notification of commencement of operations and closing of mines.

Subpart B—Ground Control

57.3000 Definitions.

SCALING AND SUPPORT—SURFACE AND UNDERGROUND

57.3200 Correction of hazardous conditions.
57.3201 Location for performing scaling.
57.3202 Scaling tools.
57.3203 Rock fixtures.

SCALING AND SUPPORT—UNDERGROUND ONLY

57.3360 Ground support use.

PRECAUTIONS—SURFACE AND UNDERGROUND

57.3400 Secondary breakage.
57.3401 Examination of ground conditions.

PRECAUTIONS—SURFACE ONLY

57.3430 Activity between machinery or equipment and the highwall or bank.

PRECAUTIONS—UNDERGROUND ONLY

57.3460 Maintenance between machinery or equipment and ribs.
57.3461 Rock bursts.

Subpart C—Fire Prevention and Control

57.4000 Definitions.
57.4011 Abandoned electric circuits.
57.4057 Underground trailing cables.

PROHIBITIONS/PRECAUTIONS/HOUSEKEEPING

57.4100 Smoking and use of open flames.
57.4101 Warning signs.
57.4102 Spillage and leakage.
57.4103 Fueling internal combustion engines.
57.4104 Combustible waste.
57.4130 Surface electric substations and liquid storage facilities.
57.4131 Surface fan installations and mine openings.
57.4160 Underground electric substations and liquid storage facilities.
57.4161 Use of fire underground.

FIREFIGHTING EQUIPMENT

57.4200 General requirements.
57.4201 Inspection.
57.4202 Fire hydrants.
57.4203 Extinguisher recharging or replacement.
57.4230 Surface self-propelled equipment.
57.4260 Underground self-propelled equipment.
57.4261 Shaft-station waterlines.
57.4262 Underground transformer stations, combustible liquid storage and dispensing areas, pump rooms, compressor rooms, and hoist rooms.
57.4263 Underground belt conveyors.

FIREFIGHTING PROCEDURES/ALARMS/DRILLS

57.4330 Surface firefighting, evacuation, and rescue procedures.
57.4331 Surface firefighting drills.
57.4360 Underground alarm systems.
57.4361 Underground evacuation drills.
57.4362 Underground rescue and firefighting operations.
57.4363 Underground evacuation instruction.

FLAMMABLE AND COMBUSTIBLE LIQUIDS AND GASES

57.4400 Use restrictions.
57.4401 Storage tank foundations.
57.4402 Safety can use.
57.4430 Surface storage facilities.
57.4431 Surface storage restrictions.
57.4460 Storage of flammable liquids underground.
57.4461 Gasoline use restrictions underground.
57.4462 Storage of combustible liquids underground.
57.4463 Liquefied petroleum gas use underground.

INSTALLATION/CONSTRUCTION/MAINTENANCE

57.4500 Heat sources.
57.4501 Fuel lines.
57.4502 Battery-charging stations.
57.4503 Conveyor belt slippage.
57.4504 Fan installations.
57.4505 Fuel lines to underground areas.
57.4530 Exits for surface buildings and structures.
57.4531 Surface flammable or combustible liquid storage buildings or rooms.
57.4532 Blacksmith shops.
57.4533 Mine opening vicinity.
57.4560 Mine entrances.
57.4561 Stationary diesel equipment underground.

WELDING/CUTTING/COMPRESSED GASES

57.4600 Extinguishing equipment.
57.4601 Oxygen cylinder storage.
57.4602 Gauges and regulators.
57.4603 Closure of valves.
57.4604 Preparation of pipelines or containers.
57.4660 Work in shafts, raises, or winzes and other activities involving hazard areas.

VENTILATION CONTROL MEASURES

57.4760 Shaft mines.
57.4761 Underground shops.

APPENDIX I TO SUBPART C OF PART 57—NATIONAL CONSENSUS STANDARDS

Subpart D—Air Quality, Radiation, Physical Agents, and Diesel Particulate Matter

AIR QUALITY—SURFACE AND UNDERGROUND

57.5001 Exposure limits for airborne contaminants.

Mine Safety and Health Admin., Labor — Pt. 57

57.5002 Exposure monitoring.
57.5005 Control of exposure to airborne contaminants.
57.5006 Restricted use of chemicals.

AIR QUALITY—SURFACE ONLY [RESERVED]

AIR QUALITY—UNDERGROUND ONLY

57.5015 Oxygen deficiency.

RADIATION—UNDERGROUND ONLY

57.5037 Radon daughter exposure monitoring.
57.5038 Annual exposure limits.
57.5039 Maximum permissible concentration.
57.5040 Exposure records.
57.5041 Smoking prohibition.
57.5042 Revised exposure levels.
57.5044 Respirators.
57.5045 Posting of inactive workings.
57.5046 Protection against radon gas.
57.5047 Gamma radiation surveys.

DIESEL PARTICULATE MATTER—UNDERGROUND ONLY

57.5060 Limit on exposure to diesel particulate matter.
57.5061 Compliance determinations.
57.5065 Fueling practices.
57.5066 Maintenance standards.
57.5067 Engines.
57.5070 Miner training.
57.5071 Exposure monitoring.
57.5075 Diesel particulate records.

Subpart E—Explosives

57.6000 Definitions.

STORAGE—SURFACE AND UNDERGROUND

57.6100 Separation of stored explosive material.
57.6101 Areas around explosive material storage facilities.
57.6102 Explosive material storage practices.

STORAGE—SURFACE ONLY

57.6130 Explosive material storage facilities.
57.6131 Location of explosive material storage facilities.
57.6132 Magazine requirements.
57.6133 Powder chests.

STORAGE—UNDERGROUND ONLY

57.6160 Main facilities.
57.6161 Auxiliary facilities.

TRANSPORTATION—SURFACE AND UNDERGROUND

57.6200 Delivery to storage or blast site areas.
57.6201 Separation of transported explosive material.
57.6202 Vehicles.
57.6203 Locomotives.
57.6204 Hoists.
57.6205 Conveying explosives by hand.

USE—SURFACE AND UNDERGROUND

57.6300 Control of blasting operations.
57.6301 Blasthole obstruction check.
57.6302 Separation of explosive material.
57.6303 Initiation preparation.
57.6304 Primer protection.
57.6305 Unused explosive material.
57.6306 Loading, blasting, and security.
57.6307 Drill stem loading.
57.6308 Initiation systems.
57.6309 Fuel oil requirements for ANFO.
57.6310 Misfire waiting period.
57.6311 Handling of misfires.
57.6312 Secondary blasting.

ELECTRIC BLASTING—SURFACE AND UNDERGROUND

57.6400 Compatibility of electric detonators.
57.6401 Shunting.
57.6402 Deenergized circuits near detonators.
57.6403 Branch circuits.
57.6404 Separation of blasting circuits from power source.
57.6405 Firing devices.
57.6406 Duration of current flow.
57.6407 Circuit testing.

NONELECTRIC BLASTING—SURFACE AND UNDERGROUND

57.6500 Damaged initiating material.
57.6501 Nonelectric initiation systems.
57.6502 Safety fuse.

EXTRANEOUS ELECTRICITY—SURFACE AND UNDERGROUND

57.6600 Loading practices.
57.6601 Grounding.
57.6602 Static electricity dissipation during loading.
57.6603 Air gap.
57.6604 Precautions during storms.
57.6605 Isolation of blasting circuits.

EQUIPMENT/TOOLS—SURFACE AND UNDERGROUND

57.6700 Nonsparking tools.
57.6701 Tamping and loading pole requirements.

MAINTENANCE—SURFACE AND UNDERGROUND

57.6800 Storage facilities.
57.6801 Vehicle repair.
57.6802 Bulk delivery vehicles.
57.6803 Blasting lines.

GENERAL REQUIREMENTS—SURFACE AND UNDERGROUND

57.6900 Damaged or deteriorated explosive material.
57.6901 Black powder.

57.6902 Excessive temperatures.
57.6903 Burning explosive material.
57.6904 Smoking and open flames.
57.6905 Protection of explosive material.

GENERAL REQUIREMENTS—UNDERGROUND ONLY

57.6960 Mixing of explosive material.

Subpart F—Drilling and Rotary Jet Piercing

DRILLING—SURFACE ONLY

57.7002 Equipment defects.
57.7003 Drill area inspection.
57.7004 Drill mast.
57.7005 Augers and drill stems.
57.7008 Moving the drill.
57.7009 Drill helpers.
57.7010 Power failures.
57.7011 Straightening crossed cables.
57.7012 Tending drills in operation.
57.7013 Covering or guarding drill holes.
57.7018 Hand clearance.

DRILLING—UNDERGROUND ONLY

57.7028 Hand clearance.
57.7032 Anchoring.

DRILLING—SURFACE AND UNDERGROUND

57.7050 Tool and drill steel racks.
57.7051 Loose objects on the mast or drill platform.
57.7052 Drilling positions.
57.7053 Moving hand-held drills.
57.7054 Starting or moving drill equipment.
57.7055 Intersecting holes.
57.7056 Collaring in bootlegs.

ROTARY JET PIERCING—SURFACE ONLY

57.7801 Jet drills.
57.7802 Oxygen hose lines.
57.7803 Lighting the burner.
57.7804 Refueling.
57.7805 Smoking and open flames.
57.7806 Oxygen intake coupling.
57.7807 Flushing the combustion chamber.

Subpart G—Ventilation

SURFACE AND UNDERGROUND

57.8518 Main and booster fans.
57.8519 Underground main fan controls.

UNDERGROUND ONLY

57.8520 Ventilation plan.
57.8525 Main fan maintenance.
57.8527 Oxygen-deficiency testing.
57.8528 Unventilated areas.
57.8529 Auxiliary fan systems.
57.8531 Construction and maintenance of ventilation doors.
57.8532 Opening and closing ventilation doors.
57.8534 Shutdown or failure of auxiliary fans.

57.8535 Seals.

Subpart H—Loading, Hauling, and Dumping

TRAFFIC SAFETY

57.9100 Traffic control.
57.9101 Operating speeds and control of equipment.
57.9102 Movement of independently operating rail equipment.
57.9103 Clearance on adjacent tracks.
57.9104 Railroad crossings.
57.9160 Train movement during shift changes.

TRANSPORTATION OF PERSONS AND MATERIALS

57.9200 Transporting persons.
57.9201 Loading, hauling, and unloading of equipment or supplies.
57.9202 Loading and hauling large rocks.
57.9260 Supplies, materials, and tools on mantrips.
57.9261 Transporting tools and materials on locomotives.

SAFETY DEVICES, PROVISIONS, AND PROCEDURES FOR ROADWAYS, RAILROADS, AND LOADING AND DUMPING SITES

57.9300 Berms or guardrails.
57.9301 Dump site restraints.
57.9302 Protection against moving or runaway railroad equipment.
57.9303 Construction of ramps and dumping facilities.
57.9304 Unstable ground.
57.9305 Truck spotters.
57.9306 Warning devices for restricted clearances.
57.9307 Design, installation, and maintenance of railroads.
57.9308 Switch throws.
57.9309 Chute design.
57.9310 Chute hazards.
57.9311 Anchoring stationary sizing devices.
57.9312 Working around drawholes.
57.9313 Roadway maintenance.
57.9314 Trimming stockpile and muckpile faces.
57.9315 Dust control.
57.9316 Notifying the equipment operator.
57.9317 Suspended loads.
57.9318 Getting on or off moving equipment.
57.9319 Going over, under, or between railcars.
57.9330 Clearance for surface equipment.
57.9360 Shelter holes.
57.9361 Drawholes.
57.9362 Protection of signalmen.

Subpart I—Aerial Tramways

57.10001 Filling buckets.
57.10002 Inspection and maintenance.
57.10003 Correction of defects.
57.10004 Brakes.

Mine Safety and Health Admin., Labor

Pt. 57

57.10005	Track cable connections.
57.10006	Tower guards.
57.10007	Falling object protection.
57.10008	Riding tramways.
57.10009	Riding loaded buckets.
57.10010	Starting precautions.

Subpart J—Travelways and Escapeways

TRAVELWAYS—SURFACE AND UNDERGROUND

57.11001	Safe access.
57.11002	Handrails and toeboards.
57.11003	Construction and maintenance of ladders.
57.11004	Portable rigid ladders.
57.11005	Fixed ladder anchorage and toe clearance.
57.11006	Fixed ladder landings.
57.11007	Wooden components of ladders.
57.11008	Restricted clearance.
57.11009	Walkways along conveyors.
57.11010	Stairstep clearance.
57.11011	Use of ladders.
57.11012	Protection for openings around travelways.
57.11013	Conveyor crossovers.
57.11014	Crossing moving conveyors.
57.11016	Snow and ice on walkways and travelways.
57.11017	Inclined fixed ladders.

TRAVELWAYS—SURFACE ONLY

57.11025	Railed landings, backguards, and other protection for fixed ladders.
57.11026	Protection for inclined fixed ladders.
57.11027	Scaffolds and working platforms.

TRAVELWAYS—UNDERGROUND ONLY

57.11036	Ladderway trap doors and guards.
57.11037	Ladderway openings.
57.11038	Entering a manway.
57.11040	Inclined travelways.
57.11041	Landings for inclined ladderways.

ESCAPEWAYS—UNDERGROUND ONLY

57.11050	Escapeways and refuges.
57.11051	Escape routes.
57.11052	Refuge areas.
57.11053	Escape and evacuation plans.
57.11054	Communication with refuge chambers.
57.11055	Inclined escapeways.
57.11056	Emergency hoists.
57.11058	Check-in, check-out system.
57.11059	Respirable atmosphere for hoist operators underground.

Subpart K—Electricity

SURFACE AND UNDERGROUND

57.12001	Circuit overload protection.
57.12002	Controls and switches.
57.12003	Trailing cable overload protection.
57.12004	Electrical conductors.
57.12005	Protection of power conductors from mobile equipment.
57.12006	Distribution boxes.
57.12007	Junction box connection procedures.
57.12008	Insulation and fittings for power wires and cables.
57.12010	Isolation or insulation of communication conductors.
57.12011	High-potential electrical conductors.
57.12012	Bare signal wires.
57.12013	Splices and repairs of power cables.
57.12014	Handling energized power cables.
57.12016	Work on electrically-powered equipment.
57.12017	Work on power circuits.
57.12018	Identification of power switches.
57.12019	Access to stationary electrical equipment or switchgear.
57.12020	Protection of persons at switchgear.
57.12021	Danger signs.
57.12022	Authorized persons at major electrical installations.
57.12023	Guarding electrical connections and resistor grids.
57.12025	Grounding circuit enclosures.
57.12026	Grounding transformer and switchgear enclosures.
57.12027	Grounding mobile equipment.
57.12028	Testing grounding systems.
57.12030	Correction of dangerous conditions.
57.12032	Inspection and cover plates.
57.12033	Hand-held electric tools.
57.12034	Guarding around lamps.
57.12035	Weatherproof lamp sockets.
57.12036	Fuse removal or replacement.
57.12037	Fuses in high-potential circuits.
57.12038	Attachment of trailing cables.
57.12039	Protection of surplus trailing cables.
57.12040	Installation of operating controls.
57.12041	Design of switches and starting boxes.
57.12042	Track bonding.
57.12045	Overhead powerlines.
57.12047	Guy wires.
57.12048	Communication conductors on power poles.
57.12050	Installation of trolley wires.
57.12053	Circuits powered from trolley wires.

SURFACE ONLY

57.12065	Short circuit and lightning protection.
57.12066	Guarding trolley wires and bare powerlines.
57.12067	Installation of transformers.
57.12068	Locking transformer enclosures.
57.12069	Lightning protection for telephone wires and ungrounded conductors.
57.12071	Movement or operation of equipment near high-voltage powerlines.

UNDERGROUND ONLY

57.12080	Bare conductor guards.

57.12081 Bonding metal pipelines to ground return circuits.
57.12082 Isolation of powerlines.
57.12083 Support of power cables in shafts and boreholes.
57.12084 Branch circuit disconnecting devices.
57.12085 Transformer stations.
57.12086 Location of trolley wire.
57.12088 Splicing trailing cables.

Subpart L—Compressed Air and Boilers

57.13001 General requirements for boilers and pressure vessels.
57.13010 Reciprocating-type air compressors.
57.13011 Air receiver tanks.
57.13012 Compressor air intakes.
57.13015 Inspection of compressed-air receivers and other unfired pressure vessels.
57.13017 Compressor discharge pipes.
57.13019 Pressure system repairs.
57.13020 Use of compressed air.
57.13021 High-pressure hose connections.
57.13030 Boilers.

Subpart M—Machinery and Equipment

57.14000 Definitions.

SAFETY DEVICES AND MAINTENANCE REQUIREMENTS

57.14100 Safety defects; examination, correction and records.
57.14101 Brakes.
57.14102 Brakes for rail equipment.
57.14103 Operators' stations.
57.14104 Tire repairs.
57.14105 Procedures during repairs or maintenance.
57.14106 Falling object protection.
57.14107 Moving machine parts.
57.14108 Overhead drive belts.
57.14109 Unguarded conveyors with adjacent travelways.
57.14110 Flying or falling materials.
57.14111 Slusher, backlash guards and securing.
57.14112 Construction and maintenance of guards.
57.14113 Inclined conveyors: backstops or brakes.
57.14114 Air valves for pneumatic equipment.
57.14115 Stationary grinding machines.
57.14116 Hand-held power tools.
57.14130 Roll-over protective structures (ROPS) and seat belts for surface equipment.
57.14131 Seat belts for surface haulage trucks.
57.14132 Horns and back-up alarms for surface equipment.
57.14160 Mantrip trolley wire hazards underground.
57.14161 Makeshift couplings.
57.14162 Trip lights.

SAFETY PRACTICES AND OPERATIONAL PROCEDURES

57.14200 Warnings prior to starting or moving equipment.
57.14201 Conveyor start-up warnings.
57.14202 Manual cleaning of conveyor pulleys.
57.14203 Application of belt dressing.
57.14204 Machinery lubrication.
57.14205 Machinery, equipment, and tools.
57.14206 Securing movable parts.
57.14207 Parking procedures for unattended equipment.
57.14208 Warning devices.
57.14209 Safety procedures for towing.
57.14210 Movement of dippers, buckets, loading booms, or suspended loads.
57.14211 Blocking equipment in a raised position.
57.14212 Chains, ropes, and drive belts.
57.14213 Ventilation and shielding for welding.
57.14214 Train warnings.
57.14215 Coupling or uncoupling cars.
57.14216 Backpoling.
57.14217 Securing parked railcars.
57.14218 Movement of equipment on adjacent tracks.
57.14219 Brakeman signals.

APPENDIX I TO SUBPART M OF PART 57—NATIONAL CONSENSUS STANDARDS

Subpart N—Personal Protection

SURFACE AND UNDERGROUND

57.15001 First aid materials.
57.15002 Hard hats.
57.15003 Protective footwear.
57.15004 Eye protection.
57.15005 Safety belts and lines.
57.15006 Protective equipment and clothing for hazards and irritants.
57.15007 Protective equipment or clothing for welding, cutting, or working with molten metal.
57.15014 Eye protection when operating grinding wheels.

SURFACE ONLY

57.15020 Life jackets and belts.

UNDERGROUND ONLY

57.15030 Provision and maintenance of self-rescue devices.
57.15031 Location of self-rescue devices.

Subpart O—Materials Storage and Handling

57.16001 Stacking and storage of materials.
57.16002 Bins, hoppers, silos, tanks, and surge piles.
57.16003 Storage of hazardous materials.
57.16004 Containers for hazardous materials.
57.16005 Securing gas cylinders.

Mine Safety and Health Admin., Labor

57.16006 Protection of gas cylinder valves.
57.16007 Taglines, hitches, and slings.
57.16009 Suspended loads.
57.16010 Dropping materials from overhead.
57.16011 Riding hoisted loads or on the hoist hook.
57.16012 Storage of incompatible substances.
57.16013 Working with molten metal.
57.16014 Operator-carrying overhead cranes.
57.16015 Work or travel on overhead crane bridges.
57.16016 Lift trucks.
57.16017 Hoisting heavy equipment or material.

Subpart P—Illumination

57.17001 Illumination of surface working areas.
57.17010 Electric lamps.

Subpart Q—Safety Programs

SURFACE AND UNDERGROUND

57.18002 Examination of working places.
57.18006 New employees.
57.18009 Designation of person in charge.
57.18010 First aid.
57.18012 Emergency telephone numbers.
57.18013 Emergency communications system.
57.18014 Emergency medical assistance and transportation.

SURFACE ONLY

57.18020 Working alone.

UNDERGROUND ONLY

57.18025 Working alone.
57.18028 Mine emergency and self-rescuer training

Subpart R—Personnel Hoisting

57.19000 Application.

HOISTS

57.19001 Rated capacities.
57.19002 Anchoring.
57.19003 Driving mechanism connections.
57.19004 Brakes.
57.19005 Locking mechanism for clutch.
57.19006 Automatic hoist braking devices.
57.19007 Overtravel and overspeed devices.
57.19008 Friction hoist synchronizing mechanisms.
57.19009 Position indicator.
57.19010 Location of hoist controls.
57.19011 Drum flanges.
57.19012 Grooved drums.
57.19013 Diesel-and other fuel-injection-powered hoists.
57.19014 Friction hoist overtravel protection.
57.19017 Emergency braking for electric hoists.

57.19018 Overtravel by-pass switches.

WIRE ROPES

57.19019 Guide ropes.
57.19021 Minimum rope strength.
57.19022 Initial measurement.
57.19023 Examinations.
57.19024 Retirement criteria.
57.19025 Load end attachments.
57.19026 Drum end attachment.
57.19027 End attachment retermination.
57.19028 End attachment replacement.
57.19030 Safety device attachments.

HEADFRAMES AND SHEAVES

57.19035 Headframe design.
57.19036 Headframe height.
57.19037 Fleet angles.
57.19038 Platforms around elevated head sheaves.

CONVEYANCES

57.19045 Metal bonnets.
57.19049 Hoisting persons in buckets.
57.19050 Bucket requirements.
57.19054 Rope guides.

HOISTING PROCEDURES

57.19055 Availability of hoist operator for manual hoists.
57.19056 Availability of hoist operator for automatic hoists.
57.19057 Hoist operator's physical fitness.
57.19058 Experienced hoist operators.
57.19061 Maximum hoisting speeds.
57.19062 Maximum acceleration and deceleration.
57.19063 Persons allowed in hoist room.
57.19065 Lowering conveyances by the brakes.
57.19066 Maximum riders in a conveyance.
57.19067 Trips during shift changes.
57.19068 Orderly conduct in conveyances.
57.19069 Entering and leaving conveyances.
57.19070 Closing cage doors or gates.
57.19071 Riding in skips or buckets.
57.19072 Skips and cages in same compartment.
57.19073 Hoisting during shift changes.
57.19074 Riding the bail, rim, bonnet, or crosshead.
57.19075 Use of open hooks.
57.19076 Maximum speeds for hoisting persons in buckets.
57.19077 Lowering buckets.
57.19078 Hoisting buckets from the shaft bottom.
57.19079 Blocking mine cars.
57.19080 Hoisting tools, timbers, and other materials.
57.19081 Conveyances not in use.
57.19083 Overtravel backout device.

SIGNALING

57.19090 Dual signaling systems.

347

57.19091 Signaling instructions to hoist operator.
57.19092 Signaling from conveyances.
57.19093 Standard signal code.
57.19094 Posting signal code.
57.19095 Location of signal devices.
57.19096 Familiarity with signal code.

SHAFTS

57.19100 Shaft landing gates.
57.19101 Stopblocks and derail switches.
57.19102 Shaft guides.
57.19103 Dumping facilities and loading pockets.
57.19104 Clearance at shaft stations.
57.19105 Landings with more than one shaft entrance.
57.19106 Shaft sets.
57.19107 Precautions for work in compartment affected by hoisting operation.
57.19108 Posting warning signs during shaft work.
57.19109 Shaft inspection and repair.
57.19110 Overhead protection for shaft deepening work.
57.19111 Shaft-sinking ladders.

INSPECTION AND MAINTENANCE

57.19120 Procedures for inspection, testing, and maintenance.
57.19121 Recordkeeping.
57.19122 Replacement parts.
57.19129 Examinations and tests at beginning of shift.
57.19130 Conveyance shaft test.
57.19131 Hoist conveyance connections.
57.19132 Safety catches.
57.19133 Shaft.
57.19134 Sheaves.
57.19135 Rollers in inclined shafts.

Subpart S—Miscellaneous

57.20001 Intoxicating beverages and narcotics.
57.20002 Potable water.
57.20003 Housekeeping.
57.20005 Carbon tetrachloride.
57.20008 Toilet facilities.
57.20009 Tests for explosive dusts.
57.20010 Retaining dams.
57.20011 Barricades and warning signs.
57.20013 Waste receptacles.
57.20014 Prohibited areas for food and beverages.
57.20020 Unattended mine openings.
57.20021 Abandoned mine openings.
57.20031 Blasting underground in hazardous areas.
57.20032 Two-way communication equipment for underground operations.

Subpart T—Safety Standards for Methane in Metal and Nonmetal Mines

GENERAL

57.22001 Scope.
57.22002 Definitions.

MINE CATEGORIZATION

57.22003 Mine category or subcategory.
57.22004 Category placement or change in placement.
57.22005 Notice and appeal of placement or change in placement.

FIRE PREVENTION AND CONTROL

57.22101 Smoking (I-A, II-A, III, and V-A mines).
57.22102 Smoking (I-C mines).
57.22103 Open flames (I-A, II-A, III, and V-A mines).
57.22104 Open flames (I-C mines).
57.22105 Smoking and open flames (IV mines).
57.22106 Dust containing volatile matter (I-C mines).

VENTILATION

57.22201 Mechanical ventilation (I-A, I-B, I-C, II-A, II-B, III, IV, V-A, and V-B mines).
57.22202 Main fans (I-A, I-B, I-C, II-A, III, V-A, and V-B mines).
57.22203 Main fan operation (I-C mines).
57.22204 Main fan operation and inspection (I-A, II-A, III, and V-A mines).
57.22205 Doors on main fans (I-A, II-A, III, and V-A mines).
57.22206 Main ventilation failure (I-A, II-A, III, and V-A mines).
57.22207 Booster fans (I-A, II-A, III, and V-A mines).
57.22208 Auxiliary fans (I-A, II-A, III, and V-A mines).
57.22209 Auxiliary fans (I-C mines).
57.22210 In-line filters (I-C mines).
57.22211 Air flow (I-A mines).
57.22212 Air flow (I-C, II-A, and V-A mines).
57.22213 Air flow (III mines).
57.22214 Changes in ventilation (I-A, II-A, III, and V-A mines).
57.22215 Separation of intake and return air (I-A, II-A, III, and V-A mines).
57.22216 Separation of intake and return air (I-C mines).
57.22217 Seals and stoppings (I-A, I-B and I-C mines).
57.22218 Seals and stoppings (III, V-A, and V-B mines).
57.22219 Seals and stoppings (II-A mines).
57.22220 Air passing unsealed areas (I-A, II-A, III, and V-A mines).
57.22221 Overcast and undercast construction (I-A, II-A, III, and V-A mines).
57.22222 Ventilation materials (I-A, I-B, I-C, II-A, III, V-A, and V-B mines).
57.22223 Crosscuts before abandonment (III mines).
57.22224 Auxiliary equipment stations (I-A and III mines).
57.22225 Auxiliary equipment stations (I-C mines).
57.22226 Testing for methane (IV mines).

Mine Safety and Health Admin., Labor § 57.2

57.22227 Approved testing devices (I-A, I-B, I-C, II-A, II-B, III, IV, V-A, and V-B mines).
57.22228 Preshift examination (I-A, I-C, II-A, III, and V-A mines).
57.22229 Weekly testing (I-A, III, and V-A mines).
57.22230 Weekly testing (II-A mines.
57.22231 Actions at 0.25 percent methane (I-B, II-B, V-B and VI mines).
57.22232 Actions at 0.5 percent methane (I-B, II-A, II-B, IV, V-B, and VI mines).
57.22233 Actions at 0.5 percent methane (I-C mines).
57.22234 Actions at 1.0 percent methane (I-A, I-B, III, V-A, and V-B mines).
57.22235 Actions at 1.0 percent methane (I-C, II-A, II-B, and IV mines).
57.22236 Actions at 1.0 percent methane (VI mines).
57.22237 Actions at 2.0 to 2.5 percent methane in bleeder systems (I-A and III mines).
57.22238 Actions at 2.0 percent methane (I-B, II-B, V-B, and VI mines).
57.22239 Actions at 2.0 percent methane (IV mines).
57.22240 Actions at 2.0 percent methane (V-A mines).
57.22241 Advance face boreholes (I-C mines).

EQUIPMENT

57.22301 Atmospheric monitoring systems (I-A, II-A, and V-A mines).
57.22302 Approved equipment (I-A and V-A mines).
57.22303 Approved equipment (I-C mines).
57.22304 Approved equipment (II-A mines).
57.22305 Approved equipment (III mines).
57.22306 Methane monitors (I-A mines).
57.22307 Methane monitors (II-A mines).
57.22308 Methane monitors (III mines).
57.22309 Methane monitors (V-A mines).
57.22310 Electrical cables (I-C mines).
57.22311 Electrical cables (II-A mines).
57.22312 Distribution boxes (II-A and V-A mines).
57.22313 Explosion-protection systems (I-C mines).
57.22314 Flow-control devices (V-A and V-B mines).
57.22315 Self-contained breathing apparatus (V-A mines).

UNDERGROUND RETORTS

57.22401 Underground retorts (I-A and I-B mines).

ILLUMINATION

57.22501 Personal electric lamps (I-A, I-B, I-C, II-A, II-B, III, IV, V-A, and V-B mines).

EXPLOSIVES

57.22601 Blasting from the surface (I-A mines).
57.22602 Blasting from the surface (I-C mines).
57.22603 Blasting from the surface (II-A mines).
57.22604 Blasting from the surface (II-B mines).
57.22605 Blasting from the surface (V-A mines).
57.22606 Explosive materials and blasting units (III mines).
57.22607 Blasting on shift (III mines).
57.22608 Secondary blasting (I-A, II-A, and V-A mines).

APPENDIX I TO SUBPART T OF PART 57—STANDARD APPLICABILITY BY CATEGORY OR SUBCATEGORY

AUTHORITY: 30 U.S.C. 811.

SOURCE: 50 FR 4082, Jan. 29, 1985, unless otherwise noted.

Subpart A—General

§ 57.1 Purpose and scope.

This part 57 sets forth mandatory safety and health standards for each underground metal or nonmetal mine, including related surface operations, subject to the Federal Mine Safety and Health Act of 1977. The purpose of these standards is the protection of life, the promotion of health and safety, and the prevention of accidents.

§ 57.2 Definitions.

The following definitions apply to this part. In addition definitions contained in any subpart of part 57 apply in that subpart. If inconsistent with the general definitions in this section, the definition in the subpart will apply in that subpart:

Abandoned areas means areas in which work has been completed, no further work is planned, and travel is not permitted.

Abandoned mine means all work has stopped on the mine premises and an office with a responsible person in charge is no longer maintained at the mine.

Abandoned workings means deserted mine areas in which further work is not intended.

Active workings means areas at, in, or around a mine or plant where men work or travel.

American Table of Distances means the current edition of "The American

§ 57.2

Table of Distances for Storage of Explosives" published by the Institute of Makers of Explosives.

Approved means tested and accepted for a specific purpose by a nationally recognized agency.

Attended means presence of an individual or continuous monitoring to prevent unauthorized entry or access. In addition, areas containing explosive material at underground areas of a mine can be considered attended when all access to the underground areas of the mine is secured from unauthorized entry. Vertical shafts shall be considered secure. Inclined shafts or adits shall be considered secure when locked at the surface.

Authorized person means a person approved or assigned by mine management to perform a specific type of duty or duties or to be at a specific location or locations in the mine.

Auxilary fan means a fan used to deliver air to a working place off the main airstream; generally used with ventilation tubing.

Barricaded means obstructed to prevent the passage of persons, vehicles, or flying materials.

Barrier means a material object, or objects that separates, keeps apart, or demarcates in a conspicuous manner such as cones, a warning sign, or tape.

Berm means a pile or mound of material along an elevated roadway capable of moderating or limiting the force of a vehicle in order to impede the vehicle's passage over the bank of the roadway.

Blast area means the area in which concussion (shock wave), flying material, or gases from an explosion may cause injury to persons. In determining the blast area, the following factors, shall be considered:

(1) Geology or material to be blasted.
(2) Blast pattern.
(3) Burden, depth, diameter, and angle of the holes.
(4) Blasting experience of the mine.
(5) Delay system, powder factor, and pounds per delay.
(6) Type and amount of explosive material.
(7) Type and amount of stemming.

Blast site means the area where explosive material is handled during loading, including the perimeter formed by the loaded blastholes and 50 feet (15.2 meters) in all directions from loaded holes. A minimum distance of 30 feet (9.1 meters) may replace the 50-foot (15.2-meter) requirement if the perimeter of loaded holes is demarcated with a barrier. The 50-foot (15.2-meter) and alternative 30-foot (9.1-meter) requirements also apply in all directions along the full depth of the hole. In underground mines, at least 15 feet (4.6 meters) of solid rib, pillar, or broken rock can be substituted for the 50-foot (15.2-meter) distance. In underground mines utilizing a block-caving system or similar system, at least 6 feet (1.8 meters) of solid rib or pillar, including concrete reinforcement of at least 10 inches (254 millimeters), with overall dimensions of not less than 6 feet (1.8 meters) may be substituted for the 50-foot (15.2-meter) distance requirement.

Blasting agent means any substance classified as a blasting agent by the Department of Transportation in 49 CFR 173.114(a) (44 FR 31182, May 31, 1979) which is incorporated by reference. This document is available for inspection at each Metal and Nonmetal Mine Safety and Health District Office of the Mine Safety and Health Administration, and may be obtained from the U.S. Government Printing Office, Washington, DC 20402.

Blasting area means the area near blasting operations in which concussion or flying material can reasonably be expected to cause injury.

Blasting cap means a detonator which is initiated by a safety fuse.

Blasting circuit means the electrical circuit used to fire one or more electric blasting caps.

Blasting switch means a switch used to connect a power source to a blasting circuit.

Blowout means a sudden, violent, release of gas or liquid due to the reservoir pressure in a petroleum mine.

Booster means any unit of explosive or blasting agent used for the purpose of perpetuating or intensifying an initial detonation.

Booster fan means a fan installed in the main airstream or a split of the main airstream to increase airflow through a section or sections of a mine.

Capped fuse means a length of safety fuse to which a blasting cap has been attached.

Mine Safety and Health Admin., Labor §57.2

Capped primer means a package or cartridge of explosives which is specifically designed to transmit detonation to other explosives and which contains a detonator.

Circuit breaker means a device designed to open and close a circuit by nonautomatic means and to open the circuit automatically on a predetermined overcurrent setting without injury to itself when properly applied within its rating.

Combustible means capable of being ignited and consumed by fire.

Combustible material means a material that, in the form in which it is used and under the conditions anticipated, will ignite, burn, support combustion or release flammable vapors when subjected to fire or heat. Wood, paper, rubber, and plastics are examples of combustible materials.

Company official means a member of the company supervisory or technical staff.

Competent person means a person having abilities and experience that fully qualify him to perform the duty to which he is assigned.

Conductor means a material, usually in the form of a wire, cable, or bus bar, capable of carrying an electric current.

Delay connector means a nonelectric short interval delay device for use in delaying blasts which are initiated by detonating cord.

Detonating cord means a flexible cord containing a solid core of high explosives.

Detonator means any device containing a detonating charge that is used to initiate an explosive and includes but is not limited to blasting caps, electric blasting caps and nonelectric instantaneous or delay blasting caps.

Distribution box means a portable apparatus with an enclosure through which an electric circuit is carried to one or more cables from a single incoming feed line; each cable circuit being connected through individual overcurrent protective devices.

Electric blasting cap means a detonator designed for and capable of being initiated by means of an electric current.

Electrical grounding means to connect with the ground to make the earth part of the circuit.

Employee means a person who works for wages or salary in the service of an employer.

Employer means a person or organization which hires one or more persons to work for wages or salary.

Emulsion means an explosive material containing substantial amounts of oxidizers dissolved in water droplets, surrounded by an immiscible fuel.

Escapeway means a passageway by which persons may leave a mine.

Explosive means any substance classified as an explosive by the Department of Transportation in 49 CFR 173.53, 173.88 and 173.100 which are incorporated by reference. Title 49 CFR is available for inspection at each Metal and Nonmetal Mine Safety and Health District Office of the Mine Safety and Health Administration, and may be obtained from the U.S. Government Printing Office, Washington, DC 20402.

Face or bank means that part of any mine where excavating is progressing or was last done.

Fire resistance rating means the time, in minutes or hours, that an assembly of materials will retain its protective characteristics or structural integrity upon exposure to fire.

Flame spread rating means the numerical designation that indicates the extent flame will spread over the surface of a material during a specified period of time.

Flammable means capable of being easily ignited and of burning rapidly.

Flammable gas means a gas that will burn in the normal concentrations of oxygen in the air.

Flammable liquid a liquid that has a flash point below 100 °F (37.8 °C), a vapor pressure not exceeding 40 pounds per square inch (absolute) at 100 °F (37.8 °C), and is known as a Class I liquid.

Flash point means the minimum temperature at which sufficient vapor is released by a liquid or solid to form a flammable vapor-air mixture at atmospheric pressure.

Geological area means an area characterized by the presence of the same ore

§ 57.2

bodies, the same stratigraphic sequence of beds, or the same ore-bearing geological formation.

Highway means any public street, public alley or public road.

High potential means more than 650 volts.

Hoist means a power driven windlass or drum used for raising ore, rock, or other material from a mine, and for lowering or raising persons and material.

Igniter cord means a fuse, cordlike in appearance, which burns progressively along its length with an external flame at the zone of burning, and is used for lighting a series of safety fuses in the desired sequence.

Insulated means separated from other conducting surfaces by a dielectric substance permanently offering a high resistance to the passage of current and to disruptive discharge through the substance. When any substance is said to be insulated, it is understood to be insulated in a manner suitable for the conditions to which it is subjected. Otherwise, it is, within the purpose of this definition, uninsulated. Insulating covering is one means for making the conductor insulated.

Insulation means a dielectric substance offering a high resistance to the passage of current and to a disruptive discharge through the substance.

Laminated partition means a partition composed of the following material and minimum nominal dimensions: ½-inch-thick plywood, ½-inch-thick gypsum wallboard, ⅛-inch-thick low carbon steel, and ¼-inch-thick plywood, bonded together in that order (IME–22 Box). A laminated partition also includes alternative construction materials described in the Institute of Makers of Explosives (IME) Safety Library Publication No. 22, "Recommendations for the Safe Transportation of Detonators in a Vehicle with Other Explosive Materials" (May 1993), and the "Generic Loading Guide for the IME–22 Container" (October 1993). The IME is located at 1120 19th Street NW., Suite 310, Washington, DC 20036–3605; 202–429–9280; *https://www.ime.org*. This incorporation by reference has been approved by the Director of the Federal Register in accordance with 5 U.S.C. 552(a) and 1 CFR part 51. Copies are available at MSHA's Office of Standards, Regulations, and Variances, 201 12th Street South, Arlington, VA 22202–5452; 202–693–9440; and at all Metal and Nonmetal Mine Safety and Health District Offices, or available for inspection at the National Archives and Records Administration (NARA). For information on the availability of this material at NARA, call 202–741–6030, or go to: *http://www.archives.gov/federal_register/code_of_federal_regulations/ibr_locations.html*.

Lay means the distance parallel to the axis of the rope in which a strand makes one complete turn about the axis of the rope.

Loading means placing explosive material either in a blasthole or against the material to be blasted.

Low potential means 650 volts or less.

Magazine means a facility for the storage of explosives, blasting agents, or detonators.

Main fan means a fan that controls the entire airflow of the mine, or the airflow of one of the major air circuits.

Major electrical installation means an assemblage of stationary electrical equipment for the generation, transmission, distribution, or conversion of electrical power.

Mantrip means a trip on which persons are transported to and from a work area.

Mill includes any ore mill, sampling works, concentrator, and any crushing, grinding, or screening plant used at, and in connection with, an excavation or mine.

Mine atmosphere means any point at least 12 inches away from the back, face, rib, and floor in any mine; and additionally, in a Category IV mine, at least 3 feet laterally away from the collar of a borehole which releases gas into a mine.

Mine opening means any opening or entrance from the surface into a mine.

Misfire means the complete or partial failure of a blasting charge to explode as planned.

Mobile equipment means wheeled, skid-mounted, track-mounted, or rail-mounted equipment capable of moving or being moved.

Multipurpose dry-chemical fire extinguisher means an extinguisher having a

Mine Safety and Health Admin., Labor § 57.2

rating of at least 2–A:10–B:C and containing a nominal 4.5 pounds or more of dry-chemical agent.

Noncombustible material means a material that, in the form in which it is used and under the conditions anticipated, will not ignite, burn, support combustion, or release flammable vapors when subjected to fire or heat. Concrete, masonry block, brick, and steel are examples of noncombustible materials.

Non-electric delay blasting cap means a detonator with an integral delay element and capable of being initiated by miniaturized detonating cord.

Outburst means the sudden, violent release of solids and high-pressure occluded gases, including methane in a domal salt mine.

Overburden means material of any nature, consolidated or unconsolidated, that overlies a deposit of useful materials or ores that are to be mined.

Overload means that current which will cause an excessive or dangerous temperature in the conductor or conductor insulation.

Permissible means a machine, material, apparatus, or device which has been investigated, tested, and approved by the Bureau of Mines or the Mine Safety and Health Administration, and is maintained in permissible condition.

Potable water means water which shall meet the applicable minimum health requirements for drinking water established by the State or community in which the mine is located or by the Environmental Protection Agency in 40 CFR part 141, pages 169–182 revised as of July 1, 1977. Where no such requirements are applicable, the drinking water provided shall conform with the Public Health Service Drinking Water Standards, 42 CFR part 72, subpart J, pages 527–533, revised as of October 1, 1976. Publications to which references are made in this definition are hereby made a part hereof. These incorporated publications are available for inspection at each Metal and Nonmetal Mine Safety and Health District Office of the Mine Safety and Health Administration.

Powder chest means a substantial, nonconductive portable container equipped with a lid and used at blasting sites for explosives other than blasting agents.

Primer means a unit, package, or cartridge of explosives used to initiate other explosives or blasting agents, and which contains a detonator.

Reverse-current protection means a method or device used on direct-current circuits or equipment to prevent the flow of current in a reverse direction.

Rock burst means a sudden and violent failure of overstressed rock resulting in the instantaneous release of large amounts of accumulated energy. Rock burst does not include a burst resulting from pressurized mine gases.

Rock fixture means any tensioned or nontensioned device or material inserted into the ground to strengthen or support the ground.

Roll protection means a framework, safety canopy or similar protection for the operator when equipment overturns.

Safety can means an approved container, of not over 5 gallons capacity, having a spring-closing lid and spout cover.

Safety fuse means a flexible cord containing an internal burning medium by which fire is conveyed at a continuous and uniform rate for the purpose of firing blasting caps or a black powder charge.

Safety switch means a sectionalizing switch that also provides shunt protection in blasting circuits between the blasting switch and the shot area.

Scaling means removal of insecure material from a face or highwall.

Secondary safety connection means a second connection between a conveyance and rope, intended to prevent the conveyance from running away or falling in the event the primary connection fails.

Shaft means a vertical or inclined shaft, a slope, incline, or winze.

Short circuit means an abnormal connection of relatively low resistance, whether made accidentally or intentionally, between two points of difference potential in a circuit.

Slurry (as applied to blasting). See "Water gel."

Storage facility means the entire class of structures used to store explosive materials. A "storage facility" used to

§ 57.1000

store blasting agents corresponds to a BATF Type 4 or 5 storage facility.

Storage tank means a container exceeding 60 gallons in capacity used for the storage of flammable or combustible liquids.

Stray current means that portion of a total electric current that flows through paths other than the intended circuit.

Substantial construction means construction of such strength, material, and workmanship that the object will withstand all reasonable shock, wear, and usage to which it will be subjected.

Suitable means that which fits, and has the qualities or qualifications to meet a given purpose, occasion, condition, function, or circumstance.

Travelway means a passage, walk or way regularly used and designated for persons to go from one place to another.

Water gel or Slurry (as applied to blasting) means an explosive or blasting agent containing substantial portions of water.

Wet drilling means the continuous application of water through the central hole of hollow drill steel to the bottom of the drill hole.

Working level (WL) means any combination of the short-lived radon daughters in one liter of air that will result in ultimate emission of 1.3×10^5 MeV (million electron volts) of potential alpha energy, and exposure to these radon daughters over a period of time is expressed in terms of "working level months" (WLM). Inhalation of air containing a radon daughter concentration of 1 WL for 173 hours results in an exposure of 1 WLM."

Working place means any place in or about a mine where work is being performed.

[69 FR 38840, June 29, 2004, as amended at 80 FR 52987, Sept. 2, 2015]

PROCEDURES

§ 57.1000 Notification of commencement of operations and closing of mines.

The owner, operator, or person in charge of any metal and nonmetal mine shall notify the nearest MSHA Metal and Nonmental Mine Safety and Health district office before starting operations, of the approximate or actual date mine operation will commence. The notification shall include the mine name, location, the company name, mailing address, person in charge, and whether operations will be continuous or intermittent. When any mine is closed, the person in charge shall notify the nearest district office as provided above and indicate whether the closure is temporary or permanent.

[51 FR 36198, Oct. 8, 1986, as amended at 60 FR 33723, June 29, 1995; 60 FR 35695, July 11, 1995; 71 FR 16667, Apr. 3, 2006]

Subpart B—Ground Control

AUTHORITY: 30 U.S.C. 811.

SOURCE: 51 FR 36198, Oct. 8, 1986, unless otherwise noted.

§ 57.3000 Definitions.

The following definitions apply in this subpart.

Travelway. A passage, walk, or haulageway regularly used or designated for persons to go from one place to another.

[51 FR 36198, Oct. 8, 1986, as amended at 69 FR 38842, June 29, 2004]

SCALING AND SUPPORT—SURFACE AND UNDERGROUND

§ 57.3200 Correction of hazardous conditions.

Ground conditions that create a hazard to persons shall be taken down or supported before other work or travel is permitted in the affected area. Until corrective work is completed, the area shall be posted with a warning against entry and, when left unattended, a barrier shall be installed to impede unauthorized entry.

§ 57.3201 Location for performing scaling.

Scaling shall be performed from a location which will not expose persons to injury from falling material, or other protection from falling material shall be provided.

§ 57.3202 Scaling tools.

Where manual scaling is performed, a scaling bar shall be provided. This bar shall be of a length and design that will allow the removal of loose material without exposing the person performing the work to injury.

§ 57.3203 Rock fixtures.

(a) For rock bolts and accessories addressed in ASTM F432–95, "Standard Specification for Roof and Rock Bolts and Accessories," the mine operator shall—

(1) Obtain a manufacturer's certification that the material was manufactured and tested in accordance with the specifications of ASTM F432–95; and

(2) Make this certification available to an authorized representative of the Secretary and to the representative of miners.

(b) Fixtures and accessories not addressed in ASTM F432–95 may be used for ground support provided they—

(1) Have been successful in supporting the ground in an area with similar strata, opening dimensions and ground stresses in any mine; or

(2) Have been tested and shown to be effective in supporting ground in an area of the affected mine which has similar strata, opening dimensions, and ground stresses as the area where the fixtures are expected to be used. During the test process, access to the test area shall be limited to persons necessary to conduct the test.

(c) Bearing plates shall be used with fixtures when necessary for effective ground support.

(d) The diameter of finishing bits shall be within a tolerance of plus or minus 0.030 inch of the manufacturer's recommended hole diameter for the anchor used. When separate finishing bits are used, they shall be distinguishable from other bits.

(e) Damaged or deteriorated cartridges of grouting material shall not be used.

(f) When rock bolts tensioned by torquing are used as a means of ground support,

(1) Selected tension level shall be—

(i) At least 50 percent of either the yield point of the bolt or anchorage capacity of the rock, whichever is less; and

(ii) No greater than the yield point of the bolt or anchorage capacity of the rock.

(2) The torque of the first bolt, every tenth bolt, and the last bolt installed in each work area during the shift shall be accurately determined immediately after installation. If the torque of any fixture tested does not fall within the installation torque range, corrective action shall be taken.

(g) When grouted fixtures can be tested by applying torque, the first fixture installed in each work place shall be tested to withstand 150 foot-pounds of torque. Should it rotate in the hole, a second fixture shall be tested in the same manner. If the second fixture also turns, corrective action shall be taken.

(h) When other tensioned and nontensioned fixtures are used, test methods shall be established and used to verify their effectiveness.

(i) The mine operator shall certify that tests were conducted and make the certification available to an authorized representative of the Secretary.

[51 FR 36198, Oct. 8, 1986, as amended at 51 FR 36804, Oct. 16, 1986; 63 FR 20030, Apr. 22, 1998]

SCALING AND SUPPORT—UNDERGROUND ONLY

§ 57.3360 Ground support use.

Ground support shall be used where ground conditions, or mining experience in similar ground conditions in the mine, indicate that it is necessary. When ground support is necessary, the support system shall be designed, installed, and maintained to control the ground in places where persons work or travel in performing their assigned tasks. Damaged, loosened, or dislodged timber use for ground support which creates a hazard to persons shall be repaired or replaced prior to any work or travel in the affected area.

PRECAUTIONS—SURFACE AND UNDERGROUND

§ 57.3400 Secondary breakage.

Prior to secondary breakage operations, the material to be broken, other than hanging material, shall be positioned or blocked to prevent movement which would endanger persons in the work area. Secondary breakage shall be performed from a location

§ 57.3401

which would not expose persons to danger.

§ 57.3401 Examination of ground conditions.

Persons experienced in examining and testing for loose ground shall be designated by the mine operator. Appropriate supervisors or other designated persons shall examine and, where applicable, test ground conditions in areas where work is to be performed, prior to work commencing, after blasting, and as ground conditions warrant during the work shift. Underground haulageways and travelways and surface area highwalls and banks adjoining travelways shall be examined weekly or more often if changing ground conditions warrant.

PRECAUTIONS—SURFACE ONLY

§ 57.3430 Activity between machinery or equipment and the highwall or bank.

Persons shall not work or travel between machinery or equipment and the highwall or bank where the machinery or equipment may hinder escape from falls or slides of the highwall or bank. Travel is permitted when necessary for persons to dismount.

PRECAUTIONS—UNDERGROUND ONLY

§ 57.3460 Maintenance between machinery or equipment and ribs.

Persons shall not perform maintenance work between machinery or equipment and ribs unless the area has been tested and, when necessary, secured.

§ 57.3461 Rock bursts.

(a) Operators of mines which have experienced a rock burst shall—
(1) Within twenty four hours report to the nearest MSHA office each rock burst which:
(i) Causes persons to be withdrawn;
(ii) Impairs ventilation;
(iii) Impedes passage; or
(iv) Disrupts mining activity for more than one hour.
(2) Develop and implement a rock burst control plan within 90 days after a rock burst has been experienced.
(b) The plan shall include—

(1) Mining and operating procedures designed to reduce the occurrence of rock bursts;
(2) Monitoring procedures where detection methods are used; and
(3) Other measures to minimize exposure of persons to areas which are prone to rock bursts.
(c) The plan shall be updated as conditions warrant.
(d) The plan shall be available to an authorized representative of the Secretary and to miners or their representatives.

Subpart C—Fire Prevention and Control

AUTHORITY: Sec. 101, Federal Mine Safety and Health Act of 1977, Pub. L. 91–173 as amended by Pub. L. 95–164, 91 Stat. 1291 (30 U.S.C. 811).

§ 57.4000 Definitions.

The following definitions apply in this subpart.

Combustible liquids. Liquids having a flash point at or above 100 °F (37.8 °C). They are divided into the following classes:

Class II liquids—those having flash points at or above 100 °F (37.8 °C) and below 140 °F (60 °C).

Class IIIA liquids—those having flash points at or above 140 °F (60 °C) and below 200 °F (93.4 °C).

Class IIIB liquids—those having flash points at or above 200 °F (93.4 °C).

Escapeway. A designated passageway by which persons can leave an underground mine.

Flash point. The minimum temperature at which sufficient vapor is released by a liquid to form a flammable vapor-air mixture near the surface of the liquid.

Main fan. A fan that controls the entire airflow of an underground mine or the airflow of one of the major air circuits of the mine.

Mine opening. Any opening or entrance from the surface into an underground mine.

Safety can. A container of not over five gallons capacity that is designed to safely relieve internal pressure when

Mine Safety and Health Admin., Labor § 57.4160

exposed to heat and has a spring-closing lid and spout cover.

[50 FR 4082, Jan. 29, 1985, as amended at 68 FR 32361, May 30, 2003; 69 FR 38842, June 29, 2004]

§ 57.4011 Abandoned electric circuits.

Abandoned electric circuits shall be deenergized and isolated so that they cannot become energized inadvertently.

§ 57.4057 Underground trailing cables.

Underground trailing cables shall be accepted or approved by MSHA as flame resistant.

[57 FR 61223, Dec. 23, 1992]

PROHIBITIONS/PRECAUTIONS/ HOUSEKEEPING

§ 57.4100 Smoking and use of open flames.

No person shall smoke or use an open flame where flammable or combustible liquids, including greases, or flammable gases are—
(a) Used or transported in a manner that could create a fire hazard; or
(b) Stored or handled.

§ 57.4101 Warning signs.

Readily visible signs prohibiting smoking and open flames shall be posted where a fire or explosion hazard exists.

§ 57.4102 Spillage and leakage.

Flammable or combustible liquid spillage or leakage shall be removed in a timely manner or controlled to prevent a fire hazard.

§ 57.4103 Fueling internal combustion engines.

Internal combustion engines shall be switched off before refueling if the fuel tanks are integral parts of the equipment. This standard does not apply to diesel-powered equipment.

§ 57.4104 Combustible waste.

(a) Waste materials, including liquids, shall not accumulate in quantities that could create a fire hazard.
(b) Waste or rags containing flammable or combustible liquids that could create a fire hazard shall be placed in the following containers until disposed of properly:
(1) Underground—covered metal containers.
(2) On the surface—covered metal containers or equivalent containers with flame containment characteristics.

§ 57.4130 Surface electric substations and liquid storage facilities.

The requirements of this standard apply to surface areas only.
(a) If a hazard to persons could be created, no combustible materials shall be stored or allowed to accumulate within 25 feet of the following:
(1) Electric substations.
(2) Unburied, flammable or combustible liquid storage tanks.
(3) Any group of containers used for storage of more than 60 gallons of flammable or combustible liquids.
(b) The area within the 25-foot perimeter shall be kept free of dry vegetation.

§ 57.4131 Surface fan installations and mine openings.

(a) On the surface, no more than one day's supply of combustible materials shall be stored within 100 feet of mine openings or within 100 feet of fan installations used for underground ventilation.
(b) the one-day supply shall be kept at least 25 feet away from any mine opening except during transit into the mine.
(c) Dry vegetation shall not be permitted within 25 feet of mine openings.

§ 57.4160 Underground electric substations and liquid storage facilities.

The requirements of this standard apply to underground areas only.
(a) Areas within 25 feet of the following shall be free of combustible materials:
(1) Electric substations.
(2) Unburied, combustible liquid storage tanks.
(3) Any group of containers used for storage of more than 60 gallons of combustible liquids.
(b) This standard does not apply to installed wiring or timber that is coated with at least one inch of shotcrete,

§ 57.4161

one-half inch of gunite, or other noncombustible materials with equivalent fire protection characteristics.

§ 57.4161 Use of fire underground.

Fires shall not be lit underground, except for open-flame torches. Torches shall be attended at all times while lit.

FIREFIGHTING EQUIPMENT

§ 57.4200 General requirements.

(a) For fighting fires that could endanger persons, each mine shall have—

(1) Onsite firefighting equipment for fighting fires in their early stages; and

(2) Onsite firefighting equipment for fighting fires beyond their early stages, or the mine shall have made prior arrangements with a local fire department to fight such fires.

(b) This onsite firefighting equipment shall be—

(1) Of the type, size, and quantity that can extinguish fires of any class which would occur as a result of the hazards present; and

(2) Strategically located, readily accessible, plainly marked, and maintained in fire-ready condition.

[50 FR 4082, Jan. 29, 1985, as amended at 50 FR 20100, May 14, 1985]

§ 57.4201 Inspection.

(a) Firefighting equipment shall be inspected according to the following schedules:

(1) Fire extinguishers shall be inspected visually at least once a month to determine that they are fully charged and operable.

(2) At least once every twelve months, maintenance checks shall be made of mechanical parts, the amount and condition of extinguishing agent and expellant, and the condition of the hose, nozzle, and vessel to determine that the fire extinguishers will operate effectively.

(3) Fire extinguishers shall be hydrostatically tested according to Table C-1 or a schedule based on the manufacturer's specifications to determine the integrity of extinguishing agent vessels.

(4) Water pipes, valves, outlets, hydrants, and hoses that are part of the mine's firefighting system shall be visually inspected at least once every three months for damage or deterioration and use-tested at least once every twelve months to determine that they remain functional.

(5) Fire suppression systems shall be inspected at least once every twelve months. An inspection schedule based on the manufacturer's specifications or the equivalent shall be established for individual components of a system and followed to determine that the system remains functional. Surface fire suppression systems are exempt from these inspection requirements if the systems are used solely for the protection of property and no persons would be affected by a fire.

(b) At the completion of each inspection or test required by this standard, the person making the inspection or test shall certify that the inspection or test has been made and the date on which it was made. Certifications of hydrostatic testing shall be retained until the fire extinguisher is retested or permanently removed from service. Other certifications shall be retained for one year.

TABLE C-1—HYDROSTATIC TEST INTERVALS FOR FIRE EXTINGUISHERS

Extinguisher type	Test interval (years)
Soda Acid	5
Cartridge-Operated Water and/or Antifreeze	5
Stored-Pressure Water and/or Antifreeze	5
Wetting Agent	5
Foam	5
AFFF (Aqueous Film Forming Foam)	5
Loaded Stream	5
Dry-Chemical with Stainless Steel Shells	5
Carbon Dioxide	5
Dry-Chemical, Stored Pressure, with Mild Steel Shells, Brazed Brass Shells, or Aluminum Shells	12
Dry-Chemical, Cartridge or Cylinder Operated, with Mild Steel Shells	12
Bromotrifluoromethane-Halon 1301	12
Bromochlorodifluoromethane-Halon 1211	12
Dry-Powder, Cartridge or Cylinder-Operated, with Mild Steel Shells [1]	12

[1] Except for stainless steel and steel used for compressed gas cylinders, all other steel shells are defined as "mild steel" shells.

§ 57.4202 Fire hydrants.

If fire hydrants are part of the mine's firefighting system, the hydrants shall be provided with—

(a) Uniform fittings or readily available adapters for onsite firefighting equipment;

(b) Readily available wrenches or keys to open the valves; and

(c) Readily available adapters capable of connecting hydrant fittings to the hose equipment of any firefighting organization relied upon by the mine.

§ 57.4203 Extinguisher recharging or replacement.

Fire extinguishers shall be recharged or replaced with a fully charged extinguisher promptly after any discharge.

§ 57.4230 Surface self-propelled equipment.

(a)(1) Whenever a fire or its effects could impede escape from self-propelled equipment, a fire extinguisher shall be on the equipment.

(2) Whenever a fire or its effects would not impede escape from the equipment but could affect the escape of other persons in the area, a fire extinguisher shall be on the equipment or within 100 feet of the equipment.

(b) A fire suppression system may be used as an alternative to fire extinguishers if the system can be manually activated.

(c) Fire extinguishers or fire suppression systems shall be of a type and size that can extinguish fires of any class in their early stages which could originate from the equipment's inherent fire hazards. Fire extinguishers or manual actuators for the suppression system shall be located to permit their use by persons whose escape could be impeded by fire.

§ 57.4260 Underground self-propelled equipment.

(a) Whenever self-propelled equipment is used underground, a fire extinguisher shall be on the equipment. This standard does not apply to compressed-air powered equipment without inherent fire hazards.

(b) A fire suppression system may be used as an alternative to fire extinguishers if the system can be manually actuated.

(c) Fire extinguishers or fire suppression systems shall be of a type and size that can extinguish fires of any class in their early stages which could originate from the equipment's inherent fire hazards. The fire extinguishers or the manual actuator for the suppression system shall be readily accessible to the equipment operator.

§ 57.4261 Shaft-station waterlines.

Waterline outlets that are located at underground shaft stations and are part of the mine's fire protection system shall have at least one fitting located for, and capable of, immediate connection to firefighting equipment.

§ 57.4262 Underground transformer stations, combustible liquid storage and dispensing areas, pump rooms, compressor rooms, and hoist rooms.

Transformer stations, storage and dispensing areas for combustible liquids, pump rooms, compressor rooms, and hoist rooms shall be provided with fire protection of a type, size, and quantity that can extinguish fires of any class in their early stages which could occur as a result of the hazards present.

§ 57.4263 Underground belt conveyors.

Fire protection shall be provided at the head, tail, drive, and take-up pulleys of underground belt conveyors. Provisions shall be made for extinguishing fires along the beltline. Fire protection shall be of a type, size, and quantity that can extinguish fires of any class in their early stages which could occur as a result of the fire hazards present.

FIREFIGHTING PROCEDURES/ALARMS/ DRILLS

§ 57.4330 Surface firefighting, evacuation, and rescue procedures.

(a) Mine operators shall establish emergency firefighting, evacuation, and rescue procedures for the surface portions of their operations. These procedures shall be coordinated in advance with available firefighting organizations.

(b) Fire alarm procedures or systems shall be established to promptly warn every person who could be endangered by a fire.

(c) Fire alarm systems shall be maintained in operable condition.

§ 57.4331 Surface firefighting drills.

Emergency firefighting drills shall be held at least once every six months for

§ 57.4360

persons assigned surface firefighting responsibilities by the mine operator.

§ 57.4360 Underground alarm systems.

(a) Fire alarm systems capable of promptly warning every person underground, except as provided in paragraph (b), shall be provided and maintained in operating condition.

(b) If persons are assigned to work areas beyond the warning capabilities of the system, provisions shall be made to alert them in a manner to provide for their safe evacuation in the event of a fire.

§ 57.4361 Underground evacuation drills.

(a) At least once every six months, mine evacuation drills shall be held to assess the ability of all persons underground to reach the surface or other designated points of safety within the time limits of the self-rescue devices that would be used during an actual emergency.

(b) The evacuation drills shall—

(1) Be held for each shift at some time other than a shift change and involve all persons underground;

(2) Involve activation of the fire alarm system; and

(3) Include evacuation of all persons from their work areas to the surface or to designated central evacuation points.

(c) At the completion of each drill, the mine operator shall certify the date and the time the evacuation began and ended. Certifications shall be retained for at least one year after each drill.

§ 57.4362 Underground rescue and firefighting operations.

Following evacuation of a mine in a fire emergency, only persons wearing and trained in the use of mine rescue apparatus shall participate in rescue and firefighting operations in advance of the fresh air base.

§ 57.4363 Underground evacuation instruction.

(a) At least once every twelve months, all persons who work underground shall be instructed in the escape and evacuation plans and procedures and fire warning signals in effect at the mine.

(b) Whenever a change is made in escape and evacuation plans and procedures for any area of the mine, all persons affected shall be instructed in the new plans or procedures.

(c) Whenever persons are assigned to work in areas other than their regularly assigned areas, they shall be instructed about the escapeway for that area at the time of such assignment. However, persons who normally work in more than one area of the mine shall be instructed at least once every twelve months about the location of escapeways for all areas of the mine in which they normally work or travel.

(d) At the completion of any instruction given under this standard, the mine operator shall certify the date that the instruction was given. Certifications shall be retained for at least one year.

FLAMMABLE AND COMBUSTIBLE LIQUIDS AND GASES

§ 57.4400 Use restrictions.

(a) Flammable liquids shall not be used for cleaning.

(b) Solvents shall not be used near an open flame or other ignition source, near any source of heat, or in an atmosphere that can elevate the temperature of the solvent above the flash point.

§ 57.4401 Storage tank foundations.

Fixed, unburied, flammable or combustible liquid storage tanks shall be securely mounted on firm foundations. Piping shall be provided with flexible connections or other special fittings where necessary to prevent leaks caused by tanks settling.

§ 57.4402 Safety can use.

Small quantities of flammable liquids drawn from storage shall be kept in safety cans labeled to indicate the contents.

§ 57.4430 Surface storage facilities.

The requirements of this standard apply to surface areas only.

(a) Storage tanks for flammable or combustible liquids shall be—

Mine Safety and Health Admin., Labor § 57.4462

(1) Capable of withstanding working pressures and stresses and compatible with the type of liquid stored;

(2) Maintained in a manner that prevents leakage;

(3) Isolated or separated from ignition sources to prevent fire or explosion; and

(4) Vented or otherwise constructed to prevent development of pressure or vacuum as a result of filling, emptying, or atmospheric temperature changes. Vents for storage of Class I, II, or IIIA liquids shall be isolated or separated from ignition sources. These pressure relief requirements do not apply to tanks used for storage of Class IIIB liquids that are larger than 12,000 gallons in capacity.

(b) All piping, valves, and fittings shall be—

(1) Capable of withstanding working pressures and stresses;

(2) Compatible with the type of liquid stored; and

(3) Maintained in a manner that prevents leakage.

(c) Fixed, unburied tanks located where escaping liquid could present a hazard to persons shall be provided with—

(1) Containment for the entire capacity of the largest tank; or

(2) Drainage to a remote impoundment area that does not endanger persons. However, storage of only Class IIIB liquids does not require containment or drainage to remote impoundment.

§ 57.4431 Surface storage restrictions.

(a) On the surface, no unburied flammable or combustible liquids or flammable gases shall be stored within 100 feet of the following:

(1) Mine openings or structures attached to mine openings.

(2) Fan installations for underground ventilation.

(3) Hoist houses.

(b) Under this standard, the following may be present in the hoist house in quantities necessary for the day-to-day maintenance of the hoist machinery:

(1) Flammable liquids in safety cans or in other containers placed in tightly closed cabinets. The safety cans and cabinets shall be kept away from any heat source, and each cabinet shall be labeled "flammables."

(2) Combustible liquids in closed containers. The containers shall be kept away from any heat source and the hoist operator's work station.

§ 57.4460 Storage of flammable liquids underground.

(a) Flammable liquids shall not be stored underground, except—

(1) Small quantities stored in tightly closed cabinets away from any heat source. The small quantities shall be stored in safety cans or in non-glass containers of a capacity equal to or less than a safety can. Each cabinet shall be labeled "flammables."

(2) Acetylene and liquefied petroleum gases stored in containers designed for that specific purpose.

(b) Gasoline shall not be stored underground in any quantity.

§ 57.4461 Gasoline use restrictions underground.

If gasoline is used underground to power internal combustion engines—

(a) The mine shall be nongassy and shall have multiple horizontal or inclined roadways from the surface large enough to accommodate vehicular traffic;

(b) All roadways and other openings shall connect with another opening every 100 feet by a passage large enough to accommodate any vehicle in the mine or alternate routes shall provide equivalent escape capabilities; and

(c) No roadway or other opening shall be supported or lined with wood or other combustible materials.

§ 57.4462 Storage of combustible liquids underground.

The requirements of this standard apply to underground areas only.

(a) Combustible liquids, including oil or grease, shall be stored in non-glass containers or storage tanks. The containers or storage tanks shall be—

(1) Capable of withstanding working pressures and stresses and compatible with the type of liquid stored;

(2) Maintained in a manner that prevents leakage;

(3) Located in areas free of combustible materials or in areas where any exposed combustible materials are

§ 57.4463

coated with one inch of shotcrete, one-half inch of gunite, or other noncombustible material with equivalent fire protection characteristics; and

(4) Separated from explosives or blasting agents, shaft stations, and ignition sources including electric equipment that could create sufficient heat or sparks to pose a fire hazard. Separation shall be sufficient to prevent the occurrence or minimize the spread of fire.

(b) Storage tanks shall be vented or otherwise constructed to prevent development of pressure or vacuum as a result of filling, emptying, or atmospheric temperature changes. Vents for storage of Class II or IIIA liquids shall be isolated or separated from ignition sources.

(c) At permanent storage areas for combustible liquids, means shall be provided for confinement or removal of the contents of the largest storage tank in the event of tank rupture.

(d) All piping, valves, and fittings shall be:

(1) Capable of withstanding working pressures and stresses;

(2) Compatible with the type of liquid stored; and

(3) Maintained in a manner which prevents leakage.

§ 57.4463 Liquefied petroleum gas use underground.

Use of liquefied petroleum gases underground shall be limited to maintenance work.

INSTALLATION/CONSTRUCTION/
MAINTENANCE

§ 57.4500 Heat sources.

Heat sources capable of producing combustion shall be separated from combustible materials if a fire hazard could be created.

§ 57.4501 Fuel lines.

Fuel lines shall be equipped with valves capable of stopping the flow of fuel at the source and shall be located and maintained to minimize fire hazards. This standard does not apply to fuel lines on self-propelled equipment.

§ 57.4502 Battery-charging stations.

(a) Battery-charging stations shall be ventilated with a sufficient volume of air to prevent the accumulation of hydrogen gas.

(b) Smoking, use of open flames, or other activities that could create an ignition source shall be prohibited at the battery charging station during battery charging.

(c) Readily visible signs prohibiting smoking or open flames shall be posted at battery-charging stations during battery charging.

§ 57.4503 Conveyor belt slippage.

(a) Surface belt conveyors within confined areas where evacuation would be restricted in the event of a fire resulting from belt-slippage shall be equipped with a detection system capable of automatically stopping the drive pulley.

(b) Underground belt conveyors shall be equipped with a detection system capable of automatically stopping the drive pulley if slippage could cause ignition of the belt.

(c) A person shall attend the belt at the drive pulley when it is necessary to operate the conveyor while temporarily bypassing the automatic function.

§ 57.4504 Fan installations.

(a) Fan houses, fan bulkheads for main and booster fans, and air ducts connecting main fans to underground openings shall be constructed of noncombustible materials.

(b) Areas within 25 feet of main fans or booster fans shall be free of combustible materials, except installed wiring, ground and track support, headframes, and direct-fired heaters. Other timber shall be coated with one inch of shotcrete, one-half inch of gunite, or other noncombustible materials.

§ 57.4505 Fuel lines to underground areas.

Fuel lines into underground storage or dispensing areas shall be drained at the completion of each transfer of fuel unless the following requirements are met:

(a) The valve at the supply source shall be kept closed when fuel is not being transferred.

Mine Safety and Health Admin., Labor § 57.4561

(b) The fuel line shall be—
(1) Capable of withstanding working pressures and stresses;
(2) Located to prevent damage; and
(3) Located in areas free of combustible materials or in areas where any exposed combustible materials are coated with one inch of shotcrete, one-half inch of gunite, or other noncombustible material with equivalent fire protection characteristics.
(c) Provisions shall be made for control or containment of the entire volume of the fuel line so that leakage will not create a fire hazard.

§ 57.4530 Exits for surface buildings and structures.

Surface buildings or structures in which persons work shall have a sufficient number of exits to permit prompt escape in case of fire.

§ 57.4531 Surface flammable or combustible liquid storage buildings or rooms.

(a) Surface storage buildings or storage rooms in which flammable or combustible liquids, including grease, are stored and that are within 100 feet of any person's work station shall be ventilated with a sufficient volume of air to prevent the accumulation of flammable vapors.
(b) In addition, the buildings or rooms shall be—
(1) Constructed to meet a fire resistance rating of at least one hour; or
(2) Equipped with an automatic fire suppression system; or
(3) Equipped with an early warning fire detection device that will alert any person who could be endangered by a fire, provided that no person's work station is in the building.
(c) Flammable or combustible liquids in use for day-to-day maintenance and operational activities are not considered in storage under this standard.

§ 57.4532 Blacksmith shops.

Blacksmith shops located on the surface shall be—
(a) At least 100 feet from fan installations used for intake air and mine openings;
(b) Equipped with exhaust vents over the forge and ventilated to prevent the accumulation of the products of combustion; and
(c) Inspected for smoldering fires at the end of each shift.

§ 57.4533 Mine opening vicinity.

Surface buildings or other similar structures within 100 feet of mine openings used for intake air or within 100 feet of mine openings that are designated escapeways in exhaust air shall be—
(a) Constructed of noncombustible materials; or
(b) Constructed to meet a fire resistance rating of no less than one hour; or
(c) Provided with an automatic fire suppression system; or
(d) Covered on all combustible interior and exterior structural surfaces with noncombustible material or limited combustible material, such as five-eighth inch, type "X" gypsum wallboard.

§ 57.4560 Mine entrances.

For at least 200 feet inside the mine portal or collar timber used for ground support in intake openings and in exhaust openings that are designated as escapeways shall be—
(a) Provided with a fire suppression system, other than fire extinguishers and water hoses, capable of controlling a fire in its early stages; or
(b) Covered with shotcrete, gunite, or other material with equivalent fire protection characteristics; or
(c) Coated with fire-retardant paint or other material to reduce its flame spread rating to 25 or less and maintained in that condition.

[50 FR 4082, Jan. 29, 1985, as amended at 50 FR 20100, May 14, 1985]

§ 57.4561 Stationary diesel equipment underground.

Stationary diesel equipment underground shall be—
(a) Supported on a noncombustible base; and
(b) Provided with a thermal sensor that automatically stops the engine if overheating occurs.

WELDING/CUTTING/COMPRESSED GASES

§ 57.4600 Extinguishing equipment.

(a) When welding, cutting, soldering, thawing, or bending—

(1) With an electric arc or with an open flame where an electrically conductive extinguishing agent could create an electrical hazard, a multipurpose dry-chemical fire extinguisher or other extinguisher with at least a 2–A:10–B:C rating shall be at the worksite.

(2) With an open flame in an area where no electrical hazard exists, a multipurpose dry-chemical fire extinguisher or equivalent fire extinguishing equipment for the class of fire hazard present shall be at the worksite.

(b) Use of halogenated fire extinguishing agents to meet the requirements of this standard shall be limited to Halon 1211 ($CBrClF_2$) and Halon 1301 ($CBrF_3$). When these agents are used in confined or unventilated areas, precautions based on the manufacturer's use instructions shall be taken so that the gases produced by thermal decomposition of the agents are not inhaled.

§ 57.4601 Oxygen cylinder storage.

Oxygen cylinders shall not be stored in rooms or areas used or designated for storage of flammable or combustible liquids, including grease.

§ 57.4602 Gauges and regulators.

Gauges and regulators used with oxygen or acetylene cylinders shall be kept clean and free of oil and grease.

§ 57.4603 Closure of valves.

To prevent accidental release of gases from hoses and torches attached to oxygen and acetylene cylinders or to manifold systems, cylinder or manifold system valves shall be closed when—

(a) The cylinders are moved;

(b) The torch and hoses are left unattended; or

(c) The task or series of tasks is completed.

§ 57.4604 Preparation of pipelines or containers.

Before welding, cutting, or applying heat with an open flame to pipelines or containers that have contained flammable or combustible liquids, flammable gases, or explosive solids, the pipelines or containers shall be—

(a) Drained, ventilated, and thoroughly cleaned of any residue;

(b) Vented to prevent pressure buildup during the application of heat; and

(c)(1) Filled with an inert gas or water, where compatible; or

(2) Determined to be free of flammable gases by a flammable gas detection device prior to and at frequent intervals during the application of heat.

§ 57.4660 Work in shafts, raises, or winzes and other activities involving hazard areas.

During performance of an activity underground described in Table C–2 or when falling sparks or hot metal from work performed in a shaft, raise, or winze could pose a fire hazard—

(a) A multipurpose dry-chemical fire extinguisher shall be at the worksite to supplement the fire extinguishing equipment required by § 57.4600; and

(b) At least one of the following actions shall be taken:

(1) Wet down the area before and after the operation, taking precaution against any hazard of electrical shock.

(2) Isolate any combustible material with noncombustible material.

(3) Shield the activity so that hot metal and sparks cannot cause a fire.

(4) Provide a second person to watch for and extinguish any fire.

TABLE C–2

Activity	Distance	Fire hazard
Welding or cutting with an electric arc or open flame		More than 1 gallon of combustible liquid, unless in a closed, metal container.
Using an open flame to bend or heat materials	Within 35 feet of—	More than 50 pounds of non-fire-retardant wood.
Thawing pipes electrically, except with heat tape		More than 10 pounds of combustible plastics.
Soldering or thawing with an open flame	Within 10 feet of—	Materials in a shaft, raise, or winze that could be ignited by hot metal or sparks.

(5) Cover or bulkhead the opening immediately below and adjacent to the activity with noncombustible material to prevent sparks or hot metal from falling down the shaft, raise, or winze. This alternative applies only to activities involving a shaft, raise, or winze.

Mine Safety and Health Admin., Labor § 57.4760

(c) The affected area shall be inspected during the first hour after the operation is completed. Additional inspections shall be made or other fire prevention measures shall be taken if a fire hazard continues to exist.

VENTILATION CONTROL MEASURES

§ 57.4760 Shaft mines.

(a) Shaft mines shall be provided with at least one of the following means to control the spread of fire, smoke, and toxic gases underground in the event of a fire: control doors, reversal of mechanical ventilation, or effective evacuation procedures. Under this standard, "shaft mine" means a mine in which any designated escapeway includes a mechanical hoisting device or a ladder ascent.

(1) *Control doors.* If used as an alternative, control doors shall be—

(i) Installed at or near shaft stations of intake shafts and any shaft designated as an escapeway under § 57.11053 or at other locations that provide equivalent protection;

(ii) Constructed and maintained according to Table C-3;

(iii) Provided with a means of remote closure at landings of timbered intake shafts unless a person specifically designated to close each door in the event of a fire can reach the door within three minutes;

(iv) Closed or opened only according to predetermined conditions and procedures;

(v) Constructed so that once closed they will not reopen as a result of a differential in air pressure;

(vi) Constructed so that they can be opened from either side by one person, or be provided with a personnel door that can be opened from either side; and

(vii) Clear of obstructions.

(2) *Mechanical ventilation reversal.* If used as an alternative, reversal of mechanical ventilation shall—

(i) Provide at all times at least the same degree of protection to persons underground as would be afforded by the installation of control doors;

(ii) Be accomplished by a main fan. If the main fan is located underground—

(A) The cable or conductors supplying power to the fan shall be routed through areas free of fire hazards; or

(B) The main fan shall be equipped with a second, independent power cable or set of conductors from the surface. The power cable or conductors shall be located so that an underground fire disrupting power in one cable or set of conductors will not affect the other; or

(C) A second fan capable of accomplishing ventilation reversal shall be available for use in the event of failure of the main fan;

(iii) Provide rapid air reversal that allows persons underground time to exit in fresh air by the second escapeway or find a place of refuge; and

(iv) Be done according to predetermined conditions and procedures.

(3) *Evacuation.* If used as an alternative, effective evacuation shall be demonstrated by actual evacuation of all persons underground to the surface in ten minutes or less through routes that will not expose persons to heat, smoke, or toxic fumes in the event of a fire.

(b) If the destruction of any bulkhead on an inactive level would allow fire contaminants to reach an escapeway, that bulkhead shall be constructed and maintained to provide at least the same protection as required for control doors under Table C-3.

TABLE C-3—CONTROL DOOR CONSTRUCTION

Location	Minimum required construction
At least 50 feet from: timbered areas, exposed combustible rock, and any other combustible material [1]	Control door that meets the requirements for a ventilation door in conformance with 30 CFR 57.8531.

§ 57.4761

TABLE C-3—CONTROL DOOR CONSTRUCTION—Continued

Location	Minimum required construction
Within 50 feet but no closer than 20 feet of: timbered areas, exposed combustible rock, or other combustible material [1] Within 20 feet of: any timbered areas or combustible rock, provided that the timber and combustible rock within the 20 foot distance are coated with one inch of shotcrete, one-half inch of gunite, or other material with equivalent fire protection characteristics and no other combustible material [1] is within that distance	Control door that serves as a barrier to the effects of fire and air leakage. The control door shall provide protection at least equivalent to a door constructed of no less than one-quarter inch of plate steel with channel or angle-iron reinforcement to minimize warpage. The framework assembly of the door and the surrounding bulkhead, if any, shall be at least equivalent to the door in fire and air-leakage resistance, and in physical strength.
Within 20 feet of: timbered areas, exposed combustible rock, or other combustible material [1]	Control door that serves as a barrier to fire, the effects of fire, and air-leakage. The door shall provide protection at least equivalent to a door constructed of two layers of wood, each a minimum of three-quarters of an inch in thickness. The wood grain of one layer shall be perpendicular to the wood grain of the other layer. The wood construction shall be covered on all sides and edges with no less than twenty-four gauge sheet steel. The framework assembly of the door and the surrounding bulkhead, if any, shall be at least equivalent to the door in fire and air-leakage resistance, and in physical strength. Roll-down steel doors with a fire-resistance rating of 1½ hours or greater, but without an insulation core, are acceptable if an automatic sprinkler or deluge system is installed that provides even coverage of the door on both sides.

[1] In this table, "combustible material" does not refer to installed wiring or track support.

[50 FR 4082, Jan. 29, 1985; 50 FR 20100, May 14, 1985]

§ 57.4761 Underground shops.

To confine or prevent the spread of toxic gases from a fire originating in an underground shop where maintenance work is routinely done on mobile equipment, one of the following measures shall be taken: use of control doors or bulkheads, routing of the mine shop air directly to an exhaust system, reversal of mechanical ventilation, or use of an automatic fire suppression system in conjunction with an alternate escape route. The alternative used shall at all times provide at least the same degree of safety as control doors or bulkheads.

(a) *Control doors or bulkheads.* If used as an alternative, control doors or bulkheads shall meet the following requirements:

(1) Each control door or bulkhead shall be constructed to serve as a barrier to fire, the effects of fire, and air leakage at each opening to the shop.

(2) Each control door shall be—

(i) Constructed so that, once closed, it will not reopen as a result of a differential in air pressure;

(ii) Constructed so that it can be opened from either side by one person or be provided with a personnel door that can be opened from either side;

(iii) Clear of obstructions; and

(iv) Provided with a means of remote or automatic closure unless a person specifically designated to close the door in the event of a fire can reach the door within three minutes.

(3) If located 20 feet or more from exposed timber or other combustible material, the control doors or bulkheads shall provide protection at least equivalent to a door constructed of no less than one-quarter inch of plate steel with channel or angle-iron reinforcement to minimize warpage. The framework assembly of the door and the surrounding bulkhead, if any, shall be at least equivalent to the door in fire and air-leakage resistance, and in physical strength.

(4) If located less than 20 feet from exposed timber or other combustibles, the control door or bulkhead shall provide protection at least equivalent to a door constructed of two layers of wood, each a minimum of three-quarters of an inch in thickness. The wood-grain of one layer shall be perpendicular to the wood-grain of the other layer. The wood construction shall be covered on all sides and edges with no less than 24-gauge sheet steel. The framework assembly of the door and the surrounding bulkhead, if any, shall be at least

Mine Safety and Health Admin., Labor §57.5001

equivalent to the door in fire and air-leakage resistance, and in physical strength. Roll-down steel doors with a fire-resistance rating of 1½ hours or greater, but without an insulation core, are acceptable provided that an automatic sprinkler or deluge system is installed that provides even coverage of the door on both sides.

(b) *Routing air to exhaust system.* If used as an alternative, routing the mine shop exhaust air directly to an exhaust system shall be done so that no person would be exposed to toxic gases in the event of a shop fire.

(c) *Mechanical ventilation reversal.* If used as an alternative, reversal of mechanical ventilation shall—

(1) Be accomplished by a main fan. If the main fan is located underground:

(i) The cable or conductors supplying power to the fan shall be routed through areas free of fire hazards; or

(ii) The main fan shall be equipped with a second, independent power cable or set of conductors from the surface. The power cable or conductors shall be located so that an underground fire disrupting power in one cable or set of conductors will not affect the other; or

(iii) A second fan capable of accomplishing ventilation reversal shall be available for use in the event of failure of the main fan;

(2) Provide rapid air reversal that allows persons underground time to exit in fresh air by the second escapeway or find a place of refuge; and

(3) Be done according to predetermined conditions and procedures.

(d) *Automatic fire suppression system and escape route.* If used as an alternative, the automatic fire suppression system and alternate escape route shall meet the following requirements:

(1) The suppression system shall be—

(i) Located in the shop area;

(ii) The appropriate size and type for the particular fire hazards involved; and

(iii) Inspected at weekly intervals and properly maintained.

(2) The escape route shall bypass the shop area so that the route will not be affected by a fire in the shop area.

APPENDIX I TO SUBPART C OF PART 57—NATIONAL CONSENSUS STANDARDS

Mine operators seeking further information in the area of fire prevention and control may consult the following national consensus standards.

MSHA standard	National consensus standard
§§ 57.4200, 57.4201, 57.4261, and 57.4262.	NFPA No. 10—Portable Fire Extinguisher. NFPA No. 11—Low Expansion Foam and Combined Agent Systems. NFPA No. 11A—High Expansion Foam Systems. NFPA No. 12—Carbon Dioxide Extinguishing Systems. NFPA No. 12A—Halon 1301 Extinguishing Systems. NFPA No. 13—Water Sprinkler Systems. NFPA No. 14—Standpipe and Hose Systems. NFPA No. 15—Water Spray Fixed Systems. NFPA No. 16—Foam Water Spray Systems. NFPA No. 17—Dry-Chemical Extinguishing Systems. NFPA No. 121—Mobile Surface Mining Equipment. NFPA No. 291—Testing and Marking Hydrants. NFPA No. 1962—Care, Use, and Maintenance of Fire Hose, Connections, and Nozzles.
§ 57.4202	NFPA No. 14—Standpipe and Hose Systems. NFPA No. 291—Testing and Marking Hydrants.
§ 57.4203	NFPA No. 10—Portable Fire Extinguishers.
§ 57.4230	NFPA No. 10—Portable Fire Extinguishers. NFPA No. 121—Mobile Surface Mining Equipment.
§ 57.4260	NFPA No. 10—Portable Fire Extinguishers.
§ 57.4261	NFPA No. 14—Standpipe and Hose Systems.
§ 57.4533	NFPA Fire Protection Handbook.
§ 57.4560	ASTM E-162—Surface Flammability of Materials Using a Radiant Heat Energy Source.

Subpart D—Air Quality, Radiation, Physical Agents, and Diesel Particulate Matter

AIR QUALITY—SURFACE AND UNDERGROUND

§ 57.5001 Exposure limits for airborne contaminants.

Except as permitted by § 57.5005—

(a) Except as provided in paragraph (b), the exposure to airborne contaminants shall not exceed, on the basis of a time weighted average, the threshold limit values adopted by the American Conference of Governmental Industrial Hygienists, as set forth and explained in the 1973 edition of the Conference's publication, entitled "TLV's Threshold Limit Values for Chemical Substances

§ 57.5002

in Workroom Air Adopted by ACGIH for 1973," pages 1 through 54, which are hereby incorporated by reference and made a part hereof. This publication may be obtained from the American Conference of Governmental Industrial Hygienists by writing to 1330 Kemper Meadow Drive, Attn: Customer Service, Cincinnati, OH 45240, *http:// www.acgih.org*, or may be examined in any Metal and Nonmetal Mine Safety and Health District Office of the Mine Safety and Health Administration. Excursions above the listed thresholds shall not be of a greater magnitude than is characterized as permissible by the Conference.

(b) *Asbestos standard*—(1) *Definitions.* Asbestos is a generic term for a number of asbestiform hydrated silicates that, when crushed or processed, separate into flexible fibers made up of fibrils.

Asbestos means chrysotile, cummingtonite-grunerite asbestos (amosite), crocidolite, anthophylite asbestos, tremolite asbestos, and actinolite asbestos.

Asbestos fiber means a fiber of asbestos that meets the criteria of a fiber.

Fiber means a particle longer than 5 micrometers (μm) with a length-to-diameter ratio of at least 3-to-1.

(2) *Permissible Exposure Limits (PELs)*—(i) *Full-shift limit.* A miner's personal exposure to asbestos shall not exceed an 8-hour time-weighted average full-shift airborne concentration of 0.1 fiber per cubic centimeter of air (f/cc).

(ii) *Excursion limit.* No miner shall be exposed at any time to airborne concentrations of asbestos in excess of 1 fiber per cubic centimeter of air (f/cc) as averaged over a sampling period of 30 minutes.

(3) *Measurement of airborne asbestos fiber concentration.* Potential asbestos fiber concentration shall be determined by phase contrast microscopy (PCM) using the OSHA Reference Method in OSHA's asbestos standard found in 29 CFR 1910.1001, Appendix A, or a method at least equivalent to that method in identifying a potential asbestos exposure exceeding the 0.1 f/cc full-shift limit or the 1 f/cc excursion limit. When PCM results indicate a potential exposure exceeding the 0.1 f/cc full-

30 CFR Ch. I (7-1-23 Edition)

shift limit or the 1 f/cc excursion limit, samples shall be further analyzed using transmission electron microscopy according to NIOSH Method 7402 or a method at least equivalent to that method.

(c) Employees shall be withdrawn from areas where there is present an airborne contaminant given a "C" designation by the Conference and the concentration exceeds the threshold limit value listed for that contaminant.

[50 FR 4082, Jan. 29, 1985, as amended at 60 FR 35695, July 11, 1995; 71 FR 16667, Apr. 3, 2006; 73 FR 11303, Feb. 29, 2008; 73 FR 66172, Nov. 7, 2008]

§ 57.5002 Exposure monitoring.

Dust, gas, mist, and fume surveys shall be conducted as frequently as necessary to determine the adequacy of control measures.

§ 57.5005 Control of exposure to airborne contaminants.

Control of employee exposure to harmful airborne contaminants shall be, insofar as feasible, by prevention of contamination, removal by exhaust ventilation, or by dilution with uncontaminated air. However, where accepted engineering control measures have not been developed or when necessary by the nature of work involved (for example, while establishing controls or occasional entry into hazardous atmospheres to perform maintenance or investigation), employees may work for reasonable periods of time in concentrations of airborne contaminants exceeding permissible levels if they are protected by appropriate respiratory protective equipment. Whenever respiratory protective equipment is used a program for selection, maintenance, training, fitting, supervision, cleaning, and use shall meet the following minimum requirements:

(a) Respirators approved by NIOSH under 42 CFR part 84 which are applicable and suitable for the purpose intended shall be furnished and miners shall use the protective equipment in accordance with training and instruction.

(b) A respirator program consistent with the requirements of ANSI Z88.2-

Mine Safety and Health Admin., Labor § 57.5037

1969, published by the American National Standards Institute and entitled "American National Standards Practices for Respiratory Protection ANSI Z88.2–1969," approved August 11, 1969, which is hereby incorporated by reference and made a part hereof. This publication may be obtained from the American National Standards Institute, Inc., 25 W. 43rd Street, 4th Floor, New York, NY 10036; http://www.ansi.org, or may be examined in any Metal and Nonmetal Mine Safety and Health District Office of the Mine Safety and Health Administration.

(c) When respiratory protection is used in atmospheres immediately harmful to life, the presence of at least one other person with backup equipment and rescue capability shall be required in the event of failure of the respiratory equipment.

[50 FR 4082, Jan. 29, 1985, as amended at 60 FR 30400, June 8, 1995; 60 FR 33723, June 29, 1995; 60 FR 35695, July 11, 1995; 71 FR 16667, Apr. 3, 2006]

§ 57.5006 Restricted use of chemicals.

The following chemical substances shall not be used or stored except by competent persons under laboratory conditions approved by a nationally recognized agency acceptable to the Secretary.

(a) Carbon tetrachloride,
(b) Phenol,
(c) 4-Nitrobiphenyl,
(d) Alpha-naphthylamine,
(e) 4,4-Methylene Bis (2-chloroaniline),
(f) Methyl-chloromethyl ether,
(g) 3,3 Dichlorobenzidine,
(h) Bis (chloromethyl) ether,
(i) Beta-napthylamine,
(j) Benzidine,
(k) 4-Aminodiphenyl,
(l) Ethyleneimine,
(m) Beta-propiolactone,
(n) 2-Acetylaminofluorene,
(o) 4-Dimethylaminobenzene, and
(p) N-Nitrosodimethylamine.

AIR QUALITY—SURFACE ONLY [RESERVED]

AIR QUALITY—UNDERGROUND ONLY

§ 57.5015 Oxygen deficiency.

Air in all active workings shall contain at least 19.5 volume percent oxygen.

RADIATION—UNDERGROUND ONLY

§ 57.5037 Radon daughter exposure monitoring.

(a) In all mines at least one sample shall be taken in exhaust mine air by a competent person to determine if concentrations of radon daughters are present. Sampling shall be done using suggested equipment and procedures described in section 14.3 of ANSI N13.8–1973, entitled "American National Standard Radiation Protection in Uranium Mines," approved July 18, 1973, pages 13–15, by the American National Standards Institute, Inc., which is incorporated by reference and made a part of the standard or equivalent procedures and equipment acceptable to the Administrator, MSHA Metal and Nonmetal Mine Safety and Health district office. This publication may be examined at any Metal and Nonmetal Mine Safety and Health Subdistrict Office of the Mine Safety and Health Administration, or may be obtained from the American National Standards Institute, Inc., 25 W. 43rd Street, 4th Floor, New York, NY 10036; http://www.ansi.org. The mine operator may request that the required exhaust mine air sampling be done by the Mine Safety and Health Administration. If concentrations of radon daughters in excess of 0.1 WL are found in an exhaust air sample, thereafter—

(1) Where uranium is mined—radon daughter concentrations representative of worker's breathing zone shall be determined at least every two weeks at random times in all active working areas such as stopes, drift headings, travelways, haulageways, shops, stations, lunch rooms, magazines, and any other place or location where persons work, travel, or congregate. However, if concentrations of radon daughters

§ 57.5038

are found in excess of 0.3 WL in an active working area, radon daughter concentrations thereafter shall be determined weekly in that working area until such time as the weekly determinations in that area have been 0.3 WL or less for 5 consecutive weeks.

(2) Where uranium is not mined—when radon daughter concentrations between 0.1 and 0.3 WL are found in an active working area, radon daughter concentration measurements representative of worker's breathing zone shall be determined at least every 3 months at random times until such time as the radon daughter concentrations in that area are below 0.1 WL, and annually thereafter. If concentrations of radon daughters are found in excess of 0.3 WL in an active working area radon daughter concentrations thereafter shall be determined at least weekly in that working area until such time as the weekly determinations in that area have been 0.3 WL or less for 5 consecutive weeks.

(b) If concentrations of radon daughters less than 0.1 WL are found in an exhaust mine air sample, thereafter:

(1) Where uranium is mined—at least one sample shall be taken in the exhaust mine air monthly.

(2) Where uranium is not mined—no further exhaust mine air sampling is required.

(c) The sample date, locations, and results obtained under (a) and (b) above shall be recorded and retained at the mine site or nearest mine office for at least two years and shall be made available for inspection by the Secretary or his authorized representative.

[50 FR 4082, Jan. 29, 1985, as amended at 60 FR 33723, June 29, 1995; 71 FR 16667, Apr. 3, 2006]

§ 57.5038 Annual exposure limits.

No person shall be permitted to receive an exposure in excess of 4 WLM in any calendar year.

§ 57.5039 Maximum permissible concentration.

Except as provided by standard § 57.5005, persons shall not be exposed to air containing concentrations of radon daughters exceeding 1.0 WL in active workings.

§ 57.5040 Exposure records.

(a) The operator shall calculate and record complete individual exposures to concentrations of radon daughters as follows:

(1) Where uranium is mined—the complete individual exposures of all mine personnel working underground shall be calculated and recorded. These records shall include the individual's time in each active working area such as stopes, drift headings, travelways, haulageways, shops, stations, lunch rooms, magazines and any other place or location where persons work, travel or congregate, and the concentration of airborne radon daughters for each active working area.

(2) Where uranium is not mined—the complete individual exposure of all mine personnel working in active working areas with radon daughter concentrations in excess of 0.3 WL shall be calculated and recorded. These records shall include the individual's time in each active working area and the concentrations of airborne radon daughters for each active working area. The operator may discontinue calculating and recording the individual exposures of any personnel assigned to work in active working areas where radon daughter concentrations have been reduced to 0.3 WL or less for 5 consecutive weeks provided that such exposure calculation and recordation shall not be discontinued with respect to any person who has accumulated more exposure than $1/12$ (one-twelfth) of a WLM times the number of months for which exposures have been calculated and recorded in the calendar year in which the exposure calculation and recordation is proposed to be discontinued.

(b) The operator shall maintain the form entitled "Record of Individual Exposure to Radon Daughters" (Form 4000–9), or equivalent forms that are acceptable to the Administrator, Metal and Nonmetal Mine Safety and Health, Mine Safety and Health Administration, on which there shall be recorded the specific information required by the form with respect to each person's time-weighted current and cumulative exposure to concentrations of radon daughters.

(1) The form entitled "Record of Individual Exposure to Radon Daughters" (Form 4000–9), shall consist of an original of each form for the operator's records which shall be available for examination by the Secretary or his authorized representative.

(2) On or before February 15 of each calendar year, or within 45 days after the shutdown of mining operations for the calendar year, each mine operator shall submit to the Mine Safety and Health Administration a copy of the "Record of Individual Exposure to Radon Daughters" (Form 4000–9), or acceptable equivalent form, showing the data required by the form for all personnel for whom calculation and recording of exposure was required during the previous calendar year.

(3) Errors detected by the operator shall be corrected on any forms kept by the operator and a corrected copy of any forms submitted to the Mine Safety and Health Administration shall be submitted to the Mine Safety and Health Administration within 60 days of detection and shall identify the errors and indicate the date the corrections are made.

(4) The operator's records of individual exposure to concentrations of radon daughters and copies of "Record of Individual Exposure to Radon Daughters" (Form 4000–9) or acceptable equivalent form or true legible facsimiles thereof (microfilm or other), shall be retained at the mine or nearest mine office for a period as specified in paragraph 9.8, ANSI N13.8–1973, or shall be submitted to the Mine Safety and Health Administration. These records, if retained by the operator, shall be open for inspection by the Secretary of Labor, his authorized representative, and authorized representatives of the official mine inspection agency of the State in which the mine is located. Paragraph 9.8, ANSI N13.8–1973, is incorporated by reference and made a part of this standard. ANSI N13.8–1973 may be examined at any Metal and Nonmetal Mine Safety and Health District Office of the Mine Safety and Health Administration, and may be obtained from the American National Standards Institute, Inc., at 25 W. 43rd Street, 4th Floor, New York, NY 10036; *http://www.ansi.org*.

(5) Upon written request from a person who is a subject of these records, a statement of the year-to-date and cumulative exposure applicable to that person shall be provided to the person or to whomever such person designates.

(6) The blank form entitled "Record of Individual Exposure to Radon Daughters" (Form 4000–9) may be obtained on request from any MSHA Metal and Nonmetal Mine Safety and Health district office.

NOTE: To calculate an individual's exposure to WLM for a given period of time, multiply the total exposure time (hours to the nearest half-hour) in an active working area by the average concentration of airborne radon daughters for the applicable active working area (average working level calculated to the nearest hundredth working level) and divide the product by the constant 173 hours per month.

An average airborne radon daughter concentration for a designated active working area shall be determined by averaging all sampling results for that working area during the time that persons are present. Any sample taken by Federal or State mine inspectors, which represents exposure to miners and reported to the operator within three days of being taken, shall be included in the average concentration; except that if the mine operator samples simultaneously with the inspector, he may use his own sample results.

[50 FR 4082, Jan. 29, 1985, as amended at 60 FR 33723, June 29, 1995; 60 FR 35695, July 11, 1995; 71 FR 16667, Apr. 3, 2006]

§ 57.5041 Smoking prohibition.

Smoking shall be prohibited in all areas of a mine where exposure records are required to be kept in compliance with standard 57.5040.

§ 57.5042 Revised exposure levels.

If levels of permissible exposures to concentrations of radon daughters different from those prescribed in 57.5038 are recommended by the Environmental Protection Agency and approved by the President, no employee shall be permitted to receive exposures in excess of those levels after the effective dates established by the Agency.

§ 57.5044 Respirators.

In environments exceeding 1.0 WL, miners shall wear respirators approved by NIOSH for radon daughters prior to July 10, 1995 or under the equivalent

§ 57.5045

section of 42 CFR part 84 and such respirator use shall be in compliance with § 57.5005.

[60 FR 30400, June 8, 1995]

§ 57.5045 Posting of inactive workings.

Inactive workings in which radon daughter concentrations are above 1.0 WL, shall be posted against unauthorized entry and designated by signs indicating them as areas in which approved respirators shall be worn.

§ 57.5046 Protection against radon gas.

Where radon daughter concentrations exceed 10 WL, respirator protection against radon gas shall be provided in addition to protection against radon daughters. Protection against radon gas shall be provided by supplied air devices or by face masks containing absorbent material capable of removing both the radon and its daughters.

§ 57.5047 Gamma radiation surveys.

(a) Gamma radiation surveys shall be conducted annually in all underground mines where radioactive ores are mined.

(b) Surveys shall be in accordance with American National Standards (ANSI) Standard N13.8–1973, entitled "Radiation Protection in Uranium Mines", section 14.1 page 12, which is hereby incorporated by reference and made a part hereof. This publication may be examined in any Metal and Nonmetal Mine Safety and Health District Office, Mine Safety and Health Administration, or may be obtained from the American National Standards Institute, Inc., 25 W. 43rd Street, 4th Floor, New York, NY 10036; http://www.ansi.org.

(c) Where average gamma radiation measurements are in excess of 2.0 milliroentgens per hour in the working place, gamma radiation dosimeters shall be provided for all persons affected, and records of cumulative individual gamma radiation exposure shall be kept.

(d) Annual individual gamma radiation exposure shall not exceed 5 rems.

[50 FR 4082, Jan. 29, 1985, as amended at 60 FR 33723, June 29, 1995; 60 FR 35695, July 11, 1995; 71 FR 16667, Apr. 3, 2006]

DIESEL PARTICULATE MATTER— UNDERGROUND ONLY

SOURCE: 66 FR 5907, Jan. 19, 2001, unless otherwise noted.

§ 57.5060 Limit on exposure to diesel particulate matter.

(a) A miner's personal exposure to diesel particulate matter (DPM) in an underground mine must not exceed an average eight-hour equivalent full shift airborne concentration of 308 micrograms of elemental carbon per cubic meter of air (308_{EC} µg/m^3). [This interim permissible exposure limit (PEL) remains in effect until the final DPM exposure limit becomes effective. When the final DPM exposure limit becomes effective, MSHA will publish a document in the FEDERAL REGISTER.]

(b)(1) Effective May 20, 2006, a miner's personal exposure to diesel particulate matter (DPM) in an underground mine must not exceed an average eight-hour equivalent full shift airborne concentration of 308 micrograms of elemental carbon per cubic meter of air (308_{EC} µg/m^3).

(2) Effective January 20, 2007, a miner's personal exposure to diesel particulate matter (DPM) in an underground mine must not exceed an average eight-hour equivalent full shift airborne concentration of 350 micrograms of total carbon per cubic meter of air (350_{TC} µg/m^3).

(3) Effective May 20, 2008, a miner's personal exposure to diesel particulate matter (DPM) in an underground mine must not exceed an average eight-hour equivalent full shift airborne concentration of 160 micrograms of total carbon per cubic meter of air (160_{TC} µg/m^3).

(c)(1) If a mine requires additional time to come into compliance with the final DPM limit established in § 57.5060 (b) due to technological or economic constraints, the operator of the mine may file an application with the District Manager for a special extension.

(2) The mine operator must certify on the application that the operator has posted one copy of the application at the mine site for at least 30 days prior to the date of application, and has provided another copy to the authorized representative of miners.

Mine Safety and Health Admin., Labor §57.5060

(3) No approval of a special extension shall exceed a period of one year from the date of approval. Mine operators may file for additional special extensions provided each extension does not exceed a period of one year. An application must include the following information:

(i) Documentation supporting that controls are technologically or economically infeasible at this time to reduce the miner's exposure to the final DPM limit.

(ii) The most recent DPM monitoring results.

(iii) The actions the operator will take during the extension to minimize exposure of miners to DPM.

(4) A mine operator must comply with the terms of any approved application for a special extension, post a copy of the approved application for a special extension at the mine site for the duration of the special extension period, and provide a copy of the approved application to the authorized representative of miners.

(d) The mine operator must install, use, and maintain feasible engineering and administrative controls to reduce a miner's exposure to or below the applicable DPM PEL established in this section. When controls do not reduce a miner's DPM exposure to the PEL, controls are infeasible, or controls do not produce significant reductions in DPM exposures, controls must be used to reduce the miner's exposure to as low a level as feasible and must be supplemented with respiratory protection in accordance with §57.5005(a), (b), and paragraphs (d)(1) through (d)(8) of this section.

(1) Air purifying respirators must be equipped with the following:

(i) Filters certified by NIOSH under 30 CFR part 11 (appearing in the July 1, 1994 edition of 30 CFR, parts 1 to 199) as a high efficiency particulate air (HEPA) filter;

(ii) Filters certified by NIOSH under 42 CFR part 84 as 99.97% efficient; or

(iii) Filters certified by NIOSH for DPM.

(2) Non-powered, negative-pressure, air purifying, particulate-filter respirators shall use an R- or P-series filter or any filter certified by NIOSH for DPM. An R-series filter shall not be used for longer than one work shift.

(3) The mine operator must provide a confidential medical evaluation by a physician or other licensed health care professional (PLHCP), at no cost to the miner, to determine the miner's ability to use a respirator before the miner is required to be fit tested or to use a respirator at the mine. If the PLHCP determines that the miner cannot wear a negative pressure respirator, the mine operator must make certain that the PLHCP evaluates the miner's ability to wear a powered air purifying respirator (PAPR).

(4) The mine operator must provide the miner with an opportunity to discuss their evaluation results with the PLHCP before the PLHCP submits the written determination to the mine operator regarding the miner's ability to wear a respirator. If the miner disagrees with the evaluation results of the PLHCP, the miner may submit within 30 days additional evidence of his or her medical condition to the PLHCP.

(5) The mine operator must obtain a written determination from the PLHCP regarding the miner's ability to wear a respirator, and the mine operator must assure that the PLHCP provides a copy of the determination to the miner.

(6) The miner must be reevaluated when the mine operator has reason to believe that conditions have changed which could adversely affect the miner's ability to wear the respirator.

(7) Upon written notification that the PLHCP has determined that the miner is unable to wear a respirator, including a PAPR, the miner must be transferred to work in an existing position in an area of the same mine where respiratory protection is not required. The miner must be transferred within 30 days of the final determination by the PLHCP.

(i) The miner must continue to receive compensation at no less than the regular rate of pay in the classification held by that miner immediately prior to the transfer.

(ii) Increases in wages of the transferred miner must be based upon the new work classification.

§ 57.5061

(8) The mine operator must maintain a record of the identity of the PLHCP and the most recent written determination of each miner's ability to wear a respirator for the duration of the miner's employment plus six months.

(e) Rotation of miners shall not be considered an acceptable administrative control used for compliance with the DPM standard.

[70 FR 32966, June 6, 2005; 70 FR 37901, June 30, 2005, as amended at 70 FR 55019, Sept. 19, 2005; 71 FR 29011, 29012, May 18, 2006; 71 FR 36483, June 27, 2006]

§ 57.5061 Compliance determinations.

(a) MSHA will use a single sample collected and analyzed by the Secretary in accordance with the requirements of this section as an adequate basis for a determination of noncompliance with the DPM limit.

(b) The Secretary will collect samples of DPM by using a respirable dust sampler equipped with a submicrometer impactor and analyze the samples for the amount of elemental carbon using the method described in NIOSH Analytical Method 5040, except that the Secretary also may use any methods of collection and analysis subsequently determined by NIOSH to provide equal or improved accuracy for the measurement of DPM.

(c) The Secretary will use full-shift personal sampling for compliance determinations.

[70 FR 32966, June 6, 2005]

§ 57.5065 Fueling practices.

(a) Diesel fuel used to power equipment in underground areas must not have a sulfur content greater than 0.05 percent. The operator must retain purchase records that demonstrate compliance with this requirement for one year after the date of purchase.

(b) The operator must only use fuel additives registered by the U.S. Environmental Protection Agency in diesel powered equipment operated in underground areas.

[66 FR 5907, Jan. 19, 2001; 66 FR 35520, July 5, 2001]

§ 57.5066 Maintenance standards.

(a) Any diesel powered equipment operated at any time in underground areas must meet the following maintenance standards:

(1) The operator must maintain any approved engine in approved condition;

(2) The operator must maintain the emission related components of any non-approved engine to manufacturer specifications; and

(3) The operator must maintain any emission or particulate control device installed on the equipment in effective operating condition.

(b)(1) A mine operator must authorize each miner operating diesel-powered equipment underground to affix a visible and dated tag to the equipment when the miner notes evidence that the equipment may require maintenance in order to comply with the maintenance standards of paragraph (a) of this section. The term *evidence* means visible smoke or odor that is unusual for that piece of equipment under normal operating procedures, or obvious or visible defects in the exhaust emissions control system or in the engine affecting emissions.

(2) A mine operator must ensure that any equipment tagged pursuant to this section is promptly examined by a person authorized to maintain diesel equipment, and that the affixed tag not be removed until the examination has been completed. The term *promptly* means before the end of the next shift during which a qualified mechanic is scheduled to work.

(3) A mine operator must retain a log of any equipment tagged pursuant to this section. The log must include the date the equipment is tagged, the date the equipment is examined, the name of the person examining the equipment, and any action taken as a result of the examination. The operator must retain the information in the log for one year after the date the tagged equipment was examined.

(c) Persons authorized by a mine operator to maintain diesel equipment covered by paragraph (a) of this section must be qualified, by virtue of training or experience, to ensure that the maintenance standards of paragraph (a) of this section are observed. An operator must retain appropriate evidence of the

Mine Safety and Health Admin., Labor § 57.5070

competence of any person to perform specific maintenance tasks in compliance with those standards for one year after the date of any maintenance, and upon request must provide the documentation to the authorized representative of the Secretary.

[66 FR 5907, Jan. 19, 2001, as amended at 67 FR 9184, Feb. 27, 2002]

EFFECTIVE DATE NOTE: At 66 FR 5907, Jan. 19, 2001, § 57.5066 was added, effective July 5, 2001, except for paragraph (b). At 66 FR 35518, July 5, 2001, the effective date of paragraph (b) was delayed pending disposition of current litigation challenging the rule. At 67 FR 9184, Feb. 27, 2002, paragraphs (b)(1) and (b)(2) were revised, effective Mar. 29, 2002.

§ 57.5067 Engines.

(a) Any diesel engine introduced into an underground area of a mine covered by this part after July 5, 2001, other than an engine in an ambulance or fire fighting equipment which is utilized in accordance with mine fire fighting and evacuation plans, must either:

(1) Have affixed a plate evidencing approval of the engine pursuant to subpart E of Part 7 of this title or pursuant to Part 36 of this title; or

(2) Meet or exceed the applicable particulate matter emission requirements of the Environmental Protection Administration listed in Table 57.5067-1, as follows:

TABLE 57.5067-1

EPA requirement	EPA category	PM limit
40 CFR 86.094-8(a)(1)(i)(A)(2)	light duty vehicle	0.1 g/mile.
40 CFR 86.094-9(a)(1)(i)(A)(2)	light duty truck	0.1 g/mile.
40 CFR 86.094-11(a)(1)(iv)(B)	heavy duty highway engine	0.1 g/bhp-hr.
40 CFR 89.112(a)	nonroad (tier, power range)	varies by power range:
	tier 1 kW<8 (hp<11)	1.0 g/kW-hr (0.75 g/bhp-hr).
	tier 1 8≤kW<19 (11≤hp<25)	0.80 g/kW-hr (0.60 g/bhp-hr).
	tier 1 19≤kW<37 (25≤hp<50)	0.80 g/kW-hr (0.60 g/bhp-hr).
	tier 2 37≤kW<75 (50≤hp<100)	0.40 g/kW-hr (0.30 g/bhp-hr).
	tier 2 75≤kW<130 (100≤hp<175)	0.30 g/kW-hr (0.22 g/bhp-hr).
	tier 1 130≤kW<225 (175≤hp<300)	0.54 g/kW-hr (0.40 g/bhp-hr).
	tier 1 225≤kW<450 (300≤hp<600)	0.54 g/kW-hr (0.40 g/bhp-hr).
	tier 1 450≤kW<560 (600≤hp<750)	0.54 g/kW-hr (0.40 g/bhp-hr).
	tier 1 kW≥560 (hp≥750)	0.54 g/kW-hr (0.40 g/bhp-hr).

NOTES:
"g" means grams.
"hp" means horsepower.
"g/bhp-hr" means grams/brake horsepower-hour.
"kW" means kilowatt.
"g/kW-hr" means grams/kilowatt-hour.

(b) For purposes of paragraph (a):

(1) The term "introduced" means any engine added to the underground inventory of engines of the mine in question, including:

(i) An engine in newly purchased equipment;

(ii) An engine in used equipment brought into the mine; and

(iii) A replacement engine that has a different serial number than the engine it is replacing; but

(2) The term "introduced" does not include engines that were previously part of the mine inventory and rebuilt.

(3) The term *introduced* does not include the transfer of engines or equipment from the inventory of one underground mine to another underground mine operated by the same mine operator.

[66 FR 5907, Jan. 19, 2001, as amended at 66 FR 27864, May 21, 2001; 67 FR 9184, Feb. 27, 2002]

§ 57.5070 Miner training.

(a) Mine operators must provide annual training to all miners at a mine covered by this part who can reasonably be expected to be exposed to diesel emissions on that property. The training must include—

(1) The health risks associated with exposure to diesel particulate matter;

(2) The methods used in the mine to control diesel particulate matter concentrations;

(3) Identification of the personnel responsible for maintaining those controls; and

§ 57.5071

(4) Actions miners must take to ensure the controls operate as intended.

(b) An operator must retain a record at the mine site of the training required by this section for one year after completion of the training.

§ 57.5071   Exposure monitoring.

(a) Mine operators must monitor, as often as necessary to effectively determine, under conditions that can be reasonably anticipated in the mine, whether the average personal full-shift airborne exposure to DPM exceeds the DPM limit specified in § 57.5060.

(b) The mine operator must provide affected miners and their representatives with an opportunity to observe exposure monitoring required by this section. Mine operators must give prior notice to affected miners and their representatives of the date and time of intended monitoring.

(c) If any monitoring performed under this section indicates that a miner's exposure to diesel particulate matter exceeds the DPM limit specified in § 57.5060, the operator must promptly post notice of the corrective action being taken on the mine bulletin board, initiate corrective action by the next work shift, and promptly complete such corrective action.

(d)(1) The results of monitoring for diesel particulate matter, including any results received by a mine operator from sampling performed by the Secretary, must be posted on the mine bulletin board within 15 days of receipt and must remain posted for 30 days. The operator must provide a copy of the results to the authorized representative of miners.

(2) The mine operator must retain for five years (from the date of sampling), the results of any samples the operator collected as a result of monitoring under this section, and information about the sampling method used for obtaining the samples.

[70 FR 32966, June 6, 2005]

§ 57.5075   Diesel particulate records.

(a) The table entitled "Diesel Particulate Matter Recordkeeping Requirements" lists the records the operator must maintain pursuant to §§ 57.5060 through 57.5071, and the duration for which particular records need to be retained.

TABLE 57.5075(a)—DIESEL PARTICULATE RECORDKEEPING REQUIREMENTS

Record	Section reference	Retention time
1. Approved application for extension of time to comply with exposure limits.	§ 57.5060(c)	Duration of extension.
2. Identity of PLHCP and most recent written determination of miner's ability to wear a respirator.	§ 57.5060(d)	Duration of miner's employment plus 6 months.
3. Purchase records noting sulfur content of diesel fuel.	§ 57.5065(a)	1 year beyond date of purchase.
4. Maintenance log	§ 57.5066(b)	1 year after date any equipment is tagged.
5. Evidence of competence to perform maintenance.	§ 57.5066(c)	1 year after date maintenance performed.
6. Annual training provided to potentially exposed miners.	§ 57.5070(b)	1 year beyond date training completed.
7. Record of corrective action	§ 57.5071(c)	Until the corrective action is completed.
8. Sampling method used to effectively evaluate a miner's personal exposure, and sample results.	§ 57.5071(d)	5 years from sample date.

(b)(1) Any record listed in this section which is required to be retained at the mine site may, notwithstanding such requirement, be retained elsewhere if the mine operator can immediately access the record from the mine site by electronic transmission.

(2) Upon request from an authorized representative of the Secretary of Labor, the Secretary of Health and Human Services, or from the authorized representative of miners, mine operators must promptly provide access to any record listed in the table in this section.

(3) An operator must provide access to a miner, former miner, or, with the miner's or former miner's written consent, a personal representative of a miner, to any record required to be

Mine Safety and Health Admin., Labor § 57.6101

maintained pursuant to § 57.5071 or § 57.5060(d) to the extent the information pertains to the miner or former miner. The operator must provide the first copy of a requested record at no cost, and any additional copies at reasonable cost.

(4) Whenever an operator ceases to do business, that operator must transfer all records required to be maintained by this part, or a copy thereof, to any successor operator who must maintain them for the required period.

[70 FR 32966, June 6, 2005; 70 FR 37901, June 30, 2005; 71 FR 29012, May 18, 2006]

Subpart E—Explosives

SOURCE: 61 FR 36801, July 12, 1996, unless otherwise noted.

§ 57.6000 Definitions.

The following definitions apply in this subpart.

Blasting agent. Any substance classified as a blasting agent by the Department of Transportation in 49 CFR 173.114a(a). This document is available at any MSHA Metal and Nonmetal Safety and Health district office.

Detonating cord. A flexible cord containing a center core of high explosives which may be used to initiate other explosives.

Detonator. Any device containing a detonating charge used to initiate an explosive. These devices include electronic detonators, electric or nonelectric instantaneous or delay blasting caps, and delay connectors. The term "detonator" does not include detonating cord. Detonators may be either "Class A" detonators or "Class C" detonators, as classified by the Department of Transportation in 49 CFR 173.53 and 173.100, which is available at any MSHA Metal and Nonmetal Safety and Health district office.

Explosive. Any substance classified as an explosive by the Department of Transportation in 49 CFR 173.53, 173.88, and 173.100. This document is available at any MSHA Metal and Nonmetal Safety and Health district office.

Explosive material. Explosives, blasting agents, and detonators.

Flash point. The minimum temperature at which sufficient vapor is released by a liquid to form a flammable vapor-air mixture near the surface of the liquid.

Igniter cord. A fuse that burns progressively along its length with an external flame at the zone of burning, used for lighting a series of safety fuses in a desired sequence.

Magazine. A bullet-resistant, theft-resistant, fire-resistant, weather-resistant, ventilated facility for the storage of explosives and detonators (BATF Type 1 or Type 2 facility).

Misfire. The complete or partial failure of explosive material to detonate as planned. The term also is used to describe the explosive material itself that has failed to detonate.

Primer. A unit, package, or cartridge of explosives which contains a detonator and is used to initiate other explosives or blasting agents.

Safety switch. A switch that provides shunt protection in blasting circuits between the blast site and the switch used to connect a power source to the blasting circuit.

Slurry. An explosive material containing substantial portions of a liquid, oxidizers, and fuel, plus a thickener.

Water gel. An explosive material containing substantial portions of water, oxidizers, and fuel, plus a cross-linking agent.

[61 FR 36801, July 12, 1996, as amended at 67 FR 38385, June 4, 2002; 68 FR 32361, May 30, 2003; 69 FR 38842, June 29, 2004; 85 FR 2027, Jan. 14, 2020]

STORAGE—SURFACE AND UNDERGROUND

§ 57.6100 Separation of stored explosive material.

(a) Detonators shall not be stored in the same magazine with other explosive material.

(b) When stored in the same magazine, blasting agents shall be separated from explosives, safety fuse, and detonating cord to prevent contamination.

§ 57.6101 Areas around explosive material storage facilities.

(a) Areas surrounding storage facilities for explosive material shall be clear of rubbish, brush, dry grass, and trees for 25 feet in all directions, except that live trees 10 feet or taller need not be removed.

§ 57.6102

(b) Other combustibles shall not be stored or allowed to accumulate within 50 feet of explosive material. Combustible liquids shall be stored in a manner that ensures drainage will occur away from the explosive material storage facility in case of tank rupture.

§ 57.6102 Explosive material storage practices.

(a) Explosive material shall be—
(1) Stored in a manner to facilitate use of oldest stocks first;
(2) Stored according to brand and grade in such a manner as to facilitate identification; and
(3) Stacked in a stable manner but not more than 8 feet high.
(b) Explosives and detonators shall be stored in closed nonconductive containers except that nonelectric detonating devices may be stored on nonconductive racks provided the case-insert instructions and the date-plant-shift code are maintained with the product.

STORAGE—SURFACE ONLY

§ 57.6130 Explosive material storage facilities.

(a) Detonators and explosives shall be stored in magazines.
(b) Packaged blasting agents shall be stored in a magazine or other facility which is ventilated to prevent dampness and excessive heating, weather-resistant, and locked or attended. Drop trailers do not have to be ventilated if they are currently licensed by the Federal, State, or local authorities for over-the-road use. Facilities other than magazines used to store blasting agents shall contain only blasting agents.
(c) Bulk blasting agents shall be stored in weather-resistant bins or tanks which are locked, attended, or otherwise inaccessible to unauthorized entry.
(d) Facilities, bins or tanks shall be posted with the appropriate United States Department of Transportation placards or other appropriate warning signs that indicate the contents and are visible from each approach.

§ 57.6131 Location of explosive material storage facilities.

(a) Storage facilities for any explosive material shall be—
(1) Located so that the forces generated by a storage facility explosion will not create a hazard to occupants in mine buildings and will not damage dams or electric substations; and
(2) Detached structures located outside the blast area and a sufficient distance from powerlines so that the powerlines, if damaged, would not contact the magazines.
(b) Operators should also be aware of regulations affecting storage facilities in 27 CFR part 55, in particular, 27 CFR 55.218 and 55.220. This document is available at any MSHA Metal and Nonmetal Safety and Health district office.

§ 57.6132 Magazine requirements.

(a) Magazines shall be—
(1) Structurally sound;
(2) Noncombustible or the exterior covered with fire-resistant material;
(3) Bullet resistant;
(4) Made of nonsparking material on the inside;
(5) Ventilated to control dampness and excessive heating within the magazine;
(6) Posted with the appropriate United States Department of Transportation placards or other appropriate warning signs that indicate the contents and are visible from each approach, so located that a bullet passing through any of the signs will not strike the magazine;
(7) Kept clean and dry inside;
(8) Unlighted or lighted by devices that are specifically designed for use in magazines and which do not create a fire or explosion hazard;
(9) Unheated or heated only with devices that do not create a fire or explosion hazard;
(10) Locked when unattended; and
(11) Used exclusively for the storage of explosive material except for essential nonsparking equipment used for the operation of the magazine.
(b) Metal magazines shall be equipped with electrical bonding connections between all conductive portions so the entire structure is at the same electrical potential. Suitable

Mine Safety and Health Admin., Labor § 57.6160

electrical bonding methods include welding, riveting, or the use of securely tightened bolts where individual metal portions are joined. Conductive portions of nonmetal magazines shall be grounded.

(c) Electrical switches and outlets shall be located on the outside of the magazine.

§ 57.6133 Powder chests.

(a) Powder chests (day boxes) shall be—

(1) Structurally sound, weather-resistant, equipped with a lid or cover, and with only nonsparking material on the inside;

(2) Posted with the appropriate United States Department of Transportation placards or other appropriate warning signs that indicate the contents and are visible from each approach;

(3) Located out of the blast area once loading has been completed;

(4) Locked or attended when containing explosive material; and

(5) Emptied at the end of each shift with the contents returned to a magazine or other storage facility, or attended.

(b) Detonators shall be kept in chests separate from explosives or blasting agents, unless separated by 4 inches of hardwood or equivalent, or a laminated partition. When a laminated partition is used, operators must follow the provisions of the Institute of Makers of Explosives (IME) Safety Library Publication No. 22, "Recommendations for the Safe Transportation of Detonators in a Vehicle with Other Explosive Materials" (May 1993), and the "Generic Loading Guide for the IME-22 Container" (October 1993). The IME is located at 1120 19th Street NW., Suite 310, Washington, DC 20036–3605; 202–429–9280; *https://www.ime.org*. This incorporation by reference has been approved by the Director of the Federal Register in accordance with 5 U.S.C. 552(a) and 1 CFR part 51. Copies are available at MSHA's Office of Standards, Regulations, and Variances, 201 12th Street South, Arlington, VA 22202–5452; 202–693–9440; and at all Metal and Nonmetal Mine Safety and Health District Offices, or available for inspection at the National Archives and Records Administration (NARA). For information on the availability of this material at NARA, call 202–741–6030, or go to: *http://www.archives.gov/federal_register/code_of_federal_regulations/ibr_locations.html*.

[61 FR 36801, July 12, 1996, as amended at 67 FR 38385, June 4, 2002; 80 FR 52988, Sept. 2, 2015]

STORAGE—UNDERGROUND ONLY

§ 57.6160 Main facilities.

(a) Main facilities used to store explosive material underground shall be located—

(1) In stable or supported ground;

(2) So that a fire or explosion in the storage facilities will not prevent escape from the mine, or cause detonation of the contents of another storage facility;

(3) Out of the line of blasts, and protected from vehicular traffic, except that accessing the facility;

(4) At least 200 feet from work places or shafts;

(5) At least 50 feet from electric substations;

(6) A safe distance from trolley wires; and

(7) At least 25 feet from detonator storage facilities.

(b) Main facilities used to store explosive material underground shall be—

(1) Posted with warning signs that indicate the contents and are visible from any approach;

(2) Used exclusively for the storage of explosive material and necessary equipment associated with explosive material storage and delivery:

(i) Portions of the facility used for the storage of explosives shall only contain nonsparking material or equipment.

(ii) The blasting agent portion of the facility may be used for the storage of other necessary equipment;

(3) Kept clean, suitably dry, and orderly;

(4) Provided with unobstructed ventilation openings;

(5) Kept securely locked unless all access to the mine is either locked or attended; and

§ 57.6161

(6) Unlighted or lighted only with devices that do not create a fire or explosion hazard and which are specifically designed for use in magazines.

(c) Electrical switches and outlets shall be located outside the facility.

§ 57.6161 Auxiliary facilities.

(a) Auxiliary facilities used to store explosive material near work places shall be wooden, box-type containers equipped with covers or doors, or facilities constructed or mined-out to provide equivalent impact resistance and confinement.

(b) The auxiliary facilities shall be—

(1) Constructed of nonsparking material on the inside when used for the storage of explosives;

(2) Kept clean, suitably dry, and orderly;

(3) Kept in repair;

(4) Located out of the line of blasts so they will not be subjected to damaging shock or flyrock;

(5) Identified with warning signs or coded to indicate the contents with markings visible from any approach;

(6) Located at least 15 feet from all haulageways and electrical equipment, or placed entirely within a mined-out recess in the rib used exclusively for explosive material;

(7) Filled with no more than a one-week supply of explosive material;

(8) Separated by at least 25 feet from other facilities used to store detonators; and

(9) Kept securely locked unless all access to the mine is either locked or attended.

TRANSPORTATION—SURFACE AND UNDERGROUND

§ 57.6200 Delivery to storage or blast site areas.

Explosive material shall be transported without undue delay to the storage area or blast site.

§ 57.6201 Separation of transported explosive material.

Detonators shall not be transported on the same vehicle or conveyance with other explosives except as follows:

(a) Detonators in quantities of more than 1,000 may be transported in a vehicle or conveyance with explosives or blasting agents provided the detonators are—

(1) Maintained in the original packaging as shipped from the manufacturer; and

(2) Separated from explosives or blasting agents by 4 inches of hardwood or equivalent, or a laminated partition. The hardwood or equivalent shall be fastened to the vehicle or conveyance. When a laminated partition is used, operators must follow the provisions of the Institute of Makers of Explosives (IME) Safety Library Publication No. 22, "Recommendations for the Safe Transportation of Detonators in a Vehicle with Other Explosive Materials" (May 1993), and the "Generic Loading Guide for the IME–22 Container" (October 1993). The IME is located at 1120 19th Street NW., Suite 310, Washington, DC 20036–3605; 202–429–9280; https://www.ime.org. This incorporation by reference has been approved by the Director of the Federal Register in accordance with 5 U.S.C. 552(a) and 1 CFR part 51. Copies are available at MSHA's Office of Standards, Regulations, and Variances, 201 12th Street South, Arlington, VA 22202–5452; 202–693–9440; and at all Metal and Nonmetal Mine Safety and Health District Offices, or available for examination at the National Archives and Records Administration (NARA). For information on the availability of this material at NARA, call 202–741–6030, or go to: http://www.archives.gov/federal_register/code_of_federal_regulations/ibr_locations.html.

(b) Detonators in quantities of 1,000 or fewer may be transported with explosives or blasting agents provided the detonators are—

(1) Kept in closed containers; and

(2) Separated from explosives or blasting agents by 4 inches of hardwood or equivalent, or a laminated partition. The hardwood or equivalent shall be fastened to the vehicle or conveyance. When a laminated partition is used, operators must follow the provisions of IME Safety Library Publication No. 22, "Recommendations for the Safe Transportation of Detonators in a Vehicle with Other Explosive Materials" (May 1993), and the "Generic Loading Guide for the IME–22 Container" (October 1993). The IME is located at 1120 19th

Mine Safety and Health Admin., Labor

Street NW., Suite 310, Washington, DC 20036–3605; 202–429–9280; *https://www.ime.org*. This incorporation by reference has been approved by the Director of the Federal Register in accordance with 5 U.S.C. 552(a) and 1 CFR part 51. Copies are available at MSHA's Office of Standards, Regulations, and Variances, 201 12th Street South, Arlington, VA 22202–5452; 202–693–9440; and at all Metal and Nonmetal Mine Safety and Health District Offices, or available for examination at the National Archives and Records Administration (NARA). For information on the availability of this material at NARA, call 202–741–6030, or go to: *http://www.archives.gov/federal_register/code_of_federal_regulations/ibr_locations.html*.

[61 FR 36801, July 12, 1996, as amended at 67 FR 38385, June 4, 2002; 80 FR 52988, Sept. 2, 2015]

§ 57.6202 Vehicles.

(a) Vehicles containing explosive material shall be—

(1) Maintained in good condition and shall comply with the requirements of subpart M of this part;

(2) Equipped with sides and enclosures higher than the explosive material being transported or have the explosive material secured to a nonconductive pallet;

(3) Equipped with a cargo space that shall contain the explosive material (passenger areas shall not be considered cargo space);

(4) Equipped with at least two multipurpose dry-chemical fire extinguishers or one such extinguisher and an automatic fire suppression system;

(5) Posted with warning signs that indicate the contents and are visible from each approach;

(6) Occupied only by persons necessary for handling the explosive material;

(7) Attended or the cargo compartment locked at surface areas of underground mines, except when parked at the blast site and loading is in progress; and

(8) Secured while parked by having—
(i) The brakes set;
(ii) The wheels chocked if movement could occur; and

(iii) The engine shut off unless powering a device being used in the loading operation.

(b) Vehicles containing explosives shall have—

(1) No sparking material exposed in the cargo space; and

(2) Only properly secured non-sparking equipment in the cargo space with the explosives.

(c) Vehicles used for dispensing bulk explosive material shall—

(1) Have no zinc or copper exposed in the cargo space; and

(2) Provide any enclosed screw-type conveyors with protection against internal pressure and frictional heat.

§ 57.6203 Locomotives.

Explosive material shall not be transported on a locomotive. When explosive material is hauled by trolley locomotive, covered, electrically insulated cars shall be used.

§ 57.6204 Hoists.

(a) Before explosive material is transported in hoist conveyances—

(1) The hoist operator shall be notified; and

(2) Hoisting in adjacent shaft compartments, except for empty conveyances or counterweights, shall be stopped until transportation of the explosive material is completed.

(b) Explosive material transported in hoist conveyances shall be placed within a container which prevents shifting of the cargo that could cause detonation of the container by impact or by sparks. The manufacturer's container may be used if secured to a nonconductive pallet. When explosives are transported, they shall be secured so as not to contact any sparking material.

(c) No explosive material shall be transported during a mantrip.

§ 57.6205 Conveying explosives by hand.

Closed, nonconductive containers shall be used to carry explosives and detonators to and from blast sites. Separate containers shall be used for explosives and detonators.

USE—SURFACE AND UNDERGROUND

§ 57.6300 Control of blasting operations.

(a) Only persons trained and experienced in the handling and use of explosive material shall direct blasting operations and related activities.

(b) Trainees and inexperienced persons shall work only in the immediate presence of persons trained and experienced in the handling and use of explosive material.

§ 57.6301 Blasthole obstruction check.

Before loading, blastholes shall be checked and, wherever possible, cleared of obstructions.

§ 57.6302 Separation of explosive material.

Explosives and blasting agents shall be kept separated from detonators until loading begins.

§ 57.6303 Initiation preparation.

(a) Primers shall be made up only at the time of use and as close to the blast site as conditions allow.

(b) Primers shall be prepared with the detonator contained securely and completely within the explosive or contained securely and appropriately for its design in the tunnel or cap well.

(c) When using detonating cord to initiate another explosive, a connection shall be prepared with the detonating cord threaded through, attached securely to, or otherwise in contact with the explosive.

§ 57.6304 Primer protection.

(a) Tamping shall not be done directly on a primer.

(b) Rigid cartridges of explosives or blasting agents that are 4 inches (100 millimeters) in diameter or larger shall not be dropped on the primer except where the blasthole contains sufficient depth of water to protect the primer from impact. Slit packages of prill, water gel, or emulsions are not considered rigid cartridges and may be drop loaded.

§ 57.6305 Unused explosive material.

Unused explosive material shall be moved to a protected location as soon as practical after loading operations are completed.

§ 57.6306 Loading, blasting, and security.

(a) When explosive materials or initiating systems are brought to the blast site, the blast site shall be attended; barricaded and posted with warning signs, such as "Danger," "Explosives," or "Keep Out;" or flagged against unauthorized entry.

(b) Vehicles and equipment shall not be driven over explosive material or initiating systems in a manner which could contact the material or system, or create other hazards.

(c) Once loading begins, the only activities permitted within the blast site shall be those activities directly related to the blasting operation and the activities of surveying, stemming, sampling of geology, and reopening of holes, provided that reasonable care is exercised. Haulage activity is permitted near the base of bench faces being loaded or awaiting firing, provided no other haulage access exists.

(d) Loading and blasting shall be conducted in a manner designed to facilitate a continuous process, with the blast fired as soon as possible following the completion of loading. If blasting a loaded round may be delayed for more than 72 hours, the operator shall notify the appropriate MSHA district office.

(e) In electric blasting prior to connecting to the power source, and in nonelectric blasting prior to attaching an initiating device, all persons shall leave the blast area except persons in a blasting shelter or other location that protects them from concussion (shock wave), flying material, and gases.

(f) Before firing a blast—

(1) Ample warning shall be given to allow all persons to be evacuated;

(2) Clear exit routes shall be provided for persons firing the round; and

(3) All access routes to the blast area shall be guarded or barricaded to prevent the passage of persons or vehicles.

(g) Work shall not be resumed in the blast area until a post-blast examination addressing potential blast-related hazards has been conducted by a person with the ability and experience to perform the examination.

Mine Safety and Health Admin., Labor § 57.6404

§ 57.6307 Drill stem loading.

Explosive material shall not be loaded into blastholes with drill stem equipment or other devices that could be extracted while containing explosive material. The use of loading hose, collar sleeves, or collar pipes is permitted.

§ 57.6308 Initiation systems.

Initiation systems shall be used in accordance with the manufacturer's instructions.

§ 57.6309 Fuel oil requirements for ANFO.

(a) Liquid hydrocarbon fuels with flash points lower than that of No. 2 diesel oil (125 °F) shall not be used to prepare ammonium nitrate-fuel oil, except that diesel fuels with flash points no lower than 100 °F may be used at ambient air temperatures below 45 °F.

(b) Waste oil, including crankcase oil, shall not be used to prepare ammonium nitrate-fuel oil.

§ 57.6310 Misfire waiting period.

When a misfire is suspected, persons shall not enter the blast area—

(a) For 30 minutes if safety fuse and blasting caps are used;

(b) For 15 minutes if any other type detonators are used; or

(c) For 30 minutes if electronic detonators are used, or for the manufacturer-recommended time, whichever is longer.

[61 FR 36801, July 12, 1996, as amended at 85 FR 2027, Jan. 14, 2020]

§ 57.6311 Handling of misfires.

(a) Faces and muck piles shall be examined for misfires after each blasting operation.

(b) Only work necessary to remove a misfire and protect the safety of miners engaged in the removal shall be permitted in the affected area until the misfire is disposed of in a safe manner.

(c) When a misfire cannot be disposed of safely, each approach to the area affected by the misfire shall be posted with a warning sign at a conspicuous location to prohibit entry, and the condition shall be reported immediately to mine management.

(d) Misfires occurring during the shift shall be reported to mine management not later than the end of the shift.

§ 57.6312 Secondary blasting.

Secondary blasts fired at the same time in the same work area shall be initiated from one source.

ELECTRIC BLASTING—SURFACE AND UNDERGROUND

§ 57.6400 Compatibility of electric detonators.

All electric detonators to be fired in a round shall be from the same manufacturer and shall have similar electrical firing characteristics.

§ 57.6401 Shunting.

Except during testing—

(a) Electric detonators shall be kept shunted until connected to the blasting line or wired into a blasting round;

(b) Wired rounds shall be kept shunted until connected to the blasting line; and

(c) Blasting lines shall be kept shunted until immediately before blasting.

§ 57.6402 Deenergized circuits near detonators.

Electrical distribution circuits within 50 feet of electric detonators at the blast site shall be deenergized. Such circuits need not be deenergized between 25 to 50 feet of the electric detonators if stray current tests, conducted as frequently as necessary, indicate a maximum stray current of less than 0.05 ampere through a 1-ohm resistor as measured at the blast site.

§ 57.6403 Branch circuits.

(a) If electric blasting includes the use of branch circuits, each branch shall be equipped with a safety switch or equivalent method to isolate the circuits to be used.

(b) At least one safety switch or equivalent method of protection shall be located outside the blast area and shall be in the open position until persons are withdrawn.

§ 57.6404 Separation of blasting circuits from power source.

(a) Switches used to connect the power source to a blasting circuit shall be locked in the open position except when closed to fire the blast.

(b) Lead wires shall not be connected to the blasting switch until the shot is ready to be fired.

§ 57.6405 Firing devices.

(a) Power sources shall be capable of delivering sufficient current to energize all electric detonators to be fired with the type of circuits used. Storage or dry cell batteries are not permitted as power sources.

(b) Blasting machines shall be tested, repaired, and maintained in accordance with manufacturer's instructions.

(c) Only the blaster shall have the key or other control to an electrical firing device.

§ 57.6406 Duration of current flow.

If any part of a blast is connected in parallel and is to be initiated from powerlines or lighting circuits, the time of current flow shall be limited to a maximum of 25 milliseconds. This can be accomplished by incorporating an arcing control device in the blasting circuit or by interrupting the circuit with an explosive device attached to one or both lead lines and initiated by a 25-millisecond delay electric detonator.

§ 57.6407 Circuit testing.

A blasting galvanometer or other instrument designed for testing blasting circuits shall be used to test the following:

(a) In surface operations—

(1) Continuity of each electric detonator in the blasthole prior to stemming and connection to the blasting line;

(2) Resistance of individual series or the resistance of multiple balanced series to be connected in parallel prior to their connection to the blasting line;

(3) Continuity of blasting lines prior to the connection of electric or electronic detonator series; and

(4) Total blasting circuit resistance prior to connection to the power source.

(b) In underground operations—

(1) Continuity of each electric detonator series; and

(2) Continuity of blasting lines prior to the connection of electric or electronic detonators.

[61 FR 36801, July 12, 1996, as amended at 85 FR 2027, Jan. 14, 2020]

NONELECTRIC BLASTING—SURFACE AND UNDERGROUND

§ 57.6500 Damaged initiating material.

A visual check of the completed circuit shall be made to ensure that the components are properly aligned and connected. Safety fuse, igniter cord, detonating cord, shock or gas tubing, and similar material which is kinked, bent sharply, or damaged shall not be used.

§ 57.6501 Nonelectric initiation systems.

(a) When the nonelectric initiation system uses shock tube—

(1) Connections with other initiation devices shall be secured in a manner which provides for uninterrupted propagation;

(2) Factory-made units shall be used as assembled and shall not be cut except that a single splice is permitted on the lead-in trunkline during dry conditions; and

(3) Connections between blastholes shall not be made until immediately prior to clearing the blast site when surface delay detonators are used.

(b) When the nonelectric initiation system uses detonating cord—

(1) The line of detonating cord extending out of a blasthole shall be cut from the supply spool immediately after the attached explosive is correctly positioned in the hole;

(2) In multiple row blasts, the trunkline layout shall be designed so that the detonation can reach each blasthole from at least two directions;

(3) Connections shall be tight and kept at right angles to the trunkline;

(4) Detonators shall be attached securely to the side of the detonating cord and pointed in the direction in which detonation is to proceed;

(5) Connections between blastholes shall not be made until immediately prior to clearing the blast site when surface delay detonators are used; and

Mine Safety and Health Admin., Labor § 57.6604

(6) Lead-in lines shall be manually unreeled if connected to the trunklines at the blast site.

(c) When nonelectric initiation systems use gas tube, continuity of the circuit shall be tested prior to blasting.

§ 57.6502 Safety fuse.

(a) The burning rate of each spool of safety fuse to be used shall be measured, posted in locations which will be conspicuous to safety fuse users, and brought to the attention of all persons involved with the blasting operation.

(b) When firing with safety fuse ignited individually using handheld lighters, the safety fuse shall be of lengths which provide at least the minimum burning time for a particular size round, as specified in the following table:

TABLE E-1—SAFETY FUSE—MINIMUM BURNING TIME

Number of holes in a round	Minimum burning time
1	2 min.[1]
2–5	2 min. 40 sec.
6–10	3 min. 20 sec.
11 to 15	5 min.

[1] For example, at least a 36-inch length of 40-second-per-foot safety fuse or at least a 48-inch length of 30-second-per-foot safety fuse would have to be used to allow sufficient time to evacuate the area.

(c) Where flyrock might damage exposed safety fuse, the blast shall be timed so that all safety fuses are burning within the blastholes before any blasthole detonates.

(d) Fuse shall be cut and capped in dry locations.

(e) Blasting caps shall be crimped to fuse only with implements designed for that purpose.

(f) Safety fuse shall be ignited only after the primer and the explosive material are securely in place.

(g) Safety fuse shall be ignited only with devices designed for that purpose. Carbide lights, liquefied petroleum gas torches, and cigarette lighters shall not be used to light safety fuse.

(h) At least two persons shall be present when lighting safety fuse, and no one shall light more than 15 individual fuses. If more than 15 holes per person are to be fired, electric initiation systems, igniter cord and connectors, or other nonelectric initiation systems shall be used.

EXTRANEOUS ELECTRICITY—SURFACE AND UNDERGROUND

§ 57.6600 Loading practices.

If extraneous electricity is suspected in an area where electric detonators are used, loading shall be suspended until tests determine that stray current does not exceed 0.05 amperes through a 1-ohm resister when measured at the location of the electric detonators. If greater levels of extraneous electricity are found, the source shall be determined and no loading shall take place until the condition is corrected.

§ 57.6601 Grounding.

Electric blasting circuits, including powerline sources when used, shall not be grounded.

§ 57.6602 Static electricity dissipation during loading.

When explosive material is loaded pneumatically into a blasthole in a manner that generates a static electricity hazard—

(a) An evaluation of the potential static electricity hazard shall be made and any hazard shall be eliminated before loading begins;

(b) The loading hose shall be of a semiconductive type, have a total of not more than 2 megohms of resistance over its entire length and not less than 1000 ohms of resistance per foot;

(c) Wire-countered hoses shall not be used;

(d) Conductive parts of the loading equipment shall be bonded and grounded and grounds shall not be made to other potential sources of extraneous electricity; and

(e) Plastic tubes shall not be used as hole liners if the hole contains an electric detonator.

§ 57.6603 Air gap.

At least a 15-foot air gap shall be provided between the blasting circuit and the electric power source.

§ 57.6604 Precautions during storms.

During the approach and progress of an electrical storm—

(a) Surface blasting operations shall be suspended and persons withdrawn

§ 57.6605

from the blast area or to a safe location; or

(b) Underground electronic or electrical blasting operations that are capable of being initiated by lightning shall be suspended and all persons withdrawn from the blast area or to a safe location.

[61 FR 36801, July 12, 1996, as amended at 85 FR 2027, Jan. 14, 2020]

§ 57.6605 Isolation of blasting circuits.

Lead wires and blasting lines shall be isolated and insulated from power conductors, pipelines, and railroad tracks, and shall be protected from sources of stray or static electricity. Blasting circuits shall be protected from any contact between firing lines and overhead powerlines which could result from the force of a blast.

EQUIPMENT/TOOLS—SURFACE AND UNDERGROUND

§ 57.6700 Nonsparking tools.

Only nonsparking tools shall be used to open containers of explosive material or to punch holes in explosive cartridges.

§ 57.6701 Tamping and loading pole requirements.

Tamping and loading poles shall be of wood or other nonconductive, nonsparking material. Couplings for poles shall be nonsparking.

MAINTENANCE—SURFACE AND UNDERGROUND

§ 57.6800 Storage facilities.

When repair work which could produce a spark or flame is to be performed on a storage facility—

(a) The explosive material shall be moved to another facility, or moved at least 50 feet from the repair activity and monitored; and

(b) The facility shall be cleaned to prevent accidental detonation.

§ 57.6801 Vehicle repair.

Vehicles containing explosive material and oxidizers shall not be taken into a repair garage or shop.

§ 57.6802 Bulk delivery vehicles.

No welding or cutting shall be performed on a bulk delivery vehicle until the vehicle has been washed down and all explosive material has been removed. Before welding or cutting on a hollow shaft, the shaft shall be thoroughly cleaned inside and out and vented with a minimum ½-inch diameter opening to allow for sufficient ventilation.

§ 57.6803 Blasting lines.

Permanent blasting lines shall be properly supported. All blasting lines shall be insulated and kept in good repair.

GENERAL REQUIREMENTS—SURFACE AND UNDERGROUND

§ 57.6900 Damaged or deteriorated explosive material.

Damaged or deteriorated explosive material shall be disposed of in a safe manner in accordance with the instructions of the manufacturer.

§ 57.6901 Black powder.

(a) Black powder shall be used for blasting only when a desired result cannot be obtained with another type of explosive, such as in quarrying certain types of dimension stone.

(b) Containers of black powder shall be—

(1) Nonsparking;

(2) Kept in a totally enclosed cargo space while being transported by a vehicle;

(3) Securely closed at all times when—

(i) Within 50 feet of any magazine or open flame;

(ii) Within any building in which a fuel-fired or exposed-element electric heater is operating; or

(iii) In an area where electrical or incandescent-particle sparks could result in powder ignition; and

(4) Opened only when the powder is being transferred to a blasthole or another container and only in locations not listed in paragraph (b)(3) of this section.

(c) Black powder shall be transferred from containers only by pouring.

(d) Spills shall be cleaned up promptly with nonsparking equipment. Contaminated powder shall be put into a container of water and shall be disposed of promptly after the granules have disintegrated, or the spill area shall be flushed promptly with water until the granules have disintegrated completely.

(e) Misfires shall be disposed of by washing the stemming and powder charge from the blasthole, and removing and disposing of the initiator in accordance with the requirement for damaged explosives.

(f) Holes shall not be reloaded for at least 12 hours when the blastholes have failed to break as planned.

§ 57.6902 Excessive temperatures.

(a) Where heat could cause premature detonation, explosive material shall not be loaded into hot areas, such as kilns or sprung holes.

(b) When blasting sulfide ores where hot holes occur that may react with explosive material in blastholes, operators shall—

(1) Measure an appropriate number of blasthole temperatures in order to assess the specific mine conditions prior to the introduction of explosive material;

(2) Limit the time between the completion of loading and the initiation of the blast to no more than 12 hours; and

(3) Take other special precautions to address the specific conditions at the mine to prevent premature detonation.

§ 57.6903 Burning explosive material.

If explosive material is suspected of burning at the blast site, persons shall be evacuated from the endangered area and shall not return for at least one hour after the burning or suspected burning has stopped.

§ 57.6904 Smoking and open flames.

Smoking and use of open flames shall not be permitted within 50 feet of explosive material except when separated by permanent noncombustible barriers. This standard does not apply to devices designed to ignite safety fuse or to heating devices which do not create a fire or explosion hazard.

§ 57.6905 Protection of explosive material.

(a) Explosive material shall be protected from temperatures in excess of 150 degrees Fahrenheit.

(b) Explosive material shall be protected from impact, except for tamping and dropping during loading.

GENERAL REQUIREMENTS—
UNDERGROUND ONLY

§ 57.6960 Mixing of explosive material.

(a) The mixing of ingredients to produce explosive material shall not be conducted underground unless prior approval of the MSHA district manager is obtained. In granting or withholding approval, the district manager shall consider the potential hazards created by—

(1) The location of the stored material and the storage practices used;

(2) The transportation and use of the explosive material;

(3) The nature of the explosive material, including its sensitivity;

(4) Any other factor deemed relevant to the safety of miners potentially exposed to the hazards associated with the mixing of the bulk explosive material underground.

(b) Storage facilities for the ingredients to be mixed shall provide drainage away from the facilities for leaks and spills.

Subpart F—Drilling and Rotary Jet Piercing

DRILLING—SURFACE ONLY

§ 57.7002 Equipment defects.

Equipment defects affecting safety shall be corrected before the equipment is used.

§ 57.7003 Drill area inspection.

The drilling area shall be inspected for hazards before starting the drilling operations.

§ 57.7004 Drill mast.

Persons shall not be on a mast while the drill-bit is in operation unless they are provided with a safe platform from which to work and they are required to use safety belts to avoid falling.

§ 57.7005 Augers and drill stems.

Drill crews and others shall stay clear of augers or drill stems that are in motion. Persons shall not pass under or step over a moving stem or auger.

§ 57.7008 Moving the drill.

When a drill is being moved from one drilling area to another, drill steel, tools, and other equipment shall be secured and the mast placed in a safe position.

§ 57.7009 Drill helpers.

If a drill helper assists the drill operator during movement of a drill to a new location, the helper shall be in sight of, or in communication with, the operator at all times.

§ 57.7010 Power failures.

In the event of power failure, drill controls shall be placed in the neutral position until power is restored.

§ 57.7011 Straightening crossed cables.

The drill stem shall be resting on the bottom of the hole or on the platform with the stem secured to the mast before attempts are made to straighten a crossed cable on a reel.

§ 57.7012 Tending drills in operation.

While in operation, drills shall be attended at all times.

§ 57.7013 Covering or guarding drill holes.

Drill holes large enough to constitute a hazard shall be covered or guarded.

§ 57.7018 Hand clearance.

Persons shall not hold the drill steel while collaring holes, or rest their hands on the chuck or centralizer while drilling.

DRILLING—UNDERGROUND ONLY

§ 57.7028 Hand clearance.

Persons shall not rest their hands on the chuck or centralizer while drilling.

§ 57.7032 Anchoring.

Columns and the drills mounted on them shall be anchored firmly before and during drilling.

DRILLING—SURFACE AND UNDERGROUND

§ 57.7050 Tool and drill steel racks.

Receptacles or racks shall be provided for drill steel and tools stored or carried on drills.

§ 57.7051 Loose objects on the mast or drill platform.

To prevent injury to personnel, tools and other objects shall not be left loose on the mast or drill platform.

§ 57.7052 Drilling positions.

Persons shall not drill from—
(a) Positions which hinder their access to the control levers;
(b) Insecure footing or insecure staging; or
(c) Atop equipment not suitable for drilling.

§ 57.7053 Moving hand-held drills.

Before hand-held drills are moved from one working area to another, air shall be turned off and bled from the hose.

§ 57.7054 Starting or moving drill equipment.

Drill operators shall not start or move drilling equipment unless all miners are in the clear.

§ 57.7055 Intersecting holes.

Holes shall not be drilled where there is a danger of intersecting a misfired hole or a hole containing explosives, blasting agents, or detonators.

[56 FR 46517, Sept. 12, 1991; 56 FR 52193, Oct. 18, 1991]

§ 57.7056 Collaring in bootlegs.

Holes shall not be collared in bootlegs.

[56 FR 46517, Sept. 12, 1991]

ROTARY JET PIERCING—SURFACE ONLY

§ 57.7801 Jet drills.

Jet piercing drills shall be provided with:
(a) A system to pressurize the equipment operator's cab, when a cab is provided; and
(b) A protective cover over the oxygen flow indicator.

§ 57.7802 Oxygen hose lines.

Safety chains or other suitable locking devices shall be provided across connections to and between high pressure oxygen hose lines of 1-inch inside diameter or larger.

§ 57.7803 Lighting the burner.

A suitable means of protection shall be provided for the employee when lighting the burner.

§ 57.7804 Refueling.

When rotary jet piercing equipment requires refueling at locations other than fueling stations, a system for fueling without spillage shall be provided.

§ 57.7805 Smoking and open flames.

Persons shall not smoke and open flames shall not be used in the vicinity of the oxygen storage and supply lines. Signs warning against smoking and open flames shall be posted in these areas.

§ 57.7806 Oxygen intake coupling.

The oxygen intake coupling on jet piercing drills shall be constructed so that only the oxygen hose can be coupled to it.

§ 57.7807 Flushing the combustion chamber.

The combustion chamber of a jet drill stem which has been sitting unoperated in a drill hole shall be flushed with a suitable solvent after the stem is pulled up.

Subpart G—Ventilation

SURFACE AND UNDERGROUND

§ 57.8518 Main and booster fans.

(a) All mine main and booster fans installed and used to ventilate the active workings of the mine shall be operated continuously while persons are underground in the active workings. However, this provision is not applicable during scheduled production-cycle shutdowns or planned or scheduled fan maintenance or fan adjustments where air quality is maintained in compliance with the applicable standards of subpart D of this part and all persons underground in the affected areas are advised in advance of such scheduled or planned fan shutdowns, maintenance, or adjustments.

(b) In the event of main or booster fan failure due to a malfunction, accident, power failure, or other such unplanned or unscheduled event:

(1) The air quality in the affected active workings shall be tested at least within 2-hours of the discovery of the fan failure, and at least every 4-hours thereafter by a competent person for compliance with the requirements of the applicable standards of subpart D of this part until normal ventilation is restored, or

(2) All persons, except those working on the fan, shall be withdrawn, the ventilation shall be restored to normal and the air quality in the affected active workings shall be tested by a competent person to assure that the air quality meets the requirements of the standards in subpart D of this part, before any other persons are permitted to enter the affected active workings.

§ 57.8519 Underground main fan controls.

All underground main fans shall have controls placed at a suitable protected location remote from the fan and preferably on the surface.

UNDERGROUND ONLY

§ 57.8520 Ventilation plan.

A plan of the mine ventilation system shall be set out by the operator in written form. Revisions of the system shall be noted and updated at least annually. The ventilation plan or revisions thereto shall be submitted to the District Manager for review and comments upon his written request. The plan shall, where applicable, contain the following:

(a) The mine name.

(b) The current mine map or schematic or series of mine maps or schematics of an appropriate scale, not greater than five hundred feet to the inch, showing:

(1) Direction and quantity of principal air flows;

(2) Locations of seals used to isolate abandoned workings;

§ 57.8525

(3) Locations of areas withdrawn from the ventilation system;

(4) Locations of all main, booster and auxiliary fans not shown in paragraph (d) of this standard.

(5) Locations of air regulators and stoppings and ventilation doors not shown in paragraph (d) of this standard;

(6) Locations of overcasts, undercasts and other airway crossover devices not shown in paragraph (d) of this standard;

(7) Locations of known oil or gas wells;

(8) Locations of known underground mine openings adjacent to the mine;

(9) Locations of permanent underground shops, diesel fuel storage depots, oil fuel storage depots, hoist rooms, compressors, battery charging stations and explosive storage facilities. Permanent facilities are those intended to exist for one year or more; and

(10) Significant changes in the ventilation system projected for one year.

(c) Mine fan data for all active main and booster fans including manufacturer's name, type, size, fan speed, blade setting, approximate pressure at present operating point, and motor brake horsepower rating.

(d) Diagrams, descriptions or sketches showing how ventilation is accomplished in each typical type of working place including the approximate quantity of air provided, and typical size and type of auxiliary fans used.

(e) The number and type of internal combustion engine units used underground, including make and model of unit, type of engine, make and model of engine, brake horsepower rating of engine, and approval number.

[50 FR 4082, Jan. 29, 1985, as amended at 60 FR 33723, June 29, 1995]

§ 57.8525 Main fan maintenance.

Main fans shall be maintained according to either the manufacturer's recommendations or a written periodic schedule adopted by the operator which shall be available at the operation on request of the Secretary or his authorized representative.

[50 FR 4082, Jan. 29, 1985, as amended at 60 FR 33723, June 29, 1995]

§ 57.8527 Oxygen-deficiency testing.

Flame safety lamps or other suitable devices shall be used to test for acute oxygen deficiency.

§ 57.8528 Unventilated areas.

Unventilated areas shall be sealed, or barricaded and posted against entry.

§ 57.8529 Auxiliary fan systems.

When auxiliary fan systems are used, such systems shall minimize recirculation and be maintained to provide ventilation air that effectively sweeps the working places.

§ 57.8531 Construction and maintenance of ventilation doors.

Ventilation doors shall be—
(a) Substantially constructed;
(b) Covered with fire-retardant material, if constructed of wood;
(c) Maintained in good condition;
(d) Self-closing, if manually operated; and
(e) Equipped with audible or visual warning devices, if mechanically operated.

§ 57.8532 Opening and closing ventilation doors.

When ventilation control doors are opened as a part of the normal mining cycle, they shall be closed as soon as possible to re-establish normal ventilation to working places.

§ 57.8534 Shutdown or failure of auxiliary fans.

(a) Auxiliary fans installed and used to ventilate the active workings of the mine shall be operated continuously while persons are underground in the active workings, *except* for scheduled production-cycle shutdowns or planned or scheduled fan maintenance or fan adjustments where air quality is maintained in compliance with the applicable standards of subpart D of this part, and all persons underground in the affected areas are advised in advance of such scheduled or planned fan shutdowns, maintenance, or adjustments.

(b) In the event of auxiliary fan failure due to malfunction, accident, power failure, or other such unplanned or unscheduled event:

(1) The air quality in the affected active workings shall be tested at least

within 2 hours of the discovery of the fan failure, and at least every 4 hours thereafter by a competent person for compliance with the requirements of the applicable standards of subpart D of this part until normal ventilation is restored, or

(2) All persons, except those working on the fan, shall be withdrawn, the ventilation shall be restored to normal and the air quality in the affected active workings shall be tested by a competent person to assure that the air quality meets the requirements of the standards in subpart D of this part, before any other persons are permitted to enter the affected active workings.

§ 57.8535 Seals.

Seals shall be provided with a means for checking the quality of air behind the seal and a means to prevent a water head from developing unless the seal is designed to impound water.

Subpart H—Loading, Hauling, and Dumping

SOURCE: 53 FR 32526, Aug. 25, 1988, unless otherwise noted.

TRAFFIC SAFETY

§ 57.9100 Traffic control.

To provide for the safe movement of self-propelled mobile equipment—

(a) Rules governing speed, right-of-way, direction of movement, and the use of headlights to assure appropriate visibility, shall be established and followed at each mine; and

(b) Signs or signals that warn of hazardous conditions shall be placed at appropriate locations at each mine.

§ 57.9101 Operating speeds and control of equipment.

Operators of self-propelled mobile equipment shall maintain control of the equipment while it is in motion. Operating speeds shall be consistent with conditions of roadways, tracks, grades, clearance, visibility, and traffic, and the type of equipment used.

§ 57.9102 Movement of independently operating rail equipment.

Movement of two or more pieces of rail equipment operating independ-ently on the same track shall be controlled for safe operation.

§ 57.9103 Clearance on adjacent tracks.

Railcars shall not be left on side tracks unless clearance is provided for traffic on adjacent tracks.

§ 57.9104 Railroad crossings.

Designated railroad crossings shall be posted with warning signs or signals, or shall be guarded when trains are passing. These crossings shall also be planked or filled between the rails.

§ 57.9160 Train movement during shift changes.

During shift changes, the movement of underground trains carrying rock or material shall be limited to areas where the trains do not present a hazard to persons changing shifts.

TRANSPORTATION OF PERSONS AND MATERIALS

§ 57.9200 Transporting persons.

Persons shall not be transported—

(a) In or on dippers, forks, clamshells, or buckets except shaft buckets during shaft-sinking operations or during inspection, maintenance and repair of shafts.

(b) In beds of mobile equipment or railcars, unless—

(1) Provisions are made for secure travel, and

(2) Means are taken to prevent accidental unloading if the equipment is provided with unloading devices;

(c) On top of loads in mobile equipment;

(d) Outside cabs, equipment operators' stations, and beds of mobile equipment, except when necessary for maintenance, testing, or training purposes, and provisions are made for secure travel. This provision does not apply to rail equipment.

(e) Between cars of trains, on the leading end of trains, on the leading end of a single railcar, or in other locations on trains that expose persons to hazards from train movement.

(1) This paragraph does not apply to car droppers if they are secured with safety belts and lines which prevent them from falling off the work platform.

(2) Brakemen and trainmen are prohibited from riding between cars of moving trains but may ride on the leading end of trains or other locations when necessary to perform their duties;

(f) To and from work areas in overcrowded mobile equipment;

(g) In mobile equipment with materials or equipment unless the items are secured or are small and can be carried safely by hand without creating a hazard to persons; or

(h) On conveyors unless the conveyors are designed to provide for their safe transportation.

§ 57.9201 Loading, hauling, and unloading of equipment or supplies.

Equipment and supplies shall be loaded, transported, and unloaded in a manner which does not create a hazard to persons from falling or shifting equipment or supplies.

§ 57.9202 Loading and hauling large rocks.

Large rocks shall be broken before loading if they could endanger persons or affect the stability of mobile equipment. Mobile equipment used for haulage of mined material shall be loaded to minimize spillage where a hazard to persons could be created.

§ 57.9260 Supplies, materials, and tools on mantrips.

Supplies, materials, and tools, other than small items that can be carried by hand, shall not be transported underground with persons in mantrips. Mantrips shall be operated independently of ore or supply trips.

§ 57.9261 Transporting tools and materials on locomotives.

Tools or materials shall not be carried on top of locomotives underground except for secured rerailing devices located in a manner which does not create a hazard to persons.

SAFETY DEVICES, PROVISIONS, AND PROCEDURES FOR ROADWAYS, RAILROADS, AND LOADING AND DUMPING SITES

§ 57.9300 Berms or guardrails.

(a) Berms or guardrails shall be provided and maintained on the banks of roadways where a drop-off exists of sufficient grade or depth to cause a vehicle to overturn or endanger persons in equipment.

(b) Berms or guardrails shall be at least mid-axle height of the largest self-propelled mobile equipment which usually travels the roadway.

(c) Berms may have openings to the extent necessary for roadway drainage.

(d) Where elevated roadways are infrequently traveled and used only by service or maintenance vehicles, berms or guardrails are not required when all of the following are met:

(1) Locked gates are installed at the entrance points to the roadway.

(2) Signs are posted warning that the roadway is not bermed.

(3) Delineators are installed along the perimeter of the elevated roadway so that, for both directions of travel, the reflective surfaces of at least three delineators along each elevated shoulder are always visible to the driver and spaced at intervals sufficient to indicate the edges and attitude of the roadway.

(4) A maximum speed limit is posted and observed for the elevated unbermed portions of the roadway. Factors to consider when establishing the maximum speed limit shall include the width, slope and alignment of the road, the type of equipment using the road, the road material, and any hazardous conditions which may exist.

(5) Road surface traction is not impaired by weather conditions, such as sleet and snow, unless corrective measures, such as the use of tire chains, plowing, or sanding, are taken to improve traction.

(e) This standard is not applicable to rail beds.

[53 FR 32526, Aug. 25, 1988, as amended at 55 FR 37218, Sept. 7, 1990]

§ 57.9301 Dump site restraints.

Berms, bumper blocks, safety hooks, or similar impeding devices shall be provided at dumping locations where there is a hazard of overtravel or overturning.

§ 57.9302 Protection against moving or runaway railroad equipment.

Stopblocks, derail devices, or other devices that protect against moving or runaway rail equipment shall be installed wherever necessary to protect persons.

§ 57.9303 Construction of ramps and dumping facilities.

Ramps and dumping facilities shall be designed and constructed of materials capable of supporting the loads to which they will be subjected. The ramps and dumping facilities shall provide width, clearance, and headroom to safely accommodate the mobile equipment using the facilities.

§ 57.9304 Unstable ground.

(a) Dumping locations shall be visually inspected prior to work commencing and as ground conditions warrant.

(b) Where there is evidence that the ground at a dumping location may fail to support the mobile equipment, loads shall be dumped a safe distance back from the edge of the unstable area of the bank.

§ 57.9305 Truck spotters.

(a) If truck spotters are used, they shall be in the clear while trucks are backing into dumping position or dumping.

(b) Spotters shall use signal lights to direct trucks where visibility is limited.

(c) When a truck operator cannot clearly recognize the spotter's signals, the truck shall be stopped.

§ 57.9306 Warning devices for restricted clearances.

Where restricted clearance creates a hazard to persons on mobile equipment, warning devices shall be installed in advance of the restricted area and the restricted area shall be conspicuously marked.

§ 57.9307 Design, installation, and maintenance of railroads.

Roadbeds and all elements of the railroad tracks shall be designed, installed, and maintained to provide safe operation consistent with the speed and type of haulage used.

§ 57.9308 Switch throws.

Switch throws shall be installed to provide clearance to protect switchmen from contact with moving trains.

§ 57.9309 Chute design.

Chute-loading installations shall be designed to provide a safe location for persons pulling chutes.

§ 57.9310 Chute hazards.

(a) Prior to chute-pulling, persons who could be affected by the draw or otherwise exposed to danger shall be warned and given time to clear the hazardous area.

(b) Persons attempting to free chute hangups shall be experienced and familiar with the task, know the hazards involved, and use the proper tools to free material.

(c) When broken rock or material is dumped into an empty chute, the chute shall be equipped with a guard or all persons shall be isolated from the hazard of flying rock or material.

§ 57.9311 Anchoring stationary sizing devices.

Grizzlies and other stationary sizing devices shall be securely anchored.

§ 57.9312 Working around drawholes.

Unless platforms or safety lines are used, persons shall not position themselves over drawholes if there is danger that broken rock or material may be withdrawn or bridged.

§ 57.9313 Roadway maintenance.

Water, debris, or spilled material on roadways which creates hazards to the operation of mobile equipment shall be removed.

§ 57.9314 Trimming stockpile and muckpile faces.

Stockpile and muckpile faces shall be trimmed to prevent hazards to persons.

§ 57.9315 Dust control.

Dust shall be controlled at muck piles, material transfer points, crushers, and on haulage roads where hazards to persons would be created as a result of impaired visibility.

§ 57.9316 Notifying the equipment operator.

When an operator of self-propelled mobile equipment is present, persons shall notify the equipment operator before getting on or off that equipment.

§ 57.9317 Suspended loads.

Persons shall not work or pass under the buckets or booms of loaders in operation.

§ 57.9318 Getting on or off moving equipment.

Persons shall not get on or off moving mobile equipment. This provision does not apply to trainmen, brakemen, and car droppers who are required to get on or off slowly moving trains in the performance of their work duties.

§ 57.9319 Going over, under, or between railcars.

Persons shall not go over, under, or between railcars unless—
(a) The train is stopped; and
(b) The train operator, when present, is notified and the notice acknowledged.

§ 57.9330 Clearance for surface equipment.

Continuous clearance of at least 30 inches from the farthest projection of moving railroad equipment shall be provided on at least one side of the tracks at all locations where possible or the area shall be marked conspicuously.

§ 57.9360 Shelter holes.

(a) Shelter holes shall be—
(1) Provided at intervals adequate to assure the safety of persons along underground haulageways where continuous clearance of at least 30 inches cannot be maintained from the farthest projection of moving equipment on at least one side of the haulageway; and
(2) At least four feet wide, marked conspicuously, and provide a minimum 40-inch clearance from the farthest projection of moving equipment.
(b) Shelter holes shall not be used for storage unless a 40-inch clearance is maintained.

§ 57.9361 Drawholes.

To prevent hazards to persons underground, collars of open drawholes shall be free of muck or materials except during transfer of the muck or material through the drawhole.

§ 57.9362 Protection of signalmen.

Signalmen used during slushing operations underground shall be located away from possible contact with cables, sheaves, and slusher buckets.

Subpart I—Aerial Tramways

§ 57.10001 Filling buckets.

Buckets shall not be overloaded, and feed shall be regulated to prevent spillage.

§ 57.10002 Inspection and maintenance.

Inspection and maintenance of carriers (including loading and unloading mechanisms), ropes and supports, and brakes shall be performed by competent persons according to the recommendations of the manufacturer.

§ 57.10003 Correction of defects.

Any hazardous defects shall be corrected before the equipment is used.

§ 57.10004 Brakes.

Positive-action-type brakes and devices which apply the brakes automatically in the event of a power failure shall be provided on aerial tramways.

§ 57.10005 Track cable connections.

Track cable connections shall not obstruct the passage of carriage wheels.

§ 57.10006 Tower guards.

Towers shall be suitably protected from swaying buckets.

§ 57.10007 Falling object protection.

Guard nets or other suitable protection shall be provided where tramways pass over roadways, walkways, or buildings.

§ 57.10008 Riding tramways.

Persons other than maintenance persons shall not ride aerial tramways unless the following features are provided.

Mine Safety and Health Admin., Labor §57.11014

(a) Two independent brakes, each capable of holding the maximum load;
(b) Direct communication between terminals;
(c) Power drives with emergency power available in case of primary power failure; and
(d) Buckets equipped with positive locks to prevent accidental tripping or dumping.

§57.10009 Riding loaded buckets.

Persons shall not ride loaded buckets.

§57.10010 Starting precautions.

Where possible, aerial tramways shall not be started until the operator has ascertained that everyone is in the clear.

Subpart J—Travelways and Escapeways

TRAVELWAYS—SURFACE AND UNDERGROUND

§57.11001 Safe access.

Safe means of access shall be provided and maintained to all working places.

§57.11002 Handrails and toeboards.

Crossovers, elevated walkways, elevated ramps, and stairways shall be of substantial construction, provided with handrails, and maintained in good condition. Where necessary, toeboards shall be provided.

§57.11003 Construction and maintenance of ladders.

Ladders shall be of substantial construction and maintained in good condition.

§57.11004 Portable rigid ladders.

Portable rigid ladders shall be provided with suitable bases and placed securely when used.

§57.11005 Fixed ladder anchorage and toe clearance.

Fixed ladders shall be anchored securely and installed to provide at least 3 inches of toe clearance.

§57.11006 Fixed ladder landings.

Fixed ladders shall project at least 3 feet above landings, or substantial handholds shall be provided above the landings.

§57.11007 Wooden components of ladders.

Wooden components of ladders shall not be painted except with a transparent finish.

§57.11008 Restricted clearance.

Where restricted clearance creates a hazard to persons, the restricted clearance shall be conspicuously marked.

[53 FR 32528, Aug. 25, 1988]

§57.11009 Walkways along conveyors.

Walkways with outboard railings shall be provided wherever persons are required to walk alongside elevated conveyor belts. Inclined railed walkways shall be nonskid or provided with cleats.

§57.11010 Stairstep clearance.

Vertical clearance above stair steps shall be a minimum of seven feet, or suitable warning signs or similar devices shall be provided to indicate an impaired clearance.

§57.11011 Use of ladders.

Persons using ladders shall face the ladders and have both hands free for climbing and descending.

§57.11012 Protection for openings around travelways.

Openings above, below, or near travelways through which persons or materials may fall shall be protected by railings, barriers, or covers. Where it is impractical to install such protective devices, adequate warning signals shall be installed.

§57.11013 Conveyor crossovers.

Crossovers shall be provided where it is necessary to cross conveyors.

§57.11014 Crossing moving conveyors.

Moving conveyors shall be crossed only at designated crossover points.

§ 57.11016 Snow and ice on walkways and travelways.

Regularly used walkways and travelways shall be sanded, salted, or cleared of snow and ice as soon as practicable.

§ 57.11017 Inclined fixed ladders.

Fixed ladders shall not incline backwards.

TRAVELWAYS—SURFACE ONLY

§ 57.11025 Railed landings, backguards, and other protection for fixed ladders.

Fixed ladders, except on mobile equipment, shall be offset and have substantial railed landings at least every 30 feet unless backguards or equivalent protection such as safety belts and safety lines, are provided.

§ 57.11026 Protection for inclined fixed ladders.

Fixed ladders 70 degrees to 90 degrees from the horizontal and 30 feet or more in length shall have backguards, cages or equivalent protection, starting at a point not more than seven feet from the bottom of the ladders.

§ 57.11027 Scaffolds and working platforms.

Scaffolds and working platforms shall be of substantial construction and provided with handrails and maintained in good condition. Floorboards shall be laid properly and the scaffolds and working platform shall not be overloaded. Working platforms shall be provided with toeboards when necessary.

TRAVELWAYS—UNDERGROUND ONLY

§ 57.11036 Ladderway trap doors and guards.

Trap doors or adequate guarding shall be provided in ladderways at each level. Doors shall be kept operable.

§ 57.11037 Ladderway openings.

Ladderways constructed after November 15, 1979, shall have a minimum unobstructed cross-sectional opening of 24 inches by 24 inches measured from the face of the ladder.

§ 57.11038 Entering a manway.

Before entering a manway where persons may be working or traveling, a warning shall be given by the person entering the manway and acknowledged by any person present in the manway.

§ 57.11040 Inclined travelways.

Travelways steeper than 35 degrees from the horizontal shall be provided with ladders or stairways.

§ 57.11041 Landings for inclined ladderways.

Fixed ladders with an inclination of more than 70 degrees from the horizontal shall be offset with substantial landings at least every 30 feet or have landing gates at least every 30 feet.

ESCAPEWAYS—UNDERGROUND ONLY

§ 57.11050 Escapeways and refuges.

(a) Every mine shall have two or more separate, properly maintained escapeways to the surface from the lowest levels which are so positioned that damage to one shall not lessen the effectiveness of the others. A method of refuge shall be provided while a second opening to the surface is being developed. A second escapeway is recommended, but not required, during the exploration or development of an ore body.

(b) In addition to separate escapeways, a method of refuge shall be provided for every employee who cannot reach the surface from his working place through at least two separate escapeways within a time limit of one hour when using the normal exit method. These refuges must be positioned so that the employee can reach one of them within 30 minutes from the time he leaves his workplace.

§ 57.11051 Escape routes.

Escape routes shall be—
(a) Inspected at regular intervals and maintained in safe, travelable condition; and
(b) Marked with conspicuous and easily read direction signs that clearly indicate the ways of escape.

§ 57.11052 Refuge areas.

Refuge areas shall be—

Mine Safety and Health Admin., Labor § 57.11059

(a) Of fire-resistant construction, preferably in untimbered areas of the mine;

(b) Large enough to accommodate readily the normal number of persons in the particular area of the mine;

(c) Constructed so they can be made gastight; and

(d) Provided with compressed air lines, waterlines, suitable handtools, and stopping materials.

§ 57.11053 Escape and evacuation plans.

A specific escape and evacuation plan and revisions thereof suitable to the conditions and mining system of the mine and showing assigned responsibilities of all key personnel in the event of an emergency shall be developed by the operator and set out in written form. Within 45 calendar days after promulgation of this standard a copy of the plan and revisions thereof shall be available to the Secretary or his authorized representative. Also, copies of the plan and revisions thereof shall be posted at locations convenient to all persons on the surface and underground. Such a plan shall be updated as necessary and shall be reviewed jointly by the operator and the Secretary or his authorized representative at least once every six months from the date of the last review. The plan shall include:

(a) Mine maps or diagrams showing directions of principal air flow, location of escape routes and locations of existing telephones, primary fans, primary fan controls, fire doors, ventilation doors, and refuge chambers. Appropriate portions of such maps or diagrams shall be posted at all shaft stations and in underground shops, lunchrooms, and elsewhere in working areas where persons congregate;

(b) Procedures to show how the miners will be notified of emergency;

(c) An escape plan for each working area in the mine to include instructions showing how each working area should be evacuated. Each such plan shall be posted at appropriate shaft stations and elsewhere in working areas where persons congregate;

(d) A fire fighting plan;

(e) Surface procedure to follow in an emergency, including the notification of proper authorities, preparing rescue equipment, and other equipment which may be used in rescue and recovery operations; and

(f) A statement of the availability of emergency communication and transportation facilities, emergency power and ventilation and location of rescue personnel and equipment.

[50 FR 4082, Jan. 29, 1985, as amended at 60 FR 33722, June 29, 1995]

§ 57.11054 Communication with refuge chambers.

Telephone or other voice communication shall be provided between the surface and refuge chambers and such systems shall be independent of the mine power supply.

§ 57.11055 Inclined escapeways.

Any portion of a designated escapeway which is inclined more than 30 degrees from the horizontal and that is more than 300 feet in vertical extent shall be provided with an emergency hoisting facility.

§ 57.11056 Emergency hoists.

The procedure for inspection, testing and maintenance required by standard 57.19120 shall be utilized at least every 30 days for hoists designated as emergency hoists in any evacuation plan.

§ 57.11058 Check-in, check-out system.

Each operator of an underground mine shall establish a check-in and check-out system which shall provide an accurate record of persons in the mine. These records shall be kept on the surface in a place chosen to minimize the danger of destruction by fire or other hazards. Every person underground shall carry a positive means of being identified.

§ 57.11059 Respirable atmosphere for hoist operators underground.

For the protection of operators of hoists located underground which are part of the mine escape and evacuation plan required under standard 57.11053, the hoist operator shall be provided with a respirable atmosphere completely independent of the mine atmosphere. This independent ventilation system shall convert, without contamination, to an approved and properly maintained 2-hour self-contained

§ 57.12001

breathing apparatus to provide a safe means of escape for the hoist operator after the hoisting duties have been completed as prescribed in the mine escape and evacuation plan for that hoist. The hoist operator's independent ventilation system shall be provided by one of the following methods:

(a) A suitable enclosure equipped with a positive pressure ventilation system which may be operated continuously or be capable of immediate activation from within the enclosure during an emergency evacuation. Air for the enclosure's ventilation system shall be provided in one of the following ways:

(1) Air coursed from the surface through a borehole into the hoist enclosure directly or through a metal pipeline from such borehole; or

(2) Air coursed from the surface through metal duct work into the hoist enclosure, although this duct work shall not be located in timber-supported active workings; or

(3) Air supplied by air compressors located on the surface and coursed through metal pipe into the hoist enclosure.

A back-up system shall be provided for a hoist enclosure ventilation system provided by either of the methods set forth in paragraphs (a) (2) and (3) of this section. This back-up system shall consist of compressed air stored in containers connected to the enclosure. This back-up system shall provide and maintain a respirable atmosphere in the enclosure for a period of time equal to at least twice the time necessary to complete the evacuation of all persons designated to use that hoist as prescribed in the mine escape and evacuation plan required under standard 57.11053; or

(b) An approved and properly maintained self-contained breathing apparatus system which shall consist of a mask connected to compressed air stored in containers adjacent to the hoist controls. The self-contained breathing system shall provide a minimum of 24 hours of respirable atmosphere to the hoist operator. In addition, the self-contained breathing system shall be capable of a quick connect with the approved 2-hour self-contained breathing apparatus above.

Subpart K—Electricity

SURFACE AND UNDERGROUND

§ 57.12001 Circuit overload protection.

Circuits shall be protected against excessive overloads by fuses or circuit breakers of the correct type and capacity.

§ 57.12002 Controls and switches.

Electric equipment and circuits shall be provided with switches or other controls. Such switches or controls shall be of approved design and construction and shall be properly installed.

§ 57.12003 Trailing cable overload protection.

Individual overload protection or short circuit protection shall be provided for the trailing cables of mobile equipment.

§ 57.12004 Electrical conductors.

Electrical conductors shall be of a sufficient size and current-carrying capacity to ensure that a rise in temperature resulting from normal operations will not damage the insulating materials. Electrical conductors exposed to mechanical damage shall be protected.

§ 57.12005 Protection of power conductors from mobile equipment.

Mobile equipment shall not run over power conductors, nor shall loads be dragged over power conductors, unless the conductors are properly bridged or protected.

§ 57.12006 Distribution boxes.

Distribution boxes shall be provided with a disconnecting device for each branch circuit. Such disconnecting devices shall be equipped or designed in such a manner that it can be determined by visual observation when such a device is open and that the circuit is deenergized, and the distribution box shall be labeled to show which circuit each device controls.

§ 57.12007 Junction box connection procedures.

Trailing cable and power-cable connections to junction boxes shall not be made or broken under load.

§ 57.12008 Insulation and fittings for power wires and cables.

Power wires and cables shall be insulated adequately where they pass into or out of electrical compartments. Cables shall enter metal frames of motors, splice boxes, and electrical compartments only through proper fittings. When insulated wires, other than cables, pass through metal frames, the holes shall be substantially bushed with insulated bushings.

§ 57.12010 Isolation or insulation of communication conductors.

Telephone and low-potential signal wire shall be protected, by isolation or suitable insulation, or both, from contacting energized power conductors or any other power source.

§ 57.12011 High-potential electrical conductors.

High-potential electrical conductors shall be covered, insulated, or placed to prevent contact with low potential conductors.

§ 57.12012 Bare signal wires.

The potential on bare signal wires accessible to contact by persons shall not exceed 48 volts.

§ 57.12013 Splices and repairs of power cables.

Permanent splices and repairs made in power cables, including the ground conductor where provided, shall be—
(a) Mechanically strong with electrical conductivity as near as possible to that of the original;
(b) Insulated to a degree at least equal to that of the original, and sealed to exclude moisture; and,
(c) Provided with damage protection as near as possible to that of the original, including good bonding to the outer jacket.

§ 57.12014 Handling energized power cables.

Power cables energized to potentials in excess of 150 volts, phase-to-ground, shall not be moved with equipment unless sleds or slings, insulated from such equipment, are used. When such energized cables are moved manually, insulated hooks, tongs, ropes, or slings shall be used unless suitable protection for persons is provided by other means. This does not prohibit pulling or dragging of cable by the equipment it powers when the cable is physically attached to the equipment by suitable mechanical devices, and the cable is insulated from the equipment in conformance with other standards in this part.

§ 57.12016 Work on electrically-powered equipment.

Electrically powered equipment shall be deenergized before mechanical work is done on such equipment. Power switches shall be locked out or other measures taken which shall prevent the equipment from being energized without the knowledge of the individuals working on it. Suitable warning notices shall be posted at the power switch and signed by the individuals who are to do the work. Such locks or preventive devices shall be removed only by the persons who installed them or by authorized personnel.

§ 57.12017 Work on power circuits.

Power circuits shall be deenergized before work is done on such circuits unless hot-line tools are used. Suitable warning signs shall be posted by the individuals who are to do the work. Switches shall be locked out or other measures taken which shall prevent the power circuits from being energized without the knowledge of the individuals working on them. Such locks, signs, or preventive devices shall be removed only by the person who installed them or by authorized personnel.

§ 57.12018 Identification of power switches.

Principal power switches shall be labeled to show which units they control, unless identification can be made readily by location.

§ 57.12019 Access to stationary electrical equipment or switchgear.

Where access is necessary, suitable clearance shall be provided at stationary electrical equipment or switchgear.

§ 57.12020 Protection of persons at switchgear.

Dry wooden platforms, insulating mats, or other electrically-nonconductive material shall be kept in place at all switchboards and power-control switches where shock hazards exist. However, metal plates on which a person normally would stand and which are kept at the same potential as the grounded, metal, non-current-carrying parts of the power switches to be operated may be used.

§ 57.12021 Danger signs.

Suitable danger signs shall be posted at all major electrical installations.

§ 57.12022 Authorized persons at major electrical installations.

Areas containing major electrical installations shall be entered only by authorized persons.

§ 57.12023 Guarding electrical connections and resistor grids.

Electrical connections and resistor grids that are difficult or impractical to insulate shall be guarded, unless protection is provided by location.

§ 57.12025 Grounding circuit enclosures.

All metal enclosing or encasing electrical circuits shall be grounded or provided with equivalent protection. This requirement does not apply to battery-operated equipment.

§ 57.12026 Grounding transformer and switchgear enclosures.

Metal fencing and metal buildings enclosing transformers and switchgear shall be grounded.

§ 57.12027 Grounding mobile equipment.

Frame grounding or equivalent protection shall be provided for mobile equipment powered through trailing cables.

§ 57.12028 Testing grounding systems.

Continuity and resistance of grounding systems shall be tested immediately after installation, repair, and modification; and annually thereafter. A record of the resistance measured during the most recent test shall be made available on a request by the Secretary or his duly authorized representative.

§ 57.12030 Correction of dangerous conditions.

When a potentially dangerous condition is found it shall be corrected before equipment or wiring is energized.

§ 57.12032 Inspection and cover plates.

Inspection and cover plates on electrical equipment and junction boxes shall be kept in place at all times except during testing or repairs.

§ 57.12033 Hand-held electric tools.

Hand-held electric tools shall not be operated at high potential voltages.

§ 57.12034 Guarding around lights.

Portable extension lights, and other lights that by their location present a shock or burn hazard, shall be guarded.

§ 57.12035 Weatherproof lamp sockets.

Lamp sockets shall be of a weatherproof type where they are exposed to weather or wet conditions that may interfere with illumination or create a shock hazard.

§ 57.12036 Fuse removal or replacement.

Fuses shall not be removed or replaced by hand in an energized circuit, and they shall not otherwise be removed or replaced in an energized circuit unless equipment and techniques especially designed to prevent electrical shock are provided and used for such purpose.

§ 57.12037 Fuses in high-potential circuits.

Fuse tongs or hotline tools, shall be used when fuses are removed or replaced in high-potential circuits.

§ 57.12038 Attachment of trailing cables.

Trailing cables shall be attached to machines in a suitable manner to protect the cable from damage and to prevent strain on the electrical connections.

§ 57.12039 Protection of surplus trailing cables.

Surplus trailing cables to shovels, cranes and similar equipment shall be—
(a) Stored in cable boats;
(b) Stored on reels mounted on the equipment; or
(c) Otherwise protected from mechanical damage.

§ 57.12040 Installation of operating controls.

Operating controls shall be installed so that they can be operated without danger of contact with energized conductors.

§ 57.12041 Design of switches and starting boxes.

Switches and starting boxes shall be of safe design and capacity.

§ 57.12042 Track bonding.

Both rails shall be bonded or welded at every joint and rails shall be crossbonded at least every 200 feet if the track serves as the return trolley circuit. When rails are moved, replaced, or broken bonds are discovered, they shall be rebonded within three working shifts.

§ 57.12045 Overhead powerlines.

Overhead high-potential powerlines shall be installed as specified by the National Electrical Code.

§ 57.12047 Guy wires.

Guy wires of poles supporting high-voltage transmission lines shall meet the requirements for grounding or insulator protection of the National Electrical Safety Code, part 2, entitled "Safety Rules for the Installation and Maintenance of Electric Supply and Communication Lines" (also referred to as National Bureau of Standards Handbook 81, Nov. 1, 1961), and Supplement 2 thereof issued March 1968, which are hereby incorporated by reference and made a part hereof. These publications and documents may be obtained from the National Institute of Science and Technology, 100 Bureau Drive, Stop 3460, Gaithersburg, MD 20899–3460. Telephone: 301–975–6478 (not a toll free number); *http://ts.nist.gov/nvl;* or from the Government Printing Office, Information Dissemination (Superintendent of Documents), P.O. Box 371954, Pittsburgh, PA 15250–7954; Telephone: 866–512–1800 (toll free) or 202–512–1800; *http://bookstore.gpo.gov,* or may be examined in any Metal and Nonmetal Mine Safety and Health District Office of the Mine Safety and Health Administration.

[53 FR 32526, Aug. 25, 1988, as amended at 60 FR 35695, July 11, 1995; 71 FR 16667, Apr. 3, 2006]

§ 57.12048 Communication conductors on power poles.

Telegraph, telephone, or signal wires shall not be installed on the same crossarm with power conductors. When carried on poles supporting powerlines, they shall be installed as specified by the National Electrical Code.

§ 57.12050 Installation of trolley wires.

Trolley wires shall be installed at least seven feet above rails where height permits, and aligned and supported to suitably control sway and sag.

§ 57.12053 Circuits powered from trolley wires.

Ground wires for lighting circuits powered from trolley wires shall be connected securely to the ground return circuit.

SURFACE ONLY

§ 57.12065 Short circuit and lightning protection.

Powerlines, including trolley wires, and telephone circuits shall be protected against short circuits and lightning.

§ 57.12066 Guarding trolley wires and bare powerlines.

Where metallic tools or equipment can come in contact with trolley wires or bare powerlines, the lines shall be guarded or deenergized.

§ 57.12067 Installation of transformers.

Transformers shall be totally enclosed, or shall be placed at least 8 feet above the ground, or installed in a transformer house, or surrounded by a substantial fence at least 6 feet high

§ 57.12068

and at least 3 feet from any energized parts, casings, or wiring.

§ 57.12068 Locking transformer enclosures.

Transformer enclosures shall be kept locked against unauthorized entry.

§ 57.12069 Lightning protection for telephone wires and ungrounded conductors.

Each ungrounded conductor or telephone wire that leads underground and is directly exposed to lightning shall be equipped with suitable lightning arrestors of approved type within 100 feet of the point where the circuit enters the mine. Lightning arrestors shall be connected to a low resistance grounding medium on the surface and shall be separated from neutral grounds by a distance of not less than 25 feet.

§ 57.12071 Movement or operation of equipment near high-voltage powerlines.

When equipment must be moved or operated near energized high-voltage powerlines (other than trolley lines) and the clearance is less than 10 feet, the lines shall be deenergized or other precautionary measures shall be taken.

UNDERGROUND ONLY

§ 57.12080 Bare conductor guards.

Trolley wires and bare power conductors shall be guarded at mantrip loading and unloading points, and at shaft stations. Where such trolley wires and bare power conductors are less than 7 feet above the rail, they shall be guarded at all points where persons work or pass regularly beneath.

§ 57.12081 Bonding metal pipelines to ground return circuits.

All metal pipelines, 1,000 feet or more in length running parallel to trolley tracks, that are used as a ground return circuit shall be bonded to the return circuit rail at the ends of the pipeline and at intervals not to exceed 500 feet.

§ 57.12082 Isolation of powerlines.

Powerlines shall be well separated or insulated from waterlines, telephone lines and air lines.

§ 57.12083 Support of power cables in shafts and boreholes.

Power cables in shafts and boreholes shall be fastened securely in such a manner as to prevent undue strain on the sheath, insulation, or conductors.

§ 57.12084 Branch circuit disconnecting devices.

Disconnecting switches that can be opened safely under load shall be provided underground at all branch circuits extending from primary power circuits near shafts, adits, levels and boreholes.

§ 57.12085 Transformer stations.

Transformer stations shall be enclosed to prevent persons from unintentionally or inadvertently contacting energized parts.

§ 57.12086 Location of trolley wire.

Trolley and trolley feeder wire shall be installed opposite the clearance side of haulageways. However, this standard does not apply where physical limitations would prevent the safe installation or use of such trolley and trolley feeder wire.

§ 57.12088 Splicing trailing cables.

No splice, except a vulcanized splice or its equivalent, shall be made in a trailing cable within 25 feet of the machine unless the machine is equipped with a cable reel or other power feed cable payout-retrieval system. However, a temporary splice may be made to move the equipment for repair.

Subpart L—Compressed Air and Boilers

§ 57.13001 General requirements for boilers and pressure vessels.

All boilers and pressure vessels shall be constructed, installed, and maintained in accordance with the standards and specifications of the American Society of Mechanical Engineers Boiler and Pressure Vessel Code.

§ 57.13010 Reciprocating-type air compressors.

(a) Reciprocating-type air compressors rated over 10 horsepower shall be equipped with automatic temperature-actuated shutoff mechanisms which shall be set or adjusted to the compressor when the normal operating temperature is exceeded by more than 25 percent.

(b) However, this standard does not apply to reciprocating-type air compressors rated over 10 horsepower if equipped with fusible plugs that were installed in the compressor discharge lines before November 15, 1979, and designed to melt at temperatures at least 50 degrees below the flash point of the compressors' lubricating oil.

§ 57.13011 Air receiver tanks.

Air receiver tanks shall be equipped with one or more automatic pressure-relief valves. The total relieving capacity of the relief valves shall prevent pressure from exceeding the maximum allowable working pressure in a receiver tank by not more than 10 percent. Air receiver tanks also shall be equipped with indicating pressure gages which accurately measure the pressure within the air receiver tanks.

§ 57.13012 Compressor air intakes.

Compressor air intakes shall be installed to ensure that only clean, uncontaminated air enters the compressors.

§ 57.13015 Inspection of compressed-air receivers and other unfired pressure vessels.

(a) Compressed-air receivers and other unfired pressure vessels shall be inspected by inspectors holding a valid National Board Commission and in accordance with the applicable chapters of the National Board Inspection Code, a Manual for Boiler and Pressure Vessel Inspectors, 1979. This code is incorporated by reference and made a part of this standard. It may be examined at any Metal and Nonmetal Mine Safety and Health District Office of the Mine Safety and Health Administration, and may be obtained from the publisher, the National Board of Boiler and Pressure Vessel Inspectors, 1055 Crupper Avenue, Columbus, Ohio 43229.

(b) Records of inspections shall be kept in accordance with requirements of the National Board Inspection Code, and the records shall be made available to the Secretary or his authorized representative.

§ 57.13017 Compressor discharge pipes.

Compressor discharge pipes where carbon build-up may occur shall be cleaned periodically as recommended by the manufacturer, but no less frequently than once every two years.

§ 57.13019 Pressure system repairs.

Repairs involving the pressure system of compressors, receivers, or compressed-air-powered equipment shall not be attempted until the pressure has been bled off.

§ 57.13020 Use of compressed air.

At no time shall compressed air be directed toward a person. When compressed air is used, all necessary precautions shall be taken to protect persons from injury.

§ 57.13021 High-pressure hose connections.

Except where automatic shutoff valves are used, safety chains or other suitable locking devices shall be used at connections to machines of high-pressure hose lines of ¾-inch inside diameter or larger, and between high-pressure hose lines of ¾-inch inside diameter or larger, where a connection failure would create a hazard.

§ 57.13030 Boilers.

(a) Fired pressure vessels (boilers) shall be equipped with water level gauges, pressure gauges, automatic pressure-relief valves, blowdown piping, and other safety devices approved by the American Society of Mechanical Engineers to protect against hazards from overpressure, flameouts, fuel interruptions and low water level, all as required by the appropriate sections, chapters and appendices listed in paragraphs (b) (1) and (2) of this section.

(b) These gauges, devices and piping shall be designed, installed, operated, maintained, repaired, altered, inspected, and tested by inspectors holding a valid National Board Commission and in accordance with the following listed sections, chapters and appendices:

§ 57.14000

(1) The ASME Boiler and Pressure Vessel Code, 1977, published by the American Society of Mechanical Engineers.

SECTION AND TITLE

I Power Boilers
II Material Specifications—Part A—Ferrous
II Material Specifications—Part B—Nonferrous
II Material Specifications—Part C—Welding Rods, Electrodes, and Filler Metals
IV Heating Boilers
V Nondestructive Examination
VI Recommended Rules for Care and Operation of Heating Boilers
VII Recommended Rules for Care of Power Boilers

(2) The National Board Inspection Code, a Manual for Boiler and Pressure Vessel Inspectors, 1979, published by the National Board of Boiler and Pressure Vessel Inspectors.

CHAPTER AND TITLE

I Glossary of Terms
II Inspection of Boilers and Pressure Vessels
III Repairs and Alterations to Boiler and Pressure Vessels by Welding
IV Shop Inspection of Boilers and Pressure Vessels
V Inservice Inspection of Pressure Vessels by Authorized Owner-User Inspection Agencies

APPENDIX AND TITLE

A Safety and Safety Relief Valves
B Non-ASME Code Boilers and Pressure Vessels
C Storage of Mild Steel Covered Arc Welding Electrodes
D-R National Board "R" (Repair) Symbol Stamp
D-VR National Board "VR" (Repair of Safety and Safety Relief Valve) Symbol Stamp
D-VR1 Certificate of Authorization for Repair Symbol Stamp for Safety and Safety Relief Valves
D-VR2 Outline of Basic Elements of Written Quality Control System for Repairers of ASME Safety and Safety Relief Valves
D-VR3 Nameplate Stamping for "VR"
E Owner-User Inspection Agencies
F Inspection Forms

(c) Records of inspections and repairs shall be kept in accordance with the requirements of the ASME Boiler and Pressure Vessel Code and the National Board Inspection Code. The records shall be made available to the Secretary or his authorized representative.

(d) Sections of the ASME Boiler and Pressure Vessel Code, 1977, listed in paragraph (b)(1) of this section, and chapters and appendices of the National Board Inspection Code, 1979, listed in paragraph (b)(2) of this section, are incorporated by reference and made a part of this standard. These publications may be obtained from the publishers, the American Society of Mechanical Engineers, 22 Law Drive, P.O. Box 2900, Fairfield, New Jersey 07007, Phone: 800–843–2763 (toll free); *http:// www.asme.org*, and the National Board of Boiler and Pressure Vessel Inspectors, 1055 Crupper Avenue, Columbus, Ohio 43229. The publication may be examined at any Metal and Nonmetal Mine Safety and Health District Office of the Mine Safety and Health Administration.

[50 FR 4082, Jan. 29, 1985, as amended at 71 FR 16667, Apr. 3, 2006]

Subpart M—Machinery and Equipment

SOURCE: 53 FR 32528, Aug. 25, 1988, unless otherwise noted.

§ 57.14000 Definitions.

The following definitions apply in this subpart.

Travelway. A passage, walk, or way regularly used or designated for persons to go from one place to another.

[53 FR 32528, Aug. 25, 1988, as amended at 69 FR 38842, June 29, 2004]

SAFETY DEVICES AND MAINTENANCE REQUIREMENTS

§ 57.14100 Safety defects; examination, correction and records.

(a) Self-propelled mobile equipment to be used during a shift shall be inspected by the equipment operator before being placed in operation on that shift.

(b) Defects on any equipment, machinery, and tools that affect safety shall be corrected in a timely manner to prevent the creation of a hazard to persons.

Mine Safety and Health Admin., Labor § 57.14101

(c) When defects make continued operation hazardous to persons, the defective items including self-propelled mobile equipment shall be taken out of service and placed in a designated area posted for that purpose, or a tag or other effective method of marking the defective items shall be used to prohibit further use until the defects are corrected.

(d) Defects on self-propelled mobile equipment affecting safety, which are not corrected immediately, shall be reported to, and recorded by, the mine operator. The records shall be kept at the mine or nearest mine office from the date the defects are recorded, until the defects are corrected. Such records shall be made available for inspection by an authorized representative of the Secretary.

§ 57.14101 Brakes.

(a) *Minimum requirements.* (1) Self-propelled mobile equipment shall be equipped with a service brake system capable of stopping and holding the equipment with its typical load on the maximum grade it travels. This standard does not apply to equipment which is not originally equipped with brakes unless the manner in which the equipment is being operated requires the use of brakes for safe operation. This standard does not apply to rail equipment.

(2) If equipped on self-propelled mobile equipment, parking brakes shall be capable of holding the equipment with its typical load on the maximum grade it travels.

(3) All braking systems installed on the equipment shall be maintained in functional condition.

(b) *Testing.* (1) Service brake tests shall be conducted on surface-operated equipment at underground mines when an MSHA inspector has reasonable cause to believe that the service brake system does not function as required, unless the mine operator removes the equipment from service for the appropriate repair;

(2) The performance of the service brakes shall be evaluated according to Table M–1.

TABLE M–1

Gross vehicle weight lbs.	Equipment Speed, MPH										
	10	11	12	13	14	15	16	17	18	19	20
	Service Brake Maximum Stopping Distance—Feet										
0–36,000	34	38	43	48	53	59	64	70	76	83	89
36,000–70,000	41	46	52	58	62	70	76	83	90	97	104
70,000–14,0000	48	54	61	67	74	81	88	95	103	111	119
140,000–250,000	56	62	69	77	84	92	100	108	116	125	133
250,000–400,000	59	66	74	81	89	97	105	114	123	132	141
Over–400,000	63	71	78	86	94	103	111	120	129	139	148

Stopping distances are computed using a constant deceleration of 9.66 FPS^2 and system response times of .5.1, 1.5, 2, 2.25 and 2.5 seconds for each of increasing weight category respectively. Stopping distance values include a one-second operator response time.

TABLE M–2—THE SPEED OF A VEHICLE CAN BE DETERMINED BY CLOCKING IT THROUGH A 100-FOOT MEASURED COURSE AT CONSTANT VELOCITY USING TABLE M–2. WHEN THE SERVICE BRAKES ARE APPLIED AT THE END OF THE COURSE, STOPPING DISTANCE CAN BE MEASURED AND COMPARED TO TABLE M–1.

Miles per hour	10	11	12	13	14	15	16	17	18	19	20
Seconds required to travel 100 feet	6.8	6.2	5.7	5.2	4.9	4.5	4.3	4.0	3.8	3.6	3.4

(3) Service brake tests shall be conducted under the direction of the mine operator in cooperation with and according to the instructions provided by the MSHA inspector as follows:

(i) Equipment capable of traveling at least 10 miles per hour shall be tested with a typical load for that particular piece of equipment. Front-end loaders shall be tested with the loader bucket empty. Equipment shall not be tested

§ 57.14102

when carrying hazardous loads, such as explosives.

(ii) The approach shall be of sufficient length to allow the equipment operator to reach and maintain a constant speed between 10 and 20 miles per hour prior to entering the 100 foot measured area. The constant speed shall be maintained up to the point when the equipment operator receives the signal to apply the brakes. The roadway shall be wide enough to accommodate the size of the equipment being tested. The ground shall be generally level, packed, and dry in the braking portion of the test course. Ground moisture may be present to the extent that it does not adversely affect the braking surface.

(iii) Braking is to be performed using only those braking systems, including auxiliary retarders, which are designed to bring the equipment to a stop under normal operating conditions. Parking or emergency (secondary) brakes are not to be actuated during the test.

(iv) The tests shall be conducted with the transmission in the gear appropriate for the speed the equipment is traveling except for equipment which is designed for the power train to be disengaged during braking.

(v) Testing speeds shall be a minimum of 10 miles per hour and a maximum of 20 miles per hour.

(vi) Stopping distances shall be measured from the point at which the equipment operator receives the signal to apply the service brakes to the final stopped position.

(4) Test results shall be evaluated as follows:

(i) If the initial test run is valid and the stopping distance does not exceed the corresponding stopping distance listed in Table 1, the performance of the service brakes shall be considered acceptable. For tests to be considered valid, the equipment shall not slide sideways or exhibit other lateral motion during the braking portion of the test.

(ii) If the equipment exceeds the maximum stopping distance in the initial test run, the mine operator may request from the inspector up to four additional test runs with two runs to be conducted in each direction. The performance of the service brakes shall be considered acceptable if the equipment does not exceed the maximum stopping distance on at least three of the additional tests.

(5) Where there is not an appropriate test site at the mine or the equipment is not capable of traveling at least 10 miles per hour, service brake tests will not be conducted. In such cases, the inspector will rely upon other available evidence to determine whether the service brake system meets the performance requirements of this standard.

[53 FR 32528, Aug. 25, 1988; 53 FR 44588, Nov. 4, 1988]

§ 57.14102 Brakes for rail equipment.

Braking systems on railroad cars and locomotives shall be maintained in functional condition.

§ 57.14103 Operators' stations.

(a) If windows are provided on operators' stations of self-propelled mobile equipment, the windows shall be made of safety glass or material with equivalent safety characteristics. The windows shall be maintained to provide visibility for safe operation.

(b) If damaged windows obscure visibility necessary for safe operation, or create a hazard to the equipment operator, the windows shall be replaced or removed. Damaged windows shall be replaced if absence of a window would expose the equipment operator to hazardous environmental conditions which would affect the ability of the equipment operator to safely operate the equipment.

(c) The operators' stations of self-propelled mobile equipment shall—

(1) Be free of materials that may create a hazard to persons by impairing the safe operation of the equipment; and

(2) Not be modified, in a manner that obscures visibility necessary for safe operation.

§ 57.14104 Tire repairs.

(a) Before a tire is removed from a vehicle for tire repair, the valve core shall be partially removed to allow for gradual deflation and then removed. During deflation, to the extent possible, persons shall stand outside of the

Mine Safety and Health Admin., Labor §57.14112

potential trajectory of the lock ring of a multi-piece wheel rim.

(b) To prevent injury from wheel rims during tire inflation, one of the following shall be used:

(1) A wheel cage or other restraining device that will constrain all wheel rim components during an explosive separation of a multi-piece wheel rim, or during the sudden release of contained air in a single piece rim wheel; or

(2) A stand-off inflation device which permits persons to stand outside of the potential trajectory of wheel components.

§57.14105 Procedures during repairs or maintenance.

Repairs or maintenance on machinery or equipment shall be performed only after the power is off, and the machinery or equipment blocked against hazardous motion. Machinery or equipment motion or activation is permitted to the extent that adjustments or testing cannot be performed without motion or activation, provided that persons are effectively protected from hazardous motion.

§57.14106 Falling object protection.

(a) Fork-lift trucks, front-end loaders, and bulldozers shall be provided with falling object protective structures if used in an area where falling objects could create a hazard to the operator.

(b) The protective structure shall be capable of withstanding the falling object loads to which it could be subjected.

§57.14107 Moving machine parts.

(a) Moving machine parts shall be guarded to protect persons from contacting gears, sprockets, chains, drive, head, tail, and takeup pulleys, flywheels, coupling, shafts, fan blades; and similar moving parts that can cause injury.

(b) Guards shall not be required where the exposed moving parts are at least seven feet away from walking or working surfaces.

§57.14108 Overhead drive belts.

Overhead drive belts shall be guarded to contain the whipping action of a broken belt if that action could be hazardous to persons.

§57.14109 Unguarded conveyors with adjacent travelways.

Unguarded conveyors next to travelways shall be equipped with—

(a) Emergency stop devices which are located so that a person falling on or against the conveyor can readily deactivate the conveyor drive motor; or

(b) Railings which—

(1) Are positioned to prevent persons from falling on or against the conveyor;

(2) Will be able to withstand the vibration, shock, and wear to which they will be subjected during normal operation; and

(3) Are constructed and maintained so that they will not create a hazard.

§57.14110 Flying or falling materials.

In areas where flying or falling materials generated from the operation of screens, crushers, or conveyors present a hazard, guards, shields, or other devices that provide protection against such flying or falling materials shall be provided to protect persons.

§57.14111 Slusher, backlash guards and securing.

(a) When persons are exposed to slushing operations, the slushers shall be equipped with rollers and drum covers and anchored securely before slushing operations are started to protect against hazardous movement before slushing operations are started.

(b) Slushers rated over 10 horsepower shall be equipped with backlash guards, unless the equipment operator is otherwise protected.

(c) This standard does not apply to air tuggers of 10 horsepower or less that have only one cable and one drum.

§57.14112 Construction and maintenance of guards.

(a) Guards shall be constructed and maintained to—

(1) Withstand the vibration, shock, and wear to which they will be subjected during normal operation; and

(2) Not create a hazard by their use.

§ 57.14113

(b) Guards shall be securely in place while machinery is being operated, except when testing or making adjustments which cannot be performed without removal of the guard.

§ 57.14113 Inclined conveyors: backstops or brakes.

Backstops or brakes shall be installed on drive units of inclined conveyors to prevent the conveyors from running in reverse, creating a hazard to persons.

§ 57.14114 Air valves for pneumatic equipment.

A manual master quick-close type air valve shall be installed on all pneumatic-powered equipment if there is a hazard of uncontrolled movement when the air supply is activated. The valve shall be closed except when the equipment is being operated.

[53 FR 32528, Aug. 25, 1988; 53 FR 44588, Nov. 4, 1988]

§ 57.14115 Stationary grinding machines.

Stationary grinding machines, other than special bit grinders, shall be equipped with—

(a) Peripheral hoods capable of withstanding the force of a bursting wheel and enclosing not less than 270°—of the periphery of the wheel;

(b) Adjustable tool rests set so that the distance between the grinding surface of the wheel and the tool rest is not greater than 1/8 inch; and

(c) A safety washer on each side of the wheel.

[53 FR 32528, Aug. 25, 1988; 53 FR 44588, Nov. 4, 1988]

§ 57.14116 Hand-held power tools.

(a) Power drills, disc sanders, grinders and circular and chain saws, when used in the hand-held mode shall be operated with controls which require constant hand or finger pressure.

(b) Circular saws and chain saws shall not be equipped with devices which lock-on the operating controls.

§ 57.14130 Roll-over protective structures (ROPS) and seat belts for surface equipment.

(a) *Equipment included.* Roll-over protective structures (ROPS) and seat belts shall be installed on—

(1) Crawler tractors and crawler loaders;

(2) Graders;

(3) Wheel loaders and wheel tractors;

(4) The tractor portion of semi-mounted scrapers, dumpers, water wagons, bottom-dump wagons, rear-dump wagons, and towed fifth wheel attachments;

(5) Skid-steer loaders; and

(6) Agricultural tractors.

(b) *ROPS construction.* ROPS shall meet the requirements of the following Society of Automotive Engineers (SAE) publications, as applicable, which are incorporated by reference:

(1) SAE J1040, "Performance Criteria for Roll-Over Protective Structures (ROPS) for Construction, Earthmoving, Forestry, and Mining Machines,", 1986; or

(2) SAE J1194, "Roll-Over Protective Structures (ROPS) for Wheeled Agricultural Tractors", 1983.

(c) *ROPS labeling.* ROPS shall have a label permanently affixed to the structure identifying—

(1) The manufacturer's name and address;

(2) The ROPS model number; and

(3) The make and model number of the equipment for which the ROPS is designed.

(d) *ROPS installation.* ROPS shall be installed on the equipment in accordance with the recommendations of the ROPS manufacturer.

(e) *ROPS maintenance.* (1) ROPS shall be maintained in a condition that meets the performance requirements applicable to the equipment. If the ROPS is subjected to a roll-over or abnormal structural loading, the equipment manufacturer or a registered professional engineer with knowledge and experience in ROPS design shall recertify that the ROPS meets the applicable performance requirements before it is returned to service.

(2) Alterations or repairs on ROPS shall be performed only with approval from the ROPS manufacturer or under

Mine Safety and Health Admin., Labor §57.14132

the instructions of a registered professional engineer with knowledge and experience in ROPS design. The manufacturer or engineer shall certify that the ROPS meets the applicable performance requirements.

(f) *Exemptions.* (1) This standard does not apply to—

(i) Self-propelled mobile equipment manufactured prior to July 1, 1969;

(ii) Over-the-road type tractors that pull trailers or vans on highways;

(iii) Equipment that is only operated by remote control; and

(2) Self-propelled mobile equipment manufactured prior to October 24, 1988, that is equipped with ROPS and seat belts that meet the installation and performance requirements of 30 CFR 57.9088 (1986 edition) shall be considered in compliance with paragraphs (b) and (h) of this section.

(g) *Wearing seat belts.* Seat belts shall be worn by the equipment operator except that when operating graders from a standing position, the grader operator shall wear safety lines and a harness in place of a seat belt.

(h) *Seat belts construction.* Seat belts required under this section shall meet the requirement of SAE J386, "Operator Restraint System for Off-Road Work Machines" (1985, 1993, or 1997), or SAE J1194, "Roll-Over Protective Structures (ROPS) for Wheeled Agricultural Tractors" (1983, 1989, 1994, or 1999), as applicable, which are incorporated by reference.

(i) *Seat belt maintenance.* Seat belts shall be maintained in functional condition, and replaced when necessary to assure proper performance.

(j) *Publications.* The incorporation by reference of these publications is approved by the Director of the Federal Register in accordance with 5 U.S.C. 552(a) and 1 CFR part 51. Copies of these publications may be examined at any Metal and Nonmetal Mine Safety and Health District Office; at MSHA's Office of Standards, Regulations, and Variances, 201 12th Street South, Arlington, VA 22202–5452; 202–693–9440; or at the National Archives and Records Administration (NARA). For information on the availability of this material at NARA, call 202–741–6030, or go to: http://www.archives.gov/federal_register/code_of_federal_regulations/ibr_locations.html. Copies may be purchased from the Society of Automotive Engineers, 400 Commonwealth Drive, Warrendale, PA 15096–0001; 724–776–4841; http://www.sae.org.

[53 FR 32528, Aug. 25, 1988; 53 FR 44588, Nov. 4, 1988, as amended at 60 FR 33722, June 29, 1995; 67 FR 38385, June 4, 2002; 68 FR 19347, Apr. 21, 2003; 80 FR 52988, Sept. 2, 2015]

§ 57.14131 Seat belts for surface haulage trucks.

(a) Seat belts shall be provided and worn in haulage trucks.

(b) Seat belts shall be maintained in functional condition, and replaced when necessary to assure proper performance.

(c) Seat belts required under this section shall meet the requirements of SAE J386, "Operator Restraint System for Off-Road Work Machines" (1985, 1993, or 1997), which are incorporated by reference.

(d) The incorporation by reference of these publications is approved by the Director of the Federal Register in accordance with 5 U.S.C. 552(a) and 1 CFR part 51. Copies of these publications may be examined at any Metal and Nonmetal Mine Safety and Health District Office; at MSHA's Office of Standards, Regulations, and Variances, 201 12th Street South, Arlington, VA 22202–5452; 202–693–9440; or at the National Archives and Records Administration (NARA). For information on the availability of this material at NARA, call 202–741–6030, or go to: http://www.archives.gov/federal_register/code_of_federal_regulations/ibr_locations.html. Copies may be purchased from the Society of Automotive Engineers, 400 Commonwealth Drive, Warrendale, PA 15096–0001; 724–776–4841; http://www.sae.org.

[53 FR 32528, Aug. 25, 1988, as amended at 67 FR 38385, June 4, 2002; 68 FR 19347, Apr. 21, 2003; 80 FR 52988, Sept. 2, 2015]

§ 57.14132 Horns and backup alarms for surface equipment.

(a) Manually-operated horns or other audible warning devices provided on self-propelled mobile equipment as a safety device shall be maintained in a functional condition.

§ 57.14160

(b)(1) When the operator has an obstructed view to the rear, self-propelled mobile equipment shall have—

(i) An automatic reverse-activated signal alarm;

(ii) A wheel-mounted bell alarm which sounds at least once for each three feet of reverse movement;

(iii) A discriminating backup alarm that covers the area of obstructed view; or

(iv) An observer to signal when it is safe to back up.

(2) Alarms shall be audible above the surrounding noise level.

(3) An automatic reverse-activated strobe light may be used at night in lieu of an audible reverse alarm.

(c) This standard does not apply to rail equipment.

§ 57.14160 Mantrip trolley wire hazards underground.

Mantrips shall be covered if there is danger of persons contacting the trolley wire.

§ 57.14161 Makeshift couplings.

Couplings used on underground rail equipment shall be designed for that equipment, except that makeshift couplings may be used to move disabled rail equipment for repairs if no hazard to persons is created.

§ 57.14162 Trip lights.

On underground rail haulage, trip lights shall be used on the rear of pulled trips and on the front of pushed trips.

SAFETY PRACTICES AND OPERATIONAL PROCEDURES

§ 57.14200 Warnings prior to starting or moving equipment.

Before starting crushers or moving self-propelled mobile equipment, equipment operators shall sound a warning that is audible above the surrounding noise level or use other effective means to warn all persons who could be exposed to a hazard from the equipment.

§ 57.14201 Conveyor start-up warnings.

(a) When the entire length of a conveyor is visible from the starting switch, the conveyor operator shall visually check to make certain that all persons are in the clear before starting the conveyor.

(b) When the entire length of the conveyor is not visible from the starting switch, a system which provides visible or audible warning shall be installed and operated to warn persons that the conveyor will be started. Within 30 seconds after the warning is given, the conveyor shall be started or a second warning shall be given.

§ 57.14202 Manual cleaning of conveyor pulleys.

Pulleys of conveyors shall not be cleaned manually while the conveyor is in motion.

§ 57.14203 Application of belt dressing.

Belt dressings shall not be applied manually while belts are in motion unless a pressurized-type applicator is used that allows the dressing to be applied from outside the guards.

§ 57.14204 Machinery lubrication.

Machinery or equipment shall not be lubricated manually while it is in motion where application of the lubricant may expose persons to injury.

§ 57.14205 Machinery, equipment, and tools.

Machinery, equipment, and tools shall not be used beyond the design capacity intended by the manufacturer, where such use may create a hazard to persons.

§ 57.14206 Securing movable parts.

(a) When moving mobile equipment between workplaces, booms, forks, buckets, beds, and similar movable parts of the equipment shall be positioned in the travel mode and, if required for safe travel, mechanically secured.

(b) When mobile equipment is unattended or not in use, dippers, buckets and scraper blades shall be lowered to the ground. Other movable parts, such as booms, shall be mechanically secured or positioned to prevent movement which would create a hazard to persons.

§ 57.14207 Parking procedures for unattended equipment.

Mobile equipment shall not be left unattended unless the controls are placed in the park position and the parking brake, if provided, is set. When parked on a grade, the wheels or tracks of mobile equipment shall be either chocked or turned into a bank or rib.

§ 57.14208 Warning devices.

(a) Visible warning devices shall be used when parked mobile equipment creates a hazard to persons in other mobile equipment.

(b) Mobile equipment, other than forklifts, carrying loads that project beyond the sides or more than four feet beyond the rear of the equipment shall have a warning flag at the end of the projection. Under conditions of limited visibility these loads shall have a warning light at the end of the projection. Such flags or lights shall be attached to the end of the projection or be carried by persons walking beside or behind the projection.

§ 57.14209 Safety procedures for towing.

(a) A properly sized tow bar or other effective means of control shall be used to tow mobile equipment.

(b) Unless steering and braking are under the control of the equipment operator on the towed equipment, a safety chain or wire rope capable of withstanding the loads to which it could be subjected shall be used in conjunction with any primary rigging.

(c) This provision does not apply to rail equipment.

§ 57.14210 Movement of dippers, buckets, loading booms, or suspended loads.

(a) Dippers, buckets, loading booms, or suspended loads shall not be swung over the operators' stations of self-propelled mobile equipment until the equipment operator is out of the operator's station and in a safe location.

(b) This section does not apply when the equipment is specifically designed to protect the equipment operator from falling objects.

§ 57.14211 Blocking equipment in a raised position.

(a) Persons shall not work on top of, under, or work from mobile equipment in a raised position until the equipment has been blocked or mechanically secured to prevent it from rolling or falling accidentally.

(b) Persons shall not work on top of, under, or work from a raised component of mobile equipment until the component has been blocked or mechanically secured to prevent accidental lowering. The equipment must also be blocked or secured to prevent rolling.

(c) A raised component must be secured to prevent accidental lowering when persons are working on or around mobile equipment and are exposed to the hazard of accidental lowering of the component.

(d) Under this section, a raised component of mobile equipment is considered to be blocked or mechanically secured if provided with a functional load-locking device or devices which prevent free and uncontrolled descent.

(e) Blocking or mechanical securing of the raised component is required during repair or maintenance of elevated mobile work platforms.

§ 57.14212 Chains, ropes, and drive belts.

Chains, ropes, and drive belts shall be guided mechanically onto moving pulleys, sprockets, or drums except where equipment is designed specifically for hand feeding.

§ 57.14213 Ventilation and shielding for welding.

(a) Welding operations shall be shielded when performed at locations where arc flash could be hazardous to persons.

(b) All welding operations shall be well-ventilated.

§ 57.14214 Train warnings.

A warning that is audible above the surrounding noise level shall be sounded—

(a) Immediately prior to moving trains;

(b) When trains approach persons, crossing, other trains on adjacent tracks; and

§ 57.14215

(c) Any place where the train operator's vision is obscured.

§ 57.14215 Coupling or uncoupling cars.

Prior to coupling or uncoupling cars manually, trains shall be brought to a complete stop, and then moved at minimum tram speed until the coupling or uncoupling activity is completed. Coupling or uncoupling shall not be attempted from the inside of curves unless the railroad and cars are designed to eliminate hazards to persons.

§ 57.14216 Backpoling.

Backpoling of trolleys is prohibited except where there is inadequate clearance to reverse the trolley pole. Where backpoling is required, it shall be done only at the minimum tram speed of the trolley.

§ 57.14217 Securing parked railcars.

Parked railcars shall be blocked securely unless held effectively by brakes.

§ 57.14218 Movement of equipment on adjacent tracks.

When a locomotive on one track is used to move rail equipment on adjacent tracks, a chain, cable, or drawbar shall be used which is capable of withstanding the loads to which it could be subjected.

§ 57.14219 Brakeman signals.

When a train is under the direction of a brakeman and the train operator cannot clearly recognize the brakeman's signals, the train operator shall bring the train to a stop.

APPENDIX I TO SUBPART M OF PART 57—NATIONAL CONSENSUS STANDARDS

Mine operators seeking further information regarding the construction and installation of falling object protective structures (FOPS) may consult the following national consensus standards, as applicable.

MSHA STANDARD 57.14106, FALLING OBJECT PROTECTION

Equipment	National consensus standard
Front-end loaders and bulldozers.	Society of Automotive Engineers (SAE) minimum performance criteria for falling object protective structures (FOPS) SAE J231—January, 1981.

MSHA STANDARD 57.14106, FALLING OBJECT PROTECTION—Continued

Equipment	National consensus standard
Fork-lift trucks	American National Standards Institute (ANSI) safety standard for low lift and high lift trucks, B 56.1, section 7.27—1983; or American National Standards Institute (ANSI) standard, rough terrain fork lift trucks, B 56.6—1987.

Subpart N—Personal Protection

SURFACE AND UNDERGROUND

§ 57.15001 First aid materials.

Adequate first-aid materials, including stretchers and blankets shall be provided at places convenient to all working areas. Water or neutralizing agents shall be available where corrosive chemicals or other harmful substances are stored, handled, or used.

§ 57.15002 Hard hats.

All persons shall wear suitable hard hats when in or around a mine or plant where falling objects may create a hazard.

§ 57.15003 Protective footwear.

All persons shall wear suitable protective footwear when in or around an area of a mine or plant where a hazard exists which could cause an injury to the feet.

§ 57.15004 Eye protection.

All persons shall wear safety glasses, goggles, or face shields or other suitable protective devices when in or around an area of a mine or plant where a hazard exists which could cause injury to unprotected eyes.

§ 57.15005 Safety belts and lines.

Safety belts and lines shall be worn when persons work where there is danger of falling; a second person shall tend the lifeline when bins, tanks, or other dangerous areas are entered.

§ 57.15006 Protective equipment and clothing for hazards and irritants.

Special protective equipment and special protective clothing shall be provided, maintained in a sanitary and reliable condition and used whenever hazards of process or environment, chemical hazards, radiological hazards, or mechanical irritants are encountered in a manner capable of causing injury or impairment.

§ 57.15007 Protective equipment or clothing for welding, cutting, or working with molten metal.

Protective clothing or equipment and face shields or goggles shall be worn when welding, cutting, or working with molten metal.

§ 57.15014 Eye protection when operating grinding wheels.

Face shields or goggles in good condition shall be worn when operating a grinding wheel.

[53 FR 32533, Aug. 25, 1988]

SURFACE ONLY

§ 57.15020 Life jackets and belts.

Life jackets or belts shall be worn where there is danger from falling into water.

UNDERGROUND ONLY

§ 57.15030 Provision and maintenance of self-rescue devices.

A 1-hour self-rescue device approved by MSHA and NIOSH under 42 CFR part 84 shall be made available by the operator to all personnel underground. Each operator shall maintain self-rescue devices in good condition.

[60 FR 30401, June 8, 1995]

§ 57.15031 Location of self-rescue devices.

(a) Except as provided in paragraph (b) and (c) of this section, self-rescue devices meeting the requirements of standard 57.15030 shall be worn or carried by all persons underground.

(b) Where the wearing or carrying of self-rescue devices meeting the requirements of standard 57.15030 is hazardous to a person, such self-rescue devices shall be located at a distance no greater than 25 feet from such person.

(c) Where a person works on or around mobile equipment, self-rescue devices may be placed in a readily accessible location on such equipment.

Subpart O—Materials Storage and Handling

§ 57.16001 Stacking and storage of materials.

Supplies shall not be stacked or stored in a manner which creates tripping or fall-of-material hazards.

§ 57.16002 Bins, hoppers, silos, tanks, and surge piles.

(a) Bins, hoppers, silos, tanks, and surge piles, where loose unconsolidated materials are stored, handled or transferred shall be—

(1) Equipped with mechanical devices or other effective means of handling materials so that during normal operations persons are not required to enter or work where they are exposed to entrapment by the caving or sliding of materials; and

(2) Equipped with supply and discharge operating controls. The controls shall be located so that spills or overruns will not endanger persons.

(b) Where persons are required to move around or over any facility listed in this standard, suitable walkways or passageways shall be provided.

(c) Where persons are required to enter any facility listed in this standard for maintenance or inspection purposes, ladders, platforms, or staging shall be provided. No person shall enter the facility until the supply and discharge of materials have ceased and the supply and discharge equipment is locked out. Persons entering the facility shall wear a safety belt or harness equipped with a lifeline suitably fastened. A second person, similarly equipped, shall be stationed near where the lifeline is fastened and shall constantly adjust it or keep it tight as needed, with minimum slack.

§ 57.16003 Storage of hazardous materials.

Materials that can create hazards if accidentally liberated from their containers shall be stored in a manner that minimizes the dangers.

§ 57.16004 Containers for hazardous materials.

Containers holding hazardous materials must be of a type approved for such use by recognized agencies.

[67 FR 42389, June 21, 2002]

§ 57.16005 Securing gas cylinders.

Compressed and liquid gas cylinders shall be secured in a safe manner.

§ 57.16006 Protection of gas cylinder valves.

Valves on compressed gas cylinders shall be protected by covers when being transported or stored, and by a safe location when the cylinders are in use.

§ 57.16007 Taglines, hitches, and slings.

(a) Taglines shall be attached to loads that may require steadying or guidance while suspended.

(b) Hitches and slings used to hoist materials shall be suitable for the particular material handled.

§ 57.16009 Suspended loads.

Persons shall stay clear of suspended loads.

§ 57.16010 Dropping materials from overhead.

To protect personnel, material shall not be dropped from an overhead elevation until the drop area is first cleared of personnel and the area is then either guarded or a suitable warning is given.

§ 57.16011 Riding hoisted loads or on the hoist hook.

Persons shall not ride on loads being moved by cranes or derricks, nor shall they ride the hoisting hooks unless such method eliminates a greater hazard.

§ 57.16012 Storage of incompatible substances.

Chemical substances, including concentrated acids and alkalis, shall be stored to prevent inadvertent contact with each other or with other substances, where such contact could cause a violent reaction or the liberation of harmful fumes or gases.

§ 57.16013 Working with molten metal.

Suitable warning shall be given before molten metal is poured and before a container of molten metal is moved.

§ 57.16014 Operator-carrying overhead cranes.

Operator-carrying overhead cranes shall be provided with—

(a) Bumpers at each end of each rail;

(b) Automatic switches to halt uptravel of the blocks before they strike the hoist;

(c) Effective audible warning signals within easy reach of the operator; and

(d) A means to lock out the disconnect switch.

§ 57.16015 Work or travel on overhead crane bridges.

No person shall work from or travel on the bridge of an overhead crane unless the bridge is provided with substantial footwalks with toeboards and railings the length of the bridge.

§ 57.16016 Lift trucks.

Fork and other similar types of lift trucks shall be operated with the:

(a) Upright tilted back to steady and secure the load;

(b) Load in the upgrade position when ascending or descending grades in excess of 10 percent;

(c) Load not raised or lowered enroute except for minor adjustments; and

(d) Load-engaging device downgrade when traveling unloaded on all grades.

§ 57.16017 Hoisting heavy equipment or material.

Where the stretching or contraction of a hoist rope could create a hazard, chairs or other suitable blocking shall be used to support conveyances at shaft landings before heavy equipment or material is loaded or unloaded.

Subpart P—Illumination

§ 57.17001 Illumination of surface working areas.

Illumination sufficient to provide safe working conditions shall be provided in and on all surface structures, paths, walkways, stairways, switch panels, loading and dumping sites, and working areas.

§ 57.17010 Electric lamps.

Individual electric lamps shall be carried for illumination by all persons underground.

Subpart Q—Safety Programs

SURFACE AND UNDERGROUND

§ 57.18002 Examination of working places.

(a) A competent person designated by the operator shall examine each working place at least once each shift before miners begin work in that place, for conditions that may adversely affect safety or health.

(1) The operator shall promptly notify miners in any affected areas of any conditions found that may adversely affect safety or health and promptly initiate appropriate action to correct such conditions.

(2) Conditions noted by the person conducting the examination that may present an imminent danger shall be brought to the immediate attention of the operator who shall withdraw all persons from the area affected (except persons referred to in section 104(c) of the Federal Mine Safety and Health Act of 1977) until the danger is abated.

(b) A record of each examination shall be made before the end of the shift for which the examination was conducted. The record shall contain the name of the person conducting the examination; date of the examination; location of all areas examined; and description of each condition found that may adversely affect the safety or health of miners.

(c) When a condition that may adversely affect safety or health is corrected, the examination record shall include, or be supplemented to include, the date of the corrective action.

(d) The operator shall maintain the examination records for at least one year, make the records available for inspection by authorized representatives of the Secretary and the representatives of miners, and provide these representatives a copy on request.

[84 FR 51401, Sept. 30, 2019]

§ 57.18006 New employees.

New employees shall be indoctrinated in safety rules and safe work procedures.

§ 57.18009 Designation of person in charge.

When persons are working at the mine, a competent person designated by the mine operator shall be in attendance to take charge in case of an emergency.

§ 57.18010 First aid.

An individual capable of providing first aid shall be available on all shifts. The individual shall be currently trained and have the skills to perform patient assessment and artificial respiration; control bleeding; and treat shock, wounds, burns, and musculoskeletal injuries. First aid training shall be made available to all interested miners.

[61 FR 50436, Sept. 26, 1996]

§ 57.18012 Emergency telephone numbers.

Emergency telephone numbers shall be posted at appropriate telephones.

§ 57.18013 Emergency communications system.

A suitable communication system shall be provided at the mine to obtain assistance in the event of an emergency.

§ 57.18014 Emergency medical assistance and transportation.

Arrangements shall be made in advance for obtaining emergency medical assistance and transportation for injured persons.

SURFACE ONLY

§ 57.18020 Working alone.

No employee shall be assigned, or allowed, or be required to perform work alone in any area where hazardous conditions exist that would endanger his safety unless he can communicate with others, can be heard, or can be seen.

§ 57.18025

UNDERGROUND ONLY

§ 57.18025 Working alone.

No employee shall be assigned, or allowed, or be required to perform work alone in any area where hazardous conditions exist that would endanger his safety unless his cries for help can be heard or he can be seen.

§ 57.18028 Mine emergency and self-rescuer training.

(a) On an annual basis, all persons who are required to go underground shall be instructed in the Mine Safety and Health Administration approved course contained in Bureau of Mines Instruction Guide 19, "Mine Emergency Training" (September 1972). The instruction shall be given by MSHA personnel or by persons who are certified by the District Manager of the area in which the mine is located.

(b) On an annual basis, all persons who go underground shall be instructed in the Mine Safety and Health Administration course contained in Bureau of Mines Instruction Guide 2, "MSA W-65 Self-Rescuer" (March 1972) or Bureau of Mines Instruction Guide 3, "Permissible Drager 810 Respirator for Self-Rescue" (March 1972). The instruction shall be given by MSHA personnel or by persons who are certified by the District Manager of the area in which the mine is located: *Provided, however,* That if a Mine Safety and Health Administration instructor or a certified instructor is not immediately available such instruction of new employees in self-rescuers may be conducted by qualified company personnel who are not certified, but who have obtained provisional approval from the District Manager. Any person who has not had self-rescuer instruction within 12 months immediately preceding going underground shall be instructed in the use of self-rescuers before going underground.

(c) All instructional material, handouts, visual aids, and other such teaching accessories used by the operator in the courses prescribed in paragraphs (a) and (b) of this section shall be available for inspection by the Secretary or his authorized representative.

(d) Records of all instruction shall be kept at the mine site or nearest mine office at least 2 years from the date of instruction. Upon completion of such instruction, copies of the record shall be submitted to the District Manager.

(e) The Bureau of Mines instruction guides to which reference is made in items (a) and (b) of this standard are hereby incorporated by reference and made a part hereof. The incorporated instruction guides are available and shall be provided upon request made to any Metal and Nonmetal Mine Safety and Health district office.

[50 FR 4082, Jan. 29, 1985, as amended at 71 FR 16667, Apr. 3, 2006]

Subpart R—Personnel Hoisting

§ 57.19000 Application.

(a) The hoisting standards in this subpart apply to those hoists and appurtenances used for hoisting persons. However, where persons may be endangered by hoists and appurtenances used solely for handling ore, rock, and materials, the appropriate standards should be applied.

(b) Standards 57.19021 through 57.19028 shall apply to wire ropes in service used to hoist—

(1) Persons in shafts and slopes underground;

(2) Persons with an incline hoist on the surface; or

(3) Loads in shaft or slope development when persons work below suspended loads.

(4) These standards do not apply to wire ropes used for elevators.

(c) Emergency hoisting facilities should conform to the extent possible to safety requirements for other hoists, and should be adequate to remove the persons from the mine with a minimum of delay.

HOISTS

§ 57.19001 Rated capacities.

Hoists shall have rated capacities consistent with the loads handled and the recommended safety factors of the ropes used.

§ 57.19002 Anchoring.

Hoists shall be anchored securely.

§ 57.19003 Driving mechanism connections.

Belt, rope, or chains shall not be used to connect driving mechanisms to man hoists.

§ 57.19004 Brakes.

Any hoist used to hoist persons shall be equipped with a brake or brakes which shall be capable of holding its fully loaded cage, skip, or bucket at any point in the shaft.

§ 57.19005 Locking mechanism for clutch.

The operating mechanism of the clutch of every man-hoist drum shall be provided with a locking mechanism, or interlocked electrically or mechanically with the brake to prevent accidental withdrawal of the clutch.

§ 57.19006 Automatic hoist braking devices.

Automatic hoists shall be provided with devices that automatically apply the brakes in the event of power failure.

§ 57.19007 Overtravel and overspeed devices.

All man hoists shall be provided with devices to prevent overtravel. When utilized in shafts exceeding 100 feet in depth, such hoists shall also be provided with overspeed devices.

§ 57.19008 Friction hoist synchronizing mechanisms.

Where creep or slip may alter the effective position of safety devices, friction hoists shall be equipped with synchronizing mechanisms that recalibrate the overtravel devices and position indicators.

§ 57.19009 Position indicator.

An accurate and reliable indicator of the position of the cage, skip, bucket, or cars in the shaft shall be provided.

§ 57.19010 Location of hoist controls.

Hoist controls shall be placed or housed so that the noise from machinery or other sources will not prevent hoistmen from hearing signals.

§ 57.19011 Drum flanges.

Flanges on drums shall extend radially a minimum of 4 inches or three rope diameters beyond the last wrap, whichever is the lesser.

§ 57.19012 Grooved drums.

Where grooved drums are used, the grooves shall be of suitable size and pitch for the ropes used.

§ 57.19013 Diesel- and other fuel-injection-powered hoists.

Where any diesel or similar fuel-injection engine is used to power a hoist, the engine shall be equipped with a damper or other cutoff in its air intake system. The control handle shall be clearly labeled to indicate that its intended function is for emergency stopping only.

§ 57.19014 Friction hoist overtravel protection.

In a friction hoist installation, tapered guides or other approved devices shall be installed above and below the limits of regular travel of the conveyance and arranged to prevent overtravel in the event of failure of other devices.

§ 57.19017 Emergency braking for electric hoists.

Each electric hoist shall be equipped with a manually-operable switch that will initiate emergency braking action to bring the conveyance and the counterbalance safely to rest. This switch shall be located within reach of the hoistman in case the manual controls of the hoist fail.

§ 57.19018 Overtravel by-pass switches.

When an overtravel by-pass switch is installed, the switch shall function so as to allow the conveyance to be moved through the overtravel position when the switch is held in the closed position by the hoistman. The overtravel by-pass switch shall return automatically to the open position when released by the hoistman.

WIRE ROPES

AUTHORITY: Sec. 101, Federal Mine Safety and Health Act of 1977, Pub. L. 91-173 as

§ 57.19019

amended by Pub. L. 95–164, 91 Stat. 1291 (30 U.S.C. 811).

§ 57.19019 Guide ropes.

If guide ropes are used in shafts for personnel hoisting applications other than shaft development, the nominal strength (manufacturer's published catalog strength) of the guide rope at installation shall meet the minimum value calculated as follows: Minimum value = Static Load × 5.0.

§ 57.19021 Minimum rope strength.

At installation, the nominal strength (manufacturer's published catalog strength) of wire ropes used for hoisting shall meet the minimum rope strength values obtained by the following formulas in which "L" equals the maximum suspended rope length in feet:

(a) *Winding drum ropes* (all constructions, including rotation resistant).

For rope lengths less than 3,000 feet: Minimum Value = Static Load × (7.0 − 0.001L)
For rope lengths 3,000 feet or greater: Minimum Value = Static Load × 4.0.

(b) *Friction drum ropes.*

For rope lengths less than 4,000 feet: Minimum Value = Static Load × (7.0 − 0.0005L)
For rope lengths 4,000 feet or greater: Minimum Value = Static Load × 5.0.

(c) *Tail ropes* (balance ropes).

Minimum Value = Weight of Rope × 7.0

§ 57.19022 Initial measurement.

After initial rope stretch but before visible wear occurs, the rope diameter of newly installed wire ropes shall be measured at least once in every third interval of active length and the measurements averaged to establish a baseline for subsequent measurements. A record of the measurements and the date shall be made by the person taking the measurements. This record shall be retained until the rope is retired from service.

[50 FR 4082, Jan. 29, 1985, as amended at 60 FR 33722, June 29, 1995]

§ 57.19023 Examinations.

(a) At least once every fourteen calendar days, each wire rope in service shall be visually examined along its entire active length for visible structural damage, corrosion, and improper lubrication or dressing. In addition, visual examination for wear and broken wires shall be made at stress points, including the area near attachments, where the rope rests on sheaves, where the rope leaves the drum, at drum crossovers, and at change-of-layer regions. When any visible condition that results in a reduction of rope strength is present, the affected portion of the rope shall be examined on a daily basis.

(b) Before any person is hoisted with a newly installed wire rope or any wire rope that has not been examined in the previous fourteen calendar days, the wire rope shall be examined in accordance with paragraph (a) of this section.

(c) At least once every six months, nondestructive tests shall be conducted of the active length of the rope, or rope diameter measurements shall be made—

(1) Wherever wear is evident;

(2) Where the hoist rope rests on sheaves at regular stopping points;

(3) Where the hoist rope leaves the drum at regular stopping points; and

(4) At drum crossover and change-of-layer regions.

(d) At the completion of each examination required by paragraph (a) of this section, the person making the examination shall certify, by signature and date, that the examination has been made. If any condition listed in paragraph (a) of this section is present, the person conducting the examination shall make a record of the condition and the date. Certifications and records of examinations shall be retained for one year.

(e) The person making the measurements or nondestructive tests as required by paragraph (c) of this section shall record the measurements or test results and the date. This record shall be retained until the rope is retired from service.

§ 57.19024 Retirement criteria.

Unless damage or deterioration is removed by cutoff, wire ropes shall be removed from service when any of the following conditions occurs:

(a) The number of broken wires within a rope lay length, excluding filler wires, exceeds either—

(1) Five percent of the total number of wires; or

(2) Fifteen percent of the total number of wires within any strand.

(b) On a regular lay rope, more than one broken wire in the valley between strands in one rope lay length.

(c) A loss of more than one-third of the original diameter of the outer wires.

(d) Rope deterioration from corrosion.

(e) Distortion of the rope structure.

(f) Heat damage from any source.

(g) Diameter reduction due to wear that exceeds six percent of the baseline diameter measurement.

(h) Loss of more than ten percent of rope strength as determined by nondestructive testing.

§ 57.19025 Load end attachments.

(a) Wire rope shall be attached to the load by a method that develops at least 80 percent of the nominal strength of the rope.

(b) Except for terminations where use of other materials is a design feature, zinc (spelter) shall be used for socketing wire ropes. Design feature means either the manufacturer's original design or a design approved by a registered professional engineer

(c) Load end attachment methods using splices are prohibited.

§ 57.19026 Drum end attachment.

(a) For drum end attachment, wire rope shall be attached—

(1) Securely by clips after making one full turn around the drum spoke;

(2) Securely by clips after making one full turn around the shaft, if the drum is fixed to the shaft; or

(3) By properly assembled anchor bolts, clamps, or wedges, provided that the attachment is a design feature of the hoist drum. Design feature means either the manufacturer's original design or a design approved by a registered professional engineer.

(b) A minimum of three full turns of wire rope shall be on the drum when the rope is extended to its maximum working length.

§ 57.19027 End attachment retermination.

Damaged or deteriorated wire rope shall be removed by cutoff and the rope reterminated where there is—

(a) More than one broken wire at an attachment;

(b) Improper installation of an attachment;

(c) Slippage at an attachment; or

(d) Evidence of deterioration from corrosion at an attachment.

§ 57.19028 End attachment replacement.

Wire rope attachments shall be replaced when cracked, deformed, or excessively worn.

§ 57.19030 Safety device attachments.

Safety device attachments to hoist ropes shall be selected, installed, and maintained according to manufacturers' specifications to minimize internal corrosion and weakening of the hoist rope.

HEADFRAMES AND SHEAVES

§ 57.19035 Headframe design.

All headframes shall be constructed with suitable design considerations to allow for all dead loads, live loads, and wind loads.

§ 57.19036 Headframe height.

Headframes shall be high enough to provide clearance for overtravel and safe stopping of the conveyance.

§ 57.19037 Fleet angles.

Fleet angles on hoists installed after November 15, 1979, shall not be greater than one and one-half degrees for smooth drums or two degrees for grooved drums.

§ 57.19038 Platforms around elevated head sheaves.

Platforms with toeboards and handrails shall be provided around elevated head sheaves.

CONVEYANCES

§ 57.19045 Metal bonnets.

Man cages and skips used for hoisting or lowering employees or other persons in any vertical shaft or any incline shaft with an angle of inclination of forty-five degrees from the horizontal, shall be covered with a metal bonnet.

§ 57.19049 Hoisting persons in buckets.

Buckets shall not be used to hoist persons except during shaft sinking operations, inspection, maintenance, and repairs.

§ 57.19050 Bucket requirements.

Buckets used to hoist persons during vertical shaft sinking operations shall—

(a) Be securely attached to a crosshead when traveling in either direction between the lower and upper crosshead parking locations;

(b) Have overhead protection when the shaft depth exceeds 50 feet;

(c) Have sufficient depth or a suitably designed platform to transport persons safely in a standing position; and

(d) Have devices to prevent accidental dumping where the bucket is supported by a bail attached to its lower half.

§ 57.19054 Rope guides.

Where rope guides are used in shafts other than in shaft sinking operations, the rope guides shall be a type of lock coil construction.

HOISTING PROCEDURES

§ 57.19055 Availability of hoist operator for manual hoists.

When a manually operated hoist is used, a qualified hoistman shall remain within hearing of the telephone or signal device at all times while any person is underground.

§ 57.19056 Availability of hoist operator for automatic hoists.

When automatic hoisting is used, a competent operator of the hoist shall be readily available at or near the hoisting device while any person is underground.

§ 57.19057 Hoist operator's physical fitness.

No person shall operate a hoist unless within the preceding 12 months he has had a medical examination by a qualified, licensed physician who shall certify his fitness to perform this duty. Such certification shall be available at the mine.

§ 57.19058 Experienced hoist operators.

Only experienced hoistmen shall operate the hoist except in cases of emergency and in the training of new hoistmen.

§ 57.19061 Maximum hoisting speeds.

The safe speed for hoisting persons shall be determined for each shaft, and this speed shall not be exceeded. Persons shall not be hoisted at a speed faster than 2,500 feet per minute, except in an emergency.

§ 57.19062 Maximum acceleration and deceleration.

Maximum normal operating acceleration and deceleration shall not exceed 6 feet per second per second. During emergency braking, the deceleration shall not exceed 16 feet per second per second.

§ 57.19063 Persons allowed in hoist room.

Only authorized persons shall be in hoist rooms.

§ 57.19065 Lowering conveyances by the brakes.

Conveyances shall not be lowered by the brakes alone except during emergencies.

§ 57.19066 Maximum riders in a conveyance.

In shafts inclined over 45 degrees, the operator shall determine and post in the conveyance or at each shaft station the maximum number of persons permitted to ride in a hoisting conveyance at any one time. Each person shall be provided a minimum of 1.5 square feet of floor space.

§ 57.19067 Trips during shift changes.

During shift changes, an authorized person shall be in charge of each trip in which persons are hoisted.

§ 57.19068 Orderly conduct in conveyances.

Persons shall enter, ride, and leave conveyances in an orderly manner.

§ 57.19069 Entering and leaving conveyances.

Persons shall not enter or leave conveyances which are in motion or after a signal to move the conveyance has been given to the hoistman.

§ 57.19070 Closing cage doors or gates.

Cage doors or gates shall be closed while persons are being hoisted; they shall not be opened until the cage has come to a stop.

§ 57.19071 Riding in skips or buckets.

Persons shall not ride in skips or buckets with muck, supplies, materials, or tools other than small hand tools.

§ 57.19072 Skips and cages in same compartment.

When combinations of cages and skips are used in the same compartment, the cages shall be enclosed to protect personnel from flying material and the hoist speed reduced to manspeed as defined in standard 57.19061, but not to exceed 1,000 feet per minute. Muck shall not be hoisted with personnel during shift changes.

§ 57.19073 Hoisting during shift changes.

Rock or supplies shall not be hoisted in the same shaft as persons during shift changes, unless the compartments and dumping bins are partitioned to prevent spillage into the cage compartment.

§ 57.19074 Riding the bail, rim, bonnet, or crosshead.

Persons shall not ride the bail, rim, bonnet, or crosshead of any shaft conveyance except when necessary for inspection and maintenance, and then only when suitable protection for persons is provided.

§ 57.19075 Use of open hooks.

Open hooks shall not be used to hoist buckets or other conveyances.

§ 57.19076 Maximum speeds for hoisting persons in buckets.

When persons are hoisted in buckets, speeds shall not exceed 500 feet per minute and shall not exceed 200 feet per minute when within 100 feet of the intended station.

§ 57.19077 Lowering buckets.

Buckets shall be stopped about 15 feet from the shaft bottom to await a signal from one of the crew on the bottom for further lowering.

§ 57.19078 Hoisting buckets from the shaft bottom.

All buckets shall be stopped after being raised about three feet above the shaft bottom. A bucket shall be stabilized before a hoisting signal is given to continue hoisting the bucket to the crosshead. After a hoisting signal is given, hoisting to the crosshead shall be at a minimum speed. The signaling device shall be attended constantly until a bucket reaches the guides. When persons are hoisted, the signaling devices shall be attended until the crosshead has been engaged.

§ 57.19079 Blocking mine cars.

Where mine cars are hoisted by cage or skip, means for blocking cars shall be provided at all landings and also on the cage.

§ 57.19080 Hoisting tools, timbers, and other materials.

When tools, timbers, or other materials are being lowered or raised in a shaft by means of a bucket, skip, or cage, they shall be secured or so placed that they will not strike the sides of the shaft.

§ 57.19081 Conveyances not in use.

When conveyances controlled by a hoist operator are not in use, they shall be released and the conveyances shall be raised or lowered a suitable distance to prevent persons from boarding or loading the conveyances.

§ 57.19083 Overtravel backout device.

A manually operated device shall be installed on each electric hoist that will allow the conveyance or counterbalance to be removed from an overtravel position. Such device shall not release the brake, or brakes, holding the overtravelled conveyance or counterbalance until sufficient drive motor torque has been developed to assure

§ 57.19090

movement of the conveyance or counterbalance in the correct direction only.

SIGNALING

§ 57.19090 Dual signaling systems.

There shall be at least two effective approved methods of signaling between each of the shaft stations and the hoist room, one of which shall be a telephone or speaking tube.

§ 57.19091 Signaling instructions to hoist operator.

Hoist operators shall accept hoisting instructions only by the regular signaling system unless it is out of order. In such an event, and during other emergencies, the hoist operator shall accept instructions to direct movement of the conveyances only from authorized persons.

§ 57.19092 Signaling from conveyances.

A method shall be provided to signal the hoist operator from cages or other conveyances at any point in the shaft.

§ 57.19093 Standard signal code.

A standard code of hoisting signals shall be adopted and used at each mine. The movement of a shaft conveyance on a "one bell" signal is prohibited.

§ 57.19094 Posting signal code.

A legible signal code shall be posted prominently in the hoist house within easy view of the hoistmen, and at each place where signals are given or received.

§ 57.19095 Location of signal devices.

Hoisting signal devices shall be positioned within easy reach of persons on the shaft bottom or constantly attended by a person stationed on the lower deck of the sinking platform.

§ 57.19096 Familiarity with signal code.

Any person responsible for receiving or giving signals for cages, skips, and mantrips when persons or materials are being transported shall be familiar with the posted signaling code.

SHAFTS

§ 57.19100 Shaft landing gates.

Shaft landings shall be equipped with substantial safety gates so constructed that materials will not go through or under them; gates shall be closed except when loading or unloading shaft conveyances.

§ 57.19101 Stopblocks and derail switches.

Positive stopblocks or a derail switch shall be installed on all tracks leading to a shaft collar or landing.

§ 57.19102 Shaft guides.

A means shall be provided to guide the movement of a shaft conveyance.

§ 57.19103 Dumping facilities and loading pockets.

Dumping facilities and loading pockets shall be constructed so as to minimize spillage into the shaft.

§ 57.19104 Clearance at shaft stations.

Suitable clearance at shaft stations shall be provided to allow safe movement of persons, equipment and materials.

§ 57.19105 Landings with more than one shaft entrance.

A safe means of passage around open shaft compartments shall be provided on landings with more than one entrance to the shaft.

§ 57.19106 Shaft sets.

Shaft sets shall be kept in good repair and clean of hazardous material.

§ 57.19107 Precautions for work in compartment affected by hoisting operation.

Hoistmen shall be informed when persons are working in a compartment affected by that hoisting operation and a "Men Working in Shaft" sign shall be posted at the hoist.

§ 57.19108 Posting warning signs during shaft work.

When persons are working in a shaft "Men Working in Shaft" signs shall be posted at all devices controlling hoisting operations that may endanger such persons.

§57.19109 Shaft inspection and repair.

Shaft inspection and repair work in vertical shafts shall be performed from substantial platforms equipped with bonnets or equivalent overhead protection.

§57.19110 Overhead protection for shaft deepening work.

A substantial bulkhead or equivalent protection shall be provided above persons at work deepening a shaft.

§57.19111 Shaft-sinking ladders.

Substantial fixed ladders shall be provided from the collar to as near the shaft bottom as practical during shaft-sinking operations, or an escape hoist powered by an emergency power source shall be provided. When persons are on the shaft bottom, a chain ladder, wire rope ladder, or other extension ladders shall be used from the fixed ladder or lower limit of the escape hoist to the shaft bottom.

INSPECTION AND MAINTENANCE

§57.19120 Procedures for inspection, testing, and maintenance.

A systematic procedure of inspection, testing and maintenance of shaft and hoisting equipment shall be developed and followed. If it is found or suspected that any part is not functioning properly, the hoist shall not be used until the malfunction has been located and repaired or adjustments have been made.

§57.19121 Recordkeeping.

At the time of completion, the person performing inspections, tests, and maintenance of shafts and hoisting equipment required in standard 57.19120 shall certify, by signature and date, that they have been done. A record of any part that is not functioning properly shall be made and dated. Certifications and records shall be retained for one year.

(Sec. 101, Pub. L. 91–173 as amended by Pub. L. 95–164, 91 Stat. 1291 (30 U.S.C. 811))

[50 FR 4082, Jan. 29, 1985, as amended at 60 FR 33722, June 29, 1995]

§57.19122 Replacement parts.

Parts used to repair hoists shall have properties that will ensure the proper and safe function of the hoist.

§57.19129 Examinations and tests at beginning of shift.

Hoistmen shall examine their hoists and shall test overtravel, deadman controls, position indicators, and braking mechanisms at the beginning of each shift.

§57.19130 Conveyance shaft test.

Before hoisting persons and to assure that the hoisting compartments are clear of obstructions, empty hoist conveyances shall be operated at least one round trip after—

(a) Any hoist or shaft repairs or related equipment repairs that might restrict or obstruct conveyance clearance;

(b) Any oversize or overweight material or equipment trips that might restrict or obstruct conveyance clearance;

(c) Blasting in or near the shaft that might restrict or obstruct conveyance clearance; or

(d) Remaining idle for one shift or longer.

§57.19131 Hoist conveyance connections.

Hoist conveyance connections shall be inspected at least once during any 24-hour period that the conveyance is used for hoisting persons.

§57.19132 Safety catches.

(a) A performance drop test of hoist conveyance safety catches shall be made at the time of installation, or prior to installation in a mockup of the actual installation. The test shall be certified to in writing by the manufacturer or by a registered professional engineer performing the test.

(b) After installation and before use, and at the beginning of any seven day period during which the conveyance is to be used, the conveyance shall be suitably rested and the hoist rope slackened to test for the unrestricted functioning of the safety catches and their activating mechanisms.

(c) The safety catches shall be inspected by a competent person at the

§ 57.19133

beginning of any 24-hour period that the conveyance is to be used.

§ 57.19133 Shaft.

Shafts that have not been inspected within the past 7 days shall not be used until an inspection has been conducted by a competent person.

§ 57.19134 Sheaves.

Sheaves in operating shafts shall be inspected weekly and kept properly lubricated.

§ 57.19135 Rollers in inclined shafts.

Rollers used in operating inclined shafts shall be lubricated, properly aligned, and kept in good repair.

Subpart S—Miscellaneous

§ 57.20001 Intoxicating beverages and narcotics.

Intoxicating beverages and narcotics shall not be permitted or used in or around mines. Persons under the influence of alcohol or narcotics shall not be permitted on the job.

§ 57.20002 Potable water.

(a) An adequate supply of potable drinking water shall be provided at all active working areas.

(b) The common drinking cup and containers from which drinking water must be dipped or poured are prohibited.

(c) Where single service cups are supplied, a sanitary container for unused cups and a receptacle for used cups shall be provided.

(d) When water is cooled by ice, the ice shall either be of potable water or shall not come in contact with the water.

(e) Potable water outlets shall be posted.

(f) Potable water systems shall be constructed to prevent backflow or backsiphonage of non-potable water.

§ 57.20003 Housekeeping.

At all mining operations—

(a) Workplaces, passageways, storerooms, and service rooms shall be kept clean and orderly;

(b) The floor of every workplace shall be maintained in a clean and, so far as possible, dry condition. Where wet processes are used, drainage shall be maintained, and false floors, platforms, mats, or other dry standing places shall be provided where practicable; and

(c) Every floor, working place, and passageway shall be kept free from protruding nails, splinters, holes, or loose boards, as practicable.

§ 57.20005 Carbon tetrachloride.

Carbon tetrachloride shall not be used.

§ 57.20008 Toilet facilities.

(a) Toilet facilities shall be provided at locations that are compatible with the mine operations and that are readily accessible to mine personnel.

(b) The facilities shall be kept clean and sanitary. Separate toilet facilities shall be provided for each sex except where toilet rooms will be occupied by no more than one person at a time and can be locked from the inside.

§ 57.20009 Tests for explosive dusts.

Dusts suspected of being explosive shall be tested for explosibility. If tests prove positive, appropriate control measures shall be taken.

§ 57.20010 Retaining dams.

If failure of a water or silt retaining dam will create a hazard, it shall be of substantial construction and inspected at regular intervals.

§ 57.20011 Barricades and warning signs.

Areas where health or safety hazards exist that are not immediately obvious to employees shall be barricaded, or warning signs shall be posted at all approaches. Warning signs shall be readily visible, legible, and display the nature of the hazard and any protective action required.

§ 57.20013 Waste receptacles.

Receptacles with covers shall be provided at suitable locations and used for the disposal of waste food and associated materials. They shall be emptied frequently and shall be maintained in a clean and sanitary condition.

§ 57.20014 Prohibited areas for food and beverages.

No person shall be allowed to consume or store food or beverages in a toilet room or in any area exposed to a toxic material.

§ 57.20020 Unattended mine openings.

Access to unattended mine openings shall be restricted by gates or doors, or the openings shall be fenced and posted.

§ 57.20021 Abandoned mine openings.

Upon abandonment of a mine, the owner or operator shall effectively close or fence off all surface openings down which persons could fall or through which persons could enter. Upon or near all such safeguards, trespass warnings and appropriate danger notices shall be posted.

§ 57.20031 Blasting underground in hazardous areas.

In underground areas where dangerous accumulations of water, gas, mud, or fire atmosphere could be encountered, persons shall be removed to safe places before blasting.

§ 57.20032 Two-way communication equipment for underground operations.

Telephones or other two-way communication equipment with instructions for their use shall be provided for communication from underground operations to the surface.

Subpart T—Safety Standards for Methane in Metal and Nonmetal Mines

AUTHORITY: 30 U.S.C. 811.

SOURCE: 52 FR 24941, July 1, 1987, unless otherwise noted.

GENERAL

§ 57.22001 Scope.

This subpart T sets forth procedures and safety standards for each metal and nonmetal underground mine subject to the Federal Mine Safety and Health Act of 1977. All metal and nonmetal mines will be placed into one of the categories or subcategories defined in this subpart. Mines shall operate in accordance with the applicable standards in this subpart to protect persons against the hazards of methane gas and dust containing volatile matter. The standards in this subpart apply to underground mines as well as surface mills at Subcategory I-C mines. These mines are also required to be operated in accordance with the other applicable health and safety standards published in 30 CFR part 57.

§ 57.22002 Definitions.

The following definitions apply in this subpart:

Competent person. A person designated by the mine operator who has sufficient experience and training to perform the assigned task.

Explosive material. Explosives, blasting agents, and detonators. Explosives are substances classified as explosives by the Department of Transportation in §§ 173.53, 173.88, and 173.100 of Title 49 of the Code of Federal Regulations (1986 Edition). Blasting agents are substances classified as blasting agents by the Department of Transportation in § 173.114(a) of Title 49 of the Code of Federal Regulations (1986 Edition). Detonators are devices containing a detonating charge used to initiate explosives. Examples of detonators are blasting caps, electric or non-electric instantaneous or delay blasting caps and delay connectors. [A copy of Title 49 is available at any Metal and Nonmetal Mine Safety and Health District Office of the Mine Safety and Health Administration].

Substantial construction. Construction of such strength, material, and workmanship that the object will withstand air blasts, blasting shock, ground movement, pressure differentials, wear, and usage which may be expected to occur in the mining environment.

[52 FR 24941, July 1, 1987, as amended at 69 FR 38842, June 29, 2004]

MINE CATEGORIZATION

§ 57.22003 Mine category or subcategory.

(a) All underground mines, and the surface mills of Subcategory I-C mines (gilsonite), shall be placed into one of

§ 57.22003

the following categories or subcategories to protect persons against the hazards of methane and dusts containing volatile matter. Categories and subcategories are defined as follows:

(1) *Category I* applies to mines that operate within a combustible ore body and either liberate methane or have the potential to liberate methane based on the history of the mine or the geological area in which the mine is located. Category I is divided into Subcategories I-A, I-B, and I-C as follows:

(i) *Subcategory I-A* applies to mines that operate within a combustible ore body and liberate methane and in which—

(A) A concentration of 0.25 percent or more methane has been detected in the mine atmosphere and confirmed by laboratory analysis; or

(B) An ignition of methane has occurred.

(ii) *Subcategory I-B* applies to mines that operate within a combustible ore body and have the potential to liberate methane based on the history of the mine or geological area in which the mine is located and in which—

(A) A concentration of 0.25 percent or more methane has not been detected in the mine atmosphere; and

(B) An ignition of methane has not occurred.

(iii) *Subcategory I-C* applies to mines in which the product extracted is combustible and the dust has a volatile matter content of 60 percent or more measured on a moisture free basis[1].

---

[1] Measured by the American Society for Testing and Materials, ASTM D 3175–82,

(2) *Category II* applies to domal salt mines where the history of the mine or geological area indicates the occurrence of or the potential for an outburst. Category II is divided into Subcategories II-A and II-B as follows:

(i) *Subcategory II-A* applies to domal salt mines where an outburst reportable under § 57.22004(c)(1) has occurred.

(ii) *Subcategory II-B* applies to domal salt mines where an outburst reportable under § 57.22004(c)(1) has not occurred, but which have the potential for an outburst based on the history of the mine or geological area in which the mine is located.

(3) *Category III* applies to mines in which noncombustible ore is extracted and which liberate a concentration of methane that is explosive, or is capable of forming explosive mixtures with air, or have the potential to do so based on the history of the mine or the geological area in which the mine is located. The concentration of methane in such mines is explosive or is capable of forming explosive mixtures if mixed with air as illustrated by Table 1 below, entitled "Relation Between Quantitative Composition and Explosibility of Mixtures of Methane and Air".

Standard Test Method for Volatile Matter in the Analysis Sample of Coal and Coke. (This document is available at any Metal and Nonmetal Mine Safety and Health District Office of the Mine Safety and Health Administration).

Table 1

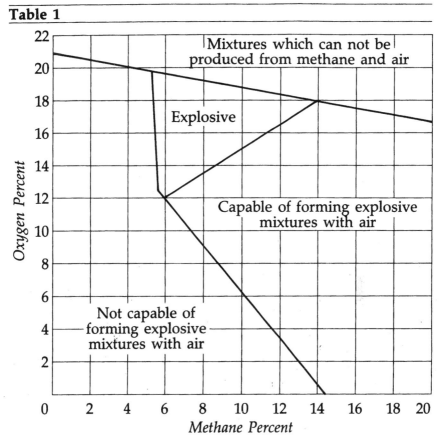

Relation Between Quantitative Composition and Explosibility of Mixtures of Methane and Air

(4) *Category IV* applies to mines in which noncombustible ore is extracted and which liberate a concentration of methane that is not explosive nor capable of forming explosive mixtures with air based on the history of the mine or the geological area in which the mine is located. The concentration of methane in such mines is not explosive nor capable of forming explosive mixtures if mixed with air as illustrated by Table 1 above, entitled "Relation Between Quantitative Composition and Explosibility of Mixtures of Methane and Air".

(5) *Category V* applies to petroleum mines. Category V is divided into Subcategories V-A and V-B as follows:

(i) *Subcategory V-A* applies to petroleum mines that operate entirely or partially within an oil reservoir; and all other petroleum mines in which—

(A) A concentration of 0.25 percent or more methane has been detected in the mine atmosphere and confirmed by laboratory analysis; or

(B) An ignition of methane has occurred.

(ii) *Subcategory V-B* applies to petroleum mines that operate outside of and

§ 57.22004

drill into an oil reservoir and in which—

(A) A concentration of 0.25 percent or more methane has not been detected in the mine atmosphere; and

(B) An ignition of methane has not occurred.

(6) *Category VI* applies to mines in which the presence of methane has not been established and are not included in another category or subcategory.

(b) Category or subcategory placement or change in placement shall include consideration of the following:

(1) The history and geology of the mine or of the geological area in which the mine is located;

(2) The ore body and host rock;

(3) The character, amount, duration, origin, and nature of methane emission and the presence of explosive dust and inert gases; and

(4) Whether or not conditions encountered during primary or access development are transient or permanent.

(c)(1) Gas samples for the purpose of category or subcategory placement or change in placement, and for determining action levels, shall be taken in the mine atmosphere. Gas samples taken to determine the nature and extent of an occurrence under § 57.22004 (c) and (d) may be taken at any location, including the source, point of entry and the mine atmosphere.

(2) Tests for methane shall be made with hand-held methanometers, methane monitors, atmospheric monitoring systems, devices used to provide laboratory analysis of samples, or with other equally effective sampling devices. However, only methane samples that have been confirmed by laboratory analysis shall be used for category or subcategory placement or change in placement.

(d) Each mine and mill shall be required to operate in accordance with the safety standards applicable to its particular category or subcategory.

§ 57.22004 Category placement or change in placement.

The Administrator for Metal and Nonmetal Mine Safety and Health (Administrator) shall be responsible for category and subcategory placement, change in placement, and notification of placement of mines.

(a) The Administrator's proposed notice of placement or change in placement shall be sent to the mine operator and the appropriate representative of miners and shall include—

(1) The category or subcategory;

(2) The reasons for placement or change in placement;

(3) The data considered;

(4) The applicable standards and a time schedule for the mine operator to achieve compliance;

(5) Whether or not conditions encountered during primary or access development are transient or permanent; and

(6) Notification of the right to appeal the Administrator's determination under § 57.22005.

(b) The operator or the representative of the miners shall have the right to request of the Administrator reassignment of the mine to a more appropriate category or subcategory if, based on operating experience, the conditions set forth in § 57.22003(b) indicate that the hazards of methane exist under circumstances more appropriately governed by a different category or subcategory. In response to such a request, the procedures set forth in paragraph (d) of this section shall apply. While the request for category or subcategory reassignment is pending, the mine shall continue to operate under the standards for the category or subcategory to which originally assigned.

(c) MSHA shall be notified as soon as possible if any of the following events occur:

(1) An outburst that results in 0.25 percent or more methane in the mine atmosphere;

(2) A blowout that results in 0.25 percent or more methane in the mine atmosphere;

(3) An ignition of methane; or

(4) Air sample results that indicate 0.25 percent or more methane in the mine atmosphere of a Subcategory I-B, I-C, II-B, V-B or Category VI mine.

(d) The Administrator shall promptly appoint an MSHA committee to investigate occurrences reported in accordance with paragraph (c) of this section or requests filed in accordance with paragraph (b) of this section. Upon completion of an investigation, the committee shall make a written report

Mine Safety and Health Admin., Labor §57.22005

of the findings. These investigations may include an evaluation of the following:

(1) Source, nature, and extent of occurrences;
(2) Conditions under which the incident occurred;
(3) Samples and tests;
(4) Physical conditions at the time of the occurrence;
(5) Charts, logs, and records related to the occurrence;
(6) Whether the occurrence is isolated, continuous, or could recur;
(7) Conditions indicating that the hazards of methane no longer exist or exist under circumstances more appropriately governed by a different category or subcategory;
(8) The geology of the mine and the geological area in which the mine is located; and
(9) Statements by witnesses, company officials, employees, and other persons having knowledge of the mine or the occurrence. Representatives of the mine operator, the miners and the appropriate State agency may participate in the investigation.

[52 FR 24941, July 1, 1987, as amended at 52 FR 41397, Oct. 27, 1987; 60 FR 33722, June 29, 1995]

§57.22005 Notice and appeal of placement or change in placement.

(a) The Administrator's determination of category or subcategory placement or change in placement shall become final upon the 30th day after it is served on the mine operator and representative of miners, unless a request for a hearing has been filed. Service of the Administrator's determination is complete upon mailing by registered or certified mail, return receipt requested.

(b) The mine operator or representative of miners may obtain review of the Administrator's determination by filing a request for a hearing with the Assistant Secretary of Labor for Mine Safety and Health, Mine Safety and Health Administration, 201 12th Street South, Arlington, VA 22202-5452 within 30 days of the Administrator's determination. Service of a request for hearing is completed upon mailing by registered or certified mail, return receipt requested. Requests for a hearing shall be in writing and contain the following information:

(1) Name, address, and mine identification number;
(2) A concise statement of the reason why the Administrator's determination is inappropriate; and
(3) A copy of the Administrator's determination.

(c) The mine operator shall post a copy of the Administrator's determination and the request for a hearing on the mine bulletin board, and shall maintain the posting until the placement becomes final.

(d) Promptly after receipt of the request for a hearing, the Assistant Secretary shall refer to the Chief Administrative Law Judge, United States Department of Labor, the following:

(1) The request for a hearing;
(2) The Administrator's determination; and
(3) All information upon which the Administrator's determination was based.

(e) The hearing shall be regulated and conducted by an Administrative Law Judge in accordance with 29 CFR part 18, entitled, "Rules of Practice and Procedure for Administrative Hearings Before the Office of Administrative Law Judges." Once the Administrative Law Judge has made an initial decision and served each party, the decision shall be final on the 30th day after service, unless discretionary review is undertaken by the Assistant Secretary or an appeal is filed by the mine operator or representative of the miners under paragraph (f) of this section.

(f) Within 30 days after service of an initial decision of an Administrative Law Judge, the Assistant Secretary for Mine Safety and Health may undertake a discretionary review of the initial decision, or the mine operator, or representative of the miners may appeal the initial decision of the Administrative Law Judge to the Assistant Secretary.

(1) The Assistant Secretary shall give notice of discretionary review to the mine operator and representative of the miners. The mine operator or representative of the miners shall give notice of an appeal to the other party. The notice shall specify the suggested

§ 57.22101

changes and refer to the specific findings of fact, conclusions of law, and terms of the initial decision to be reviewed or appealed. The Assistant Secretary shall fix a time for filing any objections to the suggested changes and supporting reasons.

(2) The Assistant Secretary shall promptly notify the Administrative Law Judge of a discretionary review or an appeal. The entire record of the proceedings shall be transmitted to the Assistant Secretary for review.

(3) The Assistant Secretary shall make the final decision based upon consideration of the record of the proceedings. The final decision may affirm, modify, or set aside in whole or in part, the findings and conclusions contained in the initial decision. A statement of reasons for the action taken shall be included in the final decision. The final decision shall be served upon the mine operator and representative of the miners.

(g) Unless a decision by the Administrator for Metal and Nonmetal Mine Safety and Health, or the initial decision of the Administrative Law Judge, is appealed within 30 days, it becomes final, and is not subject to judicial review for the purposes of 5 U.S.C. 704. Only a decision by the Assistant Secretary shall be considered final Agency action for purposes of judicial review. Any such appeal must be filed in the appropriate circuit of the United States Court of Appeal.

(h) While a final decision of category placement is pending the following procedures shall apply:

(1) Where a mine has been classified as gassy prior to the effective date of these standards, existing gassy mines standards 30 CFR 57.21001 through 57.21101 (1986 Edition) shall continue to be applicable until placement is final.

(2) Where a mine has not been classified as gassy prior to the effective date of these standards and it is placed in Categories I through V, the mine shall comply with Category VI standards (§§ 57.22231, 57.22232, 57.22236, and 57.22238) until placement is final.

(3) Where a mine has been classified in Categories I through V after the effective date of these standards and category reassignment is being considered, the mine shall comply with the standards applicable to the category to which presently assigned until category placement is final.

[52 FR 24941, July 1, 1987; 52 FR 27903, July 24, 1987, as amended at 67 FR 38385, June 4, 2002; 80 FR 52988, Sept. 2, 2015]

FIRE PREVENTION AND CONTROL

NOTE: The Category or Subcategory applicability of each standard appears in the parentheses of each standard's title line.

§ 57.22101 Smoking (I-A, II-A, III, and V-A mines).

Persons shall not smoke or carry smoking materials, matches, or lighters underground. The operator shall institute a reasonable program to assure that persons entering the mine do not carry such items.

§ 57.22102 Smoking (I-C mines).

(a) Persons shall not smoke or carry smoking materials, matches, or lighters underground or within 50 feet of a mine opening. The operator shall institute a reasonable program to assure that persons entering the mine do not carry such items.

(b) Smoking is prohibited in surface milling facilities except in designated, dust-free smoking areas.

§ 57.22103 Open flames (I-A, II-A, III, and V-A mines).

Open flames shall not be permitted underground except for welding, cutting, and other maintenance operations, and for igniting underground retorts in a Subcategory I-A mine. When using open flames in other than fresh air, or in places where methane may enter the air current, tests for methane shall be conducted by a competent person before work is started and every 10 minutes until the job is completed. Continuous methane monitors with audible alarms may be used after the initial test has been conducted as an alternative to the ten-minute interval testing requirement. Open flames shall not be used in atmospheres containing 0.5 percent or more methane.

§ 57.22104 Open flames (I-C mines).

(a) Open flames, including cutting and welding, shall not be used underground.

(b) Welding and cutting shall not be done within 50 feet of a mine opening unless all persons are out of the mine and the mine opening is covered. The cover shall be a substantial material, such as metal or wood, topped with a layer of wetted material to prevent sparks and flames from entering the mine opening.

§ 57.22105 **Smoking and open flames (IV mines).**

Smoking or open flames shall not be permitted in a face or raise, or during release of gas from a borehole until tests have been conducted in accordance with § 57.22226 and the methane level has been determined to be below 0.5 percent.

§ 57.22106 **Dust containing volatile matter (I-C mines).**

Dust containing volatile matter shall not be allowed to accumulate on the surfaces of enclosures, facilities, or equipment used in surface milling in amounts that, if suspended in air, would become an explosive mixture. An explosive mixture of dust containing volatile matter is 0.02 ounce or more per cubic foot of air.

VENTILATION

§ 57.22201 **Mechanical ventilation (I-A, I-B, I-C, II-A, II-B, III, IV, V-A, and V-B mines).**

All mines shall be ventilated mechanically.

§ 57.22202 **Main fans (I-A, I-B, I-C, II-A, III, V-A, and V-B mines).**

(a) Main fans shall be—
(1) Installed on the surface in noncombustible housings provided with noncombustible air ducts;
(2) Except in Subcategory I-A mines, provided with an automatic signal device to give an alarm when the fan stops. The signal device shall be located so that it can be seen or heard by a person designated by the mine operator.
(b) Fan installations shall be—
(1) Offset so that the fan and its associated components are not in direct line with possible explosive forces;
(2) Equipped with explosion-doors, a weak-wall, or other equivalent devices located to relieve the pressure that would be created by an explosion underground. The area of the doors or weak-wall shall be at least equivalent to the average cross-sectional area of the airway.
(c) (1) All main fan-related electrical equipment and cables located within or exposed to the forward or reverse airstream shall be approved by MSHA under the appliable requirements of 30 CFR part 18;
(2) Drive belts and nonmetallic fan blades shall be constructed of static-conducting material; and
(3) Aluminum alloy fan blades shall not contain more than 0.5 percent magnesium. [Paragraph (c)(3) of this section does not apply to Subcategory I-C mines].
(d) When an internal combustion engine is used to power a main fan or as standby power, the engine shall be—
(1) Installed in a noncombustible housing;
(2) Protected from a possible fuel supply fire or explosion; and
(3) Located out of direct line with the forward and reverse airstream provided by the fan. Engine exhaust gases shall be vented to the atmosphere so that exhaust cannot contaminate mine intake air.
(e) For Subcategory I-A mines only: Main exhaust fans shall be equipped with methane monitors to give an alarm when methane in the return air reaches 0.5 percent. The alarm shall be located so that it can be seen or heard by a person designated by the mine operator.

[52 FR 24941, July 1, 1987, as amended at 52 FR 41397, Oct. 27, 1987]

§ 57.22203 **Main fan operation (I-C mines).**

Main fans shall be operated continuously while ore production is in progress.

§ 57.22204 **Main fan operation and inspection (I-A, II-A, III, and V-A mines).**

Main fans shall be—
(a) Provided with a pressure-recording system; and
(b) Inspected daily while operating if persons are underground. Certification

§ 57.22205

of inspections shall be made by signature and date. Certifications and pressure recordings shall be retained for at least one year and made available to an authorized representative of the Secretary.

[52 FR 24941, July 1, 1987, as amended at 52 FR 41397, Oct. 27, 1987; 60 FR 33722, June 29, 1995]

§ 57.22205 Doors on main fans (I-A, II-A, III, and V-A mines).

In mines ventilated by multiple main fans, each main fan installation shall be equipped with noncombustible doors. Such doors shall automatically close to prevent air reversal through the fan. The doors shall be located so that they are not in direct line with explosive forces which could come out of the mine.

§ 57.22206 Main ventilation failure (I-A, II-A, III, and V-A mines).

(a) When there has been a main ventilation failure, such as stoppage of main fans or failure of other components of the main ventilation system, tests for methane shall be conducted in affected active workings until normal air flow has resumed.

(b) If a total failure of ventilation occurs while all persons are out of the mine and the failure lasts for more than 30 minutes, only competent persons shall be allowed underground to examine the mine or to make necessary ventilation changes. Other persons may reenter the mine after the main fans have been operational for at least 30 minutes, or after the mine atmosphere has been tested and contains less than 1.0 percent methane. Persons other than examiners shall not reenter a Subcategory II-A mine until the methane level is less than 0.5 percent.

§ 57.22207 Booster fans (I-A, II-A, III, and V-A mines).

(a) Booster fans shall be approved by MSHA under the applicable requirements of 30 CFR part 18, and be—

(1) Provided with an automatic signal device located so that it can be seen or heard by a person designated by the mine operator to give an alarm when the fan stops or when methane reaches the following levels:

(i) 1.0 percent at the fan in Subcategory I-A, Category III, and Subcategory V-A mines; and

(ii) 0.5 percent at the fan in Subcategory II-A mines.

(2) Equipped with a device that automatically deenergizes power in affected workings should the fan stop; and

(3) Equipped with starting and stopping controls located at the fan and at another accessible remote location.

(b) Booster fan installations, except for booster fans installed in ducts, shall be—

(1) Provided with doors which open automatically when all fans in the installation stop; and

(2) Provided with an air lock when passage through the fan bulkhead is necessary.

§ 57.22208 Auxiliary fans (I-A, II-A, III, and V-A mines).

(a) Auxiliary fans, except fans used in shops and other areas which have been so designed that methane cannot enter the airway, shall be approved by MSHA under the applicable requirements of 30 CFR part 18, and be operated so that recirculation is minimized. Auxiliary fans shall not be used to ventilate work places during the interruption of normal mine ventilation.

(b) Tests for methane shall be made at auxiliary fans before they are started.

§ 57.22209 Auxiliary fans (I-C mines).

Electric auxiliary fans shall be approved by MSHA under the applicable requirements of 30 CFR part 18. Tests for methane shall be made at electric auxiliary fans before they are started. Such fans shall not be operated when air passing over or through them contains 0.5 percent or more methane.

§ 57.22210 In-line filters (I-C mines).

Filters or separators shall be installed on air-lift fan systems to prevent explosive concentrations of dust from passing through the fan.

§ 57.22211 Air flow (I-A mines).

The average air velocity in the last open crosscut in pairs or sets of developing entries, or through other ventilation openings nearest the face, shall be at least 40 feet per minute. The velocity of air ventilating each face at a work place shall be at least 20 feet per minute.

§ 57.22212 Air flow (I-C, II-A, and V-A mines).

Air flow across each working face shall be sufficient to carry away any accumulation of methane, smoke, fumes, and dust.

§ 57.22213 Air flow (III mines).

The quantity of air coursed through the last open crosscut in pairs or sets of entries, or through other ventilation openings nearest the face, shall be at least 6,000 cubic feet per minute, or 9,000 cubic feet per minute in longwall and continuous miner sections. The quantity of air across each face at a work place shall be at least 2,000 cubic feet per minute.

§ 57.22214 Changes in ventilation (I-A, II-A, III, and V-A mines).

(a) Changes in ventilation which affect the main air current or any split thereof and which adversely affect the safety of persons in the mine shall be made only when the mine is idle.

(b) Only persons engaged in making such ventilation changes shall be permitted in the mine during changes.

(c) Power shall be deenergized in affected areas prior to making ventilation changes, except power to monitoring equipment determined by MSHA to be intrinsically safe under 30 CFR part 18. Power shall not be restored until the results of the change have been determined and a competent person has examined affected working places for methane.

§ 57.22215 Separation of intake and return air (I-A, II-A, III, and V-A mines).

Main intake and return air currents shall be coursed through separate mine openings and shall be separated throughout the mine, except—

(a) Where multiple shafts are used for ventilation and a single shaft contains a curtain wall or partition for separation of air currents. Such wall or partition shall be constructed of reinforced concrete or other noncombustible equivalent, and provided with pressure-relief devices.

(b) During development of openings to the surface—

(1) Ventilation tubing approved by MSHA in accordance with 30 CFR part 7 or previously issued a BC or VT acceptance number by the MSHA Approval and Certification Center may be used for separation of main air currents in the same opening. Flexible ventilation tubing shall not exceed 250 feet in length.

(2) Only development related to making a primary ventilation connection may be performed beyond 250 feet of the shaft.

[52 FR 24941, July 1, 1987, as amended at 54 FR 30508, July 20, 1989]

§ 57.22216 Separation of intake and return air (I-C mines).

The main intake and return air currents in single shafts shall be separated by ventilation tubing, curtain walls, or partitions. Ventilation tubing shall be constructed of noncombustible material. Curtain walls or partitions shall be constructed of reinforced concrete or other noncombustible equivalent, and provided with pressure-relief devices.

§ 57.22217 Seals and stoppings (I-A, I-B, and I-C mines).

All seals, and those stoppings that separate main intake from main return airways, shall be of substantial construction and constructed of noncombustible materials, except that stoppings constructed of brattice materials may be used in face areas.

§ 57.22218 Seals and stoppings (III, V-A, and V-B mines).

(a) All seals, and those stoppings that separate main intake from main return airways, shall be of substantial construction, except that stoppings constructed of brattice materials may be used in face areas.

(b) Exposed surfaces on the intake side of stoppings constructed of combustible materials or foam-type blocks shall be coated with at least one inch of construction plaster containing perlite and gypsum; at least one inch of expanded vermiculite, Portland cement and limestone; or other coatings with

§ 57.22219

equivalent fire resistance. Stoppings constructed to phenolic foam blocks at least 12 inches thick need not be coated for fire resistance. All foam-type blocks used for stopping construction shall be solid.

(c) Exposed surfaces on the fresh air side of seals constructed of combustible materials shall be coated with at least one inch of construction plaster containing perlite and gypsum; at least one inch of expanded vermiculite, Portland cement and limestone; or other coatings with equivalent fire resistance. Foam-type blocks shall not be used for seals.

§ 57.22219 Seals and stoppings (II-A mines).

(a) Exposed surfaces on the intake side of stoppings constructed of combustible materials, except brattice, shall be coated with at least one inch of construction plaster containing perlite and gypsum; at least one inch of expanded vermiculite, Portland cement and limestone; or other coatings with equivalent fire resistance.

(b) Seals shall be of substantial construction. Exposed surfaces on the fresh air side of seals constructed of combustible materials shall be coated with at least one inch of construction plaster containing perlite and gypsum; at least one inch of expanded vermiculite, Portland cement and limestone; or other coatings with equivalent fire resistance. Foam-type blocks shall not be used for seals.

§ 57.22220 Air passing unsealed areas (I-A, II-A, III, and V-A mines).

Air that has passed by or through unsealed abandoned or unsealed inactive areas and contains 0.25 percent or more methane shall—

(a) Be coursed directly to a return airway;

(b) Be tested daily for methane by a competent person; and

(c) Not be used to ventilate work places.

§ 57.22221 Overcast and undercast construction (I-A, II-A, III, and V-A mines).

Overcasts and undercasts shall be—
(a) Of substantial construction;

(b)(1) Constructed of noncombustible materials; or

(2) Where constructed of combustible materials, the outside surfaces shall be coated with at least one inch of construction plaster containing perlite and gypsum; at least one inch of expanded vermiculite, Portland cement and limestone; or other coatings with equivalent fire resistance;

(c) Kept clear of obstructions.

§ 57.22222 Ventilation materials (I-A, I-B, I-C, II-A, III, V-A, and V-B mines).

Brattice cloth and ventilation tubing shall be approved by MSHA in accordance with 30 CFR part 7, or shall bear a BC or VT acceptance number issued by the MSHA Approval and Certification Center.

[54 FR 30508, July 20, 1989]

§ 57.22223 Crosscuts before abandonment (III mines).

A means of ventilating faces shall be provided before workings are abandoned in unsealed areas, unless crosscuts are provided within 30 feet of the face.

§ 57.22224 Auxiliary equipment stations (I-A and III mines).

Battery charging stations, compressor stations, pump stations, and transformer stations shall be installed in intake air at locations which are sufficiently ventilated to prevent the accumulation of methane.

§ 57.22225 Auxiliary equipment stations (I-C mines).

Battery charging stations, compressor stations, and electrical substations shall not be installed underground or within 50 feet of a mine opening.

§ 57.22226 Testing for methane (IV mines).

Tests for methane shall be conducted in the mine atmosphere by a competent person—

(a) At least once each shift prior to starting work in each face and raise; and

(b) Upon initial release of gas into the mine atmosphere from boreholes.

§ 57.22227 Approved testing devices (I-A, I-B, I-C, II-A, II-B, III, IV, V-A, and V-B mines).

(a) Methane monitoring devices and portable, battery-powered, self-contained devices used for measuring methane, other gases, and contaminants in mine air shall be approved by MSHA under the applicable requirements of 30 CFR parts 18, 21, 22, 23, 27, and 29. Such devices shall be maintained in accordance with manufacturers' instructions, or an equivalent maintenance and calibration procedure.

(b)(1) Flame safety lamps shall not be used to test for methane except as supplementary devices.

(2) Flame safety lamps shall not be used in Subcategory I-C mines.

(c)(1) If electrically powered, remote sensing devices are used, that portion of the instrument located in return air or other places where combustible gases may be present shall be approved by MSHA under the applicable requirements of 30 CFR parts 18, 22, 23, 27, and 29.

(2) If air samples are delivered to remote analytical devices through sampling tubes, such tubes shall be provided with in-line flame arrestors. Pumping equipment and analytical instruments shall be located in intake air.

§ 57.22228 Preshift examination (I-A, I-C, II-A, III, and V-A mines).

(a) Preshift examinations shall be conducted within three hours prior to the start of the shift for which the examination is being made.

(b) Prior to the beginning of a shift following an idle shift, a competent person shall test the mine atmosphere for methane at all work places before persons other than examiners enter the mine.

(c) When one shift immediately follows another, a competent person shall test the mine atmosphere at each active working face for methane before work is started on that shift.

(d) A competent person shall test the mine atmosphere at each face blasted before work is started.

(e) Except in Subcategory I-C or Category III mines, vehicles used for transportation when examining the mine shall be approved by MSHA under the applicable requirements of 30 CFR parts 18 through 36.

[52 FR 24941, July 1, 1987, as amended at 53 FR 9615, Mar. 24, 1988]

§ 57.22229 Weekly testing (I-A, III, and V-A mines).

(a) The mine atmosphere shall be tested for methane and carbon monoxide at least once every seven days by a competent person or an atmospheric monitoring system, or a combination of the two. Such testing shall be done at the following locations:

(1) The return of each split where it enters the main return;
(2) Adjacent to retreat areas, if accessible;
(3) At least one seal of each sealed area, if accessible;
(4) Main returns;
(5) At least one entry of each intake and return;
(6) Idle workings; and
(7) Return air from unsealed abandoned workings.

(b) The volume of air (velocity in Subcategory I-A mines) shall be measured at least once every seven days by a competent person. Such measurement shall be done at the following locations:

(1) Entering main intakes;
(2) Leaving main returns;
(3) Entering each main split;
(4) Returning from each main split; and
(5) In the last open crosscuts or other ventilation openings nearest the active faces where the air enters the return.

(c) Where such examinations disclose hazardous conditions, affected persons shall be informed and corrective action shall be taken.

(d) Certification of examinations shall be made by signature and date. Certifications shall be retained for at least one year and made available to authorized representatives of the Secretary.

[52 FR 24941, July 1, 1987, as amended at 52 FR 41397, Oct. 27, 1987]

§ 57.22230 Weekly testing (II-A mines).

(a) The mine atmosphere shall be tested for methane at least once every seven days by a competent person or an atmospheric monitoring system, or a

§ 57.22231

combination of the two. Such testing shall be done at the following locations:
(1) Active mining faces and benches;
(2) Main returns;
(3) Returns from idle workings;
(4) Returns from abandoned workings; and
(5) Seals.

(b) Where such examinations disclose hazardous conditions, affected persons shall be informed and corrective action shall be taken.

(c) Certification of examinations shall be made by signature and date. Certifications shall be kept for at least one year and made available to authorized representatives of the Secretary.

[52 FR 24941, July 1, 1987, as amended at 52 FR 41397, Oct. 27, 1987; 60 FR 33723, June 29, 1995]

§ 57.22231 Actions at 0.25 percent methane (I-B, II-B, V-B, and VI mines).

If methane reaches 0.25 percent in the mine atmosphere, changes shall be made to improve ventilation, and MSHA shall be notified immediately.

§ 57.22232 Actions at 0.5 percent methane (I-B, II-A, II-B, IV, V-B, and VI mines).

If methane reaches 0.5 percent in the mine atmosphere, ventilation changes shall be made to reduce the level of methane. Until methane is reduced to less than 0.5 percent, electrical power shall be deenergized in affected areas, except power to monitoring equipment determined by MSHA to be intrinsically safe under 30 CFR part 18. Diesel equipment shall be shut off or immediately removed from the area and no other work shall be permitted in affected areas.

[52 FR 24941, July 1, 1987; 52 FR 27903, July 24, 1987]

§ 57.22233 Actions at 0.5 percent methane (I-C mines).

If methane reaches 0.5 percent in the mine atmosphere, ventilation changes shall be made to reduce the level of methane. Until methane is reduced to less than 0.5 percent, no other work shall be permitted in affected areas.

[52 FR 24941, July 1, 1987; 52 FR 27903, July 24, 1987]

§ 57.22234 Actions at 1.0 percent methane (I-A, I-B, III, V-A, and V-B mines).

(a) If methane reaches 1.0 percent in the mine atmosphere, ventilation changes shall be made to reduce methane. Until such changes are achieved—
(1) All persons other than competent persons necessary to make the ventilation changes shall be withdrawn from affected areas;
(2) Electrical power shall be deenergized in affected areas, except power to monitoring equipment determined by MSHA to be intrinsically safe under 30 CFR part 18; and
(3) Diesel equipment shall be shut off or immediately removed from the area.

(b) If methane reaches 1.0 percent at a main exhaust fan, electrical power underground shall be deenergized, except power to monitoring equipment determined by MSHA to be intrinsically safe under 30 CFR part 18, and all persons shall be withdrawn from the mine.

(c) If methane reaches 1.0 percent at a work place and there has been a failure of the main ventilation system, all persons shall be withdrawn from the mine.

[52 FR 24941, July 1, 1987, as amended at 53 FR 9615, Mar. 24, 1988]

§ 57.22235 Actions at 1.0 percent methane (I-C, II-A, II-B, and IV mines).

(a) If methane reaches 1.0 percent in the mine atmosphere, all persons other than competent persons necessary to make ventilation changes shall be withdrawn from affected areas until methane is reduced to less than 0.5 percent.

(b) If methane reaches 1.0 percent at a work place and there has been a failure of the main ventilation system, all persons shall be withdrawn from the mine.

§ 57.22236 Actions at 1.0 percent methane (VI mines).

If methane reaches 1.0 percent in the mine atmosphere, all persons other than competent persons necessary to make ventilation changes shall be withdrawn from affected areas until methane is reduced to less than 0.5 percent.

§ 57.22237 Actions at 2.0 to 2.5 percent methane in bleeder systems (I-A and III mines).

If methane reaches 2.0 percent in bleeder systems at the point where a bleeder split enters a main return split, mining shall not be permitted on ventilation splits affected by the bleeder system. If methane has not been reduced to less than 2.0 percent within 30 minutes, or if methane levels reach 2.5 percent, all persons other than competent persons necessary to take corrective action shall be withdrawn from affected areas.

§ 57.22238 Actions at 2.0 percent methane (I-B, II-B, V-B, and VI mines).

If methane reaches 2.0 percent in the mine atmosphere, all persons other than competent persons necessary to make ventilation changes shall be withdrawn from the mine until methane is reduced to less than 0.5 percent.

§ 57.22239 Actions at 2.0 percent methane (IV mines).

If methane reaches 2.0 percent in the mine atmosphere, all persons other than competent persons necessary to make ventilation changes shall be withdrawn from the mine until methane is reduced to less than 0.5 percent. MSHA shall be notified immediately.

[52 FR 24941, July 1, 1987, as amended at 52 FR 41397, Oct. 27, 1987; 60 FR 33723, June 29, 1995]

§ 57.22240 Actions at 2.0 percent methane (V-A mines).

If methane reaches 2.0 percent in the mine atmosphere, all persons other than competent persons necessary to make ventilation changes shall be withdrawn from affected areas until methane is reduced to less than 1.0 percent.

[52 FR 24941, July 1, 1987; 52 FR 27903, July 24, 1987]

§ 57.22241 Advance face boreholes (I-C mines).

(a) Boreholes shall be drilled at least 25 feet in advance of a face whenever the work place is within—

(1) 50 feet of a surveyed abandoned mine or abandoned workings which cannot be inspected; or

(2) 200 feet of an unsurveyed abandoned mine or abandoned workings which cannot be inspected.

(b) Boreholes shall be drilled in such a manner to insure that the advancing face will not accidently break into an abandoned mine or abandoned working.

EQUIPMENT

§ 57.22301 Atmospheric monitoring systems (I-A, II-A, and V-A mines).

(a) An atmospheric monitoring system shall be installed to provide surface readings of methane concentrations in the mine atmosphere from underground locations. Components of the system shall be approved by MSHA under the applicable requirements of 30 CFR parts 18, 22, 23, and 27; or be determined by MSHA under 30 CFR part 18 to be intrinsically safe or explosion-proof.

(b) Atmospheric monitoring systems shall—

(1) Give warnings on the surface and underground when methane at any sensor reaches 0.5 percent or more, and when power to a sensor is interrupted. Warning devices shall be located so that they can be seen and heard by a person designated by the mine operator; and

(2) Automatically deenergize power in affected areas, except power to monitoring equipment determined by MSHA to be intrinsically safe under 30 CFR part 18, when methane at any sensor reaches—

(i) 1.0 percent in a Subcategory I-A or V-A mine; or

(ii) 0.5 percent while persons are underground and 1.0 percent during blasting in a Subcategory II-A mine. Timing devices are permitted to avoid nuisance tripping for periods not to exceed 30 seconds, except during blasting or the ventilation time following a blast in a Subcategory II-A mine.

(c) Atmospheric monitoring systems shall be checked with a known mixture of methane, and calibrated if necessary at least once every 30 days. Certification of calibration tests shall be made by signature and date. Certifications of tests shall be retained for at least one year and made available to authorized representatives of the Secretary.

§ 57.22302 Approved equipment (I-A and V-A mines).

Equipment used in or beyond the last open crosscut shall be approved by MSHA under the applicable requirements of 30 CFR parts 18 through 36. Equipment shall not be operated in atmospheres containing 1.0 percent or more methane.

§ 57.22303 Approved equipment (I-C mines).

Only electrical equipment that is approved by MSHA under the applicable requirements of 30 CFR parts 18 through 28 or approved under 30 CFR part 29 contained in the 30 CFR, parts 1–199, edition, revised as of July 1, 1999, shall be used underground, except for submersible sump pumps.

[64 FR 43283, Aug. 10, 1999]

§ 57.22304 Approved equipment (II-A mines).

(a) Cutting and drilling equipment used at a face or bench shall be approved by MSHA under the applicable requirements of 30 CFR parts 18 through 36.

(b) While cutting or drilling is in progress, equipment not approved by MSHA under the applicable requirements of 30 CFR parts 18 through 36 shall remain at least 100 feet from the face or bench being mined.

(c) Tests for methane shall be conducted immediately before non-approved equipment is taken to a face or bench after blasting.

(d) Mine power transformers and stationary equipment not approved by MSHA under the applicable requirements of 30 CFR parts 18 through 36 shall be installed in fresh air or downwind from an atmospheric methane monitor sensor.

§ 57.22305 Approved equipment (III mines).

Equipment used in or beyond the last open crosscut and equipment used in areas where methane may enter the air current, such as pillar recovery workings, longwall faces and shortwall faces, shall be approved by MSHA under the applicable requirements of 30 CFR parts 18 through 36. Equipment shall not be operated in atmospheres containing 1.0 percent or more methane.

§ 57.22306 Methane monitors (I-A mines).

(a) Methane monitors shall be installed on continuous mining machines, longwall mining systems, and on loading and haulage equipment used in or beyond the last open crosscut.

(b) The monitors shall—

(1) Give warning at 1.0 percent methane;

(2) Automatically deenergize electrical equipment, except power to monitoring equipment determined by MSHA to be intrinsically safe under 30 CFR part 18, and prevent starting such equipment when methane levels reach 1.5 percent. Diesel equipment shall be shut off or immediately removed from the affected area; and

(3) Automatically deenergize electrical equipment when power to a sensor is interrupted. Diesel equipment shall not be operated if the monitor is inoperative.

(c) Sensing units of monitors shall be positioned at a location which provides for the most effective measurement of methane.

§ 57.22307 Methane monitors (II-A mines).

(a) Methane monitors shall be installed on continuous mining machines, longwall mining systems, bench and face drills, and undercutting machines used in or beyond the last open crosscut.

(b) The monitors shall—

(1) Give warning at 0.5 percent methane;

(2) Automatically deenergize electrical equipment, except power to monitoring equipment determined by MSHA to be intrinsically safe under 30 CFR part 18, and prevent starting such equipment when methane levels reach 1.0 percent; and

(3) Automatically deenergize the equipment when power to a sensor is interrupted.

(c) Sensing units of monitors shall be positioned at a location which provides for the most effective measurement of methane.

§ 57.22308 Methane monitors (III mines).

(a) Methane monitors shall be installed on continuous mining machines and longwall mining systems.

(b) The monitors shall—

(1) Give warning at 1.0 percent methane;

(2) Automatically deenergize electrical equipment, except power to monitoring equipment determined by MSHA to be intrinsically safe under 30 CFR part 18, and prevent starting such equipment when methane levels reach 1.5 percent; and

(3) Automatically deenergize the equipment when power to a sensor is interrupted.

(c) Sensing units of monitors shall be positioned at a location which provides for the most effective measurement of methane.

§ 57.22309 Methane monitors (V-A mines).

(a) Methane monitors shall be installed on continuous mining machines used in or beyond the last open crosscut.

(b) The monitors shall—

(1) Give warning at 1.0 percent methane.

(2) Automatically deenergize electrical equipment, except power to monitoring equipment determined by MSHA to be intrinsically safe under 30 CFR part 18, and prevent starting of such equipment when methane levels reach 1.5 percent; and

(3) Automatically deenergize the equipment when power to a sensor is interrupted.

(c) Sensing units of monitors shall be positioned at a location which provides for the most effective measurement of methane.

§ 57.22310 Electrical cables (I-C mines).

Electrical cables used to power submersible sump pumps shall be accepted or approved by MSHA as flame resistant, or be installed in continuous metal conduit or metal pipe. The ends of such conduit or pipe shall be sealed to prevent entry of explosive gas or dust.

[57 FR 61223, Dec. 23, 1992]

§ 57.22311 Electrical cables (II-A mines).

Only jacketed electrical cables accepted or approved by MSHA as flame resistant shall be used to supply power to distribution boxes and electrical equipment operating in face and bench areas.

[57 FR 61223, Dec. 23, 1992]

§ 57.22312 Distribution boxes (II-A and V-A mines).

Distribution boxes containing short circuit protection for trailing cables of approved equipment shall be approved by MSHA under 30 CFR part 18.

§ 57.22313 Explosion-protection systems (I-C mines).

Pressure-relief systems including vents, or explosion suppression systems, shall be provided on explosive dust handling and processing equipment and on facilities housing such equipment. Vents shall be installed so that forces are directed away from persons should an explosion occur. The ratio of vent size to internal size of the equipment or facility shall not be less than one square foot of vent for each 80 cubic feet of volume or space.

§ 57.22314 Flow-control devices (V-A and V-B mines).

Oil recovery drill holes that penetrate oil bearing formations shall have devices to control the release of liquid hydrocarbons and hazardous gases during the drilling process. Such devices may be recovered for reuse after the formation has been depressurized or the well or borehole has been capped or connected to a collection system.

§ 57.22315 Self-contained breathing apparatus (V-A mines).

Self-contained breathing apparatus of a duration to allow for escape from the mine and sufficient in number to equip all persons underground shall be strategically located throughout the mine. Such apparatus shall be approved by MSHA and NIOSH under 42 CFR part 84 and shall be maintained in accordance with manufacturers' specifications. This standard does not apply to double entry mining systems where

§ 57.22401

crosscut intervals do not exceed 250 feet.

[52 FR 24941, July 1, 1987, as amended at 60 FR 30401, June 8, 1995]

UNDERGROUND RETORTS

§ 57.22401 Underground retorts (I-A and I-B mines).

(a) Retorts shall be provided with—

(1) Two independent power sources for main mine ventilation fans and those fans directly ventilating retort bulkheads, and for retort blowers, and provisions for switching promptly from one power source to the other; and

(2) An alarm system for blower malfunctions and an evacuation plan to assure safety of personnel in the event of a failure.

(b) Prior to the ignition of underground retorts, a written ignition and operation plan shall be submitted to the MSHA District Manager for the area in which the mine is located. The mine operator shall comply with all provisions of the retort plan. The retort plan shall include—

(1) Acceptable levels of combustible gases and oxygen in retort off-gases during start-up and during burning; levels at which corrective action will be initiated; levels at which personnel will be removed from the retort areas, from the mine, and from endangered surface areas; and the conditions for reentering the mine;

(2) Specification and locations of off-gas monitoring procedures and equipment;

(3) Specifications for construction of retort bulkheads and seals, and their locations;

(4) Procedures for ignition of a retort and for reignition following a shutdown; and

(5) Details of area monitoring and alarm systems for hazardous gases and actions to be taken to assure safety of personnel.

[52 FR 24941, July 1, 1987, as amended at 52 FR 41397, Oct. 27, 1987; 60 FR 33723, June 29, 1995]

ILLUMINATION

§ 57.22501 Personal electric lamps (I-A, I-B, I-C, II-A, II-B, III, IV, V-A, and V-B mines).

Electric lamps used for personal illumination shall be approved by MSHA under the requirements of 30 CFR parts 19 or 20, as applicable.

EXPLOSIVES

§ 57.22601 Blasting from the surface (I-A mines).

(a) All development, production, and bench rounds shall be initiated from the surface after all persons are out of the mine. Persons shall not enter the mine until ventilating air has passed over the blast area and through at least one atmospheric monitoring sensor.

(b) After blasting, if the monitoring system indicates that methane in the mine is less than 1.0 percent, persons may enter the mine. All places blasted shall be tested for methane by a competent person before work is started.

(c) If the monitoring system indicates the presence of 1.0 percent or more methane, persons other than examiners shall not enter the mine until the mine has been examined by a competent person and the methane content has been reduced to less than 1.0 percent.

(d) Vehicles used for transportation when examining the mine shall be approved by MSHA under the applicable requirements of 30 CFR parts 18 through 36.

[52 FR 24941, July 1, 1987, as amended at 53 FR 9615, Mar. 24, 1988]

EFFECTIVE DATE NOTE: At 53 FR 9615, Mar. 24, 1988, § 57.22601 was stayed until further notice.

§ 57.22602 Blasting from the surface (I-C mines).

(a) All blasting shall be initiated from the surface after all persons are out of the mine and any connecting mines.

(b) Persons shall not enter the mine until a competent person has examined the blast sites and methane concentrations are less than 0.5 percent.

§ 57.22603 Blasting from the surface (II-A mines).

(a) All development, production, and bench rounds shall be initiated from the surface after all persons are out of the mine. Persons shall not enter the mine until the mine has been ventilated for at least 15 minutes and the ventilating air has passed over the blast area and through at least one atmospheric monitoring sensor.

(b) If the monitoring system indicates that methane in the mine is less than 0.5 percent, competent persons may enter the mine to test for methane in all blast areas.

(c) If the monitoring system indicates that methane in the mine is 0.5 percent or more, the mine shall be ventilated and persons shall not enter the mine until the monitoring system indicates that methane in the mine is less than 0.5 percent.

(d) If the monitoring system is inoperable or malfunctions, the mine shall be ventilated for at least 45 minutes and the mine power shall be deenergized before persons enter the mine. Only competent persons necessary to test for methane may enter the mine until the methane in the mine is less than 0.5 percent.

(e) Vehicles used for transportation when examining the mine shall be approved by MSHA under the applicable requirements of 30 CFR parts 18 through 36. Vehicles shall not be used to examine the mine if the monitoring system is inoperable or has malfunctioned.

§ 57.22604 Blasting from the surface (II-B mines).

All development, production, and bench rounds shall be initiated from the surface after all persons are out of the mine. Persons other than those designated by the mine operator to make methane tests shall not enter the mine until all blast areas have been tested for methane.

§ 57.22605 Blasting from the surface (V-A mines).

(a) All development and production blasting shall be initiated from the surface after all persons are out of the mine. Persons shall not enter the mine until ventilating air has passed over the blast area and through at least one atmospheric monitoring sensor.

(b) If the monitoring system indicates that methane in the mine is less than 1.0 percent, persons may enter the mine, and all places blasted shall be tested for methane by a competent person before work is started.

(c) If the monitoring system indicates the presence of 1.0 percent or more methane, persons other than examiners shall not enter the mine until the mine has been examined by a competent person and the methane level is less than 1.0 percent.

(d) Vehicles used for transportation when examining the mine shall be approved by MSHA under the applicable requirements of 30 CFR parts 18 through 36.

(e) This standard applies only to mines blasting within an oil reservoir.

§ 57.22606 Explosive materials and blasting units (III mines).

(a) Mine operators shall notify the appropriate MSHA District Manager of all nonapproved explosive materials and blasting units to be used prior to their use. Explosive materials used for blasting shall be approved by MSHA under 30 CFR part 15, or nonapproved explosive materials shall be evaluated and determined by the District Manager to be safe for blasting in a potentially gassy environment. The notice shall also include the millisecond-delay interval between successive shots and between the first and last shot in a round.

(b) Faces shall be examined for proper placement of holes, possible breakthrough, and water. Ammonium nitrate blasting agents shall not be loaded into wet holes.

(c) Multiple-shot blasts shall be initiated with detonators encased in copper-based alloy shells. Aluminum and aluminum alloy-cased detonators, nonelectric detonators, detonating cord, and safety fuses shall not be used. All detonators in a round shall be made by the same manufacturer.

(d) Nonapproved explosives shall be used only as primers with ammonium nitrate-fuel oil blasting agents. Such primers shall be placed at the back or bottom of the hole.

§ 57.22607

(e) Blast holes shall be stemmed with a noncombustible material in an amount to confine the explosive charge. Breakthrough holes shall be stemmed at both ends.

(f) Mudcaps or other nonapproved unconfined shots shall not be blasted.

(g)(1) Blasting units shall be approved by MSHA under 30 CFR part 25; or

(2) Blasting units used to fire more than 20 detonators shall provide at least 2 amperes through each detonator but not more than an average of 100 amperes through one ohm for 10 milliseconds, and provide the necessary current for at least the first 5 milliseconds with a cutoff not to exceed 10 milliseconds.

[52 FR 24941, July 1, 1987, as amended at 52 FR 41397, Oct. 27, 1987]

§ 57.22607 Blasting on shift (III mines).

When blasting on shift, tests for methane shall be made in the mine atmosphere by a competent person before blasting. Blasting shall not be done when 1.0 percent or more methane is present.

§ 57.22608 Secondary blasting (I-A, II-A, and V-A mines).

Prior to secondary blasting, tests for methane shall be made in the mine atmosphere at blast sites by a competent person. Secondary blasting shall not be done when 0.5 percent or more methane is present.

APPENDIX I TO SUBPART T OF PART 57—STANDARD APPLICABILITY BY CATEGORY OR SUBCATEGORY

Subcategory I-A

57.22101	57.22222
57.22103	57.22224
57.22201	57.22227
57.22202	57.22228
57.22204	57.22229
57.22205	57.22234
57.22206	57.22237
57.22207	57.22301
57.22208	57.22302
57.22211	57.22306
57.22214	57.22401
57.22215	57.22501
57.22217	57.22601
57.22220	57.22608
57.22221	

Subcategory I-B

57.22201	57.22231
57.22202	57.22232
57.22217	57.22234
57.22222	57.22238
57.22227	57.22401
	57.22501

Subcategory I-C

57.22102	57.22222
57.22104	57.22225
57.22106	57.22227
57.22201	57.22228
57.22202	57.22233
57.22203	57.22235
57.22209	57.22241
57.22210	57.22303
57.22212	57.22310
57.22216	57.22313
57.22217	57.22501
	57.22602

Subcategory II-A

57.22101	57.22221
57.22103	57.22222
57.22201	57.22227
57.22202	57.22228
57.22204	57.22230
57.22205	57.22232
57.22206	57.22235
57.22207	57.22301
57.22208	57.22304
57.22212	57.22307
57.22214	57.22311
57.22215	57.22312
57.22219	57.22501
57.22220	57.22603
	57.22608

Subcategory II-B

57.22201	57.22235
57.22227	57.22238
57.22231	57.22501
57.22232	57.22604

Category III

57.22101	57.22221
57.22103	57.22222
57.22201	57.22223
57.22202	57.22224
57.22204	57.22227
57.22205	57.22228
57.22206	57.22229
57.22207	57.22234
57.22208	57.22237
57.22213	57.22305
57.22214	57.22308
57.22215	57.22501
57.22218	57.22606
57.22220	57.22607

Category IV

57.22105	57.22226
57.22201	57.22227

Mine Safety and Health Admin., Labor § 58.620

57.22232
57.22235
57.22101
57.22103
57.22201
57.22202
57.22204
57.22205
57.22206
57.22207
57.22208
57.22212
57.22214
57.22215
57.22218
57.22220
57.22221

57.22239
57.22501

Subcategory V-A

57.22222
57.22227
57.22228
57.22229
57.22234
57.22240
57.22301
57.22302
57.22309
57.22312
57.22314
57.22315
57.22501
57.22605
57.22608

Subcategory V-B

57.22201
57.22202
57.22218
57.22222
57.22227
57.22231

57.22232
57.22234
57.22238
57.22314
57.22501

Category VI

57.22231
57.22232

57.22236
57.22238

PART 58—HEALTH STANDARDS FOR METAL AND NONMETAL MINES

Subpart A—General

Sec.
58.1 Scope.

Subparts B–D [Reserved]

Subpart E—Miscellaneous

58.610 Abrasive blasting.
58.620 Drill dust control.

AUTHORITY: 30 U.S.C. 811, 957, 961.

SOURCE: 59 FR 8327, Feb. 18, 1994, unless otherwise noted.

Subpart A—General

§ 58.1 Scope.

The health standards in this part apply to all metal and nonmetal mines.

Subparts B–D [Reserved]

Subpart E—Miscellaneous

§ 58.610 Abrasive blasting.

(a) *Surface and underground mines.* When an abrasive blasting operation is performed, all exposed miners shall use in accordance with 30 CFR 56.5005 or 57.5005 respirators approved for abrasive blasting by NIOSH under 42 CFR part 84, or the operation shall be performed in a totally enclosed device with the miner outside the device.

(b) *Underground areas of underground mines.* Silica sand or other materials containing more than 1 percent free silica shall not be used as an abrasive substance in abrasive blasting.

[59 FR 8327, Feb. 18, 1994, as amended at 60 FR 30401, June 8, 1995]

§ 58.620 Drill dust control.

Holes shall be collared and drilled wet, or other effective dust control measures shall be used, when drilling non-water-soluble material. Effective dust control measures shall be used when drilling water-soluble materials.

SUBCHAPTER L [RESERVED]

SUBCHAPTER M—UNIFORM MINE HEALTH REGULATIONS

PART 62—OCCUPATIONAL NOISE EXPOSURE

Sec.
62.100 Purpose and scope; effective date.
62.101 Definitions.
62.110 Noise exposure assessment.
62.120 Action level.
62.130 Permissible exposure level.
62.140 Dual hearing protection level.
62.150 Hearing conservation program.
62.160 Hearing protectors.
62.170 Audiometric testing.
62.171 Audiometric test procedures.
62.172 Evaluation of audiograms.
62.173 Follow-up evaluation when an audiogram is invalid.
62.174 Follow-up corrective measures when a standard threshold shift is detected.
62.175 Notification of results; reporting requirements.
62.180 Training.
62.190 Records.
APPENDIX TO PART 62

AUTHORITY: 30 U.S.C. 811.

SOURCE: 64 FR 49630, Sept. 13, 1999, unless otherwise noted.

§ 62.100 Purpose and scope; effective date.

The purpose of these standards is to prevent the occurrence and reduce the progression of occupational noise-induced hearing loss among miners. This part sets forth mandatory health standards for each surface and underground metal, nonmetal, and coal mine subject to the Federal Mine Safety and Health Act of 1977. The provisions of this part become effective September 13, 2000.

§ 62.101 Definitions.

The following definitions apply in this part:

Access. The right to examine and copy records.

Action level. An 8-hour time-weighted average sound level (TWA_8) of 85 dBA, or equivalently a dose of 50%, integrating all sound levels from 80 dBA to at least 130 dBA.

Audiologist. A professional, specializing in the study and rehabilitation of hearing, who is certified by the American Speech-Language-Hearing Association (ASHA) or licensed by a state board of examiners.

Baseline audiogram. The audiogram recorded in accordance with § 62.170(a) of this part against which subsequent audiograms are compared to determine the extent of hearing loss.

Criterion level. The sound level which if constantly applied for 8 hours results in a dose of 100% of that permitted by the standard.

Decibel (dB). A unit of measure of sound pressure levels, defined in one of two ways, depending upon the use:

(1) For measuring sound pressure levels, the decibel is 20 times the common logarithm of the ratio of the measured sound pressure to the standard reference sound pressure of 20 micropascals (µPa), which is the threshold of normal hearing sensitivity at 1000 Hertz (Hz).

(2) For measuring hearing threshold levels, the decibel is the difference between audiometric zero (reference pressure equal to 0 hearing threshold level) and the threshold of hearing of the individual being tested at each test frequency.

Dual Hearing Protection Level. A TWA_8 of 105 dBA, or equivalently, a dose of 800% of that permitted by the standard, integrating all sound levels from 90 dBA to at least 140 dBA.

Exchange rate. The amount of increase in sound level, in decibels, which would require halving of the allowable exposure time to maintain the same noise dose. For the purposes of this part, the exchange rate is 5 decibels (5 dB).

Hearing protector. Any device or material, capable of being worn on the head or in the ear canal, sold wholly or in part on the basis of its ability to reduce the level of sound entering the ear, and which has a scientifically accepted indicator of noise reduction value.

Hertz (Hz). Unit of measurement of frequency numerically equal to cycles per second.

Medical pathology. A condition or disease affecting the ear.

Miner's designee. Any individual or organization to whom a miner gives

Mine Safety and Health Admin., Labor §62.120

written authorization to exercise a right of access to records.

Qualified technician. A technician who has been certified by the Council for Accreditation in Occupational Hearing Conservation (CAOHC), or by another recognized organization offering equivalent certification.

Permissible exposure level. A TWA_8 of 90 dBA or equivalently a dose of 100% of that permitted by the standard, integrating all sound levels from 90 dBA to at least 140 dBA.

Reportable hearing loss. A change in hearing sensitivity for the worse, relative to the miner's baseline audiogram, or the miner's revised baseline audiogram where one has been established in accordance with § 62.170(c)(2), of an average of 25 dB or more at 2000, 3000, and 4000 Hz in either ear.

Revised baseline audiogram. An annual audiogram designated to be used in lieu of a miner's original baseline audiogram in measuring changes in hearing sensitivity as a result of the circumstances set forth in §§ 62.170(c)(1) or 62.170(c)(2) of this part.

Sound level. The sound pressure level in decibels measured using the A-weighting network and a slow response, expressed in the unit dBA.

Standard threshold shift. A change in hearing sensitivity for the worse relative to the miner's baseline audiogram, or relative to the most recent revised baseline audiogram where one has been established, of an average of 10 dB or more at 2000, 3000, and 4000 Hz in either ear.

Time-weighted average–8 hour (TWA_8). The sound level which, if constant over 8 hours, would result in the same noise dose as is measured.

§ 62.110 Noise exposure assessment.

(a) The mine operator must establish a system of monitoring that evaluates each miner's noise exposure sufficiently to determine continuing compliance with this part.

(b) The mine operator must determine a miner's noise dose (D, in percent) by using a noise dosimeter or by computing the formula: $D = 100(C_1/T_1 + C_2/T_2 + \ldots + C_n/T_n)$, where C_n is the total time the miner is exposed at a specified sound level, and T_n is the reference duration of exposure at that sound level shown in Table 62–1.

(1) The mine operator must use Table 62–2 when converting from dose readings to equivalent TWA_8 readings.

(2) A miner's noise dose determination must:

(i) Be made without adjustment for the use of any hearing protector;

(ii) Integrate all sound levels over the appropriate range;

(iii) Reflect the miner's full work shift;

(iv) Use a 90-dB criterion level and a 5-dB exchange rate; and

(v) Use the A-weighting and slow response instrument settings.

(c) *Observation of monitoring.* The mine operator must provide affected miners and their representatives with an opportunity to observe noise exposure monitoring required by this section and must give prior notice of the date and time of intended exposure monitoring to affected miners and their representatives.

(d) *Miner notification.* The mine operator must notify a miner of his or her exposure when the miner's exposure is determined to equal or exceed the action level, exceed the permissible exposure level, or exceed the dual hearing protection level, provided the mine operator has not notified the miner of an exposure at such level within the prior 12 months. The mine operator must base the notification on an exposure evaluation conducted either by the mine operator or by an authorized representative of the Secretary of Labor. The mine operator must notify the miner in writing within 15 calendar days of:

(1) The exposure determination; and

(2) the corrective action being taken.

(e) The mine operator must maintain a copy of any such miner notification, or a list on which the relevant information about that miner's notice is recorded, for the duration of the affected miner's exposure at or above the action level and for at least 6 months thereafter.

§ 62.120 Action level.

If during any work shift a miner's noise exposure equals or exceeds the action level the mine operator must

§ 62.130

enroll the miner in a hearing conservation program that complies with § 62.150 of this part.

§ 62.130 Permissible exposure level.

(a) The mine operator must assure that no miner is exposed during any work shift to noise that exceeds the permissible exposure level. If during any work shift a miner's noise exposure exceeds the permissible exposure level, the mine operator must use all feasible engineering and administrative controls to reduce the miner's noise exposure to the permissible exposure level, and enroll the miner in a hearing conservation program that complies with § 62.150 of this part. When a mine operator uses administrative controls to reduce a miner's exposure, the mine operator must post the procedures for such controls on the mine bulletin board and provide a copy to the affected miner.

(b) If a miner's noise exposure continues to exceed the permissible exposure level despite the use of all feasible engineering and administrative controls, the mine operator must continue to use the engineering and administrative controls to reduce the miner's noise exposure to as low a level as is feasible.

(c) The mine operator must assure that no miner is exposed at any time to sound levels exceeding 115 dBA, as determined without adjustment for the use of any hearing protector.

§ 62.140 Dual hearing protection level.

If during any work shift a miner's noise exposure exceeds the dual hearing protection level, the mine operator must, in addition to the actions required for noise exposures that exceed the permissible exposure level, provide and ensure the concurrent use of both an ear plug and an ear muff type hearing protector. The following table sets out mine operator actions under MSHA's noise standard.

Provision	Condition	Action required by the mine operator
§ 62.120	Miner's noise exposure is less than the action level.	None.
§ 62.120	Miner's exposure equals or exceeds the action level, but does not exceed the permissible exposure level (PEL).	Operator enrolls the miner in hearing conservation program (HCP) which includes (1) a system of monitoring, (2) voluntary, with two exceptions, use of operator-provided hearing protectors, (3) voluntary audiometric testing, (4) training, and (5) record keeping.
§ 62.130	Miner's exposure exceeds the PEL	Operator uses/continues to use all feasible engineering and administrative controls to reduce exposure to PEL; enrolls the miner in a HCP including ensured use of operator-provided hearing protectors; posts administrative controls and provides copy to affected miner; must never permit a miner to be exposed to sound levels exceeding 115 dBA.
§ 62.140	Miner's exposure exceeds the dual hearing protection level.	Operator enrolls the miner in a HCP, continues to meet all the requirements of § 62.130, ensures concurrent use of earplug and earmuff.

§ 62.150 Hearing conservation program.

A hearing conservation program established under this part must include:

(a) A system of monitoring under § 62.110 of this part;

(b) The provision and use of hearing protectors under § 62.160 of this part;

(c) Audiometric testing under §§ 62.170 through 62.175 of this part;

(d) Training under § 62.180 of this part; and

(e) Recordkeeping under § 62.190 of this part.

§ 62.160 Hearing protectors.

(a) A mine operator must provide a hearing protector to a miner whose noise exposure equals or exceeds the action level under § 62.120 of this part. In addition, the mine operator must:

(1) Train the miner in accordance with § 62.180 of this part;

(2) Allow the miner to choose a hearing protector from at least two muff types and two plug types, and in the event dual hearing protectors are required, to choose one of each type;

(3) Ensure that the hearing protector is in good condition and is fitted and maintained in accordance with the manufacturer's instructions;

(4) Provide the hearing protector and necessary replacements at no cost to the miner; and

Mine Safety and Health Admin., Labor § 62.171

(5) Allow the miner to choose a different hearing protector(s), if wearing the selected hearing protector(s) is subsequently precluded due to medical pathology of the ear.

(b) The mine operator must ensure, after satisfying the requirements of paragraph (a) of this section, that a miner wears a hearing protector whenever the miner's noise exposure exceeds the permissible exposure level before the implementation of engineering and administrative controls, or if the miner's noise exposure continues to exceed the permissible exposure level despite the use of all feasible engineering and administrative controls.

(c) The mine operator must ensure, after satisfying the requirements of paragraph (a) of this section, that a miner wears a hearing protector when the miner's noise exposure is at or above the action level, if:

(1) The miner has incurred a standard threshold shift; or

(2) More than 6 months will pass before the miner can take a baseline audiogram.

§ 62.170 Audiometric testing.

The mine operator must provide audiometric tests to satisfy the requirements of this part at no cost to the miner. A physician or an audiologist, or a qualified technician under the direction or supervision of a physician or an audiologist must conduct the tests.

(a) *Baseline audiogram.* The mine operator must offer miners the opportunity for audiometric testing of the miner's hearing sensitivity for the purpose of establishing a valid baseline audiogram to compare with subsequent annual audiograms. The mine operator may use an existing audiogram of the miner's hearing sensitivity as the baseline audiogram if it meets the audiometric testing requirements of § 62.171 of this part.

(1) The mine operator must offer and provide within 6 months of enrolling the miner in a hearing conservation program, audiometric testing which results in a valid baseline audiogram, or offer and provide the testing within 12 months where the operator uses mobile test vans to do the testing.

(2) The mine operator must notify the miner to avoid high levels of noise for at least 14 hours immediately preceding the baseline audiogram. The mine operator must not expose the miner to workplace noise for the 14-hour quiet period before conducting the audiometric testing to determine a baseline audiogram. The operator may substitute the use of hearing protectors for this quiet period.

(3) The mine operator must not establish a new baseline audiogram or a new revised baseline audiogram, where one has been established, due to changes in enrollment status in the hearing conservation program. The mine operator may establish a new baseline or revised baseline audiogram for a miner who is away from the mine for more than 6 consecutive months.

(b) *Annual audiogram.* After the baseline audiogram is established, the mine operator must continue to offer subsequent audiometric tests at intervals not exceeding 12 months for as long as the miner remains in the hearing conservation program.

(c) *Revised baseline audiogram.* An annual audiogram must be deemed to be a revised baseline audiogram when, in the judgment of the physician or audiologist:

(1) A standard threshold shift revealed by the audiogram is permanent; or (2) The hearing threshold shown in the annual audiogram indicates significant improvement over the baseline audiogram.

§ 62.171 Audiometric test procedures.

(a) All audiometric testing under this part must be conducted in accordance with scientifically validated procedures. Audiometric tests must be pure tone, air conduction, hearing threshold examinations, with test frequencies including 500, 1000, 2000, 3000, 4000, and 6000 Hz. Each ear must be tested separately.

(b) The mine operator must compile an audiometric test record for each miner tested. The record must include:

(1) Name and job classification of the miner tested;

(2) A copy of all of the miner's audiograms conducted under this part;

§ 62.172

(3) Evidence that the audiograms were conducted in accordance with paragraph (a) of this section;

(4) Any exposure determination for the miner conducted in accordance with § 62.110 of this part; and

(5) The results of follow-up examination(s), if any.

(c) The operator must maintain audiometric test records for the duration of the affected miner's employment, plus at least 6 months, and make the records available for inspection by an authorized representative of the Secretary of Labor.

§ 62.172 Evaluation of audiograms.

(a) The mine operator must:

(1) Inform persons evaluating audiograms of the requirements of this part and provide those persons with a copy of the miner's audiometric test records;

(2) Have a physician or an audiologist, or a qualified technician who is under the direction or supervision of a physician or audiologist:

(i) Determine if the audiogram is valid; and

(ii) Determine if a standard threshold shift or a reportable hearing loss, as defined in this part, has occurred.

(3) Instruct the physician, audiologist, or qualified technician not to reveal to the mine operator, without the written consent of the miner, any specific findings or diagnoses unrelated to the miner's hearing loss due to occupational noise or the wearing of hearing protectors; and

(4) Obtain the results and the interpretation of the results of audiograms conducted under this part within 30 calendar days of conducting the audiogram.

(b)(1) The mine operator must provide an audiometric retest within 30 calendar days of receiving a determination that an audiogram is invalid, provided any medical pathology has improved to the point that a valid audiogram may be obtained.

(2) If an annual audiogram demonstrates that the miner has incurred a standard threshold shift or reportable hearing loss, the mine operator may provide one retest within 30 calendar days of receiving the results of the audiogram and may use the results of the retest as the annual audiogram.

(c) In determining whether a standard threshold shift or reportable hearing loss has occurred, allowance may be made for the contribution of aging (presbycusis) to the change in hearing level. The baseline, or the revised baseline as appropriate, and the annual audiograms used in making the determination should be adjusted according to the following procedure:

(1) Determine from Tables 62–3 or 62–4 the age correction values for the miner by:

(i) Finding the age at which the baseline audiogram or revised baseline audiogram, as appropriate, was taken, and recording the corresponding values of age corrections at 2000, 3000, and 4000 Hz;

(ii) Finding the age at which the most recent annual audiogram was obtained and recording the corresponding values of age corrections at 2000, 3000, and 4000 Hz; and

(iii) Subtracting the values determined in paragraph (c)(1)(i) of this section from the values determined in paragraph (c)(1)(ii) of this section. The differences calculated represent that portion of the change in hearing that may be due to aging.

(2) Subtract the values determined in paragraph (c)(1)(iii) of this section from the hearing threshold levels found in the annual audiogram to obtain the adjusted annual audiogram hearing threshold levels.

(3) Subtract the hearing threshold levels in the baseline audiogram or revised baseline audiogram from the adjusted annual audiogram hearing threshold levels determined in paragraph (c)(2) of this section to obtain the age-corrected threshold shifts.

§ 62.173 Follow-up evaluation when an audiogram is invalid.

(a) If a valid audiogram cannot be obtained due to a suspected medical pathology of the ear that the physician or audiologist believes was caused or aggravated by the miner's occupational exposure to noise or the wearing of hearing protectors, the mine operator must refer the miner for a clinical-audiological evaluation or an

Mine Safety and Health Admin., Labor §62.190

otological examination, as appropriate, at no cost to the miner.

(b) If a valid audiogram cannot be obtained due to a suspected medical pathology of the ear that the physician or audiologist concludes is unrelated to the miner's occupational exposure to noise or the wearing of hearing protectors, the mine operator must instruct the physician or audiologist to inform the miner of the need for an otological examination.

(c) The mine operator must instruct the physician, audiologist, or qualified technician not to reveal to the mine operator, without the written consent of the miner, any specific findings or diagnoses unrelated to the miner's occupational exposure to noise or the wearing of hearing protectors.

§ 62.174 Follow-up corrective measures when a standard threshold shift is detected.

The mine operator must, within 30 calendar days of receiving evidence or confirmation of a standard threshold shift, unless a physician or audiologist determines the standard threshold shift is neither work-related nor aggravated by occupational noise exposure:

(a) Retrain the miner, including the instruction required by § 62.180 of this part;

(b) Provide the miner with the opportunity to select a hearing protector, or a different hearing protector if the miner has previously selected a hearing protector, from among those offered by the mine operator in accordance with § 62.160 of this part; and

(c) Review the effectiveness of any engineering and administrative controls to identify and correct any deficiencies.

§ 62.175 Notification of results; reporting requirements.

(a) The mine operator must, within 10 working days of receiving the results of an audiogram, or receiving the results of a follow-up evaluation required under § 62.173 of this part, notify the miner in writing of:

(1) The results and interpretation of the audiometric test, including any finding of a standard threshold shift or reportable hearing loss; and

(2) The need and reasons for any further testing or evaluation, if applicable.

(b) When evaluation of the audiogram shows that a miner has incurred a reportable hearing loss as defined in this part, the mine operator must report such loss to MSHA as a noise-induced hearing loss in accordance with part 50 of this title, unless a physician or audiologist has determined that the loss is neither work-related nor aggravated by occupational noise exposure.

§ 62.180 Training.

(a) The mine operator must, within 30 days of a miner's enrollment into a hearing conservation program, provide the miner with training. The mine operator must give training every 12 months thereafter if the miner's noise exposure continues to equal or exceed the action level. Training must include:

(1) The effects of noise on hearing;

(2) The purpose and value of wearing hearing protectors;

(3) The advantages and disadvantages of the hearing protectors to be offered;

(4) The various types of hearing protectors offered by the mine operator and the care, fitting, and use of each type;

(5) The general requirements of this part;

(6) The mine operator's and miner's respective tasks in maintaining mine noise controls; and

(7) The purpose and value of audiometric testing and a summary of the procedures.

(b) The mine operator must certify the date and type of training given each miner, and maintain the miner's most recent certification for as long as the miner is enrolled in the hearing conservation program and for at least 6 months thereafter.

§ 62.190 Records.

(a) The authorized representatives of the Secretaries of Labor and Health and Human Services must have access to all records required under this part. Upon written request, the mine operator must provide, within 15 calendar days of the request, access to records to:

Pt. 62, App.

(1) The miner, or with the miner's written consent, the miner's designee, for all records that the mine operator must maintain for that individual miner under this part;

(2) Any representative of miners designated under part 40 of this title, to training certifications compiled under §62.180(b) of this part and to any notice of exposure determination under §62.110(d) of this part, for the miners whom he or she represents; and

(3) Any former miner, for records which indicate his or her own exposure.

(b) When a person with access to records under paragraphs (a)(1), (a)(2), or (a)(3) of this section requests a copy of a record, the mine operator must provide the first copy of such record at no cost to that person, and any additional copies requested by that person at reasonable cost.

(c) Transfer of records. (1) The mine operator must transfer all records required to be maintained by this part, or a copy thereof, to a successor mine operator who must maintain the records for the time period required by this part.

(2) The successor mine operator must use the baseline audiogram, or revised baseline audiogram, as appropriate, obtained by the original mine operator to determine the existence of a standard threshold shift or reportable hearing loss.

APPENDIX TO PART 62

TABLE 62-1—REFERENCE DURATION

dBA	T (hours)
80	32.0
85	16.0
86	13.9
87	12.1
88	10.6
89	9.2
90	8.0
91	7.0
92	6.1
93	5.3
94	4.6
95	4.0
96	3.5
97	3.0
98	2.6
99	2.3
100	2.0
101	1.7
102	1.5
103	1.3
104	1.1
105	1.0
106	0.87

TABLE 62-1—REFERENCE DURATION—Continued

dBA	T (hours)
107	0.76
108	0.66
109	0.57
110	0.50
111	0.44
112	0.38
113	0.33
114	0.29
115	0.25

At no time shall any excursion exceed 115 dBA. For any value, the reference duration (T) in hours is computed by: $T = 8/2^{(L-90)/5}$ where L is the measured A-weighted, slow-response sound pressure level.

TABLE 62-2—"DOSE"/TWA$_8$ EQUIVALENT

Dose	TWA$_8$ (percent)
25	80
29	81
33	82
38	83
44	84
50	85
57	86
66	87
76	88
87	89
100	90
115	91
132	92
152	93
174	94
200	95
230	96
264	97
303	98
350	99
400	100
460	101
530	102
610	103
700	104
800	105
920	106
1056	107
1213	108
1393	109
1600	110
1838	111
2111	112
2425	113
2786	114
3200	115

Interpolate between the values found in this Table, or extend the Table, by using the formula: $TWA_8 = 16.61 \log_{10} (D/100) + 90$.

TABLE 62-3—AGE CORRECTION VALUE IN DECIBELS FOR MALES (SELECTED FREQUENCIES)

Age (years)	kHz		
	2	3	4
20 or less	3	4	5
21	3	4	5
22	3	4	5

TABLE 62–3—AGE CORRECTION VALUE IN DECIBELS FOR MALES (SELECTED FREQUENCIES)—Continued

Age (years)	kHz		
	2	3	4
23	3	4	6
24	3	5	6
25	3	5	7
26	4	5	7
27	4	6	7
28	4	6	8
29	4	6	8
30	4	6	9
31	4	7	9
32	5	7	10
33	5	7	10
34	5	8	11
35	5	8	11
36	5	9	12
37	6	9	12
38	6	9	13
39	6	10	14
40	6	10	14
41	6	10	14
42	7	11	16
43	7	12	16
44	7	12	17
45	7	13	18
46	8	13	19
47	8	14	19
48	8	14	20
49	9	15	21
50	9	16	22
51	9	16	23
52	10	17	24
53	10	18	25
54	10	18	26
55	11	19	27
56	11	20	28
57	11	21	29
58	12	22	31
59	12	22	32
60 or more	13	23	33

TABLE 62–4—AGE CORRECTION VALUE IN DECIBELS FOR FEMALES (SELECTED FREQUENCIES)

Age (years)	kHz		
	2	3	4
20 or less	4	3	3
21	4	4	3
22	4	4	4
23	5	4	4
24	5	4	4
25	5	4	4
26	5	5	4
27	5	5	5
28	5	5	5
29	5	5	5
30	6	5	5
31	6	6	5
32	6	6	6
33	6	6	6
34	6	6	6
35	6	7	7
36	7	7	7
37	7	7	7
38	7	7	7
39	7	8	8
40	7	8	8
41	8	8	8
42	8	9	9
43	8	9	9
44	8	9	9
45	8	10	10
46	9	10	10
47	9	10	11
48	9	11	11
49	9	11	11
50	10	11	12
51	10	11	12
52	10	12	13
53	10	13	13
54	11	13	14
55	11	14	14
56	11	14	15
57	11	15	15
58	12	15	16
59	12	16	16
60 or more	12	16	17

[64 FR 49630, Sept. 13, 1999, as amended at 65 FR 66929, Nov. 8, 2000]

SUBCHAPTER N [RESERVED]

SUBCHAPTER O—COAL MINE SAFETY AND HEALTH

PART 70—MANDATORY HEALTH STANDARDS—UNDERGROUND COAL MINES

Subpart A—General

Sec.
70.1 Scope.
70.2 Definitions.

Subpart B—Dust Standards

70.100 Respirable dust standards.
70.101 Respirable dust standard when quartz is present.

Subpart C—Sampling Procedures

70.201 Sampling; general and technical requirements.
70.202 Certified person; sampling.
70.203 Certified person; maintenance and calibration.
70.204 Approved sampling devices; maintenance and calibration.
70.205 Approved sampling devices; operation; air flowrate.
70.206 Bimonthly sampling; mechanized mining units.
70.207 Bimonthly sampling; designated areas.
70.208 Quarterly sampling; mechanized mining units.
70.209 Quarterly sampling; designated areas.
70.210 Respirable dust samples; transmission by operator.
70.211 Respirable dust samples; report to operator; posting.
70.212 Status change reports.
TABLE 70-1 TO SUBPART C OF PART 70—EXCESSIVE CONCENTRATION VALUES (ECV) BASED ON SINGLE, FULL-SHIFT CMDPSU/CPDM CONCENTRATION MEASUREMENTS
TABLE 70-2 TO SUBPART C OF PART 70—EXCESSIVE CONCENTRATION VALUES (ECV) BASED ON THE AVERAGE OF 5 OR 15 FULL-SHIFT CMDPSU/CPDM CONCENTRATION MEASUREMENTS

Subpart D [Reserved]

Subpart E—Dust From Drilling Rock [Reserved]

Subparts F–S [Reserved]

Subpart T—Diesel Exhaust Gas Monitoring

70.1900 Exhaust Gas Monitoring.

AUTHORITY: 30 U.S.C. 811, 813(h), 957.

SOURCE: 59 FR 8327, Feb 18, 1994, unless otherwise noted.

Subpart A—General

SOURCE: 79 FR 24972, May 1, 2014, unless otherwise noted.

§ 70.1 Scope.

This part 70 sets forth mandatory health standards for each underground coal mine subject to the Federal Mine Safety and Health Act of 1977, as amended.

§ 70.2 Definitions.

The following definitions apply in this part.

Act. The Federal Mine Safety and Health Act of 1977, Public Law 91-173, as amended by Public Law 95-164 and Public Law 109-236.

Active workings. Any place in a coal mine where miners are normally required to work or travel.

Approved sampling device. A sampling device approved by the Secretary and Secretary of Health and Human Services (HHS) under part 74 of this title.

Certified person. An individual certified by the Secretary in accordance with § 70.202 to take respirable dust samples required by this part or certified in accordance with § 70.203 to perform the maintenance and calibration of respirable dust sampling equipment as required by this part.

Coal mine dust personal sampler unit (CMDPSU). A personal sampling device approved under part 74, subpart B, of this title.

Concentration. A measure of the amount of a substance contained per unit volume of air.

Continuous personal dust monitor (CPDM). A personal sampling device approved under part 74, subpart C of this title.

Designated area (DA). A specific location in the mine identified by the operator in the mine ventilation plan under § 75.371(t) of this title where samples will be collected to measure respirable dust generation sources in the active workings; approved by the District Manager; and assigned a four-digit identification number by MSHA.

Mine Safety and Health Admin., Labor § 70.2

Designated occupation (DO). The occupation on a mechanized mining unit (MMU) that has been determined by results of respirable dust samples to have the greatest respirable dust concentration.

District Manager. The manager of the Coal Mine Safety and Health District in which the mine is located.

Equivalent concentration. The concentration of respirable coal mine dust, including quartz, expressed in milligrams per cubic meter of air (mg/m^3) as measured with an approved sampling device, determined by dividing the weight of dust in milligrams collected on the filter of an approved sampling device by the volume of air in cubic meters passing through the filter (sampling time in minutes (t) times the sampling airflow rate in cubic meters per minute), and then converting that concentration to an equivalent concentration as measured by the Mining Research Establishment (MRE) instrument. When the approved sampling device is:

(1) The CMDPSU, the equivalent concentration is determined by multiplying the concentration of respirable coal mine dust by the constant factor prescribed by the Secretary.

(2) The CPDM, the device shall be programmed to automatically report end-of-shift concentration measurements as equivalent concentrations.

Mechanized mining unit (MMU). A unit of mining equipment including hand loading equipment used for the production of material; or a specialized unit which uses mining equipment other than specified in § 70.206(b) or in § 70.208(b) of this part. Each MMU will be assigned a four-digit identification number by MSHA, which is retained by the MMU regardless of where the unit relocates within the mine. However, when:

(1) Two sets of mining equipment are used in a series of working places within the same working section and only one production crew is employed at any given time on either set of mining equipment, the two sets of equipment shall be identified as a single MMU.

(2) Two or more sets of mining equipment are simultaneously engaged in cutting, mining, or loading coal or rock from working places within the same working section, each set of mining equipment shall be identified as a separate MMU.

MRE instrument. The gravimetric dust sampler with a four channel horizontal elutriator developed by the Mining Research Establishment of the National Coal Board, London, England.

MSHA. The Mine Safety and Health Administration of the U.S. Department of Labor.

Normal production shift. A production shift during which the amount of material produced by an MMU is at least equal to 80 percent of the average production recorded by the operator for the most recent 30 production shifts or for all production shifts if fewer than 30 shifts of production data are available.

Other designated occupation (ODO). Other occupation on an MMU that is designated for sampling required by this part in addition to the DO. Each ODO shall be identified by a four-digit identification number assigned by MSHA.

Production shift. With regard to an MMU, a shift during which material is produced; with regard to a DA of a mine, a shift during which material is produced and routine day-to-day activities are occurring in the DA.

Quartz. Crystalline silicon dioxide (SiO_2) not chemically combined with other substances and having a distinctive physical structure.

Representative sample. A respirable dust sample, expressed as an equivalent concentration, that reflects typical dust concentration levels and with regard to an MMU, normal mining activities in the active workings during which the amount of material produced is equivalent to a normal production shift; or with regard to a DA, material is produced and routine-day-to-day activities are occurring.

Respirable dust. Dust collected with a sampling device approved by the Secretary and the Secretary of HHS in accordance with part 74 (Coal Mine Dust Sampling Devices) of this title.

Secretary. The Secretary of Labor or a delegate.

Valid respirable dust sample. A respirable dust sample collected and submitted as required by this part, including any sample for which the data were electronically transmitted to MSHA, and not voided by MSHA.

Subpart B—Dust Standards

SOURCE: 79 FR 24973, May 1, 2014, unless otherwise noted.

§ 70.100 Respirable dust standards.

(a) Each operator shall continuously maintain the average concentration of respirable dust in the mine atmosphere during each shift to which each miner in the active workings of each mine is exposed, as measured with an approved sampling device and expressed in terms of an equivalent concentration, at or below:

(1) 2.0 milligrams of respirable dust per cubic meter of air (mg/m^3).

(2) 1.5 mg/m^3 as of August 1, 2016.

(b) Each operator shall continuously maintain the average concentration of respirable dust within 200 feet outby the working faces of each section in the intake airways as measured with an approved sampling device and expressed in terms of an equivalent concentration at or below:

(1) 1.0 mg/m^3.

(2) 0.5 mg/m^3 as of August 1, 2016.

§ 70.101 Respirable dust standard when quartz is present.

(a) Each operator shall continuously maintain the average concentration of respirable quartz dust in the mine atmosphere during each shift to which each miner in the active workings of each mine is exposed at or below 0.1 mg/m^3 (100 micrograms per cubic meter or $\mu g/m^3$) as measured with an approved sampling device and expressed in terms of an equivalent concentration.

(b) When the equivalent concentration of respirable quartz dust exceeds 100 $\mu g/m^3$, the operator shall continuously maintain the average concentration of respirable dust in the mine atmosphere during each shift to which each miner in the active workings is exposed as measured with an approved sampling device and expressed in terms of an equivalent concentration at or below the applicable dust standard. The applicable dust standard is computed by dividing the percent of quartz into the number 10. The application of this formula shall not result in an applicable dust standard that exceeds the standard established by § 70.100(a).

Example: Assume the sampled MMU or DA is on a 1.5-mg/m^3 dust standard. Suppose a valid representative dust sample with an equivalent concentration of 1.12 mg/m^3 contains 12.3% of quartz dust, which corresponds to a quartz concentration of 138 $\mu g/m^3$. Therefore, the average concentration of respirable dust in the mine atmosphere associated with that MMU or DA shall be maintained on each shift at or below 0.8 mg/m^3 (10/12.3% = 0.8 mg/m^3).

Subpart C—Sampling Procedures

SOURCE: 79 FR 24974, May 1, 2014, unless otherwise noted.

§ 70.201 Sampling; general and technical requirements.

(a) Only an approved coal mine dust personal sampler unit (CMDPSU) shall be used to take bimonthly samples of the concentration of respirable coal mine dust from the designated occupation (DO) in each MMU as required by this part until January 31, 2016. On February 1, 2016, DOs in each MMU shall be sampled quarterly with an approved CPDM as required by this part and an approved CMDPSU shall not be used, unless notified by the Secretary to continue to use an approved CMDPSU to conduct quarterly sampling.

(b) Only an approved CMDPSU shall be used to take bimonthly samples of the concentration of respirable coal mine dust from each designated area (DA) as required by this part until January 31, 2016. On February 1, 2016:

(1) DAs associated with an MMU shall be redesignated as Other Designated Occupations (ODOs). ODOs shall be sampled quarterly with an approved CPDM as required by this part and an approved CMDPSU shall not be used, unless notified by the Secretary to continue to use an approved CMDPSU to conduct quarterly sampling.

(2) DAs identified by the operator under § 75.371(t) of this chapter shall be sampled quarterly with an approved CMDPSU as required by this part, unless the operator notifies the District Manager in writing that only an approved CPDM will be used for all DA sampling at the mine. The notification must be received at least 90 days before

the beginning of the quarter in which CPDMs will be used to collect the DA samples.

(c) Sampling devices shall be worn or carried directly to the MMU or DA to be sampled and from the MMU or DA sampled and shall be operated portal-to-portal. Sampling devices shall remain with the occupation or DA being sampled and shall be operational during the entire shift, which includes the total time spent in the MMU or DA and while traveling to and from the mining section or area being sampled. If the work shift to be sampled is longer than 12 hours and the sampling device is:

(1) A CMDPSU, the operator shall switch-out the unit's sampling pump prior to the 13th-hour of operation.

(2) A CPDM, the operator shall switch-out the CPDM with a fully charged device prior to the 13th-hour of operation.

(d) If using a CMDPSU, one control filter shall be used for each shift of sampling. Each control filter shall:

(1) Have the same pre-weight date (noted on the dust data card) as the filters used for sampling;

(2) Remain plugged at all times;

(3) Be used for the same amount of time, and exposed to the same temperature and handling conditions as the filters used for sampling;

(4) Be kept with the exposed samples after sampling and in the same mailing container when transmitted to MSHA.

(e) Records showing the length of each production shift for each MMU shall be made and retained for at least six months and shall be made available for inspection by authorized representatives of the Secretary and the representative of miners, and submitted to the District Manager when requested in writing.

(f) Upon request from the District Manager, the operator shall submit the date and time any respirable dust sampling required by this part will begin. This information shall be submitted at least 48 hours prior to the scheduled sampling.

(g) To establish a normal production shift, the operator shall record the amount of run-of-mine material produced by each MMU during each shift to determine the average production for the most recent 30 production shifts, or for all production shifts if fewer than 30 shifts of production data are available. Production records shall be retained for at least six months and shall be made available for inspection by authorized representatives of the Secretary and the representative of miners.

(h) Operators using CPDMs shall provide training to all miners expected to wear a CPDM. The training shall be completed prior to a miner wearing a CPDM and then every 12 months thereafter. The training shall include:

(1) The importance of monitoring dust concentrations and properly wearing the CPDM.

(2) Explaining the basic features and capabilities of the CPDM;

(3) Discussing the various types of information displayed by the CPDM and how to access that information; and

(4) How to start and stop a short-term sample run during compliance sampling.

(i) An operator shall keep a record of the CPDM training at the mine site for 24 months after completion of the training. An operator may keep the record elsewhere if the record is immediately accessible from the mine site by electronic transmission. Upon request from an authorized representative of the Secretary, Secretary of HHS, or representative of miners, the operator shall promptly provide access to any such training records. The record shall include:

(1) The date of training;

(2) The names of miners trained; and

(3) The subjects included in the training.

(j) An anthracite mine using the full box, open breast, or slant breast mining method may use either a CPDM or a CMDPSU to conduct the required sampling. The mine operator shall notify the District Manager in writing of its decision to not use a CPDM.

(k) MSHA approval of the dust control portion of the operator's mine ventilation plan may be revoked based on samples taken by MSHA or in accordance with this part 70.

§ 70.202 Certified person; sampling.

(a) The respirable dust sampling required by this part shall be performed by a certified person.

§ 70.203

(b) To be certified, a person shall complete the applicable MSHA course of instruction and pass the MSHA examination demonstrating competency in sampling procedures. Persons not certified in sampling, and those certified only in maintenance and calibration procedures in accordance with § 70.203(b), are not permitted to collect respirable dust samples required by this part or handle approved sampling devices when being used in sampling.

(c) To maintain certification, a person must pass the MSHA examination demonstrating competency in sampling procedures every three years.

(d) MSHA may revoke a person's certification for failing to properly carry out the required sampling procedures.

§ 70.203 Certified person; maintenance and calibration.

(a) Approved sampling devices shall be maintained and calibrated by a certified person.

(b) To be certified, a person shall complete the applicable MSHA course of instruction and pass the MSHA examination demonstrating competency in maintenance and calibration procedures for approved sampling devices. Necessary maintenance of the sampling head assembly of a CMDPSU, or the cyclone assembly of a CPDM, can be performed by persons certified in sampling or in maintenance and calibration.

(c) To maintain certification, a person must pass the MSHA examination demonstrating competency in maintenance and calibration procedures every three years.

(d) MSHA may revoke a person's certification for failing to properly carry out the required maintenance and calibration procedures.

§ 70.204 Approved sampling devices; maintenance and calibration.

(a) Approved sampling devices shall be maintained as approved under part 74 of this title and calibrated in accordance with MSHA Informational Report IR 1240 (1996) "Calibration and Maintenance Procedures for Coal Mine Respirable Dust Samplers" or in accordance with the manufacturer's recommendations, if using a CPDM. Only persons certified in maintenance and calibration can perform maintenance work on the CPDM or the pump unit of the CMDPSU.

(b) Sampling devices shall be calibrated at the flowrate of 2.0 liters of air per minute (L/min) if using a CMDPSU; at 2.2 L/min if using a CPDM; or at a different flowrate recommended by the manufacturer, before they are put into service and, thereafter, at time intervals recommended by the manufacturer or prescribed by the Secretary or Secretary of HHS.

(c) If using a CMDPSU, each sampling device shall be examined and tested by a person certified in sampling or in maintenance and calibration within 3 hours before the start of the shift on which the approved sampling devices will be used to collect respirable dust samples. This is to assure that the sampling devices are clean and in proper working condition. This examination and testing shall include the following:

(1) Examination of all components of the cyclone assembly to assure that they are clean and free of dust and dirt. This includes examining the interior of the connector barrel (located between the cassette assembly and vortex finder), vortex finder, cyclone body, and grit pot;

(2) Examination of the inner surface of the cyclone body to assure that it is free of scoring or scratch marks on the inner surface of the cyclone where the air flow is directed by the vortex finder into the cyclone body;

(3) Examination of the external hose connecting the pump unit to the sampling head assembly to assure that it is clean and free of leaks; and

(4) Examination of the clamping and positioning of the cyclone body, vortex finder, and cassette to assure that they are rigid, in alignment, firmly in contact, and airtight.

(5) Testing the voltage of each battery while under actual load to assure the battery is fully charged. This requires that a fully assembled and examined sampling head assembly be attached to the pump inlet with the pump unit running when the voltage check is made. The voltage for the batteries used in the CMDPSU shall not be lower than the product of the number of cells in the battery multiplied by

the manufacturer's nominal voltage per cell value.

(d) If using a CPDM, the certified person in sampling or in maintenance and calibration shall:

(1) Follow the pre-operational examinations, testing, and set-up procedures, and perform necessary external maintenance recommended by the manufacturer to assure the operational readiness of each CPDM within 3 hours before the start of the shift on which the sampling devices will be used to collect respirable dust samples; and

(2) Perform other required scheduled examinations and maintenance procedures recommended by the manufacturer.

(e) You must proceed in accordance with "Calibration and Maintenance Procedures for Coal Mine Respirable Dust Samplers," MSHA Informational Report IR 1240 (1996), referenced in paragraph (a) of this section. The Director of the Federal Register approves this incorporation by reference in accordance with 5 U.S.C. 552(a) and 1 CFR part 51. You may obtain a copy from the MSHA Web site at *http://www.msha.gov* and you may inspect or obtain a copy at MSHA, Coal Mine Safety and Health, 201 12th Street South, Arlington, VA 22202–5452; 202–693–9500; and at each MSHA Coal Mine Safety and Health District Office, or at the National Archives and Records Administration (NARA). For information on the availability of this material at NARA, call 202–741–6030, or go to: *http://www.archives.gov/federal_register/code_of_federal_regulations/ibr_locations.html*.

[79 FR 24974, May 1, 2014, as amended at 80 FR 52989, Sept. 2, 2015]

§ 70.205 Approved sampling devices; operation; air flowrate.

(a) Approved sampling devices shall be operated at the flowrate of 2.0 L/min if using a CMDPSU; at 2.2 L/min if using a CPDM; or at a different flowrate recommended by the manufacturer.

(b) If using a CMDPSU, each approved sampling device shall be examined each shift by a person certified in sampling during:

(1) The second hour after being put into operation to assure it is in the proper location, operating properly, and at the proper flowrate. If the proper flowrate is not maintained, necessary adjustments shall be made by the certified person. This examination is not required if the sampling device is being operated in an anthracite coal mine using the full box, open breast, or slant breast mining method.

(2) The last hour of operation to assure that the sampling device is operating properly and at the proper flowrate. If the proper flowrate is not maintained, the respirable dust sample shall be transmitted to MSHA with a notation by the certified person on the back of the dust data card stating that the proper flowrate was not maintained. Other events occurring during the collection of respirable dust samples that may affect the validity of the sample, such as dropping of the sampling head assembly onto the mine floor, shall be noted on the back of the dust data card.

(c) If using a CPDM, the person certified in sampling shall monitor the dust concentrations and the sampling status conditions being reported by the sampling device at mid-shift or more frequently as specified in the approved mine ventilation plan to assure: The sampling device is in the proper location and operating properly; and the work environment of the occupation or DA being sampled remains in compliance with the applicable standard at the end of the shift. This monitoring is not required if the sampling device is being operated in an anthracite coal mine using the full box, open breast, or slant breast mining method.

§ 70.206 Bimonthly sampling; mechanized mining units.

Until January 31, 2016:

(a) Each operator shall take five valid representative samples from the designated occupation (DO) in each mechanized mining unit (MMU) during each bimonthly period. DO samples shall be collected on consecutive normal production shifts or normal production shifts each of which is worked on consecutive days. The bimonthly periods are:

January 1–February 28 (29)
March 1–April 30
May 1–June 30

§ 70.206

July 1–August 31
September 1–October 31
November 1–December 31

(b) Unless otherwise directed by the District Manager, the DO samples shall be taken by placing the approved sampling device as specified in paragraphs (b)(1) through (b)(10) of this section.

(1) *Conventional section using cutting machine.* On the cutting machine operator or on the cutting machine within 36 inches inby the normal working position;

(2) *Conventional section blasting off the solid.* On the loading machine operator or on the loading machine within 36 inches inby the normal working position;

(3) *Continuous mining section other than auger-type.* On the continuous mining machine operator or on the continuous mining machine within 36 inches inby the normal working position;

(4) *Continuous mining machine; auger-type.* On the jacksetter who works nearest the working face on the return air side of the continuous mining machine or at a location that represents the maximum concentration of dust to which the miner is exposed;

(5) *Scoop section using cutting machine.* On the cutting machine operator or on the cutting machine within 36 inches inby the normal working position;

(6) *Scoop section, blasting off the solid.* On the coal drill operator or on the coal drill within 36 inches inby the normal working position;

(7) *Longwall section.* On the miner who works nearest the return air side of the longwall working face or along the working face on the return side within 48 inches of the corner;

(8) *Hand loading section with a cutting machine.* On the cutting machine operator or on the cutting machine within 36 inches inby the normal working position;

(9) *Hand loading section blasting off the solid.* On the hand loader exposed to the greatest dust concentration or at a location that represents the maximum concentration of dust to which the miner is exposed;

(10) *Anthracite mine sections.* On the hand loader exposed to the greatest dust concentration or at a location that represents the maximum concentration of dust to which the miner is exposed.

(c) When the respirable dust standard is changed in accordance with § 70.101, the new applicable standard shall become effective 7 calendar days after the date of the notification of the change by MSHA.

(d) If a normal production shift is not achieved, the DO sample for that shift may be voided by MSHA. However, any sample, regardless of production, that exceeds the applicable standard by at least 0.1 mg/m³ shall be used in the determination of the equivalent concentration for that MMU.

(e) When a valid representative sample taken in accordance with this section meets or exceeds the excessive concentration value (ECV) in Table 70–1 that corresponds to the applicable standard and particular sampling device used, the operator shall:

(1) Make approved respiratory equipment available to affected miners in accordance with § 72.700 of this chapter;

(2) Immediately take corrective action to lower the concentration of respirable dust to at or below the applicable respirable dust standard; and

(3) Make a record of the corrective actions taken. The record shall be certified by the mine foreman or equivalent mine official, no later than the end of the mine foreman's or equivalent official's next regularly scheduled working shift. The record shall be made in a secure book that is not susceptible to alteration or electronically in a computer system so as to be secure and not susceptible to alteration. Such records shall be retained at a surface location at the mine for at least 1 year and shall be made available for inspection by authorized representatives of the Secretary and the representative of miners.

(f) Noncompliance with the applicable standard is demonstrated during the sampling period when:

(1) Two or more valid representative samples meet or exceed the ECV in Table 70–1 that corresponds to the applicable standard and particular sampling device used; or

(2) The average for all valid representative samples meets or exceeds the ECV in Table 70–2 that corresponds

to the applicable standard and particular sampling device used.

(g) Unless otherwise directed by the District Manager, upon issuance of a citation for a violation of the applicable standard involving a DO in an MMU, paragraph (a) of this section shall not apply to that MMU until the violation is abated and the citation is terminated in accordance with paragraphs (h) and (i) of this section.

(h) Upon issuance of a citation for violation of the applicable standard, the operator shall take the following actions sequentially:

(1) Make approved respiratory equipment available to affected miners in accordance with §72.700 of this chapter;

(2) Immediately take corrective action to lower the concentration of respirable coal mine dust to at or below the applicable standard; and

(3) Make a record of the corrective actions taken. The record shall be certified by the mine foreman or equivalent mine official, no later than the end of the mine foreman's or equivalent official's next regularly scheduled working shift. The record shall be made in a secure book that is not susceptible to alteration or electronically in a computer system so as to be secure and not susceptible to alteration. Such records shall be retained at a surface location at the mine for at least 1 year and shall be made available for inspection by authorized representatives of the Secretary and the representative of miners.

(4) Begin sampling, within 8 calendar days after the date the citation is issued, the environment of the affected occupation in the MMU on consecutive normal production shifts until five valid representative samples are taken.

(i) A citation for a violation of the applicable standard shall be terminated by MSHA when:

(1) Each of the five valid representative samples is at or below the applicable standard; and

(2) The operator has submitted to the District Manager revised dust control parameters as part of the mine ventilation plan applicable to the MMU in the citation, and the changes have been approved by the District Manager. The revised parameters shall reflect the control measures used by the operator to abate the violation.

§ 70.207 Bimonthly sampling; designated areas.

Until January 31, 2016:

(a) Each operator shall take one valid representative sample from each designated area (DA) on a production shift during each bimonthly period. The bimonthly periods are:

February 1–March 31
April 1–May 31
June 1–July 31
August 1–September 30
October 1–November 30
December 1–January 31.

(b) When the respirable dust standard is changed in accordance with §70.101, the new applicable standard shall become effective 7 calendar days after the date of the notification of the change by MSHA.

(c) Upon notification from MSHA that any valid sample taken from a DA to meet the requirements of paragraph (a) of this section exceeds the applicable standard, the operator shall take five valid representative samples from that DA within 15 calendar days. The operator shall begin such sampling on the first day on which there is a production shift following the day of receipt of notification.

(d) When a valid representative sample taken in accordance with this section meets or exceeds the ECV in Table 70–1 that corresponds to the applicable standard and particular sampling device used, the operator shall:

(1) Make approved respiratory equipment available to affected miners in accordance with §72.700 of this chapter;

(2) Immediately take corrective action to lower the concentration of respirable coal mine dust to at or below the applicable standard; and

(3) Make a record of the corrective actions taken. The record shall be certified by the mine foreman or equivalent mine official, no later than the end of the mine foreman's or equivalent official's next regularly scheduled working shift. The record shall be made in a secure book that is not susceptible to alteration or electronically in a computer system so as to be secure and not susceptible to alteration. Such records shall be retained at a surface

§ 70.208

location at the mine for at least 1 year and shall be made available for inspection by authorized representatives of the Secretary and the representative of miners.

(e) Noncompliance with the applicable standard is demonstrated during the sampling period when:

(1) Two or more valid representative samples meet or exceed the ECV in Table 70–1 that corresponds to the applicable standard and the particular sampling device used; or

(2) The average for all valid representative samples meets or exceeds the ECV in Table 70–2 that corresponds to the applicable standard and the particular sampling device used.

(f) Unless otherwise directed by the District Manager, upon issuance of a citation for a violation of the applicable standard, paragraph (a) of this section shall not apply to that DA until the violation is abated and the citation is terminated in accordance with paragraphs (g) and (h) of this section.

(g) Upon issuance of a citation for violation of the applicable standard, the operator shall take the following actions sequentially:

(1) Make approved respiratory equipment available to affected miners in accordance with § 72.700 of this chapter;

(2) Immediately take corrective action to lower the concentration of respirable coal mine dust to at or below the applicable standard; and

(3) Make a record of the corrective actions taken. The record shall be certified by the mine foreman or equivalent mine official, no later than the end of the mine foreman's or equivalent official's next regularly scheduled working shift. The record shall be made in a secure book that is not susceptible to alteration or electronically in a computer system so as to be secure and not susceptible to alteration. Such records shall be retained at a surface location at the mine for at least 1 year and shall be made available for inspection by authorized representatives of the Secretary and the representative of miners.

(4) Begin sampling, within 8 calendar days after the date the citation is issued, the environment of the affected DA on consecutive normal production shifts until five valid representative samples are taken.

(h) A citation for a violation of the applicable standard shall be terminated by MSHA when:

(1) Each of the five valid representative samples is at or below the applicable standard; and

(2) The operator has submitted to the District Manager revised dust control parameters as part of the mine ventilation plan applicable to the DA in the citation, and the changes have been approved by the District Manager. The revised parameters shall reflect the control measures used by the operator to abate the violation.

§ 70.208 Quarterly sampling; mechanized mining units.

On February 1, 2016:

(a) The operator shall sample each calendar quarter:

(1) The designated occupation (DO) in each MMU on consecutive normal production shifts until 15 valid representative samples are taken. The District Manager may require additional groups of 15 valid representative samples when information indicates the operator has not followed the approved ventilation plan for any MMU.

(2) Each other designated occupation (ODO) specified in paragraphs (b)(1) through (b)(10) of this section in each MMU or specified by the District Manager and identified in the approved mine ventilation plan on consecutive normal production shifts until 15 valid representative samples are taken. Sampling of each ODO type shall begin after fulfilling the sampling requirements of paragraph (a)(1) of this section. When required to sample more than one ODO type, each ODO type must be sampled over separate time periods during the calendar quarter.

(3) The quarterly periods are:
January 1–March 31
April 1–June 30
July 1–September 30
October 1–December 31.

(b) Unless otherwise directed by the District Manager, the approved sampling device shall be worn by the miner assigned to perform the duties of the DO or ODO specified in paragraphs (b)(1) through (b)(10) of this section or

Mine Safety and Health Admin., Labor §70.208

by the District Manager for each type of MMU.

(1) *Conventional section using cutting machine.* DO—The cutting machine operator;

(2) *Conventional section blasting off the solid.* DO—The loading machine operator;

(3) *Continuous mining section other than auger-type.* DO—The continuous mining (CM) machine operator or mobile bridge operator when using continuous haulage; ODO—The roof bolting machine operator who works nearest the working face on the return air side of the continuous mining machine; the face haulage operators on MMUs using blowing face ventilation; the face haulage operators on MMUs ventilated by split intake air ("fishtail ventilation") as part of a super-section; and face haulage operators where two continuous mining machines are operated on an MMU.

(4) *Continuous mining section using auger-type machine.* DO—The jacksetter who works nearest the working face on the return air side of the continuous mining machine;

(5) *Scoop section using cutting machine.* DO—The cutting machine operator;

(6) *Scoop section, blasting off the solid.* DO—The coal drill operator;

(7) *Longwall section.* DO—The longwall operator working on the tailgate side of the longwall mining machine; ODO—The jacksetter who works nearest the return air side of the longwall working face, and the mechanic;

(8) *Hand loading section with a cutting machine.* DO—The cutting machine operator;

(9) *Hand loading section blasting off the solid.* DO—The hand loader exposed to the greatest dust concentration; and

(10) *Anthracite mine sections.* DO—The hand loader exposed to the greatest dust concentration.

(c) When the respirable dust standard is changed in accordance with §70.101, the new applicable standard shall become effective 7 calendar days after the date of notification of the change by MSHA.

(d) If a normal production shift is not achieved, the DO or ODO sample for that shift may be voided by MSHA. However, any sample, regardless of production, that exceeds the applicable standard by at least 0.1 mg/m^3 shall be used in the determination of the equivalent concentration for that occupation.

(e) When a valid representative sample taken in accordance with this section meets or exceeds the ECV in Table 70–1 that corresponds to the applicable standard and particular sampling device used, the operator shall:

(1) Make approved respiratory equipment available to affected miners in accordance with §72.700 of this chapter;

(2) Immediately take corrective action to lower the concentration of respirable dust to at or below the applicable respirable dust standard; and

(3) Make a record of the corrective actions taken. The record shall be certified by the mine foreman or equivalent mine official, no later than the end of the mine foreman's or equivalent official's next regularly scheduled working shift. The record shall be made in a secure book that is not susceptible to alteration or electronically in a computer system so as to be secure and not susceptible to alteration. Such records shall be retained at a surface location at the mine for at least 1 year and shall be made available for inspection by authorized representatives of the Secretary and the representative of miners.

(f) Noncompliance with the applicable standard is demonstrated during the sampling period when:

(1) Three or more valid representative samples meet or exceed the ECV in Table 70–1 that corresponds to the applicable standard and the particular sampling device used; or

(2) The average for all valid representative samples meets or exceeds the ECV in Table 70–2 that corresponds to the applicable standard and the particular sampling device used.

(g)(1) Unless otherwise directed by the District Manager, upon issuance of a citation for a violation of the applicable standard involving a DO in an MMU, paragraph (a)(1) shall not apply to the DO in that MMU until the violation is abated and the citation is terminated in accordance with paragraphs (h) and (i) of this section.

(2) Unless otherwise directed by the District Manager, upon issuance of a

§ 70.209

citation for a violation of the applicable standard involving a type of ODO in an MMU, paragraph (a)(2) shall not apply to that ODO type in that MMU until the violation is abated and the citation is terminated in accordance with paragraphs (h) and (i) of this section.

(h) Upon issuance of a citation for violation of the applicable standard, the operator shall take the following actions sequentially:

(1) Make approved respiratory equipment available to affected miners in accordance with § 72.700 of this chapter;

(2) Immediately take corrective action to lower the concentration of respirable coal mine dust to at or below the applicable standard; and

(3) Make a record of the corrective actions taken. The record shall be certified by the mine foreman or equivalent mine official, no later than the end of the mine foreman's or equivalent official's next regularly scheduled working shift. The record shall be made in a secure book that is not susceptible to alteration or electronically in a computer system so as to be secure and not susceptible to alteration. Such records shall be retained at a surface location at the mine for at least 1 year and shall be made available for inspection by authorized representatives of the Secretary and the representative of miners.

(4) Begin sampling, within 8 calendar days after the date the citation is issued, the environment of the affected occupation in the MMU on consecutive normal production shifts until five valid representative samples are taken.

(i) A citation for violation of the applicable standard shall be terminated by MSHA when:

(1) Each of the five valid representative samples is at or below the applicable standard; and

(2) The operator has submitted to the District Manager revised dust control parameters as part of the mine ventilation plan applicable to the MMU in the citation and the changes have been approved by the District Manager. The revised parameters shall reflect the control measures used by the operator to abate the violation.

§ 70.209 Quarterly sampling; designated areas.

On February 1, 2016:

(a) The operator shall sample quarterly each designated area (DA) on consecutive production shifts until five valid representative samples are taken. The quarterly periods are:

January 1–March 31
April 1–June 30
July 1–September 30
October 1–December 31.

(b) When the respirable dust standard is changed in accordance with § 70.101, the new applicable standard shall become effective 7 calendar days after the date of the notification of the change by MSHA.

(c) When a valid representative sample taken in accordance with this section meets or exceeds the ECV in Table 70–1 that corresponds to the applicable standard and particular sampling device used, the operator shall:

(1) Make approved respiratory equipment available to affected miners in accordance with § 72.700 of this chapter;

(2) Immediately take corrective action to lower the concentration of respirable dust to at or below the applicable respirable dust standard; and

(3) Make a record of the corrective actions taken. The record shall be certified by the mine foreman or equivalent mine official, no later than the end of the mine foreman's or equivalent official's next regularly scheduled working shift. The record shall be made in a secure book that is not susceptible to alteration or electronically in a computer system so as to be secure and not susceptible to alteration. Such records shall be retained at a surface location at the mine for at least 1 year and shall be made available for inspection by authorized representatives of the Secretary and the representative of miners.

(d) Noncompliance with the applicable standard is demonstrated during the sampling period when:

(1) Two or more valid representative samples meet or exceed the ECV in Table 70–1 that corresponds to the applicable standard and the particular sampling device used; or

(2) The average for all valid representative samples meets or exceeds the ECV in Table 70–2 that corresponds

Mine Safety and Health Admin., Labor **§ 70.210**

to the applicable standard and particular sampling device used.

(e) Unless otherwise directed by the District Manager, upon issuance of a citation for a violation of the applicable standard, paragraph (a) of this section shall not apply to that DA until the violation is abated and the citation is terminated in accordance with paragraphs (f) and (g) of this section.

(f) Upon issuance of a citation for a violation of the applicable standard, the operator shall take the following actions sequentially:

(1) Make approved respiratory equipment available to affected miners in accordance with § 72.700 of this chapter;

(2) Immediately take corrective action to lower the concentration of respirable coal mine dust to at or below the applicable standard; and

(3) Make a record of the corrective actions taken. The record shall be certified by the mine foreman or equivalent mine official, no later than the end of the mine foreman's or equivalent official's next regularly scheduled working shift. The record shall be made in a secure book that is not susceptible to alteration or electronically in a computer system so as to be secure and not susceptible to alteration. Such records shall be retained at a surface location at the mine for at least 1 year and shall be made available for inspection by authorized representatives of the Secretary and the representative of miners.

(4) Begin sampling, within 8 calendar days after the date the citation is issued, the environment of the affected DA on consecutive normal production shifts until five valid representative samples are taken.

(g) A citation for a violation of the applicable standard shall be terminated by MSHA when:

(1) Each of the five valid representative samples is at or below the applicable standard; and

(2) The operator has submitted to the District Manager revised dust control parameters as part of the mine ventilation plan applicable to the DA in the citation, and the changes have been approved by the District Manager. The revised parameters shall reflect the control measures used by the operator to abate the violation.

§ 70.210 Respirable dust samples; transmission by operator.

(a) If using a CMDPSU, the operator shall transmit within 24 hours after the end of the sampling shift all samples collected to fulfill the requirements of this part, including control filters, in containers provided by the manufacturer of the filter cassette to: Respirable Dust Processing Laboratory, Pittsburgh Safety and Health Technology Center, 626 Cochrans Mill Road, Building 38, Pittsburgh, PA 15236–3611, or to any other address designated by the District Manager.

(b) The operator shall not open or tamper with the seal of any filter cassette or alter the weight of any filter cassette before or after it is used to fulfill the requirements of this part.

(c) A person certified in sampling shall properly complete the dust data card that is provided by the manufacturer for each filter cassette. The card shall have an identification number identical to that on the cassette used to take the sample and be submitted to MSHA with the sample. Each card shall be signed by the certified person who actually performed the required examinations under 70.205(b) of this part during the sampling shift and shall include that person's MSHA Individual Identification Number (MIIN). Respirable dust samples with data cards not properly completed may be voided by MSHA.

(d) All respirable dust samples collected by the operator shall be considered taken to fulfill the sampling requirements of part 70, 71, or 90 of this title, unless the sample has been identified in writing by the operator to the District Manager, prior to the intended sampling shift, as a sample to be used for purposes other than required by part 70, 71, or 90 of this title.

(e) Respirable dust samples received by MSHA in excess of those required by this part shall be considered invalid samples.

(f) If using a CPDM, the person certified in sampling shall (1) validate, certify, and transmit electronically to MSHA within 24 hours after the end of each sampling shift all sample data file information collected and stored in the CPDM, including the sampling status conditions encountered when sampling;

§ 70.211

and (2) not tamper with the CPDM or its components in any way before, during, or after it is used to fulfill the requirements of this part, or alter any sample data files. All CPDM data files transmitted electronically to MSHA shall be maintained by the operator for at least 12 months.

[79 FR 24974, May 1, 2014, as amended at 80 FR 52989, Sept. 2, 2015]

§ 70.211 Respirable dust samples; report to operator; posting.

(a) MSHA shall provide the operator, as soon as practicable, a report with the following data on respirable dust samples submitted or whose results were transmitted electronically, if using a CPDM, in accordance with this part:

(1) The mine identification number;
(2) The locations within the mine from which the samples were taken;
(3) The concentration of respirable dust, expressed as an equivalent concentration for each valid sample;
(4) The average equivalent concentration of respirable dust for all valid samples;
(5) The occupation code, where applicable; and
(6) The reason for voiding any sample.

(b) Upon receipt, the operator shall post this data for at least 31 days on the mine bulletin board.

(c) If using a CPDM, the person certified in sampling shall, within 12 hours after the end of each sampling shift, print, sign, and post on the mine bulletin board a paper record (Dust Data Card) of the sample run. This hard-copy record shall include the data entered when the sample run was first programmed, and the following:

(1) The mine identification number;
(2) The locations within the mine from which the samples were taken;
(3) The concentration of respirable dust, expressed as an equivalent concentration reported and stored for each sample;
(4) The sampling status conditions encountered for each sample; and
(5) The shift length.

(d) The information required by paragraph (c) of this section shall remain posted until receipt of the MSHA report covering these respirable dust samples.

§ 70.212 Status change reports.

(a) If there is a change in operational status that affects the respirable dust sampling requirements of this part, the operator shall report the change in operational status of the mine, mechanized mining unit, or designated area to the MSHA District Office or to any other MSHA office designated by the District Manager. Status changes shall be reported in writing or electronically within 3 working days after the status change has occurred.

(b) Each specific operational status is defined as follows:

(1) Underground mine:
(i) *Producing*—has at least one MMU unit producing material.
(ii) *Nonproducing*—no material is being produced.
(iii) *Abandoned*—the work of all miners has been terminated and production activity has ceased.

(2) MMU:
(i) *Producing*—producing material from a working section.
(ii) *Nonproducing*—temporarily ceased production of material.
(iii) *Abandoned*—permanently ceased production of material.

(3) DA:
(i) *Producing*—activity is occurring.
(ii) *Nonproducing*—activity has ceased.
(iii) *Abandoned*—the dust generating source has been withdrawn and activity has ceased.

TABLE 70-1 TO SUBPART C OF PART 70—EXCESSIVE CONCENTRATION VALUES (ECV) BASED ON SINGLE, FULL-SHIFT CMDPSU/CPDM CONCENTRATION MEASUREMENTS

Applicable standard (mg/m³)	ECV (mg/m³)	
	CMDPSU	CPDM
2.0	2.33	2.26
1.9	2.22	2.15
1.8	2.12	2.04
1.7	2.01	1.92
1.6	1.90	1.81
1.5	1.79	1.70
1.4	1.69	1.58
1.3	1.59	1.47
1.2	1.47	1.36
1.1	1.37	1.25
1.0	1.26	1.13
0.9	1.16	1.02
0.8	1.05	0.91

Mine Safety and Health Admin., Labor § 70.1900

Applicable standard (mg/m³)	ECV (mg/m³)		Applicable standard (mg/m³)	ECV (mg/m³)	
	CMDPSU	CPDM		CMDPSU	CPDM
0.7	0.95	0.79	0.4	0.65	0.46
0.6	0.85	0.68	0.3	0.54	0.34
0.5	0.74	0.57	0.2	0.44	0.23

TABLE 70-2 TO SUBPART C OF PART 70—EXCESSIVE CONCENTRATION VALUES (ECV) BASED ON THE AVERAGE OF 5 OR 15 FULL-SHIFT CMDPSU/CPDM CONCENTRATION MEASUREMENTS

Applicable standard (mg/m³)	ECV (mg/m³) based on 5-sample average		ECV (mg/m³) based on 15-sample average	
	CMDPSU	CPDM	CMDPSU	CPDM
2.0	2.15	2.12	2.09	2.07
1.9	2.05	2.01	1.99	1.97
1.8	1.94	1.91	1.89	1.87
1.7	1.84	1.80	1.78	1.76
1.6	1.74	1.70	1.68	1.66
1.5	1.63	1.59	1.58	1.56
1.4	1.53	1.49	1.48	1.45
1.3	1.43	1.38	1.38	1.35
1.2	1.33	1.27	1.28	1.25
1.1	1.22	1.17	1.17	1.14
1.0	1.12	1.06	1.07	1.04
0.9	1.02	0.96	0.97	0.94
0.8	0.92	0.85	0.87	0.83
0.7	0.81	0.75	0.77	0.73
0.6	0.71	0.64	0.67	0.63
0.5	0.61	0.53	0.57	0.52
0.4	0.51	0.43	0.47	0.42
0.3	0.41	0.32	0.37	0.32
0.2	0.31	0.22	0.27	0.21

Subpart D [Reserved]

Subpart E—Dust From Drilling Rock [Reserved]

Subparts F–S [Reserved]

Subpart T—Diesel Exhaust Gas Monitoring

§ 70.1900 Exhaust Gas Monitoring.

(a) During on-shift examinations required by § 75.362, a certified person as defined by § 75.100 of this chapter and designated by the operator as trained or experienced in the appropriate sampling procedures, shall determine the concentration of carbon monoxide (CO) and nitrogen dioxide (NO_2):

(1) In the return of each working section where diesel equipment is used, at a location which represents the contribution of all diesel equipment on such section;

(2) In the area of the section loading point if diesel haulage equipment is operated on the working section;

(3) At a point inby the last piece of diesel equipment on the longwall or shortwall face when mining equipment is being installed or removed; and

(4) In any other area designated by the district manager as specified in the mine operator's approved ventilation plan where diesel equipment is operated in a manner which can result in significant concentrations of diesel exhaust.

(b) Samples of CO and NO_2 shall be—

(1) Collected in a manner that makes the results available immediately to the person collecting the samples;

(2) Collected and analyzed by appropriate instrumentation which has been maintained and calibrated in accordance with the manufacturer's recommendations; and

(3) Collected during periods that are representative of conditions during normal operations.

(c) Except as provided in § 75.325(j) of this chapter, when sampling results indicate a concentration of CO and/or NO_2 exceeding an action level of 50 percent of the threshold limit values (TLV®) adopted by the American Conference of Governmental Industrial Hygienists, the mine operator shall immediately take appropriate corrective action to reduce the concentrations of CO and/or NO_2 to below the applicable action level. The publication, "Threshold Limit Values for Substance in Workroom Air" (1972) is incorporated by reference and may be inspected at MSHA's Office of Standards, Regulations, and Variances, 201 12th Street South, Arlington, VA 22202-5452; 202-693-9440; at any MSHA Coal Mine Safety and Health District Office; or at the National Archives and Records Administration (NARA). For information on the availability of this material at NARA, call 202-741-6030, or go to: http://www.archives.gov/federal_register/code_of_federal_regulations/ibr_locations.html. This incorporation by reference was approved by the Director of the Federal Register in accordance with 5 U.S.C. 552(a) and 1 CFR part 51. In addition, copies of the document may be purchased from the American Conference of Governmental Industrial Hygienists, 1330 Kemper Meadow Drive, Attn: Customer Service, Cincinnati, OH 45240; 513-742-2020; http://www.acgih.org.

(d) A record shall be made when sampling results exceed the action level for the applicable TLV® for CO and/or NO_2. The record shall be made as part of and in the same manner as the records for hazards required by § 75.363 of this chapter and include the following:

(1) Location where each sample was collected;

(2) Substance sampled and the measured concentration; and

(3) Corrective action taken to reduce the concentration of CO and/or NO_2 to or below the applicable action level.

(e) As of November 25, 1997 exhaust gas monitoring shall be conducted in accordance with the requirements of this section.

[61 FR 55526, Oct. 25, 1996, as amended at 67 FR 38385, June 4, 2002; 71 FR 16667, Apr. 3, 2006; 80 FR 52989, Sept. 2, 2015]

PART 71—MANDATORY HEALTH STANDARDS—SURFACE COAL MINES AND SURFACE WORK AREAS OF UNDERGROUND COAL MINES

Subpart A—General

Sec.
71.1 Scope.
71.2 Definitions.

Subpart B—Dust Standards

71.100 Respirable dust standard.
71.101 Respirable dust standard when quartz is present.

Subpart C—Sampling Procedures

71.201 Sampling; general and technical requirements.
71.202 Certified person; sampling.
71.203 Certified person; maintenance and calibration.
71.204 Approved sampling devices; maintenance and calibration.
71.205 Approved sampling devices; operation; air flowrate.
71.206 Quarterly sampling; designated work positions.
71.207 Respirable dust samples; transmission by operator.
71.208 Respirable dust samples; report to operator; posting.
71.209 Status change reports.

Subpart D—Respirable Dust Control Plans

71.300 Respirable dust control plan; filing requirements.
71.301 Respirable dust control plan; approval by District Manager and posting.

Subpart E—Surface Bathing Facilities, Change Rooms, and Sanitary Flush Toilet Facilities at Surface Coal Mines

71.400 Bathing facilities; change rooms; sanitary flush toilet facilities.
71.401 Location of facilities.
71.402 Minimum requirements for bathing facilities, change rooms, and sanitary flush toilet facilities.
71.403 Waiver of surface facilities requirements; posting of waiver.
71.404 Application for waiver of surface facilities requirements.

Subpart F—Sanitary Toilet Facilities at Surface Worksites of Surface Coal Mines

71.500 Sanitary toilet facilities at surface work sites; installation requirements.
71.501 Sanitary toilet facilities; maintenance.

Mine Safety and Health Admin., Labor §71.2

Subpart G—Drinking Water

71.600 Drinking water; general.
71.601 Drinking water; quality.
71.602 Drinking water; distribution.
71.603 Drinking water; dispensing requirements.

Subpart H—Airborne Contaminants

71.700 Inhalation hazards; threshold limit values for gases, dust, fumes, mists, and vapors.
71.701 Sampling; general requirements.
71.702 Asbestos standard.

AUTHORITY: 30 U.S.C. 811, 813(h), 957.

SOURCE: 37 FR 6368, Mar. 28, 1972, unless otherwise noted.

Subpart A—General

SOURCE: 79 FR 24980, May 1, 2014, unless otherwise noted.

§71.1 Scope.

This part 71 sets forth mandatory health standards for each surface coal mine and for the surface work areas of each underground coal mine subject to the Federal Mine Safety and Health Act of 1977, as amended.

§71.2 Definitions.

The following definitions apply in this part.

Act. The Federal Mine Safety and Health Act of 1977, Public Law 91–173, as amended by Public Law 95–164 and Public Law 109–236.

Active workings. Any place in a surface coal mine or the surface work area of an underground coal mine where miners are normally required to work or travel.

Approved sampling device. A sampling device approved by the Secretary and Secretary of Health and Human Services (HHS) under part 74 of this title.

Certified person. An individual certified by the Secretary in accordance with §71.202 to take respirable dust samples required by this part or certified in accordance with §71.203 to perform maintenance and calibration of respirable dust sampling equipment as required by this part.

Coal mine dust personal sampler unit (CMDPSU). A personal sampling device approved under part 74, subpart B, of this title.

Concentration. A measure of the amount of a substance contained per unit volume of air.

Continuous personal dust monitor (CPDM). A personal sampling device approved under part 74, subpart C, of this title.

Designated work position (DWP). A work position in a surface coal mine and surface work area of an underground coal mine designated for sampling to measure respirable dust generation sources in the active workings. Each DWP will be assigned a four-digit number assigned by MSHA identifying the specific physical portion of the mine that is affected, followed by a three-digit MSHA coal mining occupation code describing the location to which a miner is assigned in the performance of his or her regular duties.

District Manager. The manager of the Coal Mine Safety and Health District in which the mine is located.

Equivalent concentration. The concentration of respirable coal mine dust, including quartz, expressed in milligrams per cubic meter of air (mg/m^3) as measured with an approved sampling device, determined by dividing the weight of dust in milligrams collected on the filter of an approved sampling device by the volume of air in cubic meters passing through the filter (sampling time in minutes (t) times the sampling airflow rate in cubic meters per minute), and then converting that concentration to an equivalent concentration as measured by the Mining Research Establishment (MRE) instrument. When the approved sampling device is:

(1) The CMDPSU, the equivalent concentration is determined by multiplying the concentration of respirable coal mine dust by the constant factor prescribed by the Secretary.

(2) The CPDM, the device shall be programmed to automatically report end-of-shift concentration measurements as equivalent concentrations.

MRE instrument. The gravimetric dust sampler with a four channel horizontal elutriator developed by the Mining Research Establishment of the National Coal Board, London, England.

MSHA. The Mine Safety and Health Administration of the U.S. Department of Labor.

§ 71.100

Normal work shift. (1) A shift during which the regular duties of the DWP are performed while routine day-to-day mining activities are occurring in the rest of the mine and

(2) A shift during which there is no rain, or, if rain occurs, the rain does not suppress the respirable dust to the extent that sampling results will be measurably lower, in the judgment of the person certified under this part to conduct sampling.

Quartz. Crystalline silicon dioxide (SiO_2) not chemically combined with other substances and having a distinctive physical structure.

Representative sample. A respirable dust sample, expressed as an equivalent concentration, that reflects typical dust concentration levels in the working environment of the DWP when performing normal duties.

Respirable dust. Dust collected with a sampling device approved by the Secretary and the Secretary of HHS in accordance with part 74 (Coal Mine Dust Sampling Devices) of this title.

Secretary. The Secretary of Labor or a delegate.

Surface area. A specific physical portion of a surface coal mine or surface area of an underground coal mine. These areas are assigned a four-digit identification number by MSHA.

Surface coal mine. A surface area of land and all structures, facilities, machinery, tools, equipment, excavations, and other property, real or personal, placed upon or above the surface of such land by any person, used in, or to be used in, or resulting from, the work of extracting in such area bituminous coal, lignite, or anthracite from its natural deposits in the earth by any means or method, and the work of preparing the coal so extracted, including custom coal preparation facilities.

Surface installation. Any structure in which miners work at a surface coal mine or surface work area of an underground coal mine.

Surface work area of an underground mine. The surface areas of land and all structures, facilities, machinery, tools, equipment, shafts, slopes, excavations, and other property, real or personal, placed in, upon or above the surface of such land by any person, used in, or to be used in, or resulting from, the work of extracting bituminous coal, lignite, or anthracite from its natural deposits underground by any means or method, and the work of preparing the coal so extracted, including custom coal preparation facilities.

Surface worksite. Any area in which miners work at a surface coal mine or surface work area of an underground coal mine.

Valid respirable dust sample. A respirable dust sample collected and submitted as required by this part, including any sample for which the data were electronically transmitted to MSHA, and not voided by MSHA.

Work position. An occupation identified by an MSHA three-digit code number describing a location to which a miner is assigned in the performance of his or her normal duties.

Subpart B—Dust Standards

SOURCE: 79 FR 24981, May 1, 2014, unless otherwise noted.

§ 71.100 Respirable dust standard.

Each operator shall continuously maintain the average concentration of respirable dust in the mine atmosphere during each shift to which each miner in the active workings of each mine is exposed, as measured with an approved sampling device and expressed in terms of an equivalent concentration, at or below:

(a) 2.0 milligrams of respirable dust per cubic meter of air (mg/m^3).

(b) 1.5 mg/m^3 as of August 1, 2016.

§ 71.101 Respirable dust standard when quartz is present.

(a) Each operator shall continuously maintain the average concentration of respirable quartz dust in the mine atmosphere during each shift to which each miner in the active workings of each mine is exposed at or below 0.1 mg/m^3 (100 micrograms per cubic meter or $\mu g/m^3$) as measured with an approved sampling device and expressed in terms of an equivalent concentration.

(b) When the equivalent concentration of respirable quartz dust exceeds 100 $\mu g/m^3$, the operator shall continuously maintain the average concentration of respirable dust in the mine atmosphere during each shift to which each miner in the active workings is exposed as measured with an approved sampling device and expressed in terms of an equivalent concentration at or below the applicable standard. The applicable standard is computed by dividing the percent of quartz into the number 10. The application of this formula shall not result in the applicable standard that exceeds the standard established by §71.100(a) of this section.

Example: Assume the sampled DWP is on a 1.5-mg/m³ dust standard. Suppose a valid representative dust sample with an equivalent concentration of 1.09 mg/m³ contains 16.7% of quartz dust, which corresponds to a quartz concentration of 182 µg/m³. Therefore, the average concentration of respirable dust in the mine atmosphere associated with that DWP shall be maintained on each shift at or below 0.6 mg/m³ (10/16.7% = 0.6 mg/m³).

Subpart C—Sampling Procedures

Source: 79 FR 24982, May 1, 2014, unless otherwise noted.

§71.201 Sampling; general and technical requirements.

(a) Each operator shall take representative samples of the concentration of respirable dust in the active workings of the mine as required by this part only with an approved CMDPSU. On February 1, 2016, the operator may use an approved CPDM if the operator notifies the District Manager in writing that only an approved CPDM will be used for all DWP sampling at the mine. The notification must be received at least 90 days before the beginning of the quarter in which CPDMs will be used to collect the DWP samples.

(b) Sampling devices shall be worn or carried directly to and from the DWP to be sampled. Sampling devices shall remain with the DWP and shall be operational during the entire shift, which includes the total time spent in the DWP and while traveling to and from the DWP being sampled. If the work shift to be sampled is longer than 12 hours and the sampling device is:

(1) A CMDPSU, the operator shall switch-out the unit's sampling pump prior to the 13th-hour of operation.

(2) A CPDM, the operator shall switch-out the CPDM with a fully charged device prior to the 13th-hour of operation.

(c) If using a CMDPSU, one control filter shall be used for each shift of sampling. Each control filter shall:

(1) Have the same pre-weight data (noted on the dust data card) as the filters used for sampling;

(2) Remain plugged at all times;

(3) Be used for the same amount of time, and exposed to the same temperature and handling conditions as the filters used for sampling; and

(4) Be kept with the exposed samples after sampling and in the same mailing container when transmitted to MSHA.

(d) Records showing the length of each normal work shift for each DWP shall be made and retained for at least six months and shall be made available for inspection by authorized representatives of the Secretary and the representative of miners, and submitted to the District Manager when requested in writing.

(e) Upon request from the District Manager, the operator shall submit the date and time any respirable dust sampling required by this part will begin. This information shall be submitted at least 48 hours prior to scheduled sampling.

(f) Upon written request by the operator, the District Manager may waive the rain restriction for a normal work shift as defined in §71.2 for a period not to exceed two months, if the District Manager determines that:

(1) The operator will not have reasonable opportunity to complete the respirable dust sampling required by this part without the waiver because of the frequency of rain; and

(2) The operator did not have reasonable opportunity to complete the respirable dust sampling required by this part prior to requesting the waiver.

(g) Operators using CPDMs shall provide training to all miners expected to wear the CPDM. The training shall be completed prior to a miner wearing the CPDM and then every 12 months thereafter. The training shall include:

(1) The importance of monitoring dust concentrations and properly wearing the CPDM;

(2) Explaining the basic features and capabilities of the CPDM;

(3) Discussing the various types of information displayed by the CPDM and how to access that information; and

(4) How to start and stop a short-term sample run during compliance sampling.

(h) An operator shall keep a record of the CPDM training at the mine site for 24 months after completion of the training. An operator may keep the record elsewhere if the record is immediately accessible from the mine site by electronic transmission. Upon request from an authorized representative, of the Secretary, Secretary of HHS, or representative of miners, the operator shall promptly provide access to any such training records. The record shall include:

(1) The date of training;

(2) The names of miners trained; and

(3) The subjects included in the training.

§ 71.202 Certified person; sampling.

(a) The respirable dust sampling required by this part shall be performed by a certified person.

(b) To be certified, a person shall complete the applicable MSHA course of instruction and pass the MSHA examination demonstrating competency in sampling procedures. Persons not certified in sampling, and those certified only in maintenance and calibration procedures in accordance with § 71.203(b), are not permitted to collect respirable dust samples required by this part or handle approved sampling devices when being used in sampling.

(c) To maintain certification, a person must pass the MSHA examination demonstrating competency in sampling procedures every three years.

(d) MSHA may revoke a person's certification for failing to properly carry out the required sampling procedures.

§ 71.203 Certified person; maintenance and calibration.

(a) Approved sampling devices shall be maintained and calibrated by a certified person.

(b) To be certified, a person shall complete the applicable MSHA course of instruction and pass the MSHA examination demonstrating competency in maintenance and calibration procedures for approved sampling devices. Necessary maintenance of the sampling head assembly of a CMDPSU, or the cyclone assembly of a CPDM, can be performed by persons certified in sampling or maintenance and calibration.

(c) To maintain certification, a person must pass the MSHA examination demonstrating competency in maintenance and calibration procedures every three years.

(d) MSHA may revoke a person's certification for failing to properly carry out the required maintenance and calibration procedures.

§ 71.204 Approved sampling devices; maintenance and calibration.

(a) Approved sampling devices shall be maintained as approved under part 74 of this chapter and calibrated in accordance with MSHA Informational Report IR 1240 (1996) "Calibration and Maintenance Procedures for Coal Mine Respirable Dust Samplers" or in accordance with the manufacturer's recommendations if using a CPDM. Only persons certified in maintenance and calibration can perform maintenance work on the CPDM or on the pump unit of the CMDPSU.

(b) Sampling devices shall be calibrated at the flowrate of 2.0 liters of air per minute (L/min) if using a CMDPSU, or at 2.2 L/min if using a CPDM, or at a different flowrate recommended by the manufacturer, before they are put into service and, thereafter, at time intervals recommended by the manufacturer or prescribed by the Secretary or Secretary of HHS.

(c) If using a CMDPSU, sampling devices shall be examined and tested by a person certified in sampling or in maintenance and calibration within 3 hours before the start of the shift on which the approved sampling devices will be used to collect respirable dust samples. This is to assure that the sampling devices are clean and in proper working condition. This examination and testing shall include the following:

(1) Examination of all components of the cyclone assembly to assure that they are clean and free of dust and dirt. This includes examining the interior of the connector barrel (located between

the cassette assembly and vortex finder), vortex finder, cyclone body, and grit pot;

(2) Examination of the inner surface of the cyclone body to assure that it is free of scoring or scratch marks on the inner surface of the cyclone where the air flow is directed by the vortex finder into the cyclone body;

(3) Examination of the external hose connecting the pump unit to the sampling head assembly to assure that it is clean and free of leaks; and

(4) Examination of the clamping and positioning of the cyclone body, vortex finder, and cassette to assure that they are rigid, in alignment, firmly in contact, and airtight.

(5) Testing the voltage of each battery while under actual load to assure the battery is fully charged. This requires that a fully assembled and examined sampling head assembly be attached to the pump inlet with the pump unit running when the voltage check is made. The voltage for the batteries used in the CMDPSU shall not be lower than the product of the number of cells in the battery multiplied by the manufacturer's nominal voltage per cell value.

(d) If using a CPDM, the certified person in sampling or in maintenance and calibration shall:

(1) Follow the pre-operational examinations, testing, and set-up procedures, and perform necessary external maintenance recommended by the manufacturer to assure the operational readiness of the CPDM within 3 hours before the start of the shift on which the sampling devices will be used to collect respirable dust samples; and

(2) Perform other required scheduled examinations and maintenance procedures recommended by the manufacturer.

(e) You must proceed in accordance with "Calibration and Maintenance Procedures for Coal Mine Respirable Dust Samplers," MSHA Informational Report IR 1240 (1996), referenced in paragraph (a) of this section. The Director of the Federal Register approves this incorporation by reference in accordance with 5 U.S.C. 552(a) and 1 CFR part 51. You may obtain a copy from the MSHA Web site at *http:// www.msha.gov* and you may inspect or obtain a copy at MSHA, Coal Mine Safety and Health, 201 12th Street South, Arlington, VA 22202–5452; 202–693–9500; and at each MSHA Coal Mine Safety and Health District Office, or at the National Archives and Records Administration (NARA). For information on the availability of this material at NARA, call 202–741–6030, or go to: *http:// www.archives.gov/federal_register/ code_of_federal_regulations/ ibr_locations.html.*

[79 FR 24982, May 1, 2014, as amended at 80 FR 52989, Sept. 2, 2015]

§ 71.205 **Approved sampling devices; operation; air flowrate.**

(a) Approved sampling devices shall be operated at the flowrate of 2.0 L/min, if using a CMDPSU; at 2.2 L/min, if using a CPDM; or at a different flowrate recommended by the manufacturer.

(b) If using a CMDPSU, each sampling device shall be examined each shift by a person certified in sampling during:

(1) The second hour after being put into operation to assure it is in the proper location, operating properly, and at the proper flowrate. If the proper flowrate is not maintained, necessary adjustments shall be made by the certified person.

(2) The last hour of operation to assure that it is operating properly and at the proper flowrate. If the proper flowrate is not maintained, the respirable dust sample shall be transmitted to MSHA with a notation by the certified person on the back of the dust data card stating that the proper flowrate was not maintained. Other events occurring during the collection of respirable dust samples that may affect the validity of the sample, such as dropping of the sampling head assembly onto the mine floor, shall be noted on the back of the dust data card.

(c) If using a CPDM, the person certified in sampling shall monitor the dust concentrations and the sampling status conditions being reported by the sampling device at mid-shift or more frequently as specified in the approved respirable dust control plan, if applicable, to assure: The sampling device is in the proper location and operating properly; and the work environment of

§ 71.206

the occupation being sampled remains in compliance with the applicable standard at the end of the shift.

§ 71.206 Quarterly sampling; designated work positions.

(a) Each operator shall take one valid representative sample from the DWP during each quarterly period. The quarterly periods are:
January 1–March 31
April 1–June 30
July 1–September 30
October 1–December 31.

(b) When the respirable dust standard is changed in accordance with § 71.101, the new applicable standard shall become effective 7 calendar days after the date of the notification of the change by MSHA.

(c) Designated work position samples shall be collected at locations to measure respirable dust generation sources in the active workings. The specific work positions at each mine where DWP samples shall be collected include:

(1) Each highwall drill operator (MSHA occupation code 384);

(2) Bulldozer operators (MSHA occupation code 368); and

(3) Other work positions designated by the District Manager for sampling in accordance with § 71.206(m).

(d) Operators with multiple work positions specified in paragraph (c)(2) and (c)(3) of this section shall sample the DWP exposed to the greatest respirable dust concentration in each work position performing the same activity or task at the same location at the mine and exposed to the same dust generation source. Each operator shall provide the District Manager with a list identifying the specific work positions where DWP samples will be collected for:

(1) Active mines—by October 1, 2014.

(2) New mines—Within 30 calendar days of mine opening.

(3) DWPs with a change in operational status that increases or reduces the number of active DWPs—within 7 calendar days of the change in status.

(e) Each DWP sample shall be taken on a normal work shift. If a normal work shift is not achieved, the respirable dust sample shall be transmitted to MSHA with a notation by the person certified in sampling on the back of the dust data card stating that the sample was not taken on a normal work shift. When a normal work shift is not achieved, the sample for that shift may be voided by MSHA. However, any sample, regardless of whether a normal work shift was achieved, that exceeds the applicable standard by at least 0.1 mg/m³ shall be used in the determination of the equivalent concentration for that occupation.

(f) Unless otherwise directed by the District Manager, DWP samples shall be taken by placing the sampling device as follows:

(1) *Equipment operator:* On the equipment operator or on the equipment within 36 inches of the operator's normal working position.

(2) *Non-equipment operators:* On the miner assigned to the DWP or at a location that represents the maximum concentration of dust to which the miner is exposed.

(g) Upon notification from MSHA that any valid representative sample taken from a DWP to meet the requirements of paragraph (a) of this section exceeds the applicable standard, the operator shall, within 15 calendar days of notification, sample that DWP each normal work shift until five valid representative samples are taken. The operator shall begin sampling on the first normal work shift following receipt of notification.

(h) When a valid representative sample taken in accordance with this section meets or exceeds the excessive concentration value (ECV) in Table 71–1 that corresponds to the applicable standard and particular sampling device used, the operator shall:

(1) Make approved respiratory equipment available to affected miners in accordance with § 72.700 of this chapter;

(2) Immediately take corrective action to lower the concentration of respirable coal mine dust to at or below the applicable standard; and

(3) Make a record of the corrective actions taken. The record shall be certified by the mine foreman or equivalent mine official, no later than the end of the mine foreman's or equivalent official's next regularly scheduled working shift. The record shall be

made in a secure book that is not susceptible to alteration or electronically in a computer system so as to be secure and not susceptible to alteration. Such records shall be retained at a surface location at the mine for at least 1 year and shall be made available for inspection by authorized representatives of the Secretary and the representative of miners.

(i) Noncompliance with the applicable standard is demonstrated during the sampling period when:

(1) Two or more valid representative samples meet or exceed the ECV in Table 71–1 that corresponds to the applicable standard and the particular sampling device used; or

(2) The average for all valid representative samples meets or exceeds the ECV in Table 71–2 that corresponds to the applicable standard and the particular sampling device used.

(j) Unless otherwise directed by the District Manager, upon issuance of a citation for a violation of the applicable standard, paragraph (a) of this section shall not apply to that DWP until the violation is abated and the citation is terminated in accordance with paragraphs (k) and (l) of this section.

(k) Upon issuance of a citation for violation of the applicable standard, the operator shall take the following actions sequentially:

(1) Make approved respiratory equipment available to affected miners in accordance with § 72.700 of this chapter;

(2) Immediately take corrective action to lower the concentration of respirable coal mine dust to at or below the applicable standard; and

(3) Make a record of the corrective actions taken. The record shall be certified by the mine foreman or equivalent mine official, no later than the end of the mine foreman's or equivalent official's next regularly scheduled working shift. The record shall be made in a secure book that is not susceptible to alteration or electronically in a computer system so as to be secure and not susceptible to alteration. Such records shall be retained at a surface location at the mine for at least 1 year and shall be made available for inspection by authorized representatives of the Secretary and the representative of miners.

(4) Begin sampling, within 8 calendar days after the date the citation is issued, the environment of the affected DWP on consecutive normal work shifts until five valid representative samples are taken.

(l) A citation for violation of the applicable standard shall be terminated by MSHA when the equivalent concentration of each of the five valid representative samples is at or below the applicable standard.

TABLE 71–1—EXCESSIVE CONCENTRATION VALUES (ECV) BASED ON SINGLE, FULL-SHIFT CMDPSU/CPDM CONCENTRATION MEASUREMENTS

Applicable standard (mg/m³)	ECV (mg/m³)	
	CMDPSU	CPDM
2.0	2.33	2.26
1.9	2.22	2.15
1.8	2.12	2.04
1.7	2.01	1.92
1.6	1.90	1.81
1.5	1.79	1.70
1.4	1.69	1.58
1.3	1.59	1.47
1.2	1.47	1.36
1.1	1.37	1.25
1.0	1.26	1.13
0.9	1.16	1.02
0.8	1.05	0.91
0.7	0.95	0.79
0.6	0.85	0.68
0.5	0.74	0.57
0.4	0.65	0.46
0.3	0.54	0.34
0.2	0.44	0.23

TABLE 71–2—EXCESSIVE CONCENTRATION VALUES (ECV) BASED ON THE AVERAGE OF 5 FULL-SHIFT CMDPSU/CPDM CONCENTRATION MEASUREMENTS

Applicable standard (mg/m³)	ECV (mg/m³)	
	CMDPSU	CPDM
2.0	2.15	2.12
1.9	2.05	2.01
1.8	1.94	1.91
1.7	1.84	1.80
1.6	1.74	1.70
1.5	1.63	1.59
1.4	1.53	1.49
1.3	1.43	1.38
1.2	1.33	1.27
1.1	1.22	1.17
1.0	1.12	1.06
0.9	1.02	0.96
0.8	0.92	0.85
0.7	0.81	0.75
0.6	0.71	0.64
0.5	0.61	0.53
0.4	0.51	0.43
0.3	0.41	0.32

§ 71.207

TABLE 71–2—EXCESSIVE CONCENTRATION VALUES (ECV) BASED ON THE AVERAGE OF 5 FULL-SHIFT CMDPSU/CPDM CONCENTRATION MEASUREMENTS—Continued

Applicable standard (mg/m³)	ECV (mg/m³)	
	CMDPSU	CPDM
0.2	0.31	0.22

(m) The District Manager may designate for sampling under this section additional work positions at a surface coal mine and at a surface work area of an underground coal mine where a concentration of respirable dust exceeding 50 percent of the standard in effect at the time the sample is taken, or a concentration of respirable dust exceeding 50 percent of the standard established in accordance with § 71.101, has been measured by one or more MSHA valid representative samples.

(n) The District Manager may withdraw from sampling any DWP designated for sampling under paragraph (m) of this section upon finding that the operator is able to maintain continuing compliance with the applicable standard. This finding shall be based on the results of MSHA and operator valid representative samples taken during at least a 12-month period.

§ 71.207 Respirable dust samples; transmission by operator.

(a) If using a CMDPSU, the operator shall transmit within 24 hours after the end of the sampling shift all samples collected to fulfill the requirements of this part, including control filters, in containers provided by the manufacturer of the filter cassette to: Respirable Dust Processing Laboratory, Pittsburgh Safety and Health Technology Center, 626 Cochrans Mill Road, Building 38, Pittsburgh, PA 15236–3611, or to any other address designated by the District Manager.

(b) The operator shall not open or tamper with the seal of any filter cassette or alter the weight of any filter cassette before or after it is used to fulfill the requirements of this part.

(c) A person certified in sampling shall properly complete the dust data card that is provided by the manufacturer for each filter cassette. The card shall have an identification number identical to that on the cassette used to take the sample and be submitted to MSHA with the sample. Each card shall be signed by the certified person who actually performed the required examinations under 71.205(b) of this part during the sampling shift and shall include that person's MSHA Individual Identification Number (MIIN). Respirable dust samples with data cards not properly completed may be voided by MSHA.

(d) All respirable dust samples collected by the operator shall be considered taken to fulfill the sampling requirements of part 70, 71, or 90 of this title, unless the sample has been identified in writing by the operator to the District Manager, prior to the intended sampling shift, as a sample to be used for purposes other than required by part 70, 71, or 90 of this title.

(e) Respirable dust samples received by MSHA in excess of those required by this part shall be considered invalid samples.

(f) If using a CPDM, the person certified in sampling shall (1) validate, certify, and transmit electronically to MSHA within 24 hours after the end of each sampling shift all sample data file information collected and stored in the CPDM, including the sampling status conditions encountered when sampling each DWP; and (2) not tamper with the CPDM or its components in any way before, during, or after it is used to fulfill the requirements of this part, or alter any sample data files. All CPDM data files transmitted electronically to MSHA shall be maintained by the operator for at least 12 months.

[79 FR 24982, May 1, 2014, as amended at 80 FR 52989, Sept. 2, 2015]

§ 71.208 Respirable dust samples; report to operator; posting.

(a) MSHA shall provide the operator, as soon as practicable, a report with the following data on respirable dust samples submitted or whose results were transmitted electronically, if using a CPDM, in accordance with this part:

(1) The mine identification number;

(2) The DWP at the mine from which the samples were taken;

(3) The concentration of respirable dust, expressed as an equivalent concentration for each valid sample;

(4) The average equivalent concentration of respirable dust for all valid samples;

(5) The occupation code; and

(6) The reason for voiding any sample.

(b) Upon receipt, the operator shall post this data for at least 31 days on the mine bulletin board.

(c) If using a CPDM, the person certified in sampling shall, within 12 hours after the end of each sampling shift, print, sign, and post on the mine bulletin board a paper record (Dust Data Card) of each sample run. This hard-copy record shall include the data entered when the sample run was first programmed, and the following:

(1) The mine identification number;

(2) The DWP at the mine from which the samples were taken;

(3) The concentration of respirable dust, expressed as an equivalent concentration reported and stored for each sample;

(4) The sampling status conditions encountered for each sample; and

(5) The shift length.

(d) The information required by paragraph (c) of this section shall remain posted until receipt of the MSHA report covering these respirable dust samples.

§ 71.209 Status change reports.

(a) If there is a change in operational status that affects the respirable dust sampling requirements of this part, the operator shall report the change in operational status of the mine or DWP to the MSHA District Office or to any other MSHA office designated by the District Manager. Status changes shall be reported in writing or electronically within 3 working days after the status change has occurred.

(b) Each specific operational status is defined as follows:

(1) Underground mine:

(i) Producing—has at least one mechanized mining unit producing material.

(ii) Nonproducing—no material is being produced.

(iii) Abandoned—the work of all miners has been terminated and production activity has ceased.

(2) Surface mine:

(i) Producing—normal activity is occurring and coal is being produced or processed or other material or equipment is being handled or moved.

(ii) Nonproducing—normal activity is not occurring and coal is not being produced or processed, and other material or equipment is not being handled or moved.

(iii) Abandoned—the work of all miners has been terminated and all activity has ceased.

(3) DWP:

(i) Producing—normal activity is occurring.

(ii) Nonproducing—normal activity is not occurring.

(iii) Abandoned—the dust generating source has been withdrawn and activity has ceased.

Subpart D—Respirable Dust Control Plans

Source: 79 FR 24985, May 1, 2014, unless otherwise noted.

§ 71.300 Respirable dust control plan; filing requirements.

(a) Within 15 calendar days after the termination date of a citation for violation of the applicable standard, the operator shall submit to the District Manager for approval a written respirable dust control plan applicable to the DWP identified in the citation. The respirable dust control plan and revisions thereof shall be suitable to the conditions and the mining system of the coal mine and shall be adequate to continuously maintain respirable dust to at or below the applicable standard at the DWP identified in the citation.

(1) The mine operator shall notify the representative of miners at least 5 days prior to submission of a respirable dust control plan and any revision to a dust control plan. If requested, the mine operator shall provide a copy to the representative of miners at the time of notification;

(2) A copy of the proposed respirable dust control plan, and a copy of any

proposed revision, submitted for approval shall be made available for inspection by the representative of miners; and

(3) A copy of the proposed respirable dust control plan, and a copy of any proposed revision, submitted for approval shall be posted on the mine bulletin board at the time of submittal. The proposed plan or proposed revision shall remain posted until it is approved, withdrawn, or denied.

(4) Following receipt of the proposed plan or proposed revision, the representative of miners may submit timely comments to the District Manager, in writing, for consideration during the review process. Upon request, a copy of these comments shall be provided to the operator by the District Manager.

(b) Each respirable dust control plan shall include at least the following:

(1) The mine identification number and DWP number assigned by MSHA, the operator's name, mine name, mine address, and mine telephone number and the name, address, and telephone number of the principal officer in charge of health and safety at the mine;

(2) The specific DWP at the mine to which the plan applies;

(3) A detailed description of the specific respirable dust control measures used to abate the violation of the respirable dust standard; and

(4) A detailed description of how each of the respirable dust control measures described in response to paragraph (b)(3) of this section will continue to be used by the operator, including at least the specific time, place and manner the control measures will be used.

§ 71.301 Respirable dust control plan; approval by District Manager and posting.

(a) The District Manager will approve respirable dust control plans on a mine-by-mine basis. When approving respirable dust control plans, the District Manager shall consider whether:

(1) The respirable dust control measures would be likely to maintain concentrations of respirable coal mine dust at or below the applicable standard; and

(2) The operator's compliance with all provisions of the respirable dust control plan could be objectively ascertained by MSHA.

(b) MSHA may take respirable dust samples to determine whether the respirable dust control measures in the operator's plan effectively maintain concentrations of respirable coal mine dust at or below the applicable standard.

(c) The operator shall comply with all provisions of each respirable dust control plan upon notice from MSHA that the respirable dust control plan is approved.

(d) The approved respirable dust control plan and any revisions shall be:

(1) Provided upon request to the representative of miners by the operator following notification of approval;

(2) Made available for inspection by the representative of miners; and

(3) Posted on the mine bulletin board within 1 working day following notification of approval, and shall remain posted for the period that the plan is in effect.

(e) The operator may review respirable dust control plans and submit proposed revisions to such plans to the District Manager for approval.

Subpart E—Surface Bathing Facilities, Change Rooms, and Sanitary Flush Toilet Facilities at Surface Coal Mines

§ 71.400 Bathing facilities; change rooms; sanitary flush toilet facilities.

Each operator of a surface coal mine shall provide bathing facilities, clothing change rooms, and sanitary flush toilet facilities, as hereinafter prescribed, for the use of miners employed in the surface installations and at the surface worksites of such mine. (NOTE: Sanitary facilities at surface work areas of underground mines are subject to the provisions of § 75.1712 of this chapter *et seq.*)

§ 71.401 Location of facilities.

Bathhouses, change rooms, and sanitary flush toilet facilities shall be in a location convenient for the use of the miners. Where these facilities are designed to serve more than one mine,

Mine Safety and Health Admin., Labor § 71.403

they shall be centrally located so as to be convenient for the use of all miners served by the facilities.

§ 71.402 Minimum requirements for bathing facilities, change rooms, and sanitary flush toilet facilities.

(a) All bathing facilities, change rooms, and sanitary flush toilet facilities shall be provided with adequate light, heat, and ventilation so as to maintain a comfortable air temperature and to minimize the accumulation of moisture and odors, and the facilities shall be maintained in a clean and sanitary condition.

(b) Bathing facilities, change rooms, and sanitary flush toilet facilities shall be constructed and equipped so as to comply with applicable State and local building codes. However, where no State or local building codes apply to these facilities, or where no State or local building codes exist, the facilities shall be constructed and equipped so as to meet the minimum construction requirements in the National Building Code (1967 edition) and the plumbing requirements in the National Plumbing Code (ASA A40.8–1955), which documents are hereby incorporated by reference and made a part hereof. These documents are available for examination at MSHA's Office of Standards, Regulations, and Variances, 201 12th Street South, Arlington, VA 22202–5452; 202–693–9440; and at every MSHA Coal Mine Safety and Health District Office. Copies of the National Plumbing Code (ASA A40.8–1955) may be purchased from the American National Standards Institute, Inc., 25 W. 43rd Street, 4th Floor, New York, NY 10036; *http:// www.ansi.org.*

(c) In addition to the minimum requirements specified in paragraphs (a) and (b) of this section, facilities maintained in accordance with § 71.400 shall include the following:

(1) *Bathing facilities.* (i) Showers shall be provided with both hot and cold water.

(ii) At least one shower head shall be provided where five or less miners use such showers.

(iii) Where five or more miners use such showers, sufficient showers shall be furnished to provide approximately one shower head for each five miners.

(iv) A suitable nonirritating cleansing agent shall be provided for use at each shower.

(2) *Sanitary flush toilet facilities.* (i) At least one sanitary flush toilet shall be provided where 10 or less miners use such toilet facilities.

(ii) Where 10 or more miners use such toilet facilities, sufficient flush toilets shall be furnished to provide approximately one sanitary flush toilet for each 10 miners.

(iii) Where 30 or more miners use toilet facilities, one urinal may be substituted for one flush toilet, however, where such substitutions are made they shall not reduce the number of toilets below a ratio of two flush toilets to one urinal.

(iv) An adequate supply of toilet paper shall be provided with each toilet.

(v) Adequate handwashing facilities or hand lavatories shall be provided in or adjacent to each toilet facility.

(3) *Change rooms.* (i) Individual clothes storage containers or lockers shall be provided for storage of miners' clothing and other incidental personal belongings during and between shifts.

(ii) Change rooms shall be provided with sample space to permit the use of such facilities by all miners changing clothes prior to and after each shift.

[37 FR 6368, Mar. 28, 1972, as amended at 43 FR 12319, Mar. 24, 1978; 67 FR 38385, June 4, 2002; 71 FR 16668, Apr. 3, 2006; 80 FR 52989, Sept. 2, 2015]

§ 71.403 Waiver of surface facilities requirements; posting of waiver.

(a) The Coal Mine Health and Safety District Manager for the district in which the mine is located, after consultation with the appropriate Regional Program Director, National Institute for Occupational Safety and Health, may, upon written application by the operator, and after consideration of any comments filed within 30 days after receipt of the application, waive any or all of the requirements for §§ 71.400 through 71.402 for a period not to exceed 1 year if he determines that—

(1) The operator is providing or making available, under arrangements with one or more third parties, facilities

§ 71.404

which are at least equivalent to those required by the standards, or

(2) It is impractical for the operator to meet the requirement(s) or provide the facility (facilities) for which the waiver is sought.

(b) The waiver shall be in writing and shall set forth the requirement(s) which the operator will not be required to meet or the facilities which the operator will not be required to provide and the specific reason or reasons for such waiver.

(c) Upon receipt of any waiver, the operator shall post a copy of the waiver for at least 30 days on the mine bulletin board required by section 107(a) of the Act.

(d) An extension of the waiver at the end of 1 year may be sought by the operator by filing an application pursuant to § 71.404 no later than 30 days nor more than 60 days prior to the expiration date of the waiver.

(Pub. L. No. 96-511, 94 Stat. 2812 (44 U.S.C. 3501 et seq.))

[37 FR 6368, Mar. 28, 1972, as amended at 47 FR 14696, Apr. 6, 1982; 60 FR 33723, June 29, 1995]

§ 71.404 Application for waiver of surface facilities requirements.

(a) Application for waivers of any requirements of §§ 71.400 through 71.402 shall be in writing, filed with the appropriate Coal Mine Health and Safety District Manager, and shall contain the following information:

(1) The name and address of the mine operator,

(2) The name and location of the mine, and

(3) A detailed statement of the grounds upon which the waiver is requested and the period of time for which it is requested.

(b) At the same time the application is sent to the District Manager, a copy of the application shall be forwarded to the appropriate Regional Program Director, National Institute for Occupational Safety and Health by the operator, and a copy showing the addresses of the appropriate District Manager and Regional Program Director shall be posted by the operator for at least 30 days on the mine bulletin board required by section 107(a) of the Act.

Subpart F—Sanitary Toilet Facilities at Surface Worksites of Surface Coal Mines

§ 71.500 Sanitary toilet facilities at surface work sites; installation requirements.

(a) Each operator of a surface coal mine shall provide and install at least one sanitary toilet in a location convenient to each surface work site. A single sanitary toilet may serve two or more surface work sites in the same surface mine where the sanitary toilet is convenient to each such work site.

(b) Where 10 or more miners use such toilet facilities, sufficient toilets shall be furnished to provide approximately one sanitary toilet for each 10 miners.

(c) Sanitary toilets shall have an attached toilet seat with a hinged lid and a toilet paper holder together with an adequate supply of toilet tissue.

(d) Only flush or nonflush chemical or biological toilets, combustion or incinerating toilets, sealed bag toilets, and vault toilets meet the requirements of this section. Privies are prohibited.

NOTE TO PARAGRAPH (d): Sanitary toilet facilities for surface work areas of underground mines are subject to the provisions of § 75.1712-3 of this chapter.)

[68 FR 37087, June 23, 2003]

§ 71.501 Sanitary toilet facilities; maintenance.

Sanitary toilets provided in accordance with the provisions of § 71.500 shall be regularly maintained in a clean and sanitary condition. Holding tanks shall be serviced and cleaned when full and in no case less than once each week when in use by draining or pumping or by removing them for cleaning and recharging. Transfer tanks and transfer equipment, if used, shall be equipped with suitable fittings to permit complete draining without spillage and allow for the sanitary transportation of wastes. Waste shall be disposed of in accordance with State and local laws and regulations.

Subpart G—Drinking Water

§ 71.600 Drinking water; general.

An adequate supply of potable water shall be provided for drinking purposes in each surface installation and at each surface worksite of the mine.

§ 71.601 Drinking water; quality.

(a) Potable water provided in accordance with the provisions of § 71.600 shall meet the applicable minimum health requirements for drinking water established by the State or community in which the mine is located.

(b) Where no such requirements are applicable, the drinking water provided shall conform to the Public Health Service Drinking Water Standards, 42 CFR part 72, subpart J.

§ 71.602 Drinking water; distribution.

(a) Water shall be piped or transported in sanitary containers. Water systems and appurtenances thereto shall be constructed and maintained in accordance with State and local requirements. Where no such requirements are applicable, water systems and appurtenances shall be constructed and maintained in accordance with the National Plumbing Code (ASA A40.8—1955) which is hereby incorporated by reference and made a part hereof. (For information as to the availability of this code, see § 71.402(b).)

(b) Water transported to the site shall be carried, stored and otherwise protected in sanitary containers constructed of smooth, impervious, heavy gauge, corrosion resistant materials. The containers shall be marked with the words "Drinking Water."

§ 71.603 Drinking water; dispensing requirements.

(a) Water shall be dispensed through a drinking fountain or from a water storage container with an adequate supply of single service cups stored in a clean, sanitary manner. Water shall not be dipped from inside water storage containers. Use of a common drinking cup is prohibited.

(b) Water containers shall remain sealed at all times during use and shall not be refilled with water for reuse without first being cleaned and disinfected with the use of heat or sanitizers.

(c) Drinking fountains from which water is dispensed shall be thoroughly cleaned once each week.

(d) Ice used for cooling drinking water shall not be immersed or in direct contact with the water to be cooled, unless it has been handled in a sanitary manner and unless the ice is made from the same source as the drinking water or from water of a quality equal to the source of the drinking water.

Subpart H—Airborne Contaminants

§ 71.700 Inhalation hazards; threshold limit values for gases, dust, fumes, mists, and vapors.

(a) No operator of an underground coal mine and no operator of a surface coal mine may permit any person working at a surface installation or surface worksite to be exposed to airborne contaminants (other than respirable coal mine dust, respirable dust containing quartz, and asbestos dust) in excess of, on the basis of a time-weighted average, the threshold limit values adopted by the American Conference of Governmental Industrial Hygienists in "Threshold Limit Values of Airborne Contaminants" (1972), which is hereby incorporated by reference and made a part hereof. Excursions above the listed threshold limit values shall not be of greater magnitude than is characterized as permissible by the conference. This paragraph does not apply to airborne contaminants given a "C" designation by the conference in the document. This document is available for examination at MSHA's Office of Standards, Regulations, and Variances, 201 12th Street South, Arlington, VA 22202–5452; 202–693–9440; and at every MSHA Coal Mine Safety and Health District Office. Copies of the document may be purchased from the American Conference of Governmental Industrial Hygienists, 1330 Kemper Meadow Drive, Attn: Customer Service, Cincinnati, OH 45240; 513–742–2020; http://www.acgih.org.

(b) All persons, including employees, shall be withdrawn from any area in which there is a concentration of an

§ 71.701

airborne contaminant given a "C" designation by the Conference which exceeds the threshold limit value (ceiling "C" limit) listed for that contaminant.

[37 FR 6368, Mar. 28, 1972, as amended at 39 FR 17101, May 13, 1974; 43 FR 12319, Mar. 24, 1978. Redesignated at 45 FR 80756, Dec. 5, 1980, as amended at 67 FR 38385, June 4, 2002; 71 FR 16668, Apr. 3, 2006; 80 FR 52990, Sept. 2, 2015]

§ 71.701 Sampling; general requirements.

(a) Air samples will be taken by the Secretary and will be analyzed to determine the concentrations of noxious or poisonous gases, dusts, fumes, mists, and vapors in surface installations and at surface worksites.

(b) Upon written notification by the Secretary to the operator of an underground coal mine or of a surface coal mine, the operator shall conduct any additional air sampling tests and analyses as the Secretary may from time to time require in order to ensure compliance with the standards set forth in § 71.700 in each surface installation and at each surface worksite.

(c) Where concentrations of airborne contaminants in excess of the applicable threshold limit values, permissible exposure limits, or permissible excursions are known by the operator to exist in a surface installation or at a surface worksite, the operator shall immediately provide necessary control measures to assure compliance with § 71.700 or § 71.702, as applicable.

(d) Where the operator has reasonable grounds to believe that concentrations of airborne contaminants in excess of the applicable threshold limit values, permissible exposure limits, or permissible excursions exist, or are likely to exist, the operator shall promptly conduct appropriate air sampling tests to determine the concentration of any airborne contaminant which may be present and immediately provide the necessary control measures to assure compliance with § 71.700 or § 71.702, as applicable.

[37 FR 6368, Mar. 28, 1972. Redesignated at 45 FR 80756, Dec. 5, 1980; 73 FR 11304, Feb. 29, 2008]

§ 71.702 Asbestos standard.

(a) *Definitions.* Asbestos is a generic term for a number of asbestiform hydrated silicates that, when crushed or processed, separate into flexible fibers made up of fibrils.

Asbestos means chrysotile, cummingtonite-grunerite asbestos (amosite), crocidolite, anthophylite asbestos, tremolite asbestos, and actinolite asbestos.

Asbestos fiber means a fiber of asbestos that meets the criteria of a fiber.

Fiber means a particle longer than 5 micrometers (μm) with a length-to-diameter ratio of at least 3-to-1.

(b) *Permissible Exposure Limits (PELs)*—(1) *Full-shift limit.* A miner's personal exposure to asbestos shall not exceed an 8-hour time-weighted average full-shift airborne concentration of 0.1 fiber per cubic centimeter of air (f/cc).

(2) *Excursion limit.* No miner shall be exposed at any time to airborne concentrations of asbestos in excess of 1 fiber per cubic centimeter of air (f/cc) as averaged over a sampling period of 30 minutes.

(c) *Measurement of airborne asbestos fiber concentration.* Potential asbestos fiber concentration shall be determined by phase contrast microscopy (PCM) using the OSHA Reference Method in OSHA's asbestos standard found in 29 CFR 1910.1001, Appendix A, or a method at least equivalent to that method in identifying a potential asbestos exposure exceeding the 0.1 f/cc full-shift limit or the 1 f/cc excursion limit. When PCM results indicate a potential exposure exceeding the 0.1 f/cc full-shift limit or the 1 f/cc excursion limit, samples shall be further analyzed using transmission electron microscopy according to NIOSH Method 7402 or a method at least equivalent to that method.

[73 FR 11304, Feb. 29, 2008, as amended at 73 FR 66172, Nov. 7, 2008]

PART 72—HEALTH STANDARDS FOR COAL MINES

Subpart A—General

Sec.
72.1 Scope.

Subpart B—Medical Surveillance

72.100 Periodic examinations.

Subpart C [Reserved]

Subpart D—Diesel Particulate Matter—Underground Areas of Underground Coal Mines

72.500 Emission limits for permissible diesel-powered equipment.
72.501 Emission limits for nonpermissible heavy-duty diesel-powered equipment, generators and compressors.
72.502 Requirements for nonpermissible light-duty diesel-powered equipment other than generators and compressors.
72.503 Determination of emissions; filter maintenance; definition of "introduced".
72.510 Miner health training.
72.520 Diesel equipment inventory.

Subpart E—Miscellaneous

72.610 Abrasive blasting.
72.620 Drill dust control at surface mines and surface areas of underground mines.
72.630 Drill dust control at underground areas of underground mines.
72.700 Respiratory equipment; respirable dust.
72.701 Respiratory equipment; gas, dusts, fumes, or mists.
72.710 Selection, fit, use, and maintenance of approved respirators.
72.800 Single, full-shift measurement of respirable coal mine dust.

AUTHORITY: 30 U.S.C. 811, 813(h), 957.

SOURCE: 59 FR 8327, Feb. 18, 1994, unless otherwise noted.

Subpart A—General

§ 72.1 Scope.

The health standards in this part apply to all coal mines.

Subpart B—Medical Surveillance

SOURCE: 79 FR 24986, May 1, 2014, unless otherwise noted.

§ 72.100 Periodic examinations.

(a) Each operator of a coal mine shall provide to each miner periodic examinations including chest x-rays, spirometry, symptom assessment, and occupational history at a frequency specified in this section and at no cost to the miner.

(1) Each operator shall use facilities approved by the National Institute for Occupational Safety and Health (NIOSH) to provide examinations specified in paragraph (a) of this section.

(2) The results of examinations or tests made pursuant to this section shall be furnished only to the Secretary, Secretary of Health and Human Services (HHS), and at the request of the miner, to the miner's designated physician.

(b) *Voluntary examinations.* Each operator shall provide the opportunity to have the examinations specified in § 72.100(a) at least every 5 years to all miners employed at a coal mine. The examinations shall be available during a 6-month period that begins no less than 3.5 years and not more than 4.5 years from the end of the last 6-month period.

(c) *Mandatory examinations.* For each miner who begins work at a coal mine for the first time, the operator shall provide examinations specified in § 72.100(a) as follows:

(1) An initial examination no later than 30 days after beginning employment;

(2) A follow-up examination no later than 3 years after the initial examination in paragraph (c)(1); and

(3) A follow-up examination no later than 2 years after the examinations in paragraph (c)(2) if the chest x-ray shows evidence of pneumoconiosis or the spirometry examination indicates evidence of decreased lung function. For this purpose, evidential criteria will be defined by NIOSH.

(d) Each mine operator shall develop and submit for approval to NIOSH a plan in accordance with 42 CFR part 37 for providing miners with the examinations specified in § 72.100(a) and a roster specifying the name and current address of each miner covered by the plan.

(e) Each mine operator shall post on the mine bulletin board at all times the approved plan for providing the examinations specified in § 72.100(a).

Subpart C [Reserved]

Subpart D—Diesel Particulate Matter—Underground Areas of Underground Coal Mines

SOURCE: 66 FR 5704, Jan. 19, 2001, unless otherwise noted.

§ 72.500 Emission limits for permissible diesel-powered equipment.

(a) Each piece of permissible diesel-powered equipment introduced into an underground area of an underground coal mine after May 21, 2001 must emit no more than 2.5 grams per hour of diesel particulate matter.

(b) As of July 19, 2002, each piece of permissible diesel-powered equipment operated in an underground area of an underground coal mine must emit no more than 2.5 grams per hour of diesel particulate matter.

[66 FR 5704, Jan. 19, 2001, as amended at 66 FR 15033, Mar. 15, 2001; 66 FR 27866, May 21, 2001]

§ 72.501 Emission limits for nonpermissible heavy-duty diesel-powered equipment, generators and compressors.

(a) Each piece of nonpermissible heavy-duty diesel-powered equipment (as defined by § 75.1908(a) of this part), generator or compressor introduced into an underground area of an underground coal mine after May 21, 2001 must emit no more than 5.0 grams per hour of diesel particulate matter.

(b) As of July 21, 2003, each piece of nonpermissible heavy-duty diesel-powered equipment (as defined by § 75.1908(a) of this part), generator or compressor operated in an underground area of an underground coal mine must emit no more than 5.0 grams per hour of diesel particulate matter.

(c) As of January 19, 2005, each piece of nonpermissible heavy-duty diesel-powered equipment (as defined by § 75.1908(a) of this part), generator or compressor operated in an underground area of an underground coal mine must emit no more than 2.5 grams per hour of diesel particulate matter.

(d) Notwithstanding the other provisions of this section, a generator or compressor that discharges its exhaust directly into intake air that is coursed directly to a return air course, or discharges its exhaust directly into a return air course, is not subject to the applicable requirements of this section.

[66 FR 5704, Jan. 19, 2001, as amended at 66 FR 15033, Mar. 15, 2001; 66 FR 27866, May 21, 2001]

§ 72.502 Requirements for nonpermissible light-duty diesel-powered equipment other than generators and compressors.

(a) Each piece of nonpermissible light-duty diesel-powered equipment (as defined by § 75.1908(b) of this chapter), other than generators and compressors, introduced into an underground area of an underground coal mine after May 21, 2001 must emit no more than 5.0 grams per hour of diesel particulate matter.

(b) A piece of nonpermissible light-duty diesel-powered equipment must be deemed to be in compliance with the requirements of paragraph (a) of this section if it utilizes an engine which meets or exceeds the applicable particulate matter emission requirements of the Environmental Protection Administration listed in Table 72.502–1, as follows:

TABLE 72.502–1

EPA requirement	EPA category	PM limit
40 CFR 86.094–8(a)(1)(I)(A)(2)	light duty vehicle	0.1 g/mile.
40 CFR 86.094–9(a)(1)(I)(A)(2)	light duty truck	0.1 g/mile.
40 CFR 86.094–11(a)(1)(iv)(B)	heavy duty highway engine	0.1 g/bhp-hr.
40 CFR 89.112(a)	Tier 2 nonroad	Varies by power:
	kW<(hp<11)	0.80 g/kW-hr (0.60 g/bhp-hr).
	8≤kW<19 (11≤hp<25)	0.80 g/kW-hr (0.60 g/bhp-hr).
	19≤kW<37 (25≤hp<50)	0.60 g/kW-hr (0.45 g/bhp-hr).
	37≤kW<75 (50≤hp<100)	0.40 g/kW-hr (0.30 g/bhp-hr).
	75≤kW<130 (100≤hp<175)	0.30 g/kW-hr (0.22 g/bhp-hr).
	130≤kW<225 (175≤hp<300)	0.20 g/kW-hr (0.15 g/bhp-hr).
	225≤kW<450 (300≤hp<600)	0.20 g/kW-hr (0.15 g/bhp-hr).
	450≤kW<560 (600≤hp<750)"	0.20 g/kW-hr (0.15 g/bhp-hr)

TABLE 72.502–1—Continued

EPA requirement	EPA category	PM limit
	kW≥560 (hp≥750)	0.20 g/kW-hr (0.15 g/bhp-hr)

NOTES: "g" means grams; "kW" means kilowatt; "hp" means horsepower; "g/kW-hr" means grams/kilowatt-hour; "g/bhp-hr" means grams/brake horsepower-hour.

(c) The requirements of this section do not apply to any diesel-powered ambulance or fire fighting equipment that is being used in accordance with the mine fire fighting and evacuation plan under § 75.1502.

[66 FR 5704, Jan. 19, 2001, as amended at 66 FR 15033, Mar. 15, 2001; 66 FR 27866, May 21, 2001; 70 FR 36347, June 23, 2005]

§ 72.503 Determination of emissions; filter maintenance; definition of "introduced".

(a) MSHA will determine compliance with the emission requirements established by this part by using the amount of diesel particulate matter emitted by a particular engine determined from the engine approval pursuant to § 7.89(a)(9)(iii)(B) or § 7.89(a)(9)(iv)(A) of this title, with the exception of engines deemed to be in compliance by meeting the EPA requirements specified in Table 72.502–1 (§ 72.502(b)).

(b) Except as provided in paragraph (c) of this section, the amount by which an aftertreatment device can reduce engine emissions of diesel particulate matter as determined pursuant to paragraph (a) must be established by a laboratory test:

(1) on an approved engine which MSHA has determined, pursuant to paragraph (a) of this section, to emit no more diesel particulate matter than the engine being used in the piece of diesel-powered equipment in question;

(2) using the test cycle specified in Table E–3 of § 7.89 of this title, and following a test procedure appropriate for the filtration system, by a laboratory capable of testing engines in accordance with the requirements of Subpart E of part 7 of this title; and

(3) with an aftertreatment device representative of that being used on the piece of diesel-powered equipment in question.

(c) In lieu of the laboratory tests required by paragraph (b), the Secretary may accept the results of tests conducted or certified by an organization whose testing standards are deemed by the Secretary to be as rigorous as those set forth by paragraph (b) of this section; and further, the Secretary may accept the results of tests for one aftertreatment device as evidencing the efficiency of another aftertreatment device which the Secretary determines to be essentially identical to the one tested.

(d) Operators must maintain in accordance with manufacturer specifications and free of observable defects, any aftertreatment device installed on a piece of diesel equipment upon which the operator relies to remove diesel particulate matter from diesel emissions.

(e) For purposes of §§ 72.500(a), 72.501(a) and 72.502(a), the term "introduced" means any piece of equipment whose engine is a new addition to the underground inventory of engines of the mine in question, including newly purchased equipment, used equipment, and equipment receiving a replacement engine that has a different serial number than the engine it is replacing. "Introduced" does not include a piece of equipment whose engine was previously part of the mine inventory and rebuilt.

§ 72.510 Miner health training.

(a) Operators must provide annual training to all miners at a mine who can reasonably be expected to be exposed to diesel emissions on that property. The training must include—

(1) The health risks associated with exposure to diesel particulate matter;

(2) The methods used in the mine to control diesel particulate matter concentrations;

(3) Identification of the personnel responsible for maintaining those controls; and

(4) Actions miners must take to ensure the controls operate as intended.

§ 72.520

(b)(1) An operator must keep a record of the training at the mine site for one year after completion of the training. An operator may keep the record elsewhere if the record is immediately accessible from the mine site by electronic transmission.

(2) Upon request from an authorized representative of the Secretary of Labor, the Secretary of Health and Human Services, or from the authorized representative of miners, mine operators must promptly provide access to any such training record. Whenever an operator ceases to do business, that operator must transfer the training records, or a copy, to any successor operator who must maintain them for the required period.

§ 72.520 Diesel equipment inventory.

(a) The operator of each mine that utilizes diesel equipment underground, shall prepare and submit in writing to the District Manager, an inventory of diesel equipment used in the mine. The inventory shall include the number and type of diesel-powered units used underground, including make and model of unit, type of equipment, make and model of engine, serial number of engine, brake horsepower rating of engine, emissions of engine in grams per hour or grams per brake horsepower-hour, approval number of engine, make and model of aftertreatment device, serial number of aftertreatment device if available, and efficiency of aftertreatment device.

(b) The mine operator shall make changes to the diesel equipment inventory as equipment or emission control systems are added, deleted or modified and submit revisions, to the District Manager, within 7 calendar days.

(c) If requested, the mine operator shall provide a copy of the diesel equipment inventory to the representative of the miners within 3 days of the request.

Subpart E—Miscellaneous

§ 72.610 Abrasive blasting.

(a) *Surface and underground mines.* When an abrasive blasting operation is performed, all exposed miners shall properly use respirators approved for abrasive blasting by NIOSH under 42 CFR part 84, or the operation shall be performed in a totally enclosed device with the miner outside the device.

(b) *Underground areas of underground mines.* Silica sand or other materials containing more than 1 percent free silica shall not be used as an abrasive substance in abrasive blasting.

[59 FR 8327, Feb. 18, 1994, as amended at 60 FR 30401, June 8, 1995]

§ 72.620 Drill dust control at surface mines and surface areas of underground mines.

Holes shall be collared and drilled wet, or other effective dust control measures shall be used, when drilling non-water-soluble material. Effective dust control measures shall be used when drilling water-soluble material.

§ 72.630 Drill dust control at underground areas of underground mines.

(a) Dust resulting from drilling in rock shall be controlled by use of permissible dust collectors, or by water, or water with a wetting agent, or by ventilation, or by any other method or device approved by the Secretary that is as effective in controlling the dust.

(b) *Dust collectors.* Dust collectors shall be maintained in permissible and operating condition. Dust collectors approved under Part 33—Dust Collectors for Use in Connection with Rock Drilling in Coal Mines of this title or under Bureau of Mines Schedule 25B are permissible dust collectors for the purpose of this section.

(c) *Water control.* Water used to control dust from drilling rock shall be applied through a hollow drill steel or stem or by the flooding of vertical drill holes in the floor.

(d) *Ventilation control.* To adequately control dust from drilling rock, the air current shall be so directed that the dust is readily dispersed and carried away from the drill operator or any other miners in the area.

§ 72.700 Respiratory equipment; respirable dust.

(a) Respiratory equipment approved by NIOSH under 42 CFR part 84 shall be made available to all persons as required under parts 70, 71, and 90 of this chapter. Use of respirators shall not be substituted for environmental control measures in the active workings. Each operator shall maintain an adequate supply of respiratory equipment.

(b) When required to make respirators available, the operator shall provide training prior to the miner's next scheduled work shift, unless the miner received training within the previous 12 months on the types of respirators made available. The training shall include: The care, fit, use, and limitations of each type of respirator.

(c) An operator shall keep a record of the training at the mine site for 24 months after completion of the training. An operator may keep the record elsewhere if the record is immediately accessible from the mine site by electronic transmission. Upon request from an authorized representative of the Secretary, Secretary of HHS, or representative of miners, the operator shall promptly provide access to any such training records. The record shall include:

(1) The date of training;
(2) The names of miners trained; and
(3) The subjects included in the training.

[79 FR 24986, May 1, 2014]

§ 72.701 Respiratory equipment; gas, dusts, fumes, or mists.

Respiratory equipment approved by NIOSH under 42 CFR part 84 shall be provided to persons exposed for short periods to inhalation hazards from gas, dusts, fumes, or mists. When the exposure is for prolonged periods, other measures to protect such persons or to reduce the hazard shall be taken.

[79 FR 24986, May 1, 2014]

§ 72.710 Selection, fit, use, and maintenance of approved respirators.

In order to ensure the maximum amount of respiratory protection, approved respirators shall be selected, fitted, used, and maintained in accordance with the provisions of the American National Standards Institute's "Practices for Respiratory Protection ANSI Z88.2–1969," which is hereby incorporated by reference. This publication may be obtained from the American National Standards Institute, Inc., 25 W. 43rd Street, 4th Floor, New York, NY 10036; *http://www.ansi.org*, and may be inspected at any MSHA Coal Mine Safety and Health District Office, or at MSHA's Office of Standards, Regulations, and Variances, 201 12th Street South, Arlington, VA 22202–5452; 202–693–9440; or at the National Archives and Records Administration (NARA). For information on the availability of this material at NARA, call 202–741–6030, or go to: *http://www.archives.gov/federal_register/code_of_federal_regulations/ibr_locations.html*. This incorporation by reference was approved by the Director of the Federal Register in accordance with 5 U.S.C. 552(a) and 1 CFR part 51.

[80 FR 52990, Sept. 2, 2015]

§ 72.800 Single, full-shift measurement of respirable coal mine dust.

The Secretary will use a single, full-shift measurement of respirable coal mine dust to determine the average concentration on a shift since that measurement accurately represents atmospheric conditions to which a miner is exposed during such shift. Noncompliance with the applicable respirable dust standard or the applicable respirable dust standard when quartz is present, in accordance with subchapter O of this chapter, is demonstrated when a single, full-shift measurement taken by MSHA meets or exceeds the applicable ECV in Table 70–1, 71–1, or 90–1 that corresponds to the applicable standard and the particular sampling device used. Upon issuance of a citation for a violation of the applicable standard, and for MSHA to terminate the citation, the operator shall take the specified actions in subchapter O of this chapter.

[79 FR 24986, May 1, 2014]

PART 74—COAL MINE DUST SAMPLING DEVICES

Subpart A—General

Sec.
74.1 Purpose.
74.2 Definitions.

Subpart B—Approval Requirements for Coal Mine Dust Personal Sampler Unit

74.3 Sampler unit.
74.4 Specifications of sampler unit.
74.5 Tests of coal mine dust personal sampler units.
74.6 Quality control.

Subpart C—Requirements for Continuous Personal Dust Monitors (CPDMs)

74.7 Design and construction requirements.
74.8 Measurement, accuracy, and reliability requirements.
74.9 Quality assurance.
74.10 Operating and maintenance instructions.
74.11 Tests of the continuous personal dust monitor.

Subpart D—General Requirements for All Devices

74.12 Conduct of tests; demonstrations.
74.13 Applications.
74.14 Certificate of approval.
74.15 Approval labels.
74.16 Material required for record.
74.17 Changes after certification.
74.18 Withdrawal of certification.

AUTHORITY: 30 U.S.C. 957.

SOURCE: 75 FR 17523, Apr. 6, 2010, unless otherwise noted.

Subpart A—General

§ 74.1 Purpose.

The regulations in this part set forth the requirements for approval of coal mine dust sampling devices for determining the concentrations of respirable dust in coal mine atmospheres; procedures for applying for such approval; test procedures; and labeling.

§ 74.2 Definitions.

(a) *Accuracy:* the ability of a continuous personal dust monitor (CPDM) to determine the "true" concentration of the environment sampled. Accuracy describes the closeness of a typical measurement to the quantity measured, although it is defined and expressed in terms of the relative discrepancy of a typical measurement from the quantity measured. The accuracy of a CPDM is the theoretical maximum error of measurement, expressed as the proportion or percentage of the amount being measured, without regard for the direction of the error, which is achieved with a 0.95 probability by the method.

(b) *Bias:* the uncorrectable relative discrepancy between the mean of the distribution of measurements from a CPDM and the true concentration being measured.

(c) *Coal mine dust personal sampler unit (CMDPSU):* a personal device for measuring concentrations of respirable dust in coal mine atmospheres that meets the requirements specified under Subpart B of this part.

(d) *Continuous personal dust monitor (CPDM):* a sampling device for continuously measuring concentrations of respirable dust in coal mine atmospheres that reports within-shift and end-of shift measurements of dust concentrations immediately upon the completion of the period of exposure that was monitored and that meets the requirements specified under Subpart C of this part.

(e) *ISO:* the International Organization for Standardization, an international standard-setting organization composed of representatives from various national standards-setting organizations. ISO produces industrial and commercial voluntary consensus standards used worldwide.

(f) *Precision:* the relative variability of measurements from a homogeneous atmosphere about the mean of the population of measurements, divided by the mean at a given concentration. It reflects the ability of a CPDM to replicate measurement results.

Subpart B—Approval Requirements for Coal Mine Dust Personal Sampler Unit

§ 74.3 Sampler unit.

A CMDPSU shall consist of:
(a) A pump unit,
(b) A sampling head assembly, and
(c) If rechargeable batteries are used in the pump unit, a battery charger.

§ 74.4 Specifications of sampler unit.

(a) *Pump unit:* (1) *Dimensions.* The overall dimensions of the pump unit, hose connections, and valve or switch covers shall not exceed 4 inches (10 centimeters) in height, 4 inches (10 centimeters) in width, and 2 inches (5 centimeters) in thickness.

Mine Safety and Health Admin., Labor § 74.4

(2) *Weight.* The pump unit shall not weigh more than 20 ounces (567 grams).

(3) *Construction.* The case and all components of the pump unit shall be of sufficiently durable construction to endure the wear of use in a coal mine, shall be tight fitting to minimize the amount of dust entering the pump case, and shall be designed to protect against radio frequency interference and electromagnetic interference.

(4) *Exhaust.* The pump shall exhaust into the pump case, maintaining a slight positive pressure which will reduce the entry of dust into the pump case.

(5) *Switch.* The pump unit shall be equipped with an ON/OFF switch or equivalent device on the outside of the pump case. This switch shall be protected against accidental operation during use and protected to keep dust from entering the mechanisms.

(6) *Flow rate adjustment.* Except as provided in the last sentence of this paragraph, the pump unit shall be equipped with a suitable means of flow rate adjustment accessible from outside the case. The flow rate adjuster shall be recessed in the pump case and protected against accidental adjustment. If the pump is capable of maintaining the flow rate consistency required in this part without adjustment, an external flow rate adjuster is not required.

(7) *Battery.* The power supply for the pump shall be a suitable battery located in the pump case or in a separate case which attaches to the pump case by a permissible electrical connection.

(8) *Pulsation.* (i) The irregularity in flow rate due to pulsation shall have a fundamental frequency of not less than 20 Hz.

(ii) The quantity of respirable dust collected with a sampler unit shall be within ±5 percent of that collected with a sampling head assembly operated with nonpulsating flow.

(9) *Belt clips.* The pump unit shall be provided with a belt clip which will hold the pump securely on a coal miner's belt.

(10) *Recharging connection.* A suitable connection shall be provided so that the battery may be recharged without removing the battery from the pump case or from the battery case if a separate battery case is used.

(11) *Flow rate indicator.* A visual indicator of flow rate shall be provided either as an integral part of the pump unit or of the sampling head assembly. The flow rate indicator shall be calibrated within ±5 percent at 2.2, 2.0, and 1.7 liters per minute to indicate the rate of air passing through the accompanying sampling head assembly.

(12) *Flow rate range.* The pump shall be capable of operating within a range of from 1.5 to 2.5 liters per minute and shall be adjustable over this range.

(13) *Flow rate consistency.* The flow shall remain within ±0.1 liters per minute over at least a 10-hour period when the pump is operated at 2 liters per minute with a standard sampling head assembly.

(14) *Flow restriction indicator.* The pump shall be capable of detecting restricted flow and providing a visual indication if it occurs. The flow restriction indicator shall remain activated until the cause is corrected. The pump shall shut down automatically if flow is restricted for one minute.

(15) *Duration of operation.* The pump with a fully charged battery pack shall be capable of operating for (i) not less than 8 hours at a flow rate of 2 liters per minute against a resistance of 25 inches (64 centimeters) of water measured at the inlet of the pump; and (ii) for not less than 10 hours at a flow rate of 2 liters per minute against a resistance of 15 inches (38 centimeters) of water measured at the inlet of the pump.

(16) *Low battery indicator.* The pump unit shall be equipped with a visual indicator of low battery power.

(17) *Elapsed time indicator.* The pump unit shall be capable of displaying the actual pump run time in minutes (up to 999 minutes) and retaining the last reading after the pump is shut down due to either a flow restriction described in paragraph (a)(14) of this section or low battery power described in paragraph (a)(16) of this section or at the end of the sampling shift.

(b) *Sampling head assembly.* The sampling head assembly shall consist of a cyclone and a filter assembly as follows:

§ 74.5

(1) *Cyclone.* The cyclone shall consist of a cyclone body with removable grit cap and a vortex finder and shall be constructed of nylon or a material equivalent in performance. The dimensions of the components, with the exception of the grit cap, shall be identical to those of a Dorr-Oliver 10 millimeter cyclone body, part No. 28541/4A or 01B11476–01 and vortex finder, part No. 28541/4B.

(2) *Filter assembly.* The filter assembly shall meet the following requirements:

(i) *Filter.* The filter shall be a membrane filter type with a nominal pore size not over 5 micrometers. It shall be nonhydroscopic and shall not dissolve or decompose when immersed in ethyl or isopropyl alcohol. The strength and surface characteristics of the filter shall be such that dust deposited on its surface may be removed by ultrasonic methods without tearing the filter. The filter resistance shall not exceed 2 inches (0.5 centimeters) of water at an airflow rate of 2 liters per minute.

(ii) *Capsule.* The capsule enclosing the filter shall not permit sample air to leak around the filter and shall prevent visual inspection of the filter surface or filter loading. The capsule shall be made of nonhydroscopic material. Its weight, including the enclosed filter, shall not exceed 5 grams and it shall be pre-weighed by the manufacturer with a precision of ±0.001 milligrams. Impact to the capsule shall not dislodge any dust from the capsule, which might then be lost to the weight measurement.

(iii) *Cassette.* The cassette shall enclose the capsule so as to prevent contamination and intentional or inadvertent alteration of dust deposited on the filter. The cassette must be easily removable without causing a loss or gain of capsule weight. The cassette shall be designed to prevent contaminants from entering or dust from leaving the capsule when it is not in use, and to prevent the reversal of airflow through the capsule or other means of removing dust collected on the filter.

(3) *Arrangement of components.* The connections between the cyclone vortex finder and the capsule and between the capsule and the ¼-inch (0.64 centimeters) (inside diameter) hose mentioned in paragraph (b)(5) of this section shall be mechanically firm and shall not leak at a rate of more than 0.1 liters per hour under a vacuum of 4 inches (10 centimeters) of water.

(4) *Clamping of components.* The clamping and positioning of the cyclone body, vortex finder, and cassette shall be rigid, remain in alignment, be firmly in contact and airtight. The cyclone-cassette assembly shall be attached firmly to a backing plate or other means of holding the sampling head in position. The cyclone shall be held in position so that the inlet opening of the cyclone is pointing perpendicular to, and away from, the backing plate.

(5) *Hose.* A 3-foot (91 centimeter) long, ¼-inch (0.64 centimeters) (inside diameter) clear plastic hose shall be provided to form an airtight connection between the inlet of the sampler pump and the outlet of the filter assembly. A device, capable of sliding along the hose and attaching to the miner's outer garment, shall be provided.

(c) *Battery charger.* (1) *Power supply.* The battery charger shall be operated from a 110 (VAC) (nominal), 60 Hz power line.

(2) *Connection.* The battery charger shall be provided with a cord and polarized connector so that it may be connected to the charge socket on the pump or battery case.

(3) *Protection.* The battery charger shall be fused, shall have a grounded power plug, and shall not be susceptible to damage by being operated without a battery on charge.

(4) *Charge rates.* The battery charger shall be capable of fully recharging the battery in the pump unit within 16 hours.

§ 74.5 Tests of coal mine dust personal sampler units.

(a) The National Institute for Occupational Safety and Health (NIOSH), Department of Health and Human Services, shall conduct tests to determine whether a CMDPSU that is submitted for approval under these regulations meets the requirements set forth in § 74.4.

(b) The Mine Safety and Health Administration (MSHA), Department of

Labor, will conduct tests and evaluations to determine whether the pump unit of a CMDPSU that is submitted for approval under these regulations complies with the applicable permissibility provisions of 30 CFR 18.68.

§ 74.6 Quality control.

The applicant shall describe the way in which each lot of components will be sampled and tested to maintain its quality prior to assembly of each sampler unit. In order to assure that the quality of the CMDPSU will be maintained in production through adequate quality control procedures, MSHA and NIOSH reserve the right to have their qualified personnel inspect each applicant's control-test equipment procedures and records and to interview the employees who conduct the control tests. Two copies of the results of any tests made by the applicant on the CMDPSU or the pump unit thereof shall accompany an application provided under § 74.13 of this part.

Subpart C—Requirements for Continuous Personal Dust Monitors

§ 74.7 Design and construction requirements.

(a) *General requirement.* Continuous Personal Dust Monitors (CPDMs) shall be designed and constructed for coal miners to wear and operate without impeding their ability to perform their work safely and effectively, and shall be sufficiently durable to perform reliably in the normal working conditions of coal mines.

(b) *Ergonomic design testing.* Prior to submitting an application under § 74.13, the applicant shall develop a testing protocol and test the CPDM to assure that the device can be worn safely, without discomfort, and without impairing a coal miner in the performance of duties throughout a full work shift. The results of the test shall also demonstrate that the device will operate consistently throughout a full work shift under representative working conditions of underground coal miners, including representative types and durations of physical activity, tasks, and changes in body orientation.

(1) The testing protocol shall specify that the tests be conducted in one or more active mines under routine operating conditions during production shifts.

(2) The applicant shall submit the testing protocol, in writing, to NIOSH for approval prior to conducting such testing.

(3) The applicant shall include the testing protocol and written test results in the application submitted to NIOSH as specified in § 74.13.

(4) NIOSH will advise and assist the applicant, as necessary, to develop a testing protocol and arrange for the conduct of testing specified in this paragraph.

(5) NIOSH may further inspect the device or conduct such tests as it deems necessary to assure the safety, comfort, practicality, and operability of the device when it is worn by coal miners in the performance of their duties.

(6) NIOSH may waive the requirement for the applicant to conduct testing under paragraph (b) of this section if NIOSH determines that such testing is unnecessary to assure the safety, comfort, practicality, and operability of the device when it is worn by coal miners in the performance of their duties.

(c) *Maximum weight.* A CPDM shall not add more than 2 kg to the total weight carried by the miner. CPDMs that are combined with other functions, such as communication or illumination, may exceed 2 kg provided that the total added weight carried by the miner does not exceed 2 kg.

(d) *Dust concentration range.* The CPDM shall measure respirable coal mine dust concentrations accurately, as specified under § 74.8, for an end-of-shift average measurement, for concentrations within a range from 0.2 to 4.0 mg/m^3 for respirable coal mine dust. For end-of-shift average concentrations exceeding 4.0 mg/m^3, the CPDM shall provide a reliable indication that the concentration exceeded 4.0 mg/m^3.

(e) *Environmental conditions.* The CPDM shall operate reliably and accurately as specified under § 74.8, under the following environmental conditions:

(1) At any ambient temperature and varying temperatures from minus 30 to plus 40 degrees centigrade;

(2) At any atmospheric pressure from 700 to 1000 millibars;
(3) At any ambient humidity from 10 to 100 percent relative humidity; and
(4) While exposed to water mists generated for dust suppression and while monitoring atmospheres including such water mists.

(f) *Electromagnetic interference.* The CPDM shall meet the following standards for control of and protection from electromagnetic interference.

(1) For emissions control, operators must follow: IEEE Std C95.1–2005, (IEEE Standard for Safety Levels with Respect to Human Exposure to Radio Frequency Electromagnetic Fields, 3 kHz to 300 GHz) and 47 CFR 15.1 through 15.407 (FCC Radio Frequency Devices). Persons must proceed in accordance with IEEE Std C95.1–2005 (IEEE Standard for Safety Levels with Respect to Human Exposure to Radio Frequency Electromagnetic Fields, 3 kHz to 300 GHz).

(i) The Director of the Federal Register approves this incorporation by reference in accordance with 5 U.S.C. 552(a) and 1 CFR part 51. Persons may obtain a copy from: American National Standards Institute (ANSI), 25 West 43rd Street, New York, NY 10036. *http://www.ansi.org.*

(ii) Persons may inspect a copy at MSHA, Office of Standards, Regulations, and Variances, 201 12th Street South, Arlington, VA 22202–5452, 202–693–9440, or at the National Archives and Records Administration (NARA). For information on the availability of this material at NARA, call 202–741–6030, or go to: *http://www.archives.gov/federal_register/code_of_federal_regulations/ibr_locations.html.*

(2) For immunity/susceptibility protection, operators must follow: IEC 61000–4–6, International Standard (Electromagnetic compatibility—Part 4–6: Testing and measurement techniques—Immunity to conducted disturbances, induced by radio-frequency fields), Edition 3.0, 2008–10. Persons must proceed in accordance with IEC 61000–4–6, International Standard (Electromagnetic compatibility—Part 4–6: Testing and measurement techniques—Immunity to conducted disturbances, induced by radio-frequency fields), Edition 3.0, 2008–10. The Director of the Federal Register approves this incorporation by reference in accordance with 5 U.S.C. 552(a) and 1 CFR part 51.

(i) Persons may obtain a copy from the International Electrotechnical Commission at the address provided below:

International Electrotechnical Commission, IEC Central Office, 3, rue de Varembé, P.O. Box 131, CH–1211 GENEVA 20, Switzerland. *http://www.standardsinfo.net.*

(ii) Persons may inspect a copy at MSHA, Office of Standards, Regulations, and Variances, 201 12th Street South, Arlington, VA 22202–5452, 202–693–9440, or at the National Archives and Records Administration (NARA). For information on the availability of this material at NARA, call 202–741–6030, or go to: *http://www.archives.gov/federal_register/code_of_federal_regulations/ibr_locations.html.*

(g) *Durability testing.* The CPDM shall be designed and constructed to remain safe and measure respirable coal mine dust concentrations accurately, as specified under §74.8 of this section after undergoing the following durability tests, which NIOSH will apply to test devices prior to their use in further testing under §74.8 of this-subpart:

Vibration	Mil-Std-810F, 514.5	U.S. Highway Vibration, Restrained Figure 514.5C–1.	1 Hours/Axis, 3 Axis; Total Duration = 3 Hrs, equivalent to 1,000 miles.
Drop	3-foot drop onto bare concrete surface.	In standard in-use configuration.	1 drop per axis (3 total).

(1) Persons must proceed in accordance with Mil-Std-810F, 514.5, Department of Defense Test Method for Environmental Engineering Considerations

and Laboratory Tests, 1 January 2000. The Director of the Federal Register approves this incorporation by reference in accordance with 5 U.S.C. 552(a) and 1 CFR part 51. Persons may obtain a copy from the U.S. Department of Defense at the address provided below.

ASC/ENOI, Bldg. 560, 2530 Loop Road West, Wright-Patterson AFB OH 45433–7101. http://www.dtc.army.mil/navigator/.

(2) Persons may inspect a copy at MSHA, Office of Standards, Regulations, and Variances, 201 12th Street South, Arlington, VA 22202–5452; 202–693–9440; or at the National Archives and Records Administration (NARA). For information on the availability of this material at NARA, call 202–741–6030, or go to: http://www.archives.gov/federal_register/code_of_federal_regulations/ibr_locations.html.

(h) *Reporting of monitoring results.* (1) The CPDM shall report continuous monitoring results legibly or audibly during use. A digital display, if used, shall be illuminated and shall provide a minimum character height of 6 millimeters. Other forms of display (*e.g.*, analogue) must provide comparable visibility. Auditory reporting, if used, shall be clear, have adjustable volume, and provide means for the user to obtain data reports repetitively. The CPDM shall also report end-of-shift results using computer software compatible with current, commonly used personal computer technology.

(2) The CPDM shall report results as cumulative mass concentration in units of mass per volume of air (mg/m^3) with two significant figures of accuracy rounded as customary.

(i) *Power requirements.* The power source of the CPDM shall have sufficient capacity to enable continuous sampling for 12 hours in a coal mine dust atmosphere of up to 4.0 mg/m^3. If the CPDM uses a rechargeable battery, the battery charger shall be operated from a 110 (VAC) (nominal), 60 Hz power line.

(j) *Flow stability and calibration of pump.* If a pump is used, the flow shall not vary more than ±5 percent of the calibrated flow for 95 percent of samples taken for any continuous duration for up to 12 hours. The flow calibration maintenance interval to assure such performance shall be specified in the calibration instructions for the device.

(k) *Battery check.* If the CPDM uses a rechargeable battery, the CPDM shall have a feature to indicate to the user that the device is sufficiently charged to operate and provide accurate measurements for an entire shift of 12 hours under normal conditions of use.

(l) *Integration with other personal mining equipment.* (1) If the CPDM is integrated or shares functions with any other devices used in mines, such as cap lights or power sources, then the applicant shall obtain approvals for such other devices, prior to receiving final certification of the CPDM under this section.

(2) A CPDM that is integrated with another device shall be tested, according to all the requirements under this part, with the other device coupled to the CPDM and operating.

(m) *Tampering safeguards or indicators.* The CPDM shall include a safeguard or indicator which either prevents intentional or inadvertent altering of the measuring or reporting functions or indicates that the measuring or reporting functions have been altered.

(n) *Maintenance features.* The CPDM shall be designed to assure that the device can be cleaned and maintained to perform accurately and reliably for the duration of its service life.

[75 FR 17523, Apr. 6, 2010, as amended at 80 FR 52990, Sept. 2, 2015]

§ 74.8 Measurement, accuracy, and reliability requirements.

(a) *Breathing zone measurement requirement.* The CPDM shall be capable of measuring respirable dust within the personal breathing zone of the miner whose exposure is being monitored.

(b) *Accuracy.* The ability of a CPDM to determine the true concentration of respirable coal mine dust at the end of a shift shall be established through testing that demonstrates the following:

(1) For full-shift measurements of 8 hours or more, a 95 percent confidence that the recorded measurements are

within ±25 percent of the true respirable dust concentration, as determined by CMDPSU reference measurements, over a concentration range from 0.2 to 4.0 mg/m³; and

(2) For intra-shift measurements of less than 8 hours, a 95 percent confidence that the recorded measurements are within ±25 percent of the true respirable dust concentration, as determined by CMDPSU reference measurements, over the concentration range equivalent to 0.2 to 4.0 mg/m³ for an 8-hour period.[1]

(c) *Reliability of measurements.* The CPDM shall meet the accuracy requirements under paragraph (b) of this section, regardless of the variation in density, composition, size distribution of respirable coal mine dust particles, and the presence of water spray mist in coal mines.

(d) *Precision.* The precision of the CPDM shall be established through testing to determine the variability of multiple measurements of the same dust concentration, as defined by the relative standard deviation of the distribution of measurements. The relative standard deviation shall be less than 0.1275 without bias for both full-shift measurements of 8 hours or more, and for intra-shift measurements of less than 8 hours within the dust concentration range equivalent to 0.2 to 4.0 mg/m³ for an 8-hour period, as specified under paragraph (b)(2) of this section.

(e) *Bias.* The bias of the CPDM measurements shall be limited such that the uncorrectable discrepancy between the mean of the distribution of measurements and the true dust concentration being measured during testing shall be no greater than 10 percent. Bias must be constant over the range of dust concentration levels tested, 0.2 to 4.0 mg/m³ for an 8-hour sampling period.

(f) *Testing conditions.* Laboratory and mine testing of the CPDM for accuracy, precision, bias, and reliability under diverse environmental conditions (as defined under § 74.7(e) and (g)) shall be determined using the NIOSH testing procedure, "Continuous Personal Dust Monitor Accuracy Testing," June 23, 2008, available at: *http:// www.cdc.gov/niosh/mining/pubs/ pubreference/outputid3076.htm.* All testing results shall be submitted to NIOSH in writing on the application filed under § 74.11.

(1) Persons must proceed in accordance with NIOSH testing procedure "Continuous Personal Dust Monitor Accuracy Testing," June 23, 2008. The Director of the Federal Register approves this incorporation by reference in accordance with 5 U.S.C. 552(a) and 1 CFR part 51. Persons may obtain a copy at the address below: NIOSH–Publications Dissemination, 4676 Columbia Parkway, Cincinnati, OH 45226. *http:// www.cdc.gov/niosh/mining.*

(2) Persons may inspect a copy at MSHA, Office of Standards, Regulations, and Variances, 201 12th Street South, Arlington, VA 22202–5452; 202–693–9440; or at the National Archives and Records Administration (NARA). For information on the availability of this material at NARA, call 202–741–6030, or go to: *http://www.archives.gov/ federal_register/ code_of_federal_regulations/ ibr_locations.html.*

[75 FR 17523, Apr. 6, 2010, as amended at 80 FR 52990, Sept. 2, 2015]

§ 74.9 Quality assurance.

(a) *General requirements.* The applicant shall establish and maintain a quality control system that assures that CPDM devices produced under the applicant's certificate of approval meet the required specifications and are reliable, safe, effective, and otherwise suitable for their intended use. To establish and to maintain an approval under this part, the applicant shall:

---

[1] The equivalent dust concentration range to the 8-hour range of 0.2 − 4 mg/m³ is calculated by multiplying this 8-hour range by the dividend of eight hours divided by the duration of the intrashift measurement specified in units of hours. For example, for a measurement taken at exactly one hour into the shift, the 8-hour equivalent dust concentration range would be a one-hour average concentration range of: 8 hours/1 hour × (0.2 − 4 mg/m³) = 1.6 − 32 mg/m³; for a two-hour measurement, the applicable concentration range would be calculated as: 8 hours/2 hours × (0.2 − 4 mg/m³) = 0.8 − 16 mg/m³; for a 4-hours measurement, the equivalent range would be: 0.4 − 8 mg/m³; * * * etc. A CPDM must perform accurately, as specified, for intrashift measurements within such equivalent concentration ranges.

Mine Safety and Health Admin., Labor § 74.10

(1) Submit a copy of the most recent registration under ISO Q9001–2000, American National Standard, Quality Management Systems-Requirements, published by ISO:

(i) With the application for approval under § 74.13 of this part; and

(ii) Upon request by NIOSH, subsequent to the approval of a CPDM under this part.

(2) Persons must proceed in accordance with ISO Q9001–2000, American National Standard, Quality Management Systems-Requirements. The Director of the Federal Register approves this incorporation by reference in accordance with 5 U.S.C. 552(a) and 1 CFR part 51. Persons may obtain a copy from the International Organization for Standardization at the address provided below.

International Organization for Standardization, ISO Central Secretariat, 1, ch. de la Voie-Creuse, Case Postale 56, CH–1211 GENEVA 20, Switzerland. *http://www.standardsinfo.net.*

(3) Persons may inspect a copy at MSHA, Office of Standards, Regulations, and Variances, 201 12th Street South, Arlington, VA 22202–5452; 202–693–9440; or at the National Archives and Records Administration (NARA). For information on the availability of this material at NARA, call 202–741–6030, or go to: *http://www.archives.gov/federal_register/code_of_federal_regulations/ibr_locations.html.*

(b) *Quality management audits.* Upon request, applicants or approval holders must allow NIOSH to inspect the quality management procedures and records, and to interview any employees who may be knowledgeable of quality management processes associated with the production of the CPDM. Audits may be conducted either on an occasional or periodic basis or in response to quality-related complaints or concerns.

(c) *Applicant remediation of quality management deficiencies.* An applicant or approval holder must correct any quality management deficiency identified by an audit within a reasonable time as determined by NIOSH. Failure to correct a deficiency may result in NIOSH disapproval of a pending application or, in the case of an approved device, revocation of approval until NIOSH determines that the deficiency is corrected.

[75 FR 17523, Apr. 6, 2010, as amended at 80 FR 52990, Sept. 2, 2015]

§ 74.10 **Operating and maintenance instructions.**

(a) *Contents.* The manufacturer must include operating and storage instructions and a maintenance and service life plan with each new CPDM device sold. These documents must be clearly written.

(1) Operating and storage instructions must include:

(i) An explanation of how the CPDM works;

(ii) A schematic diagram of the CPDM;

(iii) Procedures for wearing and use of the CPDM;

(iv) A one page "quick start guide" that will enable a novice to start and operate the CPDM.

(v) Procedures for calibration of the CPDM;

(vi) Procedures for inspecting the operating condition of the CPDM;

(vii) Procedures and conditions for storage, including the identification of any storage conditions that would likely impair the effective functioning of the CPDM; and

(viii) Procedures and conditions of use, including identification of any conditions of use that would likely impair the effective functioning of the CPDM.

(2) The maintenance and service life plan must address:

(i) Conditions that should govern the removal from service of the CPDM; and

(ii) Procedures that a user or others should follow when inspecting, performing maintenance and calibration, and determining when the CPDM should be removed from service.

(b) *Submission to NIOSH for approval.* A copy of the instructions and plan under paragraph (a) of this section shall be submitted to NIOSH with the application for approval of the CPDM and if substantive changes are made to the approved device or approved instructions.

§ 74.11 Tests of the continuous personal dust monitor.

(a) *Applicant testing.* The applicant shall conduct tests to determine whether a CPDM that is submitted for approval under these regulations meets the requirements specified in §§ 74.7–74.8 of this part, with the exception of durability testing, which shall be conducted by NIOSH as specified in § 74.7(g) of this part. Applicant testing shall be performed by an independent testing entity approved by NIOSH.

(b) *NIOSH testing assistance.* NIOSH will provide consultation to the applicant to identify and secure necessary testing services for meeting the requirements specified in §§ 74.7–74.8 of this part. Applicants must submit testing protocols to NIOSH prior to testing to verify that the testing protocols adequately address the requirements.

(c) *Reporting of applicant testing results.* The applicant shall include the results from testing specified under paragraph (a) of this section when submitting the application under § 74.13 of this part to NIOSH.

(d) *Intrinsic safety testing.* The applicant shall submit the CPDM to MSHA for testing and evaluation, pursuant to 30 CFR 18.68, to determine whether the electronic components of the CPDM submitted for approval meet the applicable permissibility provisions.

Subpart D—General Requirements for All Devices

§ 74.12 Conduct of tests; demonstrations.

(a) Prior to the issuance of a certificate of approval, only personnel of MSHA and NIOSH, representatives of the applicant, and such other persons as may be mutually agreed upon may observe the tests conducted. MSHA and NIOSH shall hold as confidential, and shall not disclose, principles of patentable features, nor shall MSHA or NIOSH disclose any details of the applicant's drawings or specifications or other related material.

(b) After the issuance of a certificate of approval, MSHA or NIOSH will conduct such public demonstrations and tests of the approved device as MSHA or NIOSH deem appropriate, and may reveal the protocols and results of testing considered for the approval of the device. The conduct of any additional investigations, tests, and demonstrations shall be under the sole direction of MSHA and NIOSH and any other persons shall be present only as observers.

§ 74.13 Applications.

(a) Testing of a CMDPSU will be performed by NIOSH, and testing of the pump unit of the CMDPSU will be conducted by MSHA. The applicant must submit a written application in duplicate to both NIOSH and MSHA. Each copy of the application must be accompanied by complete scale drawings, specifications, and a description of materials. Ten complete CMDPSUs must be submitted to NIOSH with the application, and one pump unit must be submitted to MSHA.

(b) Testing of a CPDM will be performed by the applicant as specified under § 74.11. The applicant must submit a written application in duplicate to both NIOSH and MSHA. Each copy of the application must be accompanied by complete scale drawings, specifications, a description of materials, and a copy of the testing protocol and test results which were provided by an independent testing entity, as specified in § 74.11(a). Three complete CPDM units must be sent to NIOSH with the application, and one CPDM device must be sent to MSHA.

(c) Complete drawings and specifications accompanying each copy of the application shall be fully detailed to identify the design of the CMDPSU or pump unit thereof or of the CPDM and to disclose the dimensions and materials of all component parts.

§ 74.14 Certificate of approval.

(a) Upon completion of the testing of a CMDPSU or the pump unit or after review of testing protocols and testing results for the CPDM, NIOSH or MSHA, as appropriate, shall issue to the applicant either a certificate of approval or a written notice of disapproval. NIOSH will not issue a certificate of approval unless MSHA has first issued a certificate of approval for either the pump unit of a CMDPSU or for the CPDM. If a certificate of approval is issued, no test data or detailed results of tests will accompany such approval. If a notice of disapproval is issued, it will be accompanied by details of the defects, resulting in disapproval, with a view to possible correction.

(b) A certificate of approval will be accompanied by a list of the drawings and specifications covering the details of design and construction of the CMDPSU and the pump unit, or of the CPDM, as appropriate, upon which the certificate of approval is based. The applicant shall keep exact duplicates of the drawings and specifications submitted to NIOSH and to MSHA relating to the CMDPSU, the pump unit thereof, or the CPDM, which has received a certificate of approval. The approved drawings and specifications shall be adhered to exactly in the production of the certified CMDPSU, including the pump unit or of the CPDM, for commercial purposes. In addition, the applicant shall observe such procedures for, and keep such records of, the control of component parts as either MSHA or NIOSH may in writing require as a condition of approval.

§ 74.15 Approval labels.

(a) Certificate of approval will be accompanied by photographs of designs for the approval labels to be affixed to each CMDPSU or CPDM, as appropriate.

(b) The labels showing approval by NIOSH and by MSHA shall contain such information as MSHA or NIOSH may require and shall be reproduced legibly on the outside of a CMDPSU or CPDM, as appropriate, as directed by NIOSH or MSHA.

(c) The applicant shall submit full-scale designs or reproductions of approval labels and a sketch or description of the position of the labels on each sampling device.

(d) Use of the approval labels obligates the applicant to whom the certificate of approval was issued to maintain the quality of the complete CMDPSU or CPDM, as appropriate, and to guarantee that the complete CMDPSU or CPDM, as appropriate, is manufactured or assembled according to the drawings and specifications upon which the certificate of approval was based. Use of the approval labels is authorized only on CMDPSUs or CPDMs, as appropriate, that conform to the drawings and specifications upon which the certificate of approval we based.

§ 74.16 Material required for record.

(a) As part of the permanent record of the approval application process, NIOSH will retain a complete CMDPSU or CPDM, as appropriate, and MSHA will retain a CMDPSU or CPDM, as appropriate, that has been tested and certified. Material not required for record purposes will be returned to the applicant at the applicant's request and expense upon receipt of written shipping instructions by MSHA or NIOSH.

(b) As soon as a CMDPSU or CPDM, as appropriate, is commercially available, the applicant shall deliver a complete sampling device free of charge to NIOSH at the address specified on the NIOSH Web page: http://www.cdc.gov/niosh/mining.

§ 74.17 Changes after certification.

(a) If the applicant desires to change any feature of a certified CMDPSU or a certified CPDM, the applicant shall first obtain the approval of NIOSH pursuant to the following procedures:

(1) Application shall be made as for an original certificate of approval, requesting that the existing certification be extended to encompass the proposed change. The application shall be accompanied by drawings, specifications, and related material.

(2) The application and accompanying material will be examined by NIOSH to determine whether testing of the modified CMDPSU or CPDM or components will be required. Testing will be necessary if there is a possibility that the modification may adversely affect the performance of the CMDPSU or CPDM. NIOSH will inform the applicant whether such testing is required.

(3) If the proposed modification meets the pertinent requirements of these regulations, a formal extension of certification will be issued, accompanied by a list of new and revised drawings and specifications to be added to those already on file as the basis for the extension of certification.

§ 74.18

(b) If a change is proposed in a pump unit of a certified CMDPSU or in electrical components of a CPDM, the approval of MSHA with respect to intrinsic safety shall be obtained in accordance with the procedures set forth in § 74.11(d).

§ 74.18 Withdrawal of certification.

Any certificate of approval issued under this part may be revoked for cause by NIOSH or MSHA which issued the certificate.

PART 75—MANDATORY SAFETY STANDARDS—UNDERGROUND COAL MINES

Subpart A—General

Sec.
75.1 Scope.
75.2 Definitions.

Subpart B—Qualified and Certified Persons

75.100 Certified person.
75.150 Tests for methane and for oxygen deficiency; qualified person.
75.151 Tests for methane; qualified person; additional requirement.
75.152 Tests of air flow; qualified person.
75.153 Electrical work; qualified person.
75.154 Repair of energized surface high voltage lines; qualified person.
75.155 Qualified hoisting engineer; qualifications.
75.156 AMS operator, qualifications.
75.159 Records of certified and qualified persons.
75.160 Training programs.
75.161 Plans for training programs.

Subpart C—Roof Support

75.200 Scope.
75.201 Definitions.
75.202 Protection from falls of roof, face and ribs.
75.203 Mining methods.
75.204 Roof bolting.
75.205 Installation of roof support using mining machines with integral roof bolters.
75.206 Conventional roof support.
75.207 Pillar recovery.
75.208 Warning devices.
75.209 Automated Temporary Roof Support (ATRS) systems.
75.210 Manual installation of temporary support.
75.211 Roof testing and scaling.
75.212 Rehabilitation of areas with unsupported roof.
75.213 Roof support removal.
75.214 Supplemental support materials, equipment and tools.
75.215 Longwall mining systems.
75.220 Roof control plan.
75.221 Roof control plan information.
75.222 Roof control plan—approval criteria.
75.223 Evaluation and revision of roof control plan.

Subpart D—Ventilation

75.300 Scope.
75.301 Definitions.
75.302 Main mine fans.
75.310 Installation of main mine fans.
75.311 Main mine fan operation.
75.312 Main mine fan examinations and records.
75.313 Main mine fan stoppage with persons underground.
75.320 Air quality detectors and measurement devices.
75.321 Air quality.
75.322 Harmful quantities of noxious gases.
75.323 Actions for excessive methane.
75.324 Intentional changes in the ventilation system.
75.325 Air quantity.
75.326 Mean entry air velocity.
75.327 Air courses and trolley haulage systems.
75.330 Face ventilation control devices.
75.331 Auxiliary fans and tubing.
75.332 Working sections and working places.
75.333 Ventilation controls.
75.334 Worked-out areas and areas where pillars are being recovered.
75.335 Seal strengths, design applications, and installation.
75.336 Sampling and monitoring requirements.
75.337 Construction and repair of seals.
75.338 Training.
75.339 Seals records.
75.340 Underground electrical installations.
75.341 Direct-fired intake air heaters.
75.342 Methane monitors.
75.343 Underground shops.
75.344 Compressors.
75.350 Belt air course ventilation.
75.351 Atmospheric monitoring systems.
75.352 Actions in response to AMS malfunction, alert, or alarm signals.
75.360 Preshift examination at fixed intervals.
75.361 Supplemental examination.
75.362 On-shift examination.
75.363 Hazardous conditions and violations of mandatory health or safety standards; posting, correcting, and recording.
75.364 Weekly examination.
75.370 Mine ventilation plan; submission and approval.
75.371 Mine ventilation plan; contents.
75.372 Mine ventilation map.
75.373 Reopening mines.
75.380 Escapeways; bituminous and lignite mines.

Mine Safety and Health Admin., Labor   Pt. 75

75.381 Escapeways; anthracite mines.
75.382 Mechanical escape facilities.
75.384 Longwall and shortwall travelways.
75.385 Opening new mines.
75.386 Final mining of pillars.
75.388 Boreholes in advance of mining.
75.389 Mining into inaccessible areas.

Subpart E—Combustible Materials and Rock Dusting

75.400 Accumulation of combustible materials.
75.400-1 Definitions.
75.400-2 Cleanup program.
75.401 Abatement of dust; water or water with a wetting agent.
75.401-1 Excessive amounts of dust.
75.402 Rock dusting.
75.402-1 Definition.
75.402-2 Exceptions.
75.403 Maintenance of incombustible content of rock dust.
75.403-1 Incombustible content.
75.404 Exemption of anthracite mines.

Subpart F—Electrical Equipment—General

75.500 Permissible electric equipment.
75.500-1 Other low horsepower electric face equipment.
75.501 Permissible electric face equipment; coal seams above water table.
75.501-1 Coal seams above the water table.
75.501-2 Permissible electric face equipment.
75.501-3 New openings; mines above water table and never classed gassy.
75.502 Permits for noncompliance.
75.503 Permissible electric face equipment; maintenance.
75.503-1 Statement listing all electric face equipment.
75.504 Permissibility of new, replacement, used, reconditioned, additional, and rebuilt electric face equipment.
75.505 Mines classed gassy; use and maintenance of permissible electric face equipment.
75.506 Electric face equipment; requirements for permissibility.
75.506-1 Electric face equipment; permissible condition; maintenance requirements.
75.507 Power connection points.
75.507-1 Electric equipment other than power-connection points; outby the last open crosscut; return air; permissibility requirements.
75.508 Map of electrical system.
75.508-1 Mine tracks.
75.508-2 Changes in electric system map; recording.
75.509 Electric power circuit and electric equipment; deenergization.
75.510 Energized trolley wires; repair.
75.510-1 Repair of energized trolley wires; training.
75.511 Low-, medium-, or high-voltage distribution circuits and equipment; repair.
75.511-1 Qualified person.
75.512 Electric equipment; examination, testing and maintenance.
75.512-1 Qualified person.
75.512-2 Frequency of examinations.
75.513 Electric conductor; capacity and insulation.
75.513-1 Electric conductor; size.
75.514 Electrical connections or splices; suitability.
75.515 Cable fittings; suitability.
75.516 Power wires; support.
75.516-1 Installed insulators.
75.516-2 Communication wires and cables; installation; insulation; support.
75.517 Power wires and cables; insulation and protection.
75.517-1 Power wires and cables; insulation and protection.
75.517-2 Plans for insulation of existing bare power wires and cables.
75.518 Electric equipment and circuits; overload and short circuit protection.
75.518-1 Electric equipment and circuits; overload and short circuit protection; minimum requirements.
75.518-2 Incandescent lamps; overload and short circuit protection.
75.519 Main power circuits; disconnecting switches.
75.519-1 Main power circuits; disconnecting switches; locations.
75.520 Electric equipment; switches.
75.521 Lightning arresters; ungrounded and exposed power conductors and telephone wires.
75.522 Lighting devices.
75.522-1 Incandescent and fluorescent lamps.
75.523 Electric face equipment; deenergization.
75.523-1 Deenergization of self-propelled electric face equipment installation requirements.
75.523-2 Deenergization of self-propelled electric face equipment; performance requirements.
75.523-3 Automatic emergency-parking brakes.
75.524 Electric face equipment; electric equipment used in return air outby the last open crosscut; maximum level of alternating or direct electric current between frames of equipment.
APPENDIX A TO SUBPART F OF PART 75—LIST OF PERMISSIBLE ELECTRIC FARE EQUIPMENT APPROVED BY THE BUREAU OF MINES PRIOR TO MAY 23, 1936

Subpart G—Trailing Cables

75.600 Trailing cables; flame resistance.
75.600-1 Approved cables; flame resistance.
75.601 Short circuit protection of trailing cables.

75.601-1 Short circuit protection; ratings and settings of circuit breakers.
75.601-2 Short circuit protection; use of fuses; approval by the Secretary.
75.601-3 Short circuit protection; dual element fuses; current ratings; maximum values.
75.602 Trailing cable junctions.
75.603 Temporary splice of trailing cable.
75.604 Permanent splicing of trailing cables.
75.605 Clamping of trailing cables to equipment.
75.606 Protection of trailing cables.
75.607 Breaking trailing cable and power cable connections.

Subpart H—Grounding

75.700 Grounding metallic sheaths, armors and conduits enclosing power conductors.
75.700-1 Approved methods of grounding.
75.701 Grounding metallic frames, casings and other enclosures of electric equipment.
75.701-1 Approved methods of grounding of equipment receiving power from ungrounded alternating current power systems.
75.701-2 Approved method of grounding metallic frames, casings and other enclosures receiving power from single-phase 110–220-volt circuit.
75.701-3 Approved methods of grounding metallic frames, casings and other enclosures of electric equipment receiving power from direct current power systems with one polarity grounded.
75.701-4 Grounding wires; capacity of wires.
75.701-5 Use of grounding connectors.
75.702 Protection other than grounding.
75.702-1 Protection other than grounding; approved by an authorized representative of the Secretary.
75.703 Grounding offtrack direct-current machines and enclosures of related detached components.
75.703-1 Approved method of grounding.
75.703-2 Approved grounding mediums.
75.703-3 Approved methods of grounding offtrack mobile, portable and stationary direct-current machines.
75.703-4 Other methods of protecting offtrack direct-current equipment; approved by an authorized representative of the Secretary.
75.704 Grounding frames of stationary high-voltage equipment receiving power from ungrounded delta systems.
75.704-1 Approved methods of grounding.
75.705 Work on high-voltage lines; deenergizing and grounding.
75.705-1 Work on high-voltage lines.
75.705-2 Repairs to energized surface high-voltage lines.
75.705-3 Work on energized high-voltage surface lines; reporting.
75.705-4 Simultaneous repairs.
75.705-5 Installation of protective equipment.
75.705-6 Protective clothing; use and inspection.
75.705-7 Protective equipment; inspection.
75.705-8 Protective equipment; testing and storage.
75.705-9 Operating disconnecting or cutout switches.
75.705-10 Tying into energized high-voltage surface circuits.
75.705-11 Use of grounded messenger wires; ungrounded systems.
75.706 Deenergized underground power circuits; idle days—idle shifts.

Subpart I—Underground High-Voltage Distribution

75.800 High-voltage circuits; circuit breakers.
75.800-1 Circuit breakers; location.
75.800-2 Approved circuit schemes.
75.800-3 Testing, examination and maintenance of circuit breakers; procedures.
75.800-4 Testing, examination, and maintenance of circuit breakers; record.
75.801 Grounding resistors.
75.802 Protection of high-voltage circuits extending underground.
75.803 Fail safe ground check circuits on high-voltage resistance grounded systems.
75.803-1 Maximum voltage ground check circuits.
75.803-2 Ground check systems not employing pilot check wires; approval by the Secretary.
75.804 Underground high-voltage cables.
75.805 Couplers.
75.806 Connection of single-phase loads.
75.807 Installation of high-voltage transmission cables.
75.808 Disconnecting devices.
75.809 Identification of circuit breakers and disconnecting switches.
75.810 High-voltage trailing cables; splices.
75.811 High-voltage underground equipment; grounding.
75.812 Movement of high-voltage power centers and portable transformers; permit.
75.812-1 Qualified person.
75.812-2 High-voltage power centers and transformers; record of examination.

HIGH-VOLTAGE LONGWALLS

75.813 High-voltage longwalls; scope.
75.814 Electrical protection.
75.815 Disconnect devices.
75.816 Guarding of cables.
75.817 Cable handling and support systems.
75.818 Use of insulated cable handling equipment.
75.819 Motor-starter enclosures; barriers and interlocks.
75.820 Electrical work; troubleshooting and testing.

Mine Safety and Health Admin., Labor

75.821 Testing, examination and maintenance.
75.822 Underground high-voltage longwall cables.
75.823 Scope.
75.824 Electrical protection.
75.825 Power centers.
75.826 High-voltage trailing cables.
75.827 Guarding of trailing cables.
75.828 Trailing cable pulling.
75.829 Tramming continuous mining machines in and out of the mine and from section to section.
75.830 Splicing and repair of trailing cables.
75.831 Electrical work; troubleshooting and testing.
75.832 Frequency of examinations; recordkeeping.
75.833 Handling high-voltage trailing cables.
75.834 Training.
APPENDIX A TO SUBPART I OF PART 75—DIAGRAMS OF INBY AND OUTBY SWITCHING

Subpart J—Underground Low- and Medium-Voltage Alternating Current Circuits

75.900 Low- and medium-voltage circuits serving three-phase alternating current equipment; circuit breakers.
75.900-1 Circuit breakers; location.
75.900-2 Approved circuit schemes.
75.900-3 Testing, examination and maintenance of circuit breakers; procedures.
75.900-4 Testing, examination and maintenance of circuit breakers; record.
75.901 Protection of low- and medium-voltage three-phase circuits used underground.
75.902 Low- and medium-voltage ground check monitor circuits.
75.902-1 Maximum voltage ground check circuits.
75.902-2 Approved ground check systems not employing pilot check wires.
75.902-4 Attachment of ground conductors and ground check wires to equipment frames; use of separate connections.
75.903 Disconnecting devices.
75.904 Identification of circuit breakers.
75.905 Connection of single-phase loads.
75.906 Trailing cables for mobile equipment, ground wires and ground check wires.
75.907 Design of trailing cables for medium-voltage circuits.
APPENDIX A TO SUBPART J OF PART 75

Subpart K—Trolley Wires and Trolley Feeder Wires

75.1000 Cutout switches.
75.1001 Overcurrent protection.
75.1001-1 Devices for overcurrent protection; testing and calibration requirements; records.
75.1002 Installation of electric equipment and conductors; permissibility.
75.1003 Insulation of trolley wires, trolley feeder wires and bare signal wires; guarding of trolley wires and trolley feeder wires.
75.1003-1 Other requirements for guarding of trolley wires and trolley feeder wires.
75.1003-2 Requirements for movement of off-track mining equipment in areas of active workings where energized trolley wires or trolley feeder wires are present; pre-movement requirements; certified and qualified persons.

Subpart L—Fire Protection

75.1100 Requirements.
75.1100-1 Type and quality of firefighting equipment.
75.1100-2 Quantity and location of firefighting equipment.
75.1100-3 Condition and examination of firefighting equipment.
75.1101 Deluge-type water sprays, foam generators; main and secondary belt-conveyor drives.
75.1101-1 Deluge-type water spray systems.
75.1101-2 Installation of deluge-type sprays.
75.1101-3 Water requirements.
75.1101-4 Branch lines.
75.1101-5 Installation of foam generator systems.
75.1101-6 Water sprinkler systems; general.
75.1101-7 Installation of water sprinkler systems; requirements.
75.1101-8 Water sprinkler systems; arrangement of sprinklers.
75.1101-9 Back-up water system.
75.1101-10 Water sprinkler systems; fire warning devices at belt drives.
75.1101-11 Inspection of water sprinkler systems.
75.1101-12 Equivalent dry-pipe system.
75.1101-13 Dry powder chemical systems; general.
75.1101-14 Installation of dry powder chemical systems.
75.1101-15 Construction of dry powder chemical systems.
75.1101-16 Dry powder chemical systems; sensing and fire suppression devices.
75.1101-17 Sealing of dry powder chemical systems.
75.1101-18 Dry powder requirements.
75.1101-19 Nozzles; flow rate and direction.
75.1101-20 Safeguards for dry powder chemical systems.
75.1101-21 Back-up water system.
75.1101-22 Inspection of dry powder chemical systems.
75.1102 Slippage and sequence switches.
75.1103 Automatic fire warning devices.
75.1103-1 Automatic fire sensors.
75.1103-2 Automatic fire sensors; approved components; installation requirements.
75.1103-3 Automatic fire sensor and warning device systems; minimum requirements; general.

75.1103-4 Automatic fire sensor and warning device systems; installation; minimum requirements.
75.1103-5 Automatic fire warning devices; actions and response.
75.1103-6 Automatic fire sensors; actuation of fire suppression systems.
75.1103-7 Electrical components; permissibility requirements.
75.1103-8 Automatic fire sensor and warning device systems; examination and test requirements.
75.1103-9 Minimum requirements; fire suppression materials and location; maintenance of entries and crosscuts; access doors; communications; fire crews: high-expansion foam devices.
75.1103-10 Fire suppression systems; additional requirements.
75.1103-11 Tests of fire hydrants and fire hose; record of tests.
75.1104 Underground storage, lubricating oil and grease.
75.1106 Welding, cutting, or soldering with arc or flame underground.
75.1106-1 Test for methane.

TRANSPORTATION, HANDLING AND STORAGE OF LIQUEFIED AND NONLIQUEFIED COMPRESSED GAS CYLINDERS

75.1106-2 Transportation of liquefied and nonliquefied compressed gas cylinders; requirements.
75.1106-3 Storage of liquefied and nonliquefied compressed gas cylinders; requirements.
75.1106-4 Use of liquefied and nonliquefied compressed gas cylinders; general requirements.
75.1106-5 Maintenance and tests of liquefied and nonliquefied compressed gas cylinders; accessories and equipment; requirements.
75.1106-6 Exemption of small low pressure gas cylinders containing nonflammable or nonexplosive gas mixtures.

FIRE SUPPRESSION DEVICES AND FIRE-RESISTANT HYDRAULIC FLUIDS ON UNDERGROUND EQUIPMENT

75.1107 Fire suppression devices.
75.1107-1 Fire-resistant hydraulic fluids and fire suppression devices on underground equipment.
75.1107-2 Approved fire-resistant hydraulic fluids; minimum requirements.
75.1107-3 Fire suppression devices; approved components; installation requirements.
75.1107-4 Automatic fire sensors and manual actuators; installation; minimum requirements.
75.1107-5 Electrical components of fire suppression devices; permissibility requirements.
75.1107-6 Capacity of fire suppression devices; location and direction of nozzles.
75.1107-7 Water spray devices; capacity; water supply; minimum requirements.
75.1107-8 Fire suppression devices; extinguishant supply systems.
75.1107-9 Dry chemical devices; capacity; minimum requirements.
75.1107-10 High expansion foam devices; minimum capacity.
75.1107-11 Extinguishing agents; requirements on mining equipment employed in low coal.
75.1107-12 Inerting of mine atmosphere prohibited.
75.1107-13 Approval of other fire suppression devices.
75.1107-14 Guards and handrails; requirements where fire suppression devices are employed.
75.1107-15 Fire suppression devices; hazards; training of miners.
75.1107-16 Inspection of fire suppression devices.
75.1107-17 Incorporation by reference; availability of publications.
75.1108 Approved conveyor belts.

Subpart M—Maps

75.1200 Mine map.
75.1200-1 Additional information on mine map.
75.1200-2 Accuracy and scale of mine maps.
75.1201 Certification.
75.1202 Temporary notations, revisions, and supplements.
75.1202-1 Temporary notations, revisions, and supplements.
75.1203 Availability of mine map.
75.1204 Mine closure; filing of map with Secretary.
75.1204-1 Places to give notice and file maps.

Subpart N—Explosives and Blasting

75.1300 Definitions.
75.1301 Qualified person.
75.1310 Explosives and blasting equipment.
75.1311 Transporting explosives and detonators.
75.1312 Explosives and detonators in underground magazines.
75.1313 Explosives and detonators outside of magazines.
75.1314 Sheathed explosive units.
75.1315 Boreholes for explosives.
75.1316 Preparation before blasting.
75.1317 Primer cartridges.
75.1318 Loading boreholes.
75.1319 Weight of explosives permitted in boreholes in bituminous and lignite mines.
75.1320 Multiple-shot blasting.
75.1321 Permit for firing more than 20 boreholes and to use nonpermissible blasting units.
75.1322 Stemming boreholes.

Mine Safety and Health Admin., Labor   Pt. 75

75.1323 Blasting circuits.
75.1324 Methane concentration and tests.
75.1325 Firing procedure.
75.1326 Examination after blasting.
75.1327 Misfires.
75.1328 Damaged or deteriorated explosives and detonators.

Subpart O—Hoisting and Mantrips

75.1400 Hoisting equipment; general.
75.1400-1 Hoists; brakes, capability.
75.1400-2 Hoists; tests of safety catches; records.
75.1400-3 Daily examination of hoisting equipment.
75.1400-4 Certifications and records of daily examinations.
75.1401 Hoists; rated capacities; indicators.
75.1401-1 Hoists; indicators.
75.1402 Communication between shaft stations and hoist room.
75.1402-1 Communication between shaft stations and hoist room.
75.1402-2 Tests of signaling systems.
75.1403 Other safeguards.
75.1403-1 General criteria.
75.1403-2 Criteria—Hoists transporting materials; brakes.
75.1403-3 Criteria—Drum clutch; cage construction.
75.1403-4 Criteria—Automatic elevators.
75.1403-5 Criteria—Belt conveyors.
75.1403-6 Criteria—Self-propelled personnel carriers.
75.1403-7 Criteria—Mantrips.
75.1403-8 Criteria—Track haulage roads.
75.1403-9 Criteria—Shelter holes.
75.1403-10 Criteria—Haulage; general.
75.1403-11 Criteria—Entrances to shafts and slopes.
75.1404 Automatic brakes; speed reduction gear.
75.1404-1 Braking system.
75.1405 Automatic couplers.
75.1405-1 Automatic couplers, haulage equipment.

WIRE ROPES

75.1429 Guide ropes.
75.1430 Wire ropes; scope.
75.1431 Minimum rope strength.
75.1432 Initial measurement.
75.1433 Examinations.
75.1434 Retirement criteria.
75.1435 Load end attachments.
75.1436 Drum end attachment.
75.1437 End attachment retermination.
75.1438 End attachment replacement.

Subpart P—Mine Emergencies

75.1500 [Reserved]
75.1501 Emergency evacuations.
75.1502 Mine emergency evacuation and firefighting program of instruction.
75.1503 Use of fire suppression equipment.
75.1504 Mine emergency evacuation training and drills.
75.1505 Escapeway maps.
75.1506 Refuge alternatives.
75.1507 Emergency Response Plan; refuge alternatives.
75.1508 Training and records for examination, maintenance and repair of refuge alternatives and components.

Subpart Q—Communications

75.1600 Communications.
75.1600-1 Communication facilities; main portals; installation requirements.
75.1600-2 Communication facilities; working sections; installation and maintenance requirements; audible or visual alarms.
75.1600-3 Communications facilities; refuge alternatives.

Subpart R—Miscellaneous

75.1700 Oil and gas wells.
75.1702 Smoking; prohibition.
75.1702-1 Smoking programs.
75.1703 Portable electric lamps.
75.1703-1 Permissible lamps.
75.1707-1 New working section.
75.1708 Surface structures, fireproofing.
75.1708-1 Surface structures; fireproof construction.
75.1709 Accumulations of methane and coal dust on surface coal-handling facilities.
75.1710 Canopies or cabs; diesel-powered and electric face equipment.
75.1710-1 Canopies or cabs; self-propelled diesel-powered and electric face equipment; installation requirements.
75.1711 Sealing of mines.
75.1711-1 Sealing of shaft openings.
75.1711-2 Sealing of slope or drift openings.
75.1711-3 Openings of active mines.
75.1712 Bath houses and toilet facilities.
75.1712-1 Availability of surface bathing facilities; change rooms; and sanitary facilities.
75.1712-2 Location of surface facilities.
75.1712-3 Minimum requirements of surface bathing facilities, change rooms, and sanitary toilet facilities.
75.1712-4 Waiver of surface facilities requirements.
75.1712-5 Application for waiver of surface facilities.
75.1712-6 Underground sanitary facilities; installation and maintenance.
75.1712-7 Underground sanitary facilities; waiver of requirements.
75.1712-8 Application for waiver of location requirements for underground sanitary facilities.
75.1712-9 Issuance of waivers.
75.1712-10 Underground sanitary facilities; maintenance.
75.1713 Emergency medical assistance; first-aid.

§ 75.1

75.1713-1 Arrangements for emergency medical assistance and transportation for injured persons; agreements; reporting requirements; posting requirements.
75.1713-2 Emergency communications; requirements.
75.1713-3 First-Aid training; supervisory employees.
75.1713-4 First-aid training program; availability of instruction to all miners.
75.1713-5 First-aid training program; retraining of supervisory employees; availability to all miners.
75.1713-6 First-aid training program; minimum requirements.
75.1713-7 First-aid equipment; location; minimum requirements.
75.1714 Availability of approved self-rescue devices; instruction in use and location.
75.1714-1 Approved self-rescue devices.
75.1714-2 Self-rescue devices; use and location requirements.
75.1714-3 Self-rescue devices; inspection, testing, maintenance, repair, and recordkeeping.
75.1714-4 Additional self-contained self-rescuers (SCSRs).
75.1714-5 Map locations of self-contained self-rescuers (SCSR).
75.1714-6 Emergency tethers.
75.1714-7 Multi-gas detectors.
75.1714-8 Reporting SCSR inventory and malfunctions; retention of SCSRs.
75.1715 Identification check system.
75.1716 Operations under water.
75.1716-1 Operations under water; notification by operator.
75.1716-2 Permit required.
75.1716-3 Applications for permits.
75.1716-4 Issuance of permits.
75.1717 Exemptions.
75.1718 Drinking water.
75.1718-1 Drinking water; quality.
75.1719 Illumination; purpose and scope of §§ 75.1719 through 75.1719-4; time for compliance.
75.1719-1 Illumination in working places.
75.1719-2 Lighting fixtures; requirements.
75.1719-3 Methods of measurement; light measuring instruments.
75.1719-4 Mining machines, cap lamps; requirements.
75.1720 Protective clothing; requirements.
75.1720-1 Distinctively colored hard hats, or hard caps; identification for newly employed, inexperienced miners.
75.1721 Opening of new underground coal mines, or reopening and reactivating of abandoned or deactivated coal mines; notification by the operator; requirements.
75.1722 Mechanical equipment guards.
75.1723 Stationary grinding machines; protective devices.
75.1724 Hand-held power tools; safety devices.
75.1725 Machinery and equipment; operation and maintenance.
75.1726 Performing work from a raised position; safeguards.
75.1727 Drive belts.
75.1728 Power-driven pulleys.
75.1729 Welding operations.
75.1730 Compressed air; general; compressed air systems.
75.1731 Maintenance of belt conveyors and belt conveyor entries.
75.1732 Proximity detection systems.

Subpart S [Reserved]

Subpart T—Diesel-Powered Equipment

75.1900 Definitions.
75.1901 Diesel fuel requirements.
75.1902 Underground diesel fuel storage—general requirements.
75.1903 Underground diesel fuel storage facilities and areas; construction and safety precautions.
75.1904 Underground diesel fuel tanks and safety cans.
75.1905 Dispensing of diesel fuel.
75.1905-1 Diesel fuel piping systems.
75.1906 Transport of diesel fuel.
75.1907 Diesel-powered equipment intended for use in underground coal mines.
75.1908 Nonpermissible diesel-powered equipment; categories.
75.1909 Nonpermissible diesel-powered equipment; design and performance requirements.
75.1910 Nonpermissible diesel-powered equipment; electrical system design and performance requirements.
75.1911 Fire suppression systems for diesel-powered equipment and diesel fuel transportation units.
75.1912 Fire suppression systems for permanent underground diesel fuel storage facilities.
75.1913 Starting aids.
75.1914 Maintenance of diesel-powered equipment.
75.1915 Training and qualification of persons working on diesel-powered equipment.
75.1916 Operation of diesel-powered equipment.

AUTHORITY: 30 U.S.C. 811, 813(h), 957.

SOURCE: 35 FR 17890, Nov. 20, 1970, unless otherwise noted.

EDITORIAL NOTE: The provisions of this part marked [Statutory Provision] appear in Title III of the Federal Coal Mine Health and Safety Act of 1969.

Subpart A—General

§ 75.1 Scope.

This part 75 sets forth safety standards compliance with which is mandatory in each underground coal mine

Mine Safety and Health Admin., Labor § 75.2

subject to the Federal Mine Safety and Health Act of 1977. Some standards also are applicable to surface operations. Regulations and criteria supplementary to these standards also are set forth in this part.

[35 FR 17890, Nov. 20, 1970, as amended at 43 FR 12319, Mar. 24, 1978]

§ 75.2 Definitions.

The following definitions apply in this part.

Act. The Federal Mine Safety and Health Act of 1977.

Active workings. Any place in a coal mine where miners are normally required to work or travel.

Adequate interrupting capacity. The ability of an electrical protective device, based upon its required and intended application, to safely interrupt values of current in excess of its trip setting or melting point.

Anthracite. Coals with a volatile ratio equal to 0.12 or less. The volatile ratio is the volatile matter content divided by the volatile matter plus the fixed carbon.

Approval documentation. Formal papers issued by the Mine Safety and Health Administration which describe and illustrate the complete assembly of electrical machinery or accessories which have met the applicable requirements of 30 CFR part 18.

Certified or registered. As applied to any person, a person certified or registered by the State in which the coal mine is located to perform duties prescribed by this part 75, except that in a State where no program of certification or registration is provided or where the program does not meet at least minimum Federal standards established by the Secretary, such certification or registration shall be by the Secretary.

Circuit-interrupting device. A device designed to open and close a circuit by nonautomatic means and to open the circuit automatically at a predetermined overcurrent value without damage to the device when operated within its rating.

Coal mine. Includes areas of adjoining mines connected underground.

Filter Self-Rescuer (FSR). A type of gas mask approved by MSHA and NIOSH under 42 CFR part 84 for escape only from underground mines and which provides at least 1 hour of protection against carbon monoxide.

Ground fault or grounded phase. An unintentional connection between an electric circuit and the grounding system.

Low voltage. Up to and including 660 volts, medium voltage means voltages from 661 to 1,000 volts; and high voltage means more than 1,000 volts.

Motor-starter enclosure. An enclosure containing motor starting circuits and equipment.

Nominal voltage. The phase-to-phase or line-to-line root-mean-square value assigned to a circuit or system for designation of its voltage class, such as 480 or 4,160 volts. Actual voltage at which the circuit or system operates may vary from the nominal voltage within a range that permits satisfactory operation of equipment.

Permissible. (1) As applied to electric face equipment, all electrically operated equipment taken into or used inby the last open crosscut of an entry or a room of any coal mine the electrical parts of which, including, but not limited to, associated electrical equipment, components, and accessories, are designed, constructed, and installed, in accordance with the specifications of the Secretary, to assure that such equipment will not cause a mine explosion or mine fire, and the other features of which are designed and constructed, in accordance with the specifications of the Secretary, to prevent, to the greatest extent possible, other accidents in the use of such equipment. The regulations of the Secretary or the Director of the Bureau of Mines in effect on March 30, 1970, relating to the requirements for investigation, testing, approval, certification, and acceptance of such equipment as permissible shall continue in effect until modified or superseded by the Secretary, except that the Secretary shall provide procedures, including, where feasible, testing, approval, certification, and acceptance in the field by an authorized representative of the Secretary, to facilitate compliance by an operator with the requirements of § 75.500 within the periods prescribed in § 75.500.

§ 75.100

(2) As applied to equipment other than permissible electric face equipment: (i) Equipment used in the operation of a coal mine to which an approval plate, label, or other device is attached as authorized by the Secretary and which meets specifications which are prescribed by the Secretary for the construction and maintenance of such equipment and are designed to assure that such equipment will not cause a mine explosion or a mine fire. (ii) The manner of use of equipment means the manner of use prescribed by the Secretary.

Qualified person. As the context requires:

(1) An individual deemed qualified by the Secretary and designated by the operator to make tests and examinations required by this part 75; and

(2) An individual deemed, in accordance with minimum requirements to be established by the Secretary, qualified by training, education, and experience, to perform electrical work, to maintain electrical equipment, and to conduct examinations and tests of all electrical equipment.

Respirable dust. Dust collected with a sampling device approved by the Secretary and the Secretary of Health and Human Services in accordance with part 74—Coal Mine Dust Personal Sampler Units of this title. Sampling device approvals issued by the Secretary of the Interior and Secretary of Health, Education, and Welfare are continued in effect.

Rock dust. Pulverized limestone, dolomite, gypsum, anhydrite, shale, adobe, or other inert material, preferably light colored, 100 percent of which will pass through a sieve having 20 meshes per linear inch and 70 percent or more of which will pass through a sieve having 200 meshes per linear inch; the particles of which when wetted and dried will not cohere to form a cake which will not be dispersed into separate particles by a light blast of air; and which does not contain more than 5 percent combustible matter or more than a total of 4 percent free and combined silica (SiO_2), or, where the Secretary finds that such silica concentrations are not available, which does not contain more than 5 percent of free and combined silica.

Secretary. The Secretary of Labor or the Secretary's delegate.

Self-Contained Self-Rescuer (SCSR). A type of closed-circuit, self-contained breathing apparatus approved by MSHA and NIOSH under 42 CFR part 84 for escape only from underground mines.

Short circuit. An abnormal connection of relatively low impedance, whether made accidentally or intentionally, between two points of different potential.

Working face. Any place in a coal mine in which work of extracting coal from its natural deposit in the earth is performed during the mining cycle.

Working place. The area of a coal mine inby the last open crosscut.

Working section. All areas of the coal mine from the loading point of the section to and including the working faces.

[57 FR 20913, May 15, 1992, as amended at 60 FR 30401, June 8, 1995; 67 FR 11001, Mar. 11, 2002]

Subpart B—Qualified and Certified Persons

§ 75.100 Certified person.

(a) The provisions of Subpart D—Ventilation of this part 75 require that certain examinations and tests be made by a certified person. A certified person within the meaning of those provisions is a person who has been certified as a mine foreman (mine manager), an assistant mine foreman (section foreman), or a preshift examiner (mine examiner). A person who has been so certified is also a qualified person within the meaning of those provisions of subpart D of this part which require that certain tests be made by a qualified person and within the meaning of § 75.1106.

(b) A person who is certified as a mine foreman, an assistant mine foreman, or a preshift examiner by the State in which the coal mine is located is, to the extent of the State's certification, a certified person within the meaning of the provisions of subpart D of this part and § 75.1106 referred to in paragraph (a) of this section.

(c)(1) The Secretary may certify persons in the categories of mine foreman, assistant mine foreman, and preshift examiner whenever the State in which persons are presently employed in these categories does not provide for such certification. A person's initial certification by MSHA is valid for as long as the person continues to satisfy the requirements necessary to obtain the certification and is employed at the same coal mine or by the same independent contractor. The mine operator or independent contractor shall make an application which satisfactorily shows that each such person has had at least 2 years underground experience in a coal mine, and has held the position of mine foreman, assistant mine foreman, or preshift examiner for a period of 6 months immediately preceding the filing of the application, and is qualified to test for methane and for oxygen deficiency. Applications for Secretarial certification should be submitted in writing to the Health and Safety Activity, Mine Safety and Health Administration, Certification and Qualification Center, P.O. Box 25367, Denver Federal Center, Denver, Colorado 80225.

(2) A person certified by the Secretary under this paragraph will be a certified person, within the meaning of the provisions for subpart D of this part and § 75.1106 referred to in paragraph (a) of this section, as long as that person continues to satisfy the requirements for qualification or certification and is employed at the same coal mine or by the same independent contractor.

[35 FR 17890, Nov. 20, 1970, as amended at 43 FR 12320, Mar. 24, 1978; 54 FR 30514, July 20, 1989]

§ 75.150 Tests for methane and for oxygen deficiency; qualified person.

(a) The provisions of Subpart D—Ventilation of this part and § 75.1106 require that tests for methane and for oxygen deficiency be made by a qualified person. A person is a qualified person for this purpose if he is a certified person under § 75.100.

(b) Pending issuance of Federal standards, a person will be considered a qualified person for testing for methane and for oxygen deficiency:

(1) If he has been qualified for this purpose by the State in which the coal mine is located; or

(2) The Secretary may qualify persons for this purpose in a coal mine in which persons are not qualified for this purpose by the State upon an application and a satisfactory showing by the operator of the coal mine that each such person has been trained and designated by the operator to test for methane and oxygen deficiency and has made such tests for a period of 6 months immediately preceding the application. Applications for Secretarial qualification should be submitted to the Health and Safety Activity, Mine Safety and Health Administration, Certification and Qualification Center, P.O. Box 25367, Denver Federal Center, Denver, Colo. 80225.

[35 FR 17890, Nov. 20, 1970, as amended at 43 FR 12320, Mar. 24, 1978]

§ 75.151 Tests for methane; qualified person; additional requirement.

Notwithstanding the provisions of § 75.150, on and after January 1, 1971, no person shall be a qualified person for testing for methane unless he demonstrates to the satisfaction of an authorized representative of the Secretary that he is qualified to test for methane with a portable methane detector approved by the Bureau of Mines or the Mine Safety and Health Administration under part 22 of this chapter (Bureau of Mines Schedule 8C).

§ 75.152 Tests of air flow; qualified person.

A person is a qualified person within the meaning of the provisions of Subpart D—Ventilation of this part requiring that tests of air flow be made by a qualified person only if he is a certified person under § 75.100 or a person trained and designated by a certified person to perform such tests.

§ 75.153 Electrical work; qualified person.

(a) Except as provided in paragraph (f) of this section, an individual is a qualified person within the meaning of §§ 75.511 and 75.512 to perform electrical work (other than work on energized surface high-voltage lines) if:

(1) He has been qualified as a coal mine electrician by a State that has a coal mine electrical qualification program approved by the Secretary; or,

(2) He has at least 1 year of experience in performing electrical work underground in a coal mine, in the surface work areas of an underground coal mine, in a surface coal mine, in a noncoal mine, in the mine equipment manufacturing industry, or in any other industry using or manufacturing similar equipment, and has satisfactorily completed a coal mine electrical training program approved by the Secretary; or,

(3) He has at least 1 year of experience, prior to the date of the application required by paragraph (c) of this section, in performing electrical work underground in a coal mine, in the surface work areas of an underground coal mine, in a surface coal mine, in a noncoal mine, in the mine equipment manufacturing industry, or in any other industry using or manufacturing similar equipment, and he attains a satisfactory grade on each of the series of five written tests approved by the Secretary and prescribed in paragraph (b) of this section.

(b) The series of five written tests approved by the Secretary shall include the following categories:

(1) Direct current theory and application;

(2) Alternating current theory and application;

(3) Electric equipment and circuits;

(4) Permissibility of electric equipment; and,

(5) Requirements of subparts F through K of this part 75.

(c) In order to take the series of five written tests approved by the Secretary, an individual shall apply to the District Manager and shall certify that he meets the requirements of paragraph (a)(3) of this section. The tests will be administered in the Coal Mine Safety and Health Districts at regular intervals, or as demand requires.

(d) A score of at least 80 percent of each of the five written tests will be deemed to be a satisfactory grade. Recognition shall be given to practical experience in that 1 percentage point shall be added to an individual's score in each test for each additional year of experience beyond the 1 year minimum requirement specified in paragraph (a)(3) of this section; however, in no case shall an individual be given more than 5 percentage points for such practical experience.

(e) An individual may, within 30 days from the date on which he received notification from the Administration of his test scores, repeat those on which he received an unsatisfactory score. If further retesting is necessary after this initial repetition, a minimum of 30 days from the date of receipt of notification of the initial retest scores shall elapse prior to such further retesting.

(f) An individual who has, prior to November 1, 1972, been qualified to perform electrical work specified in §§ 75.511 and 75.512 (other than work on energized surface high-voltage lines) shall continue to be qualified until June 30, 1973. To remain qualified after June 30, 1973, such individual shall meet the requirements of either paragraph (a) (1), (2), or (3) of this section.

(g) An individual qualified in accordance with this section shall, in order to retain qualification, certify annually to the District Manager, that he has satisfactorily completed a coal mine electrical retraining program approved by the Secretary.

[37 FR 22376, Oct. 19, 1972, as amended at 44 FR 9380, Feb. 13, 1979; 47 FR 23641, May 28, 1982]

§ 75.154 Repair of energized surface high voltage lines; qualified person.

An individual is a qualified person within the meaning of § 75.705 for the purpose of repairing energized surface high voltage lines only if he has had at least 2 years experience in electrical maintenance, and at least 2 years experience in the repair of energized high voltage surface lines located on poles or structures.

§ 75.155 Qualified hoisting engineer; qualifications.

(a)(1) A person is a qualified hoisting engineer within the provisions of subpart O of this part, for the purpose of operating a steam-driven hoist in a coal mine, if he has at least 1 year experience as an engineer in a steam-driven hoisting plant and is qualified by the State in which the mine is located as a steam-hoisting engineer; or

(2) If a State has no program for qualifying persons as steam-hoisting engineers, the Secretary may qualify

persons for this purpose if the operator of the coal mine in which such persons are employed, or the independent contractor, makes an application and a satisfactory showing that each such person has had 1 year experience in operating steam-driven hoists and has held the position of hoisting engineer for a period of 6 months immediately preceding the application. A person's qualification is valid for as long as this person continues to satisfy the requirements necessary for qualification and is employed at the same coal mine or by the same independent contractor.

(b)(1) A person is a qualified hoisting engineer within the provisions of subpart O of this part, for the purpose of operating an electrically driven hoist in a coal mine, if he has at least 1 year experience operating a hoist plant in a mine or maintaining electric-hoist equipment in a mine and is qualified by the State in which the mine is located as an electric-hoisting engineer; or

(2) If a State has no program for qualifying persons as electric-hoisting engineers, the Secretary may qualify persons for this purpose if the operator of the coal mine in which such persons are employed, or the independent contractor, makes an application and a satisfactory showing that each such person has had 1 year experience in operating electric-driven hoists and has held the position of hoisting engineer for a period of 6 months immediately preceding the application. A person's qualification is valid for as long as this person continues to satisfy the requirements for qualification and is employed at the same coal mine or by the same independent contractor.

(c) Applications for Secretarial qualification should be submitted to the Health and Safety Activity, Mine Safety and Health Administration, Certification and Qualification Center, P.O. Box 25367, Denver Federal Center, Denver, Colo. 80225.

[35 FR 17894, Nov. 20, 1970, as amended at 43 FR 12320, Mar. 24, 1978; 54 FR 30515, July 20, 1989]

§ 75.156 AMS operator, qualifications.

(a) To be qualified as an AMS operator, a person shall be provided with task training on duties and responsibilities at each mine where an AMS operator is employed in accordance with the mine operator's approved Part 48 training plan.

(b) An AMS operator must be able to demonstrate to an authorized representative of the Secretary that he/she is qualified to perform in the assigned position.

[73 FR 80612, Dec. 31, 2008]

§ 75.159 Records of certified and qualified persons.

The operator of each coal mine shall maintain a list of all certified and qualified persons designated to perform duties under this part 75.

[35 FR 17890, Nov. 20, 1970, as amended at 60 FR 33723, June 29, 1995]

§ 75.160 Training programs.

[STATUTORY PROVISION]

Every operator of a coal mine shall provide a program, approved by the Secretary, of training and retraining of both qualified and certified persons needed to carry out functions prescribed in the Act.

§ 75.161 Plans for training programs.

Each operator must submit to the district manager, of the Coal Mine Safety and Health District in which the mine is located, a program or plan setting forth what, when, how, and where the operator will train and retrain persons whose work assignments require that they be certified or qualified. The program must provide—

(a) For certified persons, annual training courses in first aid, principles of mine rescue, and the provisions of this part 75; and

(b) For qualified persons, annual courses in performance of the task which they perform as qualified persons.

[63 FR 53761, Oct. 6, 1998]

Subpart C—Roof Support

SOURCE: 53 FR 2375, Jan. 27, 1988, unless otherwise noted.

§ 75.200 Scope.

This subpart C sets forth requirements for controlling roof, face and ribs, including coal or rock bursts, in underground coal mines. Roof control

§ 75.201

systems installed prior to the effective date of this subpart are not affected so long as the support system continues to effectively control the roof, face and ribs.

§ 75.201 Definitions.

Automated temporary roof support (ATRS) system. A device to provide temporary roof support from a location where the equipment operator is protected from roof falls.

Pillar recovery. Any reduction in pillar size during retreat mining.

§ 75.202 Protection from falls of roof, face and ribs.

(a) The roof, face and ribs of areas where persons work or travel shall be supported or otherwise controlled to protect persons from hazards related to falls of the roof, face or ribs and coal or rock bursts.

(b) No person shall work or travel under unsupported roof unless in accordance with this subpart.

§ 75.203 Mining methods.

(a) The method of mining shall not expose any person to hazards caused by excessive widths of rooms, crosscuts and entries, or faulty pillar recovery methods. Pillar dimensions shall be compatible with effective control of the roof, face and ribs and coal or rock bursts.

(b) A sightline or other method of directional control shall be used to maintain the projected direction of mining in entries, rooms, crosscuts and pillar splits.

(c) A sidecut shall be started only from an area that is supported in accordance with the roof control plan.

(d) A working face shall not be mined through into an unsupported area of active workings, except when the unsupported area is inaccessible.

(e) Additional roof support shall be installed where—

(1) The width of the opening specified in the roof control plan is exceeded by more than 12 inches; and

(2) The distance over which the excessive width exists is more than 5 feet.

§ 75.204 Roof bolting.

(a) For roof bolts and accessories addressed in ASTM F432-95, "Standard Specification for Roof and Rock Bolts and Accessories," the mine operator shall—

(1) Obtain a manufacturer's certification that the material was manufactured and tested in accordance with the specifications of ASTM F432-95; and

(2) Make this certification available to an authorized representative of the Secretary and to the representative of miners.

(b) Roof bolts and accessories not addressed in ASTM F432-95 may be used, provided that the use of such materials is approved by the District Manager based on—

(1) Demonstrations which show that the materials have successfully supported the roof in an area of a coal mine with similar strata, opening dimensions and roof stresses; or

(2) Tests which show the materials to be effective for supporting the roof in an area of the affected mine which has similar strata, opening dimensions and roof stresses as the area where the roof bolts are to be used. During the test process, access to the test area shall be limited to persons necessary to conduct the test.

(c)(1) A bearing plate shall be firmly installed with each roof bolt.

(2) Bearing plates used directly against the mine roof shall be at least 6 inches square or the equivalent, except that where the mine roof is firm and not susceptible to sloughing, bearing plates 5 inches square or the equivalent may be used.

(3) Bearing plates used with wood or metal materials shall be at least 4 inches square or the equivalent.

(4) Wooden materials that are used between a bearing plate and the mine roof in areas which will exist for three years or more shall be treated to minimize deterioration.

(d) When washers are used with roof bolts, the washers shall conform to the shape of the roof bolt head and bearing plate.

(e)(1) The diameter of finishing bits shall be within a tolerance of plus or minus 0.030 inch of the manufacturer's recommended hole diameter for the anchor used.

Mine Safety and Health Admin., Labor §75.205

(2) When separate finishing bits are used, they shall be distinguishable from other bits.

(f) *Tensioned roof bolts.* (1) Roof bolts that provide support by creating a beam of laminated strata shall be at least 30 inches long. Roof bolts that provide support by suspending the roof from overlying stronger strata shall be long enough to anchor at least 12 inches into the stronger strata.

(2) Test holes, spaced at intervals specified in the roof control plan, shall be drilled to a depth of at least 12 inches above the anchorage horizon of mechanically anchored tensioned bolts being used. When a test hole indicates that bolts would not anchor in competent strata, corrective action shall be taken.

(3) The installed torque or tension ranges for roof bolts as specified in the roof control plan shall maintain the integrity of the support system and shall not exceed the yield point of the roof bolt nor anchorage capacity of the strata.

(4) In each roof bolting cycle, the actual torque or tension of the first tensioned roof bolt installed with each drill head shall be measured immediately after it is installed. Thereafter, for each drill head used, at least one roof bolt out of every four installed shall be measured for actual torque or tension. If the torque or tension of any of the roof bolts measured is not within the range specified in the roof control plan, corrective action shall be taken.

(5) In working places from which coal is produced during any portion of a 24-hour period, the actual torque or tension on at least one out of every ten previously installed mechanically anchored tensioned roof bolts shall be measured from the outby corner of the last open crosscut to the face in each advancing section. Corrective action shall be taken if the majority of the bolts measured—

(i) Do not maintain at least 70 percent of the minimum torque or tension specified in the roof control plan, 50 percent if the roof bolt plates bear against wood; or

(ii) Have exceeded the maximum specified torque or tension by 50 percent.

(6) The mine operator or a person designated by the operator shall certify by signature and date that measurements required by paragraph (f)(5) of this section have been made. This certification shall be maintained for at least one year and shall be made available to an authorized representative of the Secretary and representatives of the miners.

(7) Tensioned roof bolts installed in the roof support pattern shall not be used to anchor trailing cables or used for any other purpose that could affect the tension of the bolt. Hanging trailing cables, line brattice, telephone lines, or other similar devices which do not place sudden loads on the bolts are permitted.

(8) Angle compensating devices shall be used to compensate for the angle when tensioned roof bolts are installed at angles greater than 5 degrees from the perpendicular to the bearing plate.

(g) *Non-tensioned grouted roof bolts.* The first non-tensioned grouted roof bolt installed during each roof bolting cycle shall be tested during or immediately after the first row of bolts has been installed. If the bolt tested does not withstand at least 150 foot-pounds of torque without rotating in the hole, corrective action shall be taken.

[53 FR 2375, Jan. 27, 1988, as amended at 55 FR 4595, Feb. 8, 1990; 63 FR 20030, Apr. 22, 1998]

§75.205 Installation of roof support using mining machines with integral roof bolters.

When roof bolts are installed by a continuous mining machine with integral roof bolting equipment:

(a) The distance between roof bolts shall not exceed 10 feet crosswise.

(b) Roof bolts to be installed 9 feet or more apart shall be installed with a wooden crossbar at least 3 inches thick and 8 inches wide, or material which provides equivalent support.

(c) Roof bolts to be installed more than 8 feet but less than 9 feet apart shall be installed with a wooden plank at least 2 inches thick and 8 inches wide, or material which provides equivalent support.

§ 75.206 Conventional roof support.

(a) Except in anthracite mines using non-mechanized mining systems, when conventional roof support materials are used as the only means of support—

(1) The width of any opening shall not exceed 20 feet;

(2) The spacing of roadway roof support shall not exceed 5 feet;

(3)(i) Supports shall be installed to within 5 feet of the uncut face;

(ii) When supports nearest the face must be removed to facilitate the operation of face equipment, equivalent temporary support shall be installed prior to removing the supports;

(4) Straight roadways shall not exceed 16 feet wide where full overhead support is used and 14 feet wide where only posts are used;

(5) Curved roadways shall not exceed 16 feet wide; and

(6) The roof at the entrance of all openings along travelways which are no longer needed for storing supplies or for travel of equipment shall be supported by extending the line of support across the opening.

(b) Conventional roof support materials shall meet the following specifications:

(1) The minimum diameter of cross-sectional area of wooden posts shall be as follows:

Post length (in inches)	Diameter of round posts (in inches)	Cross-sectional area of split posts (in square inches)
60 or less	4	13
Over 60 to 84	5	20
Over 84 to 108	6	28
Over 108 to 132	7	39
Over 132 to 156	8	50
Over 156 to 180	9	64
Over 180 to 204	10	79
Over 204 to 228	11	95
Over 228	12	113

(2) Wooden materials used for support shall have the following dimensions:

(i) Cap blocks and footings shall have flat sides and be at least 2 inches thick, 4 inches wide and 12 inches long.

(ii) Crossbars shall have a minimum cross-sectional area of 24 square inches and be at least 3 inches thick.

(iii) Planks shall be at least 6 inches wide and 1 inch thick.

(3) Cribbing materials shall have at least two parallel flat sides.

(c) A cluster of two or more posts that provide equivalent strength may be used to meet the requirements of paragraph (b)(1) of this section, except that no post shall have a diameter less than 4 inches or have a cross-sectional area less than 13 square inches.

(d) Materials other than wood used for support shall have support strength at least equivalent to wooden material meeting the applicable provisions of this section.

(e) Posts and jacks shall be tightly installed on solid footing.

(f) When posts are installed under roof susceptible to sloughing a cap block, plank, crossbar or materials that are equally effective shall be placed between the post and the roof.

(g) Blocks used for lagging between the roof and crossbars shall be spaced to distribute the load.

(h) Jacks used for roof support shall be used with at least 36 square inches of roof bearing surface.

[53 FR 2375, Jan. 27, 1988, as amended at 55 FR 14228, Apr. 16, 1990; 55 FR 20137, May 15, 1990]

§ 75.207 Pillar recovery.

Pillar recovery shall be conducted in the following manner, unless otherwise specified in the roof control plan:

(a) Full and partial pillar recovery shall not be conducted on the same pillar line, except where physical conditions such as unstable floor or roof, falls of roof, oil and gas well barriers or surface subsidence require that pillars be left in place.

(b) Before mining is started in a pillar split or lift—

(1) At least two rows of breaker posts or equivalent support shall be installed—

(i) As close to the initial intended breakline as practicable; and

(ii) Across each opening leading into an area where full or partial pillar extraction has been completed.

(2) A row of roadside-radius (turn) posts or equivalent support shall be installed leading into the split or lift.

(c) Before mining is started on a final stump—

(1) At least 2 rows of posts or equivalent support shall be installed on not more than 4-foot centers on each side of the roadway; and

Mine Safety and Health Admin., Labor §75.210

(2) Only one open roadway, which shall not exceed 16 feet wide, shall lead from solid pillars to the final stump of a pillar. Where posts are used as the sole means of roof support, the width of the roadway shall not exceed 14 feet.

(d) During open-end pillar extraction, at least 2 rows of breaker posts or equivalent support shall be installed on not more than 4-foot centers. These supports shall be installed between the lift to be started and the area where pillars have been extracted. These supports shall be maintained to within 7 feet of the face and the width of the roadway shall not exceed 16 feet. Where posts are used as the sole means of roof support, the width of the roadway shall not exceed 14 feet.

§75.208 Warning devices.

Except during the installation of roof supports, the end of permanent roof support shall be posted with a readily visible warning, or a physical barrier shall be installed to impede travel beyond permanent support.

§75.209 Automated Temporary Roof Support (ATRS) systems.

(a) Except in anthracite mines and as specified in paragraphs (b) and (c) of this section, an ATRS system shall be used with roof bolting machines and continuous-mining machines with integral roof bolters operated in a working section. The requirements of this paragraph shall be met according to the following schedule:

(1) All new machines ordered after March 28, 1988.

(2) All existing machines operated in mining heights of 36 inches or more after March 28, 1989; and

(3) All existing machines operated in mining heights of 30 inches or more but less than 36 inches after March 28, 1990.

(b) After March 28, 1990 the use of ATRS systems with existing roof bolting machines and continuous-mining machines with integral roof bolters operated in a working section where the mining height is less than 30 inches shall be addressed in the roof control plan.

(c) Alternative means of temporary support shall be used, as specified in the roof control plan, when—

(1) Mining conditions or circumstances prevent the use of an ATRS system; or

(2) Temporary supports are installed in conjunction with an ATRS system.

(d) Persons shall work or travel between the support device of the ATRS system and another support, and the distance between the support device of the ATRS system and support to the left, right or beyond the ATRS system, shall not exceed 5 feet.

(e) Each ATRS system shall meet each of the following:

(1) The ATRS system shall elastically support a deadweight load measured in pounds of at least 450 times each square foot of roof intended to be supported, but in no case less than 11,250 pounds.

(2) The controls that position and set the ATRS system shall be—

(i) Operable from under permanently supported roof; or

(ii) Located in a compartment, which includes a deck, that provides the equipment operator with overhead and lateral protection, and has the structural capacity to elastically support a deadweight load of at least 18,000 pounds.

(3) All jacks affecting the capacity of the ATRS system and compartment shall have check valves or equivalent devices that will prevent rapid collapse in the event of a system failure.

(4) Except for the main tram controls, tram controls for positioning the equipment to set the ATRS system shall limit the speed of the equipment to a maximum of 80 feet-per-minute.

(f) The support capacity of each ATRS system and the structural capacity of each compartment shall be certified by a registered engineer as meeting the applicable requirements of paragraphs (e)(1) and (e)(2) of this section. The certifications shall be made available to an authorized representative of the Secretary and representative of the miners.

§75.210 Manual installation of temporary support.

(a) When manually installing temporary support, only persons engaged in installing the support shall proceed beyond permanent support.

(b) When manually installing temporary supports, the first temporary support shall be set no more than 5 feet from a permanent roof support and the rib. All temporary supports shall be set so that the person installing the supports remains between the temporary support being set and two other supports which shall be no more than 5 feet from the support being installed. Each temporary support shall be completely installed prior to installing the next temporary support.

(c) All temporary supports shall be placed on no more than 5-foot centers.

(d) Once temporary supports have been installed, work or travel beyond permanent roof support shall be done between temporary supports and the nearest permanent support or between other temporary supports.

§ 75.211 Roof testing and scaling.

(a) A visual examination of the roof, face and ribs shall be made immediately before any work is started in an area and thereafter as conditions warrant.

(b) Where the mining height permits and the visual examination does not disclose a hazardous condition, sound and vibration roof tests, or other equivalent tests, shall be made where supports are to be installed. When sound and vibration tests are made, they shall be conducted—

(1) After the ATRS system is set against the roof and before other support is installed; or

(2) Prior to manually installing a roof support. This test shall begin under supported roof and progress no further than the location where the next support is to be installed.

(c) When a hazardous roof, face, or rib condition is detected, the condition shall be corrected before there is any other work or travel in the affected area. If the affected area is left unattended, each entrance to the area shall be posted with a readily visible warning, or a physical barrier shall be installed to impede travel into the area.

(d) A bar for taking down loose material shall be available in the working place or on all face equipment except haulage equipment. Bars provided for taking down loose material shall be of a length and design that will allow the removal of loose material from a position that will not expose the person performing this work to injury from falling material.

§ 75.212 Rehabilitation of areas with unsupported roof.

(a) Before rehabilitating each area where a roof fall has occurred or the roof has been removed by mining machines or by blasting—

(1) The mine operator shall establish the clean up and support procedures that will be followed;

(2) All persons assigned to perform rehabilitation work shall be instructed in the clean-up and support procedures; and

(3) Ineffective, damaged or missing roof support at the edge of the area to be rehabilitated shall be replaced or other equivalent support installed.

(b) All persons who perform rehabilitation work shall be experienced in this work or they shall be supervised by a person experienced in rehabilitation work who is designated by the mine operator.

(c) Where work is not being performed to rehabilitate an area in active workings where a roof fall has occurred or the roof has been removed by mining machines or by blasting, each entrance to the area shall be supported by at least one row of posts on not more than 5-foot centers, or equally effective support.

§ 75.213 Roof support removal.

(a)(1) All persons who perform the work of removing permanent roof supports shall be supervised by a management person experienced in removing roof supports.

(2) Only persons with at least one year of underground mining experience shall perform permanent roof support removal work.

(b) Prior to the removal of permanent roof supports, the person supervising roof support removal in accordance with paragraph (a)(1) of this section shall examine the roof conditions in the area where the supports are to be removed and designate each support to be removed.

(c)(1) Except as provided in paragraph (g) of this section, prior to the removal of permanent supports, a row of temporary supports on no more than 5-foot centers or equivalent support shall be installed across the opening within 4 feet of the supports being removed. Additional supports shall be installed where necessary to assure safe removal.

(2) Prior to the removal of roof bolts, temporary support shall be installed as close as practicable to each roof bolt being removed.

(d) Temporary supports installed in accordance with this section shall not be removed unless—

(1) Removal is done by persons who are in a remote location under supported roof; and

(2) At least two rows of temporary supports, set across the opening on no more than 5-foot centers, are maintained between the miners and the unsupported area.

(e) Each entrance to an area where supports have been removed shall be posted with a readily visible warning or a physical barrier shall be installed to impede travel into the area.

(f) Except as provided in paragraph (g) of this section, permanent support shall not be removed where—

(1) Roof bolt torque or tension measurements or the condition of conventional support indicate excessive loading;

(2) Roof fractures are present;

(3) There is any other indication that the roof is structurally weak; or

(4) Pillar recovery has been conducted.

(g) Permanent supports may be removed provided that:

(1) Removal is done by persons who are in a remote location under supported roof; and

(2) At least two rows of temporary supports, set across the opening on no more than 5-foot centers, are maintained between the miners and the unsupported area.

(h) The provisions of this section do not apply to removal of conventional supports for starting crosscuts and pillar splits or lifts except that prior to the removal of these supports an examination of the roof conditions shall be made.

[55 FR 4595, Feb. 8, 1990]

§ 75.214 Supplemental support materials, equipment and tools.

(a) A supply of supplementary roof support materials and the tools and equipment necessary to install the materials shall be available at a readily accessible location on each working section or within four crosscuts of each working section.

(b) The quantity of support materials and tools and equipment maintained available in accordance with this section shall be sufficient to support the roof if adverse roof conditions are encountered, or in the event of an accident involving a fall.

§ 75.215 Longwall mining systems.

For each longwall mining section, the roof control plan shall specify—

(a) The methods that will be used to maintain a safe travelway out of the section through the tailgate side of the longwall; and

(b) The procedures that will be followed if a ground failure prevents travel out of the section through the tailgate side of the longwall.

§ 75.220 Roof control plan.

(a)(1) Each mine operator shall develop and follow a roof control plan, approved by the District Manager, that is suitable to the prevailing geological conditions, and the mining system to be used at the mine. Additional measures shall be taken to protect persons if unusual hazards are encountered.

(2) The proposed roof control plan and any revisions to the plan shall be submitted, in writing, to the District Manager. When revisions to a roof control plan are proposed, only the revised pages need to be submitted unless otherwise specified by the District Manager.

(b)(1) The mine operator will be notified in writing of the approval or denial of approval of a proposed roof control plan or proposed revision.

(2) When approval of a proposed plan or revision is denied, the deficiencies of the plan or revision and recommended changes will be specified and the mine operator will be afforded an opportunity to discuss the deficiencies and changes with the District Manager.

(3) Before new support materials, devices or systems other than roof bolts

§ 75.221

and accessories, are used as the only means of roof support, the District Manager may require that their effectiveness be demonstrated by experimental installations.

(c) No proposed roof control plan or revision to a roof control plan shall be implemented before it is approved.

(d) Before implementing an approved revision to a roof control plan, all persons who are affected by the revision shall be instructed in its provisions.

(e) The approved roof control plan and any revisions shall be available to the miners and representative of miners at the mine.

[53 FR 2375, Jan. 27, 1988; 53 FR 11395, Apr. 6, 1988, as amended at 60 FR 33723, June 29, 1995; 71 FR 16668, Apr. 3, 2006]

§ 75.221 Roof control plan information.

(a) The following information shall be included in each roof control plan:

(1) The name and address of the company.

(2) The name, address, mine identification number and location of the mine.

(3) The name and title of the company official responsible for the plan.

(4) A typical columnar section of the mine strata which shall—

(i) Show the name and the thickness of the coalbed to be mined and any persistent partings;

(ii) Identify the type and show the thickness of each stratum up to and including the main roof above the coalbed and for distance of at least 10 feet below the coalbed; and

(iii) Indicate the maximum cover over the area to be mined.

(5) A description and drawings of the sequence of installation and spacing of supports for each method of mining used.

(6) When an ATRS system is used, the maximum distance that an ATRS system is to be set beyond the last row of permanent support.

(7) When tunnel liners or arches are to be used for roof support, specifications and installation procedures for the liners or arches.

(8) Drawings indicating the planned width of openings, size of pillars, method of pillar recovery, and the sequence of mining pillars.

(9) A list of all support materials required to be used in the roof, face and rib control system, including, if roof bolts are to be installed—

(i) The length, diameter, grade and type of anchorage unit to be used;

(ii) The drill hole size to be used; and

(iii) The installed torque or tension range for tensioned roof bolts.

(10) When mechanically anchored tensioned roof bolts are used, the intervals at which test holes will be drilled.

(11) A description of the method of protecting persons—

(i) From falling material at drift openings; and

(ii) When mining approaches within 150 feet of an outcrop.

(12) A description of the roof and rib support necessary for the refuge alternatives.

(b) Each drawing submitted with a roof control plan shall contain a legend explaining all symbols used and shall specify the scale of the drawing which shall not be less than 5 feet to the inch or more than 20 feet to the inch.

(c) All roof control plan information, including drawings, shall be submitted on 8½ by 11 inch paper, or paper folded to this size.

[53 FR 2375, Jan. 27, 1988, as amended at 60 FR 33723, June 29, 1995; 73 FR 80697, Dec. 31, 2008]

§ 75.222 Roof control plan-approval criteria.

(a) This section sets forth the criteria that shall be considered on a mine-by-mine basis in the formulation and approval of roof control plans and revisions. Additional measures may be required in plans by the District Manager. Roof control plans that do not conform to the applicable criteria in this section may be approved by the District Manager, provided that effective control of the roof, face and ribs can be maintained.

(b) *Roof Bolting.* (1) Roof bolts should be installed on centers not exceeding 5 feet lengthwise and crosswise, except as specified in § 75.205.

(2) When tensioned roof bolts are used as a means of roof support, the torque or tension range should be capable of supporting roof bolt loads of at least 50 percent of either the yield

Mine Safety and Health Admin., Labor § 75.223

point of the bolt or anchorage capacity of the strata, whichever is less.

(3) Any opening that is more than 20 feet wide should be supported by a combination of roof bolts and conventional supports.

(4) In any opening more than 20 feet wide—

(i) Posts should be installed to limit each roadway to 16 feet wide where straight and 18 feet wide where curved; and

(ii) A row of posts should be set for each 5 feet of space between the roadway posts and the ribs.

(5) Openings should not be more than 30 feet wide.

(c) *Installation of roof support using mining machines with integral roof bolters.* (1) Before an intersection or pillar split is started, roof bolts should be installed on at least 5-foot centers where the work is performed.

(2) Where the roof is supported by only two roof bolts crosswise, openings should not be more than 16 feet wide.

(d) *Pillar recovery.* (1) During development, any dimension of a pillar should be at least 20 feet.

(2) Pillar splits and lifts should not be more than 20 feet wide.

(3) Breaker posts should be installed on not more than 4-foot centers.

(4) Roadside-radius (turn) posts, or equivalent support, should be installed on not more than 4-foot centers leading into each pillar split or lift.

(5) Before full pillar recovery is started in areas where roof bolts are used as the only means of roof support and openings are more than 16 feet wide, at least one row of posts should be installed to limit the roadway width to 16 feet. These posts should be—

(i) Extended from the entrance to the split through the intersection outby the pillar in which the split or lift is being made; and

(ii) Spaced on not more than 5-foot centers.

(e) *Unsupported openings at intersections.* Openings that create an intersection should be permanently supported or at least one row of temporary supports should be installed on not more than 5-foot centers across the opening before any other work or travel in the intersection.

(f) *ATRS systems in working sections where the mining height is below 30 inches.* In working sections where the mining height is below 30 inches, an ATRS system should be used to the extent practicable during the installation of roof bolts with roof bolting machines and continuous-mining machines with integral roof bolters.

(g) *Longwall mining systems.* (1) Systematic supplemental support should be installed throughout—

(i) The tailgate entry of the first longwall panel prior to any mining; and

(ii) In the proposed tailgate entry of each subsequent panel in advance of the frontal abutment stresses of the panel being mined.

(2) When a ground failure prevents travel out of the section through the tailgate side of the longwall section, the roof control plan should address—

(i) Notification of miners that the travelway is blocked;

(ii) Re-instruction of miners regarding escapeways and escape procedures in the event of an emergency;

(iii) Re-instruction of miners on the availability and use of self-contained self-rescue devices;

(iv) Monitoring and evaluation of the air entering the longwall section;

(v) Location and effectiveness of the two-way communication systems; and

(vi) A means of transportation from the section to the main line.

(3) The plan provisions addressed by paragraph (g)(2) of this section should remain in effect until a travelway is reestablished on the tailgate side of a longwall section.

§ 75.223 Evaluation and revision of roof control plan.

(a) Revisions of the roof control plan shall be proposed by the operator—

(1) When conditions indicate that the plan is not suitable for controlling the roof, face, ribs, or coal or rock bursts; or

(2) When accident and injury experience at the mine indicates the plan is inadequate. The accident and injury experience at each mine shall be reviewed at least every six months.

(b) Each unplanned roof fall and rib fall and coal or rock burst that occurs in the active workings shall be plotted on a mine map if it—

(1) Is above the anchorage zone where roof bolts are used;

(2) Impairs ventilation;

(3) Impedes passage of persons;

(4) Causes miners to be withdrawn from the area affected; or

(5) Disrupts regular mining activities for more than one hour.

(c) The mine map on which roof falls are plotted shall be available at the mine site for inspection by authorized representatives of the Secretary and representatives of miners at the mine.

(d) The roof control plan for each mine shall be reviewed every six months by an authorized representative of the Secretary. This review shall take into consideration any falls of the roof, face and ribs and the adequacy of the support systems used at the time.

[53 FR 2375, Jan. 27, 1988; 60 FR 33723, June 29, 1995]

Subpart D—Ventilation

AUTHORITY: 30 U.S.C. 811, 863.

SOURCE: 61 FR 9829, Mar. 11, 1996, unless otherwise noted.

§ 75.300 Scope.

This subpart sets requirements for underground coal mine ventilation.

§ 75.301 Definitions.

In addition to the applicable definitions in § 75.2, the following definitions apply in this subpart.

Air course. An entry or a set of entries separated from other entries by stoppings, overcasts, other ventilation control devices, or by solid blocks of coal or rock so that any mixing of air currents between each is limited to leakage.

AMS operator. The person(s), designated by the mine operator, who is located on the surface of the mine and monitors the malfunction, alert, and alarm signals of the AMS and notifies appropriate personnel of these signals.

Appropriate personnel. The person or persons designated by the operator to perform specific tasks in response to AMS signals. Appropriate personnel include the responsible person(s) required by § 75.1501 when an emergency evacuation is necessary.

Atmospheric Monitoring System (AMS). A network consisting of hardware and software meeting the requirements of §§ 75.351 and 75.1103–2 and capable of: measuring atmospheric parameters; transmitting the measurements to a designated surface location; providing alert and alarm signals; processing and cataloging atmospheric data; and, providing reports. Early-warning fire detection systems using newer technology that provides equal or greater protection, as determined by the Secretary, will be considered atmospheric monitoring systems for the purposes of this subpart.

Belt air course. The entry in which a belt is located and any adjacent entry(ies) not separated from the belt entry by permanent ventilation controls, including any entries in series with the belt entry, terminating at a return regulator, a section loading point, or the surface.

Carbon monoxide ambient level. The average concentration in parts per million (ppm) of carbon monoxide detected in an air course containing carbon monoxide sensors. This average concentration is representative of the composition of the mine atmosphere over a period of mining activity during non-fire conditions. Separate ambient levels may be established for different areas of the mine.

Incombustible. Incapable of being burned.

Intake air. Air that has not yet ventilated the last working place on any split of any working section, or any worked-out area, whether pillared or nonpillared.

Intrinsically safe. Incapable of releasing enough electrical or thermal energy under normal or abnormal conditions to cause ignition of a flammable mixture of methane or natural gas and air of the most easily ignitable composition.

Noncombustible structure or area. Describes a structure or area that will continue to provide protection against flame spread for at least 1 hour when subjected to a fire test incorporating an ASTM E119–88 time/temperature heat input, or equivalent. The publication ASTM E119–88 "Standard Test

Mine Safety and Health Admin., Labor § 75.310

Methods for Fire Tests of Building Construction and Materials" is incorporated by reference and may be inspected at any MSHA Coal Mine Safety and Health District Office, or at MSHA's Office of Standards, Regulations, and Variances, 201 12th Street South, Arlington, VA 22202-5452; 202-693-9440; or at the National Archives and Records Administration (NARA). For information on the availability of this material at NARA, call 202-741-6030, or go to: *http://www.archives.gov/federal_register/code_of_federal_regulations/ibr_locations.html*. In addition, copies of the document can be purchased from the American Society for Testing and Materials (ASTM), 100 Barr Harbor Drive, P.O. Box C700, West Conshohocken, PA 19428-2959; 610-832-9500; *http://www.astm.org*. This incorporation by reference was approved by the Director of the Federal Register in accordance with 5 U.S.C. 552(a) and 1 CFR part 51.

Noncombustible material. Describes a material that, when used to construct a ventilation control, results in a control that will continue to serve its intended function for 1 hour when subjected to a fire test incorporating an ASTM E119-88 time/temperature heat input, or equivalent. The publication ASTM E119-88 "Standard Test Methods for Fire Tests of Building Construction and Materials" is incorporated by reference and may be inspected at any Coal Mine Safety and Health District Office, or at MSHA's Office of Standards, Regulations, and Variances, 201 12th Street South, Arlington, VA 22202-5452; 202-693-9440; or at the National Archives and Records Administration (NARA). For information on the availability of this material at NARA, call 202-741-6030, or go to: *http://www.archives.gov/federal_register/code_of_federal_regulations/ibr_locations.html*. In addition, copies of the document can be purchased from the American Society for Testing and Materials (ASTM), 100 Barr Harbor Drive, P.O. Box C700, West Conshohocken, PA 19428-2959; 610-832-9500; *http://www.astm.org*. This incorporation by reference was approved by the Director of the Federal Register in accordance with 5 U.S.C. 552(a) and 1 CFR part 51.

Point feeding. The process of providing additional intake air to the belt air course from another intake air course through a regulator.

Return air. Air that has ventilated the last working place on any split of any working section or any worked-out area whether pillared or nonpillared. If air mixes with air that has ventilated the last working place on any split of any working section or any worked-out area, whether pillared or nonpillared, it is considered return air. For the purposes of § 75.507-1, air that has been used to ventilate any working place in a coal producing section or pillared area, or air that has been used to ventilate any working face if such air is directed away from the immediate return is return air. Notwithstanding the definition of intake air, for the purpose of ventilation of structures, areas or installations that are required by this subpart D to be ventilated to return air courses, and for ventilation of seals, other air courses may be designated as return air courses by the operator only when the air in these air courses will not be used to ventilate working places or other locations, structures, installations or areas required to be ventilated with intake air.

Worked-out area. An area where mining has been completed, whether pillared or nonpillared, excluding developing entries, return air courses, and intake air courses.

[61 FR 9829, Mar. 11, 1996; 61 FR 29288, June 10, 1996, as amended at 67 FR 38386, June 4, 2002; 69 FR 17526, Apr. 2, 2004; 71 FR 16668, Apr. 3, 2006; 80 FR 52990, Sept. 2, 2015]

§ 75.302 Main mine fans.

Each coal mine shall be ventilated by one or more main mine fans. Booster fans shall not be installed underground to assist main mine fans except in anthracite mines. In anthracite mines, booster fans installed in the main air current or a split of the main air current may be used provided their use is approved in the ventilation plan.

§ 75.310 Installation of main mine fans.

(a) Each main mine fan shall be—
(1) Installed on the surface in an incombustible housing;

§ 75.310

(2) Connected to the mine opening with incombustible air ducts;

(3) Equipped with an automatic device that gives a signal at the mine when the fan either slows or stops. A responsible person designated by the operator shall always be at a surface location at the mine where the signal can be seen or heard while anyone is underground. This person shall be provided with two-way communication with the working sections and work stations where persons are routinely assigned to work for the majority of a shift;

(4) Equipped with a pressure recording device or system. Mines permitted to shut down main mine fans under § 75.311 and which do not have a pressure recording device installed on main mine fans shall have until June 10, 1997 to install a pressure recording device or system on all main mine fans. If a device or system other than a circular pressure recorder is used to monitor main mine fan pressure, the monitoring device or system shall provide a continuous graph or continuous chart of the pressure as a function of time. At not more than 7-day intervals, a hard copy of the continuous graph or chart shall be generated or the record of the fan pressure shall be stored electronically. When records of fan pressure are stored electronically, the system used to store these records shall be secure and not susceptible to alteration and shall be capable of storing the required data. Records of the fan pressure shall be retained at a surface location at the mine for at least 1 year and be made available for inspection by authorized representatives of the Secretary and the representative of miners;

(5) Protected by one or more weak walls or explosion doors, or a combination of weak walls and explosion doors, located in direct line with possible explosive forces;

(6) Except as provided under paragraph (e) of this section, offset by at least 15 feet from the nearest side of the mine opening unless an alternative method of protecting the fan and its associated components is approved in the ventilation plan.

(b)(1) If an electric motor is used to drive a main mine fan, the motor shall operate from a power circuit independent of all mine power circuits.

(2) If an internal combustion engine is used to drive a main mine fan—

(i) The fuel supply shall be protected against fires and explosions;

(ii) The engine shall be installed in an incombustible housing and be equipped with a remote shut-down device;

(iii) The engine and the engine exhaust system shall be located out of direct line of the air current exhausting from the mine; and

(iv) The engine exhaust shall be vented to the atmosphere so that the exhaust gases do not contaminate the mine intake air current or any enclosure.

(c) If a main mine fan monitoring system is used under § 75.312, the system shall—

(1) Record, as described in paragraph (a)(4) the mine ventilating pressure;

(2) Monitor bearing temperature, revolutions per minute, vibration, electric voltage, and amperage;

(3) Provide a printout of the monitored parameters, including the mine ventilating pressure within a reasonable period, not to exceed the end of the next scheduled shift during which miners are underground; and

(4) Be equipped with an automatic device that signals when—

(i) An electrical or mechanical deficiency exists in the monitoring system; or

(ii) A sudden increase or loss in mine ventilating pressure occurs.

(5) Provide monitoring, records, printouts, and signals required by paragraphs (c)(1) through (c)(4) at a surface location at the mine where a responsible person designated by the operator is always on duty and where signals from the monitoring system can be seen or heard while anyone is underground. This person shall be provided with two-way communication with the working sections and work stations where persons are routinely assigned to work for the majority of a shift.

(d) Weak walls and explosion doors shall have cross-sectional areas at least equal to that of the entry through which the pressure from an explosion underground would be relieved. A weak wall and explosion door combination shall have a total cross-sectional area at least equal to that of the entry through which the pressure from an explosion underground would be relieved.

(e) If a mine fan is installed in line with an entry, a slope, or a shaft—

(1) The cross-sectional area of the pressure relief entry shall be at least equal to that of the fan entry;

(2) The fan entry shall be developed out of direct line with possible explosive forces;

(3) The coal or other solid material between the pressure relief entry and the fan entry shall be at least 2,500 square feet; and

(4) The surface opening of the pressure relief entry shall be not less than 15 feet nor more than 100 feet from the surface opening of the fan entry and from the underground intersection of the fan entry and pressure relief entry.

(f) In mines ventilated by multiple main mine fans, incombustible doors shall be installed so that if any main mine fan stops and air reversals through the fan are possible, the doors on the affected fan automatically close.

[61 FR 9829, Mar. 11, 1996, as amended at 61 FR 20877, May 8, 1996]

§ 75.311 Main mine fan operation.

(a) Main mine fans shall be continuously operated, except as otherwise approved in the ventilation plan, or when intentionally stopped for testing of automatic closing doors and automatic fan signal devices, maintenance or adjustment of the fan, or to perform maintenance or repair work underground that cannot otherwise be made while the fan is operating.

(b) Except as provided in paragraph (c) of this section, when a main mine fan is intentionally stopped and the ventilating quantity provided by the fan is not maintained by a back-up fan system—

(1) Only persons necessary to evaluate the effect of the fan stoppage or restart, or to perform maintenance or repair work that cannot otherwise be made while the fan is operating, shall be permitted underground;

(2) Mechanized equipment shall be shut off before stopping the fan; and

(3) Electric power circuits entering underground areas of the mine shall be deenergized.

(c) When a back-up fan system is used that does not provide the ventilating quantity provided by the main mine fan, persons may be permitted in the mine and electric power circuits may be energized as specified in the approved ventilation plan.

(d) If an unusual variance in the mine ventilation pressure is observed, or if an electrical or mechanical deficiency of a main mine fan is detected, the mine foreman or equivalent mine official, or in the absence of the mine foreman or equivalent mine official, a designated certified person acting for the mine foreman or equivalent mine official shall be notified immediately, and appropriate action or repairs shall be instituted promptly.

(e) While persons are underground, a responsible person designated by the operator shall always be at a surface location where each main mine fan signal can be seen or heard.

(f) The area within 100 feet of main mine fans and intake air openings shall be kept free of combustible material, unless alternative precautions necessary to provide protection from fire or other products of combustion are approved in the ventilation plan.

(g) If multiple mine fans are used, the mine ventilation system shall be designed and maintained to eliminate areas without air movement.

(h) Any atmospheric monitoring system operated during fan stoppages shall be intrinsically safe.

§ 75.312 Main mine fan examinations and records.

(a) To assure electrical and mechanical reliability of main mine fans, each main mine fan and its associated components, including devices for measuring or recording mine ventilation pressure, shall be examined for proper operation by a trained person designated by the operator. Examinations of main mine fans shall be made at least once each day that the fan operates, unless a fan monitoring system is used. No examination is required on

§ 75.312

any day when no one, including certified persons, goes underground, except that an examination shall be completed prior to anyone entering the mine.

(b)(1) If a main mine fan monitoring system is used, a trained person designated by the operator shall—

(i) At least once each day review the data provided by the fan monitoring system to assure that the fan and the fan monitoring system are operating properly. No review is required on any day when no one, including certified persons, goes underground, except that a review of the data shall be performed prior to anyone entering the underground portion of the mine. Data reviewed should include the fan pressure, bearing temperature, revolutions per minute, vibration, electric voltage, and amperage; and

(ii) At least every 7 days—

(A) Test the monitoring system for proper operation; and

(B) Examine each main mine fan and its associated components to assure electrical and mechanical reliability of main mine fans.

(2) If the monitoring system malfunctions, the malfunction shall be corrected, or paragraph (a) of this section shall apply.

(c) At least every 31 days, the automatic fan signal device for each main mine fan shall be tested by stopping the fan. Only persons necessary to evaluate the effect of the fan stoppage or restart, or to perform maintenance or repair work that cannot otherwise be made while the fan is operating, shall be permitted underground. Notwithstanding the requirement of § 75.311(b)(3), underground power may remain energized during this test provided no one, including persons identified in § 75.311(b)(1), is underground. If the fan is not restarted within 15 minutes, underground power shall be deenergized and no one shall enter any underground area of the mine until the fan is restarted and an examination of the mine is conducted as described in § 75.360 (b) through (e) and the mine has been determined to be safe.

(d) At least every 31 days, the automatic closing doors in multiple main mine fan systems shall be tested by stopping the fan. Only persons necessary to evaluate the effect of the fan stoppage or restart, or to perform maintenance or repair work that cannot otherwise be made while the fan is operating, shall be permitted underground. Notwithstanding the provisions of § 75.311, underground power may remain energized during this test provided no one, including persons identified in § 75.311(b)(1), is underground. If the fan is not restarted within 15 minutes, underground power shall be deenergized and no one shall enter any underground area of the mine, until the fan is restarted and an examination of the mine is conducted as described in § 75.360 (b) through (e) and the mine has been determined to be safe.

(e) Circular main mine fan pressure recording charts shall be changed before the beginning of a second revolution.

(f)(1) *Certification.* Persons making main mine fan examinations shall certify by initials and date at the fan or another location specified by the operator that the examinations were made. Each certification shall identify the main mine fan examined.

(2) Persons reviewing data produced by a main mine fan monitoring system shall certify by initials and date on a printed copy of the data from the system that the review was completed. In lieu of certification on a copy of the data, the person reviewing the data may certify electronically that the review was completed. Electronic certification shall be by handwritten initials and date in a computer system so as to be secure and not susceptible to alteration.

(g)(1) *Recordkeeping.* By the end of the shift on which the examination is made, persons making main mine fan examinations shall record all uncorrected defects that may affect the operation of the fan that are not corrected by the end of that shift. Records shall be maintained in a secure book that is not susceptible to alteration or electronically in a computer system so as to be secure and not susceptible to alteration.

(2) When a fan monitoring system is used in lieu of the daily fan examination—

(i) The certified copies of data produced by fan monitoring systems shall be maintained separate from other computer-generated reports or data; and

(ii) A record shall be made of any fan monitoring system malfunctions, electrical or mechanical deficiencies in the monitoring system and any sudden increase or loss in mine ventilating pressure. The record shall be made by the end of the shift on which the review of the data is completed and shall be maintained in a secure book that is not susceptible to alteration or electronically in a computer system so as to be secure and not susceptible to alteration.

(3) By the end of the shift on which the monthly test of the automatic fan signal device or the automatic closing doors is completed, persons making these tests shall record the results of the tests. Records shall be maintained in a secure book that is not susceptible to alteration or electronically in a computer system so as to be secure and not susceptible to alteration.

(h) *Retention period.* Records, including records of mine fan pressure and the certified copies of data produced by fan monitoring systems, shall be retained at a surface location at the mine for at least 1 year and shall be made available for inspection by authorized representatives of the Secretary and the representative of miners.

§ 75.313 **Main mine fan stoppage with persons underground.**

(a) If a main mine fan stops while anyone is underground and the ventilating quantity provided by the fan is not maintained by a back-up fan system—

(1) Electrically powered equipment in each working section shall be deenergized;

(2) Other mechanized equipment in each working section shall be shut off; and

(3) Everyone shall be withdrawn from the working sections and areas where mechanized mining equipment is being installed or removed.

(b) If ventilation is restored within 15 minutes after a main mine fan stops, certified persons shall examine for methane in the working places and in other areas where methane is likely to accumulate before work is resumed and before equipment is energized or restarted in these areas.

(c) If ventilation is not restored within 15 minutes after a main mine fan stops—

(1) Everyone shall be withdrawn from the mine;

(2) Underground electric power circuits shall be deenergized. However, circuits necessary to withdraw persons from the mine need not be deenergized if located in areas or haulageways where methane is not likely to migrate to or accumulate. These circuits shall be deenergized as persons are withdrawn; and

(3) Mechanized equipment not located on working sections shall be shut off. However, mechanized equipment necessary to withdraw persons from the mine need not be shut off if located in areas where methane is not likely to migrate to or accumulate.

(d)(1) When ventilation is restored—

(i) No one other than designated certified examiners shall enter any underground area of the mine until an examination is conducted as described in § 75.360(b) through (e) and the area has been determined to be safe. Designated certified examiners shall enter the underground area of the mine from which miners have been withdrawn only after the fan has operated for at least 15 minutes unless a longer period of time is specified in the approved ventilation plan.

(ii) Underground power circuits shall not be energized and nonpermissible mechanized equipment shall not be started or operated in an area until an examination is conducted as described in § 75.360(b) through (e) and the area has been determined to be safe, except that designated certified examiners may use nonpermissible transportation equipment in intake airways to facilitate the making of the required examination.

(2) If ventilation is restored to the mine before miners reach the surface, the miners may return to underground working areas only after an examination of the areas is made by a certified person and the areas are determined to be safe.

§ 75.320

(e) Any atmospheric monitoring system operated during fan stoppages shall be intrinsically safe.

(f) Any electrical refuge alternative components exposed to the mine atmosphere shall be approved as intrinsically safe for use during fan stoppages. Any electrical refuge alternative components located inside the refuge alternative shall be either approved as intrinsically safe or approved as permissible for use during fan stoppages.

[61 FR 9829, Mar. 11, 1996, as amended at 73 FR 80697, Dec. 31, 2008]

§ 75.320 Air quality detectors and measurement devices.

(a) Tests for methane shall be made by a qualified person with MSHA approved detectors that are maintained in permissible and proper operating condition and calibrated with a known methane-air mixture at least once every 31 days.

(b) Tests for oxygen deficiency shall be made by a qualified person with MSHA approved oxygen detectors that are maintained in permissible and proper operating condition and that can detect 19.5 percent oxygen with an accuracy of ±0.5 percent. The oxygen detectors shall be calibrated at the start of each shift that the detectors will be used.

(c) Handheld devices that contain electrical components and that are used for measuring air velocity, carbon monoxide, oxides of nitrogen, and other gases shall be approved and maintained in permissible and proper operating condition.

(d) An oxygen detector approved by MSHA shall be used to make tests for oxygen deficiency required by the regulations in this part. Permissible flame safety lamps may only be used as a supplementary testing device.

(e) Maintenance of instruments required by paragraphs (a) through (d) of this section shall be done by persons trained in such maintenance.

§ 75.321 Air quality.

(a)(1) The air in areas where persons work or travel, except as specified in paragraph (a)(2) of this section, shall contain at least 19.5 percent oxygen and not more than 0.5 percent carbon dioxide, and the volume and velocity of the air current in these areas shall be sufficient to dilute, render harmless, and carry away flammable, explosive, noxious, and harmful gases, dusts, smoke, and fumes.

(2) The air in areas of bleeder entries and worked-out areas where persons work or travel shall contain at least 19.5 percent oxygen, and carbon dioxide levels shall not exceed 0.5 percent time weighted average and 3.0 percent short term exposure limit.

(b) Notwithstanding the provisions of § 75.322, for the purpose of preventing explosions from gases other than methane, the following gases shall not be permitted to accumulate in excess of the concentrations listed below:

(1) Carbon monoxide (CO)—2.5 percent

(2) Hydrogen (H_2)—.80 percent

(3) Hydrogen sulfide (H_2S)—.80 percent

(4) Acetylene (C_2H_2)—.40 percent

(5) Propane (C_3H_8)—.40 percent

(6) MAPP (methyl-acetylene-propylene-propodiene)—.30 percent

§ 75.322 Harmful quantities of noxious gases.

Concentrations of noxious or poisonous gases, other than carbon dioxide, shall not exceed the threshold limit values (TLV) as specified and applied by the American Conference of Governmental Industrial Hygienists in "Threshold Limit Values for Substance in Workroom Air" (1972). Detectors or laboratory analysis of mine air samples shall be used to determine the concentrations of harmful, noxious, or poisonous gases. This incorporation by reference has been approved by the Director of the Federal Register in accordance with 5 U.S.C. 552(a) and 1 CFR part 51. Copies are available from MSHA's Office of Standards, Regulations, and Variances, 201 12th Street South, Arlington, VA 22202–5452; 202–693–9440; and at every MSHA Coal Mine Safety and Health District Office. The material is available for examination at the National Archives and Records Administration (NARA). For information on the availability of this material at NARA, call 202–741–6030, or go to: http://www.archives.gov/federal_register/code_of_federal_regulations/ibr_locations.html.

[80 FR 52991, Sept. 2, 2015]

§ 75.323 Actions for excessive methane.

(a) *Location of tests.* Tests for methane concentrations under this section shall be made at least 12 inches from the roof, face, ribs, and floor.

(b) *Working places and intake air courses.* (1) When 1.0 percent or more methane is present in a working place or an intake air course, including an air course in which a belt conveyor is located, or in an area where mechanized mining equipment is being installed or removed—

(i) Except intrinsically safe atmospheric monitoring systems (AMS), electrically powered equipment in the affected area shall be deenergized, and other mechanized equipment shall be shut off;

(ii) Changes or adjustments shall be made at once to the ventilation system to reduce the concentration of methane to less than 1.0 percent; and

(iii) No other work shall be permitted in the affected area until the methane concentration is less than 1.0 percent.

(2) When 1.5 percent or more methane is present in a working place or an intake air course, including an air course in which a belt conveyor is located, or in an area where mechanized mining equipment is being installed or removed—

(i) Everyone except those persons referred to in § 104(c) of the Act shall be withdrawn from the affected area; and

(ii) Except for intrinsically safe AMS, electrically powered equipment in the affected area shall be disconnected at the power source.

(c) *Return air split.* (1) When 1.0 percent or more methane is present in a return air split between the last working place on a working section and where that split of air meets another split of air, or the location at which the split is used to ventilate seals or worked-out areas changes or adjustments shall be made at once to the ventilation system to reduce the concentration of methane in the return air to less than 1.0 percent.

(2) When 1.5 percent or more methane is present in a return air split between the last working place on a working section and where that split of air meets another split of air, or the location where the split is used to ventilate seals or worked-out areas—

(i) Everyone except those persons referred to in § 104(c) of the Act shall be withdrawn from the affected area;

(ii) Other than intrinsically safe AMS, equipment in the affected area shall be deenergized, electric power shall be disconnected at the power source, and other mechanized equipment shall be shut off; and

(iii) No other work shall be permitted in the affected area until the methane concentration in the return air is less than 1.0 percent.

(d) *Return air split alternative.* (1) The provisions of this paragraph apply if—

(i) The quantity of air in the split ventilating the active workings is at least 27,000 cubic feet per minute in the last open crosscut or the quantity specified in the approved ventilation plan, whichever is greater;

(ii) The methane content of the air in the split is continuously monitored during mining operations by an AMS that gives a visual and audible signal on the working section when the methane in the return air reaches 1.5 percent, and the methane content is monitored as specified in § 75.351; and

(iii) Rock dust is continuously applied with a mechanical duster to the return air course during coal production at a location in the air course immediately outby the most inby monitoring point.

(2) When 1.5 percent or more methane is present in a return air split between a point in the return opposite the section loading point and where that split of air meets another split of air or where the split of air is used to ventilate seals or worked-out areas—

(i) Changes or adjustments shall be made at once to the ventilation system to reduce the concentration of methane in the return air below 1.5 percent;

(ii) Everyone except those persons referred to in § 104(c) of the Act shall be withdrawn from the affected area;

(iii) Except for intrinsically safe AMS, equipment in the affected area shall be deenergized, electric power shall be disconnected at the power

§ 75.324

source, and other mechanized equipment shall be shut off; and

(iv) No other work shall be permitted in the affected area until the methane concentration in the return air is less than 1.5 percent.

(e) *Bleeders and other return air courses.* The concentration of methane in a bleeder split of air immediately before the air in the split joins another split of air, or in a return air course other than as described in paragraphs (c) and (d) of this section, shall not exceed 2.0 percent.

§ 75.324 Intentional changes in the ventilation system.

(a) A person designated by the operator shall supervise any intentional change in ventilation that—

(1) Alters the main air current or any split of the main air current in a manner that could materially affect the safety or health of persons in the mine; or

(2) Affects section ventilation by 9,000 cubic feet per minute of air or more in bituminous or lignite mines, or 5,000 cubic feet per minute of air or more in anthracite mines.

(b) Intentional changes shall be made only under the following conditions:

(1) Electric power shall be removed from areas affected by the ventilation change and mechanized equipment in those areas shall be shut off before the ventilation change begins.

(2) Only persons making the change in ventilation shall be in the mine.

(3) Electric power shall not be restored to the areas affected by the ventilation change and mechanized equipment shall not be restarted until a certified person has examined these areas for methane accumulation and for oxygen deficiency and has determined that the areas are safe.

§ 75.325 Air quantity.

(a)(1) In bituminous and lignite mines the quantity of air shall be at least 3,000 cubic feet per minute reaching each working face where coal is being cut, mined, drilled for blasting, or loaded. When a greater quantity is necessary to dilute, render harmless, and carry away flammable, explosive, noxious, and harmful gases, dusts, smoke, and fumes, this quantity shall be specified in the approved ventilation plan. A minimum air quantity may be required to be specified in the approved ventilation plan for other working places or working faces.

(2) The quantity of air reaching the working face shall be determined at or near the face end of the line curtain, ventilation tubing, or other ventilation control device. If the curtain, tubing, or device extends beyond the last row of permanent roof supports, the quantity of air reaching the working face shall be determined behind the line curtain or in the ventilation tubing at or near the last row of permanent supports. When machine-mounted dust collectors are used in conjunction with blowing face ventilation systems, the quantity of air reaching the working face shall be determined with the dust collector turned off.

(3) If machine mounted dust collectors or diffuser fans are used, the approved ventilation plan shall specify the operating volume of the dust collector or diffuser fan.

(b) In bituminous and lignite mines, the quantity of air reaching the last open crosscut of each set of entries or rooms on each working section and the quantity of air reaching the intake end of a pillar line shall be at least 9,000 cubic feet per minute unless a greater quantity is required to be specified in the approved ventilation plan. This minimum also applies to sections which are not operating but are capable of producing coal by simply energizing the equipment on the section.

(c) In longwall and shortwall mining systems—

(1) The quantity of air shall be at least 30,000 cubic feet per minute reaching the working face of each longwall, unless the operator demonstrates that a lesser air quantity will maintain continual compliance with applicable methane and respirable dust standards. This lesser quantity shall be specified in the approved ventilation plan. A quantity greater than 30,000 cubic feet per minute may be required to be specified in the approved ventilation plan.

(2) The velocity of air that will be provided to control methane and respirable dust in accordance with applicable standards on each longwall or shortwall and the locations where

these velocities will be provided shall be specified in the approved ventilation plan. The locations specified shall be at least 50 feet but no more than 100 feet from the headgate and tailgate, respectively.

(d) Ventilation shall be maintained during installation and removal of mechanized mining equipment. The approved ventilation plan shall specify the minimum quantity of air, the locations where this quantity will be provided and the ventilation controls required.

(e) In anthracite mines, the quantity of air shall be as follows:

(1) At least 1,500 cubic feet per minute reaching each working face where coal is being mined, unless a greater quantity is required to be specified in the approved ventilation plan.

(2) At least 5,000 cubic feet per minute passing through the last open crosscut in each set of entries or rooms and at the intake end of any pillar line, unless a greater quantity is required to be specified in the approved ventilation plan.

(3) When robbing areas where air currents cannot be controlled and air measurements cannot be obtained, the air shall have perceptible movement.

(f) The minimum ventilating air quantity for an individual unit of diesel-powered equipment being operated shall be at least that specified on the approval plate for that equipment. Such air quantity shall be maintained—

(1) In any working place where the equipment is being operated;

(2) At the section loading point during any shift the equipment is being operated on the working section;

(3) In any entry where the equipment is being operated outby the section loading point in areas of the mine developed on or after April 25, 1997;

(4) In any air course with single or multiple entries where the equipment is being operated outby the section loading point in areas of the mine developed prior to April 25, 1997; and

(5) At any other location required by the district manager and specified in the approved ventilation plan.

(g) The minimum ventilating air quantity where multiple units of diesel-powered equipment are operated on working sections and in areas where mechanized mining equipment is being installed or removed must be at least the sum of that specified on the approval plates of all the diesel-powered equipment on the working section or in the area where mechanized mining equipment is being installed or removed. The minimum ventilating air quantity shall be specified in the approved ventilation plan. For working sections such air quantity must be maintained—

(1) In the last open crosscut of each set of entries or rooms in each working section;

(2) In the intake, reaching the working face of each longwall; and

(3) At the intake end of any pillar line.

(h) The following equipment may be excluded from the calculations of ventilating air quantity under paragraph (g) if such equipment exclusion is approved by the district manager and specified in the ventilation plan:

(1) Self-propelled equipment meeting the requirements of §75.1908(b);

(2) Equipment that discharges its exhaust into intake air that is coursed directly to a return air course;

(3) Equipment that discharges its exhaust directly into a return air course; and

(4) Other equipment having duty cycles such that the emissions would not significantly affect the exposure of miners.

(i) A ventilating air quantity that is less than what is required by paragraph (g) of this section may be approved by the district manager in the ventilation plan based upon the results of sampling that demonstrate that the lesser air quantity will maintain continuous compliance with applicable TLV®'s.

(j) If during sampling required by §70.1900(c) of this subchapter the ventilating air is found to contain concentrations of CO or NO_2 in excess of the action level specified by §70.1900(c), higher action levels may be approved by the district manager based on the results of sampling that demonstrate that a higher action level will maintain continuous compliance with applicable TLV®'s. Action levels other than those specified in §70.1900(c) shall be

§ 75.326

specified in the approved ventilation plan.

(k) As of November 25, 1997 the ventilating air quantity required where diesel-powered equipment is operated shall meet the requirements of paragraphs (f) through (j) of this section. Mine operators utilizing diesel-powered equipment in underground coal mines shall submit to the appropriate MSHA district manager a revised ventilation plan or appropriate amendments to the existing plan, in accordance with § 75.371, which implement the requirements of paragraphs (f) through (j) of this section.

[61 FR 9828, Mar. 11, 1996; 61 FR 26442, May 28, 1996; 61 FR 29288, June 10, 1996, as amended at 61 FR 55526, Oct. 25, 1996; 62 FR 34641, June 27, 1997; 79 FR 24937, May 1, 2014]

§ 75.326 Mean entry air velocity.

In exhausting face ventilation systems, the mean entry air velocity shall be at least 60 feet per minute reaching each working face where coal is being cut, mined, drilled for blasting, or loaded, and to any other working places as required in the approved ventilation plan. A lower mean entry air velocity may be approved in the ventilation plan if the lower velocity will maintain methane and respirable dust concentrations in accordance with the applicable levels. Mean entry air velocity shall be determined at or near the inby end of the line curtain, ventilation tubing, or other face ventilation control devices.

[61 FR 9828, Mar. 11, 1996; 61 FR 29288, June 10, 1996]

§ 75.327 Air courses and trolley haulage systems.

(a) In any mine opened on or after March 30, 1970, or in any new working section of a mine opened before that date, where trolley haulage systems are maintained and where trolley wires or trolley feeder wires are installed, an authorized representative of the Secretary shall require enough entries or rooms as intake air courses to limit the velocity of air currents in the haulageways to minimize the hazards of fires and dust explosions in the haulageways.

(b) Unless the district manager approves a higher velocity, the velocity of the air current in the trolley haulage entries shall be limited to not more than 250 feet per minute. A higher air velocity may be required to limit the methane content in these haulage entries or elsewhere in the mine to less than 1.0 percent and provide an adequate supply of oxygen.

§ 75.330 Face ventilation control devices.

(a) Brattice cloth, ventilation tubing and other face ventilation control devices shall be made of flame-resistant material approved by MSHA.

(b)(1) Ventilation control devices shall be used to provide ventilation to dilute, render harmless, and to carry away flammable, explosive, noxious, and harmful gases, dusts, smoke, and fumes—

(i) To each working face from which coal is being cut, mined, drilled for blasting, or loaded; and

(ii) To any other working places as required by the approved ventilation plan.

(2) These devices shall be installed at a distance no greater than 10 feet from the area of deepest penetration to which any portion of the face has been advanced unless an alternative distance is specified and approved in the ventilation plan. Alternative distances specified shall be capable of maintaining concentrations of respirable dust, methane, and other harmful gases, in accordance with the levels specified in the applicable sections of this chapter.

(c) When the line brattice or any other face ventilation control device is damaged to an extent that ventilation of the working face is inadequate, production activities in the working place shall cease until necessary repairs are made and adequate ventilation is restored.

[61 FR 9828, Mar. 11, 1996; 61 FR 29288, June 10, 1996]

§ 75.331 Auxiliary fans and tubing.

(a) When auxiliary fans and tubing are used for face ventilation, each auxiliary fan shall be—

(1) Permissible, if the fan is electrically operated;

(2) Maintained in proper operating condition;

(3) Deenergized or shut off when no one is present on the working section; and

(4) Located and operated to avoid recirculation of air.

(b) If a deficiency exists in any auxiliary fan system, the deficiency shall be corrected or the auxiliary fan shall be deenergized immediately.

(c) If the air passing through an auxiliary fan or tubing contains 1.0 percent or more methane, power to electrical equipment in the working place and to the auxiliary fan shall be deenergized, and other mechanized equipment in the working place shall be shut off until the methane concentration is reduced to less than 1.0 percent.

(d) When an auxiliary fan is stopped—

(1) Line brattice or other face ventilation control devices shall be used to maintain ventilation to affected faces; and

(2) Electrical equipment in the affected working places shall be disconnected at the power source, and other mechanized equipment shall be shut off until ventilation to the working place is restored.

§ 75.332 Working sections and working places.

(a)(1) Each working section and each area where mechanized mining equipment is being installed or removed, shall be ventilated by a separate split of intake air directed by overcasts, undercasts or other permanent ventilation controls.

(2) When two or more sets of mining equipment are simultaneously engaged in cutting, mining, or loading coal or rock from working places within the same working section, each set of mining equipment shall be on a separate split of intake air.

(3) For purposes of this section, a set of mining equipment includes a single loading machine, a single continuous mining machine, or a single longwall or shortwall mining machine.

(b)(1) Air that has passed through any area that is not examined under §§ 75.360, 75.361 or 75.364 of this subpart, or through an area where second mining has been done shall not be used to ventilate any working place. Second mining is intentional retreat mining where pillars have been wholly or partially removed, regardless of the amount of recovery obtained.

(2) Air that has passed by any opening of any unsealed area that is not examined under §§ 75.360, 75.361 or 75.364 of this subpart, shall not be used to ventilate any working place.

§ 75.333 Ventilation controls.

(a) For purposes of this section, "doors" include any door frames.

(b) Permanent stoppings or other permanent ventilation control devices constructed after November 15, 1992, shall be built and maintained—

(1) Between intake and return air courses, except temporary controls may be used in rooms that are 600 feet or less from the centerline of the entry from which the room was developed including where continuous face haulage systems are used in such rooms. Unless otherwise approved in the ventilation plan, these stoppings or controls shall be maintained to and including the third connecting crosscut outby the working face;

(2) To separate belt conveyor haulageways from return air courses, except where belt entries in areas of mines developed before March 30, 1970, are used as return air courses;

(3) To separate belt conveyor haulageways from intake air courses when the air in the intake air courses is used to provide air to active working places. Temporary ventilation controls may be used in rooms that are 600 feet or less from the centerline of the entry from which the rooms were developed including where continuous face haulage systems are used in such rooms. When continuous face haulage systems are used, permanent stoppings or other permanent ventilation control devices shall be built and maintained to the outby most point of travel of the dolly or 600 feet from the point of deepest penetration in the conveyor belt entry, whichever distance is closer to the point of deepest penetration, to separate the continuous haulage entry from the intake entries;

(4) To separate the primary escapeway from belt and trolley haulage entries, as required by § 75.380(g).

§ 75.333

For the purposes of § 75.380(g), the loading point for a continuous haulage system shall be the outby most point of travel of the dolly or 600 feet from the point of deepest penetration, whichever distance is less; and

(5) In return air courses to direct air into adjacent worked-out areas.

(c) Personnel doors shall be constructed of noncombustible material and shall be of sufficient strength to serve their intended purpose of maintaining separation and permitting travel between air courses, and shall be installed as follows in permanent stoppings constructed after November 15, 1992:

(1) The distance between personnel doors shall be no more than 300 feet in seam heights below 48 inches and 600 feet in seam heights 48 inches or higher.

(2) The location of all personnel doors in stoppings along escapeways shall be clearly marked so that the doors may be easily identified by anyone traveling in the escapeway and in the entries on either side of the doors.

(3) When not in use, personnel doors shall be closed.

(4) An airlock shall be established where the air pressure differential between air courses creates a static force exceeding 125 pounds on closed personnel doors along escapeways.

(d) Doors, other than personnel doors, constructed after November 15, 1992, that are used in lieu of permanent stoppings or to control ventilation within an air course shall be:

(1) Made of noncombustible material or coated on all accessible surfaces with flame-retardant materials having a flame-spread index of 25 or less, as tested under ASTM E162–87, "Standard Test Method for Surface Flammability of Materials Using a Radiant Heat Energy Source." This publication is incorporated by reference and may be inspected at any MSHA Coal Mine Safety and Health District Office, or at MSHA's Office of Standards, Regulations, and Variances, 201 12th Street South, Arlington, VA 22202–5452; 202–693–9440; and at the National Archives and Records Administration (NARA). For information on the availability of this material at NARA, call 202–741–6030, or go to: *http://www.archives.gov/federal_register/code_of_federal_regulations/ibr_locations.html*. In addition, copies of the document can be purchased from the American Society for Testing and Materials (ASTM), 100 Barr Harbor Drive, P.O. Box C700, West Conshohocken, PA 19428–2959; 610–832–9500; *http://www.astm.org*. This incorporation by reference was approved by the Director of the Federal Register in accordance with 5 U.S.C. 552(a) and 1 CFR part 51.

(2) Of sufficient strength to serve their intended purpose of maintaining separation and permitting travel between or within air courses or entries.

(3) Installed in pairs to form an airlock. When an airlock is used, one side of the airlock shall remain closed. When not in use, both sides shall be closed.

(e)(1)(i) Except as provided in paragraphs (e)(2), (3), and (4) of this section, all overcasts, undercasts, shaft partitions, permanent stoppings, and regulators, installed after June 10, 1996, shall be constructed in a traditionally accepted method and of materials that have been demonstrated to perform adequately or in a method and of materials that have been tested and shown to have a minimum strength equal to or greater than the traditionally accepted in-mine controls. Tests may be performed under ASTM E72–80, "Standard Methods of Conducting Strength Tests of Panels for Building Construction" (Section 12–Transverse Load–Specimen Vertical, load, only), or the operator may conduct comparative in-mine tests. In-mine tests shall be designed to demonstrate the comparative strength of the proposed construction and a traditionally accepted in-mine control. The publication ASTM E72–80, "Standard Methods of Conducting Strength Tests of Panels for Building Construction," is incorporated by reference and may be inspected at any MSHA Coal Mine Safety and Health District Office, or at MSHA's Office of Standards, Regulations, and Variances, 201 12th Street South, Arlington, VA 22202–5452; 202–693–9440; and at the National Archives and Records Administration (NARA). For information on the availability of this material at NARA, call 202–741–

Mine Safety and Health Admin., Labor §75.333

6030, or go to: *http://www.archives.gov/ federal_register/ code_of_federal_regulations/ ibr_locations.html*. In addition, copies of the document can be purchased from the American Society for Testing and Materials (ASTM), 100 Barr Harbor Drive, P.O. Box C700, West Conshohocken, PA 19428–2959; 610–832–9500; *http://www.astm.org*. This incorporation by reference was approved by the Director of the Federal Register in accordance with 5 U.S.C. 552(a) and 1 CFR part 51.

(ii) All overcasts, undercasts, shaft partitions, permanent stoppings, and regulators, installed after November 15, 1992, shall be constructed of non-combustible material. Materials that are suitable for the construction of overcasts, undercasts, shaft partitions, permanent stoppings, and regulators include concrete, concrete block, brick, cinder block, tile, or steel. No ventilation controls installed after November 15, 1992, shall be constructed of aluminum.

(2) In anthracite mines, permanent stoppings may be constructed of overlapping layers of hardwood mine boards, if the stoppings are a minimum 2 inches thick.

(3) When timbers are used to create permanent stoppings in heaving or caving areas, the stoppings shall be coated on all accessible surfaces with a flame-retardant material having a flame-spread index of 25 or less, as tested under ASTM E162–87, "Standard Test Method for Surface Flammability of Materials Using a Radiant Heat Energy Source." This publication is incorporated by reference and may be inspected at any MSHA Coal Mine Safety and Health District Office, or at MSHA's Office of Standards, Regulations, and Variances, 201 12th Street South, Arlington, VA 22202–5452; 202–693–9440; and at the National Archives and Records Administration (NARA). For information on the availability of this material at NARA, call 202–741–6030, or go to: *http://www.archives.gov/ federal_register/ code_of_federal_regulations/ ibr_locations.html*. In addition, copies of the document can be purchased from the American Society for Testing and Materials (ASTM), 100 Barr Harbor Drive, P.O. Box C700, West Conshohocken, PA 19428–2959; 610–832–9500; *http://www.astm.org*. This incorporation by reference was approved by the Director of the Federal Register in accordance with 5 U.S.C. 552(a) and 1 CFR part 51.

(4) In anthracite mines, doors and regulators may be constructed of overlapping layers of hardwood boards, if the doors, door frames, and regulators are a minimum 2 inches thick.

(f) When sealants are applied to ventilation controls, the sealant shall have a flame-spread index of 25 or less under ASTM E162–87, "Standard Test Method for Surface Flammability of Materials Using a Radiant Heat Energy Source." This publication is incorporated by reference and may be inspected at any MSHA Coal Mine Safety and Health District Office, or at MSHA's Office of Standards, Regulations, and Variances, 201 12th Street South, Arlington, VA 22202–5452; 202–693–9440; and at the National Archives and Records Administration (NARA). For information on the availability of this material at NARA, call 202–741–6030, or go to: *http://www.archives.gov/ federal_register/ code_of_federal_regulations/ ibr_locations.html*. In addition, copies of the document can be purchased from the American Society for Testing and Materials (ASTM), 100 Barr Harbor Drive, P.O. Box C700, West Conshohocken, PA 19428–2959; 610–832–9500; *http://www.astm.org*. This incorporation by reference was approved by the Director of the Federal Register in accordance with 5 U.S.C. 552(a) and 1 CFR part 51.

(g) Before mining is discontinued in an entry or room that is advanced more than 20 feet from the inby rib, a crosscut shall be made or line brattice shall be installed and maintained to provide adequate ventilation. When conditions such as methane liberation warrant a distance less than 20 feet, the approved ventilation plan shall specify the location of such rooms or entries and the maximum distance they will be developed before a crosscut is made or line brattice is installed.

§ 75.334

(h) All ventilation controls, including seals, shall be maintained to serve the purpose for which they were built.

[61 FR 9829, Mar. 11, 1996; 61 FR 20877, May 8, 1996; 61 FR 26442, May 28, 1996; 61 FR 29288, 29289, June 10, 1996, as amended at 67 FR 38386, June 4, 2002; 71 FR 16668, Apr. 3, 2006; 73 FR 80612, Dec. 31, 2008; 80 FR 52991, Sept. 2, 2015]

§ 75.334 Worked-out areas and areas where pillars are being recovered.

(a) Worked-out areas where no pillars have been recovered shall be—

(1) Ventilated so that methane-air mixtures and other gases, dusts, and fumes from throughout the worked-out areas are continuously diluted and routed into a return air course or to the surface of the mine; or

(2) Sealed.

(b)(1) During pillar recovery a bleeder system shall be used to control the air passing through the area and to continuously dilute and move methane-air mixtures and other gases, dusts, and fumes from the worked-out area away from active workings and into a return air course or to the surface of the mine.

(2) After pillar recovery a bleeder system shall be maintained to provide ventilation to the worked-out area, or the area shall be sealed.

(c) The approved ventilation plan shall specify the following:

(1) The design and use of bleeder systems;

(2) The means to determine the effectiveness of bleeder systems;

(3) The means for adequately maintaining bleeder entries free of obstructions such as roof falls and standing water; and

(4) The location of ventilating devices such as regulators, stoppings and bleeder connectors used to control air movement through the worked-out area.

(d) If the bleeder system used does not continuously dilute and move methane-air mixtures and other gases, dusts, and fumes away from worked-out areas into a return air course or to the surface of the mine, or it cannot be determined by examinations or evaluations under § 75.364 that the bleeder system is working effectively, the worked-out area shall be sealed.

(e) Each mining system shall be designed so that each worked-out area can be sealed. The approved ventilation plan shall specify the location and the sequence of construction of proposed seals.

(f) In place of the requirements of paragraphs (a) and (b) of this section, for mines with a demonstrated history of spontaneous combustion, or that are located in a coal seam determined to be susceptible to spontaneous combustion, the approved ventilation plan shall specify the following:

(1) Measures to detect methane, carbon monoxide, and oxygen concentrations during and after pillar recovery, and in worked-out areas where no pillars have been recovered, to determine if the areas must be ventilated or sealed.

(2) Actions that will be taken to protect miners from the hazards of spontaneous combustion.

(3) If a bleeder system will not be used, the methods that will be used to control spontaneous combustion, accumulations of methane-air mixtures, and other gases, dusts, and fumes in the worked-out area.

§ 75.335 Seal strengths, design applications, and installation.

(a) *Seal strengths.* Seals constructed on or after October 20, 2008 shall be designed, constructed, and maintained to withstand—

(1)(i) At least 50-psi overpressure when the atmosphere in the sealed area is monitored and maintained inert and designed using a pressure-time curve with an instantaneous overpressure of at least 50 psi. A minimum overpressure of at least 50 psi shall be maintained for at least four seconds then released instantaneously.

(ii) Seals constructed to separate the active longwall panel from the longwall panel previously mined shall be designed using a pressure-time curve with a rate of pressure rise of at least 50 psi in 0.1 second. A minimum overpressure of at least 50 psi shall be maintained; or

(2)(i) Overpressures of at least 120 psi if the atmosphere in the sealed area is not monitored, is not maintained inert, the conditions in paragraphs (a)(3)(i) through (iii) of this section are not present, and the seal is designed using a pressure-time curve with an instantaneous overpressure of at least 120 psi. A minimum overpressure of 120 psi shall be maintained for at least four seconds then released instantaneously.

(ii) Seals constructed to separate the active longwall panel from the longwall panel previously mined shall be designed using a pressure-time curve with a rate of pressure rise of 120 psi in 0.25 second. A minimum overpressure of 120 psi shall be maintained; or

(3) Overpressures greater than 120 psi if the atmosphere in the sealed area is not monitored and is not maintained inert, and

(i) The atmosphere in the sealed area is likely to contain homogeneous mixtures of methane between 4.5 percent and 17.0 percent and oxygen exceeding 17.0 percent throughout the entire area;

(ii) Pressure piling could result in overpressures greater than 120 psi in the area to be sealed; or

(iii) Other conditions are encountered, such as the likelihood of a detonation in the area to be sealed.

(iv) Where the conditions in paragraphs (a)(3)(i), (ii), or (iii) of this section are encountered, the mine operator shall revise the ventilation plan to address the potential hazards. The plan shall include seal strengths sufficient to address such conditions.

(b) *Seal design applications.* Seal design applications from seal manufacturers or mine operators shall be in accordance with paragraph (b)(1) or (2) of this section and submitted for approval to MSHA's Office of Technical Support, Pittsburgh Safety and Health Technology Center, 626 Cochrans Mill Road, Building 151, Pittsburgh, PA 15236–3611.

(1) An engineering design application shall—

(i) Address gas sampling pipes, water drainage systems, methods to reduce air leakage, pressure-time curve, fire resistance characteristics, flame spread index, entry size, engineering design and analysis, elasticity of design, material properties, construction specifications, quality control, design references, and other information related to seal construction;

(ii) Be certified by a professional engineer that the design of the seal is in accordance with current, prudent engineering practices and is applicable to conditions in an underground coal mine; and

(iii) Include a summary of the installation procedures related to seal construction; or

(2) Each application based on full-scale explosion tests or equivalent means of physical testing shall address the following requirements to ensure that a seal can reliably meet the seal strength requirements:

(i) Certification by a professional engineer that the testing was done in accordance with current, prudent engineering practices for construction in a coal mine;

(ii) Technical information related to the methods and materials;

(iii) Supporting documentation;

(iv) An engineering analysis to address differences between the seal support during test conditions and the range of conditions in a coal mine; and

(v) A summary of the installation procedures related to seal construction.

(3) MSHA will notify the applicant if additional information or testing is required. The applicant shall provide this information, arrange any additional or repeat tests, and provide prior notification to MSHA of the location, date, and time of such test(s).

(4) MSHA will notify the applicant, in writing, whether the design is approved or denied. If the design is denied, MSHA will specify, in writing, the deficiencies of the application, or necessary revisions.

(5) Once the seal design is approved, the approval holder shall promptly notify MSHA, in writing, of all deficiencies of which they become aware.

(c) *Seal installation approval.* The installation of the approved seal design shall be subject to approval in the ventilation plan. The mine operator shall—

(1) Retain the seal design approval and installation information for as long as the seal is needed to serve the purpose for which it was built.

(2) Designate a professional engineer to conduct or have oversight of seal installation and certify that the provisions in the approved seal design specified in this section have been addressed

§ 75.336

and are applicable to conditions at the mine. A copy of the certification shall be submitted to the District Manager with the information provided in paragraph (c)(3) of this section and a copy of the certification shall be retained for as long as the seal is needed to serve the purpose for which it was built.

(3) Provide the following information for approval in the ventilation plan—

(i) The MSHA Technical Support Approval Number;

(ii) A summary of the installation procedures;

(iii) The mine map of the area to be sealed and proposed seal locations that include the deepest points of penetration prior to sealing. The mine map shall be certified by a professional engineer or a professional land surveyor.

(iv) Specific mine site information, including—

(A) Type of seal;

(B) Safety precautions taken prior to seal achieving design strength;

(C) Methods to address site-specific conditions that may affect the strength and applicability of the seal including set-back distances;

(D) Site preparation;

(E) Sequence of seal installations;

(F) Projected date of completion of each set of seals;

(G) Supplemental roof support inby and outby each seal;

(H) Water flow estimation and dimensions of the water drainage system through the seals;

(I) Methods to ventilate the outby face of seals once completed;

(J) Methods and materials used to maintain each type of seal;

(K) Methods to address shafts and boreholes in the sealed area;

(L) Assessment of potential for overpressures greater than 120 psi in sealed area;

(M) Additional sampling locations; and

(N) Additional information required by the District Manager.

[73 FR 21206, Apr. 18, 2008, as amended at 80 FR 52982, Sept. 2, 2015]

§ 75.336 Sampling and monitoring requirements.

(a) A certified person as defined in § 75.100 shall monitor atmospheres of sealed areas. Sealed areas shall be monitored, whether ingassing or outgassing, for methane and oxygen concentrations and the direction of leakage.

(1) Each sampling pipe and approved sampling location shall be sampled at least every 24 hours.

(i) Atmospheres with seals of 120 psi or greater shall be sampled until the design strength is reached for every seal used to seal the area.

(ii) Atmospheres with seals less than 120 psi constructed before October 20, 2008 shall be monitored for methane and oxygen concentrations and maintained inert. The operator may request that the District Manager approve different sampling locations and frequencies in the ventilation plan, provided at least one sample is taken at each set of seals at least every 7 days.

(iii) Atmospheres with seals less than 120 psi constructed after October 20, 2008 shall be monitored for methane and oxygen concentrations and maintained inert. The operator may request that the District Manager approve different sampling locations and frequencies in the ventilation plan after a minimum of 14 days and after the seal design strength is reached, provided at least one sample is taken at each set of seals at least every 7 days.

(2) The mine operator shall evaluate the atmosphere in the sealed area to determine whether sampling through the sampling pipes in seals and approved locations provides appropriate sampling locations of the sealed area. The mine operator shall make the evaluation immediately after the minimum 14-day required sampling, if the mine ventilation system is reconfigured, if changes occur that adversely affect the sealed area, or if the District Manager requests an evaluation. When the results of the evaluations indicate the need for additional sampling locations, the mine operator shall provide the additional locations and have them approved in the ventilation plan. The District Manager may require additional sampling locations and frequencies in the ventilation plan.

(3) Mine operators with an approved ventilation plan addressing spontaneous combustion pursuant to § 75.334(f)

shall sample the sealed atmosphere in accordance with the ventilation plan.

(4) The District Manager may approve in the ventilation plan the use of a continuous monitoring system in lieu of monitoring provisions in this section.

(b)(1) Except as provided in § 75.336(d), the atmosphere in the sealed area is considered inert when the oxygen concentration is less than 10.0 percent or the methane concentration is less than 3.0 percent or greater than 20.0 percent.

(2) Immediate action shall be taken by the mine operator to restore an inert sealed atmosphere behind seals with strengths less than 120 psi. Until the atmosphere in the sealed area is restored to an inert condition, the sealed atmosphere shall be monitored at each sampling pipe and approved location at least once every 24 hours.

(c) Except as provided in § 75.336(d), when a sample is taken from the sealed atmosphere with seals of less than 120 psi and the sample indicates that the oxygen concentration is 10 percent or greater and methane is between 4.5 percent and 17 percent, the mine operator shall immediately take an additional sample and then immediately notify the District Manager. When the additional sample indicates that the oxygen concentration is 10 percent or greater and methane is between 4.5 percent and 17 percent, persons shall be withdrawn from the affected area which is the entire mine or other affected area identified by the operator and approved by the District Manager in the ventilation plan, except those persons referred to in § 104(c) of the Act. The operator may identify areas in the ventilation plan to be approved by the District Manager where persons may be exempted from withdrawal. The operator's request shall address the location of seals in relation to: Areas where persons work and travel in the mine; escapeways and potential for damage to the escapeways; and ventilation systems and controls in areas where persons work or travel and where ventilation is used for escapeways. The operator's request shall also address the gas concentration of other sampling locations in the sealed area and other required information. Before miners reenter the mine, the mine operator shall have a ventilation plan revision approved by the District Manager specifying the actions to be taken.

(d) In sealed areas with a demonstrated history of carbon dioxide or sealed areas where inert gases have been injected, the operator may request that the District Manager approve in the ventilation plan an alternative method to determine if the sealed atmosphere is inert and when miners have to be withdrawn. The mine operator shall address in the ventilation plan the specific levels of methane, carbon dioxide, nitrogen and oxygen; the sampling methods and equipment used; and the methods to evaluate these concentrations underground at the seal.

(e) *Recordkeeping.* (1) The certified person shall promptly record each sampling result including the location of the sampling points, whether ingassing or outgassing, and oxygen and methane concentrations. The results of oxygen and methane samples shall be recorded as the percentage of oxygen and methane measured by the certified person and any hazardous condition found in accordance with § 75.363.

(2) The mine operator shall retain sampling records at the mine for at least one year from the date of the sampling.

[73 FR 21207, Apr. 18, 2008; 73 FR 27730, May 14, 2008]

§ 75.337 Construction and repair of seals.

(a) The mine operator shall maintain and repair seals to protect miners from hazards of sealed areas.

(b) Prior to sealing, the mine operator shall—

(1) Remove insulated cables, batteries, and other potential electric ignition sources from the area to be sealed when constructing seals, unless it is not safe to do so. If ignition sources cannot safely be removed, seals must be constructed to at least 120 psi;

(2) Remove metallic objects through or across seals; and

(3) Breach or remove all stoppings in the first crosscut inby the seals immediately prior to sealing the area.

§ 75.338

(c) A certified person designated by the mine operator shall directly supervise seal construction and repair and—

(1) Examine each seal site immediately prior to construction or repair to ensure that the site is in accordance with the approved ventilation plan;

(2) Examine each seal under construction or repair during each shift to ensure that the seal is being constructed or repaired in accordance with the approved ventilation plan;

(3) Examine each seal upon completion of construction or repair to ensure that construction or repair is in accordance with the approved ventilation plan;

(4) Certify by initials, date, and time that the examinations were made; and

(5) Make a record of the examination at the completion of any shift during which an examination was conducted. The record shall include each deficiency and the corrective action taken. The record shall be countersigned by the mine foreman or equivalent mine official by the end of the mine foreman's or equivalent mine official's next regularly scheduled working shift. The record shall be kept at the mine for one year.

(d) Upon completion of construction of each seal a senior mine management official, such as a mine manager or superintendent, shall certify that the construction, installation, and materials used were in accordance with the approved ventilation plan. The mine operator shall retain the certification for as long as the seal is needed to serve the purpose for which it was built.

(e) The mine operator shall—

(1) Notify the District Manager between two and fourteen days prior to commencement of seal construction;

(2) Notify the District Manager, in writing, within five days of completion of a set of seals and provide a copy of the certification required in paragraph (d) of this section; and

(3) Submit a copy of quality control results to the District Manager for seal material properties specified by § 75.335 within 30 days of completion of quality control tests.

(f) *Welding, cutting, and soldering.* Welding, cutting, and soldering with an arc or flame are prohibited within 150 feet of a seal. An operator may request a different location in the ventilation plan to be approved by the District Manager. The operator's request must address methods the mine operator will use to continuously monitor atmospheric conditions in the sealed area during welding or burning; the airflow conditions in and around the work area; the rock dust and water application methods; the availability of fire extinguishers on hand; the procedures to maintain safe conditions, and other relevant factors.

(g) *Sampling pipes.* (1) For seals constructed after April 18, 2008, one non-metallic sampling pipe shall be installed in each seal that shall extend into the center of the first connecting crosscut inby the seal. If an open crosscut does not exist, the sampling pipe shall extend one-half of the distance of the open entry inby the seal.

(2) Each sampling pipe shall be equipped with a shut-off valve and appropriate fittings for taking gas samples.

(3) The sampling pipes shall be labeled to indicate the location of the sampling point when more than one sampling pipe is installed through a seal.

(4) If a new seal is constructed to replace or reinforce an existing seal with a sampling pipe, the sampling pipe in the existing seal shall extend through the new seal. An additional sampling pipe shall be installed through each new seal to sample the area between seals, as specified in the approved ventilation plan.

(h) *Water drainage system.* For each set of seals constructed after April 18, 2008, the seal at the lowest elevation shall have a corrosion-resistant, non-metallic water drainage system. Seals shall not impound water or slurry. Water or slurry shall not accumulate within the sealed area to any depth that can adversely affect a seal.

[73 FR 21207, Apr. 18, 2008]

§ 75.338 Training.

(a) Certified persons conducting sampling shall be trained in the use of appropriate sampling equipment, procedures, location of sampling points, frequency of sampling, size and condition

Mine Safety and Health Admin., Labor § 75.340

of the sealed area, and the use of continuous monitoring systems if applicable before they conduct sampling, and annually thereafter. The mine operator shall certify the date of training provided to certified persons and retain each certification for two years.

(b) Miners constructing or repairing seals, designated certified persons, and senior mine management officials shall be trained prior to constructing or repairing a seal and annually thereafter. The training shall address materials and procedures in the approved seal design and ventilation plan. The mine operator shall certify the date of training provided each miner, certified person, and senior mine management official and retain each certification for two years.

[73 FR 21208, Apr. 18, 2008]

§ 75.339 Seals records.

(a) The table entitled "Seal Recordkeeping Requirements" lists records the operator shall maintain and the retention period for each record.

TABLE—§ 75.339(a) SEAL RECORDKEEPING REQUIREMENTS

Record	Section reference	Retention time
(1) Approved seal design	75.335(c)(1)	As long as the seal is needed to serve the purpose for which it is built.
(2) Certification of Provisions of Approved Seal Design is Addressed.	75.335(c)(2)	As long as the seal is needed to serve the purpose for which it is built.
(3) Gas sampling records	75.336(e)(2)	1 year.
(4) Record of examinations	75.337(c)(5)	1 year.
(5) Certification of seal construction, installation, and materials.	75.337(d)	As long as the seal is needed to serve the purpose for which it is built.
(6) Certification of Training for Persons that Sample.	75.338(a)	2 years.
(7) Certification of Training for Persons that Perform Seal Construction and Repair.	75.338(b)	2 years.

(b) Records required by §§ 75.335, 75.336, 75.337 and 75.338 shall be retained at a surface location at the mine in a secure book that is not susceptible to alteration. The records may be retained electronically in a computer system that is secure and not susceptible to alteration, if the mine operator can immediately access the record from the mine site.

(c) Upon request from an authorized representative of the Secretary of Labor, the Secretary of Health and Human Services, or from the authorized representative of miners, mine operators shall promptly provide access to any record listed in the table in this section.

(d) Whenever an operator ceases to do business or transfers control of the mine to another entity, that operator shall transfer all records required to be maintained by this part, or a copy thereof, to any successor operator who shall maintain them for the required period.

[73 FR 21208, Apr. 18, 2008]

§ 75.340 Underground electrical installations.

(a) Underground transformer stations, battery charging stations, substations, rectifiers, and water pumps shall be housed in noncombustible structures or areas or be equipped with a fire suppression system meeting the requirements of § 75.1107–3 through § 75.1107–16.

(1) When a noncombustible structure or area is used, these installations shall be—

(i) Ventilated with intake air that is coursed into a return air course or to the surface and that is not used to ventilate working places; or

(ii) Ventilated with intake air that is monitored for carbon monoxide or smoke by an AMS installed and operated according to § 75.351. Monitoring of intake air ventilating battery charging stations shall be done with sensors not affected by hydrogen; or

(iii) Ventilated with intake air and equipped with sensors to monitor for heat and for carbon monoxide or smoke. Monitoring of intake air ventilating battery charging stations shall

§ 75.341

be done with sensors not affected by hydrogen. The sensors shall deenergize power to the installation, activate a visual and audible alarm located outside of and on the intake side of the enclosure, and activate doors that will automatically close when either of the following occurs:

(A) The temperature in the noncombustible structure reaches 165 °F; or

(B) The carbon monoxide concentration reaches 10 parts per million above the ambient level for the area, or the optical density of smoke reaches 0.022 per meter. At least every 31 days, sensors installed to monitor for carbon monoxide shall be calibrated with a known concentration of carbon monoxide and air sufficient to activate the closing door, or each smoke sensor shall be tested to determine that it functions correctly.

(2) When a fire suppression system is used, these installations shall be—

(i) Ventilated with intake air that is coursed into a return air course or to the surface and that is not used to ventilate working places; or

(ii) Ventilated with intake air that is monitored for carbon monoxide or smoke by an AMS installed and operated according to § 75.351. Monitoring of intake air ventilating battery charging stations shall be done with sensors not affected by hydrogen.

(b) This section does not apply to—

(1) Rectifiers and power centers with transformers that are either dry-type or contain nonflammable liquid, if they are located at or near the section and are moved as the working section advances or retreats;

(2) Submersible pumps;

(3) Permissible pumps and associated permissible switchgear;

(4) Pumps located on or near the section and that are moved as the working section advances or retreats;

(5) Pumps installed in anthracite mines; and

(6) Small portable pumps.

§ 75.341 Direct-fired intake air heaters.

(a) If any system used to heat intake air malfunctions, the heaters affected shall switch off automatically.

(b) Thermal overload devices shall protect the blower motor from overheating.

(c) The fuel supply shall turn off automatically if a flame-out occurs.

(d) Each heater shall be located or guarded to prevent contact by persons and shall be equipped with a screen at the inlet to prevent combustible materials from passing over the burner units.

(e) If intake air heaters use liquefied fuel systems—

(1) Hydrostatic relief valves installed on vaporizers and on storage tanks shall be vented; and

(2) Fuel storage tanks shall be located or protected to prevent fuel from leaking into the mine.

(f) Following any period of 8 hours or more during which a heater does not operate, the heater and its associated components shall be examined within its first hour of operation. Additionally, each heater and its components shall be examined at least once each shift that the heater operates. The examination shall include measurement of the carbon monoxide concentration at the bottom of each shaft, slope, or in the drift opening where air is being heated. The measurements shall be taken by a person designated by the operator or by a carbon monoxide sensor that is calibrated with a known concentration of carbon monoxide and air at least once every 31 days. When the carbon monoxide concentration at this location reaches 50 parts per million, the heater causing the elevated carbon monoxide level shall be shut down.

§ 75.342 Methane monitors.

(a)(1) MSHA approved methane monitors shall be installed on all face cutting machines, continuous miners, longwall face equipment, loading machines, and other mechanized equipment used to extract or load coal within the working place.

(2) The sensing device for methane monitors on longwall shearing machines shall be installed at the return air end of the longwall face. An additional sensing device also shall be installed on the longwall shearing machine, downwind and as close to the

cutting head as practicable. An alternative location or locations for the sensing device required on the longwall shearing machine may be approved in the ventilation plan.

(3) The sensing devices of methane monitors shall be installed as close to the working face as practicable.

(4) Methane monitors shall be maintained in permissible and proper operating condition and shall be calibrated with a known air-methane mixture at least once every 31 days. To assure that methane monitors are properly maintained and calibrated, the operator shall:

(i) Use persons properly trained in the maintenance, calibration, and permissibility of methane monitors to calibrate and maintain the devices.

(ii) Maintain a record of all calibration tests of methane monitors. Records shall be maintained in a secure book that is not susceptible to alteration or electronically in a computer system so as to be secure and not susceptible to alteration.

(iii) Retain the record of calibration tests for 1 year from the date of the test. Records shall be retained at a surface location at the mine and made available for inspection by authorized representatives of the Secretary and the representative of miners.

(b)(1) When the methane concentration at any methane monitor reaches 1.0 percent the monitor shall give a warning signal.

(2) The warning signal device of the methane monitor shall be visible to a person who can deenergize electric equipment or shut down diesel-powered equipment on which the monitor is mounted.

(c) The methane monitor shall automatically deenergize electric equipment or shut down diesel-powered equipment on which it is mounted when—

(1) The methane concentration at any methane monitor reaches 2.0 percent; or

(2) The monitor is not operating properly.

[61 FR 9829, Mar. 11, 1996, as amended at 61 FR 55527, Oct. 25, 1996]

§ 75.343 Underground shops.

(a) Underground shops shall be equipped with an automatic fire suppression system meeting the requirements of § 75.1107–3 through § 75.1107–16, or be enclosed in a noncombustible structure or area.

(b) Underground shops shall be ventilated with intake air that is coursed directly into a return air course.

§ 75.344 Compressors.

(a) Except compressors that are components of equipment such as locomotives and rock dusting machines and compressors of less than 5 horsepower, electrical compressors including those that may start automatically shall be:

(1) Continuously attended by a person designated by the operator who can see the compressor at all times during its operation. Any designated person attending the compressor shall be capable of activating the fire suppression system and deenergizing or shutting-off the compressor in the event of a fire; or,

(2) Enclosed in a noncombustible structure or area which is ventilated by intake air coursed directly into a return air course or to the surface and equipped with sensors to monitor for heat and for carbon monoxide or smoke. The sensors shall deenergize power to the compressor, activate a visual and audible alarm located outside of and on the intake side of the enclosure, and activate doors to automatically enclose the noncombustible structure or area when either of the following occurs:

(i) The temperature in the noncombustible structure or area reaches 165 °F.

(ii) The carbon monoxide concentration reaches 10 parts per million above the ambient level for the area, or the optical density of smoke reaches 0.022 per meter. At least once every 31 days, sensors installed to monitor for carbon monoxide shall be calibrated with a known concentration of carbon monoxide and air sufficient to activate the closing door, and each smoke sensor shall be tested to determine that it functions correctly.

(b) Compressors, except those exempted in paragraph (a), shall be

§ 75.350

equipped with a heat activated fire suppression system meeting the requirements of 75.1107–3 through 75.1107–16.

(c) Two portable fire extinguishers or one extinguisher having at least twice the minimum capacity specified for a portable fire extinguisher in § 75.1100–1(e) shall be provided for each compressor.

(d) Notwithstanding the requirements of § 75.1107–4, upon activation of any fire suppression system used under paragraph (b) of this section, the compressor shall be automatically deenergized or automatically shut off.

[61 FR 9829, Mar. 11, 1996, as amended at 61 FR 55527, Oct. 25, 1996]

§ 75.350 Belt air course ventilation.

(a) The belt air course must not be used as a return air course; and except as provided in paragraph (b) of this section, the belt air course must not be used to provide air to working sections or to areas where mechanized mining equipment is being installed or removed.

(1) The belt air course must be separated with permanent ventilation controls from return air courses and from other intake air courses except as provided in paragraph (c) of this section.

(2) Effective December 31, 2009, the air velocity in the belt entry must be at least 50 feet per minute. When requested by the mine operator, the district manager may approve lower velocities in the ventilation plan based on specific mine conditions. Air velocities must be compatible with all fire detection systems and fire suppression systems used in the belt entry.

(b) The use of air from a belt air course to ventilate a working section, or an area where mechanized mining equipment is being installed or removed, shall be permitted only when evaluated and approved by the district manager in the mine ventilation plan. The mine operator must provide justification in the plan that the use of air from a belt entry would afford at least the same measure of protection as where belt haulage entries are not used to ventilate working places. In addition, the following requirements must be met:

(1) The belt entry must be equipped with an AMS that is installed, operated, examined, and maintained as specified in § 75.351.

(2) All miners must be trained annually in the basic operating principles of the AMS, including the actions required in the event of activation of any AMS alert or alarm signal. This training must be conducted prior to working underground in a mine that uses belt air to ventilate working sections or areas where mechanized mining equipment is installed or removed. It must be conducted as part of a miner's 30 CFR part 48 new miner training (§ 48.5), experienced miner training (§ 48.6), or annual refresher training (§ 48.8).

(3)(i) The average concentration of respirable dust in the belt air course, when used as a section intake air course, shall be maintained at or below:

(A) 1.0 mg/m³.

(B) 0.5 mg/m³ as of August 1, 2016.

(ii) Where miners on the working section are on a reduced standard below that specified in § 75.350(b)(3)(i), the average concentration of respirable dust in the belt entry must be at or below the lowest applicable standard on that section.

(iii) A permanent designated area (DA) for dust measurements must be established at a point no greater than 50 feet upwind from the section loading point in the belt entry when the belt air flows over the loading point or no greater than 50 feet upwind from the point where belt air is mixed with air from another intake air course near the loading point. The DA must be specified and approved in the ventilation plan.

(4) The primary escapeway must be monitored for carbon monoxide or smoke as specified in § 75.351(f).

(5) The area of the mine with a belt air course must be developed with three or more entries.

(6) In areas of the mine developed after the effective date of this rule, unless approved by the district manager, no more than 50% of the total intake air, delivered to the working section or to areas where mechanized mining equipment is being installed or removed, can be supplied from the belt air course. The locations for measuring these air quantities must be approved in the mine ventilation plan.

Mine Safety and Health Admin., Labor § 75.351

(7) The air velocity in the belt entry must be at least 100 feet per minute. When requested by the mine operator, the district manager may approve lower velocities in the ventilation plan based on specific mine conditions.

(8) The air velocity in the belt entry must not exceed 1,000 feet per minute. When requested by the mine operator, the district manager may approve higher velocities in the ventilation plan based on specific mine conditions.

(c) Notwithstanding the provisions of § 75.380(g), additional intake air may be added to the belt air course through a point-feed regulator. The location and use of point feeds must be approved in the mine ventilation plan.

(d) If the air through the point-feed regulator enters a belt air course which is used to ventilate a working section or an area where mechanized mining equipment is being installed or removed, the following conditions must be met:

(1) The air current that will pass through the point-feed regulator must be monitored for carbon monoxide or smoke at a point within 50 feet upwind of the point-feed regulator. A second point must be monitored 1,000 feet upwind of the point-feed regulator unless the mine operator requests that a lesser distance be approved by the district manager in the mine ventilation plan based on mine specific conditions;

(2) The air in the belt air course must be monitored for carbon monoxide or smoke upwind of the point-feed regulator. This sensor must be in the belt air course within 50 feet of the mixing point where air flowing through the point-feed regulator mixes with the belt air;

(3) The point-feed regulator must be provided with a means to close the regulator from the intake air course without requiring a person to enter the crosscut where the point-feed regulator is located. The point-feed regulator must also be provided with a means to close the regulator from a location in the belt air course immediately upwind of the crosscut containing the point-feed regulator;

(4) A minimum air velocity of 300 feet per minute must be maintained through the point-feed regulator;

(5) The location(s) and use of a point-feed regulator(s) must be approved in the mine ventilation plan and shown on the mine ventilation map; and

(6) An AMS must be installed, operated, examined, and maintained as specified in § 75.351.

[69 FR 17526, Apr. 2, 2004, as amended at 70 FR 37266, June 29, 2005; 71 FR 12269, Mar. 9, 2006; 73 FR 80612, Dec. 31, 2008; 79 FR 24987, May 1, 2014]

§ 75.351 Atmospheric monitoring systems.

(a) *AMS operation.* Whenever personnel are underground and an AMS is used to fulfill the requirements of §§ 75.323(d)(1)(ii), 75.340(a)(1)(ii), 75.340(a)(2)(ii), 75.350(b), 75.350(d), or 75.362(f), the AMS must be operating and a designated AMS operator must be on duty at a location on the surface of the mine where audible and visual signals from the AMS must be seen or heard and the AMS operator can promptly respond to these signals.

(b) *Designated surface location and AMS operator.* When an AMS is used to comply with §§ 75.323(d)(1)(ii), 75.340(a)(1)(ii), 75.340(a)(2)(ii), 75.350(b), 75.350(d), or 75.362(f), the following requirements apply:

(1) The mine operator must designate a surface location at the mine where signals from the AMS will be received and two-way voice communication is maintained with each working section, with areas where mechanized mining equipment is being installed or removed, and with other areas designated in the approved emergency evacuation and firefighting program of instruction (§ 75.1502).

(2) The mine operator must designate an AMS operator to monitor and promptly respond to all AMS signals. The AMS operator must have as a primary duty the responsibility to monitor the malfunction, alert and alarm signals of the AMS, and to notify appropriate personnel of these signals. In the event of an emergency, the sole responsibility of the AMS operator shall be to respond to the emergency.

(3) A map or schematic must be provided at the designated surface location that shows the locations and type of AMS sensor at each location, and the intended air flow direction at these

§ 75.351

locations. This map or schematic must be updated within 24 hours of any change in this information.

(4) The names of the designated AMS operators and other appropriate personnel, including the designated person responsible for initiating an emergency mine evacuation under § 75.1501, and the method to contact these persons, must be provided at the designated surface location.

(c) *Minimum operating requirements.* AMSs used to comply with §§ 75.323(d)(1)(ii), 75.340(a)(1)(ii), 75.340(a)(2)(ii), 75.350(b), 75.350(d), or 75.362(f) must:

(1) Automatically provide visual and audible signals at the designated surface location for any interruption of circuit continuity and any electrical malfunction of the system. These signals must be of sufficient magnitude to be seen or heard by the AMS operator.

(2) Automatically provide visual and audible signals at the designated surface location when the carbon monoxide concentration or methane concentration at any sensor reaches the alert level as specified in § 75.351(i). These signals must be of sufficient magnitude to be seen or heard by the AMS operator.

(3) Automatically provide visual and audible signals at the designated surface location distinguishable from alert signals when the carbon monoxide, smoke, or methane concentration at any sensor reaches the alarm level as specified in § 75.351(i). These signals must be of sufficient magnitude to be seen or heard by the AMS operator.

(4) Automatically provide visual and audible signals at all affected working sections and at all affected areas where mechanized mining equipment is being installed or removed when the carbon monoxide, smoke, or methane concentration at any sensor reaches the alarm level as specified in § 75.351(i). These signals must be of sufficient magnitude to be seen or heard by miners working at these locations. Methane signals must be distinguishable from other signals.

(5) Automatically provide visual and audible signals at other locations as specified in Mine Emergency Evacuation and Firefighting Program of In-

30 CFR Ch. I (7-1-23 Edition)

struction (§ 75.1502) when the carbon monoxide, smoke, or methane concentration at any sensor reaches the alarm level as specified in § 75.351(i). These signals must be seen or heard by miners working at these locations. Methane alarms must be distinguishable from other signals.

(6) Identify at the designated surface location the operational status of all sensors.

(7) Automatically provide visual and audible alarm signals at the designated surface location, at all affected working sections, and at all affected areas where mechanized mining equipment is being installed or removed when the carbon monoxide level at any two consecutive sensors alert at the same time. These signals must be seen or heard by the AMS operator and miners working at these locations.

(d) *Location and installation of AMS sensors.* (1) All AMS sensors, as specified in §§ 75.351(e) through 75.351(h), must be located such that measurements are representative of the mine atmosphere in these locations.

(2) Carbon monoxide or smoke sensors must be installed near the center in the upper third of the entry, in a location that does not expose personnel working on the system to unsafe conditions. Sensors must not be located in abnormally high areas or in other locations where air flow patterns do not permit products of combustion to be carried to the sensors.

(3) Methane sensors must be installed near the center of the entry, at least 12 inches from the roof, ribs, and floor, in a location that would not expose personnel working on the system to unsafe conditions.

(e) *Location of sensors-belt air course.* (1) In addition to the requirements of paragraph (d) of this section, any AMS used to monitor belt air courses under § 75.350(b) must have approved sensors to monitor for carbon monoxide at the following locations:

(i) At or near the working section belt tailpiece in the air stream ventilating the belt entry. In longwall mining systems the sensor must be located upwind in the belt entry at a distance no greater than 150 feet from the mixing point where intake air is mixed

Mine Safety and Health Admin., Labor § 75.351

with the belt air at or near the tailpiece;

(ii) No more than 50 feet upwind from the point where the belt air course is combined with another air course or splits into multiple air courses;

(iii) At intervals not to exceed 1,000 feet along each belt entry. However, in areas along each belt entry where air velocities are between 50 and 100 feet per minute, spacing of sensors must not exceed 500 feet. In areas along each belt entry where air velocities are less than 50 feet per minute, the sensor spacing must not exceed 350 feet;

(iv) Not more than 100 feet downwind of each belt drive unit, each tailpiece, transfer point, and each belt take-up. If the belt drive, tailpiece, and/or take-up for a single transfer point are installed together in the same air course, and the distance between the units is less than 100 feet, they may be monitored with one sensor downwind of the last component. If the distance between the units exceeds 100 feet, additional sensors are required downwind of each belt drive unit, each tailpiece, transfer point, and each belt take-up; and

(v) At other locations in any entry that is part of the belt air course as required and specified in the mine ventilation plan.

(2) Smoke sensors must be installed to monitor the belt entry under § 75.350(b) at the following locations:

(i) At or near the working section belt tailpiece in the air stream ventilating the belt entry. In longwall mining systems the sensor must be located upwind in the belt entry at a distance no greater than 150 feet from the mixing point where intake air is mixed with the belt air at or near the tailpiece;

(ii) Not more than 100 feet downwind of each belt drive unit, each tailpiece transfer point, and each belt take-up. If the belt drive, tailpiece, and/or take-up for a single transfer point are installed together in the same air course, and the distance between the units is less than 100 feet, they may be monitored with one sensor downwind of the last component. If the distance between the units exceeds 100 feet, additional sensors are required downwind of each belt drive unit, each tailpiece, transfer point, and each belt take-up; and

(iii) At intervals not to exceed 3,000 feet along each belt entry.

(iv) This provision shall be effective one year after the Secretary has determined that a smoke sensor is available to reliably detect fire in underground coal mines.

(f) *Locations of sensors—the primary escapeway.* When used to monitor the primary escapeway under § 75.350(b)(4), carbon monoxide or smoke sensors must be located in the primary escapeway within 500 feet of the working section and areas where mechanized mining equipment is being installed or removed. In addition, another sensor must be located within 500 feet inby the beginning of the panel. The point-feed sensor required by § 75.350(d)(1) may be used as the sensor at the beginning of the panel if it is located within 500 feet inby the beginning of the panel.

(g) *Location of sensors—return air splits.* (1) If used to monitor return air splits under § 75.362(f), a methane sensor must be installed in the return air split between the last working place, longwall or shortwall face ventilated by that air split, and the junction of the return air split with another air split, seal, or worked out area.

(2) If used to monitor a return air split under § 75.323(d)(1)(ii), the methane sensors must be installed at the following locations:

(i) In the return air course opposite the section loading point, or, if exhausting auxiliary fan(s) are used, in the return air course no closer than 300 feet downwind from the fan exhaust and at a point opposite or immediately outby the section loading point; and

(ii) Immediately upwind from the location where the return air split meets another air split or immediately upwind of the location where an air split is used to ventilate seals or worked-out areas.

(h) *Location of sensors—electrical installations.* When monitoring the intake air ventilating underground transformer stations, battery charging stations, substations, rectifiers, or water pumps under § 75.340(a)(1)(ii) or § 75.340(a)(2)(ii), at least one sensor must be installed to monitor the mine atmosphere for carbon monoxide or smoke, located downwind and not

§ 75.351

greater than 50 feet from the electrical installation being monitored.

(i) *Establishing alert and alarm levels.* An AMS installed in accordance with the following paragraphs must initiate alert and alarm signals at the specified levels, as indicated:

(1) For § 75.323(d)(1)(ii) alarm at 1.5% methane.

(2) For §§ 75.340(a)(1)(ii), 75.340(a)(2)(ii), 75.350(b), and 75.350(d), alert at 5 ppm carbon monoxide above the ambient level and alarm at 10 ppm carbon monoxide above the ambient level when carbon monoxide sensors are used; and alarm at a smoke optical density of 0.022 per meter when smoke sensors are used. Reduced alert and alarm settings approved by the district manager may be required for carbon monoxide sensors identified in the mine ventilation plan, § 75.371(nn).

(3) For § 75.362(f), alert at 1.0% methane and alarm at 1.5% methane.

(j) *Establishing carbon monoxide ambient levels.* Carbon monoxide ambient levels and the means to determine these levels must be approved in the mine ventilation plan (§ 75.371(hh)) for monitors installed in accordance with §§ 75.340(a)(1)(ii), 75.340(a)(2)(ii), 75.350(b), and 75.350(d).

(k) *Installation and maintenance.* An AMS installed in accordance with §§ 75.323(d)(1)(ii), 75.340(a)(1)(ii), 75.340(a)(2)(ii), 75.350(b), 75.350(d), or 75.362(f) must be installed and maintained by personnel trained in the installation and maintenance of the system. The system must be maintained in proper operating condition.

(l) *Sensors.* Sensors used to monitor for carbon monoxide, methane, and smoke must be either of a type listed and installed in accordance with the recommendations of a nationally recognized testing laboratory approved by the Secretary; or these sensors must be of a type, and installed in a manner, approved by the Secretary.

(m) *Time delays.* When a demonstrated need exists, time delays may be incorporated into the AMS. These time delays must only be used to account for non-fire related carbon monoxide alert and alarm sensor signals. These time delays are limited to no more than three minutes. The use and length of any time delays, or other techniques or methods which eliminate or reduce the need for time delays, must be specified and approved in the mine ventilation plan.

(n) *Examination, testing, and calibration.* (1) At least once each shift when belts are operated as part of a production shift, sensors used to detect carbon monoxide or smoke in accordance with §§ 75.350(b), and 75.350(d), and alarms installed in accordance with § 75.350(b) must be visually examined.

(2) At least once every seven days, alarms for AMS installed in accordance with §§ 75.350(b), and 75.350(d) must be functionally tested for proper operation.

(3) At intervals not to exceed 31 days—

(i) Each carbon monoxide sensor installed in accordance with §§ 75.340(a)(1)(ii), 75.340(a)(2)(ii), 75.350(b), or 75.350(d) must be calibrated in accordance with the manufacturer's calibration specifications. Calibration must be done with a known concentration of carbon monoxide in air sufficient to activate the alarm;

(ii) Each smoke sensor installed in accordance with §§ 75.340(a)(1)(ii), 75.340(a)(2)(ii), 75.350(b), or 75.350(d) must be functionally tested in accordance with the manufacturer's calibration specifications;

(iii) Each methane sensor installed in accordance with §§ 75.323(d)(1)(ii) or 75.362(f) must be calibrated in accordance with the manufacturer's calibration specifications. Calibration must be done with a known concentration of methane in air sufficient to activate an alarm.

(iv) If the alert or alarm signals will be activated during calibration of sensors, the AMS operator must be notified prior to and upon completion of calibration. The AMS operator must notify miners on affected working sections, areas where mechanized mining equipment is being installed or removed, or other areas designated in the approved emergency evacuation and firefighting program of instruction (§ 75.1502) when calibration will activate alarms and when calibration is completed.

(4) Gases used for the testing and calibration of AMS sensors must be traceable to the National Institute of

Standards and Technology reference standard for the specific gas. When these reference standards are not available for a specific gas, calibration gases must be traceable to an analytical standard which is prepared using a method traceable to the National Institute of Standards and Technology. Calibration gases must be within ±2.0 percent of the indicated gas concentration.

(o) *Recordkeeping.* (1) When an AMS is used to comply with §§ 75.323(d)(1)(ii), 75.340(a)(1)(ii), 75.340(a)(2)(ii), 75.350(b), 75.350(d), or 75.362(f), individuals designated by the operator must make the following records by the end of the shift in which the following event(s) occur:

(i) If an alert or alarm signal occurs, a record of the date, time, location and type of sensor, and the cause for the activation.

(ii) If an AMS malfunctions, a record of the date, the extent and cause of the malfunction, and the corrective action taken to return the system to proper operation.

(iii) A record of the seven-day tests of alert and alarm signals; calibrations; and maintenance of the AMS must be made by the person(s) performing these actions.

(2) The person entering the record must include their name, date, and signature in the record.

(3) The records required by this section must be kept either in a secure book that is not susceptible to alteration, or electronically in a computer system that is secure and not susceptible to alteration. These records must be maintained separately from other records and identifiable by a title, such as the 'AMS log.'

(p) *Retention period.* Records must be retained for at least one year at a surface location at the mine and made available for inspection by miners and authorized representatives of the Secretary.

(q) *Training.* (1) All AMS operators must be trained annually in the proper operation of the AMS. This training must include the following subjects:

(i) Familiarity with underground mining systems;

(ii) Basic atmospheric monitoring system requirements;

(iii) The mine emergency evacuation and firefighting program of instruction;

(iv) The mine ventilation system including planned air directions;

(v) Appropriate response to alert, alarm and malfunction signals;

(vi) Use of mine communication systems including emergency notification procedures; and

(vii) AMS recordkeeping requirements.

(2) At least once every six months, all AMS operators must travel to all working sections.

(3) A record of the content of training, the person conducting the training, and the date the training was conducted, must be maintained at the mine for at least one year by the mine operator.

(r) *Communications.* When an AMS is used to comply with § 75.350(b), a two-way voice communication system required by § 75.1600 must be installed in an entry that is separate from the entry in which the AMS is installed no later than August 2, 2004. The two-way voice communication system may be installed in the entry where the intake sensors required by §§ 75.350(b)(4) or 75.350(d)(1) are installed.

[69 FR 17527, Apr. 2, 2004, as amended at 73 FR 80612, Dec. 31, 2008]

§ 75.352 Actions in response to AMS malfunction, alert, or alarm signals.

(a) When a malfunction, alert, or alarm signal is received at the designated surface location, the sensor(s) that are activated must be identified and the AMS operator must promptly notify appropriate personnel.

(b) Upon notification of a malfunction, alert, or alarm signal, appropriate personnel must promptly initiate an investigation to determine the cause of the signal and take the required actions set forth in paragraphs (c), (d), or (e) of this section.

(c) If any sensor installed in accordance with §§ 75.340(a)(1)(ii), 75.340(a)(2)(ii), 75.350(b), or 75.350(d) indicates an alarm or if any two consecutive sensors indicate alert at the same time, the following procedures must be followed unless the cause of the signal(s) is known not to be a hazard to miners:

§ 75.360

(1) Appropriate personnel must notify miners in affected working sections, in affected areas where mechanized mining equipment is being installed or removed, and at other locations specified in the § 75.1502 approved mine emergency evacuation and firefighting program of instruction; and

(2) All personnel in the affected areas, unless assigned other duties under § 75.1502, must be withdrawn promptly to a safe location identified in the mine emergency evacuation and firefighting program of instruction.

(d) If there is an alert or alarm signal from a methane sensor installed in accordance with §§ 75.323(d)(1)(ii) and 75.362(f), an investigation must be initiated to determine the cause of the signal, and the actions required under § 75.323 must be taken.

(e) If any fire detection components of the AMS malfunction or are inoperative, immediate action must be taken to return the system to proper operation. While the AMS component repairs are being made, operation of the belt may continue if the following conditions are met:

(1) If one AMS sensor malfunctions or becomes inoperative, a trained person must continuously monitor for carbon monoxide or smoke at the inoperative sensor.

(2) If two or more adjacent AMS sensors malfunction or become inoperative, a trained person(s) must patrol and continuously monitor for carbon monoxide or smoke so that the affected areas will be traveled each hour in their entirety, or a trained person must be stationed to monitor at each inoperative sensor.

(3) If the complete AMS malfunctions or becomes inoperative, trained persons must patrol and continuously monitor for carbon monoxide or smoke so that the affected areas will be traveled each hour in their entirety.

(4) The trained person(s) monitoring under this section must, at a minimum, have two-way voice communication capabilities with the AMS operator at intervals not to exceed 2,000 feet and report contaminant levels to the AMS operator at intervals not to exceed 60 minutes.

(5) The trained person(s) monitoring under this section must report immediately to the AMS operator any concentration of the contaminant that reaches either the alert or alarm level specified in § 75.351(i), or the alternate alert and alarm levels specified in paragraph (e)(7) of this section, unless the source of the contaminant is known not to present a hazard.

(6) Detectors used to monitor under this section must have a level of detectability equal to that required of the sensors in § 75.351(l).

(7) For those AMSs using sensors other than carbon monoxide sensors, an alternate detector and the alert and alarm levels associated with that detector must be specified in the approved mine ventilation plan.

(f) If the minimum air velocity is not maintained when required under § 75.350(b)(7), immediate action must be taken to return the ventilation system to proper operation. While the ventilation system is being corrected, operation of the belt may continue only while a trained person(s) patrols and continuously monitors for carbon monoxide or smoke as set forth in §§ 75.352(e)(3) through (7), so that the affected areas will be traveled each hour in their entirety.

(g) The AMS shall automatically provide both a visual and audible signal in the belt entry at the point-feed regulator location, at affected sections, and at the designated surface location when carbon monoxide concentrations reach:

(1) The alert level at both point-feed intake monitoring sensors; or

(2) The alarm level at either point-feed intake monitoring sensor.

[69 FR 17529, Apr. 2, 2004, as amended at 73 FR 80613, Dec. 31, 2008]

§ 75.360 Preshift examination at fixed intervals.

(a)(1) Except as provided in paragraph (a)(2) of this section, a certified person designated by the operator must make a preshift examination within 3 hours preceding the beginning of any 8-hour interval during which any person is scheduled to work or travel underground. No person other than certified examiners may enter or remain in any underground area unless a preshift examination has been completed for the

Mine Safety and Health Admin., Labor § 75.360

established 8-hour interval. The operator must establish 8-hour intervals of time subject to the required preshift examinations.

(2) Preshift examinations of areas where pumpers are scheduled to work or travel shall not be required prior to the pumper entering the areas if the pumper is a certified person and the pumper conducts an examination for hazardous conditions and violations of the mandatory health or safety standards referenced in paragraph (b)(11) of this section, tests for methane and oxygen deficiency, and determines if the air is moving in its proper direction in the area where the pumper works or travels. The examination of the area must be completed before the pumper performs any other work. A record of all hazardous conditions and violations of the mandatory health or safety standards found by the pumper shall be made and retained in accordance with § 75.363 of this part.

(b) The person conducting the preshift examination shall examine for hazardous conditions and violations of the mandatory health or safety standards referenced in paragraph (b)(11) of this section, test for methane and oxygen deficiency, and determine if the air is moving in its proper direction at the following locations:

(1) Roadways, travelways and track haulageways where persons are scheduled, prior to the beginning of the preshift examination, to work or travel during the oncoming shift.

(2) Belt conveyors that will be used to transport persons during the oncoming shift and the entries in which these belt conveyors are located.

(3) Working sections and areas where mechanized mining equipment is being installed or removed, if anyone is scheduled to work on the section or in the area during the oncoming shift. The scope of the examination shall include the working places, approaches to worked-out areas and ventilation controls on these sections and in these areas, and the examination shall include tests of the roof, face and rib conditions on these sections and in these areas.

(4) Approaches to worked-out areas along intake air courses and at the entries used to carry air into worked-out areas if the intake air passing the approaches is used to ventilate working sections where anyone is scheduled to work during the oncoming shift. The examination of the approaches to the worked-out areas shall be made in the intake air course immediately inby and outby each entry used to carry air into the worked-out areas. An examination of the entries used to carry air into the worked-out areas shall be conducted at a point immediately inby the intersection of each entry with the intake air course.

(5) Seals along intake air courses where intake air passes by a seal to ventilate working sections where anyone is scheduled to work during the oncoming shift.

(6)(i) Entries and rooms developed after November 15, 1992, and developed more than 2 crosscuts off an intake air course without permanent ventilation controls where intake air passes through or by these entries or rooms to reach a working section where anyone is scheduled to work during the oncoming shift; and,

(ii) Entries and rooms developed after November 15, 1992, and driven more than 20 feet off an intake air course without a crosscut and without permanent ventilation controls where intake air passes through or by these entries or rooms to reach a working section where anyone is scheduled to work during the oncoming shift.

(7) Areas where trolley wires or trolley feeder wires are to be or will remain energized during the oncoming shift.

(8) High spots along intake air courses where methane is likely to accumulate, if equipment will be operated in the area during the shift.

(9) Underground electrical installations referred to in § 75.340(a), except those pumps listed in § 75.340 (b)(2) through (b)(6), and areas where compressors subject to § 75.344 are installed if the electrical installation or compressor is or will be energized during the shift.

(10) Other areas where work or travel during the oncoming shift is scheduled prior to the beginning of the preshift examination.

§ 75.360

(11) Preshift examinations shall include examinations to identify violations of the standards listed below:
(i) §§ 75.202(a) and 75.220(a)(1)—roof control;
(ii) §§ 75.333(h) and 75.370(a)(1)—ventilation, methane;
(iii) §§ 75.400 and 75.403—accumulations of combustible materials and application of rock dust;
(iv) § 75.1403—other safeguards, limited to maintenance of travelways along belt conveyors, off track haulage roadways, and track haulage, track switches, and other components for haulage;
(v) § 75.1722(a)—guarding moving machine parts; and
(vi) § 75.1731(a)—maintenance of belt conveyor components.

(c) The person conducting the preshift examination shall determine the volume of air entering each of the following areas if anyone is scheduled to work in the areas during the oncoming shift:
(1) In the last open crosscut of each set of entries or rooms on each working section and areas where mechanized mining equipment is being installed or removed. The last open crosscut is the crosscut in the line of pillars containing the permanent stoppings that separate the intake air courses and the return air courses.
(2) On each longwall or shortwall in the intake entry or entries at the intake end of the longwall or shortwall face immediately outby the face and the velocity of air at each end of the face at the locations specified in the approved ventilation plan.
(3) At the intake end of any pillar line—
(i) If a single split of air is used, in the intake entry furthest from the return air course, immediately outby the first open crosscut outby the line of pillars being mined; or
(ii) If a split system is used, in the intake entries of each split immediately inby the split point.

(d) The person conducting the preshift examination shall check the refuge alternative for damage, the integrity of the tamper-evident seal and the mechanisms required to deploy the refuge alternative, and the ready availability of compressed oxygen and air.

(e) The district manager may require the operator to examine other areas of the mine or examine for other hazards and violations of other mandatory health or safety standards found during the preshift examination.

(f) *Certification.* At each working place examined, the person doing the preshift examination shall certify by initials, date, and the time, that the examination was made. In areas required to be examined outby a working section, the certified person shall certify by initials, date, and the time at enough locations to show that the entire area has been examined.

(g) *Recordkeeping.* A record of the results of each preshift examination, including a record of hazardous conditions and violations of the nine mandatory health or safety standards and their locations found by the examiner during each examination, and of the results and locations of air and methane measurements, shall be made on the surface before any persons, other than certified persons conducting examinations required by this subpart, enter any underground area of the mine. The results of methane tests shall be recorded as the percentage of methane measured by the examiner. The record shall be made by the certified person who made the examination or by a person designated by the operator. If the record is made by someone other than the examiner, the examiner shall verify the record by initials and date by or at the end of the shift for which the examination was made. A record shall also be made by a certified person of the action taken to correct hazardous conditions and violations of mandatory health or safety standards found during the preshift examination. All preshift and corrective action records shall be countersigned by the mine foreman or equivalent mine official by the end of the mine foreman's or equivalent mine official's next regularly scheduled working shift. The records required by this section shall be made in a secure book that is not susceptible to alteration or electronically in a computer system so as to be secure and not susceptible to alteration.

(h) *Retention period.* Records shall be retained at a surface location at the

Mine Safety and Health Admin., Labor § 75.362

mine for at least 1 year and shall be made available for inspection by authorized representatives of the Secretary and the representative of miners.

[61 FR 9829, Mar. 11, 1996, as amended at 61 FR 55527, Oct. 25, 1996; 62 FR 35085, June 30, 1997; 64 FR 45170, Aug. 19, 1999; 73 FR 80697, Dec. 31, 2008; 77 FR 20714, Apr. 6, 2012]

§ 75.361 Supplemental examination.

(a)(1) Except for certified persons conducting examinations required by this subpart, within 3 hours before anyone enters an area in which a preshift examination has not been made for that shift, a certified person shall examine the area for hazardous conditions and violations of the mandatory health or safety standards referenced in paragraph (a)(2) of this section, determine whether the air is traveling in its proper direction and at its normal volume, and test for methane and oxygen deficiency.

(2) Supplemental examinations shall include examinations to identify violations of the standards listed below:

(i) §§ 75.202(a) and 75.220(a)(1)—roof control;

(ii) §§ 75.333(h) and 75.370(a)(1)—ventilation, methane;

(iii) §§ 75.400 and 75.403—accumulations of combustible materials and application of rock dust;

(iv) § 75.1403—other safeguards, limited to maintenance of travelways along belt conveyors, off track haulage roadways, and track haulage, track switches, and other components for haulage;

(v) § 75.1722(a)—guarding moving machine parts; and

(vi) § 75.1731(a)—maintenance of belt conveyor components.

(b) *Certification.* At each working place examined, the person making the supplemental examination shall certify by initials, date, and the time, that the examination was made. In areas required to be examined outby a working section, the certified person shall certify by initials, date, and the time at enough locations to show that the entire area has been examined.

[61 FR 9829, Mar. 11, 1996, as amended at 77 FR 20714, 2012]

§ 75.362 On-shift examination.

(a)(1) At least once during each shift, or more often if necessary for safety, a certified person designated by the operator shall conduct an on-shift examination of each section where anyone is assigned to work during the shift and any area where mechanized mining equipment is being installed or removed during the shift. The certified person shall check for hazardous conditions and violations of the mandatory health or safety standards referenced in paragraph (a)(3) of this section, test for methane and oxygen deficiency, and determine if the air is moving in its proper direction.

(2) A person designated by the operator shall conduct an examination and record the results and the corrective actions taken to assure compliance with the respirable dust control parameters specified in the approved mine ventilation plan. In those instances when a shift change is accomplished without an interruption in production on a section, the examination shall be made anytime within 1 hour after the shift change. In those instances when there is an interruption in production during the shift change, the examination shall be made before production begins on a section. Deficiencies in dust controls shall be corrected before production begins or resumes. The examination shall include: Air quantities and velocities; water pressures and flow rates; excessive leakage in the water delivery system; water spray numbers and orientations; section ventilation and control device placement; roof bolting machine dust collector vacuum levels; scrubber air flow rate; work practices required by the ventilation plan; and any other dust suppression measures. Measurements of the air velocity and quantity, water pressure and flow rates are not required if continuous monitoring of these controls is used and indicates that the dust controls are functioning properly.

(3) On-shift examinations shall include examinations to identify violations of the standards listed below:

(i) §§ 75.202(a) and 75.220(a)(1)—roof control;

(ii) §§ 75.333(h) and 75.370(a)(1)—ventilation, methane;

§ 75.362

(iii) §§ 75.400 and 75.403—accumulations of combustible materials and application of rock dust;

(iv) § 75.1403—other safeguards, limited to maintenance of travelways along belt conveyors, off track haulage roadways, and track haulage, track switches, and other components for haulage;

(v) § 75.1722(a)—guarding moving machine parts; and

(vi) § 75.1731(a)—maintenance of belt conveyor components.

(b) During each shift that coal is produced, a certified person shall examine for hazardous conditions and violations of the mandatory health or safety standards referenced in paragraph (a)(3) of this section along each belt conveyor haulageway where a belt conveyor is operated. This examination may be conducted at the same time as the preshift examination of belt conveyors and belt conveyor haulageways, if the examination is conducted within 3 hours before the oncoming shift.

(c) Persons conducting the on-shift examination shall determine at the following locations:

(1) The volume of air in the last open crosscut of each set of entries or rooms on each section and areas where mechanized mining equipment is being installed or removed. The last open crosscut is the crosscut in the line of pillars containing the permanent stoppings that separate the intake air courses and the return air courses.

(2) The volume of air on a longwall or shortwall, including areas where longwall or shortwall equipment is being installed or removed, in the intake entry or entries at the intake end of the longwall or shortwall.

(3) The velocity of air at each end of the longwall or shortwall face at the locations specified in the approved ventilation plan.

(4) The volume of air at the intake end of any pillar line—

(i) Where a single split of air is used in the intake entry furthest from the return air course immediately outby the first open crosscut outby the line of pillars being mined; or

(ii) Where a split system is used in the intake entries of each split immediately inby the split point.

(d) (1) A qualified person shall make tests for methane—

(i) At the start of each shift at each working place before electrically operated equipment is energized; and

(ii) Immediately before equipment is energized, taken into, or operated in a working place; and

(iii) At 20-minute intervals, or more often if required in the approved ventilation plan at specific locations, during the operation of equipment in the working place.

(2) Except as provided for in paragraph (d)(3) of this section, these methane tests shall be made at the face from under permanent roof support, using extendable probes or other acceptable means. When longwall or shortwall mining systems are used, these methane tests shall be made at the shearer, the plow, or the cutting head. When mining has been stopped for more than 20 minutes, methane tests shall be conducted prior to the start up of equipment.

(3) As an alternative method of compliance with paragraph (d)(2) of this section during roof bolting, methane tests may be made by sweeping an area not less than 16 feet inby the last area of permanently supported roof, using a probe or other acceptable means. This method of testing is conditioned on meeting the following requirements:

(i) The roof bolting machine must be equipped with an integral automated temporary roof support (ATRS) system that meets the requirements of 30 CFR 75.209.

(ii) The roof bolting machine must have a permanently mounted, MSHA-approved methane monitor which meets the maintenance and calibration requirements of 30 CFR 75.342(a)(4), the warning signal requirements of 30 CFR 75.342(b), and the automatic de-energization requirements of 30 CFR 75.342(c).

(iii) The methane monitor sensor must be mounted near the inby end and within 18 inches of the longitudinal center of the ATRS support, and positioned at least 12 inches from the roof when the ATRS is fully deployed.

(iv) Manual methane tests must be made at intervals not exceeding 20 minutes. The test may be made either from under permanent roof support or from the roof bolter's work position protected by the deployed ATRS.

(v) Once a methane test is made at the face, all subsequent methane tests in the same area of unsupported roof must also be made at the face, from under permanent roof support, using extendable probes or other acceptable means at intervals not exceeding 20 minutes.

(vi) The district manager may require that the ventilation plan include the minimum air quantity and the position and placement of ventilation controls to be maintained during roof bolting.

(e) If auxiliary fans and tubing are used, they shall be inspected frequently.

(f) During each shift that coal is produced and at intervals not exceeding 4 hours, tests for methane shall be made by a certified person or by an atmospheric monitoring system (AMS) in each return split of air from each working section between the last working place, or longwall or shortwall face, ventilated by that split of air and the junction of the return air split with another air split, seal, or worked-out area. If auxiliary fans and tubing are used, the tests shall be made at a location outby the auxiliary fan discharge.

(g) *Certification.* (1) The person conducting the on-shift examination in belt haulage entries shall certify by initials, date, and time that the examination was made. The certified person shall certify by initials, date, and the time at enough locations to show that the entire area has been examined.

(2) The certified person directing the on-shift examination to assure compliance with the respirable dust control parameters specified in the approved mine ventilation plan shall:

(i) Certify by initials, date, and time on a board maintained at the section load-out or similar location showing that the examination was made prior to resuming production; and

(ii) Verify, by initials and date, the record of the results of the examination required under (a)(2) of this section to assure compliance with the respirable dust control parameters specified in the mine ventilation plan. The verification shall be made no later than the end of the shift for which the examination was made.

(3) The mine foreman or equivalent mine official shall countersign each examination record required under (a)(2) of this section after it is verified by the certified person under (g)(2)(ii) of this section, and no later than the end of the mine foreman's or equivalent mine official's next regularly scheduled working shift. The record shall be made in a secure book that is not susceptible to alteration or electronically in a computer system so as to be secure and not susceptible to alteration.

(4) Records shall be retained at a surface location at the mine for at least 1 year and shall be made available for inspection by authorized representatives of the Secretary and the representative of miners.

[61 FR 9829, Mar. 11, 1996; 61 FR 26442, May 28, 1996, as amended at 68 FR 40138, July 7, 2003; 77 FR 20715, Apr. 6, 2012; 79 FR 24987, May 1, 2014]

§ 75.363 **Hazardous conditions and violations of mandatory health or safety standards; posting, correcting, and recording.**

(a) Any hazardous condition found by the mine foreman or equivalent mine official, assistant mine foreman or equivalent mine official, or other certified persons designated by the operator for the purposes of conducting examinations under this subpart D, shall be posted with a conspicuous danger sign where anyone entering the areas would pass. A hazardous condition shall be corrected immediately or the area shall remain posted until the hazardous condition is corrected. If the condition creates an imminent danger, everyone except those persons referred to in section 104(c) of the Act shall be withdrawn from the area affected to a safe area until the hazardous condition is corrected. Only persons designated by the operator to correct or evaluate the hazardous condition may enter the posted area. Any violation of a mandatory health or safety standard found during a preshift, supplemental, on-shift, or weekly examination shall be corrected.

(b) A record shall be made of any hazardous condition and any violation of the nine mandatory health or safety

§ 75.364

standards found by the mine examiner. This record shall be kept in a book maintained for this purpose on the surface at the mine. The record shall be made by the completion of the shift on which the hazardous condition or violation of the nine mandatory health or safety standards is found and shall include the nature and location of the hazardous condition or violation and the corrective action taken. This record shall not be required for shifts when no hazardous conditions or violations of the nine mandatory health or safety standards are found.

(c) The record shall be made by the certified person who conducted the examination or a person designated by the operator. If made by a person other than the certified person, the certified person shall verify the record by initials and date by or at the end of the shift for which the examination was made. Records shall be countersigned by the mine foreman or equivalent mine official by the end of the mine foreman's or equivalent mine official's next regularly scheduled working shift. The record shall be made in a secure book that is not susceptible to alteration or electronically in a computer system so as to be secure and not susceptible to alteration.

(d) *Retention period.* Records shall be retained at a surface location at the mine for at least 1 year and shall be made available for inspection by authorized representatives of the Secretary and the representative of miners.

(e) *Review of citations and orders.* The mine operator shall review with mine examiners on a quarterly basis citations and orders issued in areas where preshift, supplemental, on-shift, and weekly examinations are required.

[61 FR 9829, Mar. 11, 1996; 61 FR 26442, May 28, 1996; 77 FR 20715, Apr. 6, 2012]

§ 75.364 Weekly examination.

(a) *Worked-out areas.* (1) At least every 7 days, a certified person shall examine unsealed worked-out areas where no pillars have been recovered by traveling to the area of deepest penetration; measuring methane and oxygen concentrations and air quantities and making tests to determine if the air is moving in the proper direction in the area. The locations of measurement points where tests and measurements will be performed shall be included in the mine ventilation plan and shall be adequate in number and location to assure ventilation and air quality in the area. Air quantity measurements shall also be made where the air enters and leaves the worked-out area. An alternative method of evaluating the ventilation of the area may be approved in the ventilation plan.

(2) At least every 7 days, a certified person shall evaluate the effectiveness of bleeder systems required by § 75.334 as follows:

(i) Measurements of methane and oxygen concentrations and air quantity and a test to determine if the air is moving in its proper direction shall be made where air enters the worked-out area.

(ii) Measurements of methane and oxygen concentrations and air quantity and a test to determine if the air is moving in the proper direction shall be made immediately before the air enters a return split of air.

(iii) At least one entry of each set of bleeder entries used as part of a bleeder system under § 75.334 shall be traveled in its entirety. Measurements of methane and oxygen concentrations and air quantities and a test to determine if the air is moving in the proper direction shall be made at the measurement point locations specified in the mine ventilation plan to determine the effectiveness of the bleeder system.

(iv) In lieu of the requirements of paragraphs (a)(2)(i) and (iii) of this section, an alternative method of evaluation may be specified in the ventilation plan provided the alternative method results in proper evaluation of the effectiveness of the bleeder system.

(b) *Hazardous conditions and violations of mandatory health or safety standards.* At least every 7 days, an examination for hazardous conditions and violations of the mandatory health or safety standards referenced in paragraph (b)(8) of this section shall be made by a certified person designated by the operator at the following locations:

(1) In at least one entry of each intake air course, in its entirety, so that the entire air course is traveled.

(2) In at least one entry of each return air course, in its entirety, so that the entire air course is traveled.

(3) In each longwall or shortwall travelway in its entirety, so that the entire travelway is traveled.

(4) At each seal along return and bleeder air courses and at each seal along intake air courses not examined under §75.360(b)(5).

(5) In each escapeway so that the entire escapeway is traveled.

(6) On each working section not examined under §75.360(b)(3) during the previous 7 days.

(7) At each water pump not examined during a preshift examination conducted during the previous 7 days.

(8) Weekly examinations shall include examinations to identify violations of the standards listed below:

(i) §§75.202(a) and 75.220(a)(1)—roof control;

(ii) §§75.333(h) and 75.370(a)(1)—ventilation, methane;

(iii) §§75.400 and 75.403—accumulations of combustible materials and application of rock dust; and

(iv) §75.1403—maintenance of off track haulage roadways, and track haulage, track switches, and other components for haulage;

(v) §75.1722(a)—guarding moving machine parts; and

(vi) §75.1731(a)—maintenance of belt conveyor components.

(c) *Measurements and tests.* At least every 7 days, a certified person shall—

(1) Determine the volume of air entering the main intakes and in each intake split;

(2) Determine the volume of air and test for methane in the last open crosscut in any pair or set of developing entries or rooms, in the return of each split of air immediately before it enters the main returns, and where the air leaves the main returns; and

(3) Test for methane in the return entry nearest each set of seals immediately after the air passes the seals.

(d) Hazardous conditions shall be corrected immediately. If the condition creates an imminent danger, everyone except those persons referred to in section 104(c) of the Act shall be withdrawn from the area affected to a safe area until the hazardous condition is corrected. Any violation of the nine mandatory health or safety standards found during a weekly examination shall be corrected.

(e) The weekly examination may be conducted at the same time as the preshift or on-shift examinations.

(f) (1) The weekly examination is not required during any 7 day period in which no one enters any underground area of the mine.

(2) Except for certified persons required to make examinations, no one shall enter any underground area of the mine if a weekly examination has not been completed within the previous 7 days.

(g) *Certification.* The person making the weekly examinations shall certify by initials, date, and the time that the examination was made. Certifications and times shall appear at enough locations to show that the entire area has been examined.

(h) *Recordkeeping.* At the completion of any shift during which a portion of a weekly examination is conducted, a record of the results of each weekly examination, including a record of hazardous conditions and violations of the nine mandatory health or safety standards found during each examination and their locations, the corrective action taken, and the results and location of air and methane measurements, shall be made. The results of methane tests shall be recorded as the percentage of methane measured by the examiner. The record shall be made by the person making the examination or a person designated by the operator. If made by a person other than the examiner, the examiner shall verify the record by initials and date by or at the end of the shift for which the examination was made. The record shall be countersigned by the mine foreman or equivalent mine official by the end of the mine foreman's or equivalent mine official's next regularly scheduled working shift. The records required by this section shall be made in a secure book that is not susceptible to alteration or electronically in a computer system so as to be secure and not susceptible to alteration.

(i) *Retention period.* Records shall be retained at a surface location at the mine for at least 1 year and shall be

§ 75.370

made available for inspection by authorized representatives of the Secretary and the representative of miners.

[61 FR 9829, Mar. 11, 1996, as amended at 77 FR 20715, Apr. 6, 2012]

§ 75.370 Mine ventilation plan; submission and approval.

(a)(1) The operator shall develop and follow a ventilation plan approved by the district manager. The plan shall be designed to control methane and respirable dust and shall be suitable to the conditions and mining system at the mine. The ventilation plan shall consist of two parts, the plan content as prescribed in § 75.371 and the ventilation map with information as prescribed in § 75.372. Only that portion of the map which contains information required under § 75.371 will be subject to approval by the district manager.

(2) The proposed ventilation plan and any revision to the plan shall be submitted in writing to the district manager. When revisions to a ventilation plan are proposed, only the revised pages, maps, or sketches of the plan need to be submitted. When required in writing by the district manager, the operator shall submit a fully revised plan by consolidating the plan and all revisions in an orderly manner and by deleting all outdated material.

(3) (i) The mine operator shall notify the representative of miners at least 5 days prior to submission of a mine ventilation plan and any revision to a mine ventilation plan. If requested, the mine operator shall provide a copy to the representative of miners at the time of notification. In the event of a situation requiring immediate action on a plan revision, notification of the revision shall be given, and if requested, a copy of the revision shall be provided, to the representative of miners by the operator at the time of submittal;

(ii) A copy of the proposed ventilation plan, and a copy of any proposed revision, submitted for approval shall be made available for inspection by the representative of miners; and

(iii) A copy of the proposed ventilation plan, and a copy of any proposed revision, submitted for approval shall be posted on the mine bulletin board at the time of submittal. The proposed plan or proposed revision shall remain posted until it is approved, withdrawn or denied.

(b) Following receipt of the proposed plan or proposed revision, the representative of miners may submit timely comments to the district manager, in writing, for consideration during the review process. A copy of these comments shall also be provided to the operator by the district manager upon request.

(c) (1) The district manager will notify the operator in writing of the approval or denial of approval of a proposed ventilation plan or proposed revision. A copy of this notification will be sent to the representative of miners by the district manager.

(2) If the district manager denies approval of a proposed plan or revision, the deficiencies of the plan or revision shall be specified in writing and the operator will be provided an opportunity to discuss the deficiencies with the district manager.

(d) No proposed ventilation plan shall be implemented before it is approved by the district manager. Any intentional change to the ventilation system that alters the main air current or any split of the main air current in a manner that could materially affect the safety and health of the miners, or any change to the information required in § 75.371 shall be submitted to and approved by the district manager before implementation.

(e) Before implementing an approved ventilation plan or a revision to a ventilation plan, persons affected by the revision shall be instructed by the operator in its provisions.

(f) The approved ventilation plan and any revisions shall be—

(1) Provided upon request to the representative of miners by the operator following notification of approval;

(2) Made available for inspection by the representative of miners; and

(3) Posted on the mine bulletin board within 1 working day following notification of approval. The approved plan and revisions shall remain posted on the bulletin board for the period that they are in effect.

(g) The ventilation plan for each mine shall be reviewed every 6 months

Mine Safety and Health Admin., Labor § 75.371

by an authorized representative of the Secretary to assure that it is suitable to current conditions in the mine.

§ 75.371 Mine ventilation plan; contents.

The mine ventilation plan shall contain the information described below and any additional provisions required by the district manager:

(a) The mine name, company name, mine identification number, and the name of the individual submitting the plan information.

(b) Planned main mine fan stoppages, other than those scheduled for testing, maintenance or adjustment, including procedures to be followed during these stoppages and subsequent restarts (see § 75.311(a)) and the type of device to be used for monitoring main mine fan pressure, if other than a pressure recording device (see 75.310(a)(4)).

(c) Methods of protecting main mine fans and associated components from the forces of an underground explosion if a 15-foot offset from the nearest side of the mine opening is not provided (see § 75.310(a)(6)); and the methods of protecting main mine fans and intake air openings if combustible material will be within 100 feet of the area surrounding the fan or these openings (see § 75.311(f)).

(d) Persons that will be permitted to enter the mine, the work these persons will do while in the mine, and electric power circuits that will be energized when a back-up fan system is used that does not provide the ventilating quantity provided by the main mine fan (see § 75.311(c)).

(e) The locations and operating conditions of booster fans installed in anthracite mines (see § 75.302).

(f) Section and face ventilation systems used and the minimum quantity of air that will be delivered to the working section for each mechanized mining unit, including drawings illustrating how each system is used, and a description of each different dust suppression system used on equipment, identified by make and model, on each working section, including:

(1) The number, types, location, orientation, operating pressure, and flow rate of operating water sprays;

(2) The maximum distance that ventilation control devices will be installed from each working face when mining or installing roof bolts in entries and crosscuts;

(3) Procedures for maintaining the roof bolting machine dust collection system in approved condition; and

(4) Recommended best work practices for equipment operators to minimize dust exposure.

(g) Locations where the air quantities must be greater than 3,000 cubic feet per minute (see § 75.325(a)(1)).

(h) In anthracite mines, locations where the air quantities must be greater than 1,500 cubic feet per minute (see § 75.325(e)(1)).

(i) Working places and working faces other than those where coal is being cut, mined, drilled for blasting or loaded, where a minimum air quantity will be maintained, and the air quantity at those locations (see § 75.325(a)(1)).

(j) The operating volume of machine mounted dust collectors or diffuser fans, if used (see § 75.325(a)(3)), including the type and size of dust collector screen used, and a description of the procedures to maintain dust collectors used on equipment.

(k) The minimum mean entry air velocity in exhausting face ventilation systems where coal is being cut, mined, drilled for blasting, or loaded, if the velocity will be less than 60 feet per minute. Other working places where coal is not being cut, mined, drilled for blasting or loaded, where at least 60 feet per minute or some other minimum mean entry air velocity will be maintained (see § 75.326).

(l) The maximum distance if greater than 10 feet from each working face at which face ventilation control devices will be installed (see § 75.330(b)(2)). The working places other than those where coal is being cut, mined, drilled for blasting or loaded, where face ventilation control devices will be used (see § 75.330(b)(1)(ii)).

(m) The volume of air required in the last open crosscut or the quantity of air reaching the pillar line if greater than 9,000 cubic feet per minute (see § 75.325(b)).

(n) In anthracite mines, the volume of air required in the last open crosscut

§ 75.371

or the quantity of air reaching the pillar line if greater than 5,000 cubic feet per minute (see § 75.325(e)(2)).

(o) Locations where separations of intake and return air courses will be built and maintained to other than the third connecting crosscut outby each working face (see § 75.333(b)(1)).

(p) The volume of air required at the intake to the longwall sections, if different than 30,000 cubic feet per minute (see § 75.325(c)).

(q) The velocities of air on a longwall or shortwall face, and the locations where the velocities must be measured (see § 75.325(c)(2)).

(r) The minimum quantity of air that will be provided during the installation and removal of mechanized mining equipment, the location where this quantity will be provided, and the ventilation controls that will be used (see § 75.325(d), (g), and (i)).

(s) The locations and frequency of the methane tests if required more often by § 75.362(d)(1)(iii) (see § 75.362 (d)(1)(iii).

(t) The locations where samples for "designated areas" will be collected, including the specific location of each sampling device, and the respirable dust control measures used at the dust generating sources for these locations (see §§ 70.207 and 70.209 of this chapter).

(u) The methane and dust control systems at underground dumps, crushers, transfer points, and haulageways.

(v) Areas in trolley haulage entries where the air velocity will be greater than 250 feet per minute and the velocity in these areas (see § 75.327(b)).

(w) Locations where entries will be advanced less than 20 feet from the inby rib without a crosscut being provided where a line brattice will be required. (see § 75.333(g)).

(x) A description of the bleeder system to be used, including its design (see § 75.334).

(y) The means for determining the effectiveness of bleeder systems (see § 75.334(c)(2)).

(z) The locations where measurements of methane and oxygen concentrations and air quantities and tests to determine whether the air is moving in the proper direction will be made to evaluate the ventilation of nonpillared worked-out areas (see § 75.364 (a)(1)) and the effectiveness of bleeder systems (see § 75.364 (a)(2)(iii). Alternative methods of evaluation of the effectiveness of bleeder systems (§ 75.364 (a)(2)(iv)).

(aa) The means for adequately maintaining bleeder entries free of obstructions such as roof falls and standing water (see § 75.334(c)(3)).

(bb) The location of ventilation devices such as regulators, stoppings and bleeder connectors used to control air movement through worked-out areas (see § 75.334(c)(4)). The location and sequence of construction of proposed seals for each worked-out area. (see § 75.334(e)).

(cc) In mines with a demonstrated history of spontaneous combustion: a description of the measures that will be used to detect methane, carbon monoxide, and oxygen concentration during and after pillar recovery and in worked-out areas where no pillars have been recovered (see § 75.334(f)(1); and, the actions which will be taken to protect miners from the hazards associated with spontaneous combustion (see § 75.334(f)(2). If a bleeder system will not be used, the methods that will be used to control spontaneous combustion, accumulations of methane-air mixtures, and other gases, dusts, and fumes in the worked-out area (see § 75.334(f)(3)).

(dd) The location of all horizontal degasification holes that are longer than 1,000 feet and the location of all vertical degasification holes.

(ee) If methane drainage systems are used, a detailed sketch of each system, including a description of safety precautions used with the systems.

(ff) Seal installation requirements provided by § 75.335 and the sampling provisions provided by § 75.336.

(gg) The alternative location for the additional sensing device if the device will not be installed on the longwall shearing machine (see § 75.342(a)(2)).

(hh) The ambient level in parts per million of carbon monoxide, and the method for determining the ambient level, in all areas where carbon monoxide sensors are installed.

(ii) The locations (designated areas) where dust measurements would be made in the belt entry when belt air is

Mine Safety and Health Admin., Labor § 75.372

used to ventilate working sections or areas where mechanized mining equipment is being installed or removed, in accordance with § 75.350(b)(3).

(jj) The locations and approved velocities at those locations where air velocities in the belt entry are above or below the limits set forth in § 75.350(a)(2) or §§ 75.350(b)(7) and 75.350(b)(8).

(kk) The locations where air quantities are measured as set forth in § 75.350(b)(6).

(ll) The locations and use of point-feed regulators, in accordance with §§ 75.350(c) and 75.350(d)(5).

(mm) The location of any diesel-discriminating sensor, and additional carbon monoxide or smoke sensors installed in the belt air course.

(nn) The length of the time delay or any other method used to reduce the number of non-fire related alert and alarm signals from carbon monoxide sensors.

(oo) The reduced alert and alarm settings for carbon monoxide sensors, in accordance with § 75.351(i)(2).

(pp) The alternate detector and the alert and alarm levels associated with the detector, in accordance with § 75.352(e)(7).

(qq) The distance that separation between the primary escapeway and the belt or track haulage entries will be maintained if other than to the first connecting crosscut outby the section loading point (see § 75.380(g)).

(rr) In anthracite mines, the dimensions of escapeways where the pitch of the coal seam does not permit escapeways to be maintained 4 feet by 5 feet and the locations where these dimensions must be maintained (see § 75.381(c)(4)).

(ss) Areas designated by the district manager where measurements of CO and NO_2 concentrations will be made (see § 70.1900(a)(4)).

(tt) Location where the air quantity will be maintained at the section loading point (see § 75.325(f)(2)).

(uu) Any additional location(s) required by the district manager where a minimum air quantity must be maintained for an individual unit of diesel-powered equipment. (see § 75.325(f)(5)).

(vv) The minimum air quantities that will be provided where multiple units of diesel-powered equipment are operated (see § 75.325(g) (1)–(3) and (i)).

(ww) The diesel-powered mining equipment excluded from the calculation under § 75.325(g). (see § 75.325(h)).

(xx) Action levels higher than the 50 percent level specified by § 70.1900(c). (see § 75.325(j)).

(yy) The locations where the pressure differential cannot be maintained from the primary escapeway to the belt entry.

[61 FR 9829, Mar. 11, 1996, as amended at 61 FR 55527, Oct. 25, 1996; 69 FR 17529, Apr. 2, 2004; 72 FR 28817, May 22, 2007; 73 FR 21209, Apr. 18, 2008; 73 FR 80613, Dec. 31, 2008; 79 FR 24987, May 1, 2014]

§ 75.372 Mine ventilation map.

(a)(1) At intervals not exceeding 12 months, the operator shall submit to the district manager 3 copies of an up-to-date map of the mine drawn to a scale of not less than 100 nor more than 500 feet to the inch. A registered engineer or a registered surveyor shall certify that the map is accurate.

(2) In addition to the informational requirements of this section the map may also be used to depict and explain plan contents that are required in § 75.371. Information shown on the map to satisfy the requirements of § 75.371 shall be subject to approval by the district manager.

(b) The map shall contain the following information:

(1) The mine name, company name, mine identification number, a legend identifying the scale of the map and symbols used, and the name of the individual responsible for the information on the map.

(2) All areas of the mine, including sealed and unsealed worked-out areas.

(3) All known mine workings that are located in the same coalbed within 1,000 feet of existing or projected workings. These workings may be shown on a mine map with a scale other than that required by paragraph (a) of this section, if the scale does not exceed 2,000 feet to the inch and is specified on the map.

(4) The locations of all known mine workings underlying and overlying the mine property and the distance between the mine workings.

§ 75.373

(5) The locations of all known oil and gas wells and all known drill holes that penetrate the coalbed being mined.

(6) The locations of all main mine fans, installed backup fans and motors, and each fan's specifications, including size, type, model number, manufacturer, operating pressure, motor horsepower, and revolutions per minute.

(7) The locations of all surface mine openings and the direction and quantity of air at each opening.

(8) The elevation at the top and bottom of each shaft and slope, and shaft and slope dimensions, including depth and length.

(9) The direction of air flow in all underground areas of the mine.

(10) The locations of all active working sections and the four-digit identification number for each mechanized mining unit (MMU).

(11) The location of all escapeways and refuge alternatives.

(12) The locations of all ventilation controls, including permanent stoppings, overcasts, undercasts, regulators, seals, airlock doors, haulageway doors and other doors, except temporary ventilation controls on working sections.

(13) The direction and quantity of air—

(i) Entering and leaving each split;

(ii) In the last open crosscut of each set of entries and rooms; and

(iii) At the intake end of each pillar line, including any longwall or shortwall.

(14) Projections for at least 12 months of anticipated mine development, proposed ventilation controls, proposed bleeder systems, and the anticipated location of intake and return air courses, belt entries, and escapeways.

(15) The locations of existing methane drainage systems.

(16) The locations and type of all AMS sensors required by subpart D of this part.

(17) Contour lines that pass through whole number elevations of the coalbed being mined. These lines shall be spaced at 10-foot elevation levels unless a wider spacing is permitted by the district manager.

(18) The location of proposed seals for each worked-out area.

(19) The entry height, velocity and direction of the air current at or near the midpoint of each belt flight where the height and width of the entry are representative of the belt haulage entry.

(20) The location and designation of air courses that have been redesignated from intake to return for the purpose of ventilation of structures, areas or installations that are required by this subpart D to be ventilated to return air courses, and for ventilation of seals.

(c) The mine map required by § 75.1200 may be used to satisfy the requirements for the ventilation map, provided that all the information required by this section is contained on the map.

[61 FR 9829, Mar. 11, 1996, as amended at 69 FR 17530, Apr. 2, 2004; 73 FR 80697, Dec. 31, 2008]

§ 75.373 Reopening mines.

After a mine is abandoned or declared inactive, and before it is reopened, mining operations shall not begin until MSHA has been notified and has completed an inspection.

§ 75.380 Escapeways; bituminous and lignite mines.

(a) Except in situations addressed in § 75.381, § 75.385 and § 75.386, at least two separate and distinct travelable passageways shall be designated as escapeways and shall meet the requirements of this section.

(b) (1) Escapeways shall be provided from each working section, and each area where mechanized mining equipment is being installed or removed, continuous to the surface escape drift opening or continuous to the escape shaft or slope facilities to the surface.

(2) During equipment installation, these escapeways shall begin at the projected location for the section loading point. During equipment removal, they shall begin at the location of the last loading point.

(c) The two separate and distinct escapeways required by this section shall not end at a common shaft, slope, or drift opening, except that multiple compartment shafts or slopes separated by walls constructed of noncombustible material may be used as separate and distinct passageways.

(d) Each escapeway shall be—
(1) Maintained in a safe condition to always assure passage of anyone, including disabled persons;
(2) Clearly marked to show the route and direction of travel to the surface;
(3) Maintained to at least a height of 5 feet from the mine floor to the mine roof, excluding the thickness of any roof support, except that the escapeways shall be maintained to at least the height of the coalbed, excluding the thickness of any roof support, where the coalbed is less than 5 feet. In areas of mines where escapeways pass through doors, the height may be less than 5 feet, provided that sufficient height is maintained to enable miners, including disabled persons, to escape quickly in an emergency. In areas of mines developed before November 16, 1992, where escapeways pass over or under overcasts or undercasts, the height may be less than 5 feet provided that sufficient height is maintained to enable miners, including disabled persons, to escape quickly in an emergency. When there is a need to determine whether sufficient height is provided, MSHA may require a stretcher test where 4 persons carry a miner through the area in question on a stretcher;
(4) Maintained at least 6 feet wide except—
(i) Where necessary supplemental roof support is installed, the escapeway shall not be less than 4 feet wide; or
(ii) Where the route of travel passes through doors or other permanent ventilation controls, the escapeway shall be at least 4 feet wide to enable miners to escape quickly in an emergency, or
(iii) Where the alternate escapeway passes through doors or other permanent ventilation controls or where supplemental roof support is required and sufficient width is maintained to enable miners, including disabled persons, to escape quickly in an emergency. When there is a need to determine whether sufficient width is provided, MSHA may require a stretcher test where 4 persons carry a miner through the area in question on a stretcher, or
(iv) Where mobile equipment near working sections, and other equipment essential to the ongoing operation of longwall sections, is necessary during normal mining operations, such as material cars containing rock dust or roof control supplies, or is to be used for the evacuation of miners off the section in the event of an emergency. In any instance, escapeways shall be of sufficient width to enable miners, including disabled persons, to escape quickly in an emergency. When there is a need to determine whether sufficient width is provided, MSHA may require a stretcher test where 4 persons carry a miner through the area in question on a stretcher;
(5) Located to follow the most direct, safe and practical route to the nearest mine opening suitable for the safe evacuation of miners; and
(6) Provided with ladders, stairways, ramps, or similar facilities where the escapeways cross over obstructions.
(7) Provided with a continuous, durable directional lifeline or equivalent device that shall be—
(i) Installed and maintained throughout the entire length of each escapeway as defined in paragraph (b)(1) of this section;
(ii) Flame-resistant in accordance with the requirements of part 18 of this chapter upon replacement of existing lifelines; but in no case later than June 15, 2009;
(iii) Marked with a reflective material every 25 feet;
(iv) Located in such a manner for miners to use effectively to escape;
(v) Equipped with one directional indicator cone securely attached to the lifeline, signifying the route of escape, placed at intervals not exceeding 100 feet. Cones shall be installed so that the tapered section points inby;
(vi) Equipped with one sphere securely attached to the lifeline at each intersection where personnel doors are installed in adjacent crosscuts;
(vii) Equipped with two securely attached cones, installed consecutively with the tapered section pointing inby, to signify an attached branch line is immediately ahead.
(A) A branch line leading from the lifeline to an SCSR cache will be marked with four cones with the base sections in contact to form two diamond shapes. The cones must be placed within reach of the lifeline.

§ 75.380

(B) A branch line leading from the lifeline to a refuge alternative will be marked with a rigid spiraled coil at least eight inches in length. The spiraled coil must be placed within reach of the lifeline (see Illustration 1 below).

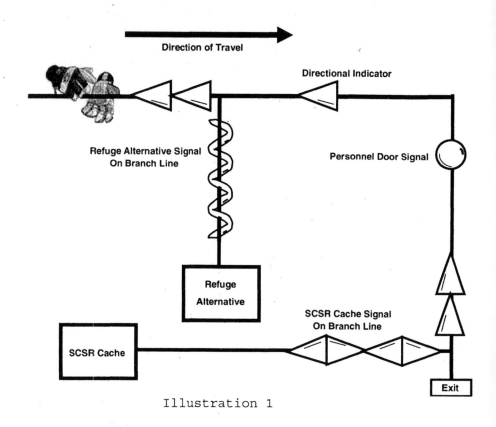

Illustration 1

(e) Surface openings shall be adequately protected to prevent surface fires, fumes, smoke, and flood water from entering the mine.

(f) *Primary escapeway.* (1) One escapeway that is ventilated with intake air shall be designated as the primary escapeway. The primary escapeway shall have a higher ventilation pressure than the belt entry unless the mine operator submits an alternative in the mine ventilation plan to protect the integrity of the primary escapeway, based on mine specific conditions, which is approved by the district manager.

(2) Paragraphs (f)(3) through (f)(7) of this section apply as follows:

(i) To all areas of a primary escapeway developed on or after November 16, 1992;

(ii) Effective as of June 10, 1997, to all areas of a primary escapeway developed between March 30, 1970 and November 16, 1992; and

(iii) Effective as of June 10, 1997, to all areas of the primary escapeway developed prior to March 30, 1970 where separation of the belt and trolley haulage entries from the primary escapeway existed prior to November 16, 1992.

(3) The following equipment is not permitted in the primary escapeway:

(i) Mobile equipment hauling coal except for hauling coal incidental to cleanup or maintenance of the primary escapeway.

(ii) Compressors, except—

(A) Compressors necessary to maintain the escapeway in safe, travelable condition;

(B) Compressors that are components of equipment such as locomotives and rock dusting machines; and

(C) Compressors of less than five horsepower.

(iii) Underground transformer stations, battery charging stations, substations, and rectifiers except—

(A) Where necessary to maintain the escapeway in safe, travelable condition; and

(B) Battery charging stations and rectifiers and power centers with transformers that are either dry-type or contain nonflammable liquid, provided they are located on or near a working section and are moved as the section advances or retreats.

(iv) Water pumps, except—

(A) Water pumps necessary to maintain the escapeway in safe, travelable condition;

(B) Submersible pumps;

(C) Permissible pumps and associated permissible switchgear;

(D) Pumps located on or near a working section that are moved as the section advances or retreats;

(E) Pumps installed in anthracite mines; and

(F) Small portable pumps.

(4) Mobile equipment operated in the primary escapeway, except for continuous miners and as provided in paragraphs (f)(5), (f)(6), and (f)(7) of this section, shall be equipped with a fire suppression system installed according to §§ 75.1107-3 through 75.1107-16 that is—

(i) Manually operated and attended continuously by a person trained in the systems function and use, or

(ii) A multipurpose dry chemical type capable of both automatic and manual activation.

(5) Personnel carriers and small mobile equipment designed and used only for carrying people and small hand tools may be operated in primary escapeways if—

(i) The equipment is provided with a multipurpose dry chemical type fire suppression system capable of both automatic and manual activation, and the suppression system is suitable for the intended application and is listed or approved by a nationally recognized independent testing laboratory, or,

(ii) Battery powered and provided with two 10 pound multipurpose dry chemical portable fire extinguishers.

(6) Notwithstanding the requirements of paragraph (f)(3)(i), mobile equipment not provided with a fire suppression system may operate in the primary escapeway if no one is inby except those persons directly engaged in using or moving the equipment.

(7) Notwithstanding the requirements of paragraph (f)(3)(i), mobile equipment designated and used only as emergency vehicles or ambulances, may be operated in the primary escapeway without fire suppression systems.

(g) Except where separation of belt and trolley haulage entries from designated escapeways did not exist before November 15, 1992, and except as provided in § 75.350(c), the primary escapeway must be separated from belt and trolley haulage entries for its entire length, to and including the first connecting crosscut outby each loading point except when a greater or lesser distance for this separation is specified and approved in the mine ventilation plan and does not pose a hazard to miners.

(h) *Alternate escapeway.* One escapeway shall be designated as the alternate escapeway. The alternate escapeway shall be separated from the primary escapeway for its entire length, except that the alternate and primary escapeways may be ventilated from a common intake air shaft or slope opening.

(i) Mechanical escape facilities shall be provided and maintained for—

(1) Each shaft that is part of a designated escapeway and is greater than 50 feet in depth; and

(2) Each slope from the coal seam to the surface that is part of a designated escapeway and is inclined more than 9 degrees from the horizontal.

(j) Within 30 minutes after mine personnel on the surface have been notified of an emergency requiring evacuation, mechanical escape facilities provided under paragraph (i) of this section shall be operational at the bottom

§ 75.381

of shaft and slope openings that are part of escapeways.

(k) Except where automatically activated hoisting equipment is used, the bottom of each shaft or slope opening that is part of a designated escapeway shall be equipped with a means of signaling a surface location where a person is always on duty when anyone is underground. When the signal is activated or the evacuation of persons underground is necessary, the person shall assure that mechanical escape facilities are operational as required by paragraph (j) of this section.

(l)(1) Stairways or mechanical escape facilities shall be installed in shafts that are part of the designated escapeways and that are 50 feet or less in depth, except ladders may be used in shafts that are part of the designated escapeways and that are 5 feet or less in depth.

(2) Stairways shall be constructed of concrete or metal, set on an angle not to exceed 45 degrees from the horizontal, and equipped on the open side with handrails. In addition, landing platforms that are at least 2 feet by 4 feet shall be installed at intervals not to exceed 20 vertical feet on the stairways and equipped on the open side with handrails.

(3) Ladders shall be constructed of metal, anchored securely, and set on an angle not to exceed 60 degrees from the horizontal.

(m) A travelway designed to prevent slippage shall be provided in slope and drift openings that are part of designated escapeways, unless mechanical escape facilities are installed.

[61 FR 9829, Mar. 11, 1996; 61 FR 20877, May 8, 1996, as amended at 61 FR 55527, Oct. 25, 1996; 69 FR 17530, Apr. 2, 2004; 71 FR 12269, Mar. 9, 2006; 71 FR 71452, Dec. 8, 2006; 73 FR 80613, Dec. 31, 2008]

§ 75.381 Escapeways; anthracite mines.

(a) Except as provided in §§ 75.385 and 75.386, at least two separate and distinct travelable passageways shall be designated as escapeways and shall meet the requirements of this section.

(b) Escapeways shall be provided from each working section continuous to the surface.

(c) Each escapeway shall be—

(1) Maintained in a safe condition to always assure passage of anyone, including disabled persons;

(2) Clearly marked to show the route of travel to the surface;

(3) Provided with ladders, stairways, ramps, or similar facilities where the escapeways cross over obstructions; and

(4) Maintained at least 4 feet wide by 5 feet high. If the pitch or thickness of the coal seam does not permit these dimensions to be maintained other dimensions may be approved in the ventilation plan.

(5) Provided with a continuous, durable directional lifeline or equivalent device that shall be—

(i) Installed and maintained throughout the entire length of each escapeway as defined in paragraph (b) of this section;

(ii) Flame-resistant in accordance with the requirements of part 18 of this chapter upon replacement of existing lifelines; but in no case later than June 15, 2009;

(iii) Marked with a reflective material every 25 feet;

(iv) Located in such a manner for miners to use effectively to escape;

(v) Equipped with one directional indicator cone securely attached to the lifeline, signifying the route of escape, placed at intervals not exceeding 100 feet. Cones shall be installed so that the tapered section points inby;

(vi) Equipped with one sphere securely attached to the lifeline at each intersection where personnel doors are installed in adjacent crosscuts;

(vii) Equipped with two securely attached cones, installed consecutively with the tapered section pointing inby, to signify an attached branch line is immediately ahead.

(A) A branch line leading from the lifeline to an SCSR cache will be marked with four cones with the base sections in contact to form two diamond shapes. The cones must be placed within reach of the lifeline.

(B) A branch line leading from the lifeline to a refuge alternative will be marked with a rigid spiraled coil at least eight inches in length. The spiraled coil must be placed within reach of the lifeline.

Mine Safety and Health Admin., Labor § 75.384

(d) Surface openings shall be adequately protected to prevent surface fires, fumes, smoke, and flood water from entering the mine.

(e) *Primary escapeway.* One escapeway that shall be ventilated with intake air shall be designated as the primary escapeway. The primary escapeway shall have a higher ventilation pressure than the belt entry unless the mine operator submits an alternative in the mine ventilation plan to protect the integrity of the primary escapeway, based on mine specific conditions, which is approved by the district manager.

(f) *Alternate escapeway.* One escapeway that shall be designated as the alternate escapeway shall be separated from the primary escapeway for its entire length.

(g) Mechanical escape facilities shall be provided—

(1) For each shaft or slope opening that is part of a primary escapeway; and

(2) For slopes that are part of escapeways, unless ladders are installed.

(h) Within 30 minutes after mine personnel on the surface have been notified of an emergency requiring evacuation, mechanical escape facilities shall be operational at the bottom of each shaft and slope opening that is part of an escapeway.

(i) Except where automatically activated hoisting equipment is used, the bottom of each shaft or slope opening that is part of a primary escapeway shall be equipped with a means of signaling a surface location where a person is always on duty when anyone is underground. When the signal is activated or the evacuation of personnel is necessary, the person on duty shall assure that mechanical escape facilities are operational as required by paragraph (h) of this section.

[61 FR 9829, Mar. 11, 1996, as amended at 71 FR 12269, Mar. 9, 2006; 71 FR 71452, Dec. 8, 2006; 73 FR 80614, Dec. 31, 2008]

§ 75.382 Mechanical escape facilities.

(a) Mechanical escape facilities shall be provided with overspeed, overwind, and automatic stop controls.

(b) Every mechanical escape facility with a platform, cage, or other device shall be equipped with brakes that can stop the fully loaded platform, cage, or other device.

(c) Mechanical escape facilities, including automatic elevators, shall be examined weekly. The weekly examination of this equipment may be conducted at the same time as a daily examination required by § 75.1400-3.

(1) The weekly examination shall include an examination of the headgear, connections, links and chains, overspeed and overwind controls, automatic stop controls, and other facilities.

(2) At least once each week, the hoist shall be run through one complete cycle of operation to determine that it is operating properly.

(d) A person trained to operate the mechanical escape facility always shall be available while anyone is underground to provide the mechanical escape facilities, if required, to the bottom of each shaft and slope opening that is part of an escapeway within 30 minutes after personnel on the surface have been notified of an emergency requiring evacuation. However, no operator is required for automatically operated cages, platforms, or elevators.

(e) Mechanical escape facilities shall have rated capacities consistent with the loads handled.

(f) Manually-operated mechanical escape facilities shall be equipped with indicators that accurately and reliably show the position of the facility.

(g) *Certification.* The person making the examination as required by paragraph (c) of this section shall certify by initials, date, and the time that the examination was made. Certifications shall be made at or near the facility examined.

§ 75.384 Longwall and shortwall travelways.

(a) If longwall or shortwall mining systems are used and the two designated escapeways required by § 75.380 are located on the headgate side of the longwall or shortwall, a travelway shall be provided on the tailgate side of that longwall or shortwall. The travelway shall be located to follow the most direct and safe practical route to a designated escapeway.

§ 75.385

(b) The route of travel shall be clearly marked.

(c) When a roof fall or other blockage occurs that prevents travel in the travelway—

(1) Work shall cease on the longwall or shortwall face;

(2) Miners shall be withdrawn from face areas to a safe area outby the section loading point; and

(3) MSHA shall be notified.

(d) Work may resume on the longwall or shortwall face after the procedures set out in §§ 75.215 and 75.222 are implemented.

§ 75.385 Opening new mines.

When new mines are opened, no more than 20 miners at a time shall be allowed in any mine until a connection has been made between the mine openings, and these connections shall be made as soon as possible.

§ 75.386 Final mining of pillars.

When only one mine opening is available due to final mining of pillars, no more than 20 miners at a time shall be allowed in the mine, and the distance between the mine opening and working face shall not exceed 500 feet.

§ 75.388 Boreholes in advance of mining.

(a) Boreholes shall be drilled in each advancing working place when the working place approaches—

(1) To within 50 feet of any area located in the mine as shown by surveys that are certified by a registered engineer or registered surveyor unless the area has been preshift examined;

(2) To within 200 feet of any area located in the mine not shown by surveys that are certified by a registered engineer or registered surveyor unless the area has been preshift examined; or

(3) To within 200 feet of any mine workings of an adjacent mine located in the same coalbed unless the mine workings have been preshift examined.

(b) Boreholes shall be drilled as follows:

(1) Into the working face, parallel to the rib, and within 3 feet of each rib.

(2) Into the working face, parallel to the rib, and at intervals across the face not to exceed 8 feet.

(3) At least 20 feet in depth in advance of the working face, and always maintained to a distance of 10 feet in advance of the working face.

(c) Boreholes shall be drilled in both ribs of advancing working places described in paragraph (a) of this section unless an alternative drilling plan is approved by the District Manager in accordance with paragraph (g) of this section. These boreholes shall be drilled—

(1) At an angle of 45 degrees to the direction of advance;

(2) At least 20 feet in depth; and

(3) At intervals not to exceed 8 feet.

(d) When a borehole penetrates an area that cannot be examined, and before mining continues, a certified person shall, if possible, determine—

(1) The direction of airflow in the borehole;

(2) The pressure differential between the penetrated area and the mine workings;

(3) The concentrations of methane, oxygen, carbon monoxide, and carbon dioxide; and

(4) Whether water is impounded within the penetrated area.

(e) Unless action is taken to dewater or to ventilate penetrated areas, boreholes shall be plugged with wooden plugs or similar devices when—

(1) Tests conducted at the boreholes show that the atmosphere in the penetrated area contains more than 1.0 percent methane, less than 19.5 percent oxygen, or harmful concentrations of carbon monoxide, carbon dioxide or other explosive, harmful or noxious gases;

(2) Tests for methane, oxygen, carbon monoxide, and carbon dioxide cannot be made because air from mine workings is flowing into the penetrated area; or

(3) Water is discharging through the boreholes from the penetrated area into the mine workings.

(f) If mining is to be conducted within 50 feet above or below an inaccessible area of another mine, boreholes shall be drilled, as necessary, according to a plan approved by the district manager.

(g) Alternative borehole patterns that provide the same protection to miners as the pattern established by paragraphs (b) and (c) of this section may be used under a plan approved by the district manager.

§ 75.389 Mining into inaccessible areas.

(a) (1) The operator shall develop and follow a plan for mining into areas penetrated by boreholes drilled under § 75.388.

(2) Mining shall not resume into any area penetrated by boreholes until conditions in the penetrated area can be determined under § 75.388 and the plan for mining-through into the area has been approved by the district manager.

(3) A copy of the procedures to be followed shall be posted near the site of the mining-through operations and the operator shall explain these procedures to all miners involved in the operations.

(b) The procedures specified in the plan shall include—

(1) The method of ventilation, ventilation controls, and the air quantities and velocities in the affected working section and working place;

(2) Dewatering procedures to be used if a penetrated area contains a water accumulation; and

(3) The procedures and precautions to be followed during mining-through operations.

(c) Except for routine mining-through operations that are part of a retreat section ventilation system approved in accordance with § 75.371(f) and (x), the following provisions shall apply:

(1) Before and during mining-through operations, a certified person shall perform air quality tests at intervals and at locations necessary to protect the safety of the miners.

(2) During mining-through operations, only persons involved in these operations shall be permitted in the mine; and

(3) After mining-through, a certified person shall determine that the affected areas are safe before any persons enter the underground areas of the mine.

Subpart E—Combustible Materials and Rock Dusting

§ 75.400 Accumulation of combustible materials.

Coal dust, including float coal dust deposited on rock-dusted surfaces, loose coal, and other combustible materials, shall be cleaned up and not be permitted to accumulate in active workings, or on diesel-powered and electric equipment therein.

[61 FR 55527, Oct. 25, 1996]

§ 75.400-1 Definitions.

(a) The term *coal dust* means particles of coal that can pass a No. 20 sieve.

(b) The term *float coal dust* means the coal dust consisting of particles of coal that can pass a No. 200 sieve.

(c) The term *loose coal* means coal fragments larger in size than coal dust.

§ 75.400-2 Cleanup program.

A program for regular cleanup and removal of accumulations of coal and float coal dusts, loose coal, and other combustibles shall be established and maintained. Such program shall be available to the Secretary or authorized representative.

§ 75.401 Abatement of dust; water or water with a wetting agent.

[STATUTORY PROVISION]

Where underground mining operations in active workings create or raise excessive amounts of dust, water or water with a wetting agent added to it, or other no less effective methods approved by the Secretary or his authorized representative, shall be used to abate such dust. In working places, particularly in distances less than 40 feet from the face, water, with or without a wetting agent, or other no less effective methods approved by the Secretary or his authorized representative, shall be applied to coal dust on the ribs, roof, and floor to reduce dispersibility and to minimize the explosion hazard.

§ 75.401-1 Excessive amounts of dust.

The term "excessive amounts of dust" means coal and float coal dust in

§ 75.402

the air in such amounts as to create the potential of an explosion hazard.

§ 75.402 Rock dusting.

[STATUTORY PROVISION]

All underground areas of a coal mine, except those areas in which the dust is too wet or too high in incombustible content to propagate an explosion, shall be rock dusted to within 40 feet of all working faces, unless such areas are inaccessible or unsafe to enter or unless the Secretary or his authorized representative permits an exception upon his finding that such exception will not pose a hazard to the miners. All crosscuts that are less than 40 feet from a working face shall also be rock dusted.

§ 75.402-1 Definition.

The term *too wet* means that sufficient natural moisture is retained by the dust that when a ball of finely divided material is squeezed in the hands water is exuded.

§ 75.402-2 Exceptions.

Exceptions granted under § 75.402 by the Secretary or his authorized representative shall be reviewed periodically.

§ 75.403 Maintenance of incombustible content of rock dust.

Where rock dust is required to be applied, it shall be distributed upon the top, floor, and sides of all underground areas of a coal mine and maintained in such quantities that the incombustible content of the combined coal dust, rock dust, and other dust shall be not less than 80 percent. Where methane is present in any ventilating current, the percent of incombustible content of such combined dust shall be increased 0.4 percent for each 0.1 percent of methane.

[75 FR 57857, Sept. 23, 2010; 76 FR 35978, June 21, 2011]

§ 75.403-1 Incombustible content.

Moisture contained in the combined coal dust, rock dust and other dusts shall be considered as a part of the incombustible content of such mixture.

§ 75.404 Exemption of anthracite mines.

[STATUTORY PROVISION]

Sections 75.401, 75.402, and 75.403 shall not apply to underground anthracite mines.

Subpart F—Electrical Equipment—General

§ 75.500 Permissible electric equipment.

[STATUTORY PROVISION]

On and after March 30, 1971:

(a) All junction or distribution boxes used for making multiple power connections inby the last open crosscut shall be permissible;

(b) All handheld electric drills, blower and exhaust fans, electric pumps, and such other low horsepower electric face equipment as the Secretary may designate on or before May 30, 1970, which are taken into or used inby the last open crosscut of any coal mine shall be permissible;

(c) All electric face equipment which is taken into or used inby the last open crosscut of any coal mine classified under any provision of law as gassy prior to March 30, 1970, shall be permissible; and

(d) All other electric face equipment which is taken into or used inby the last crosscut of any coal mine, except a coal mine referred to in § 75.501, which has not been classified under any provision of law as a gassy mine prior to March 30, 1970, shall be permissible.

§ 75.500-1 Other low horsepower electric face equipment.

Other low horsepower electric face equipment designated pursuant to the provisions of § 75.500(b) is all other electric-driven mine equipment, except low horsepower rock dusting equipment, and employs an electric current supplied by either a power conductor or battery and consumes not more than 2,250 watts of electricity and which is taken into or used inby the last open crosscut.

§ 75.501 Permissible electric face equipment; coal seams above water table.

[STATUTORY PROVISION]

On and after March 30, 1974, all electric face equipment, other than equipment referred to in paragraph (b) of § 75.500, which is taken into and used inby the last open crosscut of any coal mine which is operated entirely in coal seams located above the water table and which has not been classified under any provision of law as a gassy mine prior to March 30, 1970, and in which one or more openings were made prior to December 30, 1969, shall be permissible.

§ 75.501-1 Coal seams above the water table.

As used in § 75.501, the phrase "coal seams above the water table" means coal seams in a mine which are located at an elevation above a river or the tributary of a river into which a local surface water system naturally drains.

§ 75.501-2 Permissible electric face equipment.

(a) On and after March 30, 1971, in mines operated entirely in coal seams which are located at elevations above the water table:

(1) All junction or distribution boxes used for making multiple power connections inby the last open crosscut shall be permissible; and

(2) All handheld electric drills, blower and exhaust fans, electric pumps, and all other electric-driven mine equipment, except low horsepower rock dusting equipment, that employs an electric current supplied by either a power conductor or battery and consumes not more than 2,250 watts of electricity, which is taken into or used inby the last open crosscut shall be permissible.

(b) On and after March 30, 1974, in mines operated entirely in coal seams which are located at elevations above the water table, all electric face equipment which is taken into or used inby the last crosscut shall be permissible.

§ 75.501-3 New openings; mines above water table and never classed gassy.

(a) Where a new opening(s) is proposed to be developed by shaft, slope, or drift from the surface to, or in, any coalbed and the operator considers such proposed new opening(s) to be a part of a mine coming under section 305(a)(2) of the Act and § 75.501 the operator shall so notify the District Manager for the District in which the mine is located in writing prior to the date any actual development (in coal) through such opening(s) is undertaken. Such notification shall include the following information:

(1) Name, address, and identification number of the existing mine.

(2) A current map of the existing mine clearly setting out the proposed new opening(s), mining plan and planned interconnection, if any, with existing workings.

(3) A statement as to when the operator obtained the right to mine the coal which the proposed new opening(s) will traverse.

(4) The name of the coalbeds currently being mined and those which the new opening(s) will traverse.

(5) The expected life of the mine.

(6) The reason(s) for the proposed new opening(s) (for example, haulage, ventilation, drainage, to avoid bad roof, escapeway).

The District Manager shall require submission of any additional information he considers pertinent.

(b) The District Manager shall make a determination based on all of the information submitted by the operator as to whether the proposed new opening(s) will be considered as a part of the existing mine or as a new mine. The following guidelines and criteria shall be used by the District Manager in making his determination:

(1) The effect that the proposed new opening(s) will have on the safety of the men working in the existing mine shall be considered of primary importance.

(2) Whether the operator had a right to mine the coal which the proposed new openings will traverse prior to the date of enactment of the Act (December 30, 1969) and whether the original mining plan included mining such coal.

§ 75.502

(3) Whether, in accordance with the usual mining practices common to the particular district, the proposed new openings would have been considered a new mine or part of the existing mine. A number of factors will be considered including, but not limited to:

(i) The relationship between the coalbeds currently being mined, and those proposed to be mined;

(ii) The distance between existing openings and the proposed new opening(s);

(iii) The projected time elapsing between the start of the new opening(s) and planned interconnection, if any, with the existing mine; and

(iv) The projected tonnage of coal which is expected to be mined prior to interconnection where interconnection is planned.

The District Manager shall notify the operator in writing within 30 days of receiving all of the information, required and requested, of his determination. No informal notification shall be given.

(c) All new opening(s) shall be operated as a new mine prior to receiving a written notification from the District Manager that such new opening(s) will be considered part of an existing mine coming under section 305(a)(2) of the Act and § 75.501.

(d) Nothing in this § 75.501–3 shall be construed to relieve the operator from compliance with any of the mandatory standards contained in this Part 75.

[37 FR 8949, May 3, 1972]

§ 75.502 Permits for noncompliance.

An operator need not comply with paragraph (d) of § 75.500 or with § 75.501 during the period of time specified in a permit issued by the Interim Compliance Panel established by the Act.

§ 75.503 Permissible electric face equipment; maintenance.

[STATUTORY PROVISIONS]

The operator of each coal mine shall maintain in permissible condition all electric face equipment required by §§ 75.500, 75.501, 75.504 to be permissible which is taken into or used inby the last open crosscut of any such mine.

§ 75.503–1 Statement listing all electric face equipment.

Each operator of a coal mine shall complete and file Mine Safety and Health Administration Form No. 6-1496 entitled "Coal Operator's Electrical Survey" and Form 6–1496 Supplemental entitled "Operator's Survey of Electrical Face Equipment." Forms may be obtained from any MSHA Coal Mine Safety and Health district office. Separate forms shall be filed for each mine. Copies one and two of the completed form shall be filed with the Coal Mine District Manager for the district in which each mine is located on or before May 30, 1970. An operator must list all electric face equipment being used at each mine as of the time of filing, all such equipment being repaired, and all standby electric equipment stored at or in the mine which the operator intends to use as face equipment.

[35 FR 17890, Nov. 20, 1970, as amended at 71 FR 16668, Apr. 3, 2006]

§ 75.504 Permissibility of new, replacement, used, reconditioned, additional, and rebuilt electric face equipment.

On and after March 30, 1971, all new, replacement, used, reconditioned, and additional electric face equipment used in any mine referred to in §§ 75.500, 75.501, and 75.503 shall be permissible and shall be maintained in a permissible condition, and in the event of any major overhaul of any item of electric face equipment in use on or after March 30, 1971, such equipment shall be put in, and thereafter maintained in, a permissible condition, unless in the opinion of the Secretary, such equipment or necessary replacement parts are not available.

[38 FR 4975, Feb. 23, 1973]

§ 75.505 Mines classed gassy; use and maintenance of permissible electric face equipment.

[STATUTORY PROVISION]

Any coal mine which, prior to March 30, 1970, was classed gassy under any provision of law and was required to use permissible electric face equipment and to maintain such equipment in a permissible condition shall continue to

Mine Safety and Health Admin., Labor

§ 75.506–1

use such equipment and to maintain such equipment in such condition.

§ 75.506 Electric face equipment; requirements for permissibility.

(a) Electric-driven mine equipment and accessories manufactured on or after March 30, 1973, will be permissible electric face equipment only (1) if they are fabricated, assembled, or built under an approval, or any extension thereof, issued by the Bureau of Mines or the Mine Safety and Health Administration in accordance with schedule 2G, or any subsequent Bureau of Mines schedule promulgated by the Secretary after March 30, 1970, which amends, modifies, or supersedes the permissibility requirements of schedule 2G, and (2) if they are maintained in a permissible condition.

(b) Except as provided in paragraph (c) of this § 75.506 electric-driven mine equipment and accessories manufactured prior to March 30, 1973, will be permissible electric face equipment (1) if they were fabricated, assembled, or built under an approval, or any extension thereof, issued by the Bureau of Mines in accordance with the schedules set forth below, and (2) if they are maintained in a permissible condition.

Bureau of Mines Schedule 2D, May 23, 1936;
Bureau of Mines Schedule 2E, February 15, 1945;
Bureau of Mines Schedule 2F, August 3, 1955; and
Bureau of Mines Schedule 2G, March 19, 1968.

Copies of these schedules are available at all MSHA Coal Mine Safety and Health district offices.

(c) Electric driven mine equipment and accessories bearing the Bureau of Mines approval numbers listed in Appendix A to this subpart are permissible electric face equipment only if they are maintained in a permissible condition.

(d) The following equipment will be permissible electric face equipment only if it is approved under the appropriate parts of this chapter, or former Bureau of Mines' approval schedules, and if it is in permissible condition:

(1) Multiple-Shot Blasting Units, part 7 subpart D;
(2) Electric Cap Lamps, part 19;
(3) Electric Mine Lamps Other than Standard Cap Lamps, part 20;
(4) Flame Safety Lamps;
(5) Portable Methane Detectors, part 22;
(6) Telephone and Signaling Devices, part 23;
(7) Single-Shot Blasting Units;
(8) Lighting Equipment for Illuminating Underground Workings;
(9) Methane-Monitoring Systems, part 27; and
(10) Continuous Duty, Warning Light, Portable Methane Detectors, 30 CFR part 29 contained in the 30 CFR, parts 1–199, edition, revised as of July 1, 1999.

[35 FR 17890, Nov. 20, 1970, as amended at 63 FR 47119, Sept. 3, 1998; 64 FR 43283, Aug. 10, 1999; 71 FR 16668, Apr. 3, 2006]

§ 75.506–1 Electric face equipment; permissible condition; maintenance requirements.

(a) Except as provided in paragraph (b) of this section, electric face equipment which meets the requirements for permissibility set forth in § 75.506 will be considered to be in permissible condition only if it is maintained so as to meet the requirements for permissibility set forth in the Bureau of Mines schedule under which such electric face equipment was initially approved, or, if the equipment has been modified, it is maintained so as to meet the requirements of the schedule under which such modification was approved.

(b) Electric face equipment bearing the Bureau of Mines approval number listed in Appendix A of this subpart will be considered to be in permissible condition only if it is maintained so as to meet the requirements for permissibility set forth in Bureau of Mines Schedule 2D or, if such equipment has been modified, it is maintained so as to meet the requirements of the schedule under which the modification was approved.

(c) Notwithstanding the provisions of paragraphs (a) and (b) of this section, where the minimum requirements for permissibility set forth in the appropriate Bureau of Mines schedule under which such equipment or modifications were approved have been superseded by the requirements of this Part 75, the latter requirements shall be applicable.

§ 75.507 Power connection points.

[STATUTORY PROVISIONS]

Except where permissible power connection units are used, all power-connection points outby the last open crosscut shall be in intake air.

§ 75.507-1 Electric equipment other than power-connection points; outby the last open crosscut; return air; permissibility requirements.

(a) All electric equipment, other than power-connection points, used in return air outby the last open crosscut in any coal mine shall be permissible except as provided in paragraphs (b) and (c) of this section.

(b) Notwithstanding the provisions of paragraph (a) of this section, in any coal mine where nonpermissible electric face equipment may be taken into or used inby the last open crosscut until March 30, 1974, such nonpermissible electric face equipment may be used in return air outby the last open crosscut.

(c) Notwithstanding the provisions of paragraph (a) of this section, in any coal mine where a permit for noncompliance is in effect, nonpermissible electric face equipment specified in such permit for noncompliance may be used in return air outby the last open crosscut for the duration of such permit.

[38 FR 4975, Feb. 23, 1973]

§ 75.508 Map of electrical system.

[STATUTORY PROVISIONS]

The location and the electrical rating of all stationary electric apparatus in connection with the mine electric system, including permanent cables, switchgear, rectifying substations, transformers, permanent pumps, and trolley wires and trolley feeder wires, and settings of all direct-current circuit breakers protecting underground trolley circuits, shall be shown on a mine map. Any changes made in a location, electric rating, or setting shall be promptly shown on the map when the change is made. Such map shall be available to an authorized representative of the Secretary and to the miners in such mine.

§ 75.508-1 Mine tracks.

When mine track is used as a conductor of a trolley system, the location of such track shall be shown on the map required by § 75.508, with a notation of the number of rails and the size of such track expressed in pounds per yard.

§ 75.508-2 Changes in electric system map; recording.

Changes made in the location, electrical rating or setting within the mine electrical system shall be recorded on the map of such system no later than the end of the next workday following completion of such changes.

§ 75.509 Electric power circuit and electric equipment; deenergization.

[STATUTORY PROVISIONS]

All power circuits and electric equipment shall be deenergized before work is done on such circuits and equipment, except when necessary for trouble shooting or testing.

§ 75.510 Energized trolley wires; repair.

[STATUTORY PROVISIONS]

Energized trolley wires may be repaired only by a person trained to perform electrical work and to maintain electrical equipment and the operator of a mine shall require that such person wear approved and tested insulated shoes and wireman's gloves.

§ 75.510-1 Repair of energized trolley wires; training.

The training referred to in § 75.510 must include training in the repair and maintenance of live trolley wires, and in the hazards involved in making such repairs, and in the limitations of protective clothing used to protect against such hazards.

§ 75.511 Low-, medium-, or high-voltage distribution circuits and equipment; repair.

[STATUTORY PROVISION]

No electrical work shall be performed on low-, medium-, or high-voltage distribution circuits or equipment, except by a qualified person or by a person

Mine Safety and Health Admin., Labor § 75.516-1

trained to perform electrical work and to maintain electrical equipment under the direct supervision of a qualified person. Disconnecting devices shall be locked out and suitably tagged by the persons who perform such work, except that in cases where locking out is not possible, such devices shall be opened and suitably tagged by such persons. Locks or tags shall be removed only by the persons who installed them or, if such persons are unavailable, by persons authorized by the operator or his agent.

§ 75.511-1 Qualified person.

To be a qualified person within the meaning of § 75.511, an individual must meet the requirements of § 75.153.

§ 75.512 Electric equipment; examination, testing and maintenance.

[STATUTORY PROVISION]

All electric equipment shall be frequently examined, tested, and properly maintained by a qualified person to assure safe operating conditions. When a potentially dangerous condition is found on electric equipment, such equipment shall be removed from service until such condition is corrected. A record of such examinations shall be kept and made available to an authorized representative of the Secretary and to the miners in such mine.

[35 FR 17890, Nov. 20, 1970, as amended at 60 FR 33723, June 29, 1995]

§ 75.512-1 Qualified person.

To be a qualified person within the meaning of § 75.512, an individual must meet the requirements of § 75.153.

§ 75.512-2 Frequency of examinations.

The examinations and tests required by § 75.512 shall be made at least weekly. Permissible equipment shall be examined to see that it is in permissible condition.

§ 75.513 Electric conductor; capacity and insulation.

[STATUTORY PROVISION]

All electric conductors shall be sufficient in size and have adequate current carrying capacity and be of such construction that a rise in temperature resulting from normal operation will not damage the insulating materials.

§ 75.513-1 Electric conductor; size.

An electric conductor is not of sufficient size to have adequate carrying capacity if it is smaller than is provided for in the National Electric Code, 1968. In addition, equipment and trailing cables that are required to be permissible must meet the requirements of the appropriate schedules of the Bureau of Mines.

§ 75.514 Electrical connections or splices; suitability.

[STATUTORY PROVISION]

All electrical connections or splices in conductors shall be mechanically and electrically efficient, and suitable connectors shall be used. All electrical connections or splices in insulated wire shall be reinsulated at least to the same degree of protection as the remainder of the wire.

§ 75.515 Cable fittings; suitability.

[STATUTORY PROVISION]

Cables shall enter metal frames of motors, splice boxes, and electric compartments only through proper fittings. When insulated wires other than cables pass through metal frames, the holes shall be substantially bushed with insulated bushings.

§ 75.516 Power wires; support.

[STATUTORY PROVISION]

All power wires (except trailing cables on mobile equipment, specially designed cables conducting high-voltage power to underground rectifying equipment or transformers, or bare or insulated ground and return wires) shall be supported on well-insulated insulators and shall not contact combustible material, roof, or ribs.

§ 75.516-1 Installed insulators.

Well-insulated insulators is interpreted to mean well-installed insulators. Insulated J-hooks may be used to suspend insulated power cables

§ 75.516-2

for temporary installation not exceeding 6 months and for permanent installation of control cables such as may be used along belt conveyors.

§ 75.516-2 Communication wires and cables; installation; insulation; support.

(a) All communication wires shall be supported on insulated hangers or insulated J-hooks.

(b) All communication cables shall be insulated as required by § 75.517-1, and shall either be supported on insulated or uninsulated hangers or J-hooks, or securely attached to messenger wires, or buried, or otherwise protected against mechanical damage in a manner approved by the Secretary or his authorized representative.

(c) All communication wires and cables installed in track entries shall, except when a communication cable is buried in accordance with paragraph (b) of this section, be installed on the side of the entry opposite to trolley wires and trolley feeder wires. Additional insulation shall be provided for communication circuits at points where they pass over or under any power conductor.

(d) For purposes of this section, communication cable means two or more insulated conductors covered by an additional abrasion-resistant covering.

[38 FR 4975, Feb. 23, 1973]

§ 75.517 Power wires and cables; insulation and protection.

[STATUTORY PROVISIONS]

Power wires and cables, except trolley wires, trolley feeder wires, and bare signal wires, shall be insulated adequately and fully protected.

§ 75.517-1 Power wires and cables; insulation and protection.

Power wires and cables installed on or after March 30, 1970, shall have insulation with a dielectric strength at least equal to the voltage of the circuit.

§ 75.517-2 Plans for insulation of existing bare power wires and cables.

(a) On or before December 31, 1970, plans for the insulation of existing bare power wires and cables installed prior to March 30, 1970, shall be filed with the District Manager of the Coal Mine Safety District in which the mine is located to permit approval and prompt implementation of such plans.

(b) The appropriate District Manager shall notify the operator in writing of the approval of a proposed insulation plan. If revisions are required for approval, the changes required will be specified.

(c) An insulation plan shall include the following information:

(1) Name and address of the company, the mine and the responsible officials;

(2) Map or diagram indicating location of power wires and cables required to be insulated;

(3) Total length of bare power wires and cables required to be insulated;

(4) Schedule for the replacement or insulation of bare power wires and cables;

(5) Type of insulation to be used and the voltage rating as indicated by the manufacturer.

(d) The District Manager shall be guided by the following criteria in approving insulation plans on a mine-by-mine basis. Insulation not conforming to these criteria may be approved provided the operator can satisfy the Mine Safety and Health Administration that the insulation will provide no less than the same measure of protection.

(1) Insulation shall be adequate for the applied voltage of the circuit.

(2) When tubing is used to insulate existing power wires and cables, it shall have a dielectric strength at least equal to the voltage of the circuit. When the tubing is split for purposes of installation, the joints shall be effectively sealed. The butt ends may be sealed with a moisture resistant insulating tape.

(3) When tape is used to insulate existing power wires and cables, it shall be applied half-lapped and one thickness of the tape shall have a dielectric strength at least equal to the voltage of the circuit. The tape shall be self-adhesive and moisture resistant.

§ 75.518 Electric equipment and circuits; overload and short circuit protection.

[STATUTORY PROVISION]

Automatic circuit-breaking devices or fuses of the correct type and capacity shall be installed so as to protect all electric equipment and circuits against short circuit and overloads. Three-phase motors on all electric equipment shall be provided with overload protection that will deenergize all three phases in the event that any phase is overloaded.

§ 75.518-1 Electric equipment and circuits; overload and short circuit protection; minimum requirements.

A device to provide either short circuit protection or protection against overload which does not conform to the provisions of the National Electric Code, 1968, does not meet the requirement of § 75.518. In addition, such devices on electric face equipment and trailing cables that are required to be permissible must meet the requirements of the applicable schedules of the Bureau of Mines.

§ 75.518-2 Incandescent lamps, overload and short circuit protection.

Incandescent lamps installed along haulageways and at other locations, not contacting combustible material, and powered from trolley or direct current feeder circuits, need not be provided with separate short circuit or overload protection, if the lamp is not more than 8 feet in distance from such circuits.

§ 75.519 Main power circuits; disconnecting switches.

[STATUTORY PROVISION]

In all main power circuits, disconnecting switches shall be installed underground within 500 feet of the bottoms of shafts and boreholes through which main power circuits enter the underground area of the mine and within 500 feet of all other places where main power circuits enter the underground area of the mine.

§ 75.519-1 Main power circuits; disconnecting switches; locations.

Section 75.519 requires (a) that a disconnecting switch be installed on the surface at a point within 500 feet of the place where the main power circuit enters the underground area of a mine, and (b) that, in an instance on which a main power circuit enters the underground area through a shaft or borehole, a disconnecting switch be installed underground within 500 feet of the bottom of the shaft or borehole.

§ 75.520 Electric equipment; switches.

[STATUTORY PROVISION]

All electric equipment shall be provided with switches or other controls that are safely designed, constructed, and installed.

§ 75.521 Lightning arresters; ungrounded and exposed power conductors and telephone wires.

Each ungrounded, exposed power conductor and each ungrounded, exposed telephone wire that leads underground shall be equipped with suitable lightning arresters of approved type within 100 feet of the point where the circuit enters the mine. Lightning arresters shall be connected to a low resistance grounding medium on the surface which shall be separated from neutral grounds by a distance of not less than 25 feet.

[38 FR 4975, Feb. 23, 1973]

§ 75.522 Lighting devices.

[STATUTORY PROVISION]

No device for the purpose of lighting any coal mine which has not been approved by the Secretary or his authorized representative shall be permitted in such mine.

§ 75.522-1 Incandescent and fluorescent lamps.

(a) Except for areas of a coal mine inby the last open crosscut, incandescent lamps may be used to illuminate underground areas. When incandescent lamps are used in a track entry or belt entry or near track entries to illuminate special areas other than structures, the lamps shall be installed in weather-proof sockets located in positions such that the lamps will not come in contact with any combustible material. Lamps used in all other places must be of substantial construction and be fitted with a glass enclosure.

(b) Incandescent lamps within glass enclosures or fluorescent lamps may be used inside underground structures (except magazines used for the storage of explosives and detonators). In underground structures lighting circuits shall consist of cables installed on insulators or insulated wires installed in metallic conduit or metallic armor.

§ 75.523 Electric face equipment; deenergization.

[STATUTORY PROVISION]

An authorized representative of the Secretary may require in any mine that electric face equipment be provided with devices that will permit the equipment to be deenergized quickly in the event of an emergency.

§ 75.523–1 Deenergization of self-propelled electric face equipment installation requirements.

(a) Except as provided in paragraphs (b) and (c) of this section, all self-propelled electric face equipment which is used in the active workings of each underground coal mine on and after March 1, 1973, shall, in accordance with the schedule of time specified in paragraphs (a) (1) and (2) of this section, be provided with a device that will quickly deenergize the tramming motors of the equipment in the event of an emergency. The requirements of this paragraph (a) shall be met as follows:

(1) On and after December 15, 1974, for self-propelled cutting machines, shuttle cars, battery-powered machines, and roof drills and bolters;

(2) On and after February 15, 1975, for all other types of self-propelled electric face equipment.

(b) Self-propelled electric face equipment that is equipped with a substantially constructed cab which meets the requirements of this part, shall not be required to be provided with a device that will quickly deenergize the tramming motors of the equipment in the event of an emergency.

(c) An operator may apply to the Director of Technical Support, Mine Safety and Health Administration, Department of Labor, 201 12th Street South, Arlington, VA 22202–5452; 202–693–9440; for approval of the installation of devices to be used in lieu of devices that will quickly deenergize the tramming motors of self-propelled electric face equipment in the event of an emergency. The Director of Technical Support may approve such devices if he determines that the performance thereof will be no less effective than the performance requirements specified in § 75.523–2.

[38 FR 3407, Feb. 6, 1973, as amended at 39 FR 27557, July 30, 1974; 43 FR 12320, Mar. 24, 1978; 47 FR 28096, June 29, 1982; 67 FR 38386, June 4, 2002; 80 FR 52992, Sept. 2, 2015]

§ 75.523–2 Deenergization of self-propelled electric face equipment; performance requirements.

(a) Deenergization of the tramming motors of self-propelled electric face equipment, required by paragraph (a) of § 75.523–1, shall be provided by:

(1) Mechanical actuation of an existing pushbutton emergency stopswitch,

(2) Mechanical actuation of an existing lever emergency stopswitch, or

(3) The addition of a separate electromechanical switch assembly.

(b) The existing emergency stopswitch or additional switch assembly shall be actuated by a bar or lever which shall extend a sufficient distance in each direction to permit quick deenergization of the tramming motors of self-propelled electric face equipment from all locations from which the equipment can be operated.

(c) Movement of not more than 2 inches of the actuating bar or lever resulting from the application of not more than 15 pounds of force upon contact with any portion of the equipment operator's body at any point along the length of the actuating bar or lever shall cause deenergization of the tramming motors of the self-propelled electric face equipment.

[38 FR 3406, Feb. 6, 1973; 38 FR 4394, Feb. 14, 1973]

§ 75.523-3 Automatic emergency-parking brakes.

(a) Except for personnel carriers, rubber-tired, self-propelled electric haulage equipment used in the active workings of underground coal mines shall be equipped with automatic emergency-parking brakes in accordance with the following schedule.

(1) On and after May 23, 1989—
(i) All new equipment ordered; and
(ii) All equipment originally furnished with or retrofitted with automatic emergency-parking brakes which meet the requirements of this section.
(2) On and after May 23, 1991, all other equipment.

(b) Automatic emergency-parking brakes shall—
(1) Be activated immediately by the emergency deenergization device required by 30 CFR 75.523-1 and 75.523-2;
(2) Engage automatically within 5.0 seconds when the equipment is deenergized;
(3) Safely bring the equipment when fully loaded to a complete stop on the maximum grade on which it is operated;
(4) Hold the equipment stationary despite any contraction of brake parts, exhaustion of any non-mechanical source of energy, or leakage; and
(5) Release only by a manual control that does not operate any other equipment function.

(c) Automatic emergency-parking brakes shall include a means in the equipment operator's compartment to—
(1) Apply the brakes manually without deenergizing the equipment; and
(2) Release and reengage the brakes without energizing the equipment.

(d) On and after November 24, 1989, rubber-tired, self-propelled electric face equipment not covered by paragraph (a) of this section shall be equipped with a means incorporated on the equipment and operable from each tramming station to hold the equipment stationary—
(1) On the maximum grade on which it is operated; and
(2) Despite any contraction of components, exhaustion of any non-mechanical source of energy, or leakage.

(e) The brake systems required by paragraphs (a) or (d) of this section shall be applied when the equipment operator is not at the controls of the equipment, except during movement of disabled equipment.

[54 FR 12412, Mar. 24, 1989]

§ 75.524 Electric face equipment; electric equipment used in return air outby the last open crosscut; maximum level of alternating or direct electric current between frames of equipment.

The maximum level of alternating or direct electric current that exists between the frames of any two units of electric face equipment that come in contact with each other in the working places of a coal mine, or between the frames of any two units of electric equipment that come in contact with each other in return air outby the last open crosscut, shall not exceed one ampere as determined from the voltage measured across a 0.1 ohm resistor connected between the frames of such equipment.

[38 FR 29998, Oct. 31, 1973]

APPENDIX A TO SUBPART F OF PART 75—LIST OF PERMISSIBLE ELECTRIC FACE EQUIPMENT APPROVED BY THE BUREAU OF MINES PRIOR TO MAY 23, 1936

Motor-Driven Mine Equipment
(Approved Under Schedules 2, 2A, 2B, and 2C)

Approval No.	Date
AIR COMPRESSORS	
128	March 21, 1927.
128A	July 16, 1926.
COAL DRILLS AND DRILLING MACHINES	
Hand Drills	
109	September 19, 1922.
154	August 1, 1928.
184	February 7, 1930.
227	July 29, 1931.
254	July 15, 1933.
Post Drills	
119	April 15, 1925.
119A	Do.
225	July 10, 1931.
225A	Do.
228	August 12, 1931.
228A	February 17, 1932.
230	August 20, 1931.
230A	Do.
237	December 1, 1931.
237A	Do.

Pt. 75, Subpt. F, App. A

30 CFR Ch. I (7-1-23 Edition)

Motor-Driven Mine Equipment
(Approved Under Schedules 2, 2A, 2B, and 2C)

Approval No.	Date
Drilling Machines	
147	February 8, 1928.
147A	Do.
176	September 9, 1929.
176A	Do.
LOADING AND CONVEYING EQUIPMENT	
LOADING MACHINES	
Unmounted Type	
122	January 8, 1926.
122A	Do.
Caterpillar-Mounted Type	
150	May 11, 1928.
186	March 15, 1930.
222	May 8, 1931.
222A	July 28, 1931.
229	August 17, 1931.
229A	Do.
235	November 27, 1931.
235A	October 29, 1931.
278	January 17, 1935.
278A	Do.
283A	March 12, 1935.
284A	Do.
285A	Do.
294	September 18, 1935.
300A	May 6, 1936.
127	July 16, 1926.
127A	September 23, 1927.
Track-Mounted Type	
194	June 6, 1930.
194A	Do.
217	February 27, 1931.
217A	Do.
276	January 11, 1935.
277	January 17, 1935.
282A	March 12, 1935.
291A	July 3, 1935.
Pit-Car Loaders	
167	March 27, 1929.
167A	Do.
175	July 26, 1929.
175A	June 24, 1929.
250	December 10, 1932.
250A	Do.
252A	February 20, 1933.
CONVEYORS	
Belt Type	
236	November 19, 1931.
287A	March 12, 1935.
296A	January 6, 1936.
Chain Type	
151	May 19, 1928.
209	December 2, 1930.
240	March 12, 1932.
240A	Do.
298A	March 3, 1936.

Motor-Driven Mine Equipment
(Approved Under Schedules 2, 2A, 2B, and 2C)

Approval No.	Date
Power Units for Conveyors	
265	February 12, 1934.
265A	March 19, 1934.
390A	March 23, 1934.
Shaker Type	
247	October 21, 1932.
257A	August 11, 1933.
262A	December 8, 1933.
271	May 20, 1935.
271A	October 17, 1934.
274A	December 13, 1934.
286A	March 12, 1935.
295	September 20, 1935.
299A	April 9, 1936.
Scraper-type Loaders	
138	August 5, 1927.
138A	Do.
196	September 29, 1930.
196A	July 26, 1930.
226	July 27, 1931.
255	July 31, 1933.
256	Do.
MINING MACHINES, MACHINERY-MOVING EQUIPMENT, MISCELLANEOUS TRUCKS, AND WATER SPRAY SUPPLY UNITS	
MINING MACHINES	
Shortwall Machines	
103	November 2, 1917.
103A	Do.
105	February 9, 1922.
105A	Do.
106	Do.
106A	Do.
107	Do.
107A	Do.
108	Do.
108A	Do.
111	October 16, 1922.
111A	Do.
113	November 4, 1924.
113A	Do.
114	February 7, 1925.
114A	Do.
115	Do.
115A	Do.
153	July 31, 1928.
153A	Do.
193	June 3, 1930.
193A	Do.
197	July 31, 1930.
197A	Do.
198	August 1, 1930.
198A	Do.
201	September 8, 1930.
201A	Do.
204	October 13, 1930.
204A	December 13, 1930.
223	May 13, 1931.
223A	Do.
241	March 18, 1932.
241A	Do.
258	August 15, 1933.
259A	August 16, 1933.
260A	August 17, 1933.
273	November 30, 1934.

574

Mine Safety and Health Admin., Labor — Pt. 75, Subpt. F, App. A

Motor-Driven Mine Equipment
(Approved Under Schedules 2, 2A, 2B, and 2C)

Approval No.	Date
288	March 27, 1935.
288A	Do.
292	September 11, 1935.
292A	Do.
293A	Do.

Longwall Machines

Approval No.	Date
185	February 24, 1930.
185A	Do.
218	March 10, 1931.
218A	Do.
246	August 19, 1932.
246A	Do.
261	September 12, 1933.

Track or caterpillar mounted

Approval No.	Date
112	March 13, 1924.
112A	Do.
118	March 12, 1925.
118A	Do.
125	April 26, 1926.
125A	Do.
172	April 30, 1929.
172A	Do.
188	April 15, 1930.
188A	Do.
207	November 14, 1930.
207A	Do.
216	February 12, 1931.
216A	Do.
231	August 31, 1931.
231A	Do.
242	April 7, 1932.
244	June 18, 1932.
244A	September 20, 1932.
253A	February 25, 1933.
267	June 27, 1934.
268A	July 25, 1934.
269A	September 24, 1934.
280A	March 4, 1935.
297	January 27, 1936.
297A	Do.

Mine Pumps

Approval No.	Date
140	November 1, 1927.
140A	Do.
143	Do.
143A	Do.
144	Do.
144A	Do.
199	August 18, 1930.
199A	Do.
208	November 29, 1930.
210	December 15, 1930.
210A	Do.
211	December 17, 1930.
211A	Do.
213	December 29, 1930.
213A	Do.
214	January 2, 1931.
214A	Do.
215	Do.
215A	Do.
248	October 31, 1932.
248A	November 23, 1932.
264	January 31, 1934.
264A	Do.
272	October 23, 1934.
272A	Do.

Motor-Driven Mine Equipment
(Approved Under Schedules 2, 2A, 2B, and 2C)

Rock-Dusting Machines

Approval No.	Date
130	November 5, 1926.
137	July 2, 1927.
146	January 20, 1928.
146A	April 3, 1928.
180	October 30, 1929.
180A	January 17, 1930.
206	November 12, 1930.
279	February 14, 1935.

Room and Car-Spotting Hoists

Approval No.	Date
116	February 13, 1925.
116A	Do.
164	January 21, 1931.
164A	Do.
165	Do.
165A	Do.
169	April 5, 1929.
169A	February 26, 1934.
190	April 20, 1930.
251A	January 16, 1933.
263	January 11, 1934.
266A	February 27, 1934.

Storage-Battery Locomotives and Power Trucks
(Approved under Schedules 15, 2C, 2D, and 2E)

Gathering Locomotives

Approval No.	Date
1501	October 11, 1921.
1502	November 13, 1922.
1503	March 24, 1923.
1505	April 5, 1924.
1507	August 20, 1925.
1508	March 21, 1925.
1509	September 25, 1925.
1511	November 10, 1925.
1512	November 11, 1925.
1513	February 25, 1926.
1516	December 28, 1926.
1517	February 10, 1927.
1520	May 27, 1929.
1521	June 13, 1930.
1522	September 12, 1930.
1523	December 19, 1930.
1525	July 25, 1934.
1526	December 20, 1935.

Tandem Locomotive

Approval No.	Date
1518	November 21, 1927.

Power Trucks

Approval No.	Date
1506	May 5, 1924.
1505A	June 21, 1926.
1510C	December 31, 1926.
1514	December 18, 1926.
1515	December 28, 1926.
1512C	September 13, 1928.
1519C	April 6, 1929.
1524C	June 25, 1934.

Junction, Distribution, and Splice Boxes
(Approved under Schedules 2D and 2E)

Junction Boxes

Approval No.	Date
400	June 16, 1928.
400A	August 5, 1925.
401	May 11, 1927.

§ 75.600

Motor-Driven Mine Equipment
(Approved Under Schedules 2, 2A, 2B, and 2C)

Approval No.	Date
401A	Do.
402	Do.
402A	Do.
403	April 14, 1931.
403A	Do.
405A	December 4, 1933.

Subpart G—Trailing Cables

§ 75.600 Trailing cables; flame resistance.

[STATUTORY PROVISIONS]

Trailing cables used in coal mines shall meet the requirements established by the Secretary for flame-resistant cables.

§ 75.600-1 Approved cables; flame resistance.

Cables shall be accepted or approved by MSHA as flame resistant.

[57 FR 61223, Dec. 23, 1992]

§ 75.601 Short circuit protection of trailing cables.

[STATUTORY PROVISIONS]

Short circuit protection for trailing cables shall be provided by an automatic circuit breaker or other no less effective device approved by the Secretary of adequate current-interrupting capacity in each ungrounded conductor. Disconnecting devices used to disconnect power from trailing cables shall be plainly marked and identified and such devices shall be equipped or designed in such a manner that it can be determined by visual observation that the power is disconnected.

§ 75.601-1 Short circuit protection; ratings and settings of circuit breakers.

Circuit breakers providing short circuit protection for trailing cables shall be set so as not to exceed the maximum allowable instantaneous settings specified in this section; however, higher settings may be permitted by an authorized representative of the Secretary when he has determined that special applications are justified:

Conductor size AWG or MGM	Maximum allowable circuit breaker instantaneous setting (amperes)
14	50
12	75
10	150
8	200
6	300
4	500
3	600
2	800
1	1,000
1/0	1,250
2/0	1,500
3/0	2,000
4/0	2,500
250	2,500
300	2,500
350	2,500
400	2,500
450	2,500
500	2,500

§ 75.601-2 Short circuit protection; use of fuses; approval by the Secretary.

Fuses shall not be employed to provide short circuit protection for trailing cables unless specifically approved by the Secretary.

§ 75.601-3 Short circuit protection; dual element fuses; current ratings; maximum values.

Dual element fuses having adequate current-interrupting capacity shall meet the requirements for short circuit protection of trailing cables as provided in § 75.601, however, the current ratings of such devices shall not exceed the maximum values specified in this section:

Conductor size (AWG or MGM)	Single conductor cable		Two conductor cable	
	Ampacity	Max. fuse rating	Ampacity	Max. fuse rating
14			15	15
12			20	20
10			25	25
8	60	60	50	50
6	85	90	65	70
4	110	110	90	90
3	130	150	105	110
2	150	150	120	125
1	170	175	140	150
1/0	200	200	170	175
2/0	235	250	195	200
3/0	275	300	225	225
4/0	315	350	260	300
250	350	350	285	300
300	395	400	310	350
350	445	450	335	350
400	480	500	360	400
450	515	600	385	400
500	545	600	415	450

Mine Safety and Health Admin., Labor § 75.700-1

§ 75.602 Trailing cable junctions.

[STATUTORY PROVISION]

When two or more trailing cables junction to the same distribution center, means shall be provided to assure against connecting a trailing cable to the wrong size circuit breaker.

§ 75.603 Temporary splice of trailing cable.

[STATUTORY PROVISION]

One temporary splice may be made in any trailing cable. Such trailing cable may only be used for the next 24-hour period. No temporary splice shall be made in a trailing cable within 25 feet of the machine, except cable reel equipment. Temporary splices in trailing cables shall be made in a workmanlike manner and shall be mechanically strong and well insulated. Trailing cables or hand cables which have exposed wires or which have splices that heat or spark under load shall not be used. As used in this section, the term "splice" means the mechanical joining of one or more conductors that have been severed.

§ 75.604 Permanent splicing of trailing cables.

[STATUTORY PROVISIONS]

When permanent splices in trailing cables are made, they shall be:

(a) Mechanically strong with adequate electrical conductivity and flexibility;

(b) Effectively insulated and sealed so as to exclude moisture; and

(c) Vulcanized or otherwise treated with suitable materials to provide flame-resistant qualities and good bonding to the outer jacket.

(d) Made using splice kits accepted or approved by MSHA as flame resistant.

[35 FR 17890, Nov. 20, 1970, as amended at 57 FR 61223, Dec. 23, 1992]

§ 75.605 Clamping of trailing cables to equipment.

[STATUTORY PROVISIONS]

Trailing cables shall be clamped to machines in a manner to protect the cables from damage and to prevent strain on the electrical connections.

§ 75.606 Protection of trailing cables.

[STATUTORY PROVISIONS]

Trailing cables shall be adequately protected to prevent damage by mobile equipment.

§ 75.607 Breaking trailing cable and power cable connections.

[STATUTORY PROVISIONS]

Trailing cable and power cable connections to junction boxes shall not be made or broken under load.

Subpart H—Grounding

§ 75.700 Grounding metallic sheaths, armors, and conduits enclosing power conductors.

[STATUTORY PROVISIONS]

All metallic sheaths, armors, and conduits enclosing power conductors shall be electrically continuous throughout and shall be grounded by methods approved by an authorized representative of the Secretary.

§ 75.700-1 Approved methods of grounding.

Metallic sheaths, armors and conduits in resistance grounded systems where the enclosed conductors are a part of the system will be approved if a solid connection is made to the neutral conductor; in all other systems, the following methods of grounding will be approved:

(a) A solid connection to a borehole casing having low resistance to earth;

(b) A solid connection to metal waterlines having low resistance to earth;

(c) A solid connection to a grounding conductor, other than the neutral conductor of a resistance grounded system, extending to a low resistance ground field located on the surface;

(d) Any other method of grounding, approved by an authorized representative of the Secretary, which ensures that there is no difference in potential between such metallic enclosures and the earth.

577

§ 75.701 Grounding metallic frames, casings, and other enclosures of electric equipment.

[STATUTORY PROVISIONS]

Metallic frames, casings, and other enclosures of electric equipment that can become "alive" through failure of insulation or by contact with energized parts shall be grounded by methods approved by an authorized representative of the Secretary.

§ 75.701-1 Approved methods of grounding of equipment receiving power from ungrounded alternating current power systems.

For purposes of grounding metallic frames, casings and other enclosures of equipment receiving power from ungrounded alternating current power systems, the following methods of grounding will be approved:

(a) A solid connection between the metallic frame, casing, or other metal enclosure and the grounded metallic sheath, armor, or conduit enclosing the power conductor feeding the electrical equipment enclosed;

(b) A solid connection to a borehole casing having low resistance to earth;

(c) A solid connection to metal waterlines having low resistance to earth;

(d) A solid connection to a grounding conductor extending to a low resistance ground field located on the surface;

(e) Any other method of grounding, approved by an authorized representative of the Secretary, which ensures that there is no difference in potential between such metal enclosures and the earth.

§ 75.701-2 Approved method of grounding metallic frames, casings and other enclosures receiving power from single-phase 110–220-volt circuit.

In instances where single-phase 110–220-volt circuits are used to feed electrical equipment, the only method of grounding that will be approved is the connection of all metallic frames, casings and other enclosures of such equipment to a separate grounding conductor which establishes a continuous connection to a grounded center tap of the transformer.

§ 75.701-3 Approved methods of grounding metallic frames, casings and other enclosures of electric equipment receiving power from direct current power systems with one polarity grounded.

For the purpose of grounding metallic frames, casings and enclosures of any electric equipment or device receiving power from a direct-current power system with one polarity grounded, the following methods of grounding will be approved:

(a) A solid connection to the mine track;

(b) A solid connection to the grounded power conductor of the system;

(c) Silicon diode grounding; however, this method shall be employed only when such devices are installed in accordance with the requirements set forth in paragraph (d) of § 75.703-3; and

(d) Any other method, approved by an authorized representative of the Secretary, which insures that there is no difference in potential between such metal enclosures and the earth.

§ 75.701-4 Grounding wires; capacity of wires.

Where grounding wires are used to ground metallic sheaths, armors, conduits, frames, casings, and other metallic enclosures, such grounding wires will be approved if:

(a) The cross-sectional area (size) of the grounding wire is at least one-half the cross-sectional area (size) of the power conductor where the power conductor used is No. 6 A.W.G., or larger.

(b) Where the power conductor used is less than No. 6 A.W.G., the cross-sectional area (size) of the grounding wire is equal to the cross-sectional area (size) of the power conductor.

§ 75.701-5 Use of grounding connectors.

The attachment of grounding wires to a mine track or other grounded power conductor will be approved if separate clamps, suitable for such purpose, are used and installed to provide a solid connection.

§ 75.702 Protection other than grounding.

[STATUTORY PROVISIONS]

Methods other than grounding which provide no less effective protection may be permitted by the Secretary or his authorized representative.

§ 75.702-1 Protection other than grounding; approved by an authorized representative of the Secretary.

Under this subpart no method other than grounding may be used to ensure against a difference in potential between metallic sheaths, armors and conduits, enclosing power conductors and frames, casings and metal enclosures of electric equipment, and the earth, unless approved by an authorized representative of the Secretary.

§ 75.703 Grounding offtrack direct-current machines and the enclosures of related detached components.

[STATUTORY PROVISIONS]

The frames of all offtrack direct-current machines and the enclosures of related detached components shall be effectively grounded, or otherwise maintained at no less safe voltages, by methods approved by an authorized representative of the Secretary.

§ 75.703-1 Approved method of grounding.

In instances where the metal frames both of an offtrack direct-current machine and of the metal frames of its component parts are grounded to the same grounding medium the requirements of § 75.703 will be met.

§ 75.703-2 Approved grounding mediums.

For purposes of grounding offtrack direct-current machines, the following grounding mediums are approved:

(a) The grounded polarity of the direct-current power system feeding such machines; or,

(b) The alternating current grounding medium where such machines are fed by an ungrounded direct-current power system originating in a portable rectifier receiving its power from a section power center. However, when such a medium is used, a separate grounding conductor must be employed.

§ 75.703-3 Approved methods of grounding offtrack mobile, portable and stationary direct-current machines.

In grounding offtrack direct-current machines and the enclosures of their component parts, the following methods of grounding will meet the requirements of § 75.703:

(a) The use of a separate grounding conductor located within the trailing cable of mobile and portable equipment and connected between such equipment and the direct-current grounding medium;

(b) The use of a separate ground conductor located within the direct-current power cable feeding stationary equipment and connected between such stationary equipment and the direct-current grounding medium;

(c) The use of a separate external ground conductor connected between stationary equipment and the direct-current grounding medium; or,

(d) The use of silicon diodes; however, the installation of such devices shall meet the following minimum requirements:

(1) Installation of silicon diodes shall be restricted to electric equipment receiving power from a direct-current system with one polarity grounded;

(2) Where such diodes are used on circuits having a nominal voltage rating of 250, they must have a forward current rating of 400 amperes or more, and have a peak inverse voltage rating of 400 or more;

(3) Where such diodes are used on circuits having a nominal voltage rating of 550, they must have a forward current rating of 250 amperes or more, and have a peak inverse voltage rating of 800 or more;

(4) Where fuses approved by the Secretary are used at the outby end of a trailing cable connected to electrical equipment employing silicon diodes, the rating of such fuses must not exceed 150 percent of the nominal current rating of the grounding diodes;

(5) Where circuit breakers are used at the outby end of a trailing cable connected to electrical equipment employing silicon diodes, the instantaneous

§ 75.703–4

trip setting shall not exceed 300 percent of the nominal current rating of the grounding diode;

(6) Overcurrent devices must be used and installed in such a manner that the operating coil circuit of the main contactor will open when a fault current with a value of 25 percent or less of the diode rating flows through the diode;

(7) The silicon diode installed must be suitable to the grounded polarity of the power system in which it is used and its threaded base must be solidly connected to the machine frame on which it is installed;

(8) In addition to the grounding diode, a polarizing diode must be installed in the machine control circuit to prevent operation of the machine when the polarity of a trailing cable is reversed;

(9) When installed on permissible equipment, all grounding diodes, overcurrent devices, and polarizing diodes must be placed in explosion proof compartments;

(10) When grounding diodes are installed on a continuous miner, their nominal diode current rating must be at least 750 amperes or more; and,

(11) All grounding diodes shall be tested, examined and maintained as electrical equipment in accordance with the provisions of § 75.512.

§ 75.703–4 Other methods of protecting offtrack direct-current equipment; approved by an authorized representative of the Secretary.

Other methods of maintaining safe voltage by preventing a difference between the frames of offtract direct-current machines and the earth must be approved by an authorized representative of the Secretary.

§ 75.704 Grounding frames of stationary high-voltage equipment receiving power from ungrounded delta systems.

[STATUTORY PROVISIONS]

The frames of all stationary high-voltage equipment receiving power from ungrounded delta systems shall be grounded by methods approved by an authorized representative of the Secretary.

§ 75.704–1 Approved methods of grounding.

The methods of grounding stated in § 75.701–1 will also be approved with respect to the grounding of frames of high-voltage equipment referred to in § 75.704.

§ 75.705 Work on high-voltage lines; deenergizing and grounding.

[STATUTORY PROVISIONS]

High-voltage lines, both on the surface and underground, shall be deenergized and grounded before work is performed on them, except that repairs may be permitted, in the case of energized surface high-voltage lines, if such repairs are made by a qualified person in accordance with procedures and safeguards, including, but not limited to, a requirement that the operator of such mine provide, test, and maintain protective devices in making such repairs, to be prescribed by the Secretary prior to March 30, 1970.

§ 75.705–1 Work on high-voltage lines.

(a) Section 75.705 specifically prohibits work on energized high-voltage lines underground;

(b) No high-voltage line, either on the surface or underground, shall be regarded as deenergized for the purpose of performing work on it, until it has been determined by a qualified person (as provided in § 75.153) that such high-voltage line has been deenergized and grounded. Such qualified person shall by visual observation (1) determine that the disconnecting devices on the high-voltage circuit are in open position and (2) ensure that each ungrounded conductor of the high-voltage circuit upon which work is to be done is properly connected to the system-grounding medium. In the case of resistance grounded or solid wye-connected systems, the neutral wire is the system-grounding medium. In the case of an ungrounded power system, either the steel armor or conduit enclosing the system or a surface grounding field is a system grounding medium;

(c) No work shall be performed on any high-voltage line on the surface which is supported by any pole or structure which also supports other high-voltage lines until. (1) All lines supported on the pole or structure are deenergized and grounded in accordance with all of the provisions of this section which apply to the repair of energized surface high-voltage lines; or (2) the provisions of §§ 75.705-2 through 75.705-10 have been complied with, with respect to all lines, which are supported on the pole or structure.

(d) Work may be performed on energized surface high-voltage lines only in accordance with the provisions of §§ 75.705-2 through 75.705-10, inclusive.

§ 75.705-2 Repairs to energized surface high-voltage lines.

An energized high-voltage surface line may be repaired only when

(a) The operator has determined that:

(1) Such repairs cannot be scheduled during a period when the power circuit could be properly deenergized and grounded;

(2) Such repairs will be performed on power circuits with a phase-to-phase nominal voltage no greater than 15,000 volts;

(3) Such repairs on circuits with a phase-to-phase nominal voltage of 5,000 volts or more will be performed only with the use of live line tools;

(4) Weather conditions will not interfere with such repairs or expose those persons assigned to such work to an imminent danger; and

(b) The operator has designated a person qualified under the provisions of § 75.154 as the person responsible for carrying out such repairs and such person, in order to ensure protection for himself and other qualified persons assigned to perform such repairs from the hazards of such repair, has prepared and filed with the operator:

(1) A general description of the nature and location of the damage or defect to be repaired;

(2) The general plan to be followed in making such repairs;

(3) A statement that a briefing of all qualified persons assigned to make such repairs was conducted informing them of the general plan, their individual assignments, and the dangers inherent in such assignments;

(4) A list of the proper protective equipment and clothing that will be provided; and

(5) Such other information as the person designated by the operator feels necessary to describe properly the means or methods to be employed in such repairs.

§ 75.705-3 Work on energized high-voltage surface lines; reporting.

Any operator designating and assigning qualified persons to perform repairs on energized high-voltage surface lines under the provisions of § 75.705-2 shall maintain a record of such repairs. Such record shall contain a notation of the time, date, location, and general nature of the repairs made, together with a copy of the information filed with the operator by the qualified person designated as responsible for performing such repairs.

§ 75.705-4 Simultaneous repairs.

When two or more persons are working on an energized high-voltage surface line simultaneously, and any one of them is within reach of another, such persons shall not be allowed to work on different phases or on equipment with different potentials.

§ 75.705-5 Installation of protective equipment.

Before repair work on energized high-voltage surface lines is begun, protective equipment shall be used to cover all bare conductors, ground wires, guys, telephone lines, and other attachments in proximity to the area of planned repairs. Such protective equipment shall be installed from a safe position below the conductors or other apparatus being covered. Each rubber protective device employed in the making of repairs shall have a dielectric strength of 20,000 volts, or more.

§ 75.705-6 Protective clothing; use and inspection.

All persons performing work on energized high-voltage surface lines shall wear protective rubber gloves, sleeves, and climber guards if climbers are worn. Protective rubber gloves shall not be worn wrong side out or without protective leather gloves. Protective devices worn by a person assigned to perform repairs on high-voltage surface lines shall be worn continuously from the time he leaves the ground until he returns to the ground, and, if such devices are employed for extended periods, such person shall visually inspect the equipment assigned him for defects before each use and, in no case, less than twice each day.

§ 75.705-7 Protective equipment; inspection.

Each person shall visually inspect protective equipment and clothing provided him in connection with work on high-voltage surface lines before using such equipment and clothing, and any equipment or clothing containing any defect or damage shall be discarded and replaced with proper protective equipment or clothing prior to the performance of any electrical work on such lines.

§ 75.705-8 Protective equipment; testing and storage.

(a) All rubber protective equipment used on work on energized high-voltage surface lines shall be electrically tested by the operator in accordance with ASTM standards, Part 28, published February 1968; and such testing shall be conducted in accordance with the following schedule:

(1) Rubber gloves, once each month;
(2) Rubber sleeves, once every 3 months;
(3) Rubber blankets, once every 6 months;
(4) Insulator hoods and line hose, once a year; and
(5) Other electric protective equipment, once a year.

(b) Rubber gloves shall not be stored wrong side out. Blankets shall be rolled when not in use, and line hose and insulator hoods shall be stored in their natural position and shape.

§ 75.705-9 Operating disconnecting or cutout switches.

Disconnecting or cutout switches on energized high-voltage surface lines shall be operated only with insulated sticks, fuse tongs, or pullers which are adequately insulated and maintained to protect the operator from the voltage to which he is exposed. When such switches are operated from the ground, the person operating such devices shall wear protective rubber gloves.

§ 75.705-10 Tying into energized high-voltage surface circuits.

If the work of forming an additional circuit by tying into an energized high-voltage surface line is performed from the ground, any person performing such work must wear and employ all of the protective equipment and clothing required under the provisions of §§ 75.705-5 and 75.705-6. In addition, the insulated stick used by such person must have been designed for such purpose and must be adequately insulated and be maintained to protect such person from the voltage to which he is exposed.

§ 75.705-11 Use of grounded messenger wires; ungrounded systems.

Solely for purposes of grounding ungrounded high-voltage power systems, grounded messenger wires used to suspend the cables of such systems may be used as a grounding medium.

§ 75.706 Deenergized underground power circuits; idle days—idle shifts.

[STATUTORY PROVISIONS]

When not in use, power circuits underground shall be deenergized on idle days and idle shifts, except that rectifiers and transformers may remain energized.

Subpart I—Underground High-Voltage Distribution

§ 75.800 High-voltage circuits; circuit breakers.

[STATUTORY PROVISIONS]

High-voltage circuits entering the underground area of any coal mine shall be protected by suitable circuit breakers of adequate interrupting capacity which are properly tested and maintained as prescribed by the Secretary. Such breakers shall be equipped with devices to provide protection against under-voltage grounded phase, short circuit, and overcurrent.

§ 75.800-1 Circuit breakers; location.

Circuit breakers protecting high-voltage circuits entering an underground area of any coal mine shall be located on the surface and in no case

Mine Safety and Health Admin., Labor § 75.802

installed either underground or within a drift.

§ 75.800-2 Approved circuit schemes.

The following circuit schemes will be regarded as providing the necessary protection to the circuits required by § 75.800:

(a) Ground check relays may be used for undervoltage protection if the relay coils are designed to trip the circuit breaker when line voltage decreases to 40 percent to 60 percent of the nominal line voltage;

(b) Ground trip relays on resistance grounded systems will be acceptable as grounded phase protection;

(c) One circuit breaker may be used to protect two or more branch circuits, if the circuit breaker is adjusted to afford overcurrent protection for the smallest conductor.

§ 75.800-3 Testing, examination and maintenance of circuit breakers; procedures.

(a) Circuit breakers and their auxiliary devices protecting underground high-voltage circuits shall be tested and examined at least once each month by a person qualified as provided in § 75.153;

(b) Tests shall include: (1) Breaking continuity of the ground check conductor, where ground check monitoring is used; and

(2) Actuating at least two (2) of the auxiliary protective relays.

(c) Examination shall include visual observation of all components of the circuit breaker and its auxiliary devices, and such repairs or adjustments as are indicated by such tests and examinations shall be carried out immediately.

§ 75.800-4 Testing, examination, and maintenance of circuit breakers; record.

(a) *Recordkeeping.* The operator shall make a record of each test, examination, repair, or adjustment of all circuit breakers protecting high-voltage circuits which enter any underground area of the mine.

(b) *Record security.* These records shall be made in a secure book that is not susceptible to alteration or electronically in a computer system so as to be secure and not susceptible to alteration.

(c) *Retention and access.* These records shall be retained at a surface location at the mine for at least one year and shall be made available to authorized representatives of the Secretary, the representative of miners, and other interested persons.

[64 FR 43287, Aug. 10, 1999]

§ 75.801 Grounding resistors.

[STATUTORY PROVISIONS]

The grounding resistor, where required, shall be of the proper ohmic value to limit the voltage drop in the grounding circuit external to the resistor to not more than 100 volts under fault conditions. The grounding resistor shall be rated for maximum fault current continuously and insulated from ground for a voltage equal to the phase-to-phase voltage of the system.

§ 75.802 Protection of high-voltage circuits extending underground.

(a) Except as provided in paragraph (b) of this section, high-voltage circuits extending underground and supplying portable, mobile, or, stationary high-voltage equipment shall contain either a direct or derived neutral which shall be grounded through a suitable resistor at the source transformers, and a grounding circuit, originating at the grounded side of the grounding resistor, shall extend along with the power conductors and serve as a grounding conductor for the frames of all high-voltage equipment supplied power from that circuit.

(b) Notwithstanding the requirements of paragraph (a) of this section, the Secretary or his authorized representative may permit ungrounded high-voltage circuits to be extended underground to feed stationary electric equipment if:

(1) Such circuits are either steel armored or installed in grounded, rigid steel conduit throughout their entire length; or,

(2) The voltage of such circuits is nominally 2,400 volts or less phase-to-phase and the cables used in such circuits are equipped with metallic shields around each power conductor,

§ 75.803

and contain one or more ground conductors having a total cross sectional area of not less than one-half the power conductor; and,

(3) Upon a finding by the Secretary or his authorized representative that the use of the circuits described in paragraphs (b) (1) and (2) of this section does not pose a hazard to the miners.

(c) Within 100 feet of the point on the surface where high-voltage circuits enter the underground portion of the mine, disconnecting devices shall be installed and so equipped or designed in such a manner that it can be determined by visual observation that the power is disconnected, except that the Secretary or his authorized representative may permit such devices to be installed at a greater distance from such area of the mine if he determines, based on existing physical conditions, that such installation will be more accessible at a greater distance and will not pose any hazard to the miners.

[38 FR 4975, Feb. 23, 1973]

§ 75.803 Fail safe ground check circuits on high-voltage resistance grounded systems.

[STATUTORY PROVISIONS]

On and after September 30, 1970, high-voltage, resistance grounded systems shall include a fail safe ground check circuit to monitor continuously the grounding circuit to assure continuity and the fail safe ground check circuit shall cause the circuit breaker to open when either the ground or pilot check wire is broken, or other no less effective device approved by the Secretary or his authorized representative to assure such continuity, except that an extension of time, not in excess of 12 months, may be permitted by the Secretary on a mine-by-mine basis if he determines that such equipment is not available.

§ 75.803-1 Maximum voltage ground check circuits.

The maximum voltage used for ground check circuits under § 75.803 shall not exceed 96 volts.

§ 75.803-2 Ground check systems not employing pilot check wires; approval by the Secretary.

Ground check systems not employing pilot check wires will be approved only if it is determined that the system includes a fail safe design causing the circuit breaker to open when ground continuity is broken.

§ 75.804 Underground high-voltage cables.

(a) Underground high-voltage cables used in resistance grounded systems shall be equipped with metallic shields around each power conductor with one or more ground conductors having a total cross sectional area of not less than one-half the power conductor, and with an insulated external conductor not smaller than No. 8 (A.W.G.) or an insulated internal ground check conductor not smaller than No. 10 (A.W.G.) for the ground continuity check circuit.

(b) All such cables shall be adequate for the intended current and voltage. Splices made in such cables shall provide continuity of all components.

[38 FR 4976, Feb. 23, 1973]

§ 75.805 Couplers.

[STATUTORY PROVISIONS]

Couplers that are used with medium-voltage or high-voltage power circuits shall be of the three-phase type with a full metallic shell, except that the Secretary may permit, under such guidelines as he may prescribe, no less effective couplers constructed of materials other than metal. Couplers shall be adequate for the voltage and current expected. All exposed metal on the metallic couplers shall be grounded to the ground conductor in the cable. The coupler shall be constructed so that the ground check continuity conductor shall be broken first and the ground conductors shall be broken last when the coupler is being uncoupled.

Mine Safety and Health Admin., Labor § 75.812-1

§ 75.806 Connection of single-phase loads.

[STATUTORY PROVISIONS]

Single-phase loads, such as transformer primaries, shall be connected phase-to-phase.

§ 75.807 Installation of high-voltage transmission cables.

[STATUTORY PROVISIONS]

All underground high-voltage transmission cables shall be installed only in regularly inspected air courses and haulageways, and shall be covered, buried, or placed so as to afford protection against damage, guarded where men regularly work or pass under them unless they are 6½ feet or more above the floor or rail, securely anchored, properly insulated, and guarded at ends, and covered, insulated, or placed to prevent contact with trolley wires and other low-voltage circuits.

§ 75.808 Disconnecting devices.

[STATUTORY PROVISIONS]

Disconnecting devices shall be installed at the beginning of branch lines in high-voltage circuits and equipped or designed in such a manner that it can be determined by visual observation that the circuit is deenergized when the switches are open.

§ 75.809 Identification of circuit breakers and disconnecting switches.

[STATUTORY PROVISIONS]

Circuit breakers and disconnecting switches underground shall be marked for identification.

§ 75.810 High-voltage trailing cables; splices.

[STATUTORY PROVISIONS]

In the case of high-voltage cables used as trailing cables, temporary splices shall not be used and all permanent splices shall be made in accordance with § 75.604. Terminations and splices in all other high-voltage cables shall be made in accordance with the manufacturer's specifications.

§ 75.811 High-voltage underground equipment; grounding.

[STATUTORY PROVISIONS]

Frames, supporting structures and enclosures of stationary, portable, or mobile underground high-voltage equipment and all high-voltage equipment supplying power to such equipment receiving power from resistance grounded systems shall be effectively grounded to the high-voltage ground.

§ 75.812 Movement of high-voltage power centers and portable transformers; permit.

[STATUTORY PROVISIONS]

Power centers and portable transformers shall be deenergized before they are moved from one location to another, except that, when equipment powered by sources other than such centers or transformers is not available, the Secretary may permit such centers and transformers to be moved while energized, if he determines that another equivalent or greater hazard may otherwise be created, and if they are moved under the supervision of a qualified person, and if such centers and transformers are examined prior to such movement by such person and found to be grounded by methods approved by an authorized representative of the Secretary and otherwise protected from hazards to the miner. A record shall be kept of such examinations. High-voltage cables, other than trailing cables, shall not be moved or handled at any time while energized, except that, when such centers and transformers are moved while energized as permitted under this section, energized high-voltage cables attached to such centers and transformers may be moved only by a qualified person and the operator of such mine shall require that such person wear approved and tested insulated wireman's gloves.

[35 FR 17890, Nov. 20, 1970, as amended at 60 FR 33723, June 29, 1995]

§ 75.812-1 Qualified person.

A person who meets the requirements of § 75.153 is a qualified person within the meaning of § 75.812.

§ 75.812–2 High-voltage power centers and transformers; record of examination.

The operator shall maintain a record of all examinations conducted in accordance with § 75.812. Such record shall be kept in a book approved by the Secretary.

HIGH-VOLTAGE LONGWALLS

SOURCE: 67 FR 11001, Mar. 11, 2002, unless otherwise noted.

§ 75.813 High-voltage longwalls; scope.

Sections 75.814 through 75.822 of this part are electrical safety standards that apply to high-voltage longwall circuits and equipment. All other existing standards in 30 CFR must also apply to these longwall circuits and equipment where appropriate.

§ 75.814 Electrical protection.

(a) High-voltage circuits must be protected against short circuits, overloads, ground faults, and undervoltages by circuit-interrupting devices of adequate interrupting capacity as follows:

(1) Current settings of short-circuit protective devices must not exceed the setting specified in approval documentation, or seventy-five percent of the minimum available phase-to-phase short-circuit current, whichever is less.

(2) Time-delay settings of short-circuit protective devices used to protect any cable extending from the section power center to a motor-starter enclosure must not exceed the settings specified in approval documentation, or 0.25-second, whichever is less. Time delay settings of short-circuit protective devices used to protect motor and shearer circuits must not exceed the settings specified in approval documentation, or 3 cycles, whichever is less.

(3) Ground-fault currents must be limited by a neutral grounding resistor to not more than—

(i) 6.5 amperes when the nominal voltage of the power circuit is 2,400 volts or less; or

(ii) 3.75 amperes when the nominal voltage of the power circuit exceeds 2,400 volts.

(4) High-voltage circuits extending from the section power center must be provided with—

(i) Ground-fault protection set to cause deenergization at not more than 40 percent of the current rating of the neutral grounding resistor;

(ii) A backup ground-fault detection device to cause deenergization when a ground fault occurs with the neutral grounding resistor open; and

(iii) Thermal protection for the grounding resistor that will deenergize the longwall power center if the resistor is subjected to a sustained ground fault. The thermal protection must operate at either 50 percent of the maximum temperature rise of the grounding resistor, or 150 °C (302 °F), whichever is less, and must open the groundwire monitor circuit for the high-voltage circuit supplying the section power center. The thermal protection must not be dependent upon control power and may consist of a current transformer and overcurrent relay.

(5) High-voltage motor and shearer circuits must be provided with instantaneous ground-fault protection set at not more than 0.125-ampere.

(6) Time-delay settings of ground-fault protective devices used to provide coordination with the instantaneous ground-fault protection of motor and shearer circuits must not exceed 0.25-second.

(7) Undervoltage protection must be provided by a device which operates on loss of voltage to cause and maintain the interruption of power to a circuit to prevent automatic restarting of the equipment.

(b) Current transformers used for the ground-fault protection specified in paragraphs (a)(4)(i) and (5) of this section must be single window-type and must be installed to encircle all three phase conductors. Equipment safety grounding conductors must not pass through or be connected in series with ground-fault current transformers.

(c) Each ground-fault current device specified in paragraphs (a)(4)(i) and (5) of this section must be provided with a test circuit that will inject a primary current of 50 percent or less of the current rating of the grounding resistor through the current transformer and

Mine Safety and Health Admin., Labor § 75.818

cause each corresponding circuit-interrupting device to open.

(d) Circuit-interrupting devices must not reclose automatically.

(e) Where two or more high-voltage cables are used to supply power to a common bus in a high-voltage enclosure, each cable must be provided with ground-wire monitoring. The ground-wire monitoring circuits must cause deenergization of each cable when either the ground-monitor or grounding conductor(s) of any cable become severed or open. On or after May 10, 2002, parallel connected cables on newly installed longwalls must be protected as follows:

(1) When one circuit-interrupting device is used to protect parallel connected cables, the circuit-interrupting device must be electrically interlocked with the cables so that the device will open when any cable is disconnected; or

(2) When two or more parallel circuit-interrupting devices are used to protect parallel connected cables, the circuit-interrupting devices must be mechanically and electrically interlocked. Mechanical interlocking must cause all devices to open simultaneously and electrical interlocking must cause all devices to open when any cable is disconnected.

§ 75.815 Disconnect devices.

(a) The section power center must be equipped with a main disconnecting device installed to deenergize all cables extending to longwall equipment when the device is in the "open" position. See Figures I-1 and I-2 in Appendix A to this subpart I.

(b) Disconnecting devices for motor-starter enclosures must be maintained in accordance with the approval requirements of paragraph (f) of § 18.53 of part 18 of this chapter. The compartment for the disconnect device must be provided with a caution label to warn miners against entering the compartment before deenergizing the incoming high-voltage circuits to the compartment.

(c) Disconnecting devices must be rated for the maximum phase-to-phase voltage of the circuit in which they are installed, and for the full-load current of the circuit that is supplied power through the device.

(d) Each disconnecting device must be designed and installed so that—

(1) Visual observation determines that the contacts are open without removing any cover;

(2) All load power conductors can be grounded when the device is in the "open" position; and

(3) The device can be locked in the "open" position.

(e) Disconnecting devices, except those installed in explosion-proof enclosures, must be capable of interrupting the full-load current of the circuit or designed and installed to cause the current to be interrupted automatically prior to the opening of the contacts of the device. Disconnecting devices installed in explosion-proof enclosures must be maintained in accordance with the approval requirements of paragraph (f)(2)(iv) of § 18.53 of part 18 of this chapter.

§ 75.816 Guarding of cables.

(a) High-voltage cables must be guarded at the following locations:

(1) Where persons regularly work or travel over or under the cables.

(2) Where the cables leave cable handling or support systems to extend to electric components.

(b) Guarding must minimize the possibility of miners contacting the cables and protect the cables from damage. The guarding must be made of grounded metal or nonconductive flame-resistant material.

§ 75.817 Cable handling and support systems.

Longwall mining equipment must be provided with cable-handling and support systems that are constructed, installed and maintained to minimize the possibility of miners contacting the cables and to protect the high-voltage cables from damage.

§ 75.818 Use of insulated cable handling equipment.

(a) Energized high-voltage cables must not be handled except when motor or shearer cables need to be trained. When cables need to be trained, high-voltage insulated gloves, mitts, hooks, tongs, slings, aprons, or

§ 75.819

other personal protective equipment capable of providing protection against shock hazard must be used to prevent direct contact with the cable.

(b) High-voltage insulated gloves, sleeves, and other insulated personal protective equipment must—

(1) Have a voltage rating of at least Class 1 (7,500 volts) that meets or exceeds ASTM F496–97, "Standard Specification for In-Service Care of Insulating Gloves and Sleeves" (1997).

(2) Be examined before each use for visible signs of damage;

(3) Be removed from the underground area of the mine or destroyed when damaged or defective; and

(4) Be electrically tested every 6 months in accordance with publication ASTM F496–97. ASTM F496–97 (Standard Specification for In-Service Care of Insulating Gloves and Sleeves, 1997) is incorporated by reference and may be inspected at any MSHA Coal Mine Safety and Health District Office, or at MSHA's Office of Standards, Regulations, and Variances, 201 12th Street South, Arlington, VA 22202–5452; 202–693–9440; and at the National Archives and Records Administration (NARA). For information on the availability of this material at NARA, call 202–741–6030, or go to: *http://www.archives.gov/ federal_register/ code_of_federal_regulations/ ibr_locations.html.* In addition, copies of the document can be purchased from the American Society for Testing and Materials, 100 Barr Harbor Drive, P.O. Box C700, West Conshohocken, PA 19428–2959; 610–832–9500; *http:// www.astm.org.* This incorporation by reference was approved by the Director of the Federal Register in accordance with 5 U.S.C. 552(a) and 1 CFR part 51.

[67 FR 11001, Mar. 11, 2002, as amended at 67 FR 38386, June 4, 2002; 71 FR 16668, Apr. 3, 2006; 80 FR 52992, Sept. 2, 2015]

§ 75.819 Motor-starter enclosures; barriers and interlocks.

Compartment separation and cover interlock switches for motor-starter enclosures must be maintained in accordance with the approval requirements of paragraphs (a) and (b) of § 18.53 of part 18 of this chapter.

§ 75.820 Electrical work; troubleshooting and testing.

(a) Electrical work on all circuits and equipment associated with high-voltage longwalls must be performed only by persons qualified under § 75.153 to perform electrical work on all circuits and equipment.

(b) Prior to performing electrical work, except for troubleshooting and testing of energized circuits and equipment as provided for in paragraph (d) of this section, a qualified person must do the following:

(1) Deenergize the circuit or equipment with a circuit-interrupting device.

(2) Open the circuit disconnecting device. On high-voltage circuits, ground the power conductors until work on the circuit is completed.

(3) Lock out the disconnecting device with a padlock. When more than one qualified person is performing work, each person must install an individual padlock.

(4) Tag the disconnecting device to identify each person working and the circuit or equipment on which work is being performed.

(c) Each padlock and tag must be removed only by the person who installed them, except that, if that person is unavailable at the mine, the lock and tag may be removed by a person authorized by the operator, provided—

(1) The authorized person is qualified under paragraph (a) of this section; and

(2) The operator ensures that the person who installed the lock and tag is aware of the removal before that person resumes work on the affected circuit or equipment.

(d) Troubleshooting and testing of energized circuits must be performed only—

(1) On low- and medium-voltage circuits;

(2) When the purpose of troubleshooting and testing is to determine voltages and currents; and

(3) By persons qualified to perform electrical work and who wear protective gloves on circuits that exceed 40 volts in accordance with the following table:

Mine Safety and Health Admin., Labor § 75.824

Circuit voltage	Type of glove required
Greater than 120 volts (nominal) (not intrinsically safe)	Rubber insulating gloves with leather protectors.
40 volts to 120 volts (nominal) (both intrinsically safe and non-intrinsically safe).	Either rubber insulating gloves with leather protectors or dry work gloves.
Greater than 120 volts (nominal) (intrinsically safe)	Either rubber insulating gloves with leather protectors or dry work gloves.

(4) Rubber insulating gloves must be rated at least for the nominal voltage of the circuit when the voltage of the circuit exceeds 120 volts nominal and is not intrinsically safe.

(e) Before troubleshooting and testing a low- or medium-voltage circuit contained in a compartment with a high-voltage circuit, the high-voltage circuit must be deenergized, disconnected, grounded, locked out and tagged in accordance with paragraph (b) of this section.

(f) Prior to the installation or removal of conveyor belt structure, high-voltage cables extending from the section power center to longwall equipment and located in the belt entries must be:

(1) Deenergized; or

(2) Guarded in accordance with § 75.816 of this part, at the location where the belt structure is being installed or removed; or

(3) Located at least 6.5 feet above the mine floor.

§ 75.821 Testing, examination and maintenance.

(a) At least once every 7 days, a person qualified in accordance with § 75.153 to perform electrical work on all circuits and equipment must test and examine each unit of high-voltage longwall equipment and circuits to determine that electrical protection, equipment grounding, permissibility, cable insulation, and control devices are being properly maintained to prevent fire, electrical shock, ignition, or operational hazards from existing on the equipment. Tests must include activating the ground-fault test circuit as required by § 75.814(c).

(b) Each ground-wire monitor and associated circuits must be examined and tested at least once each 30 days to verify proper operation and that it will cause the corresponding circuit-interrupting device to open.

(c) When examinations or tests of equipment reveal a fire, electrical shock, ignition, or operational hazard, the equipment must be removed from service immediately or repaired immediately.

(d) At the completion of examinations and tests required by this section, the person who makes the examinations and tests must certify by signature and date that they have been conducted. A record must be made of any unsafe condition found and any corrective action taken. Certifications and records must be kept for at least one year and must be made available for inspection by authorized representatives of the Secretary and representatives of miners.

§ 75.822 Underground high-voltage longwall cables.

In addition to the high-voltage cable design specifications in § 75.804 of this part, high-voltage cables for use on longwalls may be a type SHD cable with a center ground-check conductor no smaller than a No. 16 AWG stranded conductor. The cables must be MSHA accepted as flame-resistant under part 18 or approved under subpart K of part 7.

§ 75.823 Scope.

Sections 75.823 through 75.834 of this part are electrical safety standards applicable to 2,400 volt continuous mining machines and circuits. A "qualified person" as used in these sections means a person meeting the requirements of § 75.153. Other standards in 30 CFR apply to these circuits and equipment where appropriate.

[75 FR 17549, Apr. 6, 2010]

§ 75.824 Electrical protection.

(a) *Trailing cable protection.* The trailing cable extending to the high-voltage continuous mining machine must be protected by a circuit-interrupting device of adequate interrupting capacity and voltage that provides short-circuit, overload, ground-fault, and under-voltage protection as follows:

(1) *Short-circuit protection.*

(i) The current setting of the device must be the setting specified in the approval documentation or 75 percent of the minimum available phase-to-phase short-circuit current, whichever is less; and

(ii) The time-delay setting must not exceed 0.050 seconds.

(2) *Ground-fault protection.*

(i) Neutral grounding resistors must limit the ground-fault current to no more than 0.5 ampere.

(ii) Ground-fault devices must cause de-energization of the circuit extending to the continuous mining machine at not more than 0.125 ampere. The time-delay of the device must not exceed 0.050 seconds.

(iii) Look-ahead circuits must detect a ground-fault condition and prevent the circuit-interrupting device from closing as long as the ground-fault condition exists.

(iv) Backup ground-fault devices must cause de-energization of the circuit extending to the continuous mining machine at not more than 40 percent of the voltage developed across the neutral grounding resistor when a ground fault occurs with the neutral grounding resistor open. The time-delay setting of the backup device must not exceed 0.25 seconds.

(v) Thermal devices must detect a sustained ground-fault current in the neutral grounding resistor and must de-energize the incoming power. The device must operate at either 50 percent of the maximum temperature rise of the neutral grounding resistor or 302 °F (150 °C), whichever is less. Thermal protection must not be dependent on control power and may consist of a current transformer and over-current relay in the neutral grounding resistor circuit.

(vi) A single window-type current transformer that encircles all three-phase conductors must be used to activate the ground-fault device protecting the continuous mining machine. Equipment grounding conductors must not pass through the current transformer.

(vii) A test circuit for the ground-fault device must be provided. The test circuit must inject no more than 50 percent of the current rating of the neutral grounding resistor through the current transformer. When the test circuit is activated, the circuit-interrupting device must open.

(3) *Under-voltage protection.* The under-voltage device must operate on a loss of voltage, de-energize the circuit, and prevent the equipment from automatically restarting.

(b) *Re-closing.* Circuit-interrupting devices must not re-close automatically.

(c) *Onboard Power Circuits.* When a grounded-phase indicator light circuit is used and it indicates a grounded-phase fault, the following corrective actions must be taken:

(1) The machine must be moved immediately to a location with a properly supported roof; and

(2) The grounded-phase condition must be located and corrected prior to placing the continuous mining machine back into operation.

[75 FR 17549, Apr. 6, 2010]

§ 75.825 Power centers.

(a) *Main disconnecting switch.* The power center supplying high voltage power to the continuous mining machine must be equipped with a main disconnecting switch that, when in the open position, de-energizes input to all power transformers.

(b) *Trailing cable disconnecting device.* In addition to the main disconnecting switch required in paragraph (a) of this section, the power center must be equipped with a disconnecting device for each circuit that supplies power to a high-voltage continuous mining machine. A disconnecting device is defined as a disconnecting switch or a cable coupler.

(c) *Disconnecting switches.* Each disconnecting switch must be labeled to clearly identify the circuit it disconnects, and be designed and installed as follows:

(1) Rated for the maximum phase-to-phase voltage of the circuit;

(2) Rated for the full-load current of the circuit that is supplied power through the device.

Mine Safety and Health Admin., Labor §75.827

(3) Allow for visual observation, without removing any covers, to verify that the contacts are open;

(4) Ground all power conductors on the load side when the switch is in the "open and grounded" position;

(5) Can only be locked out in the "open and grounded" position; and

(6) Safely interrupts the full-load current of the circuit or causes the current to be interrupted automatically before the disconnecting switch opens.

(d) *Barriers and covers.* All compartments that provide access to high-voltage circuits must have barriers and/or covers to prevent miners from contacting energized high-voltage circuits.

(e) *Main disconnecting switch and control circuit interlocking.* The control circuit must be interlocked with the main disconnecting switch in the power center so that:

(1) When the main disconnecting switch is in the "open" position, the control circuit can only be powered through an auxiliary switch in the "test" position; and

(2) When the main disconnecting switch is in the "closed" position, the control circuit can only be powered through an auxiliary switch in the "normal" position.

(f) *Interlocks.* Each cover or removable barrier providing access to high-voltage circuits must be equipped with at least two interlock switches. Except when the auxiliary switch is on the "test" position, removal of any cover or barrier that exposes energized high-voltage circuits must cause the interlock switches to automatically de-energize the incoming circuit to the power center.

(g) *Emergency stop switch.* The power center must be equipped with an externally accessible emergency stop switch hard-wired into the incoming ground-wire monitor circuit that de-energizes the incoming high-voltage in the event of an emergency.

(h) *Grounding stick.* The power center must be equipped with a grounding stick to be used prior to performing electrical work to assure that high-voltage capacitors are discharged and circuits are de-energized. The power center must have a label readily identifying the location of the grounding stick. The grounding stick must be stored in a dry location.

(i) *Caution label.* All compartments providing access to energized high-voltage conductors and parts must display a caution label to warn miners against entering the compartments before de-energizing incoming high-voltage circuits.

[75 FR 17549, Apr. 6, 2010]

§ 75.826 High-voltage trailing cables.

High-voltage trailing cables must:

(a) Meet existing trailing cable requirements and the approval requirements of the high-voltage continuous mining machine; and

(b) Meet existing ground-check conductor requirements (§ 75.804) or have a stranded center ground-check conductor not smaller than a No. 16 A.W.G.

[75 FR 17549, Apr. 6, 2010]

§ 75.827 Guarding of trailing cables.

(a) *Guarding.* (1) The high-voltage cable must be guarded in the following locations:

(i) From the power center cable coupler for a distance of 10 feet inby the power center;

(ii) From the entrance gland for a distance of 10 feet outby the last strain clamp on the continuous mining machine; and,

(iii) At any location where the cable could be damaged by moving equipment.

(2) Guarding must be constructed using nonconductive flame-resistant material or grounded metal.

(b) *Suspended cables and cable crossovers.* When equipment must cross any portion of the cable, the cable must be either:

(1) Suspended from the mine roof; or

(2) Protected by a cable crossover having the following specifications:

(i) A minimum length of 33 inches;

(ii) A minimum width of 17 inches;

(iii) A minimum height of 3 inches;

(iv) A minimum cable placement area of two and one half-inches (2½″) high by four and one-quarter inches (4¼″) wide;

(v) Made of nonconductive material;

§ 75.828

(vi) Made of material with a distinctive color. The color black must not be used; and

(vii) Made of material that has a minimum compressive strength of 6,400 pounds per square inch (psi).

[75 FR 17549, Apr. 6, 2010]

§ 75.828 Trailing cable pulling.

The trailing cable must be de-energized prior to being pulled by any equipment other than the continuous mining machine. The cable manufacturer's recommended pulling procedures must be followed when pulling the trailing cable with equipment other than the continuous mining machine.

[75 FR 17549, Apr. 6, 2010]

§ 75.829 Tramming continuous mining machines in and out of the mine and from section to section.

(a) *Conditions of use.* Tramming the continuous mining machine in and out of the mine and from section to section must be done in accordance with movement requirements of high-voltage power centers and portable transformers (§ 75.812) and as follows:

(1) The power source must not be located in areas where permissible equipment is required;

(2) The continuous mining machine must not be used for mining or cutting purposes, unless a power center is used in accordance with §§ 75.823 through 75.828 and §§ 75.830 through 75.833;

(3) Low-, medium-, and high-voltage cables must comply with §§ 75.600–1, 75.907, and 75.826, as applicable; and

(4) The energized high-voltage cable must be mechanically secured onboard the continuous mining machine. This provision applies only when using the power sources specified in paragraphs (c)(2) and (c)(3) of this section.

(b) *Testing prior to tramming.* Prior to tramming the continuous mining machine,

(1) A qualified person must activate the ground-fault and ground-wire monitor test circuits of the power sources specified in paragraph (c) of this section to assure that the corresponding circuit-interrupting device opens the circuit. Corrective actions and recordkeeping resulting from these tests must be in accordance with §§ 75.832(f) and (g).

(2) Where applicable, a person designated by the mine operator must activate the test circuit for the grounded-phase detection circuit on the continuous mining machine to assure that the detection circuit is functioning properly. Corrective actions resulting from this test must be in accordance with § 75.832(f).

(c) *Power sources.* In addition to the power center specified in § 75.825, the following power sources may be used to tram the continuous mining machine.

(1) *Medium-voltage power source.* A medium-voltage power source is a source that supplies 995 volts through a trailing cable (See Figure 1 of this section) to the continuous mining machine. The medium-voltage power source must—

(i) Not be used to back-feed the high-voltage circuits of the continuous mining machine; and

(ii) Meet all applicable requirements for medium-voltage circuits in 30 CFR 75.

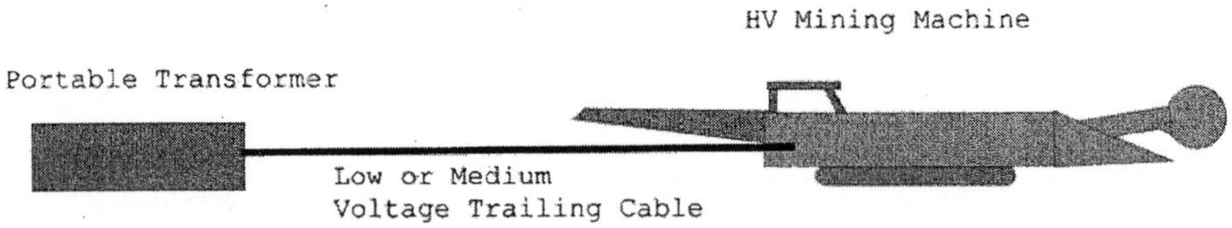

Figure 1-Power Source-75.829(c)(1) 995 volts used for tramming

(2) *Step-up transformer.* A step-up transformer is a transformer that steps up the low or medium voltage to high voltage (See Figure 2 in this section) and must meet the following requirements:

(i) The trailing cable supplying low or medium voltage to the step-up transformer must meet the applicable requirements of 30 CFR part 75;

(ii) The high-voltage circuit output of the step-up transformer supplying power to the continuous mining machine must meet the applicable provisions of §75.824;

(iii) The step-up transformer enclosure must be—

(A) Securely mounted to minimize vibration on:

(*1*) The continuous mining machine; or

(*2*) A sled/cart that must be connected to the continuous mining machine by a tow-bar and be in close proximity to the mining machine.

(B) Grounded as follows:

(*1*) Connected to the incoming ground conductor of the low- or medium-voltage trailing cable;

(*2*) Bonded by a No. 1/0 A.W.G. or larger external grounding conductor to the continuous mining machine frame; and

(*3*) Bonded by a No. 1/0 A.W.G. or larger external grounding conductor to the metallic shell of each cable coupler.

(C) Equipped with:

(*1*) At least two interlock switches for each of the enclosure covers; and

(*2*) An external emergency stop switch to remove input power to the step-up transformer.

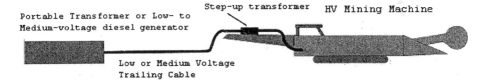

Figure 2 - Power source - 75.829(c)(*2*) 480 or 995 volts to a step-up transformer to 2300 volts for tramming

[75 FR 17549, Apr. 6, 2010]

§75.830 Splicing and repair of trailing cables.

(a) *Splices and repairs.* (1) Splicing means the mechanical joining of one or more severed conductors in a single length of a cable including the replacement of: Insulation, semi-conductive tape, metallic shielding, and the outer jacket(s).

(2) Repair means to fix damage to any component of the cable other than the conductor.

(3) Splices and repairs to high-voltage trailing cables must be made:

(i) Only by a qualified person trained in the proper methods of splicing and repairing high-voltage trailing cables;

(ii) In a workman-like manner;

(iii) In accordance with §75.810; and

(iv) Using only MSHA-approved high-voltage kits that include instructions for outer-jacket repairs and splices.

(b) *Splicing limitations.* (1) Splicing of the high-voltage trailing cable within 35 feet of the continuous mining machine is prohibited.

(2) Only four (4) splices will be allowed at any one time for the portion of the trailing cable that extends from the continuous miner outby for a distance of 300 feet.

[75 FR 17549, Apr. 6, 2010]

§75.831 Electrical work; troubleshooting and testing.

(a) *Trailing cable and continuous mining machine electrical work procedures.* Prior to performing electrical work, other than troubleshooting and testing, on the high-voltage trailing cable or the continuous mining machine, a

§ 75.831

qualified person must de-energize the power center and follow procedures specified in paragraph (1) or (2):

(1) If a trailing cable disconnecting switch is provided:

(i) Open and ground the power conductors, lock out and tag the disconnecting switch; and

(ii) Lock out and tag the plug to the power receptacle.

(2) If a trailing cable disconnecting switch is not provided and a cable coupler is used as a disconnecting device:

(i) Remove the plug from the power receptacle and connect it to the grounding receptacle;

(ii) Lock out and tag the plug to the grounding receptacle; and

(iii) Place a dust cover over the power receptacle.

(b) *Troubleshooting and testing the trailing cable.* During troubleshooting and testing, the de-energized high-voltage cable may be disconnected from the power center only for that period of time necessary to locate the defective condition. Prior to troubleshooting and testing trailing cables, a qualified person must perform the following:

(1) If a trailing cable disconnecting switch is provided:

(i) Open and ground power conductors and lock out and tag the disconnecting switch;

(ii) Disconnect the plug from the power receptacle;

(iii) Lock out and tag the plug; and

(iv) Place a dust cover over the power receptacle.

(2) If a trailing cable disconnecting switch is not provided and a cable coupler is used as a disconnecting device:

(i) Remove the plug from the power receptacle and connect it to the grounding receptacle to ground the power conductors;

(ii) Remove the plug from the grounding receptacle and install a lock and tag on the plug; and

(iii) Place a dust cover over the power receptacle.

(c) *Troubleshooting and testing limitations.* Troubleshooting and testing energized circuits must be performed only:

(1) On low- and medium-voltage circuits;

(2) When the purpose of troubleshooting and testing is to determine voltages and currents;

(3) By qualified persons; and

(4) When using protective gloves in accordance with the following table:

Circuit voltage	Type of glove required
Greater than 120 volts (nominal) (not intrinsically safe)	Rubber insulating gloves with leather protectors.
40 volts to 120 volts (nominal) (both intrinsically safe and non-intrinsically safe).	Either rubber insulating gloves with leather protectors or dry work gloves.
Greater than 120 volts (nominal) (intrinsically safe)	Either rubber insulating gloves with leather protectors or dry work gloves.

(d) *Power center electrical work procedures.* Before any work is performed inside any compartment of the power center, except for troubleshooting and testing energized circuits as specified in paragraph (c) of this section, a qualified person must:

(1) De-energize affected circuits;

(2) Open the corresponding disconnecting switch, lock it out, and tag it to assure the circuit is isolated;

(3) Visually verify that the contacts of the disconnecting switch are open and grounded; and

(4) Discharge all high-voltage capacitors and circuits.

(e) *Locking out and tagging responsibilities.* (1) When more than one qualified person is performing electrical work, including troubleshooting and testing, each person must install an individual lock and tag. Each lock and tag must be removed only by the persons who installed them.

(2) If the person who installed the lock and tag is unavailable, the lock and tag may be removed by a person authorized by the operator, provided that:

(i) The authorized person is a qualified person; and

(ii) The mine operator assures that the person who installed the lock and tag is aware that the lock and tag have been removed.

[75 FR 17549, Apr. 6, 2010]

§ 75.832 Frequency of examinations; recordkeeping.

(a) *Continuous mining machine examination.* At least once every 7 days, a qualified person must examine each high-voltage continuous mining machine to verify that electrical protection, equipment grounding, permissibility, cable insulation, and control devices are properly installed and maintained.

(b) *Ground-fault test circuit.* At least once every 7 days, and prior to tramming the high-voltage continuous mining machine, a qualified person must activate the ground-fault test circuit to verify that it will cause the corresponding circuit-interrupting device to open.

(c) *Ground-wire monitor test.* At least once every 7 days, and prior to tramming the high-voltage continuous mining machine, a qualified person must examine and test each high-voltage continuous mining machine ground-wire monitor circuit to verify that it will cause the corresponding circuit-interrupting device to open.

(d) *Trailing cable inspections.* (1) Once each day during the shift that the continuous mining machine is first energized, a qualified person must de-energize and inspect the entire length of the high-voltage trailing cable from the power center to the continuous mining machine. The inspection must include examination of the outer jacket repairs and splices for damage, and assure guarding is provided where required.

(2) At the beginning of each shift that the continuous mining machine is energized, a person designated by the mine operator must de-energize and visually inspect the high-voltage trailing cable for damage to the outer jacket. This inspection must be conducted from the continuous mining machine to the following locations:

(i) The last open crosscut;

(ii) Within 150 feet of the working place during retreat or second mining; or

(iii) Up to 150 feet from the continuous mining machine when the machine is used in outby areas.

(e) *Grounded-phase detection test.* When a grounded-phase test circuit is provided on a high-voltage continuous mining machine, a person designated by the mine operator must activate the test circuit at the beginning of each production shift to assure that the detection circuit is functioning properly.

(f) *Corrective action.* When examinations or tests of equipment reveal a risk of fire, electrical shock, ignition, or operational hazard, the equipment must be immediately removed from service or repaired.

(g) *Record of tests.* (1) At the completion of examinations and tests required under paragraphs (a), (b), and (c) of this section, the person conducting the examinations and tests must:

(i) Certify by signature and date that the examinations and tests have been conducted.

(ii) Make a record of any unsafe condition found.

(2) Any corrective action(s) must be recorded by the person taking the corrective action.

(3) The record must be countersigned by the mine foreman or equivalent mine official by the end of the mine foreman's or the equivalent mine official's next regularly scheduled working shift.

(4) Records must be maintained in a secure book that is not susceptible to alteration or electronically in a computer system so as to be secure and not susceptible to alteration.

(5) Certifications and records must be kept for at least 1 year and must be made available for inspection by authorized representatives of the Secretary and representatives of miners.

[75 FR 17549, Apr. 6, 2010]

§ 75.833 Handling high-voltage trailing cables.

(a) *Cable handling.* (1) Miners must not handle energized trailing cables unless they are wearing high-voltage insulating gloves, which include the rubber gloves and leather outer protector gloves, or are using insulated cable handling tools that meet the requirements of paragraph (c) or (d) of this section.

(2) Miners must not handle energized high-voltage cables with any parts of their bodies except by hand in accordance with paragraph (1) above.

(b) *Availability.* Each mine operator must make high-voltage insulating

§ 75.834

gloves or insulated cable handling tools available to miners handling energized high-voltage trailing cables.

(c) *High-voltage insulating gloves.* High-voltage insulating gloves must meet the following requirements:

(1) The rubber gloves must be designed and maintained to have a voltage rating of at least Class 1 (7,500 volts) and tested every 30 days in accordance with publication ASTM F496–02a, "Standard Specification for In-Service Care of Insulating Gloves and Sleeves" (2002). The Director of the Federal Register approved this incorporation by reference in accordance with 5 U.S.C. 522(a) and 1 CFR part 51. ASTM F496–02a may be obtained from the American Society for Testing and Materials, 100 Barr Harbor Drive, P.O. Box C700, West Conshohocken, PA 19428–2959, call 610–832–9500 or go to *http://www.astm.org*. ASTM F496–02a is available for inspection at any MSHA Coal Mine Safety and Health District Office, at the MSHA Office of Standards, Regulations, and Variances, 201 12th Street South, Arlington, VA 22202–5452; 202–693–9440; or at the National Archives and Records Administration (NARA). For information on the availability of this material at NARA, call 202–741–6030, or go to: *http://www.archives.gov/federal_register/code_of_federal_regulations/ibr_locations.html*.

(2) The rubber glove portion must be air-tested at the beginning of each shift to assure its effectiveness.

(3) Both the leather protector and rubber insulating gloves must be visually examined before each use for signs of damage or defects.

(4) Damaged rubber gloves must be removed from the underground area of the mine or destroyed. Leather protectors must be maintained in good condition or replaced.

(d) *Insulated cable handling tools.* Insulated cable handling tools must be:

(1) Rated and properly maintained to withstand at least 7,500 volts;

(2) Designed and manufactured for cable handling;

(3) Visually examined before each use for signs of damage or defects; and

(4) Removed from the underground area of the mine or destroyed if damaged or defective.

[75 FR 17549, Apr. 6, 2010, as amended at 80 FR 52992, Sept. 2, 2015]

§ 75.834 **Training.**

In addition to existing part 48 task training, hazard training, training for qualified persons under existing § 75.153, and annual refresher training, the following specialized training shall be provided and specified in the part 48 plan:

(a) Training for miners who perform maintenance on high-voltage continuous mining machines in high-voltage safety, testing, and repair and maintenance procedures.

(b) Training for personnel who work in the vicinity of high-voltage continuous mining machines in safety procedures and precautions for moving the high-voltage machines or the trailing cables.

[75 FR 17549, Apr. 6, 2010]

Mine Safety and Health Admin., Labor   **Pt. 75, Subpt. I, App. A**

APPENDIX A TO SUBPART I OF PART 75—DIAGRAMS OF INBY AND OUTBY SWITCHING

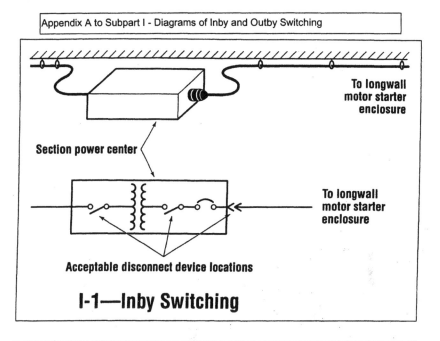

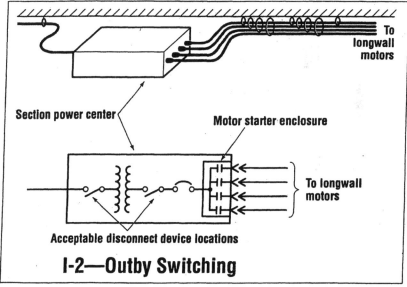

[67 FR 11001, Mar. 11, 2002; 67 FR 18823, Apr. 17, 2002]

Subpart J—Underground Low- and Medium-Voltage Alternating Current Circuits

§ 75.900 Low- and medium-voltage circuits serving three-phase alternating current equipment; circuit breakers.

[STATUTORY PROVISIONS]

Low- and medium-voltage power circuits serving three-phase alternating current equipment shall be protected by suitable circuit breakers of adequate interrupting capacity which are properly tested and maintained as prescribed by the Secretary. Such breakers shall be equipped with devices to provide protection against undervoltage, grounded phase, short circuit, and overcurrent.

§ 75.900–1 Circuit breakers; location.

Circuit breakers used to protect low- and medium-voltage circuits underground shall be located in areas which are accessible for inspection, examination, and testing, have safe roofs, and are clear of any moving equipment used in haulageways.

§ 75.900–2 Approved circuit schemes.

The following circuit schemes will be regarded as providing the necessary protection to the circuit required by § 75.900:

(a) Ground check relays may be used for undervoltage protection if the relay coils are designed to trip the circuit breaker when line voltage decreases to 40 to 60 percent of the nominal line voltage.

(b) One undervoltage device installed in the main secondary circuit at the source transformer may be used to provide undervoltage protection for each circuit that receives power from that transformer.

(c) One circuit breaker may be used to protect two or more branch circuits if the circuit breaker is adjusted to afford overcurrent protection for the smallest conductor.

(d) Circuit breakers with shunt trip, series trip or undervoltage release devices may be used if the tripping elements of such devices are selected or adjusted in accordance with the settings listed in the tables of the National Electric Code, 1968.

§ 75.900–3 Testing, examination, and maintenance of circuit breakers; procedures.

Circuit breakers protecting low- and medium-voltage alternating current circuits serving three-phase alternating current equipment and their auxiliary devices shall be tested and examined at least once each month by a person qualified as provided in § 75.153. In performing such tests, actuating any of the circuit breaker auxiliaries or control circuits in any manner which causes the circuit breaker to open, shall be considered a proper test. All components of the circuit breaker and its auxiliary devices shall be visually examined and such repairs or adjustments as are indicated by such tests and examinations shall be carried out immediately.

§ 75.900–4 Testing, examination, and maintenance of circuit breakers; record.

The operator of any coal mine shall maintain a written record of each test, examination, repair, or adjustment of all circuit breakers protecting low- and medium-voltage circuits serving three-phase alternating current equipment used in the mine. Such record shall be kept in a book approved by the Secretary.

[35 FR 17890, Nov. 20, 1970, as amended at 60 FR 33723, June 29, 1995]

§ 75.901 Protection of low- and medium-voltage three-phase circuits used underground.

[STATUTORY PROVISIONS]

(a) Low- and medium-voltage three-phase alternating-current circuits used underground shall contain either a direct or derived neutral which shall be grounded through a suitable resistor at the power center, and a grounding circuit, originating at the grounded side of the grounding resistor, shall extend along with the power conductors and serve as a grounding conductor for the frames of all the electrical equipment supplied power from that circuit, except that the Secretary or his authorized representative may permit

Mine Safety and Health Admin., Labor § 75.901

ungrounded low- and medium-voltage circuits to be used underground to feed such stationary electrical equipment if such circuits are either steel armored or installed in grounded rigid steel conduit throughout their entire length. The grounding resistor, where required, shall be of the proper ohmic value to limit the ground fault current to 25 amperes. The grounding resistor shall be rated for maximum fault current continuously and insulated from ground for a voltage equal to the phase-to-phase voltage of the system.

(b) Diesel-powered electrical generators used as an alternative to power centers for the purpose of moving equipment in, out, and around the mine, and to perform work in areas where permissible equipment is not required, must comply with the following:

(1) The diesel engine powering the electrical generator must be approved under 30 CFR part 7, subpart E.

(2) A grounding resistor rated for the phase-to-phase voltage of the system must be provided to limit the ground-fault current to not more than 0.5 amperes. The grounding resistor(s) must be located:

(i) Between the wye-connected generator neutral and the generator frame; (see Figure I in Appendix A to subpart J of this part) or

(ii) Between the wye-connected generator neutral and the generator frame and between the wye-connected transformer secondary and the transformer frame when an isolation transformer(s) is used and the generator is supplying power to the other equipment; (see Figure II in Appendix A to subpart J of this part) or

(iii) Between the wye-connected generator neutral and the generator frame when an auto-transformer is used. (see Figure III in Appendix A to subpart J of this part)

(3) Each three-phase output circuit of the generator must be equipped with a sensitive ground fault relay. The protective relay must be set to cause the circuit interrupting device that supplies power to the primary windings of each transformer to trip and shut down the diesel engine when a phase-to-frame fault of not more than 90 milliamperes occurs.

(4) Each three-phase output circuit that supplies power to equipment must be equipped with an instantaneous sensitive ground-fault relay that will cause its respective circuit interrupting device(s) to trip and cause shutdown of the diesel engine when a phase-to-frame fault occurs. The grounded-phase protection must be set at not more than 90 milliamps. Current transformers used for the ground-fault protection must be single window-type and must be installed to encircle all three phase conductors. Equipment safety grounding conductors must not pass through or be connected in series with ground-fault current transformers.

(5) Each three-phase circuit interrupting device must be provided with a means to provide short-circuit, overcurrent, grounded-phase, undervoltage, and ground wire monitoring protection. The instantaneous only trip unit for the circuit interrupting device(s) in use must be adjusted to trip at not more than 75 percent of the minimum available short circuit current at the point where the portable cable enters the equipment or the maximum allowable instantaneous settings specified in § 75.601–1, whichever is less.

(6) The equipment portable cable length(s) must not exceed the length(s) specified in 30 CFR part 18, appendix I, table 9, Specifications for Cables Longer than 500 Feet.

(7) Permanent label(s) listing the maximum circuit interrupting device setting(s) and maximum portable cable length(s) must be installed on each instantaneous trip unit or be maintained near each three-phase circuit interrupting device. The permanent label(s) must be maintained legibly.

(8) The circuit interrupting device that supplies three-phase power circuit(s) to the equipment being powered must be limited to the use of only one circuit interrupting device at a time when equipment is being moved in, out, and around the mine.

(9) The grounding system must include an MSHA-accepted ground wire monitor system that satisfies the requirements of § 75.902; or have a No. 1/0 or larger external grounding conductor to bond and ground the frames of all

599

§ 75.902

equipment to the frame of the generator.

(10) All trailing cables extending from the generator to equipment must comply with § 75.907.

(11) A strain relief device must be provided on each end of the trailing cables that extends between the generator and the piece of equipment being powered.

(12) Prior to moving each piece of equipment or performing work, a functional test of each ground fault and ground wire monitor system must be performed by a qualified electrician who meets the requirements of § 75.153. The ground-fault circuit must be tested without subjecting the circuit to an actual grounded phase condition. A record of each test must be maintained and made available to authorized representatives of the Secretary and to the miners in such mine.

[35 FR 17890, Nov. 20, 1970, as amended at 70 FR 77736, Dec. 30, 2005]

§ 75.902 Low- and medium-voltage ground check monitor circuits.

[STATUTORY PROVISIONS]

On or before September 30, 1970, low- and medium-voltage resistance grounded systems shall include a fail-safe ground check circuit to monitor continuously the grounding circuit to assure continuity which ground check circuit shall cause the circuit breaker to open when either the ground or pilot check wire is broken, or other no less effective device approved by the Secretary or his authorized representative to assure such continuity, except that an extension of time, not in excess of 12 months, may be permitted by the Secretary on a mine-by-mine basis if he determines that such equipment is not available. Cable couplers shall be constructed so that the ground check continuity conductor shall be broken first and the ground conductors shall be broken last when the coupler is being uncoupled.

§ 75.902–1 Maximum voltage ground check circuits.

The maximum voltage used for such ground check circuits shall not exceed 40 volts.

§ 75.902–2 Approved ground check systems not employing pilot check wires.

Ground check systems not employing pilot check wires will be approved only if it is determined that the system includes a fail safe design causing the circuit breaker to open when ground continuity is broken.

§ 75.902–4 Attachment of ground conductors and ground check wires to equipment frames; use of separate connections.

In grounding equipment frames of all stationary, portable or mobile equipment receiving power from resistance grounded systems separate connections shall be used when practicable.

§ 75.903 Disconnecting devices.

[STATUTORY PROVISIONS]

Disconnecting devices shall be installed in conjunction with the circuit breaker to provide visual evidence that the power is disconnected.

§ 75.904 Identification of circuit breakers.

[STATUTORY PROVISIONS]

Circuit breakers shall be marked for identification.

§ 75.905 Connection of single-phase loads.

[STATUTORY PROVISIONS]

Single-phase loads shall be connected phase-to-phase.

§ 75.906 Trailing cables for mobile equipment, ground wires, and ground check wires.

[STATUTORY PROVISIONS]

Trailing cables for mobile equipment shall contain one or more ground conductors having a cross-sectional area of not less than one-half the power conductor, and, on September 30, 1970, an insulated conductor for the ground continuity check circuit or other no less effective device approved by the Secretary or his authorized representative to assure such continuity, except that an extension of time, not in excess of 12 months may be permitted by the

Secretary on a mine-by-mine basis if he determines that such equipment is not available. Splices made in the cables shall provide continuity of all components.

§ 75.907 Design of trailing cables for medium-voltage circuits.

[STATUTORY PROVISIONS]

Trailing cables for medium-voltage circuits shall include grounding conductors, a ground check conductor, and grounded metallic shields around each power conductor or a ground metallic shield over the assembly, except that on equipment employing cable reels, cables without shields may be used if the insulation is rated 2,000 volts or more.

Appendix A to Subpart J

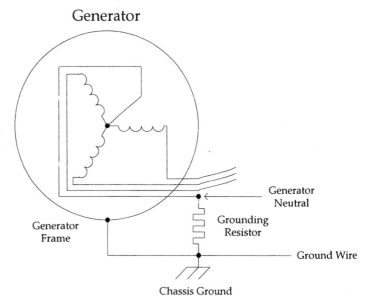

Note that grounding resistor must be mounted on the same frame with the generator.

Figure No. I

Mine Safety and Health Admin., Labor **Pt. 75, Subpt. J, App. A**

Appendix A to Subpart J

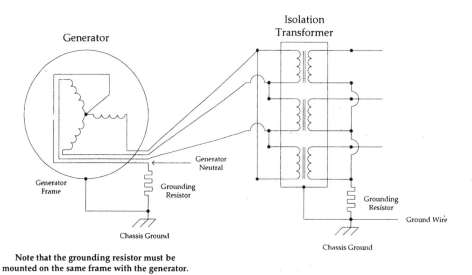

Note that the grounding resistor must be mounted on the same frame with the generator.

Figure No. II

§ 75.1000

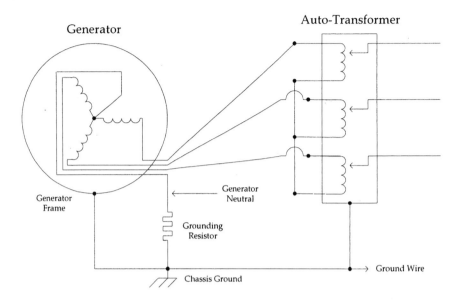

Note that the grounding resistor must be mounted on the same frame with the generator.

Figure No. III

[70 FR 77737, Dec. 30, 2005]

Subpart K—Trolley Wires and Trolley Feeder Wires

§ 75.1000 Cutout switches.

[STATUTORY PROVISIONS]

Trolley wires and trolley feeder wires, shall be provided with cutout switches at intervals of not more than 2,000 feet and near the beginning of all branch lines.

§ 75.1001 Overcurrent protection.

[STATUTORY PROVISIONS]

Trolley wires and trolley feeder wires shall be provided with overcurrent protection.

§ 75.1001-1 Devices for overcurrent protection; testing and calibration requirements; records.

(a) Automatic circuit interrupting devices that will deenergize the affected circuit upon occurrence of a short circuit at any point in the system will meet the requirements of § 75.1001.

(b) Automatic circuit interrupting devices described in paragraph (a) of this section shall be tested and calibrated at intervals not to exceed six months. Testing of such devices shall include passing the necessary amount of electric current through the device to cause activation. Calibration of such devices shall include adjustment of all associated relays to ±15 percent of the indicated value. An authorized representative of the Secretary may require additional testing or calibration of these devices.

(c) A record of the tests and calibrations required by paragraph (b) of this section shall be kept, and shall be made available, upon request, to an authorized representative of the Secretary.

[38 FR 29998, Oct. 31, 1973, as amended at 60 FR 33723, June 29, 1995]

§ 75.1002 Installation of electric equipment and conductors; permissibility.

(a) Electric equipment must be permissible and maintained in a permissible condition when such equipment is located within 150 feet of pillar workings or longwall faces.

(b) Electric conductors and cables installed in or in by the last open crosscut or within 150 feet of pillar workings or longwall faces must be—

(1) Shielded high-voltage cables supplying power to permissible longwall equipment;

(2) Interconnecting conductors and cables of permissible longwall equipment;

(3) Conductors and cables of intrinsically safe circuits; and

(4) Cables and conductors supplying power to low- and medium-voltage permissible equipment.

(5) Shielded high-voltage cables supplying power to permissible continuous mining machines.

[67 FR 11004, Mar. 11, 2002, as amended at 75 FR 17553, Apr. 6, 2010]

§ 75.1003 Insulation of trolley wires, trolley feeder wires and bare signal wires; guarding of trolley wires and trolley feeder wires.

[STATUTORY PROVISIONS]

Trolley wires, trolley feeder wires, and bare signal wires shall be insulated adequately where they pass through doors and stoppings, and where they cross other power wires and cables. Trolley wires and trolley feeder wires shall be guarded adequately:

(a) At all points where men are required to work or pass regularly under the wires;

(b) On both sides of all doors and stoppings; and

(c) At man-trip stations.

The Secretary or his authorized representatives shall specify other conditions where trolley wires and trolley feeder wires shall be adequately protected to prevent contact by any person, or shall require the use of improved methods to prevent such contact. Temporary guards shall be provided where trackmen and other persons work in proximity to trolley wires and trolley feeder wires.

§ 75.1003-1 Other requirements for guarding of trolley wires and trolley feeder wires.

Adequate precaution shall be taken to insure that equipment being moved along haulageways will not come in contact with trolley wires or trolley feeder wires.

§ 75.1003-2 Requirements for movement of off-track mining equipment in areas of active workings where energized trolley wires or trolley feeder wires are present; pre-movement requirements; certified and qualified persons.

(a) Prior to moving or transporting any unit of off-track mining equipment in areas of the active workings where energized trolley wires or trolley feeder wires are present:

(1) The unit of equipment shall be examined by a certified person to ensure that coal dust, float coal dust, loose coal oil, grease, and other combustible materials have been cleaned up and have not been permitted to accumulate on such unit of equipment; and,

(2) A qualified person, as specified in § 75.153 of this part, shall examine the trolley wires, trolley feeder wires, and the associated automatic circuit interrupting devices provided for short circuit protection to ensure that proper short circuit protection exists.

(b) A record shall be kept of the examinations required by paragraph (a) of this section, and shall be made available, upon request, to an authorized representative of the Secretary.

(c) Off-track mining equipment shall be moved or transported in areas of the active workings where energized trolley wires or trolley feeder wires are present only under the direct supervision of a certified person who shall be physically present at all times during moving or transporting operations.

(d) The frames of off-track mining equipment being moved or transported, in accordance with this section, shall be covered on the top and on the trolley wire side with fire-resistant material which has met the applicable requirements of Part 18 of Subchapter D of this chapter (Bureau of Mines Schedule 2G).

(e) Electrical contact shall be maintained between the mine track and the frames of off-track mining equipment

§ 75.1100

being moved in-track and trolley entries, except that rubber-tired equipment need not be grounded to a transporting vehicle if no metal part of such rubber-tired equipment can come into contact with the transporting vehicle.

(f) A minimum vertical clearance of 12 inches shall be maintained between the farthest projection of the unit of equipment which is being moved and the energized trolley wires or trolley feeder wires at all times during the movement or transportation of such equipment; provided, however, that if the height of the coal seam does not permit 12 inches of vertical clearance to be so maintained, the following additional precautions shall be taken:

(1)(i) Except as provided in paragraph (f)(1)(ii) of this section electric power shall be supplied to the trolley wires or trolley feeder wires only from outby the unit of equipment being moved or transported.

(ii) Where direct current electric power is used and such electric power can be supplied only from inby the equipment being moved or transported, power may be supplied from inby such equipment provided a miner with the means to cut off the power, and in direct communication with persons actually engaged in the moving or transporting operation, is stationed outby the equipment being moved.

(2) The settings of automatic circuit interrupting devices used to provide short circuit protection for the trolley circuit shall be reduced to not more than one-half of the maximum current that could flow if the equipment being moved or transported were to come into contact with the trolley wire or trolley feeder wire;

(3) At all times the unit of equipment is being moved or transported, a miner shall be stationed at the first automatic circuit breaker outby the equipment being moved and such miner shall be: (i) In direct communication with persons actually engaged in the moving or transporting operation, and (ii) capable of communicating with the responsible person on the surface required to be on duty in accordance with § 75.1600–1 of this part;

(4) Where trolley phones are utilized to satisfy the requirements of paragraph (f)(3) of this section, telephones or other equivalent two-way communication devices that can readily be connected with the mine communication system shall be carried by the miner stationed at the first automatic circuit breaker outby the equipment being moved and by a miner actually engaged in the moving or transporting operation; and,

(5) No person shall be permitted to be inby the unit of equipment being moved or transported, in the ventilating current of air that is passing over such equipment, except those persons directly engaged in moving such equipment.

(g) The provisions of paragraphs (a) through (f) of this section shall not apply to units of mining equipment that are transported in mine cars, provided that no part of the equipment extends above or over the sides of the mine car.

[38 FR 29998, Oct. 31, 1973, as amended at 60 FR 33723, June 29, 1995]

Subpart L—Fire Protection

§ 75.1100 Requirements.

[STATUTORY PROVISION]

Each coal mine shall be provided with suitable firefighting equipment adapted for the size and conditions of the mine. The Secretary shall establish minimum requirements of the type, quality, and quantity of such equipment.

§ 75.1100–1 Type and quality of firefighting equipment.

Firefighting equipment required under this subpart shall meet the following minimum requirements:

(a) Waterlines: Waterlines shall be capable of delivering 50 gallons of water a minute at a nozzle pressure of 50 pounds per square inch.

(b) Portable water cars: A portable water car shall be of at least 1,000 gallons capacity (500 gallons capacity for anthracite mines) and shall have at least 300 feet of fire hose with nozzles. A portable water car shall be capable of providing a flow through the hose of 50 gallons of water per minute at a nozzle pressure of 50 pounds per square inch.

(c) A portable chemical car shall carry enough chemicals to provide a

Mine Safety and Health Admin., Labor § 75.1100-2

fire extinguishing capacity equivalent to that of a portable water car.

(d) Portable foam-generating machines or devices: A portable foam-generating machine or device shall have facilities and equipment for supplying the machine with 30 gallons of water per minute at 30 pounds per square inch for a period of 35 minutes.

(e) Portable fire extinguisher: A portable fire extinguisher shall be either (1) a multipurpose dry chemical type containing a nominal weight of 5 pounds of dry powder and enough expellant to apply the powder or (2) a foam-producing type containing at least 2½ gallons of foam-producing liquids and enough expellant to supply the foam. Only fire extinguishers approved by the Underwriters Laboratories, Inc., or Factory Mutual Research Corp., carrying appropriate labels as to type and purpose, shall be used. After March 30, 1971, all new portable fire extinguishers acquired for use in a coal mine shall have a 2A 10 BC or higher rating.

(f)(1) Except as provided in paragraph (f)(2) of this section, the fire hose shall be lined with a material having flame resistant qualities meeting requirements for hose in Bureau of Mines' Schedule 2G. The cover shall be polyester, or other material with flame-spread qualities and mildew resistance equal or superior to polyester. The bursting pressure shall be at least 4 times the water pressure at the valve to the hose inlet with the valve closed; the maximum water pressure in the hose nozzle shall not exceed 100 p.s.i.g.

(2) Fire hose installed for use in underground coal mines prior to December 30, 1970, shall be mildew-proof and have a bursting pressure at least 4 times the water pressure at the valve to the hose inlet with the valve closed, and the maximum water pressure in the hose nozzle with water flowing shall not exceed 100 p.s.i.g.

§ 75.1100-2 Quantity and location of firefighting equipment.

(a) *Working sections.* (1) Each working section of coal mines producing 300 tons or more per shift shall be provided with two portable fire extinguishers and 240 pounds of rock dust in bags or other suitable containers; waterlines shall extend to each section loading point and be equipped with enough fire hose to reach each working face unless the section loading point is provided with one of the following:

(i) Two portable water cars; or

(ii) Two portable chemical cars; or

(iii) One portable water car or one portable chemical car, and either (*a*) a portable foam-generating machine or (*b*) a portable high-pressure rock-dusting machine fitted with at least 250 feet of hose and supplied with at least 60 sacks of rock dust.

(2) Each working section of coal mines producing less than 300 tons of coal per shift shall be provided with the following:

(i) Two portable fire extinguishers; and

(ii) 240 pounds of rock dust in bags or other suitable containers; and

(iii) At least 500 gallons of water and at least three pails of 10-quart capacity; or a waterline with sufficient hose to reach the working places; or a portable water car of at least 500-gallons capacity; or a portable, all-purpose, dry-powder chemical car of at least 125-pounds capacity.

(3) As an alternative to paragraph (a)(2) of this section, each working section with no electrical equipment at the face of an anthracite coal mine producing less than 300 tons of coal per shift shall be provided with the following:

(i) Portable fire extinguishers containing a total capacity of at least 30 pounds of dry chemical or 15 gallons of foam and located at the entrance to the gangway at the bottom of the slope; and

(ii) Portable fire extinguishers containing a total capacity of at least 20 pounds of dry chemical or 10 gallons of foam and located within 500 feet from the working face.

(b) *Belt conveyors.* In all coal mines, waterlines shall be installed parallel to the entire length of belt conveyors and shall be equipped with firehose outlets with valves at 300-foot intervals along each belt conveyor and at tailpieces. At least 500 feet of firehose with fittings suitable for connection with each belt conveyor waterline system shall be stored at strategic locations along the belt conveyor. Waterlines may be

§ 75.1100-3

installed in entries adjacent to the conveyor entry belt as long as the outlets project into the belt conveyor entry.

(c) *Haulage tracks.* (1) In mines producing 300 tons of coal or more per shift waterlines shall be installed parallel to all haulage tracks using mechanized equipment in the track or adjacent entry and shall extend to the loading point of each working section. Waterlines shall be equipped with outlet valves at intervals of not more than 500 feet, and 500 feet of firehose with fittings suitable for connection with such waterlines shall be provided at strategic locations. Two portable water cars, readily available, may be used in lieu of waterlines prescribed under this paragraph.

(2) In mines producing less than 300 tons of coal per shift, there shall be provided at 500-foot intervals in all main and secondary haulage roads:

(i) A tank of water of at least 55-gallon capacity with at least 3 pails of not less than 10-quart capacity; or

(ii) Not less than 240 pounds of bagged rock dust.

(d) *Transportation.* Each track or off-track locomotive, self-propelled mantrip car, or personnel carrier shall be equipped with one portable fire extinguisher.

(e) *Electrical installations.* At each electrical installation, the operator shall provide two portable fire extinguishers that have a nominal capacity of 5 pounds of dry chemical, or one extinguisher that has a nominal capacity of at least 10 pounds of dry chemical, and which have a 2–A:10–B:C or higher rating.

(f) *Oil storage stations.* Two portable fire extinguishers and 240 pounds of rock dust, shall be provided at each permanent underground oil storage station. One portable fire extinguisher shall be provided at each working section where 25 gallons or more of oil are stored in addition to extinguishers required under paragraph (a) of this section.

(g) *Welding, cutting, soldering.* One portable fire extinguisher or 240 pounds of rock dust shall be provided at locations where welding, cutting, or soldering with arc or flame is being done.

(h) *Powerlines.* At each wooden door through which powerlines pass there shall be one portable fire extinguisher or 240 pounds of rock dust within 25 feet of the door on the intake air side.

(i) *Emergency materials.* (1) At each mine producing 300 tons of coal or more per shift there shall be readily available the following materials at locations not exceeding 2 miles from each working section:

1,000 board feet of brattice boards
2 rolls of brattice cloth
2 hand saws
25 pounds of 8^d nails
25 pounds of 10^d nails
25 pounds of 16^d nails
3 claw hammers
25 bags of wood fiber plaster or 10 bags of cement (or equivalent material for stoppings)
5 tons of rock dust

(2) At each mine producing less than 300 tons of coal per shift the above materials shall be available at the mine, provided, however, that the emergency materials for one or more mines may be stored at a central warehouse or building supply company and such supply must be the equivalent of that required for all mines involved and within 1-hour's delivery time from each mine. This exception shall not apply where the active working sections are more than 2 miles from the surface.

[35 FR 17890, Nov. 20, 1970, as amended at 73 FR 53127, Sept. 15, 2008]

§ 75.1100-3 Condition and examination of firefighting equipment.

All firefighting equipment shall be maintained in a usable and operative condition. Chemical extinguishers shall be examined every 6 months and the date of the examination shall be written on a permanent tag attached to the extinguisher.

[35 FR 17890, Nov. 20, 1970, as amended at 60 FR 33723, June 29, 1995]

§ 75.1101 Deluge-type water sprays, foam generators; main and secondary belt-conveyor drives.

[STATUTORY PROVISIONS]

Deluge-type water sprays or foam generators automatically actuated by

Mine Safety and Health Admin., Labor § 75.1101-7

rise in temperature, or other no less effective means approved by the Secretary of controlling fire, shall be installed at main and secondary belt-conveyor drives.

§ 75.1101-1 Deluge-type water spray systems.

(a) Deluge-type spray systems shall consist of open nozzles attached to branch lines. The branch lines shall be connected to a waterline through a control valve operated by a fire sensor. Actuation of the control valve shall cause water to flow into the branch lines and discharge from the nozzles.

(b) Nozzles attached to the branch lines shall be full cone, corrosion resistant and provided with blow-off dust covers. The spray application rate shall not be less than 0.25 gallon per minute per square foot of the top surface of the top belt and the discharge shall be directed at both the upper and bottom surfaces of the top belt and to the upper surface of the bottom belt.

§ 75.1101-2 Installation of deluge-type sprays.

Deluge-type water spray systems shall provide protection for the belt drive and 50 feet of fire-resistant belt or 150 feet of nonfire-resistant belt adjacent to the belt drive.

§ 75.1101-3 Water requirements.

Deluge-type water spray systems shall be attached to a water supply. Water so supplied shall be free of excessive sediment and noncorrosive to the system Water pressure shall be maintained consistent with the pipe, fittings, valves, and nozzles at all times. Water systems shall include strainers with a flush-out connection and a manual shut-off valve. The water supply shall be adequate to provide flow for 10 minutes except that pressure tanks used as a source of water supply shall be of 1,000-gallon capacity for a fire-resistant belt and 3,000 gallons for a nonfire-resistant belt may be provided.

§ 75.1101-4 Branch lines.

As a part of the deluge-type water spray system, two or more branch lines of nozzles shall be installed. The maximum distance between nozzles shall not exceed 8 feet.

§ 75.1101-5 Installation of foam generator systems.

(a) Foam generator systems shall be located so as to discharge foam to the belt drive, belt takeup, electrical controls, gear reducing unit and the conveyor belt.

(b) Foam generator systems shall be equipped with a fire sensor which actuates the system, and each system shall be capable of producing and delivering the following amounts of foam within 5 minutes:

(1) At fire-resistant belt installations, an amount which will fully envelop the belt drive, belt takeup, electrical controls, gear reducing unit, and the conveyor belt over a distance of 50 feet; and,

(2) At nonfire-resistant belt installations, an amount which will fully envelop the belt drive, belt takeup electrical controls, gear reducing unit, and the conveyor belt over a distance of 150 feet.

(c) The foam generator shall be equipped with a warning device designed to stop the belt drive when a fire occurs and all such warning devices shall be capable of giving both an audible and visual signal when actuated by fire.

(d) Water, power, and chemicals required shall be adequate to maintain water or foam flow for no less than 25 minutes.

(e) Water systems shall include strainers with a flush-out connection and a manual shut-off valve.

§ 75.1101-6 Water sprinkler systems; general.

Water sprinkler systems may be installed to protect main and secondary belt-conveyor drives, however, where such systems are employed, they shall be installed and maintained in accordance with §§ 75.1101-7 through 75.1101-11.

§ 75.1101-7 Installation of water sprinkler systems; requirements.

(a) The fire-control components of each water sprinkler system shall be installed, as far as practicable in accordance with the recommendations set forth in National Fire Protection Association 1968-69 edition, Code No. 13, "Installation of Sprinkler Systems" and such systems' components shall be

609

§ 75.1101-8

of a type approved by the Underwriters' Laboratories, Inc., Factory Mutual Research Corp.

(b) Each sprinkler system shall provide protection for the motor drive belt takeup, electrical controls, gear reducing unit, and the 50 feet of fire-resistant belt, or 150 feet of nonfire-resistant belt adjacent to the belt drive.

(c) The components of each water sprinkler system shall be located so as to minimize the possibility of damage by roof fall or by the moving belt and its load.

§ 75.1101-8 Water sprinkler systems; arrangement of sprinklers.

(a) At least one sprinkler shall be installed above each belt drive, belt takeup, electrical control, and gear-reducing unit, and individual sprinklers shall be installed at intervals of no more than 8 feet along all conveyor branch lines.

(b) Two or more branch lines, at least one of which shall be above the top belt and one between the top and bottom belt, shall be installed in each sprinkler system to provide a uniform discharge of water to the belt surface.

(c) The water discharge rate from the sprinkler system shall not be less than 0.25 gallon per minute per square foot of the top surface of the top belt and the discharge shall be directed at both the upper and bottom surfaces of the top belt and to the upper surface of the bottom belt. The supply of water shall be adequate to provide a constant flow of water for 10 minutes with all sprinklers functioning.

(d) Each individual sprinkler shall be activated at a temperature of not less than 150 °F. and not more than 300 °F.

(e) Water systems shall include strainers with a flush-out connection and a manual shut-off valve.

§ 75.1101-9 Back-up water system.

One fire hose outlet together with a length of hose capable of extending to the belt drive shall be provided within 300 feet of each belt drive.

§ 75.1101-10 Water sprinkler systems; fire warning devices at belt drives.

Each water sprinkler system shall be equipped with a device designed to stop the belt drive in the event of a rise in temperature and each such warning device shall be capable of giving both an audible and visual warning when a fire occurs.

§ 75.1101-11 Inspection of water sprinkler systems.

Each water sprinkler system shall be examined weekly and a functional test of the complete system shall be conducted at least once each year.

§ 75.1101-12 Equivalent dry-pipe system.

Where water sprinkler systems are installed to protect main and secondary belt conveyor drives and freezing temperatures prevail, an equivalent dry-pipe system may be installed.

§ 75.1101-13 Dry powder chemical systems; general.

Self-contained dry powder chemical systems may be installed to protect main and secondary belt conveyor drives, however, where such systems are employed, they shall be installed and maintained in accordance with the provisions of §§ 75.1101-14 through 75.1101-22.

§ 75.1101-14 Installation of dry powder chemical systems.

(a) Self-contained dry powder chemical systems shall be installed to protect each belt-drive, belt takeup, electrical-controls, gear reducing units and 50 feet of fire-resistant belt or 150 feet of non-fire-resistant belt adjacent to the belt drive.

(b) The fire-control components of each dry powder chemical system shall be a type approved by the Underwriters' Laboratories, Inc., or Factory Mutual Engineering Corp.

(c) The components of each dry powder chemical system shall be located so as to minimize the possibility of damage by roof fall or by the moving belt and its load.

§ 75.1101-15 Construction of dry powder chemical systems.

(a) Each self-contained dry powder system shall be equipped with hose or pipe lines which are no longer than necessary.

(b) Metal piping and/or hose between control valves and nozzles shall have a minimum bursting pressure of 500 p.s.i.g.

(c) Hose shall be protected by wire braid or its equivalent.

(d) Nozzles and reservoirs shall be sufficient in number to provide maximum protection to each belt, belt takeup, electrical controls, and gear reducing unit.

(e) Each belt shall be protected on the top surface of both the top and bottom belts and the bottom surface of the top belt.

§ 75.1101-16 Dry powder chemical systems; sensing and fire-suppression devices.

(a) Each self-contained dry powder chemical system shall be equipped with sensing devices which shall be designed to activate the fire-control system, sound an alarm and stop the conveyor drive motor in the event of a rise in temperature, and provision shall be made to minimize contamination of the lens of any optical sensing device installed in such system.

(b) Where sensors are operated from the same power source as the belt drive, each sensor shall be equipped with a standby power source which shall be capable of remaining operative for at least 4 hours after a power cutoff.

(c) Sensor systems shall include a warning indicator (or test circuit) which shows it is operative.

(d) Each fire-suppression system shall be equipped with a manually operated control valve which shall be independent of the sensor.

§ 75.1101-17 Sealing of dry powder chemical systems.

Each dry powder chemical system shall be adequately sealed to protect all components of the system from moisture dust, and dirt.

§ 75.1101-18 Dry powder requirements.

Each dry powder chemical system shall contain the following minimum amounts of multipurpose dry powder:

Belt	Dry powder, pounds
Fire resistant	125
Non-fire resistant	250

§ 75.1101-19 Nozzles; flow rate and direction.

The nozzles of each dry powder chemical system shall be capable of discharging all powder within 1 minute after actuation of the system and such nozzles shall be directed so as to minimize the effect of ventilation upon fire control.

§ 75.1101-20 Safeguards for dry powder chemical systems.

Adequate guards shall be provided along all belt conveyors in the vicinity of each dry powder chemical system to protect persons whose vision is restricted by a discharge of powder from the system. In addition, hand-rails shall be installed in such areas to provide assistance to those passing along the conveyor after a powder discharge.

§ 75.1101-21 Back-up water system.

One fire hose outlet together with a length of hose capable of extending to the belt drive shall be provided within 300 feet of each belt drive.

§ 75.1101-22 Inspection of dry powder chemical systems.

(a) Each dry powder chemical system shall be examined weekly and a functional test of the complete system shall be conducted at least once each year.

(b) Where the dry powder chemical system has been actuated, all components of the system shall be cleaned immediately by flushing all powder from pipes and hoses and all hose damaged by fire shall be replaced.

§ 75.1102 Slippage and sequence switches.

[STATUTORY PROVISIONS]

Underground belt conveyors shall be equipped with slippage and sequence switches.

§ 75.1103 Automatic fire warning devices.

[STATUTORY PROVISIONS]

On or before May 29, 1970, devices shall be installed on all such belts which will give a warning automatically when a fire occurs on or near

§ 75.1103-1

such belt. The Secretary shall prescribe a schedule for installing fire suppression devices on belt haulageways.

§ 75.1103-1 Automatic fire sensors.

A fire sensor system shall be installed on each underground belt conveyor. Sensors so installed shall be of a type which will (a) give warning automatically when a fire occurs on or near such belt; (b) provide both audible and visual signals that permit rapid location of the fire.

§ 75.1103-2 Automatic fire sensors; approved components; installation requirements.

(a) The components of each automatic fire sensor required to be installed in accordance with the provisions of § 75.1103-1 shall be of a type and installed in a manner approved by the Secretary, or the components shall be of a type listed, approved and installed in accordance with the recommendations of a nationally recognized testing laboratory approved by the Secretary.

(b) Where applicable, and not inconsistent with these regulations, automatic fire sensors shall be installed in accordance with the recommendations set forth in National Fire Code No. 72A "Local Protective Signaling Systems" (NFPA No. 72A-1967). National Fire Code No. 72A (1967) is hereby incorporated by reference and made a part hereof. National Fire Code No. 72A is available for examination at each MSHA Coal Mine Safety and Health district office, and may be obtained from the National Fire Protection Association, 11 Tracy Drive, Avon, MA 02322; Telephone: 800-344-3555 (toll free); *http://www.nfpa.org*.

[37 FR 16546, Aug. 16, 1972, as amended at 71 FR 16668, Apr. 3, 2006]

§ 75.1103-3 Automatic fire sensor and warning device systems; minimum requirements; general.

Automatic fire sensor and warning device systems installed in belt haulageways of underground coal mines shall be assembled from components which meet the minimum requirements set forth in §§ 75.1103-4 through 75.1103-7 unless otherwise approved by the Secretary.

[37 FR 16545, Aug. 16, 1972]

§ 75.1103-4 Automatic fire sensor and warning device systems; installation; minimum requirements.

(a) Effective December 31, 2009, automatic fire sensor and warning device systems that use carbon monoxide sensors shall provide identification of fire along all belt conveyors.

(1) Carbon monoxide sensors shall be installed at the following locations:

(i) Not more than 100 feet downwind of each belt drive unit, each tailpiece transfer point, and each belt take-up. If the belt drive, tailpiece, and/or take-up for a single transfer point are installed together in the same air course, and the distance between the units is less than 100 feet, they may be monitored with one sensor downwind of the last component. If the distance between the units exceeds 100 feet, additional sensors are required downwind of each belt drive unit, each tailpiece transfer point, and each belt take-up;

(ii) Not more than 100 feet downwind of each section loading point;

(iii) Along the belt entry so that the spacing between sensors does not exceed 1,000 feet. Where air velocities are less than 50 feet per minute, spacing must not exceed 350 feet; and

(iv) The mine operator shall indicate the locations of all carbon monoxide sensors on the mine maps required by §§ 75.1200 and 75.1505 of this part.

(2) Where used, sensors responding to radiation, smoke, gases, or other indications of fire, shall be spaced at regular intervals to provide protection equivalent to carbon monoxide sensors, and installed within the time specified in paragraph (a)(3) of this section.

(3) When the distance from the tailpiece at loading points to the first outby sensor reaches the spacing requirements in § 75.1103-4(a)(1)(iii), an additional sensor shall be installed and put in operation within 24 production shift hours. When sensors of the kind described in paragraph (a)(2) of this section are used, they shall be installed and put in operation within 24 production shift hours after the equivalent distance which has been established for the sensor from the tailpiece at loading points to the first outby sensor is first reached.

(b) Automatic fire sensor and warning device systems shall be installed so as to minimize the possibility of damage from roof falls and the moving belt and its load. Sensors must be installed near the center in the upper third of the entry, in a manner that does not expose personnel working on the system to unsafe conditions. Sensors must not be located in abnormally high areas or in other locations where air flow patterns do not permit products of combustion to be carried to the sensors.

(c) Infrared, ultraviolet, and other sensors whose effectiveness is impaired by contamination shall be protected from dust, dirt, and moisture.

(d) The voltage of automatic fire sensor and warning device systems shall not exceed 120 volts.

(e) Except when power must be cut off in the mine under the provisions of §75.313, automatic fire sensor and warning device systems shall be capable of giving warning of fire for a minimum of 4 hours after the source of power to the belt is removed unless the belt haulageway is examined for hot rollers and fire as provided in paragraph (e) (1) or (2) of this section.

(1) When an unplanned removal of power from the belt occurs an examination for hot rollers and fire in the operating belts of a conveyor system shall be completed within 2 hours after the belt has stopped.

(2) When a preplanned removal of power from the belt occurs an examination for hot rollers and fire on the operating belts of a conveyor system may commence not more than 30 minutes before the belts are stopped and shall be completed within 2 hours after the examination is commenced, or the examination shall be commenced when the belts are stopped and completed within 2 hours after the belts are stopped.

[37 FR 16545, Aug. 16, 1972, as amended at 57 FR 20928, May 15, 1992; 73 FR 80614, Dec. 31, 2008]

§ 75.1103-5 Automatic fire warning devices; actions and response.

(a) When the carbon monoxide level reaches 10 parts per million above the established ambient level at any sensor location, automatic fire sensor and warning device systems shall provide an effective warning signal at the following locations:

(1) At working sections and other work locations where miners may be endangered from a fire in the belt entry.

(2) At a manned surface location where personnel have an assigned post of duty. The manned surface location must have:

(i) A telephone or equivalent communication with all miners who may be endangered and

(ii) A map or schematic that shows the locations of sensors, and the intended air flow direction at these locations. This map or schematic must be updated within 24 hours of any change in this information.

(3) The automatic fire sensor and warning device system shall be monitored for a period of 4 hours after the belt is stopped, unless an examination for hot rollers and fire is made as prescribed in §75.1103–4(e).

(b) The fire sensor and warning device system shall include a means for rapid evaluation of electrical short and open circuits, ground faults, pneumatic leaks, or other defect detrimental to its proper operational condition.

(c) Automatic fire sensor and warning devices shall include a manual reset feature.

(d) When a malfunction or warning signal is received at the manned surface location, the sensors that are activated must be identified and appropriate personnel immediately notified.

(e) Upon notification of a malfunction or warning signal, appropriate personnel must immediately initiate an investigation to determine the cause of the malfunction or warning signal and take the required actions set forth in paragraph (f) of this section.

(f) If any sensor indicates a warning, the following actions must be taken unless the mine operator determines that the signal does not present a hazard to miners:

(1) Appropriate personnel must notify miners in affected working sections, in affected areas where mechanized mining equipment is being installed or removed, and at other locations specified in the approved mine emergency evacuation and firefighting program of instruction; and

(2) All miners in the affected areas, unless assigned emergency response duties, must be immediately withdrawn to a safe location identified in the mine emergency evacuation and firefighting program of instruction.

(g) If the warning signal will be activated during calibration of sensors, personnel manning the surface location must be notified prior to and upon completion of calibration. Affected working sections, areas where mechanized mining equipment is being installed or removed, or other areas designated in the approved emergency evacuation and firefighting program of instruction must be notified at the beginning and completion of calibration.

(h) If any fire detection component becomes inoperative, immediate action must be taken to repair the component. While repairs are being made, operation of the belt may continue if the following requirements are met:

(1) If one sensor becomes inoperative, a trained person must continuously monitor for carbon monoxide at the inoperative sensor;

(2) If two or more adjacent sensors become inoperative, trained persons must patrol and continuously monitor the affected areas for carbon monoxide so that they will be traveled each hour in their entirety. Alternatively, a trained person must be stationed at each inoperative sensor to monitor for carbon monoxide;

(3) If the complete fire detection system becomes inoperative, trained persons must patrol and continuously monitor the affected areas for carbon monoxide so that they will be traveled each hour in their entirety;

(4) Trained persons who conduct monitoring under this section must have two-way voice communication capability, at intervals not to exceed 2,000 feet, and must report carbon monoxide concentrations to the surface at intervals not to exceed one hour;

(5) Trained persons who conduct monitoring under this section must immediately report to the surface any concentration of carbon monoxide that reaches 10 parts per million above the established ambient level, unless the mine operator knows that the source of the carbon monoxide does not present a hazard to miners; and

(6) Handheld detectors used to monitor the belt entry under this section must have a detection level equivalent to that of the system's carbon monoxide sensors.

[37 FR 16545, Aug. 16, 1972, as amended at 73 FR 80615, Dec. 31, 2008]

§ 75.1103-6 Automatic fire sensors; actuation of fire suppression systems.

Point-type heat sensors or automatic fire sensor and warning device systems may be used to actuate deluge-type water systems, foam generator systems, multipurpose dry-powder systems, or other equivalent automatic fire suppression systems.

[73 FR 80615, Dec. 31, 2008]

§ 75.1103-7 Electrical components; permissibility requirements.

The electrical components of each automatic fire sensor and warning device system shall:

(a) Remain functional when the power circuits are deenergized as required by § 75.706; and

(b) Be provided with protection against ignition of methane or coal dust when the electrical power is deenergized as required by § 75.313, but these components shall be permissible or intrinsically safe if installed in a return airway.

[37 FR 16546, Aug. 16, 1972, as amended at 57 FR 20929, May 15, 1992]

§ 75.1103-8 Automatic fire sensor and warning device systems; examination and test requirements.

(a) Automatic fire sensor and warning device systems shall be examined at least once each shift when belts are operated as part of a production shift. A functional test of the warning signals shall be made at least once every seven days. Examination and maintenance of such systems shall be by a qualified person.

(b) A record of the functional test conducted in accordance with paragraph (a) of this section shall be maintained by the operator and kept for a period of one year.

(c) Sensors shall be calibrated in accordance with the manufacturer's calibration instructions at intervals not to exceed 31 days. A record of the sensor calibrations shall be maintained by the operator and kept for a period of one year.

[73 FR 80615, Dec. 31, 2008]

§ 75.1103-9 Minimum requirements; fire suppression materials and location; maintenance of entries and crosscuts; access doors; communications; fire crews; high-expansion foam devices.

(a) The following materials shall be stored within 300 feet of each belt drive or at a location where the material can be moved to the belt drive within 5 minutes, except that when the ventilating current in the belt haulageway travels in the direction of the normal movement of coal on the belt, the materials shall be stored within 300 feet of the belt tailpiece or at a location where the materials can be moved to the belt tailpiece within 5 minutes.

(1) 500 feet of fire hose, except that if the belt flight is less than 500 feet in length the fire hose may be equal to the length of the belt flight. A high expansion foam device may be substituted for 300 feet of the 500 feet of the fire hose. Where used, such foam generators shall produce foam sufficient to fill 100 feet of the belt haulageway in not more than 5 minutes. Sufficient power cable and water hose shall be provided so that the foam generator can be installed at any crosscut along the belt by which the generator is located. A 1-hour supply of foam producing chemicals and tools and hardware required for its operation shall be stored at the foam generator.

(2) Tools to open a stopping between the belt entry and the adjacent intake entry; and

(3) 240 pounds of bagged rock dust.

(b) The entry containing the main waterline and the crosscuts containing water outlets between such entry and the belt haulageway (if the main waterline is in an adjacent entry) shall be maintained accessible and in safe condition for travel and firefighting activities. Each stopping in such crosscuts or adjacent crosscuts shall have an access door.

(c) Suitable communication lines extending to the surface shall be provided in the belt haulageway or adjacent entry.

(d) The fire suppression system required at the belt drive shall include the belt discharge head.

(e) A crew consisting of at least five members for each working shift shall be trained in firefighting operations. Fire drills shall be held at intervals not exceeding 6 months.

[37 FR 16546, Aug. 16, 1972]

§ 75.1103-10 Fire suppression systems; additional requirements.

For each conveyor belt flight exceeding 2,000 feet in length, where the average air velocity along the belt haulage entry exceeds 100 feet per minute, an additional cache of the materials specified in § 75.1103-9(a)(1), (2), and (3) shall be provided. The additional cache may be stored at the locations specified in § 75.1103-9(a), or at some other strategic location readily accessible to the conveyor belt flight.

[73 FR 80616, Dec. 31, 2008]

§ 75.1103-11 Tests of fire hydrants and fire hose; record of tests.

Each fire hydrant shall be tested by opening to insure that it is in operating condition, and each fire hose shall be tested, at intervals not exceeding 1 year. A record of these tests shall be maintained at an appropriate location.

[37 FR 16546, Aug. 16, 1972]

§ 75.1104 Underground storage, lubricating oil and grease.

[STATUTORY PROVISIONS]

Underground storage places for lubricating oil and grease shall be of fireproof construction. Except for specially prepared materials approved by the Secretary, lubricating oil and grease kept in all underground areas in a coal mine shall be in fireproof, closed metal containers or other no less effective containers approved by the Secretary.

§ 75.1106 Welding, cutting, or soldering with arc or flame underground.

[STATUTORY PROVISIONS]

All welding, cutting, or soldering with arc or flame in all underground areas of a coal mine shall, whenever practicable, be conducted in fireproof

§ 75.1106–1

enclosures. Welding, cutting, or soldering with arc or flame in other than a fireproof enclosure shall be done under the supervision of a qualified person who shall make a diligent search for fire during and after such operations and shall, immediately before and during such operations, continuously test for methane with means approved by the Secretary for detecting methane. Welding, cutting, or soldering shall not be conducted in air that contains 1.0 volume per centum or more of methane. Rock dust or suitable fire extinguishers shall be immediately available during such welding, cutting or soldering.

§ 75.1106–1 Test for methane.

Until December 31, 1970, a permissible flame safety lamp may be used to make tests for methane required by the regulations in this part. On and after December 31, 1970 a methane detector approved by the Secretary shall be used for such tests and a permissible flame safety lamp may be used as a supplemental testing device. A person qualified to test for methane under § 75.151 will be a qualified person for the purpose of this section.

TRANSPORTATION, HANDLING AND STORAGE OF LIQUEFIED AND NONLIQUEFIED COMPRESSED GAS CYLINDERS

§ 75.1106–2 Transportation of liquefied and nonliquefied compressed gas cylinders; requirements.

(a) Liquefied and nonliquefied compressed gas cylinders transported into or through an underground coal mine shall be:

(1) Placed securely in devices designed to hold the cylinder in place during transit on self-propelled equipment or belt conveyors;

(2) Disconnected from all hoses and gages;

(3) Equipped with a metal cap or "headband" (fence-type metal protector around the valve stem) to protect the cylinder valve during transit; and,

(4) Clearly labeled "empty" or "MT" when the gas in the cylinder has been expended.

(b) In addition to the requirements of paragraph (a) of this section, when liquefied and nonliquefied compressed gas cylinders are transported by a trolley wire haulage system into or through an underground coal mine, such cylinders shall be placed in well insulated and substantially constructed containers which are specifically designed for holding such cylinders.

(c) Liquefied and nonliquefied compressed gas cylinders shall not be transported on mantrips.

[36 FR 22061, Nov. 19, 1971]

§ 75.1106–3 Storage of liquefied and nonliquefied compressed gas cylinders; requirements.

(a) Liquefied and nonliquefied compressed gas cylinders stored in an underground coal mine shall be:

(1) Clearly marked and identified as to their contents in accordance with Department of Transportation regulations.

(2) Placed securely in storage areas designated by the operator for such purpose, and where the height of the coalbed permits, in an upright position, preferably in specially designated racks, or otherwise secured against being accidently tipped over.

(3) Protected against damage from falling material, contact with power lines and energized electrical equipment, heat from welding, cutting or soldering, and exposure to flammable liquids.

(b) Liquefied and nonliquefied compressed gas cylinders shall not be stored or left unattended in any area inby the last open crosscut of an underground coal mine.

(c) When not in use, the valves of all liquefied and nonliquefied compressed gas cylinders shall be in the closed position, and all hoses shall be removed from the cylinder.

[36 FR 22061, Nov. 19, 1971]

§ 75.1106–4 Use of liquefied and nonliquefied compressed gas cylinders; general requirements.

(a) Persons assigned by the operator to use and work with liquefied and nonliquefied compressed gas shall be trained and designated by the operator as qualified to perform the work to which they are assigned, and such qualified persons shall be specifically instructed with respect to the dangers inherent in the use of such gases in an underground coal mine.

(b) Persons who perform welding, cutting, or burning operations shall wear clothing free from excessive oil or grease.

(c) Liquefied and nonliquefied compressed gas shall be used only in well-ventilated areas.

(d) Not more than one liquefied or nonliquefied compressed gas unit, consisting of one oxygen cylinder and one additional gas cylinder, shall be used to repair any unit of equipment which is inby the loading point of any section.

(e) Where liquefied and nonliquefied compressed gas is used regularly in underground shops or other underground structures, such shops or structures shall be on a separate split of air.

(f) Where liquefied and nonliquefied compressed gas is used in any area in which oil, grease, or coal dust is present, oil and grease deposits shall, where practicable, be removed and the entire area within 10 feet of the worksite covered with a heavy coating of rock dust.

(g) Liquefied and nonliquefied compressed gas cylinders shall be located no less than 10 feet from the worksite, and where the height of the coal seam permits, they shall be placed in an upright position and chained or otherwise secured against falling.

(h) Liquefied and nonliquefied compressed gas shall not be used under direct pressure from the cylinder and, where such gases are used under reduced pressure, the pressure level shall not exceed that recommended by the manufacturer.

(i) "Manifolding cylinders" shall only be performed in well-ventilated shops where the necessary equipment is properly installed and operated in accordance with specifications for safety prescribed by the manufacturer.

[36 FR 22061, Nov. 19, 1971]

§ 75.1106–5 Maintenance and tests of liquefied and nonliquefied compressed gas cylinders; accessories and equipment; requirements.

(a) Hose lines, gages, and other cylinder accessories shall be maintained in a safe operating condition.

(b) Defective cylinders, cylinder accessories, torches, and other welding, cutting, and burning equipment shall be labeled "defective" and taken out of service.

(c) Each qualified person assigned to perform welding, cutting, or burning with liquefied and nonliquefied compressed gas shall be equipped with a wrench specifically designed for use with liquefied and nonliquefied compressed gas cylinders and a suitable torchtip cleaner to maintain torches in a safe operating condition.

(d) Tests for leaks on the hose valves or gages of liquefied and nonliquefied compressed gas cylinders shall only be made with a soft brush and soapy water or soap suds, or other device approved by the Secretary.

[36 FR 22062, Nov. 19, 1971]

§ 75.1106–6 Exemption of small low pressure gas cylinders containing nonflammable or nonexplosive gas mixtures.

Small low pressure gas cylinders containing nonflammable or nonexplosive gas mixtures, which provide for the emission of such gas under a pressure reduced from a pressure which does not exceed 250 p.s.i.g., and which is manufactured and sold in conformance with U.S. Department of Transportation Special Permit No. 6029 as a calibration test kit for methane monitoring systems, shall be exempt from the requirements of §§ 75.1106–2(c) and 75.1106–4(d), (f) and (g).

[36 FR 22062, Nov. 19, 1971]

FIRE SUPPRESSION DEVICES AND FIRE-RESISTANT HYDRAULIC FLUIDS ON UNDERGROUND EQUIPMENT

§ 75.1107 Fire suppression devices.

[STATUTORY PROVISIONS]

On and after March 30, 1971, fire-suppression devices meeting specifications prescribed by the Secretary shall be installed on unattended underground equipment and suitable fire-resistant hydraulic fluids approved by the Secretary shall be used in the hydraulic systems of such equipment. Such fluids shall be used in the hydraulic systems of other underground equipment unless

§ 75.1107-1

fire suppression devices meeting specifications prescribed by the Secretary are installed on such equipment.

§ 75.1107-1 Fire-resistant hydraulic fluids and fire suppression devices on underground equipment.

(a)(1) Unattended electrically powered equipment used underground which uses hydraulic fluid shall use approved fire-resistant hydraulic fluid.

(2) Except as provided in paragraph (a) (3) of this section, within 24 production shift hours after being installed, unattended electrically powered equipment used underground shall be equipped with a fire suppression device which meets the applicable requirements of §§ 75.1107-3 through 75.1107-16.

(3) Unattended enclosed motors, controls, transformers, rectifiers, and other similar noncombustible electrically powered equipment containing no flammable fluid may be protected:

(i) By an approved fire suppression device, or

(ii) Be located at least 2 feet from coal or other combustible materials, or

(iii) Be separated from the coal or combustible materials by a 4-inch-thick masonry firewall or equivalent; and be mounted on a minimum 4-inch-thick noncombustible surface, platform, or equivalent. The electrical cables at such equipment shall conform with the requirements of Part 18 of this chapter (Bureau of Mines Schedule 2G) or be in metal conduit.

(b) Attended electrically powered equipment used underground which uses hydraulic fluid shall use approved fire-resistant hydraulic fluid unless such equipment is protected by a fire suppression device which meets the applicable requirements of §§ 75.1107-3—75.1107-16.

(c) For purpose of §§ 75.1107—75.1107-16 the following underground equipment shall be considered attended equipment:

(1) Any machine or device regularly operated by a miner assigned to operate such machine or device;

(2) Any machine or device which is mounted in the direct line of sight of a jobsite which is located within 500 feet of such machine or device and which jobsite is regularly occupied by a miner assigned to perform job duties at such jobsite during each production shift.

(d) Machines and devices described under paragraph (c) of this section must be inspected for fire and the input powerline deenergized when workmen leave the area for more than 30 minutes.

[37 FR 15301, July 29, 1972]

§ 75.1107-2 Approved fire-resistant hydraulic fluids; minimum requirements.

Fire-resistant hydraulic fluids and concentrates required to be employed in the hydraulic system of underground equipment in accordance with the provisions of § 75.1107-1 shall be considered suitable only if they have been produced under an approval, or any modification thereof, issued pursuant to Part 35 Subchapter I of this chapter (Bureau of Mines Schedule 30), or any revision thereof.

[37 FR 15301, July 29, 1972]

§ 75.1107-3 Fire suppression devices; approved components; installation requirements.

(a) The components of each fire suppression device required to be installed in accordance with the provisions of § 75.1107-1 shall be approved by the Secretary, or where appropriate be listed as approved by a nationally recognized agency approved by the Secretary.

(b) Where used, pressure vessels shall conform with the requirements of sections 3603, 3606, 3607, 3707, and 3708 of National Fire Code No. 22 "Water Tanks for Private Fire Protection" (NFPA No. 22-1971).

(c) The cover of hose of fire suppression devices, if used on the protected equipment and installed after the effective date of this section, shall meet the flame-resistant requirements of Part 18 of this chapter (Bureau of Mines Schedule 2G).

(d) Fire suppression devices required to be installed in accordance with the provisions of § 75.1107-1 shall where appropriate be installed in accordance with the manufacturer's specifications.

[37 FR 15301, July 29, 1972]

§ 75.1107-4 Automatic fire sensors and manual actuators; installation; minimum requirements.

(a)(1) Where fire suppression devices are installed on unattended underground equipment, one or more point-type sensors or equivalent shall be installed for each 50 square feet of top surface area, or fraction thereof, of such equipment, and each sensor shall be designed to activate the first suppression system and disconnect the electrical power source to the equipment protected, and, except where sprinklers are used, there shall be in addition, a manual actuator installed to operate the system. Where sprinklers are used, provision shall be made for manual application of water to the protected equipment in lieu of a manual actuator.

(2) Two or more manual actuators, where practicable, shall be installed, as provided in paragraphs (a)(2) (i) and (ii) of this section, to activate fire suppression devices on attended equipment purchased on or after the effective date of this § 75.1107-4. At least one manual actuator shall be used on equipment purchased prior to the effective date of this § 75.1107-4.

(i) Manual actuators installed on attended equipment regularly operated by a miner, as provided in § 75.1107-1(c)(1) shall be located at different locations on the equipment, and at least one manual actuator shall be located within easy reach of the operator's normal operating position.

(ii) Manual actuators to activate fire suppression devices on attended equipment not regularly operated by a miner, as provided in § 75.1107-1(c)(2), shall be installed at different location, and at least one manual actuator shall be installed so as to be easily reached by the miner at the jobsite or by persons approaching the equipment.

(b) Sensors shall, where practicable, be installed in accordance with the recommendations set forth in National Fire Code No. 72A "Local Protective Signaling Systems" (NFPA No. 72A-1967).

(c) On unattended equipment the fire suppression device shall operate independently of the power to the main motor (or equivalent) so it will remain operative if the circuit breakers (or other protective device) actuates. On attended equipment powered through a trailing cable the fire suppression device shall operate independently of the electrical power provided by the cable.

(d) Point-type sensors (such as thermocouple, bimetallic strip, or rate of temperature rise) located in ventilated passageways shall be installed downwind from the equipment to be protected.

(e) Sensor systems shall include a device or method for determining their operative condition.

[37 FR 15301, July 29, 1972]

§ 75.1107-5 Electrical components of fire suppression devices; permissibility requirements.

The electrical components of each fire suppression device used on permissible equipment inby the last open crosscut or on equipment in the return airways of any coal mine shall be permissible or intrinsically safe and such components shall be maintained in permissible or intrinsically safe condition.

[37 FR 15302, July 29, 1972]

§ 75.1107-6 Capacity of fire suppression devices; location and direction of nozzles.

(a) Each fire suppression device shall be:

(1) Adequate in size and capacity to extinguish potential fires in or on the equipment protected; and

(2) Suitable for the atmospheric conditions surrounding the equipment protected (e.g., air velocity, type, and proximity of adjacent combustible material); and

(3) Rugged enough to withstand rough usage and vibration when installed on mining equipment.

(b) The extinguishant-discharge nozzles of each fire suppression device shall, where practicable, be located so as to take advantage of mine ventilation air currents. The fire suppression device may be of the internal injection, inundating, or combination type. Where fire control is achieved by internal injection, or combination of internal injection and inundation, hazardous locations shall be enclosed to minimize runoff and overshoot of the extinguishing agent and the extinguishing agent shall be directed onto:

§ 75.1107-7

(1) Cable reel compartments and electrical cables on the equipment which are subject to flexing or to external damage; and

(2) All hydraulic components on the equipment which are exposed directly to or located in the immediate vicinity of electrical cables which are subject to flexing or to damage.

[37 FR 15302, July 29, 1972]

§ 75.1107-7 Water spray devices; capacity; water supply; minimum requirements.

(a) Where water spray devices are used on unattended underground equipment the rate of flow shall be at least 0.25 gallon per minute per square foot over the top surface area of the equipment and the supply of water shall be adequate to provide the required flow of water for 10 minutes.

(b) Where water spray devices are used for inundating attended underground equipment the rate of flow shall be at least 0.18 gallon per minute per square foot over the top surface area of the equipment (excluding conveyors, cutters, and gathering heads), and the supply of water shall be adequate to provide the required flow of water for 10 minutes.

(c) Where water is used for internal injection on attended equipment the total quantity of water shall be at least 4.5 gallons times the number of hazardous locations; however, the total minimum amount of water shall not be less than the following:

Type of equipment	Water in gallons
(1) Cutting machines	36
(2) Continuous miners	36
(3) Haulage vehicles	22.5
(4) All other attended equipment	18.0

The rate of flow shall be not less than 7 gallons per minute.

(d) Where water is used in a combination internal injection and inundation system on attended equipment the rate of flow shall be at least 0.12 gallon per minute per square foot over the top surface area of the equipment (excluding conveyors, cutters, and gathering heads), and the supply of water shall be adequate to provide the required flow of water for 10 minutes.

(e) On equipment provided with a cable reel and an internal injection or combination-type system, the amount of water discharged into the cable reel compartments shall be approximately 25 percent of the amount required to be discharged by the system, however, such quantity need not exceed 10 gallons.

(f) Liquid chemicals may be used, as approved by the Secretary in self-contained fire suppression devices. Such liquid chemicals shall be nontoxic and when applied to a fire shall not produce excessive toxic compounds. The quantity of liquid chemicals required shall be proportionately less than water as based on equivalency ratings established by the Secretary or equivalency ratings made by a nationally recognized agency approved by the Secretary.

[37 FR 15302, July 29, 1972]

§ 75.1107-8 Fire suppression devices; extinguishant supply systems.

(a) Fire suppression systems using water or liquid chemical to protect attended equipment shall:

(1) Be maintained at a pressure consistent with the pipe, fittings, valves, and nozzles used in the system.

(2) Be located so as to be protected against damage during operation of the equipment protected.

(3) Employ liquid which is free from excessive sediment and noncorrosive to the system.

(4) Include strainers equipped with flush-out connections or equivalent protective devices and a rising stem or other visual indicator-type shutoff valve.

(b) Water supplies for fire suppression devices installed on underground equipment may be maintained in mounted water tanks or by connection to water mains. Such water supplies shall be continuously connected to the fire suppression device whenever the equipment is connected to a power source, except for a reasonable time for changing hose connections to hydrants while the machine is stopped in a ventilated passageway.

[37 FR 15302, July 29, 1972]

§ 75.1107-9 Dry chemical devices; capacity; minimum requirements.

(a) Dry chemical fire extinguishing systems used on underground equipment shall be of the multipurpose powder-type and shall include the following:

(1) The system including all hose and nozzles shall be protected against the entrance of moisture, dust, or dirt;

(2) The system shall be guarded against damage during operation of the equipment protected;

(3) Hose and pipe shall be as short as possible; the distance between the chemical container and furthest nozzle shall not exceed 50 feet;

(4) Hose, piping, and fittings between the actuator and the chemical container shall have a bursting pressure of 500 pounds per square inch (gage) or higher; the hose, piping, and fittings between the chemical container and the nozzles shall have a bursting pressure of 300 pounds per square inch (gage) or higher and

(5) The system shall discharge in 1 minute or less, for quantities less than 50 pounds (nominal)[1] and in less than 2 minutes for quantities more than 50 pounds;

(b) On unattended underground equipment, the number of pounds of dry chemical employed by the system shall be not less than 1 pound per square foot of top surface area of the equipment; however, the minimum amount in any system shall be 20 pounds (nominal). The discharge shall be directed into and on potentially hazardous locations of the equipment.

(c) On attended underground equipment, the number of pounds (nominal) employed by the system shall equal 5 times the total number of hazardous locations; however, the minimum amount in any system shall not be less than the following, except that systems on haulage vehicles installed prior to the effective date of this section may contain 20 pounds (nominal).

Type of equipment	Dry chemical pounds (nominal)
(1) Cutting machines	40
(2) Continuous miners	40
(3) Haulage vehicles	30
(4) All other attended equipment	20

(d) The amount of dry chemical discharged into the cable reel compartments of attended underground equipment shall be approximately 25 percent of the total amount required to be discharged by the system; however, the quantity discharged into cable reel compartments need not exceed 10 pounds.

[37 FR 15302, July 29, 1972]

§ 75.1107-10 High expansion foam devices; minimum capacity.

(a) On unattended underground equipment the amount of water delivered as high expansion foam for a period of approximately 20 minutes shall be not less than 0.06 gallon per minute per square foot of surface area of the equipment protected; however, the minimum total rate for any system shall be not less than 3 gallons per minute.

(b) On attended underground equipment, foam may be delivered by internal injection, inundation, or combination-type systems. Each system shall deliver water as foam for a minimum of 10 minutes. For internal injection, the rate of water application as high expansion foam shall be not less than 0.5 gallon per minute per hazardous location; however, the minimum total rate shall be not less than 2 gallons per minute. For inundation, the rate of water application as high expansion foam shall be not less than 0.05 gallon per minute per square foot of top surface area of the equipment protected; however, the minimum total rate shall be not less than 5 gallons of water per minute.

(c) In combined internal injection and inundation systems the rate of water applied as foam shall not be less than 0.035 gallon per minute per square

---

[1] Many dry chemical systems were originally designed for sodium bicarbonate before all-purpose chemical (ammonium phosphate) was shown to be more effective. Sodium bicarbonate is denser than ammonium phosphate; hence, for example, a 50-pound system designed for the sodium bicarbonate will hold slightly more by weight than all-purpose dry chemical (ammonium phosphate) by weight. The word "nominal" is used in § 75.1107-9 to express the approximate weight in pounds of all-purpose dry chemical.

§ 75.1107-11

foot of top surface area of the equipment protected; however, the minimum total rate shall not be less than 3.5 gallons of water per minute.

(d) Where internal injection is employed, the amount of water discharged as high expansion foam into the cable reel compartments of underground equipment regularly operated by a miner shall be approximately 25 percent of the total amount required to be discharged by the system; however, the quantity of water discharged as foam into the cable reel compartment need not exceed 1.5 gallons.

[37 FR 15303, July 29, 1972]

§ 75.1107-11 **Extinguishing agents; requirements on mining equipment employed in low coal.**

On mining equipment no more than 32 inches high, the quantity of extinguishing agent required under the provisions of §§ 75.1107-7, 75.1107-9, and 75.1107-10 may be reduced by one-fourth if space limitations on the equipment require such reduction.

[37 FR 15303, July 29, 1972]

§ 75.1107-12 **Inerting of mine atmosphere prohibited.**

No fire suppression device designed to control fire by total flooding shall be installed to protect unattended underground equipment except in enclosed dead-end entries or enclosed rooms.

[37 FR 15303, July 29, 1972]

§ 75.1107-13 **Approval of other fire suppression devices.**

Notwithstanding the provisions of §§ 75.1107-1 through 75.1107-12 the District Manager for the District in which the mine is located may approve any other fire suppression system or device which provides substantially equivalent protection as would be achieved through compliance with those sections: *Provided,* That no such system or device shall be approved which does not meet the following minimum criteria:

(a) Components shall be approved by the Secretary, or where appropriate be listed as approved by a nationally recognized agency approved by the Secretary.

(b) The fire suppression equipment shall be designed to withstand the rigors of the mine environment. Where used, pressure vessels shall conform with the requirements of section 3603, 3606, 3607, 3707, and 3708 of National Fire Code No. 22 "Water Tanks for Private Fire Protection" (NFPA No. 22–1971).

(c) The cover of hose of fire suppression devices, if used on the protected equipment, shall meet the flame-resistant requirements of Part 18 of this chapter (Bureau of Mines Schedule 2G).

(d) Extinguishing agents shall not create a serious toxic or other hazard to the miners.

(e) The electrical components of the fire suppression device shall meet the requirements for electrical components of the mining machine.

(f) Where used, manual actuators for initiating the operation of the fire suppression device shall be readily accessible to the machine operator. On unattended equipment, an automatic as well as a manual actuator shall be provided.

(g) On unattended equipment the fire suppression device shall operate independently of the power to the main motor (or equivalent) so it will remain operative if the circuit breakers (or other protective device) actuates. On attended equipment powered through a trailing cable the fire suppression device shall operate independently of the electrical power provided by the cable.

(h) On unattended equipment, the sensor system shall have a means for checking its operative condition.

(i) The fire suppression agent shall be directed at locations where the greatest potential fire hazard exists. Cable reel compartments shall receive approximately twice the quantity of extinguishing agent as each other hazardous location.

(j) The rate of application of the fire suppression agent shall minimize the time for quenching and the total quantity applied shall be sufficient to quench a fire in its incipient stage.

(k) The effectiveness of the quenching agent, together with the total quantity of agent and its rate of application shall provide equivalent protection to the water, dry powder, or foam systems described in §§ 75.1107–7, 75.1107–9, and 75.1107–10.

(l) The fire suppression device shall be operable at all times electrical power is connected to the mining machine, except during tramming when the machine is in a ventilated passageway, the water hose if used, may be switched from one hydrant to another in a reasonable time and except in systems meeting the minimum special criteria set forth in paragraph (m) of this section.

(m) Systems for attended equipment which are not continuously connected to a water supply shall not be approved unless they meet the following minimum criteria:

(1) The machine shall be equipped with a firehose at least 50 feet in length which is continuously connected to the machine-mounted portion of the system.

(2) Hydrants in proximity to the area where the machine is to be used shall be equipped with sufficient hose to reach the machine at any time it is connected to a power source.

(3) The machine shall be used only where the operator (or other person) will always be in ventilated air uncontaminated by smoke and hot gases from the machine fire while extending the machine-mounted hose to connect with the hydrant-mounted hose.

(4) The machine and hydrant hoses shall be readily accessible so that the connection between the machine-mounted hose and the hydrant hose can be made and water flow achieved in not more than 3 minutes under actual mining conditions for any location of the machine while electric power is connected.

(5) The rate of water flow at the machine shall provide a minimum of 0.12 gallon of water per minute per square foot of top surface area (excluding conveyors, cutters, and gathering heads). The water shall discharge to all hazardous locations on the machine.

(6) Hose, if used on the machine, in addition to meeting the flame resistant requirements for the cover of a hose provided in §§ 75.1107–3(b) and 75.1107–13(c) shall have a minimum burst pressure 4 times that of the static water pressure at the mining machine. Fabric braid hose shall have at least two braids, and wire braid hose shall have at least a single braid.

(7) In addition to the hose located at the hydrant (which is intended to be connected to the hose on the machine) the firefighting equipment required by § 75.1100–2(a) shall be maintained.

(8) A sufficient number of trained miners shall be kept on the section when the machine is in use to connect the machine hose to the hydrant hose and achieve water flow in not more than 3 minutes.

[37 FR 15303, July 29, 1972]

§ 75.1107–14 Guards and handrails; requirements where fire suppression devices are employed.

All unattended underground equipment provided with fire suppression devices which are mounted in dead end entries, enclosed rooms or other potentially hazardous locations shall be equipped with adequate guards at moving or rotating components. Handrails or other effective protective devices shall be installed at such locations where necessary to facilitate rapid egress from the area surrounding such equipment.

[37 FR 15303, July 29, 1972]

§ 75.1107–15 Fire suppression devices; hazards; training of miners.

Each operator shall instruct all miners normally assigned to the active workings of the mine with respect to any hazards inherent in the operation of all fire suppression devices installed in accordance with § 75.1107–1 and, where appropriate, the safeguards available at each such installation.

[37 FR 15303, July 29, 1972]

§ 75.1107–16 Inspection of fire suppression devices.

(a) All fire suppression devices shall be visually inspected at least once each week by a person qualified to make such inspections.

(b) Each fire suppression device shall be tested and maintained in accordance with the requirements specified in the appropriate National Fire Code listed as follows for the type and kind of device used:

§ 75.1107-17

National Fire Code No. 11A "High Expansion Foam Systems" (NFPA No. 11A—1970).
National Fire Code No. 13A "Care and Maintenance of Sprinkler Systems" (NFPA No. 13A—1971).
National Fire Code No. 15 "Water Spray Fixed Systems for Fire Protection" (NFPA No. 15—1969).
National Fire Code No. 17 "Dry Chemical Extinguishing Systems" (NFPA No. 17—1969).
National Fire Code No. 72A "Local Protective Signaling Systems" (NFPA No. 72A—1967).
National Fire Code No. 198 "Care of Fire Hose" (NFPA No. 198—1969).

(c) A record of the inspections required by this section shall be maintained by the operator. The record of the weekly inspections may be maintained at an appropriate location by each fire suppression device.

[37 FR 15304, July 29, 1972, as amended at 60 FR 33723, June 29, 1995]

§ 75.1107-17 Incorporation by reference; availability of publications.

In accordance with 5 U.S.C. 552(a), the technical publications to which reference is made in §§ 75.1107-1 through 75.1107-16, and which have been prepared by organizations other than the Bureau of Mines or the Mine Safety and Health Administration, are hereby incorporated by reference and made a part hereof. The incorporated publications are available for examination at each MSHA Coal Mine Safety and Health district office. National Fire Codes are available from the National Fire Protection Association, 11 Tracy Drive, Avon, MA 02322; Telephone: 800-344-3555 (toll free); *http://www.nfpa.org*.

[37 FR 15304, July 29, 1972, as amended at 71 FR 16669, Apr. 3, 2006]

§ 75.1108 Approved conveyor belts.

(a) Until December 31, 2009 conveyor belts placed in service in underground coal mines shall be:
(1) Approved under Part 14; or
(2) Accepted under Part 18.
(b) Effective December 31, 2009 conveyor belts placed in service in underground coal mines shall be approved under Part 14. If MSHA determines that Part 14 approved belt is not available, the Agency will consider an extension of the effective date.
(c) Effective December 31, 2018 all conveyor belts used in underground coal mines shall be approved under Part 14.

[73 FR 80616, Dec. 31, 2008]

Subpart M—Maps

§ 75.1200 Mine map.

[STATUTORY PROVISIONS]

The operator of a coal mine shall have in a fireproof repository located in an area on the surface of the mine chosen by the mine operator to minimize the danger of destruction by fire or other hazard, an accurate and up-to-date map of such mine drawn on scale. Such map shall show:
(a) The active workings;
(b) All pillared, worked out, and abandoned areas, except as provided in this section;
(c) Entries and aircourses with the direction of airflow indicated by arrows;
(d) Contour lines of all elevations;
(e) Elevations of all main and cross or side entries;
(f) Dip of the coalbed;
(g) Escapeways;
(h) Adjacent mine workings within 1,000 feet;
(i) Mines above or below;
(j) Water pools above; and
(k) Either producing or abandoned oil and gas wells located within 500 feet of such mine and any underground area of such mine; and,
(l) Such other information as the Secretary may require. Such map shall identify those areas of the mine which have been pillared, worked out, or abandoned, which are inaccessible or cannot be entered safely and on which no information is available.

§ 75.1200-1 Additional information on mine map.

Additional information required to be shown on mine maps under § 75.1200 shall include the following:
(a) Name and address of the mine;
(b) The scale and orientation of the map;
(c) The property or boundary lines of the mine;
(d) All drill holes that penetrate the coalbed being mined;

Mine Safety and Health Admin., Labor §75.1202–1

(e) All shaft, slope, drift, and tunnel openings and auger and strip mined areas of the coalbed being mined;

(f) The location of all surface mine ventilation fans; the location may be designated on the mine map by symbols;

(g) The location of railroad tracks and public highways leading to the mine, and mine buildings of a permanent nature with identifying names shown;

(h) The location and description of at least two permanent base line points coordinated with the underground and surface mine traverses, and the location and description of at least two permanent elevation bench marks used in connection with establishing or referencing mine elevation surveys;

(i) The location of any body of water dammed in the mine or held back in any portion of the mine; provided, however, such bodies of water may be shown on overlays or tracings attached to the mine maps used to show contour lines as provided under paragraph (m) of this section;

(j) The elevations of tops and bottoms of shafts and slopes, and the floor at the entrance to drift and tunnel openings;

(k) The elevation of the floor at intervals of not more than 200 feet in:

(1) At least one entry of each working section, and main and cross entries;

(2) The last line of open crosscuts of each working section, and main and cross entries before such sections and main and cross entries are abandoned;

(3) Rooms advancing toward or adjacent to property or boundary lines or adjacent mines;

(l) The elevation of any body of water dammed in the mine or held back in any portion of the mine; and,

(m) Contour lines passing through whole number elevations of the coalbed being mined. The spacing of such lines shall not exceed 10-foot elevation levels, except that a broader spacing of contour lines may be approved by the District Manager for steeply-pitching coalbeds. Contour lines may be placed on overlays or tracings attached to mine maps.

(n) The locations of refuge alternatives.

[35 FR 17890, Nov. 20, 1970, as amended at 73 FR 80697, Dec. 31, 2008]

§75.1200–2 Accuracy and scale of mine maps.

(a) The scale of mine maps submitted to the Secretary shall not be less than 100 or more than 500 feet to the inch.

(b) Mine traverses shall be advanced by closed loop methods of traversing or other equally accurate methods of traversing.

§75.1201 Certification.

[STATUTORY PROVISIONS]

Such map shall be made or certified by a registered engineer or a registered surveyor of the State in which the mine is located.

§75.1202 Temporary notations, revisions, and supplements.

[STATUTORY PROVISIONS]

Such map shall be kept up-to-date by temporary notations and such map shall be revised and supplemented at intervals prescribed by the Secretary on the basis of a survey made or certified by such engineer or surveyor.

§75.1202–1 Temporary notations, revisions, and supplements.

(a) Mine maps shall be revised and supplemented at intervals of not more than 6 months.

(b) Temporary notations shall include:

(1) The location of each working face of each working place;

(2) Pillars mined or other such second mining;

(3) Permanent ventilation controls constructed or removed, such as seals, overcasts, undercasts, regulators, and permanent stoppings, and the direction of air currents indicated;

(4) Escapeways and refuge alternatives designated by means of symbols.

[35 FR 17890, Nov. 20, 1970, as amended at 73 FR 80697, Dec. 31, 2008]

§ 75.1203 Availability of mine map.

[STATUTORY PROVISIONS]

The coal mine map and any revision and supplement thereof shall be available for inspection by the Secretary or his authorized representative, by coal mine inspectors of the State in which the mine is located, by miners in the mine and their representatives and by operators of adjacent coal mines and by persons owning, leasing, or residing on surface areas of such mines or areas adjacent to such mines. The operator shall furnish to the Secretary or his authorized representative and to the Secretary of Housing and Urban Development, upon request, one or more copies of such maps and any revision and supplement thereof. Such map or revision and supplement thereof shall be kept confidential and its contents shall not be divulged to any other person, except to the extent necessary to carry out the provisions of this Act and in connection with the functions and responsibilities of the Secretary of Housing and Urban Development.

§ 75.1204 Mine closure; filing of map with Secretary.

[STATUTORY PROVISIONS]

Whenever an operator permanently closes or abandons a coal mine, or temporarily closes a coal mine for a period of more than 90 days, he shall promptly notify the Secretary of such closure. Within 60 days of the permanent closure or abandonment of the mine, or, when the mine is temporarily closed, upon the expiration of a period of 90 days from the date of closure, the operator shall file with the Secretary a copy of the mine map revised and supplemented to the date of the closure. Such copy of the mine map shall be certified by a registered surveyor or registered engineer of the State in which the mine is located and shall be available for public inspection.

[35 FR 17890, Nov. 20, 1970, as amended at 60 FR 33723, June 29, 1995]

§ 75.1204-1 Places to give notice and file maps.

Operators shall give notice of mine closures and file copies of maps with the Coal Mine Safety and Health District Office for the district in which the mine is located.

[35 FR 17890, Nov. 20, 1970, as amended at 60 FR 33723, June 29, 1995; 71 FR 16669, Apr. 3, 2006]

Subpart N—Explosives and Blasting

SOURCE: 53 FR 46786, Nov. 18, 1988, unless otherwise noted.

§ 75.1300 Definitions.

The following definitions apply in this subpart.

Approval. A document issued by MSHA which states that an explosive or explosive unit has met the requirements of this part and which authorizes an approval marking identifying the explosive or explosive unit as approved as permissible.

Battery starting. The use of unconfined explosives to start the flow of coal down a breast or chute in an anthracite mine.

Blasting off the solid. Blasting the working face without providing a second free face by cutting, shearing or other method before blasting.

Instantaneous detonator. An electric detonator that fires within 6 milliseconds after application of the firing current.

Laminated partition. A partition composed of the following material and minimum nominal dimensions: ½-inch thick plywood, ½-inch thick gypsum wall board, ⅛-inch thick low carbon steel and ¼-inch thick plywood, bonded together in that order.

Opener hole. The first hole or holes fired in a round blasted off the solid to create an additional free face.

Permissible blasting unit. A device that has been approved by MSHA and that is used for firing electric detonators.

Permissible explosive. Any substance, compound or mixture which is approved by MSHA and whose primary purpose is to function by explosion.

Round. A group of boreholes fired or intended to be fired in a continuous sequence with one application of the firing current.

Sheathed explosive unit. A device consisting of an approved or permissible explosive covered by a sheath encased in a sealed covering and designed to be fired outside the confines of a borehole.

Short-delay electric detonator. An electric detonator with a designated delay period of 25 to 1,000 milliseconds.

§ 75.1301 Qualified person.

(a) A qualified person under this subpart is a person who—

(1) Is certified or qualified to use explosives by the State in which the mine is located provided that the State requires a demonstration of ability to safely use permissible explosives as prescribed by this subpart effective January 17, 1989; or

(2) In States that do not certify or qualify persons to use explosives required by this section, has at least 1 year of experience working in an underground coal mine that includes direct involvement with procedures for handling, loading, and preparing explosives for blasting and demonstrates to an authorized representative of the Secretary the ability to use permissible explosives safely.

(b) Persons qualified or certified by a State to use permissible explosives in underground coal mines as of May 17, 1989, are considered qualified under this section even though their State program did not contain a demonstration of ability requirement.

[35 FR 17890, Nov. 20, 1970, as amended at 56 FR 51616, Oct. 11, 1991; 60 FR 33723, June 29, 1995]

§ 75.1310 Explosives and blasting equipment.

(a) Only permissible explosives, approved sheathed explosive units, and permissible blasting units shall be taken or used underground.

(b) Black blasting powder, aluminum-cased detonators, aluminum-alloy-cased detonators, detonators with aluminum leg wires, and safety fuses shall not be taken or used underground.

(c) Explosives shall be fired only with a permissible blasting unit used in a manner consistent with its approval. Blasting units approved by MSHA that have approval labels specifying use with short-delay detonators with delay periods between 25–500 milliseconds are accepted to fire short-delay detonators up to 1,000 milliseconds, instantaneous detonators and long period delay detonators for anthracite mines.

(d) Permissible explosives and sheathed explosive units shall not be used underground when they are below the minimum product firing temperature specified by the approval. Explosives previously approved which do not specify a minimum firing temperature are permissible for use so long as the present approval is maintained.

(e) Electric detonators shall be compatible with the blasting unit and have sufficient strength to initiate the explosives being used.

§ 75.1311 Transporting explosives and detonators.

(a) When explosives and detonators are to be transported underground—

(1) They shall be enclosed in separate, substantially constructed containers made of nonconductive material, with no metal or other conductive materials exposed inside, except as specified in paragraph (d) of this section; and

(2) Each container of explosives and of detonators shall be indelibly marked with a readily visible warning identifying the contents.

(b) When explosives and detonators are transported by any cars or vehicles—

(1) The cars or vehicles shall be marked with warnings to identify the contents as explosive. The warnings shall be readily visible to miners approaching from any direction and in indelible letters;

(2) Explosives and detonators shall be transported either in separate cars or vehicles, or if in the same cars or vehicles as follows:

(i) Class A and Class C detonators in quantities greater than 1,000 shall be kept in the original containers as shipped from the manufacturer and separated from explosives by a hardwood partition at least 4 inches thick, a laminated partition or equivalent; and

(ii) Class A and Class C detonators in quantities of no more than 1,000 shall be separated from explosives by a hardwood partition at least 4 inches thick, a laminated partition or equivalent.

(3) No persons, other than those necessary to operate the equipment or to

§ 75.1312

accompany the explosives and detonators, shall be transported with explosives and detonators, and

(4) When explosives and detonators are transported using trolley locomotives—

(i) Trips carrying explosives and detonators shall be separated from all other mantrips by at least a 5-minute interval; and

(ii) Cars containing explosives or detonators shall be separated from the locomotives by at least one car that is empty or that contains noncombustible materials.

(c) When explosives and detonators are transported on conveyor belts—

(1) Containers of explosives shall be separated from containers of detonators by at least 50 feet;

(2) At least 6 inches of clearance shall be maintained between the top of any container of explosives or container of detonators and the mine roof or other obstruction;

(3) Except when persons are riding the belt to accompany explosives or detonators, a person shall be at each transfer point between belts and at the unloading location; and

(4) Conveyor belts shall be stopped before explosives or detonators are loaded or unloaded.

(d) When explosives and detonators are transported by hand they shall be carried in separate, nonconductive, closed containers.

§ 75.1312 Explosives and detonators in underground magazines.

(a) The quantity of explosives kept underground shall not be more than is needed for 48 hours of use.

(b) Except as provided in § 75.1313, explosives and detonators taken underground shall be kept in—

(1) Separate, closed magazines at least 5 feet apart; or

(2) The same closed magazine when—

(i) Separated by a hardwood partition at least 4 inches thick; or

(ii) Separated by a laminated partition; or

(iii) Separated by a device that is equivalent.

(c) Only explosives and detonators shall be kept in underground magazines.

(d) Magazines shall be substantially constructed and all interior surfaces shall be made of nonconductive material, with no metal or other conductive material exposed inside.

(e) All magazines shall be—

(1) Located at least 25 feet from roadways and any source of electric current;

(2) Located out of the direct line of the forces from blasting; and

(3) Kept as dry as practicable.

(f) Magazine locations shall be posted with indelibly marked and readily visible warnings indicating the presence of explosives.

(g) Only materials and equipment to be used in blasting shall be stored at magazine locations.

§ 75.1313 Explosives and detonators outside of magazines.

(a) The quantity of explosives outside a magazine for use in a working section or other area where blasting is to be performed shall—

(1) Not exceed 100 pounds; or

(2) Not exceed the amount necessary to blast one round when more than 100 pounds of explosives is required.

(b) Explosives and detonators outside a magazine that are not being transported or prepared for loading boreholes shall be kept in closed separate containers made of nonconductive material with no metal or other conductive material exposed inside and the containers shall be—

(1) At least 15 feet from any source of electric current;

(2) Out of the direct line of the forces from blasting;

(3) In a location to prevent damage by mobile equipment; and

(4) Kept as dry as practicable.

(c) Explosives and detonators not used during the shift shall be returned to a magazine by the end of the shift.

§ 75.1314 Sheathed explosive units.

(a) A separate instantaneous detonator shall be used to fire each sheathed explosive unit.

(b) Sheathed explosive units shall be primed and placed in position for firing only by a qualified person or a person working in the presence of and under the direction of a qualified person. To prime a sheathed explosive unit, the

Mine Safety and Health Admin., Labor § 75.1317

entire detonator shall be inserted into the detonator well of the unit and be held securely in place.

(c) Sheathed explosive units shall not be primed until immediately before the units are placed where they are to be fired. A sheathed explosive unit shall not be primed if it is damaged or deteriorated.

(d) Except in anthracite mines, rock dust shall be applied to the roof, ribs and floor within a 40-foot radius of the location where the sheathed explosive units are to be fired.

(e) No more than three sheathed explosive units shall be fired at one time.

(f) No sheathed explosive unit shall be fired in contact with another sheathed explosive unit.

§ 75.1315 Boreholes for explosives.

(a) All explosives fired underground shall be confined in boreholes except—

(1) Sheathed explosives units and other explosive units approved by MSHA for firing outside the confines of a borehole; and

(2) Shots fired in anthracite mines for battery starting or for blasting coal overhangs. No person shall go inside a battery to start the flow of material.

(b) Each borehole in coal for explosives shall be at least 24 inches from any other borehole and from any free face, unless prohibited by the thickness of the coal seam.

(c) Each borehole in rock for explosives shall be at least 18 inches from any other borehole in rock, at least 24 inches from any other borehole in coal, and at least 18 inches from any free face.

(d) No borehole that has contained explosives shall be used for starting any other hole.

(e) When blasting slab rounds off the solid, opener holes shall not be drilled beyond the rib line.

(f) When coal is cut for blasting, the coal shall be supported if necessary to maintain the stability of the column of explosives in each borehole.

§ 75.1316 Preparation before blasting.

(a)(1) All nonbattery-powered electric equipment, including cables, located within 50 feet from boreholes to be loaded with explosives or the sites where sheathed explosive units are to be placed and fired shall be deenergized or removed to at least 50 feet from these locations before priming of explosives. Battery-powered equipment shall be removed to at least 50 feet from these locations before priming of explosives.

(2) As an alternative to paragraph (a)(1) of this section, electric equipment, including cables, need not be deenergized or removed if located at least 25 feet from these locations provided stray current tests conducted prior to priming the explosives detect stray currents of 0.05 ampere or less through a 1-ohm resistor.

(i) Tests shall be made at floor locations on the perimeter, on energized equipment frames and on repaired areas of energized cables within the area between 25 to 50 feet from the locations where the explosives are to be primed.

(ii) Tests shall be conducted using a blasting multimeter or other instrument specifically designed for such use.

(3) The blasting cable or detonator circuitry shall not come in contact with energized electric equipment, including cables.

(b) Before loading boreholes with explosives, each borehole shall be cleared and its depth and direction determined.

(c) No borehole drilled beyond the depth of cut coal shall be loaded with explosives unless that portion of the borehole deeper than the cut is tamped with noncombustible material.

(d) When two working faces are approaching each other, cutting, drilling and blasting shall be done at only one working face at a time if the two faces are within 25 feet of each other.

[35 FR 17890, Nov. 20, 1970, as amended at 56 FR 51616, Oct. 11, 1991]

§ 75.1317 Primer cartridges.

(a) Primer cartridges shall be primed and loaded only by a qualified person or a person working in the presence of and under the direction of a qualified person.

(b) Primer cartridges shall not be primed until immediately before loading boreholes.

(c) Only a nonsparking punch shall be used when priming explosive cartridges.

(d) Detonators shall be completely within and parallel to the length of the cartridge and shall be secured by half-hitching the leg wires around the cartridge or secured by an equally effective method.

§ 75.1318 Loading boreholes.

(a) Explosives shall be loaded by a qualified person or a person working in the presence of and under the direction of a qualified person.

(b) When boreholes are being loaded, no other work except that necessary to protect persons shall be done in the working place or other area where blasting is to be performed.

(c) When loading boreholes drilled at an angle of 45 degrees or greater from the horizontal in solid rock or loading long holes drilled upward in anthracite mines—

(1) The first cartridge in each borehole shall be the primer cartridge with the end of the cartridge containing the detonator facing the back of the borehole; and

(2) The explosive cartridges shall be loaded in a manner that provides contact between each cartridge in the borehole.

(d) When loading other boreholes—

(1) The primer cartridge shall be the first cartridge loaded in the borehole;

(2) The end of the cartridge in which the detonator is inserted shall face the back of the borehole; and

(3) The primer cartridge and other explosives shall be pushed to the back of the borehole in a continuous column with no cartridge being deliberately crushed or deformed.

(e) An explosive shall not be loaded into a borehole if it is damaged, deteriorated or if the cartridge is incompletely filled.

(f) Explosives of different brands, types or cartridge diameters shall not be loaded in the same borehole.

(g) Only nonconductive, nonsparking tamping poles shall be used for loading and tamping boreholes. The use of nonsparking connecting devices for extendable tamping poles is permitted.

[53 FR 46786, Nov. 18, 1988; 54 FR 888, Jan. 10, 1989]

§ 75.1319 Weight of explosives permitted in boreholes in bituminous and lignite mines.

(a) The total weight of explosives loaded in any borehole in bituminous and lignite mines shall not exceed 3 pounds except when blasting solid rock in its natural deposit.

(b) The total weight of explosives loaded in a borehole less than 6 feet deep in bituminous and lignite mines shall be reduced by ½ pound for each foot of borehole less than 6 feet.

§ 75.1320 Multiple-shot blasting.

(a) No more than 20 boreholes shall be fired in a round unless permitted in writing by the District Manager under § 75.1321.

(b) Instantaneous detonators shall not be used in the same circuit with delay detonators in any underground coal mine.

(c) In bituminous and lignite mines, only detonators with delay periods of 1,000 milliseconds or less shall be used.

(d) When blasting in anthracite mines, each borehole in a round shall be initiated in sequence from the opener hole or holes.

(e) Arrangement of detonator delay periods for bituminous and lignite mines shall be as follows:

(1) When blasting cut coal—

(i) The first shot or shots fired in a round shall be initiated in the row nearest the kerf or the row or rows nearest the shear; and

(ii) After the first shot or shots, the interval between the designated delay periods of successive shots shall be at least 50 milliseconds but not more than 100 milliseconds.

(2) When blasting coal off the solid—

(i) Each shot in the round shall be initiated in sequence from the opener hole or holes; and

(ii) After the first shot or shots, the interval between the designated delay periods of successive shots shall be at least 50 milliseconds but not more than 100 milliseconds.

§ 75.1321 Permits for firing more than 20 boreholes and for use of nonpermissible blasting units.

(a) Applications for permits for firing more than 20 boreholes in a round and for the use of nonpermissible blasting units shall be submitted in writing to the District Manager for the district in which the mine is located and shall contain the following information:

(1) The name and address of the mine;

(2) The active workings in the mine affected by the permit and the approximate number of boreholes to be fired;

(3) The period of time during which the permit will apply;

(4) The nature of the development or construction for which they will be used, e.g., overcasts, undercasts, track grading, roof brushing or boom holes;

(5) A plan, proposed by the operator designed to protect miners in the mine from the hazards of methane and other explosive gases during each multiple shot, e.g., changes in the mine ventilation system, provisions for auxiliary ventilation and any other safeguards necessary to minimize such hazards;

(6) A statement of the specific hazards anticipated by the operator in blasting for overcasts, undercasts, track grading, brushing of roof, boom holes or other unusual blasting situations such as coalbeds of abnormal thickness; and

(7) The method to be employed to avoid the dangers anticipated during development or construction which will ensure the protection of life and the prevention of injuries to the miners exposed to such underground blasting.

(b) The District Manager may permit the firing of more than 20 boreholes of permissible explosives in a round where he has determined that it is necessary to reduce the overall hazard to which miners are exposed during underground blasting. He may also permit the use of nonpermissible blasting units if he finds that a permissible blasting unit does not have adequate blasting capacity and that the use of such permissible units will create any of the following development or construction hazards:

(1) Exposure to disturbed roof in an adjacent cavity while scaling and supporting the remaining roof prior to wiring a new series of boreholes;

(2) Exposure to underburden boreholes where prior rounds have removed the burden adjacent to a remaining borehole;

(3) Exposure to an unsupported roof while redrilling large fragmented roof rock following the loss of predrilled boreholes during earlier blasting operations; or

(4) Any other hazard created by the use of permissible blasting units during underground development or construction.

(c) Permits shall be issued on a mine-by-mine basis for periods of time to be specified by the District Manager.

(d) Permits issued under this section shall specify and include as a condition of their use, any safeguards, in addition to those proposed by the operator, which the District Manager issuing such permit has determined will be required to ensure the welfare of the miners employed in the mine at the time of the blasting permitted.

[35 FR 17890, Nov. 20, 1970, as amended at 60 FR 33723, June 29, 1995]

§ 75.1322 Stemming boreholes.

(a) Only noncombustible material shall be used for stemming boreholes.

(b) Stemming materials other than water stemming bags shall be tamped to fill the entire cross sectional area of the borehole.

(c) Stemming material shall contact the explosive cartridge nearest the collar of the borehole.

(d) Each borehole 4 or more feet deep shall be stemmed for at least 24 inches.

(e) Each borehole less than 4 feet deep shall be stemmed for at least half the depth of the borehole.

(f) When blasting off the solid in bituminous and lignite mines, only pliable clay dummies shall be used for stemming.

(g) The diameter of a water stemming bag shall be within ¼ of an inch of the diameter of the drill bit used to drill the borehole.

(h) Water stemming bags shall be constructed of tear-resistant and flame-resistant material and be capable of withstanding a 3-foot drop when filled without rupturing or developing leaks.

§ 75.1323 Blasting circuits.

(a) Blasting circuits shall be protected from sources of stray electric current.

(b) Detonators made by different manufacturers shall not be combined in the same blasting circuit.

§ 75.1324

(c) Detonator leg wires shall be shunted until connected into the blasting circuit.

(d) Blasting cables shall be—

(1) Well insulated, copper wire of a diameter not smaller than 18-gauge; and

(2) Long enough to permit the round to be fired from a safe location that is around at least one corner from the blasting area.

(e) Blasting cables shall be shunted until immediately before firing, except when testing for circuit continuity.

(f) Wire used between the blasting cable and detonator circuitry shall—

(1) Be undamaged;

(2) Be well insulated;

(3) Have a resistance no greater than 20-gauge copper wire; and

(4) Be not more than 30 feet long.

(g) Each wire connection in a blasting circuit shall be—

(1) Properly spliced; and

(2) Separated from other connections in the circuit to prevent accidental contact and arcing.

(h) Uninsulated connections in each blasting circuit shall be kept out of water and shall not contact the coal, roof, ribs, or floor.

(i) When 20 or fewer boreholes are fired in a round, the blasting circuit shall be wired in a single series.

(j) Immediately prior to firing, all blasting circuits shall be tested for continuity and resistance using a blasting galvanometer or other instrument specifically designed for testing blasting circuits.

[53 FR 46786, Nov. 18, 1988; 54 FR 27641, June 30, 1989]

§ 75.1324 Methane concentration and tests.

(a) No shot shall be fired in an area that contains 1.0 volume percent or more of methane.

(b) Immediately before shots are fired, the methane concentration in a working place or any other area where blasting is to be performed, shall be determined by a person qualified to test for methane.

§ 75.1325 Firing procedures.

(a) Shots shall be fired by a qualified person or a person working in the presence of and under the direction of a qualified person.

(b) Only one face in a working place shall be blasted at a time, except that when blasting cut coal up to three faces may be blasted in a round if each face has a separate kerf and no more than a total of 20 shots connected in a single series are fired in the round. A permit to fire more than 20 boreholes in a round under the provisions of 30 CFR 75.1320 and 75.1321 may not be obtained for use when blasting multiple faces.

(c) Before blasting—

(1) All persons shall leave the blasting area and each immediately adjacent working place where a hazard would be created by the blast, to an area that is around at least one corner from the blasting area;

(2) The qualified person shall ascertain that all persons are a safe distance from the blasting area; and

(3) A warning shall be given and adequate time allowed for persons to respond.

(d) All shots shall be fired promptly, after all persons have been removed to a safe location.

[35 FR 17890, Nov. 20, 1970, as amended at 56 FR 51616, Oct. 11, 1991]

§ 75.1326 Examination after blasting.

(a) After blasting, the blasting area shall not be entered until it is clear of smoke and dust.

(b) Immediately after the blasting area has cleared, a qualified person or a person working in the presence of and under the direction of a qualified person, shall examine the area for misfires, methane and other hazardous conditions.

(c) If a round has partially detonated, the qualified person shall immediately leave the area and no person shall reenter the affected area for at least 5 minutes.

§ 75.1327 Misfires.

(a) When misfires occur, only work by a qualified person to dispose of misfires and other work necessary to protect persons shall be done in the affected area.

(b) When a misfire cannot be disposed of—

(1) A qualified person shall post each accessible entrance to the area affected by the hazard of the misfire with a warning at a conspicuous location to prohibit entry; and

(2) The misfire shall be immediately reported to mine management.

[53 FR 46786, Nov. 18, 1988; 54 FR 27641, June 30, 1989]

§ 75.1328 Damaged or deteriorated explosives and detonators.

(a) Damaged explosives or detonators shall be—

(1) Placed in separate containers constructed of nonconductive and nonsparking materials; and

(2) Removed from the mine or placed in a magazine and removed when the magazine is resupplied.

(b) Damaged detonators shall be shunted, if practicable, either before being removed from the mine or placed in a magazine.

(c) Deteriorated explosives and detonators shall be handled and disposed of in accordance with the instructions of the manufacturer.

Subpart O—Hoisting and Mantrips

§ 75.1400 Hoisting equipment; general.

(a) Every hoist used to transport persons shall be equipped with overspeed, overwind, and automatic stop controls.

(b) Every hoist handling a platform, cage, or other device used to transport persons shall be equipped with brakes capable of stopping the fully loaded platform, cage, or other device.

(c) Cages, platforms, or other devices used to transport persons in shafts and slopes shall be equipped with safety catches or other no less effective devices approved by the Secretary that act quickly and effectively in an emergency. Such catches or devices shall be tested at least once every two months.

(d) Hoisting equipment, including automatic elevators, used to transport persons shall be examined daily.

(e) Where persons are transported into or out of a mine by a hoist, a qualified hoisting engineer shall be on duty while any person is underground. No such engineer, however, shall be required for automatically operated cages, platforms, or elevators.

[48 FR 53239, Nov. 25, 1983]

§ 75.1400-1 Hoists; brakes, capability.

Brakes on hoists used to transport persons shall be capable of stopping and holding the fully loaded platform, cage, or other device at any point in the shaft, slope, or incline.

§ 75.1400-2 Hoists; tests of safety catches; records.

A record shall be made in a book of the tests, required by § 75.1400, of the safety catches or other devices approved by the Secretary. Each entry shall be signed by the person making the tests and countersigned by a responsible official.

§ 75.1400-3 Daily examination of hoisting equipment.

Hoists and elevators shall be examined daily and such examinations shall include, but not be limited to, the following:

(a) *Elevators.* A visual examination of the rope for wear, broken wires, and corrosion, especially at excessive strain points such as near the attachments and where the rope rests on sheaves;

(b) *Hoists and elevators.* (1) An examination of the rope fastenings for defects;

(2) An examination of safety catches;

(3) An examination of the cages, platforms, elevators, or other devices for loose, missing or defective parts;

(4) An examination of the head sheaves to check for broken flanges, defective bearings, rope alignment, and proper lubrication; and

(5) An observation of the lining and all other equipment and appurtenances installed in the shaft.

[48 FR 53239, Nov. 25, 1983]

§ 75.1400-4 Certifications and records of daily examinations.

At the completion of each daily examination required by § 75.1400, the person making the examination shall certify, by signature and date, that the examination has been made. If any unsafe condition is found during the examinations required by § 75.1400-3, the

§ 75.1401

person conducting the examination shall make a record of the condition and the date. Certifications and records shall be retained for one year.

[48 FR 53239, Nov. 25, 1983, as amended at 60 FR 33723, June 29, 1995]

§ 75.1401 Hoists; rated capacities; indicators.

Hoists shall have rated capacities consistent with the loads handled. An accurate and reliable indicator of the position of the cage, platform, skip, bucket, or cars shall be provided.

[48 FR 53239, Nov. 25, 1983]

§ 75.1401-1 Hoists; indicators.

The indicator required by § 75.1401 of this subpart shall be placed so that it is in clear view of the hoisting engineer and shall be checked daily to determine its accuracy.

[48 FR 53239, Nov. 25, 1983]

§ 75.1402 Communication between shaft stations and hoist room.

[STATUTORY PROVISIONS]

There shall be at least two effective methods approved by the Secretary of signaling between each of the shaft stations and the hoist room, one of which shall be a telephone or speaking tube.

§ 75.1402-1 Communication between shaft stations and hoist room.

One of the methods used to communicate between shaft stations and the hoist room shall give signals which can be heard by the hoisting engineer at all times while men are underground.

§ 75.1402-2 Tests of signaling systems.

Signaling systems used for communication between shaft stations and the hoist room shall be tested daily.

§ 75.1403 Other safeguards.

[STATUTORY PROVISIONS]

Other safeguards adequate, in the judgment of an authorized representative of the Secretary, to minimize hazards with respect to transportation of men and materials shall be provided.

§ 75.1403-1 General criteria.

(a) Sections 75.1403-2 through 75.1403-11 set out the criteria by which an authorized representative of the Secretary will be guided in requiring other safeguards on a mine-by-mine basis under § 75.1403. Other safeguards may be required.

(b) The authorized representative of the Secretary shall in writing advise the operator of a specific safeguard which is required pursuant to § 75.1403 and shall fix a time in which the operator shall provide and thereafter maintain such safeguard. If the safeguard is not provided within the time fixed and if it is not maintained thereafter, a notice shall be issued to the operator pursuant to section 104 of the Act.

(c) Nothing in the sections in the § 75.1403 series in this Subpart O precludes the issuance of a withdrawal order because of imminent danger.

§ 75.1403-2 Criteria—Hoists transporting materials; brakes.

Hoists and elevators used to transport materials should be equipped with brakes capable of stopping and holding the fully loaded platform, cage, skip, car, or other device at any point in the shaft, slope, or incline.

§ 75.1403-3 Criteria—Drum clutch; cage construction.

(a) The clutch of a free-drum on a personnel hoist should be provided with a locking mechanism or interlocked with the brake to prevent accidental withdrawal of the clutch.

(b) Cages used for hoisting persons should be constructed with the sides enclosed to a height of at least six feet and should have gates, safety chains, or bars across the ends of the cage when persons are being hoisted or lowered.

(c) Self-dumping cages, platforms, or other devices used for transportation of persons should have a locking device to prevent tilting when persons are transported.

(d) An attendant should be on duty at the surface when persons are being hoisted or lowered at the beginning and end of each shift.

(e) Precautions should be taken to protect persons working in shaft sumps.

Mine Safety and Health Admin., Labor §75.1403-6

(f) Workers should wear safety belts while doing work in or over shafts.

[48 FR 53239, Nov. 25, 1983]

§75.1403-4 Criteria—Automatic elevators.

(a) The doors of automatic elevators should be equipped with interlocking switches so arranged that the elevator car will be immovable while any door is opened or unlocked, and arranged so that such door or doors cannot be inadvertently opened when the elevator car is not at a landing.

(b) A "Stop" switch should be provided in the automatic elevator compartment that will permit the elevator to be stopped at any location in the shaft.

(c) A slack cable device should be used where appropriate on automatic elevators which will automatically shut-off the power and apply the brakes in the event the elevator is obstructed while descending.

(d) Each automatic elevator should be provided with a telephone or other effective communication system by which aid or assistance can be obtained promptly.

§75.1403-5 Criteria—Belt conveyors.

(a) Positive-acting stop controls should be installed along all belt conveyors used to transport men, and such controls should be readily accessible and maintained so that the belt can be stopped or started at any location.

(b) Belt conveyors used for regularly scheduled mantrips should be stopped while men are loading or unloading.

(c) All belt conveyors used for the transportation of persons should have a minimum vertical clearance of 18 inches from the nearest overhead projection when measured from the edge of the belt and there should be at least 36 inches of side clearance where men board or leave such belt conveyors.

(d) When men are being transported on regularly scheduled mantrips on belt conveyors the belt speed should not exceed 300 feet per minute when the vertical clearance is less than 24 inches, and should not exceed 350 feet per minute when the vertical clearance is 24 inches or more.

(e) Adequate illumination including colored lights or reflective signs should be installed at all loading and unloading stations. Such colored lights and reflective signs should be so located as to be observable to all persons riding the belt conveyor.

(f) After supplies have been transported on belt conveyors such belts should be examined for unsafe conditions prior to the transportation of men on regularly scheduled mantrips, and belt conveyors should be clear before men are transported.

(g) A clear travelway at least 24 inches wide should be provided on both sides of all belt conveyors installed after March 30, 1970. Where roof supports are installed within 24 inches of a belt conveyor, a clear travelway at least 24 inches wide should be provided on the side of such support farthest from the conveyor.

(h) On belt conveyors that do not transport men, stop and start controls should be installed at intervals not to exceed 1,000 feet. Such controls should be properly installed and positioned so as to be readily accessible.

(i) Telephone or other suitable communications should be provided at points where men or supplies are regularly loaded on or unloaded from the belt conveyors.

(j) Persons should not cross moving belt conveyors, except where suitable crossing facilities are provided.

§75.1403-6 Criteria—Self-propelled personnel carriers.

(a) Each self-propelled personnel carrier should:

(1) Be provided with an audible warning device;

(2) Be provided with a sealed-beam headlight, or its equivalent, on each end;

(3) Be provided with reflectors on both ends and sides.

(b) In addition, each track-mounted self-propelled personnel carrier should:

(1) Be provided with a suitable lifting jack and bar, which shall be secured or carried in a tool compartment;

(2) Be equipped with 2 separate and independent braking systems properly installed and well maintained;

(3) Be equipped with properly installed and well-maintained sanding devices, except that personnel carriers (jitneys), which transport not more

than 5 men, need not be equipped with such sanding device;

(4) If an open type, be equipped with guards of sufficient strength and height to prevent personnel from being thrown from such carriers.

§ 75.1403-7 Criteria—Mantrips.

(a) Mantrips should be operated independently of any loaded trip, empty trip, or supply trip and should not be operated within 300 feet of any trip, including another mantrip.

(b) A sufficient number of mantrip cars should be provided to prevent overcrowding of men.

(c) Mantrips should not be pushed.

(d) Where mantrips are operated by locomotives on slopes such mantrips should be coupled to the front and rear by locomotives capable of holding such mantrips. Where ropes are used on slopes for mantrip haulage, such conveyances should be connected by chains, steel ropes, or other effective devices between mantrip cars and the rope.

(e) Safety goggles or eyeshields should be provided for all persons being transported in open-type mantrips.

(f) All trips, including trailers and sleds, should be operated at speeds consistent with conditions and the equipment used, and should be so controlled that they can be stopped within the limits of visibility.

(g) All mantrips should be under the direction of a supervisor and the operator of each mantrip should be familiar with the haulage safety rules and regulations.

(h) Men should proceed in an orderly manner to and from mantrips and no person should be permitted to get on or off a moving mantrip.

(i) [Reserved]

(j) Mantrips should not be permitted to proceed until the operator of the mantrip is assured that he has a clear road.

(k) Supplies or tools, except small hand tools or instruments, should not be transported with men.

(l) At places where men enter or leave mantrip conveyances, ample clearance should be provided and provisions made to prevent persons from coming in contact with energized electric circuits.

(m) The mine car next to a trolley locomotive should not be used to transport men. Such cars may be used to transport small tools and supplies. This is not to be construed as permitting the transportation of large or bulky supplies such as shuttle car wheel units, or similar material.

(n) Drop-bottom cars used to transport men should have the bottoms secured with an additional locking device.

(o) Extraneous materials or supplies should not be transported on top of equipment; however, materials and supplies that are necessary for or related to the operation of such equipment may be transported on top of such equipment if a hazard is not introduced.

[35 FR 17890, Nov. 20, 1970, as amended at 53 FR 46786, Nov. 18, 1988]

§ 75.1403-8 Criteria—Track haulage roads.

(a) The speed at which haulage equipment is operated should be determined by the condition of the roadbed, rails, rail joints, switches, frogs, and other elements of the track and the type and condition of the haulage equipment.

(b) Track haulage roads should have a continuous clearance on one side of at least 24 inches from the farthest projection of normal traffic. Where it is necessary to change the side on which clearance is provided, 24 inches of clearance should be provided on both sides for a distance of not less than 100 feet and warning signs should be posted at such locations.

(c) Track haulage roads developed after March 30, 1970, should have clearance on the "tight" side of at least 12 inches from the farthest projection of normal traffic. A minimum clearance of 6 inches should be maintained on the "tight" side of all track haulage roads developed prior to March 30, 1970.

(d) The clearance space on all track haulage roads should be kept free of loose rock, supplies, and other loose materials.

(e) Positive stopblocks or derails should be installed on all tracks near the top and at landings of shafts, slopes, and surface inclines.

Mine Safety and Health Admin., Labor

§ 75.1403-9 Criteria—Shelter holes.

(a) Shelter holes should be provided on track haulage roads at intervals of not more than 105 feet unless otherwise approved by the Coal Mine Safety District Manager(s).

(b) Shelter holes should be readily accessible and should be at least 5 feet in depth, not more than 4 feet in width (except crosscuts used as shelter holes) and at least the height of the coal seam where the coal seam is less than 6 feet high and at least 6 feet in height where the coal seam is 6 feet or more in height.

(c) Shelter holes should be kept free of refuse and other obstructions. Crosscuts used as shelter holes should be kept free of refuse or other materials to a depth of at least 15 feet.

(d) Shelter holes should be provided at all manually operated doors and at switch throws except: (1) At room switches, or (2) at switches where more than 6 feet of side clearance is provided. The Coal Mine Safety District Manager(s) may permit exemption of this requirement if such shelter holes create a hazardous roof condition.

(e) At each underground slope landing where men pass and cars are handled, a shelter hole at least 10 feet in depth, 4 feet in width, and 6 feet in height should be provided.

§ 75.1403-10 Criteria—Haulage; general.

(a) A permissible trip light or other approved device such as reflectors, approved by the Coal Mine Safety District Manager(s), should be used on the rear of trips pulled, on the front of trips pushed and on trips lowered in slopes. However, trip lights or other approved devices need not be used on cars being shifted to and from loading machines, on cars being handled at loading heads, during gathering operations at working faces, when trailing locomotives are used, or on trips pulled by animals.

(b) Cars on main haulage roads should not be pushed, except where necessary to push cars from side tracks located near the working section to the producing entries and rooms, where necessary to clear switches and sidetracks, and on the approach to cages, slopes, and surface inclines.

(c) Warning lights or reflective signs or tapes should be installed along haulage roads at locations of abrupt or sudden changes in the overhead clearance.

(d) No person, other than the motorman and brakeman, should ride on a locomotive unless authorized by the mine foreman, and then only when safe riding facilities are provided. No person should ride on any loaded car or on the bumper of any car. However, the brakeman may ride on the rear bumper of the last car of a slow moving trip pulled by a locomotive.

(e) Positive-acting stopblocks or derails should be used where necessary to protect persons from danger of runaway haulage equipment.

(f) An audible warning should be given by the operator of all self-propelled equipment including off-track equipment, where persons may be endangered by the movement of the equipment.

(g) Locomotives and personnel carriers should not approach to within 300 feet of preceding haulage equipment, except trailing locomotives that are an integral part of the trip.

(h) A total of at least 36 inches of unobstructed side clearance (both sides combined) should be provided for all rubber-tired haulage equipment where such equipment is used.

(i) Off-track haulage roadways should be maintained as free as practicable from bottom irregularities, debris, and wet or muddy conditions that affect the control of the equipment.

(j) Operators of self-propelled equipment should face in the direction of travel.

(k) Mechanical steering and control devices should be maintained so as to provide positive control at all times.

(l) All self-propelled rubber-tired haulage equipment should be equipped with well maintained brakes, lights, and a warning device.

(m) On and after March 30, 1971, all tram control switches on rubber-tired equipment should be designed to provide automatic return to the stop or off position when released.

§ 75.1403-11 Criteria—Entrances to shafts and slopes.

All open entrances to shafts should be equipped with safety gates at the

§ 75.1404

top and at each landing. Such gates should be self-closing and should be kept closed except when the cage is at such landing.

§ 75.1404 Automatic brakes; speed reduction gear.

[STATUTORY PROVISIONS]

Each locomotive and haulage car used in an underground coal mine shall be equipped with automatic brakes, where space permits. Where space does not permit automatic brakes, locomotives and haulage cars shall be subject to speed reduction gear, or other similar devices approved by the Secretary, which are designed to stop the locomotives and haulage cars with the proper margin of safety.

§ 75.1404–1 Braking system.

A locomotive equipped with a dual braking system will be deemed to satisfy the requirements of § 75.1404 for a train comprised of such locomotive and haulage cars, provided the locomotive is operated within the limits of its design capabilities and at speeds consistent with the condition of the haulage road. A trailing locomotive or equivalent devices should be used on trains that are operated on ascending grades.

§ 75.1405 Automatic couplers.

[STATUTORY PROVISIONS]

All haulage equipment acquired by an operator of a coal mine on or after March 30, 1971, shall be equipped with automatic couplers which couple by impact and uncouple without the necessity of persons going between the ends of such equipment. All haulage equipment without automatic couplers in use in a mine on March 30, 1970, shall also be so equipped within 4 years after March 30, 1970.

§ 75.1405–1 Automatic couplers, haulage equipment.

The requirement of § 75.1405 with respect to automatic couplers applies only to track haulage cars which are regularly coupled and uncoupled.

WIRE ROPES

SOURCE: Sections 75.1429 through 75.1438 appear at 48 FR 53239, Nov. 25, 1983, unless otherwise noted.

§ 75.1429 Guide ropes.

If guide ropes are used in shafts for personnel hoisting applications other than shaft development, the nominal strength (manufacturer's published catalog strength) of the guide rope at installation shall meet the minimum value calculated as follows: Minimum value = Static Load × 5.0.

§ 75.1430 Wire ropes; scope.

(a) Sections 75.1430 through 75.1438 apply to wire ropes in service used to hoist—

(1) Persons in shafts or slopes underground; or

(2) Loads in shaft or slope development when persons work below the suspended loads.

(b) These standards do not apply to wire ropes used for elevators.

§ 75.1431 Minimum rope strength.

At installation, the nominal strength (manufacturer's published catalog strength) of wire ropes used for hoisting shall meet the minimum rope strength values obtained by the following formulas in which "L" equals the maximum suspended rope length in feet:

(a) *Winding drum ropes* (all constructions, including rotation resistant).

For rope lengths less than 3,000 feet:
  Minimum Value = Static Load × (7.0 − 0.001L)
For rope lengths 3,000 feet or greater:
  Minimum Value = Static Load × 4.0

(b) *Friction drum ropes.*

For rope lengths less than 4,000 feet:
  Minimum Value = Static Load × (7.0 − 0.0005L)
For rope lengths 4,000 feet or greater:
  Minimum Value = Static Load × 5.0

(c) *Tail ropes* (balance ropes).

Minimum Value = Weight of Rope × 7.0

[48 FR 53239, Nov. 25, 1983; 48 FR 54975, Dec. 8, 1983]

§ 75.1432 Initial measurement.

After initial rope stretch but before visible wear occurs, the rope diameter of newly installed wire ropes shall be measured at least once in every third interval of active length and the measurements averaged to establish a baseline for subsequent measurements. A record of the measurements and the date shall be made by the person taking the measurements. This record shall be retained until the rope is retired from service.

[48 FR 53239, Nov. 25, 1983, as amended at 60 FR 33723, June 29, 1995]

§ 75.1433 Examinations.

(a) At least once every fourteen calendar days, each wire rope in service shall be visually examined along its entire active length for visible structural damage, corrosion, and improper lubrication or dressing. In addition, visual examination for wear and broken wires shall be made at stress points, including the area near attachments, where the rope rests on sheaves, where the rope leaves the drum, at drum crossovers, and at change-of-layer regions. When any visible condition that results in a reduction of rope strength is present, the affected portion of the rope shall be examined on a daily basis.

(b) Before any person is hoisted with a newly installed wire rope or any wire rope that has not been examined in the previous fourteen calendar days, the wire rope shall be examined in accordance with paragraph (a) of this section.

(c) At least once every six months, nondestructive tests shall be conducted of the active length of the rope, or rope diameter measurements shall be made—

(1) Wherever wear is evident;

(2) Where the hoist rope rests on sheaves at regular stopping points;

(3) Where the hoist rope leaves the drum at regular stopping points; and

(4) At drum crossover and change-of-layer regions.

(d) At the completion of each examination required by paragraph (a) of this section, the person making the examination shall certify, by signature and date, that the examination has been made. If any condition listed in paragraph (a) of this standard is present, the person conducting the examination shall make a record of the condition and the date. Certifications and records of examinations shall be retained for one year.

(e) The person making the measurements or nondestructive tests as required by paragraph (c) of this section shall record the measurements or test results and the date. This record shall be retained until the rope is retired from service.

[48 FR 53239, Nov. 25, 1983, as amended at 60 FR 33723, June 29, 1995]

§ 75.1434 Retirement criteria.

Unless damage or deterioration is removed by cutoff, wire ropes shall be removed from service when any of the following conditions occurs:

(a) The number of broken wires within a rope lay length, excluding filler wires, exceeds either—

(1) Five percent of the total number of wires; or

(2) Fifteen percent of the total number of wires within any strand;

(b) On a regular lay rope, more than one broken wire in the valley between strands in one rope lay length;

(c) A loss of more than one-third of the original diameter of the outer wires;

(d) Rope deterioration from corrosion;

(e) Distortion of the rope structure;

(f) Heat damage from any source;

(g) Diameter reduction due to wear that exceeds six percent of the baseline diameter measurement; or

(h) Loss of more than ten percent of rope strength as determined by nondestructive testing.

§ 75.1435 Load end attachments.

(a) Wire rope shall be attached to the load by a method that develops at least 80 percent of the nominal strength of the rope.

(b) Except for terminations where use of other materials is a design feature, zinc (spelter) shall be used for socketing wire ropes. Design feature means either the manufacturer's original design or a design approved by a registered professional engineer.

(c) Load end attachment methods using splices are prohibited.

§ 75.1436 Drum end attachment.

(a) For drum end attachment, wire rope shall be attached—

§ 75.1437

(1) Securely by clips after making one full turn around the drum spoke;

(2) Securely by clips after making one full turn around the shaft, if the drum is fixed to the shaft; or

(3) By properly assembled anchor bolts, clamps, or wedges, provided that the attachment is a design feature of the hoist drum. Design feature means either the manufacturer's original design or a design approved by a registered professional engineer.

(b) A minimum of three full turns of wire rope shall be on the drum when the rope is extended to its maximum working length.

§ 75.1437 End attachment retermination.

Damaged or deteriorated wire rope shall be removed by cutoff and the rope reterminated where there is—

(a) More than one broken wire at an attachment;

(b) Improper installation of an attachment;

(c) Slippage at an attachment; or

(d) Evidence of deterioration from corrosion at an attachment.

§ 75.1438 End attachment replacement.

Wire rope attachments shall be replaced when cracked, deformed, or excessively worn.

Subpart P—Mine Emergencies

§ 75.1500 [Reserved]

§ 75.1501 Emergency evacuations.

(a) For each shift that miners work underground, there shall be in attendance a responsible person designated by the mine operator to take charge during mine emergencies involving a fire, explosion, or gas or water inundation.

(1) The responsible person shall have current knowledge of the assigned location and expected movements of miners underground, the operation of the mine ventilation system, the locations of the mine escapeways and refuge alternatives, the mine communications system, any mine monitoring system if used, locations of firefighting equipment, the mine's Emergency Response Plan, the Mine Rescue Notification Plan, and the Mine Emergency Evacuation and Firefighting Program of Instruction.

(2) The responsible person shall be trained annually in a course of instruction in mine emergency response, as prescribed by MSHA's Office of Educational Policy and Development. The course will include topics such as the following:

(i) Organizing a command center;

(ii) Coordinating firefighting personnel;

(iii) Deploying firefighting equipment;

(iv) Coordinating mine rescue personnel;

(v) Establishing fresh air base;

(vi) Deploying mine rescue teams;

(vii) Providing for mine gas sampling and analysis;

(viii) Establishing security;

(ix) Initiating an emergency mine evacuation;

(x) Contacting emergency personnel; and

(xi) Communicating appropriate information related to the emergency.

(3) The operator shall certify by signature and date after each responsible person has completed the training and keep the certification at the mine for 1 year.

(b) The responsible person shall initiate and conduct an immediate mine evacuation when there is a mine emergency which presents an imminent danger to miners due to fire or explosion or gas or water inundation. Only properly trained and equipped persons essential to respond to the mine emergency may remain underground.

(c) The mine operator shall instruct all miners of the identity of the responsible person designated by the operator for their workshift. The mine operator shall instruct miners of any change in the identity of the responsible person before the start of their workshift.

(d) Nothing in this section shall be construed to restrict the ability of other persons in the mine to warn of an imminent danger which warrants evacuation.

[68 FR 53049, Sept. 9, 2003, as amended at 73 FR 7655, Feb. 8, 2008; 73 FR 80697, Dec. 31, 2008]

§ 75.1502 Mine emergency evacuation and firefighting program of instruction.

Each operator of an underground coal mine shall adopt and follow a mine emergency evacuation and firefighting program that instructs all miners in the proper procedures they must follow if a mine emergency occurs.

(a) *Program approval.* The operator shall submit this program of instruction, and any revisions, for approval to the District Manager of the Coal Mine Safety and Health district in which the mine is located. Within 30 days of approval, the operator shall conduct training in accordance with the revised program.

(b) *New or revised provisions.* Before implementing any new or revised approved provision in the program of instruction, the operator shall instruct miners in the change.

(c) *Instruction plan.* The approved program shall include a specific plan designed to instruct miners on all shifts on the following:

(1) Procedures for—

(i) Evacuating the mine for mine emergencies that present an imminent danger to miners due to fire, explosion, or gas or water inundation;

(ii) Evacuating all miners not required for a mine emergency response; and

(iii) The rapid assembly and transportation of necessary miners, fire suppression equipment, and rescue apparatus to the scene of the mine emergency.

(2) The use, care, and maintenance of self-rescue devices, including hands-on training in the complete donning and transferring of all types of self-rescue devices used at the mine.

(3) The deployment, use, and maintenance of refuge alternatives.

(4) Scenarios requiring a discussion of options and a decision as to the best option for evacuation under each of the various mine emergencies (fires, explosions, or gas or water inundations). These options shall include:

(i) Encountering conditions in the mine or circumstances that require immediate donning of self-rescue devices.

(ii) Using continuous directional lifelines or equivalent devices, tethers, and doors;

(iii) Traversing undercasts or overcasts;

(iv) Switching escapeways, as applicable;

(v) Negotiating any other unique escapeway conditions; and

(vi) Using refuge alternatives.

(5) Location and use of the fire suppression and firefighting equipment and materials available in the mine.

(6) Location of the escapeways, exits, routes of travel to the surface, including the location of continuous directional lifelines or equivalent devices.

(7) Location, quantity, types, and use of stored SCSRs, as applicable.

(8) A review of the mine map; the escapeway system; the escape, firefighting, and emergency evacuation plan in effect at the mine; and the locations of refuge alternatives and abandoned areas.

(9) A description of how miners will receive annual expectations training that includes practical experience in donning and transferring SCSRs in smoke, simulated smoke, or an equivalent environment and breathing through a realistic SCSR training unit or device that provides the sensation of SCSR airflow resistance and heat.

(10) A summary of the procedures related to deploying refuge alternatives.

(11) A summary of the construction methods for 15 psi stoppings constructed prior to an event.

(12) A summary of the procedures related to refuge alternative use.

(d) *Instructors.* (1) The mine operator shall designate a person who has the ability, training, knowledge, or experience to conduct the mine emergency evacuation instruction and drills in his or her area of expertise.

(2) Persons conducting SCSR donning and transferring training shall be able to effectively train and evaluate whether miners can successfully don the SCSR and transfer to additional SCSR devices.

[71 FR 71452, Dec. 8, 2006, as amended at 73 FR 80697, Dec. 31, 2008]

§ 75.1503 Use of fire suppression equipment.

In addition to the approved program of instruction required by 30 CFR

§ 75.1504

75.1502, each operator of an underground coal mine shall ensure the following.

(a) *Working section.* At least two miners in each working section on each production shift shall be proficient in the use of all fire suppression equipment available on such working section, and know the location of such fire suppression equipment.

(b) *Attended equipment.* Each operator of attended equipment specified in 30 CFR 75.1107–1(c)(1), and each miner assigned to perform job duties at the job site in the direct line of sight of attended equipment as described in 30 CFR 75.1107–1(c)(2), shall be proficient in the use of fire suppression devices installed on such attended equipment.

(c) *Maintenance shift.* The shift foreman and at least one miner for every five miners working underground on a maintenance shift shall be proficient in the use of fire suppression equipment available in the mine, and know the location of such fire suppression equipment.

[71 FR 71452, Dec. 8, 2006]

§ 75.1504 Mine emergency evacuation training and drills.

Each operator of an underground coal mine shall conduct mine emergency evacuation training and drills and require all miners to participate.

(a) *Schedule of training and drills.* Each miner shall participate in a mine emergency evacuation training and drill once each quarter. Quarters shall be based on a calendar year (Jan–Mar, Apr–Jun, Jul–Sep, Oct–Dec). In addition—

(1) A newly hired miner, who has not participated in a mine emergency evacuation training and drill at the mine within the previous 3 months, shall participate in the next applicable mine emergency evacuation training and drill.

(2) Prior to assuming duties on a section or outby work location, a foreman shall travel both escapeways in their entirety.

(b) *Content of quarterly training and drill.* Each quarterly evacuation training and drill shall include the following:

(1) Hands-on training on all types of self-rescue devices used at the mine, which includes—

(i) Instruction and demonstration in the use, care, and maintenance of self-rescue devices;

(ii) The complete donning of the SCSR by assuming a donning position, opening the device, activating the device, inserting the mouthpiece, and putting on the nose clip; and

(iii) Transferring between all applicable self-rescue devices.

(2) Training that emphasizes the importance of—

(i) Recognizing when the SCSR is not functioning properly and demonstrating how to initiate and reinitiate the starting sequence;

(ii) Not removing the mouthpiece, even to communicate, until the miner reaches fresh air; and

(iii) Proper use of the SCSR by controlling breathing and physical exertion.

(3) A realistic escapeway drill that is initiated and conducted with a different approved scenario each quarter and during which each miner—

(i) Travels the primary or alternate escapeway in its entirety, alternating escapeways each quarter;

(ii) Physically locates and practices using the continuous directional lifelines or equivalent devices and tethers, and physically locates the stored SCSRs and refuge alternatives;

(iii) Traverses undercasts or overcasts and doors;

(iv) Switches escapeways, as applicable; and

(v) Negotiates any other unique escapeway conditions.

(4) A review of the mine and escapeway maps, the firefighting plan, and the mine emergency evacuation plan in effect at the mine, which shall include:

(i) Informing miners of the locations of fire doors, check curtains, changes in the routes of travel, and plans for diverting smoke from escapeways.

(ii) Locating escapeways, exits, routes of travel to the surface, abandoned areas, and refuge alternatives.

(5) Operation of the fire suppression equipment available in the mine and the location and use of firefighting equipment and materials.

(6) Reviewing the procedures for deploying refuge alternatives and components.

(7) For miners who will be constructing the 15 psi stoppings prior to an event, reviewing the procedures for constructing them.

(8) Reviewing the procedures for use of the refuge alternatives and components.

(9) Task training in proper transportation of the refuge alternatives and components.

(c) *Annual expectations training.* Over the course of each year, each miner shall participate in expectations training that includes the following:

(1) Donning and transferring SCSRs in smoke, simulated smoke, or an equivalent environment.

(2) Breathing through a realistic SCSR training unit that provides the sensation of SCSR airflow resistance and heat.

(3) Deployment and use of refuge alternatives similar to those in use at the mine, including—

(i) Deployment and operation of component systems; and

(ii) Instruction on when to use refuge alternatives during a mine emergency, emphasizing that it is the last resort when escape is impossible.

(4) A miner shall participate in expectations training within one quarter of being employed at the mine.

(d) *Certification of training and drills.* At the completion of each training or drill required in this section, the operator shall certify by signature and date that the training or drill was held in accordance with the requirements of this section.

(1) This certification shall include the names of the miners participating in the training or drill. For each miner, this certification shall list the content of the training or drill component completed, including the escapeway traveled and scenario used, as required in paragraphs (b) and (c) of this section.

(2) Certifications shall be kept at the mine for one year.

(3) Upon request, the certifications shall be made available to an authorized representative of the Secretary and the representative of the miners.

(4) Upon request, a copy of the certification that shows his or her own training shall be provided to the participating miner.

[71 FR 71452, Dec. 8, 2006, as amended at 73 FR 80698, Dec. 31, 2008]

§ 75.1505 Escapeway maps.

(a) *Content and accessibility.* An escapeway map shall show the designated escapeways from the working sections or the miners' work stations to the surface or the exits at the bottom of the shaft or slope, refuge alternatives, and SCSR storage locations. The escapeway map shall be posted or readily accessible for all miners—

(1) In each working section;

(2) In each area where mechanized mining equipment is being installed or removed;

(3) At the refuge alternative; and

(4) At a surface location of the mine where miners congregate, such as at the mine bulletin board, bathhouse, or waiting room.

(b) *Keeping maps current.* All maps shall be kept up-to-date and any change in route of travel, location of doors, location of refuge alternatives, or direction of airflow shall be shown on the maps by the end of the shift on which the change is made.

(c) *Informing affected miners.* Miners underground on a shift when any such change is made shall be notified immediately of the change and other affected miners shall be informed of the change before entering the underground areas of the mine.

[71 FR 71452, Dec. 8, 2006, as amended at 73 FR 80698, Dec. 31, 2008]

§ 75.1506 Refuge alternatives.

(a) Each operator shall provide refuge alternatives and components as follows:

(1) Prefabricated self-contained units, including the structural, breathable air, air monitoring, and harmful gas removal components of the unit, shall be approved under 30 CFR part 7; and

(2) The structural components of units consisting of 15 psi stoppings constructed prior to an event shall be approved by the District Manager, and the breathable air, air monitoring, and harmful gas removal components of

§ 75.1506

these units shall be approved under 30 CFR part 7.

(3) Prefabricated refuge alternative structures that states have approved and those that MSHA has accepted in approved Emergency Response Plans (ERPs) that are in service prior to March 2, 2009 are permitted until December 31, 2018, or until replaced, whichever comes first. Breathable air, air-monitoring, and harmful gas removal components of either a prefabricated self-contained unit or a unit consisting of 15 psi stoppings constructed prior to an event in a secure space and an isolated atmosphere that states have approved and those that MSHA has accepted in approved ERPs that are in use prior to March 2, 2009 are permitted until December 31, 2013, or until replaced, whichever comes first. Refuge alternatives consisting of materials pre-positioned for miners to deploy in a secure space with an isolated atmosphere that MSHA has accepted in approved ERPs that are in use prior to March 2, 2009 are permitted until December 31, 2010, or until replaced, whichever comes first.

(b) Except as permitted under paragraph (a)(3) of this section, each operator shall provide refuge alternatives with sufficient capacity to accommodate all persons working underground.

(1) Refuge alternatives shall provide at least 15 square feet of floor space per person and 30 to 60 cubic feet of volume per person according to the following chart. The airlock can be included in the space and volume if waste is disposed outside the refuge alternative.

Mining height (inches)	Unrestricted volume (cubic feet) per person*
36 or less	30
>36–≤42	37.5
>42–≤48	45
>48–≤54	52.5
>54	60

*Includes an adjustment of 12 inches for clearances.

(2) Refuge alternatives for working sections shall accommodate the maximum number of persons that can be expected on or near the section at any time.

(3) Each refuge alternative for outby areas shall accommodate persons reasonably expected to use it.

(c) Refuge alternatives shall be provided at the following locations:

(1) Within 1,000 feet from the nearest working face and from locations where mechanized mining equipment is being installed or removed except that for underground anthracite coal mines that have no electrical face equipment, refuge alternatives shall be provided if the nearest working face is greater than 2,000 feet from the surface.

(2) Spaced within one-hour travel distances in outby areas where persons work such that persons in outby areas are never more than a 30-minute travel distance from a refuge alternative or safe exit. However, the operator may request and the District Manager may approve a different location in the ERP. The operator's request shall be based on an assessment of the risk to persons in outby areas, considering the following factors: proximity to seals; proximity to potential fire or ignition sources; conditions in the outby areas; location of stored SCSRs; and proximity to the most direct, safe, and practical route to an intake escapeway.

(d) Roof and rib support for refuge alternative locations shall be specified in the mine's roof control plan.

(e) The operator shall protect the refuge alternative and contents from damage during transportation, installation, and storage.

(f) A refuge alternative shall be removed from service if examination reveals damage that interferes with the functioning of the refuge alternative or any component.

(1) If a refuge alternative is removed from service, the operator shall withdraw all persons from the area serviced by the refuge alternative, except those persons referred to in §104(c) of the Mine Act.

(2) Refuge alternative components removed from service shall be replaced or be repaired for return to service in accordance with the manufacturer's specifications.

(g) At all times, the site and area around the refuge alternative shall be kept clear of machinery, materials, and obstructions that could interfere with the deployment or use of the refuge alternative.

(h) Each refuge alternative shall be conspicuously identified with a sign or marker as follows:

Mine Safety and Health Admin., Labor § 75.1507

(1) A sign or marker made of a reflective material with the word "REFUGE" shall be posted conspicuously at each refuge alternative.

(2) Directional signs made of a reflective material shall be posted leading to each refuge alternative location.

(i) During use of the refuge alternative, the atmosphere within the refuge alternative shall be monitored. Changes or adjustments shall be made to reduce the concentration of methane to less than 1 percent; to reduce the concentration of carbon dioxide to 1 percent or less and excursions not exceeding 2.5 percent; and to reduce the concentration of carbon monoxide to 25 ppm or less. Oxygen shall be maintained at 18.5 to 23 percent.

(j) Refuge alternatives shall contain a fire extinguisher that—

(1) Meets the requirements for portable fire extinguishers used in underground coal mines under this part;

(2) Is appropriate for extinguishing fires involving the chemicals used for harmful gas removal; and

(3) Uses a low-toxicity extinguishing agent that does not produce a hazardous by-product when activated.

[73 FR 80698, Dec. 31, 2008]

§ 75.1507 Emergency Response Plan; refuge alternatives.

(a) The Emergency Response Plan (ERP) shall include the following for each refuge alternative and component:

(1) The types of refuge alternatives used in the mine, *i.e.*, a prefabricated self-contained unit or a unit consisting of 15 psi stoppings constructed prior to an event in a secure space and an isolated atmosphere.

(2) Procedures or methods for maintaining approved refuge alternatives and components.

(3) The rated capacity of each refuge alternative, the number of persons expected to use each refuge alternative, and the duration of breathable air provided per person by the approved breathable air component of each refuge alternative.

(4) The methods for providing breathable air with sufficient detail of the component's capability to provide breathable air over the duration stated in the approval.

(5) The methods for providing ready backup oxygen controls and regulators.

(6) The methods for providing an airlock and for providing breathable air in the airlock, except where adequate positive pressure is maintained.

(7) The methods for providing sanitation facilities.

(8) The methods for harmful gas removal, if necessary.

(9) The methods for monitoring gas concentrations, including charging and calibration of equipment.

(10) The method for providing lighting sufficient for persons to perform tasks.

(11) Suitable locations for the refuge alternatives and an affirmative statement that the locations are—

(i) Not within direct line of sight of the working face; and

(ii) Where feasible, not placed in areas directly across from, nor closer than 500 feet radially from, belt drives, take-ups, transfer points, air compressors, explosive magazines, seals, entrances to abandoned areas, and fuel, oil, or other flammable or combustible material storage. However, the operator may request and the District Manager may approve an alternative location in the ERP if mining involves two-entry systems or yield pillars in a longwall that would prohibit locating the refuge alternative out of direct line of sight of the working face.

(12) The maximum mine air temperature at each of the locations where refuge alternatives are to be placed.

(b) For a refuge alternative consisting of 15 psi stoppings constructed prior to an event in a secure space and an isolated atmosphere, the ERP shall specify that—

(1) The breathable air components shall be approved by MSHA; and

(2) The refuge alternative can withstand exposure to a flash fire of 300 degrees Fahrenheit (°F) for 3 seconds and a pressure wave of 15 pounds per square inch (psi) overpressure for 0.2 seconds.

(c) If the refuge alternative sustains persons for only 48 hours, the ERP shall detail advanced arrangements that have been made to assure that persons who cannot be rescued within

§ 75.1508

48 hours will receive additional supplies to sustain them until rescue. Advance arrangements shall include the following:

(1) Pre-surveyed areas for refuge alternatives with closure errors of less than 20,000:1.

(2) An analysis to demonstrate that the surface terrain, the strata, the capabilities of the drill rig, and all other factors that could affect drilling are such that a hole sufficient to provide required supplies and materials reliably can be promptly drilled within 48 hours of an accident at a mine.

(3) Permissions to cross properties, build roads, and construct drill sites.

(4) Arrangement with a drilling contractor or other supplier of drilling services to provide a suitable drilling rig, personnel and support so that a hole can be completed to the refuge alternative within 48 hours.

(5) Capability to promptly transport a drill rig to a pre-surveyed location such that a drilled hole would be completed and located near a refuge alternative structure within 48 hours of an accident at a mine.

(6) The specifications of pipes, air lines, and approved fans or approved compressors that will be used.

(7) A method for assuring that within 48 hours, breathable air shall be provided.

(8) A method for assuring the immediate availability of a backup source for supplying breathable air and a backup power source for surface installations.

(d) The ERP shall specify that the refuge alternative is stocked with the following:

(1) A minimum of 2,000 calories of food and 2.25 quarts of potable water per person per day in approved containers sufficient to sustain the maximum number of persons reasonably expected to use the refuge alternative for at least 96 hours, or for 48 hours if advance arrangements are made under paragraph (c) of this section;

(2) A manual that contains sufficient detail for each refuge alternative or component addressing in-mine transportation, operation, and maintenance of the unit;

(3) Sufficient quantities of materials and tools to repair components; and

(4) First aid supplies.

[73 FR 80699, Dec. 31, 2008]

§ 75.1508 Training and records for examination, maintenance and repair of refuge alternatives and components.

(a) Persons examining, maintaining, or repairing refuge alternatives and components shall be instructed in how to perform this work.

(1) The operator shall assure that all persons assigned to examine, maintain, and repair refuge alternatives and components are trained.

(2) The mine operator shall certify, by signature and date, the training of persons who examine, maintain, and repair refuge alternatives and components.

(b) At the completion of each repair, the person conducting the maintenance or repair shall make a record of all corrective action taken.

(c) Training certifications and repair records shall be kept at the mine for one year.

[73 FR 80699, Dec. 31, 2008]

Subpart Q—Communications

§ 75.1600 Communications.

[STATUTORY PROVISIONS]

Telephone service or equivalent two-way communication facilities, approved by the Secretary or his authorized representative, shall be provided between the surface and each landing of main shafts and slopes and between the surface and each working section of any coal mine that is more than 100 feet from a portal.

§ 75.1600-1 Communication facilities; main portals; installation requirements.

A telephone or equivalent two-way communication facility shall be located on the surface within 500 feet of all main portals, and shall be installed either in a building or in a box-like structure designed to protect the facilities from damage by inclement weather. At least one of these communication facilities shall be at a location where a responsible person who is always on duty when men are underground can hear the facility and respond immediately in the event of an emergency.

[38 FR 29999, Oct. 31, 1973]

§ 75.1600-2 Communication facilities; working sections; installation and maintenance requirements; audible or visual alarms.

(a) Telephones or equivalent two-way communication facilities provided at each working section shall be located not more than 500 feet outby the last open crosscut and not more than 800 feet from the farthest point of penetration of the working places on such section.

(b) The incoming communication signal shall activate an audible alarm, distinguishable from the surrounding noise level, or a visual alarm that can be seen by a miner regularly employed on the working section.

(c) If a communication system other than telephones is used and its operation depends entirely upon power from the mine electric system, means shall be provided to permit continued communication in the event the mine electric power fails or is cut off; provided, however, that where trolley phones and telephones are both used, an alternate source of power for the trolley phone system is not required.

(d) Trolley phones connected to the trolley wire shall be grounded in accordance with Subpart H of this part.

(e) Telephones or equivalent two-way communication facilities shall be maintained in good operating condition at all times. In the event of any failure in the system that results in loss of communication, repairs shall be started immediately, and the system restored to operating condition as soon as possible.

[38 FR 29999, Oct. 31, 1973]

§ 75.1600-3 Communications facilities; refuge alternatives.

(a) Refuge alternatives shall be provided with a communications system that consists of—

(1) A two-way communication facility that is a part of the mine communication system, which can be used from inside the refuge alternative; and

(2) An additional communication system and other requirements as defined in the communications portion of the operator's approved Emergency Response Plan.

[73 FR 80700, Dec. 31, 2008]

Subpart R—Miscellaneous

§ 75.1700 Oil and gas wells.

[STATUTORY PROVISIONS]

Each operator of a coal mine shall take reasonable measures to locate oil and gas wells penetrating coalbeds or any underground area of a coal mine. When located, such operator shall establish and maintain barriers around such oil and gas wells in accordance with State laws and regulations, except that such barriers shall not be less than 300 feet in diameter, unless the Secretary or his authorized representative permits a lesser barrier consistent with the applicable State laws and regulations where such lesser barrier will be adequate to protect against hazards from such wells to the miners in such mine, or unless the Secretary or his authorized representative requires a greater barrier where the depth of the mine, other geologic conditions, or other factors warrant such a greater barrier.

§ 75.1702 Smoking; prohibition.

[STATUTORY PROVISIONS]

No person shall smoke, carry smoking materials, matches, or lighters underground, or smoke in or around oil houses, explosives magazines, or other surface areas where such practice may cause a fire or explosion. The operator shall institute a program, approved by the Secretary, to insure that any person entering the underground area of the mine does not carry smoking materials, matches, or lighters.

[35 FR 17890, Nov. 20, 1970, as amended at 60 FR 33723, June 29, 1995]

§ 75.1702-1 Smoking programs.

Programs required under § 75.1702 shall be submitted to the Coal Mine Safety District Manager for approval on or before May 30, 1970.

§ 75.1703 Portable electric lamps.

[STATUTORY PROVISIONS]

Persons underground shall use only permissible electric lamps approved by the Secretary for portable illumination. No open flame shall be permitted in the underground area of any coal mine, except as permitted under § 75.1106.

§ 75.1703-1 Permissible lamps.

Lamps approved by the Bureau of Mines or the Mine Safety and Health Administration under Part 19 or Part 20 of this chapter (Bureau of Mines Schedule 6D and Schedule 10C) are approved lamps for the purposes of § 75.1703.

§ 75.1707-1 New working section.

The term "new working section" as used in § 75.1707 means any extension of the belt or trolley haulage system in main, cross, and room entries necessary for the development of the mine on and after March 30, 1970. Room entries being developed as of March 30, 1970, with certified stop line limitations as shown on the mine map and retreating panels shall not be considered as new working sections.

§ 75.1708 Surface structures, fireproofing.

[STATUTORY PROVISIONS]

After March 30, 1970, all structures erected on the surface within 100 feet of any mine opening shall be of fireproof construction. Unless structures existing on or prior to such date which are located within 100 feet of any mine opening are of such construction, fire doors shall be erected at effective points in mine openings to prevent smoke or fire from outside sources endangering miners underground. These doors shall be tested at least monthly to insure effective operation. A record of such tests shall be kept in an area on the surface of the mine chosen by the operator to minimize the danger of destruction by fire or other hazard and shall be available for inspection by interested persons.

§ 75.1708-1 Surface structures; fireproof construction.

Structures of fireproof construction is interpreted to mean structures with fireproof exterior surfaces.

§ 75.1709 Accumulations of methane and coal dust on surface coal-handling facilities.

[STATUTORY PROVISIONS]

Adequate measures shall be taken to prevent methane and coal dust from accumulating in excessive concentrations in or on surface coal-handling facilities, but in no event shall methane be permitted to accumulate in concentrations in or on surface coal-handling facilities in excess of limits established for methane by the Secretary on and after March 30, 1971. Where coal is dumped at or near air-intake openings, provisions shall be made to avoid dust from entering the mine.

§ 75.1710 Canopies or cabs; diesel-powered and electric face equipment.

In any coal mine where the height of the coalbed permits, an authorized representative of the Secretary may require that diesel-powered and electric face equipment, including shuttle cars, be provided with substantially constructed canopies or cabs to protect the miners operating such equipment from roof falls and from rib and face rolls.

[61 FR 55527, Oct. 25, 1996]

§ 75.1710-1 Canopies or cabs; self-propelled diesel-powered and electric face equipment; installation requirements.

(a) Except as provided in paragraph (f) of this section, all self-propelled diesel-powered and electric face equipment, including shuttle cars, which is employed in the active workings of each underground coal mine on and after January 1, 1973, shall, in accordance with the schedule of time specified in paragraphs (a) (1), (2), (3), (4), (5), and (6) of this section, be equipped with substantially constructed canopies or cabs, located and installed in such a manner that when the operator is at the operating controls of such equipment he shall be protected from falls of roof, face, or rib, or from rib

Mine Safety and Health Admin., Labor §75.1710-1

and face rolls. The requirements of this paragraph (a) shall be met as follows:

(1) On and after January 1, 1974, in coal mines having mining heights of 72 inches or more;

(2) On and after July 1, 1974, in coal mines having mining heights of 60 inches or more, but less than 72 inches;

(3) On and after January 1, 1975, in coal mines having mining heights of 48 inches or more, but less than 60 inches;

(4) On and after July 1, 1975, in coal mines having mining heights of 36 inches or more, but less than 48 inches;

(5)(i) On and after January 1, 1976, in coal mines having mining heights of 30 inches or more, but less than 36 inches,

(ii) On and after July 1, 1977, in coal mines having mining heights of 24 inches or more, but less than 30 inches, and

(6) On and after July 1, 1978, in coal mines having mining heights of less than 24 inches.

(b)(1) For purposes of this section, a canopy means a structure which provides overhead protection against falls of roof.

(2) For purposes of this section, a cab means a structure which provides overhead and lateral protection against falls of roof, rib, and face, or rib and face rolls.

(c) In determining whether to install substantially constructed canopies as opposed to substantially constructed cabs, the operator shall consider and take into account the following factors:

(1) The mining method used;

(2) Physical limitations, including but not limited to the dip of the coalbed, and roof, rib, and face conditions;

(3) Previous accident experience, if any, caused by falls of roof, rib, and face, or rib and face rolls;

(4) Overhead protection, such as that afforded by a substantially constructed canopy, against falls of roof will always be required; and

(5) Lateral protection, such as that afforded by a substantially constructed cab, may also be necessary where the occurrence of falls of rib and face, or rib and face rolls is likely.

(d) For purposes of this section, a canopy or cab will be considered to be substantially constructed if a registered engineer certifies that such canopy or cab has the minimum structural capacity to support elastically: (1) A dead weight load of 18,000 pounds, or (2) 15 p.s.i. distributed uniformly over the plan view area of the structure, whichever is lesser.

(e) Evidence of the certification required by paragraph (d) of this section shall be furnished by attaching a plate, label, or other appropriate marking to the canopy or cab for which certification has been made, stating that such canopy or cab meets the minimum requirements for structural capacity set forth in paragraph (d) of this section. Written evidence of such certification shall also be retained by the operator, and shall be made available to an authorized representative of the Secretary upon request. Written evidence of certification may consist of the report of the registered engineer who certified the canopy or cab, or of information from the manufacturer of the canopy or cab stating that a registered engineer has certified that the canopy or cab meets the minimum requirements for structural capacity set forth in paragraph (d) of this section.

(f) An operator may apply to the Director of Technical Support, Mine Safety and Health Administration, Department of Labor, 201 12th Street South, Arlington, VA 22202-5452, for approval of the installation of devices to be used in lieu of substantially constructed canopies or cabs on self-propelled diesel-powered and electric face equipment. The Director of Technical Support may approve such devices if he determines that the use thereof will afford the equipment operator no less than the same measure of protection from falls of roof, face, or rib, or from rib and face rolls as would a substantially constructed canopy or cab meeting the requirements of this section.

[37 FR 20690, Oct. 3, 1972, as amended at 41 FR 23200, June 9, 1976; 43 FR 12320, Mar. 24, 1978; 47 FR 28096, June 29, 1982; 61 FR 55527, Oct. 25, 1996; 67 FR 38386, June 4, 2002; 80 FR 52992, Sept. 2, 2015]

EFFECTIVE DATE NOTE: At 42 FR 34877, July 7, 1977, the dates appearing in paragraphs (a)(5)(ii) and (a)(6) of §75.1710-1 were suspended indefinitely, effective July 1, 1977.

§ 75.1711 Sealing of mines.

[STATUTORY PROVISIONS]

On or after March 30, 1970, the opening of any coal mine that is declared inactive by the operator, or is permanently closed, or abandoned for more than 90 days, shall be sealed by the operator in a manner prescribed by the Secretary. Openings of all other mines shall be adequately protected in a manner prescribed by the Secretary to prevent entrance by unauthorized persons.

§ 75.1711–1 Sealing of shaft openings.

Shaft openings required to be sealed under § 75.1711 shall be effectively capped or filled. Filling shall be for the entire depth of the shaft and, for the first 50 feet from the bottom of the coalbed, the fill shall consist of incombustible material. Caps consisting of a 6-inch thick concrete cap or other equivalent means may be used for sealing. Caps shall be equipped with a vent pipe at least 2 inches in diameter extending for a distance of at least 15 feet above the surface of the shaft.

§ 75.1711–2 Sealing of slope or drift openings.

Slope or drift openings required to be sealed under § 75.1711 shall be sealed with solid, substantial, incombustible material, such as concrete blocks, bricks or tile, or shall be completely filled with incombustible material for a distance of at least 25 feet into such openings.

§ 75.1711–3 Openings of active mines.

The openings of all mines not declared by the operator, to be inactive, permanently closed, or abandoned for less than 90 days shall be adequately fenced or posted with conspicuous signs prohibiting the entrance of unauthorized persons.

§ 75.1712 Bath houses and toilet facilities.

[STATUTORY PROVISIONS]

The Secretary may require any operator to provide adequate facilities for the miners to change from the clothes worn underground, to provide for the storing of such clothes from shift to shift, and to provide sanitary and bathing facilities. Sanitary toilet facilities shall be provided in the active workings of the mine when such surface facilities are not readily accessible to the active workings.

[35 FR 17890, Nov. 20, 1970, as amended at 60 FR 33723, June 29, 1995]

§ 75.1712–1 Availability of surface bathing facilities; change rooms; and sanitary facilities.

Except where a waiver has been granted pursuant to the provisions of § 75.1712–4, each operator of an underground coal mine shall on and after December 30, 1970, provide bathing facilities, clothing change rooms, and sanitary facilities, as hereinafter prescribed, for the use of the miners at the mine.

§ 75.1712–2 Location of surface facilities.

Bathhouses, change rooms, and sanitary toilet facilities shall be in a location convenient for the use of the miners. Where such facilities are designed to serve more than one mine, they shall be centrally located so as to be as convenient for the use of the miners in all the mines served by such facilities.

§ 75.1712–3 Minimum requirements of surface bathing facilities, change rooms, and sanitary toilet facilities.

(a) All bathing facilities, change rooms, and sanitary toilet facilities shall be provided with adequate light, heat, and ventilation so as to maintain a comfortable air temperature and to minimize the accumulation of moisture and odors, and such facilities shall be maintained in a clean and sanitary condition.

(b) Bathing facilities, change rooms, and sanitary toilet facilities shall be constructed and equipped so as to comply with applicable State and local building codes: *Provided, however*, That where no State or local building codes apply to such facilities, or where no State or local building codes exist, such facilities shall be constructed and equipped so as to meet the minimum construction requirements of the National Building Code; and the minimum plumbing requirements of the U.S.A. Standard Plumbing Code, ASA A40.8–1955.

(c) In addition to the minimum requirements specified in paragraphs (a) and (b) of this §75.1712-3, facilities maintained in accordance with §75.1712-1 shall include the following:

(1) *Bathing facilities.* (i) Showers shall be provided with both hot and cold water.

(ii) At least one shower head shall be provided where five or less miners use such showers.

(iii) Where five or more miners use such showers, sufficient showers shall be furnished to provide approximately one shower head for each five miners.

(iv) A suitable cleansing agent shall be provided for use at each shower.

(2) *Sanitary toilet facilities.* (i) At least one sanitary flush toilet shall be provided where 10 or less miners use such facilities.

(ii) Where 10 or more miners use such sanitary toilet facilities, sufficient toilets shall be furnished to provide approximately one sanitary flush toilet for each 10 miners.

(iii) Where 30 or more miners use sanitary toilet facilities, one urinal may be substituted for one sanitary flush toilet, however, where such substitutions are made they shall not reduce the number of toilets below a ratio of two toilets to one urinal.

(iv) An adequate supply of toilet paper shall be provided with each toilet.

(v) Adequate handwashing facilities or hand lavatories shall be provided in or adjacent to each toilet facility.

(3) *Change rooms.* (i) Individual clothes storage containers or lockers shall be provided for storage of miners clothing and other incidental personal belongings during and between shifts.

(ii) Change rooms shall be provided with ample space to permit the use of such facilities by all miners changing clothes prior to and after each shift.

§ 75.1712-4 Waiver of surface facilities requirements.

The Coal Mine Safety District Manager for the district in which the mine is located may, upon written application by the operator, waive any or all of the requirements of §§75.1712-1 through 75.1712-3 if he determines that the operator of the mine cannot or need not meet any part or all of such requirements, and, upon issuance of such waiver, he shall set forth the facilities which will not be required and the specific reason or reasons for such waiver.

[35 FR 17890, Nov. 20, 1970, as amended at 60 FR 33723, June 29, 1995]

§ 75.1712-5 Application for waiver of surface facilities.

Applications for waivers of the requirements of §§75.1712-1 through 75.1712-3 shall be filed with the Coal Mine Safety District Manager and shall contain the following information:

(a) The name and address of the mine operator;

(b) The name and location of the mine;

(c) A statement explaining why, in the opinion of the operator, the installation or maintenance of the facilities is impractical or unnecessary.

§ 75.1712-6 Underground sanitary facilities; installation and maintenance.

(a) Except as provided in §75.1712-7, each operator of an underground coal mine shall provide and maintain one sanitary toilet in a dry location under protected roof, within 500 feet of each working place in the mine where miners are regularly employed during the mining cycle. A single sanitary toilet may serve two or more working places in the same mine, if it is located within 500 feet of each such working place.

(b) Sanitary toilets shall have an attached toilet seat with a hinged lid and a toilet paper holder together with an adequate supply of toilet tissue, except that a toilet paper holder is not required for an unenclosed toilet facility.

(c) Only flush or nonflush chemical or biological toilets, sealed bag toilets, and vault toilets meet the requirements of this section. Privies and combustion or incinerating toilets are prohibited underground.

[68 FR 37087, June 23, 2003]

§ 75.1712-7 Underground sanitary facilities; waiver of requirements.

If it has been determined by the Coal Mine Safety District Manager for the district in which the mine is located that sanitary toilets cannot be provided and maintained within 500 feet of

§ 75.1712-8

a working place because of the thickness of the coal seam or because of any other physical restriction in the underground workings, he may, upon written application by the operator, waive the location requirements for underground sanitary facilities with respect to such working place.

§ 75.1712-8 Application for waiver of location requirements for underground sanitary facilities.

Applications for waivers of the location requirements of § 75.1712-6 shall be filed with the Coal Mine Safety District Manager and shall contain the following information:

(a) The name and address of the mine operator;

(b) The name and location of the mine;

(c) The thickness of the coal seam in each working place in the mine for which a waiver is requested; and

(d) Other physical restrictions in the mine (for example, poor roof conditions, excessive water, timbering, etc.).

If a sanitary toilet cannot be installed within 500 feet of a working place because of physical conditions other than the thickness of the coal seam, the operator shall also include a short statement specifying areas in the mine which could be considered possible alternative sites for installation of such facilities.

§ 75.1712-9 Issuance of waivers.

Following the receipt of an application submitted in accordance with the provisions of § 75.1712-8, the Coal Mine Safety District Manager shall, if he determines that the operator cannot meet the location requirements of § 75.1712-6 with respect to any or all of the working places in the mine because of the coal seam thickness or because of other physical restriction, issue a waiver of the requirements of this section and designate an alternative site for installation of such facilities. The waiver issued shall specify each working place to which it shall apply, set forth the reasons for such waiver, and the reasons for designation of the alternative site.

§ 75.1712-10 Underground sanitary facilities; maintenance.

Sanitary toilets shall be regularly maintained in a clean and sanitary condition. Holding tanks shall be serviced and cleaned when full and in no case less than once each week by draining or pumping or by removing them to the surface for cleaning or recharging. Transfer tanks and transfer equipment used underground shall be equipped with suitable fittings to permit complete drainage of holding tanks without spillage and allow for the sanitary transportation of wastes to the surface. Waste shall be disposed of on the surface in accordance with State and local laws and regulations.

§ 75.1713 Emergency medical assistance; first-aid.

[STATUTORY PROVISIONS]

Each operator shall make arrangements in advance for obtaining emergency medical assistance and transportation for injured persons. Emergency communications shall be provided to the nearest point of assistance. Selected agents of the operator shall be trained in first-aid and first-aid training shall be made available to all miners. Each coal mine shall have an adequate supply of first-aid equipment located on the surface, at the bottom of shafts and slopes, and at other strategic locations near the working faces. In fulfilling each of the requirements of this section, the operator shall meet at least minimum requirements prescribed by the Secretary of Health and Human Services.

[35 FR 17890, Nov. 20, 1970, as amended at 47 FR 14696, Apr. 6, 1982; 60 FR 33723, June 29, 1995]

§ 75.1713-1 Arrangements for emergency medical assistance and transportation for injured persons; agreements; reporting requirements; posting requirements.

(a) Each operator of an underground coal mine shall make arrangements with a licensed physician, medical service, medical clinic, or hospital to provide 24-hour emergency medical assistance for any person injured at the mine.

Mine Safety and Health Admin., Labor § 75.1713-6

(b) Each operator of an underground coal mine shall make arrangements with an ambulance service, or otherwise provide, for 24-hour emergency transportation for any person injured at the mine.

(c) Each operator shall, on or before December 30, 1970, report to the District Manager for the district in which the mine is located the name, title and address of the physician, medical service, medical clinic, hospital or ambulance service with whom arrangements have been made, or otherwise provided, in accordance with the provisions of paragraphs (a) and (b) of this § 75.1713-1.

(d) Each operator shall, within 10 days after any change of the arrangements required to be reported under the provisions of this § 75.1713-1, report such changes to the District Manager. If such changes involve a substitution of persons, the operator shall provide the name, title, and address of the person substituted together with the name and address of the medical service, medical clinic, hospital, or ambulance service with which such person or persons are associated.

(e) Each operator shall, immediately after making an arrangement required under the provisions of paragraphs (a) and (b) of this § 75.1713-1, or immediately after any change of such arrangement, post at appropriate places at the mine the names, titles, addresses, and telephone numbers of all persons or services currently available under such arrangements to provide medical assistance and transportation at the mine.

§ 75.1713-2 Emergency communications; requirements.

(a) Each operator of an underground coal mine shall establish and maintain a communication system from the mine to the nearest point of medical assistance for use in an emergency.

(b) The emergency communication system required to be maintained under paragraph (a) of this § 75.1713-2 may be established by telephone or radio transmission or by any other means of prompt communication to any facility (for example, the local sheriff, the State highway patrol, or local hospital) which has available the means of communication with the person or persons providing emergency medical assistance or transportation in accordance with the provisions of § 75.1713-1.

§ 75.1713-3 First-Aid training; supervisory employees.

The mine operator shall conduct first-aid training courses for selected supervisory employees at the mine. Within 60 days after the selection of a new supervisory employee to be so trained, the mine operator shall certify by signature and date the name of the employee and date on which the employee satisfactorily completed the first-aid training course. The certification shall be kept at the mine and made available on request to an authorized representative of the Secretary.

[56 FR 1478, Jan. 14, 1991]

§ 75.1713-4 First-aid training program; availability of instruction to all miners.

On or before June 30, 1971, each operator of an underground coal mine shall make available to all miners employed in the mine a course of instruction in first-aid conducted by the operator or under the auspices of the operator, and such a course of instruction shall be made available to newly employed miners within 6 months after the date of employment.

§ 75.1713-5 First-aid training program; retraining of supervisory employees; availability to all miners.

Beginning January 1, 1971, each operator of an underground coal mine shall conduct refresher first-aid training courses each calendar year for all selected supervisory employees, and make available refresher first-aid training courses to all miners employed in the mine.

§ 75.1713-6 First-aid training program; minimum requirements.

(a) All first-aid training programs required under the provisions of §§ 75.1713-3 and 75.1713-4 shall include 10 class hours of training in a course of instruction similar to that outlined in "First Aid, A Bureau of Mines Instruction Manual."

§ 75.1713-7

(b) Refresher first-aid training programs required under the provisions of § 75.1713–5 shall include five class hours of refresher training in a course of instruction similar to that outlined in "First Aid, A Bureau of Mines Instruction Manual."

§ 75.1713-7 First-aid equipment; location; minimum requirements.

(a) Each operator of an underground coal mine shall maintain a supply of the first-aid equipment set forth in paragraph (b) of this § 75.1713–7 at each of the following locations:

(1) At the mine dispatcher's office or other appropriate work area on the surface in close proximity to the mine entry;

(2) At the bottom of each regularly traveled slope or shaft; however, where the bottom of such slope or shaft is not more than 1,000 feet from the surface, such first-aid supplies may be maintained on the surface at the entrance to the mine; and

(3) At a point in each working section not more than 500 feet outby the active working face or faces.

(b) The first-aid equipment required to be maintained under the provisions of paragraph (a) of this § 75.1713–7 shall include at least the following:

(1) One stretcher;
(2) One broken-back board. (If a splint stretcher combination is used it will satisfy the requirements of both (1) and (2));
(3) 24 triangular bandages (15 if a splint-stretcher combination is used).
(4) Eight 4-inch bandage compresses;
(5) Eight 2-inch bandage compresses.
(6) Twelve 1-inch adhesive compresses;
(7) One foille;
(8) Two cloth blankets;
(9) One rubber blanket or equivalent substitute.
(10) Two tourniquets;
(11) One 1-ounce bottle of aromatic spirits of ammonia or 1 dozen ammonia ampules.
(12) The necessary complements of arm and leg splints or two each inflatable plastic arm and leg splints.

(c) All first-aid supplies required to be maintained under the provisions of paragraphs (a) and (b) of this § 75.1713–7 shall be stored in suitable, sanitary, dust tight, moisture proof containers and such supplies shall be accessible to the miners.

§ 75.1714 Availability of approved self-rescue devices; instruction in use and location.

(a) Each operator shall make available to each miner who goes underground, and to visitors authorized to enter the mine by the operator, an approved self-rescue device or devices which is adequate to protect such person for 1 hour or longer.

(b) Before any person authorized by the operator goes underground, the operator shall instruct and train such person in accordance with provisions set forth in 30 CFR part 48.

[43 FR 54246, Nov. 21, 1978, as amended at 53 FR 10336, Mar. 30, 1988; 60 FR 30401, June 8, 1995; 71 FR 71454, Dec. 8, 2006]

§ 75.1714-1 Approved self-rescue devices.

The requirements of § 75.1714 shall be met by making available to each person referred to in that section a self-rescue device or devices, which have been approved by MSHA and NIOSH under 42 CFR part 84, as follows:

(a) A 1-hour SCSR;
(b) A SCSR of not less than 10 minutes and a 1-hour canister; or
(c) Any other self-contained breathing apparatus which provides protection for a period of 1 hour or longer and which is approved for use by MSHA as a self-rescue device when used and maintained as prescribed by MSHA.

[60 FR 30401, June 8, 1995]

§ 75.1714-2 Self-rescue devices; use and location requirements.

(a) Self-rescue devices shall be used and located as prescribed in paragraphs (b) through (f) of this section.

(b) Except as provided in paragraph (c), (d), (e), or (f) of this section, self-rescue devices shall be worn or carried at all times by each person when underground.

(c) Where the wearing or carrying of the self-rescue device is hazardous to the person, it shall be placed in a readily accessible location no greater than 25 feet from such person.

(d) Where a person works on or around equipment, the self-rescue device may be placed in a readily accessible location on such equipment.

(e) A mine operator may apply to the District Manager under § 75.1502 for permission to place the SCSR more than 25 feet away.

(1) The District Manager shall consider the following factors in deciding whether to permit an operator to place a SCSR more than 25 feet from a miner:

(i) Distance from affected sections to surface,

(ii) Pitch of seam in affected sections,

(iii) Height of coal seam in affected sections,

(iv) Location of escapeways,

(v) Proposed location of SCSRs,

(vi) Type of work performed by affected miners,

(vii) Degree of risk to which affected miners are exposed,

(viii) Potential for breaking into oxygen deficient atmospheres,

(ix) Type of risk to which affected miners are exposed,

(x) Accident history of mine, and

(xi) Other matters bearing upon the safety of miners.

(2) Such application shall not be approved by the District Manager unless it provides that, while underground, all miners whose SCSR is more than 25 feet away shall have a FSR approved by MSHA and NIOSH under 42 CFR part 84 sufficient to enable each miner to get to a SCSR.

(3) An operator may not obtain permission under paragraph (e) of this section to place SCSRs more than 25 feet away from miners on trips into and out of the mine.

(f) If an SCSR is not carried out of the mine at the end of a miner's shift, the place of storage shall be approved by the District Manager. A sign made of reflective material with the word "SCSRs" or "SELF-RESCUERS" shall be conspicuously posted at each SCSR storage location. Direction signs made of a reflective material shall be posted leading to each storage location.

(g) Where devices of not less than 10 minutes and 1 hour are made available in accordance with § 75.1714–1(b), such devices shall be used and located as follows:

(1) Except as provided in paragraphs (c) and (d) of this section, the device of not less than 10 minutes shall be worn or carried at all times by each person when underground, and

(2) The one-hour canister shall be available at all times to all persons when underground in accordance with a plan submitted by the mine operator and approved by the District Manager. When the one-hour canister is placed in a storage location, a sign made of a reflective material with the word "SCSRs" or "SELF-RESCUERS" shall be conspicuously posted at each storage location. Direction signs made of a reflective material shall be posted leading to each storage location.

[43 FR 54246, Nov. 21, 1978, as amended at 60 FR 30401, June 8, 1995; 69 FR 8108, Feb. 23, 2004; 71 FR 12270, Mar. 9, 2006; 71 FR 71454, Dec. 8, 2006]

§ 75.1714–3 Self-rescue devices; inspection, testing, maintenance, repair, and recordkeeping.

(a) Each operator shall provide for proper inspection, testing, maintenance, and repair of self-rescue devices by a person trained to perform such functions.

(b) After each time a self-rescue device is worn or carried by a person, the device shall be inspected for damage and for the integrity of its seal by a person trained to perform this function. Self-rescue devices with broken seals or which are damaged so that the device will not function properly shall be removed from service.

(c) All FSRs approved by MSHA and NIOSH under 42 CFR part 84, except devices using vacuum containers as the only method of sealing, shall be tested at intervals not exceeding 90 days by weighing each device on a scale or balance accurate to within + 1 gram. A device that weighs more than 10 grams over its original weight shall be removed from service.

(d) All SCSRs approved by MSHA and NIOSH under 42 CFR part 84 shall be tested in accordance with instructions approved by MSHA and NIOSH. Any device which does not meet the specified test requirements shall be removed from service.

§ 75.1714–4

(e) At the completion of each test required by paragraphs (c) and (d) of this section the person making the tests shall certify by signature and date that the tests were done. This person shall make a record of all corrective action taken. Certifications and records shall be kept at the mine and made available on request to an authorized representative of the Secretary.

(f) Self-rescue devices removed from service shall be repaired for return to service only by a person trained to perform such work and only in accordance with the manufacturer's instructions.

[43 FR 54246, Nov. 21, 1978, as amended at 47 FR 14706, Apr. 6, 1982; 56 FR 1478, Jan. 14, 1991; 60 FR 30402, June 8, 1995; 60 FR 33723, June 29, 1995]

§ 75.1714–4 Additional self-contained self-rescuers (SCSRs).

(a) *Additional SCSRs in work places.* In addition to the requirements in §§ 75.1714, 75.1714–1, 75.1714–2, and 75.1714–3 of this part, the mine operator shall provide the following:

(1) At least one additional SCSR, which provides protection for a period of one hour or longer, for each person at a fixed underground work location.

(2) Additional SCSRs along the normal travel routes for pumpers, examiners, and other persons who do not have a fixed work location to be stored at a distance an average miner could walk in 30 minutes. The SCSR storage locations shall be determined by using one of the methods found under paragraph (c)(2) of this section.

(b) *Additional SCSRs on mantrips.* If a mantrip or mobile equipment is used to enter or exit the mine, at least one additional SCSR, which provides protection for a period of one hour or longer, shall be available for each person who uses such transportation from portal to portal.

(c) *Additional SCSRs in escapeways.* When each person underground cannot safely evacuate the mine within 30 minutes, the mine operator shall provide additional SCSRs stored in each required escapeway.

(1) Each storage location shall contain at least one SCSR, which provides protection for a period of one hour or longer, for every person who will be inby that location.

(2) Storage locations shall be spaced along each escapeway at 30-minute travel distances no greater than the distances determined by—

(i) Calculating the distance an average miner walks in 30 minutes by using the time necessary for each miner in a sample of typical miners to walk a typical length of each escapeway; or

(ii) Using the SCSR storage location spacing specified in the following table, except for escapeways with grades over 5 percent.

Average entry height	Maximum distance between SCSR storage locations (in ft.)
<40 in. (Crawl)	2,200
>40–<50 in. (Duck Walk)	3,300
>50–<65 in. (Walk Head Bent)	4,400
>65 in. (Walk Erect)	5,700

(d) *Additional SCSRs in hardened rooms.* As an alternative to providing SCSR storage locations in each escapeway, the mine operator may store SCSRs in a hardened room located between adjacent escapeways.

(1) The hardened room shall be designed and constructed to the same explosion force criteria as seals.

(2) The hardened room shall include a means to provide independent, positive pressure ventilation from the surface during an emergency.

(3) The District Manager shall approve the design and construction of hardened rooms in the ventilation plan.

(4) These SCSR storage locations shall be spaced in accordance with paragraph (c) of this section.

(e) *Storage location accessibility.* All SCSRs required under this section shall be stored according to the manufacturers' instructions, in conspicuous locations readily accessible by each person in the mine.

(f) *Storage location signs.* A sign made of reflective material with the words "SCSRs" or "SELF-RESCUERS" shall be conspicuously posted at each storage location. Direction signs made of a reflective material shall be posted leading to each storage location.

[71 FR 71454, Dec. 8, 2006]

§ 75.1714-5 Map locations of self-contained self-rescuers (SCSR).

The mine operator shall indicate the locations of all stored SCSRs on the mine maps required by §§ 75.1200 and 75.1505 of this part.

[71 FR 71454, Dec. 8, 2006]

§ 75.1714-6 Emergency tethers.

At least one tether, which is a durable rope or equivalent material designed to permit members of a mine crew to link together while evacuating the mine during an emergency, shall be provided and stored with the additional SCSRs on the fixed work location and on the mobile equipment required in §§ 75.1714–4(a)(1) and (b) of this part.

[71 FR 71454, Dec. 8, 2006]

§ 75.1714-7 Multi-gas detectors.

(a) *Availability.* A mine operator shall provide an MSHA-approved, handheld, multi-gas detector that can measure methane, oxygen, and carbon monoxide to each group of underground miners and to each person who works alone, such as pumpers, examiners, and outby miners.

(b) *Qualified person.* At least one person in each group of underground miners shall be a qualified person under § 75.150 of this part and each person who works alone shall be trained to use the multi-gas detector.

(c) *Maintenance and calibration.* Multi-gas detectors shall be maintained and calibrated as specified in § 75.320 of this part.

[71 FR 71454, Dec. 8, 2006]

§ 75.1714-8 Reporting SCSR inventory and malfunctions; retention of SCSRs.

(a) *SCSR inventory.* A mine operator shall submit to MSHA a complete inventory of all SCSRs at each mine. New mines shall submit the inventory within 3 months of beginning operation.

(1) The inventory shall include—

(i) Mine name, MSHA mine ID number, and mine location; and

(ii) For each SCSR unit, the manufacturer, the model type, the date of manufacture, and the serial number.

(2) In the event that a change in the inventory occurs, a mine operator shall report the change to MSHA within the quarter that the change occurs (Jan–Mar, Apr–Jun, Jul–Sep, Oct–Dec).

(b) *Reporting SCSR problems.* A mine operator shall report to MSHA any defect, performance problem, or malfunction with the use of an SCSR. The report shall include a detailed description of the problem and, for each SCSR involved, the information required by paragraph (a)(1) of this section.

(c) *Retention of problem SCSRs.* The mine operator shall preserve and retain each SCSR reported under paragraph (b) of this section for 60 days after reporting the problem to MSHA.

[71 FR 71454, Dec. 8, 2006]

§ 75.1715 Identification check system.

[STATUTORY PROVISIONS]

Each operator of a coal mine shall establish a check-in and check-out system which will provide positive identification of every person underground, and will provide an accurate record of the persons in the mine kept on the surface in a place chosen to minimize the danger of destruction by fire or other hazard. Such record shall bear a number identical to an identification check that is securely fastened to the lamp belt worn by the person underground. The identification check shall be made of a rust resistant metal of not less than 16 gauge.

§ 75.1716 Operations under water.

[STATUTORY PROVISIONS]

Whenever an operator mines coal from a coal mine opened after March 30, 1970, or from any new working section of a mine opened prior to such date, in a manner that requires the construction, operation, and maintenance of tunnels under any river, stream, lake, or other body of water, that is, in the judgment of the Secretary, sufficiently large to constitute a hazard to miners, such operator shall obtain a permit from the Secretary which shall include such terms and conditions as he deems appropriate to protect the safety of miners working or passing through such tunnels from caveins and other hazards. Such permits shall require, in accordance with a plan to be approved by the Secretary,

§ 75.1716-1

that a safety zone be established beneath and adjacent to such body of water. No plan shall be approved unless there is a minimum of cover to be determined by the Secretary, based on test holes drilled by the operator in a manner to be prescribed by the Secretary. No such permit shall be required in the case of any new working section of a mine which is located under any water resource reservoir being constructed by a Federal agency on December 30, 1969, the operator of which is required by such agency to operate in a manner that protects the safety of miners working in such section from cave-ins and other hazards.

[35 FR 17890, Nov. 20, 1970, as amended at 60 FR 33723, June 29, 1995]

§ 75.1716-1 Operations under water; notification by operator.

An operator planning to mine coal from coal mines opened after March 30, 1970, or from working sections in mines opened prior to such date, and in such manner that mining operations will be conducted, or tunnels constructed, under any river, stream, lake, or other body of water, shall give notice to the Coal Mine Safety District Manager in the district in which the mine is located prior to the commencement of such mining operations.

§ 75.1716-2 Permit required.

If in the judgment of the Coal Mine Safety District Manager the proposed mining operations referred to in § 75.1716-1 constitute a hazard to miners, he shall promptly so notify the operator that a permit is required.

§ 75.1716-3 Applications for permits.

An application for a permit required under this section shall be filed with the Coal Mine Safety District Manager and shall contain the following general information:

(a) Name and address of the company.

(b) Name and address of the mine.

(c) Projected mining and ground support plans.

(d) A mine map showing the locations of the river, stream, lake, or other body of water and its relation to the location of all working places.

(e) A profile map showing the type of strata and the distance in elevation between the coal bed and the river, stream, lake or other body of water involved. The type of strata shall be determined by core test drill holes as prescribed by the Coal Mine Safety District Manager.

§ 75.1716-4 Issuance of permits.

If the Coal Mine Safety District Manager determines that the proposed mining operations under water can be safely conducted, he shall issue a permit for the conduct of such operations under such conditions as he deems necessary to protect the safety of miners engaged in those operations.

§ 75.1717 Exemptions.

[STATUTORY PROVISIONS]

No notice under § 75.1716-1 and no permit under § 75.1716-2 shall be required in the case of any new working section of a mine which is located under any water resource reservoir being constructed by a Federal agency as of December 30, 1969, and where the operator is required by such agency to operate in a manner that adequately protects the safety of miners.

§ 75.1718 Drinking water.

[STATUTORY PROVISIONS]

An adequate supply of potable water shall be provided for drinking purposes in the active workings of the mine, and such water shall be carried, stored, and otherwise protected in sanitary containers.

§ 75.1718-1 Drinking water; quality.

(a) Potable water provided in accordance with the provisions of § 75.1718 shall meet the applicable minimum health requirements for drinking water established by the State or community in which the mine is located.

(b) Where no state or local health requirements apply to drinking water or where no state or local minimum health requirements exist, drinking water provided in accordance with the provisions of § 75.1718 shall contain a minimum of 0.2 milligrams of free chlorine per liter of water.

Mine Safety and Health Admin., Labor § 75.1719–1

§ 75.1719 Illumination; purpose and scope of §§ 75.1719 through 75.1719–4; time for compliance.

(a) Section 317(e) of the Act (30 U.S.C. 877(e)) directs and authorizes the Secretary to propose and promulgate standards under which all working places in a mine shall be illuminated by permissible lighting while persons are working in such places §§ 75.1719 through 75.1719–4 prescribe the requirements for illumination of working places in underground coal mines while persons are working in such places and while self-propelled mining equipment is operated in the working place.

(b) Mine operators shall comply with §§ 75.1719 through 75.1719–4 not later than July 1, 1978.

[41 FR 43534, Oct. 1, 1976, as amended at 43 FR 13564, Mar. 31, 1978]

§ 75.1719–1 Illumination in working places.

(a) Each operator of an underground coal mine shall provide each working place in the mine with lighting as prescribed in §§ 75.1719–1 and 75.1719–2 while self-propelled mining equipment is operated in the working place.

(b) *Self-propelled mining equipment; definition.* For the purposes of §§ 75.1719 through 75.1719–4, "self-propelled mining equipment" means equipment which possesses the capability of moving itself or its associated components from one location to another by electric, hydraulic, pneumatic, or mechanical power supplied by a source located on the machine or transmitted to the machine by cables, ropes, or chains.

(c) The lighting prescribed in this section shall be in addition to that provided by personal cap lamps.

(d) The luminous intensity (surface brightness) of surfaces that are in a miner's normal field of vision of areas in working places that are required to be lighted shall be not less than 0.06 footlamberts when measured in accordance with § 75.1719–3.

(e) When self-propelled mining equipment specified in paragraphs (e)(1) through (e)(6) of this section is operated in a working place, the areas within a miner's normal field of vision which shall be illuminated in the working place shall be as prescribed in paragraphs (e)(1) through (e)(6) of this section.

(1) *Continuous miners and coal-loading equipment.* In working places in which continuous miners and coal-loading equipment are operated, the areas which shall be illuminated shall be as follows:
(i) The face, and
(ii) The ribs, roof, floor, and exposed surface of mining equipment, which are between the face and the inby end of the shuttle car or other conveying equipment while in position to receive material.

(2) *Self-loading haulage equipment used as a loading machine.* In working places in which self-loading haulage equipment is operated to load material, the areas which shall be illuminated be as follows:
(i) The face, and
(ii) The ribs, roof, floor, and exposed surfaces of mining equipment, which are between the face and a point 5 feet outby the machine.

(3) *Cutting and drilling equipment.* In working places in which cutting or drilling equipment is operated, the areas which shall be illuminated shall be as follows:
(i) The ribs, roof, floor, and exposed surfaces of mining equipment, which are between the face and a point 5 feet outby the machine.

(4) *Shortwall and longwall mining equipment.* In working places in which shortwall or longwall mining equipment is operated, the areas which shall be illuminated shall be as follows:
(i) The area for the length of the self-advancing roof support system and which is between the gob-side of the travelway and the side of the block of coal from which coal is being extracted, and
(ii) The control station, and the head piece and tail piece of the face conveyor, and
(iii) The roof and floor for a distance of 5 feet horizontally from the control station, head piece and tail piece.

(5) *Roof bolting equipment.* In working places in which roof bolting equipment is operated, the areas which shall be illuminated shall be as follows:
(i) *Where the distance from the floor, to the roof is 5 feet, or less:* the face, ribs, roof, floor, and exposed surfaces of

§ 75.1719-2

mining equipment, which are within an area the perimeter of which is a distance of 5 feet from the machine, when measured parallel to the floor.

(ii) *Where the distance from the floor to the roof is more than 5 feet:* the face, ribs, roof, floor, and exposed surfaces of mining equipment, which are within an area the perimeter of which from the front and sides of the machine is a distance equal to the distance from the floor to the roof and from the rear of the machine a distance of 5 feet, when measured parallel to the floor.

(6) *Other self-propelled equipment.* Unless the entire working place is illuminated by stationary lighting equipment, in working places in which self-propelled equipment is operated, other than equipment specified in paragraphs (e)(1) through (e)(5) of this section, illumination shall be provided as follows:

(i) Luminaires shall be installed on each machine operated in the working place which shall illuminate a face or rib coal surface which is within 10 feet of the front and the rear of the machine to a luminous intensity of not less than 0.06 footlamberts, and

(ii) The height and width of the area of the coal surface which shall be illuminated shall equal the height and width, respectively, of the machine on which the luminaires are installed, and

(iii) The luminaires in the direction of travel shall be operated at all times the equipment is being trammed in the working place.

(f) The Administrator, Coal Mine Health and Safety, MSHA, may specify other areas in a working place to be illuminated for the protection of miners while self-propelled mining equipment is being operated in the working place.

(g) Surface brightness of floor, roof, coal and machine surfaces in the normal visual field of a miner shall not vary more than 50 percent between adjacent fields of similar surface reflectance, and the maximum surface brightness of such surface shall not exceed 120 footlamberts when measured in accordance with § 75.1719-3.

[41 FR 43534, Oct. 1, 1976, as amended at 42 FR 18859, Apr. 11, 1977; 43 FR 43458, Sept. 26, 1978; 47 FR 28096, June 29, 1982]

§ 75.1719-2 Lighting fixtures; requirements.

(a) Lighting fixtures shall be permissible.

(b) Lighting fixtures may be installed on self-propelled machines or may be stationary lighting fixtures.

(c)(1) Electrically operated lighting fixtures shall be energized by direct current, or by sinusoidal full wave alternating current not less than 50 cycles per second (100 pulses per second), or by an equivalent power source that causes no greater flicker.

(2) Alternating current circuits supplying power to stationary lighting fixtures shall contain conductors energized at voltages not greater than 70 volts to ground. Alternating current circuits, energized at 100 volts or more and used to supply power to stationary lighting fixtures, shall originate at a transformer having a center or neutral tap grounded to earth through a proper resistor, which shall be designed to limit fault current to not more than 5 amperes. A grounding circuit in accordance with § 75.701-4 shall originate at the grounded terminal of the grounding resistor and extend along with the power conductors and serve as a grounding conductor for the frames of all equipment receiving power from the circuit. The ground fault current rating of grounding resistors shall meet the "extended time rating" set forth in the Institute of Electrical and Electronics Engineers, Inc. Standard No. 32 (IEEE Std. 32-1972) which is hereby incorporated by reference and made a part hereof. The incorporated publication is available for examination at each MSHA Coal Mine Safety and Health district office, and may be obtained from the Institute of Electrical and Electronics Engineers, Inc., Publications Office, 10662 Los Vaqueros Circle, P.O. Box 3014 Los Alamitos, CA 90720-1264 Telephone: 800-272-6657 (toll free); *http://www.ieee.org*.

(3) Machine-mounted lighting fixtures shall be electrically grounded to the machine by a separate grounding conductor in compliance with § 75.701-4.

(d) Direct current circuits in excess of a nominal voltage of 300 volts shall not be used to supply power to stationary light fixtures.

(e) Cables conducting power to stationary lighting fixtures from both alternating and direct current power sources, other than intrinsically safe devices, shall be considered trailing cables, and shall meet the requirements of Subpart G of this part. In addition, such cables shall be protected against overloads and short circuits by a suitable circuit breaker or other device approved by the Secretary. Circuit breakers or other device approved by the Secretary protecting trailing cables receiving power from resistance grounded circuits shall be equipped with a ground trip arrangement which shall be designed to deenergize the circuit at not more than 50% of the available fault current.

(f) Before shunts are removed from blasting caps, lighting fixtures and associated cables located in the same working place shall be deenergized. Furthermore, lighting fixtures shall be removed out of the line of blast and not less than 50 feet from the blasting operation unless otherwise protected against flying debris.

(g) Lighting fixtures shall be designed and installed to minimize discomfort glare.

[41 FR 43534, Oct. 1, 1976, as amended at 71 FR 16669, Apr. 3, 2006]

§ 75.1719-3 Methods of measurement; light measuring instruments.

(a) Compliance with § 75.1719-1(d) shall be determined by MSHA by measuring luminous intensity (surface brightness).

(b) In measuring luminous intensity the following procedures shall be used:

(1) In areas of working places specified in §§ 75.1719.1(e)(1) through 75.1719-1(e)(3) luminous intensity measurements of the face, ribs, roof, floor, and exposed surfaces of mining equipment, shall be made with the machine idle and located in the approximate center of the working place with the cutting, loading, or drilling head toward the face and not more than 3 feet from the face.

(2) In areas of working places specified in § 75.1719-1(e)(4) luminous intensity measurements may be made at any time longwall or shortwall mining equipment is operated except that when measurements are made in the vicinity of shearers, plows, or continuous miners, the equipment shall be idle while measurements are being made.

(3) In areas of working places specified in § 75.1719-1(e)(5) luminous intensity measurements of the face, ribs, roof, floor, and exposed surfaces of mining equipment, shall be made with the machine idle and located in the approximate center of the working place with the drilling head toward the face and a distance from the face of 5 feet, or the distance from the floor to the roof, whichever is applicable. When the machine is located in the center of the working place and the surfaces of the ribs to be illuminated are not within the perimeter of the area determined in accordance with § 75.1719-1(e)(5), the machine shall be positioned the applicable distance from the face and each rib and luminous intensity measurements made for each rib, provided, however, that luminous intensity measurements may be made of the face, roof, floor, and exposed surfaces of mining equipment with the machine so located without locating the machine in the center of the working place.

(4) In areas of working places specified in § 75.1719-1(e)(6), luminous intensity measurements of a coal surface shall be made with the machine idle and located in the approximate center of the working place with the appropriate end toward the face and not less than 9 feet nor more than 10 feet from the face.

(5) The area of surfaces to be measured shall be divided into round or square fields having an area of not less than 3 nor more than 5 square feet as illustrated by the following figure:

§ 75.1719-3

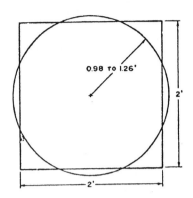

DIRECT MEASUREMENT OF LUMINOUS INTENSITY

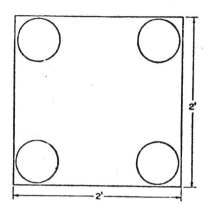

DETERMINATION OF LUMINOUS INTENSITY BY AVERAGING METHOD

(6) Measurements shall be taken with the photometer held approximately perpendicular to the surface being measured and a sufficient distance from the surface to allow the light sensing element in the instrument to receive reflected light from a field of not less than 3 nor more than 5 square feet. The luminous intensity of each such field shall be not less than 0.06 footlambert.

(7) In areas of working places where clearances are restricted to the extent that the photometer cannot be held a sufficient distance from the surface to allow the light sensing element in the instrument to receive reflected light from a field having an area of at least 3 square feet, luminous intensity shall be considered as the average of four uniformly spaced readings taken at the corners and within a square field having an area of approximately 4 square feet. In such instances, the area of each of the individual readings shall not exceed 100 square inches. The average of the four readings shall be not less than 0.06 footlambert. The method of measurement is illustrated by the following figure:

(8) Measurements shall not be made where shadows are cast by roof control posts, ventilation equipment, or other obstructions necessary to insure safe mining conditions.

(9) Where machine-mounted light fixtures are used on equipment, except self advancing roof support systems, measurements shall not be made of surfaces on or within 1 foot of a self-propelled machine.

(c) For the purpose of making illumination measurements, an authorized representative of the Secretary may require the installation of temporary roof supports or the removal of the equipment to a similar working place in which permanent roof supports have been installed.

(d) Light measuring instruments shall be properly calibrated and maintained. Instruments shall be calibrated against standards traceable to the National Institute of Standards and Technology (Formerly the National Bureau of Standards) and color corrected to the Commission Internationale de l'Eclairage (CIE) Spectral Luminous Curve. The CIE Spectral Luminous Curve is as follows:

Mine Safety and Health Admin., Labor § 75.1721

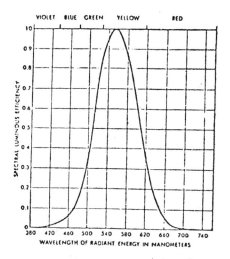

[41 FR 43534, Oct. 1, 1976, as amended at 71 FR 16669, Apr. 3, 2006]

§ 75.1719-4 Mining machines, cap lamps; requirements.

(a) Paint used on exterior surfaces of mining machines shall have a minimum reflectance of 30 percent, except cab interiors and other surfaces which might adversely affect visibility.

(b) When stationary light fixtures are used, red reflectors mounted in protective frames or reflecting tape shall be installed on each end of mining machines, except that continuous mining machines, loaders, and cutters need only have such reflectors or tape on the outby end. Reflectors or reflecting tape shall have an area of not less than 10 square inches.

(c) Each person who goes underground shall be required to wear an approved personal cap lamp or an equivalent portable light.

(d) Each person who goes underground shall be required to wear a hard hat or hard cap which shall have a minimum of 6 square inches of reflecting tape or equivalent paint or material on each side and back.

[41 FR 43534, Oct. 1, 1976]

§ 75.1720 Protective clothing; requirements.

On and after the effective date of this § 75.1720 each miner regularly employed in the active workings of an underground coal mine shall be required to wear the following protective clothing and devices:

(a) Protective clothing or equipment and face-shields or goggles when welding, cutting, or working with molten metal or when other hazards to the eyes exist from flying particles.

(b) Suitable protective clothing to cover those parts of the body exposed to injury when handling corrosive or toxic substances or other materials which might cause injury to the skin.

(c) Protective gloves when handling materials or performing work which might cause injury to the hands; however, gloves shall not be worn where they would create a greater hazard by becoming entangled in the moving parts of equipment.

(d) A suitable hard hat or hard cap. If a hard hat or hard cap is painted, nonmetallic based paint shall be used.

(e) Suitable protective footwear.

[36 FR 19497, Oct. 7, 1971, as amended at 39 FR 7175, Feb. 25, 1974]

§ 75.1720-1 Distinctively colored hard hats, or hard caps; identification for newly employed, inexperienced miners.

Hard hats or hard caps distinctively different in color from those worn by experienced miners shall be worn by each newly employed, inexperienced miner for at least one year from the date of his initial employment as a miner or until he has been qualified or certified as a miner by the State in which he is employed.

[39 FR 7175, Feb. 25, 1974]

§ 75.1721 Opening of new underground coal mines, or reopening and reactivating of abandoned or deactivated coal mines, notification by the operator; requirements.

(a) Each operator of a new underground coal mine, and a mine which has been abandoned or deactivated and is to be reopened or reactivated, shall prior to opening, reopening or reactivating the mine notify the Coal Mine Health and Safety District Manager for the district in which the mine is located of the approximate date of the proposed or actual opening of such mine. Thereafter, and as soon as practicable, the operator of such mine shall

§ 75.1722

submit all preliminary plans in accordance with paragraphs (b) and (c) of this section to the District Manager and the operator shall not develop any part of the coalbed in such mine unless and until all preliminary plans have been approved.

(b) The preliminary plans required to be submitted by the operator to the District Manager shall be in writing and shall contain the following:

(1) The name and location of the proposed mine and the Mine Safety and Health Administration mine identification number, if known;

(2) The name and address of the mine operator(s);

(3) The name and address of the principal official designated by the operator as the person who is in charge of health and safety at the mine;

(4) The identification and approximate height of the coalbed to be developed;

(5) The system of mining to be employed;

(6) A proposed roof control plan containing the information specified in § 75.220.

(7) A proposed mine ventilation plan containing the information specified in §§ 75.371 and 75.372;

(8) A proposed plan for sealing worked-out areas containing the information specified in §§ 75.371 and 75.372.

(9) A proposed program for searching miners for smoking materials in accordance with the provisions of § 75.1702; and,

(10) A proposed plan for emergency medical assistance and emergency communication in accordance with the provisions of §§ 75.1713–1 and 75.1713–2.

(c) The preliminary plans required to be submitted by the operator to the District Manager shall be in writing and shall contain the following:

(1) The proposed training plan containing the information specified in §§ 48.3 and 48.23 of this chapter, and

(2) A proposed plan for training and retraining certified and qualified persons containing the information specified in § 75.160–1.

[44 FR 9380, Feb. 13, 1979, as amended at 47 FR 23641, May 28, 1982; 57 FR 20929, May 15, 1992]

§ 75.1722 Mechanical equipment guards.

(a) Gears; sprockets; chains; drive, head, tail, and takeup pulleys; flywheels; couplings, shafts; sawblades; fan inlets; and similar exposed moving machine parts which may be contacted by persons, and which may cause injury to persons shall be guarded.

(b) Guards at conveyor-drive, conveyor-head, and conveyor-tail pulleys shall extend a distance sufficient to prevent a person from reaching behind the guard and becoming caught between the belt and the pulley.

(c) Except when testing the machinery, guards shall be securely in place while machinery is being operated.

[38 FR 4976, Feb. 23, 1973]

§ 75.1723 Stationary grinding machines; protective devices.

(a) Stationary grinding machines other than special bit grinders shall be equipped with:

(1) Peripheral hoods (less than 90° throat openings) capable of withstanding the force of a bursting wheel.

(2) Adjustable tool rests set as close as practical to the wheel.

(3) Safety washers.

(b) Grinding wheels shall be operated within the specifications of the manufacturer of the wheel.

(c) Face shields or goggles, in good condition, shall be worn when operating a grinding wheel.

[38 FR 4976, Feb. 23, 1973]

§ 75.1724 Hand-held power tools; safety devices.

Hand-held power tools shall be equipped with controls requiring constant hand or finger pressure to operate the tools or shall be equipped with friction or other equivalent safety devices.

[38 FR 4976, Feb. 23, 1973]

§ 75.1725 Machinery and equipment; operation and maintenance.

(a) Mobile and stationary machinery and equipment shall be maintained in safe operating condition and machinery or equipment in unsafe condition shall be removed from service immediately.

Mine Safety and Health Admin., Labor § 75.1731

(b) Machinery and equipment shall be operated only by persons authorized to operate such machinery or equipment.

(c) Repairs or maintenance shall not be performed on machinery until the power is off and the machinery is blocked against motion, except where machinery motion is necessary to make adjustments.

(d) Machinery shall not be lubricated manually while in motion, unless equipped with extended fittings or cups.

[38 FR 4976, Feb. 23, 1973]

§ 75.1726 Performing work from a raised position; safeguards.

(a) Men shall not work on or from a piece of mobile equipment in a raised position until it has been blocked in place securely. This does not preclude the use of equipment specifically designed as elevated mobile work platforms.

(b) No work shall be performed under machinery or equipment that has been raised until such machinery or equipment has been securely blocked in position.

[38 FR 4976, Feb. 23, 1973]

§ 75.1727 Drive belts.

(a) Drive belts shall not be shifted while in motion unless the machines are provided with mechanical shifters.

(b) Belt dressing shall not be applied while belts are in motion except where it can be applied without endangering a person.

[38 FR 4976, Feb. 23, 1973]

§ 75.1728 Power-driven pulleys.

(a) Belts, chains, and ropes shall not be guided onto power-driven moving pulleys, sprockets, or drums with the hands except on slow-moving equipment especially designed for hand feeding.

(b) Pulleys of conveyors shall not be cleaned manually while the conveyor is in motion.

(c) Coal spilled beneath belt conveyor drives or tail pieces shall not be removed while the conveyor is in motion, except where such coal can be removed without endangering persons.

[38 FR 4976, Feb. 23, 1973]

§ 75.1729 Welding operations.

Welding operations shall be shielded and the area shall be well ventilated.

[38 FR 4976, Feb. 23, 1973]

§ 75.1730 Compressed air; general; compressed air systems.

(a) All pressure vessels shall be constructed, installed, and maintained in accordance with the standards and specifications of Section VIII "Unfired Pressure Vessels," of the American Society of Mechanical Engineers Boiler and Pressure Vessel Code (1971), which is hereby incorporated by reference and made a part hereof. This document may be purchased from the American Society of Mechanical Engineers, 22 Law Drive, P.O. Box 2900, Fairfield, New Jersey 07007, Phone: 800–843–2763 (toll free); http://www.asme.org; and it is available for examination in every MSHA Coal Mine Safety and Health district office.

(b) Compressors and compressed-air receivers shall be equipped with automatic pressure-relief valves, pressure gages, and drain valves.

(c) Repairs involving the pressure system of compressors, receivers, or compressed-air-powered equipment shall not be attempted until the pressure has been relieved from that part of the system to be repaired.

(d) At no time shall compressed air be directed toward a person. When compressed air is used, all necessary precautions shall be taken to protect persons from injury.

(e) Safety chains, suitable locking devices, or automatic cut-off valves shall be used at connections to machines of high-pressure hose lines of three-fourths of an inch inside diameter or larger, and between high-pressure hose lines of three-fourths of an inch inside diameter or larger, where a connection failure would create a hazard. For purposes of this paragraph, high-pressure means pressure of 100 p.s.i. or more.

[38 FR 4976, Feb. 23, 1973, as amended at 71 FR 16669, Apr. 3, 2006]

§ 75.1731 Maintenance of belt conveyors and belt conveyor entries.

(a) Damaged rollers, or other damaged belt conveyor components, which

§ 75.1732

pose a fire hazard must be immediately repaired or replaced. All other damaged rollers, or other damaged belt conveyor components, must be repaired or replaced.

(b) Conveyor belts must be properly aligned to prevent the moving belt from rubbing against the structure or components.

(c) Materials shall not be allowed in the belt conveyor entry where the material may contribute to a frictional heating hazard.

(d) Splicing of any approved conveyor belt must maintain flame-resistant properties of the belt.

[73 FR 80616, Dec. 31, 2008]

§ 75.1732 Proximity detection systems.

Operators must install proximity detection systems on certain mobile machines.

(a) *Machines covered.* Operators must equip continuous mining machines, except full-face continuous mining machines, with proximity detection systems by the following dates. For proximity detection systems with miner-wearable components, the mine operator must provide a miner-wearable component to be worn by each miner on the working section by the following dates.

(1) Continuous mining machines manufactured after March 16, 2015 must meet the requirements in this section no later than November 16, 2015. These machines must meet the requirements in this section when placed in service with a proximity detection system.

(2) Continuous mining machines manufactured and equipped with a proximity detection system on or before March 16, 2015 must meet the requirements in this section no later than September 16, 2016.

(3) Continuous mining machines manufactured and not equipped with a proximity detection system on or before March 16, 2015 must meet the requirements in this section no later than March 16, 2018. These machines must meet the requirements in this section when placed in service with a proximity detection system.

(b) *Requirements for a proximity detection system.* A proximity detection system includes machine-mounted components and miner-wearable components. The system must:

(1) Cause a machine, which is tramming from place-to-place or repositioning, to stop before contacting a miner except for a miner who is in the on-board operator's compartment;

(2) Provide an audible and visual warning signal on the miner-wearable component and a visual warning signal on the machine that alert miners before the system causes a machine to stop. These warning signals must be distinguishable from other signals;

(3) Provide a visual signal on the machine that indicates the machine-mounted components are functioning properly;

(4) Prevent movement of the machine if any machine-mounted component of the system is not functioning properly. However, a system with any machine-mounted component that is not functioning properly may allow machine movement if it provides an audible or visual warning signal, distinguishable from other signals, during movement. Such movement is permitted only for purposes of relocating the machine from an unsafe location for repair;

(5) Be installed to prevent interference that adversely affects performance of any electrical system; and

(6) Be installed and maintained in proper operating condition by a person trained in the installation and maintenance of the system.

(c) *Proximity detection system checks.* Operators must:

(1) Designate a person who must perform a check of machine-mounted components of the proximity detection system to verify that components are intact, that the system is functioning properly, and take action to correct defects—

(i) At the beginning of each shift when the machine is to be used; or

(ii) Immediately prior to the time the machine is to be operated if not in use at the beginning of a shift; or

(iii) Within 1 hour of a shift change if the shift change occurs without an interruption in production.

(2) Check for proper operation of miner-wearable components at the beginning of each shift that the components are to be used and correct defects before the components are used.

(d) *Certifications and records.* The operator must make and retain certifications and records as follows:

(1) At the completion of the check of machine-mounted components required under paragraph (c)(1) of this section, a certified person under §75.100 must certify by initials, date, and time that the check was conducted. Defects found as a result of the check, including corrective actions and dates of corrective actions, must be recorded before the end of the shift;

(2) Make a record of the defects found as a result of the check of miner-wearable components required under paragraph (c)(2) of this section, including corrective actions and dates of corrective actions;

(3) Make a record of the persons trained in the installation and maintenance of proximity detection systems required under paragraph (b)(6) of this section;

(4) Maintain records in a secure book or electronically in a secure computer system not susceptible to alteration; and

(5) Retain records for at least one year and make them available for inspection by authorized representatives of the Secretary and representatives of miners.

[80 FR 2202, Jan. 15, 2015]

Subpart S [Reserved]

Subpart T—Diesel-Powered Equipment

SOURCE: 61 FR 55527, Oct. 25, 1996, unless otherwise noted.

§75.1900 Definitions.

The following definitions apply in this subpart.

Diesel fuel tank. A closed metal vessel specifically designed for the storage or transport of diesel fuel.

Diesel fuel transportation unit. A self-propelled or portable wheeled vehicle used to transport a diesel fuel tank.

Noncombustible material. A material that will continue to serve its intended function for 1 hour when subjected to a fire test incorporating an ASTM E119–88 time/temperature heat input, or equivalent. The publication ASTM E119–88 "Standard Test Methods for Fire Tests of Building Construction and Materials" is incorporated by reference and may be inspected at any MSHA Coal Mine Safety and Health District Office; at MSHA's Office of Standards, Regulations, and Variances, 201 12th Street South, Arlington, VA 22202–5452; 202–693–9440; or at the National Archives and Records Administration (NARA). For information on the availability of this material at NARA, call 202–741–6030, or go to: *http:// www.archives.gov/federal_register/ code_of_federal_regulations/ ibr_locations.html.* This incorporation by reference was approved by the Director of the Federal Register in accordance with 5 U.S.C. 552(a) and 1 CFR part 51. In addition, copies of the document may be purchased from the American Society for Testing and Materials (ASTM), 100 Barr Harbor Drive, P.O. Box C700, West Conshohocken, PA, 19428–2959; 610–832–9500; *http:// www.astm.org.*

Permanent underground diesel fuel storage facility. A facility designed and constructed to remain at one location for the storage or dispensing of diesel fuel, which does not move as mining progresses.

Safety can. A metal container intended for storage, transport or dispensing of diesel fuel, with a nominal capacity of 5 gallons, listed or approved by a nationally recognized independent testing laboratory.

Temporary underground diesel fuel storage area. An area of the mine provided for the short-term storage of diesel fuel in a fuel transportation unit, which moves as mining progresses.

[35 FR 17890, Nov. 20, 1970, as amended at 67 FR 38386, June 4, 2002; 71 FR 16669, Apr. 3, 2006; 80 FR 52992, Sept. 2, 2015]

§75.1901 Diesel fuel requirements.

(a) Diesel-powered equipment shall be used underground only with a diesel fuel having a sulfur content no greater than 0.05 percent and a flash point of 100 °F (38 °C) or greater. Upon request, the mine operator shall provide to an authorized representative of the Secretary evidence that the diesel fuel purchased for use in diesel-powered equipment underground meets these requirements.

(b) Flammable liquids shall not be added to diesel fuel used in diesel-powered equipment underground.

(c) Only diesel fuel additives that have been registered by the Environmental Protection Agency may be used in diesel-powered equipment underground.

§ 75.1902 Underground diesel fuel storage—general requirements.

(a) All diesel fuel must be stored in:

(1) Diesel fuel tanks in permanent underground diesel fuel storage facilities;

(2) Diesel fuel tanks on diesel fuel transportation units in permanent underground diesel fuel storage facilities or in temporary underground fuel storage areas; or

(3) Safety cans.

(b) The total capacity of stationary diesel fuel tanks in permanent underground diesel fuel storage facilities must not exceed 1000 gallons.

(c)(1) Only one temporary underground diesel fuel storage area is permitted for each working section or in each area of the mine where equipment is being installed or removed.

(2) The temporary underground diesel fuel storage area must be located—

(i) Within 500 feet of the loading point;

(ii) Within 500 feet of the projected loading point where equipment is being installed; or

(iii) Within 500 feet of the last loading point where equipment is being removed.

(3) No more than one diesel fuel transportation unit at a time shall be parked in the temporary underground diesel fuel storage area.

(d) Permanent underground diesel fuel storage facilities and temporary underground diesel fuel storage areas must be—

(1) At least 100 feet from shafts, slopes, shops, or explosives magazines;

(2) At least 25 feet from trolley wires or power cables, or electric equipment not necessary for the operation of the storage facilities or areas; and

(3) In a location that is protected from damage by other mobile equipment.

(e) Permanent underground diesel fuel storage facilities must not be located within the primary escapeway.

§ 75.1903 Underground diesel fuel storage facilities and areas; construction and safety precautions.

(a) Permanent underground diesel fuel storage facilities must be—

(1) Constructed of noncombustible materials, including floors, roofs, roof supports, doors, and door frames. Exposed coal within fuel storage areas must be covered with noncombustible materials. If bulkheads are used they must be tightly sealed and must be built of or covered with noncombustible materials;

(2) Provided with either self-closing doors or a means for automatic enclosure;

(3) Provided with a means for personnel to enter and exit the facility after closure;

(4) Ventilated with intake air that is coursed into a return air course or to the surface and that is not used to ventilate working places, using ventilation controls meeting the requirements of § 75.333(e);

(5) Equipped with an automatic fire suppression system that meets the requirements of § 75.1912. Actuation of the automatic fire suppression system shall initiate the means for automatic enclosure;

(6) Provided with a means of containment capable of holding 150 percent of the maximum capacity of the fuel storage system; and

(7) Provided with a competent concrete floor or equivalent to prevent fuel spills from saturating the mine floor.

(b) Permanent underground diesel fuel storage facilities and temporary underground diesel fuel storage areas must be—

(1) Equipped with at least 240 pounds of rock dust and provided with two portable multipurpose dry chemical type (ABC) fire extinguishers that are listed or approved by a nationally recognized independent testing laboratory and have a 10A:60B:C or higher rating. Both fire extinguishers must be easily accessible to personnel, and at least one fire extinguisher must be located

Mine Safety and Health Admin., Labor §75.1904

outside of the storage facility or area upwind of the facility, in intake air; or

(2) Provided with three portable multipurpose dry chemical type (ABC) fire extinguishers that are listed or approved by a nationally recognized independent testing laboratory and have a 10A:60B:C or higher rating. All fire extinguishers must be easily accessible to personnel, and at least one fire extinguisher must be located outside of the storage facility or area upwind of the facility, in intake air.

(3) Identified with conspicuous markings designating diesel fuel storage; and

(4) Maintained to prevent the accumulation of water.

(c) Welding or cutting other than that performed in accordance with paragraph (d) of this section shall not be performed within 50 feet of a permanent underground diesel fuel storage facility or a temporary underground diesel fuel storage area.

(d) When it is necessary to weld, cut, or solder pipelines, tanks, or other containers that may have contained diesel fuel, these practices shall be followed:

(1) Cutting or welding shall not be performed on or within pipelines, tanks, or other containers that have contained diesel fuel until they have been thoroughly purged and cleaned or inerted and a vent or opening is provided to allow for sufficient release of any buildup pressure before heat is applied.

(2) Diesel fuel shall not be allowed to enter pipelines, tanks, or containers that have been welded, soldered, brazed, or cut until the metal has cooled to ambient temperature.

§75.1904 Underground diesel fuel tanks and safety cans.

(a) Diesel fuel tanks used underground shall—

(1) Have steel walls of a minimum 3/16-inch thickness, or walls made of other metal of a thickness that provides equivalent strength;

(2) Be protected from corrosion;

(3) Be of seamless construction or have liquid tight welded seams;

(4) Not leak; and

(5) For stationary tanks in permanent underground diesel fuel storage facilities, be placed on supports constructed of noncombustible material so that the tanks are at least 12 inches above the floor.

(b) Underground diesel fuel tanks must be provided with—

(1) Devices for emergency venting designed to open at a pressure not to exceed 2.5 psi according to the following—

(i) Tanks with a capacity greater than 500 gallons must have an emergency venting device whose area is equivalent to a pipe with a nominal inside diameter of 5 inches or greater; and

(ii) Tanks with a capacity of 500 gallons or less must have an emergency venting device whose area is equivalent to a pipe with a nominal inside diameter of 4 inches or greater.

(2) Tethered or self-closing caps for stationary tanks in permanent underground diesel fuel storage facilities and self-closing caps for diesel fuel tanks on diesel fuel transportation units;

(3) Vents to permit the free discharge of liquid, at least as large as the fill or withdrawal connection, whichever is larger, but not less than 1¼ inch nominal inside diameter;

(4) Liquid tight connections for all tank openings that are—

(i) Identified by conspicuous markings that specify the function; and

(ii) Closed when not in use.

(5) Vent pipes that drain toward the tank without sagging and are higher than the fill pipe opening;

(6) Shutoff valves located as close as practicable to the tank shell on each connection through which liquid can normally flow; and

(7) An automatic closing, heat-actuated valve on each withdrawal connection below the liquid level.

(c) When tanks are provided with openings for manual gauging, liquid tight, tethered or self-closing caps or covers must be provided and must be kept closed when not open for gauging.

(d) Surfaces of the tank and its associated components must be protected against damage by collision.

(e) Before being placed in service, tanks and their associated components must be tested for leakage at a pressure equal to the working pressure, except tanks and components connected directly to piping systems, which must

669

§ 75.1905

be properly designed for the application.

(f) Safety cans must be:
(1) Limited to a nominal capacity of 5 gallons or less;
(2) Equipped with a flexible or rigid tubular nozzle attached to a valved spout;
(3) Provided with a vent valve designed to open and close simultaneously and automatically with the opening and closing of the pouring valve; and
(4) Designed so that they will safely relieve internal pressure when exposed to fire.

§ 75.1905 Dispensing of diesel fuel.

(a) Diesel-powered equipment in underground coal mines may be refueled only from safety cans, from tanks on diesel fuel transportation units, or from stationary tanks.

(b) Fuel that is dispensed from other than safety cans must be dispensed by means of—
(1) Gravity feed with a hose equipped with a nozzle with a self-closing valve and no latch-open device;
(2) A manual pump with a hose equipped with a nozzle containing a self-closing valve; or
(3) A powered pump with:
(i) An accessible emergency shutoff switch for each nozzle;
(ii) A hose equipped with a self-closing valve and no latch-open device; and
(iii) An anti-siphoning device.

(c) Diesel fuel must not be dispensed using compressed gas.

(d) Diesel fuel must not be dispensed to the fuel tank of diesel-powered equipment while the equipment engine is running.

(e) Powered pumps shall be shut off when fuel is not being dispensed.

§ 75.1905-1 Diesel fuel piping systems.

(a) Diesel fuel piping systems from the surface must be designed and operated as dry systems, unless an automatic shutdown is incorporated that prevents accidental loss or spillage of fuel and that activates an alarm system.

(b) All piping, valves and fittings must be—
(1) Capable of withstanding working pressures and stresses;
(2) Capable of withstanding four times the static pressures;
(3) Compatible with diesel fuel; and
(4) Maintained in a manner that prevents leakage.

(c) Pipelines must have manual shutoff valves installed at the surface filling point, and at the underground discharge point.

(d) If diesel fuel lines are not buried in the ground sufficiently to protect them from damage, shutoff valves must be located every 300 feet.

(e) Shutoff valves must be installed at each branch line where the branch line joins the main line.

(f) An automatic means must be provided to prevent unintentional transfer of diesel fuel from the surface into the permanent underground diesel fuel storage facility.

(g) Diesel fuel piping systems from the surface shall only be used to transport diesel fuel directly to stationary tanks or diesel fuel transportation units in a permanent underground diesel fuel storage facility.

(h) The diesel fuel piping system must not be located in a borehole with electric power cables.

(i) Diesel fuel piping systems located in entries must not be located on the same side of the entry as electric cables or power lines. Where it is necessary for piping systems to cross electric cables or power lines, guarding must be provided to prevent severed electrical cables or power lines near broken fuel lines.

(j) Diesel fuel piping systems must be protected and located to prevent physical damage.

§ 75.1906 Transport of diesel fuel.

(a) Diesel fuel shall be transported only by diesel fuel transportation units or in safety cans.

(b) No more than one safety can shall be transported on a vehicle at any time. The can must be protected from damage during transport. All other safety cans must be stored in permanent underground diesel fuel storage facilities.

(c) Safety cans that leak must be promptly removed from the mine.

Mine Safety and Health Admin., Labor §75.1908

(d) Diesel fuel transportation unit tanks and safety cans must be conspicuously marked as containing diesel fuel.

(e) Diesel fuel transportation units must transport no more than 500 gallons of diesel fuel at a time.

(f) Tanks on diesel fuel transportation units must be permanently fixed to the unit and have a total capacity of no greater than 500 gallons of diesel fuel.

(g) Non-self-propelled diesel fuel transportation units with electrical components for dispensing fuel that are connected to a source of electrical power must be protected by a fire suppression device that meets the requirements of §§75.1107–3 through 75.1107–6, and §§75.1107–8 through 75.1107–16.

(h) Diesel fuel transportation units and vehicles transporting safety cans containing diesel fuel must have at least two multipurpose, dry chemical type (ABC) fire extinguishers, listed or approved by a nationally recognized independent testing laboratory and having a 10A:60B:C or higher rating, with one fire extinguisher provided on each side of the vehicle.

(i) Diesel fuel transportation units shall be parked only in permanent underground diesel fuel storage facilities or temporary underground diesel fuel storage areas when not in use.

(j) When the distance between a diesel fuel transportation unit and an energized trolley wire at any location is less than 12 inches, the requirements of §75.1003–2 must be followed.

(k) Diesel fuel shall not be transported on or with mantrips or on conveyor belts.

(l) Diesel fuel shall be stored and handled in accordance with the requirements of §§75.1902 through 75.1906 of this part as of November 25, 1997.

[61 FR 55527, Oct. 25, 1996, as amended at 63 FR 12647, Mar. 16, 1998]

§75.1907 Diesel-powered equipment intended for use in underground coal mines.

(a) As of November 25, 1996 all diesel-powered equipment used where permissible electrical equipment is required must be approved under part 36 of this chapter.

(b) Diesel-powered equipment approved under part 36 of this chapter must be provided with additional safety features in accordance with the following time schedule:

(1) As of April 25, 1997 the equipment must have a safety component system that limits surface temperatures to those specified in subpart F of part 7 of this title;

(2) As of November 25, 1999 the equipment must have an automatic or manual fire suppression system that meets the requirements of §75.1911 of this part, and at least one portable multipurpose dry chemical type (ABC) fire extinguisher, listed or approved by a nationally recognized independent testing laboratory and having a 10A:60B:C or higher rating. The fire extinguisher must be located within easy reach of the equipment operator and be protected from damage by collision.

(3) As of November 25, 1999 the equipment must have a brake system that meets the requirements of §75.1909 (b)(6), (b)(7), (b)(8), (c), (d), and (e);

(4) As of November 25, 1997 a particulate index and dilution air quantity shall be determined for the equipment in accordance with subpart E of part 7 of this chapter; and

(5) Permissible diesel-powered equipment manufactured on or after November 25, 1999 and that is used in an underground coal mine shall incorporate a power package approved in accordance with part 7, subpart F of this chapter.

(c) As of November 25, 1999 nonpermissible diesel-powered equipment, except the special category of equipment under §75.1908(d), shall meet the requirements of §§75.1909 and 75.1910 of this part.

§75.1908 Nonpermissible diesel-powered equipment; categories.

(a) Heavy-duty diesel-powered equipment includes—

(1) Equipment that cuts or moves rock or coal;

(2) Equipment that performs drilling or bolting functions;

(3) Equipment that moves longwall components;

(4) Self-propelled diesel fuel transportation units and self-propelled lube units; or

§ 75.1909

(5) Machines used to transport portable diesel fuel transportation units or portable lube units.

(b) Light-duty diesel-powered equipment is any diesel-powered equipment that does not meet the criteria of paragraph (a).

(c) For the purposes of this subpart, the following equipment is considered attended:

(1) Any machine or device operated by a miner; or

(2) Any machine or device that is mounted in the direct line of sight of a job site located within 500 feet of such machine or device, which job site is occupied by a miner.

(d) Diesel-powered ambulances and fire fighting equipment are a special category of equipment that may be used underground only in accordance with the mine fire fighting and evacuation plan under § 75.1502.

[61 FR 55527, Oct. 25, 1996; 70 FR 36347, June 23, 2005]

§ 75.1909 Nonpermissible diesel-powered equipment; design and performance requirements.

(a) Nonpermissible diesel-powered equipment, except for the special category of equipment under § 75.1908(d), must be equipped with the following features:

(1) An engine approved under subpart E of part 7 of this title equipped with an air filter sized in accordance with the engine manufacturer's recommendations, and an air filter service indicator set in accordance with the engine manufacturer's recommendations;

(2) At least one portable multipurpose dry chemical type (ABC) fire extinguisher listed or approved by a nationally recognized independent testing laboratory with a 10A:60B:C or higher rating. The fire extinguisher must be located within easy reach of the equipment operator and protected from damage;

(3) A fuel system specifically designed for diesel fuel meeting the following requirements:

(i) A fuel tank and fuel lines that do not leak;

(ii) A fuel tank that is substantially constructed and protected against damage by collision;

(iii) A vent opening that maintains atmospheric pressure in the fuel tank, and that is designed to prevent fuel from splashing out of the vent opening;

(iv) A self-closing filler cap on the fuel tank;

(v) The fuel tank, filler and vent must be located so that leaks or spillage during refueling will not contact hot surfaces;

(vi) Fuel line piping must be either steel-wire reinforced; synthetic elastomer-covered hose suitable for use with diesel fuel that has been tested and has been determined to be fire-resistant by the manufacturer; or metal;

(vii) Fuel line piping must be clamped;

(viii) Primary fuel lines must be located so that fuel line leaks do not contact hot surfaces;

(ix) The fuel lines must be separated from electrical wiring and protected from damage in ordinary use;

(x) A manual shutoff valve must be installed in the fuel system as close as practicable to the tank; and

(xi) A water separator and fuel filter(s) must be provided.

(4) A sensor to monitor the temperature and provide a visual warning of an overheated cylinder head on air-cooled engines;

(5) Guarding to protect fuel, hydraulic, and electric lines when such lines pass near rotating parts or in the event of shaft failure;

(6) Hydraulic tanks, fillers, vents, and lines located to prevent spillage or leaks from contacting hot surfaces;

(7) Reflectors or warning lights mounted on the equipment which can be readily seen in all directions;

(8) A means to direct exhaust gas away from the equipment operator, persons on board the machine, and combustible machine components;

(9) A means to prevent unintentional free and uncontrolled descent of personnel-elevating work platforms; and

(10) A means to prevent the spray from ruptured hydraulic or lubricating oil lines from being ignited by contact with engine exhaust system component surfaces.

(b) Self-propelled nonpermissible diesel-powered equipment must have the following features in addition to those in paragraph (a):

Mine Safety and Health Admin., Labor § 75.1909

(1) A means to ensure that no stored hydraulic energy that will cause machine articulation is available after the engine is shut down;

(2) A neutral start feature which ensures that engine cranking torque will not be transmitted through the powertrain and cause machine movement on vehicles utilizing fluid power transmissions;

(3) For machines with steering wheels, brake pedals, and accelerator pedals, controls which are of automobile orientation;

(4) An audible warning device conveniently located near the equipment operator;

(5) Lights provided and maintained on both ends of the equipment. Equipment normally operated in both directions must be equipped with headlights for both directions;

(6) Service brakes that act on each wheel of the vehicle and that are designed such that failure of any single component, except the brake actuation pedal or other similar actuation device, must not result in a complete loss of service braking capability;

(7) Service brakes that safely bring the fully loaded vehicle to a complete stop on the maximum grade on which it is operated; and

(8) No device that traps a column of fluid to hold the brake in the applied position shall be installed in any brake system, unless the trapped column of fluid is released when the equipment operator is no longer in contact with the brake activation device.

(c) Self-propelled nonpermissible heavy-duty diesel-powered equipment under § 75.1908(a), except rail-mounted equipment, shall be provided with a supplemental braking system that:

(1) Engages automatically within 5 seconds of the shutdown of the engine;

(2) Safely brings the equipment when fully loaded to a complete stop on the maximum grade on which it is operated;

(3) Holds the equipment stationary, despite any contraction of brake parts, exhaustion of any nonmechanical source of energy, or leakage;

(4) Releases only by a manual control that does not operate any other equipment function;

(5) Has a means in the equipment operator's compartment to apply the brakes manually without shutting down the engine, and a means to release and reengage the brakes without the engine operating; and

(6) Has a means to ensure that the supplemental braking system is released before the equipment can be trammed, and is designed to ensure the brake is fully released at all times while the equipment is trammed.

(d) Self-propelled nonpermissible light-duty diesel-powered equipment under § 75.1908(b), except rail-mounted equipment, must be provided with a parking brake that holds the fully loaded equipment stationary on the maximum grade on which it is operated despite any contraction of the brake parts, exhaustion of any nonmechanical source of energy, or leakage.

(e) The supplemental and park brake systems required by paragraphs (c) and (d) must be applied when the equipment operator is not at the controls of the equipment, except during movement of disabled equipment.

(f) Self-propelled personnel-elevating work platforms must be provided with a means to ensure that the parking braking system is released before the equipment can be trammed, and must be designed to ensure the brake is fully released at all times while the equipment is trammed.

(g) Any nonpermissible equipment that discharges its exhaust directly into a return air course must be provided with a power package approved under subpart F of part 7 of this title.

(h) Self-propelled nonpermissible heavy-duty diesel-powered equipment meeting the requirements of § 75.1908(a) must be provided with an automatic fire suppression system meeting the requirements of § 75.1911.

(i) Self-propelled nonpermissible light-duty diesel-powered equipment meeting the requirements of § 75.1908(b) must be provided with an automatic or manual fire suppression system meeting the requirements of § 75.1911.

(j) Nonpermissible equipment that is not self-propelled must have the following features in addition to those listed in paragraph (a):

§ 75.1910

(1) A means to prevent inadvertent movement of the equipment when parked;

(2) Safety chains or other suitable secondary connections on equipment that is being towed; and

(3) An automatic fire suppression system meeting the requirements of § 75.1911.

[61 FR 55527, Oct. 25, 1996; 62 FR 34641, June 27, 1997]

§ 75.1910 Nonpermissible diesel-powered equipment; electrical system design and performance requirements.

Electrical circuits and components associated with or connected to electrical systems on nonpermissible diesel-powered equipment utilizing storage batteries and integral charging systems, except for the special category of equipment under § 75.1908(d), must conform to the following requirements:

(a) Overload and short circuit protection must be provided for electric circuits and components in accordance with §§ 75.518 and 75.518–1 of this part;

(b) Each electric conductor from the battery to the starting motor must be protected against short circuit by fuses or other circuit-interrupting devices placed as near as practicable to the battery terminals;

(c) Each branch circuit conductor connected to the main circuit between the battery and charging generator must be protected against short circuit by fuses or other automatic circuit-interrupting devices;

(d) The electrical system shall be equipped with a circuit-interrupting device by means of which all power conductors can be deenergized. The device must be located as close as practicable to the battery terminals and be designed to operate within its electrical rating without damage. The device shall not automatically reset after being actuated. All magnetic circuit-interrupting devices must be mounted in a manner to preclude their closing by force of gravity;

(e) Each motor and charging generator must be protected by an automatic overcurrent device. One protective device will be acceptable when two motors of the same rating operate simultaneously and perform virtually the same duty;

(f) Each ungrounded conductor must have insulation compatible with the impressed voltage. Insulation materials must be resistant to deterioration from engine heat and oil. Electric conductors must meet the applicable requirements of §§ 75.513 and 75.513–1, except electric conductors for starting motors, which must only meet the requirements of § 75.513;

(g) All wiring must have adequate mechanical protection to prevent damage to the cable that might result in short circuits;

(h) Sharp edges and corners must be removed at all points where there is a possibility of damaging wires, cables, or conduits by cutting or abrasion. The insulation of the cables within a battery box must be protected against abrasion;

(i) When insulated wires other than cables pass through metal frames, the holes must be substantially bushed with insulated bushings. Cables must enter metal frames of motors, splice boxes, and electric components only through proper fittings. All electrical connections and splices must be mechanically and electrically efficient, and suitable connectors shall be used. All electrical connectors or splices in insulated wire must be reinsulated at least to the same degree of protection as the remainder of the wire;

(j) The battery must be secured to prevent movement, and must be protected from external damage by position. Batteries that are not protected from external damage by position must be enclosed in a battery box. Flame-resistant insulation treated to resist chemical reaction to electrolyte must be provided on battery connections to prevent battery terminals from contacting conducting surfaces;

(k) A battery box, including the cover, must be constructed of steel with a minimum thickness of 1/8 inch, or of a material other than steel that provides equivalent strength;

(l) Battery-box covers must be lined with a flame-resistant insulating material permanently attached to the underside of the cover, unless equivalent protection is provided. Battery-box covers must be provided with a means

Mine Safety and Health Admin., Labor § 75.1911

for securing them in closed position. At least ½ inch of air space must be provided between the underside of the cover and the top of the battery, including terminals;

(m) Battery boxes must be provided with ventilation openings to prevent the accumulation of flammable or toxic gases or vapors within the battery box. The size and locations of openings for ventilation must prevent direct access to battery terminals;

(n) The battery must be insulated from the battery-box walls and supported on insulating materials. Insulating materials that may be subject to chemical reaction with electrolyte must be treated to resist such action; and

(o) Drainage holes must be provided in the bottom of each battery box.

§ 75.1911 Fire suppression systems for diesel-powered equipment and fuel transportation units.

(a) The fire suppression system required by §§ 75.1907 and 75.1909 shall be a multipurpose dry chemical type (ABC) fire suppression system listed or approved by a nationally recognized independent testing laboratory and appropriate for installation on diesel-powered equipment and fuel transportation units.

(1) The system shall be installed in accordance with the manufacturer's specifications and the limitations of the listing or approval.

(2) The system shall be installed in a protected location or guarded to minimize physical damage from routine vehicle operations.

(3) Suppressant agent distribution tubing or piping shall be secured and protected against damage, including pinching, crimping, stretching, abrasion, and corrosion.

(4) Discharge nozzles shall be positioned and aimed for maximum fire suppression effectiveness. Nozzles shall also be protected against the entrance of foreign materials such as mud, coal dust, or rock dust.

(b) The fire suppression system shall provide fire suppression and, if automatic, fire detection for the engine including the starter, transmission, hydraulic pumps and tanks, fuel tanks, exposed brake units, air compressors and battery areas on diesel-powered equipment and electric panels or controls used on fuel transportation units and other areas as necessary.

(c) If automatic, the fire suppression system shall include audible and visual alarms to warn of fires or system faults.

(d) The fire suppression system shall provide for automatic engine shutdown. If the fire suppression system is automatic, engine shutdown and discharge of suppressant agent may be delayed for a maximum of 15 seconds after the fire is detected by the system.

(e) The fire suppression system shall be operable by at least two manual actuators. One actuator shall be located on each side of the equipment. If the equipment is provided with an operator's compartment, one of the manual actuators shall be located in the compartment within reach of the operator.

(f) The fire suppression system shall remain operative in the event of engine shutdown, equipment electrical system failure, or failure of any other equipment system.

(g) The electrical components of each fire suppression system installed on equipment used where permissible electric equipment is required shall be permissible or intrinsically safe and such components shall be maintained in permissible or intrinsically safe condition.

(h) Electrically operated detection and actuation circuits shall be monitored and provided with status indicators showing power and circuit continuity. If the system is not electrically operated, a means shall be provided to indicate the functional readiness status of the detection system.

(i) Each fire suppression system shall be tested and maintained in accordance with the manufacturer's recommended inspection and maintenance program and as required by the nationally recognized independent testing laboratory listing or approval, and be visually inspected at least once each week by a person trained to make such inspections.

(j) *Recordkeeping.* Persons performing inspections and tests of fire suppression systems under paragraph (i) shall record when a fire suppression system does not meet the installation or maintenance requirements of this section.

§ 75.1912

(1) The record shall include the equipment on which the fire suppression system did not meet the installation or maintenance requirements of this section, the defect found, and the corrective action taken.

(2) Records are to be kept manually in a secure manner not susceptible to alteration or recorded electronically in a secured computer system that is not susceptible to alteration.

(3) Records shall be maintained at a surface location at the mine for one year and made available for inspection by an authorized representative of the Secretary and miners' representatives.

(k) All miners normally assigned to the active workings of the mine shall be instructed about the hazards inherent to the operation of the fire suppression systems and, where appropriate, the safeguards available for each system.

(l) For purposes of § 75.380(f), a fire suppression system installed on diesel-powered equipment and meeting the requirements of this section is equivalent to a fire suppression system meeting the requirements of §§ 75.1107-3 through 75.1107-16.

§ 75.1912 Fire suppression systems for permanent underground diesel fuel storage facilities.

(a) The fire suppression system required by § 75.1903 shall be an automatic multipurpose dry chemical type (ABC) fire suppression system listed or approved as an engineered dry chemical extinguishing system by a nationally recognized independent testing laboratory and appropriate for installation at a permanent underground diesel fuel storage facility.

(1) Alternate types of fire suppression systems shall be approved in accordance with § 75.1107-13 of this part.

(2) The system shall be installed in accordance with the manufacturer's specifications and the limitations of the listing or approval.

(3) The system shall be installed in a protected location or guarded to prevent physical damage from routine operations.

(4) Suppressant agent distribution tubing or piping shall be secured and protected against damage, including pinching, crimping, stretching, abrasion, and corrosion.

(5) Discharge nozzles shall be positioned and aimed for maximum fire suppression effectiveness in the protected areas. Nozzles must also be protected against the entrance of foreign materials such as mud, coal dust, and rock dust.

(b) The fire suppression system shall provide automatic fire detection and automatic fire suppression for all areas within the facility.

(c) Audible and visual alarms to warn of fire or system faults shall be provided at the protected area and at a surface location which is continually monitored by a person when personnel are underground. In the event of a fire, personnel shall be warned in accordance with the provisions set forth in § 75.1502.

(d) The fire suppression system shall deenergize all power to the diesel fuel storage facility when actuated except that required for automatic enclosure and alarms.

(e) Fire suppression systems shall include two manual actuators located as follows:

(1) At least one within the fuel storage facility; and

(2) At least one a safe distance away from the storage facility and located in intake air, upwind of the storage facility.

(f) The fire suppression system shall remain operational in the event of electrical system failure.

(g) Electrically operated detection and actuation circuits shall be monitored and provided with status indicators showing power and circuit continuity. If the system is not electrically operated, a means shall be provided to indicate the functional readiness status of the detection system.

(h) Each fire suppression system shall be tested and maintained in accordance with the manufacturer's recommended inspection and maintenance program and as required by the nationally recognized independent testing laboratory listing or approval, and be visually inspected at least once each week by a person trained to make such inspections.

Mine Safety and Health Admin., Labor § 75.1914

(i) *Recordkeeping.* Persons performing inspections and tests of fire suppression systems under paragraph (h) shall record when a fire suppression system does not meet the installation or maintenance requirements of this section.

(1) The record shall include the facility whose fire suppression system did not meet the installation or maintenance requirements of this section, the defect found, and the corrective action taken.

(2) Records are to be kept manually in a secure manner not susceptible to alteration or recorded electronically in a secured computer system that is not susceptible to alteration.

(3) Records shall be maintained at a surface location at the mine for one year and made available for inspection by an authorized representative of the Secretary and miners' representatives.

(j) All miners normally assigned to the active workings of the mine shall be instructed about the hazards inherent to the operation of the fire suppression systems and, where appropriate, the safeguards available for each system.

[61 FR 55527, Oct. 25, 1996; 70 FR 36347, June 23, 2005]

§ 75.1913 Starting aids.

(a) Volatile fuel starting aids shall be used in accordance with recommendations provided by the starting aid manufacturer, the engine manufacturer, and the machine manufacturer.

(b) Containers of volatile fuel starting aids shall be conspicuously marked to indicate the contents. When not in use, containers of volatile fuel starting aids shall be stored in metal enclosures that are used only for storage of starting aids. Such metal enclosures must be conspicuously marked, secured, and protected from damage.

(c) Volatile fuel starting aids shall not be:

(1) Taken into or used in areas where permissible equipment is required;

(2) Used in the presence of open flames or burning flame safety lamps, or when welding or cutting is taking place; or

(3) Used in any area where 1.0 percent or greater concentration of methane is present.

(d) Compressed oxygen or compressed flammable gases shall not be connected to diesel air-start systems.

§ 75.1914 Maintenance of diesel-powered equipment.

(a) Diesel-powered equipment shall be maintained in approved and safe condition or removed from service.

(b) Maintenance and repairs of approved features and those features required by §§ 75.1909 and 75.1910 on diesel-powered equipment shall be made only by a person qualified under § 75.1915.

(c) The water scrubber system on diesel-powered equipment shall be drained and flushed, by a person who is trained to perform this task, at least once on each shift in which the equipment is operated.

(d) The intake air filter on diesel-powered equipment shall be replaced or serviced, by a person who is trained to perform this task, when the intake air pressure drop device so indicates or when the engine manufacturer's maximum allowable air pressure drop level is exceeded.

(e) Mobile diesel-powered equipment that is to be used during a shift shall be visually examined by the equipment operator before being placed in operation. Equipment defects affecting safety shall be reported promptly to the mine operator.

(f) All diesel-powered equipment shall be examined and tested weekly by a person qualified under § 75.1915.

(1) Examinations and tests shall be conducted in accordance with approved checklists and manufacturers' maintenance manuals.

(2) Persons performing weekly examinations and tests of diesel-powered equipment under this paragraph shall make a record when the equipment is not in approved or safe condition. The record shall include the equipment that is not in approved or safe condition, the defect found, and the corrective action taken.

(g) Undiluted exhaust emissions of diesel engines in diesel-powered equipment approved under part 36 and heavy-duty nonpermissible diesel-powered equipment as defined in § 75.1908(a) in use in underground coal mines shall be tested and evaluated weekly by a person who is trained to perform this task. The mine operator shall develop and implement written standard operating procedures for such testing and evaluation that specify the following:

(1) The method of achieving a repeatable loaded engine operating condition for each type of equipment;

(2) Sampling and analytical methods (including calibration of instrumentation) that are capable of accurately detecting carbon monoxide in the expected concentrations;

(3) The method of evaluation and interpretation of the results;

(4) The concentration or changes in concentration of carbon monoxide that will indicate a change in engine performance. Carbon monoxide concentration shall not exceed 2500 parts per million; and

(5) The maintenance of records necessary to track engine performance.

(h) *Recordkeeping.* Records required by paragraphs (f)(2) and (g)(5) shall be—

(1) Recorded in a secure book that is not susceptible to alteration, or recorded electronically in a computer system that is secure and not susceptible to alteration; and

(2) Retained at a surface location at the mine for at least 1 year and made available for inspection by an authorized representative of the Secretary and by miners' representatives.

(i) Diesel-powered equipment must be maintained in accordance with this part as of November 25, 1997.

§ 75.1915 Training and qualification of persons working on diesel-powered equipment.

(a) To be qualified to perform maintenance, repairs, examinations and tests on diesel-powered equipment, as required by § 75.1914, a person must successfully complete a training and qualification program that meets the requirements of this section. A person qualified to perform these tasks shall be retrained as necessary to maintain the ability to perform all assigned diesel-powered equipment maintenance, repairs, examinations and tests.

(b) A training and qualification program under this section must:

(1) Be presented by a competent instructor;

(2) Be sufficient to prepare or update a person's ability to perform all assigned tasks with respect to diesel-powered equipment maintenance, repairs, examinations and tests;

(3) Address, at a minimum, the following:

(i) The requirements of subpart T of this part;

(ii) Use of appropriate power package or machine checklists to conduct tests to ensure that diesel-powered equipment is in approved and safe condition, with acceptable emission levels;

(iii) Proper maintenance of approved features and the correct use of the appropriate maintenance manuals, including machine adjustments, service, and assembly;

(iv) Diesel-powered equipment fire suppression system tests and maintenance;

(v) Fire and ignition sources and their control or elimination, including cleaning of the equipment;

(vi) Safe fueling procedures and maintenance of the fuel system of the equipment; and

(vii) Intake air system maintenance and tests.

(4) Include an examination that requires demonstration of the ability to perform all assigned tasks with respect to diesel-powered equipment maintenance, repairs, examinations and tests; and

(5) Be in writing. The written program shall include a description of the course content, materials, and teaching methods for initial training and retraining.

(c) *Recordkeeping.* The operator shall maintain a copy of the training and qualification program required by this section and a record of the names of all persons qualified under the program.

(1) The record of the names of qualified persons shall be made in a manner that is not susceptible to alteration, or recorded electronically in a computer system that is secure and not susceptible to alteration.

(2) The training and qualification program and record of qualified persons are to be kept at surface location of the mine and made available for inspection by an authorized representative of the Secretary and by miners' representatives.

§ 75.1916 Operation of diesel-powered equipment.

(a) Diesel-powered equipment shall be operated at a speed that is consistent with the type of equipment being operated, roadway conditions, grades, clearances, visibility, and other traffic.

(b) Operators of mobile diesel-powered equipment shall maintain full control of the equipment while it is in motion.

(c) Standardized traffic rules, including speed limits, signals and warning signs, shall be established at each mine and followed.

(d) Except as required in normal mining operations, mobile diesel-powered equipment shall not be idled.

(e) Diesel-powered equipment shall not be operated unattended.

PART 77—MANDATORY SAFETY STANDARDS, SURFACE COAL MINES AND SURFACE WORK AREAS OF UNDERGROUND COAL MINES

Subpart A—General

Sec.
77.1 Scope.
77.2 Definitions.

Subpart B—Qualified and Certified Persons

77.100 Certified person.
77.101 Tests for methane and for oxygen deficiency; qualified person.
77.102 Tests for methane; oxygen deficiency; qualified person, additional requirement.
77.103 Electrical work; qualified person.
77.104 Repair of energized surface high voltage lines; qualified person.
77.105 Qualified hoistman; slope or shaft sinking operation; qualifications.
77.106 Records of certified and qualified persons.
77.107 Training programs.
77.107-1 Plans for training programs.

Subpart C—Surface Installations

77.200 Surface installations; general.
77.201 Methane content in surface installations.
77.201-1 Tests for methane; qualified person; use of approved device.
77.201-2 Methane accumulations; change in ventilation.
77.202 Dust accumulations in surface installations.
77.203 Use of material or equipment overhead; safeguards.
77.204 Openings in surface installations; safeguards.
77.205 Travelways at surface installations.
77.206 Ladders; construction; installation and maintenance.
77.207 Illumination.
77.208 Storage of materials.
77.209 Surge and storage piles.
77.210 Hoisting of materials.
77.211 Draw-off tunnels; stockpiling and reclaiming operations; general.
77.211-1 Continuous methane monitoring device; installation and operation; automatic deenergization of electric equipment.
77.212 Draw-off tunnel ventilation fans; installation.
77.213 Draw-off tunnel escapeways.
77.214 Refuse piles; general.
77.215 Refuse piles, construction requirements.
77.215-1 Refuse piles; identification.
77.215-2 Refuse piles; reporting requirements.
77.215-3 Refuse piles; certification.
77.215-4 Refuse piles; abandonment.
77.216 Water, sediment, or slurry impoundments and impounding structures; general.
77.216-1 Water, sediment or slurry impoundments and impounding structures; identification.
77.216-2 Water, sediment, or slurry impoundments and impounding structures; minimum plan requirements; changes or modifications; certification.
77.216-3 Water, sediment, or slurry impoundments and impounding structures; inspection requirements; correction of hazards; program requirements.
77.216-4 Water, sediment or slurry impoundments and impounding structures; reporting requirements; certification.
77.216-5 Water, sediment or slurry impoundments and impounding structures; abandonment.
77.217 Definitions.

Subpart D—Thermal Dryers

77.300 Thermal dryers; general.
77.301 Dryer heating units; operation.
77.302 Bypass stacks.
77.303 Hot gas inlet chamber dropout doors.
77.304 Explosion release vents.
77.305 Access to drying chambers, hot gas inlet chambers and ductwork; installation and maintenance.
77.306 Fire protection.
77.307 Thermal dryers; location and installation; general.
77.308 Structures housing other facilities; use of partitions.
77.309 Visual check of system equipment.
77.309-1 Control stations; location.

77.310 Control panels.
77.311 Alarm devices.
77.312 Fail safe monitoring systems.
77.313 Wet-coal feedbins; low-level indicators.
77.314 Automatic temperature control instruments.
77.315 Thermal dryers; examination and inspection.

Subpart E—Safeguards for Mechanical Equipment

77.400 Mechanical equipment guards.
77.401 Stationary grinding machines; protective devices.
77.402 Hand-held power tools; safety devices.
77.403 Mobile equipment; falling object protective structures (FOPS).
77.403-1 Mobile equipment; rollover protective structures (ROPS).
77.403-2 Incorporation by reference.
77.404 Machinery and equipment; operation and maintenance.
77.405 Performing work from a raised position; safeguards.
77.406 Drive belts.
77.407 Power driven pulleys.
77.408 Welding operations.
77.409 Shovels, draglines, and tractors.
77.410 Mobile equipment; automatic warning devices.
77.411 Compressed air and boilers; general.
77.412 Compressed air systems.
77.413 Boilers.

Subpart F—Electrical Equipment—General

77.500 Electric power circuits and electric equipment; deenergization.
77.501 Electric distribution circuits and equipment; repair.
77.501-1 Qualified person.
77.502 Electric equipment; examination, testing, and maintenance.
77.502-1 Qualified person.
77.502-2 Electric equipment; frequency of examination and testing.
77.503 Electric conductors; capacity and insulation.
77.503-1 Electric conductors.
77.504 Electrical connections or splices; suitability.
77.505 Cable fittings; suitability.
77.506 Electric equipment and circuits; overload and short-circuit protection.
77.506-1 Electric equipment and circuits; overload and short circuit protection; minimum requirements.
77.507 Electric equipment; switches.
77.508 Lightning arresters, ungrounded and exposed power conductors and telephone wires.
77.508-1 Lightning arresters; wires entering buildings.
77.509 Transformers; installation and guarding.
77.510 Resistors; location and guarding.
77.511 Danger signs at electrical installations.
77.512 Inspection and cover plates.
77.513 Insulating mats at power switches.
77.514 Switchboard; passageways and clearance.
77.515 Bare signal or control wires; voltage.
77.516 Electric wiring and equipment; installation and maintenance.

Subpart G—Trailing Cables

77.600 Trailing cables; short-circuit protection; disconnecting devices.
77.601 Trailing cables or portable cables; temporary splices.
77.602 Permanent splicing of trailing cables.
77.603 Clamping of trailing cables to equipment.
77.604 Protection of trailing cables.
77.605 Breaking trailing cable and power cable connections.
77.606 Energized trailing cables; handling.
77.606-1 Rubber gloves; minimum requirements.

Subpart H—Grounding

77.700 Grounding metallic sheaths, armors, and conduits enclosing power conductors.
77.700-1 Approved methods of grounding.
77.701 Grounding metallic frames, casings, and other enclosures of electric equipment.
77.701-1 Approved methods of grounding of equipment receiving power from ungrounded alternating current power systems.
77.701-2 Approved methods of grounding metallic frames, casings and other enclosures of electric equipment receiving power from a direct-current power system.
77.701-3 Grounding wires; capacity.
77.701-4 Use of grounding connectors.
77.702 Protection other than grounding.
77.703 Grounding frames of stationary high-voltage equipment receiving power from ungrounded delta systems.
77.703-1 Approved methods of grounding.
77.704 Work on high-voltage lines; deenergizing and grounding.
77.704-1 Work on high-voltage lines.
77.704-2 Repairs to energized high-voltage lines.
77.704-3 Work on energized high-voltage surface lines; reporting.
77.704-4 Simultaneous repairs.
77.704-5 Installation of protective equipment.
77.704-6 Protective clothing; use and inspection.
77.704-7 Protective equipment; inspection.
77.704-8 Protective equipment; testing and storage.
77.704-9 Operating disconnecting or cutout switches.

Mine Safety and Health Admin., Labor Pt. 77

77.704-10 Tying into energized high-voltage surface circuits.
77.704-11 Use of grounded messenger wires; ungrounded systems.
77.705 Guy wires; grounding.

Subpart I—Surface High-Voltage Distribution

77.800 High-voltage circuits; circuit breakers.
77.800-1 Testing, examination, and maintenance of circuit breakers; procedures.
77.800-2 Testing, examination, and maintenance of circuit breakers; record.
77.801 Grounding resistors.
77.801-1 Grounding resistors; continuous current rating.
77.802 Protection of high-voltage circuits; neutral grounding resistors; disconnecting devices.
77.803 Fail safe ground check circuits on high-voltage resistance grounded systems.
77.803-1 Fail safe ground check circuits; maximum voltage.
77.803-2 Ground check systems not employing pilot check wires; approval by the Secretary.
77.804 High-voltage trailing cables; minimum design requirements.
77.805 Cable couplers and connection boxes; minimum design requirements.
77.806 Connection of single-phase loads.
77.807 Installation of high-voltage transmission cables.
77.807-1 High-voltage powerlines; clearances above ground.
77.807-2 Booms and masts; minimum distance from high-voltage lines.
77.807-3 Movement of equipment; minimum distance from high-voltage lines.
77.808 Disconnecting devices.
77.809 Identification of circuit breakers and disconnecting switches.
77.810 High-voltage equipment; grounding.
77.811 Movement of portable substations and transformers.

Subpart J—Low- and Medium-Voltage Alternating Current Circuits

77.900 Low- and medium-voltage circuits serving portable or mobile three-phase alternating current equipment; circuit breakers.
77.900-1 Testing, examination, and maintenance of circuit breakers; procedures.
77.900-2 Testing, examination, and maintenance of circuit breakers; record.
77.901 Protection of low- and medium-voltage three-phase circuits.
77.901-1 Grounding resistor; continuous current rating.
77.902 Low- and medium-voltage ground check monitor circuits.
77.902-1 Fail safe ground check circuits; maximum voltage.
77.902-2 Approved ground check systems not employing pilot check wires.
77.902-3 Attachment of ground conductors and ground check wires to equipment frames; use of separate connections.
77.903 Disconnecting devices.
77.904 Identification of circuit breakers.
77.905 Connection of single-phase loads.
77.906 Trailing cables supplying power to low-voltage mobile equipment; ground wires and ground check wires.

Subpart K—Ground Control

77.1000 Highwalls, pits, and spoil banks; plans.
77.1000-1 Filing of plan.
77.1001 Stripping; loose material.
77.1002 Box cuts; spoil material placement.
77.1003 Benches.
77.1004 Ground control; inspection and maintenance; general.
77.1005 Scaling highwalls; general.
77.1006 Highwalls; men working.
77.1007 Drilling; general.
77.1008 Relocation of drills; safeguards.
77.1009 Drill; operation.
77.1010 Collaring holes.
77.1011 Drill holes; guarding.
77.1012 Jackhammers; operation; safeguards.
77.1013 Air drills; safeguards.

Subpart L—Fire Protection

77.1100 Fire protection; training and organization.
77.1101 Escape and evacuation; plan.
77.1102 Warning signs; smoking and open flame.
77.1103 Flammable liquids; storage.
77.1104 Accumulations of combustible materials.
77.1105 Internal combustion engines; fueling.
77.1106 Battery-charging stations; ventilation.
77.1107 Belt conveyors.
77.1108 Firefighting equipment; requirements; general.
77.1108-1 Type and capacity of firefighting equipment.
77.1109 Quantity and location of firefighting equipment.
77.1110 Examination and maintenance of firefighting equipment.
77.1111 Welding, cutting, soldering; use of fire extinguisher.
77.1112 Welding, cutting, soldering with arc or flame; safeguards.

Subpart M—Maps

77.1200 Mine map.
77.1201 Certification of mine maps.
77.1202 Availability of mine map.

Subpart N—Explosives and Blasting

77.1300 Explosives and blasting.
77.1301 Explosives; magazines.
77.1302 Vehicles used to transport explosives.
77.1303 Explosives; handling and use.
77.1304 Blasting agents; special provisions.

Subpart O—Personnel Hoisting

77.1400 Personnel hoists and elevators.
77.1401 Automatic controls and brakes.
77.1402 Rated capacity.
77.1402–1 Maximum load; posting.
77.1403 Daily examination of hoisting equipment.
77.1404 Certifications and records of daily examinations.
77.1405 Operation of hoisting equipment after repairs.

Wire Ropes

77.1430 Wire ropes; scope.
77.1431 Minimum rope strength.
77.1432 Initial measurement.
77.1433 Examinations.
77.1434 Retirement criteria.
77.1435 Load end attachments.
77.1436 Drum end attachment.
77.1437 End attachment retermination.
77.1438 End attachment replacement.

Subpart P—Auger Mining

77.1500 Auger mining; planning.
77.1501 Auger mining; inspections.
77.1502 Auger holes; restriction against entering.
77.1503 Augering equipment; overhead protection.
77.1504 Auger equipment; operation.
77.1505 Auger holes; blocking.

Subpart Q—Loading and Haulage

77.1600 Loading and haulage; general.
77.1601 Transportation of persons; restrictions.
77.1602 Use of aerial tramways to transport persons.
77.1603 Trains and locomotives; authorized persons.
77.1604 Transportation of persons; overcrowding.
77.1605 Loading and haulage equipment; installations.
77.1606 Loading and haulage equipment; inspection and maintenance.
77.1607 Loading and haulage equipment; operation.
77.1608 Dumping facilities.

Subpart R—Miscellaneous

77.1700 Communications in work areas.
77.1701 Emergency communications; requirements.
77.1702 Arrangements for emergency medical assistance and transportation for injured persons; reporting requirements; posting requirements.
77.1703 First-Aid training; supervisory employees.
77.1704 First aid training program; availability of instruction to all miners.
77.1705 First aid training program; retraining of supervisory employees; availability to all miners.
77.1706 First aid training program; minimum requirements.
77.1707 First aid equipment; location; minimum requirements.
77.1708 Safety program, instruction of persons employed at the mine.
77.1710 Protective clothing; requirements.
77.1710–1 Distinctively colored hard hats or hard caps; identification for newly employed, inexperienced miners.
77.1711 Smoking prohibition.
77.1712 Reopening mines; notification; inspection prior to mining.
77.1713 Daily inspection of surface coal mine; certified person; reports of inspection.

Subpart S—Trolley Wires and Trolley Feeder Wires

77.1800 Cutout switches.
77.1801 Overcurrent protection.
77.1801–1 Devices for overcurrent protection.
77.1802 Insulation of trolley wires, trolley feeder wires and bare signal wires; guarding of trolley wires and trolley feeder wires.

Subpart T—Slope and Shaft Sinking

77.1900 Slopes and shafts; approval of plans.
77.1900–1 Compliance with approved slope and shaft sinking plans.
77.1901 Preshift and onshift inspections; reports.
77.1901–1 Methane and oxygen deficiency tests; approved devices.
77.1902 Drilling and mucking operations.
77.1902–1 Permissible diesel-powered equipment.
77.1903 Hoists and hoisting; minimum requirements.
77.1904 Communications between slope and shaft bottoms and hoist operators.
77.1905 Hoist safeguards; general.
77.1906 Hoists; daily inspection.
77.1907 Hoist construction; general.
77.1908 Hoist installations; use.
77.1908–1 Hoist operation; qualified hoistman.
77.1909 Explosives and blasting; use of permissible explosives and shot-firing units.
77.1909–1 Use of nonpermissible explosives and nonpermissible shot-firing units; approval by Health and Safety District Manager.

Mine Safety and Health Admin., Labor § 77.2

77.1910 Explosives and blasting; general.
77.1911 Ventilation of slopes and shafts.
77.1912 Ladders and stairways.
77.1913 Fire-resistant wood.
77.1914 Electrical equipment.
77.1915 Storage and handling of combustible materials.
77.1916 Welding, cutting, and soldering; fire protection.

Subpart U—Approved Books and Records [Reserved]

AUTHORITY: 30 U.S.C. 811.

SOURCE: 36 FR 9364, May 22, 1971, unless otherwise noted.

Subpart A—General

§ 77.1 Scope.

This part 77 sets forth mandatory safety standards for bituminous, anthracite, and lignite surface coal mines, including open pit and auger mines, and to the surface work areas of underground coal mines, pursuant to section 101(i) of the Federal Mine Safety and Health Act of 1977.

[36 FR 9364, May 22, 1971, as amended at 43 FR 12320, Mar. 24, 1978]

§ 77.2 Definitions.

For the purpose of this part 77, the term:

(a) *Active workings* means any place in a coal mine where miners are normally required to work or travel;

(b) *American Table of Distances* means the current edition of "The American Table of Distances for Storage of Explosives" published by the Institute of Makers of Explosives;

(c) *Barricaded* means to obstruct passage of persons, vehicles, or flying materials;

(d) *Berm* means a pile or mound of material capable of restraining a vehicle;

(e) *Blasting agent* means any material consisting of a mixture of a fuel and oxidizer which—

(1) Is used or intended for use in blasting;

(2) Is not classed as an explosive by the Department of Transportation;

(3) Contains no ingredient classed as an explosive by the Department of Transportation; and,

(4) Cannot be detonated by a No. 8 blasting cap when tested as recommended in Bureau of Mines Information Circular 8179.

(f) *Blasting area* means the area near blasting operations in which concussion or flying material can reasonably be expected to cause injury.

(g) *Blasting cap* means a detonator containing a charge of detonating compound, which is ignited by electric current, or the spark of a fuse. Used for detonating explosives.

(h) *Blasting circuit* means electric circuits used to fire electric detonators or to ignite an igniter cord by means of an electric starter.

(i) *Blasting switch* means a switch used to connect a power source to a blasting circuit.

(j) *Box-type magazine* means a small, portable magazine used to store limited quantities of explosives or detonators for short periods of time in locations at the mine which are convenient to the blasting sites at which they will be used.

(k) *Capped fuse* means a length of safety fuse to which a detonator has been attached.

(l) *Capped primer* means a package or cartridge of explosives which is specifically designed to transmit detonation to other explosives and which contains a detonator.

(m) *Certified* or *registered*, as applied to any person means a person certified or registered by the State in which the coal mine is located to perform duties prescribed by this Part 77, except that, in a State where no program of certification or registration is provided or where the program does not meet at least minimum Federal standards established by the Secretary, such certification or registration shall be by the Secretary.

(n) *Detonating cord* or *detonating fuse* means a flexible cord containing a core of high explosive.

(o) *Detonator* means a device containing a small detonating charge that is used for detonating an explosive, including, but not limited to blasting caps, exploders, electric detonators, and delay electric blasting caps.

(p) *Electrical grounding* means to connect with the ground to make the earth part of the circuit.

683

(q) *Explosive* means any chemical compound, mixture, or device, the primary or common purpose of which is to function by explosion. Explosives include, but are not limited to black powder, dynamite, nitroglycerin, fulminate, ammonium nitrate when mixed with a hydrocarbon, and other blasting agents.

(r) *Flash point* means the minimum temperature at which sufficient vapor is released by a liquid or solid to form a flammable vapor-air mixture at atmospheric pressure.

(s) *Low voltage* means up to and including 660 volts, *medium voltage* means voltages from 661 to 1,000 volts, and *high voltage* means more than 1,000 volts.

(t) *Misfire* means the complete or partial failure of a blasting charge to explode as planned.

(u) *Primer* or *Booster* means a package or cartridge of explosive which is designed specifically to transmit detonation to other explosives and which does not contain a detonator.

(v) *Qualified person* means, as the context requires, (1) An individual deemed qualified by the Secretary and designated by the operator to make tests and examinations required by this Part 77; and,

(2) An individual deemed, in accordance with the minimum requirements to be established by the Secretary, qualified by training, education, and experience, to perform electrical work, to maintain electrical equipment, and to conduct examinations and make tests of all electrical equipment.

(w) *Roll protection* means a framework, safety canopy, or similar protection for the operator when equipment overturns.

(x) *Safety can* means an approved container, of not over 5 gallons capacity, having a spring-closing lid and spout cover.

(y) *Safety fuse* means a train of powder enclosed in cotton, jute yarn, and waterproofing compounds, which burns at a uniform rate; used for firing a cap containing the detonating compound which in turn sets off the explosive charge.

(z) *Safety switch* means a sectionalizing switch that also provides shunt protection in blasting circuits between the blasting switch and the shot area.

(aa) *Secretary* means the Secretary of Labor or his delegate.

[36 FR 9364, May 22, 1971, as amended at 43 FR 12320, Mar. 24, 1978]

Subpart B—Qualified and Certified Persons

§ 77.100 Certified person.

(a)(1) The provisions of this Part 77 require that certain examinations and tests be made by a certified person. A certified person within the meaning of these provisions is a person who has been certified in accordance with the provisions of paragraph (b) of this § 77.100 to perform the duties, and make the examinations and tests which are required by this Part 77 to be performed by a certified person.

(2) A person who has been so certified shall also be considered to be a qualified person within the meaning of those provisions of this Part 77 which require that certain examinations, tests and duties be performed by a qualified person, except those provisions in Subparts F, G, H, I, and J of this part relating to performance of electrical work.

(b) Pending issuance of Federal standards, a person will be considered, to the extent of the certification, a certified person to make examinations, tests and perform duties which are required by this Part 77 to be performed by a certified person:

(1) If he has been certified for such purpose by the State in which the coal mine is located; or

(2) If this person has been certified for such purpose by the Secretary. A person's initial certification is valid for as long as the person continues to satisfy the requirements necessary to obtain the certification and is employed at the same coal mine or by the same independent contractor. The mine operator or independent contractor shall make an application which satisfactorily shows that each such person has had at least 2 years experience at a coal mine or equivalent experience, and that each such person demonstrates to the satisfaction of an

Mine Safety and Health Admin., Labor §77.103

authorized representative of the Secretary that such person is able and competent to test for oxygen deficiency with a permissible flame safety lamp, or any other device approved by the Secretary and to test for methane with a portable methane detector approved by the Bureau of Mines, MESA, or MSHA, under Part 22 of this Chapter (Bureau of Mines Schedule 8C), and to perform such other duties for which application for certification is made. Applications for certification by the Secretary should be submitted in writing to the Mine Safety and Health Administration, Certification and Qualification Center, P.O. Box 25367, Denver Federal Center, Denver, Colorado 80225.

[36 FR 9364, May 22, 1971, as amended at 43 FR 12320, Mar. 24, 1978; 54 FR 30515, July 20, 1989]

§ 77.101 Tests for methane and for oxygen deficiency; qualified person.

(a) The provisions of Subparts C, P, R, and T of this Part 77 require that tests for methane and for oxygen deficiency be made by a qualified person. A person is a qualified person for these purposes if he is a certified person for such purposes under §77.100.

(b) Pending issuance of Federal standards, a person will be considered a qualified person for testing for methane and oxygen deficiency:

(1) If he has been qualified for this purpose by the State in which the coal mine is located; or

(2) If he has been qualified by the Secretary for these purposes upon a satisfactory showing by the operator of the coal mine that each such person has been trained and designated by the operator to test for methane and oxygen deficiency. Applications for Secretarial qualification should be submitted in writing to the Mine Safety and Health Administration, Certification and Qualification Center, P.O. Box 25367, Denver Federal Center, Denver, Colo. 80225

[36 FR 9364, May 22, 1971, as amended at 43 FR 12320, Mar. 24, 1978]

§ 77.102 Tests for methane; oxygen deficiency; qualified person, additional requirement.

Notwithstanding the provisions of §77.101, on and after December 30, 1971, no person shall be a qualified person for testing for methane and oxygen deficiency unless he has demonstrated to the satisfaction of an authorized representative of the Secretary that he is able and competent to make such tests and the Mine Safety and Health Administration has issued him a current card which qualifies him to make such tests.

§ 77.103 Electrical work; qualified person.

(a) Except as provided in paragraph (f) of this section, an individual is a qualified person within the meaning of Subparts F, G, H, I, and J of this Part 77 to perform electrical work (other than work on energized surface high-voltage lines) if:

(1) He has been qualified as a coal mine electrician by a State that has a coal mine electrical qualification program approved by the Secretary; or,

(2) He has at least 1 year of experience in performing electrical work underground in a coal mine, in the surface work areas of an underground coal mine, in a surface coal mine, in a noncoal mine, in the mine equipment manufacturing industry, or in any other industry using or manufacturing similar equipment, and has satisfactorily completed a coal mine electrical training program approved by the Secretary; or,

(3) He has at least 1 year of experience, prior to the date of the application required by paragraph (c) of this section, in performing electrical work underground in a coal mine, in the surface work areas of an underground coal mine, in a surface coal mine, in a noncoal mine, in the mine equipment manufacturing industry, or in any other industry using or manufacturing similar equipment, and he attains a satisfactory grade on each of the series of five written tests approved by the Secretary as prescribed in paragraph (b) of this section.

(b) The series of five written tests approved by the Secretary shall include the following categories:

(1) Direct current theory and application;

(2) Alternating current theory and application;

(3) Electric equipment and circuits;

§ 77.104

(4) Permissibility of electric equipment; and,

(5) Requirements of Subparts F through J and S of this Part 77.

(c) In order to take the series of five written tests approved by the Secretary, an individual shall apply to the District Manager and shall certify that he meets the requirements of paragraph (a)(3) of this section. The tests will be administered in the Coal Mine Safety and Health Districts at regular intervals, or as demand requires.

(d) A score of at least 80 percent on each of the five written tests will be deemed to be a satisfactory grade. Recognition shall be given to practical experience in that 1 percentage point shall be added to an individual's score in each test for each additional year of experience beyond the 1 year requirement specified in paragraph (a)(3) of this section; however, in no case shall an individual be given more than 5 percentage points for such practical experience.

(e) An individual may, within 30 days from the date on which he received notification from the Administration of his test scores, repeat those on which he received an unsatisfactory score. If further retesting is necessary after his initial repetition, a minimum of 30 days from the date of receipt of notification of the initial retest scores shall elapse prior to such further retesting.

(f) An individual who has, prior to November 1, 1972, been qualified to perform electrical work specified in Subparts F, G, H, I, and J of this Part 77 (other than work on energized surface high-voltage lines) shall continue to be qualified until June 30, 1973. To remain qualified after June 30, 1973, such individual shall meet the requirements of either paragraph (a) (1), (2), or (3) of this section.

(g) An individual qualified in accordance with this section shall, in order to retain qualification, certify annually to the District Manager, that he has satisfactorily completed a coal mine electrical retraining program approved by the Secretary.

01(a), Federal Coal Mine Health and Safety Act of 1969; 30 U.S.C. 811(a); 83 Stat. 745)

[37 FR 22377, Oct. 19, 1972; 37 FR 28163, Dec. 21, 1972, as amended at 44 FR 9380, Feb. 13, 1979; 47 FR 23641, May 28, 1982]

§ 77.104 Repair of energized surface high-voltage lines; qualified person.

An individual is a qualified person within the meaning of § 77.704 of this part for the purpose of repairing energized surface high-voltage lines only if he has had at least 2 years experience in electrical maintenance, and at least 2 years experience in the repair of energized high-voltage lines located on poles or structures.

[36 FR 9364, May 22, 1971, as amended at 36 FR 13143, July 15, 1971]

§ 77.105 Qualified hoistman; slope or shaft sinking operation; qualifications.

(a)(1) A person is a qualified hoistman within the provisions of Subpart T of this part, for the purpose of operating a hoist at a slope or shaft sinking operation if he has at least 1 year experience operating a hoist plant or maintaining hoist equipment and is qualified by any State as a hoistman or its equivalency, or

(2) If a State has no program for qualifying persons as hoistmen, the Secretary may qualify persons if the operator of the slope or shaft-sinking operation makes an application and a satisfactory showing that the person has had 1 year of experience operating hoists. A person's qualification is valid for as long as the person continues to satisfy the requirements for qualification and is employed at the same coal mine or by the same independent contractor.

(b) Applications for Secretarial qualification should be submitted to the Mine Safety and Health Administration, Certification and Qualification Center, P.O. Box 25367, Denver Federal Center, Denver, Colo. 80225.

[36 FR 9364, May 22, 1971, as amended at 43 FR 12320, Mar. 24, 1978; 54 FR 30515, July 20, 1989]

§ 77.106 Records of certified and qualified persons.

The operator of each coal mine shall maintain a list of all certified and

Mine Safety and Health Admin., Labor

qualified persons designated to perform duties under this Part 77.

(Pub. L. No. 96-511, 94 Stat. 2812 (44 U.S.C. 3501 et seq.))

[36 FR 9364, May 22, 1971, as amended at 60 FR 33723, June 29, 1995]

§ 77.107 Training programs.

Every operator of a coal mine shall provide a program, approved by the Secretary, of training and retraining both qualified and certified persons needed to carry out functions prescribed in the Act.

§ 77.107-1 Plans for training programs.

Each operator must submit to the district manager, of the Coal Mine Safety and Health District in which the mine is located, a program or plan setting forth what, when, how, and where the operator will train and retrain persons whose work assignments require that they be certified or qualified. The program must provide—

(a) For certified persons, annual training courses in the tasks and duties which they perform as certified persons, first aid, and the provisions of this part 77; and

(b) For qualified persons, annual courses in performance of the tasks which they perform as qualified persons.

[63 FR 53761, Oct. 6, 1998]

Subpart C—Surface Installations

§ 77.200 Surface installations; general.

All mine structures, enclosures, or other facilities (including custom coal preparation) shall be maintained in good repair to prevent accidents and injuries to employees.

§ 77.201 Methane content in surface installations.

The methane content in the air of any structure, enclosure or other facility shall be less than 1.0 volume per centum.

§ 77.201-1 Tests for methane; qualified person; use of approved device.

Tests for methane in structures, enclosures, or other facilities, in which coal is handled or stored shall be conducted by a qualified person with a device approved by the Secretary at least once during each operating shift, and immediately prior to any repair work in which welding or an open flame is used, or a spark may be produced.

§ 77.201-2 Methane accumulations; change in ventilation.

If, at any time, the air in any structure, enclosure or other facility contains 1.0 volume per centum or more of methane changes or adjustments in the ventilation of such installation shall be made at once so that the air shall contain less than 1.0 volume per centum of methane.

§ 77.202 Dust accumulations in surface installations.

Coal dust in the air of, or in, or on the surfaces of, structures, enclosures, or other facilities shall not be allowed to exist or accumulate in dangerous amounts.

§ 77.203 Use of material or equipment overhead; safeguards.

Where overhead repairs are being made at surface installations and equipment or material is taken into such overhead work areas, adequate protection shall be provided for all persons working or passing below the overhead work areas in which such equipment or material is being used.

§ 77.204 Openings in surface installations; safeguards.

Openings in surface installations through which men or material may fall shall be protected by railings, barriers, covers or other protective devices.

§ 77.205 Travelways at surface installations.

(a) Safe means of access shall be provided and maintained to all working places.

(b) Travelways and platforms or other means of access to areas where persons are required to travel or work, shall be kept clear of all extraneous material and other stumbling or slipping hazards.

(c) Inclined travelways shall be constructed of nonskid material or equipped with cleats.

§ 77.206

(d) Regularly used travelways shall be sanded, salted, or cleared of snow and ice as soon as practicable.

(e) Crossovers, elevated walkways, elevated ramps, and stairways shall be of substantial construction, provided with handrails, and maintained in good condition. Where necessary toeboards shall be provided.

(f) Crossovers shall be provided where it is necessary to cross conveyors.

(g) Moving conveyors shall be crossed only at designated crossover points.

§ 77.206 Ladders; construction; installation and maintenance.

(a) Ladders shall be of substantial construction and maintained in good condition.

(b) Wooden members of ladders shall not be painted.

(c) Steep or vertical ladders which are used regularly at fixed locations shall be anchored securely and provided with backguards extending from a point not more than 7 feet from the bottom of the ladder to the top of the ladder.

(d) Fixed ladders shall not incline backwards at any point unless provided with backguards.

(e) Fixed ladders shall be anchored securely and installed to provide at least 3 inches of toe clearance.

(f) Fixed ladders shall project at least 3 feet above landings, or substantial handholds shall be provided above the landings.

§ 77.207 Illumination.

Illumination sufficient to provide safe working conditions shall be provided in and on all surface structures, paths, walkways, stairways, switch panels, loading and dumping sites, and working areas.

§ 77.208 Storage of materials.

(a) Materials shall be stored and stacked in a manner which minimizes stumbling or fall-of-material hazards.

(b) Materials that can create hazards if accidentally liberated from their containers shall be stored in a manner that minimizes the dangers.

(c) Containers holding hazardous materials must be of a type approved for such use by recognized agencies.

(d) Compressed and liquid gas cylinders shall be secured in a safe manner.

(e) Valves on compressed gas cylinders shall be protected by covers when being transported or stored, and by a safe location when the cylinders are in use.

[36 FR 9364, May 22, 1971, as amended at 67 FR 42389, June 21, 2002]

§ 77.209 Surge and storage piles.

No person shall be permitted to walk or stand immediately above a reclaiming area or in any other area at or near a surge or storage pile where the reclaiming operation may expose him to a hazard.

§ 77.210 Hoisting of materials.

(a) Hitches and slings used to hoist materials shall be suitable for handling the type of materials being hoisted.

(b) Men shall stay clear of hoisted loads.

(c) Taglines shall be attached to hoisted materials that require steadying or guidance.

§ 77.211 Draw-off tunnels; stockpiling and reclaiming operations; general.

(a) Tunnels located below stockpiles, surge piles, and coal storage silos shall be ventilated so as to maintain concentrations of methane below 1.0 volume per centum.

(b) In addition to the tests for methane required by § 77.201 such tests shall also be made before any electric equipment is energized or repaired, unless equipped with a continuous methane monitoring device installed and operated in accordance with the provisions of § 77.211-1. Electric equipment shall not be energized, operated, or repaired until the air contains less than 1.0 volume per centum of methane.

§ 77.211-1 Continuous methane monitoring device; installation and operation; automatic deenergization of electric equipment.

Continuous methane monitoring devices shall be set to deenergize automatically electric equipment when such monitor is not operating properly and to give a warning automatically when the concentration of methane

Mine Safety and Health Admin., Labor § 77.215

reaches a maximum percentage determined by an authorized representative of the Secretary which shall not be more than 1.0 volume per centum of methane. An authorized representative of the Secretary shall require such monitor to deenergize automatically electric equipment when the concentration of methane reaches a maximum percentage determined by such representative which shall not be more than 2.0 volume per centum of methane.

§ 77.212 Draw-off tunnel ventilation fans; installation.

When fans are used to ventilate draw-off tunnels the fans shall be:

(a) Installed on the surface;

(b) Installed in fireproof housings and connected to the tunnel openings with fireproof air ducts; and,

(c) Offset from the tunnel opening.

§ 77.213 Draw-off tunnel escapeways.

When it is necessary for a tunnel to be closed at one end, an escapeway not less than 30 inches in diameter (or of the equivalent, if the escapeway does not have a circular cross section) shall be installed which extends from the closed end of the tunnel to a safe location on the surface; and, if the escapeway is inclined more than 30 degrees from the horizontal it shall be equipped with a ladder which runs the full length of the inclined portion of the escapeway.

§ 77.214 Refuse piles; general.

(a) Refuse piles constructed on or after July 1, 1971, shall be located in areas which are a safe distance from all underground mine airshafts, preparation plants, tipples, or other surface installations and such piles shall not be located over abandoned openings or steamlines.

(b) Where new refuse piles are constructed over exposed coal beds the exposed coal shall be covered with clay or other inert material as the piles are constructed.

(c) A fireproof barrier of clay or inert material shall be constructed between old and new refuse piles.

(d) Roadways to refuse piles shall be fenced or otherwise guarded to restrict the entrance of unauthorized persons.

[36 FR 9364, May 22, 1971, as amended at 36 FR 13143, July 15, 1971]

§ 77.215 Refuse piles; construction requirements.

(a) Refuse deposited on a pile shall be spread in layers and compacted in such a manner so as to minimize the flow of air through the pile.

(b) Refuse shall not be deposited on a burning pile except for the purpose of controlling or extinguishing a fire.

(c) Clay or other sealants shall be used to seal the surface of any refuse pile in which a spontaneous ignition has occurred.

(d) Surface seals shall be kept intact and protected from erosion by drainage facilities.

(e) Refuse piles shall not be constructed so as to impede drainage or impound water.

(f) Refuse piles shall be constructed in such a manner as to prevent accidental sliding and shifting of materials.

(g) No extraneous combustible material shall be deposited on refuse piles.

(h) After October 31, 1975 new refuse piles and additions to existing refuse piles, shall be constructed in compacted layers not exceeding 2 feet in thickness and shall not have any slope exceeding 2 horizontal to 1 vertical (approximately 27°) except that the District Manager may approve construction of a refuse pile in compacted layers exceeding 2 feet in thickness and with slopes exceeding 27° where engineering data substantiates that a minimum safety factor of 1.5 for the refuse pile will be attained.

(i) Foundations for new refuse piles and additions to existing refuse piles shall be cleared of all vegetation and undesirable material that according to current, prudent engineering practices would adversely affect the stability of the refuse pile.

(j) All fires in refuse piles shall be extinguished, and the method used shall be in accordance with a plan approved by the District Manager. The plan shall contain as a minimum, provisions to ensure that only those persons authorized by the operator, and who have an understanding of the procedure to be used, shall be involved in the extinguishing operation.

(Secs. 101, 508, Pub. L. 91–173, 83 Stat. 745, 803 (30 U.S.C. 811, 957), Pub. L. No. 96–511, 94 Stat. 2812 (44 U.S.C. 3501 et seq.))

[36 FR 9364, May 22, 1971, as amended at 40 FR 41776, Sept. 9, 1975; 60 FR 33723, June 29, 1995]

§ 77.215-1 Refuse piles; identification.

A permanent identification marker, at least six feet high and showing the refuse pile identification number as assigned by the District Manager, the name associated with the refuse pile and the name of the person owning, operating or controlling the refuse pile, shall be located on or immediately adjacent to each refuse pile within the time specified in paragraphs (a) or (b) of this section as applicable.

(a) For existing refuse piles, markers shall be placed before May 1, 1976.

(b) For new or proposed refuse piles, markers shall be placed within 30 days from acknowledgment of the proposed location of a new refuse pile.

(Secs. 101, 508, Pub. L. 91–173, 83 Stat. 745, 803 (30 U.S.C. 811, 957))

[40 FR 41776, Sept. 9, 1975]

§ 77.215-2 Refuse piles; reporting requirements.

(a) The proposed location of a new refuse pile shall be reported to and acknowledged in writing by the District Manager prior to the beginning of any work associated with the construction of the refuse pile.

(b) Before May 1, 1976, for existing refuse piles, or within 180 days from the date of acknowledgment of the proposed location of a new refuse pile, the person owning, operating or controlling a refuse pile shall submit to the District Manager a report in triplicate which contains the following:

(1) The name and address of the person owning, operating or controlling the refuse pile; the name associated with the refuse pile; the identification number of the refuse pile as assigned by the District Manager; and the identification number of the mine or preparation plant as assigned by MSHA.

(2) The location of the refuse pile indicated on the most recent USGS 7½ minute or 15 minute topographic quadrangle map, or a topographic map of equivalent scale if a USGS map is not available.

(3) A statement of the construction history of the refuse pile, and a statement indicating whether the refuse pile has been abandoned in accordance with a plan approved by the District Manager.

(4) A topographic map showing at a scale not to exceed 1 inch = 400 feet, the present and proposed maximum extent of the refuse pile and the area 500 feet around the proposed maximum perimeter.

(5) A statement of whether or not the refuse pile is burning.

(6) A description of measures taken to prevent water from being impounded by the refuse pile or contained within the refuse pile.

(7) At a scale not to exceed 1 inch = 100 feet, cross sections of the length and width of the refuse pile at sufficient intervals to show the approximate original ground surface, the present configuration and the proposed maximum extent of the refuse pile, and mean sea level elevations at significant points.

(8) Any other information pertaining to the stability of the pile which may be required by the District Manager.

(c) The information required by paragraphs (b)(4) through (b)(8) of this section shall be reported every twelfth month from the date of original submission for those refuse piles which the District Manager has determined can present a hazard until the District Manager notifies the operator that the hazard has been eliminated.

(Secs. 101, 508, Pub. L. 91–173, 83 Stat. 745, 803 (30 U.S.C. 811, 957), Pub. L. No. 96–511, 94 Stat. 2812 (44 U.S.C. 3501 et seq.))

[40 FR 41776, Sept. 9, 1975, as amended at 57 FR 7471, Mar. 2, 1992; 60 FR 33723, June 29, 1995]

§ 77.215-3 Refuse piles: certification.

(a) Within 180 days following written notification by the District Manager that a refuse pile can present a hazard, the person owning, operating, or controlling the refuse pile shall submit to the District Manager a certification by a registered engineer that the refuse pile is being constructed or has been

Mine Safety and Health Admin., Labor

modified in accordance with current, prudent engineering practices to minimize the probability of impounding water and failure of such magnitude as to endanger the lives of miners.

(b) After the initial certification required by this section and until the District Manager notifies the operator that the hazard has been eliminated, certification shall be submitted every twelfth month from the date of the initial certification.

(c) Certifications required by paragraphs (a) and (b) of this section shall include all information considered in making the certification.

(Secs. 101, 508, Pub. L. 91-173, 83 Stat. 745, 803 (30 U.S.C. 811, 957))

[40 FR 41776, Sept. 9, 1975, as amended at 57 FR 7471, Mar. 2, 1992]

§ 77.215-4 Refuse piles; abandonment.

When a refuse pile is to be abandoned, the District Manager shall be notified in writing, and if he determines it can present a hazard, the refuse pile shall be abandoned in accordance with a plan submitted by the operator and approved by the District Manager. The plan shall include a schedule for its implementation and describe provisions to prevent burning and future impoundment of water, and provide for major slope stability.

(Secs. 101, 508, Pub. L. 91-173, 83 Stat. 745, 803 (30 U.S.C. 811, 957), Pub. L. No. 96-511, 94 Stat. 2812 (44 U.S.C. 3501 et seq.))

[40 FR 41776, Sept. 9, 1975, as amended at 60 FR 33723, June 29, 1995]

§ 77.216 Water, sediment, or slurry impoundments and impounding structures; general.

(a) Plans for the design, construction, and maintenance of structures which impound water, sediment, or slurry shall be required if such an existing or proposed impounding structure can:

(1) Impound water, sediment, or slurry to an elevation of five feet or more above the upstream toe of the structure and can have a storage volume of 20 acre-feet or more; or

(2) Impound water, sediment, or slurry to an elevation of 20 feet or more above the upstream toe of the structure; or

§ 77.216-1

(3) As determined by the District Manager, present a hazard to coal miners.

(b) Plans for the design and construction of all new water, sediment, or slurry impoundments and impounding structures which meet the requirements of paragraph (a) of this section shall be submitted in triplicate to and be approved by the District Manager prior to the beginning of any work associated with construction of the impounding structure.

(c) Before May 1, 1976, a plan for the continued use of an existing water, sediment, or slurry impoundment and impounding structure which meets the requirements of paragraph (a) of this section shall be submitted in triplicate to the District Manager for approval.

(d) The design, construction, and maintenance of all water, sediment, or slurry impoundments and impounding structures which meet the requirements of paragraph (a) of this section shall be implemented in accordance with the plan approved by the District Manager.

(e) All fires in impounding structures shall be extinguished, and the method used shall be in accordance with a plan approved by the District Manager. The plan shall contain as a minimum, provisions to ensure that only those persons authorized by the operator, and who have an understanding of the procedures to be used, shall be involved in the extinguishing operation.

(Secs. 101, 508, Pub. L. 91-173, 83 Stat. 745, 803 (30 U.S.C. 811, 957))

[40 FR 41776, Sept. 9, 1975]

§ 77.216-1 Water, sediment or slurry impoundments and impounding structures; identification.

A permanent identification marker, at least six feet high and showing the identification number of the impounding structure as assigned by the District Manager, the name associated with the impounding structure and name of the person owning, operating, or controlling the structure, shall be located on or immediately adjacent to each water, sediment or slurry impounding structure within the time specified in paragraph (a) or (b) of this section as applicable.

§ 77.216-2

(a) For existing water, sediment or slurry impounding structures, markers shall be placed before May 1, 1976.

(b) For new or proposed water, sediment, or slurry impounding structures, markers shall be placed within 30 days from the start of construction.

(Secs. 101, 508, Pub. L. 91-173, 83 Stat. 745, 803 (30 U.S.C. 811, 957))

[40 FR 41777, Sept. 9, 1975]

§ 77.216-2 Water, sediment, or slurry impoundments and impounding structures; minimum plan requirements; changes or modifications; certification.

(a) The plan specified in § 77.216, shall contain as a minimum the following information:

(1) The name and address of the persons owning, operating or controlling the impoundment or impounding structure; the name associated with the impoundment or impounding structure; the identification number of the impounding structure as assigned by the District Manager; and the identification number of the mine or preparation plant as assigned by MSHA.

(2) The location of the structure indicated on the most recent USGS 7½ minute or 15 minute topographic quadrangle map, or a topographic map of equivalent scale if a USGS map is not available.

(3) A statement of the purpose for which the structure is or will be used.

(4) The name and size in acres of the watershed affecting the impoundment.

(5) A description of the physical and engineering properties of the foundation materials on which the structure is or will be constructed.

(6) A statement of the type, size, range, and physical and engineering properties of the materials used, or to be used, in constructing each zone or stage of the impounding structure; the method of site preparation and construction of each zone; the approximate dates of construction of the structure and each successive stage; and for existing structures, such history of construction as may be available, and any record or knowledge of structural instability.

(7) At a scale not to exceed 1 inch = 100 feet, detailed dimensional drawings of the impounding structure including a plan view and cross sections of the length and width of the impounding structure, showing all zones, foundation improvements, drainage provisions, spillways, diversion ditches, outlets, instrument locations, and slope protection, in addition to the measurement of the minimum vertical distance between the crest of the impounding structure and the reservoir surface at present and under design storm conditions, sediment or slurry level, water level and other information pertinent to the impoundment itself, including any identifiable natural or manmade features which could affect operation of the impoundment.

(8) A description of the type and purpose of existing or proposed instrumentation.

(9) Graphs showing area-capacity curves.

(10) A statement of the runoff attributable to the probable maximum precipitation of 6-hour duration and the calculations used in determining such runoff.

(11) A statement of the runoff attributable to the storm for which the structure is designed and the calculations used in determining such runoff.

(12) A description of the spillway and diversion design features and capacities and calculations used in their determination.

(13) The computed minimum factor of safety range for the slope stability of the impounding structure including methods and calculations used to determine each factor of safety.

(14) The locations of surface and underground coal mine workings including the depth and extent of such workings within the area 500 feet around the perimeter, shown at a scale not to exceed one inch = 500 feet.

(15) Provisions for construction surveillance, maintenance, and repair of the impounding structure.

(16) General provisions for abandonment.

(17) A certification by a registered engineer that the design of the impounding structure is in accordance with current, prudent engineering practices for the maximum volume of water, sediment, or slurry which can be impounded therein and for the passage of runoff from the designed storm

Mine Safety and Health Admin., Labor § 77.216-3

which exceeds the capacity of the impoundment; or, in lieu of the certification, a report indicating what additional investigations, analyses, or improvement work are necessary before such a certification can be made, including what provisions have been made to carry out such work in addition to a schedule for completion of such work.

(18) Such other information pertaining to the stability of the impoundment and impounding structure which may be required by the District Manager.

(b) Any changes or modifications to plans for water, sediment, or slurry impoundments or impounding structures shall be approved by the District Manager prior to the initiation of such changes or modifications.

(Secs. 101, 508, Pub. L. 91-173, 83 Stat. 745, 803 (30 U.S.C. 811, 957))

[40 FR 41777, Sept. 9, 1975]

§ 77.216-3 **Water, sediment, or slurry impoundments and impounding structures; inspection requirements; correction of hazards; program requirements.**

(a) All water, sediment, or slurry impoundments that meet the requirements of § 77.216(a) shall be examined as follows:

(1) At intervals not exceeding 7 days, or as otherwise approved by the District Manager, for appearances of structural weakness and other hazardous conditions.

(2) All instruments shall be monitored at intervals not exceeding 7 days, or as otherwise approved by the District Manager.

(3) Longer inspection or monitoring intervals approved under this paragraph (a) shall be justified by the operator based on the hazard potential and performance of the impounding structure, and shall include a requirement for inspection immediately after a specified rain event approved by the District Manager.

(4) All inspections required by this paragraph (a) shall be performed by a qualified person designated by the person owning, operating, or controlling the impounding structure.

(b) When a potentially hazardous condition develops, the person owning, operating or controlling the impounding structure shall immediately:

(1) Take action to eliminate the potentially hazardous condition;

(2) Notify the District Manager;

(3) Notify and prepare to evacuate, if necessary, all coal miners from coal mine property which may be affected by the potentially hazardous conditions; and

(4) Direct a qualified person to monitor all instruments and examine the structure at least once every eight hours, or more often as required by an authorized representative of the Secretary.

(c) After each examination and instrumentation monitoring referred to in paragraphs (a) and (b) of this section, each qualified person who conducted all or any part of the examination or instrumentation monitoring shall promptly record the results of such examination or instrumentation monitoring in a book which shall be available at the mine for inspection by an authorized representative of the Secretary, and such qualified person shall also promptly report the results of the examination or monitoring to one of the persons specified in paragraph (d) of this section.

(d) All examination and instrumentation monitoring reports recorded in accordance with paragraph (c) of this section shall include a report of the action taken to abate hazardous conditions and shall be promptly signed or countersigned by at least one of the following persons:

(1) The mine foreman;

(2) The assistant superintendent of the mine;

(3) The superintendent of the mine;

(4) The person designated by the operator as responsible for health and safety at the mine.

(e) Before May 1, 1976, the person owning, operating, or controlling a water, sediment, or slurry impoundment which meets the requirements of § 77.216(a) shall adopt a program for carrying out the requirements of paragraphs (a) and (b) of this section. The program shall be submitted for approval to the District Manager. The program shall include as a minimum:

§ 77.216-4

(1) A schedule and procedures for examining the impoundment and impounding structure by a designated qualified person;
(2) A schedule and procedures for monitoring any required or approved instrumentation by a designated qualified person;
(3) Procedures for evaluating hazardous conditions;
(4) Procedures for eliminating hazardous conditions;
(5) Procedures for notifying the District Manager;
(6) Procedures for evacuating coal miners from coal mine property which may be affected by the hazardous condition.
(f) Before making any changes or modifications in the program approved in accordance with paragraph (e) of this section, the person owning, operating, or controlling the impoundment shall obtain approval of such changes or modifications from the District Manager.
(g) The qualified person or persons referred to in paragraphs (a), (b)(4), (c), (e)(1), and (e)(2) of this section shall be trained to recognize specific signs of structural instability and other hazardous conditions by visual observation and, if applicable, to monitor instrumentation.

(Secs. 101, 508, Pub. L. 91-173, 83 Stat. 745, 803 (30 U.S.C. 811, 957))

[40 FR 41777, Sept. 9, 1975, as amended at 57 FR 7471, Mar. 2, 1992]

§ 77.216-4 Water, sediment or slurry impoundments and impounding structures; reporting requirements; certification.

(a) Except as provided in paragraph (b) of this section, every twelfth month following the date of the initial plan approval, the person owning, operating, or controlling a water, sediment, or slurry impoundment and impounding structure that has not been abandoned in accordance with an approved plan shall submit to the District Manager a report containing the following information:
(1) Changes in the geometry of the impounding structure for the reporting period.
(2) Location and type of installed instruments and the maximum and minimum recorded readings of each instrument for the reporting period.
(3) The minimum, maximum, and present depth and elevation of the impounded water, sediment, or slurry for the reporting period.
(4) Storage capacity of the impounding structure.
(5) The volume of the impounded water, sediment, or slurry at the end of the reporting period.
(6) Any other change which may have affected the stability or operation of the impounding structure that has occurred during the reporting period.
(7) A certification by a registered professional engineer that all construction, operation, and maintenance was in accordance with the approved plan.
(b) A report is not required under this section when the operator provides the District Manager with a certification by a registered professional engineer that there have been no changes under paragraphs (a)(1) through (a)(6) of this section to the impoundment or impounding structure. However, a report containing the information set out in paragraph (a) of this section shall be submitted to the District Manager at least every 5 years.

[57 FR 7471, Mar. 2, 1992]

§ 77.216-5 Water, sediment or slurry impoundments and impounding structures; abandonment.

(a) Prior to abandonment of any water, sediment, or slurry impoundment and impounding structure which meets the requirements of 30 CFR 77.216(a), the person owning, operating, or controlling such an impoundment and impounding structure shall submit to and obtain approval from the District Manager, a plan for abandonment based on current, prudent engineering practices. This plan shall provide for major slope stability, include a schedule for the plan's implementation and, except as provided in paragraph (b) of this section, contain provisions to preclude the probability of future impoundment of water, sediment, or slurry.
(b) An abandonment plan does not have to contain a provision to preclude the future impoundment of water if the plan is approved by the District Manager and documentation is included in

the abandonment plan to ensure that the following requirements are met:

(1) A registered professional engineer, knowledgeable in the principles of dam design and in the design and construction of the structure, shall certify that it substantially conforms to the approved design plan and specifications and that there are no apparent defects.

(2) The current owner or prospective owner shall certify a willingness and ability to assume responsibility for operation and maintenance of the structure.

(3) A permit or approval for the continued existence of the impoundment or impounding structure shall be obtained from the Federal or State agency responsible for dam safety.

[57 FR 7472, Mar. 2, 1992]

§ 77.217 Definitions.

For the purpose of §§ 77.214 through 77.216-5, the term:

(a) *Abandoned* as applied to any refuse pile or impoundment and impounding structure means that work on such pile or structure has been completed in accordance with a plan for abandonment approved by the District Manager.

(b) *Area-capacity curves* means graphic curves which readily show the reservoir water surface area, in acres, at different elevations from the bottom of the reservoir to the maximum water surface, and the capacity or volume, in acre-feet, of the water contained in the reservoir at various elevations.

(c) *Impounding structure* means a structure which is used to impound water, sediment, or slurry, or any combination of such materials.

(d) *Probable maximum precipitation* means the value for a particular area which represents an envelopment of depth-duration-area rainfall relations for all storm types affecting that area adjusted meteorologically to maximum conditions.

(e) *Refuse pile* means a deposit of coal mine waste which may contain a mixture of coal, shale, claystone, siltstone, sandstone, limestone, and related materials that are excavated during mining operations or separated from mined coal and disposed of on the surface as waste byproducts of either coal mining or preparation operations. *Refuse pile* does not mean temporary spoil piles of removed overburden material associated with surface mining operations.

(f) *Safety factor* means the ratio of the forces tending to resist the failure of a structure to the forces tending to cause such failure as determined by accepted engineering practice.

(Secs. 101, 508, Pub. L. 91–173, 83 Stat. 745, 803 (30 U.S.C. 811, 957))

[40 FR 41778, Sept. 9, 1975]

Subpart D—Thermal Dryers

§ 77.300 Thermal dryers; general.

On and after July 1, 1971 dryer systems used for drying coal at high temperatures, hereinafter referred to as thermal dryers, including rotary dryers, continuous carrier dyes, vertical tray, and cascade dryers, multilouver dryers, suspension or flash dryers, and fluidized bed dryers, shall be maintained and operated in accordance with the provision of § 77.301 to § 77.306.

[36 FR 9364, May 22, 1971, as amended at 36 FR 13143, July 15, 1971]

§ 77.301 Dryer heating units; operation.

(a) Dryer heating units shall be operated to provide reasonably complete combustion before heated gases are allowed to enter hot gas inlets.

(b) Dryer heating units which are fired by pulverized coal, shall be operated and maintained in accordance with the recommended standards set forth in the National Fire Protection Association Handbook, 12th Edition, Section 9, "Installation of Pulverized Fuel Systems," 1962.

§ 77.302 Bypass stacks.

Thermal dryer systems shall include a bypass stack, relief stack or individual discharge stack provided with automatic venting which will permit gases from the dryer heating unit to bypass the heating chamber and vent to the outside atmosphere during any shutdown operation.

§ 77.303 Hot gas inlet chamber dropout doors.

Thermal dryer systems which employ a hot gas inlet chamber shall be equipped with drop-out doors at the

§ 77.304

bottom of the inlet chamber or with other effective means which permit coal, fly-ash, or other heated material to fall from the chamber.

§ 77.304 Explosion release vents.

Drying chambers, dry-dust collectors, ductwork connecting dryers to dust collectors, and ductwork between dust collectors and discharge stacks shall be protected with explosion release vents which open directly to the outside atmosphere, and all such vents shall be:

(a) Hinged to prevent dislodgment;

(b) Designed and constructed to permit checking and testing by manual operation; and

(c) Equal in size to the cross-sectional area of the collector vortex finder when used to vent dry dust collectors.

§ 77.305 Access to drying chambers, hot gas inlet chambers and ductwork; installation and maintenance.

Drying chambers, hot gas inlet chambers and all ductwork in which coal dust may accumulate shall be equipped with tight sealing access doors which shall remain latched during dryer operation to prevent the emission of coal dust and the loss of fluidizing air.

§ 77.306 Fire protection.

Based on the need for fire protection measures in connection with the particular design of the thermal dryer, an authorized representative of the Secretary may require any of the following measures to be employed:

(a) Water sprays automatically actuated by rises in temperature to prevent fire, installed inside the thermal dryer systems, and such sprays shall be designed to provide for manual operation in the event of power failure.

(b) Fog nozzles, or other no less effective means, installed inside the thermal dryer systems to provide additional moisture or an artificial drying load within the drying system when the system is being started or shutdown.

(c) The water system of each thermal dryer shall be interconnected to a supply of compressed air which permits constant or frequent purging of all water sprays and fog nozzles or other no less effective means of purging shall be provided.

§ 77.307 Thermal dryers; location and installation; general.

(a) Thermal dryer systems erected or installed at any coal mine after June 30, 1971 shall be located at least 100 feet from any underground coal mine opening, and 100 feet from any surface installation where the heat, sparks, flames, or coal dust from the system might cause a fire or explosion.

(b) Thermal dryer systems erected or installed after June 30, 1971 may be covered by roofs, however, such systems shall not be otherwise enclosed unless necessary to protect the health and safety of persons employed at the mine. Where such systems are enclosed, they shall be located in separate fireproof structures of heavy construction with explosion pressure release devices (such as hinged wall panels, window sashes, or louvers); which provide at least 1 square foot of area for each 80 cubic feet of space volume and which are distributed as uniformly as possible throughout the structure.

§ 77.308 Structures housing other facilities; use of partitions.

Thermal dryer systems installed after June 30, 1971 in any structure which also houses a tipple, cleaning plant, or other operating facility shall be separated from all other working areas of such structure by a substantial partition capable of providing greater resistance to explosion pressures than the exterior wall or walls of the structure. The partition shall also include substantial, self-closing fire doors at all entrances to the areas adjoining the dryer system.

§ 77.309 Visual check of system equipment.

Frequent visual checks shall be made by the operator of the thermal dryer system control station, or by some other competent person, of the bypass dampers, air-tempering louvers, discharge mechanism, and other dryer system equipment.

§ 77.309-1 Control stations; location.

Thermal dryer system control stations constructed after June 30, 1971, shall be installed at a location which will give to the operator of the control station the widest field of visibility of the system and equipment.

§ 77.310 Control panels.

(a) All thermal dryer system control panels constructed after June 30, 1971 shall be located in an area which is relatively free of moisture and dust and shall be installed in such a manner as to minimize vibration.

(b) A schematic diagram containing legends which show the location of each thermocouple, pressure tap, or other control or gaging instrument in the drying system shall be posted on or near the control panel of each thermal drying system.

(c) Each instrument on the control panel shall be identified by a nameplate or equivalent marking.

(d) A plan to control the operation of each thermal dryer system shall be posted at or near the control panel showing a sequence of startup, normal shutdown, and emergency shutdown procedures.

§ 77.311 Alarm devices.

Thermal dryer systems shall be equipped with both audible and visual alarm devices which are set to operate when safe dryer temperatures are exceeded.

§ 77.312 Fail safe monitoring systems.

Thermal dryer systems and controls shall be protected by a fail safe monitoring system which will safely shut down the system and any related equipment upon failure of any component in the dryer system.

§ 77.313 Wet-coal feedbins; low-level indicators.

Wet-coal bins feeding thermal drying systems shall be equipped with both audible and visual low-coal-level indicators.

§ 77.314 Automatic temperature control instruments.

(a) Automatic temperature control instruments for thermal dryer system shall be of the recording type.

(b) Automatic temperature control instruments shall be locked or sealed to prevent tampering or unauthorized adjustment. These instruments shall not be set above the maximum allowable operating temperature.

(c) All dryer control instruments shall be inspected and calibrated at least once every 3 months and a record or certificate of accuracy, signed by a trained employee or by a servicing agent, shall be kept at the plant.

§ 77.315 Thermal dryers; examination and inspection.

Thermal dryer systems shall be examined for fires and coal-dust accumulations if the dryers are not restarted promptly after a shutdown.

Subpart E—Safeguards for Mechanical Equipment

§ 77.400 Mechanical equipment guards.

(a) Gears; sprockets; chains; drive, head, tail, and takeup pulleys; flywheels; couplings; shafts; sawblades; fan inlets; and similar exposed moving machine parts which may be contacted by persons, and which may cause injury to persons shall be guarded.

(b) Overhead belts shall be guarded if the whipping action from a broken line would be hazardous to persons below.

(c) Guards at conveyor-drive, conveyor-head, and conveyor-tail pulleys shall extend a distance sufficient to prevent a person from reaching behind the guard and becoming caught between the belt and the pulley.

(d) Except when testing the machinery, guards shall be securely in place while machinery is being operated.

§ 77.401 Stationary grinding machines; protective devices.

(a) Stationary grinding machines other than special bit grinders shall be equipped with:

(1) Peripheral hoods (less than 90° throat openings) capable of withstanding the force of a bursting wheel.

(2) Adjustable tool rests set as close as practical to the wheel.

(3) Safety washers.

(b) Grinding wheels shall be operated within the specifications of the manufacturer of the wheel.

(c) Face shields or goggles, in good condition, shall be worn when operating a grinding wheel.

§ 77.402 Hand-held power tools; safety devices.

Hand-held power tools shall be equipped with controls requiring constant hand or finger pressure to operate the tools or shall be equipped with friction or other equivalent safety devices.

§ 77.403 Mobile equipment; falling object protective structures (FOPS).

(a) When necessary to protect the operator of the equipment, all rubber-tired or crawler-mounted self-propelled scrapers, front-end loaders, dozers, graders, loaders, and tractors, with or without attachments, that are used in surface coal mines or the surface work areas of underground coal mines shall be provided with substantial falling object protective structures (FOPS). FOPS which meet the requirements of the Society of Automotive Engineers (SAE) Standard J 231 shall be considered to be a "substantial" FOPS. An authorized representative of the Secretary may approve a FOPS which provides protection equivalent to SAE J 231.

(b) When necessary to protect the operator of the equipment, forklift or powered industrial trucks shall be provided with substantial FOPS. Such FOPS shall meet the requirements of the State of California, Division of Industrial Safety, General Safety Orders, Register 72, Number 6, February 8, 1972, Article 25, Section 3655—"Overhead Guards for High-Lift Rider Trucks."

(Sec. 101(a), Federal Coal Mine Health and Safety Act of 1969, as amended (83 Stat. 745; 30 U.S.C. 811(a))

[39 FR 24007, June 28, 1974]

§ 77.403-1 Mobile equipment; rollover protective structures (ROPS).

(a) All rubber-tired or crawler-mounted self-propelled scrapers, front-end loaders, dozers, graders, loaders, and tractors, with or without attachments, that are used in surface coal mines or the surface work areas of underground coal mines shall be provided with rollover protective structures (hereinafter referred to as ROPS) in accordance with the requirements of paragraphs (b) through (f) of this section, as applicable.

(b) *Mobile equipment manufactured on and after September 1, 1974.* All mobile equipment described in paragraph (a) of this section manufactured on and after September 1, 1974 shall be equipped with ROPS meeting the requirements of the Department of Labor specified in §§ 1926.1001 and 1926.1002 of Part 1926, Title 29, Code of Federal Regulations—Safety and Health Regulations for Construction.

(c) *Mobile equipment manufactured prior to September 1, 1974.* All mobile equipment described in paragraph (a) of this section manufactured prior to September 1, 1974 shall be equipped with ROPS meeting the requirements of paragraphs (d) through (f) of this section, as appropriate, no later than the dates specified in paragraphs (1), (2), and (3) of this paragraph (c), unless an earlier date is required by an authorized representative of the Secretary under paragraph (c)(4) of this section:

(1) Mobile equipment manufactured between July 1, 1971, and September 1, 1974, shall be equipped with ROPS no later than March 1, 1975.

(2) Mobile equipment manufactured between July 1, 1970, and June 30, 1971, shall be equipped with ROPS no later than July 1, 1975.

(3) Mobile equipment manufactured between July 1, 1969, and June 30, 1970, shall be equipped with ROPS no later than January 1, 1976.

(4) Irrespective of the time periods specified in paragraph (c) (1) through (3) of this section an authorized representative of the Secretary may require such mobile equipment to be equipped with ROPS at an earlier date when necessary to protect the operator of the equipment under the conditions in which the mobile equipment is, or will be operated. The authorized representative of the Secretary shall in writing advise the operator that the equipment shall be equipped with a ROPS and shall fix a time within which the operator shall provide and install the ROPS. If such ROPS is not provided and installed within the time fixed a notice shall be issued to the operator pursuant to section 104 of the Act.

Mine Safety and Health Admin., Labor § 77.403-1

(5) Nothing in this § 77.403-1 shall preclude the issuance of a withdrawal order because of imminent danger.

(d) Except as provided in paragraph (e) of this section, mobile equipment described in paragraph (a) of this section, manufactured prior to September 1, 1974, shall be deemed in compliance with this section if the ROPS is installed in accordance with the recommendations of the ROPS manufacturer or designer. The coal mine operator shall exhibit certification from the ROPS manufacturer or designer in the form of a label attached to the equipment, indicating the manufacturer's or fabricator's name and address, the ROPS model number, if any, the machine make, model or series number that the structure is designed to fit, and compliance with the applicable specification listed in paragraph (c)(1) or (2) of this section, or he shall, upon request of the authorized representative of the Secretary, furnish certification from a registered professional engineer that:

(1) The ROPS complies with the Society of Automotive Engineers (SAE) Standard J 397, "Critical Zone—Characteristics and Dimensions for Operators of Construction and Industrial Machinery" or SAE J 397a, "Deflection Limiting Volume for Laboratory Evaluation of Rollover Protective Structures (ROPS) and Falling Object Protective Structures (FOPS) of Construction and Industrial Vehicles" and the following applicable SAE Standards:

(i) J 320a, "Minimum Performance Criteria for Rollover Protective Structure for Rubber-Tired Self-Propelled Scrapers" or J 320b, "Minimum Performance Criteria for Rollover Protective Structures for Prime Movers"; or

(ii) J 394, "Minimum Performance Criteria for Rollover Protective Structure for Rubber-Tired Front-End Loaders and Rubber-Tired Dozers" or J 394a, "Minimum Performance Criteria for Rollover Protective Structures for Wheeled Front-End Loaders and Wheeled Dozers"; or

(iii) J 395, "Minimum Performance Criteria for Rollover Protective Structure for Crawler Tractors and Crawler-Type Loaders" or J 395a, "Minimum Performance Criteria for Rollover Protective Structures for Track-Type Tractors and Track-Type Front-End Loaders"; or

(iv) J 396 or J 396a, "Minimum Performance Criteria for Rollover Protective Structures for Motor Graders"; or

(v) J 167, "Protective Frame with Overhead Protection—Test Procedures and Performance Requirements"; or

(vi) J 334a, "Protective Frame Test Procedures and Performance Requirements"; or

(2) The ROPS and supporting attachments will:

(i) Show satisfactory performance by actual test of a prototype involving a roll of 720° or more; or

(ii) Support not less than the weight of the vehicle applied as a uniformly distributed horizontal load at the top of the structure and perpendicular to a vertical plane through the longitudinal axis of the prime mover, and support two times the weight of the vehicle applied as a uniformly distributed vertical load to the top of the structure;[1] or

(iii) Support the following separately applied minimum loads:

(A) 125 percent of the weight of the vehicle applied as a uniformly distributed horizontal load at the top of the ROPS and perpendicular to a critical plane through the longitudinal axis of the prime mover; and

(B) A load of twice the weight of the vehicle applied as a uniformly distributed vertical load to the top of the ROPS after complying with paragraph (d) (1) (iii) (A) of this section. Stresses shall not exceed the ultimate strength. Steel used in the ROPS must have capability to perform at 0 °F., or exhibit Charpy V-notch impact strength at 8 ft.-lb. at −20 °F. with a standard Charpy V-notch Type A specimen and provide 20 percent elongation over two inches in a standard two inch gauge length on a 0.505 inch diameter tensile specimen. Bolts and nuts shall be SAE grade 8 (reference SAE J 429d, J 429e, J

---

[1] Paragraph (d) of § 77.403-1 is based on the ROPS criteria of the U.S. Army Corps of Engineers, Safety—General Safety Requirements EM 385-1-1, Change 1, No. 21, Para. 18.A.20 (March 27, 1972), except that subparagraph (2)(ii) of this paragraph (d) is substituted for Para. 18.A.20e(2) of the Corps requirements.

§ 77.403-2

429f or J 429g and J 995, J 995a or J 995b).

(e) *Mobile equipment manufactured prior to September 1, 1974 meeting certain existing governmental requirements for ROPS.* Mobile equipment described in paragraph (a) of this section, manufactured prior to September 1, 1974 and already equipped with ROPS, shall be deemed in compliance with this section if it meets the ROPS requirements of the State of California, the U.S. Army Corps of Engineers, the Bureau of Reclamation of the U.S. Department of the Interior in effect on April 5, 1972, or the Occupational Safety and Health Administration, U.S. Department of Labor. The requirements in effect are:

(1) State of California: Construction Safety Orders 1591(i), 1596, and Logging and Sawmill Safety Order 5243, issued by the Department of Industrial Relations pursuant to Division 5, Labor Code § 6312, State of California;

(2) U.S. Army Corps of Engineers: Safety—General Safety Requirements, EM-385-1-1 (March 1967);

(3) Bureau of Reclamation, U.S. Department of the Interior: Safety and Health Regulations for Construction, Part II (September 1971); and

(4) Occupational Safety and Health Administration, U.S. Department of Labor: Safety and Health Regulations for Construction, 29 CFR 1926.1001 and 1926.1002.

(f) Field welding on ROPS shall be performed by welders who are certified by the coal mine operator or equipment distributor as being qualified in accordance with the American Welding Society Structural Welding Code AWS D1.1-73, or Military Standard MIL-STD 248, or the equivalent thereof.

(g) Seat belts required by § 77.1710(i) shall be worn by the operator of mobile equipment required to be equipped with ROPS by § 77.403-1.

(Sec. 101(a), Federal Coal Mine Health and Safety Act of 1969, as amended (83 Stat. 745; 30 U.S.C. 811(a))

[39 FR 24007, June 28, 1974. Redesignated and amended at 71 FR 16669, Apr. 3, 2006]

§ 77.403-2 Incorporation by reference.

In accordance with 5 U.S.C. 552(a), the publications to which references are made in §§ 77.403 and 77.403-1 and which have been prepared by organizations other than the Mine Safety and Health Administration (MSHA), are hereby incorporated by reference and made a part hereof. The incorporated publications are available at each MSHA Coal Mine Safety and Health district office of MSHA. The U.S. Army Corps of Engineers, Safety—General Safety Requirements and the Occupational Safety and Health Administration regulations are also available from the Information Dissemination (Superintendent of Documents), P.O. Box 371954, Pittsburgh, PA 15250-7954; Telephone: 866-512-1800 (toll free) or 202-512-1800; *http://bookstore.gpo.gov*. Bureau of Reclamation Safety and Health Regulations for Construction are available from the Bureau of Reclamation, Division of Safety, Engineering and Research Center, Denver, Colorado. SAE documents are available from the Society of Automotive Engineers, Inc., 400 Commonwealth Drive, Warrendale, PA 15096. American Welding Society Structural Welding Code D1-1-73 is available from the American Welding Society, Inc., 550 N.W. LeJeune Road, Miami, FL 33126. Military Standard MIL-STD 248 is available from the U.S. Government Printing Office, Washington, DC 20202.

(Sec. 101(a), the Federal Coal Mine Health and Safety Act of 1969, as amended (83 Stat. 745; 30 U.S.C. 811(a))

[39 FR 24008, June 28, 1974, as amended at 60 FR 35695, July 11, 1995. Redesignated and amended at 71 FR 16669, Apr. 3, 2006]

§ 77.404 Machinery and equipment; operation and maintenance.

(a) Mobile and stationary machinery and equipment shall be maintained in safe operating condition and machinery or equipment in unsafe condition shall be removed from service immediately.

(b) Machinery and equipment shall be operated only by persons trained in the use of and authorized to operate such machinery or equipment.

(c) Repairs or maintenance shall not be performed on machinery until the power is off and the machinery is blocked against motion, except where machinery motion is necessary to make adjustments.

(d) Machinery shall not be lubricated while in motion where a hazard exists, unless equipped with extended fittings or cups.

§ 77.405 Performing work from a raised position; safeguards.

(a) Men shall not work on or from a piece of mobile equipment in a raised position until it has been blocked in place securely. This does not preclude the use of equipment specifically designed as elevated mobile work platforms.

(b) No work shall be performed under machinery or equipment that has been raised until such machinery or equipment has been securely blocked in position.

§ 77.406 Drive belts.

(a) Drive belts shall not be shifted while in motion unless the machines are provided with mechanical shifters.

(b) Belt dressing shall not be applied while belts are in motion except where it can be applied without endangering a person.

§ 77.407 Power-driven pulleys.

(a) Belts, chains, and ropes shall not be guided onto power-driven moving pulleys, sprockets, or drums with the hands except on slow moving equipment especially designed for hand feeding.

(b) Pulleys of conveyors shall not be cleaned manually while the conveyor is in motion.

§ 77.408 Welding operations.

Welding operations shall be shielded and the area shall be well-ventilated.

§ 77.409 Shovels, draglines, and tractors.

(a) Shovels, draglines, and tractors shall not be operated in the presence of any person exposed to a hazard from its operation and all such equipment shall be provided with an adequate warning device which shall be sounded by the operator prior to starting operation.

(b) Shovels and draglines shall be equipped with handrails along and around all walkways and platforms.

§ 77.410 Mobile equipment; automatic warning devices.

(a) Mobile equipment such as front-end loaders, forklifts, tractors, graders, and trucks, except pickup trucks with an unobstructed rear view, shall be equipped with a warning device that—

(1) Gives an audible alarm when the equipment is put in reverse; or

(2) Uses infrared light, ultrasonic waves, radar, or other effective devices to detect objects or persons at the rear of the equipment, and sounds an audible alarm when a person or object is detected. This type of discriminating warning device shall—

(i) Have a sensing area of a sufficient size that would allow endangered persons adequate time to get out of the danger zone.

(ii) Give audible and visual alarms inside the operator's compartment and an audible alarm outside of the operator's compartment when a person or object is detected in the sensing area; and

(iii) When the equipment is put in reverse, activate and give a one-time audible and visual alarm inside the operator's compartment and a one-time audible alarm outside the operator's compartment.

(b) Alarms shall be audible above the surrounding noise levels.

(c) Warning devices shall be maintained in functional condition.

(d) An automatic reverse-activated strobe light may be substituted for an audible alarm when mobile equipment is operated at night.

[54 FR 30517, July 20, 1989]

§ 77.411 Compressed air and boilers; general.

All boilers and pressure vessels shall be constructed, installed, and maintained in accordance with the standards and specifications of the American Society of Mechanical Engineers Boiler and Pressure Vessel Code.

§ 77.412 Compressed air systems.

(a) Compressors and compressed-air receivers shall be equipped with automatic pressure-relief valves, pressure gages, and drain valves.

(b) Repairs involving the pressure system of compressors, receivers, or compressed-air-powered equipment shall not be attempted until the pressure has been relieved from that part of the system to be repaired.

§ 77.413

(c) At no time shall compressed air be directed toward a person. When compressed air is used, all necessary precautions shall be taken to protect persons from injury.

(d) Safety chains or suitable locking devices shall be used at connections to machines of high-pressure hose lines of 1-inch inside diameter or larger, and between high-pressure hose lines of 1-inch inside diameter or larger, where a connection failure would create a hazard.

§ 77.413 Boilers.

(a) Boilers shall be equipped with guarded, well-maintained water gages and pressure gages placed so that they can be observed easily. Water gages and pipe passages to the gages shall be kept clean and free of scale and rust.

(b) Boilers shall be equipped with automatic pressure-relief valves; valves shall be opened manually at least once a week to determine that they will function properly.

(c) Blowoff valves shall be piped outside the building and shall have outlets so located or protected that persons passing by, near, or under them will not be scalded.

(d) Boiler installations shall be provided with safety devices, acceptable to the Mine Safety and Health Administration, to protect against hazards of flameouts, fuel interruptions, and low-water level.

(e) Boilers shall be inspected internally at least once a year by a licensed inspector and a certificate of inspection signed by the inspector shall be displayed in the vicinity of the boiler.

Subpart F—Electrical Equipment—General

§ 77.500 Electric power circuits and electric equipment; deenergization.

Power circuits and electric equipment shall be deenergized before work is done on such circuits and equipment, except when necessary for troubleshooting or testing.

§ 77.501 Electric distribution circuits and equipment; repair.

No electrical work shall be performed on electric distribution circuits or equipment, except by a qualified person or by a person trained to perform electrical work and to maintain electrical equipment under the direct supervision of a qualified person. Disconnecting devices shall be locked out and suitably tagged by the persons who perform such work, except that in cases where locking out is not possible, such devices shall be opened and suitably tagged by such persons. Locks or tags shall be removed only by the persons who installed them or, if such persons are unavailable, by persons authorized by the operator or his agent.

§ 77.501-1 Qualified person.

A qualified person within the meaning of § 77.501 is an individual who meets the requirements of § 77.103.

§ 77.502 Electric equipment; examination, testing, and maintenance.

Electric equipment shall be frequently examined, tested, and properly maintained by a qualified person to assure safe operating conditions. When a potentially dangerous condition is found on electric equipment, such equipment shall be removed from service until such condition is corrected. A record of such examinations shall be kept.

§ 77.502-1 Qualified person.

A qualified person within the meaning of § 77.502 is an individual who meets the requirements of § 77.103.

§ 77.502-2 Electric equipment; frequency of examination and testing.

The examinations and tests required under the provision of this § 77.502 shall be conducted at least monthly.

§ 77.503 Electric conductors; capacity and insulation.

Electric conductors shall be sufficient in size and have adequate current carrying capacity and be of such construction that a rise in temperature resulting from normal operation will not damage the insulating materials.

§ 77.503-1 Electric conductors.

Electric conductors shall be sufficient in size to meet the minimum current carrying capacity provided for in the National Electric Code, 1968. All trailing cables shall meet the minimum requirements for ampacity provided in the standards of the Insulated Power Cable Engineers Association—National Electric Manufacturers Association in effect when such cables are purchased.

§ 77.504 Electrical connections or splices; suitability.

Electrical connections or splices in electric conductors shall be mechanically and electrically efficient, and suitable connectors shall be used. All electrical connections or splices in insulated wire shall be reinsulated at least to the same degree of protection as the remainder of the wire.

§ 77.505 Cable fittings; suitability.

Cables shall enter metal frames of motors, splice boxes, and electric compartments only through proper fittings. When insulated wires, other than cables, pass through metal frames, the holes shall be substantially bushed with insulated bushings.

§ 77.506 Electric equipment and circuits; overload and short-circuit protection.

Automatic circuit-breaking devices or fuses of the correct type and capacity shall be installed so as to protect all electric equipment and circuits against short circuit and overloads.

§ 77.506-1 Electric equipment and circuits; overload and short circuit protection; minimum requirements.

Devices providing either short circuit protection or protection against overload shall conform to the minimum requirements for protection of electric circuits and equipment of the National Electric Code, 1968.

§ 77.507 Electric equipment; switches.

All electric equipment shall be provided with switches or other controls that are safely designed, constructed, and installed.

§ 77.508 Lightning arresters; ungrounded and exposed power conductors and telephone wires.

All ungrounded, exposed power conductors and telephone wires shall be equipped with suitable lightning arresters which are adequately installed and connected to a low resistance grounding medium.

§ 77.508-1 Lightning arresters; wires entering buildings.

Lightning arresters protecting exposed telephone wires entering buildings shall be provided at the point where each such telephone wire enters the building.

§ 77.509 Transformers; installation and guarding.

(a) Transformers shall be of the totally enclosed type, or shall be placed at least 8 feet above the ground, or installed in a transformer house, or surrounded by a substantial fence at least 6 feet high and at least 3 feet from any energized parts, casings, or wiring.

(b) Transformer stations shall be enclosed to prevent persons from unintentionally or inadvertently contacting energized parts.

(c) Transformer enclosures shall be kept locked against unauthorized entry.

§ 77.510 Resistors; location and guarding.

Resistors, heaters, and rheostats shall be located so as to minimize fire hazards and, where necessary, provided with guards to prevent personal contact.

§ 77.511 Danger signs at electrical installations.

Suitable danger signs shall be posted at all major electrical installations.

§ 77.512 Inspection and cover plates.

Inspection and cover plates on electrical equipment shall be kept in place at all times except during testing or repairs.

§ 77.513 Insulating mats at power switches.

Dry wooden platforms, insulating mats, or other electrically nonconductive material shall be kept in place at all switchboards and power-control switches where shock hazards exist. However, metal plates on which a person normally would stand and which are kept at the same potential as the grounded, metal, non-current-carrying

§ 77.514

parts of the power switches to be operated may be used.

§ 77.514 Switchboards; passageways and clearance.

Switchboards shall be installed to provide passageways or lanes of travel which permit access to the back of the switchboard from both ends for inspection, adjustment or repair. Openings permitting access to the rear of any switchboard shall be guarded, except where they are located in buildings which are kept locked.

§ 77.515 Bare signal or control wires; voltage.

The voltage on bare signal or control wires accessible to personal contact shall not exceed 40 volts.

§ 77.516 Electric wiring and equipment; installation and maintenance.

In addition to the requirements of §§ 77.503 and 77.506, all wiring and electrical equipment installed after June 30, 1971, shall meet the requirements of the National Electric Code in effect at the time of installation.

Subpart G—Trailing Cables

§ 77.600 Trailing cables; short-circuit protection; disconnecting devices.

Short-circuit protection for trailing cables shall be provided by an automatic circuit breaker or other no less effective device, approved by the Secretary, of adequate current-interrupting capacity in each ungrounded conductor. Disconnecting devices used to disconnect power from trailing cables shall be plainly marked and identified and such devices shall be equipped or designed in such a manner that it can be determined by visual observation that the power is disconnected.

§ 77.601 Trailing cables or portable cables; temporary splices.

Temporary splices in trailing cables or portable cables shall be made in a workmanlike manner and shall be mechanically strong and well insulated. Trailing cables or portable cables with exposed wires or splices that heat or spark under load shall not be used.

§ 77.602 Permanent splicing of trailing cables.

When permanent splices in trailing cables are made, they shall be:

(a) Mechanically strong with adequate electrical conductivity;

(b) Effectively insulated and sealed so as to exclude moisture; and,

(c) Vulcanized or otherwise made with suitable materials to provide good bonding to the outer jacket.

§ 77.603 Clamping of trailing cables to equipment.

Trailing cables shall be clamped to machines in a manner to protect the cables from damage and to prevent strain on the electrical connections.

§ 77.604 Protection of trailing cables.

Trailing cables shall be adequately protected to prevent damage by mobile equipment.

§ 77.605 Breaking trailing cable and power cable connections.

Trailing cable and power cable connections between cables and to power sources shall not be made or broken under load.

§ 77.606 Energized trailing cables; handling.

Energized medium- and high-voltage trailing cables shall be handled only by persons wearing protective rubber gloves (see § 77.606-1) and, with such other protective devices as may be necessary and appropriate under the circumstances.

§ 77.606-1 Rubber gloves; minimum requirements.

(a) Rubber gloves (lineman's gloves) worn while handling high-voltage trailing cables shall be rated at least 20,000 volts and shall be used and tested in accordance with the provisions of §§ 77.704-6 through 77.704-8.

(b) Rubber gloves (wireman's gloves) worn while handling trailing cables energized by 660 to 1,000 volts shall be rated at least 1,000 volts and shall not be worn inside out or without protective leather gloves.

(c) Rubber gloves shall be inspected for defects before use on each shift and at least once thereafter during the shift when such rubber gloves are used for extended periods. All protective rubber gloves which contain defects shall be discarded and replaced prior to handling energized cables.

Subpart H—Grounding

§ 77.700 Grounding metallic sheaths, armors, and conduits enclosing power conductors.

Metallic sheaths, armors, and conduits enclosing power conductors shall be electrically continuous throughout and shall be grounded by methods approved by an authorized representative of the Secretary.

§ 77.700-1 Approved methods of grounding.

Metallic sheaths, armors, and conduits in resistance grounded systems, where the enclosed conductors are a part of the system, will be approved if a solid connection is made to the neutral conductor; in all other systems, the following methods of grounding will be approved:

(a) A solid connection to metal waterlines having low resistance to earth;

(b) A solid connection to a grounding conductor, other than the neutral conductor of a resistance grounded system, extending to a low-resistance ground field;

(c) Any other method of grounding, approved by an authorized representative of the Secretary, which ensures that there is no difference in potential between such metallic enclosures and the earth.

§ 77.701 Grounding metallic frames, casings, and other enclosures of electric equipment.

Metallic frames, casings, and other enclosures of electric equipment that can become "alive" through failure of insulation or by contact with energized parts shall be grounded by methods approved by an authorized representative of the Secretary.

§ 77.701-1 Approved methods of grounding of equipment receiving power from ungrounded alternating current power systems.

For purposes of grounding metallic frames, casings and other enclosures of equipment receiving power from ungrounded alternating current power systems, the following methods of grounding will be approved:

(a) A solid connection between the metallic frame; casing, or other metal enclosure and the grounded metallic sheath, armor, or conduit enclosing the power conductor feeding the electric equipment enclosed;

(b) A solid connection to metal waterlines having low resistance to earth;

(c) A solid connection to a grounding conductor extending to a low-resistance ground field; and,

(d) Any other method of grounding, approved by an authorized representative of the Secretary, which insures that there is no difference in potential between such metal enclosures and the earth.

§ 77.701-2 Approved methods of grounding metallic frames, casings, and other enclosures of electric equipment receiving power from a direct-current power system.

(a) The following methods of grounding metallic frames, casings, and other enclosures of electric equipment receiving power from a direct-current power system with one polarity grounded will be approved:

(1) A solid connection to the grounded power conductor of the system; and,

(2) Any other method, approved by an authorized representative of the Secretary, which insures that there is no difference in potential between such metal enclosures and the earth.

(b) A method of grounding of metallic frames, casings, and other enclosures of electric equipment receiving power from a direct-current power system other than a system with one polarity grounded, will be approved by an authorized representative of the Secretary if the method insures that there is no difference in potential between such frames, casings, and other enclosures, and the earth.

§ 77.701-3 Grounding wires; capacity.

Where grounding wires are used to ground metallic sheaths, armors, conduits, frames, casings, and other metallic enclosures, such grounding wires will be approved if:

§ 77.701-4

(a) Where the power conductor used is No. 6 A.W.G., or larger, the cross-sectional area of the grounding wire is at least one-half the cross-sectional area of the power conductor.

(b) Where the power conductor used is less than No. 6 A.W.G., the cross-sectional area of the grounding wire is equal to the cross-sectional area of the power conductor.

§ 77.701-4 Use of grounding connectors.

If ground wires are attached to grounded power conductors, separate clamps, suitable for such purpose, shall be used and installed to provide a solid connection.

§ 77.702 Protection other than grounding.

Methods other than grounding which provide no less effective protection may be permitted by the Secretary or his authorized representative. Such methods may not be used unless so approved.

§ 77.703 Grounding frames of stationary high-voltage equipment receiving power from ungrounded delta systems.

The frames of all stationary high-voltage equipment receiving power from ungrounded delta systems shall be grounded by methods approved by an authorized representative of the Secretary.

§ 77.703-1 Approved methods of grounding.

The methods of grounding stated in § 77.701-1 will be approved with respect to the grounding of frames of high-voltage equipment referred to in § 77.703.

§ 77.704 Work on high-voltage lines; deenergizing and grounding.

High-voltage lines shall be deenergized and grounded before work is performed on them, except that repairs may be permitted on energized high-voltage lines if (a) such repairs are made by a qualified person in accordance with procedures and safeguards set forth in §§ 77.704-1 through 77.704-11 of this Subpart H as applicable, and (b) the operator has tested and properly maintained the protective devices necessary in making such repairs.

§ 77.704-1 Work on high-voltage lines.

(a) No high-voltage line shall be regarded as deenergized for the purpose of performing work on it, until it has been determined by a qualified person (as provided in § 77.103) that such high-voltage line has been deenergized and grounded. Such qualified person shall by visual observation (1) determine that the disconnecting devices on the high-voltage circuit are in open position, and (2) insure that each ungrounded conductor of the high-voltage circuit upon which work is to be done is properly connected to the system grounding medium. In the case of resistance grounded or solid wye-connected systems, the neutral wire is the system grounding medium. In the case of an ungrounded power system, either the steel armor or conduit enclosing the system or a surface grounding field is a system grounding medium;

(b) No work shall be performed on any high-voltage line which is supported by any pole or structure which also supports other high-voltage lines until: (1) All lines supported on the pole or structure are deenergized and grounded in accordance with all of the provisions of this § 77.704-1 which apply to the repair of deenergized surface high-voltage lines; or (2) the provisions of §§ 77.704-2 through 77.704-10 have been complied with, with respect to all energized lines, which are supported on the pole or structure.

(c) Work may be performed on energized surface high-voltage lines only in accordance with the provisions of §§ 77.704-2 through 77.704-10, inclusive.

§ 77.704-2 Repairs to energized high-voltage lines.

An energized high-voltage line may be repaired only when:

(a) The operator has determined that,

(1) Such repairs cannot be scheduled during a period when the power circuit could be properly deenergized and grounded;

(2) Such repairs will be performed on power circuits with a phase-to-phase nominal voltage no greater than 15,000 volts;

(3) Such repairs on circuits with a phase-to-phase nominal voltage of 5,000 volts or more will be performed only with the use of live line tools; and,

(4) Weather conditions will not interfere with such repairs or expose those persons assigned to such work to an imminent danger; and,

(b) The operator has designated a person qualified under the provisions of §77.104 as the person responsible for carrying out such repairs and such person, in order to ensure protection for himself and other qualified persons assigned to perform such repairs from the hazards of such repair, has prepared and filed with the operator:

(1) A general description of the nature and location of the damage or defect to be repaired;

(2) The general plan to be followed in making such repairs;

(3) A statement that a briefing of all qualified persons assigned to make such repairs was conducted informing them of the general plan, their individual assignments, and the dangers inherent in such assignments;

(4) A list of the proper protective equipment and clothing that will be provided; and

(5) Such other information as the person designated by the operator feels necessary to describe properly the means or methods to be employed in such repairs.

§ 77.704-3 Work on energized high-voltage surface lines; reporting.

Any operator designating and assigning qualified persons to perform repairs on energized high-voltage surface lines under the provisions of § 77.704-2 shall maintain a record of such repairs. Such record shall contain a notation of the time, date, location, and general nature of the repairs made together with a copy of the information filed with the operator by the qualified person designated as responsible for performing such repairs.

§ 77.704-4 Simultaneous repairs.

When two or more persons are working on an energized high-voltage surface line simultaneously, and any one of them is within reach of another, such persons shall not be allowed to work on different phases or on equipment with different potentials.

§ 77.704-5 Installation of protective equipment.

Before repair work on energized high-voltage surface lines is begun, protective equipment shall be used to cover all bare conductors, ground wires, guys, telephone lines, and other attachments in proximity to the area of planned repairs. Such protective equipment shall be installed from a safe position below the conductors or other apparatus being covered. Each rubber protective device employed in the making of repairs shall have a dielectric strength of 20,000 volts, or more.

§ 77.704-6 Protective clothing; use and inspection.

All persons performing work on energized high-voltage surface lines shall wear protective rubber lineman's gloves, sleeves, and climber guards if climbers are worn. Protective rubber gloves shall not be worn wrong side out or without protective leather gloves. Protective devices worn by a person assigned to perform repairs on high-voltage surface lines shall be worn continuously from the time he leaves the ground until he returns to the ground and, if such devices are employed for extended periods, such person shall visually inspect the equipment assigned him for defects before each use and, in no case, less than twice each day.

§ 77.704-7 Protective equipment; inspection.

Each person shall visually inspect protective equipment and clothing provided him in connection with work on high-voltage surface lines before using such equipment and clothing, and any equipment or clothing containing any defect or damage shall be discarded and replaced with proper protective equipment or clothing prior to the performance of any electrical work on such lines.

§ 77.704-8 Protective equipment; testing and storage.

(a) All rubber protective equipment used on work on energized high-voltage surface lines shall be electrically tested by the operator in accordance with

§ 77.704-9

ASTM standards, Part 28, published February 1968, and such testing shall be conducted in accordance with the following schedule:

(1) Rubber gloves, once each month;
(2) Rubber sleeves, once every 3 months;
(3) Rubber blankets, once every 6 months;
(4) Insulator hoods and line hose, once a year; and
(5) Other electric protective equipment, once a year.

(b) Rubber gloves shall not be stored wrong side out. Blankets shall be rolled when not in use, and line hose, and insulator hoods shall be stored in their natural position and shape.

§ 77.704-9 Operating disconnecting or cutout switches.

Disconnecting or cutout switches on energized high-voltage surface lines shall be operated only with insulated sticks, fuse tongs, or pullers which are adequately insulated and maintained to protect the operator from the voltage to which he is exposed. When such switches are operated from the ground, the person using such devices shall wear protective rubber lineman's gloves, except where such switches are bonded to a metal mat as provided in § 77.513.

§ 77.704-10 Tying into energized high-voltage surface circuits.

If the work of forming an additional circuit by tying into an energized high-voltage surface line is performed from the ground, any person performing such work must wear and employ all of the protective equipment and clothing required under the provisions of §§ 77.704-5 and 77.704-6. In addition, the insulated stick used by such person must have been designed for such purpose and must be adequately insulated and be maintained to protect such person from the voltage to which he is exposed.

§ 77.704-11 Use of grounded messenger wires; ungrounded systems.

Solely for purposes of grounding ungrounded high-voltage power systems, grounded messenger wires used to suspend the cables of such systems may be used as a grounding medium.

§ 77.705 Guy wires; grounding.

Guy wires from poles supporting high-voltage transmission lines shall be securely connected to the system ground or be provided with insulators installed near the pole end.

Subpart I—Surface High-Voltage Distribution

§ 77.800 High-voltage circuits; circuit breakers.

High-voltage circuits supplying power to portable or mobile equipment shall be protected by suitable circuit breakers of adequate interrupting capacity which are properly tested and maintained and equipped with devices to provide protection against under voltage, grounded phase, short circuit and overcurrent. High-voltage circuits supplying power to stationary equipment shall be protected against overloads by either a circuit breaker or fuses of the correct type and capacity.

§ 77.800-1 Testing, examination, and maintenance of circuit breakers; procedures.

(a) Circuit breakers and their auxiliary devices protecting high-voltage circuits to portable or mobile equipment shall be tested and examined at least once each month by a person qualified as provided in § 77.103.

(b) Tests shall include:

(1) Breaking continuity of the ground check conductor where ground check monitoring is used; and,

(2) Actuating any of the auxiliary protective relays.

(c) Examination shall include visual observation of all components of the circuit breaker and its auxiliary devices, and such repairs or adjustments as are indicated by such tests and examinations shall be carried out immediately.

§ 77.800-2 Testing, examination, and maintenance of circuit breakers; record.

The operator shall maintain a written record of each test, examination, repair, or adjustment of all circuit breakers protecting high-voltage circuits. Such record shall be kept in a book approved by the Secretary.

§ 77.801 Grounding resistors.

The grounding resistor, where required, shall be of the proper ohmic value to limit the voltage drop in the grounding circuit external to the resistor to not more than 100 volts under fault conditions. The grounding resistor shall be rated for maximum fault current continuously and insulated from ground for a voltage equal to the phase-to-phase voltage of the system.

§ 77.801-1 Grounding resistors; continuous current rating.

The ground fault current rating of grounding resistors shall meet the "extended time rating" set forth in American Institute of Electrical Engineers, Standard No. 32.

§ 77.802 Protection of high-voltage circuits; neutral grounding resistors; disconnecting devices.

High-voltage circuits supplying portable or mobile equipment shall contain either a direct or derived neutral which shall be grounded through a suitable resistor at the source transformers, and a grounding circuit, originating at the grounded side of the grounding resistor, shall extend along with the power conductors and serve as a grounding conductor for the frames of all high-voltage equipment supplied power from that circuit, except that the Secretary or his authorized representative may permit other high-voltage circuits to feed stationary electrical equipment, if he finds that such exception will not pose a hazard to the miners. Disconnecting devices shall be installed and so equipped or designed in such a manner that it can be determined by visual observation that the power is disconnected.

§ 77.803 Fail safe ground check circuits on high-voltage resistance grounded systems.

On and after September 30, 1971, all high-voltage, resistance grounded systems shall include a fail safe ground check circuit or other no less effective device approved by the Secretary to monitor continuously the grounding circuit to assure continuity. The fail safe ground check circuit shall cause the circuit breaker to open when either the ground or ground check wire is broken.

§ 77.803-1 Fail safe ground check circuits; maximum voltage.

The maximum voltage used for ground check circuits under § 77.803 shall not exceed 96 volts.

§ 77.803-2 Ground check systems not employing pilot check wires; approval by the Secretary.

Ground check systems not employing pilot check wires shall be approved by the Secretary only if it is determined that the system includes a fail safe design which will cause the circuit interrupter to open when ground continuity is broken.

§ 77.804 High-voltage trailing cables; minimum design requirements.

(a) High-voltage trailing cables used in resistance grounded systems shall be equipped with metallic shields around each power conductor with one or more ground conductors having a total cross-sectional area of not less than one-half the power conductor, and with an insulated conductor for the ground continuity check circuit. External ground check conductors may be used if they are not smaller than No. 8 (AWG) and have an insulation rated at least 600 volts.

(b) All such high-voltage trailing cables shall be adequate for the intended current and voltage. Splices made in such cables shall provide continuity of all components.

§ 77.805 Cable couplers and connection boxes; minimum design requirements.

(a)(1) Couplers that are used in medium- or high-voltage power circuits shall be of the three-phase type and enclosed in a full metallic shell, except that the Secretary may permit, under such guidelines as he may prescribe, no less effective couplers constructed of materials other than metal.

(2) Cable couplers shall be adequate for the intended current and voltage.

(3) Cable couplers with any metal exposed shall be grounded to the ground conductor in the cable.

§ 77.806

(4) Couplers shall be constructed to cause the ground check continuity conductor to break first and the ground conductor last when being uncoupled when pilot check circuits are used.

(b) Cable connection boxes shall be of substantial construction and designed to guard all energized parts from personal contact.

§ 77.806 Connection of single-phase loads.

Single-phase loads, such as transformer primaries, shall be connected phase to phase in resistance grounded systems.

§ 77.807 Installation of high-voltage transmission cables.

High-voltage transmission cables shall be installed or placed so as to afford protection against damage. They shall be placed to prevent contact with low-voltage or communication circuits.

§ 77.807-1 High-voltage powerlines; clearances above ground.

High-voltage powerlines located above driveways, haulageways, and railroad tracks shall be installed to provide the minimum vertical clearance specified in National Electrical Safety Code: *Provided, however,* That in no event shall any high-voltage powerline be installed less than 15 feet above ground.

§ 77.807-2 Booms and masts; minimum distance from high-voltage lines.

The booms and masts of equipment operated on the surface of any coal mine shall not be operated within 10 feet of an energized overhead powerline. Where the voltage of overhead powerlines is 69,000 volts, or more, the minimum distance from the boom or mast shall be as follows:

Nominal power line voltage (in 1,000 volts)	Minimum distance (feet)
69 to 114	12
115 to 229	15
230 to 344	20
345 to 499	25
500 or more	35

§ 77.807-3 Movement of equipment; minimum distance from high-voltage lines.

When any part of any equipment operated on the surface of any coal mine is required to pass under or by any energized high-voltage powerline and the clearance between such equipment and powerline is less than that specified in § 77.807-2 for booms and masts, such powerlines shall be deenergized or other precautions shall be taken.

§ 77.808 Disconnecting devices.

Disconnecting devices shall be installed at the beginning of each branch line in high-voltage circuits and they shall be equipped or designed in such a manner that it can be determined by visual observation that the circuit is deenergized when such devices are open.

§ 77.809 Identification of circuit breakers and disconnecting switches.

Circuit breakers and disconnecting switches shall be labeled to show which units they control, unless identification can be made readily by location.

§ 77.810 High-voltage equipment; grounding.

Frames, supporting structures, and enclosures of stationary, portable, or mobile high-voltage equipment shall be effectively grounded.

§ 77.811 Movement of portable substations and transformers.

Portable substations and transformers shall be deenergized before they are moved from one location to another.

Subpart J—Low- and Medium-Voltage Alternating Current Circuits

§ 77.900 Low- and medium-voltage circuits serving portable or mobile three-phase alternating current equipment; circuit breakers.

Low- and medium-voltage circuits supplying power to portable or mobile three-phase alternating current equipment shall be protected by suitable circuit breakers of adequate interrupting capacity which are properly tested and maintained and equipped with devices

Mine Safety and Health Admin., Labor § 77.902-3

to provide protection against undervoltage, grounded phase, short circuit, and over-current.

§ 77.900-1 Testing, examination, and maintenance of circuit breakers; procedures.

Circuit breakers protecting low- and medium-voltage circuits serving portable or mobile three-phase alternating current equipment and their auxiliary devices shall be tested and examined at least once each month by a person qualified as provided in § 77.103. In performing such tests, the circuit breaker auxiliaries or control circuits shall be actuated in any manner which causes the circuit breaker to open. All components of the circuit breaker and its auxiliary devices shall be visually examined and such repairs or adjustments as are indicated by such tests and examinations shall be carried out immediately.

§ 77.900-2 Testing, examination, and maintenance of circuit breakers; record.

The operator shall maintain a written record of each test, examination, repair or adjustment of all circuit breakers protecting low- and medium-voltage circuits serving three-phase alternating current equipment and such record shall be kept in a book approved by the Secretary.

§ 77.901 Protection of low- and medium-voltage three-phase circuits.

(a) Low- and medium-voltage circuits supplying power to portable or mobile three-phase alternating equipment shall contain:

(1) Either a direct or derived neutral grounded through a suitable resistor at the power source;

(2) A grounding circuit originating at the grounded side of the grounding resistor which extends along with the power conductors and serves as a grounding conductor for the frames of all the electric equipment supplied power from the circuit.

(b) Grounding resistors, where required, shall be of an ohmic value which limits the ground fault current to no more than 25 amperes. Such grounding resistors shall be rated for maximum fault current continuously and provide insulation from ground for a voltage equal to the phase-to-phase voltage of the system.

(c) Low- and medium-voltage circuits supplying power to three-phase alternating current stationary electric equipment shall comply with the National Electric Code.

§ 77.901-1 Grounding resistor; continuous current rating.

The ground fault current rating of grounding resistors shall meet the "extended time rating" set forth in American Institute of Electrical Engineers Standard No. 32.

§ 77.902 Low- and medium-voltage ground check monitor circuits.

On and after September 30, 1971, three-phase low- and medium-voltage resistance grounded systems to portable and mobile equipment shall include a fail safe ground check circuit or other no less effective device approved by the Secretary to monitor continuously the grounding circuit to assure continuity. The fail safe ground check circuit shall cause the circuit breaker to open when either the ground or pilot check wire is broken. Cable couplers shall be constructed to cause the ground check continuity conductor to break first and the ground conductor last when being uncoupled when pilot check circuits are used.

§ 77.902-1 Fail safe ground check circuits; maximum voltage.

The maximum voltage used for ground check circuits under § 77.902 shall not exceed 40 volts.

§ 77.902-2 Approved ground check systems not employing pilot check wires.

Ground check systems not employing pilot check wires shall be approved by the Secretary only after it has been determined that the system includes a fail safe design causing the circuit breaker to open when ground continuity is broken.

§ 77.902-3 Attachment of ground conductors and ground check wires to equipment frames; use of separate connections.

In grounding the frames of stationary, portable, or mobile equipment

§ 77.903

receiving power from resistance grounded systems, separate connections shall be used.

§ 77.903 Disconnecting devices.

Disconnecting devices shall be installed in circuits supplying power to portable or mobile equipment and shall provide visual evidence that the power is disconnected.

§ 77.904 Identification of circuit breakers.

Circuit breakers shall be labeled to show which circuits they control unless identification can be made readily by location.

§ 77.905 Connection of single-phase loads.

Single-phase loads shall be connected phase-to-phase in resistance grounded systems.

§ 77.906 Trailing cables supplying power to low-voltage mobile equipment; ground wires and ground check wires.

On and after September 30, 1971, all trailing cables supplying power to portable or mobile equipment from low-voltage three-phase resistance grounded power systems shall contain one or more ground conductors having a cross-sectional area of not less than one-half the power conductor. Such trailing cables shall include an insulated conductor for the ground continuity check circuit except where a no less effective device has been approved by the Secretary to assure continuity. Splices made in low-voltage trailing cables shall provide continuity of all components.

Subpart K—Ground Control

§ 77.1000 Highwalls, pits and spoil banks; plans.

Each operator shall establish and follow a ground control plan for the safe control of all highwalls, pits and spoil banks to be developed after June 30, 1971, which shall be consistent with prudent engineering design and will insure safe working conditions. The mining methods employed by the operator shall be selected to insure highwall and spoil bank stability.

§ 77.1000-1 Filing of plan.

The operator shall file a copy of such plan, and revisions thereof, with the MSHA Coal Mine Safety and Health district office for the district in which the mine is located, and shall identify the name and location of the mine; the Mine Safety and Health Administration identification number if known; and the name and address of the mine operator.

(Pub. L. No. 96–511, 94 Stat. 2812 (44 U.S.C. 3501 et seq.))

[36 FR 9364, May 22, 1971, as amended at 60 FR 33723, June 29, 1995; 71 FR 16669, Apr. 3, 2006]

§ 77.1001 Stripping; loose material.

Loose hazardous material shall be stripped for a safe distance from the top of pit or highwalls, and the loose unconsolidated material shall be sloped to the angle of repose, or barriers, baffle boards, screens, or other devices be provided that afford equivalent protection.

§ 77.1002 Box cuts; spoil material placement.

When box cuts are made, necessary precautions shall be taken to minimize the possibility of spoil material rolling into the pit.

§ 77.1003 Benches.

To insure safe operation, the width and height of benches shall be governed by the type of equipment to be used and the operation to be performed.

§ 77.1004 Ground control; inspection and maintenance; general.

(a) Highwalls, banks, benches, and terrain sloping into the working areas shall be examined after every rain, freeze, or thaw before men work in such areas, and such examination shall be made and recorded in accordance with § 77.1713.

(b) Overhanging highwalls and banks shall be taken down and other unsafe ground conditions shall be corrected promptly, or the area shall be posted.

§ 77.1005 Scaling highwalls; general.

(a) Hazardous areas shall be scaled before any other work is performed in the hazardous area. When scaling of highwalls is necessary to correct conditions that are hazardous to persons in the area, a safe means shall be provided for performing such work.

(b) Whenever it becomes necessary for safety to remove hazardous material from highwalls by hand, the hazardous material shall be approached from a safe direction and the material removed from a safe location.

§ 77.1006 Highwalls; men working.

(a) Men, other than those necessary to correct unsafe conditions, shall not work near or under dangerous highwalls or banks.

(b) Except as provided in paragraph (c) of this section, men shall not work between equipment and the highwall or spoil bank where the equipment may hinder escape from falls or slides.

(c) Special safety precautions shall be taken when men are required to perform repair work between immobilized equipment and the highwall or spoil bank and such equipment may hinder escape from falls or slides.

§ 77.1007 Drilling; general.

(a) Equipment that is to be used during a shift shall be inspected each shift by a competent person. Equipment defects affecting safety shall be reported.

(b) Equipment defects affecting safety shall be corrected before the equipment is used.

§ 77.1008 Relocation of drills; safeguards.

(a) When a drill is being moved from one drilling area to another, drill steel, tools, and other equipment shall be secured and the mast placed in a safe position.

(b) When a drill helper is used his location shall be made known to the operator at all times when the drill is being moved.

§ 77.1009 Drill; operation.

(a) While in operation drills shall be attended at all times.

(b) Men shall not drill from positions that hinder their access to the control levers, or from insecure footing or staging, or from atop equipment not designed for this purpose.

(c) Men shall not be on a mast while the drill bit is in operation unless a safe platform is provided and safety belts are used.

(d) Drill crews and others shall stay clear of augers or drill stems that are in motion. Persons shall not pass under or step over a moving stem or auger.

(e) In the event of power failure, drill controls shall be placed in the neutral position until power is restored.

(f) When churn drills or vertical rotary drills are used, drillers shall not be permitted to work under suspended tools, and when collaring holes, inspecting, or during any operation in which tools are removed from the hole, all tools shall be lowered to the ground or platform.

§ 77.1010 Collaring holes.

(a) Starter steels shall be used when collaring holes with hand-held drills.

(b) Men shall not hold the drill steel while collaring holes, or rest their hands on the chuck or centralizer while drilling.

§ 77.1011 Drill holes; guarding.

Drill holes large enough to constitute a hazard shall be covered or guarded.

§ 77.1012 Jackhammers; operation; safeguards.

Men operating or working near jackhammers or jackleg drills, or other drilling machines shall position themselves so that they will not be struck or lose their balance if the drill steel breaks or sticks.

§ 77.1013 Air drills; safeguards.

Air shall be turned off and bled from the air hoses before hand-held air drills are moved from one working area to another.

Subpart L—Fire Protection

§ 77.1100 Fire protection; training and organization.

Firefighting facilities and equipment shall be provided commensurate with the potential fire hazards at each structure, enclosure and other facility (including custom coal preparation) at the mine and the employees at such facilities shall be instructed and trained annually in the use of such firefighting facilities and equipment.

§ 77.1101 Escape and evacuation; plan.

(a) Before September 30, 1971, each operator of a mine shall establish and keep current a specific escape and evacuation plan to be followed in the event of a fire.

(b) All employees shall be instructed on current escape and evacuation plans, fire alarm signals, and applicable procedures to be followed in case of fire.

(c) Plans for escape and evacuation shall include the designation and proper maintenance of adequate means for exit from all areas where persons are required to work or travel including buildings and equipment and in areas where persons normally congregate during the work shift.

(Pub. L. No. 96–511, 94 Stat. 2812 (44 U.S.C. 3501 et seq.))

[36 FR 9364, May 22, 1971, as amended at 36 FR 13143, July 15, 1971; 60 FR 33723, June 29, 1995]

§ 77.1102 Warning signs; smoking and open flame.

Signs warning against smoking and open flames shall be posted so they can be readily seen in areas or places where fire or explosion hazards exist.

§ 77.1103 Flammable liquids; storage.

(a) Flammable liquids shall be stored in accordance with standards of the National Fire Protection Association. Small quantities of flammable liquids drawn from storage shall be kept in properly identified safety cans.

(b) Unburied flammable-liquid storage tanks shall be mounted securely on firm foundations. Outlet piping shall be provided with flexible connections or other special fittings to prevent adverse effects from tank settling.

(c) Fuel lines shall be equipped with valves to cut off fuel at the source and shall be located and maintained to minimize fire hazards.

(d) Areas surrounding flammable-liquid storage tanks and electric substations and transformers shall be kept free from grass (dry), weeds, underbrush, and other combustible materials such as trash, rubbish, leaves and paper, for at least 25 feet in all directions.

§ 77.1104 Accumulations of combustible materials.

Combustible materials, grease, lubricants, paints, or flammable liquids shall not be allowed to accumulate where they can create a fire hazard.

§ 77.1105 Internal combustion engines; fueling.

Internal combustion engines, except diesels, shall be shut off and stopped before being fueled.

§ 77.1106 Battery-charging stations; ventilation.

Battery-charging stations shall be located in well-ventilated areas. Battery-charging stations shall be equipped with reverse current protection where such stations are connected directly to direct current power systems.

§ 77.1107 Belt conveyors.

Belt conveyors in locations where fire would create a hazard to personnel shall be provided with switches to stop the drive pulley automatically in the event of excessive slippage.

§ 77.1108 Firefighting equipment; requirements; general.

On and after September 30, 1971, each operator of a coal mine shall provide an adequate supply of firefighting equipment which is adapted to the size and suitable for use under the conditions present on the surface at the mine.

[36 FR 9364, May 22, 1971, as amended at 36 FR 13143, July 15, 1971]

§ 77.1108–1 Type and capacity of firefighting equipment.

Firefighting equipment required under this § 77.1108 shall meet the following minimum requirements:

(a) *Waterlines.* Waterlines shall be capable of delivering 50 gallons of water a minute at a nozzle pressure of 50 pounds per square inch. Where storage tanks are used as a source of water supply, the tanks shall be of 1,000-gallon capacity for each 1,000 tons of coal processed (average) per shift.

(b) *Fire extinguishers.* Fire extinguishers shall be:

(1) Of the appropriate type for the particular fire hazard involved;

(2) Adequate in number and size for the particular fire hazard involved;

(3) Replaced immediately with fully charged extinguishers after any discharge is made from an extinguisher; and

(4) Approved by the Underwriter's Laboratories, Inc., or the Factory Mutual Research Corp., or other competent testing agency acceptable to the Mine Safety and Health Administration.

(c) *Fire hose.* Fire hose and couplings shall meet the requirements of the Underwriter's Laboratories, Inc., or Factory Mutual Research Corp.'s specifications. Cotton or cotton-polyester jacketed hose shall be treated in accordance with the U.S. Department of Agriculture Forest Service Specification 182 for mildew resistance. The water pressure at the hose nozzle shall not be excessively high so as to present a hazard to the nozzle operator.

[36 FR 9364, May 22, 1971, as amended at 47 FR 28096, June 29, 1982]

§ 77.1109 Quantity and location of firefighting equipment.

Preparation plants, dryer plants, tipples, drawoff tunnels, shops, and other surface installations shall be equipped with the following firefighting equipment.

(a) Each structure presenting a fire hazard shall be provided with portable fire extinguishers commensurate with the potential fire hazard at the structure in accordance with the recommendations of the National Fire Protection Association.

(b) Preparation plants shall be equipped with waterlines, with outlet valves on each floor, and with sufficient fire hose to project a water stream to any point in the plant. However, where freezing conditions exist or water is not available, a 125-pound multipurpose dry powder extinguisher may be substituted for the purposes of this paragraph (b) for each 2,500 square feet of floor space in a wooden or other flammable structure, or for each 5,000 square feet of floor space in a metal, concrete-block, or other type of nonflammable construction.

(c)(1) Mobile equipment, including trucks, front-end loaders, bulldozers, portable welding units, and augers, shall be equipped with at least one portable fire extinguisher.

(2) Power shovels, draglines, and other large equipment shall be equipped with at least one portable fire extinguisher; however, additional fire extinguishers may be required by an authorized representative of the Secretary.

(3) Auxiliary equipment such as portable drills, sweepers, and scrapers, when operated more than 600 feet from equipment required to have portable fire extinguishers, shall be equipped with at least one fire extinguisher.

(d) Fire extinguishers shall be provided at permanent electrical installations commensurate with the potential fire hazard at such installation in accordance with the recommendations of the National Fire Protection Association.

(e) Two portable fire extinguishers, or the equivalent, shall be provided at each of the following combustible liquid storage installations:

(1) Near each above ground or unburied combustible liquid storage station; and,

(2) Near the transfer pump of each buried combustible liquid storage tank.

(f) Vehicles transporting explosives and blasting agents shall be equipped with fire protection as recommended in Code 495, section 20, National Fire Protection Association Handbook, 12th Edition, 1962.

§ 77.1110 Examination and maintenance of firefighting equipment.

Firefighting equipment shall be continuously maintained in a usable and operative condition. Fire extinguishers shall be examined at least once every 6 months and the date of such examination shall be recorded on a permanent tag attached to the extinguisher.

(Pub. L. No. 96-511, 94 Stat. 2812 (44 U.S.C. 3501 *et seq.*))

[36 FR 9364, May 22, 1971, as amended at 60 FR 33723, June 29, 1995]

§ 77.1111 Welding, cutting, soldering; use of fire extinguisher.

One portable fire extinguisher shall be provided at each location where welding, cutting, or soldering with arc or flame is performed.

§ 77.1112 Welding, cutting, or soldering with arc or flame; safeguards.

(a) When welding, cutting, or soldering with arc or flame near combustible materials, suitable precautions shall be taken to insure that smoldering metal or sparks do not result in a fire.

(b) Before welding, cutting, or soldering is performed in areas likely to contain methane, an examination for methane shall be made by a qualified person with a device approved by the Secretary for detecting methane. Examinations for methane shall be made immediately before and periodically during welding, cutting, or soldering and such work shall not be permitted to commence or continue in air which contains 1.0 volume per centum or more of methane.

Subpart M—Maps

§ 77.1200 Mine map.

The operator shall maintain an accurate and up-to-date map of the mine, on a scale of not less than 100 nor more than 500 feet to the inch, at or near the mine, in an area chosen by the mine operator, with a duplicate copy on file at a separate and distinct location, to minimize the danger of destruction by fire or other hazard. The map shall show:

(a) Name and address of the mine;

(b) The property or boundary lines of the active areas of the mine;

(c) Contour lines passing through whole number elevations of the coalbed being mined. The spacing of such lines shall not exceed 25-foot elevation levels, except that a broader spacing of contour lines may be approved by the District Manager for steeply pitching coalbeds. Contour lines may be placed on overlays or tracings attached to mine maps.

(d) The general elevation of the coalbed or coalbeds being mined, and the general elevation of the surface;

(e) Either producing or abandoned oil and gas wells located on the mine property;

(f) The location and elevation of any body of water dammed or held back in any portion of the mine: *Provided, however,* Such bodies of water may be shown on overlays or tracings attached to the mine maps;

(g) All prospect drill holes that penetrate the coalbed or coalbeds being mined on the mine property;

(h) All auger and strip mined areas of the coalbed or coalbeds being mined on the mine property together with the line of maximum depth of holes drilled during auger mining operations.

(i) All worked out and abandoned areas;

(j) The location of railroad tracks and public highways leading to the mine, and mine buildings of a permanent nature with identifying names shown;

(k) Underground mine workings underlying and within 1,000 feet of the active areas of the mine;

(l) The location and description of at least two permanent base line points, and the location and description of at least two permanent elevation bench marks used in connection with establishing or referencing mine elevation surveys; and,

(m) The scale of the map.

§ 77.1201 Certification of mine maps.

Mine maps shall be made or certified by an engineer or surveyor registered by the State in which the mine is located.

§ 77.1202 Availability of mine map.

The mine map maintained in accordance with the provisions of § 77.1200 shall be available for inspection by the Secretary or his authorized representative.

Subpart N—Explosives and Blasting

§ 77.1300 Explosives and blasting.

(a) No explosives, blasting agent, detonator, or any other related blasting device or material shall be stored, transported, carried, handled, charged, fired, destroyed, or otherwise used, employed or disposed of by any person at a coal mine except in accordance with the provisions of §§ 77.1301 through 77.1304, inclusive.

(b) The term "explosives" as used in this Subpart N includes blasting agents. The standards in this Subpart

Mine Safety and Health Admin., Labor § 77.1302

N in which the term "explosives" appears are applicable to blasting agents (as well as to other explosives) unless blasting agents are expressly excluded.

§ 77.1301 Explosives; magazines.

(a) Detonators and explosives other than blasting agents shall be stored in magazines.

(b) Detonators shall not be stored in the same magazine with explosives.

(c) Magazines other than box type shall be:

(1) Located in accordance with the current American Table of Distances for storage of explosives.

(2) Detached structures located away from powerlines, fuel storage areas, and other possible sources of fire.

(3) Constructed substantially of noncombustible material or covered with fire-resistant material.

(4) Reasonably bullet resistant.

(5) Electrically bonded and grounded if constructed of metal.

(6) Made of nonsparking materials on the inside, including floors.

(7) Provided with adequate and effectively screened ventilation openings near the floor and ceiling.

(8) Kept locked securely when unattended.

(9) Posted with suitable danger signs so located that a bullet passing through the face of a sign will not strike the magazine.

(10) Used exclusively for storage of explosives or detonators and kept free of all extraneous materials.

(11) Kept clean and dry in the interior, and in good repair.

(12) Unheated, unless heated in a manner that does not create a fire or explosion hazard.

(d) Box-type magazines used to store explosives or detonators in work areas shall be constructed with only nonsparking material inside and equipped with covers or doors and shall be located out of the line of blasts.

(e) Secondary and box-type magazines shall be suitably labeled.

(f) Detonator-storage magazines shall be separated by at least 25 feet from explosive-storage magazines.

(g) Cases or boxes containing explosives shall not be stored in magazines on their ends or sides nor stacked more than 6 feet high.

(h) Ammonium nitrate-fuel oil blasting agents shall be physically separated from other explosives, safety fuse, or detonating cord stored in the same magazine and in such a manner that oil does not contaminate the other explosives, safety fuse or detonating cord.

§ 77.1302 Vehicles used to transport explosives.

(a) Vehicles used to transport explosives, other than blasting agents, shall have substantially constructed bodies, no sparking metal exposed in the cargo space, and shall be equipped with suitable sides and tail gates; explosives shall not be piled higher than the side or end.

(b) Vehicles containing explosives or detonators shall be maintained in good condition and shall be operated at a safe speed and in accordance with all safe operating practices.

(c) Vehicles containing explosives or detonators shall be posted with proper warning signs.

(d) Other materials or supplies shall not be placed on or in the cargo space of a conveyance containing explosives, detonating cord or detonators, except for safety fuse and except for properly secured nonsparking equipment used expressly in the handling of such explosives, detonating cord or detonators.

(e) Explosives and detonators shall be transported in separate vehicles unless separated by 4 inches of hardwood or the equivalent.

(f) Explosives or detonators shall be transported promptly without undue delays in transit.

(g) Explosives or detonators shall be transported at times and over routes that expose a minimum number of persons.

(h) Only the necessary attendants shall ride on or in vehicles containing explosives or detonators.

(i) Vehicles shall be attended, whenever practical and possible, while loaded with explosives or detonators.

(j) When vehicles containing explosives or detonators are parked, the brakes shall be set, the motive power shut off, and the vehicles shall be blocked securely against rolling.

§ 77.1303 Explosives, handling and use.

(k) Vehicles containing explosives or detonators shall not be taken to a repair garage or shop for any purpose.

§ 77.1303 Explosives, handling and use.

(a) Persons who use or handle explosives or detonators shall be experienced men who understand the hazards involved; trainees shall do such work only under the supervision of and in the immediate presence of experienced men.

(b) Blasting operations shall be under the direct control of authorized persons.

(c) Substantial nonconductive closed containers shall be used to carry explosives, other than blasting agents to the blasting site.

(d) Damaged or deteriorated explosives or detonators shall be destroyed in a safe manner.

(e) Where electric blasting is to be performed, electric circuits to equipment in the immediate area to be blasted shall be deenergized before explosives or detonators are brought into the area; the power shall not be turned on again until after the shots are fired.

(f) Explosives shall be kept separated from detonators until charging is started.

(g) Areas in which charged holes are awaiting firing shall be guarded, or barricaded and posted, or flagged against unauthorized entry.

(h) Ample warning shall be given before blasts are fired. All persons shall be cleared and removed from the blasting area unless suitable blasting shelters are provided to protect men endangered by concussion or flyrock from blasting.

(i) Lead wires and blasting lines shall not be strung across power conductors, pipelines, railroad tracks, or within 20 feet of bare powerlines. They shall be protected from sources of static or other electrical contact.

(j) For the protection of underground workers, special precautions shall be taken when blasting in close proximity to underground operations, and no blasting shall be done that would be hazardous to persons working underground.

(k) Holes shall not be drilled where there is danger of intersecting a charged or misfired hole.

(l) Only wooden or other nonsparking implements shall be used to punch holes in an explosive cartridge.

(m) Tamping poles shall be blunt and squared at one end and made of wood, nonsparking material, or of special plastic acceptable to the Mine Safety and Health Administration.

(n) Delay connectors for firing detonating cord shall be treated and handled with the same safety precautions as blasting caps and electric detonators.

(o) Capped primers shall be made up at the time of charging and as close to the blasting site as conditions allow.

(p) A capped primer shall be prepared so that the detonator is contained securely and is completely embedded within the explosive cartridge.

(q) No tamping shall be done directly on a capped primer.

(r) Detonating cord shall not be used if it has been kinked, bent, or otherwise handled in such a manner that the train of detonation may be interrupted.

(s) Fuse shall not be used if it has been kinked, bent sharply, or handled roughly in such a manner that the train of deflagration may be interrupted.

(t) Blasting caps shall be crimped to fuses only with implements designed for that specific purpose.

(u) When firing from 1 to 15 blastholes with safety fuse ignited individually using hand-held lighters, the fuses shall be of such lengths to provide the minimum burning time specified in the following table for a particular size round:

Number of holes in a round	Minimum burning time, minutes
1	2
2 to 5	$2\frac{2}{3}$
6 to 10	$3\frac{1}{3}$
11 to 15	5

In no case shall any 40-second-per-foot safety fuse less than 36 inches long or any 30-second-per-foot safety fuse less than 48 inches long be used.

(v) The burning rate of the safety fuse in use at any time shall be measured, posted in conspicuous locations, and brought to the attention of all men concerned with blasting.

(w) Electric detonators of different brands shall not be used in the same round.

(x) Adequate priming shall be employed to guard against misfires, increased toxic fumes, and poor performance.

(y) Except when being tested with a blasting galvanometer:

(1) Electric detonators shall be kept shunted until they are being connected to the blasting line or wired into a blasting round.

(2) Wired rounds shall be kept shunted until they are being connected to the blasting line.

(3) Blasting lines shall be kept shunted until immediately before blasting.

(z) Completely wired rounds shall be tested with a blasting galvanometer before connections are made to the blasting line.

(aa) Permanent blasting lines shall be properly supported, insulated, and kept in good repair.

(bb) At least a 5-foot airgap shall be provided between the blasting circuit and the power circuit.

(cc) When instantaneous blasting is performed, the double-trunkline or loop system shall be used in detonating-cord blasting.

(dd) When instantaneous blasting is performed, trunklines, in multiple-row blasts, shall make one or more complete loops, with crossties between loops at intervals of not over 200 feet.

(ee) All detonating cord knots shall be tight and all connections shall be kept at right angles to the trunklines.

(ff) Power sources shall be suitable for the number of electrical detonators to be fired and for the type of circuits used.

(gg) Electric circuits from the blasting switches to the blast area shall not be grounded.

(hh) Safety switches and blasting switches shall be labeled, encased in boxes, and arranged so that the covers of the boxes cannot be closed with the switches in the through-circuit or firing position.

(ii) Blasting switches shall be locked in the open position, except when closed to fire the blast. Lead wires shall not be connected to the blasting switch until the shot is ready to be fired.

(jj) The key or other control to an electrical firing device shall be entrusted only to the person designated to fire the round or rounds.

(kk) If branch circuits are used when blasts are fired from power circuits, safety switches located at safe distances from the blast areas shall be provided in addition to the main blasting switch.

(ll) Misfires shall be reported to the proper supervisor and shall be disposed of safely before any other work is performed in that blasting area.

(mm) When safety fuse has been used, men shall not return to misfired holes for at least 30 minutes.

(nn) When electric blasting caps have been used, men shall not return to misfired holes for at least 15 minutes.

(oo) If explosives are suspected of burning in a hole, all persons in the endangered area shall move to a safe location and no one should return to the hole until the danger has passed, but in no case within 1 hour.

(pp) Blasted areas shall be examined for undetonated explosives after each blast and undetonated explosives found shall be disposed of safely.

(qq) Blasted areas shall not be reentered by any person after firing until such time as concentrations of smoke, dust, or fumes have been reduced to safe limits.

(rr) In secondary blasting, if more than one shot is to be fired at one time, blasting shall be done electrically or with detonating cord.

(ss) Unused explosives and detonators shall be moved to a safe location as soon as charging operations are completed.

(tt) When electric detonators are used, charging shall be stopped immediately when the presence of static electricity or stray currents is detected; the condition shall be remedied before charging is resumed.

(uu) When electric detonators are used, charging shall be suspended and men withdrawn to a safe location upon the approach of an electrical storm.

§ 77.1304 Blasting agents; special provisions.

(a) Sensitized ammonium nitrate blasting agents, and the components thereof prior to mixing, shall be mixed

§ 77.1400

and stored in accordance with the recommendations in Bureau of Mines Information Circular 8179, "Safety Recommendations for Sensitized Ammonium Nitrate Blasting Agents," or subsequent revisions.

(b) Where pneumatic loading is employed, before any type of blasting operation using blasting agents is put into effect, an evaluation of the potential hazard of static electricity shall be made. Adequate steps, including the grounding and bonding of the conductive parts of pneumatic loading equipment, shall be taken to eliminate the hazard of static electricity before blasting agent use is commenced.

(c) Pneumatic loading equipment shall not be grounded to waterlines, airlines, rails, or the permanent electrical grounding systems.

(d) Hoses used in connection with pneumatic loading machines shall be of the semiconductive type, having a total resistance low enough to permit the dissipation of static electricity and high enough to limit the flow of stray electric currents to a safe level. Wire-countered hose shall not be used because of the potential hazard from stray electric currents.

Subpart O—Personnel Hoisting

§ 77.1400 Personnel hoists and elevators.

Except as provided in § 77.1430, the sections in this Subpart O apply only to hoists and elevators, together with their appurtenances, that are used for hoisting persons.

(Sec. 101, Federal Mine Safety and Health Act of 1977, Pub. L. 91–173 as amended by Pub. L. 95–164, 91 Stat. 1291 (30 U.S.C. 811))

[48 FR 53241, Nov. 25, 1983]

§ 77.1401 Automatic controls and brakes.

Hoists and elevators shall be equipped with overspeed, overwind, and automatic stop controls and with brakes capable of stopping the elevator when fully loaded.

§ 77.1402 Rated capacity.

Hoists and elevators shall have rated capacities consistent with the loads handled.

(Sec. 101, Federal Mine Safety and Health Act of 1977, Pub. L. 91–173 as amended by Pub. L. 95–164, 91 Stat. 1291 (30 U.S.C. 811))

[48 FR 53241, Nov. 25, 1983]

§ 77.1402-1 Maximum load; posting.

The operator shall designate the maximum number of men permitted to ride on each hoist or elevator at one time; this limit shall be posted on each elevator and on each landing.

[36 FR 9364, May 22, 1971. Redesignated at 48 FR 53241, Nov. 25, 1983]

§ 77.1403 Daily examination of hoisting equipment.

Hoists and elevators shall be examined daily and such examinations shall include, but not be limited to, the following:

(a) *Elevators.* (1) A visual examination of the ropes for wear, broken wires, and corrosion, especially at excessive strain points such as near the attachments and where the rope rests on the sheaves;

(2) An examination of the elevator for loose, missing or defective parts;

(b) *Hoists and elevators.* (1) An examination of the rope fastenings for defects;

(2) An examination of sheaves for broken flanges, defective bearings, rope alignment, and proper lubrication; and

(3) An examination of the automatic controls and brakes required under § 77.1401.

(Sec. 101, Federal Mine Safety and Health Act of 1977, Pub. L. 91–173 as amended by Pub. L. 95–164, 91 Stat. 129Y (30 U.S.C. 811))

[48 FR 53241, Nov. 25, 1983]

§ 77.1404 Certifications and records of daily examinations.

At the completion of each daily examination required by § 77.1403, the person making the examination shall certify, by signature and date, that the examination has been made. If any unsafe condition is found during the examinations required by § 77.1403, the person conducting the examination shall make a record of the condition

Mine Safety and Health Admin., Labor § 77.1433

and the date. Certifications and records shall be retained for one year.

(Sec. 101, Federal Mine Safety and Health Act of 1977, Pub. L. 91–173 as amended by Pub. L. 95–164, 91 Stat. 1291 (30 U.S.C. 811))

[48 FR 53241, Nov. 25, 1983, as amended at 60 FR 33723, June 29, 1995]

§ 77.1405 Operation of hoisting equipment after repairs.

Empty conveyances shall be operated at least one round trip before hoisting persons after any repairs.

(Sec. 101, Federal Mine Safety and Health Act of 1977, Pub. L. 91–173 as amended by Pub. L. 95–164, 91 Stat. 1291 (30 U.S.C. 811))

[48 FR 53241, Nov. 25, 1983]

WIRE ROPES

AUTHORITY: Sections 77.1430 through 77.1438 issued under sec. 101, Federal Mine Safety and Health Act of 1977, Pub. L. 91–173 as amended by Pub. L. 95–164, 91 Stat. 1291 (30 U.S.C. 811).

SOURCE: Sections 77.1430 through 77.1438 appear at 48 FR 53241, Nov. 25, 1983, unless otherwise noted.

§ 77.1430 Wire ropes; scope.

(a) Sections 77.1431 through 77.1438 apply to wire ropes in service used to hoist—
(1) Persons in shafts and slopes underground;
(2) Persons with an incline hoist on the surface; or
(3) Loads in shaft or slope development when persons work below suspended loads.

(b) These standards do not apply to wire ropes used for elevators.

§ 77.1431 Minimum rope strength.

At installation, the nominal strength (manufacturer's published catalog strength) of wire ropes used for hoisting shall meet the minimum rope strength values obtained by the following formulas in which "L" equals the maximum suspended rope length in feet:

(a) *Winding drum ropes* (all constructions, including rotation resistant).

For rope lengths less than 3,000 feet:
Minimum Value = Static Load × $(7.0 - 0.001L)$
For rope lengths 3,000 feet or greater:
Minimum Value = Static Load × 4.0

(b) *Friction drum ropes*.

For rope lengths less than 4,000 feet:
Minimum Value = Static Load × $(7.0 - 0.0005L)$
For rope lengths 4,000 feet or greater:
Minimum Value = Static Load × 5.0

(c) *Tail ropes* (balance ropes).

Minimum Value = Weight of Rope × 7.0

[48 FR 53241, Nov. 25, 1983; 48 FR 54975, Dec. 8, 1983]

§ 77.1432 Initial measurement.

After initial rope stretch but before visible wear occurs, the rope diameter of newly installed wire ropes shall be measured at least once in every third interval of active length and the measurements averaged to establish a baseline for subsequent measurements. A record of the measurements and the date shall be made by the person taking the measurements. This record shall be retained until the rope is retired from service.

[48 FR 53241, Nov. 25, 1983, as amended at 60 FR 33723, June 29, 1995]

§ 77.1433 Examinations.

(a) At least once every fourteen calendar days, each wire rope in service shall be visually examined along its entire active length for visible structural damage, corrosion, and improper lubrication or dressing. In addition, visual examination for wear and broken wires shall be made at stress points, including the area near attachments, where the rope rests on sheaves, where the rope leaves the drum, at drum crossovers, and at change-of-layer regions. When any visible condition that results in a reduction of rope strength is present, the affected portion of the rope shall be examined on a daily basis.

(b) Before any person is hoisted with a newly installed wire rope or any wire rope that has not been examined in the previous fourteen calendar days, the wire rope shall be examined in accordance with paragraph (a) of this section.

(c) At least once every six months, nondestructive tests shall be conducted of the active length of the rope, or rope diameter measurements shall be made—
(1) Wherever wear is evident;
(2) Where the hoist rope rests on sheaves at regular stopping points;

§ 77.1434

(3) Where the hoist rope leaves the drum at regular stopping points; and

(4) At drum crossover and change-of-layer regions.

(d) At the completion of each examination required by paragraph (a) of this section, the person making the examination shall certify, by signature and date, that the examination has been made. If any condition listed in paragraph (a) of this standard is present, the person conducting the examination shall make a record of the condition and the date. Certifications and records of examinations shall be retained for one year.

(e) The person making the measurements or nondestructive tests as required by paragraph (c) of this section shall record the measurements or test results and the date. This record shall be retained until the rope is retired from service.

[48 FR 53241, Nov. 25, 1983; 48 FR 54975, Dec. 8, 1983; 60 FR 33723, June 29, 1995]

§ 77.1434 Retirement criteria.

Unless damage or deterioration is removed by cutoff, wire ropes shall be removed from service when any of the following conditions occurs:

(a) The number of broken wires within a rope lay length, excluding filler wires, exceeds either—

(1) Five percent of the total number of wires; or

(2) Fifteen percent of the total number of wires within any strand;

(b) On a regular lay rope, more than one broken wire in the valley between strands in one rope lay length;

(c) A loss of more than one-third of the original diameter of the outer wires;

(d) Rope deterioration from corrosion;

(e) Distortion of the rope structure;

(f) Heat damage from any source;

(g) Diameter reduction due to wear that exceeds six percent of the baseline diameter measurement; or

(h) Loss of more than ten percent of rope strength as determined by nondestructive testing.

§ 77.1435 Load end attachments.

(a) Wire rope shall be attached to the load by a method that develops at least 80 percent of the nominal strength of the rope.

(b) Except for terminations where use of other materials is a design feature, zinc (spelter) shall be used for socketing wire ropes. Design feature means either the manufacturer's original design or a design approved by a registered professional engineer.

(c) Load end attachment methods using splices are prohibited.

§ 77.1436 Drum end attachment.

(a) For drum end attachment, wire rope shall be attached—

(1) Securely by clips after making one full turn around the drum spoke;

(2) Securely by clips after making one full turn around the shaft, if the drum is fixed to the shaft; or

(3) By properly assembled anchor bolts, clamps, or wedges, provided that the attachment is a design feature of the hoist drum. Design feature means either the manufacturer's original design or a design approved by a registered professional engineer.

(b) A minimum of three full turns of wire rope shall be on the drum when the rope is extended to its maximum working length.

§ 77.1437 End attachment retermination.

Damaged or deteriorated wire rope shall be removed by cutoff and the rope reterminated where there is—

(a) More than one broken wire at an attachment;

(b) Improper installation of an attachment;

(c) Slippage at an attachment; or

(d) Evidence of deterioration from corrosion at an attachment.

§ 77.1438 End attachment replacement.

Wire rope attachments shall be replaced when cracked, deformed, or excessively worn.

Subpart P—Auger Mining

§ 77.1500 Auger mining; planning.

Auger mining shall be planned and conducted by the operator to insure against any hazard to underground workings located at or near such auger operations and all auger holes shall be located so as to prevent:

(a) The disruption of the ventilation system of any active underground mine;

(b) Inundation hazards from surface water entering any active underground mine;

(c) Damage to the roof and ribs of active underground workings; and

(d) Intersection of auger holes with underground mine workings known to contain dangerous quantities of impounded water.

§ 77.1501 Auger mining; inspections.

(a) The face of all highwalls, to a distance of 25 feet on both sides of each drilling site, shall be inspected by a certified person before any augering operation is begun, and at least once during each coal producing shift and all loose material shall be removed from the drilling site before persons are permitted to enter the drilling area. The results of all such inspections shall be recorded daily in a book approved by the Secretary.

(b) In addition, the face of all highwalls, to a distance of 25 feet on both sides of each drilling site, shall be inspected frequently by a certified person during any auger operation conducted either during or after a heavy rainfall or during any period of intermittent freezing and thawing and the results of such inspections shall be recorded as provided in paragraph (a) of this section.

(c) When an auger hole penetrates an abandoned or mined out area of an underground mine, tests for methane and oxygen deficiency shall be made at the collar of the hole by a qualified person using devices approved by the Secretary to determine if dangerous quantities of methane or oxygen-deficient air are present or being emitted. If such is found no further work shall be performed until the atmosphere has been made safe.

(d) Tests for oxygen deficiency shall be conducted with a permissible flame safety lamp or other means approved by the Secretary and all tests for methane shall be conducted with a methane detector approved by the Secretary.

(e) Internal combustion engines shall not be operated in the vicinity of any auger hole in which tests for methane or oxygen deficiency are being made.

§ 77.1502 Auger holes; restriction against entering.

No person shall be permitted to enter an auger hole except with the approval of the MSHA Coal Mine Safety and Health District Manager of the district in which the mine is located and under such conditions as may be prescribed by such managers.

[36 FR 9364, May 22, 1971, as amended at 71 FR 16669, Apr. 3, 2006]

§ 77.1503 Augering equipment; overhead protection.

(a) Auger machines which are exposed to highwall hazards, together with all those parts of any coal elevating conveyors where persons are required to work during augering operations, shall be covered with heavy gage screen which does not obstruct the view of the highwall and is strong enough to prevent injuries to workmen from falling material.

(b) No work shall be done under any overhang and, when a crew is engaged in connecting or disconnecting auger sections under a highwall, at least one person shall be assigned to observe the highwall for possible movement.

§ 77.1504 Auger equipment; operation.

(a) Persons shall be kept clear of the auger train while it is in motion and shall not be permitted to pass under or over an auger train, except where adequate crossing facilities are provided.

(b) Persons shall be kept clear of auger sections being swung into position.

(c) No person, including the auger machine operator, shall, where practicable, be stationed in direct line with a borehole during augering operations.

(d) Operator of auger equipment shall not leave the controls of such equipment while the auger is in operation.

(e) Adequate illumination shall be provided for work areas after dark.

§ 77.1505 Auger holes; blocking.

Auger holes shall be blocked with highwall spoil or other suitable material before they are abandoned.

Subpart Q—Loading and Haulage

§ 77.1600 Loading and haulage; general.

(a) Only authorized persons shall be permitted on haulage roads and at loading or dumping locations.

(b) Traffic rules, signals, and warning signs shall be standardized at each mine and posted.

(c) Where side or overhead clearances on any haulage road or at any loading or dumping location at the mine are hazardous to mine workers, such areas shall be conspicuously marked and warning devices shall be installed when necessary to insure the safety of the workers.

§ 77.1601 Transportation of persons; restrictions.

No person shall be permitted to ride or be otherwise transported on or in the following equipment whether loaded or empty:

(a) Dippers, shovels, buckets, forks, and clamshells;

(b) The cargo space of dump trucks or haulage equipment used to transport coal or other material;

(c) Outside the cabs and beds of mobile equipment;

(d) Chain, belt, or bucket conveyors, except where such conveyors are specifically designed to transport persons; and

(e) Loaded buckets on aerial tramways.

§ 77.1602 Use of aerial tramways to transport persons.

Persons other than maintenance men shall not ride empty buckets on aerial tramways unless the following features are provided:

(a) Two independent brakes, each capable of holding the maximum load.

(b) Direct communication between terminals.

(c) Power drives with emergency power available in case of primary power failure.

(d) Buckets equipped with positive locks to prevent accidental tripping or dumping.

§ 77.1603 Trains and locomotives; authorized persons.

(a) Only authorized persons shall be permitted to ride on trains or locomotives and they shall ride in a safe position.

(b) Men shall not get on or off moving equipment, except that trainmen may get on or off of slowly moving trains.

§ 77.1604 Transportation of persons; overcrowding.

(a) No man-trip vehicle or other conveyance used to transport persons to and from work areas at surface coal mines shall be overcrowded and all persons shall ride in a safe position.

(b) Supplies, materials, and tools other than small handtools shall not be transported with men in man-trip vehicles unless such vehicles are specifically designed to make such transportation safe.

§ 77.1605 Loading and haulage equipment; installations.

(a) Cab windows shall be of safety glass or equivalent, in good condition and shall be kept clean.

(b) Mobile equipment shall be equipped with adequate brakes, and all trucks and front-end loaders shall also be equipped with parking brakes.

(c) Positive-action type brakes shall be provided on aerial tramways.

(d) Mobile equipment shall be provided with audible warning devices. Lights shall be provided on both ends when required.

(e) Guard nets or other suitable protection shall be provided where tramways pass over roadways, walkways, or buildings.

(f) Guards shall be installed to prevent swaying buckets from hitting towers.

(g) Aerial tramway cable connections shall be designed to offer minimum obstruction to the passage of wheels.

(h) Rocker-bottom or bottom-dump cars shall be equipped with positive locking devices, or other suitable devices.

(i) Ramps and dumps shall be of solid construction, of ample width, have ample clearance and headroom, and be kept reasonably free of spillage.

Mine Safety and Health Admin., Labor §77.1607

(j) Chute-loading installations shall be designed so that the men pulling chutes are not required to be in a hazardous position during loading operations.

(k) Berms or guards shall be provided on the outer bank of elevated roadways.

(l) Berms, bumper blocks, safety hooks, or similar means shall be provided to prevent overtravel and overturning at dumping locations.

(m) Roadbeds, rails, joints, switches, frogs, and other elements on railroads shall be designed, installed, and maintained in a safe manner consistent with the speed and type of haulage.

(n) Where practicable, a minimum of 30 inches continuous clearance from the farthest projection of moving railroad equipment shall be provided on at least one side of the tracks; all places where it is not possible to provide 30-inch clearance shall be marked conspicuously.

(o) Track guardrails, lead rails, and frogs shall be protected or blocked so as to prevent a person's foot from becoming wedged.

(p) Positive-acting stop-blocks, derail devices, track skates, or other adequate means shall be installed wherever necessary to protect persons from runaway or moving railroad equipment.

(q) Switch throws shall be installed so as to provide adequate clearance for switchmen.

(r) Where necessary, bumper blocks or the equivalent shall be provided at all track dead ends.

§77.1606 Loading and haulage equipment; inspection and maintenance.

(a) Mobile loading and haulage equipment shall be inspected by a competent person before such equipment is placed in operation. Equipment defects affecting safety shall be recorded and reported to the mine operator.

(b) Carriers on aerial tramways, including loading and unloading mechanisms, shall be inspected each shift; brakes shall be inspected daily; ropes and supports shall be inspected as recommended by the manufacturer or as physical conditions warrant. Equipment defects affecting safety shall be reported to the mine operator.

(c) Equipment defects affecting safety shall be corrected before the equipment is used.

§77.1607 Loading and haulage equipment; operation.

(a) Vehicles shall follow at a safe distance; passing shall be limited to areas of adequate clearance and visibility.

(b) Mobile equipment operators shall have full control of the equipment while it is in motion.

(c) Equipment operating speeds shall be prudent and consistent with conditions of roadway, grades, clearance, visibility, traffic, and the type of equipment used.

(d) Cabs of mobile equipment shall be kept free of extraneous materials.

(e) Operators shall sit facing the direction of travel while operating equipment with dual controls.

(f) When an equipment operator is present, men shall notify him before getting on or off equipment.

(g) Equipment operators shall be certain, by signal or other means, that all persons are clear before starting or moving equipment.

(h) Where possible, aerial tramways shall not be started until the tramway operator has ascertained that everyone is in the clear.

(i) Dust control measures shall be taken where dust significantly reduces visibility of equipment operators.

(j) Dippers, buckets, loading booms, or heavy suspended loads shall not be swung over the cabs of haulage vehicles until the drivers are out of the cabs and in safe locations, unless the trucks are designed specifically to protect the drivers from falling material.

(k) Men shall not work or pass under the buckets or booms of loaders in operation.

(l) Tires shall be deflated before repairs on them are started and adequate means shall be provided to prevent wheel locking rims from creating a hazard during tire inflation.

(m) Electrically powered mobile equipment shall not be left unattended unless the master switch is in the off position, all operating controls are in the neutral position, and the brakes are set or other equivalent precautions are taken against rolling.

§ 77.1608

(n) Mobile equipment shall not be left unattended unless the brakes are set. The wheels shall be turned into a bank or berm, or shall be blocked, when such equipment is parked on a grade.

(o) Lights, flares, or other warning devices shall be posted when parked equipment creates a hazard to vehicular traffic.

(p) Dippers, buckets, scraper blades, and similar movable parts shall be secured or lowered to the ground when not in use.

(q) Shovel trailing cables shall not be moved with the shovel dipper unless cable slings or sleds are used.

(r) Equipment which is to be hauled shall be loaded and protected so as to prevent sliding or spillage.

(s) When moving between work areas, the equipment shall be secured in the travel position.

(t) Any load extending more than 4 feet beyond the rear of the vehicle body should be marked clearly with a red flag by day and a red light at night.

(u) Tow bars shall be used to tow heavy equipment and a safety chain shall be used in conjunction with each tow bar.

(v) Railroad cars shall be kept under control at all times by the car dropper. Cars shall be dropped at a safe rate and in a manner that will insure that the car dropper maintains a safe position while working and traveling around the cars.

(w) Railroad cars shall not be coupled or uncoupled manually from the inside of curves unless the railroad and cars are so designed to eliminate any hazard from coupling or uncoupling cars from inside of curves.

(x) Persons shall wear safety belts when dropping railroad cars.

(y) Railcars shall not be left on sidetracks unless ample clearance is provided for traffic on adjacent tracks.

(z) Parked railcars, unless held effectively by brakes, shall be blocked securely.

(aa) Railroad cars and all trucks shall be trimmed properly when they have been loaded higher than the confines of their cargo space.

(bb) When the entire length of a conveyor is visible from the starting switch, the operator shall visually check to make certain that all persons are in the clear before starting the conveyor. When the entire length of the conveyor is not visible from the starting switch, a positive audible or visible warning system shall be installed and operated to warn persons that the conveyor will be started.

(cc) Unguarded conveyors with walkways shall be equipped with emergency stop devices or cords along their full length.

(dd) Adequate backstops or brakes shall be installed on inclined-conveyor drive units to prevent conveyors from running in reverse if a hazard to personnel would be caused.

(ee) Aerial tram conveyor buckets shall not be overloaded, and feed shall be regulated to prevent spillage.

§ 77.1608 Dumping facilities.

(a) Dumping locations and haulage roads shall be kept reasonably free of water, debris, and spillage.

(b) Where the ground at a dumping place may fail to support the weight of a loaded dump truck, trucks shall be dumped a safe distance back from the edge of the bank.

(c) Adequate protection shall be provided at dumping locations where persons may be endangered by falling material.

(d) Grizzlies, grates, and other sizing devices at dump and transfer points shall be anchored securely in place.

(e) If truck spotters are used, they shall be well in the clear while trucks are backing into dumping position and dumping; lights shall be used at night to direct trucks.

Subpart R—Miscellaneous

§ 77.1700 Communications in work areas.

No employee shall be assigned, or allowed, or be required to perform work alone in any area where hazardous conditions exist that would endanger his safety unless he can communicate with others, can be heard, or can be seen.

§ 77.1701 Emergency communications; requirements.

(a) Each operator of a surface coal mine shall establish and maintain a communication system from the mine to the nearest point of medical assistance for use in an emergency.

(b) The emergency communication system required to be maintained under paragraph (a) of this section may be established by telephone or radio transmission or by any other means of prompt communication to any facility (for example, the local sheriff, the State highway patrol, or local hospital) which has available the means of communication with the person or persons providing emergency medical assistance or transportation in accordance with the provisions of paragraph (a) of this section.

§ 77.1702 **Arrangements for emergency medical assistance and transportation for injured persons; reporting requirements; posting requirements.**

(a) Each operator of a surface coal mine shall make arrangements with a licensed physician, medical service, medical clinic, or hospital to provide 24-hour emergency medical assistance for any person injured at the mine.

(b) Each operator shall make arrangements with an ambulance service, or otherwise provide for 24-hour emergency transportation for any person injured at the mine.

(c) Each operator shall, on or before September 30, 1971, report to the Coal Mine Health and Safety District Manager for the district in which the mine is located the name, title and address of the physician, medical service, medical clinic, hospital, or ambulance service with whom arrangements have been made, or otherwise provided, in accordance with the provisions of paragraphs (a) and (b) of this section.

(d) Each operator shall, within 10 days after any change of the arrangements required to be reported under the provisions of this section, report such changes to the Coal Mine Health and Safety District Manager. If such changes involve a substitution of persons, the operator shall provide the name, title, and address of the person substituted together with the name and address of the medical service, medical clinic, hospital, or ambulance service with which such person or persons are associated.

(e) Each operator shall, immediately after making an arrangement required under the provisions of paragraphs (a) and (b) of this section, or immediately after any change, of such agreement, post at appropriate places at the mine the names, titles, addresses, and telephone numbers of all persons or services currently available under such arrangements to provide medical assistance and transportation at the mine.

(Pub. L. No. 96–511, 94 Stat. 2812 (44 U.S.C. 3501 et seq.))

[36 FR 9364, May 22, 1971, as amended at 36 FR 13143, July 15, 1971; 60 FR 33723, June 29, 1995]

§ 77.1703 **First-Aid training; supervisory employees.**

The mine operator shall conduct first-aid training courses for selected supervisory employees at the mine. Within 60 days after the selection of a new supervisory employee to be so trained, the mine operator shall certify by signature and date the name of the employee and date on which the employee satisfactorily completed the first-aid training course. The certification shall be kept at the mine and made available on request to an authorized representative of the Secretary.

[56 FR 1478, Jan. 14, 1991]

§ 77.1704 **First aid training program; availability of instruction to all miners.**

On or before December 30, 1971, each operator of a surface coal mine shall make available to all miners employed in the mine a course of instruction in first aid conducted by the operator or under the auspices of the operator, and such a course of instruction shall be made available to newly employed miners within 6 months after the date of employment.

§ 77.1705 **First aid training program; retraining of supervisory employees; availability to all miners.**

Beginning January 1, 1972, each operator of a surface coal mine shall conduct refresher first aid training programs each calendar year for all selected supervisory employees and make available refresher first aid training

§ 77.1706

courses to all miners employed in the mine.

[36 FR 9364, May 22, 1971, as amended at 36 FR 13143, July 15, 1971]

§ 77.1706 First aid training program; minimum requirements.

(a) All first aid training programs required under the provisions of §§ 77.1703 and 77.1704 shall include 10 class hours of training in a course of instruction similar to that outlined in "First Aid, A Bureau of Mines Instruction Manual."

(b) Refresher first aid training programs required under the provisions of § 77.1705 shall include 5 class hours of refresher training in a course of instruction similar to that outlined in "First Aid, A Bureau of Mines Instruction Manual."

§ 77.1707 First aid equipment; location; minimum requirements.

(a) Each operator of a surface coal mine shall maintain a supply of the first aid equipment set forth in paragraph (b) of this section at or near each working place where coal is being mined, at each preparation plant and at shops and other surface installation where ten or more persons are regularly employed.

(b) The first aid equipment required to be maintained under the provisions of paragraph (a) of this section shall include at least the following:

(1) One stretcher;
(2) One broken-back board (if a splint-stretcher combination is used it will satisfy the requirements of both paragraph (b) (1) of this section and this paragraph (b) (2));
(3) Twenty-four triangular bandages (15 if a splint-stretcher combination is used);
(4) Eight 4-inch bandage compresses;
(5) Eight 2-inch bandage compresses;
(6) Twelve 1-inch adhesive compresses;
(7) An approved burn remedy;
(8) Two cloth blankets;
(9) One rubber blanket or equivalent substitute;
(10) Two tourniquets;
(11) One 1-ounce bottle of aromatic spirits of ammonia or 1 dozen ammonia ampules; and,
(12) The necessary complements of arm and leg splints or two each inflatable plastic arm and leg splints.

(c) All first aid supplies required to be maintained under the provisions of paragraphs (a) and (b) of this section shall be stored in suitable, sanitary, dust tight, moisture proof containers and such supplies shall be accessible to the miners.

§ 77.1708 Safety program; instruction of persons employed at the mine.

On or before September 30, 1971, each operator of a surface coal mine shall establish and maintain a program of instruction with respect to the safety regulations and procedures to be followed at the mine and shall publish and distribute to each employee, and post in conspicuous places throughout the mine, all such safety regulations and procedures established in accordance with the provisions of this section.

[36 FR 9364, May 22, 1971, as amended at 36 FR 13143, July 15, 1971]

§ 77.1710 Protective clothing; requirements.

Each employee working in a surface coal mine or in the surface work areas of an underground coal mine shall be required to wear protective clothing and devices as indicated below:

(a) Protective clothing or equipment and face-shields or goggles shall be worn when welding, cutting, or working with molten metal or when other hazards to the eyes exist.

(b) Suitable protective clothing to cover the entire body when handling corrosive or toxic substances or other materials which might cause injury to the skin.

(c) Protective gloves when handling materials or performing work which might cause injury to the hands; however, gloves shall not be worn where they would create a greater hazard by becoming entangled in the moving parts of equipment.

(d) A suitable hard hat or hard cap when in or around a mine or plant where falling objects may create a hazard. If a hard hat or hard cap is painted, nonmetallic based paint shall be used.

(e) Suitable protective footwear.

(f) Snug-fitting clothing when working around moving machinery or equipment.

(g) Safety belts and lines where there is danger of falling; a second person shall tend the lifeline when bins, tanks, or other dangerous areas are entered.

(h) Lifejackets or belts where there is danger from falling into water.

(i) Seatbelts in a vehicle where there is a danger of overturning and where roll protection is provided.

(Sec. 101(a), Federal Coal Mine Health and Safety Act of 1969, as amended (83 Stat. 745; 30 U.S.C. 811(a))

[36 FR 9382, May 22, 1971, as amended at 36 FR 13143, July 15, 1971; 39 FR 7176, Feb. 25, 1974]

§ 77.1710-1 Distinctively colored hard hats or hard caps; identification for newly employed, inexperienced miners.

Hard hats or hard caps distinctively different in color from those worn by experienced miners shall be worn at all times by each newly employed, inexperienced miner when working in or around a mine or plant for at least one year from the date of his initial employment as a miner or until he has been qualified or certified as a miner by the State in which he is employed.

(Sec. 101(a), Federal Coal Mine Health and Safety Act of 1969, as amended (83 Stat. 745; 30 U.S.C. 811(a))

[39 FR 7176, Feb. 25, 1974]

§ 77.1711 Smoking prohibition.

No person shall smoke or use an open flame where such practice may cause a fire or explosion.

§ 77.1712 Reopening mines; notification; inspection prior to mining.

Prior to reopening any surface coal mine after it has been abandoned or declared inactive by the operator, the operator shall notify the Coal Mine Health and Safety District Manager for the district in which the mine is located, and an inspection of the entire mine shall be completed by an authorized representative of the Secretary before any mining operations in such mine are instituted.

§ 77.1713 Daily inspection of surface coal mine; certified person; reports of inspection.

(a) At least once during each working shift, or more often if necessary for safety, each active working area and each active surface installation shall be examined by a certified person designated by the operator to conduct such examinations for hazardous conditions and any hazardous conditions noted during such examinations shall be reported to the operator and shall be corrected by the operator.

(b) If any hazardous condition noted during an examination conducted in accordance with paragraph (a) of this section creates an imminent danger, the person conducting such examination shall notify the operator and the operator shall withdraw all persons from the area affected, except those persons referred to in section 104(d) of the Act, until the danger is abated.

(c) After each examination conducted in accordance with the provisions of paragraph (a) of this section, each certified person who conducted all or any part of the examination required shall enter with ink or indelible pencil in a book approved by the Secretary the date and a report of the condition of the mine or any area of the mine which he has inspected together with a report of the nature and location of any hazardous condition found to be present at the mine. The book in which such entries are made shall be kept in an area at the mine designated by the operator to minimize the danger of destruction by fire or other hazard.

(d) All examination reports recorded in accordance with the provisions of paragraph (c) of this section shall include a report of the action taken to abate hazardous conditions and shall be signed or countersigned each day by at least one of the following persons:

(1) The surface mine foreman;

(2) The assistant superintendent of the mine;

(3) The superintendent of the mine;

(4) The person designated by the operator as responsible for health and safety at the mine; or,

§ 77.1800

(5) An equivalent mine official.

(Pub. L. No. 96–511, 94 Stat. 2812 (44 U.S.C. 3501 et seq.))

[36 FR 9364, May 22, 1971, as amended at 60 FR 33723, June 29, 1995; 63 FR 58613, Oct. 30, 1998]

Subpart S—Trolley Wires and Trolley Feeder Wires

§ 77.1800 Cutout switches.

Trolley wires and trolley feeder wires shall be provided with cutout switches at intervals of not more than 2,000 feet and near the beginning of all branch lines.

§ 77.1801 Overcurrent protection.

Trolley wires and trolley feeder wires shall be provided with overcurrent protection.

§ 77.1801-1 Devices for overcurrent protection.

Automatic circuit interrupting devices that will deenergize the affected circuit upon occurrence of a short circuit at any point in the system will meet the requirements of § 77.1801.

§ 77.1802 Insulation of trolley wires, trolley feeder wires and bare signal wires; guarding of trolley wires and trolley feeder wires.

Trolley wires, trolley feeder wires, and bare signal wires shall be adequately guarded:

(a) At all points where men are required to work or pass regularly under the wires; and

(b) At man-trip stations.

The Secretary or his authorized representative shall specify other conditions where trolley wires and trolley feeder wires shall be adequately protected to prevent contact by any person, or shall require the use of improved methods to prevent such contact. Temporary guards shall be provided where trackmen and other persons are required to work in proximity to trolley wires and trolley feeder wires.

Subpart T—Slope and Shaft Sinking

§ 77.1900 Slopes and shafts; approval of plans.

(a) Each operator of a coal mine shall prepare and submit for approval by the Coal Mine Health and Safety District Manager for the district in which the mine is located, a plan providing for the safety of workmen in each slope or shaft that is commenced or extended after June 30, 1971. The plan shall be consistent with prudent engineering design. The methods employed by the operator shall be selected to minimize the hazards to those employed in the initial or subsequent development of any such slope or shaft, and the plan shall include the following:

(1) The name and location of the mine, and the Mine Safety and Health Administration mine identification number, if known;

(2) The name and address of the mine operator;

(3) A description of the construction work and methods to be used in the construction of the slope or shaft, and whether part or all of the work will be performed by a contractor and a description of that part of the work to be performed by a contractor;

(4) The elevation, depth and dimensions of the slope or shaft;

(5) The location and elevation of the coalbed;

(6) The general characteristics of the strata through which the slope or shaft will be developed;

(7) The type of equipment which the operator proposes to use when the work is to be performed by the operator. When work is to be performed by a contractor the operator shall, as soon as known to him, supplement the plan with a description of the type of equipment to be used by the contractor;

(8) The system of ventilation to be used; and

(9) Safeguards for the prevention of caving during excavation.

(Pub. L. No. 96–511, 94 Stat. 2812 (44 U.S.C. 3501 et seq.))

[36 FR 9364, May 22, 1971, as amended at 47 FR 28096, June 29, 1982; 60 FR 33723, June 29, 1995]

§ 77.1900-1 Compliance with approved slope and shaft sinking plans.

Upon approval by the Coal Mine Health and Safety District Manager of a slope or shaft sinking plan, the operator shall adopt and comply with such plan.

§ 77.1901 Preshift and onshift inspections; reports.

(a) Examinations of slope and shaft areas shall be made by a certified person for hazardous conditions, including tests for methane and oxygen deficiency:

(1) Within 90 minutes before each shift;

(2) At least once on any shift during which men are employed inside any slope or shaft during development; and

(3) Both before and after blasting.

(b) The surface area surrounding each slope and shaft shall be inspected by a certified person and all hazards in the vicinity shall be corrected before men are permitted to enter the excavation.

(c) All hazards found during any preshift or onshift inspection shall be corrected before men are allowed to enter, or continue to work in such slope or shaft. If hazardous conditions cannot be corrected, or excessive methane concentrations cannot be diluted, the excavation shall be vacated and no person shall be permitted to reenter the slope or shaft to continue excavation operations until the hazardous condition has been abated.

(d) No work shall be performed in any slope or shaft, no drilling equipment shall be started, and no electrical equipment shall be energized if the methane content in such slope or shaft is 1.0 volume per centum, or more.

(e) Nothing in this § 77.1901 shall prevent the specific assignment of men in the slope or shaft for purposes of abating excessive methane concentrations or any other hazardous condition.

(f) The results of all inspections conducted in accordance with the provisions of paragraph (a) of this section shall be recorded in a book approved by the Secretary.

(Pub. L. No. 96-511, 94 Stat. 2812 (44 U.S.C. 3501 et seq.))

[36 FR 9364, May 22, 1971, as amended at 60 FR 33723, June 29, 1995]

§ 77.1901-1 Methane and oxygen deficiency tests; approved devices.

Tests for oxygen deficiency shall be made with a permissible flame safety lamp or other means approved by the Secretary, and tests for methane shall be made with a methane detector approved by the Secretary.

§ 77.1902 Drilling and mucking operations.

Diesel-powered equipment used in the drilling, mucking, or other excavation of any slope or shaft shall be permissible, and such equipment shall be operated in a permissible manner and shall be maintained in a permissible condition.

§ 77.1902-1 Permissible diesel-powered equipment.

Diesel-powered equipment which has been approved by the Bureau of Mines or the Mine Safety and Health Administration under Part 36 of this chapter (Bureau of Mines Schedule 31) is permissible under the provisions of this section.

§ 77.1903 Hoists and hoisting; minimum requirements.

(a) Hoists used in transporting persons and material during drilling, mucking, or other excavating operations in any slope or shaft shall have rated capacities consistent with the loads to be handled.

(b) Each hoist used in drilling, mucking, or other excavating operations shall be equipped with an accurate and reliable indicator of the position of the cage, platform, or bucket. The indicator shall be installed in clear view of the hoist operator.

(Sec. 101, Federal Mine Safety and Health Act of 1977, Pub. L. 91-173 as amended by Pub. L. 95-164, 91 Stat. 1291 (30 U.S.C. 811))

[48 FR 53242, Nov. 25, 1983; 48 FR 54975, Dec. 8, 1983]

§ 77.1904 Communications between slope and shaft bottoms and hoist operators.

(a) Two independent means of signaling shall be provided between the hoistman and all points in a slope or shaft where men are required to work. At least one of these means shall be audible to the hoistman. Signal codes used in any communication system shall be posted conspicuously at each slope and shaft.

(b) Signaling systems used for communication between slopes and shafts and the hoistman shall be tested daily.

§ 77.1905 Hoist safeguards; general.

(a) Hoists used to transport persons shall be equipped with brakes capable of stopping and holding the cage, bucket, platform, or other device when fully loaded.

(b) When persons are transported by a hoist, a second person familiar with and qualified to stop the hoist shall be in attendance, except where the hoist is fully equipped with overspeed, overwind, and automatic stop devices.

§ 77.1906 Hoists; daily inspection.

(a) Hoists used to transport persons shall be inspected daily. The inspection shall include examination of the headgear (headframe, sheave wheels, etc.), connections, links and chains, and other facilities.

(b) Prior to each working shift, and before a hoist is returned to service after it has been out of normal service for any reason, the hoist shall be run by the hoist operator through one complete cycle of operation before any person is permitted to be transported.

(c) At the completion of each daily examination required by paragraph (a) of this section, the person making the examination shall certify, by signature and date, that the examination has been made. If any unsafe condition in the hoisting equipment is present, the person conducting the examination shall make a record of the condition and the date. Certifications and records shall be retained for one year.

(Sec. 101, Federal Mine Safety and Health Act of 1977, Pub. L. 91–173 as amended by Pub. L. 95–164, 91 Stat. 1291 (30 U.S.C. 811))

[48 FR 53242, Nov. 25, 1983, as amended at 60 FR 33723, June 29, 1995]

§ 77.1907 Hoist construction; general.

If hooks are used to attach cages or buckets to the socket or thimble of a hoisting rope, the hooks shall be self-closing.

(Sec. 101, Federal Mine Safety and Health Act of 1977, Pub. L. 91–173 as amended by Pub. L. 95–164, 91 Stat. 1291 (30 U.S.C. 811))

[48 FR 53242, Nov. 25, 1983]

§ 77.1908 Hoist installations; use.

(a) Where men are transported by means of a hoist and the depth of the shaft exceeds 50 feet, the hoist rope shall be suspended from a substantial hoisting installation which shall be high enough to provide working clearance between the bottom of the sheave and the top of the cage or bucket.

(b) Where men are transported by means of a hoist and the depth of the shaft exceeds 100 feet, temporary shaft guides and guide attachments, or other no less effective means, shall be installed to prevent the cage, platform, or bucket from swinging.

(c) All guides and guide attachments, or other no less effective means, installed in accordance with paragraph (b) of this section shall be maintained to a depth of not less than 75 feet from the bottom of the shaft.

(d) Where crossheads are used, the cage, platform, or bucket shall not be hung more than 10 feet below the crosshead.

(e) Where men are required to embark or disembark from a cage, platform or bucket suspended over or within a shaft, a loading platform shall be installed to insure safe footing.

(f) During the development of each slope or shaft, either a ladder or independently powered auxiliary hoist shall be provided to permit men to escape quickly in the event of an emergency.

(g) No person shall be permitted to ride the rim of any bucket or on the top of a loaded bucket.

(h) The number of persons permitted to ride in cages, skips, or buckets shall be limited so as to prevent overcrowding.

(i) Persons shall not be permitted to ride on a cage, skip, or bucket with tools or materials, except when necessary to handle equipment while in transit. Materials shall be secured to prevent shifting while being hoisted.

(j) The speed of buckets transporting persons shall not exceed 500 feet per minute and not more than 200 feet per minute when within 100 feet of any stop.

(k) A notice of established speeds shall be posted in clear view of the hoistman.

(l) Conveyances being lowered in a shaft in which men are working shall be stopped at least 15 feet above such men and shall be lowered further only after the hoistman has received a signal that all men who may be endangered by the conveyance are in the clear.

(m) No skip or bucket shall be raised or lowered in a slope or shaft until it has been trimmed to prevent material from falling back down the slope or shaft.

(n) Measures shall be taken to prevent material from falling back into the shaft while buckets or other conveyances are being unloaded.

(o) Properly attached safety belts shall be worn by all persons required to work in or over any shaft where there is a drop of 10 or more feet, unless other acceptable means are provided to prevent such persons from falling into the shaft.

§ 77.1908-1 Hoist operation; qualified hoistman.

Hoists shall be under the control of and operated by a qualified hoistman when men are in a slope or shaft.

§ 77.1909 Explosives and blasting; use of permissible explosives and shot-firing units.

Except as provided in § 77.1909-1, only permissible explosives and permissible shot-firing units shall be used in sinking shafts and slopes.

§ 77.1909-1 Use of nonpermissible explosives and nonpermissible shot-firing units; approval by Health and Safety District Manager.

Where the Coal Mine Health and Safety District Manager has determined that the use of nonpermissible explosives and nonpermissible shot-firing units will not pose a hazard to any person during the development of a slope or shaft, he may, after written application by the operator, approve the use of such explosives and shot-firing units and issue a permit for the use of such explosives and devices setting forth the safeguards to be employed by the operator to protect the health and safety of any person exposed to such blasting.

(Pub. L. No. 96-511, 94 Stat. 2812 (44 U.S.C. 3501 et seq.))

[36 FR 9364, May 22, 1971, as amended at 60 FR 33723, June 29, 1995]

§ 77.1910 Explosives and blasting; general.

(a) Light and power circuits shall be disconnected or removed from the blasting area before charging and blasting.

(b) All explosive materials, detonators, and any other related blasting material employed in the development of any slope or shaft shall be stored, transported, carried, charged, and fired in accordance with the provision of Subpart N, "Explosives and Blasting," of this Part 77. Except as provided in paragraph (c) of this section, all shots shall be fired from the surface.

(c) Where tests for methane have been conducted and methane has not been found and only permissible blasting units are being employed, shots may be fired from an upper level of the slope or shaft.

(d) Except as provided in paragraph (c) of this section, all men shall be removed from the slope or shaft prior to blasting.

(e) Blasting areas in slopes or shafts shall be covered with mats or other suitable material when the excavation is too shallow to retain blasted material.

(f) Where it is impracticable to prepare primers in the blasting area, primers may be prepared on the surface and carried into the shaft in specially constructed, insulated, covered containers.

(g) No other development operation shall be conducted in a shaft or at the face of a slope while drill holes are being charged and until after all shots have been fired.

(h) The sides of the slope or shaft between the overhead platform and the bottom where men are working shall be examined after each blast and loose material removed.

(i) Loose rock and other material shall be removed from timbers and platforms after each blast before men are lowered to the shaft bottom.

§ 77.1911 Ventilation of slopes and shafts.

(a) All slopes and shafts shall be ventilated by mechanical ventilation equipment during development. Such equipment shall be examined before each shift and the quantity of air in the slope or shaft measured daily by a certified person and the results of such examinations and tests recorded in a book approved by the Secretary.

(b) Ventilation fans shall be:

(1) Installed on the surface;

(2) Installed in fireproof housing and connected to the slope or shaft opening with fireproof air ducts;

(3) Designed to permit the reversal of the air current, and located in an area which will prevent a recirculation of air from the slope or shaft or air contamination from any other source;

(4) Equipped with an automatic signal device designed to give an alarm in the event the fan slows or stops which can be seen or heard by any person on duty in the vicinity of the fan, except where fans are constantly attended.

(5) Offset not less than 15 feet from the shaft; and

(6) Equipped with air ducts which are fire resistant and maintained so as to prevent excessive leakage of air;

(i) Flexible ducts shall be constructed to permit ventilation by either exhausting or blowing methods and when metal air ducts are used, they shall be grounded effectively to remove static and other electrical charges;

(ii) Ducts shall extend as close to the bottom as necessary to ventilate properly.

(c) A qualified person, designated by the operator, shall be assigned to maintain each ventilating system.

(d) The fan shall be operated continuously when men are below the surface. Any accidental stoppage or reduction in airflow shall be corrected promptly; however, where repairs cannot be made immediately, development work below the surface shall be stopped and all the men not needed to make necessary repairs shall be removed to the surface.

§ 77.1912 Ladders and stairways.

(a) Substantial stairways or ladders shall be used during the construction of all shafts where no mechanical means are provided for men to travel.

(b) Landings at intervals of not more than 30 feet shall be installed.

(c) Shaft ladders shall project 3 feet above the collar of the shaft, and shall be placed at least 3 inches from the side of the shaft.

§ 77.1913 Fire-resistant wood.

Except for crossties, timbers, and other wood products which are permanently installed in slopes and shafts, shall be fire resistant.

§ 77.1914 Electrical equipment.

(a) Electric equipment employed below the collar of a slope or shaft during excavation shall be permissible and shall be maintained in a permissible condition.

(b) The insulation of all electric conductors employed below the collar of any slope or shaft during excavation shall be of the flame resistant type.

(c) Only lamps and portable flood lights approved by the Bureau of Mines or the Mine Safety and Health Administration under Part 19 and Part 20 of this chapter (Bureau of Mines Schedules 6D and 10C) shall be employed below the collar of any slope or shaft.

§ 77.1915 Storage and handling of combustible materials.

(a) Compressed and liquefied gas, oil, gasoline, and other petroleum products shall not be stored within 100 feet of any slope or shaft opening.

(b) Other combustible material and supplies shall not be stored within 25 feet of any slope or shaft opening.

(c) Pyritic slates, bony coal, culm or other material capable of spontaneous combustion shall not be used for fill or as surfacing material within 100 feet of any slope or shaft opening.

(d) Areas surrounding the opening of each slope or shaft shall be constructed to insure the drainage of flammable liquids away from the slope or shaft in the event of spillage.

(e) Oily rags, waste, waste paper, and other combustible waste material disposed of in the vicinity of any slope or shaft opening shall be stored in closed containers until removed from the area.

§ 77.1916 Welding, cutting, and soldering; fire protection.

(a) One portable fire extinguisher shall be provided where welding, cutting, or soldering with arc or flame is performed.

(b) Welding, cutting, or soldering with arc or flame within or in the vicinity of any slope or shaft, except where such operations are performed in fireproof enclosures, shall be done under the supervision of a qualified person who shall make a diligent search within or in the vicinity of the slope or shaft for fire during and after such operations.

(c) Before welding, cutting, or soldering is performed in any slope or shaft designed to penetrate into any coalbed below the surface, an examination for methane shall be made by a qualified person with a device approved by the Secretary for detecting methane. Examination for methane shall be made immediately before and periodically during welding, cutting, or soldering and such work shall not be permitted to commence or continue in air which contains 1.0 volume per centum or more of methane.

(d) Noncombustible barriers shall be installed below welding, cutting, or soldering operations in or over a shaft.

Subpart U—Approved Books and Records [Reserved]

PART 90—MANDATORY HEALTH STANDARDS—COAL MINERS WHO HAVE EVIDENCE OF THE DEVELOPMENT OF PNEUMOCONIOSIS

Subpart A—General

Sec.
90.1 Scope.
90.2 Definitions.
90.3 Part 90 option; notice of eligibility; exercise of option.

Subpart B—Dust Standards, Rights of Part 90 Miners

90.100 Respirable dust standard.
90.101 Respirable dust standard when quartz is present.
90.102 Transfer; notice.
90.103 Compensation.
90.104 Waiver of rights; re-exercise of option.

Subpart C—Sampling Procedures

90.201 Sampling; general and technical requirements.
90.202 Certified person; sampling.
90.203 Certified person; maintenance and calibration.
90.204 Approved sampling devices; maintenance and calibration.
90.205 Approved sampling devices; operation; air flowrate.
90.206 Exercise of option or transfer sampling.
90.207 Quarterly sampling.
90.208 Respirable dust samples; transmission by operator.
90.209 Respirable dust samples; report to operator.
90.210 Status change reports.

Subpart D—Respirable Dust Control Plans

90.300 Respirable dust control plan; filing requirements.
90.301 Respirable dust control plan; approval by District Manager; copy to part 90 miner.

AUTHORITY: 30 U.S.C. 811, 813(h), 957.

SOURCE: 45 FR 80769, Dec. 5, 1980, unless otherwise noted.

Subpart A—General

SOURCE: 79 FR 24988, May 1, 2014, unless otherwise noted.

§ 90.1 Scope.

This part 90 establishes the option of miners who are employed at coal mines and who have evidence of the development of pneumoconiosis to work in an area of a mine where the average concentration of respirable dust in the mine atmosphere during each shift is continuously maintained at or below the applicable standard as specified in § 90.100. The rule sets forth procedures for miners to exercise this option, and establishes the right of miners to retain their regular rate of pay and receive wage increases. The rule also sets forth the operator's obligations, including respirable dust sampling for part 90 miners. This part 90 is promulgated pursuant to section 101 of the Act and supersedes section 203(b) of the Federal Mine Safety and Health Act of 1977, as amended.

§ 90.2 Definitions.

The following definitions apply in this part:

Act. The Federal Mine Safety and Health Act of 1977, Public Law 91–173, as amended by Public Law 95–164 and Public Law 109–236.

Active workings. Any place in a coal mine where miners are normally required to work or travel.

Approved sampling device. A sampling device approved by the Secretary and Secretary for Health and Human Services (HHS) under part 74 of this title.

Certified person. An individual certified by the Secretary in accordance with § 90.202 to take respirable dust samples required by this part or certified in accordance with § 90.203 to perform the maintenance and calibration of respirable dust sampling equipment as required by this part.

Coal mine dust personal sampler unit (CMDPSU). A personal sampling device approved under part 74, subpart B, of this title.

Concentration. A measure of the amount of a substance contained per unit volume of air.

Continuous personal dust monitor (CPDM). A personal sampling device approved under part 74, subpart C, of this title.

District Manager. The manager of the Coal Mine Safety and Health District in which the mine is located.

Equivalent concentration. The concentration of respirable coal mine dust, including quartz, expressed in milligrams per cubic meter of air (mg/m³) as measured with an approved sampling device, determined by dividing the weight of dust in milligrams collected on the filter of an approved sampling device by the volume of air in cubic meters passing through the filter (sampling time in minutes (t) times the sampling airflow rate in cubic meters per minute), and then converting that concentration to an equivalent concentration as measured by the Mining Research Establishment (MRE) instrument. When the approved sampling device is:

(1) The CMDPSU, the equivalent concentration is determined by multiplying the concentration of respirable coal mine dust by the constant factor prescribed by the Secretary.

(2) The CPDM, the device shall be programmed to automatically report end-of-shift concentration measurements as equivalent concentrations.

Mechanized mining unit (MMU). A unit of mining equipment including hand loading equipment used for the production of material; or a specialized unit which uses mining equipment other than specified in § 70.206(b) or in § 70.208(b) of this chapter. Each MMU will be assigned a four-digit identification number by MSHA, which is retained by the MMU regardless of where the unit relocates within the mine. However, when:

(1) Two sets of mining equipment are used in a series of working places within the same working section and only one production crew is employed at any given time on either set of mining equipment, the two sets of equipment shall be identified as a single MMU.

(2) Two or more sets of mining equipment are simultaneously engaged in cutting, mining, or loading coal or rock from working places within the same working section, each set of mining equipment shall be identified as a separate MMU.

MRE instrument. The gravimetric dust sampler with a four channel horizontal elutriator developed by the Mining Research Establishment of the National Coal Board, London, England.

MSHA. The Mine Safety and Health Administration of the U.S. Department of Labor.

Normal work duties. Duties which the part 90 miner performs on a routine day-to-day basis in his or her job classification at a mine.

Part 90 miner. A miner employed at a coal mine who has exercised the option under the old section 203(b) program (36 FR 20601, October 27, 1971), or under § 90.3 of this part to work in an area of a mine where the average concentration of respirable dust in the mine atmosphere during each shift to which that miner is exposed is continuously maintained at or below the applicable standard, and who has not waived these rights.

Quartz. Crystalline silicon dioxide (SiO_2) not chemically combined with other substances and having a distinctive physical structure.

Representative sample. A respirable dust sample, expressed as an equivalent concentration, that reflects typical dust concentration levels in the working environment of the part 90 miner when performing normal work duties.

Respirable dust. Dust collected with a sampling device approved by the Secretary and the Secretary of HHS in accordance with part 74 (Coal Mine Dust Sampling Devices) of this title.

Secretary. The Secretary of Labor or a delegate.

Secretary of Health and Human Services. The Secretary of Health and Human Services (HHS) or the Secretary of Health, Education, and Welfare.

Transfer. Any change in the work assignment of a part 90 miner by the operator and includes: (1) Any change in occupation code of a part 90 miner; (2) any movement of a part 90 miner to or from an MMU; or (3) any assignment of a part 90 miner to the same occupation in a different location at a mine.

Valid respirable dust sample. A respirable dust sample collected and submitted as required by this part, including any sample for which the data were electronically transmitted to MSHA, and not voided by MSHA.

§ 90.3 **Part 90 option; notice of eligibility; exercise of option.**

(a) Any miner employed at a coal mine who, in the judgment of the Secretary of HHS, has evidence of the development of pneumoconiosis based on a chest X-ray, read and classified in the manner prescribed by the Secretary of HHS, or based on other medical examinations shall be afforded the option to work in an area of a mine where the average concentration of respirable dust in the mine atmosphere during each shift to which that miner is exposed is continuously maintained at or below the applicable standard. Each of these miners shall be notified in writing of eligibility to exercise the option.

(b) Any miner who is a section 203(b) miner on January 31, 1981, shall be a part 90 miner on February 1, 1981, entitled to full rights under this part to retention of pay rate, future actual wage increases, and future work assignment, shift and respirable dust protection.

(c) Any part 90 miner who is transferred to a position at the same or another coal mine shall remain a part 90 miner entitled to full rights under this part at the new work assignment.

(d) The option to work in a low dust area of the mine may be exercised for the first time by any miner employed at a coal mine who was eligible for the option under the old section 203(b) program (*http://www.msha.gov/ REGSTECHAMEND.htm*), or is eligible for the option under this part by sending a written request to the Chief, Division of Health, Coal Mine Safety and Health, MSHA, 201 12th Street South, Arlington, VA 22202–5452.

(e) The option to work in a low dust area of the mine may be re-exercised by any miner employed at a coal mine who exercised the option under the old section 203(b) program (*http:// www.msha.gov/REGSTECHAMEND.htm*) or exercised the option under this part by sending a written request to the Chief, Division of Health, Coal Mine Safety and Health, MSHA, 201 12th Street South, Arlington, VA 22202–5452. The request should include the name and address of the mine and operator where the miner is employed.

(f) No operator shall require from a miner a copy of the medical information received from the Secretary or Secretary of HHS.

[79 FR 24988, May 1, 2014, as amended at 80 FR 52993, Sept. 2, 2015]

Subpart B—Dust Standards, Rights of Part 90 Miners

SOURCE: 79 FR 24989, May 1, 2014, unless otherwise noted.

§ 90.100 **Respirable dust standard.**

After the 20th calendar day following receipt of notification from MSHA that a part 90 miner is employed at the mine, the operator shall continuously maintain the average concentration of respirable dust in the mine atmosphere during each shift to which the part 90 miner in the active workings of the mine is exposed, as measured with an approved sampling device and expressed in terms of an equivalent concentration, at or below:

§ 90.101

(a) 1.0 milligrams of respirable dust per cubic meter of air (mg/m³).

(b) 0.5 mg/m³ as of August 1, 2016.

§ 90.101 Respirable dust standard when quartz is present.

(a) Each operator shall continuously maintain the average concentration of respirable quartz dust in the mine atmosphere during each shift to which a part 90 miner in the active workings of each mine is exposed at or below 0.1 mg/m³ (100 micrograms per cubic meter or µg/m³) as measured with an approved sampling device and expressed in terms of an equivalent concentration.

(b) When the mine atmosphere of the active workings where the part 90 miner performs his or her normal work duties exceeds 100 µg/m³ of respirable quartz dust, the operator shall continuously maintain the average concentration of respirable dust in the mine atmosphere during each shift to which a part 90 miner is exposed as measured with an approved sampling device and expressed in terms of an equivalent concentration at or below the applicable standard. The applicable standard is computed by dividing the percent of quartz into the number 10. The application of this formula shall not result in an applicable standard that exceeds the standards specified in § 90.100.

Example: Assume the part 90 miner is on a 0.5 mg/m³ dust standard. Suppose a valid representative dust sample with an equivalent concentration of 0.50 mg/m³ contains 25.6% of quartz dust, which corresponds to a quartz concentration of 128 µg/m³. Therefore, the average concentration of respirable dust in the mine atmosphere associated with that part 90 miner shall be maintained on each shift at or below 0.4 mg/m³ (10/25.6% = 0.4 mg/m³).

§ 90.102 Transfer; notice.

(a) Whenever a part 90 miner is transferred in order to meet the applicable standard, the operator shall transfer the miner to an existing position at the same coal mine on the same shift or shift rotation on which the miner was employed immediately before the transfer. The operator may transfer a part 90 miner to a different coal mine, a newly-created position or a position on a different shift or shift rotation if the miner agrees in writing to the transfer. The requirements of this paragraph do not apply when the respirable dust concentration in a part 90 miner's work position complies with the applicable standard but circumstances, such as reductions in workforce or changes in operational status, require a change in the miner's job or shift assignment.

(b) On or before the 20th calendar day following receipt of notification from MSHA that a part 90 miner is employed at the mine, the operator shall give the District Manager written notice of the occupation and, if applicable, the MMU unit to which the part 90 miner shall be assigned on the 21st calendar day following receipt of the notification from MSHA.

(c) After the 20th calendar day following receipt of notification from MSHA that a part 90 miner is employed at the mine, the operator shall give the District Manager written notice before any transfer of a part 90 miner. This notice shall include the scheduled date of the transfer.

§ 90.103 Compensation.

(a) The operator shall compensate each part 90 miner at not less than the regular rate of pay received by that miner immediately before exercising the option under § 90.3.

(b) Whenever a part 90 miner is transferred, the operator shall compensate the miner at not less than the regular rate of pay received by that miner immediately before the transfer.

(c) Once a miner has been placed in a position in compliance with the provisions of part 90, paragraphs (a) and (b) of this section do not apply when the part 90 miner initiates and accepts a change in work assignment for reasons of job preference.

(d) The operator shall compensate each miner who is a section 203(b) miner on January 31, 1981, at not less than the regular rate of pay that the miner is required to receive under section 203(b) of the Act immediately before the effective date of this part.

(e) In addition to the compensation required to be paid under paragraphs (a), (b), and (d) of this section, the operator shall pay each part 90 miner the actual wage increases that accrue to the classification to which the miner is assigned.

(f) If a miner is temporarily employed in an occupation other than his or her regular work classification for two months or more before exercising the option under § 90.3, the miner's regular rate of pay for purposes of paragraph (a) and (b) of this section is the higher of the temporary or regular rates of pay. If the temporary assignment is for less than two months, the operator may pay the part 90 miner at his or her regular work classification rate regardless of the temporary wage rate.

(g) If a part 90 miner is transferred, and the Secretary subsequently notifies the miner that notice of the miner's eligibility to exercise the part 90 option was incorrect, the operator shall retain the affected miner in the current position to which the miner is assigned and continue to pay the affected miner the applicable rate of pay provided in paragraphs (a), (b), (d), and (e) of this section, until:

(1) The affected miner and operator agree in writing to a position with pay at not less than the regular rate of pay for that occupation; or

(2) A position is available at the same coal mine in both the same occupation and on the same shift on which the miner was employed immediately before exercising the option under § 90.3 or under the old section 203(b) program (36 FR 20601, October 27, 1971).

(i) When such a position is available, the operator shall offer the available position in writing to the affected miner with pay at not less than the regular rate of pay for that occupation.

(ii) If the affected miner accepts the available position in writing, the operator shall implement the miner's reassignment upon notice of the miner's acceptance. If the miner does not accept the available position in writing, the miner may be reassigned and protections under part 90 shall not apply. Failure by the miner to act on the written offer of the available position within 15 days after notice of the offer is received from the operator shall operate as an election not to accept the available position.

§ 90.104 Waiver of rights; re-exercise of option.

(a) A part 90 miner may waive his or her rights and be removed from MSHA's active list of miners who have rights under part 90 by:

(1) Giving written notification to the Chief, Division of Health, Coal Mine Safety and Health, MSHA, that the miner waives all rights under this part;

(2) Applying for and accepting a position in an area of a mine which the miner knows has an average respirable dust concentration exceeding the applicable standard; or

(3) Refusing to accept another position offered by the operator at the same coal mine that meets the requirements of §§ 90.100, 90.101 and 90.102(a) after dust sampling shows that the present position exceeds the applicable standard.

(b) If rights under part 90 are waived, the miner gives up all rights under part 90 until the miner re-exercises the option in accordance with § 90.3(e) (Part 90 option; notice of eligibility; exercise of option).

(c) If rights under part 90 are waived, the miner may re-exercise the option under this part in accordance with § 90.3(e) (Part 90 option; notice of eligibility; exercise of option) at any time.

Subpart C—Sampling Procedures

SOURCE: 79 FR 24990, May 1, 2014, unless otherwise noted.

§ 90.201 Sampling; general and technical requirements.

(a) An approved coal mine dust personal sampler unit (CMDPSU) shall be used to take samples of the concentration of respirable coal mine dust in the working environment of each part 90 miner as required by this part. On February 1, 2016, part 90 miners shall be sampled only with an approved continuous personal dust monitor (CPDM) as required by this part and an approved CMDPSU shall not be used, unless notified by the Secretary to continue to use an approved CMDPSU to conduct quarterly sampling.

(b) If using a CMDPSU, the sampling device shall be worn or carried to and from each part 90 miner. If using a CPDM, the sampling device shall be

§ 90.202

worn by the part 90 miner at all times. Approved sampling devices shall be operated portal-to-portal and shall remain operational during the part 90 miner's entire shift, which includes the time spent performing normal work duties and while traveling to and from the assigned work location. If the work shift to be sampled is longer than 12 hours and the sampling device is:

(1) A CMDPSU, the operator shall switch-out the unit's sampling pump prior to the 13th-hour of operation.

(2) A CPDM, the operator shall switch-out the CPDM with a fully charged device prior to the 13th-hour of operation.

(c) Unless otherwise directed by the District Manager, the respirable dust samples required under this part using a CMDPSU shall be taken by placing the sampling device as follows:

(1) On the part 90 miner;

(2) On the piece of equipment which the part 90 miner operates within 36 inches of the normal working position; or

(3) At a location that represents the maximum concentration of dust to which the part 90 miner is exposed.

(d) If using a CMDPSU, one control filter shall be used for each shift of sampling. Each control filter shall:

(1) Have the same pre-weight date (noted on the dust data card) as the filter used for sampling;

(2) Remain plugged at all times;

(3) Be used for the same amount of time, and exposed to the same temperature and handling conditions as the filter used for sampling; and

(4) Be kept with the exposed samples after sampling and in the same mailing container when transmitted to MSHA.

(e) The respirable dust samples required by this part and taken with a CMDPSU shall be collected while the part 90 miner is performing normal work duties.

(f) Records showing the length of each shift for each part 90 miner shall be made and retained for at least six months, and shall be made available for inspection by authorized representatives of the Secretary and submitted to the District Manager when requested in writing.

(g) Upon request from the District Manager, the operator shall submit the date and time any respirable dust sampling required by this part will begin. This information shall be submitted at least 48 hours prior to scheduled sampling.

(h) Operators using CPDMs shall provide training to all part 90 miners. The training shall be completed prior to a part 90 miner wearing a CPDM and then every 12 months thereafter. The training shall include:

(1) The importance of monitoring dust concentrations and properly wearing the CPDM;

(2) Explaining the basic features and capabilities of the CPDM;

(3) Discussing the various types of information displayed by the CPDM and how to access that information; and

(4) How to start and stop a short-term sample run during compliance sampling.

(i) An operator shall keep a record of the CPDM training at the mine site for 24 months after completion of the training. An operator may keep the record elsewhere if the record is immediately accessible from the mine site by electronic transmission. Upon request from an authorized representative of the Secretary or Secretary of HHS, the operator shall promptly provide access to any such training records. The record shall include:

(1) The date of training;

(2) The names of miners trained; and

(3) The subjects included in the training.

(j) An anthracite mine using the full box, open breast, or slant breast mining method may use either a CPDM or a CMDPSU to conduct the required sampling. The mine operator shall notify the District Manager in writing of its decision to not use a CPDM.

§ 90.202 Certified person; sampling.

(a) The respirable dust sampling required by this part shall be performed by a certified person.

(b) To be certified, a person shall complete the applicable MSHA course of instruction and pass the MSHA examination demonstrating competency in sampling procedures. Persons not certified in sampling and those certified only in maintenance and calibration procedures in accordance with § 90.203(b) are not permitted to collect

Mine Safety and Health Admin., Labor §90.204

respirable dust samples required by this part or handle approved sampling devices when being used in sampling.

(c) To maintain certification, a person must pass the MSHA examination demonstrating competency in sampling procedures every three years.

(d) MSHA may revoke a person's certification for failing to properly carry out the required sampling procedures.

§90.203 Certified person; maintenance and calibration.

(a) Approved sampling devices shall be maintained and calibrated by a certified person.

(b) To be certified, a person shall complete the applicable MSHA course of instruction and pass the MSHA examination demonstrating competency in maintenance and calibration procedures for approved sampling devices. Necessary maintenance of the sampling head assembly of a CMDPSU, or the cyclone assembly of a CPDM, can be performed by persons certified in sampling or in maintenance and calibration.

(c) To maintain certification, a person must pass the MSHA examination demonstrating competency in maintenance and calibration procedures every three years.

(d) MSHA may revoke a person's certification for failing to properly carry out the required maintenance and calibration procedures.

§90.204 Approved sampling devices; maintenance and calibration.

(a) Approved sampling devices shall be maintained as approved under part 74 of this title and calibrated in accordance with MSHA Informational Report IR 1240 (1996) "Calibration and Maintenance Procedures for Coal Mine Respirable Dust Samplers" or in accordance with the manufacturer's recommendations if using a CPDM. Only persons certified in maintenance and calibration can perform maintenance on the CPDM or the pump unit of the CMDPSU.

(b) Approved sampling devices shall be calibrated at the flowrate of 2.0 liters of air per minute (L/min) if using a CMDPSU; at 2.2 L/min if using a CPDM; or at a different flowrate recommended by the manufacturer, before they are put into service and, thereafter, at time intervals recommended by the manufacturer or prescribed by the Secretary or Secretary of HHS.

(c) If using a CMDPSU, sampling devices shall be examined and tested by a person certified in sampling or in maintenance and calibration within 3 hours before the start of the shift on which the approved sampling devices will be used to collect respirable dust samples. This is to assure that the sampling devices are clean and in proper working condition. This examination and testing shall include the following:

(1) Examination of all components of the cyclone assembly to assure that they are clean and free of dust and dirt. This includes examining the interior of the connector barrel (located between the cassette assembly and vortex finder), vortex finder, cyclone body, and grit pot;

(2) Examination of the inner surface of the cyclone body to assure that it is free of scoring or scratch marks on the inner surface of the cyclone where the air flow is directed by the vortex finder into the cyclone body;

(3) Examination of the external hose connecting the pump unit to the sampling head assembly to assure that it is clean and free of leaks; and

(4) Examination of the clamping and positioning of the cyclone body, vortex finder, and cassette to assure that they are rigid, in alignment, firmly in contact, and airtight.

(5) Testing the voltage of each battery while under actual load to assure the battery is fully charged. This requires that a fully assembled and examined sampling head assembly be attached to the pump inlet with the pump unit running when the voltage check is made. The voltage for batteries used in the CMDPSU shall not be lower than the product of the number of cells in the battery multiplied by the manufacturer's nominal voltage per cell.

(d) If using a CPDM, the certified person in sampling or in maintenance and calibration shall:

(1) Follow the pre-operational examinations, testing, and set-up procedures,

§ 90.205

and perform necessary external maintenance recommended by the manufacturer to assure the operational readiness of the CPDM within 3 hours before the start of the shift on which the sampling device will be used to collect respirable dust samples; and

(2) Perform other required scheduled examinations and maintenance procedures recommended by the manufacturer.

(e) You must proceed in accordance with "Calibration and Maintenance Procedures for Coal Mine Respirable Dust Samplers," MSHA Informational Report IR 1240 (1996), referenced in paragraph (a) of this section. The Director of the Federal Register approves this incorporation by reference in accordance with 5 U.S.C. 552(a) and 1 CFR part 51. You may obtain a copy from the MSHA Web site at *http:// www.msha.gov* and you may inspect or obtain a copy at MSHA, Coal Mine Safety and Health, 201 12th Street South, Arlington, VA 22202–5452; 202–693–9500; and at each MSHA Coal Mine Safety and Health District Office, or at the National Archives and Records Administration (NARA). For information on the availability of this material at NARA, call 202–741–6030, or go to: *http:// www.archives.gov/federal_register/ code_of_federal_regulations/ ibr_locations.html.*

[79 FR 24990, May 1, 2014, as amended at 80 FR 52993, Sept. 2, 2015]

§ 90.205 Approved sampling devices; operation; air flowrate.

(a) Approved sampling devices shall be operated at the flowrate of 2.0 L/min if using a CMDPSU; at 2.2 L/min if using a CPDM; or at a different flowrate recommended by the manufacturer.

(b) If using a CMDPSU, each approved sampling device shall be examined each shift, by a person certified in sampling during:

(1) The second hour after being put into operation to assure it is in the proper location, operating properly, and at the proper flowrate. If the proper flowrate is not maintained, necessary adjustments shall be made by the certified person. This examination is not required if the sampling device is being operated in an anthracite coal mine using the full box, open breast, or slant breast mining method.

(2) The last hour of operation to assure that the sampling device is operating properly and at the proper flowrate. If the proper flowrate is not maintained, the respirable dust sample shall be transmitted to MSHA with a notation by the certified person on the back of the dust data card stating that the proper flowrate was not maintained. Other events occurring during the collection of respirable dust samples that may affect the validity of the sample, such as dropping of the sampling head assembly onto the mine floor, shall be noted on the back of the dust data card.

(c) If using a CPDM, the person certified in sampling shall monitor the dust concentrations and the sampling status conditions being reported by the sampling device at mid-shift or more frequently as specified in the approved respirable dust control plan, if applicable, to assure: The sampling device is in the proper location and operating properly; and the work environment of the part 90 miner being sampled remains in compliance with the applicable standard at the end of the shift. This monitoring is not required if the sampling device is being operated in an anthracite coal mine using the full box, open breast, or slant breast mining method.

§ 90.206 Exercise of option or transfer sampling.

(a) The operator shall take five valid representative dust samples for each part 90 miner within 15 calendar days after:

(1) The 20-day period specified for each part 90 miner in § 90.100; and

(2) Implementing any transfer after the 20th calendar day following receipt of notification from MSHA that a part 90 miner is employed at the mine.

(b) Noncompliance with the applicable standard shall be determined in accordance with § 90.207(d) of this part.

(c) Upon issuance of a citation for a violation of the applicable standard, the operator shall comply with § 90.207(f) of this part.

§ 90.207 Quarterly sampling.

(a) Each operator shall take five valid representative samples every calendar quarter from the environment of each part 90 miner while performing normal work duties. Part 90 miner samples shall be collected on consecutive work days. The quarterly periods are:

January 1–March 31
April 1–June 30
July 1–September 30
October 1–December 31.

(b) When the respirable dust standard is changed in accordance with § 90.101, the new applicable standard shall become effective 7 calendar days after the date of notification of the change by MSHA.

(c) When a valid representative sample taken in accordance with this section meets or exceeds the excessive concentration value (ECV) in Table 90–1 that corresponds to the applicable standard and particular sampling device used, the operator shall:

(1) Make approved respiratory equipment available to affected miners in accordance with § 72.700 of this chapter;

(2) Immediately take corrective action to lower the concentration of respirable coal mine dust to at or below the applicable standard; and

(3) Make a record of the corrective actions taken. The record shall be certified by the mine foreman or equivalent mine official, no later than the end of the mine foreman's or equivalent official's next regularly scheduled working shift. The record shall be made in a secure book that is not susceptible to alteration or electronically in a computer system so as to be secure and not susceptible to alteration. Such records shall be retained at a surface location at the mine for at least 1 year and shall be made available for inspection by authorized representatives of the Secretary and the part 90 miner.

(d) Noncompliance with the applicable standard is demonstrated during the sampling period when:

(1) Two or more valid representative samples meet or exceed the ECV in Table 90–1 that corresponds to the applicable standard and the particular sampling device used; or

(2) The average for all valid representative samples meets or exceeds the ECV in Table 90–2 that corresponds to the applicable standard and the particular sampling device used.

(e) Unless otherwise directed by the District Manager, upon issuance of a citation for a violation of the applicable standard, paragraph (a) of this section shall not apply to that part 90 miner until the violation is abated and the citation is terminated in accordance with paragraphs (f) and (g) of this section.

(f) Upon issuance of a citation for a violation of the applicable standard, the operator shall take the following actions sequentially:

(1) Make approved respiratory equipment available to the affected part 90 miner in accordance with § 72.700 of this chapter.

(2) Immediately take corrective action to lower the concentration of respirable dust to at or below the applicable standard. If the corrective action involves:

(i) Reducing the respirable dust levels in the work position of the part 90 miner identified in the citation, the operator shall implement the proposed corrective actions and begin sampling the affected miner within 8 calendar days after the date the citation is issued, until five valid representative samples are taken.

(ii) Transferring the part 90 miner to another work position at the mine to meet the applicable standard, the operator shall comply with § 90.102 of this part and then sample the affected miner in accordance with § 90.206(a) of this part.

(3) Make a record of the corrective actions taken. The record shall be certified by the mine foreman or equivalent mine official, no later than the end of the mine foreman's or equivalent official's next regularly scheduled working shift. The record shall be made in a secure book that is not susceptible to alteration or electronically in a computer system so as to be secure and not susceptible to alteration. Such records shall be retained at a surface location at the mine for at least 1 year and shall be made available for inspection by authorized representatives of the Secretary and the part 90 miner.

(g) A citation for a violation of the applicable standard shall be terminated by MSHA when the equivalent concentration of each of the five valid representative samples is at or below the applicable standard.

TABLE 90–1—EXCESSIVE CONCENTRATION VALUES (ECV) BASED ON SINGLE, FULL-SHIFT CMDPSU/CPDM CONCENTRATION MEASUREMENTS

Applicable standard (mg/m³)	ECV (mg/m³)	
	CMDPSU	CPDM
1.0	1.26	1.13
0.9	1.16	1.02
0.8	1.05	0.91
0.7	0.95	0.79
0.6	0.85	0.68
0.5	0.74	0.57
0.4	0.65	0.46
0.3	0.54	0.34
0.2	0.44	0.23

TABLE 90–2—EXCESSIVE CONCENTRATION VALUES (ECV) BASED ON THE AVERAGE OF 5 FULL-SHIFT CMDPSU/CPDM CONCENTRATION MEASUREMENTS

Applicable standard (mg/m³)	ECV (mg/m³)	
	CMDPSU	CPDM
1.0	1.12	1.06
0.9	1.02	0.96
0.8	0.92	0.85
0.7	0.81	0.75
0.6	0.71	0.64
0.5	0.61	0.53
0.4	0.51	0.43
0.3	0.41	0.32
0.2	0.31	0.22

§ 90.208 Respirable dust samples; transmission by operator.

(a) If using a CMDPSU, the operator shall transmit within 24 hours after the end of the sampling shift all samples collected to fulfill the requirements of this part, including control filters, in containers provided by the manufacturer of the filter cassette to: Respirable Dust Processing Laboratory, Pittsburgh Safety and Health Technology Center, 626 Cochrans Mill Road, Building 38, Pittsburgh, PA 15236–3611, or to any other address designated by the District Manager.

(b) The operator shall not open or tamper with the seal of any filter cassette or alter the weight of any filter cassette before or after it is used to fulfill the requirements of this part.

(c) A person certified in sampling shall properly complete the dust data card that is provided by the manufacturer for each filter cassette. The card shall have an identification number identical to that on the cassette used to take the sample and be submitted to MSHA with the sample. Each card shall be signed by the certified person who actually performed the required examinations under 90.205(b) of this part during the sampling shift and shall include that person's MSHA Individual Identification Number (MIIN). Respirable dust samples with data cards not properly completed may be voided by MSHA.

(d) All respirable dust samples collected by the operator shall be considered taken to fulfill the sampling requirements of part 70, 71, or 90 of this title, unless the sample has been identified in writing by the operator to the District Manager, prior to the intended sampling shift, as a sample to be used for purposes other than required by part 70, 71, or 90 of this title.

(e) Respirable dust samples received by MSHA in excess of those required by this part shall be considered invalid samples.

(f) If using a CPDM, the person certified in sampling shall (1) validate, certify, and transmit electronically to MSHA within 24 hours after the end of each sampling shift all sample data file information collected and stored in the CPDM, including the sampling status conditions encountered when sampling each part 90 miner; and (2) not tamper with the CPDM or its components in any way before, during, or after it is used to fulfill the requirements of this part, or alter any data files. All CPDM data files transmitted electronically to MSHA shall be maintained by the operator for at least 12 months.

[79 FR 24988, May 1, 2014, as amended at 80 FR 52993, Sept. 2, 2015]

§ 90.209 Respirable dust samples; report to operator.

(a) MSHA shall provide the operator, as soon as practicable, a report with the following data on respirable dust samples submitted or whose results were transmitted electronically, if

Mine Safety and Health Admin., Labor § 90.301

using a CPDM, in accordance with this part:

(1) The mine identification number;
(2) The locations within the mine from which the samples were taken;
(3) The concentration of respirable dust, expressed as an equivalent concentration for each valid sample;
(4) The average equivalent concentration of respirable dust for all valid samples;
(5) The occupation code;
(6) The reason for voiding any sample; and
(7) The part 90 miner's MSHA Individual Identification Number (MIIN).

(b) Upon receipt, the operator shall provide a copy of this report to the part 90 miner. The operator shall not post the original or a copy of this report on the mine bulletin board.

(c) If using a CPDM, the person certified in sampling shall print, sign, and provide to each part 90 miner, a paper record (Dust Data Card) of the sample run within one hour after the start of the part 90 miner's next work shift. This hard-copy record shall include the data entered when the sample run was first programmed, and the following:

(1) The mine identification number;
(2) The location within the mine from which the sample was taken;
(3) The concentration of respirable dust, expressed as an equivalent concentration reported and stored for each sample;
(4) The sampling status conditions encountered for each sample;
(5) The shift length; and
(6) The part 90 miner's MSHA Individual Identification Number (MIIN).

(d) The operator shall not post data on respirable dust samples for part 90 miners on the mine bulletin board.

§ 90.210 Status change reports.

If there is a change in the status of a part 90 miner (such as entering a terminated, injured, or ill status, or returning to work), the operator shall report the change in the status of the part 90 miner to the MSHA District Office or to any other MSHA office designated by the District Manager. Status changes shall be reported in writing or by electronic means within 3 working days after the status change has occurred.

Subpart D—Respirable Dust Control Plans

SOURCE: 79 FR 24993, May 1, 2014, unless otherwise noted.

§ 90.300 Respirable dust control plan; filing requirements.

(a) If an operator abates a violation of the applicable standard by reducing the respirable dust level in the position of the part 90 miner, the operator shall submit to the District Manager for approval a written respirable dust control plan for the part 90 miner in the position identified in the citation within 15 calendar days after the citation is terminated. The respirable dust control plan and revisions thereof shall be suitable to the conditions and the mining system of the coal mine and shall be adequate to continuously maintain respirable dust to at or below the applicable standard for that part 90 miner.

(b) Each respirable dust control plan shall include at least the following:

(1) The mine identification number assigned by MSHA, the operator's name, mine name, mine address, and mine telephone number and the name, address and telephone number of the principal officer in charge of health and safety at the mine;
(2) The name and MSHA Individual Identification Number of the part 90 miner and the position at the mine to which the plan applies;
(3) A detailed description of the specific respirable dust control measures used to continuously maintain concentrations of respirable coal mine dust at or below the applicable standard; and
(4) A detailed description of how each of the respirable dust control measures described in response to paragraph (b)(3) of this section will continue to be used by the operator, including at least the specific time, place, and manner the control measures will be used.

§ 90.301 Respirable dust control plan; approval by District Manager; copy to part 90 miner.

(a) The District Manager will approve respirable dust control plans on a mine-by-mine basis. When approving respirable dust control plans, the District Manager shall consider whether:

§ 90.301

(1) The respirable dust control measures would be likely to maintain concentrations of respirable coal mine dust at or below the applicable standard; and

(2) The operator's compliance with all provisions of the respirable dust control plan could be objectively ascertained by MSHA.

(b) MSHA may take respirable dust samples to determine whether the respirable dust control measures in the operator's plan effectively maintain concentrations of respirable coal mine dust at or below the applicable standard.

(c) The operator shall comply with all provisions of each respirable dust control plan upon notice from MSHA that the respirable dust control plan is approved.

(d) The operator shall provide a copy of the current respirable dust control plan required under this part to the part 90 miner. The operator shall not post the original or a copy of the plan on the mine bulletin board.

(e) The operator may review respirable dust control plans and submit proposed revisions to such plans to the District Manager for approval.

SUBCHAPTER P—CIVIL PENALTIES FOR VIOLATIONS OF THE FEDERAL MINE SAFETY AND HEALTH ACT OF 1977

PART 100—CRITERIA AND PROCEDURES FOR PROPOSED ASSESSMENT OF CIVIL PENALTIES

Sec.
100.1 Scope and purpose.
100.2 Applicability.
100.3 Determination of penalty amount; regular assessment.
100.4 Unwarrantable failure and immediate notification.
100.5 Determination of penalty amount; special assessment.
100.6 Procedures for review of citations and orders; procedures for assessment of civil penalties and conferences.
100.7 Notice of proposed penalty; notice of contest.
100.8 Service.

AUTHORITY: 5 U.S.C. 301; 30 U.S.C. 815, 820, 957; 28 U.S.C. 2461 note (Federal Civil Penalties Inflation Adjustment Act of 1990); Pub. L. 114–74 at sec. 701.

SOURCE: 72 FR 13635, Mar. 22, 2007, unless otherwise noted.

§ 100.1 Scope and purpose.

This part provides the criteria and procedures for proposing civil penalties under sections 105 and 110 of the Federal Mine Safety and Health Act of 1977 (Mine Act). The purpose of this part is to provide a fair and equitable procedure for the application of the statutory criteria in determining proposed penalties for violations, to maximize the incentives for mine operators to prevent and correct hazardous conditions, and to assure the prompt and efficient processing and collection of penalties.

§ 100.2 Applicability.

The criteria and procedures in this part are applicable to all proposed assessments of civil penalties for violations of the Mine Act and the standards and regulations promulgated pursuant to the Mine Act, as amended. MSHA shall review each citation and order and shall make proposed assessments of civil penalties.

§ 100.3 Determination of penalty amount; regular assessment.

(a) *General.* (1) Except as provided in § 100.5(e), the operator of any mine in which a violation occurs of a mandatory health or safety standard or who violates any other provision of the Mine Act, as amended, shall be assessed a civil penalty of not more than $85,580. Each occurrence of a violation of a mandatory safety or health standard may constitute a separate offense. The amount of the proposed civil penalty shall be based on the criteria set forth in sections 105(b) and 110(i) of the Mine Act. These criteria are:

(i) The appropriateness of the penalty to the size of the business of the operator charged;

(ii) The operator's history of previous violations;

(iii) Whether the operator was negligent;

(iv) The gravity of the violation;

(v) The demonstrated good faith of the operator charged in attempting to achieve rapid compliance after notification of a violation; and

(vi) The effect of the penalty on the operator's ability to continue in business.

(2) A regular assessment is determined by first assigning the appropriate number of penalty points to the violation by using the appropriate criteria and tables set forth in this section. The total number of penalty points will then be converted into a dollar amount under the penalty conversion table in paragraph (g) of this section. The penalty amount will be adjusted for demonstrated good faith in accordance with paragraph (f) of this section.

(b) *The appropriateness of the penalty to the size of the business of the operator charged.* The appropriateness of the penalty to the size of the mine operator's business is calculated by using both the size of the mine cited and the size of the mine's controlling entity. The size of coal mines and their controlling entities is measured by coal production. The size of metal and

§ 100.3

nonmetal mines and their controlling entities is measured by hours worked. The size of independent contractors is measured by the total hours worked at all mines. Penalty points for size are assigned based on Tables I to V. As used in these tables, the terms "annual tonnage" and "annual hours worked" mean coal produced and hours worked in the previous calendar year. In cases where a full year of data is not available, the coal produced or hours worked is prorated to an annual basis. This criterion accounts for a maximum of 25 penalty points.

Table I—Size of Coal Mine

Annual tonnage of mine	Penalty Points
0 to 7,500	1
Over 7,500 to 10,000	2
Over 10,000 to 15,000	3
Over 15,000 to 20,000	4
Over 20,000 to 30,000	5
Over 30,000 to 50,000	6
Over 50,000 to 70,000	7
Over 70,000 to 100,000	8
Over 100,000 to 200,000	9
Over 200,000 to 300,000	10
Over 300,000 to 500,000	11
Over 500,000 to 700,000	12
Over 700,000 to 1,000,000	13
Over 1,000,000 to 2,000,000	14
Over 2,000,000	15

Table II—Size of Controlling Entity—Coal Mine

Annual tonnage	Penalty Points
0 to 50,000	1
Over 50,000 to 100,000	2
Over 100,000 to 200,000	3
Over 200,000 to 300,000	4
Over 300,000 to 500,000	5
Over 500,000 to 700,000	6
Over 700,000 to 1,000,000	7
Over 1,000,000 to 3,000,000	8
Over 3,000,000 to 10,000,000	9
Over 10,000,000	10

§ 100.3

Table III—Size of Metal/Nonmetal Mine

Annual hours worked at mine	Penalty Points
0 to 5,000	0
Over 5,000 to 10,000	1
Over 10,000 to 20,000	2
Over 20,000 to 30,000	3
Over 30,000 to 50,000	4
Over 50,000 to 100,000	5
Over 100,000 to 200,000	6
Over 200,000 to 300,000	7
Over 300,000 to 500,000	8
Over 500,000 to 700,000	9
Over 700,000 to 1,000,000	10
Over 1,000,000 to 1,500,000	11
Over 1,500,000 to 2,000,000	12
Over 2,000,000 to 3,000,000	13
Over 3,000,000 to 5,000,000	14
Over 5,000,000	15

Table IV—Size of Controlling Entity—Metal/Nonmetal Mine

Annual hours worked	Penalty Points
0 to 50,000	0
Over 50,000 to 100,000	1
Over 100,000 to 200,000	2
Over 200,000 to 300,000	3
Over 300,000 to 500,000	4
Over 500,000 to 1,000,000	5
Over 1,000,000 to 2,000,000	6
Over 2,000,000 to 3,000,000	7
Over 3,000,000 to 5,000,000	8
Over 5,000,000 to 10,000,000	9
Over 10,000,000	10

Table V—Size of Independent Contractor

Annual hours worked at all mines	Penalty Points
0 to 5,000	0
Over 5,000 to 7,000	2
Over 7,000 to 10,000	4
Over 10,000 to 20,000	6
Over 20,000 to 30,000	8
Over 30,000 to 50,000	10
Over 50,000 to 70,000	12
Over 70,000 to 100,000	14
Over 100,000 to 200,000	16
Over 200,000 to 300,000	18
Over 300,000 to 500,000	20
Over 500,000 to 700,000	22
Over 700,000 to 1,000,000	24
Over 1,000,000	25

(c) *History of previous violations.* An operator's history of previous violations is based on both the total number of violations and the number of repeat violations of the same citable provision of a standard in a preceding 15-month period. Only assessed violations that have been paid or finally adjudicated, or have become final orders of the Commission will be included in determining an operator's history. The repeat aspect of the history criterion in paragraph (c)(2) of this section applies only after an operator has received 10 violations or an independent contractor operator has received 6 violations.

(1) Total number of violations. For mine operators, penalty points are assigned on the basis of the number of violations per inspection day (VPID)(Table VI). Penalty points are not assigned for mines with fewer than 10 violations in the specified history period. For independent contractors, penalty points are assigned on the basis of the total number of violations at all mines (Table VII). This aspect of the history criterion accounts for a maximum of 25 penalty points.

§ 100.3

Table VI—History of Previous Violations-Mine Operators

Mine Operator's Overall History of Violations Per Inspection Day	Penalty Points
0 to 0.3	0
Over 0.3 to 0.5	2
Over 0.5 to 0 7	5
Over 0.7 to 0.9	8
Over 0.9 to 1.1	10
Over 1.1 to 1.3	12
Over 1.3 to 1.5	14
Over 1.5 to 1.7	16
Over 1.7 to 1.9	19
Over 1.9 to 2.1	22
Over 2.1	25

Table VII—History of Previous Violations-Independent Contractors

Independent Contractor's Overall History of Number of Violations	Penalty Points
0 to 5	0
6	1
7	2
8	3
9	4
10	5
11	6
12	7
13	8
14	9
15	10
16	11
17	12
18	13
19	14
20	15
21	16
22	17
23	18
24	19
25	20
26	21
27	22
28	23
29	24
Over 29	25

(2) Repeat violations of the same standard. Repeat violation history is based on the number of violations of the same citable provision of a standard in a preceding 15-month period. For coal and metal and nonmetal mine operators with a minimum of six repeat violations, penalty points are assigned

Mine Safety and Health Admin., Labor § 100.3

on the basis of the number of repeat violations per inspection day (RPID) (Table VIII). For independent contractors, penalty points are assigned on the basis of the number of violations at all mines (Table IX). This aspect of the history criterion accounts for a maximum of 20 penalty points (Table VIII).

Table VIII—History of Previous Violations—Repeat Violations for Coal and Metal and Nonmetal Operators with a Minimum of 6 Repeat Violations

Number of Repeat Violations Per Inspection Day	Final Rule Penalty Points
0 to 0.01	0
Over 0.01 to 0.015	1
Over 0.015 to 0.02	2
Over 0.02 to 0.025	3
Over 0.025 to 0.03	4
Over 0.03 to 0.04	5
Over 0.04 to 0.05	6
Over 0.05 to 0.06	7
Over 0.06 to 0.08	8
Over 0.08 to 0.10	9
Over 0.10 to 0.12	10
Over 0.12 to 0.14	11
Over 0.14 to 0.16	12
Over 0.16 to 0.18	13
Over 0.18 to 0.20	14
Over 0.20 to 0.25	15
Over 0.25 to 0.3	16
Over 0.3 to 0.4	17
Over 0.4 to 0.5	18
Over 0.5 to 1.0	19
Over 1.0	20

Table IX—History of Previous Violations—Repeat Violations for Independent Contractors

Number of Repeat Violations of the Same Standard	Final Rule Penalty Points
5 or fewer	0
6	2
7	4
8	6
9	8
10	10
11	12
12	14
13	16
14	18
More than 14	20

§ 100.3

(d) *Negligence.* Negligence is conduct, either by commission or omission, which falls below a standard of care established under the Mine Act to protect miners against the risks of harm. Under the Mine Act, an operator is held to a high standard of care. A mine operator is required to be on the alert for conditions and practices in the mine that affect the safety or health of miners and to take steps necessary to correct or prevent hazardous conditions or practices. The failure to exercise a high standard of care constitutes negligence. The negligence criterion assigns penalty points based on the degree to which the operator failed to exercise a high standard of care. When applying this criterion, MSHA considers mitigating circumstances which may include, but are not limited to, actions taken by the operator to prevent or correct hazardous conditions or practices. This criterion accounts for a maximum of 50 penalty points, based on conduct evaluated according to Table X.

Table X—Negligence

Categories	Penalty Points
No negligence (The operator exercised diligence and could not have known of the violative condition or practice.)	0
Low negligence (The operator knew or should have known of the violative condition or practice, but there are considerable mitigating circumstances.)	10
Moderate negligence (The operator knew or should have known of the violative condition or practice, but there are mitigating circumstances.)	20
High negligence (The operator knew or should have known of the violative condition or practice, and there are no mitigating circumstances.)	35
Reckless disregard (The operator displayed conduct which exhibits the absence of the slightest degree of care.)	50

(e) *Gravity.* Gravity is an evaluation of the seriousness of the violation. This criterion accounts for a maximum of 88 penalty points, as derived from the Tables XI through XIII. Gravity is determined by the likelihood of the occurrence of the event against which a standard is directed; the severity of the illness or injury if the event has occurred or was to occur; and the number of persons potentially affected if the event has occurred or were to occur.

Table XI—Gravity: Likelihood

Likelihood of occurrence	Penalty Points
No likelihood	0
Unlikely	10
Reasonably likely	30
Highly likely	40
Occurred	50

Table XII—Gravity: Severity

Severity of injury or illness if the event has occurred or were to occur	Penalty Points
No lost work days (All occupational injuries and illnesses as defined in 30 CFR Part 50 except those listed below.)	0
Lost work days or restricted duty (Any injury or illness which would cause the injured or ill person to lose one full day of work or more after the day of the injury or illness, or which would cause one full day or more of restricted duty.)	5
Permanently disabling (Any injury or illness which would be likely to result in the total or partial loss of the use of any member or function of the body.)	10
Fatal (Any work-related injury or illness resulting in death, or which has a reasonable potential to cause death.)	20

Table XIII—Gravity: Persons Potentially Affected

Number of persons potentially affected if the event has occurred or were to occur	Penalty Points
0	0
1	1
2	2
3	4
4	6
5	8
6	10
7	12
8	14
9	16
10 or more	18

(f) *Demonstrated good faith of the operator in abating the violation.* This criterion provides a 10% reduction in the penalty amount of a regular assessment where the operator abates the violation within the time set by the inspector.

(g) *Penalty conversion table.* The penalty conversion table is used to convert the total penalty points to a dollar amount.

TABLE 14 TO PARAGRAPH (g)—PENALTY CONVERSION TABLE

Points	Penalty ($)
60 or fewer	$159
61	173
62	186
63	203
64	220
65	238
66	258
67	280
68	302
69	328
70	354
71	385
72	418
73	453
74	488

TABLE 14 TO PARAGRAPH (g)—PENALTY CONVERSION TABLE—Continued

Points	Penalty ($)
75	530
76	576
77	621
78	674
79	731
80	792
81	858
82	927
83	1,006
84	1,089
85	1,182
86	1,280
87	1,385
88	1,501
89	1,626
90	1,762
91	1,908
92	2,065
93	2,238
94	2,425
95	2,627
96	2,846
97	3,080
98	3,340
99	3,618
100	3,920
101	4,245
102	4,599
103	4,982
104	5,396

§ 100.4

TABLE 14 TO PARAGRAPH (g)—PENALTY CONVERSION TABLE—Continued

Points	Penalty ($)
105	5,847
106	6,333
107	6,861
108	7,432
109	8,052
110	8,722
111	9,446
112	10,235
113	11,088
114	12,012
115	13,011
116	14,094
117	15,270
118	16,541
119	17,919
120	19,410
121	21,029
122	22,777
123	24,677
124	26,733
125	28,955
126	31,369
127	33,983
128	36,812
129	39,879
130	43,201
131	46,799
132	50,695
133	54,918
134	59,299
135	63,677
136	68,060
137	72,437
138	76,819
139	81,198
140 or more	85,580

(h) The effect of the penalty on the operator's ability to continue in business. MSHA presumes that the operator's ability to continue in business will not be affected by the assessment of a civil penalty. The operator may, however, submit information to the District Manager concerning the financial status of the business. If the information provided by the operator indicates that the penalty will adversely affect the operator's ability to continue in business, the penalty may be reduced.

[72 FR 13635, Mar. 22, 2007, as amended at 73 FR 7209, Feb. 7, 2008; 81 FR 43455, July 1, 2016; 82 FR 5383, Jan. 18, 2017; 83 FR 14, Jan. 2, 2018; 84 FR 219, Jan. 23, 2019; 85 FR 2299, Jan. 15, 2020; 86 FR 2970, Jan. 14, 2021; 87 FR 2336, Jan. 14, 2022; 88 FR 2218, Jan. 13, 2023]

§ 100.4 Unwarrantable failure and immediate notification.

(a) The minimum penalty for any citation or order issued under section 104(d)(1) of the Mine Act shall be $2,853.

(b) The minimum penalty for any order issued under section 104(d)(2) of the Mine Act shall be $5,703.

(c) The penalty for failure to provide timely notification to the Secretary under section 103(j) of the Mine Act will be not less than $7,133 and not more than $85,580 for the following accidents:

(1) The death of an individual at the mine, or

(2) An injury or entrapment of an individual at the mine, which has a reasonable potential to cause death.

[72 FR 13635, Mar. 22, 2007, as amended at 74 FR 68919, Dec. 29, 2009; 77 FR 76408, Dec. 28, 2012; 81 FR 43455, July 1, 2016; 82 FR 5383, Jan. 18, 2017; 83 FR 14, Jan. 2, 2018; 84 FR 220, Jan. 23, 2019; 85 FR 2299, Jan. 15, 2020; 86 FR 2970, Jan. 14, 2021; 87 FR 2336, Jan. 14, 2022; 88 FR 2218, Jan. 13, 2023]

§ 100.5 Determination of penalty amount; special assessment.

(a) MSHA may elect to waive the regular assessment under § 100.3 if it determines that conditions warrant a special assessment.

(b) When MSHA determines that a special assessment is appropriate, the proposed penalty will be based on the six criteria set forth in § 100.3(a). All findings shall be in narrative form.

(c) Any operator who fails to correct a violation for which a citation has been issued under Section 104(a) of the Mine Act within the period permitted for its correction may be assessed a civil penalty of not more than $9,271 for each day during which such failure or violation continues.

(d) Any miner who willfully violates the mandatory safety standards relating to smoking or the carrying of smoking materials, matches, or lighters shall be subject to a civil penalty of not more than $391 for each occurrence of such violation.

(e) Violations that are deemed to be flagrant under section 110(b)(2) of the Mine Act may be assessed a civil penalty of not more than $313,790. For purposes of this section, a flagrant violation means "a reckless or repeated failure to make reasonable efforts to eliminate a known violation of a mandatory health or safety standard that substantially and proximately caused, or reasonably could have been expected to cause, death or serious bodily injury."

[72 FR 13635, Mar. 22, 2007, as amended at 73 FR 7210, Feb. 7, 2008; 74 FR 68919, Dec. 29, 2009; 77 FR 76408, Dec. 28, 2012; 81 FR 43456, July 1, 2016; 82 FR 5383, Jan. 18, 2017; 83 FR 14, Jan. 2, 2018; 84 FR 220, Jan. 23, 2019; 85 FR 2299, Jan. 15, 2020; 86 FR 2970, Jan. 14, 2021; 87 FR 2336, Jan. 14, 2022; 88 FR 2218, Jan. 13, 2023]

§ 100.6 Procedures for review of citations and orders; procedures for assessment of civil penalties and conferences.

(a) All parties shall be afforded the opportunity to review with MSHA each citation and order issued during an inspection. It is within the sole discretion of MSHA to grant a request for a conference and to determine the nature of the conference.

(b) Upon notice by MSHA, all parties will have 10 days within which to submit additional information or request a safety and health conference with the District Manager or designee. A conference request may include a request to be notified of, and to participate in, a conference initiated by another party. A conference request must be in writing and must include a brief statement of the reason why each citation or order should be conferenced.

(c) When a conference is conducted, the parties may submit any additional relevant information relating to the violation, either prior to or at the conference. To expedite the conference, the official assigned to the case may contact the parties to discuss the issues involved prior to the conference.

(d) MSHA will consider all relevant information submitted in a timely manner by the parties with respect to the violation. When the facts warrant a finding that no violation occurred, the citation or order will be vacated. Upon conclusion of the conference, or expiration of the conference request period, all citations that are abated and all orders will be promptly referred to MSHA's Office of Assessments. The Office of Assessments will use the citations, orders, and inspector's evaluation as the basis for determining the appropriate amount of a proposed penalty.

§ 100.7 Notice of proposed penalty; notice of contest.

(a) A notice of proposed penalty will be issued and served by certified mail, or the equivalent, upon the party to be charged and by regular mail to the representative of miners at the mine after the time permitted to request a conference under § 100.6 expires, or upon the completion of a conference, or upon review by MSHA of additional information submitted in a timely manner.

(b) Upon receipt of the notice of proposed penalty, the party charged shall have 30 days to either:

(1) Pay the proposed assessment. Acceptance by MSHA of payment tendered by the party charged will close the case.

(2) Notify MSHA in writing of the intention to contest the proposed penalty. When MSHA receives the notice of contest, it advises the Federal Mine Safety and Health Review Commission (Commission) of such notice. No proposed penalty which has been contested before the Commission shall be compromised, mitigated or settled except with the approval of the Commission.

(c) If the proposed penalty is not paid or contested within 30 days of receipt, the proposed penalty becomes a final order of the Commission and is not subject to review by any court or agency.

§ 100.8 Service.

(a) All operators are required by part 41 (Notification of Legal Identity) of this chapter to file with MSHA the name and address of record of the operator. All representatives of miners are required by part 40 (Representative of Miners) of this chapter to file with MSHA the mailing address of the person or organization acting in a representative capacity. Proposed penalty assessments delivered to those addresses shall constitute service.

(b) If any of the parties choose to have proposed penalty assessments mailed to a different address, the Office of Assessments must be notified in writing of the new address. Delivery to this address shall also constitute service.

(c) Service for operators who fail to file under part 41 of this chapter will be upon the last known business address recorded with MSHA.

PARTS 101–103 [RESERVED]

SUBCHAPTER Q—PATTERN OF VIOLATIONS

PART 104—PATTERN OF VIOLATIONS

Sec.
104.1 Purpose and scope.
104.2 Pattern criteria.
104.3 Issuance of notice.
104.4 Termination of notice.

AUTHORITY: 30 U.S.C. 814(e), 957.

SOURCE: 78 FR 5073, Jan. 23, 2013, unless otherwise noted.

§ 104.1 Purpose and scope.

This part establishes the criteria and procedures for determining whether a mine operator has established a pattern of significant and substantial (S&S) violations at a mine. It implements section 104(e) of the Federal Mine Safety and Health Act of 1977 (Mine Act) by addressing mines with an inspection history of recurrent S&S violations of mandatory safety or health standards that demonstrate a mine operator's disregard for the health and safety of miners. The purpose of the procedures in this part is the restoration of effective safe and healthful conditions at such mines.

§ 104.2 Pattern criteria.

(a) At least once each year, MSHA will review the compliance and accident, injury, and illness records of mines to determine if any mines meet the pattern of violations criteria. MSHA's review to identify mines with a pattern of S&S violations will include:

(1) Citations for S&S violations;
(2) Orders under section 104(b) of the Mine Act for not abating S&S violations;
(3) Citations and withdrawal orders under section 104(d) of the Mine Act, resulting from the mine operator's unwarrantable failure to comply;
(4) Imminent danger orders under section 107(a) of the Mine Act;
(5) Orders under section 104(g) of the Mine Act requiring withdrawal of miners who have not received training and who MSHA declares to be a hazard to themselves and others;
(6) Enforcement measures, other than section 104(e) of the Mine Act, that have been applied at the mine;
(7) Other information that demonstrates a serious safety or health management problem at the mine, such as accident, injury, and illness records; and
(8) Mitigating circumstances.

(b) MSHA will post the specific pattern criteria on its Web site.

§ 104.3 Issuance of notice.

(a) When a mine has a pattern of violations, the District Manager will issue a pattern of violations notice to the mine operator that specifies the basis for the Agency's action. The District Manager will also provide a copy of this notice to the representative of miners.

(b) The mine operator shall post the pattern of violations notice issued under this part on the mine bulletin board. The pattern of violations notice shall remain posted at the mine until MSHA terminates it under § 104.4 of this part.

(c) If MSHA finds any S&S violation within 90 days after issuance of the pattern notice, MSHA will issue an order for the withdrawal of all persons from the affected area, except those persons referred to in section 104(c) of the Mine Act, until the violation has been abated.

(d) If a withdrawal order is issued under paragraph (c) of this section, any subsequent S&S violation will result in a withdrawal order that will remain in effect until MSHA determines that the violation has been abated.

§ 104.4 Termination of notice.

(a) Termination of a section 104(e)(1) pattern of violations notice shall occur when an MSHA inspection of the entire mine finds no S&S violations or if MSHA does not issue a withdrawal order in accordance with section 104(e)(1) of the Mine Act within 90 days after the issuance of the pattern of violations notice.

§ 104.4

(b) The mine operator may request an inspection of the entire mine or portion of the mine. MSHA will not provide advance notice of the inspection and will determine the scope of the inspection. Inspections of portions of the mine, within 90 days, that together cover the entire mine shall constitute an inspection of the entire mine for the purposes of this part.

PARTS 105-199 [RESERVED]

FINDING AIDS

A list of CFR titles, subtitles, chapters, subchapters and parts and an alphabetical list of agencies publishing in the CFR are included in the CFR Index and Finding Aids volume to the Code of Federal Regulations which is published separately and revised annually.

Table of CFR Titles and Chapters
Alphabetical List of Agencies Appearing in the CFR
List of CFR Sections Affected

Table of CFR Titles and Chapters
(Revised as of July 1, 2023)

Title 1—General Provisions

I	Administrative Committee of the Federal Register (Parts 1—49)
II	Office of the Federal Register (Parts 50—299)
III	Administrative Conference of the United States (Parts 300—399)
IV	Miscellaneous Agencies (Parts 400—599)
VI	National Capital Planning Commission (Parts 600—699)

Title 2—Grants and Agreements

SUBTITLE A—OFFICE OF MANAGEMENT AND BUDGET GUIDANCE FOR GRANTS AND AGREEMENTS

I	Office of Management and Budget Governmentwide Guidance for Grants and Agreements (Parts 2—199)
II	Office of Management and Budget Guidance (Parts 200—299)

SUBTITLE B—FEDERAL AGENCY REGULATIONS FOR GRANTS AND AGREEMENTS

III	Department of Health and Human Services (Parts 300—399)
IV	Department of Agriculture (Parts 400—499)
VI	Department of State (Parts 600—699)
VII	Agency for International Development (Parts 700—799)
VIII	Department of Veterans Affairs (Parts 800—899)
IX	Department of Energy (Parts 900—999)
X	Department of the Treasury (Parts 1000—1099)
XI	Department of Defense (Parts 1100—1199)
XII	Department of Transportation (Parts 1200—1299)
XIII	Department of Commerce (Parts 1300—1399)
XIV	Department of the Interior (Parts 1400—1499)
XV	Environmental Protection Agency (Parts 1500—1599)
XVIII	National Aeronautics and Space Administration (Parts 1800—1899)
XX	United States Nuclear Regulatory Commission (Parts 2000—2099)
XXII	Corporation for National and Community Service (Parts 2200—2299)
XXIII	Social Security Administration (Parts 2300—2399)
XXIV	Department of Housing and Urban Development (Parts 2400—2499)
XXV	National Science Foundation (Parts 2500—2599)
XXVI	National Archives and Records Administration (Parts 2600—2699)

Title 2—Grants and Agreements—Continued

Chap.

XXVII	Small Business Administration (Parts 2700—2799)
XXVIII	Department of Justice (Parts 2800—2899)
XXIX	Department of Labor (Parts 2900—2999)
XXX	Department of Homeland Security (Parts 3000—3099)
XXXI	Institute of Museum and Library Services (Parts 3100—3199)
XXXII	National Endowment for the Arts (Parts 3200—3299)
XXXIII	National Endowment for the Humanities (Parts 3300—3399)
XXXIV	Department of Education (Parts 3400—3499)
XXXV	Export-Import Bank of the United States (Parts 3500—3599)
XXXVI	Office of National Drug Control Policy, Executive Office of the President (Parts 3600—3699)
XXXVII	Peace Corps (Parts 3700—3799)
LVIII	Election Assistance Commission (Parts 5800—5899)
LIX	Gulf Coast Ecosystem Restoration Council (Parts 5900—5999)
LX	Federal Communications Commission (Parts 6000—6099)

Title 3—The President

I	Executive Office of the President (Parts 100—199)

Title 4—Accounts

I	Government Accountability Office (Parts 1—199)

Title 5—Administrative Personnel

I	Office of Personnel Management (Parts 1—1199)
II	Merit Systems Protection Board (Parts 1200—1299)
III	Office of Management and Budget (Parts 1300—1399)
IV	Office of Personnel Management and Office of the Director of National Intelligence (Parts 1400—1499)
V	The International Organizations Employees Loyalty Board (Parts 1500—1599)
VI	Federal Retirement Thrift Investment Board (Parts 1600—1699)
VIII	Office of Special Counsel (Parts 1800—1899)
IX	Appalachian Regional Commission (Parts 1900—1999)
XI	Armed Forces Retirement Home (Parts 2100—2199)
XIV	Federal Labor Relations Authority, General Counsel of the Federal Labor Relations Authority and Federal Service Impasses Panel (Parts 2400—2499)
XVI	Office of Government Ethics (Parts 2600—2699)
XXI	Department of the Treasury (Parts 3100—3199)
XXII	Federal Deposit Insurance Corporation (Parts 3200—3299)
XXIII	Department of Energy (Parts 3300—3399)
XXIV	Federal Energy Regulatory Commission (Parts 3400—3499)
XXV	Department of the Interior (Parts 3500—3599)

Title 5—Administrative Personnel—Continued

Chap.	
XXVI	Department of Defense (Parts 3600—3699)
XXVIII	Department of Justice (Parts 3800—3899)
XXIX	Federal Communications Commission (Parts 3900—3999)
XXX	Farm Credit System Insurance Corporation (Parts 4000—4099)
XXXI	Farm Credit Administration (Parts 4100—4199)
XXXIII	U.S. International Development Finance Corporation (Parts 4300—4399)
XXXIV	Securities and Exchange Commission (Parts 4400—4499)
XXXV	Office of Personnel Management (Parts 4500—4599)
XXXVI	Department of Homeland Security (Parts 4600—4699)
XXXVII	Federal Election Commission (Parts 4700—4799)
XL	Interstate Commerce Commission (Parts 5000—5099)
XLI	Commodity Futures Trading Commission (Parts 5100—5199)
XLII	Department of Labor (Parts 5200—5299)
XLIII	National Science Foundation (Parts 5300—5399)
XLV	Department of Health and Human Services (Parts 5500—5599)
XLVI	Postal Rate Commission (Parts 5600—5699)
XLVII	Federal Trade Commission (Parts 5700—5799)
XLVIII	Nuclear Regulatory Commission (Parts 5800—5899)
XLIX	Federal Labor Relations Authority (Parts 5900—5999)
L	Department of Transportation (Parts 6000—6099)
LII	Export-Import Bank of the United States (Parts 6200—6299)
LIII	Department of Education (Parts 6300—6399)
LIV	Environmental Protection Agency (Parts 6400—6499)
LV	National Endowment for the Arts (Parts 6500—6599)
LVI	National Endowment for the Humanities (Parts 6600—6699)
LVII	General Services Administration (Parts 6700—6799)
LVIII	Board of Governors of the Federal Reserve System (Parts 6800—6899)
LIX	National Aeronautics and Space Administration (Parts 6900—6999)
LX	United States Postal Service (Parts 7000—7099)
LXI	National Labor Relations Board (Parts 7100—7199)
LXII	Equal Employment Opportunity Commission (Parts 7200—7299)
LXIII	Inter-American Foundation (Parts 7300—7399)
LXIV	Merit Systems Protection Board (Parts 7400—7499)
LXV	Department of Housing and Urban Development (Parts 7500—7599)
LXVI	National Archives and Records Administration (Parts 7600—7699)
LXVII	Institute of Museum and Library Services (Parts 7700—7799)
LXVIII	Commission on Civil Rights (Parts 7800—7899)
LXIX	Tennessee Valley Authority (Parts 7900—7999)
LXX	Court Services and Offender Supervision Agency for the District of Columbia (Parts 8000—8099)
LXXI	Consumer Product Safety Commission (Parts 8100—8199)

Title 5—Administrative Personnel—Continued

Chap.	
LXXIII	Department of Agriculture (Parts 8300—8399)
LXXIV	Federal Mine Safety and Health Review Commission (Parts 8400—8499)
LXXVI	Federal Retirement Thrift Investment Board (Parts 8600—8699)
LXXVII	Office of Management and Budget (Parts 8700—8799)
LXXX	Federal Housing Finance Agency (Parts 9000—9099)
LXXXIII	Special Inspector General for Afghanistan Reconstruction (Parts 9300—9399)
LXXXIV	Bureau of Consumer Financial Protection (Parts 9400—9499)
LXXXVI	National Credit Union Administration (Parts 9600—9699)
XCVII	Department of Homeland Security Human Resources Management System (Department of Homeland Security—Office of Personnel Management) (Parts 9700—9799)
XCVIII	Council of the Inspectors General on Integrity and Efficiency (Parts 9800—9899)
XCIX	Military Compensation and Retirement Modernization Commission (Parts 9900—9999)
C	National Council on Disability (Parts 10000—10049)
CI	National Mediation Board (Parts 10100—10199)
CII	U.S. Office of Special Counsel (Parts 10200—10299)
CIV	Office of the Intellectual Property Enforcement Coordinator (Part 10400—10499)

Title 6—Domestic Security

I	Department of Homeland Security, Office of the Secretary (Parts 1—199)
X	Privacy and Civil Liberties Oversight Board (Parts 1000—1099)

Title 7—Agriculture

SUBTITLE A—OFFICE OF THE SECRETARY OF AGRICULTURE (PARTS 0—26)

SUBTITLE B—REGULATIONS OF THE DEPARTMENT OF AGRICULTURE

I	Agricultural Marketing Service (Standards, Inspections, Marketing Practices), Department of Agriculture (Parts 27—209)
II	Food and Nutrition Service, Department of Agriculture (Parts 210—299)
III	Animal and Plant Health Inspection Service, Department of Agriculture (Parts 300—399)
IV	Federal Crop Insurance Corporation, Department of Agriculture (Parts 400—499)
V	Agricultural Research Service, Department of Agriculture (Parts 500—599)
VI	Natural Resources Conservation Service, Department of Agriculture (Parts 600—699)
VII	Farm Service Agency, Department of Agriculture (Parts 700—799)

Title 7—Agriculture—Continued

Chap.	
VIII	Agricultural Marketing Service (Federal Grain Inspection Service, Fair Trade Practices Program), Department of Agriculture (Parts 800—899)
IX	Agricultural Marketing Service (Marketing Agreements and Orders; Fruits, Vegetables, Nuts), Department of Agriculture (Parts 900—999)
X	Agricultural Marketing Service (Marketing Agreements and Orders; Milk), Department of Agriculture (Parts 1000—1199)
XI	Agricultural Marketing Service (Marketing Agreements and Orders; Miscellaneous Commodities), Department of Agriculture (Parts 1200—1299)
XIV	Commodity Credit Corporation, Department of Agriculture (Parts 1400—1499)
XV	Foreign Agricultural Service, Department of Agriculture (Parts 1500—1599)
XVI	[Reserved]
XVII	Rural Utilities Service, Department of Agriculture (Parts 1700—1799)
XVIII	Rural Housing Service, Rural Business-Cooperative Service, Rural Utilities Service, and Farm Service Agency, Department of Agriculture (Parts 1800—2099)
XX	[Reserved]
XXV	Office of Advocacy and Outreach, Department of Agriculture (Parts 2500—2599)
XXVI	Office of Inspector General, Department of Agriculture (Parts 2600—2699)
XXVII	Office of Information Resources Management, Department of Agriculture (Parts 2700—2799)
XXVIII	Office of Operations, Department of Agriculture (Parts 2800—2899)
XXIX	Office of Energy Policy and New Uses, Department of Agriculture (Parts 2900—2999)
XXX	Office of the Chief Financial Officer, Department of Agriculture (Parts 3000—3099)
XXXI	Office of Environmental Quality, Department of Agriculture (Parts 3100—3199)
XXXII	Office of Procurement and Property Management, Department of Agriculture (Parts 3200—3299)
XXXIII	Office of Transportation, Department of Agriculture (Parts 3300—3399)
XXXIV	National Institute of Food and Agriculture (Parts 3400—3499)
XXXV	Rural Housing Service, Department of Agriculture (Parts 3500—3599)
XXXVI	National Agricultural Statistics Service, Department of Agriculture (Parts 3600—3699)
XXXVII	Economic Research Service, Department of Agriculture (Parts 3700—3799)
XXXVIII	World Agricultural Outlook Board, Department of Agriculture (Parts 3800—3899)
XLI	[Reserved]

Title 7—Agriculture—Continued

Chap.

XLII Rural Business-Cooperative Service and Rural Utilities Service, Department of Agriculture (Parts 4200—4299)

L Rural Business-Cooperative Service, and Rural Utilities Service, Department of Agriculture (Parts 5000—5099)

Title 8—Aliens and Nationality

I Department of Homeland Security (Parts 1—499)

V Executive Office for Immigration Review, Department of Justice (Parts 1000—1399)

Title 9—Animals and Animal Products

I Animal and Plant Health Inspection Service, Department of Agriculture (Parts 1—199)

II Agricultural Marketing Service (Fair Trade Practices Program), Department of Agriculture (Parts 200—299)

III Food Safety and Inspection Service, Department of Agriculture (Parts 300—599)

Title 10—Energy

I Nuclear Regulatory Commission (Parts 0—199)

II Department of Energy (Parts 200—699)

III Department of Energy (Parts 700—999)

X Department of Energy (General Provisions) (Parts 1000—1099)

XIII Nuclear Waste Technical Review Board (Parts 1300—1399)

XVII Defense Nuclear Facilities Safety Board (Parts 1700—1799)

XVIII Northeast Interstate Low-Level Radioactive Waste Commission (Parts 1800—1899)

Title 11—Federal Elections

I Federal Election Commission (Parts 1—9099)

II Election Assistance Commission (Parts 9400—9499)

Title 12—Banks and Banking

I Comptroller of the Currency, Department of the Treasury (Parts 1—199)

II Federal Reserve System (Parts 200—299)

III Federal Deposit Insurance Corporation (Parts 300—399)

IV Export-Import Bank of the United States (Parts 400—499)

V [Reserved]

VI Farm Credit Administration (Parts 600—699)

VII National Credit Union Administration (Parts 700—799)

VIII Federal Financing Bank (Parts 800—899)

IX (Parts 900—999)[Reserved]

Title 12—Banks and Banking—Continued

Chap.

X Consumer Financial Protection Bureau (Parts 1000—1099)
XI Federal Financial Institutions Examination Council (Parts 1100—1199)
XII Federal Housing Finance Agency (Parts 1200—1299)
XIII Financial Stability Oversight Council (Parts 1300—1399)
XIV Farm Credit System Insurance Corporation (Parts 1400—1499)
XV Department of the Treasury (Parts 1500—1599)
XVI Office of Financial Research, Department of the Treasury (Parts 1600—1699)
XVII Office of Federal Housing Enterprise Oversight, Department of Housing and Urban Development (Parts 1700—1799)
XVIII Community Development Financial Institutions Fund, Department of the Treasury (Parts 1800—1899)

Title 13—Business Credit and Assistance

I Small Business Administration (Parts 1—199)
III Economic Development Administration, Department of Commerce (Parts 300—399)
IV Emergency Steel Guarantee Loan Board (Parts 400—499)
V Emergency Oil and Gas Guaranteed Loan Board (Parts 500—599)

Title 14—Aeronautics and Space

I Federal Aviation Administration, Department of Transportation (Parts 1—199)
II Office of the Secretary, Department of Transportation (Aviation Proceedings) (Parts 200—399)
III Commercial Space Transportation, Federal Aviation Administration, Department of Transportation (Parts 400—1199)
V National Aeronautics and Space Administration (Parts 1200—1299)
VI Air Transportation System Stabilization (Parts 1300—1399)

Title 15—Commerce and Foreign Trade

SUBTITLE A—OFFICE OF THE SECRETARY OF COMMERCE (PARTS 0—29)

SUBTITLE B—REGULATIONS RELATING TO COMMERCE AND FOREIGN TRADE

I Bureau of the Census, Department of Commerce (Parts 30—199)
II National Institute of Standards and Technology, Department of Commerce (Parts 200—299)
III International Trade Administration, Department of Commerce (Parts 300—399)
IV Foreign-Trade Zones Board, Department of Commerce (Parts 400—499)
VII Bureau of Industry and Security, Department of Commerce (Parts 700—799)

Title 15—Commerce and Foreign Trade—Continued

Chap.

VIII	Bureau of Economic Analysis, Department of Commerce (Parts 800—899)
IX	National Oceanic and Atmospheric Administration, Department of Commerce (Parts 900—999)
XI	National Technical Information Service, Department of Commerce (Parts 1100—1199)
XIII	East-West Foreign Trade Board (Parts 1300—1399)
XIV	Minority Business Development Agency (Parts 1400—1499)
XV	Office of the Under-Secretary for Economic Affairs, Department of Commerce (Parts 1500—1599)

SUBTITLE C—REGULATIONS RELATING TO FOREIGN TRADE AGREEMENTS

XX	Office of the United States Trade Representative (Parts 2000—2099)

SUBTITLE D—REGULATIONS RELATING TO TELECOMMUNICATIONS AND INFORMATION

XXIII	National Telecommunications and Information Administration, Department of Commerce (Parts 2300—2399) [Reserved]

Title 16—Commercial Practices

I	Federal Trade Commission (Parts 0—999)
II	Consumer Product Safety Commission (Parts 1000—1799)

Title 17—Commodity and Securities Exchanges

I	Commodity Futures Trading Commission (Parts 1—199)
II	Securities and Exchange Commission (Parts 200—399)
IV	Department of the Treasury (Parts 400—499)

Title 18—Conservation of Power and Water Resources

I	Federal Energy Regulatory Commission, Department of Energy (Parts 1—399)
III	Delaware River Basin Commission (Parts 400—499)
VI	Water Resources Council (Parts 700—799)
VIII	Susquehanna River Basin Commission (Parts 800—899)
XIII	Tennessee Valley Authority (Parts 1300—1399)

Title 19—Customs Duties

I	U.S. Customs and Border Protection, Department of Homeland Security; Department of the Treasury (Parts 0—199)
II	United States International Trade Commission (Parts 200—299)
III	International Trade Administration, Department of Commerce (Parts 300—399)
IV	U.S. Immigration and Customs Enforcement, Department of Homeland Security (Parts 400—599) [Reserved]

Chap.	**Title 20—Employees' Benefits**
I	Office of Workers' Compensation Programs, Department of Labor (Parts 1—199)
II	Railroad Retirement Board (Parts 200—399)
III	Social Security Administration (Parts 400—499)
IV	Employees' Compensation Appeals Board, Department of Labor (Parts 500—599)
V	Employment and Training Administration, Department of Labor (Parts 600—699)
VI	Office of Workers' Compensation Programs, Department of Labor (Parts 700—799)
VII	Benefits Review Board, Department of Labor (Parts 800—899)
VIII	Joint Board for the Enrollment of Actuaries (Parts 900—999)
IX	Office of the Assistant Secretary for Veterans' Employment and Training Service, Department of Labor (Parts 1000—1099)

Title 21—Food and Drugs

I	Food and Drug Administration, Department of Health and Human Services (Parts 1—1299)
II	Drug Enforcement Administration, Department of Justice (Parts 1300—1399)
III	Office of National Drug Control Policy (Parts 1400—1499)

Title 22—Foreign Relations

I	Department of State (Parts 1—199)
II	Agency for International Development (Parts 200—299)
III	Peace Corps (Parts 300—399)
IV	International Joint Commission, United States and Canada (Parts 400—499)
V	United States Agency for Global Media (Parts 500—599)
VII	U.S. International Development Finance Corporation (Parts 700—799)
IX	Foreign Service Grievance Board (Parts 900—999)
X	Inter-American Foundation (Parts 1000—1099)
XI	International Boundary and Water Commission, United States and Mexico, United States Section (Parts 1100—1199)
XII	United States International Development Cooperation Agency (Parts 1200—1299)
XIII	Millennium Challenge Corporation (Parts 1300—1399)
XIV	Foreign Service Labor Relations Board; Federal Labor Relations Authority; General Counsel of the Federal Labor Relations Authority; and the Foreign Service Impasse Disputes Panel (Parts 1400—1499)
XV	African Development Foundation (Parts 1500—1599)
XVI	Japan-United States Friendship Commission (Parts 1600—1699)
XVII	United States Institute of Peace (Parts 1700—1799)

Title 23—Highways

Chap.

I Federal Highway Administration, Department of Transportation (Parts 1—999)

II National Highway Traffic Safety Administration and Federal Highway Administration, Department of Transportation (Parts 1200—1299)

III National Highway Traffic Safety Administration, Department of Transportation (Parts 1300—1399)

Title 24—Housing and Urban Development

SUBTITLE A—OFFICE OF THE SECRETARY, DEPARTMENT OF HOUSING AND URBAN DEVELOPMENT (PARTS 0—99)

SUBTITLE B—REGULATIONS RELATING TO HOUSING AND URBAN DEVELOPMENT

I Office of Assistant Secretary for Equal Opportunity, Department of Housing and Urban Development (Parts 100—199)

II Office of Assistant Secretary for Housing-Federal Housing Commissioner, Department of Housing and Urban Development (Parts 200—299)

III Government National Mortgage Association, Department of Housing and Urban Development (Parts 300—399)

IV Office of Housing and Office of Multifamily Housing Assistance Restructuring, Department of Housing and Urban Development (Parts 400—499)

V Office of Assistant Secretary for Community Planning and Development, Department of Housing and Urban Development (Parts 500—599)

VI Office of Assistant Secretary for Community Planning and Development, Department of Housing and Urban Development (Parts 600—699) [Reserved]

VII Office of the Secretary, Department of Housing and Urban Development (Housing Assistance Programs and Public and Indian Housing Programs) (Parts 700—799)

VIII Office of the Assistant Secretary for Housing—Federal Housing Commissioner, Department of Housing and Urban Development (Section 8 Housing Assistance Programs, Section 202 Direct Loan Program, Section 202 Supportive Housing for the Elderly Program and Section 811 Supportive Housing for Persons With Disabilities Program) (Parts 800—899)

IX Office of Assistant Secretary for Public and Indian Housing, Department of Housing and Urban Development (Parts 900—1699)

X Office of Assistant Secretary for Housing—Federal Housing Commissioner, Department of Housing and Urban Development (Interstate Land Sales Registration Program) (Parts 1700—1799) [Reserved]

XII Office of Inspector General, Department of Housing and Urban Development (Parts 2000—2099)

XV Emergency Mortgage Insurance and Loan Programs, Department of Housing and Urban Development (Parts 2700—2799) [Reserved]

Title 24—Housing and Urban Development—Continued

Chap.

XX	Office of Assistant Secretary for Housing—Federal Housing Commissioner, Department of Housing and Urban Development (Parts 3200—3899)
XXIV	Board of Directors of the HOPE for Homeowners Program (Parts 4000—4099) [Reserved]
XXV	Neighborhood Reinvestment Corporation (Parts 4100—4199)

Title 25—Indians

I	Bureau of Indian Affairs, Department of the Interior (Parts 1—299)
II	Indian Arts and Crafts Board, Department of the Interior (Parts 300—399)
III	National Indian Gaming Commission, Department of the Interior (Parts 500—599)
IV	Office of Navajo and Hopi Indian Relocation (Parts 700—899)
V	Bureau of Indian Affairs, Department of the Interior, and Indian Health Service, Department of Health and Human Services (Part 900—999)
VI	Office of the Assistant Secretary, Indian Affairs, Department of the Interior (Parts 1000—1199)
VII	Office of the Special Trustee for American Indians, Department of the Interior (Parts 1200—1299)

Title 26—Internal Revenue

I	Internal Revenue Service, Department of the Treasury (Parts 1—End)

Title 27—Alcohol, Tobacco Products and Firearms

I	Alcohol and Tobacco Tax and Trade Bureau, Department of the Treasury (Parts 1—399)
II	Bureau of Alcohol, Tobacco, Firearms, and Explosives, Department of Justice (Parts 400—799)

Title 28—Judicial Administration

I	Department of Justice (Parts 0—299)
III	Federal Prison Industries, Inc., Department of Justice (Parts 300—399)
V	Bureau of Prisons, Department of Justice (Parts 500—599)
VI	Offices of Independent Counsel, Department of Justice (Parts 600—699)
VII	Office of Independent Counsel (Parts 700—799)
VIII	Court Services and Offender Supervision Agency for the District of Columbia (Parts 800—899)
IX	National Crime Prevention and Privacy Compact Council (Parts 900—999)

Title 28—Judicial Administration—Continued

Chap.
XI Department of Justice and Department of State (Parts 1100—1199)

Title 29—Labor

SUBTITLE A—OFFICE OF THE SECRETARY OF LABOR (PARTS 0—99)
SUBTITLE B—REGULATIONS RELATING TO LABOR

I National Labor Relations Board (Parts 100—199)
II Office of Labor-Management Standards, Department of Labor (Parts 200—299)
III National Railroad Adjustment Board (Parts 300—399)
IV Office of Labor-Management Standards, Department of Labor (Parts 400—499)
V Wage and Hour Division, Department of Labor (Parts 500—899)
IX Construction Industry Collective Bargaining Commission (Parts 900—999)
X National Mediation Board (Parts 1200—1299)
XII Federal Mediation and Conciliation Service (Parts 1400—1499)
XIV Equal Employment Opportunity Commission (Parts 1600—1699)
XVII Occupational Safety and Health Administration, Department of Labor (Parts 1900—1999)
XX Occupational Safety and Health Review Commission (Parts 2200—2499)
XXV Employee Benefits Security Administration, Department of Labor (Parts 2500—2599)
XXVII Federal Mine Safety and Health Review Commission (Parts 2700—2799)
XL Pension Benefit Guaranty Corporation (Parts 4000—4999)

Title 30—Mineral Resources

I Mine Safety and Health Administration, Department of Labor (Parts 1—199)
II Bureau of Safety and Environmental Enforcement, Department of the Interior (Parts 200—299)
IV Geological Survey, Department of the Interior (Parts 400—499)
V Bureau of Ocean Energy Management, Department of the Interior (Parts 500—599)
VII Office of Surface Mining Reclamation and Enforcement, Department of the Interior (Parts 700—999)
XII Office of Natural Resources Revenue, Department of the Interior (Parts 1200—1299)

Title 31—Money and Finance: Treasury

SUBTITLE A—OFFICE OF THE SECRETARY OF THE TREASURY (PARTS 0—50)
SUBTITLE B—REGULATIONS RELATING TO MONEY AND FINANCE

Title 31—Money and Finance: Treasury—Continued

Chap.

I	Monetary Offices, Department of the Treasury (Parts 51—199)
II	Fiscal Service, Department of the Treasury (Parts 200—399)
IV	Secret Service, Department of the Treasury (Parts 400—499)
V	Office of Foreign Assets Control, Department of the Treasury (Parts 500—599)
VI	Bureau of Engraving and Printing, Department of the Treasury (Parts 600—699)
VII	Federal Law Enforcement Training Center, Department of the Treasury (Parts 700—799)
VIII	Office of Investment Security, Department of the Treasury (Parts 800—899)
IX	Federal Claims Collection Standards (Department of the Treasury—Department of Justice) (Parts 900—999)
X	Financial Crimes Enforcement Network, Department of the Treasury (Parts 1000—1099)

Title 32—National Defense

SUBTITLE A—DEPARTMENT OF DEFENSE

I	Office of the Secretary of Defense (Parts 1—399)
V	Department of the Army (Parts 400—699)
VI	Department of the Navy (Parts 700—799)
VII	Department of the Air Force (Parts 800—1099)

SUBTITLE B—OTHER REGULATIONS RELATING TO NATIONAL DEFENSE

XII	Department of Defense, Defense Logistics Agency (Parts 1200—1299)
XVI	Selective Service System (Parts 1600—1699)
XVII	Office of the Director of National Intelligence (Parts 1700—1799)
XVIII	National Counterintelligence Center (Parts 1800—1899)
XIX	Central Intelligence Agency (Parts 1900—1999)
XX	Information Security Oversight Office, National Archives and Records Administration (Parts 2000—2099)
XXI	National Security Council (Parts 2100—2199)
XXIV	Office of Science and Technology Policy (Parts 2400—2499)
XXVII	Office for Micronesian Status Negotiations (Parts 2700—2799)
XXVIII	Office of the Vice President of the United States (Parts 2800—2899)

Title 33—Navigation and Navigable Waters

I	Coast Guard, Department of Homeland Security (Parts 1—199)
II	Corps of Engineers, Department of the Army, Department of Defense (Parts 200—399)
IV	Great Lakes St. Lawrence Seaway Development Corporation, Department of Transportation (Parts 400—499)

Title 34—Education

Chap.

SUBTITLE A—OFFICE OF THE SECRETARY, DEPARTMENT OF EDUCATION (PARTS 1—99)

SUBTITLE B—REGULATIONS OF THE OFFICES OF THE DEPARTMENT OF EDUCATION

I Office for Civil Rights, Department of Education (Parts 100—199)
II Office of Elementary and Secondary Education, Department of Education (Parts 200—299)
III Office of Special Education and Rehabilitative Services, Department of Education (Parts 300—399)
IV Office of Career, Technical, and Adult Education, Department of Education (Parts 400—499)
V Office of Bilingual Education and Minority Languages Affairs, Department of Education (Parts 500—599) [Reserved]
VI Office of Postsecondary Education, Department of Education (Parts 600—699)
VII Office of Educational Research and Improvement, Department of Education (Parts 700—799) [Reserved]

SUBTITLE C—REGULATIONS RELATING TO EDUCATION

XI [Reserved]
XII National Council on Disability (Parts 1200—1299)

Title 35 [Reserved]

Title 36—Parks, Forests, and Public Property

I National Park Service, Department of the Interior (Parts 1—199)
II Forest Service, Department of Agriculture (Parts 200—299)
III Corps of Engineers, Department of the Army (Parts 300—399)
IV American Battle Monuments Commission (Parts 400—499)
V Smithsonian Institution (Parts 500—599)
VI [Reserved]
VII Library of Congress (Parts 700—799)
VIII Advisory Council on Historic Preservation (Parts 800—899)
IX Pennsylvania Avenue Development Corporation (Parts 900—999)
X Presidio Trust (Parts 1000—1099)
XI Architectural and Transportation Barriers Compliance Board (Parts 1100—1199)
XII National Archives and Records Administration (Parts 1200—1299)
XV Oklahoma City National Memorial Trust (Parts 1500—1599)
XVI Morris K. Udall Scholarship and Excellence in National Environmental Policy Foundation (Parts 1600—1699)

Title 37—Patents, Trademarks, and Copyrights

I United States Patent and Trademark Office, Department of Commerce (Parts 1—199)
II U.S. Copyright Office, Library of Congress (Parts 200—299)

Title 37—Patents, Trademarks, and Copyrights—Continued

Chap.

III   Copyright Royalty Board, Library of Congress (Parts 300—399)

IV   National Institute of Standards and Technology, Department of Commerce (Parts 400—599)

Title 38—Pensions, Bonuses, and Veterans' Relief

I   Department of Veterans Affairs (Parts 0—199)

II   Armed Forces Retirement Home (Parts 200—299)

Title 39—Postal Service

I   United States Postal Service (Parts 1—999)

III   Postal Regulatory Commission (Parts 3000—3099)

Title 40—Protection of Environment

I   Environmental Protection Agency (Parts 1—1099)

IV   Environmental Protection Agency and Department of Justice (Parts 1400—1499)

V   Council on Environmental Quality (Parts 1500—1599)

VI   Chemical Safety and Hazard Investigation Board (Parts 1600—1699)

VII   Environmental Protection Agency and Department of Defense; Uniform National Discharge Standards for Vessels of the Armed Forces (Parts 1700—1799)

VIII   Gulf Coast Ecosystem Restoration Council (Parts 1800—1899)

IX   Federal Permitting Improvement Steering Council (Part 1900)

Title 41—Public Contracts and Property Management

SUBTITLE A—FEDERAL PROCUREMENT REGULATIONS SYSTEM [NOTE]

SUBTITLE B—OTHER PROVISIONS RELATING TO PUBLIC CONTRACTS

50   Public Contracts, Department of Labor (Parts 50-1—50-999)

51   Committee for Purchase From People Who Are Blind or Severely Disabled (Parts 51-1—51-99)

60   Office of Federal Contract Compliance Programs, Equal Employment Opportunity, Department of Labor (Parts 60-1—60-999)

61   Office of the Assistant Secretary for Veterans' Employment and Training Service, Department of Labor (Parts 61-1—61-999)

62—100   [Reserved]

SUBTITLE C—FEDERAL PROPERTY MANAGEMENT REGULATIONS SYSTEM

101   Federal Property Management Regulations (Parts 101-1—101-99)

102   Federal Management Regulation (Parts 102-1—102-299)

103—104   (Parts 103-001—104-099) [Reserved]

105   General Services Administration (Parts 105-1—105-999)

Title 41—Public Contracts and Property Management—Continued

Chap.

- 109 Department of Energy Property Management Regulations (Parts 109-1—109-99)
- 114 Department of the Interior (Parts 114-1—114-99)
- 115 Environmental Protection Agency (Parts 115-1—115-99)
- 128 Department of Justice (Parts 128-1—128-99)
- 129—200 [Reserved]

SUBTITLE D—FEDERAL ACQUISITION SUPPLY CHAIN SECURITY

- 201 Federal Acquisition Security Council (Parts 201-1—201-99).

SUBTITLE E [RESERVED]

SUBTITLE F—FEDERAL TRAVEL REGULATION SYSTEM

- 300 General (Parts 300-1—300-99)
- 301 Temporary Duty (TDY) Travel Allowances (Parts 301-1—301-99)
- 302 Relocation Allowances (Parts 302-1—302-99)
- 303 Payment of Expenses Connected with the Death of Certain Employees (Part 303-1—303-99)
- 304 Payment of Travel Expenses from a Non-Federal Source (Parts 304-1—304-99)

Title 42—Public Health

- I Public Health Service, Department of Health and Human Services (Parts 1—199)
- II—III [Reserved]
- IV Centers for Medicare & Medicaid Services, Department of Health and Human Services (Parts 400—699)
- V Office of Inspector General-Health Care, Department of Health and Human Services (Parts 1000—1099)

Title 43—Public Lands: Interior

SUBTITLE A—OFFICE OF THE SECRETARY OF THE INTERIOR (PARTS 1—199)

SUBTITLE B—REGULATIONS RELATING TO PUBLIC LANDS

- I Bureau of Reclamation, Department of the Interior (Parts 400—999)
- II Bureau of Land Management, Department of the Interior (Parts 1000—9999)
- III Utah Reclamation Mitigation and Conservation Commission (Parts 10000—10099)

Title 44—Emergency Management and Assistance

- I Federal Emergency Management Agency, Department of Homeland Security (Parts 0—399)
- IV Department of Commerce and Department of Transportation (Parts 400—499)

Title 45—Public Welfare

Chap.

SUBTITLE A—DEPARTMENT OF HEALTH AND HUMAN SERVICES (PARTS 1—199)

SUBTITLE B—REGULATIONS RELATING TO PUBLIC WELFARE

II Office of Family Assistance (Assistance Programs), Administration for Children and Families, Department of Health and Human Services (Parts 200—299)

III Office of Child Support Enforcement (Child Support Enforcement Program), Administration for Children and Families, Department of Health and Human Services (Parts 300—399)

IV Office of Refugee Resettlement, Administration for Children and Families, Department of Health and Human Services (Parts 400—499)

V Foreign Claims Settlement Commission of the United States, Department of Justice (Parts 500—599)

VI National Science Foundation (Parts 600—699)

VII Commission on Civil Rights (Parts 700—799)

VIII Office of Personnel Management (Parts 800—899)

IX Denali Commission (Parts 900—999)

X Office of Community Services, Administration for Children and Families, Department of Health and Human Services (Parts 1000—1099)

XI National Foundation on the Arts and the Humanities (Parts 1100—1199)

XII Corporation for National and Community Service (Parts 1200—1299)

XIII Administration for Children and Families, Department of Health and Human Services (Parts 1300—1399)

XVI Legal Services Corporation (Parts 1600—1699)

XVII National Commission on Libraries and Information Science (Parts 1700—1799)

XVIII Harry S. Truman Scholarship Foundation (Parts 1800—1899)

XXI Commission of Fine Arts (Parts 2100—2199)

XXIII Arctic Research Commission (Parts 2300—2399)

XXIV James Madison Memorial Fellowship Foundation (Parts 2400—2499)

XXV Corporation for National and Community Service (Parts 2500—2599)

Title 46—Shipping

I Coast Guard, Department of Homeland Security (Parts 1—199)

II Maritime Administration, Department of Transportation (Parts 200—399)

III Coast Guard (Great Lakes Pilotage), Department of Homeland Security (Parts 400—499)

IV Federal Maritime Commission (Parts 500—599)

Title 47—Telecommunication

Chap.

I Federal Communications Commission (Parts 0—199)
II Office of Science and Technology Policy and National Security Council (Parts 200—299)
III National Telecommunications and Information Administration, Department of Commerce (Parts 300—399)
IV National Telecommunications and Information Administration, Department of Commerce, and National Highway Traffic Safety Administration, Department of Transportation (Parts 400—499)
V The First Responder Network Authority (Parts 500—599)

Title 48—Federal Acquisition Regulations System

1 Federal Acquisition Regulation (Parts 1—99)
2 Defense Acquisition Regulations System, Department of Defense (Parts 200—299)
3 Department of Health and Human Services (Parts 300—399)
4 Department of Agriculture (Parts 400—499)
5 General Services Administration (Parts 500—599)
6 Department of State (Parts 600—699)
7 Agency for International Development (Parts 700—799)
8 Department of Veterans Affairs (Parts 800—899)
9 Department of Energy (Parts 900—999)
10 Department of the Treasury (Parts 1000—1099)
12 Department of Transportation (Parts 1200—1299)
13 Department of Commerce (Parts 1300—1399)
14 Department of the Interior (Parts 1400—1499)
15 Environmental Protection Agency (Parts 1500—1599)
16 Office of Personnel Management, Federal Employees Health Benefits Acquisition Regulation (Parts 1600—1699)
17 Office of Personnel Management (Parts 1700—1799)
18 National Aeronautics and Space Administration (Parts 1800—1899)
19 Broadcasting Board of Governors (Parts 1900—1999)
20 Nuclear Regulatory Commission (Parts 2000—2099)
21 Office of Personnel Management, Federal Employees Group Life Insurance Federal Acquisition Regulation (Parts 2100—2199)
23 Social Security Administration (Parts 2300—2399)
24 Department of Housing and Urban Development (Parts 2400—2499)
25 National Science Foundation (Parts 2500—2599)
28 Department of Justice (Parts 2800—2899)
29 Department of Labor (Parts 2900—2999)
30 Department of Homeland Security, Homeland Security Acquisition Regulation (HSAR) (Parts 3000—3099)
34 Department of Education Acquisition Regulation (Parts 3400—3499)

Title 48—Federal Acquisition Regulations System—Continued

Chap.

51	Department of the Army Acquisition Regulations (Parts 5100—5199) [Reserved]
52	Department of the Navy Acquisition Regulations (Parts 5200—5299)
53	Department of the Air Force Federal Acquisition Regulation Supplement (Parts 5300—5399) [Reserved]
54	Defense Logistics Agency, Department of Defense (Parts 5400—5499)
57	African Development Foundation (Parts 5700—5799)
61	Civilian Board of Contract Appeals, General Services Administration (Parts 6100—6199)
99	Cost Accounting Standards Board, Office of Federal Procurement Policy, Office of Management and Budget (Parts 9900—9999)

Title 49—Transportation

SUBTITLE A—OFFICE OF THE SECRETARY OF TRANSPORTATION (PARTS 1—99)

SUBTITLE B—OTHER REGULATIONS RELATING TO TRANSPORTATION

I	Pipeline and Hazardous Materials Safety Administration, Department of Transportation (Parts 100—199)
II	Federal Railroad Administration, Department of Transportation (Parts 200—299)
III	Federal Motor Carrier Safety Administration, Department of Transportation (Parts 300—399)
IV	Coast Guard, Department of Homeland Security (Parts 400—499)
V	National Highway Traffic Safety Administration, Department of Transportation (Parts 500—599)
VI	Federal Transit Administration, Department of Transportation (Parts 600—699)
VII	National Railroad Passenger Corporation (AMTRAK) (Parts 700—799)
VIII	National Transportation Safety Board (Parts 800—999)
X	Surface Transportation Board (Parts 1000—1399)
XI	Research and Innovative Technology Administration, Department of Transportation (Parts 1400—1499) [Reserved]
XII	Transportation Security Administration, Department of Homeland Security (Parts 1500—1699)

Title 50—Wildlife and Fisheries

I	United States Fish and Wildlife Service, Department of the Interior (Parts 1—199)
II	National Marine Fisheries Service, National Oceanic and Atmospheric Administration, Department of Commerce (Parts 200—299)
III	International Fishing and Related Activities (Parts 300—399)

Title 50—Wildlife and Fisheries—Continued

Chap.

IV Joint Regulations (United States Fish and Wildlife Service, Department of the Interior and National Marine Fisheries Service, National Oceanic and Atmospheric Administration, Department of Commerce); Endangered Species Committee Regulations (Parts 400—499)

V Marine Mammal Commission (Parts 500—599)

VI Fishery Conservation and Management, National Oceanic and Atmospheric Administration, Department of Commerce (Parts 600—699)

Alphabetical List of Agencies Appearing in the CFR
(Revised as of July 1, 2023)

Agency	CFR Title, Subtitle or Chapter
Administrative Conference of the United States	1, III
Advisory Council on Historic Preservation	36, VIII
Advocacy and Outreach, Office of	7, XXV
Afghanistan Reconstruction, Special Inspector General for	5, LXXXIII
African Development Foundation	22, XV
Federal Acquisition Regulation	48, 57
Agency for International Development	2, VII; 22, II
Federal Acquisition Regulation	48, 7
Agricultural Marketing Service	7, I, VIII, IX, X, XI; 9, II
Agricultural Research Service	7, V
Agriculture, Department of	2, IV; 5, LXXIII
Advocacy and Outreach, Office of	7, XXV
Agricultural Marketing Service	7, I, VIII, IX, X, XI; 9, II
Agricultural Research Service	7, V
Animal and Plant Health Inspection Service	7, III; 9, I
Chief Financial Officer, Office of	7, XXX
Commodity Credit Corporation	7, XIV
Economic Research Service	7, XXXVII
Energy Policy and New Uses, Office of	2, IX; 7, XXIX
Environmental Quality, Office of	7, XXXI
Farm Service Agency	7, VII, XVIII
Federal Acquisition Regulation	48, 4
Federal Crop Insurance Corporation	7, IV
Food and Nutrition Service	7, II
Food Safety and Inspection Service	9, III
Foreign Agricultural Service	7, XV
Forest Service	36, II
Information Resources Management, Office of	7, XXVII
Inspector General, Office of	7, XXVI
National Agricultural Library	7, XLI
National Agricultural Statistics Service	7, XXXVI
National Institute of Food and Agriculture	7, XXXIV
Natural Resources Conservation Service	7, VI
Operations, Office of	7, XXVIII
Procurement and Property Management, Office of	7, XXXII
Rural Business-Cooperative Service	7, XVIII, XLII
Rural Development Administration	7, XLII
Rural Housing Service	7, XVIII, XXXV
Rural Utilities Service	7, XVII, XVIII, XLII
Secretary of Agriculture, Office of	7, Subtitle A
Transportation, Office of	7, XXXIII
World Agricultural Outlook Board	7, XXXVIII
Air Force, Department of	32, VII
Federal Acquisition Regulation Supplement	48, 53
Air Transportation Stabilization Board	14, VI
Alcohol and Tobacco Tax and Trade Bureau	27, I
Alcohol, Tobacco, Firearms, and Explosives, Bureau of	27, II
AMTRAK	49, VII
American Battle Monuments Commission	36, IV
American Indians, Office of the Special Trustee	25, VII
Animal and Plant Health Inspection Service	7, III; 9, I
Appalachian Regional Commission	5, IX
Architectural and Transportation Barriers Compliance Board	36, XI

Agency	CFR Title, Subtitle or Chapter
Arctic Research Commission	45, XXIII
Armed Forces Retirement Home	5, XI; 38, II
Army, Department of	32, V
Engineers, Corps of	33, II; 36, III
Federal Acquisition Regulation	48, 51
Benefits Review Board	20, VII
Bilingual Education and Minority Languages Affairs, Office of	34, V
Blind or Severely Disabled, Committee for Purchase from People Who Are	41, 51
Federal Acquisition Regulation	48, 19
Career, Technical, and Adult Education, Office of	34, IV
Census Bureau	15, I
Centers for Medicare & Medicaid Services	42, IV
Central Intelligence Agency	32, XIX
Chemical Safety and Hazard Investigation Board	40, VI
Chief Financial Officer, Office of	7, XXX
Child Support Enforcement, Office of	45, III
Children and Families, Administration for	45, II, III, IV, X, XIII
Civil Rights, Commission on	5, LXVIII; 45, VII
Civil Rights, Office for	34, I
Coast Guard	33, I; 46, I; 49, IV
Coast Guard (Great Lakes Pilotage)	46, III
Commerce, Department of	2, XIII; 44, IV; 50, VI
Census Bureau	15, I
Economic Affairs, Office of the Under-Secretary for	15, XV
Economic Analysis, Bureau of	15, VIII
Economic Development Administration	13, III
Emergency Management and Assistance	44, IV
Federal Acquisition Regulation	48, 13
Foreign-Trade Zones Board	15, IV
Industry and Security, Bureau of	15, VII
International Trade Administration	15, III; 19, III
National Institute of Standards and Technology	15, II; 37, IV
National Marine Fisheries Service	50, II, IV
National Oceanic and Atmospheric Administration	15, IX; 50, II, III, IV, VI
National Technical Information Service	15, XI
National Telecommunications and Information Administration	15, XXIII; 47, III, IV
National Weather Service	15, IX
Patent and Trademark Office, United States	37, I
Secretary of Commerce, Office of	15, Subtitle A
Commercial Space Transportation	14, III
Commodity Credit Corporation	7, XIV
Commodity Futures Trading Commission	5, XLI; 17, I
Community Planning and Development, Office of Assistant Secretary for	24, V, VI
Community Services, Office of	45, X
Comptroller of the Currency	12, I
Construction Industry Collective Bargaining Commission	29, IX
Consumer Financial Protection Bureau	5, LXXXIV; 12, X
Consumer Product Safety Commission	5, LXXI; 16, II
Copyright Royalty Board	37, III
Corporation for National and Community Service	2, XXII; 45, XII, XXV
Cost Accounting Standards Board	48, 99
Council on Environmental Quality	40, V
Council of the Inspectors General on Integrity and Efficiency	5, XCVIII
Court Services and Offender Supervision Agency for the District of Columbia	5, LXX; 28, VIII
Customs and Border Protection	19, I
Defense, Department of	2, XI; 5, XXVI; 32, Subtitle A; 40, VII
Advanced Research Projects Agency	32, I
Air Force Department	32, VII
Army Department	32, V; 33, II; 36, III; 48, 51
Defense Acquisition Regulations System	48, 2
Defense Intelligence Agency	32, I

Agency	CFR Title, Subtitle or Chapter
Defense Logistics Agency	32, I, XII; 48, 54
Engineers, Corps of	33, II; 36, III
National Imagery and Mapping Agency	32, I
Navy, Department of	32, VI; 48, 52
Secretary of Defense, Office of	2, XI; 32, I
Defense Contract Audit Agency	32, I
Defense Intelligence Agency	32, I
Defense Logistics Agency	32, XII; 48, 54
Defense Nuclear Facilities Safety Board	10, XVII
Delaware River Basin Commission	18, III
Denali Commission	45, IX
Disability, National Council on	5, C; 34, XII
District of Columbia, Court Services and Offender Supervision Agency for the	5, LXX; 28, VIII
Drug Enforcement Administration	21, II
East-West Foreign Trade Board	15, XIII
Economic Affairs, Office of the Under-Secretary for	15, XV
Economic Analysis, Bureau of	15, VIII
Economic Development Administration	13, III
Economic Research Service	7, XXXVII
Education, Department of	2, XXXIV; 5, LIII
Bilingual Education and Minority Languages Affairs, Office of	34, V
Career, Technical, and Adult Education, Office of	34, IV
Civil Rights, Office for	34, I
Educational Research and Improvement, Office of	34, VII
Elementary and Secondary Education, Office of	34, II
Federal Acquisition Regulation	48, 34
Postsecondary Education, Office of	34, VI
Secretary of Education, Office of	34, Subtitle A
Special Education and Rehabilitative Services, Office of	34, III
Educational Research and Improvement, Office of	34, VII
Election Assistance Commission	2, LVIII; 11, II
Elementary and Secondary Education, Office of	34, II
Emergency Oil and Gas Guaranteed Loan Board	13, V
Emergency Steel Guarantee Loan Board	13, IV
Employee Benefits Security Administration	29, XXV
Employees' Compensation Appeals Board	20, IV
Employees Loyalty Board	5, V
Employment and Training Administration	20, V
Employment Policy, National Commission for	1, IV
Employment Standards Administration	20, VI
Endangered Species Committee	50, IV
Energy, Department of	2, IX; 5, XXIII; 10, II, III, X
Federal Acquisition Regulation	48, 9
Federal Energy Regulatory Commission	5, XXIV; 18, I
Property Management Regulations	41, 109
Energy, Office of	7, XXIX
Engineers, Corps of	33, II; 36, III
Engraving and Printing, Bureau of	31, VI
Environmental Protection Agency	2, XV; 5, LIV; 40, I, IV, VII
Federal Acquisition Regulation	48, 15
Property Management Regulations	41, 115
Environmental Quality, Office of	7, XXXI
Equal Employment Opportunity Commission	5, LXII; 29, XIV
Equal Opportunity, Office of Assistant Secretary for	24, I
Executive Office of the President	3, I
Environmental Quality, Council on	40, V
Management and Budget, Office of	2, Subtitle A; 5, III, LXXVII; 14, VI; 48, 99
National Drug Control Policy, Office of	2, XXXVI; 21, III
National Security Council	32, XXI; 47, II
Presidential Documents	3
Science and Technology Policy, Office of	32, XXIV; 47, II
Trade Representative, Office of the United States	15, XX

Agency	CFR Title, Subtitle or Chapter
Export-Import Bank of the United States	2, XXXV; 5, LII; 12, IV
Family Assistance, Office of	45, II
Farm Credit Administration	5, XXXI; 12, VI
Farm Credit System Insurance Corporation	5, XXX; 12, XIV
Farm Service Agency	7, VII, XVIII
Federal Acquisition Regulation	48, 1
Federal Acquisition Security Council	41, 201
Federal Aviation Administration	14, I
Commercial Space Transportation	14, III
Federal Claims Collection Standards	31, IX
Federal Communications Commission	2, LX; 5, XXIX; 47, I
Federal Contract Compliance Programs, Office of	41, 60
Federal Crop Insurance Corporation	7, IV
Federal Deposit Insurance Corporation	5, XXII; 12, III
Federal Election Commission	5, XXXVII; 11, I
Federal Emergency Management Agency	44, I
Federal Employees Group Life Insurance Federal Acquisition Regulation	48, 21
Federal Employees Health Benefits Acquisition Regulation	48, 16
Federal Energy Regulatory Commission	5, XXIV; 18, I
Federal Financial Institutions Examination Council	12, XI
Federal Financing Bank	12, VIII
Federal Highway Administration	23, I, II
Federal Home Loan Mortgage Corporation	1, IV
Federal Housing Enterprise Oversight Office	12, XVII
Federal Housing Finance Agency	5, LXXX; 12, XII
Federal Labor Relations Authority	5, XIV, XLIX; 22, XIV
Federal Law Enforcement Training Center	31, VII
Federal Management Regulation	41, 102
Federal Maritime Commission	46, IV
Federal Mediation and Conciliation Service	29, XII
Federal Mine Safety and Health Review Commission	5, LXXIV; 29, XXVII
Federal Motor Carrier Safety Administration	49, III
Federal Permitting Improvement Steering Council	40, IX
Federal Prison Industries, Inc.	28, III
Federal Procurement Policy Office	48, 99
Federal Property Management Regulations	41, 101
Federal Railroad Administration	49, II
Federal Register, Administrative Committee of	1, I
Federal Register, Office of	1, II
Federal Reserve System	12, II
Board of Governors	5, LVIII
Federal Retirement Thrift Investment Board	5, VI, LXXVI
Federal Service Impasses Panel	5, XIV
Federal Trade Commission	5, XLVII; 16, I
Federal Transit Administration	49, VI
Federal Travel Regulation System	41, Subtitle F
Financial Crimes Enforcement Network	31, X
Financial Research Office	12, XVI
Financial Stability Oversight Council	12, XIII
Fine Arts, Commission of	45, XXI
Fiscal Service	31, II
Fish and Wildlife Service, United States	50, I, IV
Food and Drug Administration	21, I
Food and Nutrition Service	7, II
Food Safety and Inspection Service	9, III
Foreign Agricultural Service	7, XV
Foreign Assets Control, Office of	31, V
Foreign Claims Settlement Commission of the United States	45, V
Foreign Service Grievance Board	22, IX
Foreign Service Impasse Disputes Panel	22, XIV
Foreign Service Labor Relations Board	22, XIV
Foreign-Trade Zones Board	15, IV
Forest Service	36, II
General Services Administration	5, LVII; 41, 105
Contract Appeals, Board of	48, 61
Federal Acquisition Regulation	48, 5

Agency	CFR Title, Subtitle or Chapter
Federal Management Regulation	41, 102
Federal Property Management Regulations	41, 101
Federal Travel Regulation System	41, Subtitle F
General	41, 300
Payment From a Non-Federal Source for Travel Expenses	41, 304
Payment of Expenses Connected With the Death of Certain Employees	41, 303
Relocation Allowances	41, 302
Temporary Duty (TDY) Travel Allowances	41, 301
Geological Survey	30, IV
Government Accountability Office	4, I
Government Ethics, Office of	5, XVI
Government National Mortgage Association	24, III
Grain Inspection, Packers and Stockyards Administration	7, VIII; 9, II
Great Lakes St. Lawrence Seaway Development Corporation	33, IV
Gulf Coast Ecosystem Restoration Council	2, LIX; 40, VIII
Harry S. Truman Scholarship Foundation	45, XVIII
Health and Human Services, Department of	2, III; 5, XLV; 45, Subtitle A
Centers for Medicare & Medicaid Services	42, IV
Child Support Enforcement, Office of	45; III
Children and Families, Administration for	45, II, III, IV, X, XIII
Community Services, Office of	45, X
Family Assistance, Office of	45, II
Federal Acquisition Regulation	48, 3
Food and Drug Administration	21, I
Indian Health Service	25, V
Inspector General (Health Care), Office of	42, V
Public Health Service	42, I
Refugee Resettlement, Office of	45, IV
Homeland Security, Department of	2, XXX; 5, XXXVI; 6, I; 8, I
Coast Guard	33, I; 46, I; 49, IV
Coast Guard (Great Lakes Pilotage)	46, III
Customs and Border Protection	19, I
Federal Emergency Management Agency	44, I
Human Resources Management and Labor Relations Systems	5, XCVII
Immigration and Customs Enforcement Bureau	19, IV
Transportation Security Administration	49, XII
HOPE for Homeowners Program, Board of Directors of	24, XXIV
Housing and Urban Development, Department of	2, XXIV; 5, LXV; 24, Subtitle B
Community Planning and Development, Office of Assistant Secretary for	24, V, VI
Equal Opportunity, Office of Assistant Secretary for	24, I
Federal Acquisition Regulation	48, 24
Federal Housing Enterprise Oversight, Office of	12, XVII
Government National Mortgage Association	24, III
Housing—Federal Housing Commissioner, Office of Assistant Secretary for	24, II, VIII, X, XX
Housing, Office of, and Multifamily Housing Assistance Restructuring, Office of	24, IV
Inspector General, Office of	24, XII
Public and Indian Housing, Office of Assistant Secretary for	24, IX
Secretary, Office of	24, Subtitle A, VII
Housing—Federal Housing Commissioner, Office of Assistant Secretary for	24, II, VIII, X, XX
Housing, Office of, and Multifamily Housing Assistance Restructuring, Office of	24, IV
Immigration and Customs Enforcement Bureau	19, IV
Immigration Review, Executive Office for	8, V
Independent Counsel, Office of	28, VII
Independent Counsel, Offices of	28, VI
Indian Affairs, Bureau of	25, I, V
Indian Affairs, Office of the Assistant Secretary	25, VI
Indian Arts and Crafts Board	25, II

Agency	CFR Title, Subtitle or Chapter
Indian Health Service	25, V
Industry and Security, Bureau of	15, VII
Information Resources Management, Office of	7, XXVII
Information Security Oversight Office, National Archives and Records Administration	32, XX
Inspector General	
Agriculture Department	7, XXVI
Health and Human Services Department	42, V
Housing and Urban Development Department	24, XII, XV
Institute of Peace, United States	22, XVII
Intellectual Property Enforcement Coordinator, Office of	5, CIV
Inter-American Foundation	5, LXIII; 22, X
Interior, Department of	2, XIV
American Indians, Office of the Special Trustee	25, VII
Endangered Species Committee	50, IV
Federal Acquisition Regulation	48, 14
Federal Property Management Regulations System	41, 114
Fish and Wildlife Service, United States	50, I, IV
Geological Survey	30, IV
Indian Affairs, Bureau of	25, I, V
Indian Affairs, Office of the Assistant Secretary	25, VI
Indian Arts and Crafts Board	25, II
Land Management, Bureau of	43, II
National Indian Gaming Commission	25, III
National Park Service	36, I
Natural Resource Revenue, Office of	30, XII
Ocean Energy Management, Bureau of	30, V
Reclamation, Bureau of	43, I
Safety and Environmental Enforcement, Bureau of	30, II
Secretary of the Interior, Office of	2, XIV; 43, Subtitle A
Surface Mining Reclamation and Enforcement, Office of	30, VII
Internal Revenue Service	26, I
International Boundary and Water Commission, United States and Mexico, United States Section	22, XI
International Development, United States Agency for	22, II
Federal Acquisition Regulation	48, 7
International Development Cooperation Agency, United States	22, XII
International Development Finance Corporation, U.S.	5, XXXIII; 22, VII
International Joint Commission, United States and Canada	22, IV
International Organizations Employees Loyalty Board	5, V
International Trade Administration	15, III; 19, III
International Trade Commission, United States	19, II
Interstate Commerce Commission	5, XL
Investment Security, Office of	31, VIII
James Madison Memorial Fellowship Foundation	45, XXIV
Japan–United States Friendship Commission	22, XVI
Joint Board for the Enrollment of Actuaries	20, VIII
Justice, Department of	2, XXVIII; 5, XXVIII; 28, I, XI; 40, IV
Alcohol, Tobacco, Firearms, and Explosives, Bureau of	27, II
Drug Enforcement Administration	21, II
Federal Acquisition Regulation	48, 28
Federal Claims Collection Standards	31, IX
Federal Prison Industries, Inc.	28, III
Foreign Claims Settlement Commission of the United States	45, V
Immigration Review, Executive Office for	8, V
Independent Counsel, Offices of	28, VI
Prisons, Bureau of	28, V
Property Management Regulations	41, 128
Labor, Department of	2, XXIX; 5, XLII
Benefits Review Board	20, VII
Employee Benefits Security Administration	29, XXV
Employees' Compensation Appeals Board	20, IV
Employment and Training Administration	20, V
Federal Acquisition Regulation	48, 29

Agency	CFR Title, Subtitle or Chapter
Federal Contract Compliance Programs, Office of	41, 60
Federal Procurement Regulations System	41, 50
Labor-Management Standards, Office of	29, II, IV
Mine Safety and Health Administration	30, I
Occupational Safety and Health Administration	29, XVII
Public Contracts	41, 50
Secretary of Labor, Office of	29, Subtitle A
Veterans' Employment and Training Service, Office of the Assistant Secretary for	41, 61; 20, IX
Wage and Hour Division	29, V
Workers' Compensation Programs, Office of	20, I, VI
Labor-Management Standards, Office of	29, II, IV
Land Management, Bureau of	43, II
Legal Services Corporation	45, XVI
Libraries and Information Science, National Commission on	45, XVII
Library of Congress	36, VII
Copyright Royalty Board	37, III
U.S. Copyright Office	37, II
Management and Budget, Office of	5, III, LXXVII; 14, VI; 48, 99
Marine Mammal Commission	50, V
Maritime Administration	46, II
Merit Systems Protection Board	5, II, LXIV
Micronesian Status Negotiations, Office for	32, XXVII
Military Compensation and Retirement Modernization Commission	5, XCIX
Millennium Challenge Corporation	22, XIII
Mine Safety and Health Administration	30, I
Minority Business Development Agency	15, XIV
Miscellaneous Agencies	1, IV
Monetary Offices	31, I
Morris K. Udall Scholarship and Excellence in National Environmental Policy Foundation	36, XVI
Museum and Library Services, Institute of	2, XXXI
National Aeronautics and Space Administration	2, XVIII; 5, LIX; 14, V
Federal Acquisition Regulation	48, 18
National Agricultural Library	7, XLI
National Agricultural Statistics Service	7, XXXVI
National and Community Service, Corporation for	2, XXII; 45, XII, XXV
National Archives and Records Administration	2, XXVI; 5, LXVI; 36, XII
Information Security Oversight Office	32, XX
National Capital Planning Commission	1, IV, VI
National Counterintelligence Center	32, XVIII
National Credit Union Administration	5, LXXXVI; 12, VII
National Crime Prevention and Privacy Compact Council	28, IX
National Drug Control Policy, Office of	2, XXXVI; 21, III
National Endowment for the Arts	2, XXXII
National Endowment for the Humanities	2, XXXIII
National Foundation on the Arts and the Humanities	45, XI
National Geospatial-Intelligence Agency	32, I
National Highway Traffic Safety Administration	23, II, III; 47, VI; 49, V
National Imagery and Mapping Agency	32, I
National Indian Gaming Commission	25, III
National Institute of Food and Agriculture	7, XXXIV
National Institute of Standards and Technology	15, II; 37, IV
National Intelligence, Office of Director of	5, IV; 32, XVII
National Labor Relations Board	5, LXI; 29, I
National Marine Fisheries Service	50, II, IV
National Mediation Board	5, CI; 29, X
National Oceanic and Atmospheric Administration	15, IX; 50, II, III, IV, VI
National Park Service	36, I
National Railroad Adjustment Board	29, III
National Railroad Passenger Corporation (AMTRAK)	49, VII
National Science Foundation	2, XXV; 5, XLIII; 45, VI
Federal Acquisition Regulation	48, 25
National Security Council	32, XXI; 47, II

Agency	CFR Title, Subtitle or Chapter
National Technical Information Service	15, XI
National Telecommunications and Information Administration	15, XXIII; 47, III, IV, V
National Transportation Safety Board	49, VIII
Natural Resource Revenue, Office of	30, XII
Natural Resources Conservation Service	7, VI
Navajo and Hopi Indian Relocation, Office of	25, IV
Navy, Department of	32, VI
Federal Acquisition Regulation	48, 52
Neighborhood Reinvestment Corporation	24, XXV
Northeast Interstate Low-Level Radioactive Waste Commission	10, XVIII
Nuclear Regulatory Commission	2, XX; 5, XLVIII; 10, I
Federal Acquisition Regulation	48, 20
Occupational Safety and Health Administration	29, XVII
Occupational Safety and Health Review Commission	29, XX
Ocean Energy Management, Bureau of	30, V
Oklahoma City National Memorial Trust	36, XV
Operations Office	7, XXVIII
Patent and Trademark Office, United States	37, I
Payment From a Non-Federal Source for Travel Expenses	41, 304
Payment of Expenses Connected With the Death of Certain Employees	41, 303
Peace Corps	2, XXXVII; 22, III
Pennsylvania Avenue Development Corporation	36, IX
Pension Benefit Guaranty Corporation	29, XL
Personnel Management, Office of	5, I, IV, XXXV; 45, VIII
Federal Acquisition Regulation	48, 17
Federal Employees Group Life Insurance Federal Acquisition Regulation	48, 21
Federal Employees Health Benefits Acquisition Regulation	48, 16
Human Resources Management and Labor Relations Systems, Department of Homeland Security	5, XCVII
Pipeline and Hazardous Materials Safety Administration	49, I
Postal Regulatory Commission	5, XLVI; 39, III
Postal Service, United States	5, LX; 39, I
Postsecondary Education, Office of	34, VI
President's Commission on White House Fellowships	1, IV
Presidential Documents	3
Presidio Trust	36, X
Prisons, Bureau of	28, V
Privacy and Civil Liberties Oversight Board	6, X
Procurement and Property Management, Office of	7, XXXII
Public and Indian Housing, Office of Assistant Secretary for	24, IX
Public Contracts, Department of Labor	41, 50
Public Health Service	42, I
Railroad Retirement Board	20, II
Reclamation, Bureau of	43, I
Refugee Resettlement, Office of	45, IV
Relocation Allowances	41, 302
Research and Innovative Technology Administration	49, XI
Rural Business-Cooperative Service	7, XVIII, XLII, L
Rural Development Administration	7, XLII
Rural Housing Service	7, XVIII, XXXV, L
Rural Utilities Service	7, XVII, XVIII, XLII, L
Safety and Environmental Enforcement, Bureau of	30, II
Science and Technology Policy, Office of	32, XXIV; 47, II
Secret Service	31, IV
Securities and Exchange Commission	5, XXXIV; 17, II
Selective Service System	32, XVI
Small Business Administration	2, XXVII; 13, I
Smithsonian Institution	36, V
Social Security Administration	2, XXIII; 20, III; 48, 23
Soldiers' and Airmen's Home, United States	5, XI
Special Counsel, Office of	5, VIII
Special Education and Rehabilitative Services, Office of	34, III
State, Department of	2, VI; 22, I; 28, XI

Agency	CFR Title, Subtitle or Chapter
Federal Acquisition Regulation	48, 6
Surface Mining Reclamation and Enforcement, Office of	30, VII
Surface Transportation Board	49, X
Susquehanna River Basin Commission	18, VIII
Tennessee Valley Authority	5, LXIX; 18, XIII
Trade Representative, United States, Office of	15, XX
Transportation, Department of	2, XII; 5, L
Commercial Space Transportation	14, III
Emergency Management and Assistance	44, IV
Federal Acquisition Regulation	48, 12
Federal Aviation Administration	14, I
Federal Highway Administration	23, I, II
Federal Motor Carrier Safety Administration	49, III
Federal Railroad Administration	49, II
Federal Transit Administration	49, VI
Great Lakes St. Lawrence Seaway Development Corporation	33, IV
Maritime Administration	46, II
National Highway Traffic Safety Administration	23, II, III; 47, IV; 49, V
Pipeline and Hazardous Materials Safety Administration	49, I
Secretary of Transportation, Office of	14, II; 49, Subtitle A
Transportation Statistics Bureau	49, XI
Transportation, Office of	7, XXXIII
Transportation Security Administration	49, XII
Transportation Statistics Bureau	49, XI
Travel Allowances, Temporary Duty (TDY)	41, 301
Treasury, Department of the	2, X; 5, XXI; 12, XV; 17, IV; 31, IX
Alcohol and Tobacco Tax and Trade Bureau	27, I
Community Development Financial Institutions Fund	12, XVIII
Comptroller of the Currency	12, I
Customs and Border Protection	19, I
Engraving and Printing, Bureau of	31, VI
Federal Acquisition Regulation	48, 10
Federal Claims Collection Standards	31, IX
Federal Law Enforcement Training Center	31, VII
Financial Crimes Enforcement Network	31, X
Fiscal Service	31, II
Foreign Assets Control, Office of	31, V
Internal Revenue Service	26, I
Investment Security, Office of	31, VIII
Monetary Offices	31, I
Secret Service	31, IV
Secretary of the Treasury, Office of	31, Subtitle A
Truman, Harry S. Scholarship Foundation	45, XVIII
United States Agency for Global Media	22, V
United States and Canada, International Joint Commission	22, IV
United States and Mexico, International Boundary and Water Commission, United States Section	22, XI
U.S. Copyright Office	37, II
U.S. Office of Special Counsel	5, CII
Utah Reclamation Mitigation and Conservation Commission	43, III
Veterans Affairs, Department of	2, VIII; 38, I
Federal Acquisition Regulation	48, 8
Veterans' Employment and Training Service, Office of the Assistant Secretary for	41, 61; 20, IX
Vice President of the United States, Office of	32, XXVIII
Wage and Hour Division	29, V
Water Resources Council	18, VI
Workers' Compensation Programs, Office of	20, I, VII
World Agricultural Outlook Board	7, XXXVIII

List of CFR Sections Affected

All changes in this volume of the Code of Federal Regulations (CFR) that were made by documents published in the FEDERAL REGISTER since January 1, 2018 are enumerated in the following list. Entries indicate the nature of the changes effected. Page numbers refer to FEDERAL REGISTER pages. The user should consult the entries for chapters, parts and subparts as well as sections for revisions.

For changes to this volume of the CFR prior to this listing, consult the annual edition of the monthly List of CFR Sections Affected (LSA). The LSA is available at *www.govinfo.gov*. For changes to this volume of the CFR prior to 2001, see the "List of CFR Sections Affected, 1949–1963, 1964–1972, 1973–1985, and 1986–2000" published in 11 separate volumes. The "List of CFR Sections Affected 1986–2000" is available at *www.govinfo.gov*.

2018

30 CFR — 83 FR Page

Chapter I
- 56 Notification 15055, 17293
- 56.18002 Revised 15064
- 57 Notification 15055, 17293
- 57.18002 Revised 15065
- 100.3 (a)(1) introductory text amended; (g) Table XIV revised 14
- 100.4 (a), (b), and (c) introductory text amended 14
- 100.5 (c), (d), and (e) amended 15

2019

30 CFR — 84 FR Page

Chapter I
- 56 Notification 55500
- 56.18002 Revised 51401
- 57 Notification 55500
- 57.18002 Revised 51401
- 100.3 (a)(1) introductory text amended, (g) table XIV revised 219
- 100.4 (a), (b), and (c) introductory text amended 220
- 100.5 (c), (d), and (e) amended 220

2020

30 CFR — 85 FR Page

Chapter I
- 56 Technical correction 30627
- 56.6000 Amended 2027
- 56.6000 Regulation at 85 FR 2027 eff. date confirmed 19391
- 56.6310 (a) and (b) revised; (c) added 2027
- 56.6310 Regulation at 85 FR 2027 eff. date confirmed 19391
- 56.6407 (a) and (c) amended 2027
- 56.6407 Regulation at 85 FR 2027 eff. date confirmed 19391
- 57 Technical correction 30627
- 57.6000 Amended 2027
- 57.6000 Regulation at 85 FR 2027 eff. date confirmed 19391
- 57.6310 (a) and (b) revised; (c) added 2027
- 57.6310 Regulation at 85 FR 2027 eff. date confirmed 19391
- 57.6407 (a)(3) and (b)(2) amended 2027
- 57.6407 Regulation at 85 FR 2027 eff. date confirmed 19391
- 57.6604 (b) amended 2027
- 57.6604 Regulation at 85 FR 2027 eff. date confirmed 19391
- 75 Policy statement 41364
- 100.3 (a)(1) introductory text amended; (g) Table XIV revised 2299

30 CFR—Continued

85 FR Page

Chapter I—Continued
100.4 (a), (b), and (c) introductory text amended 2299
100.5 (c), (d), and (e) amended 2299

2021

30 CFR

86 FR Page

Chapter I
100.3 (a)(1) introductory text and (g) table XIV revised 2970
100.4 (a), (b), and (c) introductory text amended 2970
100.5 (c) through (e) amended 2970

2022

30 CFR

87 FR Page

Chapter I
100.3 (a)(1) introductory text amended; (g) table removed; (g) Table 14 added 2336

30 CFR—Continued

87 FR Page

Chapter I—Continued
100.4 (a), (b), and (c) introductory text amended 2336
100.5 (c), (d), and (e) amended 2336

2023

(Regulations published from January 1, 2023, through July 1, 2023)

30 CFR

88 FR Page

Chapter I
100 Authority citation revised 2218
100.3 (a)(1) introductory text and (g) Table 4 amended 2218
100.4 (a), (b), (c) introductory text amended 2218
100.5 (c), (d), (e) amended 2218